of the United States is again invited to participate.   The
Attorneys General of the states requiring or permitting
segregation in public education will also be permitted to
appear as *amici curiae* upon request to do so by September 15, 1954, and submission of briefs by October 1, 1954.[14]

*It is so ordered.*

based, and assuming further that this Court will exercise its equity powers to the end described in question 4 (*b*),

"(*a*) should this Court formulate detailed decrees in these cases;

"(*b*) if so, what specific issues should the decrees reach;

"(*c*) should this Court appoint a special master to hear evidence with a view to recommending specific terms for such decrees;

"(*d*) should this Court remand to the courts of first instance with directions to frame decrees in these cases, and if so, what general directions should the decrees of this Court include and what procedures should the courts of first instance follow in arriving at the specific terms of more detailed decrees?"

[14] See Rule 42, Revised Rules of this Court (effective July 1, 1954).

*Books by Richard Kluger*

WHEN THE BOUGH BREAKS (1964)

NATIONAL ANTHEM (1969)

SIMPLE JUSTICE (1976)

# Simple
## Justice

# Simple Justice

The History of
*Brown v. Board of Education*
and Black America's
Struggle for Equality

*by* Richard
Kluger

Alfred A. Knopf / New York / 1976

THIS IS A BORZOI BOOK
PUBLISHED BY ALFRED A. KNOPF, INC.

Library of Congress Cataloging in Publication Data

Kluger, Richard.
Simple justice.

Bibliography: p.
Includes index.
1.  Segregation in education—Law and legislation—
United States.  I.  Title.
KF4155.K55 1976      344′.73′0798      75–8221
ISBN 0–394–47289–6

Manufactured in the United States of America
First Edition

FOR

MATTHEW AND TEDDY

AND MINA'S GIRLS

# Contents

Illustrations appear following page 420.

# Foreword

From the start, the United States aspired to far more than its own survival. And from the start, its people have assigned themselves a nobler destiny, justified by a higher moral standing, than impartial scrutiny might confirm. Success added high luster to their character, and when Americans looked into the mirror, they admired with uncommon keenness what they saw.

Only lately, on the eve of the nation's bicentennial of independence, has the dazzle of America's achievement dimmed enough for her people to sense the need to distinguish their conceits from a set of humbling truths. Not all progress, Americans have started to see, can be measured in numbers. Not all wars can be won, and fewer still are worth the spilling of blood and surplus energies. Not all problems can be engineered out of existence without giving rise to yet more severe ones. The skies will not fall if next year's profits do not exceed this year's level. And the world is nobody's oyster forever; he who would hoard its pearls may wind up choking on them.

Material values in themselves, in short, can neither explain nor sustain the American achievement: the nation must exploit its inner resources as well if it is to linger long at the center of the global stage. This is a book about the resurrection of those inner resources.

Of the ideals that animated the American nation at its beginning, none was more radiant or honored than the inherent equality of mankind. There was dignity in all human flesh, Americans proclaimed, and all must have its chance to strive and to excel. All men were to be protected alike from the threat of rapacious neighbors and from the prying or coercive state. If it is a sin to aspire to conduct of a higher order than one may at the moment be capable of, then Americans surely sinned in professing that all men are created equal—and then acting otherwise. Nor did time close the gap between that profession and the widespread practice of racism in the land. The nation prospered mightily nonetheless, and few were willing to raise their voices and suggest that what might once have been forgiven as the excesses of a buoyant national youth had widened into systematic and undiminishing cruelty.

Some protested, to be sure. But no political leader risked all of his power and no sector of the nation's governmental apparatus was fully applied against this grave injustice—until the Supreme Court of the United States took that step. There was irony in this because the nine Justices, as has often been said, constitute the least democratic branch of the national government. Yet this, most likely, was one reason why the Court felt free to act: it is not compelled to nourish the collective biases of the electorate; it may act to curb those unsavory attitudes by the direct expedient of declaring them to be intolerable among a civilized people.

It is to these insulated nine men, then, that the nation has increasingly brought its most vexing social and political problems. They come in the guise of private disputes between only the litigating parties, but everybody understands that this is a legal fiction and merely a convenient political device. American society thus reduces its most troubling controversies to the scope—and translates them into the language—of a lawsuit. In no other way has the nation contrived to frame these problems for a definitive judgment that applies to a vast land, a varied people, a whole age.

What follows is a history of one such lawsuit (or, to be more technically accurate, five cases raising the same question and consolidated under a single title). Yet this book has not been conceived as a study of law and its permutations. It has been designed to suggest how law and men interact, how social forces of the past collide with those of the present, and how the men selected as America's ultimate arbiters of justice have chosen to define that quality with widely varying regard for the emotional content of life itself.

This is a long book because of the nature and subject of the lawsuit with which it deals. Probably no case ever to come before the nation's highest tribunal affected more directly the minds, hearts, and daily lives of so many Americans. Already, just two decades later, scholars have assigned the cases known collectively as *Brown v. Board of Education of Topeka* a high place in the literature of liberty. The decision marked the turning point in America's willingness to face the consequences of centuries of racial discrimination, a practice tracing back nearly to the first settlement of the New World. The process of ridding the nation of its most inhumane habit cannot be properly presented by dwelling on only the climactic moments of that effort.

Many unheralded people persevering in widespread communities over long, hard decades contributed to what the Supreme Court decided on the seventeenth day of May 1954. This is, in large part, their story. In a larger sense, it is a chapter in the biography of a nation that has begun to understand that history may measure its ultimate worth not by the lilt of its slogans or the might of its arsenals or its troyweights of gold, but by how evenhandedly it has dealt with all of its citizens and how consistently it has denied dignity to none.

RICHARD KLUGER
Ridgefield, Connecticut
*March 1975*

# Under Color of Law

*Part I*

. . . *we are of the humble opinion that we have the right to enjoy the privileges of free men. But that we do not will appear in many instances, and we beg leave to mention one out of many, and that is of the education of our children which now receive no benefit from the free schools in the town of Boston, which we think is a great grievance, as by woful experience we now feel the want of a common education. We, therefore, must fear for our rising offspring to see them in ignorance in a land of gospel light when there is provision made for them as well as others and yet can't enjoy them, and for not other reason can be given this they are black. . . .*

*We therefore pray your Honors that you would in your wisdom some provision would be made for the free education of our dear children. And in duty bound shall ever pray.*

—FROM A PETITION TO THE STATE LEGISLATURE OF
THE COMMONWEALTH OF MASSACHUSETTS BAY, 1787

# 1

# Together Let Us Sweetly Live

Before it was over, they fired him from the little schoolhouse at which he had taught devotedly for ten years. And they fired his wife and two of his sisters and a niece. And they threatened him with bodily harm. And they sued him on trumped-up charges and convicted him in a kangaroo court and left him with a judgment that denied him credit from any bank. And they burned his house to the ground while the fire department stood around watching the flames consume the night. And they stoned the church at which he pastored. And fired shotguns at him out of the dark. But he was not Job, and so he fired back and called the police, who did not come and kept not coming. Then he fled, driving north at eighty-five miles an hour over country roads, until he was across the state line. Soon after, they burned his church to the ground and charged him, for having shot back that night, with felonious assault with a deadly weapon, and so he became an official fugitive from justice. In time, the governor of his state announced they would not pursue this minister who had caused all the trouble, and said of him: Good riddance.

All of this happened because he was black and brave. And because others followed when he had decided the time had come to lead.

At first, he acted gingerly. Not quite six feet tall, on the slender side, with a straight-back bearing that seemed to add inches to his height and miles to his dignity, he was no candidate for martyrdom. In his fiftieth year, he had not enjoyed good health for some time. A nearly fatal bite from a black-widow spider—they could find no medical help for him for fifteen hours—and recurring bouts with influenza had drained his constitution, and the emotional demands of teaching and preaching all over the county had taken their toll as well. It was therefore natural that when he began the activities that, a few years later, were to become the profound business of the Supreme Court of the United States, he would begin in a small way.

His name was Joseph Albert DeLaine. His skin was a medium shade of brown, and his friends described him as "handsome" and "clean-cut." Ceremonial photographs in the late Forties and early Fifties show him in a well-worn black suit with a black vest, looking bright-eyed and attentive behind austere glasses. His hair was short and beginning to gray. He was convinced that it grayed rapidly after they decided to ask for the bus.

A school bus. There were thirty school buses for the white children. There was none for the black children. A muscular, soft-spoken farmer named James Gibson remembers what the chairman of the school board said when they asked for the bus. His name was Elliott, R. W. Elliott, he ran a sawmill, and he was white. Everyone who ran anything in the county was white. What he said was: "We ain't got no money to buy a bus for your nigger children." But there was always money for buses for the white children. "And you'd know it," farmer Gibson recalls, "because they was always muddyin' you up."

And so a lawsuit was filed. A black man sued white officials who he claimed were denying him and his three children the equal protection of the law as guaranteed by the Fourteenth Amendment of the Constitution of the United States. No such thing had happened before in the memory of living men in Clarendon County, South Carolina. For if you had set out to find the place in America in the year 1947 where life among black folk had changed least since the end of slavery, Clarendon County is where you might have come.

Six hundred square miles of gently rolling fields and pasture and woodland, mostly in gum trees and pine, the county lies dead center in a thirty-mile-wide plain that sweeps diagonally across the state on a northeast-southwest axis dividing the flat, marshy, tropical low country along the Atlantic coast from the sand hills farther inland and the more rugged Piedmont beyond them. The soil here is a gray-brown sandy loam on the surface, turning to a slightly sticky clay of brownish yellow or yellowish red when you plow it under. It rains a lot in Clarendon, nearly fifty inches a year, the temperature averages an agreeable 64 degrees, and the frost is out of the ground by the middle of March. It is a good place to grow things, and what they grew most of in the late Forties was just what they had always grown there since the white planters had come eighty miles up the Santee River from the coast a century and a half earlier. Cotton.

Soon after word was out that the Connecticut Yankee Eli Whitney had built an "engine" that could swiftly and inexpensively separate the cluster of fiercely clinging green seeds from the fiber of a cotton boll, South Carolina planters were the first to clamor for the machine. The state went so far as to pay the then unheard-of sum of $50,000 to make the invention available to anyone in the state who wanted to build one, with no royalty due the inventor. The cotton rush was on.

Up the Cooper River from Charleston, up the Santee from Jamestown, they came past unbroken moss-draped forest walls to plant cotton in the fertile alluvial plains that rolled away unending from the banks of the serene waterways. The Santee, a network of ramified rivers snaking 450 miles from the ramparts of the Blue Ridge in the north down to the sea, was the great commercial lifeline of its day, bisecting the richest of the cotton land. Midway between Charleston, the throbbing depot where the baled white produce was dispatched by the boatful to hungry spindles on both sides of the ocean, and the state capital of Columbia, built 120 miles to the northwest at the insistence of upland farmers, the Santee River makes a horseshoe bend that to the early planters was an ideal place to load their cargo. The Clarendon people called their river port Wright's Bluff, and each day the small hubbub at the post office, freight depot, and cotton market built there at water's edge came to a stop when a steamboat paddled around the bend, whistle blasting, to bring wares and finery from Charleston to the plantation houses and, throughout the long autumns, to return to the coast with bulging hold.

In summer, it grew hot and damp, and the anopheles mosquito came swarming out of the marshes and the swamps to infect the residents in the low-lying cotton fields close by the river. The malaria was attributed in that age not to the insects but to the "miasma," the evening mists that seeped dolorously across the moist landscape. The black men who grew the cotton were required, miasma or not, to stay in their fields, for it was commonly agreed by their owners that, their high mortality rate notwithstanding, the Africans were somehow better able to withstand the disease than white men. Having so decided, the planters then repaired ten or so miles to the north, where they built a small summer colony to be cool, healthful, and sociable, yet close enough to preserve easy contact with their riverside domains. It was called at first "The Summer Town," then simply "Summertown," and finally Summerton. In time, there were shops, a few businesses, and eventually even a once-a-day train stopping by. The population never got much above a thousand, even in season, but Summerton became the closest thing to an urban center at the southern end of the county. As river transport ebbed and the railroads took over, traffic clattered in steady wagon caravans over the ten-mile road between Summerton and the county seat of Manning to the northeast. Named for the politically influential family that eventually gave the state three governors, Manning was a relative beehive, but it never outgrew Summerton by more than two or three times, and so the county fanned out along the road linking the two little towns.

As the twentieth century came, time stood still in Clarendon County and the population rose or fell by perhaps a thousand every decade. In 1950, the population was the same as it had been forty years earlier—32,000, give or take a few hundred. The closest thing to excitement after dark in Summerton was to drive down Route 15 from Sumter to where the highway met and doglegged with the west end of Main Street, a block and a half of drab brick-front stores, a small bank, a smaller post office, and a tacky movie house. There, just off the highway and across the railroad tracks, clanking and crunching away all through the floodlit night, stood a huge shed with corrugated metal siding running its entire length of maybe 150 feet and up about forty feet to the roof. From September onward, when they started bringing in the cotton by wagon and mule, the McClary Anderson Ginnery operated around the clock. A great, ungainly contraption that hums and clatters as it eats up the yield of an entire acre—some 30,000 handpicked plants—the gin combs out the thirty-five or so seeds adhering to every boll by pressing the cotton between spiked rollers spinning in opposite directions. The seeds fall away into a jellied mass collected in pans beneath the printing-press-like rollers, and the seed-free cotton is sent whooshing upward by compressed air in foot-wide tin tubes that conduct it through a washing and drying process until the whole acre's worth of blossom is compressed into a single 500-pound-or-so bale. Then, for six or seven months of planting and fertilizing and spraying and thinning and weeding and picking and carting, an endless labor involving more than likely every able-bodied member of the family, you got paid between $100 and $200 per bale, depending on a lot of factors over which you had no control.

That was what you got if you owned the land. But most of the people in Clarendon County did not own their own land at the end of the first half of the twentieth century. Seven out of every ten people there were black, the highest percentage in the state, and almost every Negro in Clarendon lived on a farm. There were 4,000 farms in the county, and fewer than a quarter of them belonged to the people who worked them. Most of the land—as much as 85 percent, lifelong residents guessed—belonged to whites, many of them absentee owners.

If you were landless and black then, you had a choice of three ways to avoid starvation as a tenant farmer in Clarendon County. The most common way was to rent the land for an annual fee, ranging between $8 and $15 per acre. The tenant provided his own seed, fertilizer, and equipment, the last of which consisted largely of a mule (only one Clarendon farm in nine had a tractor in 1949). Or you could contract-farm, a throwback to the period just after the Civil War, whereby the black farmer was paid a dollar or two per week for his labor and, if he stayed the course through harvest time, received as a bonus the yield of a single acre, be it in cotton or produce. Or you could sharecrop, whereby the white boss provided the land, the seed, the fertilizer, and the pesticides, and the black man provided all the muscle, his own and his mules', and they divided the proceeds evenly between them. Under all three arrangements, the tenant also received a roof over his head, the better kind made of galvanized tin. Supporting the roof would be a building that you might call a cabin if you were poetic or blind, or a shack if you wished to face the physical fact. Some of them had a thin coat of paint on the outside, but most did not. Inside, they had no paint, no plumbing, no electricity. Through the walls you could see daylight and through the floorboards you could feel the breeze when it rose.

By official count of the United States government, there were 4,590 black households in Clarendon County in 1950, and the average annual income for two-thirds of them was less than $1,000. Only 280 of them earned as much as $2,000. They averaged more than five mouths to feed per household, but only every second household could claim a milk cow on the premises. Pigs were abundant, however, and so they ate pork and fatback but precious little milk, and there was scant raising of fruits or vegetables other than corn, and their diets suffered accordingly. The median age of Clarendon blacks was eighteen, youngest of any county in South Carolina, which meant there were a great many children of school age. But very few of them, in the middle of the twentieth century, attended school beyond the fourth grade. A dozen years earlier, the last time anybody had counted, 35 percent of all Negroes in Clarendon County over the age of ten were illiterate.

"We knowed it was wrong," a group of them agreed, looking back more than twenty years later, "but we didn't know how to attack it."

It was nothing short of economic slavery, an unbreakable cycle of poverty and ignorance breeding more poverty and a bit less ignorance, generation upon generation. "We had to take what was given us," says a Clarendon farmer, "or leave." And a lot of them did leave, for urban ghettos far from the sweet scents and bright sun of their native county. But wherever they went and whatever they tried to do with their lives, they were badly disabled, irreparably so for the most part, by the malnourishment that the poverty and meanness of their Clarendon birthright had inflicted upon the shaping years of their childhood. Their minds had not been fertilized half so well as their cotton, their hands had not been trained for more than steering a mule in a straight furrow. Nothing seemed to change. The land abided, eroding imperceptibly year by year but keeping them alive so long as they could work it.

For all the grim burden of the blacks, there was nothing till then that could have been labeled racial unrest. The white man, as he always had in South Carolina, held the whip hand, though the blacks were no longer his personal, disposable property. "Oh, there was a lot goin' on that we didn't like," says Joseph Richburg, a Negro teacher back then and a barber in his later years, "but everything was fine on the face of it, so long as we kept saying 'Yes, sir' and 'No, sir' and tipping our hat." And so, in Summerton, no Negro was surprised when a store clerk serving him would turn abruptly aside to attend the first white man coming through the door. The booths by the drugstore soda fountain were for whites only, and you ate your ice-cream cone on the sidewalk before or after climbing to "Buzzards' Roost," the balcony where all black moviegoers were required to sit.

"We got a good bunch of nigras here," David McClary, white owner of the main livestock, feed, and fertilizer business in town, used to tell visitors in those years. The same McClary clan that ran the big cotton gin a few hundred yards away over on Route 15.

McClary's cousin, attorney S. Emory Rogers, who for decades numbered the Board of Education in Summerton among his clients, would say in later years, "We understood each other here—the two races were living in harmony. When the man working my fields got sick, who do you think paid for his doctor?"

"Colored have made wonderful progress down here," ventured H. C. Carrigan, then in his twelfth term as mayor of Summerton. "I have several farms, and they all have Negroes on them. I sharecrop with them, and they are all as happy as can be."

"Yessir, we got good nigras in this county," echoed Charles Plowden, who ran the town bank and had 2,500 acres in cotton, corn, and soybeans. He also ran the Board of Education. And education was in very short supply among Summerton-area "nigras," however good they were in Charles Plowden's book. But after all, the banker noted, the white people paid the taxes and the white people were therefore entitled to the better schools. As with a single voice, the white taxpayers of Clarendon County agreed with that premise, though it stood in dire contradiction to the very purpose of compulsory public education as it had evolved in the United States to become the pride of the nation and the envy of the world. In Clarendon County for the school year 1949–50, they spent $179 per white child in the public schools; for each black child, they spent $43.

Schools there were the largest, costliest, and most important public enterprise, as they were and are, of course, in most American municipalities. In Clarendon County, there were then sixty-one Negro schools, more than half of them ramshackle or plain falling-down shanties that accommodated one or two teachers and their charges, and twelve schools for whites. The total value of the sixty-one black schools attended by 6,531 pupils was officially listed as $194,575. The value of the white schools, attended by 2,375 youngsters, was put at $673,850.

In charge of this dual school system was a slender, gray-haired clergyman named L. B. McCord, who three years after winning election as county superindendent of schools in 1940 was also named pastor of the Manning Presbyterian Church, the pillar of Christendom in those parts. Given the places of honor accorded to education and religion in small American communities, his dual occupation made L. B. McCord a powerful citizen indeed in Clarendon County. "He is a capable man," wrote the Manning *Times*, the county weekly, "with a keen perception of fairness to all, and the best interests of the school children of Clarendon are close to his heart."

This, though, was not the unanimous estimate of L. B. McCord. Views of him tended to diverge along racial lines. "He was a white-supremacist, is all," says Billie S. Fleming, owner of a Negro funeral home and insurance agency in Manning and perhaps the most successful black businessman in the county. "As a minister, he was fond of saying that God had intended things to be this way, and if you doubted it, he'd point to the sky and say, 'Now if you just look up at the birds, you'll see that the buzzards don't mingle with the crows, and down here dogs don't mingle with cats.' " Other blacks say he cared nothing for the caliber of the teachers in the Negro schools or the condition of the schoolhouses. "He was always shortchanging us," a former black teacher recalls. "When you came in and asked for money for, say, window sashes, he'd say something like, 'Look, you fellas do it yourselves— we can't hardly pay the teachers. Go get some boards.' "

And they did. That was how it was with Superintendent McCord. If you crossed him, you were in trouble. If you were black and you crossed him, you were in worse trouble and not long for a place on the Clarendon County public-school payroll. One of the nearly 300 teachers on that payroll in the spring of 1947 was Joseph DeLaine, a Methodist minister. He had been teaching for nine years at the little colored school in Silver, a crossroads settlement four miles due north from his home in Summerton. "I was one of McCord's good niggers," is how the Reverend DeLaine put it. And then he became something else.

In the South, people often go by the initials of their given names, and so Joseph Albert DeLaine, born on his family's 250 acres of farmland near

Manning in 1898, came soon enough to be called J.A. His father, born four years before slavery was abolished in South Carolina by the Emancipation Proclamation, also was raised in the Manning area, one of thirteen children of pious members of the African Methodist Episcopal Church (AME), and it was not unnatural that he would become a man of the cloth. By any contemporary standard, the Reverend Henry Charles DeLaine was an inspiring success. A man of strong, even features and unwavering gaze, he rose rapidly up the hierarchal ladder of the highly structured AME Church, second largest of the all-black denominations (but a very distant second numerically to the decentralized, disestablishment Baptists). He pastored at some of the larger churches in Clarendon County and the surrounding central sector of the state, spurred the building of at least three churches, became an elder of the AME and a member of the Masons, the Knights of Pythias, and the Odd Fellows—in short, a vigorous leader of many flocks. "He was a quiet, pious Christian," the AME's publication, *Voice of Missions*, would write of him. "He taught his people to be industrious and law-abiding. He was a strong advocate of human rights."

J. A. DeLaine was his father's eighth child by his second wife—there were fourteen youngsters in all and many a chore for each of them in tending the farm and keeping food on the table, especially since the man of the house had pastoring duties that kept him, by choice, from the soil. All his life J.A. would remember the supreme physical effort of his boyhood—digging deep-rooted tree stumps from the family land so they would have more room to plant. But greater effort still was required for him to pursue the one activity that would critically shape his life: he had to walk five miles to school in Manning and five miles back. And when he got there, the lessons taught were minimal. It was a time of virulent anti-Negro feeling in South Carolina, led by the toxic upcountry oratory of Senator "Pitchfork Ben" Tillman, bankrupt farmer turned raucous champion of the frustrated poor-whites of the state. Historically, times of economic travail in the decades after the Civil War were marked by an overflow of venom toward the black man. Welcome for his broad back and toothy smile in flush times, ever summonable to heave his brawn into the brutal physical labors that no self-respecting white man would undertake if a darkey were available at token wages, the Negro loomed as a thoroughly inconvenient presence in the two threadbare decades surrounding the turn of the century. The right to vote, granted the black man just a dozen years earlier by the Fifteenth Amendment, started to be taken from him in South Carolina in 1882 by a combination of legal steps and terror tactics. By the turn of the century, the Negroes of South Carolina, who had sent more of their brothers to Congress and taken a more active part in their state government than their black counterparts in any other ex-Confederate state, had been almost totally stripped of the ballot. Voteless, uneducated, yoked to the soil by what approached universal peonage, South Carolina Negroes were defenseless as a spiteful code of segregation laws was whipped through the legislature at Columbia and the black man was officially designated a lower order of being.

In the first years of the twentieth century when J. A. DeLaine was growing up on a farm midway between Charleston and Columbia, public education was a scrawny orphan of the state of South Carolina. Few cared for the blessings it might have brought in hastening the spread of democracy and its institutions. Not until 1915 did the state's business and industrial captains yield long enough to allow the passage of laws to control deforming child labor and to establish compulsory education. These measures, though, had little meaning to the fate of J. A. DeLaine and other black boys whose education was paid for by the state's meager provisions, which were never more than a fraction of the allotment for white youngsters, and the bounty of Northern philanthropists. It was hardscrabble learning, you had to walk far to get any of it, and if you were ever going to make something of yourself and get much beyond the three Rs, it would take time and money and punishing perseverance. It took J. A. DeLaine the first thirty-three years of his life.

Providence stimulated the process when he was fourteen. In Manning one day, a smaller white boy shoved one of J.A.'s sisters off the sidewalk and J.A. shoved back. The white lad injured a shoulder. A dozen black adults a month were being lynched in America just then for comparable impertinence. J.A.'s fate was declared to be twenty-five lashes. His father, the reverend, no believer in fruitless valor, urged the boy to take the punishment. A generation gap presented itself. J.A. vowed he would leave home rather than endure any white man's unwarranted lash. He went to Atlanta and worked in a steam laundry by day and attended school at night; on the job, the white boss abused him, and he fought back. By the time J.A. drifted back to Clarendon, his family's fortunes were on the upswing. His father was pastoring at Liberty Hill, four miles south of Summerton—one of the largest AME congregations in the state—and there were a grocery and funeral-casket business in Summerton and a sawmill to run, so the DeLaine children pitched in every way they could. J.A. chauffeured the family around the county in an old Model-T and before long got to know every inch of the southern half and almost every face in it. Had he been consciously preparing for a political career as lay leader of the black masses, he could not have had better training.

J.A.'s heart was set, though, on following in his father's path. His goal was a degree in theology from little Allen University in Columbia, run by the AME Church, and likely therefore to be hospitable to offspring of its own. Still, going there cost more than the family could ever put aside, and so J.A. cut grass and swept out the houses of whites for $1.25 a week per family, then went into the steam-pressing business in Columbia in his non-school hours until he compiled enough credits for a teaching license in 1925. But he would not stop there. What with odd jobs, heavy classwork, and a gradually deteriorating economic climate, which hit blacks a full two to three years before it caught up with white America, six more years were consumed before he was a Bachelor of Theology. It was 1931, and a lot of the country was falling apart. But the heart of South Carolina had been an economic disaster area for nearly three-quarters of a century, and for blacks there the times were about as they had always been. So at the age of thirty-three, the hopeful Reverend J. A. DeLaine set out to preach and teach.

He had been hired as principal and eighth-grade teacher at a 150-pupil school in Jamison, a small town about thirty-five miles southwest of Summerton across the Santee in Orangeburg County, near the state agricultural college for blacks. His pay was $50 a month plus $10 for being principal. But when he married fellow teacher Mattie Belton, thereby increasing the gross DeLaine teaching income to $110 a month, the authorities figured that was mighty uppity for one young black couple. They ordered J.A. to fire his wife and replace her with a single teacher. "I'd as soon have dug a ditch with my teeth," he says. There was the saddening spectacle, too, of the almost total failure by authorities to enforce the compulsory-school-attendance laws among black children. White landowners wanted every available pair of black hands, big or little, in the fields at harvest and planting times. School terms varied between three and six months for Negroes, depending upon the degree of enlightenment, courage, and physical stamina of the black adult population in the area. It was a dispiriting beginning for a new teacher eager for results. At the end of the first year, J.A. and Mattie had to leave Jamison and seek jobs elsewhere. And while both continued to teach for the next twenty years, Reverend DeLaine the younger found that more of his heart and mind was being drawn to teaching through the words and example of Jesus Christ.

The Christian gates to the kingdom of heaven, since the early years of the nineteenth century, did not admit blacks through the same turnstiles with whites. That Christianity remained segregated struck many—if a minority—of both races as a monstrous contradiction in terms. The brilliant, controversial theologian Joseph R. Washington, Jr., has written: "Segregation in religion is so disparaging that the insensitivity to it on the part of Negroes who are content to remain separated and on the part of whites who are delighted to have them do so is incomprehensible."

That black worshippers have been insensitive to the fact and implications of Jim Crow Christianity seems both an excessive and an unverifiable judgment. That they have been at least relatively content with it may be explained by the central place of the black church in the black community. It has had little to do with piety and a great deal to do with the deprivations that have been the lot of black America. Those with little money and scant education often devote much of their spare time to worship and group activities under religious auspices, especially in rural areas. Blacks, historically spurned in their social, economic, and political aspirations by whites, have turned naturally enough to the companionship of their own. Their church has offered them opportunities for recognition and fulfillment denied them in the white-run world. The black custodian who mops the halls in the public school Monday through Friday becomes a quite different being when he serves as principal of the Sunday School at Mt. Pisgah AME. Or the black beautician who performs with such dedication in the Elm Street Baptist choir. Their church has brightened and comforted their lives as no other haven, and it has served, by natural extension, as a social club, recreation center, meetinghouse, political headquarters, and schoolroom as well as an approved outlet for emotional repression. The man who ran the church in any black community was almost certain to be its unchallenged leader. But most black pastors, eager as any men to preserve their eminent standing, did not choose to lead very far, especially if leadership meant a collision with the white power structure that has always taken a benign—indeed, patronizing— view of black Christianity. Why, then, rock the boat?

The conversion of Reverend J. A. DeLaine from diligent pastor to outspoken rebel was no overnight thing. While his father had urged his parishioners to be "industrious and law-abiding" and give the white man minimal cause to abuse him—a message closely akin to that being broadcast by his nationally eminent contemporary Booker T. Washington—J. A. DeLaine came to the pulpit in a new and changing world that at last began to present black America with a chance to get out of the cellar. The Depression and the steps to alleviate its crushing effects finally dramatized to vast segments of the nation that grave defects had been built into the dynamic but uncontrollable American economy. And when the Second World War came, it began to dawn on more Americans than ever before that there was something severely and intolerably unjust about spending billions of dollars and hundreds of thousands of lives to fight Hitler's racist doctrines abroad while keeping black Americans—one out of every ten Americans—ignominious outcasts in their own land.

Through the Thirties and the Forties, J. A. DeLaine pastored at remote but sizable churches all over the lower half of Clarendon and in Barnwell and Bamburg counties within fifty miles to the southwest, areas with similarly heavy black population, severe poverty, and unyielding white oppression. He was not a fire-and-brimstone preacher. He was stern and serious and forceful in the pulpit, knowing that to many of his listeners, for whom reading was an ordeal and radio was largely irrelevant or prohibitively expensive, what "Rev" said on Sunday was indeed gospel. His sermons were their only ongoing form of education, and J.A. painstakingly linked his scriptural points of departure to current events that otherwise would surely have escaped the attention of hard-pressed black farmers in the backwaters of South Carolina. He did not slight Christian principles, though he saw few of them operating to the benefit of his congregants.

Or himself, really. "I think J.A. was deeply hurt," says a close and admiring relative, "because a man of his ability and dedication was denied so much in life because of his color." He did not preach that the black man's reward would be found only in Green Pastures in the Sky and that therefore his suffering was somehow providential or good for him. As the years went by, he called increasingly for his flock to seek justice with dignity in the here and now, to stand tall and live honorably and have the fortitude to endure their travail while their country was deciding when and how it would mete them their due. His AME bishop looked on at J.A.'s works and decided upon reflection that they were good.

Watching their children go off to war in faraway places of which many of them had never heard, a number of the older blacks of Clarendon County began to grow impatient with their hereditary subjugation. "The feeling around here then," one lifelong resident remembers, "was that if our youngsters could offer up their lives on the battlefield, was life so much sweeter for us here at home?" And when their sons came marching or limping home and buoyed their new mood of determination still higher, some of them now said among themselves that the time to fight back was fast approaching.

Early in June in the year 1947, Reverend J. A. DeLaine of Summerton— he had built a home there for his wife, who taught right across the street at the Scott's Branch school, and himself and their three children on a nine-acre plot off the extension of Main Street in the black outskirts of town—found himself attending a summer session at Allen University in Columbia, sixty miles from his home. One day, all the summer students were summoned to a general assembly to hear the words of a short, stocky, moonfaced Negro who made their hearts leap with his charged, unmistakable message. He earned his living by overseeing the South Carolina operations of the black-owned, black-serving Pilgrim Health and Life Insurance Company, one of the largest enterprises of its kind. This work gave him a certain amount of economic independence, which was bolstered by a relatively cosmopolitan back-ground: he had grown up in North Carolina, spent some years in New York and in the Southern industrial center of Birmingham, Alabama, and was an ordained minister without a congregation. He preached wherever he was invited and said whatever he felt. The Reverend James M. Hinton was fifty-seven years old when he addressed J. A. DeLaine and his summer classmates that June day in 1947, and for seven years he had been state president of the National Association for the Advancement of Colored People. Most people called it "the N-double A-C-P." Some people, black as well as white, just called it trouble.

Reverend Hinton's text for the day noted that the surest measure of the force with which the white man's heel was still pressing the black man's face into the mud was the schools. The colored people could not rise until they got educated, and was it not powerfully clear that the whites did not want them educated? To give the Negro anything more than the most rudimentary training was to make him restless with his lot and a competitor for your job. And who then would tend the fields for no reward beyond bare sustenance? The black schools of South Carolina were a disgrace, said Hinton. In the first place, it was an ordeal to get to them because there were no buses for black children. Was there any clearer way for the whites to say they did not want the Negro to rise above his present station? If the message was somehow not clear enough, the rickety schoolhouses themselves brought it home: small, dark, leaking all over, heated by coal stoves that sometimes smoked the children out of the building. In most places, the state or the community did not even pay for the schools to be put up or, as in Clarendon, for the coal or for even a single crayon. All it paid was the teachers' salaries, and in

Clarendon County the average white teacher earned two-thirds more than the average black one. On top of the advanced state of dilapidation of the schoolhouses was the inevitable waste of time because so many of the rural schools had only one or two teachers, who could tend to only one or several classes at a time while the rest of the crowded room went uninstructed. The N-double A-C-P had successfully launched legal action in other Southern states, most notably Virginia, to end such inequities, Hinton explained, and now the effort should begin in South Carolina.

The way to start, NAACP strategists had agreed, was with buses. It would be the least inflammatory step, and the hardest request for the whites to deny. But South Carolina was not Virginia, and any step, especially the first, was likely to be greeted with enmity and perhaps violence. "No teacher or preacher in South Carolina has the courage," J. A. DeLaine heard James Hinton declare, "to find a plaintiff to test the legality of the discriminatory bus-transportation practices in this state." But he wished that one did.

It was not just a matter of the teacher's or preacher's courage; it was the courage required by the man he might find to bring the case. It would take someone with the proper legal standing—a *bona fide* taxpayer of good moral character who could claim a legitimate disability in his children's behalf. Nobody had to add that whoever would lend his name to such a cause might die for it.

The Reverend DeLaine was pastoring that year on the Pine Grove circuit, which consisted of two churches on the southeastern edge of the county. Between them, they had maybe 900 members. "Rev" knew them and they knew him. Along with the Reverend E. E. Richburg, a younger, taller, and somewhat more learned man who pastored at the big Liberty Hill Church where J.A.'s father had served for nine years, DeLaine was one of the two best-known and most respected black ministers in the county.

He knew that they had had a bad bus problem on their hands in the area he was pastoring down close by the Santee River ever since it had been dammed up right near that spot in the early Forties as part of a massive hydroelectric project under the New Deal. It had cost $65 million—probably as much as all the other public works in South Carolina put together—and was supposed to lure new industry to the state and provide a broad new inland waterway to carry products down the Santee-Cooper system to Charleston. No one had seemed to remember, though, that trucks and trains were a good deal faster and cheaper than boats for transporting most goods. Or that hydroelectric power was hardly more efficient or economical than coal, which was abundant throughout most of the East. Or that new industry was not likely to settle in an area where the labor supply was so poorly educated. The whole thing proved a massive white elephant.

Just before the Santee Dam at the end of the lake, about ten miles downstream from the horseshoe bend where the old plantation port of Wright's Bluff had once stood, the waters backed up into inlets and feeder streams and caused minor flooding in the area for long stretches of the year. It did not seem minor, however, if you lived around the tiny black community of Jordan, where some of the low-lying roads were inundated. To cross them in certain seasons en route to school, the Negro children had to row a boat. And then, if they were attending high school, they had to proceed nine miles any way they could to Scott's Branch in Summerton. Most didn't bother. Something clearly had to be done.

Reverend DeLaine and a committee of two others were authorized by the board of Pine Grove Church to seek relief from county officials, and so the angular black Methodist minister went to Manning to call on the angular white Presbyterian minister who ran the county schools. L. B. McCord, the reverend-superintendent, cordially explained that Negroes did not pay much in taxes and it was not fair to expect the white citizens to shoulder a yet heavier economic burden by providing bus transportation for the colored. The answer was no. Reverend DeLaine decided to write to the state superintendent of education in Columbia, and the state superintendent wrote back that this was a county matter and he could not interfere in it. Then Reverend DeLaine wrote to the Attorney General of the United States, Tom Clark, in Washington. In time, Clark's office wrote back, urging him to pursue the matter with local officials.

And so the black farmers in the Jordan area dug deep into their overalls and bought a secondhand bus to carry their children to school. "It wasn't the best," recalled Joseph Lemon, who farmed seventy acres for his living, "but it was a school bus." Then they asked Superintendent-Reverend L. B. McCord if the county would provide gasoline for the bus. He said no. They had to buy their own gas for their own bus, and it cost them dear. The bus also managed to break down a lot.

The Sunday after James Hinton had declared that the NAACP wanted to launch a court case against the kind of whites-only bus policy practiced by the Clarendon County schools, J. A. DeLaine got up early and drove with his oldest son to the 160-acre farm of the Pearson brothers, Levi and Hammitt, out in Jordan. Levi Pearson was a short, wiry man with very dark skin. He was about fifty years old, and though he did not attend either of the churches that Reverend DeLaine pastored, the two men had known each other a long time. "I knew Levi's daddy, too," the minister recalled. He explained it all to the farmer, especially the risks: the NAACP did not want to get the whites thinking that a mass protest movement was afoot nor did it want to endanger any more blacks than necessary. At the moment, all they needed was one name, one man, so they could act.

Levi Pearson had three children attending the Scott's Branch high school nine miles from his farm, and he had chipped in for the bus that kept breaking down. Levi listened closely to what J.A. was telling him, and he mulled it and mulled it. And then he decided to stick his neck out. The two men shook hands, and the minister drove off to preach his sermon that morning with an extra sense of mission.

There were meetings in Columbia then in the small law office of Harold R. Boulware, a tall, bluff, city-shrewd attorney in his mid-thirties who had received his legal training at Howard University in Washington, from which a small cadre of smart, well-trained black civil-rights lawyers had begun to emerge in the early Thirties. Boulware drew up a two-page petition in Levi

Pearson's name. Dated July 28, 1947, it declared that he was the father of Daisy Pearson, age eighteen, James Pearson, age fifteen, and Eloise Pearson, age twelve, and prayed that "school bus transportation be furnished, maintained and operated out of the public funds in School District Number 26 of Clarendon County, South Carolina, for use of the said children of your Petitioner and other Negro school children similarly situated." It was submitted to County Superintendent of Education McCord, to the chairman of the District No. 26 school board, and to the secretary of the State Board of Education.

Three and a half months passed without a word from the superintendent or the chairman or the secretary, though they were reminded by mail about the petition on several occasions. Early in November, Harold Boulware wrote to the chairman of the school board to advise that Levi Pearson had retained his services and to request a hearing. When three more weeks passed without a word, Boulware wrote Superintendent McCord and requested a hearing. But there was nothing to hear except the hostility in the air.

Lawyer Boulware knew his business. He had successfully argued a series of cases in the mid-Forties for black teachers in Charleston and Columbia who sought the same pay as their white counterparts. Since that precise issue had been ruled upon by the United States Court of Appeals for the Fourth Circuit in Richmond in 1940 and upheld by the Supreme Court, Boulware's victory broke no new legal ground. But in South Carolina, nothing was automatic. When the black teachers' association of the state had asked the South Carolina legislature to equalize their pay just after the Supreme Court had upheld the Fourth Circuit opinion making the step mandatory in 1941, the lawmakers bared their teeth. "We would like to see them make us give the Negroes more money," said a state senator from Georgetown County. On adjournment day, the legislature voted a $152,000 supplementary appropriation for the white teachers of the state and turned the Negro petitioners away without a dime.

So the teachers had had to sue, and by 1947 most of the city school systems in the state were offering equal pay for black teachers, though rural areas, comprising the bulk of the state, remained massively opposed to any such fissures in the white-supremacist barricades. Now, in like fashion, Levi Pearson would have to go to court to get his children a bus. But he had no professional association behind him, as the teachers had. Or neighbors. Reverend DeLaine's involvement was shrouded as well, for it was suspected that the school officials would fire him faster than a cracker's whip from his teaching job at the school in Silver if word got back to them. The reverend, moreover, considered himself an unwell man, not up to the official burdens of a long fight against an entrenched foe. And yet he was eager for the confrontation. He wrote to State NAACP President Hinton in February of 1948:

> When the Bus Transportation case breaks to the public it will give great courage to many who are waiting on leadership. . . . Who will take the leadership is a problem to me. There are a number of folks about in the county who want to do something but don't have the ability to take the leadership. . . .

Many questions are being asked me about when the Bus Transportation case will start. I had a pretty good sentiment worked up for financial help but everything is growing cold and wandering now. The lawyer told me that it would be filed in January.

It was filed on March 16, 1948, in the United States District Court in Florence County, adjacent to Clarendon on the northeast. It asserted that Levi Pearson's children were suffering "irreparable damage" and were threatened with more of the same and asked the court to issue a permanent injunction "forever restraining and enjoining the defendants . . . from making a distinction on account of race or color" in providing free bus service for white schoolchildren while denying it to Negroes. The complaint was signed by the attorneys for the plaintiff—Harold Boulware of Columbia first, and below him Thurgood Marshall, the NAACP's top lawyer in New York. Marshall's office had scrutinized the legal papers, suggesting language drawn from similar cases it had pursued earlier in Virginia and Maryland. The whole thing had taken more time than Reverend DeLaine had hoped. Then again, he was entitled to his impatience: thirty-six years had passed since the day he had been expected to take twenty-five lashes for defending his sister from a white boy's shove.

The news broke the next day in the Columbia *State.* Levi Pearson was an immediate hero among his people, though the jubilation did not rise above a whisper. They all understood the risks. He was the obvious choice to serve as acting president of the new branch that the NAACP sought to plant in the county in the wake of local enthusiasm over the bus case. The feisty little farmer agreed, and J. A. DeLaine became the branch secretary of what was, practically speaking, an undercover operation. A more open arrangement would have been suicidal in Clarendon County.

It was too late for caution now, though. And when planting time came to Clarendon that spring, Levi Pearson found that his credit had been cut off by every white-owned store and bank in the county. He had had enough put aside for seed for the cotton, tobacco, oats, and wheat plantings, but there was not enough for fertilizer. He had to cut down some of his timber and sell it for cash. But when the pickup man came from the mill—the mill that belonged to R. W. Elliott, head of grammar school board No. 22 in the Summerton area—and learned why the timber was being sold, he drove away and left it lying there.

The case of *Pearson v. County Board of Education* was scheduled in Charleston for June 9. "Please do not make any other commitments for the week beginning Monday, June 7, 1948," Harold Boulware wrote Levi Pearson on May 28. The warning proved unnecessary. On June 8, the case was thrown out of court. L. B. McCord and his fellow white county school officials had checked Levi Pearson's tax receipts more rigorously than the Negro attorney. Pearson's farm was almost precisely on the line between School District No. 5, to which he paid his property taxes, and School Districts No. 26 for the Scott's Branch high school and No. 22 for the grammar school—the ones his children attended. He was held to have no legal standing to bring the case.

"I think that's when my hair turned white," Reverend DeLaine remembered. It was a long drive home to Summerton, and not many days before they heard that Clarendon's state senator was snortingly telling white cronies around the county courthouse in Manning that "our niggers don't even know where they live." In his excitement beforehand, the "Rev" had advised his people that the law was clear and "they're going to have to transport us out of the woods." And then to lose on sloppy homework. "We were mighty discouraged," he said.

That autumn, Levi Pearson could not find a white farmer with a harvester, as he always had done in the past, to bring in the crop. He had had to borrow from hard-pressed blacks to buy fertilizer in the spring. And now he had to sit and watch his harvest of oats and beans and wheat rot in the fields.

Finally they told him that if he would just forget about the buses and the N-double A-C-P and tend to his own, everything would be taken care of again. But Levi Pearson would not give up.

They had to begin all over again the following spring. This time, the stakes were higher, and the whites were watching.

DeLaine and Pearson headed a small group of Clarendon blacks summoned to Columbia in March of 1949 for a skull session with top state and national officials of the NAACP, led by Thurgood Marshall, whose record of success as a civil-rights lawyer had begun to turn him into a legend. Chagrined by the setback in the bus case the previous year, Marshall was too seasoned a battler to be discouraged for very long. To tie a test case to a single plaintiff was always risky business: it was too easy to find some disqualifying ground, as they had with Levi Pearson, or to intimidate the plaintiff into dropping out. And then you were nowhere. They had not sought more than a single plaintiff in the bus case to spare the Clarendon black community the wrath of the whites. But this time they would seek a firm, unified group of twenty plaintiffs, and this time they would not settle for a few battered buses. The black schools of Clarendon were a plain disgrace—anyone could see it—and this time the Negroes were going to ask for equal treatment from top to bottom: buses, buildings, teachers, teachers' salaries, teaching materials. Everything the same. Anything less was patently in violation of the Fourteenth Amendment, Thurgood Marshall explained. Now if the Clarendon group thought it could assemble twenty sturdy plaintiffs who would stay the course, the large man from New York told them, the NAACP would bring a major test case there. If not, it would take the fight elsewhere—and now.

The Clarendon people went off during a coffee break to huddle among themselves. No one strengthened DeLaine's backbone more than his close friend, the Reverend J. W. Seals, a small, bespectacled, warmly humorous man who lacked DeLaine's education but gave away very little to him in the way of dedication. "Now don't you get down, J.A.," said Seals, who pastored at St. Mark's in Summerton, next door to DeLaine's home. Before, they had asked for just one man, and J.A. had brought them Levi; now they wanted twenty, and they would get twenty.

So much for bravado. In the event, the task very nearly proved impossible. The infant branch of the NAACP lacked experience in civil affairs and political action, but the Reverends DeLaine and Seals, looking not unlike a black Mutt and Jeff, kept at it. They organized a series of four informational meetings at churches around the county during the next few months, including an overflow session at Summerton to hear from the executive secretaries of the Virginia and South Carolina NAACP state organizations. It was a kind of excitement no one in the county had ever witnessed before. But no one was rushing to sign up as plaintiff in the equalization test case. Most of them, after all, were tenant farmers who might be tossed off their land at any time. And word from the whites was beginning to circulate that that was precisely what would happen to anyone who signed up: he'd be a homeless hero. Farmers who owned their land had the depressing example of Levi Pearson staring them in the face. And teachers and those in other occupations could ponder the equally disturbing fate of the principal of the Scott's Branch school, who, after eighteen years of service, was summarily fired on the suspicion that he had inspired or strongly encouraged the Pearson bus suit. Add to these potent deterrents a labyrinth of overlapping school districts and apparently conflicting jurisdictions, and you had a political jungle thick enough to puzzle a Talleyrand, let alone a group of earnest but fearful novices. It would take something else to forge them into an action-ready phalanx. And when it came, the Reverend DeLaine seized the day.

To replace the fired principal at Scott's Branch, the school board installed a black man without a college degree but with long experience doing the white man's bidding. His black teaching colleagues at the school found him arrogant to them, pathetic in his efforts to cotton up to white officials, and, by year's end they concluded, more than likely crooked. There had been two school fund-raising rallies and eight entertainment programs that produced well over $1,000—a great deal of money in a town like Summerton in 1949—and nobody knew where the money went after the principal had collected it. He charged out-of-district seniors $27 in tuition and local students fees of $2.50 before he would hand over their state certificates of completion—plain extortion, so far as the youngsters and their families were concerned—and when some of the children declined to pay, he threatened to impound their transcripts and had uncomplimentary remarks inserted in some of their term records. On top of which it was charged that he was not on hand nine-tenths of the time to teach his mathematics classes, classes whose pupils had paid extra for teaching materials in algebra and geometry and got neither the materials nor a refund. In short, he was a bully, a thief, and a malingerer in the eyes of the black community, and probably a traitor to his race: they suspected he had funneled much of the ill-got money to white officials who let him keep the rest. The charges against the principal, later endorsed in sworn statements by some of the faculty, were drawn up by a group of two dozen or so members of the graduating class and sent to white school officials. There was no response.

DeLaine, whose wife, Mattie, had been teaching at Scott's Branch for more than a dozen years and kept him apprised of the scandal, dropped a match in ready tinder. Parents, students, teachers, school officials, and the alleged culprit were summoned to a mass meeting called for the first Sunday in June at Reverend Seals's St. Mark's Church next to the school. Neither the accused principal nor any white official showed up, but some 300 blacks gathered and, as DeLaine later recounted the occasion, "a flame of anger" was in them. If they acted in concert and presented their charges to the whites as an official petition of the black community, surely something would be done about it. But who would be their leader? From the packed church, the call came for J. A. DeLaine. He declined on account of his having been involved in the Pearson case: another leader might get a better reception from the whites. He suggested a strong-armed farmer named Eddie Ragin, who with his brother William was later to provide food, transportation, and yeoman support as the struggle intensified. "Not me!" said Eddie Ragin. "I can say Gee and Haw fine to my mules and plow a furrow good enough, but let's get us an educated person to do our talkin'." And again the cry came for J. A. DeLaine. Again he declined, noting that his health had prevented him from preaching for the past eighteen months and that he needed the income from his teaching job, for they all understood that his job would be taken away if he did as they asked. He suggested another of the five preachers in the room to be their leader—the one he knew to be least willing. In doing so, he was not without political guile, for J. A. DeLaine had decided, before organizing this angry churchful of his people, that subterranean leadership would never embolden the black community. Frustrated by the results since first hearing James Hinton's rousing challenge two years earlier, piqued by whispers he had overheard that his health was not as precarious as he let on, J. A. DeLaine now crossed his private Rubicon. He would lead them, out front, if they really wanted him.

The minister he had deferred to declined the honor, and for a third time the call came, now more insistent: "DeLaine! DeLaine!" He rose from the back of the room and said to them that he would not do it unless they were ready, unless they had grit to go to the local school board and then the county school board and then the state education department—"and every time they'll turn us down." And then they would fight in the courts with the help of the N-double A-C-P, they would fight it all the way up to the Supreme Court of the United States, and unless they were all willing to stand with him against whatever would come during the lengthy process, he would not do it. But if they would do this thing, which was the right thing to do for their children—if they would use this occasion to insist that the white people provide them with decent schools to which they were entitled—he would be their leader. And they shouted back to him yes, that was what they wanted. So he went up inside the chancel rail and he led them.

They formed a small grievance committee, of which he was chairman.

His brother in Christ, Reverend E. E. Richburg of Liberty Hill, who ran the largest AME church in Clarendon County with well over a thousand members but had held back from the protest movement until now, was secretary. The committee, according to the Reverend Richburg's minutes, "was instructed to ask for the privilege to help in the selection of a suitable principal and teachers to put over our children," then an offering was collected of $10.82. For the Doxology, they sang "Together Let Us Sweetly Live, Together Let Us Die."

Two days after the parents' action committee submitted its petition of grievances and sought a hearing from the white school trustees, J. A. DeLaine was advised that his services as a teacher at the little school up in Silver on the Sumter Road would not be required the following fall.

Had the white authorities moved to minimize the uprising, it might have been swiftly quelled. Instead, and in rancor, they turned their backs and refused to explore the legitimacy of the Negro complaints. After a local school trustees' meeting on the subject toward the end of June, no response or action was forthcoming, as DeLaine had predicted. He took his case to the county board, and when that too proved fruitless, the "Rev" got into his old Ford—for there were only 101 homes with telephones in the entire county, and very few of them were owned by blacks—and plowed the dusty summer roads gathering affidavits from parents and teachers and pupils. Then he took the lot of them and drove the sixty miles to Columbia to see the man in charge of supervising Negro education throughout the state. The fat was in the fire now.

As summer wore on, word trickled out from the white man's redoubt, the county courthouse in Manning, that the State Department of Education was riled by the Clarendon dispute and wanted it settled before it turned into something bigger. The county board was petulant. Requests via registered mail for a public hearing were returned unopened to DeLaine's committee. One of the black girls who signed an affidavit against the principal was branded a slut. No action was taken as summer wore on, and the black community grew edgy. To brace their spirits, DeLaine sent a leaflet to parents the first part of September, urging them not to pay the usual fee for fuel and supplies or anything else "until an UNDERSTANDING and AGREEMENT is made between the Parent Committee and those who are in Authority." It added:

> Money paid to a school should be used for the benefit of the CHILDREN of that school, and the parents should know how it is spent. . . . A Principal who receives his SALARY from monies appropriated for PUBLIC INSTRUCTION should be glad to let the PARENTS know what is being done with the monies they pay or give, unless it is going in the "RAT HOLE" or the "PRIVATE SINKING FUND."
>
> Seemingly, an effort is made at Summerton to keep the parents IGNORANT OF THE SCHOOL AFFAIRS and also to keep them DIVIDED; ONE GROUP AGAINST ANOTHER. By such METHODS the past practices may be continued in the future or made worse. Little gifts and nice talk should be carefully watched and proven.
>
> If Parents want assurance for a "BETTER DEAL" they must stand together for the future good of their children and community.

And they did. Among those greatly annoyed by this sudden show of consolidated protest was the superintendent of schools for District No. 22, encompassing the Summerton area—H. B. Betchman, who had run things his own way there for more than twenty years. "I don't see what you niggers want," one of the black residents remembers him saying at the time, " 'cause you got more than we got." "That," the black farmer adds, "was just natural-born falsifyin'." To the embattled Negro community, H. B. Betchman was "a nasty-talkin' man like all the rest" and a poor-white tool of school-board attorney Emory Rogers, the short, florid, well-educated Summerton lawyer whose family roots in the area went back more than two centuries. Between his own holdings and those of his relatives, such as cousin David McClary, who owned the feed business and cotton gin, and cousin Charles Plowden, who owned the Summerton bank, the power of the old plantation stock was perpetuated and mobilized.

On September 23, 1949, Reverend L. B. McCord bit the bullet and sent a notice to Reverend J. A. DeLaine that as superintendent of education and chairman of the county school board, he was officially setting a hearing on the charges against the Scott's Branch principal in the county courthouse eight days hence. "You are at liberty to present witnesses to prove the charges," the notice said.

When the hearing was over, the accused principal, who failed to produce records to refute the charges, was out of his job. He was, after all, a Negro, and his dismissal was trivialized by the whites as an intramural hassle among the blacks. Two days later, the ousted principal left Summerton. But he would yet take his revenge.

Monday of the following week, Superintendent Betchman invited Reverend DeLaine to his office at the white elementary school on Church Street. With its red-brick solidity and graceful cupola, it was easily the most stately building in Summerton. The superintendent handed DeLaine the transcript for his son Joseph that had been withheld since his graduation at Scott's Branch in June. Then he offered the reverend the principal's job at the black school. No fees whatever would be charged except for the rent of books—a notable concession, since the county previously had charged each black pupil $7 a year for coal and other sundries that the white got free. But there was a catch: he would have to call off the fight for more improvements in the black schools. "Ninety percent of the people are following you, DeLaine," the superintendent said, "and they deserve better leadership than to get them into a fight with the white people. The whites provide the money and the jobs that keep them going."

"In my heart I said I would never do it," J. A. DeLaine later wrote. "From my tongue I told him that there were other grown people who might even turn to fight me. Then he would be holding me responsible for their conduct while they [would] be looking upon me as a traitor."

The superintendent was not satisfied with that. "You've got to stop them, DeLaine," he snapped. "I'm holding you responsible."

So charged, the reverend produced a thick wad of postcards from his pocket and handed them to Betchman. Each bore an invitation to a mass meeting to carry the fight for decent schools into the courtroom.

"What does this mean?" asked the superintendent, anger rising.

"I don't know any further than what the words say," DeLaine answered, repocketed the cards, and went about his business.

Later that week, the superintendent appointed DeLaine's wife, Mattie, to serve as acting principal of Scott's Branch in a transparent maneuver to compromise the reverend's protest activities. It was to no avail. "There was a fire here that no water was gonna put out," says one of the black farmers who now began to sign the NAACP petition. By November 11, DeLaine had the twenty names that Thurgood Marshall said they needed to go to court. It had taken eight months to get them.

Legal custom dictates that in a suit with many plaintiffs, the case is called after the first name on the complaint. Heading the list of Clarendon Negroes, given in alphabetical order, was Harry Briggs, then a thirty-four-year-old Navy veteran with five children. A short, chunky man with heavy eyebrows over large, expressive eyes, he was the son of sharecroppers and had spent all his life, except for the years away in the South Pacific, in Summerton. For fourteen years, he had worked at the Carrigan service station on Main Street, right across from the Piggly Wiggly, pumping Sinclair gas, repairing tires, and greasing cars. They did not let him do body work. "I knowed everybody in town," Harry Briggs recalls, and everybody knew that, the year before, he had taken out a small loan from the Summerton bank and bought a small lot from Reverend DeLaine right near the Scott's Branch school and built himself a small house. Harry, Jr., and the other Briggs kids could walk just across the street to get to school. It was into the Briggs parlor that many of the petitioners trooped to sign their names to the legal forms after Reverend DeLaine's October rally at nearby St. Mark's Church. Not a leader, Summerton blacks said of Harry Briggs, but a solid man.

"We figured anything to better the children's condition was worthwhile," he remembers. "There didn't seem to be much danger to it. But after the petition was signed, I knew it was different. The white folks got kind of sour. They asked me to take my name off the petition. My boss, he said did I know what I was doin' and I said, 'I'm doin' it for the benefit of my children.' He didn't say nothin' back. But then later—it was the day before Christmas—he gave me a carton of cigarettes and then he let me go. He said, 'Harry, I want me a *boy*—and I can pay him less than you.' "

Harry's wife, Liza, had been working for six years as a chambermaid at a Summerton motel over on Route 15 when they caught up with her. "They told me that they were under a lot of pressure to get me and one of the other women working there to take our names off the petition," she says, "or the motel wasn't going to get its supplies delivered any more." Liza Briggs told them that her name was not on the petition, and they said no, but her husband's was and she'd better tell him to take it off. She said he was old enough to have a mind of his own and that she wouldn't do that. They gave her a week's notice.

The Briggs family stayed on in the county for four years, trying to farm twenty rented acres while the legal fight over the schools came to a boil. But in time they cut off Harry's credit at the Summerton bank, so he went up to Sumter, twenty-three miles north, and got a loan there, until they found out who Harry Briggs was and they, too, called the money in.

The Briggses were not the only petitioners who suffered. Bo Stukes was let go at his garage, and James Brown was fired as a driver-salesman for Esso, though his boss commended him for never having come up a penny short in ten years on the job. Teachers got fired, Negroes had great trouble getting their cotton ginned that harvest season, and Mrs. Maisie Solomon not only got thrown out of her job at the motel but also tossed off the land her family rented and had to take rapid refuge with other blacks. John Edward McDonald, a thirty-one-year-old veteran of Iwo Jima and Okinawa, couldn't get any financing for a tractor to farm his hundred acres, and Lee Richardson, who had a hefty debt outstanding at McClary's feed store as he did every year at that time, was told to pay up at once. They knew that he had no spare money just then; that was why he owed them in the first place. McClary's people were about to seize Richardson's two mules as payment when the blacks in town hurriedly passed the hat for him. A few years later, David McClary told an inquiring Northern newspaperman: "When you're in business, you give a lot of credit. You have to collect sometime. That foreclosure had nothing to do with that petition he signed."

As the fates would have it, Harry Briggs's cow got loose and stepped heavily on a gravestone in the McClary family plot. The town's sole policeman came and arrested the cow. The whites thought that was funny as hell. Harry Briggs had to sweat plenty before he got his precious cow back.

Up in Manning, at the Fleming-DeLaine funeral home, Billie Fleming learned that black sharecroppers on some farms were no longer allowed to bring their dead to his funeral parlor. Fleming was Reverend DeLaine's nephew; J.A.'s father had put the family into the casket-selling business long years before. One family brought in a dead infant for burial soon after the lawsuit was filed, Fleming recalls, but had to switch the small body to another home when the white boss, who paid the bill, found out.

The weight of reprisal grew. The black ministers rose to the occasion. "We ain't asking for anything that belongs to these white folks," persisted the Reverend J. W. Seals of St. Mark's. "I just mean to get for that little black boy of mine everything that any other South Carolina boy gets—I don't care if he's as white as the drippings of snow."

"You're just like mules," asserted the Reverend Richburg of Liberty Hill AME, "you don't know your own strength." And he urged his people to launch an economic boycott against the Clarendon whites, whom they heavily outnumbered. Such militance was beyond the Negroes of Summerton, but the very idea stirred them.

In January of 1950, the Reverend DeLaine let go with his strongest words to date. They were in a three-page open letter, mimeographed and widely passed around town. Part of it said:

Is this the price that free men must pay in a free country for wanting their children trained as capable and respectable American citizens? . . . Shouldn't officials employ the dignity, foresight, and intelligence in at least the honest effort to correct outstanding evils?

. . . Is it a credit for Summerton to wear the name of persecuting a segment of its citizens? Shall we suffer endless persecution just because we want our children reared in a wholesome atmosphere? What some of us have suffered is nothing short of Nazi persecution.

He was writing the truth, and they made him pay for it. He was subjected to menacing incidents on the highway, a hair-trigger confrontation on Main Street, threats by mail from people signing themselves "the Ku Klux Klan." His wife and nieces lost their teaching jobs. And then, out of the blue, DeLaine was named in a $20,000 slander suit by the black principal who had been charged with abuse of office at the Scott's Branch school and let go by the white county school board the previous October. When the case came to trial, the reverend-superintendent-chairman of the county school board, L. B. McCord, supported the claim of the disreputed ex-principal that J. A. DeLaine had concocted the case out of whole cloth and put the Negro community up to hounding the principal out of town. It came down to Reverend McCord's word against Reverend DeLaine's. Only white men were on the jury. The ex-principal was awarded $2,700 in damages. J. A. DeLaine vowed to himself that he would pay it only when there was no fight left within him.

There were reports now in April that a black youngster had been kicked to death by a notorious white bigot who caught him urinating in plain view on the side of the road to Manning. DeLaine wrote to the Federal Bureau of Investigation about the report, but the rest of the black community, sensing the heightening tactics of terrorism, clammed up tight. Witnessing all of this, Reverend DeLaine's superior, AME Bishop Frank Madison Reid, ordered him out of the county. He was put in charge of St. James Church in Lake City, thirty-five miles northeast of Summerton. It was one of the churches his father had founded.

On Saturdays, the man they called the "Rev" came home to his embattled people in Clarendon and kept their spirits flying. "The black man in the county had had nothing to look forward to until then," says Billie Fleming. "Without the schools, there was no way to break out." Adds a black farmer who had a hand in that remarkable agrarian uprising, "We just got tired of workin' the man's fields."

And so for the first time any of them could remember, they had hope as well as a heavier burden of fear. Their yearnings had been gathered up and committed to paper and were being directed by able lawyers of their own race to the courts of the government of the United States. They would need all the hope the "Rev" could generate, for the better part of another year would pass before their lawsuit would come to trial in Charleston. When it did, it would be known as *Briggs v. Elliott*—after Harry Briggs, the former gas-station attendant they would never let become a mechanic, and Roderick W. Elliott, flinty chairman of School District No. 22 and owner of the sawmill whose pickup man would not take away the trees that Levi Pearson had cut down to pay for his urgently needed fertilizer.

The outcome of the case, and four others that eventually joined it for consideration together by the highest tribunal in the land, would change America profoundly. The injustice it sought to end had persisted since the settlement of the New World.

# 2

# Original Sin

Slavery as practiced in the American South, it is now generally acknowledged, was probably as severe as any form of it in recorded history. This is especially so if one considers that the African blacks were not brought to America for punitive reasons: they had committed no transgressions against the people who purchased and then savaged them. If the system was to work in a sparsely settled land, white repression had to strain the limits of black endurance.

A slave had no legal standing. He could take no action to control his sale. He could not be a party to a lawsuit. He could not offer testimony except against another Negro. He could not swear an oath that would be legally binding. He could make no contract. He could not, generally speaking, own property other than the most insignificant of personal items. And if perchance he did come into possession of negotiable goods, he could not sell them without a permit. Nor could he hire out his own spare time (generally Saturday afternoon and Sunday except during harvest time) or otherwise seek employment. He could not have whiskey in his cabin or live alone or possess a weapon. He was not to quarrel or fight or use foul words or blow horns or beat drums. His movements and communication were rigidly restricted. No slave was to be off the plantation premises without a permit stating his destination and the time he was due back. After "hornblow," usually eight o'clock at night in winter and nine in summer, he was confined to his cabin, and the curfew was enforced by inspections and night watches that knew no rights of privacy. A slave had no privacy. Nor could more than five of them convene outside their cabins unattended by a white man without the meeting being deemed "unlawful assembly." No slave could preach except to fellow slaves and then only on his master's premises and in the presence of a white.

Of life's necessities, the slave had not many more than the minimum. His weekly food rations consisted almost unvaryingly of a peck of cornmeal, three or four pounds of meat—usually pork or bacon—and some molasses. Now and then, some fruits or vegetables would be thrown in. This starchy, high-energy diet staved off hunger and produced the appearance of good health, but it was in fact seriously deficient in protein and left the slave prone to disease and low in stamina. His clothing was of rough fiber—calicos, osnaburgs, linsey-woolseys, kerseys—and spare: two pairs of cotton shirts and pants in the spring, two shirts and a single pair of woolen pants and a jacket in the fall, and one pair of shoes the year long. The women would get two dozen yards of fabric a year and needle, thread, and buttons. Children got perhaps four shirts "made very long" but never any shoes. Considering the variety and severity of the weather to which they were exposed and the grueling work they performed each day, it was the rare bondsman whose wardrobe was anything more than rags and tatters at season's end. Their cabins were crude and cramped and dark and dirty; the loosely fitting clapboards had no insulation and winter penetrated in gusts. Total cost of maintaining a slave in such circumstances has been put at about $25 a year in antebellum currency.

Added to these endless indignities was the illegitimate state of the slave family. A century after emancipation, learned papers and eminent sociologists would speak of the matriarchal nature of the black family and the inconstant and undependable nature of the Negro father—all as if these were new and bespoke a basic weakness in the character of the race. For more than two centuries, the white masters of the South strove to institutionalize this very destabilizing condition. Slave marriages were recognized by neither church nor state. No black man could protect his conjugal rights or defend the marriage bed. No slave was ever prosecuted for fornication, adultery, or bigamy. Black couples might share not the blessed sacrament of marriage that their white exemplars took as a matter of custom and obligation but "only that concubinage with which . . . their condition is compatible." A slave father had no rights he could enforce nor ultimate authority over the children he sired, nor could he protect the mother of his children except by throwing himself on the mercy of his master. Denied all responsibility, he became irresponsible. He might come and go as whim dictated, visiting his woman's cabin two or three times a week perhaps and expressing limited interest at best in his offspring. Besides, he might be sold at any time and transported hundreds of miles to another world. It was not a life that invited enduring emotional relationships.

While the demands upon their bodies were excessive, the minds of the slaves were left frankly free to atrophy. All slaveholders agreed that the thinking slave was a potentially rebellious slave. Among the more insistently enforced sections of the black codes was the prohibition against teaching a slave to read or write or giving him or her pamphlets, not excluding the Bible or religious tracts. So apprehensive were members of the slavocracy about the great mischief that literacy might stir that in many states it was illegal to teach free as well as enslaved Negroes. And slave schools, of course, were unknown. No art or culture was permitted to touch their lives as both had done in Africa. Only the swing of the seasons brought variety to their days. Life was lived in limbo between their ancestral past, surviving only in traces amid their speech and song and dance, and the alien present, its pleasing prizes tantalizingly nearby but impassably barred to them by the white man's upraised arm.

At its creation, the United States of America was unlike any nation that had gone before it. It came into the world largely unencumbered by the limitations of custom and necessity that clamped a vise of despair upon the lives of most people on earth. In America, men would have the chance to put into practice what others had only dreamed of. In America, there were space and time and nature's bounty, and if there was travail as well, men were resolved to establish a government that might reduce the perils of survival without unduly burdening the free play of their energies. During a dozen years of painful gestation, Americans asked themselves what kind of government would achieve that purpose. At once, they determined that it had to be conceived in liberty and so they set that as their first task. But liberty for whom? Like a great many other entries in the glossary of American aspirations, liberty proved not only elusive in the quest but, once in hand, also prone to tarnishing. For the exalted ideals that Americans select to enshrine and codify have invariably outstripped their convictions. And so it was with liberty. Liberty meant, of course, liberty for white men. But nobody thought it quite seemly to put the matter thus.

On June 10, 1776, the Continental Congress appointed five of its members as a committee to draw up a Declaration of Independence. Four of them—John Adams of Massachusetts, Roger Sherman of Connecticut, Robert Livingston of New York, and Benjamin Franklin of Pennsylvania—agreed that the fifth member, thirty-three-year-old Thomas Jefferson of Virginia, had the most felicitous pen of the lot of them and assigned him the task of composing the document. He did it well, and his words of outrage and resolve, duly edited by his colleagues but unmistakably of his phrasing, have ever since riled despots and stirred their victims to rise up against them throughout the globe. Inspired principally by the writings of the English philosopher-statesman John Locke a century earlier, Jefferson wrote the now immemorial lines

> We hold these truths to be self-evident, that all men are created equal, that they are endowed by their Creator with certain inalienable Rights, that among these are Life, Liberty and the pursuit of Happiness.—That to secure these rights, Governments are instituted among Men, deriving their just powers from the consent of the governed,—That whenever any Form of Government becomes destructive of these ends, it is the Right of the People to alter or to abolish it. . . .

It was not lost upon the young Virginia squire who wrote them that while charging the British Crown with a wide range of intolerable oppressions, the American colonies were permitting yet more unendurable practices to be inflicted upon their Negro slaves. For in addition to his gifts as statesman, diplomat, author, philosopher, scientist, architect, lawyer, cartographer, geographer, engineer, educator, and violinist, Thomas Jefferson was a farmer who owned 10,000 acres in plantation land and as many as 100 slaves. Yet he professed deep loathing of slavery and took steps throughout his career to have it brought to an end. Among them was a hypocritical charge, in his original draft of the Declaration, that the King of England was a prime promoter of the slave trade. But Jefferson's language was so sharply chastising that, had it been included in the Declaration, it would have deeply undermined continuation of slavery once the colonies had severed ties to the alleged instigator of the loathsome practice. And this the slaveholding South was not prepared to consider; the offending words were struck from the great document.

The omission has not been much dwelt upon by Fourth of July orators over the ensuing generations, but it was widely recognized at the time as a self-indulgence of sizable dimension. Five years before the Declaration, Massachusetts had outlawed the future importation of slaves to her shores. A small but growing corps of artists, intellectuals, social commentators, and reformers was now stepping forward to denounce slavery as a barbaric and unmitigated evil. Newspapers and pamphlets were full of protest over the glaring inconsistency between professed egalitarianism and the ongoing fact of slavery. The ends of humanitarianism and economics dovetailed during the two decades following the Declaration as changed patterns in trading and new farming techniques required fewer slaves. State after state took steps to check the cruel system that had done so much to line the purses of Americans and expose their reputations, amid their exultant cries for liberty, to the charge of massive hypocrisy. Pennsylvania in 1780 passed a law providing for the eventual abolition of slavery. Massachusetts in 1783 abolished it altogether. Connecticut and Rhode Island in 1784 followed Pennsylvania's pattern. New York in 1785 and New Jersey the next year passed manumission acts of a broad nature, while Virginia and North Carolina enacted measures to facilitate the process. And by 1794 every state had passed legislation banning the import of new slaves.

The linchpin of the Declaration of Independence was the demand for government based on "the consent of the governed." Like the other resonant words in what was, after all, a revolutionary document and not a blueprint for nationhood, their specific meaning was not clear or very much in debate. In fact, the great majority of the newly free American people were voteless. The disenfranchised included all slaves, indentured servants, and women and the mass of men who did not own enough property to qualify as voters under the various state regulations. Though the requirements tended to be more restrictive in the Southern states, disenfranchisement by economic test was common in all states. In New York City in 1790, for example, only 1,209 residents out of 30,000 met the property qualification to vote for state senators, who in turn voted to designate the United States Senators from the state. Propertyless mechanics in Pennsylvania and Georgia were entitled to vote, but such exceptions were rare indeed. Charles Beard, in *An Economic Interpretation of the Constitution of the United States*, asserts that no more than 160,000 Americans (out of nearly four million) were in any way connected with the process of drafting and ratifying the Constitution—that is, in electing the men who chose the fifty-five delegates to the convention in Philadelphia in 1787 and passed judgment on their handiwork—and that the vote on ratification was cast by not more than one-sixth of the adult males in all thirteen states. There was no talk at Philadelphia about such ideas as universal suffrage, the rights of labor, the equality of women, free public education—concepts that would have been as alien to the delegates as wireless telegraphy or the internal-combustion engine.

What should not have been alien to them, however, were the principles of human equality so glowingly asserted just eleven years earlier by that similar group of delegates sitting in the very same place. Yet there was no talk now that all men were created equal. Or should be treated equally before the law. Or have equal opportunity to scale life's cliffs of adversity. No such language did they write into the Constitution. No such egalitarian rights were guaranteed. The purposes as stated in the Preamble—to "establish Justice, insure domestic Tranquility, provide for the common Defence, promote the general Welfare, and secure the Blessings of Liberty to ourselves and our Posterity"—were glittering enough generalities, but everything hinged on who "We the People" were and what proportion of them were to enjoy those blessings of liberty. The prospects were not encouraging for the mass of propertyless Americans. The members of the Philadelphia Convention which drafted the Constitution represented the wealthy, the influential, and the greater portion of the educated men of the country who shared what Woodrow Wilson would call "a conscious solidarity of interests." The last thing they wanted was a nation ruled by majority. Majorities were given to unruly, fickle, and imprudent conduct not useful in establishing stable governments. No, power belonged in the hands of the propertied, who were bound to wield it for the mutual benefit of all because their stakes were the highest of all.

Fifteen of the delegates to the Constitutional Convention owned slaves. And since slaves were the principal form of property other than realty in the states they represented, any effort by the convention to abolish the right to slaveholding would have been furiously opposed. If abolition were to come eventually, each state would have to decide the question itself; no national government would or could force it upon the great planters and their allies.

Neither the word "slave" nor "black" nor "Negro" nor "African" nor "colored" was therefore written anywhere in the document those men composed that very long summer. Considering that the subject of slavery was perhaps the most inflammable question on the agenda and provoked sharp exchanges each time it came up, one is tempted to conclude that the lack of any direct allusion to it in the final version of the Constitution was testimony to either the statesmanlike discreetness or the lily-livered mendacity of the delegates. Some 675,000 slaves were then residing in the thirteen states, all but about 7 percent of them in the five southernmost ones and almost half the total living in Virginia alone. Nearly one American in every five was a slave. Even if his master could have been persuaded or paid to part with him, what place could the black man have occupied in this struggling nation if he were free as any white? That he had been brought here against his will was undeniable, but it was also now a matter of history that could not be undone by words on paper. That, unshackled, he too might add his strength and spirit to the building of a great country was a notion that few men had the courage or vision to contemplate in 1787. The slave was simply not equipped to function as a free and responsible member of society. That he had been studiously maintained in such a condition by his master was not a matter on the agenda, nor would anyone place it there.

The convention bogged down early over how the states would be represented in the new government—whether equally or proportionately to size, whether in a legislature with one house or two. Before the first great compromise of the summer could be worked out (namely, a bicameral legislature, the upper house composed of two Senators from each state, the lower house proportioned according to the population of the states), the weight to be given to the slave population had to be determined. As discussion began on an equitable ratio of representation, John Rutledge and Pierce Butler of South Carolina proposed that the basis be "according to the quotas of contributions." In other words, whoever contributed the most in taxes to the national government would have the largest say in its operation. Before that plutocratic fancy could be voted on, it was suggested that each state be represented under the same formula that the Continental Congress had applied in 1783 in determining what each should contribute to the confederated government then existing:

> in proportion to the whole number of white and other free Citizens and inhabitants of every age, sex, and condition, including those bound to servitude for a term of years, and three fifths of all other persons not comprehended in the foregoing description, except Indians, not paying taxes in each State.

The words "three fifths of all other persons" were universally understood to mean the slaves. Now, in Philadelphia, as the various plans of representation were shuffled on and off the floor throughout June and July, the South Carolina delegates tried to improve on the "three fifths" bargain in the confidence that they could lose little in the effort. When it was suggested that an official census be taken at regular intervals as the basis for representation, with the three-fifths principle applying, Butler and Charles Cotesworth Pinckney were up in their places at once and asserting that "blacks be included . . . equally with Whites." The labor of a Carolina slave was as productive and valuable as that of a free man in Massachusetts, they pointed out, and since wealth was the "great means of defence and utility to the Nation," it ought to count as much—especially, Butler added in a telltale aside that disclosed his delegation's view of the true value of the union, "in a Government which was instituted principally for the protection of property, and was itself to be supported by property."

Only Georgia and Delaware went along. Because the margin against was so heavy, South Carolina suddenly faced the possibility that its offensive proposal might backfire: the delegates moved to reconsider their earlier decision to count three-fifths of the slaves as inhabitants. But James Wilson of Pennsylvania, for one, did not see what principle could be invoked in defense of the three-fifths device. Either slaves were citizens and should count equally with whites in determining the population basis or they were property, in which case they should not count at all. On a vote, six states—one short of a majority—came out against counting any slaves in determining the basis for representation. South Carolina had nearly turned victory into defeat. When it was then proposed that taxes be proportioned among the states according to their representation, only wealthy South Carolina and slave-hungry Georgia agreed, on the proviso that all of their bondsmen be counted as inhabitants. But the other slave states would not buy the bargain, and North Carolina and Virginia proposed that the convention retreat to the sensible original basis of compromise: a slave was three-fifths of a free white man. James Madison, whose performance as philosopher, strategist, and legal technician at Philadelphia has come to be regarded by history as masterful, explained the compromise in *The Federalist, No. 54* in a tone that reveals something of his own lack of fondness for slavery:

> . . . In being compelled to labor not for himself, but for a master; in being vendible by one master to another master; and in being subject at all times to being restrained in his liberty, and chastised in his body, by the capricious will of another, the slave may appear to be degraded from the human rank, and classed with those irrational animals, which fall under the legal denomination of property. . . . The Federal Constitution therefore, decides with great propriety on the case of our slaves, when it views them in the mixt character of persons and of property. This is in fact their true character.
>
> . . . Let the compromising expedient of the Constitution be mutually adopted, which regards them as inhabitants, but as debased by servitude below the equal level of free inhabitants, which regards the *slave* as divested of two fifths of the *man.*

There it was, stated in the most reasonable, and monstrous, fashion. White supremacy and black degradation were institutionalized within the very framework of the new government. The convention moved on to other trying business.

It was late August when the slavery issue exploded anew. A delegate from Maryland proposed that the importation of slaves be taxed. Not only was the institution itself denounced as dishonorable but its continuing traffic, it was said, would enhance the position of the slave states in the House of Representatives while increasing the peril of black insurrection in those same states, which would naturally turn to the United States to help quell it. The gauntlet had been flung in South Carolina's face.

The state's ex-governor, John Rutledge, rose in all his majesty to answer. He tended to speak too rapidly to be rated an outstanding orator, but this day he spoke with what Madison noted as "cold precision." If Virginia, most populous state in the Union and leader of the Southern bloc, was consumed by ambivalence toward its widespread practice of slavery and could not square it with the ennobling principle of men's natural rights, South Carolina suffered no such pangs of conscience. "Religion and humanity have nothing to do with this question," declared Rutledge. "Interest alone is the governing principle with nations. The true question at present is whether the Southern states shall or shall not be parties to the Union. If the Northern states consult their interest, they will not oppose the increase of slaves which will increase the commodities of which they will become the carriers." The next day,

George Mason of Virginia lashed back, denouncing the slave trade as "the infernal traffic" and adding:

> The present question concerns not the importing states alone but the whole Union. . . . Slavery discourages arts and manufactures. The poor despise labor when performed by slaves. They prevent the immigration of whites, who really enrich and strengthen a country. They produce the most pernicious effect on manners. Every master of slaves is born a petty tyrant. They bring the judgment of heaven on a country. As nations can not be rewarded or punished in the next world they must in this. By an inevitable chain of causes and effects, providence punishes national sins, by national calamities.

Young Charles Pinckney of South Carolina stood firm in rebuttal. If slavery were wrong, he asked, why had it been "justified by the example of all the world"? He cited Greece, Rome, and other ancient societies as practitioners. His older cousin, Charles Cotesworth Pinckney, added with passion that his state and Georgia could not manage without their slaves, though Virginia would grow rich by the cessation of the slave trade since the Old Dominion had more blacks than it needed and would dispose of them to other states in a market of rising prices.

The matter was referred to committee for compromise, and so it was that though every state except Georgia had already passed a law outlawing or suspending the overseas slave trade, the Constitution of the United States would speak in conciliatory terms on the subject in deference to the unbending stand of the delegates from Charleston:

> The Migration or Importation of such Persons as any of the States now existing shall think proper to admit, shall not be prohibited by the Congress prior to the Year one thousand eight hundred and eight, but a Tax or duty may be imposed on such Importation, not exceeding ten dollars for each Person.

Almost as an afterthought, Butler persuaded the delegates to go along with a discreetly worded fugitive-slave provision—a custom that could claim honorable antecedents as far back as Hammurabi's Code, which had prescribed death for harboring a fugitive or helping a slave escape. With scarcely a whimper, the third and final veiled allusion to slavery was added to the Constitution:

> No Person held to Service or Labour in one State, under the Laws thereof, escaping into another, shall, in Consequence of any Law or Regulation therein, be discharged from such Service or Labour, but shall be delivered up on Claim of the Party to whom such Service or Labour may be due.

Discretion, though, did not veil the intent of the provision: no state could get away with encouraging slaves to escape and then harboring them within its borders.

Thus, the framers of the Constitution failed in any way to mitigate the condition of the slave and thereby consolidated the hold of his tormentor. In the fundamental conflict between human rights and property rights that was implicit in the slave question, the men who cast the mold of basic national policy did not hesitate to select the latter. They saw no choice—or would not, at any rate, admit to any for fear of the consequences. And so they passed the conflict on to other generations.

Having won its freedom and established its form of government, the nation over which George Washington presided in uneasy eminence now had to figure out how to make a living. In the South, tobacco, once the glory of the region, had been overproduced, flooding European markets and badly depleting the soil at home; it was no longer a profitable crop. Indigo had declined with the end of British bounties, and the rice crops were down sharply since the intricate dike and drainage systems needed to produce sizable harvests had fallen into disrepair during the war. Without staples to ship, the South had begun to feel slavery a great black albatross around its neck.

The South, though, was not about to surrender its whole way of life and devote itself to harvesting hominy and rutabagas by the googol. It knew perfectly well the remedy for its ailment. Even before 1800, steam-powered cotton mills were dotting Lancashire and consuming all the cotton that the West Indies, Brazil, India, and other growing regions could send it. All they needed was cotton, and the Southern states of America knew it.

Eli Whitney's separating machine—the cotton gin—was patented in March of 1794 and did the work of fifty pairs of hands. Within a year, the upland fields of Georgia and South Carolina were blooming with white. Cotton was selling for a lofty forty cents a pound. Planter after planter turned eagerly to the new crop. What had been a 9,000-bale curiosity in 1791 had become a 79,000-bale harvest by 1800. Planters had a product now that the world wanted, and they would grow it with abandon. They would beat back the forest with their mules and plows and black men, they would ford the Mississippi and send steamboats down it to the Gulf, they would feed the railroads and spur the nation's growth and build an empire within it and live grandly. In time, the Cotton Belt would cover almost 300 million acres of black earth in a huge arc running 1,600 miles in length and 300 miles in width from eastern North Carolina to western Texas. By 1822, cotton production reached half a million bales; by 1831, a million; by 1840, two million; by 1852, three million; by 1860, more than five million—all but one-fifth of it exported to Britain and the Continent.

The growing sentiment to emancipate the slaves that had been detectable in many places, most notably Pennsylvania and Virginia, at the time the Constitution was being drafted and ratified soon dimmed. In the South Carolina Piedmont, where there had been 15,000 slaves in 1790, there would be more than 25,000 in 1800 and nearly 50,000 by 1810. In Mississippi, where there had been 3,489 slaves officially recorded in 1800, there were 136,621 by 1840. The Southern way west was thus paved by and with black men. The slavocracy, moreover, moved west stride for stride, and state for state, with the free-soilers; there was a symmetry to it that cannot be mistaken as the nation turned from the deliberations at Philadelphia and began its march across the continent.

Six of the original thirteen states practiced slavery—Maryland, Delaware, Virginia, the Carolinas, and Georgia—and by 1800 the sides were evened at eight to eight after Vermont was granted statehood in 1791 and slaveholding Kentucky and Tennessee joined in 1792 and 1796 respectively. Ohio in 1803 became the first of the five free-soil states to be carved from the old Northwest Territory, where Congress had banned the practice in 1787. Louisiana, where slavery had long been sanctioned by the French, became in 1812 the first of the states to be carved from the new Louisiana Purchase lands. Then, taking turns to keep the slave- and free-state sides in equilibrium, came Indiana in 1816, Mississippi in 1817, Illinois (a part, like Indiana, of the Northwest Territory) in 1818, and Alabama in 1819. That brought the count to eleven slave and eleven free states in the year 1820. When Missouri, the second of the former Louisiana Purchase territories to apply for admission, sought entrance as a slaveholding state, the North abruptly put on the brake. Missouri would give the slave states control of the Senate—a prospect the North was not prepared to accept without a fight. Tensions rose throughout the nation as Congress sought a compromise. The timely decision by Maine to break off from Massachusetts kept the sides in parity: Missouri would enter as a slave state, Maine as a free state, and slavery would henceforth be prohibited in the remaining portion of the Louisiana Purchase territory north of Missouri's southern boundary, Missouri itself excepted. On the face of it, the North had the better of the Missouri Compromise, since by far the greater portion of the Louisiana Territory lay in the slave-free zone, but the climate and the soil there would likely have proven largely inhospitable to plantation agriculture and slave labor.

The crisis averted, the country paused in its pell-mell adolescent growth for a decade and caught its breath. It was then, though, that isolated individuals and a few small groups began lighting the candles of abolition anew. An itinerant saddler named Benjamin Lundy began editing a sheet called the *Genius of Universal Emancipation* in 1821, and if it did not move mountains, its very name was at least a thin pennant in the wind. There were other pennants soon, with names like the *Manumission Intelligencer*, the *Emancipator*, and the *Patriot*, and then in January of 1831 a former assistant of Lundy named William Lloyd Garrison brought out the first number of his *Liberator* and there was a disturbing new voice in the land. Garrison's militancy stirred the first wave in a crusade almost quasi-religious in its liturgy: slavery was wrong because it plainly violated the teachings of Christ that all men were created in the image of God and were therefore brothers. And it was plainly wrong because it violated the most basic, inalienable, and self-evident right in the American credo—that of personal liberty. Its perpetrators were arrogant tyrants intoxicated with their power and ought to be brought down. Garrison's New England Anti-Slavery Society was formed the same year as the *Liberator* and was soon spawning similar action and lecture groups. If the South was inclined at first to dismiss the movement as staffed by ranting dervishes, it abruptly stopped when Nat Turner's insurrection near Norfolk that same year took sixty white lives and had to be put down by state and federal troops. Garrison applauded the uprising, and the slaveholders understood that they had a true incendiary on their hands. The South grew vigilant as it had never been before.

Its impulse to expand, however, was only slowed, not quelled, by such concerns. And so the perilous seesaw contest between the sections went on in the Thirties—Arkansas came into the Union as a slave state under the Missouri Compromise and Michigan as a free state under the Northwest Territory laws—and picked up momentum in the Forties. When Wisconsin joined the Union as the fifth and last of the Northwest Territory states in 1848, it brought the count of free-soil and slave states back to fifteen on each side. That year, gold was discovered in California, which now loomed as a gleaming trophy to both sides. A new crisis was at hand amid a growing sense of foreboding about the eventual fate of a Union half dedicated to slavery and half proclaiming its insistence on universal liberty.

The Compromise of 1850—California would enter as a free state, the other new territories would be organized without mention of slavery in their charters (leaving the ultimate decision to the residents at the time of statehood), a toughened fugitive-slave law would take effect, and slave trading would henceforth cease in the District of Columbia—proved a mark-time measure that satisfied neither side. South Carolina and other Deep South states talked secession. In the North, the underground railway carried growing numbers of runaway slaves, dogged by pursuers bent on exercising their employers' constitutional right to reclaim fleeing property. Fervor rose on both sides, stoked by such fuel as *Uncle Tom's Cabin*, appearing in book form in 1852 and soon rending hearts in stage versions as well. It sold an astonishing 300,000 copies in the first year alone—a one-woman outcry that carried across the land. That same year, the city of Rochester, New York, asked its most eminent citizen to deliver the Fourth of July oration. It proved a notable occasion because of both the speaker, who was an ex-slave, and what he said. Tall, straight, muscular, with flashing eyes and a voice of oak that rolled out its phrases in driving cadence, the thirty-five-year-old abolitionist leader Frederick Douglass rose and declared:

> What to the American slave is your Fourth of July? I answer, a day that reveals to him more than all other days of the year, the gross injustice and cruelty to which he is the constant victim. To him your celebration is a sham; your boasted liberty an unholy license; your national greatness, swelling vanity; your sounds of rejoicing are empty and heartless; your denunciation of tyrants, brass-fronted impudence; your shouts of liberty and equality, hollow mockery; your prayers and hymns, your sermons and thanksgivings, with all your religious parade and solemnity, are to him mere bombast, fraud, deception, impiety, and hypocrisy—a thin veil to cover up crimes that would disgrace a nation of savages. There is not a nation of the earth guilty of practices more shocking and bloody than are the people of these United States at this very hour.

Within two more years, the lull won by the Compromise of 1850 was in smithereens. The Kansas-Nebraska Act, a gesture of appeasement to the seething South, allowed the territories of Kansas and Nebraska—part of the Louisiana Purchase lands that were north of Missouri's southern boundary and therefore free soil under the 1820 compromise—to be organized with the question of slavery to be determined by the territorial legislatures. The congressional prohibition was at an end. Kansas would be the staging ground for civil war. Both sides sponsored parties of settlers in a race to prevail. The South proclaimed that its residents' constitutional right to possess property could not be stripped from them in any of the territories—and slaves were property. But the South failed to appreciate how passionately hostile the free-soil settlers were toward slavery and the whole plantation system. It had little to do with humanitarian motives. Rather, the new immigrants saw the grand opportunity before them—here was free, open land and plenty of it; nothing like it remained in Europe—but to be thrown into direct competition with slaves would almost surely mean the eventual absorption of Western land by the plantation system. There could be no coexistence. It was the same attitude essentially as the one that workmen in the North had long displayed toward free Negroes, whom they feared and resented as job rivals and a depressant on wage levels. And so neither the working masses of the North nor the homesteading farmers of the West demanded that slavery be ended and the black man be enfranchised and otherwise granted political equality.

The black man's prospect was thus scarcely more inviting outside the South than within it. North and South, he was classified as a lower form of human life and therefore fair game for continual debasement. He was held accountable, in short, for what had been done to him. Beyond the abolitionist circle, few Northerners believed that the slave, once freed, could be meshed politically, socially, or economically with the dominant white society. Free blacks were generally denied political equality and were everywhere denied social equality. They were disenfranchised in Delaware in 1792, in Kentucky in 1799, in Maryland and Ohio in 1799, and in New Jersey in 1807. Between 1814 and 1861, they were either denied the vote or drastically restricted in their access to it in Connecticut, New York, Rhode Island, Tennessee, North Carolina, Pennsylvania, Indiana, Illinois, Michigan, Iowa, Wisconsin, Minnesota, and—after the bleeding there was over—Kansas. In New York, for example, free Negroes could vote only if they met a discriminatory property qualification of $250; no such qualification was required of whites. By custom, Negroes were excluded from jury service throughout the North. They were either kept off of or assigned to Jim Crow sections of public conveyances of every sort, from stagecoach to steamboat; most theaters, restaurants, and public lodgings were closed to them, and in those churches that continued to practice interracial worship the black man prayed in pews put aside for him, usually as far aside as possible.

While Kansas was being turned into a battleground over the permissibility of slavery there, the legal issue was being confronted by the Supreme Court of the United States. Five of the nine members were from slave states, including the frail, deeply respected, eighty-year-old Chief Justice, Roger Brooke Taney of Maryland, then in his twenty-first year on the high court. The son of a tobacco-plantation owner, he had many years before manumitted his own slaves. In an opinion delivered on March 6, 1857, two Justices from the North joined their Southern brethren to strike down an act of Congress for only the second time in the nation's history. The first time, in *Marbury v. Madison*, the principle of judicial supremacy—the Court's power to overrule statutes it finds inimical to the Constitution—was inferentially established. Now, in *Dred Scott v. Sanford*, the Court made a finding scarcely less momentous. The Missouri Compromise of 1820 was invalid, Taney declared in accepting the basic Southern position of the 1850s, because no citizen could be deprived of his property without due process of law as guaranteed by the Fifth Amendment. And a slave was undeniably property. Congress could therefore not outlaw slavery in any territory under its jurisdiction. Moreover, the plaintiff before the Court, Dred Scott himself, a slave who had sued his owner on the ground that his temporary residence on free soil had removed his slave status, was not entitled to sue because he was not a citizen, nor in fact was any Negro, Taney wrote. The heart of the matter, his long, careful opinion said, was the status of the black man at the time the Declaration of Independence proclaimed the equality of all men:

> . . . it is too clear for dispute, that the enslaved African race were not intended to be included, and formed no part of the people who framed and adopted this declaration; for if the language, as understood in that day, would embrace them, the conduct of the distinguished men who framed the Declaration of Independence would have been utterly and flagrantly inconsistent with the principles they asserted; and instead of the sympathy of mankind, to which they so confidently appealed, they would have deserved and received universal rebuke and reprobation.
>    . . . They perfectly understood the meaning of the language they used, and how it would be understood by others; and they knew that it would not in any part of the civilized world be supposed to embrace the negro race, which, by common consent, had been excluded from civilized Governments and the family of nations, and doomed to slavery. . . . The unhappy black race were separated from the white by indelible marks, and laws long before established, and were never thought of or spoken of except as property, and when the claims of the owner or the profit of the trader were supposed to need protection.

The old Chief Justice then added the words that sealed the stamp of white supremacy on the great document, which he said was adopted under the general agreement that Negroes were

> beings of an inferior order, and altogether unfit to associate with the white race, either in social or political relations; and so far inferior that they had no rights which the white man was bound to respect.

And so the South moved toward the apex of its power. It possessed nearly four million slaves to do its drudgery. Cotton was blooming as never before. The federal government had proven pliable to Southern interests. In fact, it had nearly become a Southern plaything. Since the nation was founded, the South had provided 11 out of 15 Presidents, 17 out of 28 Justices of the Supreme Court, 14 out of 19 Attorneys General, 21 out of 34 Speakers of the House, and 80 out of 134 foreign ministers. And it dominated the Army and Navy. Now the Supreme Court had sanctioned its views regarding slavery, and the South could anticipate a boundless future either as a semi-independent section of the Union or, if the Union failed to pay it proper homage, as a separate nation, funded by its great annual cotton crop, with territorial ambitions not necessarily restricted by the Rio Grande.

Or so it seemed if you did not look very hard. And many in the South did not look at all. If they did, they refused to believe that the structure they had so grandly erected was about ready to split apart at the seams. It would have been hard to invent a more wasteful economic system. At its base was the black slave, who had no hope of improving his lot in life and thus no reason to work harder than he needed to in order to survive. To register their resistance, the bondsmen malingered whenever they could, fought any change in their work quotas, put rocks or dirt at the bottom of their baskets to fatten loads lightened by loafing, and used a whole range of guerrilla tactics—from busting tools and mistreating animals to taking out their fury on the cotton itself by damaging young plants and picking "trashy" bolls. If the system was wasteful of labor, it was still more wasteful of the Southland's earth itself. The soil, light to begin with, was steadily pounded by the heavy rainfall of the region, and cotton and other cash crops failed to bind the topsoil. The cheap wrought-iron plows given the slaves in the 1840s and after stirred the ground to a depth of only a few inches. The net effect of these factors was to rob the soil of its fertility and invite severe erosion. Corrective measures were readily available, to be sure, but in the long run it was cheaper not to bother restoring the land, for land was in far greater supply—half a nation of it, as the South kept adding states during the first fifty years of the century—than either labor or cold cash for the mountains of fertilizer it would have taken to make much headway against the chronic erosion. It was easier just to keep devouring new land, bring in the heaviest cash crops as fast as they could be harvested for as long as the land held out, and then move on.

Each new expansion of the cotton kingdom required massive infusions of capital to buy land, move slaves and supply them, and otherwise underwrite the time period when fields were being readied for production. Much of the seed money came from Northern and British financiers, and at interest rates that were far more predictable than the price of cotton grown on the new land. Here was a steady drain on the South's profits. And once the harvests were brought in, the planters found themselves too often at the mercy of the market. Their single-crop economy had no elasticity to cope with reverses like dropping prices or rising interest rates. And profits were siphoned off on all sides by willful failure to diversify: the South paid far more than it should have for food imported from the West and for what basic manufactured goods it imported from the North when instead it should have been accumulating capital to supply these needs locally and to develop labor-saving technology. But that was precisely what the planters did not want to do. Labor was their capital, and their capital was in their slaves. They kept putting their profits into slavery, going increasingly into debt to do so if they had to, for slaves were the very root of their power as men, the source of their increasingly bloated pride, the foundation of their claims to a uniquely admirable civilization. They would do anything to keep their slaves, for without them they would be like other men.

For all their political power, social charm, and apparent prosperity, then, the men who owned and ruled the South were living beyond their means. It was a way of life they loved too much to tolerate criticism of its values or its financial soundness. They would not take the steps necessary to integrate their region into the national economy—one in which a dynamic home market would absorb a major part of production, capital could accumulate and build more efficient means of production, and agriculture could demand its fair share of the profits earned by the nation's overall productive performance. Instead, they sought to keep adding territory because that was the only way to keep the whole gaudy contraption from breaking down. The South *had* to keep growing, and so its political performance on the national level was perforce brilliant and determined. Its spokesmen maneuvered with a sureness that had shaded into arrogance. They would have their own way or they would go their own way. They did not fully understand how they had been manipulated by Northern financiers, shippers, railroads, and other commercial interests that were using the South's great white harvest to offset the enormous quantity of goods that the nation, especially the West, was importing. The cotton crop served, in effect, as America's collateral for its overseas credits, and so the businessmen of the North were not gladly going to suffer the South's willful departure from the Union. Yet neither were the infant industrialists of Connecticut and Pennsylvania going to tear down tariff walls they needed to protect themselves from foreign competition in order to placate Southern planters who, as chronic exporters and importers, ardently favored free-trade policies. Nor were the new farmers clearing and plowing the prairies about to let the slavemasters push them into a corner of the Western plains as the poor whites had been shoved aside in the South. Nor were the abolitionists ready to accept the Supreme Court's holding that the sway of slavery could not legally be contained.

The moment of inevitable collision had come. It had many manifestations—economic, political, social, moral—but its underlying cause was the system of labor that ambitious settlers had hit upon two centuries earlier when it was clear that their own limbs would not suffice to wrench wealth speedily enough from the new land.

History has lifted no chief of state to a more exalted eminence than the angular sixteenth President of the United States. Men have come to venerate him as the incomparable exemplar of selfless leadership, as much spiritual as political in essence. He sits there in Washington still, like God Himself in judgment of us all, an enormous graven image in marble and a living spirit most especially to black Americans, who have beatified his memory and credited him with the deliverance of their race from bondage.

Iconography aside, Abraham Lincoln was a man of his time and place and station. He was not a passionate freedom fighter or a believer in the equality of all men of all races. Lincoln's own words belie his latter-day reputation. In his series of seven stump debates with Stephen Douglas for the latter's senatorial seat in 1858, the tall man won much applause for declaring his unequivocal opposition to social and political equality for Negroes. He did not approve of their voting. Or holding office. Or serving on juries. Or, to be sure, marrying whites. He favored their ultimate resettlement back in Africa, but so long as they remained in America ". . . there must be the position of superior and inferior, and I as much as any other man am in favor of having the superior position assigned to the white race." In the White House, he held to his views. He told a delegation of visiting free black leaders that in his judgment most white Americans did not want the black man to remain on their shores. His opposition to slavery and its cruelties was firm, but he came into the presidency emphasizing that he had no wish to end the practice where it prevailed—only to prevent its spread. His entire purpose was to preserve the Union. But the South was unified and militant, the North divided and uncertain. Lincoln was a minority President, a nobody-much from out of the West, and homely as sin. A fratricidal war to keep the long-sparring halves of the country together was beyond the endurance of a badly splintered electorate, the South assumed. Preservation of the Union was simply too abstract a ground to fight upon, and so it would be a swift and successful rebellion, after which the Confederacy and the Union might deal with one another as equals.

But it soon became clear that it would not be a short contest. The South had a mission and better generals. The North had far more people and money. Lincoln's moderate position on the aims of the war gave way as the ghastly killing mounted. Since, at bottom, the black man was the issue, he would have to be freed if a war of this magnitude were to be morally justified. Lincoln proposed a constitutional amendment to accomplish the task. It provided for gradual, voluntary emancipation, culminating no later than the year 1900. The slaveholding states would administer the process themselves, and the federal government would cooperate in reimbursing slaveholders for the loss of their mortal property and in helping colonize the freed slaves. But the country was moving swiftly to a far more radical view of the issue. Lincoln's amendment was not seriously entertained by Congress. He could not hold the anti-slavery forces in check. Men's passions rose with the body count. The war had passed the stage of a police action. The next step would move the sides beyond any hope of reconciliation.

He delayed it as long as he could. He twice overruled field commanders who had issued edicts of abolition in their war zones. He pondered the obviously troubling matter of constitutional authority for the step. The Constitution had left the lawfulness of slavery up to the separate states. The only legal ground Lincoln could plausibly stand on in issuing the Emancipation Proclamation was that of war-emergency power in his role as commander-in-chief, and so he used it on the first day of the year 1863. Technically, it is true, it did not free anybody within Lincoln's territorial command. It applied only to those slaves in rebel states, excluding parts of Virginia and Louisiana then under Union control. It did not mention the rest of the Union, for there would have been no military justification for such a step. But it did confirm what was happening on the battlefield: it formally invited freed slaves to join the Union army—a step they had taken right along.

Emancipation as a war measure only would not suffice, and for the better part of the next two years Congress debated the wording and implications of a constitutional amendment to free the slaves forever. What rights were to be enjoyed by the freedmen? Were they to become citizens like any other despite their obvious disabilities? Was there perhaps some intermediate stage of citizenship through which the black people ought to evolve? From the language of the Thirteenth Amendment as finally proposed by resolution of Congress on the last day of January 1865, such questions seem not to have been confronted:

> SECTION 1. Neither slavery nor involuntary servitude, except as a punishment for crime whereof the party shall have been duly convicted, shall exist within the United States, or any place subject to their jurisdiction.

> SECTION 2. Congress shall have power to enforce this article by appropriate legislation.

In fact, the sweep of the amendment had been debated endlessly, and the prevailing view was that by emancipation, every freed black man would stand equal before the law with every white one—except in the matter of voting. Even the most radical of the Republicans and abolitionists, not excluding Horace Greeley and William Lloyd Garrison, were not willing to go that far. By the second section of the amendment, Congress was empowered to take active steps against any state that perpetuated the practice of slavery or the deprivation of rights resulting from it. Opponents of the amendment were left shaken by the very sweep of the measure. It would revolutionize the Constitution, not amend it, they said. It was a wholesale, unwarrantable invasion of the rights of the states and a grievous extension of the power of the central government beyond any bounds ever envisioned for it. The entire federal compact was imperiled by the step. Yet it passed Congress overwhelmingly and was ratified within ten months by twenty-seven states. The niceties of the thus redefined federal compact were dwarfed by the enormity of the conflict just ended. And so the law of the land, seventy-eight years after it was first drawn, now held that the black man was five-fifths of a human being. Beyond that, the language itself did not go, whatever the framers and opponents of the new amendment chose to read into it in the early months of 1865.

Ranged against those few words on paper were two centuries of custom. The black man was clearly going to need help to make his freedom a fact as well as a right. He could scarely look for that help from the people who had subjugated him, and so he looked North and to the Yankee troops in his midst.

Soon after passing the Thirteenth Amendment, Congress took the first step. It was a modest one, given the size of the problem presented by the sudden casting adrift of four million black souls with very few pennies to their names. It was a new creature of the War Department, and its manifold functions were reflected in its inelegant name: The Bureau of Refugees, Freedmen, and Abandoned Lands—for short, the Freedmen's Bureau. Upon it was heaped an unimaginable number of chores: provision of food, clothing, and medical care for refugees both white and black; their resettlement on abandoned or confiscated lands where available; overseeing the transition of freedmen to the status of workingmen with full contractual rights in dealing with landlords; and the establishment of schools to achieve at least marginal literacy as rapidly and as widely as possible. The bureau was given one year to function after the war ended and very meager funding. But it was a start, at least—a place for the bewildered freedman to turn. A month after the bill was enacted, Lee surrendered to Grant at Appomattox. Five days later, Abraham Lincoln was dead. The fate of the black man's transition from slavery to liberty now passed into the hands of a man from Tennessee who, it turned out, did not much favor it.

Andrew Johnson, a spiritual and political descendant of Andrew Jackson, hated slavery more for what it had done to the poor-whites of the South than to those in actual bondage. He had favored the war because, frankly, it had "freed more whites than blacks." An avowed foe of the planters, the new President nevertheless soon showed himself to be an easy mark for the fallen masters of the Confederacy. To regain admission to the Union and its seats in Congress, each state of the late Confederacy was obliged only to summon a constitutional convention—to qualify as a participant one had merely to take a non-blood oath of allegiance to the Union or to have been formally pardoned by the President—that would repeal its acts of secession, repudiate the Confederate debt, and abolish slavery in conformity with the Thirteenth Amendment. The planters and other scarcely remorseful Confederates who quickly took command of the new governments saw that this piddling business was disposed of in a fashion that ranged from perfunctory to occasionally outright defiant (South Carolina, for example, refused to repudiate the Confederate debt). By December of 1865, Andrew Johnson reported to Congress that his plan for reconstruction had been accomplished. Congress listened to the President, reviewed reports to it by investigators it had sent South, and concluded that neither the President nor the former Confederate States of America understood what the war had been all about and who had won it.

Aside from abolishing slavery, the South would voluntarily make no provision at all for the Negro. His liberation had cost the plantocracy between two and three billion dollars, using the pre-war auction-block price per head as the basis for calculation. That was a great deal of value to lose overnight. The very sight of a former slave was reminder to his former owner that the world had changed drastically. Those proud heads born to command had been made to bend. They did not like the sensation. Whites of all classes viewed any deviation from the antebellum fashion of subservience as a display of impudence by the Negro and did not hesitate to beat him for it. He was, after all, no longer the property of a white man. The journalist Carl Schurz reported back to the Senate:

> Wherever I go—the street, the shop, the house, the hotel, or the steamboat—I hear the people talk in such a way as to indicate that they are yet unable to conceive of the Negro as possessing any rights at all. . . . To kill a Negro, they do not deem murder; to debauch a Negro woman, they do not think fornication; to take the property away from a Negro, they do not consider robbery. The people boast that when they get freedmen's affairs in their own hands, to use their own expression, "the niggers will catch hell."
>
> The reason of all this is simple and manifest. The whites esteem the blacks their property by natural right, and however much they admit that the individual relations of masters and slaves have been destroyed . . . they still have an ingrained feeling that the blacks at large belong to the whites at large.

State policy followed private conviction. None of the states reconstructed under the Johnson plan gave the freedman the vote or any other form of participation in the civic life of his state. Nor did any of the state governments make provisions for the education of the freedman. The prevailing view was that a little learning would spoil the Negro for hard work, and if he were not available to till the fields, it was not readily apparent who would be.

Beyond such sins of omission, the so-called reconstructed states of the South displayed their active truculence by imposing a series of tightly restrictive laws on the movement and behavior of their former slaves. These Black Codes were designed to fasten the Negro to the very misfortune he sought to escape. To seek more attractive work terms, a freedman would of course have had to leave his old plantation in search of a new arrangement, but the moment he did so, he was liable to charges of vagrancy and a fine. The fine might be paid by any landholder, who could then command the alleged vagrant's services—a form, that is, of involuntary servitude proscribed by the newly effective Thirteenth Amendment. In Florida, any Negro failing to fulfill his employment contract or who was impudent to the owner of the land he worked was subject to being declared a vagrant and punished accordingly. In Louisiana, the black laborer had to enter into a written contract within the first ten days of the year and, having done so, "shall not be allowed to leave his place of employment until the fulfillment of his contract, unless by consent of his employer . . . and if they do so leave, without cause or permission, they shall forfeit all wages earned to the time of abandonment." Mississippi simply re-enacted its old slave codes *en masse*. And South Carolina, as usual, set the standard of vehemence for the South. No "person of color" was permitted to enter and reside in the state unless he posted a bond within twenty days of arriving, guaranteed by two white property owners, for $1,000 "conditioned for his good behavior, and for his support." Any Negro who wished to work in the state at an occupation other than farmer or servant had to be especially licensed, had to prove his or her fitness for the work, and pay an annual tax ranging from $10 to $100. To do farm work, a Negro in South Carolina had to have a written contract, attested to by white witnesses; failure to obtain one before commencing to work was a misdemeanor punishable by a fine of from $5 to $50. Contracting Negroes were known as "servants" and the contractors as "masters." Labor was from sunrise to sunset; servants were to be quiet and orderly and to go to bed at a reasonable time. Masters might discharge servants for disobedience, drunkenness, disease, or any of a number of other reasons, none requiring corroboration. A master could command a servant to aid him in defense of his own person, family, or property. The right to sell farm products "without having written evidence from such master, or some person authorized by him, or from the district judge or a magistrate, that he has the right to sell such product" was strictly forbidden.

Such measures, President Johnson told the Senate with a straight face in December of 1865, "confer upon freedmen the privileges which are essential to their comfort, protection, and security." But Congress would not acquiesce in that judgment. The South had been handed an olive branch and, in the fury of defeat, had shaped it into a whip. A less willful people would perhaps have known what the South had failed to appreciate: if it did not rein in its excessive intolerance of the free black man, the North would force it to do so.

After December of 1865, Johnson was a President who presided in name only. Congress formed the powerful Joint Committee of Fifteen to monitor the rest of the reconstruction process. Its dominant voice belonged to the seventy-three-year-old Pennsylvanian Thaddeus Stevens, a founder of the Republican Party, who declared that America did not stand for "white man's government" and to say as much was "political blasphemy, for it violates the fundamental principles of our gospel of liberty. This is man's government; the government of all men alike." Lincoln would have put it more eloquently, no doubt, and would perhaps have proven a man for all seasons, while Stevens was portrayed by his detractors as a crotchety old bachelor bitter over his lifelong condition as a cripple and vindictive toward the South ever since Lee's army had destroyed his ironworks in Caledonia, Pennsylvania. Whether by animus or conviction, Stevens was moved to drive Congress to act.

The Thirteenth Amendment had nationalized the right to freedom. And it made Congress the instrument to enforce that right. Congress began to do so early in 1866 by two acts of legislation—the extension of the Freedmen's Bureau Bill and the first Civil Rights Act. The two acts shared a premise: freedmen were to be protected in their "civil rights and immunities" by the government of the United States and not left to the unmerciful ministrations of the states. In the case of the Freedmen's Bureau Bill, the protection would be carried out by agents of the federal bureau; in the case of the Civil Rights Bill, by the federal courts. Nor were those "rights and immunities" left as generalized pledges. Both of the bills contained a section specifying in identical language the guaranteed rights that, when taken together, were aimed directly at destroying the plainly vicious Black Codes. Among them were the right to make and enforce contracts; the right to buy, sell, and own real and personal property; the right to sue, be parties in a legal action, and give evidence; and most sweeping and basic of all, the right to "full and equal benefit of all laws and proceedings for the security of person and estate." As a package, these rights embodied the basic tenet of abolitionist theory—that liberty was inseparable from equality—and transformed it into law.

In the profound congressional debates over the two bills, their proponents argued that the Thirteenth Amendment plainly mandated that there could no longer be one set of rules governing the conduct of black men and another for whites. Any statute that was not equal to all was an encroachment on the liberty of American society as a whole. Congress was henceforth to be the bulwark against such inequities. Conservatives, reversing their earlier position, now argued that the operation of the amendment had never been thought to be wider than "to cover the relation which existed between the master and his Negro African slave . . . and the breaking up of it." Any wider application of the amendment, the minority argued, exceeded the power it conveyed to the federal government and threatened to alter radically and irreparably the very nature of the federal compact.

But Congress was clearly ready to take revolutionary steps in the federal-state relationship. Both the Freedmen's Bureau and Civil Rights bills were passed, vetoed by President Johnson, and passed again over his veto. Still, the conservatives had made their point. Doubts lingered as to the constitutionality of the radical new laws. Thaddeus Stevens and others guiding the process of what came to be called Radical Reconstruction felt that it was essential to place these newly won rights of the freedman beyond the power of congressional majorities that might shift in the future, fasten a far more restrictive interpretation on the Thirteenth Amendment, and overturn such measures as the Freedmen's Bureau and Civil Rights bills. Another constitutional amendment was therefore required. It would in effect do again what the majority in Congress thought it had done in shaping the Thirteenth Amendment in the first place—give the freed black people of America the same rights as everyone else. This time, though, the language would be far more explicit and sweeping and place the rights guaranteed beyond all constitutional doubt. Certainly the new amendment was revolutionary. Without doubt it was changing the previous division of powers between the state and federal governments. Without doubt it promoted the United States as an interloper between every state and its inhabitants. And without doubt its language asserted that the black man was not only no longer a slave but could not be shunted into some indeterminate limbo between slavery and full citizenship. On June 13, 1866, Congress proposed the Fourteenth Amendment to the Constitution. The first section declared:

> All persons born or naturalized in the United States, and subject to the jurisdiction thereof, are citizens of the United States and of the State wherein they reside. No State shall make or enforce any law which shall abridge the privileges or immunities of citizens of the United States; nor shall any State deprive any person of life, liberty, or property, without due process of law; nor deny to any person within its jurisdiction the equal protection of the laws.

The fifth and final section of the amendment gave Congress the same power to enforce it "by appropriate legislation" as the federal legislature had received under the second section of the Thirteenth Amendment. Deciding what was "appropriate" would, in short order, provoke heated disagreement. Indeed, the debate has never been settled.

The middle three sections of the new amendment were plainly and intentionally punitive. No former state or federal officeholder who had violated his oath to the Constitution by joining the late Confederate rebellion could now hold state or federal office until Congress lifted the ban by a two-thirds vote at some future date. Furthermore, and excruciatingly painful to many of the South's most ardent defenders, neither the United States nor any state government was to honor any debt incurred "in aid of insurrection or rebellion against the United States, or any claim for the loss or emancipation of any slave; but all such debts, obligations and claims shall be held illegal and void." Holders of Confederate currency and bonds were out of pocket an estimated $3 billion. And they would never get it back. Added to the reported value of their emancipated slaves and confiscated property, the total financial bloodbath cost the South, according to a later report to the House of Representatives, some $5.2 billion. For the first fifty years of the nation's history, total federal governmental expenditures had come to little more than $1 billion. The federal budget would not run as high as $5 billion in a peacetime year until the New Deal. The unrecoverable losses of the financiers of the Confederacy, then, were of a stupendous proportion and left the region supine before the impending economic takeover by the North.

Though a constitutional amendment does not require the President's approval, Andrew Johnson made his disapproval of the Fourteenth Amendment widely known. The South did not need his advice, of course, to see that the full weight of defeat that it had so far avoided would now come crashing down upon it. As if it had a real option in the matter, ten of the eleven states in the Confederacy refused to ratify the Amendment that they saw as suicidal. Only Tennessee acceded. Three state legislatures rejected the amendment unanimously. The South's defiance now helped hand the Radical Republicans almost total control of the machinery of government in the United States. In the 1866 elections, they won every state legislature, every gubernatorial contest, and more than two-thirds of the seats in both houses of Congress, thereby assuring the party of enough strength to overcome any presidential veto.

The new Congress went right to work. In March of 1867 it passed the First Reconstruction Act. The ten Southern state governments that had failed to ratify the Fourteenth Amendment were ordered disbanded, the states were divided into five military districts, and high civil and military officials of the Confederacy were barred from the state conventions that were to be summoned to pass new constitutions, ratify the Fourteenth Amendment, and—most traumatic of all for the white South—give the black man the right to vote. Only when these steps had been taken would Union bayonets be withdrawn and the South's congressional delegations be seated again in Washington. Three other Reconstruction measures were slammed through in the next twelve months to detail how the process of political rehabilitation was to be carried out, and to leave little to the imagination of reluctant ex-Confederates.

Nothing about the program infuriated the South more than the obligation to let the freedmen vote. It was a step that had caused sharp debate in the North, where many feared that the Negro would be easily manipulated by his former master or readily intimidated into voting against the Republican ticket. Ninety-five percent of the blacks, after all, could not read. The massive Republican election victory in 1866, however, emboldened the shapers of Radical Reconstruction. The fickleness of the public did not have to be impressed upon them. The Republican Party, if it was to retain power, needed the black vote. Thaddeus Stevens saw no sin in admitting as much: "I believe, on my conscience, that on the continued ascendancy of [my] party depends the safety of this great nation. If impartial"—he meant Negro—"suffrage is excluded in the rebel States then every one of them is sure to send a solid rebel"—he meant Democratic—"representation to Congress, and cast a solid rebel electoral vote." A Democratic Congress and President were sure to follow.

Less candidly acknowledged was the stake of Northern business interests in perpetuating Republican economic policies. At war's end, the nation was on the threshold of unparalleled prosperity. It had raw materials, a growing capability to process and manufacture them, and a transportation system flinging its iron tentacles in every direction. By 1868, the railroad had spanned the continent. The Eastern financiers who controlled most of this frenetic activity wanted no barriers in their way—surely nothing like a renewal of the rural-agrarian alliance of Southern and Western interests that had dominated national politics in the decades leading up to the Civil War. Thus, the Congress that was busily dismantling Andrew Johnson's balsa-wood reconstruction of the South was also using its newly won power to enhance the interests of Eastern money and the rising middle class that was beginning to feed off it. There were tariffs to protect iron and wool manufacturers, among others. The railroads were handed enormous bounties, thousands of square miles of open land on both sides of their trackage, and a variety of other subsidies that, however well rationalized as being in the national interest, were blatant giveaways. Timber and mineral rights on federal lands were sold to private enterprises that paid scandalously little for them. A new national banking and monetary system was established and aimed at providing the maximum benefit to the capital-supplying interests. A sound paper currency was created and secured by government bonds, and a prohibitive federal tax discouraged circulation of notes issued by often irresponsible state banks. To protect and extend such measures, the business bloc piloting the Republican ship was persuaded that black votes were essential.

Unquestionably, some members of the abolitionist wing of the party and others with a primarily humanitarian interest favored Negro enfranchisement as the morally correct action, as the final step in the conversion of the American black from a bondsman to truly a freedman. That the measure was more of a political and economic device, and a punitive slap at the South, than the culminating ritual in the anointment of the Negro as citizen is testified to by the Republicans' reluctance to extend the vote to Negroes in the rest of the nation. Not until after the 1868 election returns had been verified did the party introduce the Fifteenth Amendment in February of 1869. Thirteen months later, it had been ratified by twenty-nine states, and to the law of the land were now added the words:

> SECTION 1. The right of citizens of the United States to vote shall not be denied or abridged by the United States or by any State on account of race, color, or previous condition of servitude.
>
> SECTION 2. The Congress shall have power to enforce this article by appropriate legislation.

Congress was shortly obliged to use its enforcement power as the South exploded in wrath over the humiliating new amendment. The Ku Klux Klan rode out in force and other terrorist groups struck when more than 700,000 former slaves registered as voters and the flower of Confederate manhood was itself banned from the polls by the Fourteenth Amendment. To blunt the reign of terror, Congress passed stiff election-enforcement bills against the Klan and empowered the Army to combat it and oversee the polling process.

Enactment of black suffrage and laws to enforce the right were the high-water mark of Radical Reconstruction. As much as could be done by laws for the ex-slave had now been done, it was widely felt outside the South. A long, sometimes bitter legislative fight under the direction of abolitionist Senator Charles Sumner of Massachusetts, Thaddeus Stevens' comrade-in-arms through the early stages of the Reconstruction drive, was necessary before Congress voted the Civil Rights Act of 1875 under the enforcement provision of the Fourteenth Amendment. It was the last plank in a decade of remarkable legislation that may be said to have marked the true completion of the American Revolution. The new act of 1875 asserted that all people regardless of race or color were guaranteed "the full and equal enjoyment of the accommodations . . . of inns, public conveyances on land or water, theatres and other places of public amusement" and that no one was to be disqualified for jury service because of race, color, or previous condition of servitude. But Sumner had lost his fight to have unsegregated schools included among the rights guaranteed by the bill. Given the rudimentary nature of the public school system in the nation at the time, it did not seem a critical issue. So much else had been won in just ten tumultuous years. The Constitution had been amended three times and dozens of supporting bills had been passed by Congress to provide the black man with freedom, equality, and the vote.

# 3

# The Special Favorite of the Laws

"The most piteous thing amid all the black ruin of war-time," W. E. B. Du Bois would write a generation afterward, "amid the broken fortunes of the masters, the blighted hopes of mothers and maidens, and the fall of an empire,—the most piteous thing amid all this was the black freedman who threw down his hoe because the world called him free. What did such a mockery of freedom mean? Not a cent of money, not an inch of land, not a mouthful of victuals,—not even ownership of the rags on his back. Free!"

Having spent a great deal of money and blood to win the war, the nation would invest no more to provide a livelihood for the four million black people it had set at liberty. They were to be cast adrift without an oar—without a boat, really. And they were powerfully ignorant, besides. Next to land, the Negro's great hunger was for learning. Enough of it, anyway, to start him on the process of discovery of the great world he knew dimly to exist beyond the next plantation. "It was a whole race trying to go to school," Booker T. Washington would recall of those days in his autobiography, *Up from Slavery.* "Few were too young, and none too old, to make the attempt to learn. As fast as any kind of teachers could be secured, not only were day-schools filled, but night-schools as well. The great ambition of the older people was to try to learn to read the Bible before they died." Reading, writing, and ciphering were nearly the entire curriculum at•the more than 4,000 little schools opened all over the South by the Freedmen's Bureau. Over five years, nearly 250,000 people attended them. But in 1870 the bureau was shut down and its work mostly abandoned. It was the most extraordinary governmental effort at mass uplift in the nation's history; not until the New Deal would its like be tried. Yet only a little more than $5 million—$1.25 per capita—was spent to compensate for 200 years of ignorance enforced on a whole transplanted people. It was a pitiful amount for a cause of such urgency and magnitude. True, the Freedmen's Bureau schools had inspired the Reconstruction legislatures of the South to provide for public education programs, but there would be little local or state money to pay for them for decades, and white property owners, hard pressed to hold on, were disinclined in the extreme to be taxed in behalf of their late bondsmen, whose need for learning they found dubious in the first place. What organized learning the freedmen could find thereafter was provided largely by Northern philanthropy. Heroic white schoolmarms braved merciless taunts and other stigmata to bring learning to some of the most benighted crannies and far-off corners of the Southland. But it was a drop in the bucket. His liberators were leaving the freedman to wither on the vine.

Could he not start over elsewhere in the nation? With no material resources and little or no education, he was welcome nowhere. Not in the West, as the free-soilers had made clear to free Negroes in the pre-war decades. Not in the cities of the North, as a resolution of New York's Tammany Hall had made clear in 1862: "We are opposed to emancipating Negro slaves unless on some plan of colonization in order that they may not come in contact with the white man's labor." It was the same all over. Few labor unions wanted Negroes, and white employers used them whenever convenient to undercut demands of white laborers for better working conditions. Blacks were desperate for decent employment, but their disaffiliation with the growing white labor movement in the North served only to widen the estrangement. In the towns and small cities of the South, white craftsmen and workers wanted no part of skilled black competition—men trained in slavery as blacksmiths or bricklayers or cabinetmakers—at a time when the regional economy was prostrate.

Without land, without learning, with nowhere else really to turn, the helpless freedman shortly saw that his freedom was an empty husk. There was nothing else to do but go back to his old master on the old plantation. But both master and plantation had undergone severe changes.

It was hardly a plantation system at all any more. Between one-third and one-half of the old plantation land had passed into the hands of new owners, often absentee ones who cared only about the income from it. They might be lumber speculators or railroad companies or insurance outfits in the North or English syndicates or, more and more, wholesale supply merchants. What had happened as the war went on and then Confederate debts were voided by the victorious federal government was that the South had run out of money. Nowhere in the region could capital accumulate. A new system had to be devised if the region was to rouse itself from defeat and gloom. The one that developed proved to be among the most unfortunate and extortionate financial arrangements ever invented by man.

Some black workers were able to sign on simply as contract workers at a stipulated monthly wage—usually somewhere between $9 and $15 for men and perhaps half that for women—plus food, shelter, and fuel. Since cash was in short supply, sharecropping was more common: the black worker would get his basic needs plus from one-fourth to one-half of the crop. But by far the most common arrangement was the insidious new lien system that soon blanketed the South, covering poor-white as well as black farmers, and hardly less destructive of men and soil than slavery itself had been. The principals in the system were the landless freedman, the bankrupt planter or absentee landlord, and that new cock of the walk, the supply merchant.

Typically, the freed slave would lease fifty acres—or if he were a workhorse, a hundred—from the planter or landlord. Then he would come, hat in anxious hand, to the merchant to arrange a "furnish." Any white man who could scrape together several hundred dollars, and preferably a thousand or more, had only to convince a couple of Yankee wholesalers to extend him credit in turn, so he could open a store or expand the one he had. In no time, a line of penniless black farmers would be forming at the door, eager to obtain credit. Collateral was the next season's cotton crop on the land the farmer had just rented, but neither the rate of interest nor the size of the loan itself was stipulated. Instead, the farmer was furnished what he needed—clothes, side pork, fertilizer, plowpoints, a wagon, whatever—provided it did not exceed, in the merchant's judgment, what the black man's crop would be good for. The farmer was required to sign a contract saying he would deal exclusively with the merchant; he could not spread his business around or shop for the best prices and rates. From that moment on, the farmer had lost control over the fruits of his own labor. And he had to pay like the devil for the privilege. During the growing season, whenever the farmer needed rations or to see a doctor or to have his mule shod, his account with the merchant would be charged for the cost—and then some. The credit price generally ranged from 30 to 60 percent higher—and sometimes more—than the cash price the farmer would have paid. The local merchant himself was gouged by wholesalers and other credit suppliers all the way up the line, who justified the usury, not altogether implausibly, by declaring that the risks they were taking were extraordinary and they had to cover themselves. Once the mortgaged crop was ready for market, the hovering merchant took possession of it, sold it at any price he wished without having to answer to the farmer, then paid the planter or landlord the rent the farmer owed, subtracted the farmer's interest-choked supply bill from the remainder, and if there were by any chance something left over, it would be paid to the hapless black farmer. Generally, the farmer would wind up in the hole, already owing the merchant on the following year's crop. Nor could the farmer second-guess the merchant or challenge his arithmetic and expect to get away with it. Thus, most of the black men of the South, within a few years of their emancipation, had been reduced to a state of helpless peonage. So much for the Thirteenth Amendment.

The legal rights of economically crippled people have probably always been frail in every land that called itself free, but the vulnerability of the weak has been especially acute in the United States, where good economics has so often determined what is good law. No better example of the price of economic dependency may be culled from American history than the sustained erosion of the Negro's civil rights. The degenerative process began almost as soon as he got them and, while the rest of the nation turned its eyes and contemplated instead its golden destiny, gangrene rapidly set in.

By the time Ulysses S. Grant began his second term in the White House, the uproar over equality for the black man had reached its terminal stage in Congress. It would require nearly three more years of debate to pass the last major piece of Reconstruction legislation. Meanwhile, the job of reconciling the country's new moral and constitutional commitments to the Negro with its undiluted distaste for him as a human being fell to that esteemed broker of national disputes, the Supreme Court of the United States.

Just why the American people, as rambunctious and criminally inclined as any on earth, have come to hold their Supreme Court in such reverential regard is hard to say. Public estimate of it has fluctuated with events, of course, but as time has gone on, more rather than less power has come to reside in the marble mausoleum it occupies a few blocks from the Capitol. No other tribunal on earth rivals it. No other government reserves the last word for the judiciary to pronounce.

Perhaps the Court has won such vast hegemony precisely because Americans believe that its nine life-membership Justices are beyond the rough-and-tumble of everyday politics. In this, they would be mistaken, for any close reading of the Court's history reveals its constant intimacy with the political process, though usually at one or two removes from the killing ground. Or perhaps Americans retain a latent admiration, as has often been suggested, for the trappings of monarchy—witness their fondness for political dynasties—and thus the cloistered proceedings and ceremonial bearing of the Justices fill a subconscious hunger. Or perhaps Americans simply wish to think that the Court, as the nation's arbiter of last resort, is composed of men both wise and incorruptible in a world where men possessing abundant deposits of either quality are rare.

All these reasons, no doubt, contribute to the Court's mystique, but at a functioning level the real explanation is probably much grainier. Lawyers have had an extraordinary degree of power in American life from the beginning. Lawyers have been the American peerage. They designed the nation and saw that it worked. Their business is the nation's business. Early on, the American obsession was with land, and so lawyers were consumed by matters of realty—titles and surveys and credit and interest. Then it was property in the larger sense of goods to be manufactured and crops to be traded, and lawyers fretted over the sanctity of contracts and negotiable instruments. Then it was commerce and industry, and lawyers pondered government regulation and tax policies and labor negotiations. Lawyers were on all sides of all questions, and it was they, generally and not entirely inappropriately, who made the laws. As a group, it is no surprise, they have been steadfastly conservative. It is in the very nature of the profession, which places a premium on rational behavior by the people it deals with and on stabilizing activity by the government it largely staffs. And so the nation's most strategically placed and politically potent panel of lawyers—the Supreme Court—has reflected this agenda of national interests and philo-sophical disposition. The Court's tilt for the nation's first century and a half was toward the stability of the economy and the maintenance of domestic tranquility. It did not act by whim. It spoke in tones of priestly certitude. And it built upon itself and its appearance of rectitude. In a nation where the frontier changed almost daily and the pace of events outstripped any man's understanding, here was an institution that exemplified solidity. Here was a rudder for all the mainsails that took to the American wind.

Installed in the federal machinery as a safeguard against runaway majorities and tyrannical officeholders, the Court spent a feeble first decade as the national government struggled to gain identity and direction. Starting in 1800, though, two successive Chief Justices of massive ability transformed the Court into a critical component of the rapidly surging young nation. John Marshall moved with craft and deliberateness along two parallel tracks—to establish the supremacy of the Court over Congress and of the federal government over the states. In each goal, he had the support of the men of means who founded the country and enshrined property rights above all others. Chief Justice Marshall exploited every chance to strengthen the federal system and lubricate the economic workings of the country. Thus, he led the Court in rulings that states could not violate the sanctity of contracts, that corporations had a life beyond the men who made them, that commercial enterprises could not be unduly hamstrung by punitive local regulations, and that the states could not tax creations of the federal government. As to Congress, if it were free to ignore the limitations placed upon it by the Constitution, why bother to have a Constitution at all? The wise men who made it had had good reason, for this was to be a government of limited powers, and someone ultimately had to say what those limits of power were. That someone, clearly, was the Supreme Court. It was clear, at any rate, to John Marshall.

His successor, Roger Taney, spoke for other, countervailing interests— for the general welfare of the community as opposed to the special interests of private property, for the rights and needs of the states as opposed to the federal government, for rural sectors and agrarian enterprises as opposed to the cities and the bankers. Yet he failed to quell his own partisanship, reaching out in *Dred Scott* to settle issues far beyond the dictates of judicial restraint and nearly extinguishing the Court's place of honor. Certainly it was stilled for the duration of the war, as the presidency siphoned off its power. When uneasy peace returned, Congress emerged as the dominant branch of government while the Court lay low, recuperating and stamping its approval on highly controversial war and Reconstruction measures in the name of patriotism.

But the Court did not long remain in eclipse. The nation was weary of wrangling over war and its strident aftermath, and as it turned its primary attention back to economic affairs, it tacitly looked to the Court to serve as caretaker of the black man's newly awarded rights. By the Seventies, abolitionist passion had run its course, and men of genuinely humanitarian conviction had come to feel that the freedman had been handed all the rights it was within government's power to bestow. The rest, it was said, was up to the Negro himself. The nation had fought a cruel and costly war in his behalf and, by a decade of legislation, had now strongly reinforced the federal mandate to protect him—and any other citizen—from potential abuse by the people and government of the state in which he resided. So much legal hardware had been added to the national government's machinery, in fact, that some sober political observers began to fear that the federal equation had been thrown permanently out of kilter by the Civil War amendments and their enforcement measures. The states might soon become more shadow than sovereign if the amendments were expansively interpreted when they came before the Supreme Court in test cases.

The test was not long in coming, and it came at a moment when the Court was faced with a particularly hazardous course of adjudication. Nearly half the nation was still under military occupation. Industry and the railroads were collecting wealth and power in such concentrated strength that measures would have to be taken to curb them before long. The electorate was growing, and with it came new problems and needs. Country crossroads were becoming towns, and towns were becoming cities, and the nation moved west without enough money to go around. In every phase of American life, clashing economic, social, and political interests would have to be resolved. The job would fall to the Supreme Court as it emerged from its nearly parasitic relationship with the Grant administration at the end of the short Chief Justiceship of the once ambitious Salmon P. Chase.

The Court's dominant figure at that juncture was a robust physician-turned-lawyer named Samuel F. Miller out of Keokuk, Iowa, nominated to the Court by Abraham Lincoln in 1862 as its first member from west of the Mississippi. A big, hearty, fiery man who said what he meant and would not truck with big-city palaver, Miller was an authentic grass-roots liberal, a dedicated abolitionist who had given his personal notes to raise funds for the Union. A man of relatively little legal education, he was more a gregarious humanist and pragmatist of generous impulses than a lawyer's lawyer. He had been strongly nationalistic in his attitudes during his first decade on the bench and approved federal confiscation of rebel property as a necessary war measure. In short, the Negro could hardly have hoped for a more compassionate Justice to write the opinion of the Court when it was called upon in 1873 for the first time to define the reach of the centerpiece of Reconstruction—the majestic Fourteenth Amendment. Samuel Miller wrote the opinion and nearly consigned the amendment to the trash heap.

On the face of it, the *Slaughterhouse Cases* had nothing to do with the rights of Negroes. The Louisiana legislature in 1869 had granted one corporation a twenty-five-year exclusive franchise to conduct all the butchering business in three of the state's parishes. Health considerations were cited as the reason for granting the monopoly, though reports were rampant that carpetbagger lawmakers had been bribed. Whatever the machinations behind it, the official monopoly prompted a lawsuit by rival slaughterhouses that claimed a thousand butchers had been deprived of their natural right to earn a living—and thus of their privileges and immunities as guaranteed by the first section of the thus far untested Fourteenth Amendment.

It was fitting that the first test of the amendment should have an economic framework, for the amendment that had been designed to assure the Negro of his civil rights would come to be called upon far more often as a license to corporations and other businesses seeking to avoid government regulation. Justice Samuel Miller was no special friend of big or small businesses, but he did bring to the Court the yen for individualism of the hard-riding frontiersman, and as the nation now moved into its post-war phase, he scrutinized the federal-state relationship with stern eyes. He was frankly worried about the power of Congress and its capability of recklessness. He believed that great governmental power ought to be exercised with great restraint, and that once the war crisis had passed, a new equilibrium ought to be established between the states and the national government. "All loose construction of authority is dangerous," he said; "all construction of authority too limited to serve the purpose for which it is given is injurious." He now applied that oracular pronouncement to the Fourteenth Amendment, and in his fashion he chose to view it on the narrowest possible grounds. For the Negro standing on those grounds, the *Slaughterhouse* decision was the beginning of a long nightmare.

The key to Miller's opinion was in the first two sentences of the amendment itself:

> All persons born or naturalized in the United States, and subject to the jurisdiction thereof, are citizens of the United States and of the State wherein they reside. No State shall make or enforce any law which shall abridge the privileges or immunities of citizens of the United States . . .

Miller chose to break the two sentences apart and not read them in the sequence in which they were put down. The first sentence, he said, was written to establish beyond question the citizenship of the Negro. But he did not interpret the second sentence to mean that no state could interfere with the basic rights of all American citizens. Instead, he read it restrictively. The second sentence, Miller said, was more important in the case at hand, for in it "the distinction between citizenship of the United States and the citizenship of a State is clearly recognized and established. . . . It is quite clear, then, that there is a citizenship of the United States, and a citizenship of a State, which are distinct from each other. . . ." The clarity was in the eye of the beholder, for there was no evidence in the debates surrounding the passage of the amendment or the 1866 Civil Rights Act from which it sprang that its framers envisioned such a duality of citizenship. Their avowed purpose was, on the contrary, to establish the supremacy of federally guaranteed rights and fortify them against invasion by the states in the way that the Black Codes, for example, had grossly invaded the rights of freedmen. So far as the five-to-four majority of the Supreme Court was concerned, however, it was "not the purpose of the Fourteenth Amendment . . . to transfer the security and protection of . . . civil rights . . . from the states to the federal government." Then what had been the purpose of the amendment? To place under federal guarantee and protection those privileges and immunities "which arise out of the nature and essential character of the national government" as distinguished from the privileges and immunities of citizens of the states, which "embrace generally those fundamental civil rights for the security and establishment of which organized society is instituted, and they remain . . . under the care of the state governments."

Maddeningly, the Court declined in its *Slaughterhouse* opinion to go further in defining "the privileges and immunities of citizens of the United States which no state can abridge, until some case involving those privileges may make it necessary to do so." Evidently stung by charges of vagueness, Justice Miller elaborated with a few examples: the rights of national citizenship he and his four brethren had in mind included the right to vote in federal elections, the right to go to the seat of government and gain access to federal buildings, the right to petition the federal government for redress of grievances, the right of access to seaports, the high seas, and navigable streams, and the like. Was it possible that Congress and the nation had fought a great war and undergone agonizing recuperation with force-fed medicine to establish such rights as these—rights that were implicit in the supremacy clause of the original Constitution? So the Court held. And so the licensing of slaughterhouses in Louisiana was declared to have nothing to do with men's rights under the Fourteenth Amendment. Whether the license had been rightly or wrongly granted was up to the courts of Louisiana to determine.

So the federal-state pendulum was given a sharp shove from Washington back toward the components of the Union. The federal government had not been handed a passkey to barge in on the states' authority to manage "those fundamental civil rights for the security and establishment of which organized society is instituted." And what exactly were those rights? Nobody exactly knew. Did the *Slaughterhouse* ruling imperil the Civil Rights Act of 1870, which had basically re-enacted the 1866 act under the enforcement provision of the Fourteenth Amendment and guaranteed such privileges as the right to make and enforce contracts, the right to buy, sell, and own real and personal property, and the right to sue, be parties to a suit, and give evidence in court? It was not yet clear, and the Court's narrow five-to-four vote in the case left the question dangling.

It began to be answered the following year when President Grant nominated an industrious but humdrum lawyer from the Midwest to become the seventh Chief Justice of the United States. Morrison R. Waite, a Yale graduate and the son of a chief justice of the Connecticut Supreme Court, had moved to Ohio to get ahead on his own and soon become a pillar of Toledo. An expert in realty law and attorney to railroads and other corporate interests, Waite came to Washington as a strong believer in states' rights. The people, the real people, lived out there in the states, and their governments were closest to their needs. Unbridled power in the central government was a menace to be checked, and Morrison Waite voted to do so during a productive fourteen-year tenure that would see him deliver more than a thousand opinions of the Court. In his preference for state power to federal, Waite was a throwback to Roger Taney. Unfortunately for the Negro, Waite also resembled Taney in his negative attitude toward civil rights. The new Chief Justice was to write two opinions that would go far to undo the right to vote that the Negro thought he had been guaranteed by the Fifteenth Amendment.

The circumstances of his enfranchisement in the South almost guaranteed that the right would be wrenched away from the Negro at the earliest opportunity. The vote was not given to him as it had been in the North—with grudging recognition that it was due him, however inferior, unruly, or divisive a citizen he might prove. There, he was a citizen, whatever else he was. In the South, he was a black man, whatever else he was, and he had been empowered to vote at the very same time that the best elements in the community—the great landowners and statesmen and captains of the Confederacy—had been denied the vote. The freedman's vote, moreover, was cast under the gaze of federal troops. It was coercive democracy. And it had patently been jammed down the South's gullet as a punitive measure, intended to humiliate the proud white man who had climbed so high on the black man's back. As the Republican Congress swiveled its attention to economic matters after the adoption of the Fifteenth Amendment, the process of restoring men of the Old South to positions of elective leadership began in earnest. It could be done only by discouraging the black vote.

In 1871, Congress repealed its early requirement under Radical Reconstruction that acknowledged ex-Confederates had to take an ironclad oath of allegiance to the Union and, in effect, disavow their earlier overt acts. The next year, it followed up with a general amnesty restoring full political rights to all but a few hundred former officials of the C.S.A. At once, the drowsing Democratic Party, stalwart defender of states' rights and rugged individualism, revived and began to win elections. By 1874, the United States House of Representatives had gone Democratic. By 1875, the Conservatives had rewon Alabama, Texas, and Arkansas. The fiercest remaining battlegrounds as the elections of 1876 approached were states with great numbers of Negro voters who resisted the tide of white supremacy that was again flowing in upon them—Mississippi, South Carolina, Louisiana, and Florida. The fury of the electoral—and racial—contests in the last three of them would decide who the next President was to be.

Black voters under Radical Reconstruction elected hundreds of black officials to state and local office and sent one United States Senator and ten Representatives to Congress, though only in South Carolina did they serve in numbers even approaching fair representation of any state's Negro population. The large infusion of black voting threatened to turn the rickety oligarchy of state government into a far more democratic and humanitarian mechanism. Throughout the South, Reconstruction governments extended the franchise to many men of both races by reducing property qualifications. They opened the jury box to thousands who had not been admitted before. They instituted public school systems, even if of a skeletal nature. They reduced the hold of the old plantocracy on county government and introduced home rule. They abolished the whipping post and the branding iron and other barbarous forms of punishment and greatly reduced the number of crimes that could cost a man his life. Unquestionably, some radical lawmakers, including a number of blacks, had their hand in the till, but in general the record was a positive one: the laws passed by the radical legislatures were therapeutic and long overdue—a judgment supported by the fact that the Reconstruction constitutions remained in force in many states long after the coalition of Negroes, scalawags, and carpetbaggers that devised them had been routed.

Yet throughout the South now, white men practiced violence and extra-legal acts to keep the Negro from voting. The Ku Klux Klan rode under other names, but it rode. Black voters saw their crops and homes and barns burned, and organized whites patrolled polling places and later whipped or even lynched Negroes who voted Republican. The federal voting-enforcement act of 1871 brought some relief in the form of supervisory military observers, but the arm of federal law could not reach enough places. In Louisiana in 1874, conservative whites were nearly ready to use organized force to overturn the Radical Republican government as armed "White Leagues" clashed with government officials repeatedly. By 1875, Mississippi was on the verge of civil war, with the governor's black militia ranged against white "protective" troops that paraded proudly and did not hesitate to shoot when challenged. In South Carolina, pistol-packing "Red Shirts" held rallies and inveighed against the tyranny of radicals who had run the state long enough. And in Washington, shortly before the fateful campaign of 1876 began, the United States Supreme Court handed down two decisions that did nothing to douse the political tinder.

It was just six years after the Fifteenth Amendment had been adopted when Chief Justice Morrison Waite wrote a jolting opinion of the Court that made the federal guarantee of the right to vote all but worthless. The case of *United States v. Reese* had been brought in behalf of a black man otherwise qualified who went to register to vote in Lexington, Kentucky, but when he offered payment of the compulsory head tax—that is, a form of poll tax—it was refused. When he showed up to vote on election day and was again refused, he turned to federal authorities, who had the local white election officials duly indicted. It seemed an obvious example of denial of the right to vote, in a manner prohibited by the Fifteenth Amendment. Here was exactly the kind of situation the framers of the amendment had envisioned: arbitrary refusal of the black man's constitutional rights as a full-fledged citizen. The Supreme Court, however, disagreed. According to Chief Justice Waite, the Fifteenth Amendment did not confer on the Negro—or anyone—the right of suffrage. Only a state could grant that right to its citizens. What the amendment did say was that no state may *deny* any would-be voter the right to vote because of his race or color. It was not a positive grant allowing Congress to regulate or control all interference with a citizen's right to vote; Congress was limited to passing enforcement laws protecting a citizen "from discrimination in the exercise of the election franchise." In other words, the Negro who had been turned away at the polls had to prove that he had been prevented from voting specifically because of his race. That there could have been no other conceivable reason was not a factor the Court felt it proper to consider.

In a companion case, Waite doubled the strength of the Court's blow. A riotous group of about 100 whites had broken up a political rally of Negroes in Louisiana, and two of them were indicted under the federal acts enforcing the Fifteenth Amendment. The case, titled *United States v. Cruikshank*, involved rights thought to have been granted blacks under both the Fourteenth and Fifteenth amendments. Not so, said the Court. Invoking its ruling in *Reese*, it held that "the right of suffrage is not a necessary attribute of national citizenship" and that conviction of the Louisiana rioters could not be upheld because the indictment against them failed to charge that the rioters had harassed the Negroes because of their race. So much for the Fifteenth Amendment. As to the Fourteenth Amendment, Chief Justice Waite agreed that it did indeed prohibit any *state* from depriving a citizen of life, liberty, privileges, and immunities, due process of law, and equal protection of the laws, "but this adds nothing to the rights of one citizen against another. It simply furnishes an additional guaranty against any encroachment by the states upon the fundamental rights which belong to every citizen as a member of society." In other words, a state was not allowed to deny any citizen within its jurisdiction equal protection of its laws, but a mob that broke up the meeting of Negro voters was not the state. It was a group of private individuals, and what they did was not "state action." And only state action—that is, action by the state itself in the form of a law or in the person of a public official—was covered by the Fourteenth Amendment. In short, it was not the federal government's business if a state failed to prevent a mob from interfering with a Negro group's right to assemble peaceably.

Here were two cases almost custom-tailored for adjudication under the great new Civil War amendments and their supporting legislation. Two states had defaulted in their obligations to protect the rights of their citizens, and the highest court of the federal government was asked to correct the obvious error. Yet the Court declined and offered rulings that were, at best, examples of judicial hairsplitting. The *Reese* and *Cruikshank* decisions of 1875 were to prove just the tip of a distinctly jagged iceberg.

By the time of the 1876 presidential election contest between Democrat Samuel J. Tilden and Republican Rutherford B. Hayes, abolitionist, radical, and free-soil elements had gradually receded within the Republican Party, which in the North passed now into the controlling hands of bankers, industrialists, would-be tycoons, and other believers in the gospel of gold. Reformers were gravitating to the Democrats. In the South, Republicanism still depended upon the votes of landless freedmen and an egalitarian platform to which the rest of the party paid little heed. But the force taking command of Southern politics—men known as Redeemers (as in the redemption of white supremacy)—included not only the planter-statesmen of pre-war days but men far more business-oriented and practical in their political aims.

To win, Hayes needed the electoral votes of the three states where the returns were fiercely contested—South Carolina, Louisiana, and Florida, the only three where the Republicans still hung on in force. An enormously complicated negotiation ensued. Under it, the South would cast its congressional votes to certify the Republican slate of presidential electors in the three contested states. Hayes, as President, would turn on the federal spigot for the South and give its leaders a large measure of control over federal patronage. Among the direct benefits to the region would be a federal-government guarantee of the interest payment on a massive bond issue by the Texas and Pacific Railroad to build 2,500 miles of main and trunk lines linking the South and West—a long-held dream of the region; the interest guaranteed would come to nearly $250 million. By far the most important psychological and political part of the Hayes compromise package, of course, was the withdrawal of all federal troops from the South. It was far better, said the new President, for the white man and the black man of the South to make their peace together than to live in constant tension under the surveillance of a federal garrison.

Back in the saddle, Southern Democrats moved at once to make sure they would not be unhorsed again. The Negro began to be disenfranchised by a series of measures that may have been technically legal in some instances but by and large were plainly criminal. Polling places would be set up far from black residential districts. Or they would be changed at the last minute without black voters being advised of the fact. Or strategic access roads would be blocked or ferries shut down. Stuffing of Democratic ballot boxes was common. Gerrymandered election districts to nullify pockets of black voting strength were reshuffled five times within seventeen years in Virginia. Added to the list of crimes that would cost a convicted Southern citizen his vote was petty larceny, of which a significant number of Negroes were found guilty. Redeemer pledges of fairness to the Negro notwithstanding, South Carolina came up with a trailblazing disenfranchisement technique in an 1882 law requiring that special ballots and boxes be placed in every polling place for each contested office so that voters had to put their ballots in the correct boxes or lose their vote—and no voter could be helped through the maze by election officials in attendance. By an 1894 statute no less intimidating, Virginia required the would-be voter to show his registration and poll-tax certificates at the polls or be denied a ballot. If he got a ballot, he found it remarkably confusing since candidates were listed not by party but by the name of the office they sought. And if others were on line, the voter had no more than two and a half minutes allotted to him in the voting booth. All these devices were designed to prove a particular burden to marginally literate voters. By 1889, Henry W. Grady, part owner of the largest newspaper in the South, the Atlanta *Constitution*, and the region's most articulate booster, would remark, "The Negro as a political force has dropped out of serious consideration."

Men without a vote have a hard time preserving their other civil rights. The Supreme Court did not make matters any easier for the Negro now, even when it seemed to be endorsing provisions of the Reconstruction program.

A principal gain under that program, implicit in the Fourteenth Amendment and made explicit under the 1875 Civil Rights Act, was the right to a fair jury trial. Such a right had been present in the Constitution virtually from the beginning. The Sixth Amendment in the Bill of Rights guaranteed to the accused in all criminal proceedings the right to "a speedy and public trial, by an impartial jury of the State and district wherein the crime shall have been committed." The Fourteenth Amendment and the 1875 follow-up legislation had pounded the point home. Their purpose in this connection was quite obviously to integrate Negroes into the jury system in order to assure the black man of an impartial trial and thereby counteract a presumed hostility of white jurors toward black defendants. The obligation of state and local jurisdictions to establish such impartial trial machinery would seem to have been clear beyond a question. The Supreme Court, however, in three decisions handed down in 1879, beclouded the situation and added a burden to the Negro.

The law of West Virginia limited service on grand and trial juries to white males; the language of the statute was explicit, and no proof of hostility was therefore required by the Supreme Court, which said in overturning it in *Strauder v. West Virginia* that the Fourteenth Amendment prohibited denial of due process and equal protection of the laws:

> What is this but declaring that the law in the states shall be the same for the black as for the white; that all persons, whether colored or white, shall stand equal before the laws of the states and, in regard to the colored race, for whose protection the Amendment was primarily designed, that no discrimination shall be made against them by law because of their color? The words of the Amendment, it is true, are prohibitory, but they contain a necessary implication of a positive immunity, or right, most valuable to the colored race—the right to exemption from unfriendly legislation against them distinctively as colored—exemption from legal discriminations, implying inferiority in civil society, lessening the security of their enjoyment of rights others enjoy, and discriminations which are steps toward reducing them to a subject race.

Inspiriting words. They would have to be invoked over and over by Negro plaintiffs in ensuing years, for, despite the clarity of the *Strauder* opinion, the indisputable right of every American citizen standing trial before an impartial jury was regularly ignored throughout the South for the better part of a century. A decision handed down at the same time as *Strauder* helps explain why.

In *Virginia v. Rives*, two Negroes charged with capital crimes had been indicted and tried by all-white juries. The wording of the Virginia state law did not limit jury service to white male citizens as the West Virginia statute did, and so the black defendant in Virginia faced with an all-white jury could not claim that the state law was being violated. The absence of a Negro on the jury panel was not, in and of itself, evidence of discrimination. The defendant had to claim and prove that officials in charge of the jury-selection process had discriminated against prospective, qualified Negro jurors. The defendants in this case did accuse the jury commissioners of discrimination and demanded that Negroes be named to their jury—a request that was denied. Federal Judge Alexander Rives then invoked the 1875 Civil Rights Act and claimed federal jurisdiction of the case upon the complaint of the black defendants. The state of Virginia sued to regain jurisdiction. The Supreme Court ruled for Virginia. By a vote of seven to two, it said that it could not be claimed that either the constitution or the laws of Virginia explicitly denied Negroes the right of jury service and therefore the obligation rested with the black defendant to claim and prove that discrimination had been practiced in the jury selection. If the trial judge refused to grant such a claim and order a Negro added to the jury, the black defendant could appeal to the state's highest court. Not until rejected by that tribunal as well could the suit come before the federal courts on the jury question—an expensive, time-consuming, and altogether discouraging process for the black man on trial.

In a related third case decided the same day, the Court brushed aside the argument of a Virginia judge who had acknowledged acting in defiance of the state's non-discriminatory jury-selection law but who claimed that Congress and the federal government had no right or power to interfere with a state judicial officer whose actions were not "state action" but merely those of an individual—an obvious appeal to the Court's tremulous logic in *United States v. Cruikshank*. But in that case the discriminatory party had been a red-eyed mob bent on violence, not a state judge. "We do not perceive how holding an office under a State, and claiming to act for the State, can relieve the holder from obligation to obey the Constitution of the United States," said the Court in *Ex parte Virginia*, "or take away the power of Congress to punish his disobedience."

On the face of it, then, the three jury cases added up to a gain, certainly in rhetoric, for the Negro, but they did little to affect the continuing prevalence of all-white juries. For the Court did not rule that such juries were, by the very fact of their pure whiteness, illegally constituted and that all their acts were therefore void. Barring a challenge, such juries could continue to function. Negroes did challenge them, repeatedly, but probably no constitutional issue would have to be more frequently litigated. The Department of Justice, which could have sought enforcement of the 1875 provision, chose to sit on its law books. And so the Negro, though his rights to a fair jury trial had been confirmed by the Supreme Court, was guaranteed instead, thanks in part to his spreading disenfranchisement throughout the South, state judicial systems composed entirely of white sheriffs, white prosecutors, white juries, and white judges. The practical effect of such an arrangement was greatly to encourage violence by whites against blacks.

The Supreme Court's permissiveness toward the disregard of Negro claims for a fair shake from Southern police and courts was underscored by an 1883 opinion. An armed mob had taken a group of Negroes from the custody of a Tennessee sheriff and killed one of them and beaten others. No doubt this was not a civilized way to administer the criminal-justice process, the Court indicated in *United States v. Harris*, but it found no violation of the Negroes' rights to equal protection of the law under the Fourteenth Amendment. Expanding on its ruling in *Cruikshank*, the Court declared the language of the amendment to be clear beyond doubt: it said that "No State" shall deprive a citizen of equal protection, and no state had done so in this instance. A mob had. Indeed, the state laws forbade such a denial of rights, and the amendment imposed no duty and conferred no rights upon Congress to intrude. If citizens of the state abused black men—or even murdered them as they had in the *Harris* case—it was up to the state to bring the criminals to justice. If the state was lax about it, if it did not much seem to mind that black men were being seized and beaten and killed by lawless thugs, that was unfortunate for black men. And so they kept being seized and beaten and killed and could not turn for protection to the Fourteenth Amendment, which had been passed for that express purpose. It had begun to look very much as if an unspoken part of the 1877 Compromise that produced the Hayes election was that officials of the federal government, including the Justices of the Supreme Court, would keep their distance from the South's handling—however perverse—of the Negro's civil rights.

In the decade after he came to the Court, Chief Justice Waite was joined by five new appointees, and the lineup of Justices by 1883 included only two holdovers from before 1870—Samuel Miller and Stephen J. Field, both named by Lincoln. All but Field were Republicans, all were from the North or West, and all were presumed friendly, to one extent or another, toward the intent of the Civil War amendments.

Certainly this would seem to have been true of Justice Joseph P. Bradley, who had run for Congress in New Jersey as a Lincoln Republican in 1862. A prominent lawyer for railroads and insurance companies, he had proven a proficient technical craftsman since coming to the high court and a constitutional logician of superior intellect. In 1873, he was part of the vocal four-judge minority that had dissented from the Court's highly restrictive reading of the Fourteenth Amendment in the *Slaughterhouse Cases*. But a decade later he wrote an eight-to-one decision of the Court that would soon leave Reconstruction legislation an empty vessel.

The *Civil Rights Cases* of 1883, on the legality of the public-accommodations section of the 1875 act, came from various parts of the country at a time when more than a hundred test cases were making their way through the courts. Segregation was by no means universal in the South or elsewhere, and in most communities operators of restaurants, inns, theaters, and public conveyances decided for themselves just whom they would serve. In each of the *Civil Rights Cases*, the federal government was pressing an action in behalf of the Negroes offended under the 1875 statute.

That statute carried no weight in these cases, Justice Bradley declared, and exceeded the authority granted Congress under the Fourteenth Amendment. Invoking the increasingly familiar state-action argument, the eight-man majority opinion said that the amendment outlawed discriminatory action only when taken by the states themselves and not by private persons. "It would be running the slavery argument into the ground," wrote Bradley, "to make it apply to every act of discrimination which a person may see fit to make as to the guests he will entertain, or as to the people he will admit into his coach or cab or car, or admit to his concert or theatre, or deal with in other matters. . . ." The Justice was here performing some sleight of hand, since the law he was invalidating had made no mention of "guests" that private individuals may wish to "entertain"—presumably on their own property. Nor did Bradley choose to note that coaches and cabs and theaters and the like all existed for the very purpose of serving the public, and the public meant all citizens. Instead, Bradley held that the excluded Negroes had suffered private wrongs to their "social rights," not the invasion of their political or civil rights by the state or under state authority. Sooner or later, he added, for the black man emerging from slavery, "there must be some stage in the progress of his elevation when he takes the rank of a mere citizen, and ceases to be the special favorite of the laws, and when his rights, as a citizen or a man, are to be protected in the ordinary modes by which other men's rights are protected."

The sole voice of dissent on the Court did not make itself heard for some time. So disturbed by the majority opinion in the *Civil Rights Cases* was Justice John Marshall Harlan, the former slaveholder from Kentucky who had joined the Union camp during the war, that he took weeks to put his thoughts on paper. He would write yet more memorable and prophetic dissents in his day, but the words he issued in rebuke of his colleagues in the closing weeks of 1883 aptly conveyed a sense of sadness flecked with irony over the declining fate of the freed Negro at the national bar of justice. The Civil War amendments had not been passed to sustain him as "a special favorite of the laws," as Justice Bradley had implied, but to include the Negro as "part of the people for whose welfare and happiness government is ordained." But if the obligation to protect his privileges and immunities were henceforth to rest not upon the federal government but on the states, "we shall enter upon an era of constitutional law, when the rights of freedom and American citizenship cannot receive from the nation that efficient protection which heretofore was unhesitatingly accorded to slavery and the rights of the master."

As it nudged the black man to the sidelines of the civic arena, the white South was faced with a growing economic cleavage that shortly sundered its racial solidarity. Starting with the Panic of 1873, tight credit, overexpanded cotton production, and falling prices combined to cause a wave of foreclosures that sent many a white farmer into the fields as another man's tenant—a severe blow to his pride as an independent yeoman and a hell of a fellow. The Northeast, moreover, intensified its exploitive pressure upon the Southern whites by treating the region more and more as a colonial appendage. Instead of merely squeezing profits out of the processing, shipping, and financing of the cotton crop, Yankee financiers began to invade the South directly, buying up land and resources and sending in their lieutenants to oversee the operations. Nearly two-thirds of the South's workers were thus employed in low-value-creating jobs in the production of raw materials for extractive industries such as agriculture, forestry, and mining, which were characterized by absentee ownership. Still, bankrupt Southern communities fell over themselves to attract Northern investors, who liked the region's combination of abundant natural resources, cheap energy, and tractable labor that could be paid in pennies per hour—$2.50 for a seventy-hour week (plus housing and a few fringe benefits) was standard pay for mill hands of that era—and counted on not to strike.

All along the line, then, Southerners found themselves in a tributary position to outside capital that seemed to thrive on the fatal weaknesses of the plantation-system legacy. The burden fell most heavily on the small farmers of both races who made up the bulk of the population. Broke and frustrated, they turned with an unaccustomed snarl upon the white Southerners who were running things—the Redeemers, that curious mixture of old Bourbon aristocrats and the new breed of merchants, industrialists, and local representatives of Northern capital. The lot of them were seen as agents perpetuating a system that was increasingly intolerable. Poor-white farmers and workers began to see that perhaps they had a good deal to gain by discarding allegiance to white solidarity and uniting politically with the blacks. The white Southern Farmers' Alliance had branches in every state by 1889 and took as its ally the Colored Farmers' National Alliance and Cooperative Union, which claimed a million members by 1891. Together, they threw their weight behind many of the causes supported by the Populist Party and demanded that the federal government stop serving the exclusive interests of industrial wealth and corporate privilege. Government's larger responsibility was to the welfare of the people.

White Southerners rallying behind the Populist banner were suddenly eager to enlist the voting strength of black men whom they had just as eagerly been shoving out of polling places a few years earlier. Opposing conservatives, fearful of losing control of government built largely on massive disenfranchisement of the Negro, responded in kind, and now both sides were courting the black voter, bribing him when practical, and otherwise placing him in a pivotal position. But strength was lacking for a genuine agrarian revolution, and by 1896 the white backlash came whacking down on the last vestiges of black electoral power. Nervous Southern Democrats saw that the Negro was ever ready to install himself as a potent political force between white classes and factions, and once confirmed in that role, he would be enthroned as the veritable arbiter of Southern politics. The Negro had to be disabused of further fancy notions that he was entitled to the same rights as any white man and was therefore as good. Rebellious poor-whites, fearful that they themselves might be deprived of the vote if they persisted in the Populist cause, went along with the new movement to close white ranks. Increasing economic rivalry between the races in a lean time sparked new hate and anxiety among white men who found comfort nowhere else but in the color of their skin. It was no trick at all for them to persuade themselves that the black man was the cause, and not the fellow victim, of their degradation. White supremacy had all the fuel it needed.

Mississippi had led the way by calling a state constitutional convention in 1890 for the avowed purpose of disenfranchising the Negro. Out of it came a new suffrage law that required a two-dollar poll tax, excluded voters convicted of bribery, burglary, theft, or bigamy, and barred anyone who could not read any section of the state constitution or understand it when read aloud and give a reasonably good interpretation of it back to the reader. This last interpretive feature was a new refinement in the maturing art of disenfranchisement, and since it left a great deal of discretion to white election officials, 123,000 black voters in Mississippi were defunct practically overnight. After the Populist scare, the rest of the South followed suit. In 1895, South Carolina's convention adopted voting requirements of a one-dollar poll tax, two years of residence, and the ability to read and write the constitution or ownership of property valued at $300. Louisiana joined the movement in 1898, adding as a fillip the infamous "grandfather clause" that provided for the permanent registration of all men whose fathers or grandfathers had been qualified to vote as of January 1, 1867—just before the First Reconstruction Act mandating the Negro vote was passed by the Radical Republican Congress. Negroes who wanted to vote would have to meet prohibitive educational and property requirements. The effect of the new law was immediately evident: 130,344 Negroes had been registered in Louisiana in 1896; by March of 1900, two years after the new constitution, just 5,320 Negroes remained registered.

In 1898, the Supreme Court of the United States passed judgment on such schemes. Speaking through Justice Joseph McKenna, who had just moved to the bench after serving as William McKinley's Attorney General for a year, the Court ruled in *Williams v. Mississippi* that such codes, alleged to disenfranchise Negroes, "do not, on their face, discriminate between the white and Negro races, and do not amount to a denial of equal protection of the law . . . and it has not been shown that their actual administration was evil but only that evil was possible under them." In other words, as in the *United States v. Reese* decision, those who would do in the Negro were absolved from their heinous acts so long as they did not proclaim their intentions to the world in so many words. It was a hard sort of justice for its black victim to fathom.

By 1910, every Southern state had followed the lead of Mississippi and South Carolina in reducing the black man to a political cipher. The Fifteenth Amendment lay mortally wounded beside him.

The Fourteenth had fared hardly better. In the hands of the Supreme Court, it had been twisted nearly unrecognizable within twenty years of the end of the Civil War. It seemed part of a pattern of abandonment. Federal troops had folded their tents and gone home. The national government had shaken hands with the white masters of the South and ordained them to conduct racial matters as those forcibly retired slavedrivers saw fit. The black man was left severely vulnerable.

It should have surprised no one, therefore, when he began to be lynched. In the twenty years following the Supreme Court's decision in the *Civil Rights Cases*, 3,000 lynchings occurred. Almost certainly many others went unreported. The number of lynchings alone, though, tells only a small part of the story. Because they were carried out with impunity—it was the exceedingly rare white man who was tried for participating in a lynching, and a conviction was unheard of—no black man anywhere any time could feel secure. He always had to be on his mettle or risk providing the kindling for the quickly stirred mob's Saturday-night spectacle.

By 1892, lynchings had climbed to an unofficial figure of 231, the most ever in a single year. The widespread barbarism seemed to activate Southern hormones in less disreputable—but no less obvious—displays of hate as well: by 1892, the first segregation laws were in force in no fewer than nine Southern states, which now required railroad companies to assign colored passengers to cars separate from whites. The legalized degradation of the Negro in the form of a state-mandated caste system had begun. But here, beyond a speck of doubt, were cases of "state action"—laws duly enacted by state legislatures setting blacks apart from the rest of the population. If the Fourteenth Amendment could yet provide any sanctuary for the black man, surely it would cover this development. Surely laws openly discriminatory against the Negro were a denial of equal protection. Hadn't the Court made that plain by the ringing language of the *Strauder* decision as early as 1879?

The Court's answer would come in the closing years of the nineteenth century. For the Negro's dwindling hopes under the great amendment passed in the afterglow of what had become a holy war, it would prove the *coup de grâce.*

In 1895, the city of Atlanta, Georgia, stood as a symbol of the politically restored and economically reviving South. In the three decades since the warlock Sherman had ordered his troops to put it to the torch, the city had been entirely rebuilt. It was turning into the rail and industrial hub of the burgeoning Southeast as the whole region lured the likes of the Mellons and the Rockefellers, who sent their agents roving through Dixie for new treasures. J. Pierpont Morgan had just organized the Southern Railway system.

To celebrate the rise of the New South and stir yet more investor interest, Atlanta decided to throw itself a party. Grandly called the Atlanta Cotton States and International Exposition, it was the closest thing to a world's fair the South had ever seen. Its organizers included the most progressive thinkers of the region, several of whom persuaded the rest that the fairground exhibitions ought to include a pavilion devoted to the progress the colored folks had made since achieving freedom. Such a display would reassure outsiders that the South was kindly disposed to its black population and coping well with the racial question. And if amity prevailed, the South was all that much better a place to put your money to work.

Having gone that far, the exposition leaders then took the risky additional step of deciding to invite a Negro to address the opening ceremonies in September of 1895. It would have to be just the right fellow, of course. The press from all over the world would be covering the event, and never before, in anyone's memory, had a colored man shared a prominent public platform with white men in the South. The acknowledged grand old man of his people, Frederick Douglass, had died in Washington that February. But that stormy petrel would surely not have been the sort to serve this purpose. Their choice was a beautifully mannered ex-slave whose good work among his people at the school he had built over in Tuskegee, Alabama, was fast bringing him fame and admiration among Southerners of both races.

Booker T. Washington—the "T." was for his old master's name of Taliaferro; the "Washington" he had selected himself—was thirty-nine years old when he boarded the train for Atlanta and the speech that would make him a national figure overnight. The heat was bad on September 18, 1895, and the three-hour procession to launch the exposition drained him. He had been nervous for days, and now as he entered the great exposition hall as the chosen spokesman of his race, he shook off his anxiety and took heart at what he would remember as "the vigorous cheers from the colored portion of the audience." Newspapermen would wire back stories that the black educator had stood straight and proud and that the sun streaming into the hall reflected off his face as the governor of Georgia introduced him with the words, "We have with us today a representative of Negro enterprise and Negro civilization." And then Booker T. Washington spoke the words of accommodation that amounted to surrender. First he apologized for the apparent overreaching of his race:

> . . . Ignorant and inexperienced, it is not strange that in the first years of our new life we began at the top instead of at the bottom; that a seat in Congress or the state legislature was more sought than real estate or industrial skill; that the political convention of stump speaking had more attractions than starting a dairy farm or truck garden.

Then he urged his race to be realistic: "Cast down your bucket where you are," and added:

> Our greatest danger is that in the great leap from slavery to freedom we may overlook the fact that the masses of us are to live by the productions of our hands, and fail to keep in mind that we shall prosper in proportion as learn to dignify and glorify common labor and put brains and skill into the common occupations of life . . . to draw the line between the superficial and the substantial, the ornamental geegaws of life and the useful. No race can prosper till it learns that there is as much dignity in tilling a field as in writing a poem. It is at the bottom of life we must begin, and not at the top.

To his white listeners, he respectfully recommended kindliness toward the black people of the South who, with the education of their head, hand, and heart,

> will buy your surplus land, make blossom the waste places in your fields, and run your factories. While doing this, you can be sure in the future, as in the past, that you and your families will be surrounded by the most patient, faithful, law-abiding and unresentful people that the world has seen. . . .

Then, to clinch the bargain he thought he was negotiating, he declared,

> . . . in our humble way, we shall stand by you with a devotion that no foreigner can approach, ready to lay down our lives, if need be, in defense of yours, interlacing our industrial, commercial, civil, and religious life with yours in a way that shall make the interests of both races one. In all things that are purely social we can be as separate as the fingers, yet one as the hand in all things essential to mutual progress.

He concluded his call for amity between the races by assuring his rapt audience that he would do his best to muzzle the discontent in his own people.

> The wisest among my race understand that the agitation of questions of social equality is the extremest folly, and that progress in the enjoyment of all the privileges that will come to us must be the result of severe and constant struggle

rather than of artificial forcing. . . . It is important and right that all privileges of the law be ours, but it is vastly more important that we be prepared for the exercises of these privileges. The opportunity to earn a dollar in a factory just now is worth infinitely more than the opportunity to spend a dollar in an opera-house.

The governor of Georgia rushed across the stage to shake the hand of this superbly understanding and reasonable colored man who would ask for nothing for his people until they had demonstrated their readiness for the gifts of full citizenship. The hall rang with approval. Crowds eager to shake Booker Washington's hand thronged him on the streets of downtown Atlanta, and at every train stop on the way home to Tuskegee more crowds turned out for a glimpse of the new black hero of the South, the first to be held as such in biracial regard. The editor of the Atlanta *Constitution* wrote: "The whole speech is a platform upon which blacks and whites can stand with full justice to each other." Until his death twenty years later, Booker Washington would reign as the uncrowned king of black America. Frederick Douglass was gone, and the scepter of leadership had now been taken up by a very different sort of Negro out of sympathy for the words of the dead Douglass: "If there is no struggle, there is no progress. Those who profess to favor freedom, and yet deprecate agitation, are men who want crops without plowing up the ground. . . . Power concedes nothing without a demand. It never did and never will. . . ."

In the year that Booker Washington genuflected to the white man at Atlanta, the United States was dominated by conservative thought as it had never been. The industrial goliaths had been born or were about to be, and the men behind them believed that the economically strong should be free to prey upon the economically weak without interference of government; in short, they favored the survival of the fittest. The old wounds of war had been largely patched up, and a thriving alliance of businessmen from both North and South had moved decisively to turn back the wild-eyed threat of Populism and assure continuation of its own orderly pillage. Conservative Presidents cooperated fully, and the men they named to the Supreme Court for the most part supported government's distant stance.

Since the *Civil Rights Cases* decision in 1883, the Court had been substantially remade. By 1895, only three members of the Waite Court survived—clear-headed Samuel Miller, proud old Stephen Field, and the conscience-stricken Kentuckian, John Marshall Harlan. In the Chief Justice's chair now sat the most obscure man ever named to the position—Melville Weston Fuller, the first Democrat to preside since Roger Taney. Fuller's distinctions included the only mustache ever worn till then by a Chief Justice, a hack political background devoid of exposure to federal issues, a legal practice built upon representing his father-in-law's big Chicago bank, a social philosophy unswervingly dedicated to the divinity of profits, and a long-standing record of hostility to the cause of the Negro. Believing "it is the duty of the people to support the government and not of the government to support the people," he efficiently administered the proceedings of the Court as it converted the Fourteenth Amendment from a sword to win the black man equal protection of the laws into a shield to assure corporations that their rates, prices, and profits would not be unduly regulated without due process of law.

Fuller's seventh year as head of the Court—1895—was to see it at the height of its consecrated conservatism. In that year, it ruled that the nation's first federal income tax (of 2 percent on all incomes over $4,000) was unconstitutional; that the holding company with a lock on 98 percent of the sugar sold and refined in the nation was not in violation of the Sherman Antitrust Act of 1890; and that an injunction was justified against the officers of the American Railway Union for striking the Pullman Company and that the union's president, Eugene Victor Debs, should be sent to prison. The prospects of the Negro, then, were somewhat less than glowing in the year 1896 when the Supreme Court, headed by a man who had once fought for a constitutional amendment to prevent federal interference with the practice of slavery, took up a case on the legality of state-required segregation of the races.

Entitled "An Act to promote the comfort of passengers," the law in question was passed by the Louisiana legislature on July 10, 1890, and stated that "all railway companies carrying passengers in their coaches in this State, shall provide equal but separate accommodations for the white, and colored, races, by providing two or more passenger coaches for each passenger train, or by dividing the passenger coaches by a partition so as to secure separate accommodations." Any passenger not honoring the arrangement was liable to a fine of $25 or not more than twenty days in jail. Discrimination of this sort had been practiced erratically in the South prior to 1887, when Florida passed the first railway-segregation act. Before then, Negroes had generally been forbidden in first-class cars, though in some of the coastal states there were frequent exceptions, and had generally been allowed to mix with white passengers in second-class or "smoking" cars. Each railroad set its own rules, and nowhere had a state law required segregation of this sort. But Florida's enactment of such a law was followed by one in Mississippi the following year and in Texas the year after that. The Jim Crow era had begun.

The Negro community in New Orleans was a highly vocal and visible one, and the rich mixture of black, French, Indian, and Anglo-Saxon stock made Louisiana a racial *bouillabaisse* unlike any other state in the nation. Negroes passing as whites were common, and ancestral lines were often so tangled and untraceable that many no longer bothered to fret about how racially pure or polluted their blood was. The 1890 legislature that passed the railway-segregation law contained eleven Negro members, and the colored community at large entered strong protest against the bill, saying that it would be a "license to the evilly-disposed that they might with impunity insult, humiliate, and otherwise maltreat inoffensive persons, and especially women and children who should happen to have a dark skin." But the swing to racism had picked up momentum in Louisiana, which under Radical Reconstruction in 1869 had passed a law *forbidding* public carriers to segregate its passengers—precisely the opposite of what it now legalized in 1890. The 1869 law was overturned by the United States Supreme Court in 1877 in the case of *Hall v. DeCuir*, which held Louisiana's anti-segregation statute to be an invasion of the right of Congress to regulate interstate commerce, even though the law had limited its reach to conveyances within the state. A white passenger boarding a segregated carrier outside of Louisiana, the Court indicated, would be obliged to share the coach or car or cabin with colored passengers once the conveyance entered Louisiana, and that was not the sort of regulation a state ought to be making, for "If the public good requires such legislation, it must come from Congress and not from the states." Yet when Mississippi passed legislation for the precisely opposite purpose in 1888—that is, to make segregation on trains *mandatory* within its state borders—the Supreme Court ignored its own ruling in *Hall v. DeCuir* and found no intrusion on interstate commerce. What Mississippi did within its borders was Mississippi's business, the Court said, and so the state was upheld in its prosecution of the Louisville, New Orleans & Texas Railway for failing to install separate facilities for Negroes. But the Court ducked the more profound question of whether Negro passengers had to submit to such state-imposed segregation and ride in separate cars.

The Negroes of Louisiana were determined to test the new law. Its implications were expansive and deeply unsettling. Railroad officials approached by the black protest group were found to be sympathetic. They had put separate "Colored" cars on their passenger trains as the law prescribed, but they urged their conductors not to enforce the law with much vigor. The added cost of the separate cars was an obvious factor in the railroad's lack of enthusiasm for the segregation statute. "They want to help us," one of the black leaders reported back, "but dread public opinion." And so on June 7, 1892, after two years of agitation and false starts, an exceedingly light-skinned Negro named Homer Adolph Plessy boarded an East Louisiana Railway train for a run from New Orleans to Covington, about thirty miles north of the city near the Mississippi border. Plessy took a seat in a car reserved for whites and was promptly asked by the conductor to move to the car for colored passengers—almost certainly a prearranged action in view of the railroad's professed distaste for the segregation law and of Plessy's "seven-eighths Caucasian" coloration. When Plessy refused to move, he was arrested by a detective standing by and soon hailed before Judge John H. Ferguson of the Criminal District Court for the Parish of New Orleans, who ruled against Plessy's argument that the segregation law was a violation of the Fourteenth Amendment and therefore void. Ferguson's ruling was appealed to the Louisiana Supreme Court, which granted the petition for Plessy to take his case to the Supreme Court of the United States.

The Supreme Court did not get around to handing down its opinion in *Plessy* until 1896. To write it, Chief Justice Fuller chose one of the Court's dimmer lights, Massachusetts-born Henry Billings Brown. Brown was thoroughly grounded in federal law and procedures after having served as a United States marshal, a United States Attorney, and a United States District judge for Eastern Michigan. And his own earlier private practice had given him added perspective. Since being appointed to the Supreme Court by Benjamin Harrison, Brown had proven a steady, useful member, relatively free of ideological ballast. His guy wires were fastened to unadorned, conservative, Anglo-Saxon, Protestant, white, middle-class values that were probably close to the national consensus as a computer might have determined it. While a federal District judge, he had occasionally sat on Southern courts and been charmed by the cordiality extended to him. During the Civil War, he declined to serve in the Union army, instead hiring a substitute as the law permitted. Nothing in his background, then, suggested an opinion friendly—or particularly unfriendly—to the hopes of Homer Plessy and the race he represented. Six of Brown's fellow Justices joined in his remarkable opinion. A seventh, Justice David Brewer, did not participate in the case—why is not known, for members of the Court are not required to explain why they choose not to sit on a case. The usual assumption is that something in the Justice's pre-Court experience or off-the-bench life might tend to prejudice his thinking in the case. Justice Brewer, at any rate, had written the opinion of the Court upholding the Mississippi railway-segregation law and, it is more likely than not, would have endorsed Justice Brown's opinion in *Plessy*. Only one Justice dissented from the Court majority.

The nub of the case was whether Plessy had been denied his privileges, immunities, and equal protection of the law under the Fourteenth Amendment. But it was not at all clear, Justice Brown wrote, just what rights were covered by the Fourteenth Amendment. No doubt it had been written to establish the citizenship of the Negro, but as the Court had defined it in the *Slaughterhouse Cases*, the citizenship of the Negro—and of everybody else—was really dual: he was a citizen of his state and of the United States. *Slaughterhouse* "did not call for any expression of opinion as to the exact rights it was intended to secure to the colored race" but was meant generally "to protect from the hostile legislation of the States the privileges and immunities of citizens of the United States, as distinguished from those of citizens of the States." Distinguished how? And by whom? The Court had never said. Justice Brown now filled the void:

> The object of the amendment was undoubtedly to enforce the absolute equality of the two races before the law, but in the nature of things it could not have been intended to abolish distinctions based upon color, or to enforce social, as distinguished from political equality, or a commingling of the two races upon terms unsatisfactory to either.

It would be onerous work to find a more unsupported or unsupportable sentence in the annals of American jurisprudence. The universally acknowledged, exhaustively documented intention of the framers of the Fourteenth Amendment had been to remove degradation of the Negro from the realm of legitimate legislative ends. Aside from the vaporous words "but in the nature of things," nowhere in the balance of the opinion was any justification offered for the flat statement that the amendment "could not have been intended to abolish distinctions based upon color." The contrast cited between "political" and "social" equality, moreover, rested upon no words written in the amendment itself or spoken during the congressional debates over it. Justice Brown went on:

> Laws permitting, or even requiring, [racial] separation in places where [the races] are liable to be brought into contact do not necessarily imply the inferiority of either race to the other, and have been generally, if not universally, recognized as within the competency of the state legislatures in the exercise of their police power. . . .

If they did not imply the inferiority of one of the two races, then what *did* such laws of enforced separation imply? What else could they conceivably have implied? Perhaps if such laws had been submitted by plebiscite for the approval of each racial group, a favorable vote by each race would have signified the mutually agreeable character of such separation. But no such step was undertaken or obviously ever contemplated by the lawmakers fashioning the Louisiana separate-railroad-car requirement. It was imposed by the whites upon the blacks on the sheer strength of numbers and willfulness.

Brown then began to document his argument:

> . . . The most common instance of this [state-sanctioned separation of the races] is connected with the establishment of separate schools for white and colored children, which has been held to be a valid exercise of the legislative power even by courts of States where the political rights of the colored race have been longest and most earnestly enforced.
> One of the earliest of these cases is that of *Roberts v. City of Boston.* . . .

It was perhaps fitting that Justice Brown, a native of the little Berkshire village of South Lee, Massachusetts, should stake an important part of his case on a decision by the Supreme Judicial Court of Massachusetts made in 1849. The *Roberts* case had been a sensation in its day. Five-year-old Sarah Roberts would leave home and walk past five elementary schools for white children only on her way to the Smith Grammar School, which the city of Boston had maintained as a public school for Negroes since 1820. An evaluation committee had reported to the city that the Smith School was badly run down—"the school rooms are too small, the paint is much defaced," and the equipment "has been so shattered and neglected that it cannot be used until it has been thoroughly repaired"—and Sarah Roberts' father tried repeatedly to place her in one of the nearby schools available to white children. Rebuffed in each instance, he turned to the courts and selected as attorney Charles Sumner, whose eloquence and fervor would soon win him wide distinction in the United States Senate and a reputation as slavery's most implacable enemy. Sumner argued the case before a court headed by the most highly regarded state jurist of his age—Chief Justice Lemuel Shaw, whose scholarship and legal acumen had had a shaping impact on American law for twenty years.

Citing passages from the Massachusetts constitution that courts of a later era were to liken to the equal-protection clause of the Fourteenth Amendment, Sumner declared that every form of discrimination in civil and political institutions was thereby outlawed. For the Boston school committee to segregate Negro children was to "brand a whole race with the stigma of inferiority and degradation," and for the school committee to do that would be to place itself above the state constitution. No, if the committee were going to impose discriminatory classifications, these must bear a reasonable relationship to the legitimate business of education: children might be classified by age, by sex, or by moral and intellectual fitness in assigning them to schools and classrooms—but not by race or color. A segregated school, said Sumner, could not be considered as the equivalent of the white schools because of the inconvenience and the stigma of caste that mandatory attendance of it imposed on the Negro child. A public school was just that—a place for the benefit of all classes meeting together on equal terms. Segregation, moreover, injured the white pupils as well: "Their hearts, while yet tender with childhood, are necessarily hardened by this conduct, and their subsequent lives, perhaps, bear enduring testimony to this legalized uncharitableness."

Sumner was probably never more eloquent. Judge Shaw, though, was unpersuaded. His decision would be cited as precedent by a dozen state courts and by the United States Supreme Court on at least three occasions by way of justifying state-approved segregation of the races. Sumner's invocation of "the great principle" that all persons ought to stand equal before the law, Shaw wrote, was "perfectly sound" and "animates the whole spirit of our constitution of free government." But, he went on, dooming Sarah Roberts' plea,

> when this great principle comes to be applied to the actual and various conditions of persons in society, it will not warrant the assertion, that men and women are legally clothed with the same civil and political powers, and that children and adults are legally to have the same functions and be subject to the same treatment; but only that the rights of all, as they are settled and regulated by law, are equally entitled to the paternal consideration and protection of the law, for their maintenance and security. What these rights are, to which individuals, in the infinite variety of circumstances by which they are surrounded in society, are entitled, must depend upon laws adapted to their respective relations and conditions.

Yet the judge failed to suggest, and certainly to demonstrate, that the discrimination practiced by the Boston school committee had any foundation in reason. School segregation, he said, was for the good of both races—as if asserting as much made it so.

Whatever the wisdom or lack of it in the Shaw opinion, it is important to note that in citing it prominently and at length in the text proper and not as a footnote in his *Plessy* opinion, Justice Brown was playing fast and loose with history, for he wrote of the *Roberts* case, "Similar [segregation] laws have been enacted by Congress under its general power of legislation over the District of Columbia . . . as well as by the legislatures of many of the States, and have been generally, if not uniformly, upheld by the courts." In fact, Congress passed a law of a somewhat different kind, one that did not require segregation of the schools but permitted local custom to dictate. More to the point, Justice Brown conveniently neglected to mention that the state legislature of Massachusetts voted to prohibit school segregation just six years after Shaw's opinion in *Roberts*. Still more to the point, between the *Roberts* and *Plessy* cases a war was fought that enabled passage of the Fourteenth Amendment, which mandated equality of the races. To cite so prominently a state case that predated the amendment by twenty years and to ignore the historic circumstances of and motives for the passage of the amendment were, at best, tendentious tactics by Justice Brown. The seven other precedents he cited in the state courts had only hazy relevance. In the California case of *Ward v. Flood*, decided in 1874, for instance, the issue before the state court was not whether segregated schools were permissible but whether Negro children might be excluded from the public schools in the absence of schools specifically set aside for them. (The California court said no.) In the Kentucky case of *Dawson v. Lee* decided in 1884, the issue under litigation was whether tax revenues from whites could be used solely for white schools and from blacks for black schools. (The Kentucky court held that such taxation would result in inferior schools for Negro children and was thus unconstitutional.) And those state cases that were legitimately parallel to the Louisiana statute under challenge in *Plessy* were for the most part decided in the years just after the Fourteenth Amendment was adopted and there was as yet no Supreme Court law on the question to guide the state and federal district courts.

But Justice Brown was just entering his quagmire. The opinion grew stickier as it proceeded:

> The distinction between laws interfering with the political equality of the negro and those requiring the separation of the two races in schools, theatres, and railway carriages has been frequently drawn by this court.

In fact, the only relevant distinction the Court had drawn was in the *Civil Rights Cases*, where it held that discriminatory practices by private parties operating businesses specified in the 1875 Civil Rights Act—inns, conveyances, places of entertainment—were not "state action" under the Fourteenth Amendment and so did not violate it. Patently, the Louisiana statute mandating separate railroad cars was not a private act of discrimination but an instance of "state action" taken by a duly elected legislature. Nothing daunted, Justice Brown plowed ahead to demonstrate the fragility of his own premise by citing the Court's decisions on laws "requiring the separation of the two races" as if they supported his proposition that the issue had long been settled.

First he noted the Court's 1877 decision in *Hall v. DeCuir*, striking down the 1869 Louisiana statute *prohibiting* segregation on public carriers because it was said to intrude on congressional supervision of interstate commerce. Yet there was not a word in that opinion about equal protection or the Fourteenth Amendment. "Much nearer, and, indeed, almost directly in point," said Justice Brown, was the Court's opinion in *Louisville, New Orleans & Texas Railway v. Mississippi*, in which the Justices upheld the

Mississippi state law of 1888 requiring segregated passenger cars—a decision that had also in fact entirely avoided consideration of how the racial prohibition affected the rights and privileges guaranteed against state deprivation by the Fourteenth Amendment; instead, the Court held that since the segregation statute in question applied solely to commerce within the state of Mississippi, it did not poach on the power given to Congress under Article I of the Constitution to regulate interstate commerce. Such reasoning was totally irrelevant to the question of whether the segregation law offended the rights of the segregated black citizens of Mississippi, who under the Fourteenth Amendment had been promised equal protection of the laws of Mississippi. The pressing issue in both the Mississippi case and *Plessy* was not the power of Congress to regulate interstate commerce but the legitimacy of the power each state legislature had exercised in classifying its citizens by race and separating them by force while they rode trains that traveled entirely within the borders of their state.

Having propped up a straw man, Justice Brown then had no trouble in brushing him aside. The real issue, he perceived now, was whether a state could segregate passengers who remained within its borders. "Similar statutes for the separation of the two races upon public conveyances," Brown wrote by way of establishing the legitimacy of the Louisiana law, "were held to be constitutional" in eleven state and lower federal cases that he cited. Unfortunately, not one of the eleven cases reached the constitutional issue presented to the Court in *Plessy*. And a number of them could in no plausible way be read to relate to the legality of the Louisiana law. The most that can be said about the eleven citations as a group, aside from their disclosure that Justice Brown was not very conscientious about his homework, is that they all dealt with public conveyances of one sort or another. Beyond that, the similarity is either remote or nonexistent. The first case cited *(West Chester and Pennsylvania Railroad Company v. Miles)*, for instance, was decided before the ratification of the Fourteenth Amendment and did not involve any constitutional or statutory question but the matter of the reasonableness of racial separation under a regulation imposed by the railroad, not the state. In another case, the issue was whether the separate facilities provided for Negroes were adequate—not whether the law itself was valid. In a third case, the issue was whether the management of a steamer traveling from Maryland to Virginia had taken proper pains to protect "a well-behaved, educated minister of the Christian religion" who was allegedly set upon by his fellow passengers because his dark skin offended them. Only one of the cases cited, moreover, even involved the constitutionality of a state statute, and in that case the New York courts had held that a law prohibiting the exclusion of any citizen from a place of amusement because of race did not violate the federal constitutional provision protecting the property rights of the owner. In short, an entirely different legal issue was involved.

Having dealt with legal precedent in so cavalier a fashion, Justice Brown then began to confront the key to the case with some candor. Was the railway-segregation law a justifiable exercise of the state's police power? The answer, he said, was that "every exercise of the police power must be reasonable, and extend only to such laws as are enacted in good faith for the promotion for the public good, and not for the annoyance or oppression of a particular class." And he cited in support the Court's enlightened decision in *Yick Wo v. Hopkins*, an 1886 case that invalidated a San Francisco municipal statute prohibiting laundry businesses from being conducted in wooden buildings. The law had been passed ostensibly as a safety measure, but the Court saw in it instead an arbitrary classification—in this case, aimed at the owners of laundries, almost all of whom were Chinese and almost all of whom operated in wooden buildings. Here was plainly racial bias, for,

> Though the law itself be fair on its face and impartial in appearance, yet, if it is applied and administered by public authority with an evil eye and an unequal hand, so as practically to make unjust and illegal discriminations between persons in similar circumstances, material to their rights, the denial of equal justice is still within the prohibition of the Constitution.

In citing *Yick Wo*, Justice Brown seemed to think he was buttressing his ultimate finding in support of the Louisiana segregation statute, for he remarked that the San Francisco laundry case was concerned with a statute that sought "to make an arbitrary and unjust discrimination against the Chinese race." And did he not find that the Louisiana law in *Plessy* was a similarly arbitrary and unjust discrimination against a racial group? He did not, explaining:

> So far, then, as a conflict with the Fourteenth Amendment is concerned, the case reduces itself to the question whether the statute of Louisiana is a reasonable regulation, and with respect to this there must necessarily be a large discretion on the part of the legislature. In determining the question of reasonableness it is at liberty to act with reference to the established usages, customs and traditions of the people, and with a view to the promotion of their comfort, and the preservation of the public peace and good order. Gauged by this standard, we cannot say that a law which authorizes or even requires the separation of the two races in public conveyances is unreasonable. . . .

His support for this line of thinking was "the acts of Congress requiring separate schools for colored children in the District of Columbia, the constitutionality of which does not seem to have been questioned, [and] the corresponding acts of state legislatures." Leaving aside the fact that Congress had not *required* segregated schools, we are left to understand that Justice Brown was saying the practice of segregation in Louisiana was not a violation of the Fourteenth Amendment because various other states were also practicing segregation. And this was all right so long as it was in keeping with the "established usages, customs and traditions of the people." What "established usages, customs and traditions" of Louisiana did the Justice have in mind? If he meant segregation in public conveyances as a private policy of the carriers, he was on exceedingly thin ice. Jim Crow transportation practices varied widely in the South and were by no means the universal practice. In many places, second-class coaches had long been shared by white and colored passengers. Nor could it be contended that segregation as a state-mandated practice was an established usage, custom, or tradition of any venerability. Of the eight Southern states that had Jim Crow transportation laws at the time of the *Plessy* decision, seven had had them for eight years or less. What Justice Brown must have been alluding to, then, was the relative social standing of the two races as it had evolved during more than two centuries in which the enslavement and debasement of the Negro had become the established usage, custom, and tradition of the white people of Louisiana. No one, of course, had bothered to ask the slaves how they felt about the traditional practice. Justice Brown, in short, would make no provision for the fact or purpose or result of the Civil War. He wrote as if the South had won. And as if, when it failed to acknowledge its loss and instead passed its Black Codes, the nation had not imposed Radical Reconstruction upon it in the belief that nothing short of compulsion would bring the South to alter its "established usages, customs and traditions" of treating the Negro as a marginal form of humanity.

As to the "preservation of the public peace and good order" which Justice Brown said the state legislature might wish to consider in passing a racial-segregation law, no one involved in the case had suggested that such was in fact the reason for passing the law. Evidence of public disorder because of racial mingling on trains did not exist, nor had any other reasonable basis for such a statute been put forth at the time of its passage.

Nearing the end of his extraordinary performance, Justice Brown then struck perhaps the most remarkable note of all:

> We consider the underlying fallacy of the plaintiff's argument to consist in the assumption that the enforced separation of the two races stamps the colored race with a badge of inferiority. If this be so, it is not by reason of anything found in the act, but solely because the colored race chooses to put that construction upon it.

Of all the words ever written in assessment of the *Plessy* opinion, none have been more withering than those offered sixty-four years after the decision by Yale law professor Charles L. Black, Jr., who, among other points, cited the two sentences above in a footnote and then added: "The curves of callousness and stupidity intersect at their respective maxima."

Justice Brown could support his claim of what amounted to black paranoia only by proposing a few final *non sequiturs,* among them that "Legislation is powerless to eradicate racial instincts or to abolish distinctions based upon physical differences. . . . If the civil and political rights of both races be equal one cannot be inferior to the other civilly or politically. If one race be inferior to the other socially, the Constitution of the United States cannot put them upon the same plane." In other words, Justice Brown seemed to be saying, since laws cannot affect how men think about and react to their racial differences, there can be no harm in laws that are based upon and emphasize those differences. Furthermore, so long as all men are proclaimed by statute to be treated equally by the state, then they indeed are treated equally by the state. If some men feel they are not treated equally merely because the law requires them to be separated from the rest of the citizenry, such a feeling can be of no concern to the state. Finally, if some men are truly inferior to others, the state may not be held accountable, for laws—it is well known—can not disturb mankind's more unruly habits.

Justice Brown and seven of his eight brethren had tortured truth to make the shoe fit: racially separate facilities, so long as they were equal, could legally be ordained by the state; segregation was not discrimination. To reach that conclusion, the Court had to indulge in a willful reading of human nature and to abuse case law, common law, and common sense. In dismissing the wound men suffer when forcefully separated from their fellow citizens for no reason beyond the pigmentation of their skin, the Supreme Court was reduced to pretending that the resulting pain was self-inflicted, the result of an overly fragile psychological makeup. It was unfortunate, said the Justices, but that was life.

In his nearly thirty-four years on the Supreme Court, Justice John Marshall Harlan heard 14,226 cases. In 745 of them, he was designated to write the opinion of the Court. In 100 of them, he wrote separate concurring opinions. In 13,074 of them, he endorsed the majority opinion. In but 316 of them, he dissented. It is upon those dissents, though, that Justice Harlan's reputation largely rests.

In many ways, he was a deeply conservative man. Few surpassed him in his belief in the sanctity of property, and he thought the Constitution ought to be followed closely and courts ought to tread with utmost caution upon the discretionary acts of legislatures—a philosophy strongly shared by his colleague Justice Oliver Wendell Holmes during Harlan's latter years on the Court. Though opposed to secession in the years of his young manhood, Harlan had argued loudly for the preservation of slavery and fought against the Thirteenth Amendment. Some students of his life and writings believe that his transformation from slaveholder into eloquent defender of the black man's rights is traceable to the brutalities he saw inflicted upon Negroes in his native Kentucky during the post-Civil War years—beatings, lynchings, terror tactics beyond any conceivable justification. Whatever the causes, they were more than latently present when he wrote his lonely dissent in *Plessy v. Ferguson.* He cut through Justice Brown's suggestion that nothing malevolent was implied in the segregation law:

> Everyone knows that the statute in question had its origin in the purpose, not so much to exclude white persons from railroad cars occupied by blacks, as to exclude colored people from coaches occupied by or assigned to white persons. . . . The thing to accomplish was, under the guise of giving equal accommodation for whites and blacks, to compel the latter to keep to themselves while travelling in railroad passenger coaches. No one would be so wanting in candor as to assert the contrary.

No one except the seven members of the Supreme Court who voted in the majority to uphold the Louisiana law. Justice Harlan then noted the contagious nature of segregation:

> . . . If a State can prescribe, as a rule of civil conduct, that whites and blacks shall not travel as passengers in the same railroad coach, why may it not so

regulate the use of the streets of its cities and towns as to compel white citizens to keep on one side of the street and black citizens to keep on the other? . . . [I]f this statute of Louisiana is consistent with the personal liberty of citizens, why may not the State require the separation in railroad coaches of native and naturalized citizens of the United States, or of Protestants and Roman Catholics?

After considering the questionable wisdom of using the "reasonableness" of a statute as the ground for judging its legality, he went to the heart of the matter:

The white race deems itself to be the dominant race in this country. And so it is, in prestige, in achievements, in education, in wealth and in power. . . . But in view of the Constitution, in the eye of the law, there is in this country no superior, dominant, ruling class of citizens. There is no caste here. Our Constitution is color-blind, and neither knows nor tolerates classes among its citizens. In respect of civil rights, all citizens are equal before the law. The humblest is the peer of the most powerful. The law regards man as man, and takes no account of his surroundings or of his color when his civil rights as guaranteed by the supreme law of the land are involved.

The immediate and long-term consequences of the Court's majority opinion were not hard to foresee, he said:

The present decision, it may well be apprehended, will not only stimulate aggressions, more or less brutal and irritating, upon the admitted rights of colored citizens, but will encourage the belief that it is possible, by means of state enactments, to defeat the beneficent purposes which the people of the United States had in view when they adopted the recent amendments of the Constitution. . . . Sixty millions of whites are in no danger from the presence here of eight millions of blacks. The destinies of the two races, in this country, are indissolubly linked together, and the interests of both require that the common government of all shall not permit the seeds of race hate to be planted under the sanction of law.

He then termed the arbitrary separation of the races "a badge of servitude wholly inconsistent" with civil freedom and the principle of equality before the law. And he charged Justice Brown's opinion with inappropriate references to state cases, noting,

Some, and the most important, of them are wholly inapplicable, because rendered prior to the adoption of the last amendments of the Constitution, when colored people had very few rights which the dominant race felt obliged to respect. Others were made at a time when public opinion was dominated by the institution of slavery; when it would not have been safe to do justice to the black man. . . . Those decisions cannot be guides in an era introduced by the recent amendments of the supreme law.

Finally, he saw that *Plessy* would be used to justify a plague of discriminatory legislation throughout the nation:

If laws of like character should be enacted in the several States of the Union, the effect would be in the highest degree mischievous. Slavery, as an institution tolerated by law would, it is true, have disappeared from our country, but there would remain a power in the States, by sinister legislation, to interfere with the full enjoyment of the blessings of liberty; to regulate civil rights, common to all citizens, upon the basis of race; and to place in a condition of legal inferiority a large body of American citizens. . . .

Yet even Harlan was to prove capable of grievous pettifoggery on the racial issue. Three years after *Plessy* was decided, the Supreme Court had before it for the first time a case involving separate schools for white and black children. The year was 1899. In Richmond County, Georgia, the board of education maintained a high school for white boys, a high school for white girls, and a high school for Negroes. Finding that there were too many black children of grade-school age to be accommodated in the existing buildings, the board decided to solve the problem by turning the Negro high school into a grade school. This left Negro children without a high school to attend. The board advised them to attend church-affiliated schools. Parents of the black children went to court to prevent the operation of any white high school in the county until Negro children were provided with equal facilities, as required by the opinion in *Plessy*. Their case came before the Supreme Court as *Cumming v. Richmond County Board of Education*. The Court upheld the school board:

> It was said at the argument that the vice in the common school system of Georgia was the requirement that the white and colored children of the state be educated in separate schools. But we need not consider that question in this case. No such issue was made in the pleadings. . . . While all admit that the benefits and burdens of public taxation must be shared by citizens without discrimination against any class on account of their race, the education of people in schools maintained by state taxation is a matter belonging to the respective states, and any interference on the part of Federal authority with the management of such schools cannot be justified except in the case of a clear and unmistakable disregard of rights secured by the supreme law of the land. We have here no such case to be determined.

There was no dissenting opinion. The opinion of the Court was written by Justice John Marshall Harlan.

By the close of the nineteenth century, then, the Supreme Court had nullified nearly every vestige of the federal protection that had been cast like a comforting cloak over the Negro upon his release from bondage. Even his sole demonstrated friend among the Justices was an unreliable champion. Once more, the black man seemed to have no rights that the white man was bound to honor.

# 4

# Not Like Bales of Hay

The toxins of racism flourished as never before throughout America during the first fifteen years of the twentieth century. It infected the entire nation and was openly acknowledged as official policy of the United States government soon after the first Southern-born President since the Civil War—Thomas Woodrow Wilson—took office in 1913. Fifty years after Appomattox, the black man in America had reason to lament his ever having been freed, for by 1915 he was despised and ridiculed as he had never been in slavery.

This outpouring of aggressive hatred may have been released by the continuing, severe economic problems in the South, but it was marked there as everywhere by a lapse in restraining decency and replaced by what C. Vann Woodward has called "permissions-to-hate" granted by people and institutions at the apex of society. The Republican Party, which a generation earlier had fired the nation's spirit and directed a crusade to make all men free, piped a quite different anthem at the close of the nineteenth century as America buoyantly assumed command of eight million colored people in the Caribbean and Pacific as a result of the Spanish-American War.

The press sat in the front row of the imperialist-racist claque. Many of its members came whooping around the pyre with blood in their eye. *The Nation* labeled America's newly conquered victims "a varied assortment of inferior races" who could not, of course, be allowed to vote. The editor of the *Atlantic Monthly* saw the analogy at once. "If the stronger and cleverer race is free to impose its will upon 'new-caught, sullen peoples' on the other side of the globe," he asked rhetorically, "why not in South Carolina and Mississippi?" In the spring of 1900, the *New York Times* noted that such thinking had saturated the nation: "Northern men . . . no longer denounce the suppression of the Negro vote as it used to be denounced in the reconstruction days. The necessity of it under the supreme law of self-preservation is candidly recognized."

There was nothing gentlemanly about the vilification of the Negro in the press. It was a paper lynching. The *Saturday Evening Post*, for example, opened its pages to Thomas Dixon, Jr., whose novels on the Reconstruction period were written in venom. His biggest success was *The Clansman: An Historical Romance of the Ku Klux Klan*, published in 1905 and the inspiration a decade later of the first great creative and box-office success in the infant art of the motion picture—*The Birth of a Nation.* Dixon's books were orgies of hatred. His Negro characters, when they were not clowns, all seemed to be either contemplating or swiftly fleeing after the rape of a white woman.

Periodicals of high repute volleyed epithets like "darkey," "mammy," "buck," and "high yaller" across their pages—"nigger" was very nearly honorific, by comparison—and black characters bore such mocking names as Lady Adelia Chimpanzee and the ever popular Abraham Lincum. Current songs at the turn of the century and shortly thereafter contributed to the abuse with such knee-slapping titles as "If the Man in the Moon Were a Coon," "Go Way Back and Sit Down," "All Coons Look Alike to Me" (subtitled: "A Darkey Misunderstanding"), and "By the Watermelon Vine, Lindy Lou."

If popular culture had lost all its inhibitions with regard to racial courtesy—and, indeed, pandered to its opposite—the presumably more refined academic community was not far behind. As early as 1884, the future dean of Harvard's Lawrence Scientific School cited the Negro's "animal nature" and his innate and allegedly uncontrollable immorality as good reasons for disenfranchising the race. By 1896, a widely circulated report written by a statistician for the Prudential Life Insurance Company and published by the American Economic Association argued that the Negro's "race traits and tendencies" naturally caused his high incidence of tuberculosis, syphilis, scrofula, and other diseases that science would soon recognize as social and not congenital in origin; no improvement in his environment, the report said, would affect his health record, since the root of the problem was the black man's "immense amount of immorality." By the beginning of the new century, the wave of books preaching racial determinism and the unimprovability of the Negro, starting with Charles Carroll's *"The Negro a Beast" or "In the Image of God"* in 1900, turned into a flood, and scholars of large and small eminence contributed to it. Paul B. Barringer, chairman of the faculty at the most eminent center of higher learning in the South—the University of Virginia—told the Southern Education Association meeting in Richmond in 1900 that the Negro's learning ought to be limited to "a Sunday-school training" since his principal function in life was as an incomparable "source of cheap labor for a warm climate; everywhere else he is a foreordained failure, and as he knows this he despises his own color."

Scholars in the North were scarcely more charitable. At New York's Columbia University, which took the lead in the development of sociology and cultural anthropology, Professor Franklin Henry Giddings dwelt on such racist concepts as "consciousness of kind" in his *Principles of Sociology* while his colleague in the history department William H. Dunning was characterizing the enfranchisement of the freedman as a "reckless . . . species of statecraft." The most damning—and intellectually stunting— words of all came from Yale's wide-ranging guru, William Graham Sumner, whose studies in political science and sociology blended scholarship with polemics and a dash or more of divinity. The result was a finding in favor of the free play of capitalism and against soft-on-poverty social quackery promoted by do-gooders and bunglers in or out of government. His 1907 work, *Folkways*, was seized upon at once by Southerners and others convinced of the irremedial backwardness of the Negro and the futility of efforts to improve him. Sumner asserted that "stateways cannot change folkways," and that Reconstruction legislation had been a vain and foolish attempt to sway the white Southerner from his beliefs; folkways were "uniform, universal in the group, imperative and invariable." It was all foreordained, and though "[a] man may curse his fate because he is born of an inferior race," his "imprecations" will go unanswered. A vastly more formidable piece of work, because of the exhaustive research and use of sources that went into it, was Ulrich Bonnell Phillips's *American Negro Slavery*, a monumental recasting of the institution into a kindly and therapeutic practice—a blessing to a race of backward man-children. It was all but unanimous, then. The black man was a second-rate human being. Famous scholars testified to it. Few politicians, North or South, challenged it. The Supreme Court had said it couldn't help it. And the best people everywhere saw small virtue in opposing the swollen tide of racism. Thus, instead of efforts to improve the Negro's lot and make him a more worthy member of the national community, the drive to ostracize him intensified.

In the South, where under slavery the races had lived in close touch and the mastery of the white man was at all times explicit, the free black man was now shoved farther out of the way lest physical mingling be taken as a tacit sign of unacknowledged equality. Stripping the Negro of his civil rights by statute and custom in a fashion sanctioned by the nation's highest court was not enough. Jim Crow, begun on passenger trains, spread rapidly. In 1900, the Richmond *Times* asked that rigid segregation be "applied in every relation of Southern life." The *News and Courier* in Charleston, South Carolina, the oldest newspaper in the South, had ridiculed racial separation in 1898 in the wake of the *Plessy* decision; Jim Crow railroad cars, it said disapprovingly, would soon prompt Jim Crow streetcars and restaurants and saloons, and before long the courts would Jim-Crow the jury box and the witness stand and boast "a Jim Crow Bible for colored witnesses to kiss." Just eight years later, the same newspaper saw things differently: "Segregation of the races is the only radical solution of the negro problem in this country." Special Bibles for colored witnesses were not long in coming. That same year—1906—Montgomery, Alabama, passed the first Jim Crow streetcar law. Restaurants and saloons and boardinghouses throughout the South soon sprouted signs declaring which race they served. Transportation depots and theaters were plainly marked so that black and white travelers and audiences might never be exposed to one another in social intercourse. Public washrooms and water fountains were rigidly demarcated to prevent contaminating contact with the same people who cooked the white South's meals, cleaned its houses, and tended its children.

Having validated racial separation by its narrow, if popular, reading of the Civil War amendments, the Supreme Court contributed importantly to its spread by a decision in 1908. In the *Civil Rights Cases* in 1883, the Court had decided that the states had not been empowered to prevent private discrimination, even by businesses said to be open to the public at large. In *Plessy*, the Court had said that the states themselves could discriminate by segregating the races on public conveyances, in schools, and presumably elsewhere when members of both races would otherwise be thrown into contact against their will. Now, in *Berea College v. Kentucky*, the Court endorsed a far more lethal idea: all contact, whether obligatory and indiscriminate as it would be in biracial public schools or voluntary and selective as it would be in biracial private schools, could be outlawed by the state.

Berea was a brave little college that had prided itself on its racially mixed student body since its founding in 1859. The state of Kentucky finally found the biracial school not to its taste and passed a law saying that any institution could teach members of both races at the same time only if they were taught separately in classes conducted at least twenty-five miles apart. The law was as broad as it was vile, applying to "any person, corporation, or association of persons," though everyone knew it was aimed at just one small maverick college. Berea sued. Kentucky's Supreme Court held the twenty-five-mile separation a bit excessive, but otherwise not only approved the balance of the new state law but applauded its aims. God created the races dissimilar, the court noted, and any interracial association "at all, under certain conditions, leads to the main evil, which is amalgamation. . . . [F]ollowing the order of Divine Providence human authority ought not to compel these widely separated races to intermix."

That Berea College, a totally private institution, did not compel anyone to attend it was simply glided over by the Kentucky court. And when the Supreme Court of the United States took the college's case on appeal, it received a brief from the state of Kentucky that trafficked openly and insistently with racist doctrine:

> If the progress, advancement and civilization of the twentieth century is to go forward, then it must be left, not only to the unadulterated blood of the Anglo-Saxon-Caucasian race, but to the highest types and geniuses of that race. . . .

Berea answered that it had been formed "to promote the cause of Christ" and while it had always recognized the inherent differences in the races, it deemed these as irrelevant to its purpose. And its purpose, it said, was protected amply by the Constitution.

Not quite, said the Supreme Court in a seven-to-two decision that marked its almost total surrender to the states' drive to extinguish not merely the civil rights of Negroes but many of the private prerogatives of white and black people alike. The Kentucky statute was not as harsh as it may have seemed, the Court in effect said, because it did not prevent Berea from teaching students of each race in the same place but at different times, or at the same time but in different places. That being the case, it could not be said that the corporate charter granted to the college by the state had been substantially impaired. Had the college functioned not as a corporation, which thus made it a creature of the state licensing it, but as a private association of individuals, a different order of constitutional question would have presented itself. The Court, though, was not in the habit of passing on broader matters than it needed to, and so it sidestepped the denial of personal liberty at issue in the case—the right of the citizen to free association in his private dealings.

But the high court had done quite enough for one day to spur racial segregation. It had flashed the green light, and in state after state, city after city, town after town, Jim Crow laws went on the books throughout the South and ended biracial attendance in barbershops and baseball parks, in auditoriums and pool halls, at circuses and domino matches. Georgia had put through the first "separate-park law" in 1905, and five years later Baltimore passed the first municipal ordinance restricting where Negroes might live within its city limits. By 1912, three cities in North Carolina had similar laws, and then Richmond, Norfolk, and Roanoke went along the next year, and so did Atlanta. Louisville drew up its version in 1914, and two years later St. Louis and Dallas had authorized residential segregation. School segregation was universal by then in the South and sanctioned by three Supreme Court decisions—*Plessy*, *Cumming*, and *Berea*—just so long as the separate facilities provided each race were equal. Separate-but-equal schools, however, proved a myth from the moment they were approved. In 1910, eleven Southern states spent an average of $9.45 on each white child enrolled in their public schools and $2.90 on each black child. And the disparity grew. By 1916, the per-capita outlay for black children dropped a penny to $2.89, but the white per-capita expense rose to $10.32. And the more heavily Negro any given county's population, the larger the gap in the per-pupil outlay.

The private sector of the economy promoted Jim Crow practices at every turn. Insurance companies charged Negroes higher premiums than whites. Banks discriminated in issuing mortgages on black-owned property. And labor unions showed notorious contempt toward Negroes seeking membership. At best, Negroes could hope for Jim Crow auxiliary units, separate from the main white organization, as Samuel Gompers, president of the American Federation of Labor, proposed in 1900. Ten years later, presumably because job-famished blacks had been used on several occasions as strikebreakers, Gompers wanted no part of black union members because they could not "understand the philosophy of human rights." As Negroes began to abandon the hopeless toil of tenant farming and thronged the cities of the South in the first years of the twentieth century, they inevitably depressed wages— seventy-five cents a day or less was typical—and invited repression from working-class whites. When new industries opened up anywhere, the black man found himself at the end of the job line, especially in fields where mechanization was replacing the skills and handicrafts that the marginally literate or frankly illiterate Negro had to offer.

Up North, European immigration continued heavy—the annual total of arrivals from overseas exceeded the entire Northern resident population of blacks—and blocked a mass migration of Negroes from the South. In the Deep South, sharecropping seemed life's fate for hundreds of thousands.

Starting in 1910, that fate grew even drearier with the arrival from Central America of the tiny traveler known to entomologists as *Anthonomus grandis.* One-fifth of an inch long, the weevil did its damage in a life cycle that ran just twenty days and left the devoured cotton bolls still attached to the plants. What the supply merchant didn't get of his crop, went the black man's lament, the weevil did. Add to nature's ravages a series of floods that paralyzed much of the South in 1915 and the plight of the Negro farmer began to take on a truly Job-like cast.

For all his woe, the Negro in America took heart briefly in the first years of the century at the arrival in the White House of a young, progressive, and idealistic President. In office just a month, Theodore Roosevelt astonished and pleased the Negro community by inviting Booker T. Washington to the White House for a discussion and luncheon. The white South was predictably horrified. The Richmond *Dispatch* said that it deplored the President's taste and henceforth distrusted his wisdom. Roosevelt must have concluded there was little mileage, and fewer votes, in honoring black men and thereby inducing apoplexy among whites. During the balance of his years in the White House, he did appoint a well-qualified Negro as Collector of the Port of Charleston and, by way of rebuking the white community of a little Mississippi town for forcing an old black postmistress out of her long-held job, he closed down the post office altogether for a number of months before agreeing to name a white man to run it. Beyond these episodes, which altered the course of national events hardly a centimeter but did boost Negro morale at a singularly welcome moment, nothing that could be called a Negro policy was ever formulated by Roosevelt's administration. On trips to the South, his conciliatory remarks increasingly brought comfort to the prejudices of the region. When he ran for President under the Bull Moose banner in 1912, his independent party's convention spurned a platform proposal for ending Jim Crow and disenfranchising laws and refused to seat black delegates. The cracker vote came first.

No Negroes were disappointed, at least, by Roosevelt's successor, William Howard Taft, whose indifference to the civic status of black Americans was as vast as his torso. At the very outset of his administration in 1909, he pledged to the white South that he would appoint no federal officials to their region who would offend their sensibilities. Nor were there any luncheons with Booker T. Washington or any other colored person whose lips might soil the White House linen. Taft's tolerance of the South's ongoing disfigurement of the Negro as a human being reached the zenith of heartlessness during the summer of 1911 when one of the more barbaric lynchings of the era was literally staged in Livermore, Kentucky. A Negro charged with murdering a white man was seized and hauled to the local theater, where an audience was invited to witness his hanging. Receipts were to go to the murdered white man's family. To add interest to the benefit performance, seatholders in the orchestra were invited to empty their revolvers into the swaying black body while those in the gallery were restricted to a single shot. And so it happened. Sadism was riding bareback and unimpeded through the South. Presented with resolutions protesting such blots on civilization and calling upon him to ask Congress to end lynch law by stern measures to enforce the Fourteenth Amendment, President Taft declined the honor. It was a matter for the states to handle, he said. That they were not doing so was plain to see. That the White House was morally bankrupt when it came to the black man's plight was even plainer.

Taft, at least (and at most), took no action to reduce the already shriveled standing of the Negro. His successor, amid a flurry of reassuringly high-minded pledges to deal fairly with blacks, approved actions that belied his words. Woodrow Wilson, a native Virginian, wasted little time introducing segregation into the national government. At a Cabinet meeting in April 1913, just three months after the inauguration, the Postmaster General's proposal to bring official racism into the federal administration on the premise that "segregation was best for the negro and the Service" was approved without dissent. Wilson said on the occasion that he had made "no promises in particular to negroes, except to do them justice." He did not wish to see the Negro's "position" reduced, but favored the adjustment of the segregation matter "in a way to make the least friction." The Bureau of the Census, the Bureau of Printing and Engraving, and the Department of the Treasury would shortly follow the Post Office in adopting segregation. Black men's desks were curtained off, cafeteria tables were assigned racially, and federal toilets were marked "Whites Only" and "Colored." Before the end of the Wilson administration, segregation would be extended to the galleries of the United States Senate and the lunchroom of the Library of Congress. Nor was official racism restricted to Washington. The newly named Collector of the Internal Revenue for Georgia, for example, fired blacks of unquestionable competence from their civil-service career posts and replaced them with whites of dubious credentials. "There are no government positions for Negroes in the South," he was quoted as declaring. "A Negro's place is in the cornfield."

It is hardly surprising, then, that during the Wilson years Congress was besieged by bills seeking to impose yet wider discriminations on the Negro. It was as if the racist bloc were trying to rip the de-energized Civil War amendments out of the Constitution for good. No fewer than six bills were introduced for Jim Crow streetcars in the District of Columbia. There were bills to exclude Negroes from commissions in the Army and Navy, to impose racial separation on all federal employees, and to bar immigration of Negro aliens entirely despite their ability to pass the mandatory literacy test. The last proposal actually passed the Senate by a 29–25 vote, though it was massively defeated in the House as liberal lobbies assailed the measure with fury. Woodrow Wilson did nothing to help. He turned down a carefully conceived proposal by leading Northern reformers for a federal commission to study the Negro question. It would be misunderstood in the South as accusatory, he said, and therefore exacerbate the already heated emotional climate. He declined to speak out against lynching. He would not address colored audiences. He did not overrule the wholesale firing of black federal employees. And his administration's adoption of Jim Crow rules, he insisted, was not a movement against Negroes but a step in their favor, for, as he explained, "by putting certain bureaus and sections . . . in the charge of negroes we are rendering them more safe in their possession of office and less likely to be discriminated against." When militant William Monroe Trotter, editor of Boston's Negro newspaper, the *Guardian*, headed a delegation of blacks who called upon the President late in 1914 to protest his segregationist policies, Wilson employed his usual rebuttal that separation was "not humiliating but a benefit." When Trotter respectfully declined to agree, the President of the United States showed his group the door.

In 1915, then, the Negro was at his nadir. Late in the year, Booker T. Washington died at the age of fifty-nine. His soft-spoken policies of conciliation had been reduced to ashes by a strident racism that seemed ascendant in every sphere of American life. Other black voices, though, now began to be raised.

William Edward Burghardt Du Bois grew up in the small town of Great Barrington in the southwestern corner of Massachusetts—a slender, light-brown boy in a community with only a handful of Negroes. In him, he would say later, was "a flood of Negro blood, a strain of French, a bit of Dutch, but thank God! no Anglo-Saxon." With funds collected from a number of churches, he embarked upon a course of higher education unlike any ever obtained till then by an American black. At Fisk University on the heights above Nashville, Tennessee, he was thrilled and reassured by being among so many young people of color. There was joy in them that he found contagious, he would later write, and he learned to dance with them and sing with them, and in summertime he went out beyond the railroads and stagecoach lines "to where men lived and died in the shadow of one blue hill" and taught school and lived in log cabins built before the Civil War. "We read and spelled together," he would recall, "wrote a little, picked flowers, sang, and listened to stories of the world beyond the hill." He saw the seemingly unbreakable cycle of ignorance and penury and despair among those isolated people, but there was pride and grace as well that could be coaxed from them by anyone treating them as semi-human.

After Fisk, he won a scholarship to Harvard, where he studied with monkish dedication under the giants of American philosophy, William James and George Santayana, and did well enough to be chosen one of five commencement speakers. His subject was Jefferson Davis, president of the Confederacy. "Under whatever guise," Du Bois declared, "however a Jefferson Davis may appear as man, as race, or as a nation, his life can only logically mean this: the advance of a part of the world at the expense of the whole." The civilization that spawned Jefferson Davis, he said, "represents a field for stalwart manhood and heroic character, and at the same time for moral obtuseness and refined brutality." Du Bois was the star of the ceremonies and, as one of his professors would write, "altogether the best black man that has come to Cambridge."

A foundation grant of $750 paid his way for a year's study at the

University of Berlin. The money let him travel and absorb a whole new world, and he studied amid a galaxy of the greatest scholars on the Continent. After two years abroad, the splendidly trained young scholar came back to Harvard—a lonely, terribly proud black man who carried himself with a dignity reinforced by the props of his European stay: a high hat, white gloves, and a cane. They would become his trademark. He was a little below medium height, had a long bladelike nose, a stiletto of a tongue, a well-tended Vandyke beard, and coloring and physiognomy that bespoke his richly mixed ancestry. Most of all, he had a glorious pen. There was power and precision and poetry in it. He put it to work now on his doctoral thesis, titled *The Suppression of the African Slave Trade in the United States.* The hypocrisy and self-interest that had marked the barbaric practice he documented in subdued but nonetheless denunciatory language. The university press published the study, a tribute to its excellence. At the age of twenty-seven, William E. B. Du Bois was awarded the degree of Doctor of Philosophy by Harvard University—the first man of his race to earn his doctorate at the premier seat of learning in America. It was 1895, the same year that Booker T. Washington was standing up before multitudes in Atlanta and asserting that the Negro would tread the earth humbly and with love for his white betters if he were just allowed to make a modest living.

For all his academic equipment and bundle of degrees, no white college would take Du Bois on its faculty. No black man taught then at any white-run university. Very few blacks, in fact, taught at black colleges. He was lucky to latch on to a job teaching Latin and Greek for $800 a year at little Wilberforce in Ohio, a small colored denominational college. Cocky, brilliant, ambitious to lead his people, he found the little college stultifying. He taught German and English composition and a bit of world history in addition to classics, but the school had no interest in the subject Du Bois most wished to pursue—sociology. It was being used against the Negro by quasi-scholars as well as authentic ones; if only rigorous scientific methods were applied to studying the race, much could be done to sweep away the myths on which racism fed.

The only place that would have him and his ideas was the University of Pennsylvania on terms that must have galled him, though he claimed otherwise. Philadelphia was going through one of its periodic reform movements, and the university had agreed as a civic gesture to undertake a thorough study of the rampant criminality in the city's heavily Negro Seventh Ward. Du Bois was hired for $900 a year and given a rank even below the lowest subaltern in the academic hierarchy—"assistant instructor." He had no office, no contact with students, almost none with the faculty except one professor of sociology who supervised his work, and his name was omitted from the university catalogue for that year. He had no research assistants or tape recorders—just his legs and a note pad—and he was not an instant favorite among the colored population of the neighborhood, who, he understood, had no fondness for "being studied like a strange species." He spoke, he said, to 5,000 of them. He composed endless memoranda, consulted the rarest of books and records, mapped the district, classified its conditions, assembled a history of the black man in the city for the previous two centuries, and when he was done he turned it into a volume of nearly 1,000 pages that combined the rigor of scientific investigation with the insight of social psychology. Published in 1898, *The Philadelphia Negro* was the first treatise on the pathological effects of urban life on blacks. It argued that the alarming prevalence of crime and vice in Negro neighborhoods was not the product of natural moral degeneracy but the predictable symptom of pervasive poverty, ignorance, illness, and lack of economic opportunity. It was an insight that was ahead of its time and not popular with those who sponsored Du Bois's work.

It helped earn him his heart's desire. Atlanta University, among the best of the black schools in the nation, invited him to direct a new program of study on the conditions of Negro life, and for the next thirteen years, on a budget of $5,000 annually, he turned the program into the most vital sector of the university's curriculum. Each year, he ran a massive scholarly conference devoted to a single aspect of black life and drew scholars and laymen to the university from all over the country. Each conference was turned into an annual report in the Atlanta University Publications series—on such subjects as "Mortality Among Negroes in Cities," "The Negro in Business," "The Negro Church," "Notes on Negro Crime," "The Negro American Family," and "The Common School and the Negro American"—and brought praise from ranking outside academicians for the level of scholarship and the pathbreaking methodology. Du Bois kept at his work with an enthusiasm that communicated itself to the farm boys and city-tenement girls who had to meet the exacting academic standards of the Harvard Ph.D. with the European walking stick. He wanted the best that was in them, and he inspired them to produce it. Wrote the university president: "He taught them the nobility and sacredness of their manhood—endowed, as they were, with all the inherent rights and possibilities of development enjoyed by humanity anywhere." By his early thirties, Du Bois was recognized as the intellectual leader of his race.

It was not possible for him to remain above the battle while his people were being brutalized under sanction of law. Besides, there was little interest among white social scientists in his scholarly works and there were simply too few blacks with the training to use them. Without abandoning his academic position, Du Bois now turned his facile pen and agile mind to the practice of agitation and propaganda. He wrote with such energy, compassion, and authority that a Chicago publisher, A. C. McClurg & Co., asked him to gather up some of his pieces into a book. Such collections, then as now, were almost certain money-losers, but the publisher was hoping to capitalize on the international success of Booker T. Washington's autobiography, *Up from Slavery*, issued in 1901 after being serialized in the weekly magazine *Outlook*. It had proven so popular that magazine editors and book publishers panted for works under Washington's byline, and a corps of ghost writers was put to work cranking out inoffensive and sincere pieces of uplift that were snatched up for publication. An annual letter under the regal title "To My People" was released to the press as Tuskegee became what Du Bois called "the capital of the Negro nation" and Washington its resident monarch. His visit with Teddy Roosevelt at the White House had been the coronation. It was with careful calculation, then, that Du Bois added an essay to the articles he had already written. He titled it "Of Booker T. Washington and Others" and placed it third in the modest-sized volume of essays and sketches that was published in 1903 under the title *The Souls of Black Folk.* Its impact on the literate black world was immediate and explosive. Its challenge to the values and methods of Booker Washington was imperative and unconcealed:

> . . . So far as Mr. Washington preaches Thrift, Patience, and Industrial Training for the masses, we must hold up his hands and strive with him, rejoicing in his honors and glorying in the strength of this Joshua called of God and of man to lead the headless host. But so far as Mr. Washington apologizes for injustice, North or South, does not rightly value the privilege and duty of voting, belittles the emasculating effects of caste distinctions, and opposes the higher training and ambition of our brighter minds,—so far as he, the South, or the Nation, does this—we must increasingly and firmly oppose them.

The immediate point of contention was how much and what kind of education the Negro should seek. It was no abstract debate. In urging the higher education of "a Talented Tenth" of the black people who through their broad cultural background could guide the race "into a higher civilization," Du Bois was not self-servingly proposing an intellectual elite but was declaring that white leadership could obviously not be depended upon if American blacks were ever to achieve a destiny of their own beyond mass peonage and political ostracism. Washington's appeal was to the masses, who he said ought to be trained as skilled workers whose diligence would earn them fair salaries, allow them to acquire property, and in due time win them the respect of the dominant race. On the face of it, there was nothing mutually exclusive about the two positions. But in Washington's call for forbearance and self-improvement, Du Bois saw confession of black inferiority and contrition for an assumed turpitude. Washington's speeches and writings, while not entirely ignoring the disenfranchisement and other civil debasements of the Negro, did not assault these obviously appalling developments but tended to excuse them and emphasize instead the shortcomings of the Negro. The inference he left was obvious: the fault for their condition rested largely with the black people themselves. Du Bois would not accept that argument. The low condition of the American Negro was due largely to the prejudice that had prevailed against him from the start and kept him low; Booker Washington, for whatever his reasons, had just exactly reversed the matters of cause and effect. The white benefactors of Tuskegee and Washington's philosophy, moreover, sought to perpetuate the Negro's station in life, as Du Bois viewed it, because what most of these Northern philanthropists really wanted was an able-bodied, simple-minded black force that would stay in the South, labor mightily at modest wages to produce the raw materials for the capitalist industrial machine, and serve as a bulwark against the spreading union movement with its infestation of socialist thought from Europe. The black man, though, had more to offer America than muscle, Du Bois insisted. He wrote in the opening selection of *The Souls of Black Folk*:

> . . . We the darker ones come even now not altogether empty-handed: there are to-day no truer exponents of the pure human spirit of the Declaration of Independence than the American Negroes; there is no true American music but the wild sweet melodies of the Negro slave; the American fairy tales and folk-lore are Indian and African; and, all in all, we black men seem the sole oasis of simple faith and reverence in a dusty desert of dollars and smartness. Will America be poorer if she replace her brutal dyspeptic blundering with light-hearted but determined Negro humility? or her coarse and cruel wit with loving jovial good humor? or her vulgar music with the soul of the Sorrow Songs?

It was one thing to challenge Booker Washington; it was another to mobilize an opposing camp. Du Bois needed allies. Yet more outspoken than Du Bois was Monroe Trotter of Boston, also a Harvard man, whose *Guardian* was the most acerbic voice in the black press and lost no opportunity to denounce Washington. One July evening in 1905, Trotter and his colleagues came loaded for bear to an address Washington was to give at a Boston church. Before long, the whole place was a shouting, scuffling mob scene, and Trotter, among others, was taken off to jail. The *New York Times* called the episode "disgraceful and lamentable" and blamed it on agitators who were "all for war and for a rush into full equality of every kind, deserved or undeserved."

It was more than Du Bois could bear. Though he was not in Boston at the time, he believed Trotter to be "an honest, brilliant, unselfish man" who deserved better than to be tossed into the hoosegow for his troubles. From Atlanta, he sent out a call to a carefully culled list of black men for a meeting to be held later that summer "for organized determination and aggressive action on the part of men who believe in Negro freedom and growth." Fifty-nine men responded favorably to the idea. Du Bois hired a small hotel on the Canadian side of the river near Niagara Falls, once an important terminus on the underground railroad, and twenty-nine men showed up for the spirited meeting. Among the eight points in the program they agreed to were universal manhood suffrage, the abolition of all segregation laws, and "the recognition of the highest and best human training as the monopoly of no race." Incorporated as "The Niagara Movement," the protest group was promptly pilloried in the Negro press for envying Booker Washington and being ashamed of its own blackness.

Du Bois was not readily discouraged. He nursed his little group along. It numbered just 170 members in thirty-four states after a year and confined itself to distributing pamphlets and doing a bit of lobbying. At its second annual gathering, the group issued the manifesto that Du Bois had prepared and that Trotter, his co-leader in the Niagara Movement, endorsed. In a nation used to the dulcet blandishments of Booker Washington, the Niagarites' remonstrance came like the crack of a rifle: "We will not be satisfied to take one jot or tittle less than our full manhood rights. We claim for ourselves every single right that belongs to a freeborn American, political, civil, and social; and until we get these rights we will never cease to protest and assail the ears of America." As to the Bookerites' gospel of salvation through work and manual training, the Niagara people declared:

> We want our children educated. . . . And when we call for education, we mean real education. We believe in work. We ourselves are workers, but work is not necessarily education. Education is the development of power and ideal. We want our children trained as intelligent human beings should be and we will fight for all time against any proposal to educate black boys and girls simply as servants and underlings, or simply for the use of other people. They have a right to know, to think, to aspire.

A few people were beginning to listen. But little money was raised, and potential white supporters were pointedly discouraged from participating by the Bookerite organization. There was never more than a few hundred dollars in the treasury. The third annual meeting, held at Boston's Faneuil Hall, rallied support for the movement from descendants of the abolitionist movement, and the famed white lawyer Moorfield Storey, secretary to Senator Charles Sumner during the most momentous days of the Reconstruction Congresses and a vocal foe of American imperialism and political corruption, addressed the group. It was the first support it had won from whites of real eminence. In between these annual rallies, though, the movement sputtered. It was simply too far-flung, unfocused, and impoverished to do more than issue occasional statements of angry eloquence.

Shortly after the Niagara Movement's annual meeting in 1908, a race riot of extraordinary severity occurred in Springfield, the capital of Illinois. Two Negroes were lynched, four white men murdered, and some seventy others injured as nearly 5,000 militiamen had to be summoned to restore peace. When it was over, more than 2,000 blacks had fled the city in terror—a principal goal of the rioting ringleaders, none of whom was punished. The city itself seemed in no way contrite over the episode, part of an epidemic of such violence that had gone on unchecked across the nation for a dozen years. This one seemed particularly poignant to liberals, for it had occurred in the city where Abraham Lincoln had made his home and lay buried.

A month after the Springfield riot, an article about it ran in a liberal monthly magazine, the *Independent*, under the title "The Race War in the North." Its author, William English Walling, was a wealthy Southerner whose family had once owned slaves. He himself was a socialist and settlement-house worker married to a Russian Jewish immigrant who had once been imprisoned in her mother country for revolutionary activity. Traveling to Springfield to research his article, Walling was less troubled by the townspeople's lack of shame over their widely practiced racial persecution than he was by their continuing efforts to drive away the black families that stayed on after the riot. The local newspaper had encouraged a riotous atmosphere before the event by linking crime to race, and now in the aftermath of violence, the paper, the *Illinois State Journal*, labeled the outbreak as inevitable and attributed it to the black residents' "misconduct, general inferiority, or unfitness for free institutions." Walling saw that if race-baiters could take charge of Springfield, Illinois, they could take charge anywhere in America. "Who realizes the seriousness of the situation?" he asked rhetorically. "What large and powerful body of citizens is ready to come to [the Negro's] aid?"

A white social worker named Mary White Ovington, then living in a Negro tenement where she had devoted four years to gathering data for a study on the condition of black New Yorkers, read Walling's piece on the Springfield riot and wrote him at once. Like Walling, she was a socialist with a wealthy family background. In time, the two of them met, and Miss Ovington, a descendant of abolitionists, proposed that they proceed at once with Walling's idea of founding a national biracial organization of "fair-minded whites and intelligent blacks." They set the centennial anniversary of Lincoln's birth—February 12, 1909—as the moment to launch their drive. And they invited into their founding group a man with the power and wealth to assure that the project would not be ignored—Oswald Garrison Villard, president of the New York *Evening Post* and grandson of the most renowned of the abolitionists, William Lloyd Garrison.

Villard took the lead at once and drafted the text of the organizing group's "Call" for a national conference later that spring. The Lincoln's Birthday appeal, signed by sixty prominent whites and blacks, was a good deal less passionate than the manifesto of the Niagara Movement, but it made its points forcefully: the Negro was voteless, segregated, and badly educated; the Supreme Court had failed to uphold his basic liberties—the *Berea College* decision was cited as an example—and the spread of lawless attacks upon him "even in the Springfield made famous by Lincoln" was a national scandal. "Silence under these circumstances means tacit approval," Villard wrote. "Discrimination once permitted cannot be bridled. . . ." Among the signers were the social worker Jane Addams of Chicago, the philosopher John Dewey, the writers William Dean Howells and Lincoln Steffens, Rabbi Stephen S. Wise, the presidents of Mount Holyoke College and Western Reserve University, and just one man who came from south of Washington, D.C.—Professor W. E. B. Du Bois of Atlanta, Georgia.

Of the 1,000 people invited to attend what was designated as the National Negro Conference on May 31, 1909, at Cooper Union in New York, 300 came, and instead of platitudes they were exposed to a great deal of hard-edged information. Leading scientists presented detailed evidence contradicting the widely purveyed belief that Negroes were inherently inferior to whites because their brains were structured differently. Men and apes had different brain structures, studies showed, but not white men and black men. The term "race" itself was a loose and imprecise one, designating only certain shared physical traits and no more. A prominent Columbia economist asserted that environmental shortcomings, not any inherent inferiority, had held back the Negro. John Dewey declared his belief that every human being, given a fair and equal opportunity to develop, would make a worthwhile contribution to society. And Du Bois argued, as he had in *The Souls of Black Folk*, that the South's three-pronged pitchfork—disenfranchisement, education restricted to vocational training, and curtailment of civil liberties—was humiliating the Negro and imposing on him "a new slavery."

Mostly, it proved to be a white man's show. Attending black militants led by Trotter were suspicious of the organizers' genuineness and bickered endlessly over the precise wording of the resolutions adopted by the conference, which denounced, among other failures, President Taft's unwillingness to enforce the Fifteenth Amendment. Tension reached such a pitch that Villard seriously considered abandoning the whole enterprise. Du Bois, though, functioned effectively as a moderating force, and when the last session of the two-day meeting broke up well after midnight, the conference had given birth to what would rapidly become the most important civil-rights organization in the country.

By the second annual conference a year later, the groundwork had been done. A name had been settled on—the National Association for the Advancement of Colored People. After the working sessions had heard lively remarks about the hitherto unmentionable subject of intermarriage from speakers Clarence Darrow, the famed attorney, and Columbia anthropologist Franz Boas, the NAACP got down to its principal business. Item one on the agenda was to hire a prominent Negro on a full-time basis and in a position of high responsibility, or else the whole venture would lose its point. The man chosen for the task could hardly wait to begin.

At first, they wanted to give Du Bois the title of chairman of the executive committee. But such a job would have involved a great deal of fund-raising and glad-handing—precisely the sort of work that the often waspish Du Bois wanted as little to do with as possible. The chairman's title went to the gracious Southerner William Walling, whose article on the Springfield riot had set the whole enterprise in motion. The presumably honorary title of national president was accepted by Moorfield Storey, the Boston barrister and champion of humanitarian causes who had lent his stature to the Niagara Movement a few years earlier. And Du Bois, the only black among the ranking officials, took the title of director of publicity and research. His job, really, was what he wanted: to found and edit a monthly journal that would carry the new organization's message to black folk throughout the land and spark an uprising that white men could not ignore.

He remembered James Russell Lowell's poem "The Present Crisis" and thought it apt. He would call the magazine *The Crisis* and under its name on the cover run the words "A Record of the Dark Race." He was not supposed to take up his new assignment until October of 1910, but he came in August. In November, the first issue of *The Crisis* appeared. Its circulation was 1,000. A year later, it was 10,000. Ten years later, it was more than 100,000. Despite constant carping from the Bookerite forces, despite no funding from the NAACP beyond his own salary and free office space, despite fierce feuds over his freedom to run the magazine as he wished, *The Crisis* succeeded even beyond Du Bois's expectations. And he was a man who aimed high. From the start, his was the voice of the NAACP.

He ran *The Crisis* for twenty-four years. The best of it came during that first decade, and that was when black America needed it most. It worked because Du Bois was brilliantly equipped to make it work. And it worked because it dealt intelligently and urgently with the doings of the black world. It digested and analyzed contemporary events from the special perspective of the Negro reader. It suggested current books and articles worth reading. It followed the progress of the race in a popular column that Du Bois devised called "Along the Color Line," a potpourri of black doings all over, and it inculcated pride of achievement in its "Men of the Month" profiles. But the pulsebeat of *The Crisis* was its editorial column, where Du Bois let his anger over racial injustice and the shattered promises of the American creed cascade down the page without let-up. He wished to shame white America and bestir black America. And to help, he added a column called "The Burden," listing the most flagrant examples of racial discrimination he could unearth, especially lynchings, which never ended in the punishment of the lynchers. Nothing generated his explosive anger like a lynching, an act of mass hysteria that seemed to him so bestial and intolerable that he would flay both the perpetrators and the submissive victims alike. In the September issue of 1911, for example, he wrote of a Sunday-night lynching by fire on the grounds of a church in Coatsville, Pennsylvania:

> Let the eagle scream! Again the burden of upholding the best traditions of Anglo-Saxon civilization has fallen on the sturdy shoulders of the American republic. Once more a howling mob of the best citizens in a foremost state of the Union has vindicated the self-evident superiority of the white race. . . . It must warm the hearts of every true son of the republic to read how the brawn and sinew of Coatsville rallied to the great and glorious deed. It deserves a poem; think of the hoary farmers, toilworn with the light of a holy purpose in their eyes and pitchforks in their hands. . . .
>
> Ah, the splendor of the Sunday night dance. The flames beat and curled against the moonlit sky. The church bells chimed. The scorched and crooked thing, self-wounded and chained to his cot, crawled to the edge of the ash with a stifled groan, but the brave and sturdy farmers pricked him back with the bloody pitchforks until the deed was done.
>
> . . . Some foolish people think of punishing the heroic mob, and the governor of Pennsylvania seems to be real provoked. We hasten to assure our readers that nothing will be done. . . . But let every black American gird up his loins. The great day is coming. We have crawled and pleaded for justice and we have been cheerfully spit upon and murdered and burned. We will not endure it forever. If we are to die, in God's name let us perish like men and not like bales of hay.

Du Bois cherished his role and carried it out like a holy charge. In the process, he managed to alienate a great many people who he felt were not helping the black struggle—and of whom he said as much. He renewed his dispute with Booker Washington at the very beginning of *The Crisis* by sharply rebuking speeches and remarks the Tuskegee leader delivered in London and elsewhere in Europe on the sunny state of race relations in America. He charged wide segments of the Negro press with bad writing, unreliable reporting, sensation-mongering, and venality. He offered harsh words on the death of Robert C. Ogden, the very model of reputedly enlightened white philanthropy, who as head of the privately run Southern Education Board probably dispensed more funds for the education of Negroes than any other man in America. But funds alone were no answer to Du Bois, who wrote that "a self-conscious, self-helping Negro was beyond Mr. Ogden's conception" and that Ogden wanted blacks to do well but only in the positions "he was sure . . . they ought to occupy." Du Bois blasted old-line black colleges as well, including Wilberforce, where he had taught, and raised holy hell by denouncing black church leadership as inadequate to its task. Negro ministers, he found, were consumed by trivialities and their own personal influence among their congregants; their sermons were out of date and provided no leadership.

For every enemy his sharpshooting earned, there were hundreds of new subscribers. Du Bois became a celebrity. He lectured widely and every appearance helped in the building of NAACP branches. By 1915, the year Booker Washington died, the balance of power in the black world had moved from Tuskegee toward the small office on New York's lower Fifth Avenue where *The Crisis* was edited.

Two other events made the year of Booker Washington's death a pivotal one in the painful journey of black America.

During the hundred preceding years, nearly 35 million immigrants had come to the United States from Europe. Exceedingly few of them came to the South. That was where the black people were, and everyone in Europe knew the blacks did all the work in the South. So the immigrants went to the North and West and took every job they could find, and the blacks stayed in the South. By 1915, though, the cumulative onslaught of hate and flood and the weevil and the Klan, of Jim Crow and pauperism and diurnal drudgery, had brought the black multitudes to the dead end of hope. No road went anywhere better than where they were. And then, suddenly, the steady influx of Europeans ended. The Great War had begun. New industries were born in the North, and with the end of immigration, jobs went begging. Black men came to take them. Nearly 1.5 million Negroes would move out of the South in the next fifteen years—an average of 100,000 annually. In 1910, there were fewer than 100 black men working in five steel plants in Pittsburgh; by 1923, there were nearly 17,000 working in twenty-three of them. In 1915, the Great Migration got under way.

That year, too, the National Association for the Advancement of Colored People authorized a lawyer to represent its membership for the first time before the Supreme Court of the United States. It was in this arena that, after Du Bois had made his mark, the NAACP would do its most vital work. The first effort before the Court was more a glad omen than a thrilling triumph. After so many setbacks to the Negro's rights administered by that tribunal, though, any victory was a jubilee.

Even while it was getting organized, it was evident that the NAACP would perform a highly valuable service if it could toss a legal lifeline to Negroes in distress. Since thousands of them got into one or another kind of scrape with the law each year, the association could obviously not begin to provide legal-defense assistance for the entire race. But there were no more than several hundred even marginally trained black lawyers throughout the nation, and few black men in trouble had enough money to hire competent counsel. That was one of the reasons they were so often unjustly harassed by lawmen—their helplessness before the mystifying processes of criminal justice. So the problem was a large one, and a small, new organization run on a charity basis at first, as the NAACP had to be, could not get involved in a court case unless the legal issues at stake went well beyond the flawed or spotless character of the black defendant. A case would have to demonstrate the likelihood that flagrant injustice had been done in violation of the Constitution, not merely of a state law. In short, it would have to provide a national object lesson to all who would deprive the black man of his rights.

In 1910 an illiterate Negro farmhand named Pink Franklin left the property of a South Carolina landowner who had given him an advance on his paltry wages. A black farmer in such circumstances would have to repay the wages advanced him, of course, and the South Carolina Supreme Court and the Supreme Court of the United States had both ruled that detaining a man against his will under such circumstances constituted peonage and violated the Thirteenth and Fourteenth amendments. Even though Pink Franklin had acted entirely within his rights, the landowner had a warrant sworn out for his arrest. To serve it, two police officers with drawn pistols marched into the cabin occupied by the black farmer, his wife, Sad Franklin, and their small son. It was before daylight and the policemen did not state their business and Franklin did not know who they were. Everybody but the boy got shot, and a few hours later one of the policemen died. Franklin, barely escaping being lynched, was soon enough convicted by the prevailing form of South Carolina justice and sentenced to die. While it is questionable whether any lawyers might have fared better under the circumstances, eminent white attorneys who reviewed the defense and appeals made in Franklin's behalf by his two colored lawyers found them severely inadequate. The Supreme Court upheld Franklin's conviction, and the just-organized NAACP could do no more than to ask Booker Washington to help it appeal to the governor of South Carolina for clemency. Nine years later, after repeated efforts by the NAACP, Pink Franklin was set free.

Pink Franklin's case brought the NAACP to the attention of a Columbia professor of literature named Joel Elias Spingarn, son of a wealthy, Austrian-born tobacco merchant prominent in the New York Jewish community. Spingarn contributed to the Franklin defense effort and eventually resigned his professorship to devote full time to the NAACP, which became his principal life's work. The Franklin case, while thus attracting favorable publicity and new enlistees for the association, also showed the limitations of the rescue-operation approach to the legal defense of the Negro. A more stable, planned approach was required. In January of 1911, when a New York branch of the NAACP was established in Harlem, one of its first steps was to set up a legal-vigilance committee to seek out, publicize, and prosecute cases of injustice to Negroes in the metropolitan area. Under the leadership of Joel Spingarn's brother, Arthur, an attorney, a number of cases were brought against policemen charged with brutality toward innocent Negroes, and several victories were achieved as well against public places of entertainment, including Palisades Amusement Park, for barring Negroes from admission. Such efforts were instructive, but when the Harlem branch failed to prosper after a couple of years, the legal work was turned over to the national office, where it was felt that local people ought to deal with local problems as they came up around the country; a national organization ought to deal with national issues, not run a local legal-aid bureau. The NAACP leadership sought a "class action," a case that would be brought in the name of one plaintiff or a small group of plaintiffs but really affect many others "similarly situated."

An Oklahoma election-law case that was to come before the Supreme Court provided the sort of test that the NAACP was looking for. Shortly after Oklahoma was admitted to the Union in 1908, it amended its constitution to make it very difficult for Negroes to vote. Among the barriers was a "grandfather clause" that said no one lineally descended from a voter qualified as of 1866 could be denied the vote even if he were illiterate. Since there was nothing magical about 1866 except that it was the last year before Reconstruction measures gave the Negro the vote in the ex-Confederate states, the purpose of the "grandfather clause" was transparent, and was meant to be. When a pair of Oklahoma election officials named Guinn and Beal upheld the state law and prevented a group of Negroes from voting under the "grandfather clause," a conscientious United States Attorney pressed charges and won a United States District Court ruling against the officials for violating the 1871 federal act passed to enforce the Fifteenth Amendment. On appeal to the Supreme Court, however, the case of *Guinn v. United States* did not look very promising from the Negro's standpoint.

For one thing, the high court had been ruling against him consistently for forty years, regardless of the shifting coalitions and changing personalities of its members. And the Court was now presided over by a man whose background seemed almost to guarantee his hostility to any effort to improve the black man's voting opportunities.

Edward Douglass White had gone off from his Louisiana family's 1,600-acre beet-sugar plantation as a sixteen-year-old to fight for the Confederate cause and later, as a young lawyer, had joined the Redeemer ranks and fought as hard as he knew how against the yoke of Reconstruction. After the Hayes-Tilden Compromise of 1877, White was rewarded by being named to the Louisiana Supreme Court at the age of thirty-three. The vicissitudes of politics sent him to the United States Senate in 1891, where his most notable achievement was a two-day filibuster against a piece of moderate regulatory legislation that would have done away with speculative bidding on agricultural commodities—a procedure that had produced rampant graft. That he himself was a beneficiary of the permissive rules made no difference as the big man with the round red face and thick long hair maneuvered his girth tirelessly around the chamber and bellowed against unjust invasion of states' rights by the proposed federal law. He was the very model of the often caricatured fatuous Southern Congressman.

Appointed to the Supreme Court in 1894 by Grover Cleveland as a political compromise after the Senate had rejected the President's first two nominees, White sat with neither more nor less distinction than most of his modestly talented colleagues. By 1915, he was the only holdover from the Court that had authorized separate-but-equal segregation in the *Plessy* decision of 1896. Of the colleagues who sat with him now to hear the Oklahoma "grandfather clause" case, only two were jurists of any real distinction. The brilliant and acerbic Oliver Wendell Holmes had been a legal scholar and the dominant figure of the Massachusetts bar; he was viewed as a progressive in the sense that he opposed thwarting the will of reform-minded legislatures except in dire instances of their abuse of power. Charles Evans Hughes came to the bench after a celebrated career in New York State as a legislative investigator whose findings led to the cleaning up of the insurance and natural-gas industries and then to his election as a two-term, reform-minded governor of rare efficiency. After just six years on the Court, Hughes would resign to run against Woodrow Wilson and lose one of the closest presidential elections in history. Holmes and Hughes aside, the White Court was made up of men lacking notable credentials. They came mostly from small towns and favored the Court's historic dedication to the sanctity of property rights above personal rights and the granting of maximum liberty to private enterprise. There were important breaks in this pattern, though, as the Court began selectively to uphold such public-interest legislation as the Pure Food and Drug Act of 1906, the Mann Act of 1910 aimed at outlawing interstate prostitution, and various state workmen's-compensation programs. White became the first man elevated from the ranks of the Associate Justices to the Chief's chair when President Taft picked him to succeed Melville Fuller in 1911; he was also the first Catholic to serve as Chief Justice. Much of his own energy and that of the Court he headed for the next ten years would be consumed by hammering out remarkably arbitrary and inconsistent decisions on the power of government to regulate industry.

It was, then, a conservative Court, trailing well behind the Wilsonian philosophy of the "New Freedom" and not much concerned with civil rights. Any chance that the Justices might overturn the "grandfather clause" seemed to hang on how vigorously the case would be argued for the United States by the Wilson administration, which had given scant evidence of friendship to the Negro. Nor was there much hope for zeal on the Negro's behalf in the man who would argue the government's case, Wilson's newly named Solicitor General, John W. Davis. A moderate from West Virginia, son of a state legislator who had vigorously opposed ratification of the Fifteenth Amendment, and himself a man with no record of concern for the Negro's condition, Davis had made his debut before the Court just the day previous to the *Guinn* argument; it was clear to everyone present that he was a superb advocate. But that maiden performance was in an antitrust case, and Davis had held a strong interest as a state legislator and United States Representative in battling monopolies. Race was something else again.

The NAACP was a party to the case only as an *amicus curiae*, a friend of the court, admitted by the consent of both parties and the court itself. No one from the civil-rights organization actually argued before the Court, but the Justices accepted its legal brief endorsing the government's position; it was written by the NAACP's eminent president, Moorfield Storey. The Boston attorney, a past president of the American Bar Association and a tower of respectability, no doubt won special attention for—if not approval of—the NAACP position that the Oklahoma voting law offended the Fourteenth as well as the Fifteenth Amendment in that it denied to the state's Negroes equal protection of the law.

Oklahoma's case was spiritedly argued before the Court by former United States Senator Joseph Bailey of Texas, a doctrinaire devotee of states' rights, who leaned far over the lectern toward the Justices' bench in his almost physical entreaty to them to let the law stand. But it was the calm, dignified, and relentless Solicitor General who was in command. He moved slowly to his place before the Justices, who were still smitten with his debut the previous day, and he methodically demonstrated that Oklahoma stood in violation of the Constitution. It would not do to argue, as the state had, that under certain circumstances members of every race were entitled to vote; the Fifteenth Amendment provided that under no condition may a member of any race be *excluded* from voting for racial reasons, and such an exclusion was the patent purpose of Oklahoma's "grandfather clause." The amendment was designed to protect even "the humblest member" of the Negro race, declared John W. Davis, and any state law to the contrary, no matter how well costumed, would have to fall.

And it did fall. By a unanimous vote, delivered by Chief Justice Edward Douglass White. It was the first time in forty-five years since its adoption that the Fifteenth Amendment had been used by the Court to overturn a state law.

In the spirit of racial rancor and defiance of the law that characterized that era, Oklahoma promptly moved to nullify the Court's decision. It passed a new election law that bestowed permanent registration status on anyone who had voted in 1914 under the now invalidated law and granted others (meaning, for the most part, Negroes) a twelve-day period to get their names on official voter lists or be disenfranchised for life. The insolent new law was not brought back before the Supreme Court for twenty-two years. For practical purposes, then, the *Guinn* victory proved a hollow one. But the obvious subterfuge of the "grandfather clause" had at least been struck down. The open rout of the black man had finally been slowed.

# 5

# Coming of Age
# in Nigger Heaven

Anyone seeking an instant index of good works and perseverance by black Americans in that troubled time had only to dip into the grab-bag department called "Along the Color Line" in the latest issue of *The Crisis.* There were dozens of little one-paragraph items that testified to the pride and hope that, however muffled, had by no means died among the colored masses.

The May 1915 issue was typical. Park facilities were going to be provided for Negroes in El Paso, Texas, and Lexington, Kentucky. Colored railway mail clerks in Chicago had just organized an affiliate of the National Postal Alliance. Colored teachers were about to replace white teachers in the colored schools of Richmond, Virginia. A black man was named postmaster of Boley, Oklahoma. Dr. Booker T. Washington had toured the state of Louisiana the previous month. And then there was this item:

> Charles H. Houston, a colored senior of Amherst College, has been elected to the Phi Beta Kappa.

Not many Negroes made it to first-rate colleges like Amherst—a handful a year at most—and the achievement of high scholastic honor at one of them instantly marked a young black person as a potential leader of the race. Every Phi Beta Kappa key worn by a Negro was a truncheon to beat back the charge of racial inferiority. In Charlie Houston's case, the Phi Beta key was extra baggage: even at age twenty, he was a man of striking self-possession. A solidly constructed six-footer, he had the kind of good looks that seemed almost sculpted in the evenness of the facial planes and the graceful proportions of the features. The cheekbones were strong but not flaring, the jawline was pronounced but not accentuated, the nose and lips were more than a trace African, and his skin bore a burnished coppery pigmentation as if there were American Indian stock in his lineage. His eyes were almost too pretty for a man's face, but there was nothing unmanly about his bearing, and his deep baritone made his a yet more arresting presence. Charlie Houston was smart as a whip and handsome as a movie star—had there been any black movie stars—and he had never known a day of real poverty.

His goals included neither money nor personal power, and because his ambitions proved remarkably selfless, he nearly succeeded in promoting himself into oblivion. Yet Charles Houston became the critical figure who linked the passion of Frederick Douglass demanding black freedom and of William Du Bois demanding black equality to the undelivered promises of the Constitution of the United States. If the Negro was ever to achieve equal justice under law, he would have to act as his own claimant. No white attorney would give his life to the effort—and that was what it would cost.

Brains were no recent arrival on the Houston family tree. Family legend held that Charles Houston's paternal grandfather earned constant reproof from his illiterate Kentucky master, who would come upon the slave pondering an ill-got book, wrench it from his hands, toss it in the fire, and administer a thrashing. Good books made bad slaves. One thrashing too many drove Thomas Jefferson Houston off into the night, and two weeks later he came back by dark, soundlessly collected the rest of his family, and headed for the free state of Illinois, where he joined the perilous work of smuggling out other slaves on the underground railroad.

Legend or not, Houston family lore added that grandfather Tom traveled with Ulysses S. Grant as an aide-de-camp during the Civil War and was an honorary pallbearer when they brought Abraham Lincoln's body home to Springfield. Then he took his family to Evansville, Indiana, where the schools were reported good and open to blacks, and spent his life as a Baptist preacher and a cabinetmaker. Tom's wife, Catherine, added to the family purse by working as hairdresser to the local ritz, and so they were able to save a little and seek bright futures for their five children. Economic and educational opportunities drew the family to Washington, the one metropolis in the country where blacks were relatively prosperous and not excessively vilified. Catherine Houston promptly became hairstylist to the wives and daughters of Congressmen, Cabinet members, and other officials, and thereby helped her youngsters make their way faster and higher than most black families managed. Four of the five children won distinction in the professions.

Their oldest boy, William, had taught school back in Indiana and made it up to principal in Paducah, Kentucky, but his dream was to be a lawyer. He took the civil-service examination in Washington, won a clerk's job in the War Department, and enrolled in Howard University's law classes, conducted at night in that era. Moonlighting all the way, he completed his legal study in the minimum of three years, was admitted to practice in the District of Columbia, and took as his wife the former Miss Mary Hamilton of Xenia, Ohio. Her father, a free Negro, had left South Carolina to make a new life in the Midwest, where he became owner of a large farm and put Mary and two other daughters through nearby Wilberforce College.

The future was promising in Washington as William Houston opened his law office. More than 10 percent of nearly 25,000 federal employees in the District were Negroes, and there were perhaps twenty-five other black lawyers making a living in town. In the whole country in the 1890s, no more than 600 to 700 black lawyers were members of the bar, and though the ones in Washington were not hired by the government, a distinct black upper class and a broadening middle class existed in the city and meant a man like William Houston could earn his keep practicing law. Other black lawyers supplemented their income in ways that detracted from their dignity and added nothing to their professional ability; Houston was able to teach law part-time at Howard and thus keep growing in his knowledge.

William and Mary Houston had been married three years when their only child was born on September 3, 1895. Charles Hamilton Houston was a dearly loved child. His mother gave up teaching for more lucrative work sewing and hairdressing, and from her visits to the finest homes in Washington she came away determined that her son should have every advantage his parents could provide—every advantage a white child had. She sent him to private nursery school to spur his learning readiness. She provided piano lessons in time and surrounded him with books and offered all the supportive love a child could bear. His tie to his father was equally strong; in the future they would share a law office and when William Houston would write a letter to his grown son, Charles, he would begin it, "My dear boy." It was the kind of warm cocoon that enveloped few urban blacks in Washington or any other town, where everyday sights jarred loose the security of Negro children and replaced self-esteem with self-loathing.

But it could not be hidden from little Charlie Houston that black people in Washington were treated differently from whites. Segregation was pervasive, by custom if not by law. The housing shortage was appalling, with thousands living in alleys where disease was rampant. Young black men with college educations had to take jobs as bellhops and busboys. Decent young black women sold their bodies as prostitutes and many others sold theirs as domestics. To express their displeasure over the separate bathing areas provided along the Potomac during the stifling summer, black militants of the day were reduced to staying away. Even the proudest blacks, though, could not avoid segregation when the school term began. Washington was one of the very few places in the country where Jim Crow schools were both separate and equal—or nearly equal. They would grow less so as the District's black population jumped sharply in the twentieth century, but when Charles Houston went to grade school and high school, a black teacher earned perhaps 10 percent less than a white teacher and taught perhaps only five or six more pupils per class. This relatively small differential served to graft the segregated system to the community without protest from black parents and especially from black teachers who would otherwise have been thrown onto the job market, for almost nowhere in America then did black teachers teach white pupils. So Charlie Houston went to all-black schools in Washington and probably suffered little disadvantage in the quality of teachers or facilities available to him. The M Street High School he attended was roomy, well equipped, and built only three years before he was born. Nearly all of its teachers had degrees from leading Northern colleges and instilled their own intellectual appetites among the student body. Examinations showed that M Street High's student body outperformed its white counterpart at other high schools in the District; more than likely, it was the finest all-black secondary school in America. Charlie Houston was class valedictorian. At the age of sixteen, he went off to college in Massachusetts.

At Amherst, where black students were not entirely a novelty, young Houston proved a precocious scholar. He was friendly enough, but reserved and indulged in little levity. He had a fine memory and a gift for clear written and oral expression, both of which he harnessed in his studies. Besides winning membership in Phi Beta Kappa, he was selected as one of several class valedictorians at graduation. His topic, by way of declaring his pride of race at a time it was being badly battered by events elsewhere in the nation, was the life and work of Paul Laurence Dunbar, the Negro poet who had died nine years earlier at the age of thirty-four. Dunbar was the first American poet to make significant use of Negro folk culture in verse of enduring value. Charles Houston was not fleeing from his people into the embrace of white America.

He would be a lawyer like his father, but better. He would go to Harvard. That took money the family did not have, though, and so Charlie taught English for a couple of years back in Washington—one year at Howard University, the other at his old high school, renamed now after Paul Dunbar. It was a time to take stock, and what Houston saw around him at the height of Woodrow Wilson's reign in Washington would have depressed any young gifted colored man rash enough to nourish ambitions as large as his talent. Half as many Negroes were federal employees as there had been twenty-five years earlier. Federal Jim Crow was spreading to the private sector. Civic groups meeting to plan how to make better use of the city's recreational facilities did not bother to invite a single Negro organization. Residential segregation grew stronger. About the only place left where biracial activity was sanctioned was the White House lawn for one day only—when black and white District youngsters were allowed to mingle for Easter egg-rolling exercises.

With so many grievances, the local branch of the NAACP grew rapidly under strong leadership and became the largest in the nation. In 1917, it finally had something to cheer about. The national NAACP came before the Supreme Court in an effort to overturn the residential segregation laws that had spread all over the South since Baltimore inaugurated the practice in 1910. At issue specifically was the 1914 statute put through in Louisville, Kentucky, where segregationist city fathers had artfully applied cosmetics to the mean face of legalized hatred. The law was euphemistically titled an "ordinance to prevent conflict and ill-feeling between the white and colored races . . . to preserve the public peace and promote the general welfare by making reasonable provisions requiring . . . the use of separate blocks for residence, places of abode, and places of assembly by white and colored people respectively." If a block had a majority of white residents on it, no blacks could move in, and the reverse arrangement also applied, thus seeming to impose equal restrictions on both races and presumably honor the Fourteenth Amendment. The net effect was to freeze blacks into fixed neighborhoods and encourage whites there to sell out and reduce racial mixing to a minimum.

Joel Spingarn, then chairman of the NAACP board of directors, traveled to Louisville to run a mass meeting aimed at sparking a Negro counterattack against ghettoization. A local branch was started to conduct the fight, and funds were raised, but suspicion that the money was being misused caused the Louisville organization to fall apart. Such a lack of cohesion and leadership, coupled with not unjustified fears of white reprisals, hampered many branches. But the main office in New York hustled staff people out to Louisville to repair the damage in the greater interest of beating back the new, tightly enmeshing ghetto law. The fight was finally joined in a case titled *Buchanan v. Warley*. The trial judge threw it out of court and ruled that the law was unquestionably constitutional. The Kentucky appeals court, invoking its own ruling in the *Berea College* case, re-endorsed the prohibition of racial intermingling even on a voluntary basis and said that for blacks and whites to live next to one another was even worse than their attending school together. The state was entitled to use its police power "to prevent the mixing of the races in cross breeding." To the argument that the new law would pen Negroes into the least desirable parts of the city, the court said that the blacks could fix up their neighborhoods just as whites had done, and besides, now they could have the benefit of leadership by the better class of blacks, who would, perforce, be available to help "their less fortunate fellows" in the task of de-uglification. Here, quite simply, was the highest court of the state of Kentucky declaring that a law to establish on American soil the medieval practice of walling off racial and religious pariahs was an excellent means for achieving civic improvement among members of the benighted race.

Since more than a dozen other cities had similar, if less artful, statutes, the test case was followed with close interest as it came before the Supreme Court. Again the NAACP was represented by its national president, Moorfield Storey, who had agreed to argue the case without fee. The Court sat on the case for seven months after the oral arguments and then it ruled unanimously: the Louisville law that dictated where members of each race might live was illegal. Purity of the races and social harmony were dismissed by the Court as irrelevant to the main issue, which it saw as a very simple one. The original Civil Rights Act of 1866, which led directly to the framing of the Fourteenth Amendment and was then re-enacted in 1870 after ratification of the amendment, asserted: "All citizens of the United States shall have the same right in every state and territory as is enjoyed by white citizens thereof to inherit, purchase, lease, sell, hold and convey real and personal property." The Louisville law stood in plain violation of that federal statute. As to *Berea*, that case had involved merely a state's power to amend a corporate charter. The NAACP had wiped away its first Jim Crow law.

The victory would prove short-lived, precisely as the "grandfather clause" triumph had. But it was sweet while it lasted. Handsome young Charlie Houston was not in Washington to celebrate the Court's ruling. A few months earlier, he had gone off to war.

Or at least to Iowa. The place was called Fort Des Moines, and it was opened to train colored officers for the United States Army. On the face of it, a Jim Crow army camp to train a Jim Crow army was the ultimate betrayal of the

American creed. But sensitive young Negroes like Charlie Houston, fully aware of the irony of going to war to make the world safe for Jim Crow, grimly headed off to segregated training camps.

He and many fellow black cadets had applied for artillery training when they got to Fort Des Moines, but they were all given infantry training and nothing but. After receiving their commissions as infantrymen, many of the young black officers were nevertheless shipped to artillery regiments at Camp Dix, New Jersey, where, not surprisingly, they failed to perform well. Their failure was in turn used against them to demonstrate their inability to serve in the artillery, which had been a whites-only branch until that war.

Despite such open displays of hostility, the Negro did not boycott the war effort. The remarkable thing about the nearly 370,000 blacks called to serve a nation that so methodically debased them was how willingly, even eagerly, they went to risk their necks. Many no doubt must have calculated that they had nothing better to do with their lives, but there was almost certainly more to it than that. It was a test of their collective manhood, a chance to show their white countrymen that they were no less competent than they and, for all their deprivations, no less loyal. And if they did the job, surely they could no longer be denied their equal manhood and civil rights by a grateful nation.

Their thanks from the French proved to be warmth, medals, and respect as men among equals. From their white American countrymen, their thanks were memos to the French protesting fraternization. And denial of absentee ballots to Negro voters and would-be voters in the 1918 elections. And post-war investigation of reports that blacks were raping Mademoiselle from Armentières with Dionysian ferocity.

Houston was commissioned a first lieutenant in the infantry, remained in the States with his regiment until June of 1918, and then resigned his commission to go to artillery school. He was shipped to France as a second lieutenant in September, just a few weeks shy of the Armistice. He was to be neither a dead hero nor a live one. He remained overseas until the following February. In April, he was mustered out. He had looked terribly handsome in his uniform. In Washington, President Wilson led a massive parade early in 1919 to honor America's fighting men—the white ones. The District of Columbia's "1st Separate Battalion" of black soldiers had done superbly in combat and twenty-five of its members had won the Croix de Guerre, but no black troops paraded with Woodrow Wilson. The "1st Separate" came home two months after the white soldiers, and there were no parades.

Charlie Houston came home to Washington a month after the "1st Separate." In the fall, he would begin Harvard Law School.

In the interim, Houston's world was not quiet. Washington and dozens of other places across the country were ripped by the bloodiest riots in American history.

The "Red Summer" of 1919 had been building up for years—for 300 years, one could argue. The more immediate origin was the great northward flow of Negroes beginning in 1915 and accelerating with the American war effort at home and overseas. The Pennsylvania Railroad alone signed on 10,000 black men from Georgia and Florida. Some 75,000 Negroes were hired to work the coal mines of the North—in Illinois and Pennsylvania and Ohio and West Virginia. More than 25,000 went to work building ships for the war. And still they kept coming, in broken-down flivvers and Jim Crow trains and on freights and on foot. Some in the South were glad to see them depart. More calculating heads felt otherwise as white homes went without servants and fields went fallow and the black man's dollar was spent somewhere else. Southerners began to fine white employment agents who raided the cities and countryside like the carpetbaggers of half a century earlier, and for the first time the region acknowledged how central a place the Negro occupied in its daily life. Those blacks who stayed behind—the vast majority—were hardly coddled, but everyone understood that at last an escape hatch had opened and was beckoning. The notion of their being spurned for the North irritated many whites in the South. The sight of black soldiers added to their ill temper. On the receiving end of the great black exodus, tensions also began running high. There were not enough housing or recreation facilities, organized labor bristled at the influx of so many blacks into war industries, and white men not used to sharing workbenches and lunch breaks with black men did not always take kindly to the innovation.

The first explosion came in East St. Louis, Illinois, in July of 1917, just three months after America entered the war—from a dispute over the hiring of Negroes by a factory holding government contracts. Blacks were clubbed, stabbed, and hanged, at least 40 of them, though some accounts say 200, and thousands were routed from their homes. The lynchings spread and the Klan rode during 1918. The coming of peace to the trenches of Europe brought no abatement in the race war at home. Reports of black soldiers strutting on the Champs-Elysées with the pick of French womanhood at their disposal—it was either that or reports that they were on a raping binge, it did not matter which as long as it amounted to interracial fornication—were heard throughout the South, and returning black servicemen, however heavily beribboned for valor, were more likely to get pounced on than given a hearty welcome. When job layoffs began, the racist thermometer soared. Blacks were tired of being the last hired and the first fired and they fought now to hold down their newly won positions. A wave of strikes added tinder. Restless, idle men carried chips the size of oaks on their shoulders, and the natural letdown of morale after a war strained the remaining props of civility. Black Americans, their backbones strengthened by the war experience, dug in to resist. In May of 1919, Du Bois asserted in a *Crisis* editorial entitled "Returning Soldiers":

> . . . We stand again to look America squarely in the face. . . . We sing: this country of ours, despite all its better souls have done and dreamed, is yet a shameful land. . . .
>
> It *steals* from us.
>
> It organizes industry to cheat us. It cheats us out of our land; it cheats us out of our labor. It confiscates our savings. It reduces our wages. It raises our rent. It

steals our profit. It taxes us without representation. It keeps us consistently and universally poor, and then feeds us on charity and derides our poverty.

Du Bois and other black leaders frankly urged their people to take up arms if the hovering mood of racism were converted to violence. The onset of hot weather was the trip wire. Blood flowed first in Longview, Texas, and shortly after in Washington. In Chicago, the mayhem ran on for thirteen days despite the presence of the militia. Thirty-eight died there and more than 500 were injured, but while black casualties outnumbered white in Chicago as in Washington and Omaha and Knoxville and two dozen other cities, Negro resistance was felt everywhere.

The violent summer ended in early October with the worst kind of white brutality and a particularly blatant attempt at lynch law deep in the Black Belt country of Arkansas. That the attempt, itself prompted by new black militancy, was narrowly foiled by the NAACP was yet another sign of hope, if one chose to make a virtue out of a checked malignancy.

Phillips County in Delta country bordering the Mississippi was typical cotton country; indeed, it was a textbook case of the lingering lien system that kept black farmers broke and desperate. The county's population was three-quarters black, and for every Negro farmer who owned his land, nine others were tenants. A world war had made no difference to the immemorial ways of Phillips County. Nor had the slow awakening of black resistance penetrated till now. Colored croppers and tenants were advised, year after year, that they had ended up the season in debt to their landlords or the supply merchant, and the few intrepid souls who had dared ask for an itemized accounting of their supply bill or for proof of the price received for the crops they had raised were generally beaten and sometimes lynched.

But now in 1919 a twenty-six-year-old black Army veteran had come home to Phillips County and organized its frustrated blacks into a group with the almost laughably ambitious name of the Farmers Progressive Household Union of America. It sounded vaguely Bolshevik and rather menacing to the white community, but no one took it very seriously at first. Its avowed purpose was to demand reforms in the accounting methods between black tenants and white landlords—a step that could be achieved only by collective action. The black farmers pooled their funds, hired a pair of white lawyers from Little Rock to incorporate, set up a number of rituals including passwords and related devices to keep their doings from the ears of the plantation owners, and generally acted as if they meant business. The Negroes called a mass meeting in a church in the little village of Hoop Spur so that legal steps could be mapped out and the fortitude of would-be complainants determined. At once, whites in the county grasped the stakes involved. Black insurrection was at hand, even if legal and peaceful, and it had to be stamped out.

A deputy sheriff and a colleague stopped their car near the Negro church where the meeting was going on—the car had broken down, it was later claimed, to shift the blame for what ensued to the black farmers—and suddenly the crowded church was being strafed with gunfire. Some of the black farmers, who had come to the meeting armed, answered in kind, and when the shooting stopped, the deputy sheriff was dead and his companion wounded. The black toll that night was never separated from the figures for the slaughter that followed. The sheriff swore in 300 deputies, and the governor of Arkansas summoned 500 federal troops; together, the white avengers swept the county for seven days, rounding up every black farmer they found. Those who resisted were shot. The Arkansas *Gazette* estimated that twenty-five Negroes and five whites were killed in the rundown; Walter White, the young assistant secretary of the NAACP sent a few weeks later to conduct an undercover investigation, reported that the Negro death toll was closer to 200.

Every Negro who had not escaped the slaughter through woods and swamps—or been killed trying—was herded into a stockade, where a star-chamber court of white landlords and merchants determined which of the captives would stand trial for conspiracy and the killing of whites. "Good niggers" who rued the day the protest group was organized and now agreed to work for nothing for specified lengths of time for specified employers—in other words, to be forcibly returned to slavery—were released. Seventy-nine "bad niggers" would have no part of the surrender. A dozen ringleaders were put on trial for their lives before an all-white jury after an all-white grand jury had indicted them—this in a county where blacks outnumbered whites three to one.

The attorney assigned to the case was denied access to his black clients before the trial and put no defense witnesses on the stand. Armed mobs prowled around the courthouse in the little town of Elaine, Arkansas, ready to make off with the wretched defendants if the promises of swift justice made by local civic and business leaders were not fully honored. The outcome was never in doubt. The first defendant's trial lasted forty-five minutes. The jury deliberated five minutes and brought in a verdict of guilty of murder in the first degree, with its mandatory death sentence. The others received similar treatment from the kangaroo court. Numbed by the spectacle, thirty-six of the other defendants caved in and pleaded guilty on a second-degree murder charge. The local Rotary Club, the American Legion, and other civic-minded groups demanded speedy executions.

While the cases were being appealed to the Arkansas Supreme Court, blue-eyed, blond-haired, fair-skinned Walter White of the NAACP home office arrived on the scene with credentials as a newsman for the Chicago *Daily News*, which had agreed to run his report on Phillips County's brand of justice.

White's articles captured the entire nation's attention. Plain old American racism was one thing, but the kind of butchering they were trying to pull off down in Arkansas under color of law was enough to make the Statue of Liberty turn red. Money for the black farmers' appeal came pouring in to the NAACP—$50,000 before the case, known as *Moore v. Dempsey*, was finally decided by the Supreme Court of the United States in 1923 after three years of appeals. The essence of the Negroes' case was that their trial had been farcical, that the community had been dominated by a mob which made its intentions overwhelmingly plain, that the jury had been all white, that such evidence as there was against the defendants had been extracted from other arrested blacks who had been beaten with chains to make them confess—in sum, that if the words of the Constitution had a grain of meaning, the defendants had been deprived of due process of law under the Fourteenth Amendment in just about every way possible.

The Supreme Court's problem was its own decision eight years earlier in the case of Leo Frank, a Jewish factory owner in Atlanta tried for murder under hysterical conditions similar to those in Phillips County. By a seven-to-two vote, the Court had held then that so long as the forms of legal process were honored, the Justices might not second-guess the outcome of a case as adjudicated in state courts. Moorfield Storey, now in his seventy-eighth year, came before the Court once again for the NAACP—an august, masterly figure with only a corona of snow-white hair remaining—and frankly told the Justices he thought they had erred grievously in the *Frank* case and that here was the moment to correct the record.

It was not an auspicious moment to ask the Supreme Court to reverse a decision of only eight years' standing. The new Chief Justice, William Howard Taft, was probably the most committed judicial conservative ever to head the Court, and with him on the high bench were four men of virtually Paleolithic perspective—Willis Van Devanter of Wyoming, a federal judge named to the Court by Taft himself in 1911; James Clark McReynolds of Tennessee, a disaster as Woodrow Wilson's first Attorney General and a man of scarcely veiled racist and anti-Semitic sentiments; George Sutherland of Utah, a skilled corporation lawyer turned politician and the brains, such as they were, behind Warren G. Harding; and Pierce Butler of Minnesota, who had saved his powerful railroad clients millions by his forceful advocacy of their views, and whom they in turn had made rich. Thus, Moorfield Storey started out with a five-man majority that sanctified the principle of legal precedent and would presumably reject his admirably candid but distasteful proposal that the *Frank* ruling be reversed. One of the two dissenters in *Frank,* however, was Justice Holmes, whose magisterial impatience with those who held an expansive view of civil rights did not diminish his insistence on the imperative right to fair trial. He had sat on the highest courts of Massachusetts and the United States for more than forty years, and he knew well that merely questionable judgment by the courts below did not warrant reversal on appeal. "But if the case is that the whole proceeding is a mask," he wrote and carried the Taft Court with him now in *Moore v. Dempsey,* "that counsel, jury and judge were swept to the end by an irresistible wave of public passion, and that the state courts failed to correct the wrong," then the convicted Arkansas Negroes had indeed been deprived of due process of law. And Holmes so found, Justices McReynolds and Sutherland dissenting.

Two years later, the twelve condemned men and the sixty-seven given life terms were set free by the state of Arkansas—testament to the total fabrication of the charges. The NAACP victory dealt a blow to mob justice. It publicized the continuing brutal exploitation of poor farmers, black *and* white, in the South, and it made Walter White a nationally known figure and heir apparent to direct the work of the NAACP.

Shock from the summer's rioting had begun to ebb in Washington, Jim Crow ruled more firmly than ever in that showplace of American democracy, and Woodrow Wilson lay gravely ill in the White House in the fall of 1919 as Charles Houston left his home in the nation's capital for the three-year course of study at Harvard University's School of Law, the largest, most competitive, and probably the best law school in the country.

From the start, it was evident that he had a mind ideally contoured for a career at law. He relished the kind of abstract thinking needed to shape the building blocks of the law. He had a clarity of thought and grace of phraseology, a retentive brain, a doggedness for research, and a drive within him that few of his colleagues could match or understand. After his first year, he was elected to the *Harvard Law Review*, an honor that went to the highest-ranking members of the class. It was more than an honor, though, for the quality of writing and thinking that went into the monthly magazine carried its editors far beyond the demands of normal classroom work. And none of the editors was more purposeful than the first black man ever to serve on the staff.

Early in his Harvard days, Houston was drawn by the swirl of nervous energy, noisy intellect, and joyous combat surrounding the bantam dynamo of the law-school faculty—Professor Felix Frankfurter. Just back from Washington, where he had spent several years as a government lawyer investigating severe instances of high-handed treatment of labor, Frankfurter began his second stint at Harvard with fresh enthusiasm. The intensity and roving brilliance of the man were turning him into a legend. He became Charles Houston's mentor and exemplar. A perpetual-motion machine, Frankfurter would be challenging and exhausting his students in the classroom one hour and pursuing any of a dozen extracurricular causes the next. When he was not fighting totalitarian abuses by government in those years Houston saw him close-up, Felix Frankfurter was lending counsel to the American Civil Liberties Union, of which he was a founder, or the NAACP, on whose legal advisory committee he served. Or he was investigating the nature of crime in Cleveland at that city's invitation, or negotiating in London at the side of Zionist leader Chaim Weizmann, or arguing for the legality of a minimum-wage law before the United States Supreme Court, or writing articles for the *New Republic*, or hassling with Harvard President Abbott Lawrence Lowell over the imposition of a Jewish quota on the university's admissions policies. For all that, he was a peerless teacher, in or out of the classroom, and those of his students to whom he took a fancy were often invited to the childless home he made with his wife, Marion. Charles Houston was "one of my students whom I saw intimately," Frankfurter would later recall. No doubt Houston knew that the Viennese-born professor was the only Jew on the law-school faculty and had overcome a good deal of hostility in the pursuit of his provocative activities; no doubt Frankfurter saw in the young colored man a brilliance and a dedication that, if properly nurtured, would produce a badly needed leader of his race.

Houston graduated in the top 5 percent of his class and decided to stay on another year to work with Frankfurter for the graduate degree of Doctor of Juridical Science. Back home in Washington, they had just dedicated the Lincoln Memorial. The Negroes in the crowd were allotted a special section far off from the platform and across a road.

Houston's year as an advanced scholar of the law was used not only to polish his skills but to broaden his outlook. Frankfurter stressed the uses of history, economics, and sociology in the practice of law and close awareness of contemporary events—a lesson he had learned early from his own mentor, Louis Dembitz Brandeis, then seated on the Supreme Court. "What I care about profoundly," Frankfurter wrote a few years after Houston had left Cambridge, "is that men should know what they think and why they think it." He saw that emerging confidence now in Charlie Houston and helped him win the law school's Sheldon Traveling Fellowship, worth $1,800, after he was awarded his doctorate in 1923. Houston studied in Spain and traveled to Italy, was dubbed Doctor of Civil Law by the University of Madrid, and came home to Washington as the best-educated black American ever to study the law. In training, brilliance, and sense of mission at a comparable stage of life, he greatly resembled Du Bois, a generation his senior and then at the height of his influence, but Houston disciplined the racial fury at work inside him, whereas Du Bois had been likely to let his rage smolder a little and then go off like a firecracker in a deep canyon.

Admitted promptly to the District of Columbia bar, Houston joined his father's already busy law office in 1924. It was not the kind of practice likely to bring a man instant fame or fortune, but for the next five years he worked hard at turning himself into a thoroughly professional lawyer with a passion for getting the little things right. Mostly there were personal-injury cases, commercial matters involving small businesses, wills, and domestic problems, and an occasional criminal case assigned by the courts. In between, he found time to teach at Howard law school. His father was a congenial taskmaster, the firm was prospering, Charlie had married Margaret Gladys Moran of Baltimore, and their future among Washington's black first families seemed secure. More than likely, he would have acquired considerable wealth if he had stayed in private practice, using his technician's skills to the hilt. But he had long since resolved to put his gifts to work helping lift the Negro from the ever more sordid slums of second-class citizenship.

Black America seemed sadly apathetic to its own plight. Negro masses, mystics, and radicals had been badly burned by the brief flickering of Marcus Moziah Garvey, whose black nationalist movement in the early Twenties—"Up, you mighty race," he cried, and "Africa for the Africans at home and abroad!"—brought hundreds of thousands flocking to him, coins at the ready. Mountebank or saint, Garvey sounded an echoing note that profoundly disturbed NAACP and other civil-rights activists who saw in Garveyism the triumph of Negro despair rather than the rising of black pride. Back-to-Africa seemed like a plausible idea not because black Americans stemmed from there but because white Americans were so toweringly hostile to them. Financial manipulations, the likes of which went unnoticed (and unpursued) on white Wall Street, ruined Garvey's African Orthodox Church, with its black Jesus and black Virgin Mother, and he himself was ingloriously shipped back to his native Jamaica in 1927. The ethereal Father Divine, preaching love and free eats, created his own brand of resonance, but it offered nothing to the leaderless militants. The NAACP itself marked time. To most blacks, it seemed either too conservative or too radical in its aims, and its gifted executive secretary, James Weldon Johnson, was perhaps a better poet and man of letters than an organizer of mass movements. And understandably, for it was a period when black artists enjoyed great vogue for the first time in the nation's history; writers and poets like Langston Hughes and Claude McKay and Countee Cullen were being read, jazz and the blues were elevated to an art form, Louis Armstrong and Duke Ellington and "Bojangles" Robinson became headline entertainers, and the Charleston and the Black Bottom (or gimpy imitations thereof) were the rage from Albany to Abilene. White novelist Carl Van Vechten convinced the country that Harlem, with its bright lights, cool cabarets, free love, and freer violence, was *Nigger Heaven*, as he titled his 1926 novel. It made Harlem into a nighttime tourist attraction; by daylight, though, the place was far more sordid than exotic.

Everywhere in the nation, the basic facts of black life continued grim. A 1928 government report showed that blacks were dying on the average fourteen years before whites and that there was one hospital bed available for every 139 white Americans and one for every 1,941 black Americans in the land. The American Federation of Labor steadfastly refused to accept Negroes into its ranks—a stand reaffirmed at its 1927 national convention. Not only did the AFL stiff-arm would-be black members, but it helped sabotage A. Philip Randolph's heroic efforts to obtain recognition, minimum pay (instead of smiling pretty for tips), and decent working conditions for his Brotherhood of Sleeping Car Porters from the Pullman Company; it would take him a dozen years to win. All along the labor front, the Negro walked a tightrope. He continued to land jobs mostly in the vulnerable unskilled areas, working the sawmills and blast furnaces, on the docks and in the fields and at the white man's home, while being denied positions as retailers, clerks, salesmen, or skilled laborers. This lopsided distribution of blacks across the economic landscape left the Negro worker in demand only where white labor was unavailable or where the black man would work cheaper or was plainly better qualified than white applicants who had been rejected for superior grades of work. In sum, the black labor supply continued to be of only marginal utility, and while there was work for many during the boom times of the Twenties, the inevitable result of production slippage would be massive Negro layoffs. The hardest times of all were just around the bend.

In Charles Houston's Washington, the upper tiers of the black community were at pains to avoid fretting about the state of the needy lower echelons. Since lightness of skin color, here as elsewhere, had been the passport of many to escape the hoi polloi of their own race, many of the palest-skinned Washington Negroes sought to break the Jim Crow taboos by passing as whites. The "Harlem Renaissance" that had activated racial pride and produced black achievement in the arts in New York and a few other urban centers scarcely touched black Washington, where those who could afford it applied bleaches to their skin and straighteners to their hair in the apparent hope that one morning they would wake up white. This spiritual depression that preceded the economic one was abetted by the attitude of the federal government that could not have escaped the attention of a race-conscious young black attorney like Charles Houston.

In the White House, Calvin Coolidge may on occasion have donned Indian feathers, but he was never seen doing the Charleston in the East Wing or having fellow New Englander William Du Bois in for tea. Down Pennsylvania Avenue, Congress remained in thrall to avowed racists who deftly batted aside repeated efforts by liberal lawmakers to get an anti-lynching measure passed during the Twenties. And the Supreme Court under William Howard Taft made things worse yet with three rulings during the latter part of the raucous decade, including one hometown case that strongly promoted the practice of residential segregation.

Thirty white people owning twenty-five parcels of land on S Street between 18th Street and New Hampshire Avenue in Washington signed a mutual covenant in 1921, restricting sale, lease, or occupancy of the properties to whites only. The following year, Mrs. Irene Corrigan, one of the signers, contracted to sell her parcel to a prominent Negro physician and his wife. John J. Buckley, another party to the white covenant, promptly sued Mrs. Corrigan for breaching the neighborhood agreement. This she had surely done, but the question of law involved, as NAACP lawyers who handled her would-be purchaser's case saw it, was whether the Negro couple were about to be deprived of property without due process of law, in violation of the Fifth and Fourteenth amendments. A battery of eight NAACP attorneys, headed by Moorfield Storey and including for the first time two Negroes (William Lewis of Boston and James A. Cobb of Washington, who would shortly become a municipal judge for the District of Columbia), brought the case before the Supreme Court early in 1926.

The Taft Court, for all its Neanderthal characteristics, took on a surprising civil-libertarian cast during the nine years it sat, as evidenced early on by its decision in the Arkansas case of *Moore v. Dempsey*. Before the Twenties ended, the Court would take a series of bold steps establishing that such personal liberties as freedom of speech, the press, religion, and assembly, which had been guaranteed against infringement by Congress under the First Amendment, were similarly entitled to protection from infringement by the states under the Fourteenth Amendment. This protection of personal rights from state usurpation was, of course, precisely what the framers of the Fourteenth Amendment had thought they were unequivocally establishing in the wake of the Black Codes and other actions against the freedmen right after the Civil War. The Taft Court, in other words, now chose to advance the cause of civil liberties by taking a giant step backward to the original intent of the Fourteenth Amendment.

The Court's newly found vigilance against state deprivations of life and liberty under the due-process language of the Fourteenth Amendment was welcomed across almost the entire political spectrum. For so long as only procedural questions of a factual kind were at issue—e.g., did this citizen receive a fair trial?—there was little problem in defining just what "due process of law" meant. But in the last decade of the nineteenth century, the Supreme Court had begun taking a suddenly expansive view of the words "liberty" and "property" and redefining "due process" itself in a way that was almost certainly far beyond any intention of the framers of the Fourteenth Amendment. "Property" was held to mean not only realty or personal possessions but ownership of any business or enterprise. "Liberty" was held to include "freedom of contract" by employers. Thus, when states began to regulate rates charged by railroads in response to pleas by the public, the Court began to intrude by judging whether a railroad complaining of harsh treatment by a state regulatory body had been deprived of a fair return on its "property" under the due-process provision of the Fourteenth Amendment. Similarly, when states began to pass laws regulating minimum pay, maximum working hours, and other conditions of labor, the Court began to intrude by considering whether the states were thus depriving employers of their "liberty" under the Fourteenth Amendment by limiting their freedom of contract. In such cases, the very words "due process" were amplified by the Court to mean not merely whether the proper procedures and forms had been followed by the state legislatures in drawing up the statutes, but whether the *substance* of the laws and regulations was reasonable and intelligent public policy. Lawyers and legal scholars refer to this expanded concept as "substantive due process," and what it did that was extraordinary was to substitute the Court's estimate of what is reasonable and prudent public policy for that of the legislature, be it state or federal. The result was an enormous increase in the Court's power to shape legislative policy by overruling laws that offended the political, economic, and social views of the Justices.

The dominant public philosophy—and principal priority—of the Supreme Court under Chief Justice Taft in the Twenties remained what it had been for almost the entire life of the institution: to defend private property against unjustified intrusions upon it by government. But with the growth of the modern corporation, and its accompanying surge in power by means of vast accumulations of capital, the suspicion arose—and then turned into wide conviction—that it was not private property that needed the protection so much as the public interest. Companies that drove out competition and charged all the traffic would bear, that treated labor like disposable tissues, that sold adulterated products, that had no interests whatever beyond their profit margins—these were seen as menaces to the commonwealth and thus in need of curbing. In the heightening conflict between the public interest as defined by legislators and the rights of property owners to seek maximum return on their investments with minimum government regulation, the Supreme Court remained a fortress for the defense of private enterprise, and "substantive due process" became its handiest weapon.

Chief Justice Taft saw bomb-throwers and Bolsheviks behind every piece of social-welfare legislation that had come along since Woodrow Wilson began pushing his "New Freedom." The Old Freedom was good enough for the Tafts and the Sutherlands of the high court. Starting in 1920, the Court threw out more laws during the ensuing ten years than it had in the previous fifty. Not only did Felix Frankfurter lose the case he argued before the Justices for upholding a minimum-wage law for women in industry, but such measures as a standard-weight bread law to protect consumers, a bill to control exploitation of jobless workers by unemployment agencies, and a variety of new tax provisions were struck down by the Court, with Justices Holmes and Brandeis generally dissenting. Thus, if NAACP lawyers arguing the restrictive-covenant case of *Corrigan v. Buckley* believed that the Court was likely to prefer the civil-rights claims of their black clients to the private-property rights of Mr. Buckley and his white neighbors on S Street, they were in for a letdown.

Unanimously the Court approved racially restrictive covenants as typified by the Washington case. Citing the holding in the *Civil Rights Cases* of 1883 that private invasion of individual rights was not prohibited by the Fourteenth Amendment, the Court found the NAACP position to be "entirely lacking in substance or color of merit." It was obvious, the Justices said, that nothing in the Constitution prevented private parties "from entering into contracts respecting the control and disposition of their own property."

For the first time before that tribunal, the NAACP had suffered a major setback. Its victory over residential segregation laws in *Buchanan v. Warley* nine years earlier was now rendered almost worthless. Voters who had been barred by the Court from passing laws to ghettoize Negroes could achieve the same effect by drawing up private agreements with the assurance that these would be upheld and enforced by the law of the land. So pervasive was the effect of the pro-covenant ruling that federal agencies thereafter accepted segregated housing as a socially stabilizing policy and the Federal Housing Administration would for years insist on such Jim Crow arrangements as a condition for granting mortgage insurance.

A year after the Corrigan disaster, the Supreme Court ruled in a case to which no Negro was a party but which served nevertheless to consolidate the Court's previous findings on school segregation and to reinforce the practice in a way that suggested the entire question was no longer open to debate.

In Bolivar County, Mississippi, hard by the great river in the northwest sector of the state, Americans of Chinese ancestry were rare, and so the superintendent of schools in the Rosedale district was momentarily per-plexed when Martha Lum, aged nine, presented herself bright and early one weekday morning in 1924 for enrollment in the white school. By noon, however, the superintendent had recovered sufficiently to summon the child and point out to her that she was a little yellow girl—a fact of which she was more than likely aware—and as such was not permitted to attend school with white children. Yellow, after all, was a color. Martha Lum's father, a merchant and taxpayer who knew the condition of Negro schools in

Mississippi, resolved to fight for his daughter's right to attend white schools. He fought all the way to the Supreme Court.

But the Court was unanimously disposed against the Chinese family's claim to exemption from the laws of Mississippi. More than that, it found such laws none of its business. In his opinion, in *Gong Lum v. Rice* in late 1927, Chief Justice Taft wrote: "Were this a new question, it would call for very full argument and consideration; but we think that it is the same question that has been many times decided to be within the constitutional power of the state Legislature to settle, without intervention of the federal courts. . . ."

In fact, Mr. Lum had not challenged the legality of segregated schools. He had asked only that his daughter not be classified as colored and sent to the Negro schools. Nor had any other case ever been decided by the Supreme Court in which school segregation itself was directly upheld. But here was the Chief Justice asserting that the question "has been many times decided" and citing in support fifteen cases decided by various state courts. The first of them was *Roberts v. City of Boston*, which pre-dated the Fourteenth Amendment by nearly twenty years and had been invalidly cited as precedent in many of the other state cases Taft now invoked. *Roberts* had also been the chief basis of the Court's grossly flawed ruling in *Plessy v. Ferguson*, which Taft now went on to cite as further support for his claim that school segregation was old-hat and perfectly legal so far as the Court was concerned. In fact, *Plessy* had dealt only with a Louisiana law requiring separate-but-equal facilities on passenger trains. The Court's passing remark in the *Plessy* decision that the establishment of separate schools "has been held to be a valid exercise of the legislative power" was simply that, a passing remark—what the law calls *obiter dictum*—that did not directly confront the question of how such schools squared with the Fourteenth Amendment.

But there was little doubt left by Taft's decision in *Gong Lum* how he and the Court would have ruled had the case been framed in a way to challenge the legality of dual systems of education. He cited at length Justice Harlan's unanimous opinion in the 1899 case of *Cumming v. Richmond County Board of Education* in which the Court rejected a demand by Negro parents that the board shut down the county's white high school until the black high school was reopened. Legal scholars would note that the black plaintiffs in *Cumming* had erred badly in seeking the punitive relief they did instead of either challenging the entire practice of segregated schools or insisting that the *Plessy* decision obliged the county to maintain a black high school if it ran a white one. So, too, legal strategists would point out that plaintiff Lum had taken the wrong tack and should have attacked the whole system or insisted that the colored schools be brought up to par with the white ones so his daughter would not suffer by being classified as colored. But all such academic second-guessing ignores the simple lesson that Chief Justice Taft chose to draw from Harlan's *Cumming* opinion and glued right into place in writing *Gong Lum*: "The right and power of the state to regulate the method of providing for the education of its youth at public expense is clear." There was no folderol about equal protection of the laws.

And so by taking *Cumming*, the most vacillating opinion on racial matters ever written by John Marshall Harlan the Elder, adding to it fifteen state cases on school segregation either decided before passage of the Fourteenth Amendment or in possible conflict with it, and for ballast bringing in *Plessy*, one of the most loosely reasoned and arbitrary opinions ever to come down from that high bench, the Court had now blessed Jim Crow education without evident reserve. Southern lawyers added the *Berea College* ruling and saw a line of Supreme Court precedents—*Plessy* in 1896, *Cumming* in 1899, *Berea* in 1908, and *Gong Lum* in 1927—that seemed to have declared segregated schools an inviolable institution. And since the South encountered neither moral pangs nor legal obstacles when it allocated to black schools only a fraction of the funds it gave to the white ones under the so-called separate-but-equal doctrine, the Southern Negro faced exceedingly bleak prospects in hoping his children might obtain a better education than he himself had been permitted.

Just how unhelpful the Supreme Court was proving to be in protecting the Negro's rights was demonstrated in another 1927 decision, one that on the face of it had gone in favor of the black plaintiff. In 1921, the Court had ruled that a Michigan candidate for the Senate could not be indicted under a federal corrupt-practices act for overspending to finance his primary election campaign. Primaries were not a basic enough part of the election process, the Court had said, for Congress to assume power to limit campaign outlays. Down in Texas, reigning racists saw in the ruling a new, improved mechanism, free from tampering by federal authorities, to disenfranchise the Negro. The statute they passed was quite direct about its intent: "In no event shall a negro be eligible to participate in a Democratic primary election in the State of Texas." It was right there in the language of the law: a citizen was being deprived of his right to vote because of his race—a seemingly indisputable violation of the Fifteenth Amendment. Dr. A. L. Nixon of El Paso, a Negro, challenged the Texas law that eventually came before the Supreme Court in *Nixon v. Herndon* in 1927. For the last time, the NAACP was represented by Moorfield Storey, then eighty-two years old.

Circumnavigating, the Court ignored the Fifteenth Amendment but still found in Dr. Nixon's favor. It was as if a man on fire had preferred to pat out the flames with a damp sponge instead of plunging into the nearby swimming pool. "States may do a good deal of classifying that it is difficult to believe rational," wrote Justice Holmes, citing the Fourteenth Amendment's suddenly rediscovered guarantee of equal protection of the laws, "but there are limits, and it is too clear for extended argument that color cannot be made the basis of a statutory classification affecting the right set up in this case." The Texas law was found in error because it denied specifically to the Negro the right to vote in a primary. Texas Democrats took the Holmes opinion to mean only that the state itself could not disqualify black voters, and so the state legislature promptly met and the power to prescribe voting qualifications was handed over to the state executive committee of each party. The Democratic committee just as promptly convened and limited the right to vote in primaries to "all white Democrats who are qualified under the constitution and laws of Texas."

By the close of the third decade of the twentieth century, then, segregation of the Negro and other blatant denials of his rights as a citizen were more pervasive in the United States than they had been in 1900. And the Supreme Court, despite skilled arguments before it in the black man's behalf by white lawyers of the highest ability, continued to interpret the Constitution in ways that legitimized his banishment.

"The young American Negro is practically asleep," Kelly Miller, the ranking black intellectual in the nation after Du Bois, declared in 1927 to a large gathering of Negro college fraternity members. Born the son of a free tenant farmer and a slave mother in deepest South Carolina, Miller had been connected with Washington's Howard University for almost fifty years—as student, professor, dean of the College of Arts and Sciences, and lightning rod for the white men who presided over the place—and his words were therefore hardly those of a crank or gadfly to his race. "The white race has furnished leaders for us," he went on, disapprovingly. "No man of one group can ever furnish leadership to people of another group, unless he is willing to become naturalized into the group he seeks to lead."

But that drowsy indifference was about to end. And Miller's beloved Howard University would now become the command post of black militancy and, welded to NAACP headquarters in New York, part of a double-edged drive for black equality that would gather strength and confidence for the next three decades. Here at Howard, a jumble of inelegant buildings two miles north of the Capitol, and in New York, at the NAACP's similarly shopworn suite of offices, a corps of committed black men began to replace the handful of white patrons who had comforted Afro-America but could no more fight its fight than don its coloration.

It began with a fearless, granite-willed, thoroughly despotic ordained Baptist minister who was appointed at the age of thirty-six as the first Negro president of Howard University. He came in 1926 and in no time had the place in an uproar. His name was Mordecai W. Johnson. He had a fleshy face, hyphens for eyes, menacingly dark brows, a thin and decidedly fixed mouth, and skin that could have got him into the National Theatre downtown any night—or day—of the year. He was a man no one ever accused of being weak.

The institution he inherited was a mishmash of secondary-school and college undergraduate departments and ten more or less professional and graduate schools, almost none of them accredited except the medical and dental schools. Collectively, the place had earned the unenviable nickname among black highbrows of "Dummies' Retreat." And yet it was the closest thing in the whole nation to a real university for Negroes. No graduate or professional school in the South accepted black students, and few colored youngsters had the training or money to attend Northern colleges. A great many of America's black doctors, dentists, lawyers, nurses, pharmacists, engineers, and social workers were trained at Howard. And yet it had been an academic slum since its founding in 1867 as an outgrowth of the Freedmen's Bureau.

It started in a former beer-and-dance hall, purchased for $12,000, with a student body ranging in age from thirteen to thirty. In its first five years, the bureau pumped in more than $500,000 to get it established, and after the bureau itself had been shuttered, its former head and the namesake of the new college, General Oliver O. Howard, took over the presidency of the struggling place for five critical years. Convinced by all the reports he had received over the years from the bureau's widely dispersed agents that neither the South nor the federal government wanted or expected the freedman to succeed, Howard had called for the creation of a college open to all races and charging modest fees. Nothing in its charter specified that it was to serve Negroes primarily, but that was everywhere understood to be its mission. After Howard left the school, its real travail began. Philanthropy made up the early deficits, and then Congress began its mingy annual allocations in 1879 with a grant of $10,000. Every year, there was a squabble over the appropriation as unreconstructed Southern lawmakers grumbled over what they called the pointlessness of subsidizing higher learning for Negroes. By the turn of the century, Howard was largely a hand-to-mouth operation, a glorified high school in many ways, and in need of every one of the $35,000 that Congress was then providing annually.

Mordecai Johnson was a fresh, stinging wind as he whirled into office after ministering for some years in Charleston, West Virginia. A native of Tennessee, he had begun his education in the preparatory department at Atlanta Baptist College, taken his bachelor's degree at the University of Chicago, studied for the ministry at Harvard and Rochester Theological Seminary, and sandwiched in two years of teaching at Morehouse College, the new name for Atlanta Baptist. He had moved with ease between white and black America, and he knew what had to be done if Howard University was ever to mean anything in the struggle for the betterment of the Negro. He found and fired the deadwood. He hired and encouraged excellent, outspoken Negro scholars such as E. Franklin Frazier in sociology, Ralph Bunche in political science, Charles R. Drew in medicine, and John Hope Franklin and Rayford W. Logan in history. The year he became its president, Howard University received $216,000 from Congress; when he left thirty-four years later, it got $7 million and would get $12 million the year after. Before he came, Congress had appropriated a total of about $900,000 for buildings and other capital expenditures; by the time he left, the total was nearing $42 million. And he did not do it by eating humble pie before Congressmen and other white warhorses. In fact, he seemed to make a point of delivering at least one pugnacious speech a year noting how little America was doing to improve the lot of its deprived masses—words that generally brought one more Dixiecrat or conservative Congressman howling to his feet to demand the ouster of Mordecai Johnson. He raised faculty salaries and academic standards, toughened admission requirements, and insisted on a crash program to have the graduate and professional schools accredited. In one area, he was told there was a special need for swift and drastic overhaul—the law school. And Mordecai Johnson listened because the man who told him was Louis Brandeis, Associate Justice of the Supreme Court of the United States.

With the haunted, brooding look of a biblical prophet—his law clerks would refer to him as "Isaiah" in his later years—Brandeis had passed seventy by the time Mordecai Johnson came to Washington. The first Jew named to the high court, Brandeis sometimes appeared radical in contrast to the men of mildewed perspective who had long composed the rank and file of the Court. Far more receptive to social experimentation than his colleagues on the bench, a proven defender of the underdog before and after coming to the Court, a master technician of the law, and a philosopher with a passion to assemble facts and grasp the dynamics of an intensely mobile society, Brandeis did not hesitate to offer a little advice to the new president of Howard University. "I can tell most of the time when I'm reading a brief by a Negro attorney," he said. "You've got to get yourself a real faculty out there or you're always going to have a fifth-rate law school. And it's got to be full-time and a day school."

It might take years, decades, even generations to build a law school—to enlist a competent faculty, to assemble a big enough library, to attract promising students, to develop the courses and traditions and intellectual rigor. Johnson wanted it done overnight. There were nearly 12 million Negroes in America and no more than 1,100 of them were lawyers. Of those, fewer than 100 had been trained at ranking law schools. The black man could not continue to depend on the charity of white attorneys to obtain justice. A few whites had served nobly and out of a sense of humanitarian duty—such as Moorfield Storey. But Storey was old now, and there was work to be done. The initiative had to be taken along the legal front.

Mordecai Johnson scouted for the ideal man. He had to be a scholar of the best training, a craftsman of high reputation, young enough to relate to his students but seasoned enough to command their respect. He had to be forceful, driven—and black.

Johnson did not have far to look. Charles Houston had been teaching part-time at the law school for five years while devoting most of his time to the firm of Houston & Houston. The dean of the school was a retired white judge of small eminence; the vice dean was a sitting municipal judge, James Cobb, a Negro. The rest of the faculty was lackluster. At the age of thirty-four, Charlie Houston was just the man to turn the place upside down.

He moved into an office in the small brick townhouse at 420 Fifth Street Northwest that served as the law school in July of 1929. His salary was $4,500—hardly a fortune but enough to allow him to devote full time to the school. In the six years he stayed, he both built a creditable law school and injected enormous momentum into a social movement that has not yet ended.

# 6

# Exhibit A

At a moment when the national economy began falling apart and the Negro, scarcely the beneficiary of America's bounty even in good times, was viewed as more expendable than ever, only a fool or a man of extraordinary determination would have undertaken the battle for racial justice. Charles Houston was no fool. "He had a soldier's faith that winning the fight is all that matters," his second cousin and closest associate at Howard, William Henry Hastie, has written, "that every battle must be fought until it is won and without pause to take account of those stricken in the fray. He reflected that conviction in a slogan which he gave to his students: 'No tea for the feeble, no crape for the dead.'"

A law school for Negroes was different from a medical school for Negroes or, say, an engineering school for Negroes. Hearts and lungs and glands worked the same way inside Negroes as in whites. And the principles of thermodynamics or the properties of the hypotenuse did not vary with the color of the man contemplating them. But the laws of the United States did not operate to provide equal justice for whites and blacks, and so it would not do just to learn about them in general and in principle. Charles Houston set out to teach young Negroes the difference between what the laws said and meant and how they were applied to black Americans. His avowed aim was to eliminate that difference.

Heads rolled. There was no other way to do it. Houston shut down the night school—the same school that had allowed his father to earn a degree while working full-time as a government clerk forty years earlier—and overall enrollment dropped off sharply. Never a large law school, it used to grant degrees to about two dozen a year before Houston took over; in 1922, it had graduated a peak of fifty-eight. By 1930, it was down to twenty, and by 1933, it had dropped off to eleven. But the smaller it got under Houston's command, the better it got. He toughened admission standards, built up the pitifully inadequate library, and performed a painful purge of the faculty. One popular but inadequate full professor was reduced to the rank of instructor (but not fired lest he go hungry in the Depression), six part-timers resigned or were eased out, and alumni started protesting to Mordecai Johnson. But Howard's president had little interest in nostalgia for a place that had never been half what it was supposed to be or might have been. He was going down the line with Charlie Houston.

And so Houston cleaned house and brought in top-flight young black legal scholars like Bill Hastie, whose credentials besides being a second cousin were remarkably like Houston's: a Phi Beta Kappa graduate of Amherst who went on to excel at Harvard Law School and then start private practice in Washington. Though Hastie was nine years younger, the two were close and their intellects meshed. "Charlie was the philosopher and the architect," says a close associate, "and Bill more of the legal strategist, linking goals to means." Houston was the better speaker and the inspiring leader; Hastie was the better writer and keener classroom analyst and teacher. They were reinforced by such men as Leon A. Ransom, who had graduated first in his class from Ohio State University's law school and brought with him a photographic memory and an old-shoe disposition that made him both a fine law professor and a boon companion at the poker table to fellow faculty members and students alike. And there were outside advisors and consultants such as the young black Texas lawyer James Madison Nabrit, Jr., who, when he was not representing Indians leasing oil wells, was fending off Ku-Kluxers who disapproved of the fight he and his law associates were waging, especially in the voting-rights area. Nabrit, a graduate of Northwestern Law School, was in early touch with the Howard law faculty and in a few years would join it, organize the first civil-rights law course in the country, and help turn Howard into a clearinghouse for the legal fight that picked up full momentum as the Thirties lengthened.

"The real problem in those days," says Nabrit, who would eventually succeed Mordecai Johnson as president of Howard, "was that we didn't have the facilities to argue these [civil rights] cases as well as we might have. We didn't have the lawbooks, we didn't have the precedent cases, we didn't have the sample briefs and records of procedure, and we couldn't use the facilities or contacts of the bar associations since they wouldn't let us belong." Even before Nabrit himself arrived at Howard, the materials started coming in from all over the country as black lawyers volunteered to dispatch records of litigation in which they had been involved. In time, the law library became a data bank on bias in America, organized by subject and state—briefs, position papers, memos, and opinions on segregated education, disenfranchisement practices, separate but unequal teachers' salaries, police brutality, Jim Crow transportation, how not to sell or rent housing to Negroes. And to this storehouse of vital information Houston added the front-line experience of great lawyers and scholars whom he imported as guest lecturers—men such as Dean Roscoe Pound of Harvard Law School and Clarence Darrow. For all these helpful teaching aids, though, the school worked because of the driving purposefulness of one man.

"He was hard-crust," recalls Houston's best-known pupil, Thurgood Marshall, who came to Howard in 1930. "First off, you thought he was a mean so-and-so. He used to tell us that doctors could bury their mistakes but lawyers couldn't. And he'd drive home to us that we would be competing not only with white lawyers but really well-trained white lawyers, so there just wasn't any point in crying in our beer about being Negroes. And I'll tell you—the going was rough. There must have been thirty of us in that class when we started, and no more than eight or ten of us finished up. He was so tough we used to call him 'Iron Shoes' and 'Cement Pants' and a few other names that don't bear repeating. But he was a sweet man once you saw what he was up to. He was absolutely fair, and the door to his office was always open. He made it clear to all of us that when we were done, we were expected to go out and do something with our lives."

Thurgood Marshall, lanky, cheerful, and plainly ambitious, graduated first in the Howard law class of 1933. Right behind him came an even taller young fellow of equally high spirit who had a head going very rapidly bald—a Virginian named Oliver W. Hill, who would lead the NAACP legal fight in his state and become the first Negro ever to serve on the city council of Richmond, capital of the old Confederacy. "He was a man you either liked intensely or hated," Hill says of Houston, whose good looks, eloquence, and iron will left his students more than a little awed. The work load alone was enough to make him a scourge—eighteen or twenty class hours a week, Hill calculates—and he made sure his students came to class prepared to recite and that their "casebooks" were orderly and up to date or he would point them toward the bus terminal. "Oh, he was a *tough* disciplinarian," says Hill, but Houston had more than good work habits on his mind. "He kept hammering at us all those years that, as lawyers, we had to be social engineers or else we were parasites." It would not do merely to become skilled technicians of the law, though all else would fail if they did not first achieve thorough technical competence. "In all our classes," says Edward P. Lovett, another early student under Houston, "whether it was equity or contracts or pleadings, stress was placed on learning what our rights were under the Constitution and statutes—our rights as worded and regardless of how they had been interpreted to that time. Charlie's view was that we had to get the courts to change—and that we could and should no longer depend upon high-powered white lawyers to represent us in that effort."

Howard Law School became a living laboratory where civil-rights law was invented by teamwork. There were probably never more than fifty or sixty students enrolled at any one time, and that was all right with Houston, who was not after numbers but intensive training of young minds that shared his dream. They all worked on real briefs for real cases and accompanied Houston and other faculty members to court to learn procedure and tactics. "Frankly," says a Howard law graduate who went on to become a federal judge, "the purpose there then was to learn how to bend the law to the needs of blacks." Beyond that highly result-oriented outlook was Houston's belief that a law case was a splendid opportunity to lead and teach the black population in whatever community the case arose. It was largely for that reason that he preferred to argue in local, county, and state courts rather than in federal jurisdictions, where the judges were more likely to be favorably disposed—or at least less hostilely disposed—to black lawyers with black clients. It was a strategy that Hastie, Nabrit, and others disapproved of, and their views would eventually convince Houston.

He was not an easy man to convince. "Charlie would dominate anything he was part of by the sheer weight and activity of his mind," says Nabrit. "He did nothing with levity. His work was his only real interest in life, and he brought the full force of his personality to it." There were some who considered him stiff and unapproachable. Even his warmest admirers acknowledged that Houston was no hail-fellow-well-met. The closest thing to a funny story about him is a recollection by Wilmington, Delaware, attorney Louis L. Redding, long-time local counsel for the NAACP and a Harvard Law School graduate a few years behind Houston. "I knew him by reputation, of course," says Redding. "He wired me once asking whether I would serve on the Howard law faculty. I said no, and he wired right back: 'TOO BAD YOU WON'T AVAIL YOURSELF OF OPPORTUNITY TO CONTINUE YOUR EDUCATION.' " Such playfulness was rare in the man. It was not so much that he was humorless or aloof as that he was preoccupied. "He was full of his mission," a younger colleague says.

Houston's reputation grew rapidly, particularly when he began to appear in court more often as the decade went on. White scholars of liberal inclination were the first to recognize the transformation he was working at Howard and the quality of his own and his students' craftsmanship. "He was an imposing-looking man and a topnotch lawyer," says Walter Gellhorn of Columbia University Law School, a veteran civil-libertarian. "No one ever patronized him as 'good—for a Negro.' He was Exhibit A for those who believed in and fought for egalitarianism." Gellhorn's Columbia colleague Herbert Wechsler, one of the nation's ranking legal scholars and a leading authority on criminal law, served as law clerk to Supreme Court Justice Harlan Fiske Stone for the 1931 Term and came to know Houston a bit. "He was a charming, delightful man," Wechsler recalls. "He seemed moderate in his manner but his determination was evident."

It had to be, for outside of his safe harbor at black Howard, Houston was just another colored man as far as the laws and practices of the federal government were concerned. One noon hour, as Wechsler hurried out from the Court, then housed in the old Senate Office Building, he bumped into Houston, who had come by to file a petition for a rehearing. "I proposed that we have lunch in the Capitol," Wechsler would remember more than forty years afterward, "and he said no, we couldn't do that, but we might go over to Union Station for a bite. I hadn't realized . . ."

Everyone, though, at Howard realized. Houston's task was precisely to translate that unforgettable realization of racial caste and second-class citizenship into action-oriented learning. The whole university was gearing up along these lines. "There was great ferment at the place," says Kenneth B. Clark, the social psychologist, who entered Howard as an undergraduate in 1932. "The school was a creation of American racism. There was a disproportionate number of excellent black minds on the campus—men like Ralph Bunche, Franklin Frazier, Alain Locke, Charlie Houston, Abram Harris, all giants in their field—because they were denied places on faculties of white universities that, like the whole academic structure, were permeated by racism. They gave Howard enormous drive and purpose."

Militant dissatisfaction with the plight of blacks was what drove the place and ignited students such as Clark, who did not care at all for the idea that the likes of Charles Houston could not eat lunch with the likes of Herbert Wechsler in the restaurants at the Capitol of the United States. Clark organized a group of about twenty Howard students who went over to the Capitol and picketed, got arrested and carted away in a van to the stationhouse, where their belts were removed and they were all booked. Clark, who was regularly causing a rumpus as editor of the *Hilltop*, the campus newspaper, recalls that the Capitol Hill Twenty were denied "the martyrdom of staying in jail overnight or longer" when a big, red-faced desk sergeant ordered their names taken off the books and suggested the students deserved medals for what they had done. Mordecai Johnson was less forgiving, at least in public. The president, claiming the protesters might have jeopardized Howard's congressional appropriation by their efforts, had to issue a statement of public disavowal. "Ralph Bunche and others on the faculty discipline committee had to fight like hell to see that we were not suspended or harassed," Clark relates.

It was a time for learning as much outside the classroom as in it. Clark, for one, was particularly struck by Bunche, who taught political science at Howard on and off starting in 1928. If he later became every closet racist's Negro-I-wouldn't-mind-living-next-door-to and an internationally acclaimed peacemaker, Bunche was a highly militant and decidedly pessimistic scholar of strong leftward political tilt in the Thirties. Indeed, any Negro who thought about it then and was not ready to urge a major economic overhaul on the nation simply did not understand the black man's isolation as surplus labor, disposable at industry's whim and unacceptable to the union movement. Bunche scoffed at Du Bois and the NAACP as misguided in their efforts to seek political, social, and legal equality. The civil-rights activists, he felt, were destined to become less militant with each new small sign of success. "Extreme faith is placed in the ability of these instruments of democratic government to free the minority from social proscription and civic inequality," he wrote. "The inherent fallacy of this belief rests in the failure to appreciate the fact that the instruments of the state are merely the reflections of the political and economic ideology of the dominant group, that the political arm of the state cannot be divorced from its prevailing economic structure, whose servant it must inevitably be." It was the old story. So long as white workers could be kept convinced that their economic stake in America depended on the subjugation of the black worker, all labor would remain an exploited class. And playing up the schism as always was a virulent racism. Bunche, as Kenneth Clark remembers him, "forcefully articulated that racism was to be understood not in terms of the black man's deficiencies but in terms of the white man's."

It was the sort of lesson that Clark and other bright young Negroes had come to hear. Clark could have gone to New York's City College for free, but to a generation newly race-conscious and race-proud, a school like Howard, "where blacks had the main responsibility," as Clark puts it, was a strong lure. "The whole atmosphere of the place was heady, and every scholar was eager to relate classroom work to social action."

Charges of Communist infiltration at Howard erupted in the early

Thirties and peaked during the first half of 1935 as students organized mass rallies to support the Communist-backed legal defense of the Scottsboro Boys, nine black teenagers who had been sentenced to death in Alabama for the alleged rape of two white young women of questionable virtue and even more dubious veracity. On top of that, some 300 Howard students struck to protest war and fascism, and the university itself sponsored a large colloquium on the economic condition of the Negro, during which socialist sentiment, among other kinds, was aired. Congressional attacks and bills to investigate alleged radicalism on black campuses brought swift and sharp reply from Mordecai Johnson, by then an established maverick. If obtaining annual funds from Congress meant that his university had to give up any degree of its academic freedom, declared the Baptist minister-turned-educator, why, then Howard University would not accept any appropriation at all and the students and faculty might as well all pack up and "go back to the cornfield." Finally, black America had an educator who not only did not need to bow and scrape before white benefactors but quite plainly would not have dreamed of doing so.

Such a release from servility brought with it what William Hastie calls "a remarkably buoyant atmosphere" that reached into every part of the university. At the law school in particular, where the social consequences of the curriculum were constantly placed before teachers and students, the awakening brought with it high spirits, and the best and brightest young students—men such as Thurgood Marshall and Oliver Hill—were eager to be on their way. "They did not let personal hardship or racial issues distort their personalities," Hastie says of the two honor graduates of the class of '33.

Charlie Houston had worked a small revolution. The law school had a whole new curriculum, mostly new and young faculty people, and a small but spirited student body that was thriving on the intellectual demands being made of it. By 1931, just two years after Houston's arrival, the school had won full accreditation from the American Bar Association (only whites admitted), and the Association of American Law Schools had elected Howard to membership "without qualification." They had their pedigree now. The next step was settling upon a battle plan.

Even as Charles Houston began his labor of transforming Howard Law School from a part-time, shoestring operation into a select academy for black lawyers, the NAACP was losing its own great appellate champion. Moorfield Storey, president of the association from the start and its counsel in all five NAACP appearances before the Supreme Court, died in 1929 at the age of eighty-four. The organization's legal burden now fell largely into the dedicated hands of Arthur Spingarn, its chief volunteer attorney and head of the national legal committee, for which he had enlisted a roster of eminent civil-libertarians. Spingarn was a competent lawyer with a Manhattan practice of his own, but he was not a profound thinker or a notably skilled advocate. When the opportunity now arose to swing the NAACP over to the legal offensive, Spingarn was the first to endorse it, though inevitably other men would get to carry the banner.

In 1922, a twenty-one-year-old Harvard undergraduate named Charles Garland had chosen not to accept his share of the estate left by his father, a Boston millionaire. Believing that it was wrong for anyone to be handed a fortune he had done nothing to create, young Garland announced, "I am placing my life on a Christian basis," and gave some $800,000 to establish a foundation for the support of liberal and radical causes.* He tarried long enough to see it christened the American Fund for Public Service before he himself took up a farmer's life.

The Garland Fund, as it came to be known for short, was administered by a group of liberal lawyers, writers, politicians, and other activists including James Weldon Johnson, then general secretary of the NAACP; Roger N. Baldwin, founder of the American Civil Liberties Union (ACLU); attorney Morris L. Ernst; Lewis S. Gannett, the literary critic; and socialist Norman Thomas. Johnson took a leave from his job at the NAACP to head the fund, and in 1929 joined with Ernst and Gannett to form a special committee on Negro work practices and problems. Noting that America's 12 million blacks constituted the largest group of unorganized workers—they might as well have said "citizens"—in the nation "and the most significant and at present most ineffective bloc of the producing class," the committee recommended that the Garland Fund finance "a large-scale, widespread, dramatic campaign to give the Southern Negro his constitutional rights, his political and civil equality, and therewith a self-consciousness and self-respect which would inevitably tend to effect a revolution in the economic life of the country. . . ." A grant of $100,000 to the NAACP to carry out such a legal campaign was suggested, along with a memorandum of proposed legal strategy, especially in the education area. Taxpayers' suits were urged, to assure equal as well as separate public schools in the seven states that most flagrantly discriminated against Negroes in their school allocations—Alabama, Arkansas, Florida, Georgia, Louisiana, Mississippi, and South Carolina. The suits, expected to cost an average of $2,000 each, would

> (a) make the cost of a dual school system so prohibitive as to speed the abolishment of segregated schools; (b) serve as examples and give courage to Negroes to bring similar actions; (c) [cause] cases . . . [to] be appealed by [local] authorities, thus causing higher court decisions to cover wider territory; (d) focus as nothing else will public attention north and south upon vicious discrimination.

Not everyone at the Garland Fund was enthusiastic about the idea. Indeed, the man who had most experience in such undertakings—Roger Baldwin of the ACLU—was the most skeptical. He was convinced that the legal approach would misfire "because the forces that keep the Negro under subjection will find some way of accomplishing their purposes, law or no law." Along with such thinkers as Ralph Bunche, Baldwin favored "the

---

* Among the organizations assisted during the nineteen years of its existence were the United Mine Workers of America, the Rand School of Social Science, the League for Industrial Democracy, the magazine The New Masses, the American Birth Control League, the Sacco-Vanzetti Defense League, Vanguard Press, the Brotherhood of Sleeping Car Porters, and, as indicated, the NAACP. In 1923, Garland's grandfather left him half a million dollars more, which he also gave to his foundation. Contemporary news reports suggested he was eccentric. In retrospect, a kinder word would seem in order.

union of white and black workers against their common exploiters." But the committee report carried anyway, the $100,000 was earmarked for the effort, and the first $8,000 transferred to the NAACP for drawing up a detailed blueprint of the legal campaign. But who should undertake the vital assignment? It would be the first time that the NAACP had enough money to proceed in a planned, sustained fashion. Spingarn, as head of the association's national legal committee, asked member Felix Frankfurter for advice. Frankfurter suggested they consult with the new black dean at Howard Law School, for it was time now to involve Negro lawyers in shaping long-range strategy.

Houston nominated a man whom Frankfurter fully endorsed, perhaps not least of all because Nathan Ross Margold resembled him in so many outward ways. Like Frankfurter, Margold was a European-born Jew—he had come from Jassy, Rumania, at the age of two—who grew up in New York City, graduated from City College, and excelled at Harvard Law School. Like Frankfurter, he was a small man of slight build with a high-pitched voice and an intense manner. And, like Frankfurter, he was a brilliant man of the law. He had been a year behind Charles Houston at Harvard and worked with him for one year on the *Harvard Law Review*; both were devoted admirers of Frankfurter. After two years of private practice in New York, Margold was named an Assistant United States Attorney for the Southern District of New York, later taught at Harvard for a year, and then returned to private practice in New York, where he was involved in a wide variety of public-service work, including serving as counsel to the New York Transit Commission in its fight to maintain a five-cent fare. In 1930, he became special counsel to the Pueblo Indian tribes in pressing their land-title claims. That same year he was retained by the NAACP to frame the legal drive financed by the Garland Fund grant.

Nathan Margold did not think much of the strategy suggested by the original Garland Fund memo. But its instincts were right, he seemed to say in devoting the major share of his own book-length report to combating discrimination in public schools. To go after the problem as proposed in the fund's original memo—by launching one suit in each of the seven most discriminatory states in an effort to force officials to provide equalized school facilities—would be like trying to empty a swimming pool with an eye-dropper. There were thousands upon thousands of school districts in the South, and a suit that proved Negroes received less than equal funds and facilities in one district would have no governing effect on the neighboring one unless the state laws themselves were challenged in the process. And the suggested equalization drive would have to be waged not only district by district but also year by year, for such *mandamus* actions—that is, a court writ compelling a public official to perform his legally prescribed duty— might be directed only against the disposition of funds actually on hand at the time the proceeding was initiated. It was an unthinkable approach, wrote Margold:

> . . . the very multiplicity of suits which would have to be brought is itself appalling. . . . It would be a great mistake to fritter away our limited funds on

sporadic attempts to force the making of equal divisions of school funds in the few instances where such attempts might be expected to succeed. At the most, we could do no more than to eliminate a very minor part of the discrimination during the year our suits are commenced. We should not be establishing any new principles, nor bringing any sort of pressure to bear which can reasonably be expected to retain the slightest force beyond that exerted by the specific judgment or order that we might obtain. And we should be leaving wholly untouched the very essence of the existing evils.

On the other hand, if we boldly challenge the constitutional validity of segregation *if and when accompanied irremediably by discrimination,* we can strike directly at the most prolific sources of discrimination [italics added].

But how? Had not all the Supreme Court's rulings on school segregation, from *Plessy v. Ferguson* in 1896 to *Gong Lum v. Rice* in 1927, upheld the practice? Actually, no, said Margold, scrutinizing the opinions with a fresh eye and a new legal compass. The question had never been confronted directly. Partly that was due to the bungling of plaintiffs. Partly it was due to the Court's preference for dealing with most issues on as narrow a ground as possible. In *Plessy,* Margold contended, the Court had countenanced racial segregation only so long as the separate facilities were equal. But what if the facilities were not equal? And what if a state's schools were habitually operated in a way that failed to provide equal educational facilities for Negroes? Neither of these questions challenged the essential legality of segregation itself. In this sense, Margold was playing it cautious. His plan, he said, was not "trying to deprive Southern states of their acknowledged privilege of providing separate accommodations for the two races." His target was segregation "as *now provided and administered.*" Theoretical equality was splendid, but what would the Supreme Court say if presented with a case in which the theory had never been put into practice?

Readily available data gathered by the NAACP convinced Margold he was on the right track. The disparity between black and white school expenditures actually recorded in 1930 showed beyond a doubt that segregated schools were light-years away from equality. South Carolina was spending ten times as much on the education of every white child as it was on every Negro child. Florida, Georgia, Mississippi, and Alabama were spending five times as much. And North Carolina, Maryland, Virginia, Texas, and Oklahoma were spending twice as much. "Surely it is impossible to account for these wide margins of discrimination except on the ground of race prejudice," Margold declared, "and it is inconceivable that the Supreme Court of the United States will shut its eyes to this fact, in a proper case, and sustain the constitutional validity of statutory provisions under which such startling discrimination can be accomplished."

But what would be "a proper case"? It would be no trick to bring suits, as the Garland Fund memo had proposed, in any jurisdiction where the black school system was being demonstrably shortchanged in violation of the separate-but-equal doctrine. This, though, as Margold himself had shown, would require a great deal of litigation—endless amounts of it. But suppose it could be shown that school officials in segregating states were under no statutory obligation to provide what the Court had said they must provide if they wished to operate segregated schools—namely, equal schools? Margold examined the school-segregation laws of the Southern states and made a fascinating discovery. The seven worst-offending states in terms of unequal school allocations had exactly this sort of open-ended statute. Six of the state laws called for a division of funds between white and colored schools, but did not specify the proportions of the division. Any division at all would do, just so long as all the money did not go to one race. South Carolina, the seventh state, did not require *any* division of school funds.

Such laws could be struck down as unconstitutional, Margold asserted. The Court had shown the way in *Yick Wo v. Hopkins*, the 1886 case in which a San Francisco law against operating laundries in wooden buildings was held void because it granted power to public officials without apparent rhyme or reason and provided no guidelines for its application. "When we consider the nature and the theory of our institutions of government," the Court had said, ". . . we are constrained to conclude that they do not mean to leave room for the play of action of purely personal and arbitrary power." Beyond that, the San Francisco case provided another ground for hoping to overturn the segregation laws in those states where equal expenditures were mandated by law but not practiced by men. If a law, though fair on its face, was held to have been "applied and administered by public authority with an evil eye and an unequal hand, so as practically to make unjust and illegal discriminations between persons in similar circumstances," it was a denial of equal protection under the Court's *Yick Wo* ruling.

So here was a two-pronged weapon with which to attack and eliminate separate-and-*un*equal schools. One prong, in theory, would void segregation laws in seven states that had not safeguarded the Negro from unequal school expenditures. The other prong, in theory, would outlaw the practice of segregation in states where inequality was habitual and therefore discriminatory and therefore in violation of equal protection. No doubt suits pursuing such strategy, Margold recognized, would stir "intense opposition, ill-will and strife." But, after all, he was not proposing an attack on segregation "under any and all circumstances," and unless the NAACP was prepared to attack and destroy "the constitutional validity of Southern school systems as they exist and are administered at the present time, then . . . we cannot proceed at all."

The Margold Report was a remarkable document. Not that its reasoning was without flaw or that its suggestions were all followed. What it did do was open up vistas, especially at places like Howard Law School. It stood back from the flow of litigation and projected a counter-flow. It did not restrict itself to narrow or obscure arguments. It stayed very close to the Court's own precedents but tried to find some that the Court had not chosen to recall—or had chosen to ignore—in sustaining segregation practices. Margold felt the Court was not eager to promote school segregation into an honored principle of American law. It would duck the matter as long as it could, hoping the states would eventually act in good faith. Margold proposed forcing the issue, but on the least risky terrain possible.

William Hastie remembers that the Margold Report became the Bible of the NAACP legal drive: it did not have to be taken literally to be inspiring. Thurgood Marshall regards Margold as a man who was ahead of his time. "His report stayed with me," he says. "It's still with me."

At its heart, the Margold Report of 1931 was a conservative instrument. But it was conceived against the background of an exceedingly conservative Supreme Court. Abrupt reversals of precedent were hardly likely in any court including four men who seemed refugees from a time capsule—Justices Van Devanter, McReynolds, Sutherland, and Butler. Margold was therefore proposing an end-run on segregation. By moderate Supreme Court decisions requiring the South to draw up fair laws and to administer them in a way to provide truly equal schools, the NAACP would improve Negro education and in the process put so much financial pressure on the white community that in time it would be forced to abandon the far more costly dual system and integrate the schools. On paper, it made sense. But Charles Houston did not plunge ahead.

For one thing, times were bad everywhere in the nation, and especially in the South. School budgets were being slashed and marginal facilities being shut down. NAACP associates and Southern white liberals who were invited to comment on Margold's proposals praised their aims, but expressed fear that any effort to push the South to spend more on Negro schools would be like trying to squeeze blood from the proverbial turnip—only this turnip might turn into a club and be used to batter the colored population, not nourish it. There were other problems obvious to Houston that had to be confronted before any massive legal drive could be undertaken. They would need black plaintiffs in whose names the actions could be brought, but these would not be easy to enlist. The black masses were still ignorant of their rights, for the most part. Those who were not were also the ones most likely to be better off economically and educationally—and therefore the ones least inclined to rock the boat, to risk financial reprisals and perhaps violence by the white community. Racial tension was on the rise once more, as it always seemed to be when the economy sputtered. And, of course, there was the other matter that Houston was then attending to: developing competent black lawyers to wage the fight that no white men could be expected to sustain for as long as the effort was likely to require.

For the moment, then, the Margold Report stayed in the drawer—the top drawer—while Houston went about his business one step at a time. But Margold's ideas were always on his mind, and before long he had evolved a variation on the New York lawyer's strategy that seemed to have all of its advantages and few of its problems. The black attack ought to begin in the area where the whites were most vulnerable and least likely to respond with anger. That segregation had produced blatantly discriminatory and unequal school systems, Houston calculated, was most obvious at the level of graduate and professional schools: aside from Howard itself and Meharry Medical College in Nashville, there were *no* graduate or professional schools at any black college in the South. A Negro in Georgia or South Carolina who wanted to become a lawyer or doctor or architect or engineer or biochemist would have to travel hundreds or thousands of miles from home and undergo heavy financial privation to obtain a training available to whites within their home state. Here was an area where the educational facilities for blacks were neither separate nor equal but non-existent. The Supreme Court, unyielding as it had been on the education question, would have trouble turning its back on so plain a discrimination and denial of equal protection. The South would either have to build and operate separate graduate schools for blacks or admit them to white ones. The first alternative, while costly, would not require the sort of massive expenditure that would be likely to engender a violent backlash; the second alternative—admitting Negroes to existing graduate and professional schools—was unthinkable on the face of it, but, in view of the relatively small number of Negroes who would be involved and their maturity, the step was not likely to prove convulsive. At the very least, a legal drive at the graduate level promised to result in improved all-black facilities; at the most, it would demonstrate that blacks and whites could attend school together to the mutual benefit of the students as well as the state treasury. If bones rattled in every Confederate cemetery, well, that would pass in a few nights; for their living progeny, the upset might take a bit longer to subside. And if the process were to prove bloody, well, much blood had already been spilled and for little gain in the Negro's rights. The point now was to establish a real beachhead. If graduate schools were peaceably desegregated, then the NAACP could turn to undergraduate colleges. And then secondary schools. And grade schools. Each new gain would help the advance to the next stage. That the South would know this, too, and therefore fight accordingly in the courts, Houston had no doubt.

Nathan Margold remained in the hire of the NAACP just long enough to see the limitations of his own provocative strategy.

In 1932, for the only time during his three-year connection with the civil-rights organization, Margold represented it in the Supreme Court in a case again involving the white primary election in Texas. In 1927, the Court had ruled in *Nixon v. Herndon* that a state law explicitly banning Negroes from the primary violated the Fourteenth Amendment. The state then moved to divest itself of authority in the matter by granting to the executive committees of the state's political parties the power to determine who qualified as a voter. The Democratic executive committee promptly decided that only whites were qualified, and there the law stood until Dr. Nixon, the black physician from El Paso, chose to renew his fight against disenfranchisement.

He took his case to the young Houston law firm of Nabrit, Atkins and Wesley. Nabrit was James Nabrit, Jr., the future president of Howard. Carter Wesley had studied law with Nabrit at Northwestern, and Jack Atkins had learned law at Yale. All three were black, smart, and ambitious. Wesley and Atkins had made an early success in the law as partners in Oklahoma and moved to Texas to open other ventures, including a newspaper, a real-estate firm, and an insurance company, while Nabrit handled the bulk of the legal work. Starting with Dr. Nixon's second case, the three black lawyers launched a fight that lasted more than twenty years before white Texans were forced to relent.

Nabrit's firm, as expected, lost the first round in the Texas courts, and Nathan Margold took the case titled *Nixon v. Condon* to the Supreme Court for the NAACP. Holmes had spoken for a one-sided majority in the 1927 decision, and his successor on the high court, Justice Benjamin Cardozo, wrote the Court's opinion in the new appeal, but Dr. Nixon's margin of victory was lowered to a narrow five-to-four. The device adopted by Texas to circumvent the earlier ruling against a white primary was unsatisfactory, Cardozo held. The state Democratic executive committee was a "committee and nothing more" and it had no power except that conferred upon it by the state, which minutely regulated the primary election procedures. The committee's power to exclude Negroes from the primary was therefore statutory in origin—that is, it was a form of state action—and unconstitutional.

The Democrats of Texas were nothing if not resourceful. Instead of relying on the authority of merely the executive committee, which the Court had just ruled to be inadequate, they called a statewide convention within a few weeks of the Cardozo decision and resolved that "all white citizens" qualified to vote under the state constitution and laws were eligible for party membership and "entitled to participate in its deliberations"—that is, to vote in the party primary. Dr. Nixon was still out in the cold, along with every other black Democrat in Texas. And since in that era the Democratic primary there was in effect the decisive election contest, the black voter had no voice at all in that state.

Nathan Margold's victory had turned to ash. And was it any more likely that the South's school-segregation laws, if overturned by the Court's order in cases brought under the Margold Report strategy, would be revised and administered in a way to provide equal educational facilities for the Negro? It began to look as if Roger Baldwin of the ACLU, Ralph Bunche at Howard, and other critics of a massive legal campaign to ease racial discrimination had been justified in their skepticism.

Still, the NAACP had hope. The Garland Fund allocated another $10,000 to the legal effort in 1933, but that turned out to be almost all of the originally budgeted $100,000 that remained. The stock-market crash had eaten up the rest of the value of the fund's securities. Now there was no money for the sort of vast legal assault originally projected.

Nathan Margold that year became the Solicitor for the Department of the Interior under Harold L. Ickes as the New Deal burst upon Washington. For the time being, the NAACP's legal effort was reduced, as one long-time staff member puts it, to "Arthur Spingarn running around with a lot of papers in his pocket." By then, leadership of the association had passed from the ailing James Weldon Johnson, whose value to the race had been more effectively expressed in creative writing than in political activism, to the far more flamboyant figure of Walter Francis White, a former insurance salesman from Atlanta.

Blue-eyed, fair-haired Walter White looked no more like a Negro than F. Scott Fitzgerald did. In his conservative business suits with matching vests, White seemed more of a Boston banker than the skilled, charming, and indefatigable publicist that he essentially was, at ease with the white liberal establishment whose favor he courted to keep the NAACP solvent. For all his gifts as a political operator in the outside world, he was not a greatly beloved figure within the higher reaches of the NAACP organization. Du Bois, whom White shuffled out of the NAACP hierarchy on two occasions—partly because the old man's overbearing ego had made him increasingly difficult to work with, partly because his steadily more leftward political tilt was beginning to embarrass the distinctly non-radical organization—would later call the NAACP executive secretary "absolutely self-centered and egotistical . . . one of the most selfish men I ever knew . . . often absolutely unscrupulous." There was the growing suspicion, too, that White was a white man passing as a Negro and using his marginal negritude as a passport to the white power structure.

Whatever his shortcomings, Walter White was a shrewd enough social analyst to see that the courts were the arena where the black man's fight for equal rights might be most effectively waged as the threadbare Thirties got under way. He would remain a law buff and amateur attorney throughout his twenty-three-year reign at the NAACP, to the great annoyance of the lawyers who were to work with and for the association. He had a way of running press conferences and making speeches which seemed to imply that he was the chief legal strategist for the NAACP and the lawyers simply carried on their activities at his behest. In fact, he knew his limitations. One of his first goals upon taking command of the association was to enlist a crack attorney to replace Nathan Margold and provide the kind of full-time legal counsel the NAACP badly needed but had never had. He knew just whom he wanted for the position. "The ideal person," he wrote to Roger Baldwin, one of the NAACP's legal advisors, in July of 1933, "is Mr. Charles H. Houston . . . of the Howard University Law School. . . ."

Two years were to pass before White would get his man. For the moment, he had to function in fact as his own prime legal policy-maker—a perilous arrangement, White would shortly discover, as the NAACP moved into the national spotlight as it had never done before.

By early 1930, it was clear that the great crash on Wall Street had portended economic chaos on a national scale. Suffering was widespread, but it came most swiftly and painfully to the Negro. Those areas of the economy that were the first to contract—the ones involving the extraction of raw materials from the earth and the heavy, messy work of processing them, along with household jobs and other forms of personal service—were where most Negroes worked. In the cities, they were laid off by the tens of thousands. In the country, their pauperdom grew still more severe. By 1934, nearly 40 percent of working-age blacks would be categorized as incapable of self-support. By 1935, some 65 percent of employable Negroes in Atlanta were in need of public relief, and in Norfolk the figure was still higher. The matter of civil rights seemed to recede as the nation in general, and the black man in particular, fell under the creeping shadow of despondency.

Just what steps government was prepared to take—and would be judged capable of taking under the Constitution—to rebuild the American economy and check its worst abuses was to emerge as the great legal issue of the Thirties. Before it was done, the Supreme Court would demonstrate for all the nation to see that its members were as much partisan political combatants as high priests handing down holy writ from the mountaintop.

The judicial revolution began with the deaths on March 8, 1930, of both recently retired Chief Justice Taft and sitting Associate Justice Edward T. Sanford, a political moderate who regularly voted with Taft. That left the arch-conservative quartet of Justices Van Devanter, McReynolds, Sutherland, and Butler aligned against the formidable progressive trinity of Holmes, the Court's eighty-nine-year-old Nestor; the brilliant if unpredictable Brandeis; and the scholarly pragmatist Harlan Fiske Stone, Calvin Coolidge's principal contribution to the preservation of American liberty. The first four were nearly inflexible in adhering to the supremacy of property rights over the intrusion of government regulatory policies claimed to be in the public interest. Little matter that great social changes had all but compelled massive governmental monitoring of industry's predatory instincts, which, left largely untended thanks in no small measure to the Court's past decisions, had contributed importantly to the national crack-up. Binding the liberal triad was the equally firm belief in judicial self-restraint— the conviction that the Justices ought not to allow their own social and political preferences to thwart the right of legislatures to curb the consequences of runaway free enterprise. With the Court thus severely divided and its power to thwart public-interest legislation well established, concern ran high over whom Herbert Hoover would name to hold the balance of power on the great tribunal.

The debris of panic had already begun to tumble down upon him as Hoover reached into the past to pick the splendidly qualified Charles Evans Hughes to head the Court. In turn a reformist legislative investigator, a highly acclaimed governor of New York, an Associate Justice on the Court for an earlier six-year spell, a narrowly defeated presidential candidate, and Secretary of State for five accomplished years, Hughes was beyond cavil an outstanding public servant and a man of progressive and humanitarian impulses. Yet his nomination as Chief Justice produced a surge of protest from liberal, radical, labor, and reformist forces. For in addition to his acknowledged credentials, Hughes bore what at the moment was the stigma of having been a $400,000-a-year Wall Street lawyer for the five years since he had left Washington. He had become the mouthpiece of corporations, representing them before the Supreme Court among other places, and a man who, in the view of Senator George Norris of Nebraska, "looks through glasses contaminated by the influence of monopoly, as it seeks to get favors by means which are denied to the common, ordinary citizen." To hand the Chief's chair to Hughes seemed to many progressives a step certain to perpetuate the business community's traditional hegemony over the Court at a time when open-mindedness would be critically required.

As Senate debate ended, it was evident that much of the enmity directed at the Hughes nomination had stemmed from the record of the Taft Court, which had clipped Congress's wings by invalidating nineteen pieces of progressive legislation in ten years—about half as many congressional acts as had been voided by the Court in the preceding 131 years of its life. Hughes suffered from resentment, too, over the lethargic policies of the Hoover administration at a time of growing crisis. The nominee himself was more commended than pilloried. Charles Evans Hughes became the ninth Chief Justice of the United States by a Senate vote of 52 to 26.

But when Hoover then proposed to fill the vacancy created by Justice Sanford's death with a young and little-known Republican federal judge from North Carolina, the Senate rebelled.

John Johnston Parker, a large man of unusually genial manner, was the grandson of a Confederate soldier who fell at Chancellorsville and the son of a small-town merchant who fought a losing battle against poverty like so many others in the post-Civil War South. Taught industry and thrift and reared as a churchgoing member of the Episcopal Church, to which he retained lifelong devotion, young John Parker was in the American grain of poor-but-proud strivers. He worked his way through the University of North Carolina, partly by selling suits "all wool and a yard wide" for an out-of-town clothier, and emerged as a young man marked for leadership: he had been elected president of his class for several years and his academic record earned him Phi Beta Kappa membership. He excelled at the university's law school, opened a successful law practice, and soon became a trial lawyer of the first rank with a firm he headed in Charlotte.

In 1910, when he was just twenty-five, the Republicans nominated Parker for Congress; in 1916 they ran him for attorney general of the state, and in 1920 for governor. There being about as many Republicans as there were elephants in North Carolina at that time, John Parker did not fare well at the polls, but everyone agreed he was a decent, smart, God-fearing fellow. In 1925, he was rewarded with a seat on the United States Court of Appeals for the Fourth Circuit, covering Maryland, Virginia, West Virginia, and the Carolinas. That was just one level below the Supreme Court. Parker proved a highly competent judge, hard-working, notably courteous and fair in the courtroom, and the author of commendably clear and sound opinions. After North Carolina and several other states in the South had gone Republican in the 1928 presidential election, Herbert Hoover went on the lookout for a moderate Southerner whom he could name to the Supreme Court. In early April of 1930, he sent the Senate the name of John J. Parker.

At NAACP headquarters in New York, the sirens went off. The Carolinas were Klan country, and about the last thing the Negro needed just then was another advocate of Jim Crowism on the nation's court of last resort. The one Southerner already on the Court—McReynolds—had no hood attached to his judicial robe, but, short of that, the evidence of his votes on the bench and his demeanor off of it had established him as a documented enemy of the interests of the colored people. And often McReynolds carried his three hyper-conservative brethren with him. Add someone from North Carolina to that bloc and the Negro's hope of obtaining relief from the judicial branch of the federal government would be as slender as it was in the other two branches. Walter White ordered a prompt investigation of Judge John Parker.

The first response was almost encouraging. Southern contacts reported that Parker was hardly a raving racist, on or off the bench. And in January of that very year, he had ruled in favor of a Negro resident of Richmond who had tried to buy a home in a white neighborhood and found himself thwarted by a municipal housing ordinance of a kind plainly outlawed by the Supreme Court's decision thirteen years earlier in the Louisville case of *Buchanan v. Warley*. Parker at least knew the law and obeyed it when it had been unequivocally stated above. But then Walter White received a telegram with disturbing news about the judge's past. He telephoned at once for corroboration, and his informant quickly sent an associate to the files of the Greensboro, North Carolina, *Daily News*, where he surreptitiously cut out an article dated April 19, 1920, and mailed the clipping to NAACP headquarters. It cooked John Parker's goose.

In accepting the Republican gubernatorial nomination, the newspaper reported, Parker had told the party convention that year that he approved of a pending state constitutional amendment which would add a "grandfather clause" to the North Carolina voting laws—in plain violation of the Supreme Court's decision in *Guinn v. United States* in 1915. Beyond that *prima facie* evidence of anti-black bias, Parker was reported to have said:

> The Negro as a class does not desire to enter politics. The Republican Party of North Carolina does not desire him to do so. We recognize the fact that he has not yet reached that stage in his development when he can share the burdens and responsibilities of government. This being true, and every intelligent man in North Carolina knows it is true, the attempt of certain petty Democratic politicians to inject the race issue into every campaign is most reprehensible. I say it deliberately, there is no more dangerous or contemptible enemy of the state than men who for personal and political advantage will attempt to kindle the flame of racial prejudice or hatred. . . . The participation of the Negro in politics is a source of evil and danger to both races and is not desired by the wise men in either race or by the Republican Party of North Carolina.

Walter White sent Parker a telegram asking him if the newspaper report was accurate and, if so, whether he still felt the same way a decade later. After waiting seventy-two hours without an answer, White took his story to the NAACP board of directors, which authorized him to fight the Parker nomination. President Hoover, apprised of the 1920 speech and Parker's apparent unrepentance, was asked to withdraw the nomination. Hoover angrily rejected the NAACP request. White then appeared before a Senate Judiciary subcommittee and let his bomb go off. Senator Lee S. Overman of North Carolina, chairman of the subcommittee, was incensed. Didn't White know that "niggras vote freely throughout North Carolina"? Not easily cowed, White said that that was not so and the Senator knew it as well as he and there was ample documentation to refute such rhetorical flatulence. Other Senators seemed at best mildly interested in White's memorandum of opposition; at worst they were resentful that a Negro organization would dare speak up to oppose the nomination of a federal judge to the Supreme Court. That evening, White's office sent out telegrams to every NAACP branch, with special emphasis on those in the North and in border states where Negro voting was a growing political factor, and urged telegraphic protests to their home-state Senators by the branches and by every church, labor, civic, and fraternal group and any other living organisms they could enlist. Mass meetings were quickly called, and W. E. B. Du Bois, in his twentieth year as editor of *The Crisis*, legal-committee head Arthur Spingarn, and White himself hit the speaking circuit.

Organized labor, meanwhile, had done its own poking around in John Parker's closet and come up with a lively skeleton. In 1927, the United Mine Workers of America (UMW) had tried to enlist members from among the thousands of workers in West Virginia who had signed "yellow dog" contracts with the Red Jacket Consolidated Coal and Coke Company and other outfits. Under such agreements, the workers pledged as a condition of employment that they would not join a union; as a result, of course, they could not benefit from collective bargaining and had to take what wages the companies offered—or go hungry. When UMW agents tried to sign up Red Jacket workers, the company won an injunction against the union; the union appealed to the Fourth Circuit Court, and Judge Parker wrote an opinion sustaining the injunction. John L. Lewis, stentorian president of the union, now sent a protest letter from his office in Indianapolis to every member of the Senate. William Green, president of the American Federation of Labor, added his opposition. The telegrams, letters, and petitions trickled in. And then the trickle turned to a torrent. Constituents telephoned from back home or came to visit their Senators' offices. What had begun as a routine matter was now a donnybrook.

Parker hesitated and then sent a letter to Senator Overman defending himself. On the labor matter, he said, he had simply followed two rulings of the Supreme Court, which had upheld the legality of "yellow dog" contracts: "I had no latitude or discretion in expressing my opinion or views of my own, but [I] was bound by these decisions to reach the conclusion and render the decision that I did." As to the charges of racism, "My effort then [in 1920] was to answer those who were seeking to inject the race issue into the campaign under a charge that the Republican party in North Carolina intended to organize the colored people and restore the conditions of the Reconstruction era. I knew the baneful effect of such a campaign and sought to avoid it." At no time, he said, had he tried to deny Negroes the right to participate in elections where they were qualified to do so.

The labor issue was muted by the judge's rebuttal. But the racist tag stuck. He had not denied the substance of his remarks a decade earlier that the Negro was unfit for participation in the political process and that his presence in that arena was evil and dangerous. Oswald Garrison Villard, a founder of the NAACP, denounced the Parker nomination in *The Nation.* The Washington *Post* and the Scripps-Howard chain joined the opposition. Some of Parker's defenders denied the NAACP charges against him and that he had ever said the things attributed to him. Overnight, Walter White had the Greensboro newspaper clipping photostated and placed on the desk of every Senator and sent to the White House and to every newspaper correspondent of consequence in Washington. The anti-Parker bloc of liberal Senators enlisted recruits from Southern moderates who feared the judge's elevation might drive a wedge into the solidly Democratic South and encourage the Republicans to still stronger showings than those of 1928. Hard-lining racists were not concerned about such nuances. Their lobbyists swarmed over Capitol Hill asking whether any self-respecting lawmaker from Dixie would accept the dictates of some "nigger advancement society." It was going to be close.

Packed galleries followed the seesaw tally. Senator Thomas Schall, blind and seriously ill, returned to Washington from his home in Minnesota and entered the chamber to vote against confirmation. The final tabulation showed 39 votes for confirmation, 41 against.

"The first national demonstration of the Negro's power since Reconstruction days," the *Christian Science Monitor* said of Parker's defeat. The Montgomery, Alabama, *Advertiser* credited the NAACP with doing in the North Carolinian: "He had other effective opposition, but it was this organization that broke his back."

Hoover, stunned, sent the Senate the safe name of Owen J. Roberts, a Philadelphia lawyer who had prosecuted espionage cases for the government during the First World War and accepted a similar assignment in the Teapot Dome scandal in 1924. Roberts was speedily approved by the Senate. He turned out to be the pivotal member of the Hughes Court as the Chief Justice joined the progressive bloc a good deal more often than liberals who had opposed his nomination had expected. Meanwhile, John J. Parker remained a fixture on the Fourth Circuit Court, voting to uphold New Deal legislation, when the occasion arose, far more often than Justice Owen Roberts did on the Supreme Court. In civil-rights cases as well, Roberts proved to be no friend of the Negro, while Parker supported the Negro position in several important cases heard by his court. Parker stayed on the federal bench twenty-eight years after he had been rejected by the Senate; liberals and conservatives, whites and blacks all agreed that he had been the very model of a federal judge.

When the NAACP, which had denied him his place on the Supreme Court, came into federal court in Charleston, South Carolina, twenty-one years later to open the climactic round of its long fight to end segregation, the presiding judge would turn out to be John J. Parker.

Most of the mileage he had gained in the Parker fight of 1930 Walter White lost the next year. The NAACP's foe this time was on the left side of the political spectrum, not the right.

White had read in the newspapers about the nine black teenagers, most of them illiterate drifters, who had been taken off a freight train at Paint Rock, Alabama, on March 25, 1931, charged with gang-raping two white young women who were also on board, and arraigned for trial at the Jackson County courthouse in Scottsboro, a small trading center in the middle of farm country. On the basis of the allegations alone, White must have calculated that the Scottsboro Boys' chances of escaping with their lives were slim, for no crime was more objectionable to the South than a black man despoiling the flower of white womanhood. And a group rape was all the more savage and reprehensible. That the lynchers in such a Deep South community had not already clawed the black boys to pieces was probably a gain in law-abiding practices. What the NAACP did not need just then was to go to the defense of a gang of rapists—if indeed they were that—so long as the formalities of the judicial process were honored at the trial. The nearest NAACP branch had been in Chattanooga, about a hundred miles away, but it was practically defunct at the moment. A black minister from that city telephoned White in New York and said that the Negro churches in the city had passed the hat, since some of the defendants had come from there, and raised a little money to hire a local white attorney to defend the boys. The man was competent enough, White was told, and to get anyone at all other than court-appointed counsel was no easy trick. Would the NAACP help finance the defense?

White was noncommittal. He wanted a better idea of the defendants' guilt or innocence. Could they please send up a transcript of the trial the moment one became available? As the trial went ahead, White got a call from the great defense attorney Clarence Darrow, an NAACP advisor, who said he had been contacted by the International Labor Defense (ILD), a civil-rights group affiliated with the Communist Party, which had asked him to serve as chief counsel in appealing the expected guilty verdict at Scottsboro. White warned Darrow to stay away from involvement with the Communist-front group and said that the NAACP had the situation well in hand—a claim he was to make repeatedly in the ensuing weeks. He was whistling in the dark. The Chattanooga defense attorney proved a disaster. He conferred with the defendants for just half an hour before going into court to face the all-white jury. In no time, the boys were accusing each other of the alleged rape while insisting on their own innocence—a sure ticket to their common doom. Their lawyer failed to cross-examine some key witnesses, failed to press the ones he did face, failed to deliver a closing statement, failed to protest that the town was one giant armed mob out there in the courthouse square—and failed to order the transcript that Walter White had asked for because the lawyer's retainer was so skimpy and he was not sure he would be reimbursed. By the time White discovered all this, the ILD had moved in.

Scottsboro quickly became a round-the-world byword for injustice in the American South. The speed of the trial, the number and age of the defendants, the severity of the punishment—death in the electric chair—and reports that the alleged victims of the crime were worldly-wise girls who had sold their bodies to men of both races—all these factors stirred protest over the outcome. And the *Daily Worker*, the voice of the American Communist Party, trumpeted the loudest, while ILD lawyers traveled to Chattanooga, won the confidence of the black churchmen who had helped the boys and did not know of the ILD's Red affiliation, and then went to Alabama to win the defendants' approval to represent them in the appeal. Walter White moved belatedly now to get the NAACP into the case, but all he succeeded in doing was confusing the convicted and frightened boys, beset by relays of lawyers from both groups who wanted to represent them but could not and would not work together. Every time White asserted that the ILD was using the case merely to ballyhoo the virtues of international Communism, the *Daily Worker* shouted back that the NAACP, working with "pliant Negro preachers," was a group of "traitors to the Negro masses and betrayers of the Negro liberation struggle" who were helping "lead the boys to the electric chair." Respectability in the eyes of the liberal white establishment was the guideline to every NAACP policy, the Communists charged, and soon the black press across the nation had picked up the theme and was accusing the association of worrying more about not tainting itself with Communism than about the fate of the Scottsboro Boys. At rallies to answer such charges, NAACP speakers found themselves heckled or shouted down by ILD operatives.

Walter White had simply not been prepared for the fury of the Red attack. Until just a few years earlier, Communism had been preoccupied with establishing its hold in Russia. But at the Sixth World Congress of the Communist International, held in Moscow in 1928, the low state of the American Negro was noted and seized upon as fit business for the party. In 1930, it published a manifesto proclaiming "the right of self-determination" of blacks in the United States and that "The Communist Party must stand up with all strength and courage for the struggle to win independence and for the establishment of a Negro republic in the Black Belt." The party's propaganda apparatus geared up for the effort, and the Scottsboro case was a perfect opportunity to push the cause. What was happening to these poor black youngsters was testimony of the Negro's degradation: he was without rights and without a job and America was failing him as it had always failed and abused him. The party was skillful at fishing in troubled waters, and here it got more than one bite. Growing destitute by the thousands, black Americans did not flee the siren song of the Soviets. But neither did they succumb to it. The Negro had never been invited to show much interest in political ideology or the higher reaches of dogma. Apathy and skepticism were his ruling emotions in the face of efforts to politicize him; he was at heart a quite conservative human being: he did not want a new revolution in America; he just wanted America to let him share fairly in the results of the last one.

Walter White had failed, for the moment, to attune himself to the yearnings of his race. In the Scottsboro confrontation, he had chosen to stand on ceremony, and the Communists shot his platform out from under him.

The next time he saw a chance to throw the NAACP behind the fate of a Negro facing lynch law, he did not hesitate. The chance came even as the

Scottsboro agony was landing in the laps of the Justices of the Supreme Court. This time, though, White had Charles Houston to help him.

Mrs. Agnes Boeing Illsley, a handsome, wealthy widow of a year's duration, was viewed by her little town of Middleburg in the fox-hunting territory of rural Loudoun County, Virginia, as a woman of great charm and gentility. A member of the local hunt club, she rode regularly to hounds. She also evidently enjoyed taking a belt of liquor from time to time, for on the evening of January 12, 1932, she attended an anti-Prohibition meeting in town, returning by car to the smaller of the two houses on her property shortly before midnight. Her companion and housekeeper, Mrs. Mina Buckner, lived in and slept in a room across the hall. Shortly after they had retired, someone broke in and bludgeoned them both to death. Just why they had been killed was a mystery. Jewelry and furs in clear view had not been taken. There was no evidence of attempted rape. The women had no known enemies.

Expert investigators were summoned from Washington forty miles southeast of the site of the crime. Microscopic examination of Mrs. Illsley's fingers revealed the presence of what police said were "bits of Negro hair and flesh beneath the nails." Other clues were picked up in her car, found abandoned in a coal yard outside of Alexandria. Suspicion began to settle on a short, quite dark Negro of about thirty named George Crawford, an ex-convict who had worked for Mrs. Illsley as a chauffeur and gardener the year before and was reported seen in the woods outside of Middleburg the afternoon before the murder. Crawford's one-time girl friend was brought in and questioned, and while police told reporters that the colored woman denied any knowledge of the crime or Crawford's whereabouts, she had in fact received a note from him asking for food the afternoon before the crime—information she later testified to. Others, too, said they had seen Crawford in the vicinity. The alarm went out. Twenty-five thousand circulars were distributed across the country describing Crawford, who had twice been convicted of larceny, as cunning, dangerous, and likely to be armed. Meanwhile a Loudoun County grand jury returned an indictment against him. A year later in Boston, police booked him on a robbery charge, took his fingerprints, ran a check on criminals wanted in other jurisdictions, and put in a call to the prosecutor's office in Leesburg, seat of government in Loudoun County, Virginia.

This time Walter White did not wait for any transcript. He sent an NAACP staff investigator to Boston, where Crawford asserted his innocence and listed witnesses to his presence in that city at the time of the double murder in Middleburg. White decided to put the NAACP into the case. At issue was more than the criminal question, for the Virginia grand jury that had indicted Crawford contained no Negroes and the jury that would try him was unlikely to contain any. NAACP lawyers saw only one strategy to save Crawford's skin: he must not be removed from the jurisdiction of Massachusetts.

In United States District Court in Boston, the Loudoun County prosecutor argued that Virginia had the undeniable constitutional right to extradite the accused murderer and put him on trial. Charles Houston joined the Boston lawyers representing the NAACP, who argued that Crawford's constitutional rights to a fair jury trial were no less pressing. Edward Lovett, who studied under Houston at Howard and later was an associate in his law firm, accompanied him to Boston for the hearing before Judge James A. Lowell. "I remember Charlie telling him that we had a Constitution of the United States," Lovett says, "and it was under that that Crawford was being sought by Virginia and it was under that that Crawford was being denied his rights by Virginia—and you can't spit and whistle at the same time, is how he put it."

The Boston judge ruled for the NAACP, but the United States Court of Appeals for the First Circuit reversed him, and the Supreme Court declined to hear the case. Virginia officials traveled to Boston to bring back their man. While there, they confronted Crawford with the fruits of their own investigative efforts and during a night of long interrogation extracted a confession from the accused man. Crawford implicated another Negro, who, according to the alleged confession, had done the actual killing after first suggesting a break-in and robbery "because things looked so quiet and unguarded there." Presented the next morning with a typescript of his confession, though, Crawford would not sign it. He had talked with NAACP lawyers in the interim and they had convinced him the confession was his death warrant. He would take his chances standing trial in Virginia.

It was agreed by Houston and Walter White that efforts ought to be made to quash the indictment against Crawford on the ground that an all-white jury in a case involving a Negro defendant was a violation of due process of law. Though the NAACP's challenge of Crawford's extradition on the same point had not been successful in the Court of Appeals, the question was by no means foreclosed. Indeed, parallel developments down in Alabama, where the Scottsboro Boys' fate had taken several sensational turns, made it imperative that the Virginia jury system now be challenged.

The United States Supreme Court had thrown out the results of the first Scottsboro trial because of the undue haste with which it was conducted. The Alabama court, moreover, had failed to provide the defendants with adequate counsel, and in a case where capital punishment was involved, such a failure represented denial of due process, the Court ruled. A new trial was held in March of 1933 before another all-white jury. But this time one of the two alleged rape victims denied that she had been attacked by the Negro defendants, denied that she had seen her traveling companion raped, and admitted that she had been coached in what to say by her friend, who in turn had told several white boys with them on the train that they might be charged with violating the Mann Act if they did not corroborate the girls' story. One of the white boys confirmed the girl's courtroom confession. But the other girl stuck to her story, and the jury again convicted the first black defendant to stand retrial. The new trial judge grimly re-sentenced the boy to death. But shortly thereafter he said that the prosecution's proof had been inadequate, that the evidence as presented was quite clearly on the side of the defense, and he ordered that a third trial be held. It was conducted in the weeks just before George Crawford's trial in Virginia was scheduled, and a third all-white jury again found the black defendants guilty. Exactly one week before the Crawford trial opened, a death sentence was again pronounced on the first two of the Scottsboro Boys. By now, it was clear that the exclusion of Negroes from the grand and trial juries had fatally affected the chances of the black defendants in the Alabama case. It again was appealed to the Supreme Court on that issue. And the issue, as Houston saw it, was no different in Virginia.

But who should handle Crawford's case? If all-white juries were the unvarying practice in Virginia, all-white lawyers were no less the rule. No black attorney had ever set foot inside the Loudoun County courthouse so far as anyone knew, and in the state as a whole the situation was hardly better. In fact, in the entire South the appearance of a black lawyer in a courtroom of any signficance was almost unheard of. It was a matter not only of white hostility toward such a display of black arrogance but also the consequent inexperience of Negro attorneys, who could not learn their craft if they were kept away from court and were therefore rarely hired to conduct business or cases of any importance. Able Negro attorneys were graduating in increasing numbers from leading Northern law schools, and Howard itself was about to graduate men of the caliber of Thurgood Marshall and Oliver Hill; such men were badly needed throughout the South, where Negroes' rights were daily violated in nearly every community. Somewhere, some time, someone had to break the taboo. And if it was going to mean anything, the case would have to be one of great prominence and the black attorney a man of unquestioned competence. After several efforts to enlist a leading white lawyer to defend Crawford—whose life, after all, was at stake and who could not be used as a guinea pig to advance the training of the black legal fraternity—it was clear to Walter White that the moment was at hand for the NAACP to sanction the switchover to black counsel in cases it was conducting in the South or anywhere else. And though the man's experience in handling criminal cases was negligible, it was also apparent to White that the best Negro lawyer in America was right beside him. Charlie Houston would run the case, and his fellow professor at Howard, Leon Ransom, would assist, along with Edward Lovett and another young colored attorney from Washington.

It did not take Houston long to discover that winning friends and influencing people in Loudoun County would not be easy. "Crawford had been accused of committing a pretty heinous crime," Lovett recounts, "and right in the middle of redneck country. No black lawyer had ever been seen in that courthouse before. And the way some of those guys looked at you around there, it was pretty plain they'd wring your neck if you crossed them—and maybe even if you didn't."

Loudoun County Negroes were not notably more hospitable. Houston and his team ranged all over the rural community trying to assemble a list of black citizens legally qualified and clearly competent to serve on grand and trial juries. No colored family would let them stay the night out of fear of reprisal, though a black barber with a white clientele let the Negro attorneys eat their lunches in the back of his shop. Houston concentrated on ministers, teachers, and other professional or obviously respectable people, but few were eager to volunteer their names. Out of nearly 4,000 Negroes in the county, the defense team was lucky to come up with a couple of dozen names to place before the courts. Meanwhile, Houston had learned that county juries were selected from the property-tax rolls, which were in two parts—white and colored. The jury commissioners consulted only the former in compiling their lists.

The coming of black lawyers to the county was big news in Loudoun and given major play by the Leesburg weekly, the Loudoun *Times-Mirror*. By the time argument was heard on the defense plea against the Crawford indictment, the paper was running a feature story headlined "Houston, Crawford Attorney, One of Leaders of Race in Nation," and noting his academic distinctions and membership on the District of Columbia's Board of Education, to which he had by then been appointed. Six telegraphers stood by in a Leesburg store converted temporarily into press headquarters as reporters flocked to the hearing from all over the state and throughout the East. The governor of Virginia was on hand. Crawford was brought into the courthouse shackled and guarded by twenty-five state policemen armed with rifles, clubs, and tear-gas guns. Half the reported 600 spectators were Negroes, many of them imported from Washington. If Walter White and Charlie Houston had ever wanted a showcase for black lawyers to strike back against unjust legal procedures, to stiffen the spines of local Negroes who had been cowed for generations by entrenched white supremacy, and to demonstrate that colored lawyers properly educated and trained were every bit as competent as white ones, they had found it.

Key to the hearing would be the testimony of Virginia Circuit Court Judge J. R. H. Alexander, who had selected the grand jury that indicted Crawford and now quite properly disqualified himself from sitting on the case, since the legality of the all-white grand jury was under challenge. On the bench was James L. McLemore, a competent jurist from the city of Suffolk in the southeast corner of the state near the North Carolina border, who had been assigned to the case by the governor.

Houston would question more than twenty witnesses before the hearing was done, but his case hinged on how he did with Judge Alexander. The judge testified that Negroes were not omitted from grand juries in Loudoun because of their race. He said the roster for the jury that returned the Crawford indictment had been drawn from the county tax list.

"Did you or did you not consider the Negro population?" Houston asked.

"I considered the population as a whole," Alexander answered. "I didn't know whether they were white or colored."

Houston knew better. He pressed the judge. Were Negroes' names on any of the lists from which the jurors were chosen? Alexander dodged the question. Those selected were well qualified, he said. He knew each juror personally and had taken into account their individual reputations for honesty, reliability, and intelligence. The list as a whole consisted of people of more than average intelligence and of good repute—"substantial citizens," in other words—and this was the kind of person who ought to be a grand juror.

Were there no such colored people in all of Loudoun County?

Well, said the judge, he knew of just two colored men in the county who met the statutory qualifications and there might be others unknown to him, but he had drawn up the lists without any thought of or reference to race. He simply picked grand jurors who met the qualifications prescribed by law. Later, though, Houston caught him in the self-contradictory acknowledgment that he had given some consideration to Negroes but was unable to find any colored people he knew to be qualified. Still later, on cross-examination by the county prosecutor, Alexander would testify that the race question "never entered my mind" in drawing up the 1933 grand-jury list, that he had sought the advice of no one, and that he reviewed the name of every qualified voter, "both white and colored," until he had compiled the required total of 480. That he referred to the county voting list was in further contradiction to his earlier testimony that he had used the property list as the basis for selecting the jurors.

Houston moved in closer. Wasn't it a fact that Negroes were never chosen to sit on Loudoun juries?

To his knowledge, said Judge Alexander, that was so. The practice was to use whites only.

Houston asked why.

Well, said Alexander, he himself had few business and no social relations with Negroes, and so he did not know any colored people well enough to determine if they might be qualified to serve as grand jurors.

Houston kept his temper under careful check. "Lose your temper, lose your case," he would tell his law-school classes, and now he had to heed his own preachment. Methodically he summoned thirteen Negroes from the county and established by their matter-of-fact testimony that they were substantial citizens by any standard of the community—save one—and met all the statutory requirements to serve as jurors.

In his summary, Houston felt no constraint to soft-pedal Judge Alexander's gentlemanly racism. But he chose his words with great care. He referred to the judge as "a slow and reluctant witness"—which was about as close to personal rebuke as it was safe for him to venture in that courtroom. There were two basic questions before them, he went on. Were there Negroes qualified for jury service living in Loudoun County? "Yes!" Houston shouted, his rich voice exploding over every head in the jammed chamber. Were such Negroes excluded from jury service solely because of their race? "Yes!" the black lawyer shouted again. "All the testimony here today shows that there have been no Negroes on grand juries or trial juries in Virginia, so their deliberate exclusion must be admitted by the commonwealth [the state]. Public policy in Virginia is that Negroes are not to serve on juries." Judge Alexander's jury selections were based on his own narrow orbit of acquaintances, Houston charged. The judge had been "revolving around a closed circle—a wheel excluding all Negroes. In other words, a caste system is prevalent in Virginia and the South."

They were powerful words, and nobody in the courtroom had ever heard their like spoken by a Negro in the South before. The county prosecutor responded that the jurors selected were all qualified, that no county Negroes were comparably qualified, and that no Negro's constitutional rights had been invaded by the selection process. But it was Houston's words that hung in the air as the hearing adjourned and George Crawford was taken back to jail in Alexandria without incident.

Next day, the court ruled against Houston. Negroes were not excluded from the grand-jury roster because of their race, Judge McLemore found. Nothing in the hearing testimony suggested that Judge Alexander had not acted honestly and legally, and if his list "includes no colored people among the 48 men selected, the list is still a perfectly good list." It was the old story: the absence of a Negro on a jury was not in and of itself evidence of discrimination.

There were repeated reports that Houston would appeal the grand-jury ruling or that Negroes might be among the 300 names on the list from which the trial jury would be selected. But neither happened, and Crawford's trial opened on schedule. Houston calculated that he might win the battle and lose the war if he appealed; even if Negroes were included on either the grand- or the trial-jury list, there was still no known obligation on the county's part to call them for actual service. To charge that all-white juries were *per se* unconstitutional in cases involving Negroes would have been to raise an issue that the trial court was not competent to rule on; indeed, it was just that question that was about to be raised by the Scottsboro attorney in his new appeal to the Supreme Court. Right now, Houston had a murder trial to win, and his best hope was not to rile up the local gentry unduly. Aware of the weakness of his case, Houston was maneuvering to save Crawford's life.

Just how weak Crawford's case was became apparent as the four-day trial unfolded. The alibi witnesses that Crawford once claimed would bear him out had evaporated. His former lover and other Loudoun Negroes testified against him, placing him in the county the day before the murder. And then there was the withdrawn confession that Crawford had made to the Loudoun prosecutor who had gone to Boston to bring back the colored prisoner. The text of the confession could not be introduced into the proceedings, but the prosecutor was allowed to testify as to what Crawford had allegedly told him in Boston. The details of the confession, even though rescinded, were convincing. Then there was the damaging matter of the two prior terms Crawford had served in the state penitentiary in Richmond.

The best Houston could do was try to punch holes in the prosecution's case, since the evidence against Crawford was largely circumstantial. He pounced on conflicting medical opinion and other testimony over the murder weapon and stressed that the prosecution had not in fact produced any weapon. Houston's colleague Leon Ransom had spent weeks researching human pathology to prepare himself for questioning the Washington medical examiner who had declared that the bits of hair and skin found under Mrs. Illsley's fingernails had come from a Negro. At the trial, Ransom seemed to shake the pathologist with his technical command of the subject and probing questions that drove the judge to ask for "testimony the jury can understand." Finally, Ransom succeeded in getting the medical examiner to admit that the particles of hair and flesh *might* have come from a white person.

Despite all their best efforts, Houston feared the worst from the all-white, all-male jury. He had challenged the composition of the trial jury just as he had the grand jury, but the nine farmers, two bankers, and a merchant were impaneled anyway. And now at the end it seemed likely that they had heard nothing to make them doubt George Crawford's withdrawn confession. In his summary, Houston argued that the state had not proven its case but that if the jury chose to believe the withdrawn confession, it ought to spare the life of the man he called "a poor, homeless dog" so that if his accomplice were ever caught, Crawford would be available to testify against him. A death sentence seemed imminent.

The jury deliberated for two hours. After four votes, it came in with a verdict: guilty—with a life sentence recommended.

By prevailing standards of Virginia, and Southern, justice, Houston and his team had done superbly. Jury members later told the press that Houston's moving appeal for Crawford had saved him from the electric chair. Beyond that, the entire conduct of the trial was the kind of breakthrough in courtesy and fair procedure that Houston and White had hoped to win. At no time during the trial had the state's lawyers referred to the defendant's race. There was no petty bickering between counsel. The Richmond *News-Leader*, one of the state's two most powerful papers, said that the group of Howard defense lawyers "demonstrated to the Virginia public that there are negro lawyers in the country who can be courageous without being obsequious, lawyers who can make a fight without arousing racial antagonisms. That of itself gave to the trial a certain educational value." And Virginius Dabney, the best-known political commentator in the state, wrote of Houston: "The dignity, the poise and the ability with which this 36-year-old honor graduate of Amherst and Harvard conducted the defense impressed everyone." There was even talk that around the state some Negroes might soon be added to grand-jury lists.

On reflection, Houston chose not to appeal Crawford's conviction and sentence. A new jury, even a biracial one, might recommend the death penalty. A year later, in the spring of 1935, the Supreme Court ruled on the Scottsboro Boys' appeal by ILD-paid attorney Samuel Leibowitz that all-white juries were illegal as they had been constituted in this case. Chief Justice Hughes was struck by testimony of a jury commissioner that no Negro in his county had been found to be competent to serve on a jury—almost precisely the same testimony that Judge Alexander had given in the Loudoun County courthouse upon examination by Houston. "We find it impossible to accept such a sweeping characterization of the lack of qualifications of Negroes," Hughes wrote for the Court. "For this long-continued, unvarying and wholesale exclusion of Negroes from jury service, we find no justification consistent with the constitutional mandate." The original indictment was set aside and the case had to begin all over—for the fourth time.

The Court had not ruled that all-white juries were in themselves illegal in communities with a sizable black population or were illegal whenever a black defendant was on trial. But it had said that a persistent pattern of excluding Negroes was in itself conclusive evidence of discrimination and therefore intolerable. While each such case would still have to be fought on its own merits, the Court had put up a signpost of major significance in both its Scottsboro rulings. If a state did not act to assure due process of law in its courts, then the Supreme Court was obliged to invoke the Fourteenth Amendment and exercise its supervisory function in this regard. The mere forms of the judicial process would no longer do; the courtroom was no place for charades.

Though Houston might have had as strong a case as Leibowitz had he appealed Crawford's conviction by an all-white jury, there were extenuating circumstances that had dictated Houston's decision. The malevolence of the Alabama juries was in the record and so self-evident that one of the trial judges had insisted on a retrial; no such picture had emerged in Loudoun County, Virginia. Besides, the Scottsboro Boys were almost certainly innocent; it is unlikely that any of his lawyers thought George Crawford was.

# 7

# The Raw Deal

In the midst of Charles Houston's involvement in the Crawford case, a pair of the first crop of young blacks to emerge from Howard University's rugged, retooled law mill gave a premature push to the anti-Jim Crow fight that Nathan Margold had blueprinted for the NAACP and that Walter White wanted Houston to wage at the earliest possible moment.

One March morning in 1933, a twenty-four-year-old resident of Durham, North Carolina, named Thomas Raymond Hocutt, who worked as an assistant headwaiter at the Washington Duke Hotel, filed an application for admission to the school of pharmacy at the beautiful University of North Carolina. The university was the pearl of the state's relatively progressive public education system, probably the most modern in the South, but never in its 144 years of operation had a Negro student been enrolled there.

Hocutt was advised that black residents of the state could pursue college studies at five institutions set aside for their exclusive use—two junior colleges for teacher training, one four-year teachers' college, one agricultural and technical college, and North Carolina College for Negroes. Hocutt had attended the last of these schools for a time, but it did not offer a course of study in pharmacy. Rejected by the all-white University of North Carolina, which ran the only public school of pharmacy in the state, Hocutt filed suit in Durham County Superior Court. His two young attorneys, Howard law-school alumni Conrad Pearson and Cecil McCoy, had wasted little time in getting into the fight against racial injustice in a fashion urged by Houston.

When Pearson wrote to Walter White at NAACP headquarters in New York seeking financial help to wage Hocutt's pioneering legal action, White directed the matter to Houston, who had become his chief informal legal advisor. Pearson had the makings of a fine lawyer, Houston knew, but he did not want to risk losing the very first round of the attack on school segregation because of inexperienced counsel. For here was an opportunity to activate the premise of the Margold Report as modified by Houston's less theoretical strategy of attacking the white citadel of school segregation where it was most vulnerable—at the graduate- and professional-school level. Thomas Hocutt's case could provide the classic example. North Carolina either had to admit him to its lily-white university or supply him and any other qualified colored resident of the state with a school of pharmacy all their own.

In view of the ailing economy and his own heavy schedule of duties, Houston had not wanted to launch the drive against school segregation just yet. And he would have preferred a border state as the arena for the opening clash rather than a mid-South state such as North Carolina. Still, the terrain could have been worse. And one couldn't pick and choose one's plaintiffs those days: there were too few willing to risk the fight and possible reprisals. It was a case that Houston should have handled himself, since a setback at the start might curdle enthusiasm for the full-scale drive he anticipated, but the Crawford extradition proceedings required his shuttling to Boston and he still had a law school to run. He recommended that the NAACP cooperate with Pearson's efforts but dispatch his cousin and colleague at Howard, Bill Hastie, to oversee the case. White had heard warm words from Felix Frankfurter about Hastie, and so the young lawyer was assigned the task.

William Hastie—you would never guess from looking at or speaking to him in later years—grew up on a chicken farm on the outskirts of Knoxville, Tennessee. The streetcars and the theaters were segregated there, and so the proud Hasties walked or rode bicycles, except in emergencies, and never went to the theater. His father, a federal government clerk, moved the family to Washington, where he went to work for the bureau then handling veterans' affairs, and Bill went to the same Dunbar High School that his second cousin Charlie Houston had attended. In fact, he did almost everything Charlie Houston did, only a fraction or so better. He graduated first in his high-school class and went on to Amherst, where he won election to Phi Beta Kappa in his junior year, ran the hundred-yard dash for the Amherst track team in ten seconds—"I think I owe my success in track to having spent my entire boyhood on a bicycle," he surmised long after—and graduated *magna cum laude* with prizes in mathematics and physics. His excellence in those abstract sciences testified to a mind of exceptional clarity, honed to slice through masses of data to the nucleus of any problem presented to him. It was a mind of lightning responses but not one given to large creative lunges. At Harvard, he made the *Law Review* just as cousin Charlie had and learned, too, from Felix Frankfurter. Beyond his academic distinctions, Hastie displayed high gentility that still did not prevent his being snubbed by the fraternities at Amherst, where blacks traditionally were welcomed to the academic life but pointedly omitted from the socializing. Bill Hastie did not need Sigma Chi to teach him etiquette, for he had matured rapidly into what one white admirer calls "a polished, assimilated gentleman—a black WASP, in fact."

Back home in Washington in 1930, Hastie joined the law firm of Houston & Houston, picking up some of the slack created by Charlie's departure to run Howard Law School, where Bill also taught part-time. The two young Amherst-Harvard men were a formidable pair of lawyers and legal strategists. Though their paths would diverge soon enough, they stayed in constant touch and, with their upcoming protégé, Thurgood Marshall, argued or masterminded almost every major lawsuit for black rights throughout the country during the next twenty-five years. "Charlie was the earthier of the two," says a mutual friend; Hastie was the keener analyst and, on the face of it, the less emotional. In time, both of them would be viewed as highly controversial and, to government officials and other whites in the power establishment, somewhat combustible personalities, but Hastie was cooler and less self-punishing in the process of protest. "He had an excellent mind, superb in its grasp of a problem and the ways it might be pursued," says James Nabrit, Jr., who has known Hastie long and well. "It took him a while, though, to overcome a slight defensiveness that stemmed from fretting about what his old Harvard law professors might say about how to handle a case."

And in fact Hastie had gone back to Harvard to get his degree as Doctor of Juridical Science and was finishing up when Houston and White summoned him to handle the NAACP's interests in the case of Thomas Hocutt. Hastie readily accepted the challenge. Arriving in Durham a week or so before the court hearing, he found that North Carolina might have enjoyed relatively peaceful race relations, but no one was putting up statues . of Harriet Beecher Stowe in front of its county courthouses. More to the point was the mood of the black population itself. Militancy had not taken root, and the prevailing feeling was that because North Carolina blacks were relatively well off, agitation—especially if stirred by out-of-staters—would backfire and hurt the amicable status quo.

Principal spokesman for Negro conservatism in the state was the president of its leading colored school—Dr. James E. Shepard of North Carolina College for Negroes, the school Hocutt had attended. Black rebellion would jeopardize his position with the state legislature, which funded the Negro college, and thereby hurt all colored people in the state, Shepard confided to other black leaders. Three years earlier, when North Carolina whites had needed a Negro spokesman to speak up so Congress would know that the charge of racism had been unfairly draped on Supreme Court nominee John Parker, they had turned to Dr. James Shepard, who obliged them, though no other black leader of note collaborated. And now it was Dr. Shepard, Hastie discovered upon his arrival in Durham, who was more of an obstacle to Hocutt's legal efforts than any white official. For the rules of the university stated that any applicant who had attended another school or college after secondary school had to supply "the recommendation of the last school attended"—and in Hocutt's case that was Dr. Shepard's college. But James Shepard, most eminent black educator in the state, was not about to participate in an effort to desegregate the University of North Carolina. He would not recommend Hocutt or supply his transcript.

In court, there was no avoiding the roadblock Dr. Shepard had put in the way. Hastie had to counter the university's claim that Hocutt's academic qualifications had not been proven, and it was here that disaster struck. The principal of his old high school testified that Hocutt had shown good character and completed his course credits as required; but on cross-examination he acknowledged that Hocutt's grades had barely been high enough for promotion. As to his work at North Carolina College for Negroes, there was no record, of course, although Pearson's group had put out word that Hocutt was an honor student in his college work. On the witness stand, however, he was pounced upon by the state's lawyers, who asked him to read to the court his high-school record. Whether unnerved or unskilled, Hocutt had great difficulty in pronouncing his words and stumbled awkwardly a few times. The defense had made its point. Hocutt, said the state lawyers in their turn, was "a reluctant colored man, poorly prepared and thoroughly disqualified," being made the instrument of agitators who sought to force the university to admit Negroes. It was all a scheme to promote social equality and intermarriage, asserted the state's attorney general.

Hocutt's right to admission to the university, the judge concluded, was "not of a public character"—that is, the university had the discretion to determine who might be admitted to its student body—and the most that Hocutt's lawyers could have asked of the court was to direct university officials to consider Hocutt's application "in good faith without regard to the fact that he is a person of African descent." But his lawyers had not asked that; they had asked more than that. And more than that he could not grant. The judge added that Hocutt had not supplied the required evidence of his qualifications for admission or established his clear legal right to it. But there was a ray of light in the decision, from the NAACP standpoint. The court declared that the duty of the university to admit Negroes to its professional schools "as long as the state fails to provide equal opportunity for training in said professions in the state supported negro schools . . . is not determined or sought to be determined in this judgment."

They had made too many mistakes. Hocutt had not been the ideal plaintiff in whose name to bring such a case. The suit itself had been drawn too narrowly. And the opposition of Dr. Shepard had tied their hands almost from the start. Under the circumstances, there seemed no point in appealing —unless Shepard could be persuaded to relent or was sued to release Hocutt's records. But such an intra-racial squabble would likely put the NAACP out of business in North Carolina. Better to retreat with honor and fight another day.

There was some honor in the case, especially for Hastie. "The universal agreement in Durham," said the Greensboro *Daily News*, "is that the lawyer has handled his case in admirable taste and with first-rate ability." Walter White would later write in his autobiography that the trial judge had told him Hastie's performance was one of the most brilliant he had witnessed in twenty-two years on the bench.

The Crawford and Hocutt cases, while not precisely ringing triumphs in terms of measurable results, had sent morale soaring among the whole Howard law group. Together, the cases had demonstrated the high competence and cool courage of black counsel arguing freely in Southern courtrooms. Their outcomes seemed to release Charles Houston's churning intellect and great energy. He would never feel at home as an organization man, and Mordecai Johnson's imperious ways did not make the prospect of an extended academic career at Howard any more enticing. Houston had essentially achieved what had been asked of him in rebuilding the law school, and now there was so much else to be out and doing.

His cousin William Hastie had shown the way by joining the Department of Interior as Assistant Solicitor under Nathan Margold in 1933. All around him, Houston sensed the mood of hope that the administration of Franklin D. Roosevelt had begun to bring to the economically beleaguered country. Washington was suddenly an exhilarating place, not just another segregated Southern city where the national government happened to be housed. His hometown was now the great national forum where the black man could most forcefully argue his case. The new federal officials would at least listen. And so, by 1934, Charles Houston began to phase himself out of Howard's law school, though he would remain its principal back-seat counselor, and gravitated toward the world of Walter White and the NAACP.

Houston seemed to be everywhere now, doing everything—a one-man lobby against the continued debasement of the Negro. His law-school affiliation opened many doors and allowed him to agitate without seeming to. His appointment in 1933 to the District of Columbia's Board of Education had made him interracially respectable. And the Crawford case had made him a celebrity. People would listen to him. To the whites, he was a credit to his race; to the blacks, he was the living answer to white supremacy. He began to speak out now with unaccustomed sharpness.

In February 1934, he appeared in Richmond at the annual conference of the Virginia Commission on Interracial Cooperation, a typical hearts-and-flowers gathering at which the governor of the state presided and dispensed the usual quota of homilies about the prevalence of racial harmony in Virginia as contrasted with other states. Then he introduced Houston, who promptly demurred. Virginia had to share the blame with the rest of the white South, the black scholar-lawyer declared, for the sorry state of the Negro, who was worse off now under the so-called economic-recovery program than he had been before. Why did the white South impose lower wages upon blacks in the textile and steel industries and in the laundry business when blacks had to pay just as much for food as white men? And why did the federal government sanction industrial codes that approved such wage differentials? New home-loan and farm-mortgage laws, similarly rigged against the Negro, were reducing the colored race to a landless, jobless class. NRA, he said with bitter wryness, stood for "Negro Robbed Again."

Later in the year, he went after General Douglas MacArthur, then Chief of Staff of the United States Army. Overwhelming evidence indicated, Houston wrote, that "the army has constantly discriminated and is even now discriminating against colored officers and colored troops." When MacArthur sent back an I-appreciate-your-interest-in-the-national-defense letter grandly denying military bigotry, Houston let him have it with both barrels. Was it not true that the colored soldiers at Fort Riley were there to rub liniment on the Ninth Cavalry's horses and oil the mounted equipment instead of learning to operate either? And that the colored soldiers attached to Fort Myer's machine-gun troop were trained to mop up barracks and not mow down enemy ranks? And that the colored troops of the Second Squadron at the general's beloved West Point performed out-of-sight police and fatigue duty and were never seen to drill on the hallowed parade grounds? Why were "75 per cent of the colored troops" performing service duty? And as to colored officers: well, every time one ranked high enough to warrant seniority and control over any number of white officers, he was "shunted away from regiments into detached service." Houston released the exchange to the press.

That summer, he toured the massive works of the Tennessee Valley Authority and discovered massive discrimination against Negroes. Reporting on his findings in *The Crisis*, he blasted the TVA as "lily-white reconstruction." Blacks were limited to the traditional dirty jobs reserved for them in any industrial enterprise—as drillers, powder men, and concrete-pourers in the field of dam-building. No Negroes were given inside jobs as clerks or office workers. No Negroes were employed as foremen. No Negroes were allowed to participate in the job-training or social rehabilitation programs. And most assuredly no Negroes were invited to settle in the snug brick homes in the new "model" communities that housed TVA workers. The government-funded TVA was going along with all the Jim Crow ways of the region. The New Deal had to be made to understand that "the economic wage slavery and social suppression cursing the South today are absolutely incompatible with a real return to prosperity."

By early in 1935, it had been announced that Houston would leave Howard at the end of the spring term and take up duties as special counsel to the NAACP. At once, he was shuttled over to Capitol Hill to offer knowledgeable testimony to the Senate Finance Committee on how the proposed new economic-security program would shortchange the black population. Most Negroes still earned their bread as domestic and agricultural workers, and the old-age-assistance plan pointedly omitted them by its requirement of forty weeks of employment a year for five years running in a given community. Houston labeled the bill "a sieve" through which black workers would drop, as intended. The program would benefit only organized labor, although it was well known that when sharecroppers and tenant farmers tried to organize, as they had in Phillips County, Arkansas, and a hundred other places, they were generally thrown off the land, often assaulted, and sometimes killed. No doubt some would say that Negroes make small tax payments to their communities, he noted in anticipation of the point, and should therefore not receive social-security benefits on a par with the white man. "If we have not paid more taxes," Houston declared firmly, "it is because we have been denied more work. What we want now is equal work opportunity."

When he was not making such pronouncements from every available platform, Charlie Houston was out in the community pushing whatever social-action cause he thought would do good. He helped raise funds for the Scottsboro defense after Communist domination of that effort dwindled and the NAACP joined a wide-based coalition to finance the seemingly endless litigation. He helped organize picketing against a national conference on crime that was felt to be dominated by racist thinking. He helped organize a group of young black lawyers, professors, and other professionals who called themselves the New Negro Alliance and took out after white employers in colored neighborhoods who refused to hire colored people.

In the middle of all this, Charles Houston argued and won his first case before the Supreme Court of the United States. It was the first time a black lawyer had represented the NAACP before the high court and won.

It was, as such things go, an easy case. But arguing before the Supreme Court for the first time can be a traumatizing experience for anyone. "He wasn't nervous at all," remembers Edward Lovett, Houston's younger associate in the family law firm. "He'd been trained awfully well." The case combined the principal features of both the Crawford and Scottsboro trials. A Negro named Jess Hollins had been convicted of rape in Sapulpa, Oklahoma, in 1931 by an all-white jury and sentenced to die. NAACP attorneys in the area intervened just three days before the scheduled execution and appealed on the ground that no Negroes had served on juries in Okmulgee County, Oklahoma, where the trial had been held, within the memory of man. By the time Houston appeared to plead Hollins's case before the Supreme Court, the Justices had ruled favorably in the second Scottsboro appeal of *Norris v. Alabama*: Negroes could not be habitually prohibited from jury service; where they were, black defendants could claim denial of due process. Arguing against the attorney general of Oklahoma, Houston so claimed. On May 13, 1935, the Supreme Court ruled in his favor in the case of *Hollins v. Oklahoma*. It was a *per curiam* decision in which the Court did not bother with a written opinion but simply cited a previous decision on the same point—in this case, the Scottsboro holding. It made up a little for the outcome in Loudoun County.

For all these facets of his work, Houston performed one function that almost no one else knew about but was probably far more important than all the others put together. He became Walter White's brains. Not that White was notably deficient in that area, but he had not half the knowledge or contacts that he needed in the one place where the NAACP should have been strongest—Washington. It would have made far more sense to move the organization's headquarters to the capital, but tradition and the proximity of most of its big contributors kept the NAACP in New York. In the second half of 1934, White began leaning heavily on Houston's advice and lifelong familiarity with Washington. White could be a haughty commander within the walls of his organization, but he did not command Charlie Houston. The two men had what Houston's junior law partner, Joseph Waddy, calls "a cordial and productive relationship." They spoke on the telephone or wrote to each other nearly every day for a number of years—"Walter White wouldn't make a move without consulting Charlie," Waddy suggests—and every so often White would come down from New York for a day-long session with Houston, who would then work late into the night catching up with his regular business.

The tone of their surviving correspondence suggests why the partnership worked so well. It was an exchange between equals, and while White rarely credited Houston in public (and scarcely mentioned him in his autobiography), he deferred to the attorney's thinking on many problems and did not hesitate to put his suggestions into action. White listened to almost every idea Houston came up with because most of them were both practical and aimed at extending the NAACP's sway. Houston suggested the possibility of opening up branches on black college campuses, where race pride was presumably high and readily mobilized. He urged that more effort be made to have association officials attend statewide conferences of ministers: it was "the chance to reach the 'leaders' of the masses . . . in a way that nothing else will." He proposed that documentary motion pictures of the plight of the Negro be made for showing to legislative committees, branch members, and outside power groups, and he himself began shooting sixteen-millimeter film on every trip to the South. But it was Houston's sensitivity to the political scene that made his command post especially valuable to White. The lawyer kept close track of the progress of bills in Congress and knew the racial implications of each. He knew who had what power and what levers might activate it. And he knew protocol and Washington's brand of etiquette. His advisory letters to White were really battle-front memos. They might take the form of simply listing priorities for the NAACP chief, as in a short letter to him dated September 13, 1934:

> . . . May I suggest that when you come to Washington you put down the following things on your agendum, plus the talk with Mrs. Roosevelt:
> 1. FERA, with a special emphasis on southern rural relief,
> 2. Homestead Subsistence,
> 3. AAA, with reference to cotton and tobacco,
> 4. A.F. of L., Negroes in unions, and
> 5. War Department, re Army discrimination.

More typical would be advisory letters of a substantive nature, laying out Houston's reading of the political landscape, his suggested strategy, and the thinking behind the strategy. And it would all be done with compelling clarity and forthrightness.

In February of 1935, for example, just before Houston's appearance before the Senate Finance Committee on the economic-security bill, he wrote White that his reconnoitering on Capitol Hill disclosed that the House version of the sweeping measure would definitely cut out agricultural and domestic workers from the old-age annuity (shortly to become known as Social Security) and unemployment benefits. The fight would have to be made on the floor of each house. Houston was aware that White's ultimate legislative passion was not for the economic-relief measure but for the perennial anti-lynching bill. It was again locked up in committee, but in this session, thanks to the massive Democratic majorities sent to Congress by the 1934 election results, White was nursing real hopes for action. Houston, while understanding and admiring White's fifteen-year fight for federal action to curb lynching, knew the barbaric practice had fallen off sharply and saw that the association's priority should now be given to the economic-security bill. He wrote White:

> It seems to me you now have an opportunity to do one of the greatest jobs since the [Judge John] Parker fight. Here is where Labor will be aggressively with you.

I think you should swing all the force of the Association and its Branches behind this fight. . . . It is a chance to get lined up right on a vital economic issue; and to draw to you a lot of people who are somewhat lukewarm to the anti-lynching bill.

What I fear is that with the activity of the national office [i.e., White] centering so much around the anti-lynching bill, there are not enough irons in the fire, and that the success of the [Roosevelt] administration may tend to be judged on one issue alone. From my view this is bad strategy. There should be a three-ringed fight going on at all times.

Further lots of us feel that a fight for anti-lynching legislation without just as vigorous a battle for economic independence is to fight the manifestation of the evil and ignore its cause.

He was no office-bound operative. Charlie Houston liked to get out and around, for all his lack of folksiness, and find out how things sat in the hinterland. In the late fall of 1934, he took a typically grueling four-week trip that reflected his strategic role as liaison between the largely mute black folk of the South and the spokesmen of the race such as Walter White who, operating out of New York and huddling with white patrons much of the time, inevitably lost touch with the colored masses and their needs. By then, Houston had yielded to White's overtures to come to work for the NAACP, but on his tour he would travel under the auspices of the law school, seeking applicants, because he would be more welcome that way.

Driving south in his old Graham-Paige with Eddie Lovett, he ranged from Richmond, Virginia, to Augusta, Georgia, with most of the four weeks allotted to the Carolinas. It was no sightseeing tour. He was booked well ahead of time to speak in college chapels, to inspect local public schools, to meet with state officials, to rally NAACP branch officials, to address church meetings and tobacco workers and schoolteachers. To open white as well as colored doors, he took with him letters of introduction from Interior Secretary Ickes and Secretary of Agriculture Wallace, obtained at Houston's instigation by Walter White. His schedule for November 26, when Houston was in Charlotte, North Carolina, was typical:

Inspection and photographing school buses.
Booker Washington high school teachers.
Grand jury report, Feb. 1934.
Conference [with] Felton, State Supervisor Negro Ed.
Re-inspection Mt. Arat School, Richburg.
Johnson C. Smith [College] pictures                 7:00 PM
Charlotte Branch NAACP                        8:00 PM

In South Carolina, he took a lot of film of the condition of black schools and added footage the next spring. By June of 1935, he had blocked out a detailed scenario of a documentary with the working title "Examples of Educational Discrimination Among Rural Negroes in South Carolina." Sample scenes from the eleven-page proposal suggest how carefully he had gathered the data and how acutely disturbed he was by the findings:

PLEASANT GROVE SCHOOL, CHESTER COUNTY

Pleasant Grove offers grades 1 through 7. But November 15, 1934, no pupils had registered for the 7th grade as the older children were still out gathering the crops. (Reel I, Scene 3)

> Enrolment November 15, 1934, 75 students. Enrolment January 24, 1935, after the crops were in, 156 students. Compulsory attendance laws are not enforced as regards Negro school children.

. . . .

d. The Broom Brigade (Reel I, Scene 6)

> The County furnishes nothing except teachers and two tons of coal per year. Negroes have to provide their own blackboards, erasers, crayon, stoves, extra fuel, and make most of the repairs on the building.

e. The teacher had to raise money to buy her bell and horn by selling candy around the neighborhood. (Reel I, Scene 9)

. . . .

g. The only toilet facilities (Reel I, Scene 8)

> No pit, no lime; just ashes from the stoves to cover the waste.

. . . .

MT. ARAT SCHOOL BUILDING, CHESTER COUNTY (Reel I, Scene 25)

. . . .

e. Road scene

> For toilet facilities the boys have to cross railroad and highway to get to the woods.

. . . .

g. The student body. 68 pupils packed into one room, 20 x 16 feet, on seven benches. No tables, no desks, no stove. One chair, one open fireplace. (Reel I, Scene 31)

. . . .

i. Richburg School, white, about two miles from Mt. Arat School. Grades 1 through 11; six rooms, six teachers. Assembly hall, piano, individual desks. Three buses to transport children. Two Negro women janitresses clean entire building and make 6 fires daily for wages of $4.00 per month each. (Reel I, Scene 33)

. . . .

MOORE'S POND SCHOOL, RICHLAND COUNTY, housed in Negro church 9 miles out of Columbia on U.S. Highway No. 21. The County furnishes wood, pays the teacher's salary of $40.00 per month for the 4 month term, and gives the Church $1.00 per week as rent. (Reel II, Scene 22)

. . . .

a. The nearest drinking water is across the highway at the abandoned gasoline station. (Reel II, Scene 23)

b. The children sit inside crowded together on benches. No desks, no chairs, one old piece of blackboard. (Reel II, Scene 24)

c. Cracks in the door are half inch wide. The cracks in the floor are so wide that pencils often roll through to the ground when dropped. (Reel II, Scene 25)

d. Abandoned white school about a mile away. Curtains still at the windows. The building is full of desks and other school equipment not in use. The white children are transported 17 miles into Columbia to school; but the authorities will not permit the Negroes to use either the abandoned building or the abandoned equipment. (Reel II, Scene 26)

. . . .

IV. There can be no consolidation of rural schools without transportation.

A. In 1932–33 South Carolina spent $331,932.00 transporting 29,624 white children to elementary school, but only $628.00 transporting 87 Negroes to elementary school.

B. As long as Negro children are denied transportation and have to trudge along in the mud and dust to school, consolidated schools are out of the question and the one-room school will persist. (Reel II, Scene 6)*

It was not unnatural, then, that when formal announcement of Houston's joining the NAACP staff was made in the spring of 1935, stress was placed on the pitiable school conditions he would try to tackle. He had been selected, the announcement said, "as special counsel to handle a legal campaign against unequal educational facilities and some phases of Jim Crow transportation. . . . Mr. Houston will work under a joint committee of the NAACP and the American Fund for Public Service [the Garland Fund]." There was little of the Garland money left by that point, but Walter White set aside $6,000 of it for Houston's salary. Now White would have his principal field advisor right at hand in the New York headquarters.

They needed him badly. Du Bois had quit the NAACP the year before in anger and frustration. After two dozen years, the bright light had dimmed but it was still burning and still needed when the end came. Du Bois was always a proud, cantankerous man who had found it painful to compromise, but too many negative factors piled up now as he grew old. He respected Walter White's vigor and appreciated his charm, yet he had never fully trusted the "white" Negro who now led the organization that Du Bois had been instrumental in founding. There was the lingering suspicion that the glib younger man was more interested in building a personal fiefdom than in advancing the race. And the board of directors that backed White struck Du Bois as "still mainly conservative" and representative mostly of "capital and investment" while Du Bois himself was swinging increasingly toward labor and socialism and thought that was where the black folk belonged. Then, too, *The Crisis* was no longer paying its way as it had from the start—a result of Depression economics—and now he was answerable to the association for the magazine's editorial positions after so many years of freedom. Finally, the basic philosophical posture he had begun to assume on the race question was at odds with the core concept of the NAACP—namely, unmitigated opposition to segregation. That was all very well in the abstract, Du Bois had concluded, but in real life such a policy was working insidiously to undermine, not enhance, black pride. What Du Bois called "clear and incontrovertible facts" showed that most Negroes attended black schools and black churches, lived in black neighborhoods, and associated with black friends, and it was going to be that way for many decades to come. Why disparage these institutions by insisting on the desirability of their dissolu-

* Extensive inquiries of NAACP officials, Houston's closest associates, and his son, as well as examination of the NAACP records and archives at the Library of Congress, have failed to uncover what use was ever made of the film or what became of it.

tion? In view of ongoing white enmity, it was imperative that black culture and social institutions be improved, not disbanded or denounced as automatically inferior. He wrote critically in *The Crisis* of White's "unsound explanation" of the NAACP's historic stand on segregation, and the board of directors passed a censuring motion that foreclosed such intramural wrangling in the pages of the magazine. Du Bois resigned and, at the age of sixty-six, returned to teach at Atlanta University. Charles Houston's arrival at NAACP headquarters would help compensate for the loss.

Far more troubling to Walter White than the departure of Du Bois was the fate of his perennially committee-locked anti-lynching bill. He had put more of his life into this single cause than any other. His 1929 investigatory book on the subject, *Rope and Faggot*, had earned him a reputation as a social reformer and he had risked his neck more than once in the effort. By 1935, the portents for action on Capitol Hill seemed good. The Seventy-Fourth Congress was composed of 69 Democrats and 2 Progressives against 25 Republicans in the Senate; in the House, the Democrats' edge was 319 to 103, with 10 independents. It was an overwhelming party advantage—except, of course, that the Democrats of the South continued to oppose benefits for the Negro, and their unrelenting hostility meant that Congress was in fact closely divided on any matter remotely touching the race question. The NAACP's champions in Congress managed to get the bill sprung from the stranglehold of the Senate Judiciary Committee and reported to the floor, where the filibusterers began at once to bleed it to death. There was only one chance to save it. Walter White wangled a visit to the White House.

It was a warm spring Sunday, and he met the President on the porch of the south portico with Mrs. Roosevelt in attendance. Senator Joe Robinson had told him the anti-lynching bill was unconstitutional, the President said—an invasion of states' rights. White reeled off the collective opinion of many lawyers, prominently including Charles Houston, that countered Robinson's view. Roosevelt listened, raised another objection he had heard, listened again while White smoothly rebutted it, then finally admitted the real reason why he would not throw his enormous prestige into the fight. Only White's memory of that explanation survives:

> "I did not choose the tools with which I must work," he [Roosevelt] told me. "Had I been permitted to choose them I would have selected quite different ones. But I've got to get legislation passed by Congress to save America. The Southerners by reason of the seniority rule in Congress are chairmen or occupy strategic places on most of the Senate and House Committees. If I come out for the anti-lynching bill now, they will block every bill I ask Congress to pass to keep America from collapsing. I just can't take that risk."

Even with the most popular President in modern times on his side and top-heavy majorities in Congress loyal to the White House, the Negro could not muster support for the most elementary guarantee of social justice: that his nation would not permit hate-contorted creatures to slay him without due process of law. The number of black men lynched had never been the main argument against the ghastly rite. It was the fact that the killings were carried off with impunity that was so chilling. No Negro could rest easy in a state whose law-enforcement officials, from the governor down, failed to search out lynchers and bring them to trial. No state in the South had officials who pursued lynchers with zeal. If the federal government could not yet be persuaded to impose constraints on this unacknowledged butchery, what was black life worth in America? Asked to defend it, Franklin Delano Roosevelt, who had done more than his thirty-one predecessors combined to help white men who needed help, said, "I just can't take that risk."

More than ever, then, the Negro's hopes were in the hands of the courts. Especially the Supreme Court. But in 1935, more than ever, the Supreme Court quenched those hopes with a unanimous decision. It was a decision generally overlooked amid all the other momentous ones the Court was then handing down by way of disconnecting the New Deal's intravenous feeding of the stricken economy. But it finished off the judicial degradation of the Negro that began with the *Slaughterhouse* decision and peaked in *Plessy v. Ferguson.* The final nail in the coffin of the American creed was labeled *Grovey v. Townsend* and it came from Texas.

William Grovey, a Negro, had requested an absentee ballot from the county clerk of Harris County, Texas, for the Democratic primary election to be held in July of 1934. Pursuant to the new rules of the party adopted in general convention in 1932 to circumvent the Court's opinion in *Nixon v. Condon,* invalidating the whites-only stricture of the party's executive committee as a veiled form of state action, the state official refused Grovey's request. Carter Wesley and J. Alston Atkins, the Negro attorneys from Texas who, with James Nabrit, had handled the first two white-primary cases that NAACP lawyers eventually won on appeal to the Supreme Court, now came to Washington to argue Grovey's case. Logic and precedent were on their side. The Court was not.

Ignoring, as it had in the previous Texas cases, the unmistakable command of the Fifteenth Amendment against a racial test for voting, the Court concerned itself solely with whether the acts of the Democratic Party, alleged to be a private organization, constituted state action within the meaning of the Fourteenth Amendment. Grovey's lawyers presented a mountain of evidence to show that state laws defined and regulated the conduct of the party primary every inch of the way. From the style of the ballots to the specifications for the voting booths to the method of tabulation of the votes, the rules and personnel involved in the running of primary elections were identical with those in the general elections. No matter, said the Court. It was a party function. Party funds paid for holding the election. Party people counted the votes. And the state law recognized the sovereignty of the party's state convention to decide who could participate in its primaries. To the argument that as a practical matter the Negro's exclusion from the Democratic primary left him totally disenfranchised because the results of the general election, in which he might qualify to vote, were a foregone conclusion, the Court gave the back of its hand. To argue that, it said, was "to confuse the privilege of membership in a party with the right to vote for one who is to hold public office."

Here was judicial sophistry at its most flagrant. The Democratic Party was not a private country club or a fraternal order that wore funny hats. It was a vast congregation of citizens whose business was at all points infused with the public interest. It was sanctioned, aided, and abetted by state laws. If the Democratic Party chose to engage in discriminatory practices that served to deprive citizens of the only vote that really mattered, solely on account of the color of their skin, the state that supervised the electoral proceedings of that party was plainly implicated. The Court's unanimous opinion to the contrary was written by Justice Owen Roberts, the man Herbert Hoover chose after the Senate, with a vigorous push by Walter White and the NAACP, turned down John J. Parker of North Carolina.

The white primary was now dignified as constitutional. Other states soon adopted it. Not a single Justice of the Supreme Court denied its legality. Not a single Congressman sought to overturn it under powers specifically granted to the federal legislature by the Fifteenth Amendment. And so long as Negroes were without the ballot in the states where four out of every five black Americans lived, their lobbyists such as Walter White might win sympathy but little more from the consummate politician in the White House.

The size and severity of the task confronting Charles Houston as he took command of the NAACP's effort to combat the legalized ostracism of the colored people was definitively recorded in a new publication that had begun to appear in 1932—the *Journal of Negro Education*, another sign of Mordecai Johnson's determination to turn Howard University into the nation's clearinghouse for black culture and social action. Rarely has a scholarly publication served a more immediately useful practical purpose.

Brainchild of a Mississippi-born Howard professor of psychology and education named Charles H. Thompson, the *Journal* won initial backing from the university when Johnson saw it as a way to document the burden Howard was carrying for black America and its consequent need for ever greater funding by Congress. The new quarterly journal would be gentlemanly propaganda, whatever else it was. But Charles Thompson was too fine a scholar to leave it at that. Though he had almost no money except to pay the printing bills and postage, he launched the *Journal* as a means of fully documenting the condition of Negro schools and exploring the implications of segregated education. Thompson's magazine now seized the torch that had been let fall when *The Crisis* lost its founder. The *Journal* was, to be sure, far less polemical than *The Crisis* had ever been, but it served a similar purpose: to inform, to arouse, to inspire.

Thompson cajoled free but nonetheless worthy articles from many educational experts across the country, white as well as Negro, though the emphasis was on the latter. Howard University contributed office space, clerical help, and about one-third of Thompson's salary. The result was a magazine that began with 1,000 copies distributed free and in time became an invaluable chronicle of almost every development in black education of any consequence—in the classroom, in the courtroom, in the press, in books, in professional associations, in state legislatures and Congress, in curriculum development, and in the learning process itself—with 25,000 paid and heavily thumbed copies going out every quarter to help black America make the best of a bad deal.

One of the four issues of Thompson's *Journal* each year came out in July, after school was over, and was devoted to a single subject, explored from many angles. In 1935, the *Journal*'s "yearbook," as Thompson called these special numbers, was devoted to "The Courts and the Negro Separate School." Most of its knowledgeable contributors seemed convinced that it was hopeless to challenge the laws that had by now institutionalized school segregation.

The statistics alone were enough to dishearten the most unwavering partisan. School segregation, the *Journal* showed, had been the subject of litigation 113 times in twenty-nine states and the District of Columbia. Forty-four of the cases raised the question directly: were segregated schools constitutional? Forty-four times the answer was yes. In seven cases, the authority of school officials to determine who shall be admitted to a school was challenged, and seven times the authority was upheld. Only where segregation was practiced in the absence of a statute or was financed by separate tax collections so that each race funded its own schools did the court rulings work consistently to the Negro's benefit. The best he could hope for, then, was true enforcement of the separate-but-equal doctrine. The *Journal* tabulations showed how far short of this principle the performance fell. The average white child had two-and-one-half times as much spent on him each school year as the average Negro youngster. White teachers got paid more than twice as much. A number of Northern states—like Illinois, New Jersey, Ohio, and Pennsylvania—permitted some communities within their borders to segregate their public schools without statutory authority. In seventeen of the nineteen states that authorized school segregation, there was no state-supported school at which a Negro could pursue graduate or professional education, while Missouri and West Virginia provided tuition for a few Negroes out-of-state; more than 11,000 white students pursued graduate- or professional-school study in those nineteen states.

Beyond the numbers and precedents were the social dynamics of the segregated system that the *Journal*'s contributors saw as even more discouraging. Ralph Bunche, listed as associate professor of political science at Howard, asserted that the courts placed the burden of proof of discrimination upon the Negro, who had been forced "to substitute the complicated, arduous and expensive processes of litigation for the ballot box"—to little avail. The states of the South had made manifest their refusal to insure the Negro's legal rights, and in scores of decisions "the highest courts of the land have amply demonstrated their willingness to acquiesce in the prevailing attitudes of the dominant population. . . ." Thanks to "the adroitness of white legislators," the courts had been able to hand down what passed as "legally sound opinions and still permit popular abuses of the Negro's rights to persist." The Constitution, he was saying, was no better or worse than the people interpreting it, and Negroes who still believed that the document was "a sort of protective angel hovering over us . . . keeping a constant vigil over the rights of all America's children" were naïve in the extreme.

Du Bois weighed in from Atlanta with the most provocative piece in the *Journal,* a characteristic effort blending data and philippic, titled "Does the Negro Need Separate Schools?" It took the position that had led to his parting company with the NAACP: realistically, the Negro had to accept separate schools for the moment—it was either that or nothing in many places—and he had jolly well better stop looking in through white-school-house windows like a destitute orphan on Christmas Eve and start turning his own schools into first-rate ones. Du Bois argued that "as long as American Negroes believe that their race is constitutionally and permanently inferior to white people, they necessarily disbelieve in every possible Negro Institution." Accepting race hatred "as a brutal but real fact," they ought to forgo "using a little child as a battering ram" to get into white schools and consider that child's own soul. The crying need was not for separate schools or biracial schools, but for the Negro to put aside his "inner paralysis and lack of self-confidence" and replace them with "a firm and unshakable belief that twelve million American Negroes have the inborn capacity to accomplish just as much as any nation of twelve million anywhere in the world ever accomplished. . . ." Almost as a postscript, he added:

> I know that this article will forthwith be interpreted by certain illiterate "nitwits" as a plea for segregated Negro schools and colleges. It is not. . . . It is saying in plain English: that a separate Negro school, where children are treated like human beings, trained by teachers of their own race, who know what it means to be black in the year of salvation of 1935, is infinitely better than making our boys and girls doormats to be spit and tramped upon and lied to by ignorant social climbers, whose sole claim to superiority is ability to kick "niggers" when they are down.

In his commendable zeal to bolster sagging black pride, Du Bois ignored a question that psychologists and social scientists were beginning to ponder in earnest: how do you instill pride in segregated schoolchildren—indeed, how do you imbue them with even rudimentary values of good citizenship—when the very fact of their separation overwhelms nearly every other aspect of their education and belies any claim of pride? On the answer to that question would hang the fate of legalized segregation in the United States. It was explored well ahead of its time by perhaps the least-known contributor to Thompson's remarkable 1935 *Journal* yearbook—Howard Hale Long, then the assistant superintendent in charge of research for the public schools of Washington, D.C. Titled "Some Psychogenic Hazards of Segregated Education of Negroes," his article was cautious and tentative, but what it said made the views of Bunche, Du Bois, and others tending toward black-separatism seem like defeatist petulance. The essence of the problem, Long ventured, was to describe "certain phenomena which result from segregated education of Negroes and thereby, in part, to determine whether the real harm does not lie in the rather neglected field of pauperized and gnarled personality development." Foreshadowing the debate that would rock behavioral science a generation later, he added:

> There is a growing belief that the almost ineradicable architecture of the response pattern is laid down early in childhood and that in a few years the construct becomes so set that fundamental changes become very difficult if not impossible. . . .
>
> To look forward to a life apart from the general populace in the midst of which one must live with limited choice and opportunity, regardless of ability, is a dysgenic factor of first importance. It chills ambition in embryo. Ability is left undeveloped because of a lack of stimulus, or its development is diverted into compensatory channels. More often mediocrity is accepted as the standard so that there is a toneless effort—a what's-the-use attitude. . . .

Set apart from the white community, without hope of reaching real goals, the black child feels crushed before he begins. "For him the symptoms of unavoidable limitation are as ubiquitous as the air he breathes," Long explained. "He is reminded of it whether in home, school, theatre, or on the streets." The high rate of delinquency was almost certainly related to this sense of isolation and "absence of wholesome goals." And even if he subscribed to such goals, the colored citizen soon found himself "surrounded by a highly organized social and economic structure in which he is not allowed to compete on equal terms." Deep and corrosive feelings of inferiority generally followed, and to survive, the Negro understandably resorted to fantasy, hedonism, regression to juvenile responses in the face of unbearable difficulty, or aggression born of despair.

Appropriately, the one really positive note in the whole issue of the *Journal* was sounded by its editor. Charles Thompson lashed back at the Jeremiahs and finally gave Charlie Houston something to cheer about. Since voteless Negroes had no voice in the administration of their schools, he said, discrimination had become far worse during the previous thirty years. What could be done about it? Neither migration nor revolution was practical. Appealing to the white man's sense of fair play was hardly more likely to prove availing. In the long run, the answer would have to be the Negro's rewinning the ballot, but there seemed no point in looking over Jordan like that. In the foreseeable future, the only real remedy to the severe abuses of the segregated school system lay in the courts. No doubt hostile state legislatures could and probably would move to cancel out the effect of court decisions they did not like. No doubt a public that still felt a rope and tree were all the law the Negro was entitled to would evade or ignore court decisions that ordered the betterment of black schools. But the likelihood of such defiance of the rule of law was not reason enough to give up without trying—and trying again—any more than fear of reprisal justified sitting on their hands, Thompson declared. Even unfavorable decisions by the courts had some value: they dramatized Negro discontent and might cause a twinge of white consciences.

As to the alleged merits of the separate school, Thompson implied that Du Bois—without naming him—was just whistling in the dark. There was no evidence to date that black children in segregated schools performed better academically or developed more wholesome personalities than those in integrated schools. All the arguments, he felt, were on the side of ending separate schools:

> In the first instance, I think most of us would agree that to *segregate* is to *stigmatize,* however much we may try to rationalize it. . . . For we all know that segregation is practically always initiated by the whites, and initiated on the basis that Negroes are inferior and undesirable. Thus, when Negroes allow themselves to be cajoled into accepting the status defined by the separate school, they do something to their personalities which is infinitely worse than any of the discomforts *some* of them *may* experience in a mixed school.

But the Supreme Court of the United States had pointedly and specifically rejected such an interpretation in *Plessy v. Ferguson,* where it had said "the underlying fallacy" of the segregated plaintiff's argument was "the assumption that the enforced separation of the two races stamps the colored race with a badge of inferiority. If this be so, it is not by reason of anything found in the act, but solely because the colored race chooses to put that construction upon it." Without citing *Plessy,* Thompson was challenging its central premise as a great lie. No one else was then saying that—no lawyer, anyway, for what seemed obvious to Charles Thompson about the motive, purpose, and effect of segregation had been brutally denied by the Supreme Court nearly forty years before and never re-examined since. Thompson added knowingly:

> In the second instance, the separate school is generally uneconomical, and frequently financially burdensome. . . . Consequently, where sufficient funds are not available to support decent schools for both whites and Negroes, and even in many cases where they are sufficient, it is the Negro school that suffers, and there is very little that is done about it. Those who argue that the separate school with equal facilities is superior to the mixed school with prejudice should know that the separate school, or separate anything, with equal facilities is a fiction.

In short, he was saying in layman's language that everyone knew that the separate-but-equal principle was as much a myth in operation as the Court's claim in *Plessy* that segregation was not discrimination. In a few strokes of the pen, Thompson had sketched the principal arguments for attacking segregation itself as unconstitutional that would in time be carried into the highest court in the land by lawyers for the NAACP.

The most successful of those black attorneys was then making his first appearances in the courtrooms of the nation.

# 8

# Uncle Fearless's Nephew

A friend of the family could still readily summon up a mental daguerreotype of the boy more than half a century later. "I have a very clear picture of Thurgood," recalls Odell Payne, whose husband, the Reverend A. J. Payne, has presided over the Enon Baptist Church in West Baltimore for more than fifty years. "He was a jolly boy who always had something to say." But what she remembers best is a different snapshot. "I can still see him coming down Division Street every Sunday afternoon around one o'clock. He'd be wearing knee pants with both hands dug way into his pockets and be kicking a stone in front of him as he crossed over to Dolphin Street to visit his grandparents at their big grocery store on the corner. He was in a deep study, that boy, and it was plain something was going on inside him."

Such moments of sustained contemplation were, if not rare, at least not characteristic of the youngster, who by all reports was an outgoing, much-loved child somewhat on the raucous side. His parents, each half-white and perhaps more, worked hard and steadily—his father as head steward at an exclusive Chesapeake Bay boat club, his mother as a highly regarded elementary-school teacher—and thereby qualified as candidates for the cautious, color-conscious mulatto aristocracy of black Baltimore. But their direction, while upward-mobile, was not toward the showy status of the black bourgeoisie with its implied defensiveness. The Will Marshalls were transitional figures in the history of the American Negro, for they would not settle for what modest comforts they could accumulate within a ghetto culture. They were proud of who and what they were, yet they became, in their fashion, race-conscious rebels against the cold grip of white supremacy.

The Marshall family tree is ripe with tales of rebellion and displays of moxie. Its progenitor in pluckiness was a slave forebear whose name has not survived but whose legendary orneriness has been proclaimed with great relish by Thurgood Marshall to almost anyone who has ever known him for any time. The story changes a bit with the passing decades and no two newspaper, magazine, or book accounts of Marshall's career agree on the details, but what matters was the verve of the man who Marshall delightedly —and in private—insists was "the baddest nigger in the whole state of Maryland." Some of his descendants like to claim that the fellow, probably Thurgood's great-grandfather on his mother's side, came from the more cultured tribes in Sierra Leone, "but we all know," says his great-grandson, "that he really came from the toughest part of the Congo." Wherever it was, he is supposed to have tagged around after a Marylander who was there on a hunting expedition—hunting slaves, more than likely—and brought him back to his Eastern Shore plantation, where the African grew into a singularly truculent slave. "Look," his exasperated master is said to have said finally, "I brought you over here myself, so I guess I can't very well shoot you. But you're so vicious I can't with good conscience sell you to another owner—I can't even *give* you away." There was nothing for it but to hand the slave his freedom on the proviso he get as far away as possible from his distraught ex-owner. "And that," Marshall winds up the official account, "is the only time Massuh didn't get an argument from the old boy." Unofficially —because Marshall is so aware of Southern sensibilities—the old boy almost certainly married a white woman, settled down as a free Negro not terribly far from his old slave home, and lived without chains ever after.

Marshall's grandparents on both sides demonstrated the same streak of cussedness in the face of adversity. His namesake, Grandpa Thoroughgood Marshall, who shipped out with the United States merchant marine for many years, was supposedly the possessor of the not very veiled alias of Thornygood Marshall in order to obtain a second pension from the government. The alternate first name may simply have been a matter of errant penmanship. At any rate, Grandfather Marshall settled down and opened a successful market. "It was a great big store," says Thurgood's Aunt Elizabeth Marshall, who lived on the third floor above it, "on the corner of Dolphin and Division streets," in the heart of a growing black area. "It catered to the whole neighborhood—vegetables, groceries, everything—and a lot of people would telephone in their orders even then." The lady of the store, Grandmother Annie Marshall, was well known for her spunk. Since the corner of Dolphin and Division was a busy spot, the electric company found it necessary to install a power pole on the sidewalk directly in front of the Marshalls' grocery. Annie Marshall would have none of it and shooed the utility's workmen away on the ground that it was her sidewalk and she wanted no pole in the middle of it. The company went and got a court order. When the workmen came back, Annie was hunkered in a kitchen chair placed right over the designated spot on the sidewalk. And there she stayed, defying the world. "This went on for days and weeks," her grandson has recounted on more than one occasion, "and finally Grandma Annie emerged as the victor of what may have been the first successful sitdown strike in Maryland."

The census-takers were similarly victimized by Annie Marshall, who had more than a little of the spirited colleen in both her looks and her manner and naturally aroused the interest of the government's enumerators who were charged with the task of classifying people as white or colored. "She never knew her real name, her age, her parents, or her race," says Thurgood Marshall. "All she knew was that she had been raised by a Negro family in Virginia—and she never changed her story, no matter what the census-takers threatened."

The sea, groceries, and a penchant for quirky names ran on his maternal side as well. Grandfather Isaiah Olive Branch Williams brought back a fondness for Shakespeare and opera from his sailing days before opening his Baltimore grocery and siring six children named, in order of their arrival, Avonia Delicia and Avon (a girl and boy after the Bard's river), Denmedia Marketa (for the family store!), Norma Arica (Thurgood's mother, named for Bellini's 1831 opera *Norma*, which Isaiah is said to have seen performed in the Chilean port of Arica), Fearless Mentor and Ravine Silestria (because they sounded nice, probably). Old Isaiah bought himself a house with a white neighbor who was not pleased at the arrival of colored. For some years, the neighbor made his displeasure known by a chronic crabbiness. There came a time, though, when the fence between the two properties needed mending, and the white man suggested they make a joint venture of it. "After all," he said, "we belong to the same church and are going to the same heaven." At which Isaiah Olive Branch Williams is said to have forsaken his middle names and replied: "I'd rather go to hell." Such grit also prompted him to take the lead in calling the black community to a large public rally in the 1870s to protest brutal behavior toward Negroes by Baltimore police—a rare showing of united action by the city's traditionally quiescent colored population.

Norma Williams, seventeen when she married William Canfield Marshall in 1904, gave birth the next year to William Aubrey and three years after that to Thoroughgood. They stopped their family at two boys ("He was enough," recalls the younger brother of the older). Their mother was the stabilizing force in the household. "She was a very strong person," says Elizabeth Marshall, "a leader who went all out for her boys and had a great influence on them." Like her mother before her and half a dozen other relatives on the Williams side of the family, Norma Marshall went into the teaching profession, training at a local school, Coppin Normal, and pursuing graduate credits at Morgan, the leading black college in Maryland, and at Columbia University when the Marshalls moved to New York City in 1909 for five years before returning to Baltimore. A music-fancier like her father, she sang and played piano, took part in occasional amateur theatricals, saw to it that the family attended St. James Episcopal Church, and in general brought cultivation and stability to the Marshall home at 1838 Druid Hill Avenue. She taught for a total of thirty-five years at two public schools not far from home, but she did not teach during the years when her two boys were growing up and benefited most from her presence.

Partly, that was because their father, Will Marshall, was taken away from home with some frequency by his job as a dining-car waiter on the Baltimore & Ohio Railroad, preferably on the New York-Washington run. Things improved when he signed on as a waiter at the Gibson Island Club, a favorite sailing and watering hangout for Washington power brokers and camp followers, located on a V-shaped peninsula twenty miles southeast of Baltimore on Chesapeake Bay. The one road into the place had a chain across it. In time, Will Marshall became the head steward there and caught more than a glimpse of the powerful white men who ran the country. He was not a well-educated man, but he was intensely interested in the world around him and loved to plunge into spirited debates about its rights and wrongs with his wife and two boys. On days off, he would sometimes haunt the courtrooms of Baltimore, occasionally taking his younger son with him. Eventually, Will Marshall became the first Negro to serve on a grand jury in the city of Baltimore. The first two days he sat on it, he was struck by the habit of some of his fellow grand jurors of inquiring whether the party under investigation was white or colored. If colored, the likelihood of indictment jumped sharply, Marshall noted. The next time the matter came up, he moved that the question of race be omitted from consideration: what, after all, did it have to do with whether someone deserved to be indicted? There was a flash of tension. Then the foreman ruled with Marshall. The racial question was never raised again—at least not while Will Marshall was in the room.

It was a warm, supportive home life, and Druid Hill Avenue was probably one of the better places in America for a Negro to grow up in the second and third decades of the twentieth century. West Baltimore had been a mixed neighborhood until then, with whites still dominant and blacks relegated to side streets and back alleys. But Druid Hill, with its three-story row houses of short stoops, arched doorways, and alternating red-brick and stone façades, was an open street at the beginning of the century. "If you were Negro and got there, well then you were somebody," says one long-time neighborhood resident.

It was not a place of open hostility between the races. There were few gangs or gang wars. Drugs were not known. Druid Hill was a neat, clean street. And little Thoroughgood Marshall was about as well protected from the world's cruelties as urban black parents could manage. But, as his Aunt Elizabeth puts it, "He wasn't any Mama-dress-me-and-send-me-to-Sunday-School sort of boy. He was always a smart, alert little fella, full of life and laughter." And gab. Everyone who knew him growing up agrees that he was a vocal, happily disputatious lad, encouraged to express himself at the family's dinner-table colloquia about everything under the sun. A favorite subject—and complaint—was his distinctive monicker. Surely there was not another Thoroughgood in the whole city, perhaps in the whole country, and maybe even in the whole world, but it was a powerfully long name for a second-grader to spell. They shortened it to Thurgood and even at that he was the only Thurgood at the grammar school on Division Street—and very possibly the only one in the world.

By the time he entered the old colored high school on Pennsylvania Avenue, a dingy but still serviceable place that had no auditorium or gymnasium and only a tiny, brick-paved yard in the rear for a playground, he was shaping into a passably good scholar. His mother made sure his homework got done, and for good measure there was Uncle Cyrus Marshall, who taught mathematics at the high school and kept an eye out for his sprouting nephew. He gave Thurgood an A in algebra and announced to the family that the boy had the keenest mind of any student he had ever taught. "Of course, he might have been a little bit prejudiced," acknowledges Cyrus Marshall's widow, Elizabeth. Thurgood's American-history teacher, no relation and perhaps a trifle more disinterested observer, called him "a good, earnest, argumentative student." An angel he was not. In fact, he first made the acquaintance of the Constitution of the United States while still in grade school because of a tendency to cut up. His principal made him stay after school and memorize a portion of the sacred writ each time he was caught breaking rules. His parents were not pleased with the crime, but the punishment suited them just fine. "Before I left that school," Marshall claimed in later years, "I knew the whole thing by heart."

No claim was made that the command lessons turned the boy into either a precocious constitutional scholar or a junior militant. But he came to an early enough understanding of racial inequality through the teachings of his parents, especially lean, light-skinned, blue-eyed Will Marshall, who frequently told his son he would rather sleep in the streets than betray his principles. One of his principles, firmly fixed in young Thurgood's mind, was: "Anyone calls you nigger, you not only got my permission to fight him—you got my orders to fight him."

It was always understood at the Marshall home that the brothers were to make something of themselves. Aubrey would be a doctor. That was pretty well settled. He went off to Lincoln University, a small school in Oxford, Pennsylvania, just across the Mason-Dixon Line and about thirty miles from Baltimore. A liberal-arts college with an all-black student body of about 300 and an all-white faculty, Lincoln was one of a handful of Negro colleges that met the academic standards of white higher education. Aubrey Marshall did well there and went on to become a doctor—a chest surgeon and specialist in tuberculosis, a disease that then hit Negroes with particular severity. Just what direction Thurgood would take was more of a concern. Dentistry had been broached by his parents, and while it seemed an honorable enough profession, it stirred little interest in him. His maternal grandmother, Mary Eliza Williams, would take no chances. She summoned Thurgood to her kitchen one day and announced she was going to teach him to cook. "I'm all with your parents in wanting you to be a professional man," she said to him, "but I want to be sure you can always earn a dollar. You can pick up all that other stuff later, but I bet you never saw a jobless Negro cook." And in fact Marshall developed into a passably good cook over the years, with a special gift for she-crab soup and a reported yen for dishes featuring horseradish. But it was not a gift a man might live by.

The career decision was held in abeyance as he finished up at the rundown high school, which was closed for good the year Thurgood graduated ("They were just waitin' till we got out," he says) and replaced by a new, much larger school named, inevitably, for native Marylander Frederick Douglass. His grades were superior but not so high as to make him scholarship material for an Ivy League college or any other Eastern school of the first rank. Besides, Lincoln University had come to be called "Black Princeton": it had been founded by a Princeton graduate, was staffed with a considerable number of Princeton alumni, had adopted Princeton colors of orange and black as its own, and, like Princeton, was an all-male college in a small town and emphasized the liberal arts. That Negroes were not welcome at Princeton itself provided an ironic undertow to the parallel. Thurgood's brother had enjoyed Lincoln, and his parents frankly preferred that their younger boy not yet open himself to the wounds sure to be inflicted by the white world. It was 1925 and Thurgood Marshall went off to Lincoln.

These were his last carefree years. Most of the students were on their own for the first time and insulated for the moment from the more somber problems of the race. It was as cosmopolitan a group of young blacks as was gathered anywhere in the world, in all likelihood; on campus with Marshall were students from Africa, Asia, and all over the United States, among them Kwame Nkrumah, who would become president of Ghana; Nnamdi Azikiwe, who would become president of Nigeria; and Cabell "Cab" Calloway, who grew up in Baltimore with Thurgood, dropped out of Lincoln, and quickly became a star entertainer with his rendition of "Minnie the Moocher," which swept the country in the Depression year of 1931. Strong in its academic requirements, Lincoln exercised few social restraints on its heady young men, who rather prided themselves in being the pick of the black world. They all worked summers—Thurgood as a baker and a bellhop and a dining-car waiter—for tuition and spending money, and they played as much as they studied, and at a decibel level one might expect in a community of young, randy males. It was a splendid place for the flourishing of the uninhibited young Thurgood Marshall. By all accounts, he seemed to major in pinochle, a joyful source of additional income to him, and during the traditional hazing of freshmen in his sophomore year he showed such zeal in the rite of shaving the newcomers' heads to the scalp line that he and a group of others were thrown out of school. He spent a sobering couple of weeks before being reinstated and thereafter directed his energies into more constructive activities.

He excelled on the college debating team and became so comfortable speaking in public that at a pep rally one autumn day when the Lincoln football team was going through a particularly disastrous season, he reportedly jumped up on stage and for twenty minutes or so produced an impromptu rapid-fire oration of such spellbinding quality that the team marched out and gave its best performance of the year—a scoreless tie—for which Thurgood duly claimed credit. He posted a B average in his academic work while encouraging the firm conviction among his classmates that he never cracked a book. Without doubt, he at least wrinkled a few, steeping himself for the first time in the growing body of literature of black America—Du Bois especially, and Carter Woodson's *The Negro in American History*, and Jerome Dowd's *The American Negro*, the black poets and novelists such as Claude McKay and Langston Hughes of the then blooming Harlem Renaissance, and the works of such white curiosity-seekers as Carl Van Vechten, whose *Nigger Heaven* left Marshall, a Harlem resident from the age of two to six, highly skeptical. Out of class, away from their white professors, the black young men of Lincoln would project their private ambitions against their common backdrop of racial animosity and inequality. Pride and shame mingled in them, and occasionally the tension between the two would lead to an overt act, such as the time Marshall and a handful of

Lincoln friends piled into a roadster, drove to the nearby town of Oxford, and defied the local movie theater's rule of Negroes-in-the-balcony-only. It was not exactly an act of daredeviltry: Oxford, after all, had only one potbellied policeman for its few thousand souls and was located just sixty miles due east of the battlefield at Gettysburg, not exactly the heart of Klan country. Still, such acts were rare in that day anywhere in America.

Banged up from a leg injury in an intramural football game, he lost more than a semester of school in the middle of his college career while he recuperated and "tried to sell insurance and failed and messed around doin' other things and flopped at them, too, that spring term." He was eager now to get moving, and the first signs of self-discipline appeared. For one thing, he married a University of Pennsylvania undergraduate named Vivian Burey in September of 1929, the beginning of his senior year. They were both twenty-one. The young couple took a small apartment in Oxford, and Vivian Marshall, better known on campus and thereafter as "Buster," did secretarial work to help pay the bills. The marriage, which would last until her death twenty-five years later, had a stabilizing effect on Thurgood that was recognized by his mother, who welcomed the couple into the Marshall home, assigned them Thurgood's old room, and gave them the run of the house while they accumulated enough to set up on their own. That would take a little time, though. Thurgood had decided on law school.

All during his senior year, the idea had been growing in him. He loved speaking in public and thinking on his feet and dealing with people face to face, and he would graduate with honors from Lincoln—surely evidence that he was nobody's fool. The law was at the root of American life, and practicing it offered the widest scope possible for his ambitions. His father encouraged Thurgood's thinking; as a lawyer, he could help himself and the race as well.

Life would have been a good deal easier for the newlyweds if Marshall could have attended the University of Maryland's law school in Baltimore. But there seemed to be no point in applying. Maryland was a Jim Crow state, and its schools were segregated from top to bottom. He had heard good things, though, about Howard University's law school, then being sharply upgraded under a new dean. And Washington was only an hour's ride away on the train. He became a commuter, rising with the sparrows in order to make his 8 a.m. class and returning to Baltimore in mid-afternoon to one of the half-dozen or so part-time jobs he picked up to help pay the tuition and transportation. His mother insisted on selling her engagement ring and wedding band to help meet their expenses.

The moment he fell under the tutelage of Charles Houston, Thurgood Marshall was certain he had made the right choice of career. Within a week, he knew "this was it. This was what I wanted to do for as long as I lived." It remained to be seen whether he would make the grade. He applied himself as he had never done before. "He had come down here from Lincoln with the reputation as something of a playboy," recalls Oliver Hill, who adds with warmth that he and Marshall rapidly became both bosom pals and fierce rivals for class leadership. Marshall headed a faction of about half the class that had belonged to Alpha Phi Alpha, a national black fraternity that traditionally enrolled many campus standouts, and Hill headed up the independents. But as Houston's academic regimen took hold and the fearful attrition rate mounted, the two tall factionalists grew into fast friends and would remain such afterward. "He was happy-go-lucky on the face of it," says Hill, "always with some lie to tell, but he managed to get a lot of work done when nobody was looking."

He used every minute of his daily commute for studying. "I got through simply by overwhelming the job," he once said, and added, with characteristic hyperbole: "I was at it twenty hours a day, seven days a week." His weight dropped from a none too paunchy 170 to a downright skeletal 130. But his course work sparkled. William Hastie, then a young faculty member at the law school, has not forgotten the performance that Marshall and Hill turned in working in tandem during the first year for a course in the preparation of appellate briefs and moot-court argument. "Their brief was better than many I've seen since by practicing lawyers," Hastie remembers. "I would have been willing to say unequivocally then and there that they were going to turn out to be darned fine lawyers."

As the top-ranking student in his class, Marshall qualified for the plum of the student jobs—assistant in the law library. The job had the negative effect of lengthening Marshall's day till 8 p.m. and often an hour or two later; rarely did he crawl into bed before midnight, only to rise with the birdsong. But the job had compensations. It paid for his tuition during the second and third years at law school. More important, it threw him into almost daily contact with Houston. "He idolized Charlie," says a law-school colleague, and the mentor responded warmly to the diligence and obvious aptitude of his acolyte. Houston taught him how to use the law books, how to structure research, how to think like a lawyer. And then he put him to work checking out citations and looking up cases for whatever Houston was handling in the courtroom just then. Marshall eavesdropped at many a planning session in the school library for the Crawford and Hocutt cases, among others. It was the young man's basic training in the law, and he was clearly thriving on it.

Complementing his applied intellect in the process of becoming a creditable lawyer was a remarkable native canniness. He read character the way Charlie Houston could read a law book. It was Thurgood Marshall's great natural gift. And he learned a thing or two about his own character and what traits it would require for the ends he had in mind. Early on, he developed a kind of pragmatic view of the law and of life itself. He had his principles and he would fight like hell for them. But any man who ran around the battlefront waving his flag all day was a dead duck, he understood. And any man who had to fight with one arm tied behind his back—as almost every Negro had to who challenged custom in the racial arena—was often well advised not to fight at all if his one good arm wasn't feeling awfully strong that day.

There was the time during his law-school years, for example, when he was working as a summer waiter at the Gibson Island Club, where his father was the head steward. He recounted the incident long afterward to a professor and NAACP advisor, who would retell it with the sort of detail that suggests Marshall had implanted it in his memory forever. "It was a marvelous story," says the professor, "the way he told it in that off-stage dialect of his. 'There I was,' Thurgood said, 'workin' at the club, when in came a United States Senator from out West—a very crude fellah, a very vulgah individual—with a bevy of beautiful women on his arm. He takes a seat with his party and he looks around for a waiter and he spots ole Thurgood. "Hey, nigger!" he yells over. Now I hear what he say, and I didn't like the i-dea of his callin' me that, not one bit. But ah go on over anyway, and he says, "Nigger, I want service at this table!" So ah give him the service an' he is always callin' me nigger all during the meal an' ah'm likin' it less an' less. But when he gets up to go, he leaves me a twenty-dollah tip. Now this crude fellah keeps comin' into the club and keeps on callin' me nigger—and keeps on leavin' me twenty-dollah tips. In a few days, I got myself almost enough money to pay off all my bills. After about the third day of mah takin' care of this fellah, Senator "Cotton Ed" Smith [of South Carolina], who is a member of the club, overhears what this other Senator is callin' me, and he beckons me ovah to his table sorta friendly-like and he says, "Thurgood, what's that Senator callin' you?" An' ah say, "He's callin' me 'Boy,' Senator." Senator Ed, he looks kinda skeptical and he say, "You *sure* that's all he's callin' you?" An' ah say, "Oh, ah'm sure that's all he's callin' me, Senator." Now 'course Senator Smith he don't know this other in-div-id-ual is givin' me the twenty dollahs each time. Well, now, that evenin' my daddy is standin' in the doorway of the dinin' room an' he hears this fellah callin' me that and sees me runnin' right over there takin' good care of him. So my daddy he calls me over and says, "Thurgood, you are fired! And you are a disgrace to the colored people!"' '

"Thurgood paused then," says the professor retelling the story, "and waited for me to take the bait. A look of disapproval must have passed over my face. He saw it and then he said, 'Naturally I explained to my daddy what it was all about.' Then Thurgood leaned toward me and said, 'Between you, me, an' the lamp-post, Robert, any time you wanna call me nigger, you just put your twenty dollahs down on this table. And you can keep doin' it all day.' Then his eyes narrowed and his voice suddenly hardened and he said, 'But the second you run outa them twenties, Robert, I'M GONNA BUST YOU IN THE NOSE!'"

Years later, when he was famous, Baltimore's Negro weekly newspaper, the *Afro-American*, would run a profile on Thurgood Marshall and note that he had passed the state bar examination with one of the highest marks ever recorded. Marshall wrote in promptly to set the record straight. The truth of the matter, he said, was that his bar-examination score was, "as I remember it, less than one point above the passing mark of 210."

The law, happily, did not require the new attorney to post his bar-exam score below his name on the shingle he hung out. Nor, on the other hand, were his fine grades at Howard of any account now as Marshall turned down the chance to go to Harvard Law School on a fellowship and earn a graduate degree. Eager to begin lawyering, he rented a small office at 4 Redwood Street in east Baltimore on the fringe of the downtown business area. To lend it a bit of distinction, his mother contributed the Oriental rug from off the parlor floor of the Marshall home.

It was not a good time to open a law practice—or much of anything else. The Depression was about at its low point. And Baltimore was not precisely a mecca for colored attorneys. "There may have been eight, ten of us—maybe a dozen at most—in town then," recalls A. Briscoe Koger, a Howard law-school graduate who had begun practicing in Baltimore in the Twenties. "It wasn't a question of how much business you did, because no one did very much. It was mostly the honor of being a lawyer—of actually having passed the bar and gotten the license. It was a matter of pride, almost. What business you got would be small property matters or some little two-for-nothing misdemeanor. Negroes weren't anxious to have Negro lawyers. The feeling was that whites could get more for them, that they had more influence, and the white lawyers, frankly, fed the feeling. It was a vicious circle because we didn't gain enough confidence or respect because we didn't handle enough cases of anything but a petty criminal or minor property nature. I had to write some insurance and sell real estate to keep my shingle hanging."

At the end of his first year, Thurgood Marshall was practicing more economy than law. His total earnings were minus $1,000. To keep their spirits up, he would bring sandwiches for lunch one day and his secretary would bring them the next; that way, when not much else was going on, there was always the suspense of one of them not knowing what was for lunch. It wasn't only that business for a new Negro attorney was slow; it was that when it came, its bearers generally couldn't pay much of anything. But he took everything that walked through the door: people dispossessed for failing to meet their mortgage payments, people evicted for failing to pay the rent, people brutalized by police or charged with excessive penalties for minor law infractions, plus run-of-the-mill commercial business like wills and deeds. He handled it all with as much skill as he could command. And he did not begrudge the non-paying client his services.

It was not the route to riches, but it surely brought him fame of a sort: Thurgood Marshall, the little man's lawyer. It was only a matter of time before word spread about his competence as well as his generosity of spirit. In effect, provision of his services *gratis* or close to it was the best (and only) advertisement a struggling black attorney could have. Along with the negligence and probate cases, he began to pick up some solid clients. One was the biggest steam laundry in town. There were some building associations, some labor matters, and then there was the prosperous Murphy family, some of whose members had been steady customers for years at his grandfather Marshall's grocery.

The Murphys were about the most powerful black family in Baltimore. John H. Murphy, Sr., a whitewasher by trade, had purchased type fonts and a small press and put out a little Sunday School newspaper in his cellar as a spare-time activity in the closing years of the nineteenth century. Eventually he borrowed $200 from his wife and bought out an embryonic weekly called the *Afro-American*, to become known in Baltimore and elsewhere in black America as simply the *Afro*. At its start, it had a circulation of 250. By his death in 1922, it was challenging the older black weeklies for national circulation leadership. Fifty years later, it would sell 150,000 copies a week in five separate editions, published out of a bustling office on Baltimore's Eutaw Street. It has always been an all-Negro operation, from the composing room to the newsboys. "How can our own people ever expect to operate complicated machinery," John Murphy would ask in those early days, explaining his on-the-job training program for scarce black printers, "unless they get a chance at it in our own plants?"

Leadership of the *Afro* passed to John Murphy's son, Carl. A Harvard graduate, he did advanced work at the University of Jena in Austria and taught German at Howard, but when he applied to Baltimore's Johns Hopkins to continue his scholarly work, he was rejected on racial grounds. He was a small, very light-skinned man with an unassuming manner, and while he did not throw his weight around, he was nevertheless a power in Jim Crow Baltimore. "He could move mountains," says a well-placed older member of the town's black community. "He was the greatest man we had."

Carl Murphy took it unkindly when his own civil rights were tramped upon. Once, he sued the Baltimore & Ohio Railroad for segregating him unlawfully on a ferry crossing. Another time, he went after the city when one of its finest falsely arrested him and failed to allow him counsel in the course of coping with the alleged minor traffic violation. By the mid-Thirties, Carl Murphy was ready to throw himself into the civil-rights cause. His chosen instrument for the effort was a young, long-legged attorney who shared his sense of mission. "They were very close," Elizabeth Murphy Moss, who became executive vice president and treasurer of the *Afro*, remembers of the tie between Thurgood Marshall and her father, who died in 1967. The fledgling lawyer did not conduct himself like a novice. "He gave you the impression that he had taken time to think over what he said," Mrs. Moss adds. "He exuded confidence and seemed very solid—a born leader. His very size helped give that impression, that and his outgoing personality. He was a bundle of applied energy—and never a stuffed shirt. He was the model of what you wanted your own son to turn out to be."

Young Marshall also demonstrated early another knack that would enhance his career: he listened. It was not simply that he was deferential; rather, he never thought he knew all the answers. His way to wisdom was to hear out others who might or might not know any more than he did and then to sift it all through his own mental strainer. He never tried to score points as an original or especially creative thinker; his skill was in figuring out who made the most sense—or what parts of other people's ideas to seize upon and fuse into a prudent plan of action. Morris Ernst, the civil-liberties lawyer and NAACP legal advisor, who first got to know him in the Thirties, attributes much of Marshall's precocious success to a related trait: knowing not only when to listen but what to ask. "Knowing the right questions may be more important than thinking you know the answers," says Ernst. "He understood that there may not be any big answers and you try to accomplish what you can, one thing at a time." Adds a younger former associate of Marshall who watched him work in later years: "He'll take ideas from a chimneysweep if they sound right to him."

In 1934, Carl Murphy's office was the site for the rebirth of the Baltimore branch of the NAACP. It had declined over the years to a few dozen members, but a determined, forty-five-year-old housewife named Lillie M. Jackson decided to change all that. A devout churchgoer, Lillie Jackson had a loud voice and convictions to go with it. She had little trouble in getting Carl Murphy to bankroll the first stages of the rebuilding process, but money was always short because black Baltimore was not inclined to chip in to support an even semi-militant group. Financial problems fazed Lillie Jackson not the slightest. "I know the funds are not in yet," she would tell the officers of the Baltimore branch, of which she had got herself elected president, "but we must go ahead with our work on faith because God's storehouse is full."

It was largely from that divine source that Thurgood Marshall was compensated at first in his capacity as legal counsel to the Baltimore branch. But to be designated as the official lawyer in town for the principal Negro-rights group was honor enough in the beginning. Lillie Jackson would come to call him "my boy" and he would affectionately refer to her as "Ma Jackson," and with the backing of Carl Murphy, they made the Baltimore NAACP a civic force and a new byword in the black community. They were after recruits in the beginning. "I remember when I was a kid," Marshall has said, "we used to say that NAACP stood for the National Association for the Advancement of *Certain* People." It was to be no elite, effete club now under Lillie Jackson's consecrated leadership. Everyone was welcome, and Thurgood Marshall was her young apostle, going to the neighborhoods and speaking everywhere he could to stir black interest.

"The prevailing feeling here then among too many," says the Reverend A. J. Payne of the big Enon Baptist Church, one of the largest Negro congregations in Baltimore, "was that segregation was segregation, and it was going to be that way till kingdom come. The Negro's place was fixed, and few had the nerve to try to change it. Some very fine men in the community were just plain afraid. Young Marshall, though, was different. He showed his courage and his tenacity, and the people liked him, the common people and the professional people both. He spoke around at the churches a lot, and when he talked it would be about our rights. He'd say that, Jim Crow or no Jim Crow, we were free citizens and as such we had rights but we were going to have to fight to get them. People in the community looked up to him. He was never arrogant and always accessible. You knew that he had the ability—it just registered. Other lawyers didn't have the impress that young Thurgood did."

Negro attorney Briscoe Koger agrees. Koger, who was born in 1891 and opened his struggling practice a decade before Marshall appeared on the scene, blames the timidity of older blacks in that era on their economic vulnerability. "There was a great deal of anxiety and desire in the area of civil rights," he says, "but not much movement. People didn't have the confidence to proceed. But Marshall had a powerful personality—a lot on the stick—he projected himself and clearly believed in himself and made others believe, too. Most of the rest of us doubted ourselves, and we didn't fight as hard as he did. Old-timers had the feeling that here finally was a leader. Everybody was in his corner. Others had none of the assurance and power that whites are accustomed to, but Thurgood Marshall had that."

It was one thing to talk a good game; it was another to get out and play it. People were more worried then about where their next meal was coming from than anything else, and one of Marshall's first efforts was to help lead an NAACP picketing campaign against the white merchants along Pennsylvania Avenue who refused to hire black salespeople, though most of their customers were colored. It was a tactic that had been used successfully in Washington by the New Negro Alliance, which Charles Houston had helped organize, and now in Baltimore young blacks coming out of high school without a job in sight were desperate enough to stand up and protest with placards. White shopkeepers fought back by bringing the NAACP into court. Reverend Payne, active in the picketing drive, remembers the teamwork of Houston, who argued the case in Baltimore's federal courthouse, and Marshall, who undertook prodigious amounts of homework locating appropriate statutes. The courtroom was jammed throughout the trial, the minister recalls, and the presiding judge complimented the black lawyers from the bench in ruling in their favor.

Soon Marshall found himself devoting more and more time to NAACP activities. He organized local efforts to persuade Maryland Congressmen to back the federal anti-lynching bill. He won a manslaughter conviction in a controversial case where the defendant had been tried for burglary and murder. He worked closely with Lillie Jackson in rallying the black teachers of Maryland to support lawsuits to bring their salaries up to the level of white teachers. There was strong fear of reprisals among the teachers until a strategy was devised to raise a trust fund to protect any plaintiffs who might be fired once the suits got off the ground. It was delicate missionary work. So, too, was the handling of a rape case in Frederick County in the western part of the state, adjacent to Loudoun County, Virginia. He asked for a token annual retainer of $25 to pay for his NAACP legal stationery, postage, and telephone calls (and to head off possible charges that he was stirring up litigation in the NAACP's name); reimbursement of any actual out-of-pocket traveling costs while investigating cases as directed to by the Baltimore branch; and a *per diem* payment of $5 "for actual legal work including research, investigation and appearances in court. . . . [This payment] *is not to be considered as a fee* but rather as an expense to cover overhead . . . such as office, secretary, etc., which must be paid while the Counsel is out of his office and, therefore, not in a position to handle private business which pays for this." No longer a dollar-a-year man, he was still one of the better bargains in town.

Then he took on the white establishment and really put himself on the legal map for the first time.

As early as December 1933, only a few months after he opened his office, Thurgood Marshall began preparing his first major civil-rights case.

The loss of the Hocutt suit against the University of North Carolina the previous spring rankled the Howard colony of black lawyers. Marshall soon generated support among young Negroes then gravitating toward the NAACP for making the law school at the University of Maryland the target for the next attempt to crack segregation. He turned for help to the man best qualified to give it. "Dear Charlie," he wrote Houston in early January of 1934. "Trust you had a good Christmas etc. I hate to worry you so much about this University of Maryland case. When are we to get together on it? Things are very slow just now and I would like very much to get started as soon as possible." But he was not about to go off half-cocked to challenge the Goliath of racism with a rubber band and a paper clip.

Houston was very busy in 1934, winding down his work at Howard but cranking up for his NAACP assignment and half a dozen collateral undertakings, yet he was anxious to set in motion his version of the Margold strategy. The goal would be, as Margold had suggested, not to attack the constitutionality of segregation itself but to challenge its legality *as it was practiced* by showing that nothing remotely approaching equal educational opportunities was offered Negroes in segregating states—and *that* was unconstitutional. No Supreme Court ruling to date had dampened his hopes that such a tactic might work, though the composition of the Court was still not very encouraging. The four troglodyte Justices were getting old, to be sure—they averaged seventy-two, with Van Devanter the oldest at seventy-four and Butler the youngest at sixty-eight—but none of them seemed enfeebled, and all it would take was one other vote from the moderate wing of the Court to sink the Margold strategy. Houston knew he had to be careful.

Nothing firm was decided as 1934 lengthened and Thurgood Marshall's eagerness for combat grew. Nine Negroes had applied and been turned down by the University of Maryland Law School since the beginning of 1933. Marshall was not the only one who saw the opportunity to fight back. After all, there was nothing in the Maryland state laws that required the segregation of colleges, nor did the charter or rules of the university itself prohibit the admission of Negro students. The bias of the people running the university was what was maintaining its Jim Crow status, and bias could be challenged in court. Among those who shared this view was Belford V. Lawson, Jr., an ambitious young colored attorney in Washington who was an organizer of the New Negro Alliance and an assistant counsel to Alpha Phi Alpha, the black fraternity that beyond its social function served to promote civil rights. In mid-1934, the fraternity allocated several hundred dollars to launch a legal drive to open up the University of Maryland, located at College Park, only a few miles northeast of the District of Columbia line, and Lawson was designated to coordinate the effort. He lined up the New Negro Alliance and the Washington branch of the NAACP as allies to the fraternity's effort and then sent off a letter to the Baltimore NAACP inviting its participation. With the initiative in the matter about to be snatched from him, Marshall fired off a note to Houston in mid-October that put the matter directly to his mentor:

> What about the University of Maryland case? B. V. Lawson has been writing me and seems to think that the fraternity is going to try the case along with the local branches of the NAACP. I am up a tree as to just what is going to be done.

Houston still held off. Marshall's plan to act against the law school, which was situated in Baltimore and not on the College Park campus, made far more sense to Houston than a frontal assault on the university, including its undergraduate divisions. It was crucial for the NAACP's legal drive to post a major victory as soon as possible; moral victories like Hocutt and Crawford would no longer do. The plan was to build a string of precedents, one victory leading to and supporting the next. The place to begin, Houston was convinced, was at the graduate-school level. And law schools were the most promising target of all, because judges were of course themselves lawyers who would be most inclined to grasp the absurdity of a separate-but-equal law school for Negroes. In a properly framed case brought in a moderate Southern state, no court would order the opening of a colored law school or the closing down of the white one. The court's choice would be either to order the admission of qualified black applicants to the lily-white law schools or to sanction the new out-of-state scholarship funds that several of the Southern legislatures had passed or were contemplating to provide Negroes with professional or graduate study not available at the black colleges within the state. Such exporting of a state's obligation to provide equal protection was plainly evasive of the Fourteenth Amendment, Houston believed, and could be challenged successfully right up to the Supreme Court.

While Houston held off a decision on the Maryland case, Lawson was ready to move ahead. He invited Marshall and an older Baltimore attorney named William Gosnell to a strategy meeting in Washington late in November. Marshall did not want to be finessed into participating as a third-stringer in someone else's case; besides, the up-and-coming Baltimore NAACP wanted to take on its hometown law school and not have to fuss with a lot of Washington people. Marshall pursued Houston, who was out of town, for advice. Houston wired back from Augusta, Georgia: "ATTEND LAWSON'S MEETING GET FACTS BUT BE CAREFUL ABOUT COMMITMENTS." Marshall was still wary, and Gosnell went to Lawson's meeting without him. Gosnell agreed to seek suitable plaintiffs in the Baltimore area, and within a fortnight he had come up with an ideal candidate—Donald Gaines Murray, a twenty-year-old Baltimore resident who had graduated from Amherst the previous June and whose grandmother was the widow of the Baltimore bishop of the African Methodist Episcopal Church. A well-qualified, nice-looking fellow from a prominent black family. Lawson was enthusiastic. He would proceed without the NAACP.

His hand forced, Houston now acted decisively. He was not one for dividing counsel's responsibility with others. When he was on a case, it was *his* case to win or lose. "He was a very virile, awfully strong guy," Marshall says. "He was very nice and very sweet, but when he set his mind, that was it." Houston had set his mind to get Donald Murray into the Maryland law school. Maryland was the most promising state in which to bring such a case, and Murray had qualifications that Hocutt had lacked. Houston gave Marshall the go-ahead to work out the law in the case. Lawson was left out in the cold.

Even before then, and at Gosnell's suggestion, Donald Murray had written to the president of the University of Maryland, Raymond A. Pearson, asking about admission to the law school. Within a week, Pearson sent a chilly form-letter reply that spoke volumes:

> Under the general laws of this State the University maintains the Princess Anne Academy as a separate institution of higher learning for the education of Negroes. In order to insure equality of opportunity . . . the 1933 Legislature passed Chapter 234, creating partial scholarships at Morgan College or institutions outside of the State for Negro students who may desire to take professional courses or other work not given at the Princess Anne Academy.
>
> Should you desire to make application for such scholarship, notify me, and I will see that such application is duly filed.

It was a sorry joke to call Princess Anne Academy, a small, glorified high school run as an extension of the university on the Eastern Shore, an "institution of higher learning." And of course neither it nor Morgan had a law school. Worse still, the bill passed by the Maryland legislature authorizing the establishment of out-of-state scholarships for Negroes was an empty shell; no funds had been allocated for the purpose. One might well have accused President Pearson of mendacity without risking a slander suit.

With Houston and Marshall now his lawyers, Murray followed through. Late in January, he filed a formal application to the law school and enclosed the required two-dollar handling fee. On February 9, 1935, the university's registrar wrote back:

> President Pearson instructed me today to return to you the application form and the money order, as the University does not accept Negro students, except at the Princess Anne Academy.

It was not satisfactory. In a carefully worded registered letter composed with aid of counsel and sent to every member of the university's Board of Regents, Murray wrote on March 5:

> . . . I am a citizen of the State of Maryland and fully qualified to become a student at the University of Maryland Law School. No other State institution affords a legal education. The arbitrary action of the officials of the University of Maryland in returning my application was unjust and unreasonable and contrary to the Constitution and laws of the United States and the Constitution and laws of this State. I, therefore, appeal to you as the governing body of the University to accept the enclosed application and money order and to have my qualifications investigated within a reasonable time. . . . I am ready, willing and able to meet all requirements as a student, to pay whatever dues are required of residents of the State and to apply myself diligently to my work.

All it got him was another letter from President Pearson, returning the two-dollar money order again and referring Murray to his earlier letter. But this time, in a helpful aside that must have brought a bitter smile to Houston's lips, the president of the University of Maryland called to Murray's attention "the exceptional facilities open to you for the study of law in Howard University in Washington" and noted its fine accreditation and lower cost than Maryland's law school. How right he was about Howard would shortly be brought home to him during an hour and a half on the witness stand under interrogation by the black dean of that black law school.

The case was styled *Murray v. Pearson*, though it came to be referred to as *Murray v. Maryland.* And while Thurgood Marshall was widely credited as the plaintiff's chief counsel, he unhesitatingly sets the record straight: "I worked the case out on the ground and I drew the pleadings since there was some intricate old Maryland common law involved, but outside the legwork, I did very little. The court presentation was his [Houston's] doing. The fact is, I never was chief counsel in a case that Charlie took part in."

It was argued in June in Baltimore City Court before Judge Eugene O'Dunne, who was amused at the outset when Marshall moved Houston's admission to the Maryland bar. The judge said he had often heard of law-school deans moving the admission of their former students, but this was the first time he had ever seen the process reversed. It was just a warm little aside, but it was an omen for what lay ahead during a very long day in court. Will and Norma Marshall were on hand to see their son's first major case. Mostly, they saw Charles Houston reduce the defense to rubble.

Donald Murray had been arbitrarily and wrongfully refused by the law school, Houston declared at the opening. He was fully qualified for admission, and neither state law nor the university charter barred him. Before an assistant attorney general of Maryland named Charles T. LeViness III could respond for the university, the judge asked him if Murray's race was the acknowledged reason for his rejection. Yes, said LeViness, that was public policy. The judge asked what public policy had to do with the state of the law. Why, the state had built an elaborate educational apparatus, including a junior college, for the benefit of its colored people, said the assistant attorney general, and gave funds to help run a private college for colored. And only recently the state had established fifty out-of-state scholarships of $200 each for Negro youngsters who wished to pursue courses of study not available at Maryland's colored colleges. He neglected to say that the legislature had failed to make that $10,000 appropriation for out-of-state scholarships until after Donald Murray had taken the University of Maryland to court. And suppose, the judge wanted to know, a colored youngster did not want to go out-of-state to pursue his studies? Well, said LeViness, one had to be practical about such things; one could not build a separate professional school every time a colored youngster announced his intentions.

Houston opened by calling Raymond Pearson, president of the university. It was a revealing display. Princess Anne Academy for Negroes offered substantially the same caliber of education during its two-year course as the

University of Maryland did during its first two years, said Dr. Pearson, and the competence of the faculty was comparable "in some instances." If that were so, asked Houston, was it true that the University of Maryland faculty had only one member with a master's degree and none with a doctorate, as was the case at Princess Anne? Well, no, said President Pearson. Did he know, Houston asked, whether the title of "Doctor" used by the principal of Princess Anne was merely honorific or earned by an advanced degree? No, said President Pearson, he didn't know. Did he believe, Houston asked, that the single table, small batch of test tubes, and glass butterfly case that made up the chemistry and biology laboratory equipment *in toto* at Princess Anne was adequate? Yes, he did. Then why was so much more equipment available at the university? Because more advanced courses were offered there. Would he admit Mexicans, Japanese, Indians, and Filipinos to the university as he would whites? If they were residents of the state, they would probably be admitted, yes, said the president. Then why, Houston asked, were members of Donald Murray's race not admitted to the university? Pearson retreated into obfuscation. He personally had no objection to Negroes attending the university, but state policy was against it; besides, scholarships had been set up for colored students in cases such as Murray's. But no money had yet been allocated for those scholarships at the time he rejected Murray and suggested he apply for one, wasn't that true? Well, yes, said President Pearson. And if Murray had accepted his recommendation to attend Howard University's law school, wasn't it true that he would not have received any money from the state of Maryland for that purpose? Yes, admitted Pearson, and Houston dismissed him.

Next, he put on his own opposite number at the University of Maryland—Roger Howell, dean of the law school. Howell acknowledged that the curriculum at his law school was built largely around study of the Maryland state codes and that of the eighteen people on the faculty, twelve were either local judges or private attorneys of prominence from the area. Clearly, anyone who wished to practice law in Baltimore, as Murray had testified to be his preference, was being deprived of valuable training if he was not allowed to attend the Maryland law school. Howell contested this conclusion by Houston and, in answer to a question from the bench, said there would not be sufficient demand to justify a separate law school for Negroes in Maryland. What would the dean say, then, about those states that practiced Jim Crow on the railroad—should there not be separate cars for Negroes even if only a few of them choose to travel? "How would you let them ride—in an oxcart?" asked the judge. The dean was nonplused. "Well," he said, "if the oxcart were about as good as the cars, I think that I would."

With an apparent friend presiding, Houston was not going to let the chance pass to underscore the inequality of black and white schooling in the state, even if the testimony were not directly relevant to his case. He summoned the state superintendent of colored schools—a white man—who declared that educational opportunities in Maryland for both races were "substantially" the same. But wasn't the school year for colored children a month shorter? Yes, said the superintendent. And weren't there proportionately many more one-room schoolhouses for colored children than for white? Yes, said the superintendent. And wasn't it true, Houston asked, that white teachers were paid more than colored teachers with the exact same level of certification and teaching experience? Yes, said the superintendent, but he didn't see how that could affect the quality of education colored teachers would give colored pupils. Wouldn't it be more difficult for teachers on lower salaries to pursue advanced degrees? Perhaps, said the superintendent, but it was well known that it cost colored teachers less to live.

After examining a handful of other state officials, Houston wound up by producing a member of the newly created state commission to administer the out-of-state scholarships for Negroes. For the fifty grants available, the commissioner said, they had already received 380 applications—and the program had only been announced a few months earlier.

Thurgood Marshall came on at the close. His assignment was to cope with the constitutional issues at stake and reassure a municipal court at the bottom of the judicial ladder that it would be on solid footing if it ordered Murray admitted to the Maryland law school. Since no such court-ordered instance of desegregation was on the books anywhere, Marshall's task was not simple.

What he and Houston had settled on, with an obvious eye on appealing Murray's case as high as necessary, was to take the Supreme Court at its word the last time it had spoken on the question of school segregation. Marshall sketched out the course of *Gong Lum v. Rice,* the Court's unanimous ruling of eight years earlier, upholding Mississippi's right to segregate and assign the Chinese-American plaintiff's daughter to a "colored" school. But, Marshall noted, Chief Justice Taft had left the door open to the sort of question presented in Murray's case. "Had the petitioner alleged specifically that there was no colored school in Martha Lum's neighborhood, a different question would have been presented," wrote Taft. In other words, the "separate" part of the separate-but-equal doctrine of segregation had been legitimized by the Court on several occasions, Marshall was arguing, but its position on cases where the facilities offered blacks were inarguably not equal—as in the absence of a law school open to Negroes in the state of Maryland—had never been directly tested. Marshall had also uncovered a California case that seemed closely related to the Murray situation. An Indian child had been denied admission to the only locally maintained public school in the district on the ground that the federal government was supplying a school for Indian children. But the California courts held that the presence of the federally financed school did not relieve the local school authorities of their constitutional duty of equal protection: they either had to open a separate school for Indians or admit the Indian child to the white school.

Marshall's performance was doubly impressive when compared to the bumbling job by the assistant attorney general. LeViness was out of his depth in trying to decipher Supreme Court rulings on segregation and use them in support of Maryland's position. He said that *Cumming v. Richmond County Board of Education,* the 1899 case in which Negroes had sued to close down a white high school until the colored one in their area was reopened, was highly pertinent. But of course Donald Murray was not suing to have the University of Maryland close down its law school; he just wanted to get in. Judge O'Dunne told LeViness he was wrong. LeViness then invoked *Plessy v. Ferguson* in defense of the Maryland custom of segregated schools. But Murray's lawyers had not challenged Maryland's right to establish a colored school system. They had challenged the inequality of the system as administered, and nothing in *Plessy* countenanced that; it specifically cited equal facilities as a precondition to sanctioning the separation of the races. The bench asked LeViness: "Does the state mean to contend that Murray should not be admitted because of custom?" The state's attorney wriggled on the skewer. Well, he meant that it was too soon to tell how much demand there might be by Negroes for legal education and that the out-of-state scholarships established by the state might meet the *Plessy* requirement of equal facilities. And besides, separate facilities did not imply inferiority. He did not say what they did imply.

A few minutes before five o'clock on June 25, 1935, Judge Eugene O'Dunne of the Baltimore City Court issued a writ of *mandamus* ordering President Raymond Pearson to admit Donald Gaines Murray, colored, to the law school at the University of Maryland.

The state's attorney asked to speak. "I wish to be quoted as saying that I hope that Mr. Murray leads the class in the law school," said Charles LeViness. Such sentiments notwithstanding, the state of Maryland shortly appealed O'Dunne's decision. Many felt the Negro victory would be short-lived.

Might it not be in everyone's interests, the attorney general of Maryland asked the Maryland Court of Appeals in petitioning it to reverse the *Murray* decision, if the case could be heard before the next regular session of the court in October? Surely it would not be good for Mr. Murray to enroll and begin law classes, only to find himself expelled by court order.

The court was unmoved, and so, in the words of Baltimore's most eminent man of letters and dispenser of vitriol, "there will be an Ethiop among the Aryans when the larval Blackstones assemble next Wednesday." And that was as it should be, H. L. Mencken added in his column in the Baltimore *Sun*, for he could see no reason why the law-school faculty and students should object "to the presence among them of a self-respecting and ambitious young Afro-American, well prepared for his studies by four years of hard work in a Class A college." It would be "brutal" and "absurd" for the Court of Appeals to turn him out. Mencken scoffed at the university's proposal that Murray attend Howard. "The regents might just as well advise him to go to Addis Ababa or Timbuctoo," he wrote. "He wants to get his training, not in Washington, but here in Baltimore, where the laws and procedure of Maryland are at the bottom of the teaching and where he plans to practice. . . ." The real fear of the university officials, Mencken contended, was that if Murray opened the door to Negro students, many of them would apply to the undergraduate school, "the so-called College of Arts" in College Park. That was downright silly, said the Sage of Baltimore, because "the College of Arts is a fifth-rate pedagogical dump patronized largely by the children of Washingtonians, and it would be easy to bring the Princess Anne Academy, which is for colored students, up to equality with it."

Lest anyone get the idea that the state's most enlightened social commentator was about to propose the wholesale abandonment of Jim Crow, Mencken concluded otherwise. "I am not arguing here for mixing the races in public schools," he wrote, for "in the present state of public opinion in Maryland it would probably be most unwise, no matter what may be said for it in the abstract." And anyway, the separation of the races in the schools was resented only "by a small faction of colored people"—how he arrived at that estimate, Mencken did not indicate—and "inasmuch as virtually all the whites of the State are in favor of it, it is not likely to be abandoned in the near future."

If that was the view of race relations held by the most liberal thinker in the least militant Jim Crow state, how mountainous the barriers must have looked just then to the new special counsel to the NAACP, surveying the legal horizon from the canyons of Manhattan. But Charlie Houston was not twiddling his thumbs while waiting for the Maryland high court to decide the *Murray* appeal. He whipped off a fighting broadside titled "Educational Inequalities Must Go!" for the October number of *The Crisis*. The ultimate objective of the NAACP's new legal drive was the abolition of all forms of segregation in public education, Houston declared. In places where Jim Crow was too well entrenched to be assaulted frontally, the drive would aim at "absolute equality. . . . If the white South insists upon its separate schools, it must not squeeze the Negro schools to pay for them." The NAACP stood ready to help whenever called. It recognized that inequalities in Negro education were "merely part of the general pattern of race prejudice in American life. . . . One of the greatest tragedies of the Depression has been the humiliation and suffering which public authorities have inflicted upon trained Negroes, denying them employment at their trades on public works and forcing them to accept menial low-pay jobs as an alternative to starvation." There was a big job ahead, then, for the NAACP, and schools were the key to it in the view of the association because

> It conceives that in equalizing educational opportunities for Negroes it raises the whole standard of American citizenship, and stimulates white Americans as well as black. Fundamentally, the NAACP is not a special pleader; it merely insists that the United States respect its own Constitution and its own laws.

The Maryland Court of Appeals agreed. In January of 1936, it said, in ruling on the *Murray* decision, "Compliance with the Constitution cannot be deferred at the will of the state. Whatever system is adopted for legal education now must furnish equality of treatment now." O'Dunne's opinion was upheld. Murray was confirmed as a student in good standing at the Maryland law school. And the wisdom of bringing the case in Maryland in the first place was evidenced by the state's decision not to appeal to the Supreme Court of the United States. It was, after all, only a quite small dent in the stout wall separating the races.

When he took his seat in the middle of the room in which all first-year classes were taught at the University of Maryland Law School, Donald Murray was greeted with indifference. After a day, the fellows sitting next to him shook his hand, wished him well, and offered to be of help if they could. No one ever hit him, pushed him, razzed him, or otherwise made life unpleasant for him.

# 9

# Stalking the Law of the Jungle

The admission of Donald Murray to law school did not itself save the Negro race. Its immediate by-products, though, were considerable.

The Maryland Legislature, perhaps to discourage a wave of Donald Murrays, sharply raised its outlay for Negro higher education. The funds for out-of-state scholarships that had been at issue in the Murray case were tripled. The state colored teachers' college at Bowie was given more than $250,000 for new buildings. Morgan College, the private black school, had its annual appropriation doubled and received a $100,000 grant to put up a gymnasium. Weighing the court's decision in *Murray*, the neighboring state of Virginia authorized—but did not yet fund—graduate study at its principal college for Negroes and allocated money for out-of-state scholarships. Missouri, too, set up out-of-state funding.

To black morale in the Baltimore area, the legal victory was a strong tonic. NAACP membership in the local branch leaped from the few dozen when "Ma" Jackson took over in 1934 to more than 1,500 by the end of 1936.

"Don't Shout Too Soon" was the title of a cautionary article by Charlie Houston in *The Crisis*. The subheading read, "Victory in the University of Maryland test case does not mean the battle for educational equality for Negroes is over, warns the chief counsel in the legal campaign." Indeed, it was just beginning. Qualified applicants had been denied entry at the white state universities in Virginia, Tennessee, and Missouri since Murray made it at Maryland. The Richmond *Times-Dispatch* hollered that the first black in the door at the University of Virginia would be a giant step toward miscegenation.

In late 1935, even before the Court of Appeals ruled for Murray, Marshall and the Baltimore NAACP had picked their next target. It seemed a lot more important in many ways than the Murray case. In Baltimore County, which formed an arc on the east, north, and west of the city, there were ten high schools for white children and no high schools for colored children. Though Negroes made up nearly 10 percent of the county's population, white school officials contended that the wide but thin dispersal of blacks made it impossible to open a centrally located high school for them. Instead, black youngsters who wanted to continue their education past the seventh grade were given a test to see if they qualified for admission to Frederick Douglass High School for colored in Baltimore. About half those tested were judged qualified and their tuition to the city school was paid by the county, which did not, however, provide the black students with transportation from their outlying homes, nearly ten miles from the school on average. White youngsters were automatically admitted to high school after seventh grade. The colored grade schools in the county, moreover, were a disgrace in many instances: the roofs leaked, the floors were rotten, the playgrounds were non-existent, and the approach roads were quagmires in wet weather. The whole arrangement, it seemed undeniable to Marshall and the Baltimore-area NAACP leaders, was meant to discourage black education. If Donald Murray had been denied equal protection by the failure of the state to provide a law school open to him, how much more pressing was the case of several thousand Baltimore County youngsters offered broken-down grade schools and no high schools?

Marshall brought a petition signed by leading county blacks to a regular session of the board of education meeting at Towson. The petition was flatly rejected. An appeal to the State Board of Education proved no more fruitful. After the Court of Appeals announced its decision in *Murray* early in 1936, Marshall was ready to act. But what relief action should be asked in behalf of the black seventh-grade girl Marshall had found to serve as plaintiff? There were three choices: (1) sue to force the county to equalize the black schools—a step that would likely require massive data to prove the inequalities, and even then the availability of Douglass High in the city might be held adequate for black needs; (2) sue to close the white high schools in the county until equal black facilities were provided—a course that had all the perils of the first alternative plus the unfavorable precedent of the *Cumming* decision by the Supreme Court in 1899; and (3) sue to gain the black plaintiff admission to the white high school nearest her home—in effect, the same remedy won for Donald Murray. Marshall chose the third course. In hindsight only, it was a blunder.

The case was heard in September in the State Circuit Court, where the judge ruled that the county board of education had the power to determine the basis upon which students might enter high school. Marshall went right to the Maryland Court of Appeals. Surely the state's high court would see the analogy to *Murray*, in which it had ruled for the Negro plaintiff's rights—and the county-high-school case was a far more flagrant instance of inequality. The appellate court mulled the case for months, and then in June of 1937 it ruled: Marshall had sought the wrong remedy. He should have sued not to gain admission of the plaintiff to the white high school but to require the county to pay her tuition to the colored high school in Baltimore without the obligation to pass an entrance examination. Whether the county should have provided a high school for Negro children was not considered.

It was Thurgood Marshall's first civil-rights loss. It was not a pleasing sensation. There was too much else to do, though, to let it get him down. By then, he was officially Charles Houston's assistant, plying between New York and Baltimore and points south.

In May of 1936, a few months after *Murray* had been resolved, Marshall had made a drastic appraisal of his financial situation and discovered, as he wrote Houston in New York, that "things are getting worse and worse." He appealed to Houston and Walter White to see if there was any way he "could be assured of enough to tide me over, then in return, I could do more on these cases." It could not have been an easy letter for so proud a man to write. But there was no point in deceiving himself: either he was to be a full-time, all-out civil-rights lawyer or he would be a lawyer who would do what he could on occasion to forward the race.

Houston and White talked it over. It was already becoming clear that Maryland and then Virginia would be the critical laboratories for the NAACP campaign to overcome Jim Crow in the South. The two states were close to Washington, for one thing. They were relatively less hostile to black aspirations, for another. And the NAACP itself was making major strides in both places—an important consideration in seeking plaintiffs and community support for the legal drive for equal rights. Negro teachers in Maryland, for example, were proving receptive to the salary-equalization drive then shaping up under Marshall and Lillie Jackson. Houston was increasingly weighted down with other business in the New York headquarters; to have an alert and energetic younger man such as Marshall in the field, especially in the Maryland-Virginia territory where he was at home, made good sense. He was hired for $2,400 a year plus expenses.

It was like a finishing school for Marshall. His regard for Houston could occasionally border on dependency—a not unwise recognition by a young lawyer of his own callowness. And Houston never wearied of being the teacher. For all his skills as a lawyer, he was a teacher most of all. He could be a philosopher one moment and a meticulous technician the next, but at all points he was a pragmatist and taught his charges to be, too. He wrote Marshall, for example, to take pains not to antagonize his opposing counsel in the *Murray* appeal "because you may have to come back to him on this question of the judgment not conforming to the prayers. At the same time, I do not want any of our rights to be lost by default. Handle the matter diplomatically but I think that whatever you finally decide upon, you should put it in writing so as to have a record."

Houston was compulsive in his work habits and preached them to assistants like Marshall and to Edward Lovett, who worked with him in his Washington law office. "He used to work like hell and way into the night," says Lovett. "There was a certain minimum standard he set for himself and those who worked with him, and beyond that it was just a matter of polishing. But the trick was to get up to that minimum standard." Another one-time assistant, Juanita Kidd Stout, remembers his advising her, "Regardless of how small a case may be, act as though it will end in the Supreme Court." Spottswood W. Robinson III, who, like Mrs. Stout, eventually became a federal judge, recalls that Houston helped train him as a young NAACP lawyer in Virginia. "One thing he taught me," says Robinson, "was to read over the record the night before arguing a case, so I'd have all the facts and rebuttal arguments at my fingertips in the courtroom. He was always, without fail, doing that." Robinson, who worked closely with him on several cases, was struck, too, by the perfectionist drive in the older lawyer.

He remembers Houston laboring long in crafting his briefs for important cases; then he would park himself in the back room at his firm's office at 615 F Street Northwest, clamp on a green eyeshade, arm himself with a container of freshly sharpened pencils and snub-nosed black crayons, and mark up his brief until it was disfigured nearly beyond recognition. Sometimes the process took all night—or several nights—but he would not quit until he felt he had something worthy of himself. Confidence was the crucial ingredient for Houston, and it was perhaps the most difficult lesson of all to teach young blacks in that period. He wrote one student: "The most important thing now, as fast as conditions are changing, is that no Negro tolerate any ceiling on his ambitions or imagination. Good luck and don't have any doubts; you haven't time for such foolishness."

Thurgood Marshall thrived under the tutelage of Charles Houston. They worked closely for only a few years, but there was an immediate intimacy and understanding, born of their close association in the Thirties, whenever they worked together thereafter. "You have to understand that we had absolutely no money at all in those days," Marshall recounts. When they were on the road, filing lawsuits in the courthouses of the South, "Charlie would sit in my car—I had a little old beat-up '29 Ford—and type out the briefs. And he could type up a storm—faster than any secretary—and not with just two fingers going. I mean he used 'em all. We'd stay at friends' homes in those days—for free, you understand. I think the whole budget for the legal office then was maybe $8,000—that was for two lawyers and a secretary." And when they could not find a friend's home, they would put up at grimy hotels or something a little better if they could find it in the land of Jim Crow, and Houston and Marshall would jaw over bourbon about life and law far into the night. They were quite different as men and as lawyers. Where Houston was a private and somewhat remote man of deep intellectual fiber, Marshall was a constantly engaging extrovert who used ideas as steppingstones down a path of ever widening possibilities. Where Houston was smart, Marshall was shrewd. Where Houston was a fine writer and superb draftsman of legal briefs, Marshall was gifted with the spoken word, full of humor or fire as the occasion demanded, whether in a courtroom or before a packed house of overalled black farmers in a remote church. They shared a largeness of stature—both were formidable-sized men, with Houston the shorter and stockier of the two—and gesture. Each was a firecracker of energy and dedication to the task they shared.

At first, and really throughout the two years they worked together as full-time NAACP lawyers, Houston was a taskmaster who expected Marshall to snap to when his orders came down. Houston's manner was hortatory but never imperious, and Marshall did not feel himself a functionary with a law degree. Soon enough, he demonstrated his own skill as a leader and tactician with political savvy. In October of 1937, he made a swing through Virginia and North Carolina, mainly to line up plaintiffs for teachers' salary-equalization cases; his field reports to Houston and Walter White were intelligence briefings on the state of black militancy wherever he had been. In Petersburg, Virginia, he noted simply, "No franchise questions in immediate vicinity.

Negroes just do not vote." Of South Boston, a town of about 5,000 in tobacco country just north of the Carolina border, he wrote:

> . . . School situation is terrible. Principal of elementary school is gardener and janitor for the county superintendent of schools and is a typical uncle tom. New addition to high school at Halifax but not equipped. Elementary schools terrible. Question of voting has not arisen because so few register.
> Spoke at mass meeting and stressed school questions and voting questions. Negroes in this community very lax and inactive. President of [NAACP] branch fighting almost alone.

Regular meetings once or twice a year of all the NAACP branches, known as "the state conference," had lapsed in Virginia, and Marshall urged their renewal despite the laggard ways of the state NAACP president. He suggested the session be scheduled simultaneously with the annual meeting of the black teachers' association in the state, so that a joint committee of teachers and NAACP operatives could "handle the teachers' salary case and at the same time start the conference with a definite program around this case. Virginia could be built up around this case." In North Carolina, he encountered both hope and hostility. In Winston-Salem, for example, he found that

> only those Negroes are permitted to register who are "all right" Negroes. Others are refused. No one will bring a case on the question. Had the president of the branch . . . call a meeting of his executive committee. Stressed the point to them and told them that they should start a program to break this down. We will have to keep behind this branch. Winston-Salem Negroes have money—they all work in factories and make good money. They have a bus company on the streets owned and operated by Negroes. Branch should be strong. They want a speaker for mass meeting but do not have the money. Winston-Salem should be one of the main spots for the franchise fight.

Trying to organize teachers for the equal-pay fight, he ran into choppy waters. Those opposed to the move, Marshall reported, were claiming that the NAACP was a glory-seeking interloper and that North Carolina blacks could handle their own problems. Nevertheless, the state's 6,000 black teachers were "tired of waiting" and wanted action from the NAACP "or anyone else." Their main problem was a state teachers' association "controlled by . . . leaders who give no consideration to the rank and file." Marshall proposed a battle plan whereby the NAACP would stay out of the picture until teachers' committees were set up around the state and funds collected to finance the salary case and support anyone fired as a result. The branches had all been contacted and would stand by, "ready to cooperate when the case breaks and to use the case" as a way to revive interest in their activities. "This procedure," Marshall was sure after all his *sub rosa* talks, "is the only type that will work."

Already he was shaping up as an accomplished guerrilla fighter.

Established in his office at NAACP headquarters in New York at 69 Fifth Avenue near 13th Street, Charles Houston did not precisely take New York by storm. He had his detractors on both ends of the political spectrum and would for the rest of his life. There were some who thought he was too radical and questioned the propriety of his representing Communists in civil-liberties actions, as he did on several occasions before and after but not during his time at the NAACP national office. "There was this fellow in Baltimore," Edward Lovett recalls, "who couldn't get anyone to handle his case, and Charlie finally agreed to take it, even though he was told it might hurt him. His concern wasn't limited to the well-being of the Negro. He was fighting for equality of treatment of all minorities." Others saw him as too much of a conservative, who settled for small gains while the severe afflictions of the race continued unabating.

Some who lacked Houston's learning or cultivation envied him and called him snooty; some who lacked neither—such as Du Bois—resented his closeness to Walter White, a man probably more welcomed in the white world than in the colored world he claimed to represent. Nor did Houston go out of his way to cultivate friends in the black press. Henry Lee Moon, who later became NAACP publicity director, was a reporter on the *Amsterdam News* in the late Thirties when the editorial staff of the Harlem weekly threw up a picket line and struck in an effort to install an American Newspaper Guild unit and union shop. "Charlie was against it," Moon remembers. "I think he felt that it wasn't right, all of us being black and the paper being kind of poor. But Walter White and Roy Wilkins [White's assistant and a former editor of the black Kansas City *Call*] and I, we were out on the picket line. No hard feelings against Charlie, though."

Some, if not all, of these factors conspired to put Houston's private life, which he kept remarkably private, on the front page of the *Amsterdam News* of February 8, 1936. "DIVORCE SEEN/FOR HOUSTONS," said the one-column headline to the piece that ran above the centerfold, a testament to the eminence of its subject or the hostility of the editors, or both. Houston's first marriage—to Margaret Moran, whom friends have described as an older woman—had not been a love story for the ages. Some acquaintances suggest that he was married to his work more than his wife and she in time expressed her resentment. Whatever the details, which Houston chose never to disclose, he married Henrietta Williams the year after the newspaper report of his impending divorce and settled down with the second Mrs. Houston in a first-floor apartment at 227 West 149th Street, in the center of Harlem. They were happily married for the rest of Houston's life, though the pace of his work never truly slowed. Charles, Jr., was a product of the second marriage.

His courtroom appearances were by no means the principal part of his new job. He served as a steadying gyroscope to the flamboyant Walter White, who turned to him constantly for advice on policy and organization. Houston was not bashful about supplying it. In May 1936, for example, he sent White a brisk memo on the entire structure of the NAACP, which had seemed spongy to the lawyer. "If the Association is to function effectively and get the benefit of its numbers, it must be divided and sub-divided into smaller units very much after the fashion of an army," he wrote. In time, the proposal was essentially adopted.

But most of Houston's effort was addressed to protest and watchdog activity in the form of written and spoken pronouncements on racial inequality. He used every forum at his disposal. In *The Crisis*, he wrote on "How to Fight for Better Schools" and said that before real progress could be made, the Negro masses must be convinced that "they are part of the public which owns and controls the schools." He blueprinted the steps local people could take in pushing their school boards for equal funding and facilities, and he wound up: "Do not lose heart if victory does not come at once. Persevere to the end." In a Nashville courtroom, representing a young colored man seeking admission to the pharmacy school at the University of Tennessee, he declared in words carried across the country on the Associated Press wire and run in hundreds of newspapers: "This case may mean nothing in 1937, but in A.D. 2000 somebody will look back on the record and wonder why the South spent so much money in keeping rights from Negroes rather than granting them. . . . [W]e'll all be better off when instead of spending money in lawsuits we spend it for social advancement." At a church-sponsored interracial conference in Philadelphia, he thundered that the only solution to the race problem was to provide Negroes with "complete industrial and social opportunity."

His forensic gifts aside, Houston continued to be of greatest value to White as a pathfinder through the Washington political labyrinth. White's access to the chambers of power was enhanced by Houston's appointment in early 1937 as an unpaid consultant to Harry Hopkins, head of the mammoth Works Progress Administration. There was a great deal of racial inequity in the WPA's way of dispensing food, clothing, and work opportunities to the needy, and Houston had denounced openly discriminatory policies such as wage differentials between whites and blacks in federally funded jobs or federally approved industrial codes. Still, by the later part of the Thirties more than a million Negroes owed their livings to the WPA, and Houston's designation as an advisor to the New Deal's huge economic-rescue operation added to his strategic usefulness to the NAACP.

His credentials as a student of the Constitution were another invaluable asset. He was always on the lookout for new bills in Congress that might further damage the Negro's hard-pressed civil rights. Useful, too, was Houston's cold-eyed estimate of the NAACP's effectiveness as a lobbying center. In the aftermath of a 1938 filibuster that once again smothered a federal anti-lynching bill *in utero*, Houston suggested that a scattering of telegrams and letters to Senators was far short of the impassioned plea in the name of humanity that NAACP branches might have wrung from their communities by a sustained, graphic publicity campaign. Lobbying help from church-affiliated groups such as the YWCA and the Federal Council of Churches was no doubt adding arrows to the NAACP quiver, but they were more feather than point. The NAACP needed muscular help and ought to turn to the labor movement for it—a proposal that must have struck White as semi-utopian in view of the union movement's allergy to the Negro.

The main front, for Houston, remained the courtroom. While his other NAACP duties contrived to reduce his activities in the legal arena, he went to Columbia, Missouri, in July of 1936 to argue one of the three cases that would compose his monument as a civil-rights advocate. From the Missouri case would stem a full-scale assault on segregation in all the nation's schools.

Victory in the *Murray* case had been a breakthrough but no more. It had to be reinforced and then expanded. "We all recognized that Maryland was a border state, and you couldn't assume that states in the deeper South would follow the precedent," remarks William Hastie. "But as a result of *Murray*, local NAACP branches around the country started referring cases to the national office." One of them came from the St. Louis branch.

Colored lawyers were scarce in Missouri; there were only forty-five in the whole state, and thirty of those practiced in St. Louis. A total of just three Negro attorneys had been admitted to the Missouri bar in the previous five years, and there were fewer black practitioners in the state in 1936 than there had been ten years earlier. Something had to be done about it. The president of the St. Louis NAACP and one of the branch's directors, both lawyers, decided to launch a test case. Their plaintiff, a twenty-five-year-old St. Louis resident named Lloyd Lionel Gaines, did not have to be dragooned into participation. He had graduated from Missouri's state-supported black college, Lincoln University,* in June 1935 and wanted to go to law school. Lincoln, though, had no law school; it was, in fact, not a university at all but had merely been empowered to become one by the state legislature, should the need ever arise among the state's black population. The law school at the University of Missouri, a Jim Crow institution, refused Gaines's application and instructed him to apply either to Lincoln, which in theory could provide him with a legal education, or to an out-of-state law school. If he chose the latter course, the state would pay any tuition charge in excess of what Gaines would have paid if enrolled at the Missouri law school.

It was almost exactly like the Murray case, except for two factors. Missouri, unlike Maryland, said it had every intention of maintaining Lincoln University as a first-rate school, on a par with the white university, and had been a leader among the segregating states in providing quality higher education for Negroes. If they wanted a law school, then the state would build them a law school, but there was no point in building one if no colored applicants showed any interest. Let Gaines apply to Lincoln, and wheels would begin turning. The out-of-state subsidy, furthermore, was a *bona fide* offer—not an empty vessel as the scholarship program had been in Maryland when Murray was applying to the law school there—and if Gaines chose not to wait until Lincoln could meet his needs, the state would pay the extra tuition charge, if any. The state said nothing, of course, about paying Gaines's extra traveling and living expenses that would be necessitated by his attending an out-of-state law school.

The NAACP attorneys in St. Louis worked the case up and brought it to Charles Houston. Suit was entered in the Missouri circuit court for a

---

* Not to be confused with Lincoln in Pennsylvania, the college Thurgood Marshall attended.

*mandamus* writ against the registrar of the University of Missouri, S. W. Canada. The case was styled *Missouri ex rel. Gaines v. Canada.**

Houston had been hoping for a sizable turnout of blacks at the courthouse in Columbia to show officials and the white public that the case had sparked genuine interest among the Negroes of Missouri. When court opened at 9 a.m. on the morning of July 10, though, few of the promised throng from the St. Louis area were on hand. In fact, neither Gaines nor Houston nor the local Negro lawyers serving as Houston's co-counsel were on hand. Houston, staying in St. Louis to research the case for several days before the trial, had arisen at 4:15 a.m. to prepare for the 120-mile drive to Columbia, but by the time Gaines and the lawyers had been assembled and had a snack it was six o'clock. A detour for thirty miles on U.S. Highway 40 turned the drive into a steeplechase. Houston & Company showed up in court at 9:15, breathless and moist in the morning heat. The thermometer was flirting with 100 degrees.

The heat, the distance, the lack of public transportation, and the fact that there had been a pair of lynchings in the Columbia area not long before had all contributed to the scarcity of colored faces in the courtroom audience. There was no lack of rustic white faces, however. Surrounding Boone County was suffering a serious drought, and dozens of farmers had come to town in their overalls to see officials at the county relief agencies located in the courthouse. When the backlog of farmers piled up, the overflow went upstairs to watch the colored lawyers perform. One hundred or so students attending summer school at the University of Missouri, located in Columbia, also crowded into court, and before long the jammed room was a hotbox.

Yet it was not a hostile crowd, Houston thought. The opposing white counsel shook hands cordially all around and shared a single table in front of the witness stand with their colored adversaries—an arrangement "odd to us," Houston reported afterward in an office memo. "All during the trial we were looking down one another's throats. For private conference at the table we almost had to go into a football huddle." At the outset, "the Court and all concerned agreed to remove coats, so we had a shirtsleeve trial." There was not a single hostile demonstration or outburst during it, and nobody in court called Lloyd Gaines anything other than "Mr. Gaines." The courtroom was unsegregated. During recess, Houston noted, some of the farmers "looked a little strange at us drinking out of the same fountain and using the same lavatories with them, but they did not say anything."

The hearing itself went less satisfactorily. The university's lawyers,

* The term *"ex rel."* is an abbreviation of *ex relatione*, which is defined by the fourth edition of *Black's Law Dictionary* this way: "Legal proceedings which are instituted by the attorney general (or other proper person) in the name and behalf of the state, but on the information and at the instigation of an individual who has a private interest in the matter, are said to be taken 'on the relation' *(ex relatione)* of such person, who is called 'the relator.'" Lloyd Gaines's case was instituted not by the attorney general, however, but by Houston, who exercised the plaintiff's prerogative of captioning his suit and was apparently indulging in the then permitted formalism of invoking the state of Missouri as the party he believed legally obliged to act in Gaines's behalf in directing the state university to stop denying him his right of admission. The somewhat poetic practice has disappeared, and today the case would be called simply *Gaines v. Canada.*

skillful private practitioners from a top Kansas City firm, were "driving and dramatic" in their opening presentation, in Houston's judgment. Gaines's remedy, they declared, obviously lay with the officials of black Lincoln University, which was built to provide the kind of study this laudably ambitious young Negro now sought. Houston himself had his hands full trying to pry any acknowledgment from the university officials he put on the stand that the Missouri law school was a particularly good place to be trained if you wanted to be a lawyer in Missouri. Other state officials were no more helpful. "It is beyond expectation that the court will decide in our favor, so we had just as well get ready for the appeal," Houston wrote his office.

He was right. The court ruled against Gaines. His appeal would take nearly two and a half years to travel to the Supreme Court of the United States. By the time he argued it, Charles Houston was no longer working full-time for the NAACP.

Despite a robust physique—in 1938 he carried 200 pounds on his six-foot frame—he had never been a particularly hardy man. When he was in the Army, a touch of tuberculosis had been detected and arrested. But an inguinal hernia suffered while in service lingered, and though he was advised to have it operated on ten years later, he dismissed the suggestion because the condition did not bother him sufficiently, he said. In 1928, he had suffered a breakdown, and now in 1938 he was again on the verge of nervous exhaustion. His work did not inflict the normal anxieties suffered by a private person with merely high goals and only twenty-four hours a day to achieve them. Charlie Houston was always a spokesman, always engineering, always on exhibit as an exemplar of his race. It was a killing regimen for a man of his hyper-kinetic temperament. "Telling him to slow down," says Houston's later associate Joseph Waddy, "was like talkin' to the wind."

In March 1938, he made his only appearance before the Supreme Court as the NAACP's full-time attorney. It was a reprise of the all-white jury case, *Hollins v. Oklahoma*, he had successfully argued in his first appearance before the Court three years earlier. The Paducah, Kentucky, Colored Civic League had brought him the problems of nineteen-year-old Joe Hale, charged with murdering a white woman and convicted by a jury in McCracken County, where no Negro had served as a juror in more than fifty years. Since there were 8,000 Negroes in the county, of whom 700 fully qualified under Kentucky law for jury service, the Court had little trouble in setting aside the conviction. Joining in the unanimous decision was the newest member of the Court and the first to come from the Deep South in twenty-six years—Justice Hugo Lafayette Black of Alabama. He had also voted for the black plaintiff in another case that first term on the bench, a suit successfully brought by the New Negro Alliance to defend its right to picket a Washington, D.C., grocery chain that had refused to hire blacks at stores in colored areas. It was a hopeful sign, especially considering that Black was Franklin Roosevelt's first appointment to the Court.

By the time the Court's decision in *Hale v. Kentucky* came down in April 1938, Charles Houston had decided to go home to Washington and resume private practice. The firm of Houston & Houston was nearly in a state of dissolution by then. Houston's father, William, had been appointed an Assistant Attorney General of the United States, and their partner and relative William Hastie had been named the previous year to the United States District Court for the Virgin Islands—the nation's first Negro federal judge. For the senior Houston, appointment to the Justice Department was more of a reward for decades as a model civic leader than an invitation to share in policy-framing. For the precociously ascendant Hastie, elevation from the Solicitor's office at Interior to the lowest rung on the federal judicial ladder was an unmistakable portent. Charles Houston, though, neither sought nor won a federal position. His new dream was to put Houston & Houston back on its feet and then turn it into a haven for public-interest lawyers who might have fallen from grace in their communities for championing unpopular causes.

"I have had the feeling all along that I am much more of an outside man than an inside man; that I usually break down under too much routine," he wrote his father on April 14. "Certainly for the present, I will grow much faster and be of much more service if I keep free to hit and fight wherever circumstances call for action." As an afterthought, he noted that in the previous ten tumultuous years his financial situation had not improved. "I will come home with debts practically closed out, more insurance and no money saved. But I would not give anything for the experience that I have had."

The feeling was mutual at NAACP headquarters. Recalls Roy Wilkins, later to succeed Walter White as executive secretary of the NAACP: "Charlie was never afraid to challenge an idea. He operated from the certainty of his own intellect. He knew that when the chips were down, he had what it takes in that sharp, brilliant mind of his. Walter was slightly different—he didn't have that same certainty. Charlie Houston passed through here and left a lot of sparks."

Between the time Charles Houston threw himself against the tide of white supremacy in a steaming Missouri courtroom in the summer of 1936—while in Berlin throngs watched a black American sprinter kick cinders on Teutonic claims of racial supremacy—and the final adjudication of the *Gaines* case at the end of 1938, America had undergone a bloodless revolution. At its center was the issue of the power and reach of the Supreme Court. The question came down to whether the Justices, in their priestly raiment and putatively higher wisdom, could stymie the rest of government in its earnest effort to meet the needs of a public under severe economic distress.

One of the basic justifications for the establishment of the Supreme Court had been to shield property-owners and creditors from the grasp of the landless, the luckless, the reckless, the penniless, the unscrupulous, and other unsavory multitudes. For if a man were not free to apply his energy, ingenuity, courage, and ruthlessness to the quest for maximum rewards—and be sheltered by the new national government in the accumulation of those rewards—then there would be no way to carve a great republic from the wilderness. The membership of legislatures was always shifting with the popular will, but a Supreme Court of Justices with life tenure might repulse lawmakers who would seek to defile the sanctity of private property in the name of some fancied public interest.

In theory, this conception of a judicial breakwater against a tide of potentially rampaging masses was a reassuring one. But in practice the Court worked to institutionalize the hold of the past upon the present. The Justices remained in place long after the men who had appointed them had passed from office. They were answerable to no one beyond themselves. They were disposable only by death or extreme dereliction of duty. And they were not obliged to conform their conceptions of the nation's laws and needs to the pleasure of the voting masses. The Court was a defiantly undemocratic body that viewed as its highest duty the need to strike down the errant acts of willful majorities. The Holmesian doctrine that, on the contrary, the Court's highest duty was to restrain itself and acquiesce in the determination of public policy by legislative will—except in the most glaring transgressions of constitutional limits—had never captured more than two or three adherents among the Justices. Power meanwhile kept flowing to the Court. And so long as confidence in the economic future of the great land did not flag, the Court's allegiance to the preferred position of property rights was unshakable. In the first century and a half of its existence, the Supreme Court of the United States had rarely been the protector of any but the conservative and wealthy interests in the land.

But by the onset of the 1930s that allegiance had become untenable. The American economy lay distraught and disorganized, its confidence shattered, and an increasingly impoverished citizenry groped in desperation for a way out. In doggedly holding that business must not yield to government intrusion, even in the name of stilling chaos and restoring the semblance of an orderly marketplace, the Court threatened both to forestall the return of economic well-being to the nation and to promote the pauperization of the American masses. A collision between Court and country became inevitable.

The bills hurriedly carpentered by Congress and the state legislatures to repair the worst damage of the Depression began to come before the Court in 1934. Before long, it was clear that the radical relief programs of the New Deal would be sustained by, at best, a precarious majority of the Justices or be rudely overturned in a conservative charge led by the doomsday foursome of Van Devanter, McReynolds, Sutherland, and Butler. The first test was a New York state law to adjust the price of milk when it ran amuck. Here was undeniable tampering—in the name of babies and the public interest—with the laws of supply and demand. The conservative four could not win over a single member from the rest of the Court, which thus narrowly upheld the milk-pricing statute.

The doctrinal confrontation escalated. By the same five-to-four vote, the Court upheld a statute tampering with an even more firmly fixed verity in the American economic firmament: the sanctity of contractual obligations. At issue was a Minnesota law granting a moratorium on farm foreclosures.

Landless farmers, like milkless infants, constituted a national emergency, and so the majority on the Court was willing to stretch things a bit. The Minnesota law, the five Justices voting to affirm it held, would not diminish or alter any debtor's ultimate obligation; all it would do was alter the method and timing of meeting it—a necessity in view of the hard times engulfing so large a portion of the people. Hard cheese, said the right-wing bloc. The nation had suffered through economic travail before, noted Justice Sutherland, and, thanks to "self-denial and painful effort," had ultimately corrected its problems. "If the provisions of the Constitution be not upheld when they pinch as when they comfort," Sutherland added in a classic defense of *laissez-faire*, "they may as well be abandoned."

By early 1935, the conservatives were being joined by the moderate Justices. With only Cardozo dissenting, the Court threw out an act of Congress to stabilize the oil industry after its leaders had sought a federally imposed quota on the production within any given state in order to prevent ruinous price-slashing across the nation. Then, by a single vote—Chief Justice Hughes's—the Court avoided fiscal chaos. It upheld the 1933 joint resolution of Congress declaring unenforceable and against public policy any contract that called for the repayment of a loan in gold. Such a requirement had been common to corporate and government bonds when the Roosevelt administration, to bolster the plummeting dollar in world currency markets, devalued it and Congress declared such debts payable in any legal tender—meaning the devalued dollar.

In May 1935, the ax fell. The first blow was struck by gyrating Justice Owen Roberts, who had swung between the conservative and moderate poles of the Court since joining it in 1930. Now he delivered the five-to-four opinion that scuttled the Railroad Retirement Act, a forerunner of the Social Security Act's old-age payment, on the ground that it forced the railroads to contribute to the pension kitty for their employees. Such a step, Roberts said sniffishly, smacked of "the contentment and satisfaction" theory of society and was not a safety measure stemming from the right of Congress to regulate interstate commerce but was "really and essentially related solely to the social welfare of the workers."

Three weeks later, the Court struck three times against the New Deal on the same day, and it did so unanimously. A federal bankruptcy act designed to keep farmers afloat by allowing them to buy back their foreclosed property at a devalued price (and on the installment plan, with only token interest charges) was denounced by Brandeis as class legislation that transferred the property of creditors to debtors without compensation—precisely the sort of Robin Hood tactics the Constitution had been designed to prevent. Then the Court denied President Roosevelt the power to fire a member of the Federal Trade Commission who had been appointed to the post by President Hoover and was at odds with New Deal philosophy. But most vital of all that day was the Court's unanimous decision to shoot down the blue eagle of the National Recovery Administration, one of the two foundation stones of the New Deal.

Pushing through a sweeping industrial-recovery law, Congress had empowered the new agency to relieve rampant joblessness by a series of codes that provided for shorter work hours, a minimum pay scale, and the end of unfair trade practices and price-cutting within each industry covered. In short order, the New Deal's NRA czar had framed codes governing 541 industries from automobiles to pants-pressing, and the blue-eagle insignia of participation flew like a patriotic phoenix above the plants and mills of the nation. The only way the complex industrial codes could be thrashed out in time to be useful in the emergency and revised as necessary, Congress agreed, was to leave their specific provisions and enforcement in the hands of the President and his administration. No, said the Supreme Court, that was a legislative function of great magnitude and could not be delegated by Congress under the Constitution. That cut the heart out of the whole program.

Over the summer of 1935, the Justices moved from their modest quarters in the old Senate chamber on the second floor of the Capitol into the outsized Corinthian mausoleum that became the Court's permanent home on the east side of Capitol Hill. The move may have inspired delusions of Olympian divinity, for that fall term the Justices proceeded to dismantle most of the rest of Franklin Roosevelt's handiwork. They pulled down the Agricultural Administration Act, the second of the economic keystones of the New Deal and a measure that had worked well to bolster depressed farm prices and curb overproduction by means of a subsidy program. The act, said Roberts for the Court's six-to-three majority, was an underhanded device by Congress to gain control over farm production, which, unlike interstate commerce, was not subject to regulation by the federal lawmakers. Justice Stone was furious at what he called Roberts's "tortured construction of the Constitution" and delivered his memorable chastisement of the majority:

> While unconstitutional exercise of power by the executive and legislative branches of the government is subject to judicial restraint, the only check upon our own exercise of power is our own sense of self-restraint. . . . For the removal of unwise laws from the statute books appeal lies not to the courts but to the ballot and to the processes of democratic government. . . . Courts are not the only agency of government that must be assumed to have capacity to govern.

But the four conservative Justices, joined by Roberts and sometimes Hughes, kept right on chopping away throughout the term. A law regulating the output and pricing of soft coal was ruled an infringement of states' rights, even though the major coal-producing states filed *amicus* briefs urging the Court to uphold the law. In the spring of 1936, the Court scrapped the Municipal Bankruptcy Act, a realistic effort to meet the needs of more than 2,000 communities that were unable to fulfill their obligations to bond-holders.

Finally, and suicidally, the Justices voted five-to-four to kill the New York minimum-wage law for women. Roberts once again joined the four hatchet men on the Court's right when they proclaimed, just as other Court majorities had been proclaiming for fifty years, that such humanitarian measures undercut private employers' "freedom of contract." Said Justice

Butler blandly for the majority: "In making contracts of employment, generally speaking, the parties have equal right to obtain from each other the best terms they can by private bargaining." Here was the high-water mark of social Darwinism and the ultimate display of hardheartedness by the Court. Writing in 1941, the same year he himself donned Justice's robes, Robert H. Jackson labeled Justice Butler's revealing remark a declaration of "the freedom of the sweat shop":

> This, of course, meant that the weak must bear the consequences of their weakness, and the strong may drive the best bargain that their strength and labor's necessities make possible. Labor relations were to be governed by the law of the jungle, and the state might not protect even women and children from exploitation.

The Court had outreached itself, just as it had in formulating the *Dred Scott* decision nearly eighty years before in the only comparable national showdown. What made his setbacks by the Court especially galling to Roosevelt was the narrowness of the majority's margin. The swing of just one vote, or two to be safe, was all he had needed to preserve the New Deal. But none of the Justices had died or retired during Roosevelt's first term, though six of them were over seventy. They were indeed "the Nine Old Men," as they had been lampooned and decried by the Court's critics for hamstringing the nation's economic recovery. In view of the severity of the ideological split within the Court, any Justice who now departed from the new marble palace on Capitol Hill seemed unlikely to go any way other than feet first.

Roosevelt took his plight to the people in the presidential election of 1936. They gave him 61 percent of the popular vote and 523 electoral votes to 8 for Alfred M. Landon. The Senate lineup was 76 Democrats to 16 Republicans, and there were 331 Democrats against 89 Republicans in the House. It was the most lopsided political triumph in the history of the United States. The people had given the President his own marble palace.

Shortly after his second inauguration, Roosevelt aimed his great counter-blow at the Court. Called a judiciary-reorganization bill, the therapeutic measure provided that when any federal judge reached the age of seventy after serving for ten years and did not retire within six months, the President would be empowered to name an additional judge to the same court, though at no time might the Supreme Court number more than fifteen members. His enemies—and even many of his admirers who felt he was tinkering with something too basic in the machinery of federalism—tagged the plan "court-packing" and a fierce national row erupted over who was the more overweening in the exercise of power, the Court or the President. There is no telling what even that Congress, top-heavy with New Dealers, would have done with the President's bill to curb the Court, but its very framing served the purpose Roosevelt intended.

Less than two months after the bill was introduced, the Court upheld a minimum-wage law of the state of Washington that was substantially the same as the New York law the Justices had overturned the previous year. Justice Roberts had abandoned the conservative camp, and Hughes wrote the five-to-four opinion. Such minimum-wage laws, as well as measures against the sweat shop and child labor, were at last recognized as necessary, humane, and justifiable under the police powers of the states. In short order, the Court upheld the revised railroad-workers' retirement law and the patched-up bill to help farmers hold on to their mortgaged lands—both measures that the Court had earlier invalidated—and then approved the National Labor Relations Act, state laws banning injunctions against picketing, state and federal social-security laws, the Fair Labor Standards Act, and a good many other pieces of public-welfare legislation. The era of judicial nullification had ended. Thirty-seven years into it, the Supreme Court of the United States decided by a narrow vote that the twentieth century was constitutional.

Though it lacked the court-packing provision Roosevelt had sought before Justice Roberts switched judicial gear, a bill to reform the federal courts was passed by Congress in 1937 and helped speed the rejuvenation of the Supreme Court. The act provided that retiring Justices would continue to receive full salary and might be called on to sit in the circuit courts when those calendars grew crowded. Willis Van Devanter, then seventy-eight years old, was the first to take advantage of the new arrangement. After twenty-six dogmatic years, the conservative from Wyoming left the Court. In his place, Roosevelt named Hugo Black, a liberal from Alabama whose record suggested he thought people mattered even more than money.

The disclosure by the Northern press that Black had been a member of the Ku Klux Klan for two years before running for the Senate could not have brought comfort to Negroes across the country who did not know much about the rest of the new Justice's career. A little research might have suggested what time was to prove: the black man had never had a better friend on the Supreme Court than this lean, courtly son of the Deep South. The offspring of a small-town shopkeeper, he began to practice law in the industrial metropolis of Birmingham, and from the start showed concern for the abused rights of blacks. One of his first clients was a Negro ex-convict who, in the custom of the day, was leased out to work while serving time but was held for fifteen days beyond his sentence period without pay—as a slave, that is. Black sued for damages and, remarkably enough, won a judgment of $137.50. As a police-court judge, he did not treat Negro defendants more harshly than whites—a trait noted in the local press, which did not pillory him for it. His obvious competence led to his appointment as county prosecutor, and in that role he exposed the torture chamber that police were operating in the Birmingham suburb of Bessemer; many of the victims of the police brutality were black, including one seventy-year-old who had been strapped to a door and beaten to the brink of death. In time, Black developed into perhaps the foremost trial lawyer in Alabama, with a private practice that stressed personal-injury claims and included labor-union business. As he could honestly say when running for the Senate in 1926, "I am not now, and never have been, a railroad, power company, or corporation lawyer."

His first term in the Senate was not a spectacular one. Its highlight was his spirited protest against customs controls over the import of allegedly obscene or subversive publications—a position that foreshadowed his nearly religious defense of First Amendment rights while he was a Justice. When the New Deal came to power, he was among its most devoted supporters in Congress. He was a principal architect of the Fair Labor Standards Act, setting minimum wages and maximum hours and outlawing child labor, and his Senate investigations disclosed fraud and corruption in airline and shipping companies receiving federal subsidies for carrying the mail. He won acclaim as a reformer by uncovering the brass-knuckled practices of public-utility holding companies in their efforts to prevent the federal government from dissolving them, and by showing how big money in general lobbied in a variety of guises to gain its ends. Hugo Black had won his spurs as an authentic defender of the underdog. He was fifty-one years old when he was named to the Supreme Court. He would serve there for thirty-four years and one month.

Only a few months after Black took his seat for the first time, seventy-six-year-old George Sutherland of Utah stepped down after sixteen years on the Court. Half of the mastodons were gone now. In Sutherland's place, Roosevelt named his long-suffering Solicitor General, Stanley Forman Reed of Kentucky, who had argued and lost the government's side when the Court skewered the NRA and AAA among other New Deal agencies. A man of kindly disposition, Reed had come up East from the rich tobacco country around Maysville, just south of the Ohio River in eastern Kentucky, and gone to Yale for his bachelor's degree, Virginia and Columbia for his law degree, and the Sorbonne to combine a honeymoon and graduate study. Such exposure to cosmopolitanism did not sour him on small-town Kentucky life. Back home, he became a highly successful lawyer whose clients included the Chesapeake & Ohio Railroad and a large tobacco-growers' cooperative. As a progressive state legislator, he introduced child-labor and workmen's-compensation bills in the Assembly. A moderate Democrat in politics, a conventional legal thinker of informed but hardly flaming social views, and a civilized gentleman by any standard of the day, he was summoned to Washington by Herbert Hoover in 1929 and named general counsel to the Federal Farm Board. As the Depression deepened, he was chosen chief counsel to the Reconstruction Finance Corporation (RFC), the Old Deal's chief weapon to combat the economic nosedive by means of loans to banks, farmers, and other businessmen. His solid performance as a government lawyer won him holdover status under Roosevelt and then elevation to the Solicitor General's job at Justice in 1935 and leadership of the New Deal's defense of its recovery programs against the bloodletting of the Court. By the time he took his own seat on the Court, Reed had become a confirmed believer in government power when wielded discerningly in the public interest.

Over the summer of 1938, Justice Benjamin Cardozo died. Cardozo, like Brandeis, was a Jew, and Roosevelt hesitated at naming the man he had settled on to succeed Cardozo—Professor Felix Frankfurter of Harvard, one of the most intimate and reliable of the President's back-door braintrusters.

He had helped draft some of the New Deal's most complex legislation and counseled Roosevelt on key speeches, personnel, and other vital matters, but the President wished to wait until Brandeis had indicated his readiness to retire. Two Jews on the Roosevelt Court were evidently one too many. Brandeis, though, was not eager to be shoved aside. He would not indicate his retirement plans until the beginning of 1939, and so as the Supreme Court convened on November 9, 1938, to hear *Missouri ex rel. Gaines v. Canada*, the most important civil-rights case since *Grovey v. Townsend* three years earlier, there were only eight sitting Justices—the moderate-liberal bloc of Hughes, Stone, Brandeis, Black, and Reed; the moderate-conservative, Roberts; and the two surviving arch-conservatives, McReynolds and Butler. All but the two newcomers had joined in the *Grovey* decision, so disastrous to the Negro's cause in its approval of the Texas white-primary scheme. Would the new libertarian mood of the Court envelop civil-rights cases as well as economic matters? *Gaines* would be the first test.

Charles Houston was not asking for the moon. Arguing before the Court, he did not challenge the holy writ of *Plessy v. Ferguson* and the legitimacy of separate-but-equal schools. But he insisted that the Court enforce the principle. If Missouri offered its white citizens a law school, then it had to offer its black citizens a law school every bit as good. That was what separate-but-equal meant. Anything short of that was pantomime justice. He had the Maryland courts' disposition of *Murray* to back him. And no decision of the Supreme Court conflicted with Houston's view. It seemed an airtight case. But then so had the black plaintiff's in *Grovey*. Houston had learned to take nothing for granted.

A month after the case was heard, Chief Justice Hughes read the six-to-two opinion of the Court. It went along with Houston's reading of the *Plessy* doctrine. Missouri's efforts to establish a university for Negroes on the same basis as the ones for whites was certainly "commendable," but the fact remained that

> instruction in law for negroes is not now afforded by the state, either at Lincoln University or elsewhere within the state, and that the state excludes negroes from the advantages of the law school it has established at the University of Missouri.

The Court understood that law schools in surrounding states might be every bit as good as the one in Missouri, which, it was further granted, might offer no special advantage to anyone who planned to practice law in Missouri. But all that was beside the point.

> The basic consideration is not as to what sort of opportunities other states provide, or whether they are as good as those in Missouri, but as to what opportunities Missouri itself furnishes to white students and denies to Negroes solely upon the ground of color. The admissibility of laws separating the races in the enjoyment of privileges afforded by the State rests wholly upon the equality of the privileges which the laws give to the separated groups within the State. . . . By the operation of the laws of Missouri a privilege has been created for white law students which is denied to Negroes by reason of their race. The white resident is afforded legal education within the State; the Negro resident having

the same qualifications is refused it there and must go outside of the State to obtain it.

Nor did it matter that there was slight demand by Negroes for legal education, for the petitioner's right was "a personal one. It was as an individual that he was entitled to the equal protection of the laws, and the State was bound to furnish him within its borders facilities for legal education" equal to those offered whites regardless of whether any other Negro sought the same opportunity. In the future law school that might or might not be opened by Lincoln University, the Court saw no satisfactory remedy; it said that "we cannot regard the discrimination as excused by what is called its temporary character." Lloyd Gaines was entitled to admission to the University of Missouri's school of law.

Justice McReynolds could not stomach this alarming development. In a dissent concurred in by his antediluvian colleague, Justice Butler, McReynolds remarked:

> For a long time Missouri had acted on the view that the best interest of her people demands separation of whites and Negroes in schools. Under the opinion just announced, I presume she may abandon her law school and thereby disadvantage her white citizens without improving petitioner's opportunities for legal instruction; or she may break down the settled practice concerning separate schools and thereby, as indicated by experience, damnify both races. . . .

*Gaines* was an enormous milestone. If Missouri had either to build a separate law school for colored students or desegregate the white one, did not the same principle apply to the colored high-school students of, say, Baltimore County, Maryland, who were deprived of equal facilities within the county? Shouldn't it apply to colored students in any county in America that failed to provide a high school for them? Could not the case serve as the basis for suits against any jurisdiction that failed to provide equal public-school facilities for Negroes anywhere along the educational ladder? And why would the principle be limited to physical facilities? Why wouldn't the separate-but-equal rule now reinforced by *Gaines* apply to the salaries of teachers and the length of the school term and the availability of bus transportation, all of which presently worked to the disadvantage of Negroes? And why should the principle be restricted to the field of education? Should it not apply as well to parks and libraries and hospitals? If blacks could be kept out of such facilities by Jim Crow, then were they not entitled to ones of their own?

# 10

# One of the Gang

Thurgood Marshall was just thirty years old when they gave him the job that made him, by definition, the most important Negro lawyer in the United States. He did not think of himself that way—at least not out loud—but the fact was that no other attorney had behind him financial resources, though skimpy, and organizational weight, though more flab than muscle in most locales, to devote full time to the pursuit of black America's civil and human rights.

His real apprenticeship in the field was spent not in courtrooms at Charlie Houston's elbow but in ranging his native state of Maryland in his old Ford trying to convince school officials that it was not justice to pay white janitors $960 a year and black elementary-school teachers $621 a year. Throughout the South, black teachers earned about half of what white ones did, and while the pay discrimination was comparable in other professional and job categories, teachers were of special importance because there were so many of them, because they were generally leaders in their community, and because they were paid by the government, which in theory was not supposed to discriminate against anyone on account of race. Between 1935 and 1938, Thurgood Marshall was the NAACP's fast-moving ambassador to nearly every one of Maryland's twenty-three counties as he urged colored teachers to organize and demand parity of pay.

Maryland was relatively more secure than the rest of the South because its black teachers were given job tenure after several years of satisfactory performance, but still Marshall's mission did not earn him warm welcomes in most counties, and only when the legal papers were filed did the school boards take his presence seriously. Some, such as Montgomery County, Washington's northern suburbia, yielded readily to Marshall's prodding, but most resisted and tried to intimidate black plaintiffs.

By the time he succeeded to Houston's job in the NAACP's New York headquarters in mid-1938, Marshall had won equal-pay agreements from nine Maryland county school boards. It was hand-to-hand combat, a war he had fought personally and now had to turn from for other tasks. To pursue the fight county by county, in and out of local courts, might have taken all his time for five more years. Instead, he made his first major break with the legal strategy favored by Houston: he went into federal court to get a ruling that would have statewide applicability. He sued the state board of education in the name of black principal Walter Mills from Anne Arundel County, on the ground that state funds were being used to supplement county education outlays and thereby to perpetuate the grossly unequal pay scales.

The United States District Court in Maryland held in March 1939 that the Anne Arundel County principal's suit against the state was improper since state school officials did not set the salary schedules. The proper course, said the court, would have been to sue a given county school board. For trying to kill too many birds with a single stone, Marshall was back where he had started. But still, if he could get a federal-court ruling even in a single county that unequal salaries violated the Constitution, he would have an invaluable precedent in trying to get the rest of the counties of the state to go along; if he lost in the federal District Court, he could appeal it all the way in light of the *Gaines* opinion. Marshall took the Anne Arundel case back to the District Court, naming the county school board as defendant. In November 1939, Judge W. Calvin Chesnut gave the NAACP drive the wedge it needed. The evidence of discrimination was overwhelming, said the judge. Not one of the 91 Negro teachers in Anne Arundel received as much pay as any of the 243 white teachers with similar qualifications and experience. Such discrimination, Chesnut said, "violated the supreme law of the land." The county school board chose not to appeal, and the governor prepared to ask the legislature to outlaw racial pay differentials for teachers throughout the state. The Maryland phase of the operation would now be mostly mopping up by local lawyers. Marshall himself moved his bridgehead across the Potomac, where the fighting was more hazardous. Virginia gave its black teachers no tenure, and so the enlistment of plaintiffs would be more difficult, too.

Prudence dictated bringing the Virginia cases in the relatively more progressive cities rather than in rural areas, and so the first suit was brought against the school board in the state's biggest city, Norfolk. Marshall drove down from New York—nearly 500 miles—several times to work out the details in alien terrain. His expense vouchers for those sorties verify just how frugal the NAACP field operation was; he would spend less than a dollar a meal on average and never more than two dollars for a room. It was no joyride. And no sooner was the Norfolk case mounted than the school board there refused to renew the plaintiff's teaching contract. "I am now firmly convinced," Marshall wrote Bill Hastie, who had left his Virgin Islands judgeship to become dean of Howard Law School, "that we have no case and that it will be necessary to file a new one."

To prevent the continual firing of any teachers who would agree to serve as plaintiffs, Marshall filed the new case jointly in the names of the Norfolk Teachers' Association and Melvin O. Alston, a teacher for five years at the city's Booker T. Washington High School. Alston's salary was $921; white teachers in his category received $1,200. The case was brought in the United States District Court for Virginia under the same approach as the Anne Arundel suit in Maryland. But the federal court in Virginia, which was not obliged to conform its ruling to that of the parallel court in Maryland, handed Marshall a setback. Alston and his fellow black teachers had no right to bring such an action, said the court, because they had knowingly and willingly accepted contracts with the Norfolk school board which they now sought to challenge as invalid. It was a demonic decision. What it really said was that the black teachers could not obtain relief in the courts because once they signed contracts, they could not then challenge them—and if they failed to sign contracts, then of course they had no legal standing as teachers and still could not sue. Heads we win, tails you lose, the white authorities had ruled in *Alston.*

Meanwhile in other Virginia cities where cases were being organized, school officials were proving no less resistant, and in some counties black groups were informally advised that if their teachers persisted in the equal-pay fight, badly needed new buildings or repairs in old ones would not materialize. It was a handy way to splinter the colored community and reduce its resolve. Marshall saw which way the wind was blowing and knew he needed a victory badly. He took the *Alston* case to the United States Court of Appeals for the Fourth Circuit. It was the highest court before which he had ever argued. Presiding over it was the man the NAACP had ten years earlier prevented from taking a seat on the Supreme Court of the United States—Judge John J. Parker.

If there remained any hard feelings in the man, Marshall could not detect them. After the arguments in the federal courthouse in Richmond, Parker and his two judicial colleagues on the case came down from the bench and shook hands with the attorneys as was their wont after every case they heard. Because few, if any, black lawyers had come before the Fourth Circuit Court of Appeals and witnessed the judicial ritual, word quickly spread in the black world that Marshall had been accorded a unique tribute by the judges who had come off the bench especially to commend the young Negro attorney for his performance. The story no doubt gained credence from Parker's decision in June 1940. The District Court's ruling against Alston and the black teachers of Norfolk was reversed. Statutory discrimination on account of race had been ruled unconstitutional by the Supreme Court as long ago as 1879 in *Strauder v. West Virginia,* Parker wrote, and Judge Chesnut's ruling in the Anne Arundel suit was proper. More than that, the Norfolk teachers were well within their legal rights to band together and take concerted action as co-plaintiffs—a sharp rebuff to the District Court, which had denied the group's claim to stand as legitimate plaintiffs. It would make future cases of this type much easier to bring.

Marshall's victory in *Alston* was topped off on November 4, 1940, when the Supreme Court declined to take the case on appeal by the Norfolk school board. For all practical purposes, *Alston* was the law of the land. Marshall had moved the front lines well inland from the beachhead that he had helped Houston win in *Murray* and *Gaines.* Litigation over equal pay would continue in other Virginia cities for five years as white resisters stalled compliance with the Norfolk ruling as long as possible, and in Newport News the NAACP finally had to obtain a contempt-of-court ruling against the defiant school board. But *Alston* stood as a beacon to the black teachers of the South as, one by one, white school boards recognized their obligation. In Virginia, the fight would escalate from a demand by blacks for equal pay for their teachers to insistence upon equal school facilities and bus transportation for their children. It was a glacially slow process, but without doubt there was movement discernible now.

The New Deal of Franklin Roosevelt had brought relief to the most extreme forms of pain suffered by the Negro as the Thirties drew to a close. The gains were almost all at the subsistence level, and they were achieved not because the Roosevelt administration had evidenced any special devotion to racial equality but because it became the first government of the United States to sponsor massive assistance programs for those on the underside of society. And in its drive to prevent the nation's poor from being submerged by despair, the New Deal did not leave out the neediest Americans of all, its scorned and segregated colored people.

They shared in the alphabet-soup relief agencies' bounty, but always as second-class citizens. They participated in the AAA's farm-subsidy allotments and in the voting to establish regional production quotas, but many landlords took advantage of their illiterate black sharecroppers and withheld federal payments. Under the NRA industrial codes, which generally allowed blacks to be paid less than whites for the same work, few colored workers complained for fear of being fired, but when the minimum wage rose to twenty-five cents an hour toward the end of the decade, many blacks lost their advantage as cheap labor and were replaced by whites at equal or higher wages. Civil Service Commission data disclosed that blacks held about 10 percent of all federal government jobs across the country by 1938—just about their fair proportion—but almost all of them were mail carriers, janitors, or in other unskilled occupations and almost none was in the white-collar clerical area that made up most of the Civil Service roster.

By 1939, Thurgood Marshall was advising Walter White, "From the complaints we have received it appears . . . that a definite policy has been established of replacing Negroes in Civil Service with whites" whenever black jobholders resigned or retired. And advancement was sharply restricted. In the Customs Service in New York, Marshall reported, not a single Negro had been promoted in five years. Black youngsters had been liberally enrolled in the job-training and student-work programs of the National Youth Administration—an openness encouraged, no doubt, by the access of its Negro division head, Mary McLeod Bethune, to the White House. And 200,000 Negro boys, many refugees from city ghettos, had joined the Civilian Conservation Corps during its nine-year life as a Jim Crow fresh-air fund. In WPA projects as well, many blacks found work. More than one-quarter of all WPA hands in the South were colored by 1940, but there were only eleven black supervisors in fourteen Southern states compared to 10,333 white supervisors. Blacks benefited considerably, too, from the Public Works Administration as it put up colored schools and hospitals in the South, but in nothing approaching the Negro's proportionate share. The Federal Housing Administration and related agencies helped many blacks find better shelter, though generally along segregated lines and often in areas where Jim Crow had not been practiced before. In the older branches of government, official racism still held sway. The Navy continued to accept black enlistees only as mess men, and the Secretary of War advised the NAACP at the end of 1938, "Since no colored units of the air corps are provided for in the Army of the United States, it is impossible for the War Department to accept colored applicants at air corps schools."

Segregation was more deeply entrenched than ever. Black disenfranchisement continued nearly universal in the Deep South. Ralph Bunche's studies concluded that no more than 2.5 percent of the Negroes of voting age in South Carolina, Georgia, Alabama, Florida, Mississippi, Louisiana, Arkansas, and Texas cast ballots in the presidential election of 1940, and the figures in the other Southern states were not substantially better. Without the vote, colored citizens were unable to command their fair share of public services, and so Negro neighborhoods throughout the South lacked adequate streets and street lighting, sewage and garbage disposal, and health, education, and recreation facilities. More than 70 percent of Southern black men in non-farm jobs were doing unskilled work—the corresponding figure for whites was 20 percent—but none of the federal programs was directed at upgrading the skills of this outsized pool of black brawn. On the Southern farms, the New Deal had saved many colored families from destitution, but the money pumped into the Black Belt mostly fertilized the bank accounts of landholders. It is scarcely surprising that with the revival of industrial output in the North, the exodus from the South would resume.

By 1940, one out of every four American blacks was living in the North or West. But Eden was nowhere to be found. Black unemployment nationwide that year was at 22 percent and holding, while the white rate of 13 percent was going down. Fifteen percent of the white males in the country did not live beyond their forty-fifth birthday; for Negroes, the figure was 36 percent. And crime among blacks, whose rights as citizens and aspirations as human beings were regularly ignored and often brutally destroyed, grew worse. By 1940, Negroes committed proportionally six times as many homicides, four times as many robberies, and seven times as many assaults as whites. White cruelty and disparagement had bred black lawlessness. Segregation of Negroes as a lower order of being was an accomplished fact, sanctioned by the nation's highest court.

As America edged toward war again, though, signs were growing that Franklin Roosevelt viewed the Negro's dilemma with far more compassion than any President before him had. He was still not willing to abandon his alliance with Southern Congressmen who stood as an unbreachable barrier to meaningful federal action against white supremacy, but for the first time the President's office was truly open to black leaders, and nearly every department had its Negro advisor or section head. There were occasional symbolic acts that suggested human caring in high places, such as the decision to allow the concert by black contralto Marian Anderson, originally scheduled for Constitution Hall in Washington and then canceled by the Daughters of the American Revolution who owned the building, to be held on Easter Sunday of 1939 on the steps of the Lincoln Memorial under the auspices of the Department of the Interior. At the Justice Department,

Attorney General Frank Murphy set up the first Civil Rights Section. Under increasing pressure for its discriminatory policies, the War Department agreed to open its ranks to blacks in proportion to their share of the population, Reserve Officers Training Corps units were installed at four black colleges, and William Hastie was named as civilian aide to the department in 1940. And as the nation's defense industries began to tool up, the President yielded to demands by black leaders, of whom A. Philip Randolph was foremost, that Negro workers be hired by plants holding government contracts. Roosevelt's executive proclamation in June of 1941 against discrimination in hiring practices was followed up by the establishment of the Fair Employment Practices Committee, a toothless wonder that nevertheless served to embarrass many a lily-white employer into taking colored workers for fear of being labeled bigoted in a time of national emergency.

Most fateful by far of Franklin Roosevelt's acts in their effect on the colored people of the country were his appointments to the Supreme Court. With Black and Reed, ideological New Dealers, the President had assured himself of a progressive majority, or at least one unlikely to renew the debacle of the mid-Thirties. His next batch of appointments changed the Court's political outlook from moderate-progressive to progressive-liberal.

Felix Frankfurter took Cardozo's seat in the early weeks of 1939. Shortly after, Brandeis retired and in his place the President picked the youngest man to be named to the Court in 128 years—William Orville Douglas, the forty-year-old chairman of the Securities and Exchange Commission. Viewed by Wall Street as anti-business when he came to the SEC in 1935 from Yale, where he had been a prominent professor in the law school and precocious authority on corporate finance, Douglas showed himself to be a tough but fair customer in pushing for full disclosure of financial data of publicly traded companies and other steps to prevent foul play in the money market. He would rapidly distinguish himself as perhaps the most steadfast defender of civil rights and civil liberties ever to sit on the Court. If he had any rivals for that distinction, they were Hugo Black, who preceded him by two years, and Frank Murphy, a passionate liberal, who replaced Pierce Butler in 1940. In his previous positions as mayor of Detroit, governor of Michigan, governor general of the Philippines, and Attorney General of the United States, Murphy had evidenced exemplary concern for the rights of minority groups. His coming left only the obsidian-hearted McReynolds on the far right of the Court, and he would be gone in another year.

The Roosevelt Court began to make its weight felt in civil-rights cases almost at once, though there were no new major doctrinal pronouncements.

Justice Black spoke for a unanimous Court in the 1939 case of *Pierre v. Louisiana*, the latest in the lengthening list of decisions throwing out convictions by all-white juries in communities where blacks had been systematically excluded from serving. The next year, Black again spoke for the Court in the criminal-justice area. Four Negroes accused of murdering a white fish peddler in Pompano, Florida, pleaded guilty after being detained for five days without access to counsel or friends. Since no evidence of physical compulsion in the confessions was presented, Florida juries voted a conviction at a trial and retrial and the Florida Supreme Court upheld the verdict. In *Chambers v. Florida*, brought to the United States Supreme Court by the NAACP, Thurgood Marshall's brief and Leon Ransom's argument before the Justices asserted that such "sunrise confessions," extracted under conditions of extreme fatigue and mental duress, were no more voluntary than if they had been won at gunpoint. Agreeing, Justice Black inserted in his majority opinion an aside that caught the new humanitarian fervor of the liberal members. The defendants in most such cases of abuse by the state, he wrote, seemed invariably to be Southern blacks because "they who have suffered most from secret and dictatorial proceedings have almost always been the poor, the ignorant, the numerically weak, the friendless and the powerless."

In 1939, Justice Frankfurter wrote the majority opinion in *Lane v. Wilson*, the long-delayed sequel to the 1915 decision in *Guinn v. United States* outlawing Oklahoma's notorious "grandfather clause." The unrepentant Oklahoma legislature had sought to blunt the effect of the Court's ruling by passing a new law that said anyone who failed to register during a two-week period in the spring of 1916 would be perpetually barred from voting, except those who had been eligible to vote in 1914—that is, under the discredited "grandfather clause" law. It was a clumsy, outrageous piece of legislation that had nevertheless stood untested before the Court until James Nabrit, by then moved from his Texas law practice and installed as a mainstay at Howard Law School, brought the case under the NAACP flag. Speaking for a six-to-two majority (McReynolds and Butler dissenting), Frankfurter wrote that "the opportunity thus given Negro voters to free themselves from the effects of discrimination to which they should never have been subjected was too cabined and confined." Here was a clear violation of the Fifteenth Amendment, which, he remarked acidly, "nullifies sophisticated as well as simpleminded modes of discrimination."

Then in 1941 a unanimous Court carried the principle established in *Gaines* over into the area of interstate transportation. On a train headed south from Chicago, black Congressman Adrian Mitchell of Illinois had been ordered to surrender his place in a well-equipped car as it crossed into Arkansas and to move into a smoker without toilets, running water, or other comforts that the first car offered. In *Mitchell v. United States*, the Jim Crow doctrine in public transportation as framed in *Plessy* was challenged directly, but the Court, through Chief Justice Hughes, limited its position to what it had found in *Gaines*: where separate facilities are authorized by law, they must be equal; otherwise they are discriminatory and unlawful. What made *Mitchell* noteworthy, aside from the unanimity of the Court, was the fact that though the United States government was the nominal defendant—Mitchell had first taken his complaint to the Interstate Commerce Commission, which rejected it—Attorney General Murphy appeared in the case as a friend of the Court on the side of the black Congressman. And in a matter of months Murphy himself would be on the Court.

"I want you to know that the Memphis Branch is 100% for you," read the thank-you letter to Thurgood Marshall after one of his swift passages through the South in 1939 with stopoffs at any NAACP group within shouting distance, "and we welcome your return anytime it may be convenient for you to do so at our expense."

He was building a constituency across the country. It had begun as early as 1935 when he served as secretary of the National Lawyers Guild, the colored counterpart of the then Jim Crow American Bar Association. He thrived on movement and good company and laughter without ever losing sight of his main mission. "Everybody loved Thurgood," says a veteran in the NAACP national office. "Where Houston was aloof, Marshall had the common touch. He had great energy and warmth and was clearly an emerging leadership figure—someone who might one day challenge Walter White for supremacy in the organization."

The idea occurred also to Walter White, who in 1939 promoted Marshall right out of the parent organization and into a tiny enclave all his own. Set up to take advantage of new laws granting tax-exempt status to non-profit organizations that did not have a lobbying function as their principal purpose, the offshoot was formally called the NAACP Legal Defense and Educational Fund, Inc. That was, everyone agreed, rather a mouthful. For short, it was called the Legal Defense Fund. For shorter, it became "the Inc. Fund." In time, it would be just "the Fund."

At the start, the Fund was Marshall and a secretary. He was still very much under Walter White's sway and remained in the same suite of offices. At just over thirty, he lacked the seasoning and scholarship that Houston had, and he knew it. He gladly leaned on his ex-professors—especially the solid, easy-going Leon Ransom and the more astringent and brilliant Bill Hastie, who with Jim Nabrit were the heart of the Howard law faculty now. From this nucleus, he would build over the next fifteen years a network of advisors, most of them from Harvard, Yale, and Columbia law schools, who would supplement the basic but ever shifting Howard group and provide the Legal Defense Fund with a sizable reservoir of readily tapped brain power. It was not the sort of approach that Houston, certain of his legal ground, would or did entertain. Marshall, thrown into the breach as a commander while still little more than a fledgling, did not try to play the hero. He did not rush to take the toughest cases or argue before the highest courts. He had little pride of authorship and knew his limits as a writer of legal briefs. "I never hesitated to pick other people's brains—brains I didn't have," he reflects. "After a while, you'd get to know who was best at what kind of thing."

The trick was in getting people to want to give of themselves. It was a skill of enormous use not only within the Fund office in thrashing out a legal strategy but out on the chicken-and-greens circuit where the drive for black equality began to gather momentum. And it was out there that Marshall emerged as more politician than constitutional lawyer and communicated in his special fashion. "Before he came along," observes Charles Thompson, editor of the *Journal of Negro Education*, "the principal black leaders—men like Du Bois and James Weldon Johnson and Charles Houston—didn't talk the language of the people. They were upper-class and upper-middle-class Negroes. Thurgood Marshall was *of* the people. He knew how to get through to them. Out in Texas or Oklahoma or down the street here in Washington at the Baptist church, he would make these rousing speeches that would have 'em all jumping out of their seats. He'd explain what he was up to with his law cases in language they could all understand. 'We ain't gettin' what we should,' was what it came down to, and he made them see that. That was his secret. He knew how to deal with commoners and kings with equal effectiveness."

"Thurgood was always one of the gang," adds NAACP publicist Henry Lee Moon, who has known him for more than thirty years. "He never put barriers between himself and the less exalted. And he could get up and pitch when he wanted to. Charlie Houston wasn't like that—he was quite deliberate when he spoke."

For more than a dozen years starting in 1939, Thurgood Marshall got up and pitched all over America. He pitched mostly to black and less frequently to interracial audiences, and always in homey, hopeful, and bantering but earnest phrases—his "jes'-folks" style, as one not overly friendly ex-associate calls it. "The reason white folks don't wanna open up the schoolhouse door," he would say by way of mocking the most common excuse for segregation, "is they say that'll lead straight to the bedroom door. Well, now, that other door's been open a mighty long time." Of the white flight to suburbia, he would say, "They can run—but they can't hide." Speaking to law students to demystify the section of the Constitution to which he had devoted the best part of his professional life, he would say, "The Fourteenth Amendment was no more or less than a codification of the Judeo-Christian ethic."

Like any public speaker in demand, he survived by building each talk around a few basic stories with an unmistakable moral. Because he was on the road so much, he had no trouble replenishing his supply of handy homilies that, properly delivered, had a rousing effect. In the early Fifties, he was fond of invoking a Columbia, South Carolina, minister while proposing to his listeners that "we need to feel in our own minds that we are the equal of anybody on the face of the globe. Anybody. The only way to do that is to feel in our own minds that we are not only as good as anybody but that we are better than the average one we pass as we walk down the street. As Reverend Adams says, he likes to think that when the Lord created him, He did not do it on a Saturday when He was tired out and did not have much with which to work. He said he preferred to think that the Lord made him early on Monday morning when He had the best materials to work with and all the energy He needed. . . ."

Only a man with remarkable *joie de vivre* could have stood the pace or invited it in the first place. "He loves to have a drink, to tell a story, to pat asses, to be hearty company," says a longtime associate. In a feature piece on him in his fifth year as the NAACP's top lawyer, Carl Murphy's admiring *Afro-American* described the thirty-five-year-old, six-feet-one-inch, 185-pounder whose accompanying publicity photograph showed a matinee-idol Marshall with wavy black hair, soulful eyes, and trim mustache. "Thurgood

Marshall is the amazing type of man," said the *Afro* in 1944, "who is liked by other men and probably adored by women. He carries himself with an inoffensive self-confidence, and seems to like the life he lives. He wears and looks especially well in tweed suits."

The more he was on the road, the more the legends grew. In time, even a friendly newsman would say of him in print that Marshall was known to polish off three cocktails before the main course came at lunch. Such stories displeased him, for he was neither boozer nor philanderer nor vaudevillian. A former Fund attorney who found Marshall "a skillful con artist in his way" acknowledged the efficacy of his methods: "People trusted him. They felt he related to them. And whites in power accepted him as well because he presented himself as a sort of transitional figure—enough of a joking, friendly Tom but still aggressively standing up in court and scoring his points. A militant, too serious black man would have gotten their backs up. If they gave him their respect by not fighting what he wanted quite as hard as they might have, he had to reciprocate by wearing something of a Tom's face. A number of black guys didn't like him for that. Maybe it was jealousy. But he was getting the job done."

The job was not so much winning his cases as getting a fair hearing on the record as the basis for subsequent appeal to higher and, he hoped, friendlier courts. More often than not, he would lose at the local level, but more often than not he would come away with half a loaf in places where the last black attorney to show his face in court had been tarred and feathered afterward. Hostile judges might have cut short his presentations and sustained every objection of local white lawyers opposing him, but few did. His low-key lawyering won him respect, and rarely was he treated as less than a gentleman in the courtroom, except by an occasional clerk or bailiff who might call him by his first name. Marshall would return the compliment. On more than one occasion, friendly white court officials would find a bottle of bourbon from him in their locker.

He handled every kind of case in every kind of place in the years when there were still too few black lawyers with enough talent and courage to stand up to racism and call it what it was. He would fight for equal teachers' salaries in angry Little Rock or defend three Negroes charged with murder in a Klan-infested county in Florida or argue against South Carolina's truculent denial to blacks of court-ordered voting rights, and he would not weigh the personal risks. "He was a very courageous figure," says NAACP labor affairs director Herbert Hill, not a sentimental man. "He would travel to the courthouses of the South, and folks would come for miles, some of them on muleback or horseback, to see 'the nigger lawyer' who stood up in white men's courtrooms."

The risks were real enough, though, and they were almost always present because he was almost always showing up in trouble spots. Characteristically, he would play down the peril of his work, no doubt to spare his wife and associates concern but also to keep his own nerve cool. A favored role he would assign himself in anecdotes of his travels was that of the shrewd but not overly valorous Negro swiftly calculating the odds against him in a confrontation with white bullies and deciding not to offer himself as cannon fodder. In one account of a Southern trip, he told how he had stopped off at a small Mississippi town and was contemplating an overnight stay: "I was out there on the train platform, trying to look small, when this cold-eyed man with a gun on his hip comes up. 'Nigguh,' he said, 'I thought you oughta know the sun ain't nevah set on a live nigguh in this town.' So I wrapped my constitutional rights in cellophane, tucked 'em in my hip pocket . . . and caught the next train out of there."

Usually, in fact, he stayed and fought. In 1938, soon after he took over Houston's New York office at the NAACP, Marshall journeyed to Texas to investigate an episode involving a sixty-five-year-old black president of a junior college who had been summoned for jury duty in Dallas, refused to have himself excused as court officials had firmly suggested, was dragged from the central jury room by two white men, and, despite his pleas to court guards and attendants for help, was thrown down the front steps of the courthouse. A small, slight man, he picked himself off the ground, squared his shoulders, marched back up the steps through a dozen threatening whites, and took his place again in the jury room. Local blacks were furious, and their anger fueled yet greater white hostility. Marshall strode into the middle of the scene, gauged the intensifying emotional climate, and called the office of Governor James Allred in Austin. A relative moderate on race issues, Allred was astonished at the brashness of the unknown young colored lawyer operating out of New York who had come all the way to Texas to tell them what justice was all about. He agreed to see Marshall promptly, and by the end of the interview he was disarmed. The Texas Rangers were ordered out to stand watch at the Dallas courthouse for further displays of unlawfulness, the FBI was summoned to investigate the earlier incident, and future intrusion against Negroes called for jury service, it was announced, would not be tolerated. No one could remember the last time a Southern governor had demonstrated quite as much enthusiasm for enforcement of the law.

Marshall did not have to travel two-thirds of the way across the country to find danger. Ted Poston, the Negro newspaperman, recalled a hair-raising evening he spent with the lawyer in a Long Island suburb twenty-five miles from Times Square. As a reporter on the *Amsterdam News*, Poston had come to know Marshall socially; later he moved to the New York *Post*, where he was the only black newsman in town, but at first he was paid as a space reporter—only for what actually ran in the paper. Sensing a story, Marshall called Poston "and invited me to go out to the Island with him to check into reports that police were terrorizing blacks in the Freeport area, a center of KKK activity. What we heard was that some of the police were Klan members or the sons of members. The idea of a lawyer being that interested and involving himself in a case to that degree fascinated me, so I went with him and saw what a really courageous guy he was. We started off carefully interviewing victims of this police brutalization—Thurgood's idea was to gather as many affidavits as possible so he could get a restraining order to close down the Klan activities in the area. Things went fine for a while, but then we got to one guy's home who told us he'd just had a call from the guy we'd seen ahead of him who said the cops had come looking for us and were headed after us right then. So we had to keep dodging them all night like that—even passed 'em a few times going in the opposite direction. I wanted to get out of there fast, but all Thurgood did was make more and more outlandish jokes about what they'd do to us if they ever caught up with us. Finally, we had enough statements, so we stashed 'em in a spare tire and drove out of there without honoring the speed laws. I was damned scared and damned tired when I got home—and never did file a story on it." But Marshall presented his findings to the state attorney general, who brought heavy pressure on local officials to end the terror tactics.

His closest call probably came on a November night in 1946 while he was driving on a highway in Maury County in the middle of Tennessee, where he had just unofficially won the prize as least popular Negro in America from local police. Marshall had been summoned to defend twenty-five blacks charged with assault to commit murder. After a series of night raids by local police resulting in beatings and frame-up arrests in the colored neighborhood of the small city of Columbia, the blacks had organized a resistance movement. From hiding places in a row of one-story shops, they had repulsed a further raid with a fusillade that wounded four of the invading police. Not only did Marshall succeed in getting the trial switched to a town thirty miles away, but he also got twenty-three of the twenty-five defendants acquitted. At a new trial back in Columbia, one of the two remaining defendants had just been acquitted, and Marshall and two other lawyers for the defense were driving back after dark to Nashville, where they were staying, when three patrol cars sirened them to a halt. Out piled patrolmen, constables, and a deputy sheriff with raised guns and a search warrant. It was a dry county, and police later said they had been tipped off that Marshall and his associates were carrying liquor in the car. A search uncovered nothing, and Marshall was allowed to drive on. He was stopped a second time and his driver's license checked, and again he was let go. But on the third try they arrested him for drunk driving and sped off with him to Columbia. At one point, the patrol car carrying Marshall swung off onto a side road, but returned to the highway when the other lawyers following in Marshall's car remained in close pursuit.

In Columbia, Marshall was ordered out of the patrol car and told to cross the street unaccompanied to the magistrate's office. Marshall knew better. The toll of black men shot in the back while "escaping" custody was well imprinted on his mind. Escorted into the office of the magistrate, an aggressive teetotaler renowned for his skill at sniffing out even a trace of alcohol on a man's breath, Marshall breathed—"as hard as I could"—into the nostrils of the human drunkometer, who pronounced him clean and ordered him released. "After that," Marshall said, "I really needed a drink." Temperance prevailed, though, and a good thing, for while Marshall was under custody, his colleagues had returned to the colored section of town called Mink Slide and switched cars so they could head back up to Nashville without further harassment. As a decoy, their original car left Mink Slide in another direction. It was overtaken by police and its driver beaten, Marshall learned the next day. He wired United States Attorney General Tom Clark and requested a federal investigation of the entire incident. Then he returned to court in Columbia the following week and won acquittal for the last of the twenty-five defendants.

Some Tom.

Black Americans did not possess the rights for which they and their nation fought the Second World War, and they knew it. Yet in nearly every way, things went better with them than during the First World War. The draft was run far more equitably. The Army opened up every branch to colored soldiers, including the Air Corps, and accepted them at officer-candidate schools on a more or less integrated basis. The Navy welcomed 165,000 Negroes, made a few of them officers, and had special praise for the black construction battalions of the "Seabees" who kept U.S. forces hopscotching across the Pacific. Even the rednecked "leathernecks" relented and 17,000 broke the color line in the Marines for the first time. Black women joined the Army WACs and, after initial resistance, the Navy WAVEs. For the most part, black service units were led by black officers and monitored by black military police. And before the war was over, black and white platoons fought side by side in Germany.

But it was still Jim Crow who waved the flag of freedom. Though Negroes were serving widely in capacities other than menial, their units were still segregated, including the black WACs. Blacks were accepted at officer-candidate schools, but only a stiff directive by Secretary of the Army Henry Stimson got them graduated in numbers approaching their fair share of commissions. The Army Air Force flatly refused to accept blacks at flight-training and other officers' schools on an integrated basis—a defiance that led William Hastie to denounce the Air Force for "reactionary policies and discriminatory practices" and resign as civilian aide to Secretary Stimson. In authorizing integrated regiments near the end of the war, Army brass hedged its bet by limiting the mixture to all-black platoons fighting next to all-white ones instead of desegregating down to the foxhole level. At military posts and training centers, blacks were widely discriminated against, on and off base. Sadistic drill instructors and other non-commissioned whip-crackers were legion. Negro newspapers were often forbidden and seized as if subversive. Bus service was often denied colored troops on leave until whites had been accommodated. Post exchanges were segregated in many places, with shoddy merchandise palmed off on blacks, and recreational facilities were often separated. Efforts by Negroes to resist segregation triggered riots at a number of camps. Courts-martial were convened readily to handle proud resisters known as troublemakers or simply "bad niggers," and Walter White uncovered "innumerable instances where Negro soldiers were . . . sentenced to long terms for minor offenses while white soldiers who were clearly guilty of much graver crimes were either acquitted or meted out light punishment."

But civilian black protest had not been silenced in the name of mindless patriotism. Negro newspapers did not hesitate to suggest that Uncle Sam in a helmet still looked very much like Simon Legree. The Pittsburgh-based *Courier* perhaps best caught the irony of the black war effort in its "Double V" slogan—for victory at home as well as abroad. The Congress of Racial Equality (CORE) was born in 1943 and launched its career of direct, non-violent activism by staging anti-Jim Crow sit-ins in Chicago, Baltimore, and St. Louis. Among other targets of protest was the infuriating Red Cross practice of separating Negro from white contributions to blood banks for the aid of wounded servicemen—a division made all the more distasteful by the fact that the plasma-preserving process that made blood banks practical had been largely developed by a Negro, Dr. Charles Drew of Howard University.

It was on the labor front that the greatest strife, and the greatest progress, occurred. The Depression had been routed by the war boom, and manpower-starved industries welcomed colored workers where they had not been wanted or where there had been no jobs before. FEPC surveillance helped open up aircraft plants and shipyards with war contracts to thousands of Negroes, and more than 100,000 blacks were in the metal industries. With jobs plentiful, organized labor looked far more kindly on colored recruits, especially in the ranks and even higher councils of big industrial unions such as the United Auto Workers, the United Steelworkers, the National Maritime Union, and affiliates of the Congress of Industrial Organizations. Brotherhood was only tolerated, though, not rhapsodized, and racial tension rose in industrial centers where the influx of blacks was swiftest and community facilities were inadequate so that the races were colliding instead of mingling.

The most pressing case was Detroit, where raw racism crested in 1943. As blacks moved into a federally financed project at a time when decent housing was hard to find in the congested Motor City, whites attacked them and vandalized the property while police looked on with folded arms. A bit later, when three blacks were to be promoted at a Packard plant producing engines for bombers and PT boats, 25,000 whites staged a wildcat strike. Ku-Kluxers and other rabid racists had their soapboxes all over town and their sympathizers in every plant, and it was plain that big trouble was brewing. It came on a warm June night when short tempers and vicious rumors of violent acts sent mobs of whites into the streets, stoning Negro cars, yanking Negroes out of streetcars, and beating Negro pedestrians without provocation. It went on for two days as thirty-four were killed, twenty-five of them Negroes—and seventeen of them by policemen; three-quarters of the 600 injured were colored, as were 85 percent of the more than 1,800 arrested.

Thurgood Marshall joined Walter White in speeding to Detroit and trying to put a lid on the violence and then investigate the nature of equal protection of the laws, Detroit-style. Marshall was plainly shocked by the openness and massiveness of police brutality in a Northern city. Canvassing victims, piecing together accounts of atrocity, hurrying to trouble spots where the blood was still warm and welts rising, he concluded that the police had not merely stood aside as whites clawed at unarmed blacks but had joined the fray and even led it. NAACP efforts spurred no punishment or even official reprimands in Detroit, but an extensive report of the episode by White and Marshall was published in pamphlet form and added to the nationwide shock over the surfacing of so much subterranean hate on the home front.

Racism in labor became a consuming concern of the NAACP as the war lengthened, and Marshall went to court to fight it. The most unrelenting practitioners of bias were the independent craft unions and affiliates of the American Federation of Labor, whose long-standing antipathy to blacks has never died. A prominent example that Marshall challenged was the International Brotherhood of Boilermakers, Iron Shipbuilders and Helpers of America.

The Boilermakers had never admitted qualified colored workers to their ranks and at the outset of the war were disinclined to change their policy. But as shipyards were swamped with orders, the union had to bend or sacrifice its closed-shop contract with the companies. Negroes were admitted not to the regular locals but to all-black "auxiliaries" that had no business agents or grievance committees of their own, provided members with half the insurance benefits of the white locals, and were totally under the thumb of the international union's president, who could unilaterally and without appeal suspend any auxiliary member or officer. It was clear that once shipbuilding contracts declined, the black "auxiliaries" would be hit by the first layoffs and lose any semblance of job security.

When West Coast shipbuilders took on black workers who declined to accept second-class union membership, the Boilermakers flexed their muscles and demanded that the companies lay off the non-union help. The NAACP flashed the FEPC for help and, when the union proved resistant, went to court for a federal injunction against the union's discriminatory practices. The union stalled and in some places used subterfuge to keep blacks from equal membership. In the shipyards of Providence, Rhode Island, the union welcomed blacks in order to gain designation as the bargaining agent for all workers; Negroes paid the same initiation fees and dues and expected the same rights. But the Boilermakers' international moved to nullify equality by mailing "auxiliary" union cards to new colored members, pushing for local officers who would downgrade Negroes, and refusing to count the votes of black members in the Providence local elections. Marshall went to court in Rhode Island in January of 1944 and won an injunction against the international's ceaseless meddling and discrimination.

But it was a draining kind of battle that never seemed to end. Having won a court injunction against the union in Providence, an FEPC anti-bias directive against it for its activities on the West Coast, and an appeal to it from the White House for fair play, Marshall was unable to budge the union's basic policy. At their annual national convention in 1944, the Boilermakers voted unanimously to keep their locals all-white. It was not a total loss: Negro auxiliary lodges were granted a measure of self-rule and equal insurance benefits. And that, the union presumed, beat chopping cotton.

It was left to Charles Houston to gain the Negro's first major legal triumph over union racism. His opponent was the wealthiest, laziest, and most frankly bigoted batch of unions in the entire labor movement.

Having cast off from both Howard University and the NAACP after brilliant but relatively brief full-time careers at each, Charlie Houston became somewhat less visible in the civil-rights movement but hardly a hermit. He kept close ties both to Howard, where his cousin Bill Hastie ran the law school from 1939 to 1946, and to Walter White and Thurgood Marshall in New York. He stayed on the NAACP's legal-advisory committee and functioned as something of a senior statesman to the younger black lawyers who were coming on now, but gradually he became what he wanted—his own man, pursuing those civil-rights matters he wanted to, in the fashion he thought best, from his own law office in Washington.

Much of what he did was behind the scenes, such as his strategic part in convincing the Department of Interior to strike a blow for racial democracy by in effect sponsoring the Marian Anderson concert in 1939; earlier he had made an eloquent but fruitless plea to the District of Columbia school board to allow the concert at a white high school. He pursued or helped pursue a great many race cases dealing with, among other matters, segregation of military trainees, discrimination against black passengers by taxicab operators, Jim Crow arrangements on interstate carriers, and bias in labor, especially by railroad unions. For all that, he lacked the knack of self-promotion that came so naturally to a freer spirit like Thurgood Marshall. And he would not campaign for favor or honors. In time, he was offered a judgeship on the Municipal Court for the District of Columbia, a position for which he was warmly endorsed by his old law professor Justice Felix Frankfurter, responding to an inquiry about his capability by Attorney General Francis Biddle:

> Houston would make an admirable judge. He has the necessary professional training, a sense of justice seasoned with an understanding of human nature, a kindly yet firm disposition, and a strong devotion to the public zeal. To put him on the bench would be not a sentimental gesture to our colored fellow citizens, but merely a striking declaration that the public is not to be denied the services of a man unusually equipped to be a judge because of his color.

Yet Houston never became a judge. Whether he felt the municipal bench was not very exalted and wished to wait for something higher or he truly did not want to wear the confining robes of a magistrate is not clear. Whatever the reason, Houston was a partisan fighter by nature and a man to whom the sedentary life of a judge might have seemed a jail sentence. More in keeping with his gifts and temperament was his appointment in 1944 to the President's Fair Employment Practices Committee, of which he was one of two Negro members. Almost predictably, he would quit the FEPC twenty months later and charge the Truman administration, then six months in office, with paying no more than lip service to job equality.

After *Gaines*, Houston did not appear before the Supreme Court again until 1944, when he represented a client whom he had served as counsel on retainer since 1939—the beleaguered black railroad workers, against whom the closed white train brotherhoods had been practicing what amounted to industrial genocide for the previous sixty years.

Black men had worked the railroads since the beginning. Before the Civil War, most of the hot, dirty work of firemen was done on the Southern railroads by slaves, owned either by the rail companies or by their white engineers. After the war and especially after the Hayes-Tilden Compromise of 1877, the Southern lines expanded as Northern capital was. pumped into Dixie and white railwaymen from the North followed. The white firemen found the messy, hazardous working conditions worse than on the Northern roads and the pay lower: a fireman earned only half as much as an engineer for twice the work, much of it menial, and black firemen had to tend not only the engine but the engineer as well, functioning as his valet on the job. To gain better pay, working conditions, and seniority rules and hold the gains made in the North, the Brotherhood of Locomotive Firemen and Enginemen had to make a choice in expanding into the South: either welcome Negroes as full-fledged members to present management with a united labor front or throw the Negroes off the trains as rapidly as it could and keep the unions all-white. In 1884, the Brotherhood wrote "white" into its own constitutional requirements for membership. Before long, the other three railway unions constituting the "Big Four" of the industry—the Brotherhood of Railroad Trainmen, the Brotherhood of Locomotive Engineers, and the Order of Railway Conductors—wrote identical whites-only rules into their bylaws and set out on an organized, bareknuckled program to drive Negroes entirely out of their job categories. Pressure was put on the railroad lines to sign contracts guaranteeing that no new blacks would be hired and those non-union blacks already employed would either be fired or never promoted regardless of seniority or skill.

As the nation's industrial expansion raced on into the twentieth century, most of the carriers agreed to the Big Four demands; business was too good to risk a strike—and, after all, it was only colored men whose livelihoods were at stake. The big coal carrier, the Norfolk & Western, for example, yielded to union demands in a secret agreement in 1909 and did not hire a Negro fireman or brakeman thereafter. In 1910, the union trainmen and conductors got most of the railroads in the South to agree to hire no more blacks as baggagemen, flagmen, or yard foremen. During the First World War, the Baltimore & Ohio and the New Haven lines, which had adhered to the whites-only policy, were hard put to find enough firemen in view of war-induced manpower shortages and asked the Brotherhood's permission to hire black firemen to tide them over the emergency. The white trainmen answered no, explosively, and the full might of the Big Four threatened to come crashing down on any line that sought to bring in colored workers, war or no war.

Because the railroads were vital to the increasingly interdependent American economy, the train unions were able to win more liberal pay scales and working conditions than any other labor group. And the need for high safety standards and maximum alertness by crews encouraged short hours and featherbedding that was in most cases unjustifiable except by union intransigence. On a fast freight, a fireman or brakeman in the 1940s might make his run in two or three hours and be done for the day. A brakeman might do no more than thirty minutes of physical labor on any given run. And the cushier the jobs got and the better the pay, the less inclined the Big Four were to let blacks stay on the gravy train.

No job category better demonstrated the complicity of railroad management in perpetuating the Big Four bias than the colored train porters, who on the head end of passenger trains did all the braking work, handled mail, baggage, and all passenger needs, and swept out the coaches en route, but because they were black they were classified as porters and paid half a brakeman's salary. So it was, too, on Pullmans, where in many cases Negroes performed all the duties of conductors but were categorized "porter-in-charge" and paid a porter's wage. On diners as well, blacks were sometimes called "waiter-in-charge" though they did everything a steward did except earn his pay. Houston would write of this practice that "the only difference was that the steward had a white face and a black coat, while the waiter-in-charge had a black face and a white coat."

The concerted drive by the Big Four largely succeeded. Since 1928, no major American railroad had hired a Negro fireman, brakeman, switchman, flagman, or yardman. In 1920, there were still 6,500 colored firemen on the trains; by 1940, the number had dropped to 2,263. Black brakemen, switchmen, and yardmen had dropped from 8,275 to 2,739 in the period. The Big Four white unions by then had more than 400,000 members. Nearing extinction, the few thousand blacks left decided to fight back. The Colored Railway Trainmen & Locomotive Firemen organized out of Roanoke, Virginia, and hired Charles Houston as their counsel.

The plight of the ageing black railroadmen moved Houston deeply as he threw his energies into litigation to prevent further and faster attrition in their ranks. "Our office must have handled fifteen cases for them," Joseph Waddy, Houston's law partner, recalls. "I remember once we were in the home of a black brakeman in Roanoke, gathering information for a suit attacking the Brotherhood of Trainmen for misrepresenting their position to the Norfolk & Western. There must have been fifteen or twenty brakemen sitting around with us, all of them fifty years old or more, and there was this one old-timer who must have been seventy and was all white-haired, who was carrying on about how they had to save these jobs for their children and grandchildren, so there would be other generations of black men on the railroads. And then the old-timer used this phrase that filled Charlie up emotionally. He said they also had to save the jobs for themselves and protect 'these old heads blooming for the grave.' Charlie never forgot that. The railroadmen loved him. They'd do anything he asked."

He asked them to stand with him in the Supreme Court. The Second World War had brought no abatement in the Big Four's practices. When the Atlantic Coast Line, where Negroes had worked as firemen since the line was opened, could find no more white firemen as the labor shortage tightened, the company asked union approval to hire blacks. The Brotherhood threatened to strike on the spot. Summoned to a four-day FEPC hearing in Washington on job bias on the railroads, the Big Four thumbed their noses and sent no representatives. And their powerful lobby, the oldest in the capital, let Congressmen know that if the federal government ordered the color bar removed from their constitutions, the unions could not be held responsible for the subsequent actions of their members. "To me a fascist is a fascist," Houston wrote in *The Crisis* of such tactics, "whether he wears a black shirt or blue overalls. I think a closed union with a closed shop is a form of fascism and should be prohibited by law."

In 1943, Houston went to court in a case filed in the name of black fireman B. W. Steele, who worked in Alabama on the Decatur-Montgomery division of the Louisville & Nashville Railroad. By seniority, Steele had been entitled to be put on a passenger run, but as a result of what Houston called "a secret, fraudulent agreement" between the railroad and the Brotherhood of Firemen in 1941, under which the line agreed to chop the number of black firemen and soon end their employment altogether, the black fireman was assigned to a lower-paying run and then to a switch engine, the toughest job available. Since Steele's dilemma was identical to that of several thousand other black railwaymen, Houston framed Steele's suit as a "class action" in the name of others "similarly situated" and brought it against twenty-one other railroads besides the Louisville & Nashville that had similar contracts with the trainmen's Brotherhood. He also asked $50,000 in damages for Steele from the Brotherhood "for loss of wages, destruction of vested seniority preference rights and breach of its duty under the Railway Labor Act." Houston argued the case in December of 1943 before the Alabama Supreme Court, whose chief justice remarked that it was the first time in his twenty-nine years on that tribunal that a Negro lawyer had appeared before it. The pleasantries over, the Alabama high court then ruled against the black railroad workers.

Without dissent, the Supreme Court of the United States reversed. Under the Railway Labor Act, the Court said in *Steele v. Louisville & Nashville Railroad*, a majority union cannot enter into contracts that discriminate against the non-member minority workers because the law "imposes upon the statutory representative of a craft at least as exacting a duty to protect equally the interests of a member of the craft as the Constitution imposes upon a legislature to give equal protection to the interests of those for whom it legislates." In other words, because the government had thought it was in the national interest to make the majority union the exclusive bargaining agent with railroad management, the government could insist that the union not put a knife to the throat of non-members already on the job.

Justice Murphy, feeling the Court's opinion in *Steele* failed to stress the constitutional and humanitarian debasement involved, declared in concurrence:

> . . . The cloak of racism surrounding the actions of the Brotherhood in refusing membership to Negroes and in entering into and enforcing agreements discrimi-

nating against them, all under the guise of Congressional authority, still remains. No statutory interpretation can erase this ugly example of economic cruelty against colored citizens of the United States. . . . A sound democracy cannot allow such discrimination to go unchallenged. Racism is far too virulent today to permit the slightest refusal, in the light of a Constitution that abhors it, to expose and condemn it wherever it appears in the course of a statutory interpretation.

That brought a smile to those old heads blooming for the grave.

In the same year that Houston won *Steele*, his star pupil came before the Supreme Court with a major case for the first time. Thurgood Marshall could not have picked a tougher challenge. He was asking the Court to strike down the Texas primary-election procedures that had been approved just nine years earlier in *Grovey v. Townsend*. Not only had they been approved—they had been approved by a unanimous Court. And of the two men who in 1944 survived from the Court that handed down *Grovey* without dissent, one had become Chief Justice and the other was the Justice who had written the *Grovey* decision. Marshall's prospects seemed less than glittering.

Since the *Grovey* decision in 1935, the Court had passed on voting rights three times without notably altering the arrangements whereby so many barriers stood between the Negro and the polls that only a relative handful of blacks—2 to 3 percent of those over twenty-one—voted in the South, where most colored Americans continued to live. In 1937, the Court had unanimously turned back a challenge by a white voter to the constitutionality of the poll tax. No privilege or immunity protected by the Fourteenth Amendment was injured by poll taxes so long as everyone in the jurisdiction imposing them had to pay up. That such a tax fell with punitive weight upon the poorest members of the community and served to discourage exercise of the franchise by them was no business of the Court. In 1939, it had voided Oklahoma's callous effort to get around the Court's 1915 decision striking down the "grandfather clause"—a result pleasing to the NAACP but one that merely confirmed a ruling first made a generation earlier and then blatantly defied by a state legislature. To celebrate it would have been like asking the Negro to rejoice that slavery had not been re-imposed. But in 1941 the Court decided a case brought by the United States government that Thurgood Marshall thought provided the basis for a new attempt to have the white primary, by far the most effective device to disenfranchise Negroes, declared illegal.

A number of qualified, registered white Democrats in Louisiana had complained to the Justice Department that their ballots in the primary election for federal offices in 1940 had not been counted, and the government, in *United States v. Classic*, moved against the party's election supervisors and charged corrupt practices. This step seemed to be in conflict with *Grovey*, where the Court had held that a primary election was basically a party's own business, did not constitute state action, and could therefore not be the subject of complaint before the courts. Not so, said the government's attorney, Herbert Wechsler, who argued that "election officials who willfully alter or falsely count and certify ballots" in a primary election were performing acts under color of state law. In 1941, the Court agreed, finding that under a part of Article I of the Constitution—"The times, places, and manner of holding elections for Senators and Representatives shall be prescribed in each State by the legislature thereof; but the Congress may at any time by law make or alter such regulations"—Congress could regulate primary as well as general elections "where the primary is by law made an integral part of the election machinery." And since the Louisiana Democratic primary, similar to the one in Texas and other one-party states of the South, was in fact more important than the general election, which merely rubber-stamped the primary results, the Court held that federal criminal codes governing corrupt actions by election officials could be applied in the Louisiana case.

To Thurgood Marshall and his advisors, the *Classic* decision looked like a significant departure from *Grovey*. If the way primaries were run in the solidly Democratic South was plainly a form of state action, how could they be conducted to the exclusion of black voters? That was in clear violation of the Fifteenth Amendment. To strengthen his hand in taking such an argument before the Justices, Marshall went to the federal government for help. If the Justice Department, which had brought and won *Classic*, would now stand by the NAACP as an *amicus curiae* urging the outlawing of the white primary, the chances of the Court's reversing its unimaginable ruling in *Grovey* would be greatly improved. Marshall's case was brought in behalf of a Houston Negro named Lonnie E. Smith against election judge S. E. Allwright, who had denied Smith the vote in the 1940 primary and was upheld by the Texas courts, which cited *Grovey* as ruling precedent. After *Classic* had come down from the Court and Marshall petitioned it to hear *Smith v. Allwright*, he paid a visit to Attorney General Biddle and Assistant Attorney General Herbert Wechsler. Would the government come in on Smith's side? It might make all the difference.

"Well, I thought it over," recalls Wechsler, who argued *Classic* before the Court, "and my advice to Biddle was not to go in with Marshall. There were two reasons. For one thing, we had narrowed the grounds in *Classic* in order to win it—it applied only to those white registered Democrats whose votes hadn't been counted. And Justice Roberts, who wrote *Grovey*, was very shaky on *Classic*. I felt that if we came in with Marshall and asked the Court to extend *Classic*, our role could be actually hurtful." (Writing on the same point in the *Harvard Law Review* in 1959, Wechsler said that the Court, in holding that the right of a qualified voter to participate in federal elections extended to primaries, "did not, of course, deal with the scope of party freedom to select its members. The victim of the fraud in *Classic* was a member of the Democratic Party, voting in a primary in which he was entitled to participate, and the only one in which he could.") Beyond the legal issue, as Wechsler saw it, there was the delicate political problem Marshall's request presented. "We were a governmental department," Wechsler says, "and we had to get along with the Senate Judiciary Committee, which was dominated by the Southerners—and this seemed an unnecessary fight. When I told Thurgood that the answer would be no, he took it very well. He said, 'I'm sorry, we'd like to have you with us, but we'll just have to go it alone. I see your position.' That was one of his great virtues—seeing things from the other fellow's side. He was a good, tough advocate who functioned without having to feel that his opponents were either knaves or fools."

Marshall was banking on the Court itself and its strikingly liberal cast as the 1943–44 term unfolded. Harlan Stone, a man of deep learning who believed the prime purpose of the law was to serve society's most pressing needs and not to provide a club for judges who would wield it in the name of values of their own devising, had succeeded the conservative Hughes as Chief Justice in 1941. McReynolds's old seat was now held by ardent Roosevelt-supporter Wiley Rutledge, a former law-school dean of high benevolence and at least middling scholarship, who had put in four years on the Court of Appeals for the District of Columbia and would prove a reliable addition to the Court's liberal wing of Black, Douglas, and Murphy. To the seat vacated by Stone in moving over to the Chief's spot, Roosevelt named one of the most gifted—and mercurial—men ever to sit on the Court: Robert Houghwout Jackson.

Springing from yeomanry of hard-won wealth in upstate New York, Jackson was blessed with a mind both deep and agile, a tongue fluid in motion yet content at rest, and a pen with more grace and bite than any other ever wielded by a member of the Court. At eighteen, he had taken one year of law at a small school in Albany and then apprenticed himself to a firm in the little city of Jamestown, where he built a highly successful practice handling every kind of law including criminal cases but specializing in commercial matters for small companies and local tradespeople. A Democrat in Republican country, he made the acquaintance early on of another wealthy upstate Democrat then serving as Assistant Secretary of the Navy under Woodrow Wilson—Franklin Roosevelt. Fond of his trotting horses, thirty-foot cruiser, and the good manorial life that his applied intellect and independent character had won for him, Jackson reluctantly accepted Roosevelt's summons to Washington to become interim chief counsel of the temporarily befuddled Bureau of Internal Revenue in 1934. A patroon and an individualist, he was never a knee-jerk liberal nor a team player in the New Deal professing an egalitarian spirit he did not feel. As he moved up to head the tax division and then the antitrust division at Justice, he would not commit his principles as lawyer and square shooter to the political meat grinder—he did not flinch, for example, from going after labor as well as big business for breaking antitrust laws, though such a step was hardly in cadence with New Deal policy. Succeeding Reed as Solicitor General, Jackson proved a masterful advocate, with only one loss in twenty-four arguments before the Court, and a technically superior overseer of government litigation. Briefly Attorney General, he was considered for the Chief Justiceship, though he was only forty-nine; on reflection, Roosevelt promoted Stone and named Jackson as an Associate Justice. A confidant and fishing crony of the President, he harbored ambitions to succeed him in the White House or, failing that, to gain the Chief's chair on the Court after

Stone relinquished it. The country-gentleman lawyer had moved far and fast in Washington in just seven years.

"For the two years from 1943 to 1945," wrote Fred Rodell, of Yale Law School, in *Nine Men,* his spirited and partisan-liberal profile of the high tribunal, "the Court was—without even a close competitor—the most brilliant and able collection of Justices who ever graced the high bench together; the least of them would have stood out on many Courts of the past." Such men, Thurgood Marshall believed, could be counted on to view the white primary with fresh eyes and enlightened judgment.

It was Marshall's second appearance before the Court. In 1943, he had argued and won *Adams v. United States,* involving three black soldiers convicted by a federal District Court of rape on the premises of a Louisiana military base; the NAACP lawyer won dismissal from a unanimous Court on the narrow technical ground that the federal government had failed to file its claim of jurisdiction over the base with the state's governor. It had been an ideal case for Marshall to try out his wings before the august Supreme Court. No transcendent race question had been at stake as there now was in *Smith v. Allwright.* At his side in arguing the Texas voting case was Marshall's Gibraltar, the unflappable Bill Hastie. The NAACP team's task was no doubt lightened by the failure of any Texas official to appear for the oral argument before the Court, though the state filed an *amicus* brief, which is all it evidently felt was required because *Grovey* had sealed the issue so tightly nine years before. Still, there was high drama in it for Marshall, who had not rushed his career as a Supreme Court advocate, especially in view of the added burden any NAACP lawyer carried in speaking for thousands and perhaps millions of black Americans who had no other voice in the councils of government. "Arguing before that Court," Marshall acknowledges years later, "is much more than most people realize. It takes something out of you."

Marshall and Hastie leaned heavily on *Classic,* Wechsler's restrictive view of it notwithstanding. The Texas primary, they argued, was run almost exactly like the one in Louisiana and thus, under *Classic,* the right to vote in it was protected by the Constitution. Election judges such as Allwright were obliged under Texas law to exercise certain police duties, such as preserving order and administering oaths, and thus fell under the net as performers of state action. As to the *Grovey* holding that a party convention could set its own rules for membership and voting in its primaries without poaching on the functions of the state, Marshall and Hastie said *Classic* had held otherwise. "Once the state's relationship to the enterprise in which the offending persons are engaged is established," their brief declared, it did not matter that the party approved *en masse* of the offense. What mattered was whether the acts of the party officials offended the requirements of the Constitution.

On April 3, 1944, the Supreme Court voted eight-to-one to outlaw the Texas white primary. Justice Reed spoke for the Court. In states such as Texas, he said, *Classic* had established that the delegation of state functions to a political party—such as fixing qualifications for voting in a primary—

made the party's action potentially the state's action. And the Texas primary was honeycombed with procedures and duties required of the party by the state. Such duties "do not become matters of private law because they are performed by a political party." The Court's inescapable conclusion was that the state "endorses, adopts and enforces the discrimination against the Negroes, practiced by a party entrusted by Texas law" to decide who may vote in its primary. Under the Constitution, the people's power to elect federal officials "is not to be nullified by a state through casting its electoral process in a form which permits a private organization to practice racial discrimination. . . ."

The decision in *Smith v. Allwright*, slaying the white primary, was cause to rejoice. And indeed Marshall's Fund office in New York was the scene of such high and wet spirits that he ordered all phone calls to him to be directed through an ever ascending chain of secretaries instead of put right through to him as was office custom. This was not just an ordinary office party. Next morning, a bleary Marshall solemnly took a phone call from Justice Frank Murphy, who said he had tried to reach Marshall the previous afternoon to extend his best wishes and invite him to lunch but for some reason had been unable to get through the secretarial blockade. "I apologized profusely," Marshall later recounted, "and Murphy agreed that a guy had the right to get drunk at a time like that." Marshall still got his luncheon invitation.

Three months later, addressing the NAACP national conference in Chicago with the gusto of Joshua at Jericho, Marshall declared that they all had just begun to fight. Bigots could no longer scare them. In every state in the Deep South, Negroes had come out to vote that spring in the no-longer-white primaries, and affidavits of their rejection by white election officials in Alabama, Georgia, and Florida had already been sent on to the Department of Justice. "There is no reason why a hundred clear cases of this sort should not be placed before the United States Attorneys and the Attorney General every year," Marshall declared, "until the election officials discover that it is both wiser and safer to follow the United States laws than to violate them." It was time, too, that the Justice Department started prosecuting obvious and continuing violations of Federal law and Supreme Court decisions against all-white jury systems. "One whole-hearted prosecution of a judge or other official for excluding Negroes from jury service," Marshall said, "would do more to make this . . . law a reality than dozens of other cases merely reversing the conviction of individual defendants." They all had work to do, he said and urged local branches to demand action and bring cases to the Fund, because "the NAACP can move no faster than the individuals who have been discriminated against. . . . We must not be delayed by people who say, 'The time is not ripe,' nor should we proceed with caution for fear of destroying the status quo. People who deny us our civil rights should be brought to justice now."

The rhetoric grew stronger as the war ended.

In the spring of 1946, Marshall and Hastie were back before the Supreme Court to argue the case of Irene Morgan, a black woman who had boarded a Greyhound bus in Gloucester County in tidewater Virginia en route to

Baltimore. Ordered to the back of the bus, as state law required, Miss Morgan refused on the ground that she was an interstate passenger and not subject to Virginia's statute. The bus driver disagreed. Irene Morgan was arrested and fined ten dollars.

Marshall fought the case in the courts of Virginia, which rejected his argument that the Supreme Court's nineteenth-century holding in *Hall v. DeCuir* supported Miss Morgan's claim. That decision had wiped away a Louisiana law that *prohibited* segregation on interstate carriers because it overreached state authority: such a restriction, said the 1877 Court, might tend to place an undue burden on interstate commerce, which at any rate was under the supervision of Congress, according to the Constitution. Well, argued Marshall and Hastie, if state laws *forbidding* Jim Crow practice on interstate carriers were illegal, then surely state laws *requiring* segregation under the same circumstances—as in the case of the Virginia statute Miss Morgan was challenging—were just as illegal. The NAACP brief appealing *Morgan v. Virginia* to the Supreme Court reflected the new confidence and high hopes of the men who wrote it and their awareness of the fresh moral mandate visited upon the country by the birth of the United Nations. It concluded:

> . . . Today we are just emerging from a war in which all of the people of the United States were joined in a death struggle against the apostles of racism. . . . How much clearer, therefore, must it be today than it was in 1877, that the national business of interstate commerce is not to be disfigured by disruptive local practices bred of racial notions alien to our national ideals, and to the solemn undertakings of the community of civilized nations as well.

The Court agreed in a seven-to-one vote (Justice Jackson was off in Nuremberg at President Truman's request, serving as chief prosecutor in the Nazi war-crimes trial). But the Court's ruling was carefully worded to apply only to interstate passengers on buses. Intrastate Jim Crow laws were left very much intact. Nevertheless, *Morgan* marked the first transportation case to be brought to the Court by the NAACP, and it was a victory, however limited and difficult to enforce. In fact, most bus lines continued to segregate on all Southern runs, interstate or not. But Marshall's stock soared. Later that year, the chief counsel of the Legal Defense Fund was given the NAACP's highest tribute, the Spingarn Medal, named for longtime NAACP head Joel Spingarn, who had died in 1939 and been succeeded by his brother Arthur. The medal went each year to the Negro who "shall have reached the highest achievement in his field of activity."

# 11

# A Foot in the Door

For a dozen remarkable years that had tested their economic, social, and emotional resiliency, the American people had lived under emergency conditions, and with the survival of the nation as a world leader at stake, they had thrived on all the adversity. Class and regional barriers were being breached everywhere, and in the building and supplying of the most massive and lethal war machine the world had ever seen, the Negro had demonstrated, as he was not allowed to in the Depression, that he could amount to a great deal more than the white man's burden if America would give him half the chance.

The Supreme Court had become the sole instrument of government to insist that that chance now be granted. This was something new under the American sun. The remarkably gifted men Franklin Roosevelt had designated as Justices included no apologists for Babbittry, no recent transfers from the suspicious provinces, no envoys from the truculent strongholds of corporate capitalism. They were all men who had served in the New Deal ranks. They all believed that the troubled times the nation was undergoing required the decisive intervention of government. They all understood that the paths to private gain and public good often diverged and that no amount of mythifying could turn Americans into a nation of Good Samaritans.

Thus freed from the stranglehold that the Court had traditionally exercised upon it, American government extended its sway at an exponential rate in the late Thirties. The waging of a far-flung war added a patriotic motive to the expansion of federalism, and those who opposed it were readily dismissed as backwoodsmen or plutocrats who plain didn't want their wings clipped. The era of super-government and the onset of the welfare state were accomplished facts by the end of World War Two.

So much new power was rich with possibilities for abuse, and as the Forties unfolded, the first fumes of totalitarianism were in the air. The preservation of civil liberties, those freedoms assured under the Bill of Rights and the Fourteenth Amendment, sometimes became downright inconvenient to a government that felt justified in minimizing opposition. To what extent the courts ought to intervene in the name of protecting civil liberties by curbing the excesses of the majority became the explosive issue that caused the Roosevelt Court to splinter badly.

It was no easy question to reconcile philosophically. If the courts—under the flag of Holmesian liberalism—should stand aside and yield to popular will and public necessity when weighing the lawfulness of *economic* regulations, weren't the courts similarly obliged to accept public policies that reduced or narrowly construed civil liberties? State action in both areas was undertaken in the name of the greatest good for the greatest number. To condone it in one instance and not the other was surely inconsistent and perhaps damnably hypocritical. Did the decision about when to keep judicial hands off and when to lay judicial hands on overzealous governments finally turn on whose ox was being gored?

Justice Harlan Stone gingerly ventured an answer as early as 1938. In a footnote to an opinion of the Court of otherwise minor importance, he took the by then ascendant view that the Court ought not to review regulatory legislation unless it seemed utterly outlandish and without justification. But, Stone added, "There may be narrower scope" for granting any law the benefit of doubt if "on its face" it appears to collide with any of the prohibitions pinpointed by the Constitution "such as those of the first ten Amendments." Such laws, as well as those that rigged the political process itself in a way to prevent the repeal of unjust or no longer desirable laws, were perhaps open to "more exacting judicial scrutiny" than other laws.

As war neared, it grew more impolitic to hew to such an argument. Indeed, in 1940 Stone dissented alone in a case that well illustrated the dilemma. The law in Pennsylvania required all schoolchildren to pledge allegiance to the American flag at the start of the day. Youngsters of the Jehovah's Witnesses declined to obey the law in the conviction that their first and highest allegiance was to God. Coerced, they went to court to defend their First Amendment freedom of worship. Speaking for the Court, Justice Frankfurter argued that no infringement of religious freedom could reasonably be charged to the Pennsylvania legislature "in providing for this universal gesture of respect for the symbol of our national life." Besides, said Frankfurter, a fierce apostle of judicial restraint, for the Justices to pass on the likes of state and local flag-salute regulations "would in effect make us the school board for the country." As he wrote to Stone in private: "All my bias and pre-disposition are in favor of giving the fullest elbow room to every variety of religious, political, and economic view. . . . [But] I want to avoid the mistake comparable to that made by those whom *we* criticized when dealing with the control of property"—namely, usurping the responsibility of the people and their representatives for determining democratically what was best for America.

Stone was not impressed. For the Court to swing from one extreme to the other was not enlightened—and certainly not compassionate—adjudication. After becoming Chief Justice, he elevated his cautious footnote of 1938 into a full-fledged doctrine in another dissenting opinion involving the Jehovah's Witnesses, who served as judicial guinea pigs in a series of significant civil-liberties cases in the period. The Court majority, in the 1942 case of *Jones v. Opelika*, had upheld a municipal license tax on booksellers that had been levied against the proselytizing literature of the Witnesses. To Stone, this was a covert means of discouraging the Witnesses' form of worship. The

First Amendment was not confined, he wrote, to safeguarding freedom of speech and religion from direct attempts to wipe them out. "On the contrary, the Constitution, by virtue of the First and Fourteenth Amendments, has put these freedoms in a preferred position," and regulations that struck at them indirectly were no less pernicious than those that assaulted them head-on. Indeed, those taking the back-door approach required the greater vigilance by the Court.

By 1943, Stone's "preferred position" doctrine seemed to have commended itself to a majority of the Court, which now agreed with his earlier dissent in the compulsory flag-salute decision and, when another case on the question arose, overturned the Pennsylvania law. Where legislatures could not be expected to correct oppressive laws and where laws bore down on rights of minorities that were politically powerless to combat them, the preferred-freedoms doctrine held that the courts had a special responsibility to intervene. This endorsement of judicial activism was the wedge that drove the New Deal Court to pieces. Justice Frankfurter, heading the wing of the Court that saw great potential mischief in such a doctrine, became increasingly critical of it and was sometimes sharp in expressing concern over the jurisdictional ambitions of others on the Court. For if the Court overreached itself anew as it had in the pre-1937 days of the New Deal, it would soon lose its standing as ultimate arbiter of the nation's laws. Judicial power was to be husbanded against the day it was truly needed—not frittered away on any pretext.

The line between governmental abuse of civil liberties and governmental toleration of social injustice grew increasingly hard to define in the view of the Roosevelt Court's four judicial-activists: Black, who read the Bill of Rights and the Fourteenth Amendment as iron commands to protect individual rights; Douglas, impatient with judicial nitpicking and almost offhand in his flinty resolve to repulse state abuse of personal liberties; Murphy, the visceral liberal, bordering on the injudicious in his fervor for equal justice under law; and Rutledge, a bit cumbersome about it but even more unwavering in his avowal of civil liberties and equal rights. It was a foursome every bit as committed to using the strategic influence of the Court to promote a just society as the old reactionary quartet of Van Devanter, McReynolds, Sutherland, and Butler had been determined to use the Court to freeze the values of the past.

Ranged against Roosevelt's activists was the trio dedicated to judicial restraint. The peppery Frankfurter rarely tired of explaining to his brethren why he dared not indulge his humanitarian impulses in misguided do-gooding that would serve only to erode the Court's lofty standing. Indeed, some commentators have suggested that the brilliant little jurist so venerated the traditions of the Court that his conviction had turned to idolatry and his usefulness on the Court to dysfunction. His colleague Robert Jackson often came out with the same result but by a different route. Far less self-conscious and prolix than the garrulous ex-Harvard professor, Jackson could not help letting the patrician in him show from time to time. He was almost cynical in some of his withering opinions that seemed to suggest that his libertarian fellow Justices were laboring under utopian delusions. Solving crimes was a higher social good to him than immaculate avoidance of intruding upon the rights of suspects. The Jehovah's Witnesses could pray their hearts or lungs out just so long, he ruled, as they did not do it from a truck loudspeaker beside a small park in a small city on a quiet Sunday afternoon. Jackson and Frankfurter were joined on the right wing of the Court by Stanley Reed, the Kentuckian who had never truly been a New Deal firebrand, though he strongly favored a more equitable social order and a better shake for the workingman. A lawyer whose mind lacked the cutting edge of many of his colleagues' and who was therefore often disposed to take the judicial path of least resistance, Reed increasingly cast his vote in behalf of the powers and policies of the federal government, which he believed the legitimate if not divinely inspired repository of the public good.

The holdover Justices from the pre-Roosevelt Court—Stone and Roberts—veered to the left and right wings respectively, and the result during the first half of the Forties was a Court often narrowly divided, especially in civil-liberties cases. Stone, as an Associate Justice, had chafed under the whip hand with which his predecessor, Chief Justice Hughes, had directed the weekly closed-door conferences of the Court at which the cases were discussed and decided. Exchanges were often truncated and philosophical differences rarely explored as Hughes sought to prevent fissures among the Justices from showing. In the five years he was to preside over the Court on which he had already served for seventeen years, Stone did not try to muzzle any of his colleagues in robes. It was a grand assortment of minds and temperaments, but as a Court it was an uncoordinated group of soloists who seemed to be forever backing and filling in the name of judicial statesmanship.

When Roberts, considerably to the right of the judicial-restraint bloc with which he was generally associated, retired in 1945, President Harry Truman made the first of his four appointments to the high court. Without exception, they would prove to be men of kindly disposition and limited intellect. They hung together in their votes on the Court as if glued, and in their solidarity they would come to control it. For the civil-libertarians, the takeover by the Truman appointees produced a judicial Dunkirk.

There were many reasons why Harry Truman, a political partisan if there ever was one, reached across party lines to pick a Republican—Harold Hitz Burton, the junior Senator from Ohio—to take Roberts's place on the Court. By common consent, the trim, blue-eyed Midwesterner with the high forehead and small, even features had a cooperative disposition, a mind both open and fair, and an outlook that reflected the moderate social views of the American heartland. As a state legislator, Cleveland city attorney, and then two-term mayor of the metropolis on Lake Erie, Burton got along well with New Dealers, and in the Senate he turned out to be progressive in domestic affairs and an avowed internationalist who pushed early for the establishment of a united-nations organization. On top of that, he hit it off with the other members of Senator Harry Truman's special committee to investigate defense contracts—a group whose performance did much to boost Truman's stock and earn him second place on the 1944 national Democratic ticket. In the White House now, Truman was advised that it would be an act of prudence to extend an olive branch to the cranky opposition by picking a Republican to replace Republican Justice Roberts. No member of the GOP had been selected since Roberts himself fifteen years earlier. A pedigreed Republican of New England abolitionist stock, Harold Burton was no ardent right-winger. Indeed, in comparison to Ohio's other Republican leviathans, conservative ex-Governor John W. Bricker and high-buttoned senior Senator Robert A. Taft, Burton was practically a Spartacus. Besides, Ohio was a bellwether state, and it would do Truman no harm to pick a popular Buckeye for the Court with apparent disregard for party labels. Besides that, Ohio's Democratic governor could then name a Democrat to Burton's Senate seat.

Justice Burton slid unassumingly onto the high bench. His coming did little to alter the precarious balance of power. Lacking in strong philosophical commitments, he voted a little less conservatively than Roberts had, but not much. He tended to side with the Frankfurter-Jackson-Reed faction in often supporting government action in preference to individual rights, and he dissented in several labor cases in which the majority favored the worker's side. But Thurgood Marshall and the NAACP legal staff were concerned by the newcomer's first civil-rights vote in 1946. In *Morgan v. Virginia*, Burton dissented alone, contending that each state should be free to make its own segregation laws on motor carriers operating within its borders—hardly a promising debut by Burton from the Negro's standpoint.

Rancor, publicly aired, soiled the spotless marble palace of the Justices that year. Jackson openly denounced Black for sitting and voting in a case in which one of the litigants, the United Mine Workers, was represented by Black's former law partner. Each Justice abides by his own conscience in deciding whether the circumstances in any given case might prevent him from rendering an unbiased opinion. In Black's case, the partnership had been short to begin with and had ended nineteen years earlier, and the two men had scarcely been in touch since. Still, Jackson and Frankfurter felt that Black had acted unethically, and they issued a short, cryptic memorandum to that effect from the bench when the case was decided in 1945. Reports of squabbling on the Court were leaking to the public, and by the time Harlan Stone died in April of 1946, it seemed clear that harmony would not be won by elevating a member of either faction on the Court to the Chief's chair. Robert Jackson had coveted that chair. Franklin Roosevelt had seriously considered naming him to it in 1941. And when Harry Truman chose his mournful-faced Secretary of the Treasury, Fred M. Vinson, to be the thirteenth Chief Justice of the United States, Jackson let his frustration boil over. He wrote to the Senate and House Judiciary committees giving his side of the feud among the Justices. It was shockingly injudicious conduct that Black chose not to dignify by rebuttal. Jackson had been prompted by the belief that Black had blocked his selection as Chief by lobbying with Truman to pick Reed or anyone else for the post. Frankfurter, Jackson's closest ally on the Court, was reported to have spoken up similarly against the elevation of Black's close ally, Douglas. For Jackson, the ambitious brahmin, the episode meant the premature decline of his influence. Whatever the truth behind the schism, Fred Vinson was inheriting a fratricidal Court. His skill at spreading balm was one reason he got the job.

He came out of the little town of Louisa, Kentucky, near the West Virginia line at the eastern end of the state. Son of the town jailkeeper, young Vinson was the beneficiary of his family's determination that he receive a college education and make something of himself, and off he went to Centre College over in Danville in the middle of the state, where he starred as shortstop and captain of the baseball varsity. He even had a fling at semi-professional baseball for a few months in the local Blue Grass League, but his academic record—he graduated from the Centre College law school in 1911 with the best grades anyone had ever earned there—suggested he might do well in a more stable field. For ten years, he practiced law in and around his little hometown on the banks of the Big Sandy River, serving as municipal attorney for a spell and following the sports pages persistently. The latter habit he never lost, and it was said in his Washington years that he could summon up the current batting average of any major-leaguer a good deal faster than he could cite legal precedent. After two years as common-wealth attorney for his section of the state, he was elected to Congress in 1924 for the first of six terms, interrupted only by the Republican sweeep of 1928. By 1931, he had earned a spot on the strategic House Ways and Means Committee, and with the coming of the New Deal the young Democrat came into his own.

Social fervor was not a trait Fred Vinson wore on his sleeve, but the caring was there. "He was proudest, I think, of being the floor leader in the House during the fight for the Social Security program," says his son, Fred Vinson, Jr. "He was a humanist and a doer, not one of your theoretical liberals. When I was growing up and Dad sent us some clippings of his speeches on the Social Security bill, my mother told me how one day soon after he had first been elected to Congress, they were driving along a back road together and they saw this gnarled old-timer scratching away at his flat field. 'Someday,' Dad said, turning to her, 'I'm going to try to do something to help that old fella.'" Whether the vignette is more fanciful than *verbatim,* the younger Vinson cannot attest, but the reformist instinct it suggests was borne out by his father's legislative record. He was a marvel with figures, and in the early era of the New Deal a sharp pencil point and a strong urge to rid the country of the fiscal blues made him a key lawmaker in shaping such landmark measures as the Fair Labor Standards Act, the National Labor Relations Act, the Vinson-Guffey Coal Acts, and reciprocal trade agree-ments, besides the Social Security bill. In 1936, his skills were rewarded with the chairmanship of the special House subcommittee on revenue legislation. Fred Vinson was the reigning fiscal genius of the lower house. But his gifts were not merely technical. There was a warmth that the man radiated, and a knack for being able to disagree during high-powered backroom debates without being disagreeable about it.

In 1938, he began five years of unremarkable but solid service on the United States Court of Appeals for the District of Columbia, just one rung below the Supreme Court. His high technical competence as a legal draftsman helped a great deal, and his opinions were notable for their common sense and clarity. No one, though, mistook him for the next Oliver Wendell Holmes. In 1942, he was tapped by Chief Justice Stone to serve as chief judge of a newly created emergency appeals court to review the rulings of the Office of Price Administration, the domestic hot spot of wartime Washington. He handled that judicial assignment so well that one day a year later, while Vinson was in his chambers talking with a brother judge, the President telephoned him. Would he give up his lifetime place on the federal bench to become Director of Economic Stabilization? It was about the toughest job in town. In effect, with the President absorbed by military affairs, Vinson became czar of the American economy, then bursting at the seams in an effort to keep the fighting machine rolling. Inflationary pressures were staggering, and from all sides came appeals to lift the lid on upward price and wage pressures, but Vinson held fast, and he did so with tact and grace. He had become a Solomon among the bureaucrats.

As the war neared its end, he was named Director of War Mobilization and Reconversion, another key post, but then all at once Franklin Roosevelt was gone and the unassuming, chipper little man from Missouri was in the oval office, overwhelmed by events and unaccustomed to wielding the sort of massive responsibility that had now been thrust upon him. Harry Truman had always liked Fred Vinson's down-to-earth ways, and the lonely President turned to the kindly, competent Kentuckian as a principal advisor during his early ordeal of power. As Secretary of Treasury, Vinson swiftly became the strongest figure in the Truman Cabinet and a poker-playing crony besides. When Chief Justice Harlan Stone died, the President did not have to look far for a successor. Was any man in America better prepared for the job? Small-town lawyer, state attorney, veteran Congressman, high federal judge, national administrator of the most sensitive sorts of wartime policy, Fred Moore Vinson seemed the ideal man to restore peace to the Supreme Court and to preside over it with dignity, knowledge, and compassion.

For all his charm, gentle humor, and long-practiced skill at smoothing ruffled feathers, the job of pacifying and unifying the Supreme Court was beyond Fred Vinson as he took the Chief's chair at the beginning of the October 1946 term. It might have been beyond any man just then. If that long, saggy face of his with its bushy brows, heavy pouches beneath the eyes, and drooping nose gave him a doleful countenance, what he encountered in his effort to take command of the Court did nothing to brighten it. Cold War and chronic crisis gripped Washington, and Chief Justice Vinson believed that the federal government had to be free to wield power as its leaders thought best if the nation was to contend successfully with the enormously complex social, political, and economic problems of the post-war world. And so he voted on the Court. His strong pro-government stance drew fellow Kentuckian Reed and Justice Burton within his orbit of influence. Frankfurter and Jackson, while steadfast in adhering to the tenets of judicial restraint, found the Vinson bloc rather too slavish in taking the government line and too cavalier in skewering civil liberties. Frankfurter and Jackson became a centrist bloc by themselves, though Frankfurter steadily pursued influence with the new Chief. The judicial activists remained united in a libertarian bloc that would survive just two years longer. The anxiety they registered over the judicial philosophy of the new Chief Justice was prompted by such opinions as two he wrote in 1947. In *Harris v. United States*, Vinson spoke for a five-to-four majority that sustained a conviction based on evidence obtained in a search without a warrant; in *United States v. United Mine Workers*, he said the President had been justified in seizing the nation's coal mines in order to break a strike, and that a federal injunction ordering the miners back to work—in apparent violation of the Norris–La Guardia Act outlawing injunctions in labor disputes—was permissible in cases of properties taken by the government to head off "such a serious threat to orderly constitutional government, and to the economic and social welfare of the nation." In civil-liberties cases, Vinson supported state governments in preference to individual rights 80 percent of the time; the federal government he supported 90 percent. It was almost as if Fred Vinson were still a member of Harry Truman's Cabinet.

The Justices whose conflicting views Vinson had hoped to reconcile were anything but sheep. They were independent personalities with deep convictions, and at least four of them—Black, Douglas, Frankfurter, and Jackson— had markedly greater intellectual ability than their new Chief. Not surprisingly, then, the Court grew more, not less, fractured. Before 1935, the Court had rarely decided fewer than 85 percent of its cases unanimously. By Vinson's first term, only 36 percent of the cases were decided unanimously; by his third term, the figure had dropped to 26 percent—and it would keep on dropping. In Vinson's last year, the sardonic Jackson was prompted to remark, "Rightly or wrongly, the belief is widely held by the practicing profession that this Court no longer respects impersonal rules of law but is guided in these matters by personal impressions which from time to time may be shared by a majority of the Justices."

The crying need among Negroes as the war ended was not jobs but housing. Even those who could afford to buy their own places or rent at the going rates in white neighborhoods were firmly told to keep out.

Federal housing programs were officially and insistently segregated. The Federal Housing Administration, which in time would insure billions of dollars of construction by builders of millions of dwelling units, had never insured a non-segregated project. The FHA underwriting manual pulled no punches about its support of bias: "If a neighborhood is to retain stability, it is necessary that properties shall continue to be occupied by the same social and racial classes." To help sustain Jim Crow housing, the FHA drew up and urged the adoption of a model racially restrictive covenant, of the type sanctioned by the Supreme Court in the 1926 case of *Corrigan v. Buckley*. To avoid the charge of racism, the FHA said that its federal housing projects would be built on a strictly separate-but-equal basis, as the law insisted. But in public housing, as in public education, the *Plessy* principle was all theory and no practice. Thurgood Marshall told an NAACP gathering in 1944 how the Negro fared under FHA policies. In Detroit, he noted, racially separate projects had been built and "by the first of this year every single white family in the area eligible for public housing had been accommodated and there were still some 800 'white' units vacant with 'no takers.' At the same time there were some 5,000 Negroes inadequately housed and with no units open to them. This is the inevitable result of 'separate but equal' treatment."

In the 1926 *Corrigan* decision upholding a restrictive covenant in the District of Columbia, the Supreme Court had not touched on the related question of whether court enforcement of a covenant was not in fact a form of state action and therefore a violation of the equal-protection and due-process clauses of the Constitution. Repeatedly, the question had been sent to the Court, and each time the Justices had declined to hear the case. Nevertheless, the pace of litigation in the area rose as more blacks broke the color bar and more whites went to court to drive them back to the ghetto. During the war years, more than twenty covenant suits had been filed in the Los Angeles area alone, and Chicago had had almost as many. Toward the end of the war, a group of Howard lawyers including Hastie and Ransom defended a black federal employee who had been enjoined from occupying covenanted premises in Washington. They won a dissenting opinion from one of the three Court of Appeals judges on the case, but it went no higher. Only two members of the Supreme Court—Murphy and Rutledge—had voted to hear the appeal; four were necessary under the rules of the Court.

The effort intensified after the war. Test cases were soon launched before state and local courts by NAACP branch lawyers in Detroit, St. Louis, and Chicago, among other cities, but the model of aggressive litigation was provided by Charles Houston, who brought the case of James Hurd against Frederic and Lena Hodge, white Washington homeowners who wished to keep colored people from moving to the block on Bryant Street in the North Capitol area where they had lived since 1909. Blacks had made inroads into the area, bounded on the southeast by Union Station and the northwest by Howard University, though the Washington Real Estate Board had done its best to repulse them. Its code of ethics provided that no member in good standing could sell a home to a Negro in a white part of the city. Still, the Hodges' block had slowly become surrounded by many where Negroes were living. Houston argued that the covenant was now pointless. But he went far beyond that. He put Lena Hodge on the witness stand and demonstrated how mindless racism can be when called upon to justify itself:

Q. . . . Now, suppose, Mrs. Hodge, it was a very, very light Negro, say 99 percent so-called white blood. . . .

A. It would still be a Negro, I think.

Q. And it would not make any difference?

A. No.

Q. If you got a person in the block who was supposed to be white and that person was undesirable, in the sense of untidy or something like that, you couldn't do anything about it?

A. No, certainly we couldn't.

Q. And you would prefer that untidy white person to a Negro, no matter how educated or cultured?

A. As long as they are white. I would prefer them.
Q. No Negro, no matter how—or whether he might be Senator or Congressman, it would not make any difference to you?
A. It wouldn't make any difference.
Q. Even if the white man just came from jail, you would prefer him?
A. Because he is white and I am white.


Houston used every maneuver he knew. He challenged the qualifications of the presiding United States District Court judge because the home he rented was covered by a covenant. He put experts on the witness stand to demonstrate the absurdity of racial labeling. An anthropologist from Catholic University said that visible physical traits were by no means a reliable test for determining racial classification. A bacteriologist from George Washington University stated that neither blood tests nor any other kind of chemical test had been devised that could determine racial identity. E. Franklin Frazier, the Howard sociologist, offered constantly interrupted testimony on the dismal social effects of segregated housing. Houston had his clients testify to the hardship they had undergone in finding the home that the Hodges now sought to take from them.

Nothing helped. Houston lost *Hurd v. Hodge* in the District Court in 1946. The following spring he would lose it before the Court of Appeals as well. Was there any reason to believe the Supreme Court would now take it up on application for a writ of *certiorari*? * The Court had turned down a similar case in the District of Columbia just two years earlier, and even though Houston had now created a far more extensive record in the trial court, it was far from certain that he had added anything solid to the issue. And if he appealed anew to the Supreme Court and got turned down anew, all he would have succeeded in doing was strengthening the Justices' adamancy about sticking with the 1926 *Corrigan* ruling. Nor had the other test cases mounted by the NAACP branch lawyers—*Shelley v. Kraemer* in St. Louis and *McGhee v. Sipes* in Detroit—fared any better in the lower courts. Their only hope seemed to reside in the Supreme Court, and that hope was none too robust. Neither of the newcomers, Justice Burton and Chief Justice Vinson, was noted for devotion to civil rights. The latter had voted to uphold

---

* The Constitution and Congress have mandated select categories of cases to be heard by the Supreme Court; otherwise, the Court on its own decides when it will grant a writ of *certiorari*—that is, an order to the lower court that last heard the case to send up the certified record of the proceedings. Most applications to the Court to grant "cert," as the law profession calls it, are in fact denied. Denial may mean merely that the Justices do not believe that a substantial federal or constitutional question has been raised by the case. Or it may mean the issue in the case has been before it earlier and there is nothing to add to the Court's earlier holdings. Or it may mean that the Justices feel the issue is too hot or too sweeping to handle—for example, it may raise a major political issue that the Court feels is beyond its jurisdiction. Court members and commentators have many times declared that denial of *certiorari* implies neither approval nor disapproval of the decision below, but repeated denial of "cert" on the same question, as in the restrictive-covenant cases, opened the Court to the inference that it did not wish to entertain arguments that might lead to the reversal of its decision in *Corrigan v. Buckley*, upholding the legality of private discrimination in housing. Other than by *certiorari*, cases in which a state law is challenged as unconstitutional may be sent to the Supreme Court "on appeal" in a process discussed in the next chapter.

housing covenants while he was on the U.S. Court of Appeals for the District of Columbia.

To figure out how best to get the Court to take one of the covenant cases, NAACP lawyers convened early in 1947 at Howard, which now increasingly became the favorite bivouac of the black legal corps. The Detroit lawyers felt their case was ripe for appeal and urged the Legal Defense Fund to assume direction of it from that point on. But Marshall and Houston still hoped that they might win one of the other pending cases in the lower courts. It was agreed that they would reassemble in a few months and determine which case or cases offered the most promising candidate for appeal.

Discipline within the black legal ranks, though, was not monolithic. Neither Marshall nor Houston could prevent St. Louis attorney George Vaughn from filing—prematurely, in the Fund's view—a petition for *certiorari* with the Supreme Court to review *Shelley v. Kraemer*. Vaughn was an able enough attorney at the municipal-court level, but he was not an experienced appellate lawyer and he was not familiar with the new kinds of sociological material that Houston and others were now introducing into the legal record in civil-rights cases. That he believed *Shelley* could be won on the ground that racial housing covenants violated the anti-slavery provisions of the Thirteenth Amendment—and that such an approach had every bit as much validity as the Fourteenth Amendment arguments that had been fruitlessly pursued for years—was a telltale sign to Marshall that he himself could no longer hold back while less informed and less able lawyers forced the issue on the wrong legal grounds. If *Shelley* alone was taken by the Court and argued by Vaughn, or if *Shelley* alone went up for "cert" and was denied, the whole battle against covenants might be set back for an incalculable number of years. "Thurgood was very reluctant to push the restrictive-covenant cases at the Supreme Court level," recalls Franklin Williams, who was a junior lawyer at the Fund in those days and believes Marshall was less than bold in his leadership. "If the initiative had not come from outside the Fund office—from Loren Miller in California and the branch people in Detroit and St. Louis—Marshall might have let it go then," Williams suggests. "But the lawyers outside the Fund made it clear that they were going to fight their cases all the way, with or without Marshall."

Less than three weeks after Vaughn petitioned the Supreme Court to hear *Shelley*, Thurgood Marshall came in with the Fund appeal of the Detroit case. Houston appealed *Hurd v. Hodge* over the summer. On the last Monday of the term, the Supreme Court agreed to hear the cases the following fall.

To have a prayer of winning in the face of so many defeats for so many years in so many lower courts, the black lawyers needed something approximating divine intervention. And, astonishingly, they got it. It came not from heaven, though, but from the White House.

Franklin Roosevelt may have opened the White House door wide to Negroes, but Harry S. Truman risked his future tenancy there in their behalf—and because of his own conception of what America was all about.

No President before or since Lincoln had put his political neck on the chopping block to help the colored people of the nation.

A series of lynchings and a flood of hate literature in 1946 drove civil-rights and civil-liberties groups to renewed efforts to stir the federal government into action. Walter White tried to bring his anti-lynching bill back from the dead, and labor and church groups rallied to the cause, but chances of getting an effective bill through Congress, where white-suprema-cists still reigned, remained slim. After some delays, White was able to obtain an audience with the President, but he had no reason to anticipate any more success in this instance than he had had with Presidents Coolidge, Hoover, and Roosevelt. But when White finished his recitation of the latest atrocities and the pox of hatred that seemed to be sweeping the land, the President's face was grim. "My God," he said in his flat Midwestern tone, "I had no idea it was as terrible as that. We've got to do something!"

That was the most concern anyone around the White House had shown toward black rights since Eleanor Roosevelt had moved out. They had to rally public opinion first of all, Truman said, and his staff people present suggested that a special citizens' committee be appointed to study the whole area and recommend a remedial program. *Oh, my stars,* thought Walter White, *another runaround.* Besides, congressional Dixiecrats would never consent to establishing and funding such a commission. The devil with that, said Truman; he would create it by executive order and pay for it out of the President's contingency fund. And it was done. Fifteen more or less notable Americans, including the presidents of General Electric and Lever Brothers, the presidents of Dartmouth and the University of North Carolina, officers of the CIO and AFL, representatives of the major religious denominations, and even a Negro or two were named to the President's Committee on Civil Rights, which convened early in 1947 and was asked not to dawdle. Among its members was civil-liberties lawyer and author Morris Ernst, longtime friend and advisor of the NAACP, who was struck by the initiative being shown in the matter by a President from a segregationist state. "I asked him how come he was doing more on this anti-lynching business than FDR had," recalls Ernst, then a Democratic stalwart with ready access to the party's top level, "and the President said, 'Well, when I came back from the Army after the First World War and went back to my hometown, there were regular meetings of the KKK going on—and it scared the shit out of me. And I'm still scared!' I think that was typical of the man: a single event might have a shaping effect on his pragmatic outlook on life and politics. To show the priority he meant the Civil Rights Committee to have, he said to me, 'And you'll hold your meetings in the Cabinet Room.'"

Harry Truman soon made it clear that he was not just going through the motions. At the end of June 1947, just a week after the Supreme Court had agreed to hear the restrictive-covenant cases, the President of the United States addressed the thirty-eighth annual conference of the NAACP assembled before the Lincoln Memorial. "The extension of civil rights today means not protection of the people *against* the government, but protection of the people *by* the government," Truman declared. "We must make the federal government a friendly, vigilant defender of the rights and equalities of all Americans. And again I mean all Americans." No President had ever dared say such a thing.

While the President's Committee on Civil Rights was going about its deliberations, Thurgood Marshall, Charles Houston, and the other Negro lawyers involved were drawing up their appeal briefs for the Supreme Court arguments in the covenant cases that collectively would come to be called *Shelley v. Kraemer.* They jumped at the chance they now saw of turning the President's outspoken words to their advantage. Walter White wrote to the Attorney General of the United States, Tom C. Clark, and urged him to put federal muscle behind the President's sentiments by filing an *amicus* brief for the government that called on the Court to strike down restrictive covenants. Under federal law and Supreme Court rules, the Attorney General or the Solicitor General could file a brief or appear before the Justices almost any time the government felt it had an interest in a case, even if it were not a party to the litigation. But it had never done so in a civil-rights case in which only private citizens were the litigants, as was true in *Shelley*, though the issue at stake was of course suffused with public policy considerations. Other activist groups added their encouragement to the Attorney General, who stalled on his decision throughout the summer and seemed to be bucking the matter to his new Solicitor General, Philip B. Perlman. Neither man had ever evidenced much interest in the problems of black America. But both were pretty fair practicing politicians.

Tom Campbell Clark's father, William, grew up in Mississippi cracker country and attended Ole Miss, as the Johnny Reb university at Oxford was belovedly known throughout the South, before heading with his family to Texas and a law career. A hard-core white supremacist, he sired a son who would become one of the more repressive Attorneys General in American history and would himself sire a son who would in turn become one of the more liberal Attorneys General in American history. Remarks Ramsey Clark of his grandfather's politics, "We got out some of his speeches one time, and they showed he could out-Bilbo Bilbo." Tom Clark did well to grow up in the Klan-tainted atmosphere of Texas politics and still escape the lingering miasma of bigotry. After the University of Texas Law School, he went into practice with his father, within five years got elected civil district attorney for Dallas County, and thereafter ingratiated himself with the moderate wing of the state party, headed by the two congressional powerhouses, Senator Tom Connally and Representative Sam Rayburn. Under their patronage, he came to the Justice Department in 1937 and for the next six years handled journeyman's chores there—war claims, antitrust actions, and the like—and two sensitive matters that colored his future. He uncomplainingly helped direct one of the home front's least palatable acts of wartime repression, the evacuation of Japanese-Americans from their West Coast homes. And he prosecuted many of the war-contract frauds uncovered by Harry Truman's Senate investigating committee; in the process, the jaunty junior Senator from Missouri befriended the quick-to-smile young Texan in the bow tie. They worked together at the 1944 Democratic convention to promote Sam

Rayburn into Henry Wallace's number-two spot on the ticket. When the usual shoot-out erupted within the Texas delegation, Rayburn urged Clark to turn the tables and push for Truman's nomination as Vice President. By the time Roosevelt died, Clark had risen to Assistant Attorney General in charge of the antitrust division and then the criminal division. He was ready for bigger things, and as an uneasy Harry Truman moved to surround himself with a Cabinet and close advisors of his own down-home style, he asked polished Easterner Francis Biddle to step aside as Attorney General for genial Tom Clark.

Out of office, years later, Harry Truman would have unkind things to say about Tom Clark's intelligence, but while in power he did not hesitate to get every inch of mileage he could out of the Texan's fealty to him and his key connections in Congress. Clark became an able administration hatchet man at Justice, himself arguing the coal-seizure case against the mineworkers and pressing antitrust and other visible policy matters. Most of all, he became Truman's favorite wind-up Cold Warrior as the nation began looking under its bedsprings for domestic Communists. Clark was a leading advocate of the loyalty-test program for government employees. He pushed the President to have the FBI, which was nominally under Clark's direction, conduct the investigative phase of the program, and he had his department compile the first Attorney General's pink-list of allegedly Communist, Communist-front, fellow-traveling, or otherwise subversive organizations, none of which could appeal the merits of its being thus designated. The witch-hunt was on, and Tom Clark, earnestly believing in the Red Peril, stirred the pot. When Harry Truman's enemies accused the President of being soft on Communism, Tom Clark went to the microphone to prove it was otherwise. If non-government organizations would just pursue the Communists in their midst with the same zeal the Truman administration had shown, the country would be a lot safer. By 1948, Clark was prosecuting the top leaders of the American Communist Party for preaching Marx and Lenin.

When he received Walter White's request that he put the government on the Negro's side in the restrictive-covenant cases before the Supreme Court, Tom Clark was on the spot. Aside from pursuing an occasional voting-irregularity case or investigating a report of brutality at a federal prison, the civil-rights unit at the Justice Department was still pretty much the Tinker Toy it had been when Frank Murphy set it up in 1940. But it was plain to Clark that the Cold War which had driven him to hound Communists in the name of patriotism obliged the President and his government to come to the aid of the Negro in that same name. Clark talked it over with Solicitor General Philip Perlman, a conservative Democrat from Baltimore who, like Clark himself, had been criticized as essentially a glad-handing political hack. Both knew that Harry Truman's Fair Deal was in trouble with the electorate. Congress was under Republican control for the first time since Hoover had been President. The Negro vote was becoming increasingly important in the industrial swing states of the North. The President was talking civil rights as if he meant it. Undersecretary of Interior Oscar Chapman had written Clark to suggest he get into *Shelley*, and the very able attorney Philip Elman in Perlman's office was strongly urging both the Attorney General and the Solicitor General to jump into civil rights with both feet. But Clark and Perlman waited for the President's Committee on Civil Rights to weigh in with its report.

Called *To Secure These Rights*, the report was issued on October 29, 1947. It was almost as vigorous and straightforward a denunciation of racism in America as the NAACP itself might have composed. It called for the elimination of segregation from American life, and among its forty concrete suggestions for federal action was the proposal that the Justice Department enter the legal fight against restrictive covenants, especially "when severe housing shortages are already causing hardship for many people of the country. . . ." A week later, Solicitor General Perlman summoned his best brief-writer, Philip Elman, and told him, "We're going in."

"My impression is that Tom Clark made the decision to put the government into *Shelley*," says Elman, who had to postpone his honeymoon and hurriedly assemble a crew to help write the historic government brief. Beyond the constitutional issues, Elman enlisted statements from other government agencies in support of the brief's basic contention that government support of restricted housing was against the national interest. So suggested the Housing and Home Finance Agency, the United States Public Health Service, the Interior Department's Indian Service, and the Secretary of State, whose legal advisor, Ernest Gross, stated for the record that "the United States has been embarrassed in the conduct of foreign relations by acts of discrimination taking place in this country." Elman worked all this into the Solicitor General's brief, along with the contention that overcrowded, debasing ghettos promoted by the covenants "cannot be reconciled with the spirit of mutual tolerance and respect for the dignity and rights of the individual which give vitality to our democratic way of life."

When Chief Justice Fred Vinson finished reading his copy of the government's brief, he wrote a note to himself on the front. It said: "certainly has heart appeal—But this is for the *head*."

Charles Houston went for the head. He discarded a number of the points that he had belabored in the trial court and instead loaded his brief to the Court with economic and sociological arguments. More than 150 articles, reports, and books were cited, and charts and maps were interlaced in the brief that Houston carefully stitched together with help from the brainiest and most painstaking of the younger Howard law graduates, Spottswood Robinson, who was beginning to make a name for himself in Virginia just as Thurgood Marshall had in Maryland the decade before. In its blend of law and applied social research, the brief was probably the most ambitious and masterly of Houston's career. In New York, the Legal Defense Fund staff, with Marshall at the helm and Loren Miller, the best civil-rights lawyer on the West Coast, imported to do the bulk of the drafting, worked up an equally ambitious brief for the Detroit case. In their freewheeling use of sociological and medical data—among the sources cited were the *American Journal of Public Health*, the *New England Journal of Medicine*, *Mental Hygiene*, and a 1939 paper titled *Mental Disorders in Urban Areas: An*

*Ecological Study of Schizophrenia and Other Psychoses*—the Fund was barging into territory that had first been explored in a presentation before the Supreme Court by Louis Brandeis, arguing the 1908 case of *Muller v. Oregon,* in which he fought to defend the state's law imposing a maximum ten-hour day on laundresses for reasons of health and public welfare. Even though Du Bois, its principal Negro founder and long its leading light, had been exploring and quantifying data on the social effects of discrimination more than half a century earlier, the NAACP legal arm had never ventured to offer a "Brandeis brief" before *Shelley* seemed to necessitate the step. "As soon as we had it all together," says Marian Wynn Perry, a former Department of Labor lawyer who worked at the Fund between 1945 and 1949, "Thurgood saw its worth at once." Marshall would no longer try to shoehorn his cases into the often cramped and distorting logic of straight legal precedent. Men did not live by law alone.

The difficulty of trying to predict the Justices' decision after the covenant cases were heard at the beginning of 1948 was compounded by the fact that three of them—Reed, Jackson, and Rutledge—did not sit on the case. The inference most widely drawn was that they themselves owned or occupied premises covered by restrictive covenants. The black lawyers had surmised that such arrangements by the Justices had complicated their efforts to get a case on appeal before the Court and might affect the ultimate vote. But which way? If a Justice had in fact signed a covenant himself, he was unlikely, as a morally consistent human being, to vote on the Court to hold such a covenant illegal or unenforceable. But if those who had signed covenants excused themselves from sitting on the case, didn't that mean that the votes likeliest to uphold the enforceability of covenants had in effect been voided? And yet Rutledge, as a Court of Appeals judge, had voted to strike down the covenants. And Reed had written the opinion of the Court in *Smith v. Allwright* with its expansive view of "state action."

The Chief Justice wrote the opinion of the Court, handed down at the beginning of May 1948. The six sitting Justices all agreed—in itself a rare enough event, but particularly noteworthy in view of the Court's prior record of avoidance on this question. "These are not cases, as has been suggested, in which the states have merely abstained from action, leaving private individuals free to impose such discriminations as they see fit," said Vinson. "Rather, these are cases in which the states have made available to such individuals the full coercive power of government to deny to petitioners, on the grounds of race, or color, the enjoyment of property rights in premises which petitioners are willing and able to acquire and which the grantors are willing to sell." Nor was it sufficient to argue in response, as the defense lawyers had, that under the separate-but-equal doctrine such covenants ought to be honored by courts whether they were drawn by whites to exclude blacks or by blacks to exclude whites. "Equal protection of the laws is not achieved," Vinson suggested in one of his rare aphoristic utterances, "through indiscriminate imposition of inequalities." Someone long before had said it more pithily: two wrongs don't make a right.

On its face, *Shelley* was a major victory for blacks. It also had the advantage, from the Court's point of view, of not overturning any earlier decision. Instead, it threaded the needle with legalistic precision. In the 1926 decision of *Corrigan v. Buckley*, the Court had held that restrictive covenants were a form of private, not state, action and, though discriminatory, were therefore legal. Now, in *Shelley*, the Court did not even disturb the *Corrigan* holding: restrictive covenants were still private and legal acts of discrimination, but they were unenforceable by resort to the courts.

Had it been disposed to wipe away the housing disability on broader grounds of public policy or perhaps even criminal conspiracy, the Court might well have found them. The Justices were of no such mind. In effect, though, they had pulled the plug on covenanters, and the results were measurable. According to the 1950 census, of the 3,887 residential blocks in the District of Columbia, non-white accommodations had spread into 459 more than in 1940. In Chicago, it was estimated by the local Commission on Human Relations that within four years of the *Shelley* decision, 21,000 colored families purchased or rented homes in areas formerly barred to them. But neither *Shelley* nor any other decision of the Court had yet weakened the power of the states to segregate under the separate-but-equal doctrine.

A month after *Shelley* came down, Harry Truman dropped a bomb of his own on the tormentors of the Negro. On the strength of the ringing report by his Committee on Civil Rights, the President called on Congress to make lynching a federal offense, to outlaw the poll tax, to end segregation on all interstate transportation, to set up a permanent FEPC to prevent discriminatory hiring practices, to enforce fair elections, and to create a permanent civil-rights commission. Later in 1948, he went beyond entreaties to the legislative branch and issued executive orders ending all discrimination in federal employment and, more stunning yet, all segregation in the armed forces. The FHA, too, was told to end its ban on the insurability of racially mixed housing.

That summer, the President paid for his unflinching stand in behalf of black America. Southern delegates bolted the Democratic convention in Philadelphia because the civil-rights plank in the party platform included most of the provisions Truman had called upon Congress to enact in his February message. The Dixiecrat ticket headed by Governor J. Strom Thurmond of South Carolina cost the Democrats thirty-nine electoral votes. On the left, the Progressive ticket headed by former Vice President Henry Wallace attracted a million popular votes that almost certainly would have gone to the Democrats. The people had had sixteen uninterrupted years of New Deal and Fair Deal, and there was much talk about the therapeutic value of throwing out the rascals in Washington.

Despite the defections on his political right and left, despite the gloomy forecasts of pollsters, despite the grinding burden of his office, Harry Truman went out and licked the pants off dapper Tom Dewey and rewon the White House for four more years. During them, the fight to end segregation would come to a boil.

# 12

# The Spurs of Texas
# Are Upon You

It took a nervy Swedish economist to put down on paper what no white American had ever done—to document, analyze, and excoriate the nation's continuing mistreatment and evident hatred of the Negro. Published in two volumes in 1944, Gunnar Myrdal's *An American Dilemma* was a milestone in sociology, cultural anthropology, and two-fisted investigative reporting once known as muckraking. Its very size, range, and completeness made its findings seem almost inarguable, and its understated but plainly detectable sense of moral revulsion caused civil-rights groups to seize up the book as a bible and white-supremacists to put down its author as a meddling socialist and anti-American.

Myrdal had not spared blacks for what he felt was a degree of complicity in their own subjugation, and his evaluation of the NAACP's efforts to combat racism was, at most, only moderately complimentary. A more militant posture, he suspected, would have boomeranged. In the future, though, he looked for—seemed to demand, even—heightened effort. "The whole system of discrimination in education in the South is not only tremendously harmful to the Negroes," he wrote, "but it is flagrantly illegal, and can easily be so proven in the courts. The main organization for guarding civil liberties for Negroes, the N.A.A.C.P., has not waged, up to now, an extensive legal campaign against school discrimination."

A more generous assessment of the NAACP legal effort since Nathan Margold had first blueprinted a legal-action plan more than a dozen years earlier would have been that, given the meager financial resources available —Thurgood Marshall worked within a $25,000-a-year budget for his whole staff and all expenses during the late Thirties—NAACP lawyers had launched a spirited and relatively successful counterattack before the war to improve the quality of black education, but that the war had inevitably made wholesale litigation seem like special pleading and therefore unpatriotic and imprudent for the time being. No one at the NAACP believed it had done more than scratched the surface in the pre-war *Gaines* and *Alston* victories. Just how far it had to go in the education area was apparent from the data disseminated as the post-war legal drive for equal schools went into motion.

In 1945, the South was spending twice as much to educate each white child as it was per black child. It was investing four times as much in white school plants, paying white teachers salaries 30 percent higher, and virtually ignoring the critical logistics of transporting rural Negroes to their school-houses. In 1944, the seventeen segregating states spent a total of $42 million busing white children to their schools; on transporting colored children, they spent a little more than one million dollars. In the *Journal of Negro Education*, editor Charles Thompson noted in 1947 that the median years of schooling in the segregating states and the District of Columbia was 8.4 for whites and 5.1 for blacks. The percentage of whites finishing high school was four times that of blacks. In February 1947, President Mordecai Johnson of Howard University came before the House Subcommittee on Appropriations and declared that the situation was even worse at the college level. The segregating states spent $86 million of public funds on white colleges and $5 million on black colleges, and as a result, "in no one of these states is there anything approaching a first-class university opportunity available to Negroes." Almost a decade after the *Gaines* decision, there was still no institution in the South where a Negro could pursue studies for a doctorate. Excluding Howard University, there was one accredited medical school in the South for Negroes, but twenty-nine for whites. There was one accredited school of pharmacy for Negroes, but twenty for whites. There was one provisionally accredited law school for Negroes, but forty for whites. There was no accredited engineering school for Negroes, but thirty-six for whites.

About one-fourth of the entire Negro population was functionally illiterate in 1946, according to Ambrose Caliver, the senior specialist in Negro education in the U.S. Office of Education and, with Charles Thompson, probably the leading national authority on the subject. Poor health and family disorganization continued to cause low school-attendance and high pupil-dropout rates, Caliver noted, and almost all those young blacks who did advance intellectually had to work while studying, to the detriment of their schoolwork or their health or both. The South, he added, was still in thrall to a colonial and extractive economy, hobbled by wasteful use of land, absentee ownership, discriminatory freight rates, and lack of technical development—its chronic lamentations. And the continuing hold of the cotton economy was still causing severe poverty, lack of initiative, dietary deficiency, poor housing and sanitation, widespread disease, and extreme cultural deprivation.

However easy Gunnar Myrdal thought it was to prove in the courtroom that blacks were educationally disadvantaged, it was another thing for Thurgood Marshall to convert statistics into a judicial mandate. He had to begin in 1946 by recovering ground that had been lost during the war years.

Colleges were flooded with returning veterans able to pay tuition with their GI Bill benefits, and college-starved Negroes were hit hard by segregation. There were just too few spots available to meet the tremendous demand for graduate and undergraduate study. Howard, by far the biggest and best black university in America, had 7,000 enrolled students in 1947, but was turning away applicants by the legion. The Howard medical school could accept only 70 new students out of well over 1,000 qualified applicants; the pharmacy and dentistry schools could add only 50 each, though more than ten times as many applied. The only solution was to open up the all-white universities, at least at the graduate level, or insist that the Southern states build separate and equal facilities, no matter what the financial burden on the still beleaguered region. In the Depression, the NAACP had hesitated to push the South all the way. Now those inhibitions were gone. And there were enough willing plaintiffs.

Between 1946 and 1950, the principal arena of legal confrontation on the school question was the Southwest. The first plaintiff was no ex-GI at all, but the shy, slender, and pretty twenty-one-year-old daughter of a black clergyman. Ada Lois Sipuel had done superior work at the State College for Negroes in Langston, Oklahoma, and applied to the University of Oklahoma Law School, the only law school in the state. Miss Sipuel's qualifications were acknowledged, but she was turned down because a separate law school for Negroes with "substantially equal" facilities would soon be opened. That a younger generation of Oklahomans disapproved of Jim Crow education was suggested by the astonishing spectacle of white students who had heard of Miss Sipuel's effort and welcomed her to the campus when she came in person to deliver her application; summarily rejected, she was taken to luncheon by a group of the young whites and encouraged not to give up.

To Thurgood Marshall, it looked like a replay of the *Gaines* case, not to mention his own baptism in civil-rights litigation in *Murray v. Pearson.* Hadn't the Supreme Court made it thunderously clear that Oklahoma and every segregating state had to offer Negro students the same educational opportunity it offered whites? Wasn't that the unequivocal finding in *Gaines*? But Oklahoma did not much cotton to the dictates of the Supreme Court. It had crudely circumvented the Court's 1915 decision outlawing the Oklahoma "grandfather clause" and got away with it for twenty-four years. Oklahoma was so vehement in its opposition to biracial schools that its laws called for a fine of from $100 to $500 a day against any institution that instructed whites and blacks together, and any student attending such a school could be fined five to twenty dollars a day.

Marshall had to bring in heavy equipment as he went to court to fight Ada Sipuel's case against the Oklahoma University Board of Regents. He imported leading professors from Harvard, Chicago, Columbia, and Wisconsin law schools to testify in the District Court of Cleveland County, Oklahoma, that to establish an all-black law school, cut off from the dominant white population, was to stage a travesty of legal education. The extended implications of launching Jim Crow graduate and professional schools bordered on the ludicrous. One of the NAACP expert witnesses, Walter Gellhorn of Columbia, recalls chatting during a recess in the Sipuel trial with Mac Q. Williamson, the attorney general of Oklahoma, who was arguing the state's case to retain Jim Crow. "I was saying to him how I thought that even if they were eventually able to persuade the Supreme Court that the facilities of the Negro law school were equal," says Gellhorn, "what was the state going to do when a Negro applied for a medical education— build him a whole medical school? He suddenly saw a flash of light, I guess, and struck his forehead with his palm as the revelation hit. 'Oh, my God,' he said, 'suppose one of them wanted to be a petroleum engineer! Why, we've got the biggest petroleum-cracking laboratory in the country here.' And I think the fire went out of his case after that."

But not out of the court, which ruled that the university did not have to open a black law school until it had enough applicants to make one practicable. Meanwhile, Miss Sipuel could wait. In April of 1947, the Oklahoma Supreme Court upheld the trial court, and Marshall took his case, captioned *Sipuel v. Oklahoma State Board of Regents*, to the United States Supreme Court. His own rising expectations and quickened resentment were reflected in the NAACP brief, which did not merely settle for invoking *Gaines* as a controlling precedent but went after the whole separate-but-equal doctrine for the first time. Miss Sipuel was entitled to immediate admission to the white law school, Marshall's brief said, and "the full extent of the evil inherent" in the *Plessy*-sanctioned form of segregation was evident here, where the state claimed it as a complete defense without even having made the pretense of establishing a separate law school. "Classifications and distinctions based on race or color have no moral or legal validity in our society," the brief declared. "Segregation in public education helps to preserve a caste system which is based upon race and color. It is designed and intended to perpetuate the slave tradition. . . . Equality, even if the term be limited to a comparison of physical facilities, is and can never be achieved . . . the terms 'separate' and 'equal' can not be used conjunctively in a situation of this kind; *there can be no separate equality.*"

The NAACP attack, however, was not a frontal one. It was not yet ready to challenge the segregation laws of Oklahoma or any state. For the moment, all Marshall was doing was invoking the Margold strategy: *as practiced* by the segregating South, the separate-but-equal principle was a false coin. The doctrine itself was counterfeit, too, devised as a constitutional axiom and perpetuated by the Court without stringent examination. Myrdal's *An American Dilemma* and several dozen other works of social science were quoted in denunciation of Jim Crow practices, and yet it was a somewhat loose and unfocused legal brief, better in its polemics than its logic.

Marshall argued *Sipuel* before the Supreme Court during the first week of 1948 and just a week before he had to return for the argument in the restrictive-covenant cases. A mere four days after the Justices heard *Sipuel*, they handed down a unanimous, unsigned *per curiam* opinion that said Oklahoma had to provide Ada Sipuel with a legal education "in conformity with the equal protection clause of the Fourteenth Amendment and provide it as soon as it does for applicants of any other group." It sent the case back to the Oklahoma high court, which ordered the university either to admit Miss Sipuel to the white law school or to open up a separate one for her or to suspend the white law school until it saw fit to open one for Negroes. Miffed, the Oklahoma Board of Regents promptly created a separate law school overnight by ordering a small section of the state capitol in Oklahoma City roped off for colored students and assigning three law teachers to attend to the instruction of Miss Sipuel "and others similarly situated."

Ada Sipuel would have no part of the outrage, and more than a thousand students and professors on campus held a protest rally over the benighted tactics of the university overlords. Declared one law-school professor: "It is a fake, it is a fraud, and . . . I think it is indecent." Marshall came right back to the Supreme Court to claim that the university's solution had defiled the Court's mandate. But he went further. A separate law school, let alone the roped-off overnight special, could not comply with any reasonable definition of equality, for the essence of a law school was to be found not in mere physical facilities but in the free exchange of ideas and attitudes of representatives of all groups. "Exclusion of any one group on the basis of race," Marshall argued, "automatically imputes a badge of inferiority to the excluded group." But the Court was not ready to go that far. In a seven-to-two decision in February 1948, it held that the original Sipuel case "did not present the issue of whether a state might satisfy the equal protection clause . . . by establishing a law school for Negroes." The Oklahoma courts had not acted in defiance of the Court's earlier decision nor had the university in setting up its roped-off "law school" in the state capitol. Only Justices Murphy and Rutledge dissented.

All that *Sipuel* established, then, was that a state had to offer something or other that passed for a school to meet the separate-but-equal test—and it had to do so promptly. *Sipuel* was the judicial ratification of tokenism, and it did nothing to advance the NAACP drive for truly equal schools, let alone the end of segregated ones. By any hardheaded standard, it was a setback.

Thurgood Marshall fought harder now.

The South began to talk about setting up regional graduate and professional schools for colored students only, real ones well equipped and staffed and paid for on a shared basis by the segregating states. It seemed a possible solution to the dilemma posed by *Gaines*. For if or when the Supreme Court went beyond its holding in *Sipuel* and insisted that separate graduate schools had to be really equal in educational value, the South would have to spend millions it could ill afford to preserve Jim Crow education—or let the blacks into the law schools and engineering schools and the rest, and there would be no end of it. For the moment, though, the Court had spared the South from any major policy decision, and the region dug in, ready to repulse the next Negro assault.

The sovereign state of Texas had been so displeased by remarks of Homer Rainey, president of the University of Texas, to the effect that more generous educational facilities ought perhaps to be provided for the state's colored population that he was tossed out of his job. A former head of the U.S. Office of Education, Dr. Rainey had no doubt acquired his un-Texan notions by moseying around the federal corral for too long. In his place, the university's board of regents picked Theophilus Shickel Painter, who would shortly win a place in history by being sued by a black mailman who wanted to become a lawyer. At the time, there were 7,701 white lawyers in Texas and 23 black ones. One more of the latter could hardly have mattered, except that this letter carrier, who bore the unfortunate name of Heman Marion Sweatt, wanted to get his legal education at the all-white university's big law school in Austin, by far the best one in that part of the country. Sweatt applied in

February 1946, a few weeks before Ada Sipuel did in Oklahoma, and was similarly rejected on racial grounds. But the outcome of his case, after a fight of more than four years in four different courts, would be very different from hers.

At first, the district court in Travis County, where Austin was located, seemed to promise justice to Heman Sweatt. After the first hearing there in June of 1946, the judge gave the state six months to establish a law school at colored Prairie View University, an academic hovel that offered college credit for mattress-making, broom-making, and other minimal vocational skills, or it would have to admit Sweatt to the white law school at Austin. The colored school, formerly known as Prairie View State Normal and Industrial Colleges for Negroes, was a university in name only, so designated by a state with a fetish for giantism and a reluctance to acknowledge it was treating its gifted young blacks as intellectual lepers. In response to the court order, the state stuck with the fiction that Prairie View was a university, rented a few rooms in Houston, about forty miles southeast of the Prairie View campus, hired two Negro lawyers to serve as its faculty, and called the arrangement the Prairie View law school. The Travis County District Court, reconsidering Sweatt's case in December as scheduled, found that the makeshift arrangement in Houston provided substantial equality to the Negro applicant despite its deficiencies in a few areas, such as the absence of a student body, a trained faculty, and a library.

By the time Sweatt's complaint was heard by the Court of Civil Appeals the following March, the Texas legislature had shown that it had a heart as big as all outdoors by appropriating three million dollars to create a new, "first class" Texas State University for Negroes. Of the total, $100,000 was to go at once to the establishment and maintenance of a law school. The Houston excuse for a law school was abandoned and a new and better one was temporarily created in downtown Austin in an office building eight blocks away from the University of Texas Law School and just across the street from the state capitol. It consisted of three smallish basement rooms, three part-time faculty members who were first-year instructors at the Texas law school the rest of the time, and a library of 10,000 books plus access to the state law library in the capitol. Classes were to begin for Heman Sweatt on March 10, 1947, if he chose to attend.

Sweatt chose instead to go back to court. Before the appeals judge, both parties agreed that a trial should be conducted in Travis County Court to determine if the one-man law school offered true equality. Since the same court had previously held that the makeshift school in Houston had met the test, the outcome of a full-dress hearing seemed foreordained. But Thurgood Marshall was building a record for the scrutiny of the only court in America that ultimately mattered. To do so, he had to fight on whatever ground was available.

He came loaded for bear to the humid, crowded courtroom in Austin. "I think we've humored the South long enough," Marshall told the New York *Post*'s Texas stringer in a dispatch for consumption up North, "and it's only by law suits and legislation that we'll ever teach reactionaries the meaning of the Fourteenth Amendment. . . . This is going to be a real showdown fight against Jim Crow in education." He was thirty-nine by then and smoking two packs of cigarettes a day. The pressure on him was constant. His duties as he defined them drew him regularly outside the courtroom to rally community support for whatever case he was arguing and for the larger goals of the NAACP. Nearly 2,000 white university people showed up at such a mass meeting in Austin in mid-May just before the Sweatt trial began, by way of demonstrating support for Marshall's efforts. A temporarily all-white NAACP branch, the only one in the country, had been launched on campus and enlisted 200 dues-paying members. At the giant rally, the young ex-GI who was president of the student body stood and said he thought democracy and Christianity ought to be practiced as well as preached at the university, and that no Negro who entered it would be mistreated or ostracized. His view won roaring approval and was seconded by the widely admired J. Frank Dobie, the state's leading man of letters, chairman of the university's English department and the closest thing in Texas to Mr. Chips.

Biracism, though, was not applauded over at the state capitol. To hold the segregationist line, the state dispatched to the Travis County court Attorney General Price Daniel, who would subsequently serve as United States Senator for three years and governor of Texas for eight—and prove a white-supremacist throughout all of them. His family owned land and the newspaper in the town of Liberty in easternmost Texas not far from Louisiana. "That's Deep South," notes Ronnie Dugger, a founder of the liberal *Texas Observer*, a political weekly published out of Austin. "Daniel was an ally of racists and a states'-rights man all the way. The most you could say for him was that he was not a real good hater."

Throughout the five-day trial of *Sweatt v. Painter*, Price Daniel was a tiger. He objected every time Marshall or his two associates, James Nabrit, Jr., and Dallas attorney W. J. Durham, blinked too hard. He went after the NAACP witnesses as if they were cattle rustlers. And he had schooled his own witnesses so well that Marshall met resistance every inch of the way. Marshall put heavy pressure on the dean of the law school, the law librarian, and other officials, but all contended they were doing right by any Negro law-school applicant. After Sweatt himself testified that "I don't believe equality can be given on the basis of segregation" and he had therefore refused to enroll at the basement law school set up to meet his application, Daniel charged that this view represented an about-face from Sweatt's original willingness to attend the Prairie View "law school" in Houston, a position he had taken in a deposition at the first court hearing in mid-1946. Daniel tried to blame the change on Thurgood Marshall's entry into the case as *agent provocateur*, but Sweatt fended him off, saying he had not understood that Prairie View's law school would necessarily be segregated. Daniel kept pressing the point, over the objections of Sweatt's local counsel, Durham. Finally, Marshall objected with vehemence. He cited a 1942 case, conducted by Charles Houston to desegregate the University of Missouri School of Journalism, in which "the Attorney General of Missouri put up the same type of smokescreen to the effect that the case wasn't the plaintiff's case but belonged to a public organization. . . ." The court in Missouri ruled, ". . . if the appellant has the legal right and actually expects to attend the university, her motives for doing so are immaterial." The Travis County judge, Roy C. Archer, agreed. But Price Daniel persisted:

> . . . our purpose here is not to show his [Sweatt's] motive for wanting to attend a law school. Our purpose is to lead up to a connected chain of events motivating him not to attend the separate school that has been offered to him, and, therefore, showing bad faith. . . .

He pushed Sweatt to admit that the NAACP was paying most of the costs of the case. When Durham objected that such a line of questioning was "completely immaterial," Daniel opened up again:

> I want to prove as to what was said and done about that matter about finances for the case, for the purpose of showing that the National Association for the Advancement of Colored People had as much control and management of this case . . . as he does himself, and that they have the further purpose of following that up with a concerted program to boycott this law school and keep other students out.

Clearly, Texas was vulnerable in its claim of having established an equal law school for blacks if no students had enrolled in it. And here was this incendiary Marshall and his colored advancement group doing their utmost to discourage Negroes from attending the bargain basement of American law schools.

The judge's willingness to let such diversionary and demagogic remarks be sprayed around his courtroom burned Marshall up. But he never lost his grip. James Nabrit, his co-counsel in the Sweatt trial, recalls: "He had the rare ability to know when and where to draw the line in his fervor. He was fuming over the judge in Austin, and he said to me before court began one morning, 'I'm gonna tell that judge what I think of him today.' I told him to take it easy. He said nothing in court, but after the case was over and we were all heading for the cars, there was Thurgood standing over in the corner apparently muttering to himself. When he came back to join us, I asked him what that was all about, and he said, 'I told you I was gonna tell that judge what I thought of him—and I just did.' He could do that. Once I was with him in a case in Louisville, and the attorney general of Kentucky kept calling our client by his first name—which was Lyman. Thurgood got up and said he resented it in behalf of his client and that everyone else in court was referred to as 'Mister' with his surname. The point was made and heeded until a little later the judge himself said, 'What did Lyman say to that point?' When I asked Thurgood later why he hadn't protested a second time after the judge had done that, he said, 'I was talkin' to the judge, too, the first time.' In court, he would fight with everything at his disposal, but he didn't waste his effort. And he finally didn't really care if the whites much liked him or not. He was trying to sell his wares, but he was less cold-blooded about it than Charlie Houston or Bill Hastie or myself. In his somewhat more offhanded way, he'd fight for every chip."

Marshall fought now by bringing into court a string of experts who branded the state's basement law school for blacks as a subterfuge. Earl Harrison, dean of the law school at the University of Pennsylvania, asserted: ". . . a very important facility of a modern law school consists of one's classmates. In other words, it isn't enough to have a good professor. It is equally essential that there be a well-rounded, representative group of students in the classroom to participate in the . . . discussion which centers around previous decisions of the courts."

Marshall then moved to get on the record that state-imposed racial separation was both scientifically unjustifiable and socially destructive. His instrument was one of the best-known and most highly respected scholars in the nation—Robert Redfield, chairman of the department of anthropology and for a dozen years the head of social sciences at the University of Chicago. He had a doctorate in *both* anthropology and law and was perhaps the only scholar in America with such credentials. He had studied racial differences for twenty years. As soon as Marshall's line of inquiry became clear, the attorney general of Texas was on his feet objecting "because this lawsuit involves only education in law and procedure." Marshall, threatened with the loss of testimony of one of the aces in his deck, was determined not to let the issue be narrowed. More in ardor than in order, the sentences came tumbling out of him with a directness and a conviction that riveted his listeners. Lest there be any mistake about it, he said, Sweatt was challenging the constitutionality of the laws of Texas as they deprived him of admission to the white law school because of his race, and "we have a right to put in evidence to show that segregation statutes in the state of Texas and in any other state, actually when examined—and they have never been examined in any lawsuit that I know of yet—have no line of reasonableness. There is no understandable factual basis for classification by race, and under a long line of decisions by the Supreme Court, not on the question of Negroes, but on the Fourteenth Amendment, all courts agree that if there is no rational basis for the classification, it is flat in the teeth of the Fourteenth Amendment." The judge relented.

Redfield proved a brilliant witness whose every word suggested a cool, considered judgment with great authority behind it. Were there basic differences in the learning abilities of the two races? Scholars in the field, the Chicago professor replied, had begun with "a rather general presumption . . . that inherent differences in intellectual ability or capacity to learn existed between Negroes and whites, and have slowly, and I think convincingly, been compelled to come to the opposite conclusion. . . ." More to the point, Redfield declared that research results "make it very probable that if such differences are later shown to exist, they will not prove to be significant for any educational policy or practice"—such as segregation, which he said "prevents the student from the full, effective and economical coming to understand the nature and capacity of the group from which he is segregated." Beyond that, "it intensifies suspicion and distrust between Negroes and whites, and suspicion and distrust are not favorable conditions either for the acquisition and conduct of an education, or for the discharge of the duties of a citizen."

On vigorous cross-examination by Price Daniel, Redfield turned back the attorney general's thrusts so well that his answers were sometimes stronger than they had been on direct examination. Thus, when Daniel asked him if he did not agree that segregation, long enforced in Southern localities, could be ended only "by a gradual change instead of forcing it upon the community," Redfield said simply, "I think that all change should not come on any more rapidly than it is consistent with the general welfare." Daniel thought he had an easy mark on his hands and moved in.

Q. Yes, sir. In other words, you will agree with the other eminent educators in your field . . . that it is impossible to force the abolition of segregation upon a community that had had it for a long number of years, in successfully obtaining the results that are best?

A. No, I don't agree to that.

Q. Do you think the laws should be changed tomorrow?

A. I think that segregation is a matter of legal regulation. Such a law can be changed quickly.

Q. Do you think it has anything to do with the social standing in the community?

A. Segregation in itself is a matter of law, and that law can be changed at once, but if you mean the attitude of the people with respect to keeping away from people of another race, then perhaps I have another answer. . . . I think in every community there is some segregation that can be changed at once, and the area of higher education is the most favorable for making the change.

A little later, Daniel thought he had a trump card to show that the articulate anthropologist's views were dwarfed by far weightier authority.

Q. Doctor, are you acquainted with the Encyclopædia Britannica, the publication by that name?

A. I have a set. I don't look at it very often.

Q. You are from the University of Chicago?

A. Yes.

Q. Is that publication now published under the auspices of that university?

A. Yes.

Q. Have you read the article therein on education and segregation of the races in American schools?

A. If I have, I don't remember it.

Q. You don't remember it. Have you written any articles for the Encyclopædia Britannica?

A. No, we are just beginning a revision of anthropological articles, and it seems there has to be a very drastic change.

Q. Do you know who wrote the articles in the Encyclopædia Britannica on the subject of higher education for Negroes and segregation?

A. I don't remember such articles.

Q. Do you recognize the Encyclopædia Britannica and the articles on such subjects as an authority in the field?

A. No, I do not.

Q. You do not?

A. No, sir.

Off the witness stand, Robert Redfield persisted in opposing the state of Texas. "The courtroom was integrated at the beginning," recalls Charles Thompson, who followed Redfield to the witness stand, "but then it began to get more crowded and the whites coming in later on couldn't find room. A big white policeman—this fella must have been seven feet tall—came in and saw the whites standing against the wall and then started telling our people, 'Come on now, you know better than that.' It was a state court, remember, and so he began to segregate the audience to make room for the whites. But Dr. Redfield and the dean of Penn law school, they wouldn't move when the fellow told them to. They said they wanted to stay right where they were—with us."

A month after the trial ended, the court ruled against Sweatt. It would take the better part of three years before *Sweatt v. Painter* crawled up the judicial ladder to the Supreme Court of the United States. Heman Sweatt, meanwhile, continued his appointed rounds as a postman, and as the hands of history touched the midpoint of the twentieth century, Texas remained fastidiously Jim Crow.

Charlie Houston's teaching that local and state courts provided a far more intimate stage for dramatizing the issues at stake in a civil-rights case had no doubt been correct—up to a point. It was a far surer way to rally the local black community and a more promising one for jabbing the conscience of the local white community. The federal courts seemed remote and almost antiseptic by comparison. But since most of the municipal, county, and state courts, particularly in the South, were unfavorably disposed toward the Negro's aching grievances, NAACP lawyers and other counsel to black litigants were becoming deeply enmeshed in the appeal process. At its worst and most exhausting, as in *Sweatt*, the glacially creeping cycle seemed like something out of grossest Kafka.

To speed the process, the NAACP Legal Defense Fund turned now to the federal courts. After the Supreme Court had washed its hands of *Sipuel* and while *Sweatt* was slowly making its way up to it, Marshall agreed to take on one more graduate-school case that a number of his advisors were not very sanguine about. It would prove to be a vital link in the chain of cases he had been pursuing since 1935.

George W. McLaurin had long before earned his master's degree and in 1948 applied to the graduate school of the University of Oklahoma to earn his doctorate in education. A few years later, Marshall recounted the graduate-school desegregation campaign to a group of black newspaper executives: "The Dixiecrats and the others said it was horrible. The only thing Negroes were trying to do, they said, was to get social equality. As a matter of fact, there would be intermarriage, they said. The latter theory was the reason we deliberately chose Professor McLaurin. We had eight people who had applied and who were eligible to be plaintiffs, but we deliberately picked Professor McLaurin because he was sixty-eight years old and we didn't think he was going to marry or intermarry. . . . They could not bring that one up on us, anyhow."

The university nevertheless rejected George McLaurin, and to speed his case, the Fund approached the federal courts by an avenue it had not traveled before. Generally, a three-step process is involved in cases that ultimately reach the Supreme Court by the federal route. Jurisdiction of the federal courts covers cases on questions peculiarly national in character and usually hinging on interpretation of the Constitution and other federal laws. Under Article III of the Constitution, federal courts also may consider cases in which the federal government itself is a party, cases between two or more states, cases between citizens of different states, and admiralty and maritime cases. Federal suits usually begin in the United States District Courts, of which every state has at least one. The more populous states are divided into two or more federal judicial districts, each served by a District Court. Trials are held before a single District judge, whose decision was at one time automatically appealable directly to the United States Supreme Court. Too much of the high court's time, though, was spent weighing such routine appeals, and in 1891 Congress created an intermediate level of eleven Courts of Appeals with jurisdiction over "circuits" composed of the District Courts; the circuits vary in size from the Ninth, which covers nine entire Western states, to the one in the District of Columbia, which covers the smallest geographic area but handles the heavy flow of cases involving the federal government. Each Court of Appeals is made up of at least three judges, who sit together on cases before them. Since the Judicial Reform Act of 1925, the Supreme Court has had almost unlimited discretion in which cases it wishes to hear on appeal from the circuit courts—a plea it grants in relatively few cases, so that the Circuit Courts of Appeals have increasingly become the framers of judicial doctrine in federal law.

A novel feature of the appeals machinery, relatively little used before World War Two, allows the three-step process to be shortened in instances when an injunction is sought against enforcement of a federal, state, or municipal law on the ground that it is in conflict with the Constitution. In such cases, a special three-judge District Court is summoned by the chief judge of the Circuit Court of Appeals and usually consists of two District Court judges and one Court of Appeals judge. On the theory that the issue at stake in such a case is of a more urgent nature than in other cases, appeal of a decision by such a three-judge District Court goes directly to the Supreme Court without intermediate review. As judicial matters generally go, such a process is downright streamlined. Thus, the Legal Defense Fund brought *McLaurin v. Oklahoma State Regents for Higher Education* straight to a special three-judge federal District Court in August 1948. The special District Court handed down its opinion the very next month, ruling just as the Supreme Court had after the first round of *Sipuel*: "the state is under the constitutional duty to provide the plaintiff with the education he seeks as soon as it does for applicants of any other group."

Oklahoma was in no hurry to comply. The governor agreed to recommend to the next session of the legislature, convening early in 1949, that Negroes seeking courses of study not available at the state's colored college might be admitted to the regular colleges and universities of the state. That sounded fair enough, and something of an advance over the roped-off "law school" in the state capitol that had been proposed to meet Ada Sipuel's needs. But there was a catch, as McLaurin discovered soon after returning to court in November to demand and win immediate admission to the state university. He became a fully matriculated graduate student at the University of Oklahoma, all right, but in accordance with the legislature's hurry-up revision of the state laws, all such instruction of colored students was to be given "on a segregated basis" within the university. And so sixty-eight-year-old George McLaurin was made to sit at a desk by himself in an anteroom outside the regular classrooms where his course work was given. In the library, he was assigned a segregated desk in the mezzanine behind half a carload of newspapers. In the cafeteria, he was required to eat in a dingy alcove by himself and at a different hour from the whites.

It was surely Oklahoma's most inventive contribution to legalized bigotry since the adoption of the "grandfather clause." The state was punishing George McLaurin for requiring it to honor his rights as a citizen. In so doing, it had resolved to shame him as a man. Marshall went back to court. McLaurin's "required isolation from all other students, solely because of the accident of birth," he argued, "creates a mental discomfiture, which makes concentration and study difficult, if not impossible." The regulations scarred McLaurin with "a badge of inferiority which affects his relationship, both to his fellow students and to his professors." McLaurin himself came before the special three-judge District Court and said that it was "quite strange and humiliating to be placed out in that position."

Yet the court turned McLaurin down. A few hundred stigmata a day firm up a man's soul.

Marshall appealed straight to the Supreme Court. Before *McLaurin* was heard by the Justices in April 1950—on the same day as *Sweatt*—Oklahoma modified the ordeal it had imposed on its least-likely-to-succeed student. McLaurin was now admitted to the classroom with white students. But his seat was surrounded by a railing marked "Reserved for Colored." Nauseated by the spectacle, white students tore the sign down until officials settled for assigning McLaurin to an unmarked row set aside for him and any other colored student who might enroll in quest of similar humiliation. They also let McLaurin onto the main floor of the library, but restricted him to his own table. And they let him eat in the cafeteria at the same time as whites, but still at his own place, which became endearingly known to McLaurin and his sympathizers as "The Jug." Such restrictions, Oklahoma contended in its brief to the Court, were merely nominal. They were necessary if the university was to conform to the state's separate-but-equal laws.

But were separate-but-equal laws finally defensible? McLaurin's case now seemed to present that question in sharp relief. It could not be claimed, as in all the preceding graduate-school cases, that McLaurin had been denied equal educational facilities in terms of measurable factors—curriculum, faculty, size and condition of buildings, per-student outlay. In all these, McLaurin had been granted equality. All that was left was segregation itself. Did the very fact of it cause him to receive an inferior educational opportunity? Did it produce such mental anguish that, as he claimed, he could not focus properly on his schoolwork? Or was the "badge of inferiority" he wore imposed on him, as the Supreme Court had said in *Plessy*, "not by reason of anything found in the act [of separation], but solely because the colored race chooses to put that construction on it"? Here, thought Thurgood Marshall, was the ideal case to show up that contention for what it was.

The Supreme Court that would decide *Sweatt* and *McLaurin* had taken a decidedly less libertarian swing during the summer of 1949 with the deaths of the two ardent, if not overly accomplished, judicial-activists—Frank Murphy and Wiley Rutledge.

To replace Murphy, President Truman named his devoted Attorney General, Tom Clark, the first Texan to serve on the high court. Civil-libertarians took one look at Clark's record at the Justice Department and groaned: he had launched sweeping security checks throughout the federal apparatus, stepped up wiretapping, disseminated lists of allegedly subversive groups that were given no chance to challenge the smear label, turned down many aliens with strong cases for citizenship on the remotest suspicion of Red sympathies, directed the relocation of Japanese-Americans in wartime, and personally argued a major Supreme Court case against the United Mine Workers' right to strike. To liberals, Tom Clark looked like a potential disaster area on the Court. In manner and outlook, he was much like Fred Vinson, and predictably the new Justice joined the Chief in almost every vote during his first few terms on the Court.

Less concern but no higher enthusiasm was voiced by liberals over Truman's fourth and final appointee to the Court, Sherman Minton of Indiana, who took Rutledge's chair. By almost any standard, "Shay" Minton would rank near the bottom of the list of 100 men who have served as Justices of the United States Supreme Court. Built like a heavyweight boxer, the broad-shouldered Hoosier with the square, doughy face came to the United States Senate in 1934 and was assigned a seat next to another freshman Senator, Truman of Missouri. A lonely figure during those bustling New Deal days when Eastern intellectuals and old-time pols ran Washington and viewed the small man from Missouri as the plaything of Kansas City's Pendergast political machine, Harry Truman took to "Shay" Minton, and the two remained friends well after the Indiana voters turned him out of the Senate in 1940. He served as a White House aide to the President for a year and then, for his loyalty and New Deal votes in the Senate, where he had represented a conservative and isolationist state that dumped him, he was named a judge on the United States Court of Appeals for the Seventh Circuit, encompassing Indiana, Illinois, and Wisconsin. His opinions on the bench were pedestrian and sometimes tended to miss the substantive point of a case. That Minton was not exactly a bright ornament of the American judiciary hardly discouraged Harry Truman, who, for all his grit and for all the outstanding men he picked for other offices, somehow felt compelled to staff the Supreme Court with men whose chief recommendation for the post,

Vinson perhaps excepted, was their friendship with him. On the Court, Minton proved even more slavish than the other Truman appointees in voting to uphold government power, often at the expense of individual liberties and private interests—a position that would have pegged him as a judicial liberal in the Thirties, when he in fact had spoken out in behalf of Roosevelt's court-packing plan.

This, then, was the new Truman-Vinson Court that would pass on the most critical civil-rights cases to come before the high tribunal in the twentieth century. Vinson, frustrated for three long terms in his desire to take command of a splintered Court, now had a virtual majority. The three other Truman appointees, none of them particularly brainy or reflective and all devoid of leadership qualities, gathered beneath the Chief Justice's wing, where Stanley Reed had already found comfort. Black and Douglas anchored the other end of the Court, where their rarely compromised defense of individual liberties and ready assaults on perceived abuses of government power led them into frequent dissent. Frankfurter and Jackson fluctuated between the two poles, opting whenever possible for the Court's avoidance of the political thicket and the bogs of federal policy. As a practical matter, that meant more often than not allowing federal and state power wide orbit, but the Frankfurter-Jackson position proclaimed devotion to judicial restraint rather than the belief that the government was entitled to virtually limitless license to protect the national security, as the Truman appointees often seemed on the brink of proposing.

Where the Vinson Court would come out on Negro rights was by no means clear to Thurgood Marshall. The loss of Murphy and Rutledge, two fast friends of the NAACP's legal crusade, was obviously a blow. Tom Clark, to be sure, had put the government into *Shelley* on the Negro's side, but there was little other evidence of his concern for civil rights and a good deal of evidence of his indifference to civil liberties. There were reports, moreover, that the government's entry into *Shelley* was more the doing of Solicitor General Perlman than of Attorney General Clark. But Marshall saw a friend in Clark. "He was never funny on this score—on race," he says twenty-five years later. Minton had almost no track record at all in dealing with Negro rights in his three federal positions before coming to the Court, though his denunciation of the Klan, then active in Indiana, was thought to have contributed to his Senate re-election setback in 1940.

Where Chief Justice Vinson himself would come out on Negro rights also defied easy prediction. It was tempting to read a great deal into his *Shelley* opinion, but on close examination, *Shelley* stood on sandy ground. It had been more clever than principled, and a later dissent by Vinson on a sequel case involving the right of signers of restrictive covenants to collect damages from other signers who broke them would suggest just how unsteady the Chief Justice had been in relying on the "state action" device in the first place. In the long run, Thurgood Marshall's best hope for carrying the Truman appointees with him in the crucial graduate-school cases might be the very thing that made them seem such hangdog Justices in comparison to the Roosevelt appointees—their devotion to the power and policies of the federal government. And Harry Truman had given strong evidence by then of where he stood on civil rights. He had staked the Presidency on that stance and he had won, perhaps more in spite of than because of his pro-Negro efforts. It was not unthinkable that the politically attuned Justices he had selected felt they owed him their allegiance on racial questions.

Harry Truman made one other judicial appointment in 1949 of special interest to black America. He named William H. Hastie to the United States Court of Appeals for the Third Circuit. It was the highest rank in the American judiciary ever held by a Negro, and it was just one rung below the Supreme Court.

Bill Hastie, at forty-five years of age, had not risen so far and so fast by playing it safe. As a District Court judge in the Virgin Islands in the late Thirties, he had had his run-ins with U.S. military brass over their encrusted Jim Crow preferences. As dean of Howard Law School from 1939 to 1946, he had stood up to the high-handedness of Mordecai Johnson, who seemed to grow more imperious as the years passed. And though he had been somewhat controversial as a District judge and had ended his wartime stint as aide to Secretary of War Stimson by resigning in protest over Jim Crow practices, Hastie was picked as the first black governor of the Virgin Islands in 1946—which made him the first black governor of any American state or territory—and Truman later visited him there as Hastie's official guest, to the chagrin of congressional Dixiecrats. As governor, Hastie had his differences with his lieutenant governor on the racial front and ended up as no special favorite of local blacks, who made up 95 percent of the islands' population but still found the governor's equalitarian beliefs rather too advanced and a discomfort to resident whites with money. "He was very controversial and political, and he didn't draw the line in his positions the way Thurgood did," says James Nabrit. "He'd speak out—and he was always right in his views, even if it meant losing favored jobs and positions."

Now, with Hastie gone and Charlie Houston relatively remote, the burdens on Marshall grew. After the war, the cases began to pile into the Fund. Many of them involved personal or private instances of prejudice that could not be combated in the courtrooms of the nation. Many came in barely literate letters that were themselves testament to the failure of the system. Others came from the travels of Walter White, who would blithely pledge the Legal Defense Fund's help in matters that Marshall's hard-pressed office either could not or preferred not to pursue. The relationship between the two men, degenerating ever since the Fund was broken off into a separate unit in 1939, had become, at best, an armed truce a decade later. White's detractors suggested that he saw in the younger Marshall a fast-rising contender to his widely acknowledged position as unofficial spokesman for the colored people of America. The NAACP head seemed to go to some lengths to keep the spotlight on himself in the steady stream of press releases that flowed from headquarters, and he edged into Marshall's domain every time the attorney won another case. After one such victory under the NAACP banner, White called a press conference—a prerogative not open to the Legal Defense

Fund's decorous general counsel—and started sounding off on the legal implications of the court decision. In a rare show of public annoyance, Marshall interrupted him to ask, "What law school did you attend again, Mr. Executive Secretary?"

White seemed more and more of a figurehead as Marshall's list of real accomplishments lengthened and people began to call him "Mr. Civil Rights." And the better Marshall did, the greater the pressure got. He was always on the move, often grabbing only three or four hours of sleep a night. The Fund was no longer a one-man show. Marshall had begun to bring in dedicated young people to help him late in the war years. His key assistant was a limber, quiet, and strongly self-disciplined Negro lawyer named Robert Lee Carter, who came to the Fund in 1944 at the age of twenty-seven after a stormy career in the Army Air Force. Carter's insistence that black officers were entitled to every privilege that white officers enjoyed got him branded a troublemaker and almost tossed out of service altogether until Bill Hastie intervened with Washington higher-ups. Carter had followed the same academic route as Marshall—first Lincoln University and then Howard Law School, where Hastie was dean and noted his work with high approval. He was a natural for Marshall's staff. "He was very hard-working, very thorough, very bright," says a knowledgeable associate of those years, "but he was not a philosopher, not well read or broadly based like Houston or Hastie. He was a partisan, a doer, a man deeply concerned with results. He carried the heaviest burden, getting the work out and the briefs in on time. In that office, Bob Carter was the keel and Thurgood was—I don't know, the wind maybe."

Carter freed his outgoing boss to roam the country with the comfort of knowing that the wheels were still turning back in New York. "And that was important," remarks James Nabrit, "because if the courts or our opponents could catch us up on a procedural miscue—a missed deadline, say—there was every chance we'd be ruled out of a case on a technicality." In later years, Carter would come to resent the staff-man role, but during the late Forties and early Fifties he was a totally dedicated trouper. "Thurgood was pleasant and easy to work with—he is not a grim man—and he expressed a great deal of loyalty to those in his professional family," says Carter. "He'd be generous with praise for his staff, though almost never in person. You'd hear about it by what he said to others. He wanted me to play the role of gadfly in the strategy sessions. I was younger and more radical than many of the people Thurgood would have in, I guess, but he'd never let them shut me up. And I was always pushing for us to go further. It was easy for me to do, though, because it was Thurgood who had the ultimate responsibility."

How Marshall exercised that responsibility met with disapproval in many ways from the other man in the office during the 1945–50 span—tall, handsome, glib Franklin Williams, a Negro honors graduate from Fordham Law School who joined the Fund at the age of twenty-eight and brought along a precociously developed ego. A debonair native New Yorker, Williams saw in the suave Walter White a leader cut more to his mold than the earthy Marshall, who could flick on his Rastus dialect without skipping a consonant. "Walter liked me and respected me as a dynamic young guy in the office," says Williams, "and Thurgood probably thought I was in league with Walter—and since I did hang out with him, I suppose I was." With a friend in power, Williams did not hesitate to second-guess Marshall on how he ran the office. Within a year of his arrival, he was dispatching a long, detailed, and pompous memorandum urging "a more businesslike manner" in the office, "[e]limination of wasted time and expeditious handling of cases and incidental matters," and a regular weekly staff meeting after hours to avoid "the ever-present danger that busy men, preoccupied with different problems, may grow apart and lose touch." Not incidentally, he was eager to be assigned more responsibility. More important, Williams thought Marshall was cautious to a fault in taking on thorny cases. "He knew where cases had to move," Williams comments, "which ones would and should move, and how to move them, but more often than not cases were taken on reluctantly. Thurgood had to be convinced of victory beyond a reasonable doubt before he said yes."

Despite his reservations, Williams grew to admire Marshall's method of operation: "He had great success in picking people's brains and manipulating them in the interests of the cause. He'd get a lot of outside lawyers together in a room, and he'd be talking and laughing and drinking along with the rest of them and getting everybody relaxed and open, and he'd seem to be having such a good time with them that you wouldn't think he was listening. But after they'd left, there it all was—he'd had the benefit of all their brains, which was his strategy in the first place. Frankly, it was a little embarrassing —until I came to understand what he was up to."

The rest of the Fund staff then was female. Marian Wynn Perry, a white Brooklyn College graduate with experience in government and private practice, had met Marshall and Carter while working with the Lawyers Guild and came to work at the Fund the same day Williams did in 1945. Having helped draft New York State's FEPC law, Mrs. Perry specialized in labor and employment matters, an area that Williams, saddled primarily with court-martial cases, sought to share with her. Tensions persisted between the two throughout their four years at adjacent desks. It was there, too, between Mrs. Perry and the young black law student who came to clerk with Marshall in 1945 and stayed on at the Fund for twenty years—Constance Baker Motley. Pleasant, taciturn Connie Motley passed the bar in 1948 and became the resident expert on housing matters. "She was a plodder," says a colleague of the period, "but she knew her stuff." In addition, there were four secretaries and a white research assistant, Annette Peyser, in the Fund office, which still functioned as a sub-duchy within the main NAACP headquarters, by then located in an office building on West 40th Street between Fifth and Sixth Avenues overlooking Bryant Park and the main branch of the New York Public Library, a convenient resource.

There was human electricity all around. Walter White felt threatened by Thurgood Marshall. Marshall was constantly on the go. Williams was making his complaints known and reaching for power. The white women— Peyser, Perry, and Walter White's secretary—were, in Perry's words, "walking on eggs." And yet there was a remarkable *esprit* at the Fund and a great deal of work of high competence got churned out. Just how competent the group was may be inferred from the fact that three of the five lawyers then in the office would go on to become federal judges, and Frank Williams would become by turn a key NAACP operative on the West Coast, a top man in the Peace Corps, American ambassador to Ghana, and the holder of impressive positions in the world of education.

Everyone at the Fund set to work on the briefs in *Sweatt* and *McLaurin* as it became clear that Texas was waging an all-out fight in defense of segregation. The state had learned a lesson in *Smith v. Allwright* in 1944 when it had felt the white primary was so well protected by prior Supreme Court rulings that there was no need to send an attorney to argue the question before the Justices. Not only did Texas submit a fighting and skillful brief to the Court in *Sweatt*, but it enlisted the backing of eleven other states, whose attorneys general joined in a forceful *amicus* brief reaffirming segregation and the rights of the states to deal with schools and racial matters as the customs and preferences of their region dictated. *Sweatt* seemed to have the makings of a landmark case, to judge by the energy of the Southern defense.

By late 1949 at the Legal Defense Fund office, Marian Perry had been succeeded by a twenty-five-year-old lawyer just out of Columbia who would one day succeed Thurgood Marshall as chief counsel—Jack Greenberg. White and Jewish, possessor of a firm jaw and a no-nonsense manner, Greenberg added a first-rate analytical mind to the staff and felt no discomfort amid what to outsiders seemed strictly a black man's world. His work at the Fund Greenberg saw as beyond special pleading for the Negro; basic human rights were being fought for, and there was no better spot in American law in which to help wage that fight.

New and untried, Greenberg did only minor work in the graduate cases, though within a year of his arrival he would win a major college-desegregation case in the state courts of Delaware. Carter, Williams, James Nabrit at Howard, and Chicago law professor William Robert Ming, Jr., who had taught at Howard for ten years, mostly under Hastie's deanship, and put in four more years in Washington as a government lawyer, did the bulk of the drafting on the *Sweatt* brief. It was by no means just another legal document. After considerable internal debate and outside consultation, the Fund brief took a far stronger position than it had done in more or less exploratory fashion in *Sipuel*: it urged the Supreme Court to reverse its earlier holdings on *Plessy v. Ferguson* and rule now that segregation had no place in education.

But the Fund's overall presentation to the Court, while more aggressive than any in the past, still hedged its bet in refusing to strike at segregation itself as the heart of its case. Marshall was clinging to the original Margold concept: segregation was illegal because, as practiced, it never provided equality for Negroes. The NAACP continued to stress the consequences of segregation rather than its constitutional standing. Marshall's reading of the Court left him with the queasy sense that a frontal attack on segregation, not merely as practiced but as conceived, might well backfire. The Court in *Sipuel* two years earlier had chosen to construe the issue as narrowly as possible and claimed that it had not been presented with the question of whether a separate law school could ever provide equality; it then went along with Oklahoma's makeshift arrangements for the Negro plaintiff. *Sweatt* now raised the issue squarely with regard to law schools, but all the Court had to do, really, to satisfy the NAACP position was rule that *Plessy* meant what it said and that Texas had to provide Heman Sweatt with a truly equal law school or let him into the white one. The Court, in short, had paid lip service to *Plessy* on a number of occasions, but never had it ruled that the separate school facilities actually provided for a black student fell short of the *Plessy* standard of equality and therefore violated the Constitution. In *Sweatt*, all the statistical support necessary for such a holding was now being brought to the Court's attention. Marshall's first job, he felt, was to win on any ground that he could, and winning within the confines of the *Plessy* doctrine was the safest way.

But Marshall had been in the fight too long not to see that he could spend the rest of his life trying to prove that white school boards in a thousand counties were failing to provide an equal-but-separate education for their resident Negroes. Thus, in its *Sweatt* brief the NAACP Legal Defense Fund took its hardest swipe yet at *Plessy*. But Marshall went further. Through the Lawyers Guild, Marshall had met white Yale law professor Thomas I. Emerson perhaps a dozen times and knew him as a firm supporter of racial equality. Emerson had come to Washington as a young lawyer in the early New Deal days and worked in a number of fast-moving agencies and administrative bodies including the NRA, the Social Security Board, the National Labor Relations Board, and the OPA. Marshall filled Emerson in on the *Sweatt* case and asked him to consider drafting an *amicus* brief in behalf of a committee of leading law professors across the country. It was not to be just another *amicus* brief chiming in with the main NAACP position, but rather an all-out assault on *Plessy* and a full-scale denunciation of segregation itself. It would go well beyond the NAACP brief and talk to the Court with the full weight and authority of some of the nation's top legal scholars. "There had been a long-standing difference of opinion within the Fund as to how far they ought to go on *Plessy* at that time," Emerson recalls. "This seemed a good solution."

The solution was called the Committee of Law Teachers Against Segregation in Legal Education, and the brief submitted in its name and written by Emerson and his Yale colleagues John Frank and David Haber was eventually signed by 187 law professors from leading schools across the country. Their remarks addressed to the Court bore an almost man-to-man tone as the professors rehearsed the history of the Fourteenth Amendment and *Plessy* and suggested what the NAACP dared not: the Court itself had deprived the Negro of his rights, and the time had come for the Court to restore them. "Laws which give equal protection are those which make no *discrimination* because of race in the sense that they make no *distinction* because of race," the professors wrote. "As soon as laws make a right or responsibility dependent solely on race, they violate the 14th Amendment. Reasonable classifications may be made, but one basis of classification is completely precluded; for the Equal Protection clause makes racial classifications unreasonable per se."

More forcefully than the NAACP brief, the professors charged that the Court had avoided squarely facing the question of whether segregation in education was reasonable. On several occasions, *Gaines* most recently, it had mistakenly said that the point had been settled. "The result is that if segregation in education is legal, it is a rule of law that came from no place."

Only after the legal theory had been extensively presented did the law professors dwell on the specifics of Sweatt's case and assert that "in countless ways separate legal education cannot be equal legal education." Not the least of the reasons was that "By sending Sweatt to a raw, new law school without alumni or prestige, Texas deprives him of economic opportunity which its white students have." It was vital that Negroes have the chance to become able lawyers, said the professors. "If they have the ability to rise above the cotton picking, the manual labor, and the domestic service to which our white society has consigned their race, it is almost as important to them as life itself that they have the opportunity to do so." The scholars closed on a decidedly unscholastic note—one that Thurgood Marshall would perhaps have found it impolitic to sound: "The treatment of our Negro minority is a moral responsibility of our white majority, and it is important that the American conscience be freed of wrongdoing. This Court, as the expounder of the Constitution, is one of the custodians of that conscience."

Texas fought back with a tough-minded brief that made maximum use of its initial advantage: the law as pronounced by the Court in the past was on its side. None of the cases cited by Sweatt's attorneys, said Price Daniel's brief for Texas, had held that "a state may not constitutionally provide education for its white and Negro students at separate schools where equal education is furnished to both groups." Texas was reinforced by a "Brief of the States of Arkansas, Florida, Kentucky, Georgia, Louisiana, Mississippi, North Carolina, Oklahoma, South Carolina, Virginia and Tennessee, *Amici Curiae* in Support of Respondents." Dixie was willing to yield nothing other than the admission that it might not have honored the *Plessy* doctrine to the letter. But past failure to meet standards of equality did not require throwing the baby out with the bathwater. *Plessy* was fixed law. It simply had to be better enforced, and the states stood ready to do so.

In the battle of the *amicus* briefs, Texas appeared to enjoy the advantage of support by eleven sovereign states while Sweatt's principal allies were 187 law professors, linked in an *ad hoc* committee, who in effect were telling the Supreme Court to recant for past errors. In the end, though, Marshall won the backing of another important friend of the Court who would even the scales against the massed impact of the Southern bloc—the government of the United States.

Tom Clark, who as Attorney General had put the government into *Shelley* on the Negro side in 1948, was himself a Justice now. His successor, former Senator and former Democratic National Chairman J. Howard

McGrath of Rhode Island, shared a number of Tom Clark's traits. He was close to Harry Truman, he was intensely political, he was not known as a heavy thinker, and he had not strained himself in behalf of advancing Negro rights. But the two Clark lieutenants who had played a large part in swinging the Justice Department behind the NAACP effort in the restrictive-covenant cases—Solicitor General Philip Perlman and his principal assistant in the civil-rights area, Philip Elman—were still in their jobs and still pushing for government involvement in the slowly flowering civil-rights movement. Perlman, reluctant at first, had given what one close confederate calls "a real Fourth of July speech" to the Supreme Court in presenting the government's position as *amicus* in *Shelley*. As *Sweatt* and *McLaurin* now came before the Court, Perlman and Elman were busy getting the government to take a critical position in another segregation case that would affect the two NAACP graduate-school cases as well.

Elmer Henderson was a black employee of the federal government who, in the course of his duties, had to take a Southern Railway train from Washington to Georgia in 1942. The one table set aside for Negroes in the dining car was not enough to handle the needs of colored passengers, and Henderson went unfed. He sued. In time, the railroad changed its regulations a little, but their effect was still the same: a Negro passenger had to eat at a table set aside for him at the end of the diner and separated from the rest of the car by curtains. "It was as if you were a pig or some kind of animal," said Henderson's attorney, Belford Lawson of Washington, who brought the case of *Henderson v. United States* with the financial backing of the Negro fraternity Alpha Phi Alpha. It was one of the very few civil-rights cases argued in that era outside of the NAACP umbrella, and it was brought by the same lawyer, with the same fraternity in back of him, whom Thurgood Marshall had collided with in taking charge of his first important civil-rights case, *Murray v. Maryland*, sixteen years earlier. Because the Southern Railway's dining-car regulations had been approved by the Interstate Commerce Commission, Lawson brought the action against the federal government on the charge that both the Constitution and the Interstate Commerce Act had been violated when Henderson was discriminated against solely because of his race. The antitrust division of the Justice Department had coped successfully with the case in the lower federal courts in defending the ICC on the ground that the separate-but-equal holding of *Plessy* had essentially been met by the railroad's provision of space for Negro passengers in the same dining car with the same food as whites. But when Lawson appealed to the Supreme Court, the Solicitor General's office took charge of the government's case. Perlman and Elman had had enough of *Plessy* and the pretense that the government of the United States could continue in good conscience to defend the degradation of black Americans.

"There was something of a hassle," Elman remembers, "but we decided we were going into the Court and confessing error. McGrath backed Perlman—in fact, he wanted to argue the case himself—and in *Henderson* the government argued for the first time that *Plessy* was wrong and that the

Court should overrule it." And then the Justice Department gave Thurgood Marshall a needed lift. It filed *amicus* briefs in both *Sweatt* and *McLaurin* saying what it had said in *Henderson: Plessy* must go.

The Court decided all three cases on the same day.

Just before the Justices spoke in response to the most spirited NAACP effort yet to breach the walls of segregation, Charlie Houston died. He was fifty-four.

Officially, he was only remotely involved with the NAACP during the Forties. At the beginning of the decade, he had relinquished his title of "special counsel" to the organization, but he stayed in touch as chairman of the NAACP's national legal committee, an advisory panel, and argued a number of important cases that might otherwise have been handled by Thurgood Marshall or his assistants, had they had the time. Besides Houston's Supreme Court triumphs in the railway-labor case of *Steele v. Louisville & Nashville* in 1944 and the restrictive-covenant case of *Hurd v. Hodge* in 1948, he also handled a good deal of civil-rights litigation in the lower courts, and while the results varied, they all advanced the black man's claim for equal justice. In 1945, for example, he went to court to force Baltimore's publicly supported Enoch Pratt Free Library, an important cultural resource in the community, to open its training course to young Negroes. By 1947, he was spearheading a drive in Washington launched by the parents and teachers of Browne Junior High School against the overcrowded and otherwise inferior conditions that prevailed in the separate Negro schools of the District of Columbia. And only a week before his death on April 22, 1950, he won his last case. Or, to be more precise, he had asked his star pupil to handle it for him; the case involved the very same opponent that Houston and his pupil had faced when they first joined forces.

Houston was in the hospital, trying to combat a relapse from the heart attack that floored him in October 1949, and he asked Thurgood Marshall to take over as counsel in *McCready v. Byrd*, a case brought by a Negro seeking admission to the University of Maryland's School of Nursing. Marshall, though pressed by the workload of *Sweatt*, *McLaurin*, and dozens of other NAACP cases, could not refuse his old mentor. "It was the same university we had opposed together in *Murray*, of course," Marshall recalls, "but the defendants, they had a mighty peculiar i-dea about that. Their defense was that a different principle was involved from the one in *Murray* because that case had involved a law school and this one involved a nursing school. So I said to the judge, 'Judge, I agree with that—the law school and the nursing school are different, and I can *prove* it.' And the judge looked interested. So I said, 'I can prove it because I went to law school—and I didn't come out a nurse.' And that took care of that case."

Charlie Houston would never have said such a thing in a courtroom. In style and personality, they proved very different men. "Charlie was sort of the Vince Lombardi type," says James Nabrit, lapsing into the metaphor of sports that Americans are wont to use in unconsciously trivializing their great men on life's other playing fields. "He was a tough, excellent technician who drove you to produce to the limit of your ability. Thurgood was more of a Knute Rockne type."

The volcano inside Charles Houston did not sputter out with the years. It was active until the moment he died, and it was visible in many places besides the courtroom. He made nationwide headlines when he quit the FEPC at the end of 1945 with a sharp slap at the President of the United States. The Fair Employment Practices Committee had voted in November of that year to issue a cease-and-desist order to the Capital Transit Company of the District of Columbia aimed at its practice of denying employment to Negroes as conductors, motormen, bus operators, and traffic checkers. Truman, without notice to the FEPC, ordered the decision held up and then declined to see Houston or any of the committee members who had promptly asked for an audience at the White House. The President's action, Houston said in his letter of resignation, had served to condone discrimination, not to eliminate it.

The following year, Houston began writing a weekly column for Carl Murphy's *Afro-American* and used it as a klaxon to stir the black masses to action. Calling the column "The Highway," changing it to "Along the Highway," and then to the yet more prosaic "Our Civil Rights," he wrote with strength and directness and a candor that could sometimes annoy or bite too hard. Once, for example, he pointedly attacked the standards of health care maintained by the Freedmen's Hospital, an institution affiliated with Howard University that was staffed largely by Negroes and served Negro patients primarily. "Contaminated food, inferior service and unsanitary conditions do not mean that Negroes are unable to run a first class hospital," he wrote. "It means merely that some Negroes cannot run hospitals—that Negroes should lose false pride and stop tolerating incompetence because it is black." He thought the segregated hospital was a victim of its own racial exclusivity and was hampering the professional growth of the attending physicians. Such outspoken criticism no doubt earned him unpopularity with some sections of the black community of Washington that had been his home most of his life, and yet only the year before he died his friends accumulated more than 20,000 signatures for a petition seeking his appointment to the District of Columbia's governing Board of Commissioners; among the principal backers of the move was the dean of the Howard Medical School. Harry Truman, who had done a good deal in the interim to show Houston he had been wrong in his estimate of the President's racial conscience, did not forget the black lawyer's sharp words when quitting the FEPC four years earlier. Houston was not named to the District board.

In the view of some who knew him well, Charlie Houston remained bitter throughout his life over the discrimination to which his race was subjected. Says Joseph Waddy, who was his partner during most of Houston's post-NAACP days, "I remember one time when his wife brought their son, little Charlie, down to the office while she went off somewhere, and the little fella was playing around till Charlie had to go to the drugstore for something and he took the boy along. While Charlie was being taken care of, the boy climbed up on a stool by the soda fountain, and the man behind the fountain said to him, 'Get down from there, you little nigger—you got no business here.' When they got back to the office, we had to take Charlie into the back room and give him a sedative."

"He got less honor and remuneration than almost anyone else involved in this fight," says Charles Thompson. "He was a philanthropist without money." He shook off influenza and pneumonia and kept going, and he thought he could shake off the heart attack that came in 1949 the same way. He went first to Bethesda Naval Hospital, but as his recuperation lengthened he transferred to Freedmen's Hospital, nearer to his family and friends. Doctors told him to stop working for six months, but he didn't know how. Finally released from the hospital, he went back to his office and renewed the routine. His heart could not take it. In the hospital again, he kept on working. Waddy was with him at the end. His father, William, with whom he had been professionally associated for twenty-six years, had just left their office on his way to pay his ailing son a visit. He arrived too late.

No one paid him deeper homage than Houston's cousin, United States Court of Appeals Judge William Hastie, who won the medals in the family. Writing in the *Journal of Negro History*, Hastie said, "He guided us through the legal wilderness of second-class citizenship. He was truly the Moses of that journey. He lived to see us close to the promised land of full equality under the law, closer than even he dared hope when he set out on that journey and so much closer than would have been possible without his genius and his leadership."

That June in Boston, the NAACP posthumously presented Houston with its highest tribute, the Spingarn Medal. That he could have been overlooked for so many years while he was alive testified to the uncelebrated and self-contained way in which he did his work. Charles Houston was not a noisy man. Few black Americans have ever heard of him, and fewer whites.

During the early part of May 1950, the Chief Justice of the United States, Fred M. Vinson, was writing the opinion of the Supreme Court in both *Sweatt v. Painter* and *McLaurin v. Oklahoma Board of Regents*. Kentuckian Vinson was a man of moderate political and social views. He placed stability in government high among the public virtues. He was not disposed to scuttle the Court's fifty-four-year-old precedent of *Plessy v. Ferguson.*

He sent his draft of the *Sweatt* and *McLaurin* opinions to the print shop in the basement of the Court and dispatched copies to his judicial brethren. Justice Felix Frankfurter sent Vinson a note after reviewing the opinions and agreeing with some changes proposed by Justice Stanley Reed:

Dear Chief:
. . . They [Reed's suggestions] are, after all, in the spirit of your opinions in that they seek to accomplish the desired result without needlessly stirring the kind of feelings that are felt even by truly liberal and high-minded Southerners like Jonathan Daniels *[sic]*. The problem is a perfect instance for requiring the wisdom of Bishop Phillips Brooks who, when a friend chided him for being so orthodox in his ecclesiastical dress although so heretical in his views, replied: "If the other fellow is willing to take my ideas, I am ready to wear his clothes."

> . . . It seems to me desirable now not to go a jot or tittle beyond the *Gaines* test. The shorter the opinion, the more there is an appearance of unexcitement and inevitability about it, the better.

Given the doctrinal divisions and personality clashes within the Court, Frankfurter held the balance of power without the vestments of leadership. The Truman appointees were a solid bloc behind Vinson, but they needed Reed to make a majority, and Reed got on well enough in terms of judicial philosophy with the two other believers in judicial restraint from the Roosevelt group—Frankfurter and Jackson—to keep the Court's alliances in flux. Frankfurter, indefatigable in working to promote his own views among his brethren on the bench, had voted consistently on the side of Negro plaintiffs in cases brought to the Court by the NAACP. He saw now that the civil-rights drive to which he had once been a counselor had reached the point of no return. The Negro lawyers were pushing the Court to declare segregation itself illegal. Few customs in American life had become more firmly entrenched than the separation of the races throughout the South. It was a practice hateful to Frankfurter, the Austrian Jew who had come to America at the age of twelve and believed that he had indeed found the promised land. And yet could the Court take it upon itself to intrude boldly into the fiercely defended social arrangements of so proud and so vast a region of the nation? The Court, moreover, in a lengthening chain of holdings, had implicated itself in the practice by doing or saying nothing to cast a shadow on its constitutionality. His note to Vinson endorsing the Chief Justice's opinion confirms the great caution Frankfurter felt the Court must exercise in entering upon the booby-trapped no-man's-land between *Plessy* and real equality for colored Americans.

Frankfurter displayed his cautionary bent still more by proposing a slight change in the draft of Vinson's *McLaurin* opinion:

> I have an emendation—from last paragraph of Stanley [Reed]'s letter, to which he agrees. He wrote: "These are handicaps to an effective education." I would make it: "These are handicaps to graduate instruction."
> . . . Perhaps these minor suggestions will commend themselves to you. I hope very much we can get an all-but unanimous, if not a unanimous, Court in the final form of your opinion.

Yet more symptomatic of the Court's great caution on the race question was the subdued response to Vinson's narrowly drawn opinion by the Court's most eloquent libertarian. Hugo Black, who so often was on the opposite side from Vinson in the Court's voting, was solidly with him now. He sent back his copy of the Chief's opinion in *Sweatt* with a note reading, ". . . I sincerely hope it can obtain a unanimous approval—. Certainly I shall say nothing unless some one writes in a way that [illegible but looks like 'moves'] me to express separate views—. Full Court acceptance of this and the McLaurin opinion should add force to our holdings."

Vinson got his unanimous Court. He read his opinions in the two graduate cases on June 5. Almost his first words dashed whatever hopes Thurgood Marshall may have harbored for a sweeping opinion. The two cases, Vinson said, presented different aspects of the same general question, which was to what extent the equal-protection clause of the Fourteenth Amendment limited the power of a state to distinguish between students of different races in professional and graduate education in a state university. The NAACP had framed its case far more broadly than that, but the Court was not buying it, Vinson now made clear:

> Broader issues have been urged for our consideration, but we adhere to the principle of deciding constitutional questions only in the context of the particular case before the Court. . . . Because of this traditional reluctance to extend constitutional interpretations . . . much of the excellent research and detailed argument presented in these cases is unnecessary to their disposition.

The history of the case disclosed that three years after it had been set up just for Sweatt, who chose not to attend it, the Negro law school in Texas had a faculty of five full-time professors, twenty-three students, a library of 16,000 books serviced by a full-time staff, a practice court, and a legal-aid association. But Vinson declared: "Whether the University of Texas Law School is compared with the original or the new law school for Negroes, we cannot find substantial equality in the educational opportunities offered white and Negro law students by the state." He cited the measurable categories for comparison and then added:

> What is more important, the University of Texas Law School possesses to a far greater degree those qualities which are incapable of objective measurement but which make for greatness in a law school. Such qualities, to name but a few, include reputation of the faculty, experience of the administration, position and influence of the alumni, standing in the community, traditions and prestige. It is difficult to believe that one who had a free choice between these law schools would consider the question close.

*Sipuel*, Vinson said, had not presented the issue of whether a state might not meet its constitutional obligation by establishing a separate law school for Negroes. Here in *Sweatt*, the issue was clearly raised by the Negro plaintiff seeking "a legal education equivalent to that offered by the state to students of other races. Such education is not available to him in a separate law school as offered by the state. We cannot, therefore, agree with respondents [Texas] that the doctrine of *Plessy v. Ferguson* . . . requires affirmance of the judgment below."

Heman Sweatt was ordered admitted to the University of Texas Law School. It was the first time the Supreme Court had ordered a black student admitted to a school previously for white students on the ground that the colored school established by the state failed to offer equal educational opportunity.

The war was hardly won, however. For Vinson added, after dismissing the claim by Texas and its Southern allies that *Plessy* demanded Sweatt's exclusion from the white law school: "Nor need we reach petitioner's contention that *Plessy v. Ferguson* should be re-examined in the light of contemporary knowledge respecting the purposes of the Fourteenth Amendment and the effects of racial segregation." *Plessy* was still the law.

But *McLaurin*, it had been felt at the NAACP Legal Defense Fund, would not allow the Justices to sidestep *Plessy* quite so nimbly. The fact of his segregation *within* the otherwise all-white University of Oklahoma seemed to rule out the need for the Court to consider the equality part of the separate-but-equal formula, for George McLaurin had incontestably been given equal educational facilities; it was the stigma of his separation that was at issue—the legality of segregation itself.

The Court found otherwise. Without doubt, McLaurin had been given a raw deal, and "the restrictions placed upon him were such that he had been handicapped in his pursuit of effective graduate instruction. Such restrictions impair and inhibit his ability to study, to engage in discussions and exchange views with other students, and in general, to learn his profession." Then Vinson's opinion offered this eye-opening paragraph:

> Our society grows increasingly complex, and our need for trained leaders increases correspondingly. Appellant's case represents, perhaps, the epitome of that need, for he is attempting to obtain an advanced degree in education, to become, by definition, a leader and trainer of others. Those who will come under his guidance and influence must be directly affected by the education he receives. Their own education and development will necessarily suffer to the extent that his training is unequal to that of his classmates. State-imposed restrictions which produce such inequalities cannot be sustained.

What the Court had just said was that the restrictions on George McLaurin were inequalities and had to end. It did not use the word "segregation" because it chose not to. Nor did it go on to reach the conclusion that its own logic seemed to demand: if the students whom McLaurin was to teach in the future would be deprived to the extent that his training had been handicapped by state-imposed restrictions, would the same thing not be true many times over of the students themselves who were taught in separate schools—a severe form of state-imposed restriction? Wasn't segregation in and of itself just such a restriction and no more worthy of being sustained than the indignities piled on George McLaurin inside the white university he attended? The Court left the question dangling.

But the Court ended on a note that seemed to offer black litigants strong hope in the future. To the state's claim that removing McLaurin's restrictions would not make him any less of a social pariah on campus, the Court said that was beside the point, because

> There is a vast difference—a Constitutional difference—between restrictions imposed by the state which prohibit the intellectual commingling of students, and the refusal of individuals to commingle where the state presents no such bar. . . . The removal of the state restrictions will not necessarily abate individual and group predilections and choices. But at the very least, the state will not be depriving appellant of the opportunity to secure acceptance by his fellow students on his own merits.

So Oklahoma had to stop tormenting McLaurin, but here, too, nothing was said that disturbed *Plessy*'s deep moorings. And the same held true of the Court's third civil-rights decision of that day. It threw out the Southern

Railway's discriminatory dining-car regulations in ruling for the Negro position in *Henderson v. United States.* Special tables for black passengers were not permissible, and every ticketholder entitled to use the diner must be equally free to do so. "The curtains, partitions and signs emphasize the artificiality of a difference in treatment which serves only to call attention to a racial classification of passengers holding identical tickets and using the same public dining facility," said the Court, which cited its earlier decision that day in *McLaurin* as precisely analogous. *Henderson,* too, was a unanimous opinion, and it was written by Justice Burton, who had hitherto seemed somewhat reluctant in his commitment to civil rights.

It had been a big day. For the first time, the Court had asserted that separate-but-equal education was not a mere slogan. The equality had to be real or the separation was constitutionally intolerable. That was what *Sweatt* had accomplished. And if separate facilities were not provided, no individual or group might suffer restrictions or harassments within the biracial school. That was what *McLaurin* did. And *Henderson* extended *McLaurin* to interstate transportation. And the Court did these things without ever raising its voice above a matter-of-fact level or in any way chastising the South. Note, for example, the words "individual and group predilections and choices" in the closing lines of *McLaurin,* cited above, as a way of avoiding the accusatory word "prejudices." The Court, moreover, was massed behind all three decisions handed down that day—a rare show of unanimity by the Vinson Court and one that stressed its understanding of the explosive nature of racial feeling in white America.

But as Thurgood Marshall and his staff assessed the day's work by the Court, there was a decidedly gloomy side to it as well. All the Justices had really done was to declare that the Court meant what it had said in *Plessy* more than half a century earlier. Unless the Court could be forced now to confront the legality of segregation itself, NAACP lawyers might have to spend the next half-century arguing cases of unequal educational facilities one by one. Meanwhile, segregation would go on. If the issue were forced, though, and the Supreme Court chose not to uproot *Plessy,* the cost of defeat might be higher still. Segregation would be reinforced as the law of the land and the Negro's yearning for equality might be stifled for new generations.

The decision, finally, was Thurgood Marshall's to make. In making it, he turned now to the black folk down in the fields of Clarendon County, South Carolina.

# Part II

# The Courts Below

*Hereditary bondsmen! Know ye not*
*Who would be free themselves must strike the blow?*

—BYRON

# 13

# On the Natural Inferiority of Bootblacks

In the dank July gloaming, the air was heavy with the mouth-watering aroma of fresh fish frying. The rich smell assaulted the nostrils of the white man as he got out of his car and made his way over crumbling sidewalk toward the old clapboard house that had been in urgent need of painting for so long that it seemed to have acquiesced in its own denuding. Ethel's Restaurant and Fish Fry was an institution in the black backwater of Scotlandville, where the Mississippi makes a sharp bend sinister just north of Baton Rouge, the capital of Louisiana, about fifty miles upriver from New Orleans. Louisiana State University was in Baton Rouge, at the south end of town along the river—"Kingfish" Huey Long's gift to higher education. At the other end of town in Scotlandville stood black Southern University, probably the biggest colored college in the country outside of Howard. The white man had been tipped off that a bunch of Negroes was huddling at Ethel's Fish Fry, conspiring to break the color line at LSU.

He made his way through the barefoot children capering in the dust in front of the building. The little girls had their hair done up with paper butterflies known locally as *papillotes.* A handful of black grownups, restful in the fading twilight, watched the white intruder move past the tall weeds growing around the front stoop of the ramshackle restaurant and head for the rear entrance as if he knew precisely what he was looking for.

A low hum of voices floated out the screen door from the darkened back room. His footfalls in the dusk caused the sound to ebb, and as he climbed the wooden steps and knocked on the screen door, bellied out from too many kicks, nothing at all was heard within. The white man peered into the room and made out four or five shadowy shapes, unmoving.

"Who's that?" finally came a muffled voice.

Warren Rogers, number-two man in the Associated Press's Baton Rouge bureau, identified himself.

The silence thickened. By the remnant of daylight, Rogers could make out the table around which the men sat frozen, their murmured exchanges interrupted. Slowly one of the men climbed to his feet and came to the door, blocking the uninvited visitor's view. Rogers recognized him: A. P. Tureaud, Sr., one of the very few black lawyers in the whole state and the local counsel of the NAACP. In Louisiana, the NAACP conducted its business in back rooms after dark.

"What do you want?" Tureaud asked in as neutral a tone as he could manage.

"I want to talk to Thurgood Marshall," said the AP man.

More silence. Bad silence, thought Rogers. There was scant communication between the races in Louisiana in July 1950, and here was a group of Negroes plotting boldly and in the process of being discovered at it by a white newsman. Rogers expected the panel door behind the screen door to be slammed tight.

"What about?" the colored lawyer said at last.

"About those students you're going to register at LSU tomorrow."

Stunned silence. Then a mighty sigh. "Let him in," said Thurgood Marshall.

Sweat-soaked in shirt sleeves and galluses, the big man presided over the table of picked-clean fish bones. Strained introductions were quickly offered, but hostility hung in the air for another moment until Marshall exploded in a loud, thigh-slapping laugh. "You caught us!" he said, making a flash calculation of the weapons at his disposal. "Now, we'll talk," he said, "if you promise not to write anything in advance. We need the surprise. Okay?"

Conned into collaborating, Rogers was the only newsman on hand the next morning when Tureaud led a dozen young blacks to the office of the registrar of Louisiana State, where, frightened but determined, they filled out the registration blanks for admission to various graduate and professional schools of the university. A few days later, the Board of Supervisors at LSU turned them all down. Promptly, Tureaud and Marshall filed suit in the name of one of the dozen young Negroes, Roy Samuel Wilson, who had applied to the LSU law school. To keep Negroes out, the state legislature had shortly before set up a colored law school at Southern University, but it was missing a few things, like a library. Also a faculty member qualified to teach the Napoleonic legal code, peculiar to Louisiana, so that no black law graduate of Southern would be able to practice in the state. With the decision in *Sweatt* just a month behind him, Marshall took Roy Wilson's case straight into a three-judge federal District Court, won handily, and had the Supreme Court swiftly affirm in a *per curiam* opinion that did not bother to elaborate on its holding in *Sweatt*. Fried fish may have tasted no better on the other side of the college color line in Baton Rouge, but for the first time a Negro was permitted to cross it and find out.

Nearly a year would pass between the Supreme Court's decisions in *Sweatt* and *McLaurin* and the opening of the showdown round of the segregation fight in a federal courtroom in Charleston, South Carolina, but there was little time in the interim for Thurgood Marshall to relax, pat himself on the back, and regroup his forces for the big assault. He did not think in terms of stage-managing a major production. He played his cards one at a time, never wanting the game to ride on any single hand. He and his collaborators would play in fish-fry parlors and any other handy grotto all over the South in a steadily widening effort to breach the walls of white supremacy.

Besides Texas and LSU, law schools were desegregated now at the University of Virginia in a decision by a three-judge District Court and at the University of North Carolina in a decision by the United States Court of Appeals for the Fourth Circuit, then presided over by one of the most illustrious of the university's alumni, Judge John J. Parker. At the University of Maryland, where graduate-school desegregation had begun fifteen years earlier, the segregationists were not giving up gracefully but they were losing, department by department. The Supreme Court upheld the Maryland state court's ruling in Charles Houston's last case to admit Negroes to the school of nursing, and the state courts now ordered the diehard university to admit blacks to its graduate department of sociology since no comparable course of study was elsewhere available to Maryland Negroes. The equally begrudging University of Missouri began, though, to acknowledge that it finally understood what the *Gaines* case, which it had lost a dozen years earlier, was all about, and admitted a colored student to its school of mining without a court fight.

But the Red Sea was not about to part. The handful of graduate-school victories affected only a fraction of the black elite, and new ones were slow in coming as the state courts declined to fall in line automatically behind the *Sweatt* and *McLaurin* decisions, which on their face did nothing to tamper with the separate-but-equal principle of *Plessy*. The Florida Supreme Court, for example, ruled against five Negroes who sought entry to the University of Florida's schools of law, pharmacy, chemical engineering, and agriculture; the state hurriedly established separate black schools and said they offered substantially equal educational opportunities. The road ahead looked endless.

But even on that road, real enforcement of the separate-but-equal rule was beginning to open things up. In their gloomier moments, the black lawyers feared that segregation itself as a legally sanctioned practice had been more deeply entrenched than ever, thanks to *Sweatt* and *McLaurin*, yet just two months after those decisions came down, the NAACP won a little-heralded case with large implications. A state court in Delaware had listened to an appeal by ten black plaintiffs seeking admission as undergraduates to the University of Delaware. Young Jack Greenberg of the Legal Defense Fund office, working with Wilmington NAACP lawyer Louis Redding, put together an overwhelming case on the comparative merits of the white university and the Delaware State College for Negroes. The latter, like Prairie View in Texas and most of the black state colleges of the South and border states, was an academic shanty. The black college in Delaware gave its faculty no tenure and paid it less than public-school teachers, had a library with only 16,000 books (about one-tenth the size of the one at the white university), and had recently lost its academic accreditation. The curriculum was pitifully skimpy, too, and in a visit to the two campuses the Delaware judge found any resemblance between the physical plants of the white and black colleges to be purely coincidental. "Under the present state of the decisions of the United States Supreme Court construing the equal protection clause of the United States Constitution," wrote Delaware's Court of Chancery Judge Collins J. Seitz, "I do not believe I am entitled to conclude that segregation alone violates that clause. I therefore pass over plaintiffs' first contention that a segregated school cannot be an equal school." But on finding actual, gaping inequality between the college facilities offered the two races, Seitz ordered the colored applicants admitted to the white state university. For the first time, the color line had been broken at the undergraduate level. If Delaware wanted to bring its black college up to par with the white one, then theoretically it could resegregate. But, as Houston and Margold had calculated nearly twenty years earlier, Jim Crow would prove exorbitantly expensive to segregating states once the courts decided that real equality, as well as real separation, had to be enforced.

Out in Missouri, the state Supreme Court took *Plessy* even further. It held that a black St. Louis high-school student was entitled to be given the same course in aeromechanics offered at the white high school—and if the course were not given at his school, he could go to the white one for it. The equality principle was now beyond argument, even as the legitimacy of segregation itself seemed to be. The prospect was that equality, when challenged in the courts, would be enforced up and down the academic ladder, from law school to kindergarten, though decades might be consumed in the course of litigation.

The issue extended beyond schools as well. The *McLaurin* decision seemed a sharp blade for chopping away at every form of Jim Crow practice. If under the "combined facilities" provision of *McLaurin* a Negro could no longer be stigmatized at a racially mixed college, why upon entering a bus or streetcar shared with whites should he be required to sit in the back? *McLaurin*, if applied beyond the classroom, seemed to say that in any area of public life, Negroes had to be offered separate facilities every bit as good as the white ones or they had to be admitted *without restrictions* to racially combined facilities. Either separate buses for blacks or fully integrated biracial buses. The first signs from the Supreme Court suggested that the Justices fully understood the potential reach of *McLaurin*. Citing both it and *Sweatt*, the Court directed the Florida Supreme Court to reconsider a Miami ordinance that allowed Negroes to play on the municipal golf course only one day a week; the city's argument that six times as many whites as Negroes used the course was deemed irrelevant. And a Missouri federal court ruled that Negroes must be given equal access to outdoor swimming pools supported by municipal funds in St. Louis. *Plessy* was finally coming into its own—fifty-four years late.

In his heart, Thurgood Marshall knew the fight against *Plessy* ought to be pressed to the limit. Segregation was an unmitigated evil, and no black man anywhere in America was free of its scar so long as the Supreme Court tolerated it. But was the Court now ready to meet the Legal Defense Fund's direct challenge of segregation *per se* as unconstitutional? Marshall's head was less certain than his heart, and his doubts were held as well by law-review commentators and other knowledgeable observers. Philip Elman, then an Assistant Solicitor General, who had clerked for Frankfurter and remained on close terms with the Justice, was perhaps the most knowledgeable and strategically placed Court-watcher in Washington. "With Vinson as Chief Justice," says Elman in retrospect, "it was too early for Marshall to go for overruling segregation *per se.*" That Marshall clearly understood the risks has been testified to by Alfred H. Kelly, a white historian at Wayne State University, who worked closely with him in 1953 and wrote in 1962:

> Marshall later admitted that the NAACP was at this point at a kind of crossroads. The legal gap between the Sweatt and McLaurin cases on the one hand and an outright destruction of the Plessy precedent appeared to be appallingly wide, and he and his colleagues were not at all sure they could cross it. Might it not be well to "go along" with the Southern procedure, at least in part? At this stage of the game, Marshall later told the author, if the school boards in key Southern states had shown a general disposition to accept any kind of gradualist program combining more adequate schools with some primary and secondary desegregation, the Association [NAACP] might well have agreed to cooperate, at least for a time.

No trace of such irresoluteness was to be found in Marshall's public remarks at the time. Indeed, the week after *Sweatt* and *McLaurin* came down from the Court, he summoned dozens of leading civil-rights lawyers and constitutional-law professors to a major policy session at NAACP headquarters to ponder the best way "to end segregation once and for all." And while no one in the NAACP camp questioned the desirability of that goal, feeling was by no means unanimous that the straight route to it was the wisest one. Recalls Herbert Hill, director of labor affairs for the NAACP: "There was lots of resistance in the branches because real progress toward equalization was now beginning to be made in schools and other facilities like parks, libraries, and swimming pools. The dissidents said, 'You mean that you want us to oppose all this?' And the answer was not only yes but that the new equal facilities ought to be shut down and that the black community ought to settle for nothing less than integrated facilities only. It was a big lurch." The NAACP was by then a huge network of people of sharply varying degrees of militancy; an unpopular or too rigid policy on segregation might well have left Marshall far out on a limb. And if the Supreme Court chose to cut off that limb, the whole race might take a tumble along with its star courtroom advocate. "He wasn't conservative," says Oliver Hill, the Richmond lawyer and NAACP stalwart, "but he was cautious. His prevailing sense, I think, was that we just couldn't afford to lose a big one."

One man who sharply disagreed with the cautious approach was Howard University mainstay James Nabrit, who later in the Fifties would take over direction of the law school and, shortly thereafter, succeed Mordecai Johnson as president. "We had nothing to lose by an outright assault on segregation," argues Nabrit. "I thought it was a fallacy to say, as some were saying, that if we lost before the Court on overturning segregation *per se,* we'd be set back a generation. Separate-but-equal was still there, and if we lost, we could come back into court the next day arguing *Plessy*. There was a serious difference of opinion between my thinking and that of Thurgood and some of his associates on this point. And, after all, the NAACP got its funds from many people who wanted these cases won, even if on the wrong grounds. Thurgood understood my argument—I think he was convinced of it back in 1950—but he had a constituency out there."

The equally well respected voice of Charles Thompson was added to Nabrit's in the Howard camp. In the autumn 1950 number of the *Journal of Negro Education*, Thompson wrote that the debate over strategy was in a sense academic "since it appears that we will have to fight each case as it comes up in order to find one which will confront the Court with the general issue of segregation. Moreover, we can not afford to allow the ground already gained to be lost by default."

Thompson, though, was basically more a cheerleader than a strategist as the legal effort intensified and Marshall sought a way to hedge his bet, to be militant without becoming foolhardy. Nabrit's approach looked too risky to Marshall, who did not think it good law to argue against the constitutionality of *Plessy* one day and, if he lost, to come back the next day pleading for equal facilities under *Plessy* before the same Justices. He reached out now toward a wider circle of advisors, including a number of younger men with excellent credentials who were still more cautious than Marshall himself. Two of them were rare finds, for they had just finished clerking for Supreme Court Justices and were now associated with the high-powered, liberal New York law office of Paul, Weiss, Rifkind, Wharton & Garrison, the only interfaith, interracial Wall Street firm in town. One of them was Louis H. Pollak, who had clerked for Justice Rutledge and would later serve as dean of Yale Law School. Pollak was by no means sanguine about the chances of a direct attack on *Plessy*. "If it had been my responsibility to decide how to proceed in the wake of *Sipuel, Sweatt*, and *McLaurin*," he says, "I would not have had the courage to go after segregation *per se*—and certainly not at the public-school level. I would first have tried to erode the separate-but-equal doctrine at places where attendance was not compulsory [i.e., the college level]."

Of even greater value to Marshall was the cold-eyed counsel of thirty-year-old William T. Coleman, Jr., who had clerked the year before for Felix Frankfurter. He was the first Negro ever to serve as law clerk to a Justice, and, in view of Frankfurter's didactic bent, it was good for Coleman that he had come well prepared. A *summa cum laude* graduate of the University of Pennsylvania, a *magna cum laude* graduate of Harvard Law School who had served as a *Harvard Law Review* editor, a Harvard Business School graduate for good measure, Coleman withal had been unable to find a job with a law firm in his hometown of Philadelphia, but landed a position there as law clerk to one of the judges for the Court of Appeals for the Third Circuit—a job he handled with distinction for two years before Justice Frankfurter summoned him to Washington. The jurist's vitality amazed Coleman. "He was interested in everything," the stocky lawyer recalls. "By eight in the morning, he had read five newspapers. He'd already have discussed foreign affairs with the Australian Prime Minister and taken a stroll with Dean Acheson. By the time we law clerks arrived at the office at nine, he'd be ready to give us a seminar on government until ten or eleven." Coleman worked closely with the Justice on his opinions and acquired insight into his mental processes while stretching his own. "Frankfurter would never say to us, 'I want you to support this or that opinion.' He would say, 'What do you think of this case?' Or, 'Have you read these cases? They'll interest you, I think.' " When Coleman left Frankfurter's service, the Justice wrote him, "What I can say of you with great confidence is what was Justice Holmes's ultimate praise of a man: 'I bet on him.' I bet on you, whatever choice you may make and whatever the Fates may have in store for you." In time, Coleman cracked every color bar in Philadelphia, was made a partner in its most powerful law firm, joined the previously all-white Midday Club, was named the first black director of Pan American World Airways, became president of the Legal Defense Fund, and entered the Cabinet of President Gerald R. Ford. But in 1950, all his superb training and credentials notwithstanding, he still could not get a job as a Philadelphia lawyer, and so he was glad to sign on with the Paul, Weiss firm in New York. For Thurgood Marshall, the articulate, immensely brainy Coleman was a gem of special magnitude in the collection of superior intellects with which he was now surrounding himself. Not only did Coleman bring his own rare gifts with him, but he had the unspoken added advantage of offering Marshall intimate knowledge of the thought processes of the pivotal Justice on the Court that would decide the future of segregation in America.

It was Coleman's nuanced mind, along with that of Judge William Hastie and Richmond lawyer Spottswood Robinson, that helped Marshall arm himself with a two-string bow as he carried the segregation fight into its critical stage. "It wasn't really a debate," Coleman recalls of the Fund's planning sessions. "We were saying that we'd still hedge on the strategy— that is, in any given case we'd argue that at the very least these facilities are unequal and therefore unconstitutional—but equality, so long as the facilities were separate, was not equality at all. There had to be an identity of facilities for equal protection to prevail. This is what we meant by the second string to our bow. We'd ask for integration forthwith, not at some vague future date, because that was the only way to grant equality—now. We never brought a case after that where we'd concede equality without integration, but it was done within the traditional framework so that at the very least we could fall back on the equal-facilities argument. The point was that if we didn't win on constitutional grounds by getting *Plessy* reversed, we'd at least get the remedy we sought: integrated schools forthwith." In short, the NAACP would argue that black public schools violated the Fourteenth Amendment because they were (1) demonstrably unequal to and (2) separate from the white schools of the community.

On the face of it, Thurgood Marshall came down for boldness. At an NAACP conference of forty-three lawyers and fourteen branch and state conference presidents held at the end of June 1950, it was resolved that pleadings in all future education cases would "be aimed at obtaining education on a non-segregated basis and that no relief other than that will be acceptable. . . . Further, that all lawyers operating under such rule will urge their client[s] and the branches of the Association involved to insist on this final relief." Marshall brought the resolution to the board of directors of the NAACP and asked that it be adopted as official policy. The goal now, he declared, was to break up segregation, and nothing less would do. The board approved Marshall's stand. It was perhaps the most militant position the NAACP had ever taken in its forty-two-year history.

Once the official position had been established, there was little opposition to it in the branches. "A lot of the black communities around the country had the bit between their teeth by then," remarks William Hastie. "They were just fed up with what we called 'doghouse education,' and it was clear that the segregation fight was going to be pushed at the secondary- and elementary-school level, NAACP or not. It would have been futile to try damming the tide of human emotion that had been let loose."

By the later part of 1950, then, Thurgood Marshall had escalated the stakes dramatically. But he kept hoping that the Supreme Court would not think the change nearly so extreme as he himself recognized it to be. The Legal Defense Fund would keep working to open up the colleges at the graduate and undergraduate level within the *Plessy* doctrine, but the new battleground was the public schools, and to win there, Marshall had armed himself with the bristling and loudly proclaimed intension of destroying *Plessy* and everything it represented. Yet the misgivings he bore—the gnawing sense that he could have a field day by backtracking to prove the grossly inferior condition of black schools and thereby driving the courts to force equalization on the South within the safe and tested *Plessy* formula— surfaced the very first time he walked into a courtroom to challenge the legality of segregated public schools.

Probably no other courts in the nation invite the same degree of personal quirkiness in the judges who run them as the United States District Courts.

The Supreme Court speaks with the voice of at least five men and often all nine of its members. Below it, the Courts of Appeals speak with the voice of at least two and often three judges. But each District Court speaks with the sole voice of the individual judge presiding over it. Yet, like the federal judges above him, the District Court judge has life tenure—in contrast to most state-court judges—and with that tenure, in theory, comes independence of the political tides of his community. Nor is the District Court judge obliged to heed the rulings of other District Court judges. The District judge conducts the bread-and-butter business of the federal judiciary. It is he who creates the principal trial record in most federal court proceedings. He decides what evidence may or may not be admitted, he speeds or delays the proceedings, he makes the finding of facts, he hands down the first decision on the law, and he proposes the remedies to a case. Yet none of his work is final; all of it is subject to automatic appeal. It is this combination of security, independence, and power without final responsibility for saying what the law is that produces widely varying and unpredictable opinions at the District Court level. And while most District judges stick closely to precedent as set by the appellate courts above them, some District judges have proven far more willing than others to risk making new interpretations when the precedents are ambiguous on the points of law before them. Thus, a potential litigant is well advised to consider the judicial philosophy and temperament of the District judge before whom he chooses to bring an action, for while it is true that District Court opinions are readily and regularly reversed, the momentum in a case begins here and the record created can be fatally affected by a hostile District judge.

The Reverend Joseph A. DeLaine, Levi Pearson, Harry Briggs, and the other black residents of benighted Clarendon County, South Carolina, who went into the federal courts in the late Forties to obtain better schools for their children had the benefit of lawyers who were well aware of the importance of bringing their case before a friendly federal judge. Indeed, if there had not been one in their neck of those very lonely and very hostile woods, it is doubtful that the NAACP would have taken on the case of *Briggs v. Elliott*, when it did.

Julius Waties Waring had been the lean, long-legged, long-faced embodiment of Charleston's aristocratic faith for the first sixty-one years of his not particularly eventful life. He breathed establishment values from every pore. His lineage in the stately little port city ran back through at least eight generations of Episcopalians to the seventeenth century, when Charleston was a prosperous, colorful clearinghouse for the whole lower South. Among his ancestors, he said, were many "fine, decent slaveholders" including his father, a railroad-company man, and uncles who fought for the Confederacy. Born in 1880, Waring was nursed through childhood by an ex-slave toward whom the family was kindly disposed. "Most of the Negroes I knew were ex-slaves," he would recall toward the end of his life, "and you loved them and were good to them. We didn't give them any rights, but they never asked for any rights, and I didn't question it. I was raised in the atmosphere that we ought to take care of these people."

The ascent of Negro-baiting Ben Tillman during Waties Waring's formative years had poisoned the murky racial atmosphere of South Carolina. It also caused the sharp shift of power from Charleston, which had never really recovered from the Civil War, and the sleepy low country it commanded to the increasingly industrialized upcountry in the western sector of the state. Its former luster now threadbare, its gentility strained but still recognizable, the Charleston in which Waring came of age lived largely—as its residents themselves would quip—on rice and recollections. Proud of its role in the making of the Confederacy, it was neither addled by its secessionist ambitions of yore nor seriously infected by the racism that had swept the state beginning with the restoration of white supremacy after the 1877 Compromise. Always a cosmopolitan enclave amid the xenophobic tropical provinces of the nation, the city seemed a singularly comforting womb to young Waties Waring, who showed no eagerness to discover the world beyond it. He went to a private school there and graduated from the

College of Charleston, where the toploftiest of the fraternities reigned over the social life, a reproduction in miniature of the exclusivism that shaped the thinking of the adult community. "Pretty nice if you belong to it," Waring would say in his seventy-sixth year, "but it's really a terrible social system." Charleston never bothered its pretty little head brooding on such matters. "It has a charm, a fashion," Waring noted, "but it doesn't think much, and it doesn't think outside of its pattern."

He read law and clerked with upper-crust firms on the Broad Street main stem, got a nice little practice going, made the right political connections, and found himself named Assistant United States Attorney for the Eastern District of South Carolina by the Wilson administration. His superior, preferring the salary and fame to the work, stayed home in Columbia, the state capital, and gave Waring a free hand to run the office as he chose. Soon he was a big man politically as well as socially in Charleston, and on the strength of his unexceptionable record as a government lawyer, he was able to build a private practice in the Twenties around corporate and criminal matters. But he never amassed a great deal of money from his lawyering, perhaps because he lacked drive, perhaps because he was generally judged to be an amiable, competent, but basically rather plodding lawyer.

More deeply than ever now, he settled into the magnolia-scented society life of cliquish Charleston. He married a hometown belle of Episcopalian upbringing no less impeccable than his own. He moved into one of the lovely old landmark homes south of Broad Street in the most picturesque section of town—a two-story, gray-white house with a distinctive fan-shaped window over the big arched front doorway at 61 Meeting Street, just a block and a half from the municipal crossroads of Broad and Meeting. Four blocks to the south was the Battery with its promenade overlooking the historic harbor. There was no more convenient and stylish address in Charleston, though there were many more imposing homes. He was a member in good standing of the Charleston Light Dragoons, a sort of silver-spoon American Legion that traced its origins back to well before the American Revolution, and the yet more elitist St. Cecilia Society, whose principal function was to give one or at most two formal, ultra-exclusive cotillions a year at the Hibernian Hall a few doors from the Waring home on Meeting. The St. Cecilia bashes, to which admission was by hand-delivered engraved invitation only, featured dance "cards" in the old fluttering-fan style, a strict prohibition on smoking and divorced persons, and breakfast by dawn's pearly light.

In the Thirties, Waties Waring dirtied his hands just a bit in municipal politics and became the corporation counsel—that is, the city attorney—for Charleston under eight-year Mayor Burnet Rhett Maybank, who turned the county Democratic Party into a Tammany Hall with palmettos out front. Maybank's ambitions were big and his reach for power undisguised. He had inherited a nearly bankrupt city when he came to Charleston city hall, and Waring pushed for the adoption of scrip to tide the treasury over the crisis; the debt-moratorium scheme worked. Soon the city's credit rating was fully restored, and both Maybank and Waring were well regarded. Waring became a fixture at all-white Democratic Party functions and once served as campaign manager for veteran United States Senator "Cotton Ed" Smith, whose racist rhetoric made Klan kleagles sound like Boy Scouts by comparison. A party regular, a solid citizen, an authentic aristocrat as such things were measured in Charleston, Waties Waring got his reward in 1941 when Senator Smith and his new junior colleague in Washington, Burnet Maybank, agreed that Waring should fill the vacancy as United States judge for the Eastern District of South Carolina. He was sixty-one. His chambers and courtroom were just a few hundred yards from his home. He seemed about as safe and unthreatening a figure as the white-supremacist county-courthouse rings that ruled the state could have hoped for in that position of potential federal encroachment upon their sovereignty.

Waring's conversion came gradually. It began with a peonage case. Many South Carolina farmers winked at the practice of detaining Negroes against their will by force or dire threats, to work for nothing or close to it. Sometimes the colored man would be held just overnight or perhaps a few days; sometimes it would be for weeks or even months. The practice went on unchecked because white man's justice paid it little heed. If occasionally a case came to court, the worst that might happen was that the perpetrator was ordered to cease and desist. But when a case came before him in the United States District Court in Charleston, Waties Waring did not let it pass. A young Negro had been held in a cabin overnight against his will, and Waring ordered his tormentor sent to jail for violating the Thirteenth Amendment. There was more shock than grumbling as word fanned out across the low country that the abusive practice was no longer being countenanced.

Then Waring started changing a few things in his own courtroom. The list of potential jurors who might be seated in his court had traditionally carried the designation "(c)" beside the names of the two or three colored people who were generally put on it in token obedience to the due-process clause. Thus distinguished, they were easily avoided by the clerks and lawyers selecting the juries. Waring ended the practice, and Negroes occasionally began to appear on the federal jury in Charleston. By custom, the public seating area of his courtroom had been segregated. Waring ordered that ended. He named a Negro, John Fleming, as his court bailiff—John the Bailiff, as he quickly became known in black legal circles across the country, for there were few black court officers anywhere in America and probably none elsewhere in the South.

In 1945, Waties Waring's conversion quickened. In May, he handed down a decision favoring a black teacher from Columbia who had sued to win a salary equal to what white teachers received. The legal issue in the case had been resolved in the *Alston* decision five years earlier, but South Carolina was not precisely falling over itself to improve the condition of its black residents. The salary case had fed Judge Waring's growing discomfort with the racial situation "because every time you looked into one of these things, the less reason you [could] see for resistance to what we commonly call the American creed of equality of all citizens of this country. . . . The whole thing worried me a great deal, and I knew the thing was coming to a showdown someday—and probably was coming in my state. The question arose as to whether I should dodge it or meet it."

The question was answered by another decision Waring made the month after the salary case. He divorced his wife of thirty-two years and married a twice-previously-wed native of Detroit two weeks later. The first Mrs. Waring moved to New York. The second Mrs. Waring moved right into 61 Meeting Street. Polite Charleston was stunned. So unthinkable was the idea of shedding marriage partners that South Carolina had no divorce law at the time; Mrs. Waring had gone to Florida to obtain the decree. Outside Charleston, Judge Waring was still cordially received, but at home the doors began to close on him and his new beloved. There would be no more St. Cecilia's balls for the eminent judge. And it was just as well, the Warings decided, because the social climate of the town was suffocating and bigoted. They began to read—books like Myrdal's *An American Dilemma* and Cash's *The Mind of the South*. For sixty-five years, Waties Waring had known all these things he read now, but the sight of them in print proved an overwhelming indictment of the life he had so enjoyed and the ways of injustice he had unblinkingly condoned. He condoned them no longer. He started to travel more, sitting in federal courts with overcrowded dockets in places as far away as New York and California. His rage grew.

In 1946, he presided in a case that chilled the nation. Isaac Woodward, a black soldier returning from three years in the Army, including fifteen months fighting in the jungles of the South Pacific, had been discharged at a camp in Georgia and boarded a bus for reunion with his North Carolina family. En route, Woodward asked the bus driver to stop so he might go to the toilet. Returning to the bus, the war veteran was cursed out for taking too long; the bus driver summoned the police chief of the small South Carolina town and had Woodward arrested for allegedly being drunk and disorderly. Woodward vehemently denied the charges, but the constable took him off anyway and in an alley beat him with a blackjack and drove the end of his nightstick into the Negro's eyes. Woodward was kept in jail overnight without medical treatment. In the morning, he could not see. They let him wash up and paraded him before the local judge, who promptly found him guilty and fined him fifty dollars. By the time Woodward reached the Army hospital in Spartanburg, both his corneas were found to have been damaged beyond repair.

When the blind ex-soldier told his story in the federal court presided over by Waring in Columbia, the police official denied it. Woodward had grabbed his gun, he said, and threatened to kill him, so he had swung his nightstick mightily at the Negro to subdue him. The jury nodded. The United States Attorney charged with arguing the case against the law-enforcement official had failed to obtain any witnesses to Woodward's conduct or condition on the bus other than the bus driver—a remarkable dereliction of duty, Waring believed. "I was shocked by the hypocrisy of my government . . . in submitting that disgraceful case," he said privately afterward. When the defense lawyer began to utter racist remarks, Waring shut him off at once. But the jury needed no goading. The police chief was promptly found not guilty. The courtroom cheered.

Isaac Woodward's case was publicized throughout America by the NAACP. It was one of the cases of brutality that Walter White called to the attention of Harry Truman and thereby helped spur the President's appeal for sweeping civil-rights reforms. For Judge Waties Waring, the Woodward case moved his philosophical conversion to the point of no return. In 1947, he collided head-on with the prevailing racial attitudes of his native place.

There were two racial cases, and he heard them back to back. The first was relatively unexplosive. A Negro represented by the NAACP had sued the state because no public college offered him a law degree. The *Sweatt* case was still at the trial stage in Texas, and there had been no Supreme Court decision on the question since *Gaines* in 1938. Waring ruled, in *Wrighten v. Board of Trustees of University of South Carolina*, that the state had either to offer the plaintiff a decent law education at the State College for Negroes at Orangeburg or to admit him to the white law school or, if it did neither, to close down the white law school. The state chose the first alternative, claiming it would allocate $200,000 to open a law program for blacks at Orangeburg.*

The *Wrighten* decision was quietly received. It affected, after all, only a handful of colored. But the decision Waring delivered right after it raised the roof. Negroes in South Carolina had been effectively disenfranchised for more than half a century. A key tool in that denial of basic American rights was the white primary election. When Thurgood Marshall prevailed before the Supreme Court in *Smith v. Allwright*, striking down the Texas white primary in 1944, South Carolina was jolted and then defiant. Governor (later Senator) Olin Johnston summoned a special session of the state legislature, which thought it could foil the intent of the Court's holding by carefully stripping away every law that had anything to do with primary elections. The South Carolina lawmakers repealed some 150 statutes on the theory that no court could thereafter hold that a primary election was "state action" if there were no state laws on the books that said a word about primaries. But aside from the massive erasure, nothing changed. The Democrats said they were a private club, and they went right on holding their primaries as they had before. Only those free, white, and over twenty-one were permitted to vote in the primary. George Elmore, a colored resident of Columbia, challenged the new allegedly state-free primary in the United States District Court.

Thurgood Marshall argued Elmore's case. Waties Waring did not take much convincing. In his decision, he invoked *Smith v. Allwright* as governing and struck down South Carolina's transparent white-primary subterfuge, declaring:

> It is time for South Carolina to rejoin the Union. It is time to fall in step with the other states and to adopt the American way of conducting elections. . . . Racial distinctions cannot exist in the machinery that selects the officers and lawmakers of the United States.

* In fact, all the state did in that era was to establish a single professorship of law, not a program of legal education.

Furious white South Carolinians, led by the venomously hissing Charleston crowd that Waties Waring had run with all his life, said of their turncoat judge, "He's got a union *he* should rejoin"—meaning, of course, his first wife. It did not matter that Waring's decision to open the primary to Negroes was firmly upheld by the Court of Appeals in a ringing opinion by none other than North Carolina's John J. Parker, who had lost his place on the Supreme Court seventeen years earlier for a campaign speech he had once made urging that the Negro be kept out of politics. It did not matter that the Supreme Court of the United States declined to hear an appeal of the *Elmore* decision. All South Carolina knew was that J. Waties Waring was now "the guy who let the nigger vote."

The state's Democrats convened in 1948 in a last-gasp resistance effort. It would be all right for Negroes to vote in the primary, the convention decided, provided each of them first took the following oath:

> I . . . solemnly swear that I believe in and will support the principles of the Democratic Party of South Carolina, and that I believe in and will support the social and educational separation of the races.
> I further solemnly swear that I believe in the principles of States' Rights, and that I am opposed to the proposed so-called FEPC law.

It would be democracy by thought control.

The whole mess landed back in Waring's lap in mid-1948 as the registration deadline neared. He not only did not back off from his original decision indicting his state as a relic of the Dark Ages; he lashed out now with all the vigor and outrage at his command. The majesty of the federal judiciary was not going to be spurned, he said. In *Elmore*, "the law was clearly and succinctly stated and anyone who can read the English language must have known what it meant. . . . It's a disgrace and a shame that you have to come into court and ask a judge to tell you to be American citizens. The law of the land is supposed to be obeyed." And then, leveling a finger at the Democratic county chairmen who had been named co-defendants in the case, Waring told them that the oath they proposed was illegal and that they were to register qualified Negroes just as they registered whites and if they did not do that, he would hold them personally in contempt of court and punish them by fine or imprisonment. He would sit in his courtroom all day on primary day, he added, and make good his threat at once.

Thirty thousand Negroes voted that primary day. It was the best news black South Carolina had had since Reconstruction. "I've done lots of things in life that were careless and poor and dull and bad," Judge Waring said eight years later, "but I had one opportunity, and I think it was a great stroke of fortune that came down my alley."

Other things came down his alley, too, now. Like vicious mail. Like obscene phone calls. Like threats of impeachment proceedings by the South Carolina congressional delegation. The lower house of the state legislature actually resolved to buy the Warings one-way tickets out of the state to any destination of their choice—preferably Hell. On the street, the whites cut him dead. Youngsters taunted his wife, and grownups would occasionally block her passage. But pretty, exuberant Elizabeth Avery Waring would not relent. She went down to the YMCA and told Charleston Negroes that Southern whites were "sick, confused, decadent people . . . full of pride and complacency, introverted, morally weak and low. . . ." She gave out copies of her remarks to anyone who wanted them, and requests came in from all over the nation. The Warings began to exchange home visits with black residents of Charleston—a notion utterly alien and detestable to the St. Cecilia's crowd—and Mrs. Waring was featured on the nationally televised interview program *Meet the Press*, where she explained her views and defended her husband's judicial opinions. Judge Waring had crossed his Rubicon on a skyrocket.

Someone planted a flaming cross on the lawn in front of the Warings' house one evening when they were away. In early October of 1950, though, they were home playing canasta in their living room when three pistol shots rang through the night, a large lump of concrete crashed through the front window just above the Warings' heads, and another hit the front door. "You can expect this sort of thing in South Carolina," the judge told the wire services. "It's a state dominated by the Klan—a crime-committing Klan that goes unpunished." And he flayed the Dixiecrat movement, headed by South Carolina's Governor Thurmond, as "the dying gasp of white supremacy and slavocracy. . . . South Carolina and aristocratic Charleston show savage sentiments against not only the American creed but the creed of true religion."

Old-line Charlestonians shook their heads in regret. The assault on the judge's home was reprehensible, but he had been asking for it for some years now. Spurned socially for divorcing his first wife, they said, the judge had seized upon the racial issue to gain his revenge on the community. Such nuances were lost out in the rural areas. Up in Bennettsville, the county seat of outlying Marlboro County, the *Pee Dee Advocate* editorialized: "We see by the papers that somebody in Charleston hurled a few chunks of concrete through a window and door at the residence of federal Judge J. Waties Waring. Unfortunately, the judge was not hit."

It was a month after the night attack on his residence that the NAACP came into Judge Waring's courtroom to argue the first public-school segregation case. Thurgood Marshall knew he had a friend on the bench and had shaped his pleadings with that friendliness in mind. Waring, however partisan he had become on the racial question, was still more judge than advocate, and he did not let Marshall forget it at the pre-trial hearing on November 17, 1950.

The judge knew all about life in Clarendon County. He had driven through it innumerable times en route to Columbia or up to Florence, where he held court a couple of days a year. "Rather poor farming land," Waring called it. "A very backward county, one of the most backward counties of the state. It's ruled by a small white minority very limited in their viewpoint and education." The county had "a large population of Negroes, most of whom are dreadfully ignorant and poor, with very little opportunities. . . . You could drive through Clarendon County, as I often did . . . , and see these awful-looking little wooden shacks in the country that were the Negro schools. The white schools were nothing to be really enthusiastic about, but they were fairly respectable-looking. In the towns, they were generally of brick and some of them had chimneys, running water, and things of that kind. The Negro schools were just tumbledown, dirty shacks with horrible outdoor toilet facilities."

To end "doghouse education" in Clarendon County, Thurgood Marshall had a choice to make. He could bring the case of Harry Briggs and the other harassed blacks of Clarendon County before Waring in the United States District Court on the ground that R. W. Elliott, the sawmill owner who was chairman of the Board of Trustees of School District No. 22, and his adamantly white-supremacist associates had failed to provide adequate school facilities for the colored pupils within their jurisdiction. That looked like an open-and-shut case. The evidence was overwhelming that Clarendon's blacks had been denied equal protection of the law as required by the *Plessy* doctrine. And in view of Waring's earlier rulings on equalization of teachers' salaries, peonage, the law-school case, and the white primary, it seemed unthinkable that the judge would turn down the blacks' plea to replace what Waring knew to be their "pretty dreadful schools." But Thurgood Marshall had just finished successfully pushing the NAACP hierarchy to discard the equalization approach in all future litigation. *Plessy*, even honored to the letter, would no longer do. Segregation itself was the target now. The change of tactics had been made with much fanfare and, in Marshall's case, with deep but unpronounced concern. *Briggs v. Elliott* was a good example of why he was uneasy. It would be relatively easy to win an equalization suit in front of a friendly judge such as Waring or perhaps before any of a number of not rabidly bigoted Southern jurists. But to attack segregation itself was almost to insure negative decisions in every lower court until the Supreme Court itself faced the question directly. Nor was it clear whether Waring was jurisdictionally permitted to hear a suit attacking segregation itself. To bring such action, Marshall would have to direct it not only against the handful of stonehearted crackers who ran the Clarendon schools but also against the laws of South Carolina that required segregation of the schools. Under the Judiciary Act of 1937, cases challenging the constitutionality of state laws were to be heard by special three-judge District Courts that the NAACP had first used in *McLaurin*. The intention of the procedure had been both to speed up final adjudication of such important questions of law and to relieve an individual District Court judge of the sole responsibility of pronouncing that a state statute was in conflict with the Constitution.

Thus, if Marshall were to draw up the *Briggs* case pleadings to challenge the very practice of segregation in South Carolina and not merely the gross inequities in how it was practiced in Clarendon County, he would probably have to come before a three-judge District Court, of whom the black man's friend, J. Waties Waring, would be but one member. A second member would automatically be another District Court judge for South Carolina named George Bell Timmerman, a Bible-quoting fundamentalist and an outspoken advocate of white supremacy. The third member of the three-judge court would be the chief judge of the Fourth Circuit of the Court of Appeals—the eminent John J. Parker. Even Walter White, who twenty years earlier had led the NAACP assault on Parker's nomination to the Supreme Court, acknowledged that John Parker had proven as fair-minded and generous-spirited a Southerner as had ever sat on the federal bench, Justice John Marshall Harlan of Kentucky excepted. Twice before, Thurgood Marshall had won major appeals before Parker—the *Alston* decision, reversing the District Court in Virginia on equal salaries for Negro teachers, and the *Elmore* decision, upholding Waring's ruling on the South Carolina white primary. And both decisions had in effect been affirmed by the Supreme Court, which chose not to hear them on appeal. Though Parker had written these and other decisions favorable to black litigants, none of his opinions had broken new ground in defining or redefining the civil rights of colored Americans. He was a hard-headed, clear-thinking, relatively enlightened grandson of the Confederacy unafflicted by the regional fever that so often produced hallucinations over the outcome of the Civil War. Yet, for all John Parker's uprightness, it did not seem plausible to Thurgood Marshall that the judge would have the judicial temerity to overrule *Plessy* when anyone at all sensitive to the question knew that the Supreme Court itself was taking a hyper-cautious approach. It was likely, then, that a three-judge District Court of Parker, Waring, and Timmerman would refuse to rule school segregation in South Carolina unconstitutional; at best, Marshall might get a spirited dissent out of Waring.

There was the even stickier question of how the Clarendon case would look to the Supreme Court if Marshall appealed the defeat he would likely suffer in the three-judge court. He would be coming before the Justices not merely to ask that separate schools in Clarendon County be declared unlawful. He would be asking not that a relatively few Negroes be admitted to the all-white schools of a predominantly white community, but that the white children be mingled among the predominantly black enrollment in a county that was more than 70 percent Negro. It would have been hard to find a more perilous test case. How much wiser it would have been to launch the attack on segregation in a border state, a Southern city, or any community where the white reaction would be less dire than in the old plantation country of rural Clarendon County in the Carolina black belt. But the colored people around Summerton, under the leadership of Reverend J. A. DeLaine, had shown too much courage for Marshall to turn his back on them now. DeLaine had been dismissed as a teacher. Levi Pearson's crops had rotted in the field because he could not get credit for machines to harvest them. Harry Briggs had been fired as a gas-station attendant, his wife had been fired as a motel maid, and many other blacks in the Summerton area were feeling the lash of white resentment. Their case had to be fought now. Marshall weighed all these factors and chose the cautious legal course, though it meant skirting the new strategy he himself had asked the NAACP to sanction. He would not directly challenge the state segregation law.

Judge Waring was fully aware of Marshall's dilemma. Marshall's restless lieutenant in the Fund office, Franklin Williams, had represented Isaac Woodward, the blinded war veteran, in the 1946 case presided over by Waring, who was heartsick over the outcome. Williams, who ushered Woodward around the country to fund-raising rallies, helped fertilize a friendship between Waring and Walter White during the judge's periodic trips north. Williams's impatience with Marshall's wariness in assaulting *Plessy* was communicated to White, his patron now at NAACP headquarters, and White was not hesitant about confiding to the judge that he feared Marshall was indecisive about taking the plunge. Having taken his own private plunge by now, Waring was not overly tolerant of Marshall's chosen strategy when he appeared before the judge at the start of the *Briggs* proceedings.

At the pre-trial hearing, Marshall gambited. He was indeed attacking the state's segregation laws themselves, he said. Waring was not biting. "Well, I pointed out to him," he recalled a few years later, "right there from the bench, that in my opinion the pleadings didn't raise the issue. I said, 'You've partially raised the issue, but of course can and may do what has been done so very, very often heretofore: decide a case on equal facilities. . . . It's very easy to decide this case on that issue.' "

Marshall, as the judge recalled the moment, again said he thought the issue of segregation itself had been raised clearly enough in his pleadings, and Waring told him flatly that it had not been. Then he would like to amend his pleadings, Marshall conceded. That would only complicate the whole proceeding, said Waring, who suggested that the case be dismissed without prejudice and a new case filed, directly charging that the South Carolina segregation laws "are unconstitutional, and that'll raise the issue for all time as to whether a state can segregate by race in its schools. He [Marshall] looked rather astonished, but said, 'Yes.' I said, 'Very good. I'll sign an order dismissing without prejudice, and I'll expect you to file a suit bringing that issue clearly before the court.' "

The confrontation had made Marshall look either incompetent or craven. He was neither. He had simply tried to maneuver through very difficult terrain and found one of his routes cut off. *Briggs* would have to be heard now by a three-judge court. Marshall's right-hand man, Robert Carter, dutifully explained away the matter to the expert witnesses he had lined up for the now postponed *Briggs* trial by putting the onus for the delay on Waring. In identically worded letters, he wrote:

. . . When, at the conference, the Judge became aware of the theory of our case—that is, that segregation was unconstitutional—he, apparently, did not feel that he alone could order the School Board to admit Negroes into the white schools. All that he felt that he alone could do would be to order the School Board to provide separate equal facilities if the evidence showed that the Negro schools were inferior. In his opinion our attack on segregation would have to be made before a special three-judge court.

We think the Judge is wrong, [and] there was no need to proceed to trial if all we could get was an order to secure equal facilities. . . .

But there is no doubt that such a version of the pre-trial hearing was a face-saving one. Three weeks after the hearing, Marshall himself wrote to Franklin Williams, who was by then installed in San Francisco as the NAACP's main operative on the West Coast: "We had drafted the pleadings to make an attack on segregation without raising the issue of the constitutionality of the segregation statute in order to escape the necessity of having a three-judge court." He added that he was sure Williams knew "why we preferred a one-judge proceeding instead of the three-judge proceeding in this particular case."

Carter, reflecting on the matter two decades later, summed up the mixed blessing of Waring's involvement in the case: "His behind was on the block, and I guess he wanted ours to be, too. He was measuring Thurgood's dedication. Thurgood was not dragging his feet in this. We were struggling to find the right way."

That way was to convince the Supreme Court it had to take judicial notice that state-ordained segregation was plainly an act of discrimination—and thus constitutionally indefensible.

Most of the white South denied that contention. Implicit in the denial was the profound conviction that the Negro in his natural state was inferior to the white man; all that segregation did was to corroborate nature's doing.

Back in 1896, when the Court handed down *Plessy*, most of the nation shared the South's estimate of the black man. When the Justices said in their opinion that segregation "did not stamp the colored race with a badge of inferiority," America saw no cynicism in that judgment. The Court, to be sure, had been disingenuous in its suggestion that the inferiority was solely in the minds of the segregated blacks. Had the *Plessy* Court chosen candidly to declare the prevailing view of the day among white Americans of every station, it would have said that no badge was necessary to proclaim what was self-evident. Keeping blacks separate, everyone understood, would prevent contamination of white blood by the defective genes of colored people, whose unfortunate traits stemmed from their tribal origins in densest Africa and were incurably fixed upon the race from generation unto generation. Why speak of "badges of inferiority" when their very blackness bespoke their low and brutish nature? All literature, folklore, and custom of the English-speaking peoples reinforced the notion that the African's tawny hide was a primal stain. Black was bad. Black was evil. Black was sinister. Blackness was baseness. The devil was black; Satan was the Prince of Darkness. Witches practiced black magic. The plague was the black death. Melancholy was the black humor. An unprincipled scoundrel was called a blackguard. When things were at their worst, they were said to look blackest. And white was all the things that black was not: it was God, it was good, it was virtue, honor, health. The Bible, Shakespeare, Milton, Melville—the masters of the King's English all promoted the easy imagery of black as vile and white as purity and thereby fed a deep and potent racism that well served all who would enslave the black men of Africa.

The degradation into which the Negro had fallen since his release from bondage—the ignorance and lassitude of the Southern blacks who clung beetlingly to the exhausted land, the moral corruption and physical filth of the urban sties into which blacks North and South had herded—was viewed as continuing proof of black inferiority. Segregation, by law in the South and by custom and economic coercion in the North, was still sanctioned in 1950 because few white Americans questioned *why* black people had fared so poorly in the fourscore and seven years since their emancipation. Other minorities had coped with ignorance and poverty and managed to prevail. The continuing derelict state of colored people in America, the story-book land of opportunity, *had* to be their own fault. It was in their blood. If survival went to the fittest, the blacks of America were plainly unfit. And their unattractive characteristics—sloth, dishonesty, low intelligence, high temper, and foul odor, to name a few of the alleged problems—naturally enough had caused widespread prejudice against them and compounded the problem. Few whites yet acknowledged that the low state and bad habits of the Negro might, on the contrary, stem from that very prejudice, which had always operated against him in white America. Few, that is, would grant that Negro inferiority might be not a fact of nature so much as the result of willful public and private policy. George Bernard Shaw, writing in *Man and Superman* seven years after the *Plessy* decision, skewered the prevailing arrangement by noting that "the haughty American Nation . . . makes the negro clean its boots and then proves the moral and physical inferiority of the negro by the fact that he is a bootblack."

By the time *Plessy* was decided by the Supreme Court, the paragon of informed and compassionate social thought in America was William Graham Sumner, the theologian turned Yale sociologist, who wrote of the black man in bondage:

> The slave acted only under two motives, fear and sensuality. Both made him cowardly, cringing, cunning, and false, and at the same time fond of good eating and drinking and of sensual indulgence. As he was subject to the orders of others, he lacked character, and this suited his master all the better.

Sumner's immensely influential book *Folkways*, issued ten years after *Plessy*, saw such ingrained traits as ineradicable by laws and the schemes of well-meaning reformers. Sumner's disciples and the growing crop of social scientists and their co-workers in the laboratory sought to demonstrate the inferiority of the Negro by clinical showings of lower mentality and cranial capacity. In 1906, a young scholar at Johns Hopkins published a study titled "Some Racial Peculiarities of the Negro Brain" in the *American Journal of Anatomy* in which the researcher claimed that Negro skulls were smaller than those of whites and their brains less convoluted and otherwise deficient. (A sharp rebuttal by the Hopkins researcher's laboratory director ran in the same journal three years later, but rebuttals rarely command as much attention as original charges.) By the second decade of the twentieth century, anti-Negro feeling in America was at its zenith and the social scientists had developed intelligence tests that were being avidly used to demonstrate the mental inferiority of blacks. As early as 1913, tests on the Binet-Simon Scale showed that more than twice as many blacks as whites were retarded in their mental age, and during the latter part of the decade G. O. Ferguson demonstrated in a wide series of tests that Negro schoolchildren were only 75 percent as able as white ones. IQ tests of more than 100,000 World War One draftees added to the seemingly irrefutable indictment: over 85 percent of the Negroes were found to score below the average of the white soldiers. When it was noted that Northern blacks scored higher than Southern whites, the test-givers answered that this was due to the high mixture of white blood among the colored subjects and the likelihood that, thanks to "selective migration," the brightest Southern blacks had bestirred themselves and moved North. These Northern Negroes, in other words, were the exceptions that proved the rule.

William Sumner's successor as race-*meister* of the American academy, Dr. William McDougall, professor of psychology at Harvard, did not need intelligence tests to convince him of the superiority of the white race. His *Introduction to Social Psychology*, first issued in 1908 and destined to run through two dozen subsequent editions, was the dominant textbook of its day. That intelligence was wholly or largely a matter of heredity and that such biological imperatives justified the existing social arrangements (i.e., white over black) were perhaps open to debate, but just barely. Racial instincts and such concepts as "the universal consciousness of kind" were said to be proper subjects of psychology, a discipline now thought to be useful to the effective political leader as well as to the scholar. By the early Twenties, McDougall was pamphleteering on the superiority of the Nordic peoples and inveighing, along with the rest of the growing racist academic lobby, to shut down America's open immigration policy before Mediterranean, Slavic, and other inferior stocks produced physical "disharmonies," not to mention disfigurements of character as well, when blended with the good blood of old Americans. Among the most outspoken of the race lobbyists was the president of the American Museum of Natural History, a blueblood named Henry Fairfield Osborn, a reputable paleontologist who had studied anatomy in England under Thomas Henry Huxley and met all the great biologists of his time, including Darwin. Assuming command of the museum in 1908 and remaining as its head for twenty-five years, Osborn was little troubled by the technical difficulties being encountered by those immersed in the infant science of cultural anthropology—men who acknowledged the accuracy of intelligence tests results but were beginning to question whether those results might be better explained by the Negro's heredity or by his environmental deprivations. "In the United States," wrote Osborn blithely, "we are slowly waking to the consciousness that education and environment do not fundamentally alter racial values." The politicians took note. Running for President in 1920, Warren Harding declared, "There is abundant evidence of the dangers which lurk in racial differences," and came out strongly for restrictive immigration. His successor, Calvin Coolidge, wrote as Vice President in 1922 that the laws of biology had demonstrated that Nordic peoples deteriorate when mixed with other races. Only with the passage of the immigration act of 1924, favoring English, Irish,

German, and Scandinavian newcomers, did the epidemic of quasi-scientific racism begin to lose its virulence. The Chicago *Tribune*, sentinel of the American heartland, called the 1924 immigration law as "epoch-making" as the Declaration of Independence.

But as the social sciences gathered momentum, the suspicion grew that the race theorists had imposed a predetermined set of values on the evidence they gathered. Even the intelligence tests, it was warily suggested, reflected the social biases of the white test-givers. What scientific evidence was there really that intelligence was a characteristic largely determined by racial inheritance? One of America's most outspoken, and least scientific, equalitarians, Mark Twain, wrote with bite and mockery of the deep racist strain in a white America that accepted the theory of natural Negro inferiority. In his 1894 novel *Pudd'nhead Wilson*, he endorsed social conditioning as far more potent than racial heritage in his story of a white child and a fair-skinned Negro child who were switched in infancy with the result that the pale Negro grew up spouting the full litany of white supremacy and the white turned into the very model of the bootlicking servant.

Study of the relationship between biological inheritance and social process in the shaping of a human being began to become a legitimate science in the United States soon after the arrival here, almost simultaneously with the *Plessy* decision, of a brilliant German physicist who in his twenty-ninth year became an American citizen. Before Franz Boas, most students of race relied on casual, if not fanciful, observation of scientific evidence. Boas, beginning with an intensive study of Eskimos in remote Baffin Land, brought a Prussian discipline and a physicist's precision to the gathering and weighing of data in the field. His preconception that Eskimo culture would prove readily explainable as a natural response to the environment was shattered by his discovery that many of their conventions were man-made and stood in apparent defiance of the Eskimos' physical setting. Only by exhaustive studies of their language, folk beliefs, and customs could the rationale behind much of their otherwise inexplicable behavior be decoded. No easy formulas would do. Working in America as an anthropometrist, Boas later directed a massive study of 17,000 immigrants and their children, showing that offspring do not necessarily reproduce the cranial and other features of their parents if they grow up in a different environment—a result that made all efforts to classify races on the basis of brain size and shape appear scientifically preposterous. By 1899, Boas was professor of anthropology at Columbia. By 1901, he was also curator of the American Museum of Natural History. By 1908, he was lending his name to the establishment of the NAACP. In 1911, he published his classic work *The Mind of Primitive Man*, and the entire study of race was revolutionized among serious scholars of the subject. It would no longer do to judge other cultures or alien strains within one's own culture as if they all represented stages of progression from primitive to sophisticated. Invariably, such a standard was saturated by the observer's tendency to weigh the ideas and customs of the subject group by the degree to which they coincided with those of his own culture. Properly, the true anthropologist should study the thoughts, feelings, actions, and institutions of another culture on its own terms. Culture, not racial inheritance, was the principal shaping force in determining the mental and temperamental characteristics of a people. The more closely the Boas school of psychologists and anthropologists studied the results of the intelligence tests that racists claimed proved the natural inferiority of Negroes, the more convinced they became that no racial scale of intelligence could be scientifically authenticated.

By the last half of the Twenties, the counterattack on racism was in full swing among social scientists. In 1927, E. B. Reuter was writing in *The American Race Problem* that the gap between Negro and white scores on IQ and related tests was not due to inborn inferiority but was "subject to a more immediate, complete, and adequate explanation on the grounds of a difference in education and in educational opportunity." T. J. Woofter, Jr., of the University of North Carolina suggested in 1928 that many colored children given intelligence tests were "merely pedagogically retarded, not mentally deficient," and that, transferred to a more favorable setting, "these tend to progress faster and to catch up with their normal grade." In 1927, Boas declared, without much fear of contradiction, "All our best psychologists recognize clearly that there is no proof that the intelligence tests give an actual insight into the biologically determined functioning of the mind." Studies of American Indian children underscored the role of family wealth and parental occupation in intelligence ratings. A disciple of Boas at Columbia—social psychologist Otto Klineberg—studied intelligence and other mental proficiency-rating tests and in the early Thirties conducted experiments that dealt a hard blow to racist theorists who clung to the World War One test results. To explore the racist contention that the superior test performance of Northern blacks was due to selective migration of the brightest Southern blacks, Klineberg studied more than 3,000 Harlem schoolchildren over a number of years on the premise that if the racists were right, the length of the youngsters' residence in New York should have made no appreciable difference in their test scores. Klineberg's results were striking: ". . . the lowest scores are obtained by the groups which have most recently arrived from the South. There is a close, though by no means perfect, relationship between length of residence in New York and 'intelligence,' either as measured by test score or by school grade. There can be no doubt that an improvement in 'environment,' with everything that this implies, can do a great deal to raise the intelligence-test scores."

Behavioral and neurological testing produced insights of new kinds which suggested that the teachings of Franz Boas had begun to triumph. In 1926, the *Psychological Review* carried a study that speculated on why Negro children of all ages played school and invented classroom situations much more frequently than whites even though the colored children were "conspicuously unsuccessful in academic endeavor." The play-school activity, the experimenters suggested, may have symbolized to the colored children the kind of knowledge, power, and prestige they were unable to achieve in the real world. "This form of make-believe play may be a compensatory activity." Other tests exploded stereotyped racial characteristics. A 1931 study in the *Journal of Applied Psychology* found only slight differences in the musical abilities of children of the two races. Klineberg even reported on clinical experiments that had been conducted by others to compare the aroma of perspiration collected in test tubes from the bodies of white and black students who had just finished exercising in a gymnasium. The white nostrils that were then invited to quiver above the sweat samples detected no differences along racial lines. Though physiologists had shown that Negroes have more sweat glands than whites, it was the social psychologists who finally reached the not very profound conclusion that white belief in powerful Negro bodily aroma was inspired—to the extent that the phenomenon may have existed at all—not by a natural-born funk that ran with the genes but by the lack of bathing facilities and laggard sanitary habits among poor people living in warm climates who also tended not to have very large wardrobes or much chance to wash the clothes they owned.

By the mid- and late Thirties, long-held racist theories were under assault throughout the academic world. Melville J. Herskovits, an anthropologist who taught at Columbia and Howard before moving to Northwestern to establish the university's program in African studies, began publishing his extraordinary fieldwork, conducted in the Boas manner throughout central Africa and among the black peoples of the Caribbean. In his 1941 publication of *The Myth of the Negro Past*, Herskovits challenged the prevailing notion that earlier generations of Americans who had enslaved millions of Africans had in the process rescued them from lives of brutish savagery. On the contrary, said Herskovits, tribal cultures of great social, political, and economic complexity had existed in Africa for centuries, and African music, wood-carving, metalwork, weaving, and basketry were of a beauty to compare with any on earth. Nearly all vestiges of that cultural heritage, aside from a few folklore traditions and traces of the old languages, had been systematically obliterated among the New World blacks over their centuries in bondage. Equally eye-opening was the very different kind of fieldwork of John Dollard, a Yale psychologist raised and educated in the Midwest, who made an intensive study of Southern folkways and published his findings in 1937. In *Caste and Class in a Southern Town*, Dollard argued that the continuing exploitation of Negroes by whites in the community he investigated had its roots in an unquenched desire for revenge against the North after the Civil War and had long since settled into a social pattern that produced undeniable advantages to the whites; Dollard called them "the economic gain," "the sexual gain," and "the prestige gain." "In a larger sense," he wrote, "the [Civil] War has been continued by this hostility against Negroes. . . . [I]t is equally obvious that the threat of Negro competition to the middle-class trustees of southern culture would also arouse, and appear to legitimate, aggression against Negroes." In other words, segregation and other "badges of inferiority" placed upon the Negro by the South had more to do with the psychological needs of the whites and the advantages they gained from the process than with any intrinsic inferiority or warranted demotion of the blacks.

Black sociologists such as Franklin Frazier at Howard and Charles S. Johnson at Fisk, less passionate than Du Bois but writing now at a time when their work began to find an audience as his had not in an age of monolithic bias, added their reports from the field. The housing of rural Negroes, Johnson wrote in *Shadow of the Plantation* in 1934, was as much cause as effect of their depressed state: "The crowding-together of families in these small rooms destroys all privacy, dulls the desire for neatness and cleanliness, and renders virtually impossible the development of any sense of beauty. It is a cheerless condition of life with but few avenues of escape even for those who keep alive a flickering desire for something better."

The most spectacular measure of the revolution in the social sciences, though, was the appearance of a pair of books by native Southerners whose love of their region did not blind them to the pressing need to mend its aberrant thinking. Howard Washington Odum, a native of Georgia, had gone north to study at Columbia, which, Franz Boas aside, was a hotbed of racist sentiment in the social-science faculties. Odum's 1910 doctoral dissertation on *Social and Mental Traits of the Negro*, published as a volume in the Columbia University Studies in History, Economics and Public Law, was a compendium of every shallow, thoughtless prejudice of its time. Among other assertions, it found:

> . . . The Negro has little home conscience or love of home, no local attachment of the better sort. . . . He has no pride of ancestry, and he is not influenced by the lives of great men. The Negro has few ideals and perhaps no lasting adherence to an aspiration toward real worth. He has little conception of the meaning of virtue, truth, honor, manhood, integrity. He is shiftless, untidy, indolent. . . . He does not know the value of his word or the meaning of words in general. . . . He recognizes no causal relation between stability and prosperity. . . .
>
> The young educated negroes are not a force for good in the community but for evil. . . . They feel manual labor is beneath their dignity; they are fitted to do no other. They sneer at the idea of work and thus spread dissatisfaction among the members of their race. . . . The negro woman constitutes a serious feature of the situation. She fails to assist the men in a better struggle, she is inefficient and indisposed to be faithful. She is a hindrance to the saving of money and the industrial development of the family.

Any notion of equality of the races was nonsense to Odum, who concluded his scholarly essay with a masterstroke of old plantation logic: "What the future attitude of the whites will be toward the Negro will depend largely on the Negro's ability to prove his worth and his assistance to the whites."

A quarter of a century later, installed at the University of North Carolina, the same Howard Odum would be regarded as one of the most liberal and objective social scientists in the South. His 1936 publication, *Southern Regions of the United States*, a massive inventory of the physical and human resources of the section, was packed with revealing data, clear thinking, and an agenda for urgent reforms. High upon that list, Odum declared, was the need to stop leaning on the black man. Social scientists had long erred grievously in their assumption that "race was an entity in itself, a purely physical product rather than the result of long developed folk-regional culture." They had erred, too, in assuming that the races were inherently different, that some were superior and some were inferior, and that the Negro race as an inferior one was naturally available for exploitation and discrimination. "On the contrary," Odum now wrote of the black man, "there is ample evidence to indicate many manifestations of superiority, of extraordinary personality and survival qualities, of capacity for intellectual and social achievement. . . . His inequalities of opportunity everywhere strike at the heart of any working democracy." He then invoked the conclusions of the Commission on Interracial Cooperation, an Atlanta-based philanthropic group of liberal Southerners devoted to reducing racial tensions in the region. Odum and a Chapel Hill colleague, sociologist Guy B. Johnson, were mainstays of the Interracial Commission, which asserted that "it is time for the leaders of the white race to make an honest effort to be fair to the Negro . . . it is a matter of simple justice to a people who have earned well the right to have a voice in their own government. . . ."

But Howard Odum did not restrict his panoramic study of Southern dysfunction to the race problem. He won high regard because he saw that racial concerns served as both a crutch to the region and an excuse to avoid tending to its severe economic ailments. Here was a land perhaps more abundantly blessed by nature than any other in the world, and yet the South was ill-fed, ill-housed, ill-clothed, and ill-educated. Its economy was un-planned and desperately unbalanced. Sixty percent of its land was eroded, and there were neither tools nor will to preserve it. Why was the South so deficient in dairy cows, why did it have to buy food and hay from other regions, when it had the lushest pastures in America? Why should California vegetable growers and poultrymen ship their lettuce and eggs to the New York markets while the farmers of the much nearer Carolinas did not? The South had people enough and the land was rich enough to supply all the food for sustenance, the wood for housing, the cotton for clothing, and the minerals for industry that any area on earth needed to gain self-sufficiency, if only Southerners would end their enslavement to the cotton economy and their reliance on cheap labor as an enticement to outside capital.

Such views were shared by Odum's gifted colleagues in the social sciences at North Carolina—Guy Johnson, T. J. Woofter, and Rupert B. Vance among them—and made the university a shrine for progressive young Southerners and a patron of activist scholarship. For individual brilliance, though, no work by a loyal son of the South exceeded the scorching version of the region's history and psyche presented by Wilbur J. Cash's *The Mind of the South*, published in 1941. A native of South Carolina who later worked on a Chicago newspaper and contributed to H. L. Mencken's *American Mercury* before settling down as an editor of the Charlotte, North Carolina, *News*, Cash performed literary open-heart surgery on his native land as he cut away the myths and the bluster in an effort to explain why the South was more neurotic than exotic. Never before had a Southerner written with such unforgiving candor of the region's collective malaise, of its lack of personal restraint and the "inviolability of whim," of its distrust of and contempt for authority, of its divorce of pride from diligent effort and industrious achievement, of the "vastly ego-warming distinction" it claimed between the lowest white man and every black, of the historic and continuing manipulation of the poor-whites, of the suppression of dissent, of the hatred of criticism, of the sadism and angry impatience and taste for cruelty that were slavery's legacy to the master class, and of the mentality that for long decades encouraged lynching as a chivalric ritual.

What little respectability remained in the racist camp of the social sciences was buried with the 1944 publication of Myrdal's mountainous study, *An American Dilemma*. Written with the aid of a task force of scholars and researchers, including Ralph Bunche, Otto Klineberg, Melville Herskovits, Howard Odum, and Guy Johnson, Myrdal's indictment of the race problem was so comprehensive that it became the principal frame of reference for almost all literature in the field. And it said things with a dispassionate directness that demanded attention. Himself an economist, Myrdal was perhaps at his best in discussing the economic impact of racism. His chapter on "Economic Inequality" begins with this indicting paragraph:

> The economic situation of the Negroes in America is pathological. Except for a small minority enjoying upper or middle class status, the masses of American Negroes, in the rural South and in the segregated slum quarters in Southern and Northern cities, are destitute. They own little property; even their household goods are mostly inadequate and dilapidated. Their incomes are not only low but irregular. They thus live from day to day and have scant security for the future. Their entire culture and their individual interests and strivings are narrow.

Myrdal's value was that he not only indicted; he explained why the Negro remained in such a state of severe distress. The essence of the problem was what he called "the vicious circle of cumulative causation." From the beginning, American whites had exploited Negroes. That was what they had been brought here for, and the tradition was sanctioned by law. "When slavery disappeared, caste remained," wrote Myrdal. "Within this framework of adverse tradition the average Negro in every generation has had a most disadvantageous start. Discrimination against Negroes is thus rooted in this tradition of economic exploitation." When the Negro no longer served as an economic convenience—when he demanded treatment like any other human being—immigrant white labor in the North and poor-white labor in the South were given the good jobs and the blacks were consigned to the human slag heap. "The vicious circle works here, too," Myrdal explained; "the very fact that the masses of Negroes, because of economic discrimination—partly caused by social inequality—are prevented from entering even the bottom of the occupational hierarchy, are paid low wages and, consequently, are poor gives in its turn motivation for continued social discrimination." Because Negroes were badly off, in other words, dominant whites saw no need to treat them decently: "Negroes are given inadequate education, health protection, and hospitalization"; such basic public services as garbage removal and police protection were "neglected or withheld while vice is often allowed. All this must keep the Negro masses inferior and provide reasons for further discrimination in politics, justice and bread-winning." And the cycle spun on through the generations. "Since Negroes are seldom in demand for jobs for which education is necessary, there certainly is nothing surprising in the conclusion that they, unlike whites, usually fail to improve their opportunities by staying in school longer." Unmotivated and thus uneducated, young blacks dropped out by the tens of thousands. Their respect for law and order "constantly undermined by the frequent encroachments upon Negro rights and personal integrity," their attitudes conditioned by a prevailing belief in some sectors of the white community that Negroes are born criminals, young blacks abandoned hope of ever joining the mainstream of American society and sharing in its rewards. Self-esteem turned to self-loathing, and widespread anti-social behavior followed. Colored people were plainly aliens in their own nation. And segregation worked to institutionalize that alienation and widen the gap between the races.

As Thurgood Marshall sought to convince the Supreme Court to sweep aside the conniving legalisms of past decisions upholding Jim Crow law, he therefore had the benefit of a half-century evolution in the social sciences that declared segregation to be both a cause and a result of the victimization of black America. It was time to tell the Court what it had so long denied in keeping *Plessy* on the books: segregation was the approval of man's inhumanity to man. Nothing could have been more obvious, but to admit as much seemed to require more moral stamina than white America could or would summon. If Negroes tested out as inferior, said the social scientists, it was plainly because whites kept them that way. And so it was to the social scientists that Marshall and the NAACP lawyers now turned as they prepared to argue that racial separation caused severe psychological damage and anti-social tendencies among members of the segregated group. Such effects denied the victims equal protection of the laws. And when those so denied were children, the sin was multiplied and their lives misshapen beyond repair.

# 14

# The Doll Man
# and Other Experts

The Atlantic Coast Line Railroad in those days ran half a dozen trains daily out of New York that stopped at Charleston, South Carolina. The only convenient one, though, for the three black men who boarded it together on Wednesday, May 23, 1951, was the Palmetto, the overnighter that left Pennsylvania Station at 1:30 in the afternoon and was due at the City Market station in Charleston at 8:00 the next morning.

The top two attorneys for the NAACP Legal Defense Fund, Thurgood Marshall and Robert Carter, would have flown to Charleston, but their traveling companion did not relish the prospect. "Thurgood and Bob tried to convince me," recalls Kenneth B. Clark, a slender, fastidious man of high though carefully controlled intensity, "but I just wasn't flying in those days. I told them to go on ahead, but they said no, we'd all go down by train. It turned out to be a fascinating trip."

It also turned out to be the pivotal moment of Kenneth Clark's career. A thirty-seven-year-old social psychologist who was then an assistant professor at City College of New York, Clark would become the best-known and most highly regarded black social scientist in the nation, the first black full professor at City College, a militant member of the New York Board of Regents that oversees public education throughout the state, and the author of many works, *Dark Ghetto* the best known of them, that would be assigned reading in sociology, anthropology, and black-studies courses at almost every American university. But on that spring afternoon in 1951, Ken Clark was not yet any of those things, and Thurgood Marshall was plainly taking a chance on him.

If he was apprehensive to start with, Marshall was not entirely put at ease by the box that Clark lugged onto the train with him and stowed out of the way in the overhead rack. The box contained the tools of Clark's particular trade: dolls. There were four of them, each about a foot high and sexually neuter. Dressed only in diapers, they were identical except for one thing: two of them were pink and two of them were brown. They had cost fifty cents each at a five-and-ten on 125th Street, where Clark had bought them himself. He and his wife, Mamie, who was also a psychologist, had used the dolls for several years in developing a series of projective tests that disclosed how early in life black children came to understand that success, security, beauty, and status all wear a white skin in America. The effect of that realization on the self-images of the colored youngsters tested was profound, the Clarks had discovered. It was just such findings in clinical psychology that the Legal Defense Fund needed as it prepared for the rescheduled trial of *Briggs v. Elliott*, directed now at overturning segregation itself and not merely winning equal schools for the black children of Clarendon County.

"I told the staff that we had to try this case just like any other one in which you would try to prove damages to your client," recounts Thurgood Marshall. "If your car ran over my client, you'd have to pay up, and my function as an attorney would be to put experts on the stand to testify to how much damage was done. We needed exactly that kind of evidence in the school cases. When Bob Carter came to me with Ken Clark's doll test, I thought it was a promising way of showing injury to these segregated youngsters. I wanted this kind of evidence on the record."

Carter, who had done graduate work in law at Columbia, had gone first to an established star in the field of race studies—Columbia's Otto Klineberg, whose work debunking the "selective migration" theory of performance on intelligence tests by Northern Negroes was well known to the NAACP lawyer. Advised that the NAACP's case would rest on the theory that school segregation itself contributed heavily to the psychic damage of black children, Klineberg directed Carter to the young Negro psychologist who had earned his doctorate at Columbia. It was Kenneth Clark's specialty. And his life.

Reared in the Panama Canal Zone, Clark was five years old when his mother moved him and his two-year-old sister into a tiny Harlem tenement and, though she had been an accomplished seamstress in Panama, took a job as a sweat-shop worker in the garment center. Kenneth's father, a passenger agent with the United Fruit Company, did not want to lose his status as the token black with an inside job and had refused to leave Panama so his children might seek wider horizons in the States. His mother became one of the early shop stewards in the International Ladies' Garment Workers Union's fight for recognition, but she did not stint on her children's upbringing. Small Ken Clark was made to do his lessons and directed toward life's higher goals. When one of his school advisors made the mistake of writing his mother and suggesting that the boy be entered in a vocational school to learn a trade, "Mama stormed into school, more the shop steward than the lady she usually was," Clark has recounted, "and told my counselor, 'I don't give a damn where you send *your* son, but *mine* isn't going to any vocational school.' Naturally I was embarrassed and thought she'd messed things up for me, but she hadn't. They sent me to George Washington High School—without any further discussion with Mama on the subject."

He went on to Howard University, where he became the controversial editor of the student newspaper, the *Hilltop*, and prospered intellectually under such faculty members as Bunche, Frazier, and literary critic turned philosophy professor Alain Leroy Locke, the ex-Rhodes Scholar who had played an important role in popularizing the Harlem Renaissance in the arts during the Twenties. A psychology major, Clark met a mathematics major named Mamie Phipps, daughter of a comfortable Hot Springs, Arkansas, physician, and persuaded her to switch to his field and, a few years later, to marry him. Kenneth took his master's degree at Howard and taught there for a year while Mamie finished her bachelor's work. One of the subjects he taught was abnormal psychology and one of the students he taught was his wife—"She was an excellent student," he remarks dryly, "and got an A in the course." For her fieldwork in the course, Mamie Clark began studying black Washington schoolchildren and the effects of race on their sense of self-identity. Kenneth was fascinated and joined in. As early as 1939, the couple began publishing their findings in the *Journal of Social Psychology.* By 1940, they had moved to New York, where Clark earned his doctorate at Columbia and his wife pursued her work on racial identity while working on her master's at City College.

The transfer to New York gave the Clarks the chance to compare the effect of segregated and racially mixed schools upon black children. "Children were asked to show the experimenter which one of a series of drawings of white and colored boys, animals, and a clown they considered to be themselves," the Clarks reported in an article titled "Segregation as a Factor in the Racial Identification of Negro Pre-School Children" that appeared in the Spring 1940 issue of the *Journal of Experimental Education.* The evidence showed that segregated black children in Washington seemed a good deal more aware of their color than Negro children in the racially mixed schools of New York. What the effects of that awareness were, the Clarks were not ready to conclude, but they pursued their field investigations steadily while Kenneth worked with the Carnegie Corporation study of the Negro headed by Myrdal (of which *An American Dilemma* was the ultimate product), taught at Hampton Institute in Virginia while holding a fellowship from the Rosenwald Foundation, and served as a research analyst traveling around the country to study Negro morale for the Office of War Information before being appointed an instructor in psychology at City College in 1942. Mamie Clark meanwhile earned her Ph.D. at Columbia, put in volunteer work in the psychiatric clinic of the city Children's Court, and became a psychologist at an armed-forces think tank. At the end of the war, the Clarks pooled their brain power and growing concern with the pathology of racism and established a child-guidance project in Harlem called the Northside Testing and Consultation Center. In time, the enterprise became known as the Northside Center for Child Development, took on biracial cases, and attracted municipal and federal funding.

Through it all, their researches continued. To pinpoint the nature and development of the damage that racism caused, the Clarks worked out a pair of test techniques. One was the doll test. There was nothing very subtle about it. They showed Negro children in the three-to-seven-year-old range four identical dolls, two of them brown and two white, and to test the children's awareness of their negritude, asked them to (1) "Give me the white doll," (2) "Give me the colored doll," and (3) "Give me the Negro doll." Three-quarters of the children correctly identified the dolls. Then came the emotionally loaded questions. The children were told: (1) "Give me the doll you like to play with" or "the doll you like best," (2) "Give me the doll that is the nice doll," (3) "Give me the doll that looks bad," and (4) "Give me the doll that is a nice color." The majority of the Negro children tested—in such varying communities as Philadelphia, Boston, Worcester, Massachusetts, and several cities in Arkansas—indicated "an unmistakable preference for the white doll and a rejection of the brown doll." That was true even of the three-year-olds.

In addition to the doll test, the Clarks worked with a coloring test that produced equally disturbing findings. The subject child was given a piece of paper with outline drawings of a leaf, an apple, an orange, a mouse, a girl, and a boy on it and a box of twenty-four colored crayons that included black, brown, white, yellow, pink, and tan. If the child correctly colored the leaf, apple, orange, and mouse, he or she was asked to color in the two children. If the child was a boy, he was told, "See this little boy? Let's make believe he is you. Color this little boy the color that you are." After he was done, the boy would be told, "Now, this is a little girl. Color her the color you like little girls to be." The Negro children with very light skin pigment tended to color the drawings white and yellow. But 15 percent of the children with medium-brown skin and 14 percent of the dark-brown children also colored the figures of themselves with white or yellow crayon or an outlandish color such as red or green. When asked to add the colors they preferred in members of the opposite sex, 52 percent of the children crayoned the drawings white or in a bizarre or apparently irrelevant color.

"We were really disturbed by our findings," Kenneth Clark recalls, "and we sat on them for a number of years. What was surprising was the degree to which the children suffered from self-rejection, with its truncating effect on their personalities, and the earliness of the corrosive awareness of color. I don't think we had quite realized the *extent* of the cruelty of racism and how hard it hit." The interviewing and testing proved a moving and shaping experience for Clark. "Some of these children, particularly in the North, were reduced to crying when presented with the dolls and asked to identify with them. They looked at me as if I were the devil for putting them in this predicament. Let me tell you, it was a traumatic experience for me as well."

In 1950, one of Clark's former professors at Howard, Alain Locke, was serving as an advisor to a semi-cultural jamboree known as the White House Midcentury Conference on Youth. Noting that no provision had been made for a panel discussion or report on problems of minority-group children, Locke got Clark commissioned to write a report that was published five years later in revised form as a book called *Prejudice and Your Child*. Clark's White House report summarized the findings he and his wife had made in their doll and coloring tests, but scarcely claimed a monopoly on such test techniques. Among others they credited were Marian J. Radke and Helen G. Trager, who had run a more ambitious series of similar tests as part of what was known as the Philadelphia Early Childhood Project. In an article titled "Children's Perceptions of the Social Roles of Negroes and Whites" in the *Journal of Psychology* in 1950, Radke and Trager went a good deal further than the Clarks had. They had tested both Negro and white children by presenting them with eight-inch brown and white cardboard dolls; clothing that was typed as dress-up, work, and shabby and that fitted all the dolls interchangeably; and a pair of painted plywood houses, one a red-brick-and-white-trim single-family house with a lawn and trees depicted, the other a rundown multiple-family dwelling of red-brown shown adjacent to an alley. The Radke-Trager findings corroborated—indeed, they considerably elaborated on—the published and unpublished work of the Clarks. Among the results the two women obtained with the Philadelphia test group were that 57 percent of the Negro children and 89 percent of the white children preferred the white cut-out doll; that 60 percent of the white children outfitted the brown dolls in shabbier clothing than they put on the white dolls; and that 82 percent of the white children and two-thirds of the colored children placed the Negro doll in the tenement. Clark might have strengthened his White House Conference report and the subsequent book with a more generous use and attribution of such revealing work by others in the field, but the thrust of his writing was clear enough. The mold of racial prejudice, with its fixed social expectations, was set at an appallingly early age. If anything was to be done about the problem, it would have to be done very early before despair and self-hatred took their fatal toll.

Kenneth Clark's report was used as the basis for a decorous panel at the White House Conference—"and then I forgot about it. It was a monograph. A few people knew about it, but there was little publicity. A few months later, Bob Carter called me and I asked him up to my office. He was remarkably clear and direct and candid, saying that they had gone to Klineberg first, who told him about my monograph. None of them down there [at the Legal Defense Fund office] knew about it, and Bob asked whether I thought I could help."

The problem was in trying to isolate the psychological damage caused specifically by segregation in the schools as singled out from other manifestations of prejudice in society as a whole. Such a distinction was impossible to make, but what was beyond dispute was the great shaping effect of the early school years on the lives of Americans, whatever their color. No other people in history had invested so many of its resources and so much of its hope in its schools. As the nation's best-known social philosopher, John Dewey, wrote, it had become

> the office of the school environment to balance the various elements in the social environment, and to see to it that each individual gets an opportunity to escape from the limitations of the social group in which he was born, and to come into living contact with a broader environment.

It was precisely this "living contact" that was intolerable to the white-supremacist, segregating South. It was not that admission of Negroes to the same schools with whites meant automatic admission to the same social class, though that fear was expressed. It was that such mingling would raise black aspirations and unfit them for their long-held place on the underside of society. And so long as blacks occupied that underside, no whites—however modest their IQ or income or family pedigree—could occupy it. Indeed, any real improvement in the education of blacks threatened the very basis of white supremacy and the long-harbored assumption of Negro inferiority. Wrote Dollard in 1937:

> . . . the school training of Negroes makes them more skillful in dealing with whites, arouses latent wishes for advancement and personal dignity, and increases their demands on the caste system. Our type of education stands against the ideas of luck, chance, and magic which help to distort the reality picture of the lower-class Negro. . . . [T]he schools carry the pattern of impulse renunciation along with them and in this way they prepare Negroes for middle-class status.

But the provision of better schools for black children could not, by itself, compensate for the deprivations they so often suffered before ever setting foot inside a classroom. The root of the retardation in learning that so many Negro pupils suffered all the way up the educational ladder was found in their failure to learn to read properly in the first and second grades. Researchers noted that the home environment of lower-class black youngsters provided little of the sensory or intellectual stimulation vital to maximum learning benefits from conventional kindergarten and first-grade programs that stress reading readiness and then the basic building-block skills in literacy. Black homes, often badly overcrowded, were found to have high noise levels that forced children unconsciously to tune out sounds—a sanity-preserving function that unfortunately served also to lower their hearing acuity and the ability to distinguish subtle differences in sounds essential in learning how to read. Black lower-income households, moreover, are often non-verbal; sustained conversations using a vocabulary rich in standard English may be infrequent. Black parents, fatigued by heavy physical labor or otherwise beaten down by the precarious aspects of ghetto life, often fail to encourage their children during the first but vital stages of schooling. And many black families cannot afford to provide children with toys, books, magazines, paper, and writing implements, all of which serve to stimulate the learning process. It was a handicap that got them off on the wrong foot and caused them to fall farther behind at each grade level. Their reading disabilities invariably reinforced the negative images that so many black schoolchildren had of themselves and produced frustration and self-hate that led in turn to withdrawal from further intellectual striving. Bored and hostile, they would then linger on the fringes of the "blackboard jungle" until dropping out at the earliest possible moment.

It was all part of the vicious circle that Myrdal and a growing number of other social scientists saw trapping the Negro. The poisoned fruit of prejudice worked its toxic effect on each succeeding generation of Negroes: where and how could the chain of environmental deprivation be broken? Segregation itself, so long as it bore the imprimatur of the Supreme Court, was the place to begin, for it most assuredly fastened "the badge of inferiority" to the Negro and served to keep it there more effectively than any other public policy or private practice permitted by the collective conscience of the American people.

Robert Carter read Dr. Kenneth Clark's White House Conference monograph and saw in it an Aladdin's lamp. "He was enormously enthusiastic," Clark recalls. "In fact, I wondered if I weren't getting a bit of a snow job when he came back to me and said, 'It's just what we're looking for. It's almost as if it were written for us.' Within a few days, he came to my office with a blueprint of what they wanted me to do—and he was clear as a bell about it: (1) be a witness in the *Briggs* case, (2) enlist other social scientists, as prestigious as possible, to testify, and (3) work directly with the NAACP lawyers in going over the briefs as they dealt with the social-science material. And he wanted me to get started yesterday."

Clark did not hesitate. He had met Thurgood Marshall socially and occasionally visited the NAACP offices. "I both admired their work and was critical of it, much as the young people today may feel about the establishment people," Clark recounted twenty years later. "I had some doubts about the effectiveness of the legal approach in curing the basic problems, but I guess I was envious that they were actually doing something specific to improve things while I was off in the scholarly area, vaguely wishing to be part of what they were doing." When the chance came, he took it.

By no means all the lawyers in the elite corps Thurgood Marshall was enlisting for the massive assault on segregation were enthusiastic about Kenneth Clark's participation. In fact, his dolls were the source of considerable derision, and the social-science approach itself was viewed as unlikely to sway the Justices. "Of all the debunkers, I was the most debunking," acknowledges William Coleman, whose clerkship for Felix Frankfurter had left him extremely dubious about the usefulness of Clark's techniques. "Jesus Christ, those damned dolls! I thought it was a joke." But Thurgood Marshall was taking all the help he could get. "Thurgood kept his options open," Clark recalls. "He played the role of conductor beautifully. It was clear that Bob Carter was the most persistent, consistent advocate of the involvement of the social scientists at the trial level. Bob was way out on the limb, pretty much by himself. Most of the other lawyers felt this approach was, at best, a luxury and irrelevant. Thurgood didn't tip his hand, except that he did let Bob and me go ahead with the dolls. By the time we actually went to Charleston, the battle had been basically won."

The three black men looked out at the overcast sky as their train clacked down the Jersey corridor toward the Southland. One would call them "black" only after the polarizing language born of heightened racial pride made the word almost obligatory a dozen or so years later. Then there would be serious talk about changing the name of the NAACP because "colored people" is what Toms called themselves. But in May 1951 things were different. It was still a time when the lighter a man's skin, the higher his social status was in many sectors of black America. "BE LIGHTER! Be Lovelier! Be Loved! With Dr. Fred Palmer's New Double-Strength SKIN WHITENER," urged a large advertisement in that week's issue of the *Amsterdam News*, the

Harlem weekly. It was only one of many such ads that ran in nearly every Negro periodical, including the NAACP's monthly *Crisis.*

The three Negroes riding the Palmetto down to Charleston were in fact not "black" at all but slightly varying shades of light brown. Robert Carter, the younger of the two lawyers, had perhaps the deepest tone of the three. Kenneth Clark's was a barely detectable shade lighter. The palest brown of the three was the big man. Thurgood Marshall was a burly six-foot-two, and his youthful, loose-jointed ranginess had given way to signs of an unmistakably thickening middle as he approached his forty-third birthday. It was his face, though, rather than his bulk that was his most arresting feature. It was a long face with remarkable mobility, and its owner worked it like an actor to register a disarming range of moods and emotions. Among its features were a somewhat beaked nose and an unobtrusive mustache beneath, both of which seemed to recede in prominence as the face filled out with the years. What struck one most about Thurgood Marshall's face, though, were the eyes: heavy-lidded, somewhat sleepy, and yet very watchful. Behind tortoise-shell eyeglasses, they took on an owlish cast that could make his overall countenance appear decidedly dour. Publications over the years described him variously as a grumpy-seeming maharajah, a lazy panther, and "a disheveled bear of a man" who often needed a haircut, his pants pressed, and cigarette ashes brushed off his lapels. Gone was the Dapper Dan described so admiringly by the *Afro* seven years earlier in the afterglow of his triumph in *Smith v. Allwright.* There was too little time now to fuss about his grooming, and so his rumpled raiment overflowed the large-boned slouch he would slip into on his endless round of train, plane, bus, and car rides, of church suppers and NAACP pep rallies, of backroom strategy huddles in the fish-fry parlors of the South.

Sandwiched in the middle of the six months between the abortive *Briggs* hearing before Judge Waring the previous November and the *Briggs* trial that was to begin the last week in May, Marshall had put in an exhausting six weeks in Korea in response to urgent requests by mail to the NAACP from Negro soldiers who claimed that they had been unjustly court-martialed or otherwise unduly convicted and sentenced. Black soldiers convicted on charges ranging from being lost from their units to "disobedience" and "misbehavior" in the face of the enemy were receiving sentences of from ten years at hard labor to death.

What he found happening to black GIs on the other side of the world followed a painfully familiar pattern. Though President Truman had ordered the armed forces desegregated in 1948, military brass had dragged its feet implementing the rule. And since a disproportionately high ratio of officers were Southern whites, biracial fighting units were not proving a popular innovation. Indeed, the nation's most widely admired hero-general of the Second World War, Dwight Eisenhower, had testified before the Senate Armed Services Committee in 1948 that he believed racial segregation should not be discontinued at the platoon level or below. Thus, a division, brigade, regiment, or company of American soldiers was said to have been desegregated at the time of the Korean War if it numbered in its ranks small

all-black units—troops or squads of them, but not whites and blacks marching side by side or fighting out of the same foxholes. Nor had General Douglas MacArthur, the Far East commander, taken forceful steps to reduce military segregation within his command, though he had a career-long record of lip service to the valor of the black fighting man. Charles Houston had called him on it in the early Thirties.

In Korea and Tokyo, Thurgood Marshall studied the records of the court-martial proceedings and, going right up to the front lines in some cases, interviewed witnesses to the alleged acts of non-valor. He concluded that many of the convicted black soldiers had been tried under circumstances making it highly improbable that impartial justice would be dispensed. Few of the men had had adequate time to prepare their defense. In four cases in which life sentences were given, two of the trials had lasted fifty minutes each, one had lasted forty-four minutes, and one forty-two minutes. One soldier charged with "misbehavior in front of the enemy" testified that he had sprained his ankle and was unable to keep up with his outfit; he was given a sentence of fifty years.

At the bottom of the problem, Marshall soon saw, was the undiminished bias that still ruled the military, made white commanders quick to find fault with black troops, and produced low morale among the still essentially segregated Negro soldiers. Marshall gave a full report to MacArthur. The general was said to be quite aware of the situation. Marshall was unconvinced. On his return to New York, he held a press conference, divulged the essence of his findings of racism under MacArthur's command, and noted that not one Negro was attached to the general's headquarters in Tokyo. Not long after Marshall's return, the Army reduced the sentences for twenty of the thirty-two convicted black soldiers whose cases the lawyer had examined, and Marshall pressed the whole question of justice for black GIs with the Secretary of the Army in a meeting aimed at revising court-martial procedures. It had been a fruitful trip.

Korea was behind him now, though, as he unwound for a few hours on the train that was bearing them below the Mason-and-Dixon Line—Marshall liked to call it "the Smith-and-Wesson line"—toward the most fateful courtroom rendezvous of his career.

In Washington, the dining car was put on the train. Almost every black man working on it knew Thurgood Marshall. His father had worked the trains as a waiter for many years before landing his job at the Gibson Island Club, and young Thurgood had come to know the men and the work. To help pay his way through college, the then lanky Thurgood took summer jobs in the dining cars of the Baltimore & Ohio. The pants they gave him when he first reported for work ended midway up his shins. He complained of the poor fit to the head steward. "Boy," said the steward, "we can get a man to fit the pants a lot easier than we can get pants to fit the man. Why don't you just kind of scroonch down in 'em a little more?" Added Marshall, telling the story long after: "I scroonched."

Over dinner, Marshall and Carter pointed out to Kenneth Clark that, thanks to the *Henderson* decision of the previous June, they and any other

Negroes on interstate trips no longer had to eat at tables curtained off at the end of the dining car. "We joked a lot on that ride," Clark remembers, "but it's a mistake to think of Thurgood as a comedian. He had this unique capacity to deal with profoundly serious matters and then alleviate the mood with a remark that cut to the human predicament at the core of the problem." A Negro lawyer who worked with him for many years cites an example of just such a quip. The legal talk had become very heavy one afternoon and the others around the table were feeling stymied when Marshall fell back and said, "I wonder if a colored man can claim denial of equal protection if he's turned down by a white prostitute." Such a musing served as a kind of emotional thermostat and prevented NAACP skull sessions from becoming deadended. It also said something serious about both race and sexual relations in America.

After dinner, the train pulled into Richmond, where Marshall's group was joined by a blade-thin young Negro of a color lighter than any of them. His ascetic looks and soft-spoken manner suggested that he was more scholar than advocate, and there were those who said even then that Spottswood W. Robinson III, the NAACP's thirty-four-year-old lawman in Virginia, would someday make an outstanding law-school dean or federal judge. In time, he would become both.

Robinson shared a compartment with Carter, and Thurgood Marshall and Kenneth Clark retired for the evening to a nearby room. "For the first time," says Clark, "I saw the battle fatigue in Thurgood. I had known him on and off for ten years, and till then I had always thought he was inexhaustible and that he would just naturally keep on fighting. But he said to me then, 'You know, Kenneth, sometimes I get awfully tired of trying to save the white man's soul.' I said something innocuous back, like, 'You have no choice.' And he said, 'I'm not so sure.' He was resolved, of course, to see the segregation case through—'and then I've got to rest,' he said. I sensed the complexity of the man for the first time then."

"No one else could have survived," says a former member of the Legal Defense Fund staff in tribute to Marshall's generalship. It was not only the physical burden of the work, of course, but its psychological demands as well. Marshall was a man on a mental tightrope. "I think he had an awful lot of veiled hostility toward whites, but he kept it under control," adds his ex-associate. "He never lost track of where he was, once he set foot inside a courthouse. I remember one time when the head clerk of the Supreme Court—the United States Supreme Court—brought in sandwiches for the white attorneys during the lunch break in a case Thurgood was arguing. We looked in through the door and saw the white tablecloth being spread out, we saw that nice linen, and then we had to pile into cabs and go over to 'The Indian Reservation' to eat—that was what we called the black part of town. We were angry and hurt, but there was nothing to do but shrug it off."

That ability to absorb such psychological punishment kept Thurgood Marshall in one piece. "I ride in the for-colored-only cabs and in the back of the street-cars—quiet as a mouse," he told interviewers. "I eat in Negro cafés and don't use white washrooms. I don't challenge the customs personally because I figure I'm down South representing a client—the NAACP—and not myself." Since his client was paying him a less than princely annual salary in 1951 of $8,748.30 for his extraordinarily taxing labors, it is not unreasonable to surmise that Thurgood Marshall had come to think of the NAACP cause as identical with his own. And the way he best served both was not to strive for premature martyrdom. Myrdal wrote in *An American Dilemma* of the president of an NAACP branch in one of the smaller capitals of the Deep South whose outlook essentially mirrored Marshall's. The branch head, a postal clerk for much of his long life and therefore relatively immune from economic reprisal, had cautiously fought for Negro interests in his city for many years. Myrdal asked the old gent if there were other black civil-rights groups in the community, and the NAACP man said yes, there was the League for Civil Improvement. Myrdal asked him why the duplicated effort.

> "Sir, that is easily explainable. The NAACP stands firm on its principles and demands our rights as American citizens. But it accomplishes little or nothing in this town, and it arouses a good deal of anger in the whites. On the other hand, the League for Civic Improvement is humble and 'pussy-footing.' It begs for many favors from the whites, and succeeds quite often. The NAACP cannot be compromised in all the tricks that Negroes have to perform down here. But we pay our dues to it to keep it up as an organization. The League for Civic Improvement does all the dirty work."
>
> "Would you please tell me who is president of this League of Civic Improvement? I should like to meet him."
>
> "I am. We are all the same people in both organizations."

It was just that blend of militant radical-idealist and wily pragmatist that kept Marshall afloat. And unwittingly or by design, he reached into the folk traditions of the black people for the tools that made him so effective at his special trade: humor and dialect. Charles S. Johnson and Willis D. Weatherford, in their 1934 book *Race Relations*, remark on the manipulative use of humor by slaves in the interest of their own survival: "The master says to a young slave, 'You scoundrel, you ate my turkey,' and the slave replies, 'Yes, suh, Massa, you got less turkey, but you sho' got more nigger.' The slave lives to eat another turkey and the master has another entertaining story." Marshall never yes-suhed the Massa in any such abject fashion, but he achieved similar effects by often making himself the butt of a steady recital of funny stories. Around the Clerk's Office at the Supreme Court, where it did not hurt to have friends who could occasionally expedite matters or pass on a helpful piece of information, the white deputies would fondly recall long afterward the funny stories Marshall dispensed any time he was in the building. A typical farewell throwaway line of his went: "Well, gotta go down to South Carolina from here. Last time I was there, they told me they were gonna run me out of town on a rail. Better get my runnin' shoes on. . . ." A variation on that from his storehouse of self-effacing lines went: "I've got back trouble, you know—a big yellow stripe down the middle." But the humor did not have to be turned on himself to serve Marshall's ends. He genuinely loved to laugh. It was a great big knee-thwacking kind of laughter that came up out of the belly until the plastic face exploded with glee as its owner told the latest slightly off-color story he had picked up on the road. A typical one went: These two fellows were down in the locker room after golf, taking a shower. As they started to dress, one of them pulls a girdle out of his locker, garter fasteners and all, and starts slipping it on. The other fella says, "My God, when did you start wearing *that?*" The first fella says, "Ever since my wife found it in the glove compartment." It was leftover vaudeville and the kind of stuff Marshall could get off to a biracial group gathered in the corridors of a Southern courthouse. The very laughter that greeted it bespoke a man-to-man equality between yarn-spinner and listener. And that was where Marshall wanted to be—neither above nor below the whites he dealt with on a daily basis. He used his Southern dialect the same way. It plainly disarmed, if not unnerved, the proper and not-so-proper whites who heard it. Outside of court, he was forever dropping the final *g* from words, saying "ax" for "ask" and "substantual" instead of "substantial," and he could "dese" and "dat" with the broadest minstrel-show mimic. Says Henry Moon, former NAACP publicity director: "It was all part of his strategy. He never wanted them to think, 'Now this here nigger thinks he's smarter than I am.'" It was not a trait, of course, that Marshall invented. Myrdal remarks, "In the South a few educated Negroes do it [use dialect] to avoid appearing 'uppity' in the eyes of the whites." But it was not just the whites Marshall was concerned with; as Myrdal also noted, "Negroes seem to be proud of their dialect, and frequently speak it even when they know how to speak perfect English. Some upper class Negroes do this to retain prestige and a following among lower class Negroes." That textbook explanation serves as well as any to explain Thurgood Marshall's regular use of the folk language in his private dealings. He did not lapse into it—he embraced it whole-heartedly. It was the language of the unlettered black people of America, and it was for them mainly that he worked.

"He had a terribly deep and real affection for the little people—the people he called the Little Joes," says Marian Wynn Perry, the white lawyer who worked with him in the late Forties, "and the affection was returned. I never saw him put a little person down. At a national convention, some little fellow might ask a not very penetrating question and Roy Wilkins or someone else on the rostrum might wave him off. But Thurgood would send me to find the fellow or go see him himself because he knew that question was terribly important to this Little Joe, even if not to anyone else. He had this enormous ability to relate. He was not only *of* them—he was *with* them."

In extreme contrast stood the haughty personality of that other magnetic spokesman of the black folk who had risen to prominence as an NAACP standard-bearer—W. E. B. Du Bois. At the age of eighty-three, moreover, Du Bois was still active. Even as Marshall and his colleagues were speeding toward Charleston, in fact, the old man who had given such eloquent voice to the yearnings of black America for more than six decades was standing trial for having failed to register as an alleged enemy agent. If convicted, he faced a five-year jail sentence. It was the peak of the McCarthy witch-hunts, and

Du Bois had sinned by serving as a leader of an *ad hoc* leftist group called the Peace Information Center, which had distributed literature for an international colloquium and propaganda festival known as the Paris Congress of Peace, branded as subversive by the House Un-American Activities Committee. Du Bois's real sin was that, in his declining years, he had given up hope that the American capitalist system would ever treat the black man as other than economic fodder. The intellectual process that had begun for him at Atlanta University at the close of the nineteenth century with his first tentative probing of Marxism left him now, in the ninth decade of his life, an irreparably alienated black American. He was an elitist who suffered for and with the masses without ever joining them. His leftward lurch beyond the orbit of the American system, though, was a gesture that discomfited the far more demotic and resilient Thurgood Marshall, who was no less pained than Du Bois by what he saw.

It was hard to avoid succumbing to Du Bois's brand of earned despair if you were fighting for justice for the Negro in May of 1951. You got weary, as Thurgood Marshall put it to Kenneth Clark, from trying to save the white man's soul—especially since he was so unappreciative of the effort.

In May of 1951, the state of Texas did not allow interracial boxing matches.

Florida did not permit white and black students to use the same editions of some textbooks.

In Arkansas, white and black voters could not enter a polling place in the company of one another.

In Alabama, a white woman was forbidden to nurse a black man in a hospital.

North Carolina required racially separate washrooms in its factories. South Carolina required them in its cotton mills. Four states required them in their mines.

In six states, white and black prisoners could not be chained together.

In seven states, tuberculosis patients were separated by race.

In eight states, parks, playgrounds, bathing and fishing and boating facilities, amusement parks, racetracks, pool halls, circuses, theaters, and public halls were all segregated.

Ten states required separate waiting rooms for bus and train travelers.

Eleven states required Negro passengers to ride in the backs of buses and streetcars. Eleven states operated separate schools for the blind.

Fourteen states segregated railroad passengers on trips within their borders. Fourteen states segregated mental patients.

And in May of 1951 seventeen states required the segregation of public schools, four other states permitted the practice if local communities wished it, and in the District of Columbia the custom had prevailed for nearly ninety years.

School District No. 22 in Clarendon County, South Carolina, was just one of the 11,173 school districts in the United States that segregated their schoolchildren. But what the courts said about the legality of segregation there would affect the fate of all 11.5 million school-age children in the segregating states. It would affect every other form of segregation as well, and the pride and standing in the eyes of their fellow Americans of all 15 million Negroes in the nation.

The Palmetto raced through the night into the Carolinas.

"My God," Kenneth Clark exclaimed as they were counting their luggage on the railroad platform in Charleston, "I left my dolls on the train!" And off he flew in pursuit.

Spottswood Robinson, the Virginian in their midst, eyed Thurgood Marshall and Robert Carter with high suspicion as their fourth companion disappeared into the hissing trackside tumult. No one had bothered to fill Robinson in on Professor Clark's testing techniques and the dime-store apparatus essential to it. "I know these psychology people are a little strange to begin with," Robinson needled, having noted the real anxiety in Clark's face as he hurried back into the train, "but what kind of fellow is this one exactly?"

A panting Clark returned in triumph, Robinson was reassured that the dolls were for business and not pleasure, and the whole group piled into taxis and descended on a two-story brick-and-stucco house at 184 Smith Street, about a mile from the federal courthouse, that was to be their operational headquarters for the next week. The house belonged to Reginald and Eva Boone, lifelong residents of Charleston and active members of the local NAACP. The large game-room basement, actually on ground level, and an attached garage were turned over to Marshall and his group, and the traffic in and out never stopped. Eva Boone hired a cook to handle the overflow of lawyers, reporters, expert witnesses, stenographers, NAACP hands, and other local well-wishers who thronged her place and mooched meals at the big table set up in the garage, where many of the skull sessions were held because the temperature was well into the eighties throughout the week and a breeze came through out there.

Uncharacteristically, the FBI checked in by telephone to ask if everything was in order and any protection was required. "It was a long block and we lived right in the middle of it, with friends on all sides," Reginald Boone recalls. "We had no concern about our safety." Kenneth Clark, though, who was not allowed to linger in the comfort of the NAACP's Charleston beehive, was mightily concerned about safety. He and his dolls had a rendezvous in the backcountry, and the prospect had badly worried his wife, a native of Arkansas, before he left New York. Clark himself had never been to South Carolina before and rarely to any place as remote and hostile to his cause as Clarendon County. He was scared to death, he later confided.

"After we'd settled in at the Boone house and had a real nice meal," Clark remembers, "we started talking specifically about our plans for the week. You could see the tremendous psychological investment these men all had in the case—and of course my own life hasn't been the same since. After a while, I naturally started asking who was going to go over to Clarendon County with me—Thurgood or Bob or who? They said no one. I thought they were kidding, of course, and said so. They said, 'No, we're here to prepare for the trial and—well, you know, it's dangerous over there. The white fellas are *rough* over there.' It began to dawn on me then that maybe they weren't kidding. Now, I didn't know my way around the area, so Thurgood said don't worry, they'd have a chauffeur for me, someone who knows the county. The next morning I still think maybe they're kidding when this young fellow Montgomery of the South Carolina NAACP appears and Thurgood introduces us. But even as I walk out the door to get into that car, I'm half-believing Thurgood or Bob is going to climb in with me. All that happened, though, was that Thurgood called me over to one side, gave me a fifty-dollar bill, and said, not exactly sheepishly, 'Look, if you get into trouble over there, you might try showing this to them or to their leader—it might help.' Aside from my travel expenses, that is the only money that ever passed between the NAACP and me."

Eugene Montgomery was no ordinary chauffeur. A cool, soft-spoken Negro of twenty-eight, he had come out of Atlanta University's School of Social Work three years earlier and signed on as the South Carolina NAACP's executive secretary. Under the whip hand of James Hinton, the roly-poly ace insurance salesman and sometime preacher who was president of the state NAACP organization, Montgomery built up the number of branches in South Carolina from 30 to 130 with a total membership of about 15,000. After decades of cowed silence, the black people of South Carolina were aroused if not militant, and their newfound activism was one reason Thurgood Marshall felt committed to proceed with the Clarendon County case despite its unpromising circumstances.

Gene Montgomery had helped hold the harassed black residents of the Summerton area in line as the white community struck back in the face of the *Briggs* suit. Their leader, the Reverend J. A. DeLaine, had been reassigned to a parish in Lake City by the state's AME hierarchy in the interests of his safety, and Montgomery's toughness and reassurance were essential in the troubled months before the trial was held. At the last minute, word reached the NAACP listening posts that a counter-petition opposing the all-out assault on segregation in the revised pleadings of the *Briggs* suit was circulating, with white complicity, among Clarendon blacks. "We had an information apparatus over there that would have made the FBI look sick," says Montgomery, who was dispatched to check out the potentially devastating development. "I practically lived in the county during that time, and the whites by then knew all about me. Every time I crossed the county line, there was this fella sittin' in a cotton field with a shotgun. They knew when my car was comin'. Somehow I never felt physically endangered, though. I had a job to do—and I had to be professional about it."

Part of that job was to orient strangers to the Clarendon racial climate. "Montgomery's idea of putting me at ease on the ride over to Summerton," Kenneth Clark says, "was to tell me all the awful things that had been going on over there—the threats, the reprisals, and the rest. He did a pretty damned good job of preparing me, too, because I'd of course never had to make my tests under such difficult circumstances. He had me terrorized by the time we got to Summerton."

Their first stop was the office of the superintendent of schools for School District No. 22, H. B. Betchman, whom local Negroes viewed as the mean-talking henchman of the white-supremacist power structure in the area. "Betchman started being palsy-walsy with me," Clark recalls, "talking about our having something in common because he'd spent a summer session studying at Columbia, and then remarking that we both knew that the little black fellas around there couldn't compete with the whites. On the way out the door, he pointed out some loose masonry to me, as if to show that the white school wasn't in any better shape than the colored one. Then suddenly, and right in front of me, in a tone totally different from the sort of man-to-man one he'd been using with me, he turns to Gene and says, 'Montgomery, didn't I tell you I didn't want to see you around here any more in this county? I'd hate to have to get my boys to do something to you.' It was the first time I had ever heard anyone threaten another person like that, so openly and matter-of-factly. I thought that he must be joking, it was so unreal. In fact, if he'd pulled a gun out and shot Gene on the spot, my reaction probably would have been, 'Now what a dumb thing that was to do.' When we got back to the car to drive over to the Scott's Branch school, I asked Gene if Betchman had been kidding. 'Hell, no,' he said, 'he's threatened me a lot of times.' "

At Scott's Branch, the combination Negro elementary and high school just beyond the railroad tracks and the Summerton town line where the DeLaine and Briggs families lived, the colored children had been prepared for Clark's visit. Thurgood Marshall had telephoned down to Harold Boulware, the able and strong-willed black attorney in Columbia who had been the local legal operative in the *Briggs* case from the start, and told him about Clark and his doll tests. He added, "He's also the smartest damned man I know." Boulware passed the word to Montgomery, who then made the testing arrangements with the local black school people under an order by Judge Waring of the United States District Court. Sixteen children had been arbitrarily selected from the classroom rosters and stood by now as the light-brown professor from faraway New York arrived with his dolls. "When I got through testing the first youngster," Clark recounts, "I heard some light commotion down the hall. I looked out of the classroom and here came two big Negroes in overalls leading a little six- or seven-year-old child between them to my door. They told me they had been assigned the responsibility to make sure that nobody and nothing interfered with the testing. I said, 'You mean you're my bodyguards?' and they said that was right. A little later, Betchman came by and stuck his head in the door to say something—I think maybe it was his idea of a pleasantry—and the fact is that I did feel a whole lot better knowing those two fellows were right outside the door there."

Of the sixteen black children between six and nine years old whom Clark tested, ten said they preferred the white doll to the Negro one. Eleven of them said the Negro doll was the one that looked "bad." Nine of them said the white doll was the "nice" one. All sixteen correctly identified the white one as white and the colored one as colored, yet seven of the sixteen children picked the white doll when asked to select the one most like themselves. All these responses matched almost precisely the ratios that Clark and his wife had obtained in their tests over the years. Here, too, there were moments of anguish as there always were when he administered the tests. Clark asked one dark-brown girl of seven—"so dark brown that she was almost black"—to take the coloring test that he generally gave along with the doll test. "When she was asked to color herself," Clark would testify in court the following week, "she was one of the few children who picked a flesh color, pink, to color herself. When asked to color a little boy the color she liked little boys to be, she looked all around the twenty-four crayons and picked up a white crayon and looked up at me with a shy smile and began to color. She said, 'This doesn't show.' So she pressed a little harder . . . in order to get the white crayon to show."

Clark did not complete his testing the first afternoon and had to come back the next day. "The fact that our side was playing for keeps really sank in to me after the tests were over that first day. I figured that I'd be sleeping right there in Summerton, but Montgomery said, 'No, sir, my instructions are to take you to Sumter for the evening'—that was about twenty-five miles away in the next county. I finally realized that nobody was joking in all this."

Matthew J. Whitehead had made the trip to Clarendon County for the NAACP the month before. A native of Rocky Mount, North Carolina, where his father had run a taxi service, a restaurant, and a poolroom, Whitehead came to Summerton better armed emotionally for his ordeal than Clark had.

Assistant registrar and associate professor of education at Howard University, Whitehead had been recommended by Charles Thompson, who said he was well qualified to evaluate the schools in Clarendon County and testify in court on the relative merits of the provisions for each race. Though segregation itself was the object of the NAACP suit, the second string in its bow continued to be the inequality of schools as run in Clarendon in violation of the *Plessy* principle. At the very least, Marshall would hope to win an equalization order from the courts, and if he could not get an opinion that overturned *Plessy*, he could try to prove that segregation as administered in South Carolina *never* resulted in equality and therefore had to fall. Either way, he needed a careful field investigation in Clarendon. It was not a popular assignment. Several specialists had turned down Robert Carter's invitation, but Matthew Whitehead saw the request as a duty. "Somebody had to do it," he says. He remembers how the blacks in Summerton reassured him. "They told me there was nothing to fear down there—and besides, there's only one time you can die."

When he drove over to Superintendent Betchman's office at the white elementary school to present his credentials for his court-approved survey, Whitehead recalls, "I got out of my car and it was recess time at the school. I asked a little eight- or nine-year-old boy if he could tell me where to find Mr. Betchman. He said, 'Yes, sir,' and took my hand and led me across the little campus, into the building, and up the stairs, right into the superintendent's office. There he said, 'Mr. Betchman, here's a nigger come to see you.' Mr. Betchman got pretty red in the face. Now that little fella didn't mean anything by it—he was just saying what he'd been taught."

Matthew Whitehead was told that he was the first Negro visitor ever permitted inside the two white schools of District No. 22. His findings, dispatched promptly by mail to the Legal Defense Fund office in New York, suggested why. The total value of the buildings, grounds, and furnishings of the two white schools that accommodated 276 children was four times as high as the total for the three Negro schools that accommodated a total of 808 students. The white schools were constructed of brick and stucco; the colored schools were all wooden. At the white elementary school, there was one teacher for each 28 children; at the colored schools, there was one teacher for each 47 children. At the white high school, there was only one class with an enrollment as high as 24; at the Scott's Branch high school for Negroes, classes ranged from 33 to 47. Besides the courses offered at both schools, the curriculum at the white high school included biology, typing, and bookkeeping; at the black high school, only agriculture and home economics were offered. There was no running water at one of the two outlying colored grade schools and no electricity at the other one. There were indoor flush toilets at both white schools but no flush toilets, indoors or outdoors, at any of the Negro schools—only outhouses, and not nearly enough of them. Whitehead also found:

> Open galvanized buckets with dippers inserted furnished drinking water for the children who attended the two Negro elementary schools whereas the children in the two white schools were rid of this health hazard by having fountains.
>
> . . . For the two white schools . . . there is bus transportation available. . . . Although the three Negro schools are located in isolated, unimproved areas, the children have no transportation whatever. At the Rambay elementary school this investigator found that two little Negro boys in the first grade, age six, walked each day a round trip of ten miles in order to get to school.
>
> . . . The white schools have a lunchroom with a paid attendant and other workers in charge, but nowhere in the Negro schools could there be found by this investigator any signs of a lunchroom.
>
> Janitorial services were available for both white schools, but there was no such service at any of the Negro schools. These chores were performed by the Negro teachers and students. . . .
>
> . . . At the Rambay School . . . there was not a single desk in the whole school. . . . In contrast . . . in each of the white schools there was a desk for every child.
>
> At the Summerton Elementary School [for whites] there was a spacious auditorium which provided for expression of students in aesthetics, group assemblies, moving pictures, types of demonstrations, etc. . . . At the Summerton High School there was a combination gymnatorium which made provisions for the values listed above. At all three Negro schools there was the absence of any type room for such valuable group instruction, and the provision for developing creative ability through the arts.

This pattern of handing out a pittance for the colored schools had prevailed in the state since the beginning of the century. Back in 1915, the state school superintendent had been viewed as softheaded for asking whether it was too much to spend one dollar per black pupil for every five dollars spent per white child. Twenty years later, when Charles Houston toured the state schools and took pictures of them for the NAACP, the situation was just as bad. Now, nearly two decades after that, another NAACP investigator found that little had changed, at least in the rural districts, where the preponderance of the black people of South Carolina still lived. In fact, the more black people per county in proportion to whites, the worse off each black pupil was, and the more the children of the whites benefited. The effect was most apparent with the distribution of funds given to each county by the state. Such funds would be allocated on the basis of total student enrollment in each county, regardless of race. In heavily black counties like Clarendon, the white officials took pains to count every single colored youngster, and perhaps then some, in order to get as big a slice of the state-aid melon as possible. But once the all-white county board of education had its hands on the state money, it could divide it up among the schools any way it liked; the way it liked was that black children got a fraction of what they were entitled to on a per-capita basis and white children got a good deal more than they were entitled to. Sometimes the money was divided half for the white schools and half for the colored schools despite the vastly greater enrollment in the latter. The effect was to shortchange the blacks severely.

At the very time Whitehead's report on the appalling conditions in Clarendon County reached Thurgood Marshall's desk, officials in South Carolina were deciding that they had better do something about such gross inequities before the courts ordered them to do it. The implications of the *Sweatt* and *McLaurin* decisions of the previous year were not lost on the more enlightened leaders of the state. The governor's chair at Columbia, moreover, had been occupied of late by a pair of men who were remarkably liberal by South Carolina standards, though the rest of the country placed them far to the right on the political spectrum. J. Strom Thurmond, who had been governor from 1946 to 1950, not only did not stoop to the racial demagoguery that had been standard since the hate-spewing days of Ben Tillman but he actually pushed through a number of measures that benefited the black people. He had done away with the poll tax, he had launched large-scale public building projects, and he had appointed a Negro to the state hospital board, all without the skies falling. Constitutionally ineligible to serve a second term, Thurmond was succeeded by one of the best-known and most experienced political figures in the nation—James Francis Byrnes.

Most South Carolina politicians of high aspiration used the governor's job as a steppingstone to the United States Senate. But Governor Jimmy Byrnes, who was seventy-two years old when he took office, had already been to the Senate for ten years. He had also been to the House as a Congressman from South Carolina for a dozen years before that. Franklin Roosevelt named him to the Supreme Court in 1941, but Byrnes, who loved the wheeling and dealing of backroom power politics and the excitement of the hustings, yielded his judicial robes after just a year on the high court and came to the White House to be what Roosevelt called his "Assistant

President." Byrnes, whose enthusiasm for the New Deal had been at best lukewarm though he admired the President's leadership, proved an adroit broker between the liberal and conservative wings of the Democratic Party. After serving as Director of War Mobilization and Director of Economic Stabilization, he was picked by Harry Truman, who had known him in the Senate, to be his first Secretary of State. It was not a felicitous selection. Byrnes was neither a creative thinker nor an agile statesman. His health, too, was not good and his relations with the President declined. After a year and a half, he was replaced by George C. Marshall. Byrnes lingered in Washington for a few years, practicing law, seeing old friends, and giving an occasional speech that reflected his growing dissatisfaction with the civil-rights policies of the Fair Deal and what he characterized as its increasing fondness for socialistic programs. Though he did not join Strom Thurmond's Dixiecrat crusade for the presidency in 1948, Byrnes had opened a law office back in South Carolina and began to be looked to as the statesman who could preserve states' rights and segregation against the ever more menacing federal steamroller and at the same time provide relatively progressive leadership for a state now eager to rid itself of chronic poverty and cultural backwardness. He ran for governor as a moderate, was silent on the race question, and won easily.

Byrnes was hardly a friend of the Negro, but he opposed the more blatant forms of white repression. Soon after winning the governorship, he prevailed upon the state legislature to pass an anti-mask law by way of discouraging the Klan. His principal act of humanity, however, was revealed in his inaugural address in January 1951. "It must be our goal to provide for every child of this state, white or colored," he declared, "at least a grade school education. . . . We must have a state school building program." Local funding could not do the job by itself. What was required was a massive state program: $75 million in bonds to be issued over a twenty-year period and to be paid for by revenues from a new 3 percent state sales tax. "One cannot speak frankly on this subject," Governor Byrnes added, "without mentioning the race problem. It is our duty to provide for the races substantial equality in school facilities. We should do it because it is right. For me that is sufficient reason."

A former Justice of the Supreme Court, Byrnes understood very well the trend of the Court's decisions on racial matters. If conditions as bad as those in Clarendon were allowed to remain, the federal courts might indeed be obliged to intervene and command the state to equalize—and perhaps even to desegregate as the quickest, fairest means to equalize. South Carolina, in short, was trying to keep one step ahead of the law. Under Byrnes's insistence, the state legislature passed the most ambitious school program in South Carolina's history. It provided for school-building under the bond program, state operation of school transportation, and higher teachers' salaries paid on an equal basis to both races. Lest all this state activity be taken as a sign by South Carolina's overwhelmingly conservative electorate that their venerable solon in the statehouse was a closet Bolshevik with a secret fondness for his black comrades, Byrnes's aides noted that the sales tax which would pay for the $75-million school-building program was not a form of public financing favored by liberals. More to the point, Byrnes himself spoke up to chase the specter of desegregation as the date neared for arguing *Briggs v. Elliott.* Now that the legislature had passed his hurry-up program to equalize the schools provided for both races, the governor of South Carolina wanted one thing understood: if the federal courts were perchance to order the state to abandon segregation in its schools, he would ask the state legislature to abandon public education. South Carolina was under no obligation by the Constitution to provide public schooling for its children, and if its provision of truly equal-but-separate facilities for both races did not satisfy the federal courts, well—that would be that. Segregation came before education. Such teeth-rattling militancy more than satisfied the white-supremacist masses, who were advised that if the courts thought the governor was bluffing and called him on his threat, ways would be found to funnel state money to private, segregated school systems.

Byrnes, moreover, was fully aware of how racial inequality was being used against America by her enemies. One prominent white South Carolina political figure recalls that Byrnes cited just that point in pushing his big school-equalization program through the state legislature: "He told us how Molotov, at one of the foreign ministers' meetings, had needled him about racial trouble in Georgia at a moment when the United States was protesting Soviet high-handedness and ruthlessness in Eastern Europe." Equal treatment of the races met the moral imperatives that ruled Jimmy Byrnes. Separation of the races remained for him no less of an imperative.

At the NAACP's Legal Defense Fund office in New York, number-two man Bob Carter had little time to worry about the last-minute maneuverings in the South Carolina political cockpit. Carter had fought hard to put Kenneth Clark and the whole psychological dimension into *Briggs* and for months had been working to enlist a roster of eminent sociologists and psychologists willing to travel to Charleston and tell the federal judges that segregation caused irreparable damage to black children. It was no easy task to find those experts.

The Fund lawyers were of course free to cite any leading authorities they wanted in the briefs they might submit to the court, but expert testimony delivered in person, if it withstood cross-examination and rebuttal as anthropologist Robert Redfield's had in the *Sweatt* trial, was likely to have greater impact on the judicial mind. Kenneth Clark and Matthew Whitehead were set to testify on their findings in Clarendon County, but they were not enough. Neither was a leading figure in his field, neither had a book to his credit, and both were Negroes whose professional objectivity in this instance would be open to question by a court of Southern white judges. Carter wanted authorities with impeccable credentials to elaborate on the specific findings that Clark and Whitehead would report to the court.

The most impressive and effective professional educator that the NAACP could have put on the stand in Charleston was John Dewey's genial follower at Columbia Teachers College, William H. Kilpatrick. Some 35,000 of the best school superintendents, principals, headmasters, and teachers in America had passed under the tutelage of the engaging, green-eyed professor with the big shock of white hair and the dulcet tones of his native Georgia still readily detectable in his speech. Kilpatrick would not have sounded like a wise-guy carpetbagger down for the day to lecture the rednecks; on the contrary, he came on in public like a good old country boy running his down-home school district without a lot of newfangled notions. In fact, the Dewey-Kilpatrick approach to schooling had been exceedingly newfangled. The school, they held, was the laboratory for social experimentation, the seedbed for tomorrow's society, and its purpose was not merely to jam a lot of memorized data into the slowly yielding gray matter of its young charges but to teach them as well how to cope with the problems they would confront in the world beyond the reach of the schoolhouse bell. Here was the perfect witness for the NAACP. Carter wrote him an earnest letter asking him to testify.

The great Kilpatrick was cordial in response. He approved of the NAACP's efforts to secure admission of Negroes to graduate and profes-sional schools "and I have rejoiced in your success along these lines." He looked forward to the day when segregation would cease everywhere. "But I must confess," he added, "that I seriously doubt the wisdom of seeking to have the Courts attempt to abolish at this stage the existing segregation in the elementary and secondary schools. I fear the results in the South would put back the long-run cause. I think some time is necessary first to digest the change at the highest level." In view of that belief he preferred not to testify.

Scarcely less troubling was the response Carter received from Elsa E. Robinson, a well-regarded psychologist at New York University's Graduate School of Arts and Science. After studying the experimental evidence on the effects of segregation, and after consulting with a number of her colleagues, she wrote back, "I have come to the conclusion that there is as yet no scientifically verified material of an empirical nature which bears directly on the issue." Such a judgment both challenged the value of the fieldwork by Kenneth and Mamie Clark and the likes of the Radke-Trager study of racial attitudes among Philadelphia schoolchildren, and raised the prospect that South Carolina might have little trouble finding a competent social scientist to rebut Clark and any other social psychologists the NAACP might troop to the witness stand.

There were other problems as well. Some superbly qualified scholars proved to be bashful or reluctant about testifying. Clark had strongly recommended to Carter that he go after Gordon W. Allport, who had been a prominent psychologist at Harvard for more than twenty years, served as president of the American Psychological Association, written many articles for leading scholarly journals on the nature of prejudice, and was doing a major book on the subject. Allport was at the apex of the social-science establishment. He wrote back congratulating Carter on the "admirable" fight the NAACP was waging to end segregation. "Unfortunately," he added, "I feel certain that I would not be the type of effective witness you need." He referred Carter to Columbia's Otto Klineberg, who of course was the first scholar Carter had approached. Carter pressed Allport to reconsider and got a polite but firm no.

The best-known, and perhaps most controversial, psychologist in the South was Joseph Banks Rhine, who ran Duke University's parapsychology laboratory. His 1934 book *Extra-Sensory Perception* and subsequent works *New Frontiers of the Mind* and *The Reach of the Mind* had introduced the acronym ESP into the language and made J. B. Rhine an international academic celebrity. Carter wrote him, and the message came back: "I wish I could be of help. . . . I am not, however, an expert on the educational and psychological issues that would be involved." Rhine, too, recommended Klineberg, who he supposed "would best qualify as an expert on relative racial abilities."

Carter had in fact prevailed upon Klineberg to testify and had not hesitated to use his name in trying to line up other top scholars. But in mid-May, just two weeks before the *Briggs* trial was due to open in Charleston, Carter got a jolting note in which Klineberg, "with very deep regret," backed out of his promise to testify. The last half of May, when the academic year wound up at Columbia, had become dreadfully jammed up with engagements and there were Ph.D. examinations that had to be conducted then, Klineberg wrote. Besides, he told Carter, the NAACP undoubtedly had engaged enough leading psychologists so that his absence would scarcely be felt.

Carter was successful in getting a number of lesser lights to agree to testify—an associate professor from Teachers College instead of William Kilpatrick; the dean of a little-known sectarian West Virginia college that had just admitted Negroes for the first time; psychologist Helen Trager, then a Vassar lecturer, whose articles on the racial-attitude tests she and others had run with Philadelphia children dovetailed with the fieldwork by the Clarks—but he had not landed a really big name. He came close, however, when he bagged David Krech, a forty-two-year-old psychologist on leave— and glad of it—from the University of California. For Krech, who had been born in Poland to Joseph and Sarah Krechevsky, had come to America at the age of three and been naturalized at sixteen, the invitation from the NAACP was a way of paying back his adopted land and yet reminding it that it had still not made good on its great promise of equality for all men. Beyond that but related to it, he was moved by the question of nascent McCarthyism which by then was savaging the academic community.

Krech, co-author of a 1948 textbook titled *Theory and Problems of Social Psychology* that had been well received and would be widely adopted for college use over the next fifteen years, possessed a growing reputation in his quarter of the academic world. He was named a Fulbright Professor for the 1949–50 school year and taught at Oslo University. While he was on leave from California, the Berkeley campus was in a howl over the decision by the university regents asking every faculty member to sign an oath proclaiming loyalty to America and denying membership in the Communist Party, past or present. Most faculty members viewed the oath as both an insult and an invasion of academic freedom. Some refused to sign and were fired as a result. Some resigned in protest. Some hid out as visiting professors. Krech, when his year in Norway was up, reluctantly faced the prospect of returning to Berkeley and the trial of conscience: to sign the oath or not to sign. A last-minute transatlantic telephone call from a younger friend, Harvard psychologist Jerome S. Bruner, produced an invitation to Krech to spend the following academic year as a visiting professor at Cambridge. Off he trekked to Harvard, within ready reach of the NAACP's recruitment drive for *Briggs* and more than eager "to strike a blow for Truth and Beauty (as Truth and Beauty were perceived in those more innocent times)," Krech remarks. "I thought the irony of it most marvelous."

Carter took a cram course in social-psychology readings, including Krech's textbook, so that he could at least begin to talk the language of the scholars. As the trial neared, he wrote Krech: ". . . If the state shows that reactions [to prejudice among Northern and Southern Negro children] are the same in the absence of segregation, then our case has been seriously damaged unless we can show that (1) segregation is a prop which sustains racial prejudice or, to borrow your phrase, is an environmental support to prejudice; and (2) that segregation in public schools in the South is a major cause [of prejudice] throughout the country; and (3) the abolition of segregated public schools will help abate prejudice in this country. It seems to me then that in No. 2 the cart is before the horse, but I believe that you would be able to justify this approach by virtue of your conclusion that the Negroes' status in this country as contrasted to his role in South America is a historical accident. . . ." Krech, pleased with the homework Carter had done, wrote back reassuringly. He had a clear picture of what the NAACP wanted and it presented no problems of intellectual integrity for him. Prejudice and segregation fed each other in a vicious circle, he said, as the poor educational facilities provided for Negro children affected negatively their intellectual and personality traits. "Thus segregation and inadequate schooling may create a situation which will seem to 'justify' prejudice and segregation and inferior-status treatment," Krech added. "The state, then, through its practices, is deliberately creating less well-equipped citizens, minority groups, pre-conditions for prejudice. . . ." This was exactly the sort of thing Carter had been looking for.

Nothing could have prevented David Krech from showing up on schedule in Charleston. He joined the briefing sessions in the basement of the Boone home, where the lawyers coached him, Kenneth Clark, and the other social psychologists on how to respond in the event their competence as experts was challenged by the lawyers for the state. What struck Krech, though, was not the drill dealing with his part of the proceedings but the commanding presence in the room of Thurgood Marshall. "He was completely relaxed and seemed to be enjoying himself hugely," Krech recalls, "as he would pose a question—often enough in a deliberate Negro dialect—that he anticipated the state might ask in the next day's court session. One of his staff members would suggest a possible reply and perhaps cite a precedent or two. Marshall would then lay into that staff member, spell out counter-arguments, refer to counter-citations, and completely destroy, or so I thought, the staff member's answer. The staff would then offer a rebuttal, Marshall would rebut the rebuttal, and this went on and on—between beer and sandwiches and coffee—to Marshall's seemingly huge amusement."

But Marshall had no illusions about the job ahead. He had stated his estimate of the Supreme Court's position in an article that very month in the *Annals*, the quarterly publication of the American Academy of Political and Social Science. "The Court's present strategy may be to breach the pattern of segregation area by area by dealing with specific problems as they are presented," Marshall wrote. "It may feel that in whittling away the legal foundation upon which segregation is based, in this fashion, the protection offered to civil rights may be more palatable to the community and hence more lasting." This was a cagey and realistic reading of the Court's posture. What it required was clear to Marshall: "The problem is carefully to marshal overwhelming evidence of the inequalities inherent in segregation in the particular areas involved, and thereby demonstrate that an extension of the principles of the *Sweatt* and *McLaurin* cases is timely."

Rumors and reports circulated throughout black South Carolina about what the other side was up to. While Gene Montgomery had uncovered no traces of a counter-petition by Clarendon Negroes favoring the maintenance of segregated schools provided they were equalized, reports continued to come in of efforts by the state to put prominent black figures on the witness stand who would speak out against mingling the races. Negro teachers throughout the state were said to be a source of considerable disgruntlement over the prospect of lost jobs due to desegregation. In March, the *Lighthouse & Informer*, the Negro weekly in Columbia, attacked "grumbling" among colored teachers in the wake of Byrnes's threat to shut the schools rather than desegregate them. While the teachers in Clarendon had been among the most active collaborators in the suit, elsewhere a gap seemed to be widening between the profession and the rest of the black community, to judge by the sharpness of the *Lighthouse* remonstrance: "As to teachers themselves, their poor showing in replacing money spent for better salaries for them in Charleston and Columbia, their shiftlessness, their utter lack of appreciation for the fine civic work of the NAACP, have lessened public sympathy for the profession. Most of them are as worthless to aiding fights for the race as the most worthless of citizens." At a time when racial solidarity was especially needed, signs of rancor, born of fear and insecurity, were growing. Word was out that Governor Byrnes had summoned Frank Madison Reid, bishop of the African Methodist Church for South Carolina, to discuss the *Briggs* case and urge him to speak out for a gradualist—which was to say segregationist —position so long as he could assure his flock that the state was earnestly going about its equalization program. On top of that possibility there was the uncertainty of what the state was planning for the courtroom. "Jimmy Byrnes and others are arranging for a sizable list of experts in an effort to counteract our experts," Marshall wrote to Robert Redfield in April, urging his appearance at Charleston. Redfield, who agreed to come as a rebuttal witness, was curious to know whom he would have to rebut, but Marshall wrote him two weeks before the trial, "Unfortunately, we do not yet know the names of the witnesses to be produced by the other side but I assume they will do their best. They are not worrying about expenses and are shaking the South apart trying to get as high calibre witnesses as they possibly can. We should really have a full trial."

Finally, of course, there was the opposition legal team, which the NAACP expected to defend South Carolina's preferred way of life with skill and ardor. The team turned out to be one man, a fifty-year-old Charleston attorney. He was said to be the best in the state.

"If it came to a choice between arguing or following up a case and getting in a good round of golf," says a veteran South Carolina newspaper editor, "Bob Figg would probably have played golf. He was smart as a whip—and lazy as can be." That was about as severe an assessment as anyone ever made of the public performance of Robert McCormick Figg, Jr., who had served for a dozen years as district solicitor (that is, prosecuting attorney) for Charleston and Berkeley counties and, by most accounts, kept crime within his jurisdiction under reasonable check. Figg's family, Virginia people, had moved to Charleston when he was fourteen. His father had come to be supervisor of the Charleston Naval Shipyard, one of the more important bourgeois posts in the city, and it was natural that every effort would have been made to turn young Robert into a proper Charlestonian. He was sent to a local military academy in keeping with the city's long martial tradition and at the age of nineteen won his bachelor's degree from the somewhat inbred if not precisely provincial College of Charleston. After two years of studying law at Columbia, he was admitted to the South Carolina bar and proceeded to become an exemplary young attorney, a devoted Mason and Knight of Pythias, the city handball champion, and a booster in such good standing that the ruling circle in town soon began to forget that the Figgs were, as these things were calculated in Charleston, *arrivistes.*

By the time Bob Figg entered politics at thirty-one, his claim to a leadership position in the community was secure. Running for the state legislature in 1932, he placed second on the list of candidates and was chosen to chair the Charleston County legislative delegation. He stayed for only one two-year term, winning credit as the principal architect of a bill establishing a state control board that put the banks of South Carolina back on their feet after the national bank holiday of 1933; he was also known as an advocate of legalized 3.2 beer, the Santee-Cooper power project, and the policies and aspirations of Charleston's Mayor Burnet Maybank. With the blessings of the Maybank machine, Figg won the key job of district solicitor and held on to it for three elective terms. Toward the end of the first one, he was subjected to criticism in the state press for failing to acknowledge the degree of crime in Charleston. "There was a feeling in some quarters that the problem was getting a fast shuffle," remarks William D. Workman, who was a Charleston newspaper reporter and editor before rising to be editor of the Columbia *State,* "and that few cases were followed up in the solicitor's office." Figg fought back. He came before the Charleston Rotarians and declared that he had driven the gambling and lottery interests from the area, that the city was as clean of crime as any community of comparable size if one took into account the high and criminally prone Negro population, and that the whole attack was an attempt to discredit Maybank's gubernatorial drive by detracting from the job he had done in rebuilding Charleston's pride and financial stability. There had been no major crimes in the city, Figg asserted, adding that "in five years I don't recall but one white homicide." The consensus was that Bob Figg was a dedicated if not terribly dynamic public servant, and when he had a case in hand, he was a crack courtroom prosecutor. And he never let the pressure turn him into a law-and-order bully. The best way to fight crime, he would say at many a public forum, was not by harsh punishment but by community-wide preventive measures; he called for psychiatric care for repeating offenders.

Leaving office in 1947, gentleman Bob Figg became one of the most successful lawyers in the state, with special competence in handling the affairs of governmental clients, among which he in time would number the South Carolina State Ports Authority, the Charleston County Council, and the Charleston County Board of Education. His interest in politics remained high. Waties Waring credited Figg with dreaming up the scheme enacted by the South Carolina legislature that wiped away all laws dealing with state supervision of primary elections as a means of getting around the Supreme Court's ruling in *Smith v. Allwright*—a device Waring struck down in his 1947 decision of *Rice v. Elmore*. By 1948, Figg was taking an active part as a fund-raiser in Governor Thurmond's States Rights Democratic Party campaign for the presidency and was denouncing Harry Truman's leadership of the regular Democrats for his reputed abandonment of the rights of individual citizens and local self-government. In the eyes of the miniature but nonetheless potent white power structure that ran Clarendon County, Bob Figg had been just the man to get hold of when the restless local blacks started sending for legal help from up North. Gracious, dignified, seasoned, smart, he was clearly no Klan type, but neither was there anything in Figg's background to suggest he was at all soft on segregation.

Small, peppery S. Emory Rogers, who ran the southern end of Clarendon County out of his law office on Summerton's Main Street, kept Figg closely posted on racial developments beginning in 1947. Rogers, whose own holdings, family ties, and legal practice put him into cotton, banking, and the supply business, was no backwoods lawyer in galluses. By pedigree and education, in fact, he had far greater claim to membership in the South Carolina aristocracy than Figg. His ancestors had come to the state as early as 1735 and the family tree numbered several Northerners of eminence, including an original patentee of a section of Harlem in New York—"of all places," says Rogers, smiling—and a Yale Divinity School graduate who came South to bring light to the heathen blacks. A native of Summerton, Rogers graduated Phi Beta Kappa from Washington and Lee in Virginia, studied psychology for a time at Columbia, and taught at the University of Pittsburgh and Georgia Tech before deciding on a career at law. He earned his Bachelor of Laws degree at the University of North Carolina, where he roomed at the home of Professor Howard W. Odum and worked as a part-time associate at Odum's Institute for Social Science Research. Yet throughout his life Rogers would remain firmly convinced of the natural born thickness of the Negro's skull and his general inferiority to the white man. The Constitution, he was sure, was never intended to grant rights to the black man. Of the abolition of slavery by Northern tormentors, he would comment in his sixty-ninth year: "In the Civil War, you took our wealth away from us after having sold it to us in the first place."

Such views steeled him for the fight he would wage as attorney for the board of trustees for Clarendon County School Board No. 22 in Summerton; in a larger sense, he was the attorney for indigenous white supremacy. Folks like Bob Figg and Jimmy Byrnes were city dwellers who for the most part could and did ignore the colored people. In Clarendon County, the colored people could not be ignored; they had to be mastered. Town attorney of Summerton for more than twenty years as well as attorney for the local school board, Main Street czar Emory Rogers never laughed off the *Briggs* suit, even in its original version with Levi Pearson as plaintiff seeking bus service for his children. It was not mere luck that Pearson's case had been thrown out of court on a technicality; the white courthouse crowd had discovered, by combing through the black farmer's tax-payment records, that he lacked legal standing to bring the action. No, the Clarendon blacks were proving too persistent for comfort in their pursuit of something more than what the whites had felt like giving them, and Rogers went to Figg's office in Charleston to ask him to argue the case in federal court.

Figg was receptive. "It wasn't just the whites who resented the idea of desegregation," he remarked two decades later. "Many of the black parents did, too. They were geared to the soil. They needed their youngsters to help with the harvest." Governor Byrnes took the same tack. "Except for the professional agitators," he declared, "what the colored people want, and what they are entitled to, is equal facilities in their schools." Those "professional agitators," of course, were primarily operatives of the NAACP. Byrnes's attorney general, Tolliver Cleveland Callison, loudly denounced the NAACP as subversive—the surefire code word of the day for gross perfidy—and a menace because it "has been able to brainwash millions of Negroes. . . ." Just what basis Figg, Byrnes, Callison, and other white leaders had for their statements that the blacks of South Carolina generally did not support the aims of the *Briggs* suit, none of them ever volunteered. Byrnes did confer with Bishop Reid of the AME and several other Negro leaders in an effort to persuade at least one of them to stand up in court and oppose the NAACP position as beyond the aspirations of their people, but he found no takers. Figg was sure it was fear that held them back. Recounting the governor's efforts to win over black leaders, Figg wrote to a friend in Spartanburg, "The impression I got was that they [the Negro leaders] knew that they would be cut to pieces by their people and destroy their leadership. They want better facilities, but they are alarmed at the idea of mixed schools, and yet they feel that they would undoubtedly turn the whole situation over to the NAACP if they undermined their own capacity for leadership of the colored people of this state."

Still more nagging a problem to the South Carolina whites planning the *Briggs* defense was their failure to line up a scholar of national reputation who would testify in court on the wisdom of preserving segregation if the state provided genuine equalization. The logical man for the job, and perhaps the only man, was Howard Odum. His loyalty to his region was beyond question, and he had won nationwide esteem in the academic world for his insistence that no real progress would come to Dixie until the white man stopped regarding the black man as a lower order of animal life. The Arkansas *Gazette*'s executive editor, native South Carolinian Harry S. Ashmore, himself a leading moderate, called Odum "the South's ranking sociologist," and few would have argued with that estimate. At the end of April 1951, just a month before the *Briggs* trial was due to open, Odum gave a characteristic address to the Southern Sociological Society gathered in Atlanta. Titled "The Mid-Century South: Looking Both Ways," Odum's talk called for "mature and quick action on a statesmanlike basis" to solve the South's racial problems by remedying "the inexcusable situation with reference to brutalities, injustices, inequalities and discrimination." He urged the introduction of "Operation Equal Opportunity" into all phases of public education and immediate "non-segregation in all university education on the graduate and professional level." What made Odum so alluring to Figg and Byrnes as a spokesman was his insistence that Jim Crow laws ought not to be convulsively wrenched away. "The above agenda for equalizing educational opportunities," Odum added, "assumes the normal status and processes of segregation *and* non-segregation consistent with the development and administration of educational systems everywhere. It assumes a certain inevitable continuity of the subsystem featuring primarily segregation in the public schools but with both non-segregation and segregation modes and privileges in institutions of higher learning. This is necessary to insure equality of opportunity for the extraordinary Negro institutions, teachers, students, and administrative officers in ways which will give maximum recognition and opportunity for Negro professional folk and students." Once you cut through all his academic verbiage, Howard Odum had something to offer everyone in the segregation showdown.

Rogers, who knew Odum from his law-school days in Chapel Hill, traveled with Figg to the sociologist's office at the University of North Carolina to persuade him to appear for the *Briggs* defense. Odum was the great white hope for rebuffing the assorted experts that Thurgood Marshall's crew was certain to import for the trial at Charleston. But Odum did not want the role. Figg recounted the interview:

> . . . I spent considerable time at Chapel Hill with Dr. Odum and Dr. Guy Johnson, who headed up the Myrdal Racial Relations Survey in this part of the country. They both felt very strongly that at the present time and under present conditions it would be disastrous to force mixed schools in South Carolina, or any other State now having legal segregation. They felt even more strongly that they should not take the witness stand. Dr. Odum said that he had never testified, had constantly refused even before congressional committees, and that because of his years of liberal work in race relations and many statements of one kind or

another, the other side would probably tear him to pieces. Dr. Johnson is a trustee of Howard University, and has been given many honors and awards because of his work in race relations. I gathered that he did not want to face the barrage of dead cats which would be thrown in his direction by the colored press and our "liberal" brothers in the North, for which I could not blame him. . . .

Rogers recalls that Odum also felt that his testifying on the segregationist side would reflect badly on the University of North Carolina. All the South Carolina lawyers got for their troubles was a copy of Odum's recent talk to brother Southern sociologists in Atlanta.

Their failure to land Odum, Johnson, or any other racial moderate from the academic world did not particularly perturb Figg as he prepared his case. For the man presiding over the *Briggs* trial—Judge John Parker—was cut from the same cloth as Howard Odum. And Parker would hold the balance of power in the court's decision. Judge Waring, in Figg's view, was a tragic figure, striking back bitterly at his native community because it had ostracized him after he had "coldbloodedly" got rid of his first wife. Surely, Waring would vote with the blacks. Indeed, Figg and Attorney General Callison had toyed with the idea of asking that Waring be disqualified from sitting on the *Briggs* case on the ground that he failed to demonstrate proper judicial conduct. On reflection, though, Callison acknowledged that in non-racial matters he had brought before Waring, the judge's conduct had been quite satisfactory. They would just have to mark Waring off as a lost vote and pair him with Judge George Bell Timmerman, whose vote was equally certain in favor of segregation. Seventy years old, like Waring, and a lifelong organization Democrat, like Waring, Timmerman had never wandered far from the fold of white supremacy. A native of Edgefield, where Ben Tillman rose to power at about the time Timmerman was born, the judge never dropped into the depths of Tillmanite vituperation while practicing his somewhat genteel brand of racism, typified by utterances like: "God made people and endowed them with the talent of race in the expectation that they would use and improve that talent, not abase, mongrelize or bury it." Callison confided to Figg in February of 1951 that he was alarmed over an illness then afflicting Timmerman and added that "if he should be unable to sit on this case we would be most unfortunate." But the illness passed, and that left the decision in the capable hands of the presiding judge. "We were trying the case to Judge Parker," says Figg, "and there was no more liberal judge, not just in the South but in the whole country."

Parker was indeed relatively liberal because he believed the never-say-die racists would eventually have to yield. He was liberal in the sense that he thought the Negro was entitled to equality but not overnight. Such a man was a potential menace in the eyes of ex-Governor Strom Thurmond, who wrote Figg just before the *Briggs* trial that he was "greatly concerned" over two of the three judges who were to hear the case. Thurmond was so worried, he said, that he urged Figg to consider defaulting in the case so that only the Clarendon district would be affected—to make the Summerton area a sacrificial lamb and not risk a major defeat in the Supreme Court.

In effect, Figg had already decided on a double-edged strategy that would come close to meeting Thurmond's concern by recasting the case to cut the ground from under Thurgood Marshall. First, he had urged the greatest practicable swiftness in the passage of the governor's $75-million school-construction program. By the time the *Briggs* trial began, Figg had to be able to stand up in court and say that the funding arrangement was an accomplished fact, fully approved by the legislature, not some blue-sky hope. With Byrnes pushing hard all the way, Figg won the race against the calendar. The newly created State Educational Finance Commission, which was to administer the school-building program, opened its doors just three weeks before *Briggs* was argued. The governor sat as the *ex officio* chairman of the commission and made it clear to its director—a man named Crow—that the first funds distributed by the commission were to go to improving the colored schools in Clarendon County. Without a public announcement that might tip Figg's hand, Clarendon school officials began at once to confer with the new funding agency.

But Figg went a step further. At the last minute, he decided his case would be immeasurably strengthened—and the NAACP's weakened—if he came to court and admitted straight out that the colored school facilities were unequal. This was a sharp about-face from the Clarendon white community's repeated insistence that it was providing adequately for the Negro schoolchildren, that the white schools were themselves in a sad state of disrepair due to the limited resources of the population, and that if the outlying black schools lacked electricity or running water, it was not because of prejudice but because neither power nor water lines served the remote areas in question. But Figg looked, with a colder eye than the Clarendon whites, at the same data that Matthew Whitehead had uncovered on his fact-finding mission to Summerton for Thurgood Marshall's office, and it was plain that John Parker would not buy the claim of equal facilities. The state, moreover, was now ready and legally empowered to help Clarendon's whites meet the problem by building the blacks decent schools. Why should the state therefore risk a possible ruling by the court that segregation as practiced in Clarendon County inevitably meant inequality and was therefore unconstitutional? Far better to confess past sins and promise immediate remedy.

"I called Governor Byrnes and told him I thought that the findings of fact were going to be such that we ought to admit," Figg recalls. "I said, 'They'll drench us with unfavorable testimony.' When I told him that the total equipment in the home-economics class at the black high school was a single sewing machine—and that it was broken—he said he saw the point and agreed with my recommendation."

And so when Bob Figg went to the United States District Court on the morning of May 28, 1951, to defend segregation as South Carolina's way of life, he had an ace up his sleeve.

# 15

# Charleston Detour

The little caravan of old cars formed up at dawn next to St. Mark's Church in Summerton. Between two and three dozen Clarendon colored people—no one remembers how many for sure—piled in for the two-hour drive to Charleston. Mrs. Harry Briggs went. It was a hot day and the drive would be long and the cars cramped and no one knew if there would be room in court for all of them once they got there. "There must have been eight people in my car," farmer James Gibson recalls, and yet nobody minded the crowding terribly much. "I never did get to sit down in the courtroom," Gibson adds, "but I never got tired standing that day. The fact that Judge Waring was up there meant that we were going to get a hearing."

Negroes from the whole eastern half of South Carolina began streaming into Charleston soon after sunrise and kept coming all morning. They came in cars and buses and even a few horse-and-buggies. Well before the squat, three-story federal building that housed the court opened for business, the juncture of Broad and Meeting streets was filled with arriving blacks in a semi-festive mood. They lined the steps into and the sidewalk next to the granite fortress of a building that was put up in 1896, the year *Plessy* was decided, at a cost of $885,000. Its style was Monumental Victorian, with a little bit of everything else thrown in. Every entrance and window on the first floor was arched, every window on the second floor was crowned with a pediment, every window on the third floor with a cornice; the northern façade facing Broad Street and the eastern one facing Meeting each was topped with a neo-classic pediment of no particular elegance, and a tower with a heavy balustrade and a flagpole lumbered an additional story into the sky at the northeast corner of the building. A lean shadow fell across it from the soaring white steeple of St. Michael's Episcopal, just across Meeting Street.

Because the bottom floor of the federal building housed the Charleston post office, the doors opened shortly after seven o'clock and the waiting Negroes began filing in two abreast. To those who had not been in it before, it seemed a grand building. Polished red-brown marble, richly mottled throughout, covered the bottom half of the walls, and gleaming brass fixtures and graceful grillwork added to the palatial air. Slowly the black line climbed the huge main stairway leading to the balcony-like second and third floors from which you could look down on the filigreed skylight that shut off the post office on the ground floor from the rest of the bustling building. On the second floor, the line snaked along the hall to the federal courtroom in the southwest corner of the building, as far from the street noises as possible, and stopped before the two sets of double mahogany doors, one at the back of the small chamber and one at the rear of the side wall. No more than 150 would be able to be seated inside. But the line, stretching all the way down the hall and stairway and lobby and front steps, numbered more than 500, and still they were coming.

"The discipline was terrific," reporter Ted Poston of the New York *Post* remembered. "Everyone knew how important an occasion it was and that an incident of any kind could have been badly disruptive and damaging. Whenever a seat became available, the line just inched forward." Some, like James Gibson, never made it and just stood as the line operated like a human telegraph, relaying the latest developments via quick whispers out the courtroom door and all the way down to the front steps and street, where the crowd never thinned. The few women on line with children in their arms were given priority to the several benches in the hallways. And Liza Briggs was guaranteed a seat in the courtroom throughout the day. The case, after all, was known by her family's name, and the family had suffered enough for the honor.

John the Bailiff, the black bailiff, called the special three-judge session of the United States District Court for the Eastern District of South Carolina to order promptly at ten o'clock. John J. Parker, square-faced, bespectacled chief judge of the Court of Appeals for the Fourth Circuit, presided. To his right sat Waties Waring, an outcast in his own community beyond the great double doors at the other end of the courtroom. To his left sat the recuperated George Bell Timmerman, the white man's judge. A moment after Judge Parker asked counsel on both sides if they were ready, Robert Figg was on his feet and taking his surprise initiative.

> FIGG: If the Court please, I wanted to make a statement on behalf of defendants that it is conceded that inequalities in the facilities, opportunities and curricula in the schools of this district do exist. We have found that out from investigating authorities.
> JUDGE PARKER: You will do that when you make your opening statement.
> FIGG: I just thought that if we made the record clear and clarified the answer in this case at this time, it would serve perhaps to eliminate the necessity of taking a great deal of testimony.

The stunned look on Thurgood Marshall's face told Figg he had achieved his desired effect. The last thing the NAACP legal chieftain wanted was to have his case ruled moot and all his carefully assembled witnesses sent home. But Parker let Figg elaborate on his quick first thrust and in effect deliver his opening statement even before the plaintiff's counsel, who customarily led off.

Yes, it was true, declared Figg, the educational provisions for colored pupils in the defendant school district were not substantially equal to those offered white youngsters, but no malice was involved in the long-evolving process during which the differences had grown. Indeed, if time allowed, causes and explanations could be given "which we feel certain would sustain the good faith of the trustees in their effort to carry out the difficult and often thankless functions devolved upon them." The root of the problem was in the almost entirely agricultural economy of Clarendon County, which, like so many other rural parts of South Carolina, had been unable to keep pace in recent years with the larger and urban school districts in their provisions for the children of both races. To end that disparity, Figg explained, Governor Byrnes had presented and the state legislature had now adopted "legislation of a broad and sweeping nature." Collection of the new sales tax to finance the school program would start just a few weeks hence, and the defendant trustees had already requested a survey by the director of the new State Educational Finance Commission "so that they may formulate and submit to proper authorities a plan to bring about as speedily as possible equality of buildings, equipment, facilities and other physical aspects of the district." All the defendants were therefore asking was that the court give them "a reasonable time" to turn their plans into reality and retain jurisdiction over the case "in the event the defendants should fail to comply with the constitutional standards prescribed in the applicable decisions."

In effect, Figg was asking the Negroes of Clarendon County, who had first filed suit for better facilities three years and two months earlier, to wait still longer because now the state had finally heard their grievances and was hereby acknowledging them. Figg's concession, though, in no way addressed itself to the merits or evils of segregation itself, and that of course was what the suit was primarily about. Figg's was a diversionary action, based on the premise that half a loaf was a good deal more than the blacks of Clarendon, or most of the other rural places of the state, had ever been offered before.

Thurgood Marshall was not about to budge, though his surprise over Figg's maneuver was plain. The defendants' statement, he asserted, "has no bearing on this litigation at this stage. I think it is an effort to prevent the plaintiffs in this case from developing their case in the only fashion which will enable us to present a full and complete case." To show the unconstitutional nature of the state's segregation statutes as applied in Clarendon, said Marshall, "we must be able to show the inequalities as they actually exist."

Parker acknowledged the point and waved Marshall on. His first witness was one of the defendants, Clarendon's superintendent of education, L. B. McCord, the grizzled old cracker who doubled as minister of the Presbyterian Church in Manning, the county seat. McCord held a tight rein on the school system and never made any bones about his belief that the good Lord intended the races to be separate. On the witness stand, he proved a tough customer for Marshall, who fenced with the white official for a few minutes, trying to soften him up with bland questions about his authority and the state's ultimate jurisdiction over his domain. Then he tried to close in some.

Q. Do you enforce the state segregation laws? Do you know what laws I am speaking about?
A. I think I do.

Q.  Do you enforce those laws?
A.  I enforce all laws. I know nothing but the law.
Q.  It is true, is it not, that Negroes in Clarendon County attend one group of schools and people who are not Negroes attend other schools. Is that correct?
A.  That is true.
Q.  Why is that true?
A.  Well, I couldn't answer it exactly. You would have to ask the children why. None of them have ever asked me to go to one school or the other.
Q.  Well, isn't it a fact that you do it because of the state statute?
A.  It is the law, the Constitution.

Painfully, Marshall went on to establish that though there were nearly three times as many black pupils as white pupils attending Clarendon public schools, current expenditures for the black schoolchildren totaled $282,000 and those for the far-outnumbered whites totaled $395,000. Why was so much more spent per white child, Marshall asked. "Well, the only explanation that I could give, possibly, is this," replied the superintendent-minister. "It is not, I don't think, because of the color, because we have certain white schools [where] considerably less is spent per pupil than certain other white schools." That was no answer at all to his question, so Marshall worked his way back to it as McCord danced away from the impact of the numbers. For a second time, McCord was evasive. Finally, Marshall insisted that the question had not been answered, and Judge Parker allowed as much. McCord replied: "I will answer the question again, and I will answer just this way. In Clarendon County we have 60-odd Negro schools, whereas we have, I think, just about a dozen white schools, and [in] all of the rural schools, whether white or Negro, the expenditures isn't anything like in proportion to the larger schools." It was nothing but doubletalk. Marshall threw up his hands and handed the witness over to Figg, who, not surprisingly, had no questions.

Spottswood Robinson's examination of Roderick W. Elliott, the gruff sawmill owner who served as chairman of the District No. 22 school trustees—and whose name provided the second half of the title of the case—proved no more obliging. Elliott had trouble hearing Robinson's questions and more trouble still framing intelligible answers. He did not know the geographical boundaries of the school district, he said, though he had been its chairman for twenty-five years. He was not aware to what extent the district fell under the jurisdiction of Superintendent McCord's office. After Robinson doggedly tried to extract from him the number and names of the schools in his district, Parker intervened, said all that had been established in the pleadings, and urged Robinson to get to the heart of the matter. But the lanky Virginia lawyer saw how fruitless it would be to keep after the old man, who was either genuinely ignorant about the details of his public responsibility or even more gifted than McCord at dodging any question put to him.

Robert Carter then moved forward from the plaintiffs' counsel table and got the NAACP case moving with a crisp examination of Matthew

Whitehead, the Howard professor of education who had surveyed the Clarendon schools. That he was a black man in a South Carolina courtroom confronting the white officialdom of the state with its grave misdeeds in no way cowed Whitehead. "We thought he had the guts to stand up there and speak out," Carter recalls, and Whitehead did not falter.

After his long string of credentials as an expert had been given, the Howard professor coolly ticked off the inequalities affecting every aspect of the colored schools he had visited. The grounds were poorer, the buildings were made of less durable materials, their cost and value were much lower, the size of their classes was much larger, they lacked such instructional and visual aids as decent blackboards, charts, maps, globes, slides, stereopticans, an auditorium, a music room, all of which the white schools had. There was no running water at two of black grade schools, only an outdoor well, an open galvanized bucket, a dipper and glasses—"and these buckets were not at all covered. They were open to germs, etc." There were no lunchrooms at the colored schools, though he saw lunch being served at the white schools when he went through them with Mr. Betchman and Mr. Rogers. At the Rambay school for Negroes, said Whitehead, there were no desks at all but "two long tables that were not surfaced by way of shellac or any type of furniture wood curing that would make those accessible to students for easy writing." The toilet facilities at the Negro schools drew Whitehead's deepest censure. "They were not of the type which the State Department of Health of South Carolina describes as privies," he said. "It is what they describe as earth toilets."

> JUDGE WARING:   Was there any running water for flushing them?
> A.   There was no running water at all, nor any urinals in any of these places for boys. At Scott's Branch School, the same situation prevailed, only to a greater degree of disgust on the part of one who made such a survey, to see 694 students serviced by two toilets for boys and two toilet seats for girls, of the same out-of-door type of construction, no running water, no urinals. . . .

In view of such conditions, did Whitehead believe the children in the Negro schools were getting equal classroom instruction as compared with the white children? "Not at all," he answered.

Having begun the morning with a blanket acknowledgment of the inequalities Whitehead had just documented, Figg nevertheless proceeded to try to undermine the expert witness's testimony by suggesting the mitigating circumstances that could have produced those sorry conditions. Wasn't it unfair, for example, in calculating the number of colored pupils in each class, to go by the enrollment figures instead of the actual daily attendance, which in fact amounted to about only two-thirds of those enrolled? The truancy rate, that is, was 33 percent for blacks. Well, said Whitehead, he had checked that out and had been advised that "there was no enforcement by way of students remaining in school. And the reason I raised the question was because I was able to see myself that there were any number of students who should have been in school, being of school age, who were in the fields plowing and working and what-not as we made the tours from school to school." In other words, the white school officials hardly cared that the black children were not getting the schooling the state said they should. Figg wanted to know if Whitehead had bothered to find out that there was no electricity or running water and sewerage at several of the colored schools because neither existed in the remote countryside surrounding them. "No," said Whitehead. "The reason I wouldn't do that is because I would assume the fact that the school was operated as a public school, and that there were certain responsibilities on the Board of Education [to] insure health and safety." Well, now, as to the lack of desks at the Rambay school and those unvarnished tables provided instead, was that really such a hardship?

> Q. Wasn't it the kind of equipment that might be used with [a] school population that might have a large enrollment but a fluctuating attendance because of the agricultural occupations of the parents of the school children?
> A. I regret, sir, that I could not agree with you. They could not be used anywhere except in a kitchen.
> Q. In a what?
> A. In a kitchen. There were cracks. They were supposed to be used for instructional purposes for students to write on and read on, and there were actually holes in the tables. The lady who taught the first grade at the school showed me three chairs which she had just received that had been sent over from the white school, that were dilapidated and the children could not sit in them. Other chairs had spokes and rounds out in them and the bottoms were out in many of them. . . .

Wasn't the white elementary school also in poor condition? No, not poor, said Whitehead. Couldn't he see that it needed a good deal of work done to it? No, said Whitehead, he could not. Wasn't the interior of the colored Scott's Branch school generally similar in layout to the Summerton elementary school? No, said Whitehead. Figg kept trying, and Whitehead kept batting the questions back with denials or counter-claims that served to strengthen the charges. At one point, Figg asked if the principal of one of the black elementary schools was "a colored man." "The principal," said Whitehead calmly, "is a Negro."

He remained on the stand for forty-five minutes that would stay with him for the rest of his life. Twenty years later, when he was dean of the District of Columbia Teachers College, he remembered his emotions as he came off the stand: "I felt good. It was all now down there on the record, and I could see it multiplied throughout the South. And you could see it on the faces of the people in the courtroom—a sort of sigh of relief that it had finally all come out."

To reinforce Whitehead's strong performance, Carter next put on his enlistee from Teachers College, Columbia—Harold McNally—who qualified as a specialist in educational psychology and administration. Having just heard Dr. Whitehead's recitation of the facilities at the colored schools in Clarendon, did Professor McNally think the students there could receive an education comparable to that offered at the white schools? Definitely not, said McNally. There was the matter of money, for one thing. Research by many experts in the field had "established a strong relationship between the quality of education and the cost of education"—a conclusion not easily gainsaid. The per-pupil load carried by each teacher was another major factor, since modern education stressed the need for individualized instruction and "knowledge of the nature and needs of each pupil"—the Dewey-Kilpatrick philosophy of schooling, in other words. The sharp contrast in the provision of physical facilities relating to health—the drinking water and toilet facilities, in particular—was another determinant of an inferior learning process because "in the modern conception of education, all the experiences the child has in the school constitute his education. And, it would seem to me that if you have poor health facilities provided children, they are learning poor health habits as well as being exposed to health hazards."

On cross-examination, all Figg wanted to know was whether McNally had himself ever studied any school system in South Carolina. He had not. Or elsewhere in the South? He had not. Had he made any inquiry into "the factors and facts, the problems and what-not which have motivated those states in establishing separate schools for the two races"? He had not. "That's all," said Figg with a pinch of disdain.

But Carter's next witness, Ellis O. Knox, like Whitehead a professor of education at Howard University, had indeed had experience studying the school systems in segregated communities, especially his participation in a recent major survey in Washington under the auspices of Congress—and Carter established this credential promptly. He had also conducted surveys of school systems in ten other major cities during the past two decades. In view of his wide experience, Carter asked him, did Professor Knox believe that Negro children attending a segregated school with facilities equal to the white schools in their community could obtain equal classroom instructional opportunities? It was exactly the same question that Carter had put to his previous witness, but this time Figg objected.

JUDGE PARKER: Well, what he's asking him is whether or not in his opinion it is discriminating against the Negro children to segregate them in schools. That is what he's asking him. Why isn't that competent?

FIGG: We think it's irrelevant and immaterial. It's been settled that the states can provide public schools and that they may provide separate schools for the different races. And his opinion is irrelevant and immaterial under the legal situation as laid down in the [Supreme Court's] decisions. That is a political matter for the legislature under our situation and not for witnesses on the witness stand.

The entire question of the legality of segregation, Figg was arguing, was beyond dispute. Judge Parker overruled him somewhat airily, and Knox was allowed to answer. But the witness seemed flustered as he concluded that segregated schools, as far as he had seen, never provided Negro pupils with educational opportunities equal to those offered whites.

Figg waded in on cross-examination. Knox had made school surveys in

Texas, he noted. Didn't his observations there suggest that segregation was not necessarily all bad? Weren't there "ways of life and emotionalisms and what-not to be taken into account as a practical matter" in weighing the desirability of segregated schools? Knox would not accept the drift of the question:

> . . . We must take into account the ways of life and emotionalisms, but I do not want to, in any sense of the word, say that we should not control emotionalisms and direct our ways and lives in terms of our democratic goals at all times.

Figg kept probing. He sought and won acknowledgment that the state's new school-funding program should prove "a distinct aid to the development of education in rural sections," but Knox granted him no more and was dismissed.

It was then that Robert Carter introduced into the case the element he had spent the better part of a year preparing—the testimony of social psychologists. He began with Kenneth Clark.

Clark had never before testified as an expert, but he seemed calm and soft-spoken as he began to testify. "I wouldn't allow myself to be concerned with ego," he remarks. "I knew I wasn't dissembling or trying to force the evidence I had at my disposal. I was just stating what I had learned over the years." From the very beginning, he had told Carter that he did not think it was possible to isolate the effect of school segregation as a factor in the psychological damage that Negro children suffered from the collective impact of prejudice. In that case, Carter had said, perhaps the NAACP couldn't use him. Then don't, said Clark, determined not to sacrifice his professional integrity. On reflection, Carter saw that any other posture would have made Clark a pliant reed. "He proved to be a very stubborn, very self-confident, very precise man," says Carter, looking back, and that was precisely the sort of man he had to have to command a court's attention.

After sketching out his background and projective test methods with dolls and coloring crayons, Clark gave the essence of his findings as presented in his White House conference paper of the previous year: "I have reached the conclusion from the examination of my own results and from an examination of the literature in the entire field that discrimination, prejudice and segregation"—good to his word, he refused to single out school segregation—"have definitely detrimental effects on the personality development of the Negro child." He went on:

> The essence of this detrimental effect is a confusion in the child's concept of his own self-esteem—basic feelings of inferiority, conflict, confusion in his self-image, resentment, hostility towards himself, hostility towards whites, intensification of . . . a desire to resolve his basic conflict by sometimes escaping or withdrawing.

Citing a recent survey by a pair of social scientists on the effects of segregation, Clark said 90 percent of the psychologists, anthropologists, and sociologists questioned "agree that segregation definitely has negative detrimental effects on the personalities of those individuals who are the victims of segregation," and 82 percent agreed that segregation also had negative effects on the segregating group by inducing guilt feelings.

> Another problem is confusion in the mind of the child—confusion concerning basic moral ideology—and a conflict which is set up in the child who belongs to the segregating group in terms of having the same people teach him democracy, brotherhood, love of his fellow man, and teaching him also to segregate and to discriminate. Most of these social scientists believe that this sets off in the personalities of these children a fundamental confusion in the entire moral sphere of their lives.

Clark then applied his general statements to the specific test results he obtained in Clarendon County: eleven of the sixteen Negro children thought the brown doll looked "bad"; ten of them considered the white doll the "nice" one—though a few moments later he said, in perhaps his only slip, that nine had chosen the white doll as the nice one; and seven of the sixteen picked the white doll as the one like themselves.

> The conclusion which I was forced to reach was that these children in Clarendon County, like other human beings who are subjected to an obviously inferior status in the society in which they live, have been definitely harmed in the development of their personalities; that the signs of instability in their personalities are clear, and I think that every psychologist would accept and interpret these signs as such.

It was a careful, low-key recitation, all the more stark for Clark's modulated manner. The psychologist hurriedly caught his breath and then braced himself for a relentless cross-examination. "I wasn't prepared for Mr. Figg's Southern gentility," he recalls.

Figg had sized up Clark's testimony and decided it would not adversely affect his case. He snipped away, trying to trivialize it rather than bludgeon it into inconsequence. No, Clark said, nobody else was present in the room while he tested each youngster. Yes, Clark said, he and his wife primarily had developed these particular tests, which had been given to about 400 children all together over the years. There was only a single sharp exchange between them as Figg tried to invoke the racist ideology of William Graham Sumner and other early sociologists that had prevailed half a century earlier but had been almost totally discredited by the academic world in the past two decades.

> Q. Do you recognize the psychology that people, based upon the "universal consciousness of kind," social heritage and the degree of visibility of differences between the races and so forth—enters into the problem of dealing with the existence of two different races in great numbers in a particular area?
>
> A. I do not recognize that at all, sir.
>
> Q. You don't recognize that?
>
> A. I do not recognize it as a principle which should govern democratic relations.
>
> Q. Do you recognize that there is an emotional facet in the problem of two different races living in large numbers together in the same area?

A. I have just given you results which indicate the consequences of that kind of emotional tension.

Confronted with a determined and obviously quick-witted witness with expertise in an area that Figg knew relatively little about, the defense attorney did not force the issue. "You don't cross-examine in a probing way if you're not sure what the answers are going to be," notes Figg, who by then had had a dozen years' experience as a state prosecutor and knew the territory. "I was concerned about findings of fact, and once we determined that his testimony was based on very few children, that there were no witnesses to the tests, and that this was his own test method and not a well-established one, I didn't press the matter. His numbers were small and unimposing, so why should I have pushed it? In the courtroom, his manner was quiet and matter-of-fact. Nobody took it seriously."

The essence of Kenneth Clark's testimony, though, would be taken very seriously indeed before *Briggs* was finally resolved. And while Figg was no doubt correct in leaving the substance of Clark's testimony unchallenged, latter-day commentators have demonstrated how vulnerable it might have proven to a pointed cross-examination. There was the size of Clark's sampling, for one thing. Sixteen children were not very many, to start with, and if even one or two of them had undergone atypical experiences or traumas in their young lives, the overall test results would have been thrown out of kilter. Then there was the question of fuzzy terminology in his tests. What was meant by a "good" doll and what was a "bad" one? What was a "nice" doll? Why could only one of the dolls be "nice," as the question put to the children clearly implied? And was it at all surprising that many of the children answered the final question in the series—"Which doll is like you?"—by picking the white doll after having previously designated it as the "nice" doll?

Clark's interpretations of the answers seemed "predetermined" in the view of New York University law professor Edmond Cahn, who wrote in a 1955 *New York University Law Review* analysis: ". . . For example, if Negro children say a *brown* doll is like themselves, [Clark] infers that segregation has made them conscious of race; yet if they say a *white* doll is like themselves, he infers that segregation has forced them to evade reality." A yet more damaging point, which would be hurled back at Clark before the *Briggs* litigation was over, was explored by Ernest van den Haag, a professor of social philosophy at New York University, who did some homework on Clark's studies that Figg could not have performed on his feet in the courtroom. In a chapter titled "Racial Identification and Preference in Negro Children" that Clark had contributed to a 1947 textbook, *Readings in Social Psychology*, edited by Theodore Newcomb and Eugene Hartley, the Negro psychologist had contrasted the results he had obtained from his doll and coloring tests of 134 colored children in the segregated schools of Pine Bluff, Arkansas, with 119 colored children in the unsegregated schools of Springfield, Massachusetts. The segregated Southern children, Clark wrote, were "less pronounced in their preference for the white doll" and when asked to hand their interrogator "the doll that looks like you," 39 percent of the unsegregated Springfield children picked the white doll compared with only 29 percent in the segregated schools of Arkansas. In his 1955 book *Prejudice and Your Child*, Clark similarly reported on the crayon test that "Nearly 80 percent of the southern children colored their preferences brown, whereas only 36 percent of the northern children did." In terms of the effects of segregation on the self-esteem and self-rejection of colored children, such findings were, at the very least, highly ambiguous and open to sharply varying interpretations. Van den Haag wrote that "if Professor Clark's tests do demonstrate damage to Negro children, then they demonstrate that the damage is *less* with segregation and *greater* with congregation." Clark had by no means proven or even offered evidence "to indicate that preference for, or identification with, a doll different in color from oneself indicates personality disturbance." If a dark-haired white child identified a blond doll as "nice" or "the good doll," would that prove he or she had suffered injury or psychic damage somehow? "Perhaps the main point," wrote Edmond Cahn tellingly, "is that this test does not purport to demonstrate the effects of *school* segregation, which is what the court was being asked to enjoin. If it disclosed anything about the effects of segregation on the children, their experiences at school were not differentiated from other causes. Considering the ages of the children [six to nine], we may conjecture they had not been long at school."

Such criticism hardly came as a surprise to Clark. In his pre-trial discussions with the NAACP lawyers, he had faced up to such problems. At worst, though, most of the criticism came down to the suggestion that Clark's tests did not definitively prove anything; they only suggested interpretations, and these were open to argument. The finding that Southern segregated black children showed much less inclination to reject the brown doll seemed a spot of special vulnerability, which Clark of course chose to avoid in his courtroom testimony. "Thurgood Marshall was very worried about that point," Clark comments. "But I believe, and I so argued at the time, that what the findings show is that the black children of the South were more adjusted to the feeling that they were not as good as whites and, because they felt defeated at an early age, did not bother using the device of denial. But that's not health. Adjusting to a pathology is not health. The way the Northern kids were fighting it can be seen as a better sign. The little Southern children would point to the black doll and say, 'Oh, yeah, that's me there—that's a nigger—I'm a nigger,' and they said it almost cheerfully. In the Northern cities, the question clearly threw the kids into a much more emotional state and often they'd point to the white doll."

Marshall had weighed the risks of Clark's findings and decided that on balance they demonstrated injury to segregated Negro youngsters. "I wanted this kind of evidence on the record," he had said. And as court recessed for lunch on the first day of the *Briggs* trial, Kenneth Clark had put it there.

Waties Waring had come early that morning to the court he had presided over for the previous decade. He arrived an hour before court was due to begin and found, to his astonishment, that "corridors were jammed to such an extent that the marshal had set up ropes" to cordon the crowd off "so that there would be a passageway for the judges and officials to get to their offices and to the courtroom, because otherwise it would have been impassable."

Though the crowd had behaved well during the morning session, its patience snapped momentarily as court reconvened in the afternoon. The big double doors at the back of the courtroom, through which spectators entered and which were then left open so the nearby standees in the hall could hear the proceedings, had been shut during the noon recess and the courtroom cleared. There were not dozens but hundreds of people packed behind the big double doors as the judges filed back onto the bench. "When the marshal went to open the door," as Waring recalled the moment, "there was a press of humanity out there in the corridor, and the doors wouldn't open. There was almost a mob scene, and the marshal and his deputies were kind of quarreling around, [saying] 'Get back, get back,' and so on. Finally the marshal looked up to the bench and he said, 'These people aren't behaving out there—I can't let them in.' I said, 'Open those doors and let the people in.' " Then, according to the Charleston *News and Courier*: "For ten minutes the crowd pushed and shoved, trying to elbow into the room while the shrill cries of women rose above the tumult. Three U.S. marshals sought to stem the flow of human forms . . . but it was left to Thurgood Marshall, lawyer for the National Association for the Advancement of Colored People, to restore order. His shouts of 'Please, Please!' caused the confusion to subside somewhat. . . ."

To Waring, the unruly interlude was understandable and excusable. "These were people from the country," he commented afterward. "They had come there on a pilgrimage. There were battered-looking automobiles parked all around the courthouse. People showed a great desire. . . . They had never known before that anybody would stand up for them, and they came there because they believed the United States District Court was a free court—and believed in freedom and liberty. I really feel that. To me it was a very heartening thing."

Carter got little mileage out of his afternoon witnesses. James L. Hupp, dean of West Virginia Wesleyan College and a professor of education and psychology there, repeated the view of earlier witnesses that segregation hindered the social development of schoolchildren, but when he began to testify on what had happened when black students were admitted to his college a few years earlier, Figg objected: events in West Virginia scarcely applied to conditions in South Carolina. Carter argued that Figg had been "raising the question that there would be a great deal of emotional tension involved in a situation in which Negroes and whites were thrown together for the first time in a school system . . . and we were called upon to meet it." To Judge Parker, Carter was barking up the wrong tree. "It's not the function of the court to determine what is the best educational policy," he said. "It is the function of the court to see that all men are given their rights." With that,

Carter got his witness quickly to report that the Negroes arriving at his campus had been accepted "with open arms"—an image not calculated to lighten the hearts of white South Carolinians.

The last NAACP witness of the day Figg succeeded in getting driven from the stand. Carter had thought it would be useful to bring in an expert from a Southern school, but he had little luck in finding one who would stand up in court and speak out against segregation and thereby risk his job. He finally found a relatively obscure, thirty-two-year-old assistant professor of political science at the University of Louisville named Louis Coleridge Kesselman, who had published a book in 1948 about the politics of the FEPC. Most of the other witnesses Carter had enlisted were either well known in their fields or strongly recommended by Ken Clark. Kesselman had been recommended by outsiders, and Carter was uneasy, for, as he wrote an NAACP contact in Louisville, "It is imperative that we have a southerner, but it is also imperative that our case not be embarrassed by the political identification of any of these people who testify." The last thing Carter needed was to have the essence of a witness's testimony obscured by innuendos of sharply leftist leanings, which were about as popular as leprosy in the South at that time and scarcely more welcome in the rest of the nation.

Nothing pink surfaced in the background of native Ohioan Kesselman, who had been an arbitrator and economist with the National War Labor Board while serving as an instructor on the Ohio State faculty during the war. A problem arose only after Carter put him on the witness stand, but it had nothing to do with Kesselman's political preferences—only his credentials as an expert, to which Figg objected. Carter explained, a trifle lamely, that the witness was an expert in the science of government and equipped to testify "whether or not an idea is developed in the child or in the people as to support democratic institutions." Judge Parker was skeptical. Any lawyer or person with government experience would be just as qualified by that standard, he said and asked Marshall to comment. The exchange that followed did little to advance the cause of social science in America:

> MARSHALL: May it please the court, what we have been trying to do is to present as many experts in the field with as many different reasons why we consider that segregation in and of itself is injurious to the child who is segregated. . . . Professor Kesselman, we hoped, would be able to testify as to the effect insofar as the study of government and the development of necessary fundamentals. . . .
>
> PARKER: Are you going to offer any more witnesses along this line?
>
> MARSHALL: No, sir. The other witnesses are *real* scientists.

Thus garlanded, Kesselman was allowed to testify. But not for long. He launched into a civics lesson on the effects of segregation on citizenship; Parker cut him off. Carter was obliged to excuse his witness, later apologizing to him for not having done a better job of pre-trial preparation.

Figg's initial decision that morning to admit the inequalities of the colored schools in Clarendon had thrown off the carefully calculated timetable that Marshall and Carter had worked out with their witnesses.

They had expected Figg to challenge their early witnesses on the equality issue and to offer more biting and exhaustive cross-examination, thereby consuming a good deal more of the clock than he had. The rest of the NAACP witnesses were due in overnight, including Robert Redfield from Chicago and Theodore Newcomb from the University of Michigan, and so Marshall was obliged to ask the court either to adjourn for the day or to let the defense begin its case. The court chose the latter. Figg's defense, as it turned out, was remarkably short.

E. R. Crow, the director of South Carolina's brand-new State Educational Finance Commission, testified glowingly on the details of Governor Byrnes's school-building program and how it might affect the situation in Clarendon. Marshall jumped in and objected to testimony on the state's intentions. Parker acknowledged Marshall's position that Fourteenth Amendment rights existed in the present, not the indefinite future, "but what this court may do in its decree might depend on whether they were making efforts in good faith to better the condition of these people." Crow was allowed to explain that more than $500,000 would be made available to Clarendon to rebuild its school system and eradicate the inequalities. Figg, noting Crow's experience as the former superintendent of schools in the city of Sumter, then asked his witness whether it would be wise policy at the present time for South Carolina students to attend racially mixed schools. Crow said, "The feeling of separateness between the races . . . would make it impossible to have peaceable association with each other in the public schools." Would mixing the races improve the education that both races received in South Carolina or make it worse? "In my opinion," said Crow, taking his cue from the earlier pronouncements of Governor Byrnes, "it would eliminate public schools in most, if not all, of the communities of the state." And was a violent emotional reaction likely should the races be mixed? "There would be, I am sure," said Crow.

Mr. Marshall had a few questions for Mr. Crow.

Since Negroes made up 40 to 45 percent of the population of South Carolina, were there any Negroes on Mr. Crow's new commission? No, said Crow.

Did the commission employ any Negroes? No, not yet.

Under the enabling legislation by which the new commission was to operate, was there any provision guaranteeing what percentage would go to the Negro schools—and wasn't it, as a matter of fact, "entirely possible for the Negro schools not to get a nickel of it"? That would be in defiance of the stated purposes of the act, said Crow. "Is there anything in the act to prevent that from happening?" Marshall demanded. Crow insisted that the commission was directed "to proceed to guarantee equal educational advantages and opportunities to all the children of the state." Then this exchange:

Q.  Mr. Crow, how much study have you done on the question of racial tension?
A.  If you mean formal study to qualify myself as an expert, I have done none.
Q.  I mean any kind of study, Mr. Crow.
A.  I would not say any study especially, but I have observed conditions and

people in South Carolina all of my life, but I have not studied racial tensions as such.

Q. Do you know of any situation in which previously segregated schools were mixed?

A. In South Carolina?

Q. In any place.

A. I have never been connected with any schools outside of this state, and I have never known of any in this state that come under your question.

Q. How do you draw your conclusion as to what will happen if they are mixed?

A. Because of my knowledge of what people say, from [what] their expressions with reference to this issue are.

Q. You are speaking of white people?

A. Mainly.

Q. How many Negroes do you know?

A. That would be impossible to answer. I know a great many Negroes.

Q. Well, approximately how many?

A. I couldn't answer that. I couldn't answer as to how many white people I know. That is an impossible question. I do not know how many Negroes I know.

Q. Do you know anything about the Negroes' beliefs in this thing?

A. Probably so, yes.

Q. You think so?

A. Yes, sir.

Q. Do you know what the Negroes' reaction would be to mixed schools?

A. Well, I have heard—.

Q. Of your own knowledge, now.

A. I could not predict what they would do, but I have an opinion that is based upon what a number of Negro school administrators have said to me that if this issue should be settled on a voluntary basis, that you would have a continuance of substantially the same situation.

Q. You are speaking of Negro public school administrators?

A. Yes, sir.

Q. Are any of the administrators you are talking about not employed by white school boards and responsible to them?

A. All the school administrators I know are employed by white school boards . . . but as I have stated, a good many Negroes, Negro school administrators have said that if they remained free to choose the schools to which they would go, they would prefer to have schools of their own race.

Q. Can you give me the names of some of those administrators?

A. No, sir.

Q. You don't remember their names?

A. No, sir.

As to Crow's contention that the public schools of the state would be abandoned if it was ordered that they be racially mixed, Marshall wanted to know whether that meant the white people of South Carolina would deprive their own children of an education for this reason. "I didn't say they would do that," said Crow. Well, what did he say? Crow said he meant that in his view the state legislature and local communities would no longer levy taxes for public schools if segregation were ended. Would Crow's view of the perils of desegregation be tempered by the peaceful way graduate and professional schools had handled the matter elsewhere in the South? That was quite a different thing from public schools, Crow contended, because few people were involved in the graduate schools, which functioned at a level of maturity where a good deal of the hostile feeling between the races was eliminated. What about the fact that Indiana had just recently outlawed segregation? Indiana had a very different ratio of the two races, said Crow, and the comparison was not useful. Suppose the ratio in Clarendon County were 95 percent white and 5 percent Negro—would that change Crow's feeling about the question? No, said Crow. Then the ratio of Negroes in the population was not really the basis of Crow's opinion, was it?

> A. The question you have asked me is in my opinion will the elimination of segregation be fraught with undesirable results, and I said that I thought it would. That may not be stating your question exactly, but that is still my answer.
> Q. As a matter of fact, Mr. Crow, isn't your opinion based on the fact that you have all your life believed in segregation of the races, isn't that reason the real basis of your opinion?
> A. That wouldn't be all.
> Q. Is that part of it?
> A. I suppose that is part of it.
> MARSHALL: Your witness.

Figg wound up with a humdrum examination of District No. 22 Superintendent Betchman in order to counter the testimony that Whitehead had offered in the morning on the equalities of the black schools. One of his problems, Betchman noted, was that Negro parents "want us to keep the schools closed until [they] can get the cotton picked, and sometimes that runs us a little late." Had he made strong effort under the state's compulsory-education law to counter the high rate of absenteeism among the colored pupils? "We insist upon that," said Betchman, "and we have our teachers . . . teach the bad results of absenteeism, and also insist that the teachers go around quite a bit among the people—it is hard for me to ever find them, so the teachers do what they can about it."

Finally, Judge Parker called a halt to the tedious questioning: "In the light of your admission this morning, what is the significance of all this, Mr. Figg?" The defense counsel said he saw the judge's point. Court was adjourned. It was 4:30 p.m.

David Krech went on first thing the next morning. "My opinion is that legal segregation of education is probably the single most important factor to wreak harmful effect on the emotional, physical and financial status of the Negro child," he asserted. By defining people in terms of race, Krech explained, the law promoted racial prejudice. This was so because people, except for mental defectives, cannot long maintain an attitude or belief unless there are some objective, concrete supports for that belief. We believe, for example, that there are trees, but how long would we continue to believe in trees if we never saw one? "Legal segregation, because it is legal, because it is obvious to everyone," he said, "gives what we call in our lingo environmental support for the belief that Negroes are in some way different from and inferior to white people, and that in turn, of course, supports and strengthens beliefs of racial differences, of racial inferiority."

The courtroom stirred when toward the end of his direct testimony Krech said he did not agree with those who said that the white man who was prejudiced against the Negro had no cause for his prejudice. In most cases, the Negro was indeed inferior to the white man—because the white man had made him that way through the practice of legalized segregation. On the other hand, Krech asserted, "There is no psychologist that I know of who would maintain that there is any biological, fundamental difference between the two groups of people. . . ." In his cross-examination, Figg settled for establishing that Krech was born in Poland, had spent most of his life in the North, and had done no field research in a state where segregation was practiced. Then he let the California scholar go. "I was a bit disappointed that he did not badger me or challenge me more than he did," says Krech, who recalls having worked himself into an aggressive "Come on, I dare you!" state of mind.

But Figg did put Carter's last witness through some hoops. Helen Trager, a fortyish educational consultant, recounted the extensive testing she had carried on with a number of colleagues in Philadelphia on the awareness of racial differences among schoolchildren. Though her group had used a number of techniques similar to those of Kenneth and Mamie Clark, the study seemed more carefully thought out and the results more convincing. The nub of her findings was that "the Negro children, unlike the white children, showed a tendency to expect rejection. This expectation of rejection increased sharply from five to eight years old"—the early school years. "A child who expects to be rejected," she explained, "who sees his group held in low esteem, is not going to function well, he is not going to be a fully developed child, he will be withdrawn, or aggressive in order to win the acceptance he doesn't get."

Figg tried to counter by arguing that schools themselves were not a major factor in the consciousness of group differences that Mrs. Trager had found so acute.

Q. It came out of the homes, didn't it?
A. It came out of many things, not just the home.
Q. At the age of five, the chances are that it came mostly out of the home, isn't that true?
A. . . . it was not always the home, although we know the home is an important factor in the learning of children. It was the playground. It was what they saw on the bus. It was what they knew about where their father worked—or couldn't work. It was all of their learning in the total community in the society of their five-year-oldness, and they were aware of many things, and their sources included church and shop and marketplace.

Figg kept after her. He quoted Myrdal and Du Bois, in highly selective and untypical passages, to show that they did not necessarily favor racially mixed schools or believe that most Negroes favored them. Trager was not impressed, though in her candor she yielded some ground to Figg. At the end, however, when Carter had her on redirect examination, she strongly sounded the keynote of the NAACP's case against segregation; in the process, she excited a rare show of life out of Judge Timmerman.

> TIMMERMAN: Assuming all you say is of consequence, do you think those conditions [leading to emotional damage of and self-rejection by Negro children] arise first in the home or first in the school?
> A. I think unquestionably they arise in the home first because the first years in a child's life are in the home. I think the place, however, where education can take place—and must, if we are to diminish the amount of hostility and fear that children of all groups have toward each other—is the school.

Carter was out of witnesses. His last two were still en route, and Judge Parker was frankly impatient. He had heard quite enough experts already. Were these last two really essential? Carter huddled with Marshall. Professor Newcomb of Michigan was likely to go over the same ground that David Krech had discussed with vigor. And Professor Redfield was to be a rebuttal witness, but Figg had not introduced anything into the case that required rebutting. At a little after 11:30 a.m., Thurgood Marshall, who had turned most of the trial work over to Carter, reclaimed the floor and delivered his summation. It was one of the better efforts of his career.

There was little factual dispute in the case, in view of the defense's concessions, Marshall noted. What was at issue was the law. Yes, separate-but-equal had been on the books for a long time, but "progressive development of the law" had produced a steady series of decisions by the Supreme Court in recent years and led to the end of segregation at graduate and professional schools in the South without any resulting disruptions on the campuses involved. Yes, public schools were different from universities, but the inequities in South Carolina were such that the step had to be taken. "In South Carolina you have admitted inferiority of Negro schools. All your state officials are white. All your school officials are white. It is admitted. That's not just segregation. It's exclusion from the group that runs everything. The Negro child is made to go to an inferior school; he is branded in his own mind as inferior. This sets up a roadblock in his mind which prevents his ever feeling he is equal. You can teach such a child the Constitution, anthropology, and citizenship, but he knows it isn't true." The defense had introduced no evidence of the reasonability of the South Carolina segregation law, whereas the plaintiffs' expert witnesses had plainly shown the damage done by it. Clarendon County was "violating the law every day it operates this school system." The defense, in opening, had asked for time to correct the inequalities, "but I know of no statute that permits anyone to come into court and ask time to stop doing something which is unlawful. . . . There is no relief for the Negro children of Clarendon County except to be permitted to attend existing and superior white schools."

A vast body of legal precedent, replied Figg, said that South Carolina was allowed to run its schools as it saw fit. The state recognized the problem of inequality, but "problems of race are not soluble by force but by the slow processes of community experience." Segregation had existed in many Northern states prior to 1861, and the Congress that passed the Fourteenth Amendment clearly did not intend to outlaw school segregation by the states or it would not itself have enacted legislation allowing separate schools in the District of Columbia. Separate schools, then, were undeniably legal, but just as undeniably they did have to be truly equal. The best schools in Columbia, South Carolina, were the Negro schools because they were the newest ones, and the state's new building program would provide the $40 million it was going to take to bring the colored schools of the state up to equality.

Judge Parker had a question: "What decree do you suggest the court ought to enter in the light of your admissions?" Figg had in mind "a reasonable time" for the plans to be drawn up and implemented; meanwhile the court would retain jurisdiction over the case.

> JUDGE PARKER: Well, I'm not much impressed with that. You have come into court here and admitted that facilities are not equal, and the evidence shows it beyond all peradventure. Now it seems to me it's not for the court to wetnurse the schools. Assuming that segregation is not abolished by the decree, it would be proper for this court to direct an equalization of educational facilities. And we wouldn't tell you how to do it . . . all we can do is to tell you to do what the Constitution enjoins upon you. Now what I'm asking you is: what sort of decree ought to be entered with that end in view?
>
> FIGG: I think, if your honor pleases, that the decree should take into account the fact that school buildings cannot be built overnight. . . .

Figg did not want to be pinned down. Whatever deadline he might have picked, the court might prove more lenient still; better to remain silent or vague in reply. Besides, the longer he could get the court to retain jurisdiction, the better, he later acknowledged, for "it would delay for months any chance of the plaintiffs appealing from an adverse opinion to the Supreme Court of the United States." Whatever the court settled on, though, Figg said, "you can't pass laws on the mores of a people, their culture, their traditions, their cumulative heritage. You can't have such changes suddenly or by decree; one has to grow up to them. And you can't write off the happenings of the past 75 or 80 years because they have grown into the lives of the people." Great progress had been made in education in the South of late, but it would be undone if segregation were now forcibly removed. He had been talking with Dr. Howard Odum—the magic name!—just the other day about that, and Dr. Odum said, "Why, that would upset twenty-five years of work that I have done in the field of race relations." There will come a time, said Figg, when "this problem will disappear as it disappeared in times past in the other states, which have been permitted to deal in their own time with the problem of their legislative functions." But now was not the time to end segregation in South Carolina.

Marshall had the last word. After eighty years of effort, he said, "the best South Carolina can show this court in good faith today is that Negroes are forty million dollars behind the white schools." Education, though, was more than mortar and bricks. It was everything a child learns. And what segregation had taught the Negro child caused him "lasting, not temporary, injury." Equal education meant "Negroes must be offered the exact [same] thing. If the white child is permitted to obtain an education without mental roadblocks, the Negro child must be permitted." It was the responsibility of the court "to end this injustice now."

Court was adjourned. Some of the black spectators surged forward to grasp Thurgood Marshall's hand. Out in the corridor, New York *Post* newsman Ted Poston reported finding "a white-haired, dark-faced old patriarch who had attended the Reconstruction schools for his only two years of schooling. . . . 'We ain't asking the white folks to give us anything new,' he observed quietly. 'We're just asking 'em to give back what they stole from us in the first place.' "

Back in Charleston, the three judges met in chambers. "It was a long talk," Judge Waring recalled five years afterward, "but hardly much discussion. Judge Timmerman is a rigid segregationist. I was and am an equally rigid anti-segregationist. And Judge Parker is an extremely able judge who knows the law, and follows the law, but quite unwillingly, in the Southern country. He just set his feet on *Plessy v. Ferguson* and said, 'We can't overrule.' . . . Of course my position was . . . we didn't have to overrule *Plessy*."

On June 21, three weeks after the two-day trial in Charleston ended, Judge Parker's opinion was handed down, Judge Timmerman concurring.

"The problem of segregation at the common school level is a very different one" from that presented in *Sweatt* and *McLaurin*, the most recent instances in which the Supreme Court had spoken on the question, said Parker. At the public-school level, "as good education can be afforded in Negro schools as in white schools and the thought of establishing professional contacts does not enter into the picture." At this level, moreover, education was compulsory, and the state entered into a compact with the parent in training the child—"a delicate field and one fraught with tensions and difficulties." Testimony in the case just heard differed as to whether racially mixed schools in South Carolina would produce better education and understanding in the community or result in racial friction and tension. The determination of which view was correct was not a question of constitutional right "but of legislative policy, which must be formulated, not in *vacuo* or with doctrinaire disregard of existing conditions, but in realistic approach to the situations to which it is to be applied." The states' regulation of their public schools, provided and paid for by their citizens, was not to be interfered with unless constitutional rights were clearly being infringed. But

> when seventeen states and the Congress of the United States have for more than three quarters of a century required segregation of the races in the public schools, and when this has received the approval of the leading appellate courts of the country including the unanimous approval [in *Gong Lum v. Rice*] of the Supreme Court of the United States at a time when that court included Chief Justice Taft and Justices Stone, Holmes and Brandeis, it is a late day to say that such segregation is violative of fundamental constitutional rights. It is hardly

reasonable to suppose that legislative bodies over so wide a territory, including the Congress of the United States, and great judges of high courts have knowingly defied the Constitution for so long a period or that they have acted in ignorance of the meaning of its provisions. The constitutional principle is the same now that it has been throughout this period; and if conditions have changed so that segregation is no longer wise, this is a matter for the legislatures and not the courts. The members of the judiciary have no more right to read their ideas of sociology into the Constitution than their ideas of economics.

The plaintiffs' plea for an injunction abolishing segregation of the races in the schools of South Carolina was therefore denied. But the defendants were directed "promptly" to furnish equal educational facilities to the Negro pupils within their district and to report back to the court "within six months" on the progress that had been made toward that end.

Judge J. Waties Waring filed a twenty-page dissent, his last important opinion as a sitting judge. *Plessy v. Ferguson* was irrelevant to *Briggs*, he wrote, since the 1896 case had dealt with segregation on railroads. Schools were an entirely different matter, as recent decisions of the Supreme Court, such as *Sweatt* and *McLaurin*, had made clear. The only real issue before the court was whether there was a rational basis for segregation, which was undeniably founded on prejudice.

> . . . There is absolutely no reasonable explanation for racial prejudice. It is all caused by unreasoning emotional reactions and these are gained in early childhood. Let the little child's mind be poisoned by prejudice of this kind and it is practically impossible to remove these impressions, however many years he may have of teaching by philosophers, religious leaders or patriotic citizens. If segregation is wrong, then the place to stop it is in the first grade and not in graduate colleges.
>
> . . . [S]egregation in education can never produce equality and . . . is an evil that must be eradicated. This case presents the matter clearly for adjudication, and I am of the opinion that all of the legal guideposts, expert testimony, common sense and reason point unerringly to the conclusion that the system of segregation in education adopted and practiced in the state of South Carolina must go and must go now.
>
> *Segregation is per se inequality.*

Waties Waring moved out of South Carolina not long after writing those words. He made his home in New York for the next seventeen years. At his death in 1968, the Charleston *News and Courier*, then edited by his nephew Thomas, who disagreed sharply with his uncle's racial views, wrote: "He was a judge of uncommon ability that was recognized and admired by all regardless of opinion. On retirement . . . he chose to leave the land of his forefathers in a self-imposed exile from which he now returns to be buried." Fewer than a dozen white people attended the graveside service at Magnolia Cemetery on the northern outskirts of Charleston. But on hand were more than 200 Negroes who had formed a motorcade from St. Matthew's Baptist Church, where the NAACP conducted a memorial service.

"He's dead," says James Gibson, the black farmer from Clarendon County, "but living in the minds of the people here still."

# 16
# Prairie Fire

No one at the NAACP's Legal Defense Fund office in New York had been holding his breath awaiting the decision in *Briggs*. Judge Parker would have had to set aside practical and theoretical questions of great difficulty in order to find legalized segregation a moral crime of no longer tolerable iniquity. So remote did such an outcome seem to Thurgood Marshall and his staff that well before the *Briggs* opinion came down, they were hurrying to complete arrangements for school-segregation suits in other—and, they hoped, more vulnerable—communities, so that when they appealed the question anew to the Supreme Court, they might present a record of pervasive and undeniable injustice, whatever its variations in degree of severity. Thus, on the very day the *Briggs* decision was issued, NAACP lawyers were flying west to complete preparations for the next segregation-case trial, due to open the following week in the capital city of Kansas.

Racism, by whatever name, had never been limited to the American South. The complicity of the Northern states in allowing slavery to thrive as an American institution was clear. The profound disrespect for the free Negro in the North and West, as disclosed in disenfranchising and many other humiliating laws, as well as fear and hatred of him as an economic rival, were no less plain in the antebellum period. Once emancipated and therefore the less pitiable to those so inclined, the black man faced rising antagonism. His relatively slow migration out of the South seemed not to affect the tide of antipathy in either the sector losing him and resenting it or the sector receiving him and suspecting he had nothing to offer but his troubles.

By 1950, more than 28 percent of the Negroes in America lived outside the states of the old Confederacy, and the percentage was rising fast. Most of them lived in the great industrial metropolises where jobs and racial companionship were thought to be most readily available. As early as 1940, eleven cities included Negro populations of more than 100,000. Their concentration there gave them the beginnings of real political power, but they were largely isolated from and by the white population—scarcely less so than they had been in the South and perhaps even more so. Racial animosity, then, followed a common pattern, North and South, though the laws of the South were a good deal more brutal about it. Whatever the laws outside the

South, it was the rare place where the Negro was not viewed as second-class humanity. He was so considered in Topeka, Kansas.

In the decade preceding the Civil War, the 50 million acres of rich and rolling terrain that made up the Kansas Territory became the staging ground of the great conflict over the permissible reach of slavocracy. Until then, Kansas had been the vast midland corridor on the way west. By the 1850s, traffic in goods and people grew heavier over the Oregon and Santa Fe trails that carried the intrepid wagon trains across hundreds of miles of Kansas prairie toward the gold and new life in the Far West.

Those who stopped off to stay in Kansas were few at first, though the land in the eastern third of the state was surely as lush—fertile, well watered, timbered, with gentle hills and lovely little valleys—as any they would find elsewhere on the continent. The charms of Kansas soil were most apparent, perhaps, to its immediate neighbors to the east, the slaveholding interests of the state of Missouri, who had harnessed black muscle power in the counties along the Missouri River to grow tobacco and hemp among other crops. Under the Missouri Compromise of 1820, it was the southern border of Missouri that was to mark the northern extent of slavery in any state—except for Missouri itself—carved from the Louisiana Purchase lands. All of the Kansas Territory lay north of that line and thus slavery was presumably outlawed in it. Nevertheless, slaveholders and pro-slavery outriders advanced across the Missouri and began to stake their claims and work the endless virgin land that was Kansas. Fearful of the continuing spread of the cotton kingdom and its dehumanizing slavery, abolitionist groups in New England began to sponsor emigrant parties to settle the Kansas Territory and fight for its development as a free state. Though small in number, such anti-slavery groups established the free-soil communities of Lawrence and Topeka west of Kansas City by fifty and seventy-five miles respectively. The free-soilers were reinforced by growing numbers of homesteaders from Illinois, Ohio, and other Midwestern states looking for greener pastures. What they were not looking for was competition with slave labor. It denigrated their own struggle with the soil. It thrived on vast holdings that few of the free-state settlers could afford. It threatened to drive them into the backlands, as it had done to the poor-white farmers of the Old South. While the nation as a whole hung in combustible equilibrium, half slave country and half free, agents of these passionately conflicting interests met head-on in Kansas. The result was chaos.

The course of national war was more than likely assured by the passage of the Kansas-Nebraska Act. There is no less attractive or more savage chapter in the development of democracy in America than the seven-year spectacle of "bleeding Kansas" between the 1854 act authorizing "squatter sovereignty" and the state's admission to the Union a few months before the outbreak of war at Fort Sumter. The actual death rate was remarkably low—most historians count no more than fifty-five fatalities over the slavery conflict in Kansas, including John Brown's bloody foray at Pottawatomie Creek and the pro-slavery sacking of Lawrence—but the corruption of the democratic process was almost complete. The first territorial legislature, found to have been elected largely by pro-slavery residents of Missouri, voted promptly to restrict officeholding to pro-slavers. A rump state convention dominated by free-soilers then met in Topeka and passed a territorial constitution that amply reflected the prevailing Republican sentiment: no slavery—and free Negroes as well were to be excluded from Kansas. The black man, of whatever status, was to keep out. President Buchanan sided with the pro-slavery group, though its ready use of electoral fraud, violence, and other extra-legal chicanery was well documented and the majority of residents was increasingly opposed to slavery.

Territorial governors came and went, caught in an impossible vise. High commodity prices brought on by wars in Europe and the steadily growing trans-Atlantic clipper trade fed land speculation as westward migration intensified and Congress threw open the territory to full-scale settlement without bothering first to ratify treaties with the Indians, provide for proper land surveys, or otherwise oversee and prevent a disorderly land grab. Counties were organized illegally, bonds were sold fraudulently, and the ballot box was regularly stuffed by the pro-slavers, who grew more desperate and wanton as the decade wore on. Finally, a strong governor authenticated an anti-slavery constitution that carried in a territorial plebiscite by a ratio of ten to one, and on the strength of it Kansas renewed its application to Congress for statehood. Under its new constitution, Kansas would not absolutely bar free Negroes; rather, as Iowa and Minnesota had done, it would merely deny them the vote. For more than a year, as the drums of war began to sound unmistakably, Congress would not act on statehood for Kansas. But the line had been drawn. Only after secession—almost immediately after—did Kansas become the thirty-fourth state. Its contribution in manpower to the Union war effort proved proportionately greater than that of any other state.

From the end of the war to 1890, Kansas grew swiftly and prospered in an age of rowdy, wide-open frontier life and endless, uncertain contest with the earth itself. With Southern lawmakers absent, Congress put through the Homestead Act of 1862, granting 160 acres to every hardy settler who would hunker down on those dry, treeless, wind-whipped grasslands that made up the western two-thirds of Kansas. The sod was so hard on the great plains that new steel plows had to be developed to break it, and in places it could be penetrated only with an ax. But corn and then wheat flourished there, and machines were developed to let the homesteaders cultivate vast, undulating vistas of grain. The railroads came and functioned as the great land developers and promoters. Handed a subsidy of more than seven million acres, one-seventh of the state, the railroads served as bankers and brokers as they ballyhooed the glories of the Sunflower State and sold off their vast holdings as fast as they could find customers. The cattlemen added to the Kansas boom, but by 1890 the open range was gone and the cattle-drive days were over. Gone, too, were the Indians and the buffalo. Where there had been 108,000 people in Kansas in 1860, thirty years later—despite the wind and the dust and the snowstorms that strafed the great plains, despite drought and cyclones and plagues of grasshoppers and the gyrating prices that farmers got for their wheat—there were more than 1,400,000 people in Kansas, and the state had become the granary of the nation. Fewer than 50,000 of these Kansans were Negro.

The boom tailed off sharply, and Kansas thereafter added people at an exceedingly modest rate. By the middle of the twentieth century, it would number no more than 2.1 million residents. Though it endured much of the same economic travail that confronted the equally agricultural South, Kansas was far more prosperous and prudent than the hard-hit states of the fallen Confederacy. Populism took command in Kansas for a time, just as it did in the South, as farmers everywhere put aside their cherished individualism and locked arms against the confiscatory policies of Eastern and Northern creditors, railroad managers, and other monopoly-minded manipulators of the American economy. But Kansas, unlike the South, had taken steps from the start to prevent its exploitation as a mere colony of the urban East. For one thing, it did not depend overly on a single great crop, promoting its own impoverishment by overproduction. In time, Kansas would supply one-fifth of the nation's wheat, but it grew many other things—corn and oats and alfalfa and beef and poultry—and fed itself, as the South had not, and processed its grain in mills and its beef in meatpacking plants, as the South had not processed the fruit of its soil. Kansans went into hock to buy the latest and best threshers and combines and increase the yield of their land, as the South had never wanted to mechanize under slavery and thereafter was too poor to manage it. Kansas improved its railroads and waterways and bridges and quickly built highways for the coming of the automobile, so that there was no remote backcountry as there was throughout the South; no matter where you were in Kansas, you could get your produce to market. By the third generation after statehood, Kansas was long past its hayseed era. Industry flowered now. In less than a century, by pluck and thrift and a massive outlay of human energy, rootless Kansans had turned their great garden on the plains into a remarkably productive, balanced, and stable society whose deep-rootedness and plain-spokenness were among the most attractive features of the American character as it had taken hold out there in midcontinent.

For all that, there were those who found Kansas a spiritually dreary place and its residents a joyless lot. It was perhaps not surprising that people who made their living from the earth should prove something less than playful, but in their dedication to life's sodbusting chores, dour Kansans seemed to be sounding a collective lamentation over the devil's multiple distractions. Fundamentalist religion and puritanical sexuality found ready soil in Kansas. Alcohol and tobacco were legislated against early, and it was there that Carry Nation first smote demon rum, not to mention any saloon mirror she could reach. One of the state's most gifted and astute native sons, psychiatrist Karl Augustus Menninger of Topeka, has commented lovingly on the peculiarities of his fellow Jayhawkers, whose fanaticism he has said was due "not so much to puritanical self-righteousness, the desire to reform and inhibit, as to a wish to identify themselves with the best, the most idealistic and fruitful ways of life. And because they feel pathetically unequal to maintaining these ideals and to living at the high pitch at which they conceive other more gifted people to be living, they fence themselves about and reinforce their tense strivings with laws and prohibitions."

Nowhere had the moral ambiguity of Kansans been more suspect than in their treatment of Negroes. John Brown's incendiary wrath would later be portrayed in a dominant mural installed in the capitol at Topeka, but no such righteousness swept over the first state legislature, which promptly provided for the establishment of separate-but-equal schools for the offspring of its unenfranchised black citizens. In subsequent sessions, the legislature limited the power to establish such schools to cities "of the first class" (i.e., over 7,000 people). Shortly after ratifying the Fourteenth Amendment in 1867, the Kansas lawmakers extended, rather than reduced, segregated schooling. It was now permitted in second-class cities as well (any town with more than 1,000 residents). But nine years later, for reasons not disclosed in any public debates recorded, the school laws of Kansas were recodified and all mention of separate schools was omitted. Desegregation began, and not without difficulty. The superintendent of public instruction in Wyandotte County, where nearly one-third of the state's colored population then lived, reported in 1876: "There are a large number of colored pupils in this county, and where they predominate, or attend schools in considerable numbers, these mixed schools are not a success." The same session of the legislature that wiped out the permissive school-segregation provision also passed a civil-rights statute, still standing more than a century later, outlawing racial distinctions in "any state university, college, or other school of public instruction" or in any licensed place of public accommodation or amusement or public conveyance. That profession of equality was the high-water mark for tolerance. The civil-rights law was repeatedly violated by countless inns, hotels, restaurants, and theaters, and the desegregation of schools lasted just three years.

In 1879, steamboats loaded with black refugees, many of them destitute but bearing circulars promising them free land and provisions for a year, came up the Missouri River from Louisiana, Mississippi, and Tennessee and put in at Wyandotte, just outside Kansas City on the Kansas side of the river. At first, the "Exodusters," as these wayfarers wearing bandanas and lugging battered suitcases came to be called, were greeted kindly, but as their numbers mounted to an eventual total of nearly 8,000, violence threatened. The state government rallied to bring relief and help disperse the blacks to settlements throughout Kansas. That same year, the state legislature granted to first-class cities, then defined as those with more than 15,000 residents, the authority to resegregate their elementary schools. A specific exception was made for high schools, "where no discrimination shall be made on account of color." The wording of the law itself thus made it clear that Kansas knew that the establishment of separate schools was an unmistakable act of discrimination. The 1879 law remained unchanged until 1905, when Kansas City was allowed to open a separate high school for Negroes.

In 1903, a colored man by the name of William Reynolds tried to enroll his son in a school set aside for whites only in Topeka. He was refused and brought suit against the board of education. The Supreme Court of Kansas, citing *Plessy, Roberts v. City of Boston*, and numerous other state cases upholding school segregation, politely and unanimously told Mr. Reynolds that Topeka was well within its rights.

Forty-eight years passed before another colored man tried to enroll his child in a school set aside for whites only in Topeka. He, too, was refused and brought suit against the board of education. This time, though, the black plaintiff was joined by a dozen more colored parents, rallied by the local branch of the NAACP and represented by lawyers from the national organization's main office in New York. The suit was not a popular one in the black community of Topeka, where surprise was registered that the principal plaintiff in the action should have turned out to be a quiet, distinctly unmilitant welder in the Santa Fe repair shops who served also as a part-time pastor at the leading black church in town. Except for his time in military service, he had lived all his thirty-two years in Topeka with no involvement in the troublemaking NAACP, so why he should now become a rebel was something of a puzzle to those who knew Oliver Brown.

After a twenty-mile straightaway that bisects the pancake-smooth country-side, the Kansas Turnpike veers to the southwest and bypasses the capital city. To reach it, the visiting motorist swings off the interstate express at the East Topeka interchange, climbs a slow-access rise, and circles onto state highway 40, where if he comes by night he will first glimpse the 300-foot-high dome of the capitol glowing pale green in the western sky. It is a very large structure of beige marble that took Kansas nearly forty years to complete, and if its French Renaissance grandeur and Corinthian detail seem somehow misplaced out there above the fruited plain, one must not mock Kansans for putting on airs, for they do little enough preening. Indeed, the capitol is not even the most striking architectural feature of the Topeka skyline if one arrives by day, any more than are the new towering boxes of glass and steel that house the leading banks and utility companies in the downtown nexus. One's eye, rather, is drawn off to the north, across the Kansas River (known locally as the Kaw), to a double row of massive cylinders, each a soaring column and linked to the next like mammoth piston chambers in some unearthly engine. Hundreds of yards long, the whole apparatus seems to gleam silver in the sunlight, but that is a trick of nature, for the cylinders are made of concrete and contain, when full, 40 million bushels of wheat and corn and rye and oats and milo and barley and not a few soybeans. The C-G-F Grain Elevator was the second largest in the world when built, and more than any fancified government building, it says what Topeka and Kansas are about.

One could have argued plausibly that Topeka in 1951 was the ideal American city. Or perhaps one might call it as close to a metropolis as Thomas Jefferson would have tolerated in the great American heartland. Its size was pleasingly modest. It claimed a few over 100,000 residents within its 125-square-mile city limits, of whom not quite 7.5 percent were Negro—

almost the precise percentage of black residents for the state as a whole. The city had grown a substantial 15 percent during the Forties and ranked third in size in the state, behind brawling Wichita to the southwest, which was more than twice as big, and still more industrialized Kansas City to the east, which was just a few thousand larger. Compared to either of those cities, Topeka was downright bucolic. It had wide streets and almost no traffic congestion. People knew each other.

But Topeka has never been a cowtown. The presence of the state government and its relatively trim bureaucracy assured it of a certain built-in importance. Its municipal university, Washburn, has been a serviceable and unpretentious city college, running night and day, summer and winter, with a special interest in training yeoman lawyers and teachers. If Washburn did not suit the aspiring Topekan, Kansas University was just twenty miles due east in Lawrence and Kansas State sixty miles due west in Manhattan. In 1951, the town was proud of its new 200,000-volume public library, and the State Historical Society Museum was a superior research facility. Few small cities boasted as refreshing a spot as Gage Park, with its well-kept zoo (featuring performing elephants and the only known giraffes in all of Kansas), a minitrain for children, and a rose garden with no fewer than a hundred varieties of blossom. There were a dozen smaller parks as well and half a dozen public swimming pools and Lake Shawnee for boating. The prettiest building in the city was old Topeka High School, with its Gothic tower, at Tenth and Polk (the principal north-south streets in town are named for the Presidents). Two blocks from Topeka High stands the most imposing of the more than 100 churches in the community—Grace Episcopal Cathedral, a mixture of Kansas stone and Bavarian wood. What Topeka has had more of, though, than anything else—and almost certainly than any other community its size—is hospitals. Big ones, like Topeka State Hospital and small ones like the Capper Foundation for Crippled Children. There were St. Francis for Catholics, the Veterans Administration Hospital for veterans, the Santa Fe Railroad's own hospital for its employees across the country, the State Rehabilitation Center for the Blind, and, most notable of all, the institutions for the mentally ill: Stormont-Vail Hospital, Kansas Neurological Institute, and out on its campuslike spread at the west end of town, the world-famous Menninger Foundation, which bills itself as "a non-profit center for treatment and prevention, research and professional education in psychiatry." Something on the order of 10,000 people are involved in this medical sub-community, long the biggest industry in town and all the more remarkable for the degree of cooperation said to exist among the various professional staffs. The Menningers are the best known of the Topeka healers, and they have not limited their efforts to building their own empire. Through their efforts, among others, the local VA hospital was rebuilt as the biggest psychiatric facility for veterans in the nation, and the Kansas legislature was goaded into providing funds that took mental-health care in the state out of medieval bedlam and lifted it close to national leadership. All this activity brought a certain sophistication to Topeka, as well as professional people of highly varied backgrounds from distant places.

They have something else in Topeka that has made it a good place to live and work. They have a variety of businesses that has brought high economic stability to the community. Besides a lot of non-cyclical jobs in state, county (Topeka is also the seat of Shawnee County), and municipal government and the medical field, the town has been the headquarters of the Atchison, Topeka and Santa Fe Railroad since it was founded in the 1870s; rarely has it carried fewer than 3,000 to 4,000 people on its local payroll, including hundreds in the huge repair shops down by the riverside. Goodyear put up a big plant after the war that at its peak was turning out 25,000 tires a day. Later came Forbes Air Force Base just south of town, bringing 6,000 or so new consumers into the area. The city's rail and highway facilities and its location almost at dead center of the continental United States made it a natural warehousing depot, and not only for grain. On top of which were dozens of banking and insurance companies centered in or doing business out of the capital city. Topeka, in short, was a solid place, a steady place, though no one ever called it a particularly exciting, beautiful, or culturally stimulating place. Remarks a long-time Menninger psychiatrist who worked hard for civic causes but has since left Topeka: "It is a town that seemed to me largely contented with itself, a town that could not bring itself to act imaginatively in its own behalf."

Perhaps more than most communities, Topeka was long dominated by a handful of conservative business leaders—prominent among them the presidents of Merchants National Bank, First National of Topeka, Capitol Federal Savings & Loan, and Kansas Power & Light, the manager of the local Sears, and the owner of the biggest clothing store in town (and widely known to be the only Jewish member of the Topeka Country Club, where the big civic decisions in town were thrashed out over highballs). This tight circle of Goldwater Republicans generally declined to admit members of the Menninger-Washburn cultural community to its inner council and indeed viewed with alarm almost anything that smacked of liberalism or foreign infiltration of the Topekan psyche. One of the town's top bankers was introduced in an elevator in the Jayhawk Hotel to Alexander Kerensky, the ex-premier of Russia, a documented anti-Bolshevik and a resident of the United States since 1940, who had come to Topeka to speak at Washburn; the banker turned his back on Kerensky. The municipal spirit tended to be aroused only by such clear and present threats to Americanism and by those projects that promised substantial economic reward. The country-club group had thus been highly visible and active in Topeka's efforts to bring in the VA hospital, the Air Force base, and the Goodyear plant. That was good business. And good business was good citizenship. Beyond that, each man was on his own. That was what made America great. For those who couldn't cope—well, that's what the Menninger crowd was there for.

Whatever else it was in 1951, Topeka was also a Jim Crow town. It had been one as long as anyone could remember.

There were no separate waiting rooms at the train and bus stations, and Negroes did not have to ride in the back of the local buses, but in most other ways it was segregated by law and, more effectively, by custom. There were eighteen elementary schools for whites and four for blacks. There was one colored hotel, the Dunbar, and all the rest were for whites. Almost no restaurants downtown served colored customers. Before the Second World War, a number of the better beaneries in town had a sign in the window reading: "Negroes and Mexicans served in sacks only," meaning they could take out food in bags but not eat on the premises. One movie theater in town admitted colored people to its balcony. Another, called the Apex, was for colored only. The other five movie houses were for whites only. The swimming pool at Gage Park was off-limits to colored, except one day a year when they were allowed in for a gala picnic.

Worse yet was the employment picture. Blacks had won some jobs at the Santa Fe shops during a strike in the early Twenties, but there were few black union members in Topeka and fewer held white-collar positions of any kind. A black clerk at a retail shop or a black stenographer at an insurance company was almost unknown. Mrs. Inza Brown, who had been a legal secretary to the only black lawyer in town for thirteen years in the Twenties and Thirties, won a civil-service job at the State Department of Health, where, as she remembers, "They didn't know what to do with a black woman, so they lent me out to the city health department. In two years there, I was never offered a cup of coffee from the office coffee wagon. I had to go around the corner to get some. Topeka was one prejudiced town then, let me tell you."

Unwelcomed by most white employers, Topeka blacks retreated into their own world and tried to make do. The principal black businesses in town were beauty and barber shops, barbecue restaurants, after-hours bars, and whorehouses. A black-owned drugstore started up and, serving black clientele only, folded after a year. Few colored retailers could command credit from the banks; few could get management experience at any white-owned store. A hundred or so professionals made a living in town—black teachers teaching black children, black preachers serving black churches, a few physicians tending the black sick. The only other work blacks had a corner on in Topeka was the most menial sort: the janitorial jobs in the statehouse, the mop-up work at the hotels, the maids and laundresses and cooks and gardeners and chimneysweeps of the white people. A black laborer was much more likely to find an honest day's work in Detroit or Pittsburgh or back South.

Until the Second World War, black Topeka took it all quietly. Things were worse elsewhere, they said. The head of the local NAACP branch, who had been a lieutenant in the First World War and was the first Negro to work in the Topeka post office, was no firebrand. "We've got to learn to crawl before we can walk," he was wont to say with the solemnity of Booker Washington. The war, though, began to change things on both sides of the color line. Says Tom Lee Kiene, a native Topekan who served seventeen years on the staff of the Topeka *Capital-Journal* before becoming its executive editor in 1959: "Blacks who participated in civic drives selling war bonds or raising money for the Red Cross began to come to banquets—it seemed the patriotic thing to ask them—and we whites started remarking to each other that it didn't seem to spoil our dinners."

In the black community, a few enlightened discontents began to emerge, like Lucinda Todd, an ex-schoolteacher who had been forcibly retired by the then common rule that married women could not teach. Mrs. Todd was especially sensitive to the education her daughter, Nancy, received and was increasingly disturbed when she found that it was not as rich as that offered white youngsters. She had wanted her daughter to play the violin, for example, but there was no musical instruction at any of the black schools. Then one day she saw a notice in the newspaper about a concert by the grade-school orchestra representing all eighteen schools in town, and she exploded. "I got on the phone to the music supervisor," she remembers, "and told him there were twenty-two grade schools in town, not eighteen, and why weren't the black children offered music instruction?" She was directed to the coordinator of black schools in Topeka, who assured her that colored folks did not want music instruction and could not afford to buy the instruments. She brought her case to the Board of Education and won it. There was another time—in 1944, she places it—when Mrs. Todd bought a ticket to the Grand movie theater, the one that admitted Negroes to a section of the balcony, and when she climbed up there the two dozen or so seats reserved for colored were filled, so she took a seat right across the aisle in the white section. A policeman came and told her that she could not do that and would have to sit in the colored section or nowhere. They gave her her money back. "They did things like that all the time," Lucinda Todd recalls. Soon she became active in the NAACP, was elected secretary of the branch, and once had Walter White as an overnight guest in her residence.

But there were few such proud and angry Negroes in Topeka who were ready to do something about their degraded standing in the community. Things would pick up after the war, everybody said. It was no time to rock the boat. In fact, though, very little opened up after the war. Remembers Negro attorney Charles Scott, who went to Washburn Law School after military service prior to joining his father's firm: "You'd look up and down Kansas Avenue early in the morning, and all you could see were blacks washing windows. That wasn't anything, but at least it was work. There was still no chance for a black man to become a bank teller or a store clerk or a brick mason. The few blacks with union jobs at Goodyear almost never advanced, and people were retiring from the Santa Fe shops after holding the same job for twenty or twenty-five years. A lot of hopes got dashed."

The 1950 U.S. Census documents the job plight of Topeka Negroes:

|  | White | Non-white |
|---|---|---|
| Bookkeepers (female) | 541 | 2 |
| Stenographers, secretaries and typists | 2,225 | 16 |
| Bus drivers | 86 | 1 |
| Electricians | 215 | 1 |
| Salesmen and sales clerks in retail trade | 2,158 | 11 |
| Accountants and auditors | 425 | 1 |

| | | |
|---|---|---|
| Plumbers and pipefitters | 197 | 4 |
| Compositors and typesetters | 214 | 2 |
| Pharmacists | 71 | 2 |
| Dentists | 57 | 2 |
| Managers, officials, proprietors (self-employed) | 1,600 | 30 |
| Managers, officials, proprietors (salaried) | 1,684 | 32 |
| Janitors, porters, charwomen | 293 | 318 |
| Private household workers (living out) | 320 | 347 |
| (living in) | 120 | 14 |

What did the black children of Topeka have, then, to look forward to as adults in their own community? It was a question that concerned another group of Negroes in town who were not only not members of the NAACP but stayed as clear of the civil-rights group as possible.

Mamie Luella Williams was, by wide assent, the best black teacher in Topeka.

Tall, straight-backed, passionately dedicated to her calling, devout in her Catholic faith, she taught grade school in Topeka for forty-two years. She taught three generations of some families and two generations of many others. Among the latter were Oliver Brown, the welder in the Santa Fe repair shops who later turned to the ministry, and his daughter, who would become the most famous of Mamie Williams's pupils—Linda Smith (*née* Brown). "She was a brilliant woman," recalls Mrs. Smith, "a staunch, old-time teacher who really made you apply yourself. She explained a subject well and then stuck with you until she made sure you understood it thoroughly. I respected her a great deal."

Mamie Williams was born in Greenwood, South Carolina, one of the bigger hill towns in the upcountry, in 1895, the year Ben Tillman dictated a new constitution for the state that virtually disenfranchised Negroes. Her grandfather had been a tenant farmer, and prospects were not much brighter for her father. Her mother had had the advantage of attending a private school run by Northern white teachers and sponsored by a church group, and she taught Mamie to read at the age of three, the same year the family picked up and moved west to Topeka and a new life. Her father found jobs in the construction field and later settled on the steadier position as custodian at the Kansas Supreme Court. He was always interested in politics and helped turn his daughter Mamie into an active Republican worker in later years, "but he didn't really have the education to aspire to big things occupationally." He had managed to go as far as the sixth grade back in South Carolina—a lot higher than most of his colored contemporaries. Mamie's mother was determined that her two daughters should get all the learning they could.

The family settled in the Monroe Street neighborhood, one of Topeka's several pocket ghettos, just west of the Santa Fe tracks between the capitol and what would become the Mid-America Fairgrounds. There were perhaps thirty-five black youngsters in the immediate area, and almost all of them were pushed hard by their parents to persevere at school. "We didn't spend a lot of time looking for signs of mistreatment and prejudice," Miss Williams remarks in retrospect. "We were consciously trying to improve ourselves. One of the sayings you would hear a lot was that Lincoln lived in a dirt house but he wasn't a dirt man." At sixteen, she became one of three black girls among the ninety-two to graduate from Topeka High School that year. At Washburn University, about a mile and a half from her home, Mamie Williams won departmental honors in mathematics and German and studied Greek as well. There were no other Negroes among the ninety in Washburn's graduating class of 1915. She went down to the high-school department at little Lane College in Jackson, Tennessee, about sixty miles out of Memphis, and taught everything—English, rhetoric, algebra, Latin, history—and kept growing intellectually. In 1918, she went home to Topeka and a teaching job at the colored Buchanan School about a dozen blocks from where she lived. Scraping and skimping, she put aside enough money to ride the New York Central to New York for four summers of study at Columbia University. "I loved it there—the freedom of it," she remembers. "I explored everything I could—the theater, concerts, the city . . ." And she perfected her skills. Columbia was the last word in educational psychology and theory. She was taught how to respect the teachings of the home, yet build upon them and supplant them when required. She learned how to cultivate pupil interest in every subject "from a toad frog on up to God."

Mamie Williams became a master teacher. A forceful taskmaster and disciplinarian, she was no ogre. Her classroom was never a place for rote learning, and she readily acknowledged that "children with their sincerity and candor can teach adults something new every day." She was a great one for mottos. One of her favorites was: "Life is infinitely rich in fine and adequate compensations. Never a door is shut but several windows are opened." Mamie Williams was a window-opener. She designed special projects of the kind she had heard about at Columbia. One of the most popular was a communal lesson in self-government: the whole school was organized like a state, with a constitution, by-laws, officers, and a legislative council. There were campaign speeches and elections, rousing inauguration ceremonies, and regular legislative reports to be filed and posted on the bulletin board in every classroom. And she organized a "Little Theater" project for which her pupils dramatized stories they had read together in class. One time, she turned her classroom into an art gallery; those who liked to draw contributed their own works, the others brought in what they liked from magazines or other sources, and everyone was excited and stimulated and learned how widely human notions of beauty can vary. Yet Mamie Williams had time to participate widely in her community, and it was not a community defined by the color of her skin. She was on the public-affairs committee of the Topeka YWCA, she worked with the American Association of University Women, she put her faith into practice in fellowship work at the Assumption Catholic Church, she became historian and chaplain of the

Shawnee County Women's Republican Club. She traveled summers and lectured with slides when she got home. She would eventually be sent by the governor of Kansas as one of three representatives from her state to a conference in Washington of the President's Commission on the Status of Women. And in 1968 she was invited to the Inaugural Ball of the President of the United States. The invitation hangs framed in the foyer of the house she has lived in on Quincy Street since 1928.

The very suggestion that her pupils were any the worse off for attending all-black schools riled Mamie Williams. What mattered most in determining the quality of education the colored schoolchildren of Topeka received were the skill and dedication of their teachers. At two of the four black schools in town, more of the teachers held master's degrees than at any of the white grade schools, and their devotion to their work was exemplary. In 1941, a group of Topeka Negroes nevertheless opposed the creation of junior high schools for whites and sued the all-white Board of Education. Mamie Williams was called to testify. They asked her "a lot of unnecessary questions" aimed at establishing that the Negro curriculum was not equal to the one in the white schools and that the teacher load, of both subjects and students, was too heavy. She was not an enthusiastic witness. As she would write for a local Negro newspaper, "Those who are socially informed about people can help them best." Freely translated, that meant colored teachers gave more of themselves to educating colored children than white teachers were likely to. She was saying to her people: We teachers are important. Unspoken was the fear that if the junior high schools were opened to blacks, black teachers would be fired. It was no feckless thought. The courts ruled for the black plaintiff in *Graham v. Board of Education of Topeka* and the junior high schools were integrated. Eight black teachers were promptly fired. Mamie Williams was not among them. Rather, she went up the ladder. Soon she became assistant principal of the Washington School and then the principal. But she still carried her regular teaching load and got no more pay for the honor.

The brief uprising that led to the integration of Topeka's junior high schools did not please the dominant white-supremacist element in the community. In 1942, a new superintendent of schools was brought in who would shortly spellbind the city's civic and commercial establishment with his silver tongue, ambassadorial smoothness, and the iron hand he clamped on the school system. He also made it unmistakably clear that he favored the continuing separation of the races in the elementary schools, and his agents moved forcefully to squelch interracial chumminess at the junior-high and high-school levels. For the black teachers and students of Topeka, the coming of Kenneth McFarland was a dark day. That he would soon become a nationally known and ceaselessly traveling evangelist of four-square Americanism, speaking to Rotary Clubs and Chambers of Commerce across the land under the sponsorship of *Reader's Digest* and later the General Motors Corporation, was an irony no harder for Topeka blacks to swallow than the pledge of allegiance their children offered every morning to the land that brought liberty and justice to all.

Kenneth McFarland had spent almost all of his first thirty-five years in the southern tier of his state that some called the Balkans of Kansas. It was oil and mining country, and the little town of Caney, where he grew up, hard by the Oklahoma border about 140 miles due south of Topeka, was in the poorest sector of the state and the one where anti-black feeling had historically run deepest. He had a strong mother who told him God had put her on earth to bring him up right and she would brook no sass from the boy. He was thirteen before he set foot in Coffeyville, the closest town of any size; it was just seventeen miles from his home. But Ken McFarland determined early on that he would not live an insular existence. He won his bachelor's degree at the age of twenty over at the state teachers' college in Pittsburg, seventy miles to the east on the Missouri line, and then started his swift and restless climb up the professional ladder. He taught history for just a year at a high school on the other end of his native Montgomery County, then became—at twenty-one—superintendent of schools in tiny Quincy, about forty miles farther north near Eureka, for three years while he earned his master's degree from Columbia during summers in New York. At twenty-four, he was chosen high-school principal in Anthony, the seat of Harper County in south central Kansas, and two years later he was promoted to superintendent. But he kept reaching. In 1935, when he was twenty-eight, he was summoned to run the schools in Coffeyville, then a town of 17,000—and the first of the communities in which he had served that was large enough to have legally segregated schools. During his seven-year stretch in Coffeyville, Ken McFarland began to win friends and influence people with his gifts as an orator—he had a thoroughly self-assured manner, a smooth Midwestern voice of the approximate tone and pitch of Hubert Humphrey's, and a delivery that could rattle off gags with the rapidity of Bob Hope, yet thunder with the power and conviction of Billy Graham. He became Dr. McFarland in 1941, winning his doctorate at Stanford. It was no accident that the ambitious Kansas educator had traveled to great universities on the opposite coasts of the nation to earn his advanced degrees. In 1942, he made it to the capital of his state.

Before he arrived, power to run the Topeka schools had been dispersed among committees of the school board. Kenneth McFarland won that power almost at once. "All departments and divisions of the school system were unified under the superintendent, who alone was responsible to the Board for the execution of its policies," according to school-board archives. He was tall, lean, handsome, and prematurely gray, his dark suits, commanding manner, hard line on segregation, and no-frills approach to education made him a prompt favorite with the most conservative element in town.

"He had a powerful need to please," remarks Harry Levinson, who lived in Kansas for twenty-eight years, most of them in Topeka, where he was director of the division of industrial mental health at the Menninger Foundation and was deeply involved in civic causes. Levinson, who later became a professor at the Harvard Business School, says of McFarland: "He had a certain charismatic quality and the kind of educational mentality that likes to pick ex-coaches as principals and administrators. There was a low level of intellectual expectation, though in certain para-education areas like music and journalism there were excellent programs in the higher grades. He was not a thoughtful man, and his educational orientation was vocational." In the view of Ray Morgan, a native Topekan who has covered state and local politics since 1947 and has for years been chief Kansas correspondent for the Kansas City (Missouri) *Star*, McFarland's philosophy "was pretty representative of the entrenched community interests of the town at that time. He was viewed as an efficient school administrator—probably there was a sense that the schools had been a bit too heavily oriented toward college preparation, and he modified that—and a complex man with a great sense of humor and a solid mid-America background. There was talk of running him for governor in the late Forties. Some of his critics thought he was far right politically and a charlatan in his patriotic speeches. I don't think that. I think he was sincere and basically a kind man."

"Kind," though, is not a word Topeka Negroes use to describe the superintendency of Dr. Kenneth McFarland. "Arrogant," "demagogic," and "racist" are the words leading members of the black community use, including those who taught under him. "The power of a school system is in its personnel," McFarland stated as his policy as soon as he took office. "Instructors . . . should work under nearly ideal conditions, secure in office tenure during service, drawing satisfactory salaries, assured of retirement funds, judged professionally for their work." But black Topeka teachers who did not go along with the segregationist line or who otherwise challenged the system faced a swift ax. "Your performance was evaluated each year fifty percent on your teaching and fifty percent on your attitude," says Mamie Williams, "and that was their way of keeping you in line. Since nobody had tenure then and most of the teachers were unmarried women dependent on their salaries for their livelihood, you went along."

The superintendent's main means of controlling incipient militancy within the black school community was a large Negro teacher of often glowering countenance named Harrison Caldwell, who had gone to teachers' college with McFarland and served under him in Coffeyville as overseer of the colored schools. Caldwell, says Mamie Williams, was "a difficult, dictatorial man. The first night after he took over running the Negro schools, he began lambasting the colored teachers. 'There are only two decent teachers among you,' he said and charged us with general inefficiency. Then he got a few of the more pliant old teachers to introduce a motion to separate the black teachers from the Topeka Teachers Association, and it carried." Fear was high because of the eight black teachers fired in the wake of the junior-high-school integration before McFarland arrived, and Caldwell traded heavily on it. Any messing with the NAACP was out. Integration, Caldwell stressed, would mean the end of all black teaching jobs in Topeka. Besides, it would not be good for the race. He was not a subtle persuader. "During the war," recalls J. B. Holland, who began teaching in Topeka in 1940 and served as principal of three schools before retiring in June of 1974, "I was advised by Caldwell that if I saw things his way, I could be kept out of the military. I chose the military." Adds Merrill Ross, a coach, teacher, and later principal in the Topeka system, "He used to delve into your personal life and try to control it. He tried to head off my marriage and then later tried to intrude on it." Ross became convinced that Caldwell was working actively to keep the grade schools racially separate in order to retain his own position of power. "He was a con man, a bigot, but quite articulate, and a number of people in the community admired him. I know, because I had crossed with him, and many teachers didn't trust me because of what Harrison said of me." Mamie Williams made the mistake of asking Caldwell if she wasn't entitled to a small raise for serving as both teacher and principal at the Washington School. "His attitude toward me changed after that," she says.

At the integrated high school, Caldwell played a malevolent version of Father Flanagan to the black students. Outside the classroom, every effort was made to keep the races apart. Caldwell prowled the cafeteria on the lookout for interracial tables. The black students had their own student advisory council and were excluded from the regular school government. After the whites had attended chapel, what the Negro students derided as "the nigger bell" sounded and the black youngsters trooped in to one of Caldwell's "good-nigger assemblies." Recalls Samuel C. Jackson, who attended Topeka High in the Forties and would later become a top official in the federal Department of Housing and Urban Development (HUD) and one of the most highly placed blacks in the Nixon administration: "Caldwell would tell us not to rock the boat and how to be as little offensive to whites as possible—to be clean and study hard and accept the status quo—and things were getting better. Those who went along got the good after-school and summer jobs, the scholarships, and the choice spots on the athletic teams."

Integrated Topeka High maintained two basketball teams, the Trojans with their black-and-gold uniforms for the white boys and the Ramblers in red and green for the Negro boys. There were separate swimming, wrestling, golf, and tennis teams as well, and separate cheerleaders and pep clubs. Worst of all, the black high-school students received no encouragement to hone their talents and aspire to their maximum potential as breadwinners and citizens. Indeed, the black girls were urged to avoid taking typing and stenography since they were left to understand that few jobs requiring these skills would be waiting for them in the community. "Many of the black kids felt resigned to conditions," says Sam Jackson, who later headed up the Topeka NAACP, "and certainly their parents were."

McFarland himself kept his distance and seemed a formidable, menacing figure to the black teachers. "Dr. Mac was a brilliant man," says Merrill Ross. "He could stand up there and introduce ninety teachers without notes and remember all their names and what schools they taught at. But he was a vain and selfish man—a prejudiced man who believed there would be far fewer problems if the races were kept separate." Says Mamie Williams: "He was full of his own superiority." Adds Sam Jackson: "He was an astute and effective leader of the status quo position," which held that Topeka was not ready for integration. He took pains to assure the Board of Education that Negroes received precisely the same educational opportunities that white students did. "He was a very strong man," says Jackson, "a vigorous foe of change—and a bigot."

It is a charge that McFarland might challenge by citing almost any of the literally thousands of public speeches he has given over more than three decades in hundreds of American communities. Starting in the late Forties, even while serving in his post as Topeka's school superintendent, he began hopscotching the country as a "guest lecturer" sponsored first by *Reader's Digest* and then by General Motors and the American Trucking Associations. He would later give as many as 200 speeches a year, his book titled *Eloquence in Public Speaking* would sell more than 50,000 hardcover copies for Prentice-Hall, and a Grand Rapids, Michigan, company would vigorously market eight records of his speeches (sample titles: "Liberty Under Law," "Let's Sell Success," "The MAN in SalesMAN") that bill McFarland as "America's Foremost Speaker." His talks were slick displays of showmanship, full of clean jokes (like "This one fella says, 'How long have you worked for the company?' and the other fella says, 'Ever since the day they threatened to fire me' "), hollow sloganeering ("Let's turn facts into a philosophy of living"), and unquestionably sincere outcries against the moral decline of the breed ("The erosion of individual character is America's greatest internal threat!"). Against Communism, he long urged his listeners to wage "total war" because "we are right and they are wrong" and "we must learn what can't be compromised and what must be conserved" because truth yoked to courage will prevail. On the racial question, he eagerly invoked Booker Washington, who he said told his followers that the way to gain equality is to earn it, to get a job and work at it. McFarland strongly opposed what he believed to be the increasingly widespread idea that "the individual is no longer responsible for his own economic welfare or his moral conduct." Poverty, he declared in his law-and-order plea, was no license to commit crime. "In the Sermon on the Mount," McFarland would note, "Jesus never told his listeners, 'You've got a bad deal.' He wasn't for getting the people out of the slums—he was for getting the slums out of the people!" Equality in America means "equality of opportunity—that's *all* that's guaranteed by our system. Not happiness but the *pursuit* of happiness."

That segregation and the economic racism rampant in Topeka in his years as its most dynamic public official constituted a brutal denial of the equality of opportunity he so fervently trumpeted seemed not to occur to Dr. Kenneth McFarland. By the late Forties, though, a new generation of black Topekans was ready to press the point. It owed its inspiration to a bent little man who nearly alone had fought white supremacy in the area for more than thirty years.

Late in the summer of 1896, the year that *Plessy v. Ferguson* was decided, a handsome, thirty-nine-year-old Congregationalist minister named Charles M. Sheldon wrote another of the sermon-stories that he would read in weekly installments to his Topeka flock. This new one proved especially popular. It dealt with the arrival of a shabby stranger in an unnamed town, but recognizably like Topeka, who was looking for a job and was instead spurned by everyone he approached, including the Reverend Henry Maxwell. The following Sunday, the stranger came forward immediately after Reverend Maxwell delivered his eloquent sermon on the need to follow the way of Jesus and offered his own scorching rebuke to the very proper, and now quite bug-eyed, parishioners. "What do you mean when you sing, 'I'll go with Him, with Him all the way'? Do you mean you are suffering and denying yourselves and trying to save lost, suffering humanity just as I understand Jesus did?" Not at all, the speaker charged, flaying his listeners for their cold, cold indifference to "the people outside the church who die in tenements, and walk the streets for jobs, and never have a piano or a picture in the house, and grow up in misery and drunkenness and sin." The stranger then collapsed and breathed his last at the reverend's home three days later. Profoundly shaken, the clergyman invites members of his church to join him in an extraordinary experiment: for a year they would live their lives the way they supposed Jesus would. A small group takes him up on the idea, beginning with the newspaper editor, who spikes a long dispatch on the previous night's championship boxing match, an un-Christian spectacle if there ever was one. Rich people help poor people in the town's worst neighborhood, and the big railroad company is disclosed to have been engaging in highly unethical practices that must be uncovered at whatever personal expense.

It was in fact a quite badly written religious soap-opera, but it had a poignancy that pleased Reverend Sheldon's listeners. It found another warm reception on the pages of a Chicago religious weekly called the *Advance*, which serialized it but failed to obtain proper copyright protection. And that was unfortunate, for Sheldon's little novel, which he titled *In His Steps*, was soon pirated and published in many editions all over the world. Sales estimates range from a low of 8 million copies to more than 20 million copies in all languages. Sheldon received royalties on very few of them; one exception is the edition still kept in print by the Grosset & Dunlap publishing company. Historian Eric F. Goldman has suggested that the book's great success "in a decade swinging toward reform" may have stemmed from "its reformer's insistence that Christianity means not fear of God but love of the distressed."

Reverend Sheldon practiced what he preached. He made a point of visiting the Negro sections of Topeka and providing what succor he could. In the process, he came across a colored lad named Elisha Scott, who had been born in 1890, the youngest of a brood of thirteen, to a family that had come to Topeka with perhaps fifty other "Exoduster" families from a settlement outside of Memphis. The Scotts settled on Lane Street in the west Topeka section that came to be called T-Town (for Tennessee), and the mother hired herself out as a domestic and the father and the youngsters sold coal by the bushel and herded cattle, and somehow they got by. The Reverend Sheldon spotted young Elisha, who seemed a quick-witted and deserving lad, and after inviting him to his church and meeting with his family, the minister got the boy some decent clothing to replace his well-worn hand-me-downs, put a bit of spending silver in his pocket, and helped get him enrolled and pay his tuition at Kansas Technical Institute, an all-black vocational school. It had been Reverend Sheldon's hope that Elisha might follow in his steps to the ministry, but the young man's interest turned to law while he attended Washburn. He was the only Negro in his graduating class. Nobody held his hand as he began to earn his living in 1916.

He was five and a half feet tall and had dark-brown skin and a deep voice that he loved to use in a courtroom—"he could make one word sound like a paragraph," remembers his daughter-in-law, Berdyne—and he was almost never without his spectacles, wire-frame granny ones and later shell-frame ones that he was finally buried in. As a lawyer, he was a quick study. Much of his early practice was criminal work, defending clients such as the fastidious madam of the nearby whorehouse who burst into his office after she had been raided and complained, "But why did they *do* that? I just had all the girls checked out at the city health clinic and there's absolutely *nothing* wrong with any of them!" Many of his clients were white, especially those whose regular attorneys knew them all too well and fobbed them off on the little colored lawyer in the oversized double-breasted suits.

However thorny the client or hopeless his case, Elisha Scott gave him a run for his money. He had a real knack for selecting a jury, a flair at cross-examining, and a gift for dredging up obscure Kansas statutes to save his clients' hides. He could be truly inventive in the defense of his clients' civil liberties, like the time he represented a seventeen-year-old boy who had allegedly confessed to forgery, and Scott insisted that the burden was on the state to prove that the confession had been obtained without coercion and only after the defendant had been advised of all his constitutional rights—a view upheld on appeal by the Kansas Supreme Court. Or he could be shamelessly emotional, quoting scripture lavishly and falling to his knees dramatically during two- and three-hour-long summations, like the time he begged for mercy for an old former slave charged with first-degree murder of his son-in-law. There were extenuating circumstances that could not be ignored, said Scott: the victim had beaten his wife many times and the defendant had warned him repeatedly to stop or face the loss of his life. "Do not send this poor old man who did only what he thought was right," his lawyer pleaded, "to spend his last years in the bondage of the jailhouse as he spent his early years in the bondage of the plantation." Family legend holds that the jury spent no more than two minutes bringing in a not-guilty verdict on the first-degree murder charge.

He broke through financially in the Twenties by representing a lot of Negro and Indian clients in Oklahoma and Texas who had bought, been given, or been driven off to backland, much of it swampy or without access, that turned out to be the richest oil-producing pieces of earth in the country. The whites, as whites were wont, tried to take the land back or rent it for a song. "Some of these places there'd be thirty wells pumping away at back," remembers Inza Brown, Elisha Scott's secretary in those days, "and all the owners got would be fifty dollars a month in royalties." Scott tried to negotiate better deals for some of his clients, but as often as not his efforts went unappreciated. "We'd get run out of some communities because the people didn't want any trouble," says Mrs. Brown. But those he did represent won concessions, which Scott often had to go to court to get them. In time, the oil companies decided to get the pesky colored lawyer on their side. For a spell, Sun Oil put him on its payroll at $500 a week plus expenses while Elisha tried to buy up oil-rich land from blacks, Indians, and poor-whites at fair prices. In the process, he picked up a lot of new clients, opened a second office in Tulsa, and began to make a little hay.

But there was no way he could or would forget his race. When Negroes rioted in Tulsa, the NAACP called on Scott to defend the arrested blacks. It was a time when he found himself having to sleep in chicken coops for safety's sake, and he would carry what fees he got from other clients in a paper bag because "the banks belonged to the white people" and he was not one of their favorites. Back in Topeka, the Klan got after him for representing a colored worker who had been involved in strikebreaking at the Santa Fe shops. "The Klan was very much in evidence then," says Elisha's second son, John, who recalls that when he was a small boy "we'd watch 'em march down Lincoln, hoods and all. One Sunday afternoon, we went over to a field to see them drilling and marching. It was just like a Legion parade." Their father tried to avoid arousing hostile whites needlessly, though there were times when he shaved it close. Once he had successfully brought suit against a cattle rustler, and a group of white cowboys sidled over to his car outside the courthouse and threatened to rough up the black lawyer. "Well, now," said Elisha, "I've known you boys for a good long time and I know you don't want to really do that," and he kept on talking and talking until one of his would-be assailants finally said, "You know, Scott, you're right—he was a bad old boy, that one you done in."

His fame grew. Mail started to come in addressed simply "Colored Lawyer, Topeka." His impassioned defenses in murder trials drew big crowds. By 1930, he was well-known enough to run for the Republican nomination for attorney general of Kansas—the first Negro to seek state-wide office. He polled 45,000 votes, exactly half the winner's total, to finish third in a four-man race. That didn't hurt business, either. What did, though, was the disorder of his desk. It was a total mess that only he could tunnel through, and when his secretary tried to straighten it or find something on it, Scott would explode. "I'd get fired at least once a month," Inza Brown remembers, "and then he'd call me back the next morning and demand, 'Where are you?' and I'd remind him I'd been fired and he'd say, 'Well, you'd better get down here in a hurry.'" He was on the go all the time, his office and home were open twenty-four hours a day, and he would sometimes forget to feed himself, just as he would forget many of the items that he tossed into the paper stew that collected on his desk. The government, among others, was not amused and twice charged him with failure to pay his income tax. He had to argue hard to hang on to the big house that the family had owned for years and that meant so much to him since his wife's death had left him a widower at thirty-eight. His sister Viola, known to the family as Aunt Duck, took over rearing his three boys, who grew accustomed to having famous visitors stop by for a meal or an overnight stay—people like Dr. Du Bois, Walter White, Charles Houston, or the ex-heavyweight champion Jack Johnson, whose tax problems Elisha had handled and who would come to town for fight exhibitions. It was a close-knit family, and however busy Elisha was or the boys became as they grew, they would all always try to get home for dinner together, a custom that continued for years even after the younger Scotts had married.

In time, Elisha Scott's more eccentric traits, as well as his proven skills (including the ability in his prime years to dictate a deed with every "whereas" in place), turned him into a legendary black Clarence Darrow of the Southwest. He was always paying fines for being out of order. There was the time he lost a case over title to a piece of real estate that he decided was too small to be really bothered about. "To hell with it!" he yelled when the decision was announced, jumped up, jammed his papers into the overstuffed old briefcase he dragged around with him, and growled over shoulder: "Why, I could pee halfway across the thing!" The judge snapped, "Scott, you're out of order!" "Yes, sir," said Scott, moving to the door, "and if I weren't, your honor, I could pee *all* the way across it!"

There was the matter, too, of his drinking. He was a sociable, funny man who loved to play poker when he found the time, but his drinking, everyone knew, was habitual. He was a sipper, not a belter, and he sipped all his adult life, starting first thing in the morning, when he would reach for a little bourbon. He carried a Listerine bottle filled with it wherever he went, including the courtroom. Once, opposing counsel, who did not know of Scott's fondness for the stuff, rose in court and declared with all the righteousness of an ardent Kansas dry, "Your honor, I do believe I smell alcohol in this court." Whereupon Elisha got up, walked over to the other lawyer, gave a big sniff, and said, "He's right, your honor, I smell it, too."

His habits could be maddening. A 1937 memo in the NAACP files from Thurgood Marshall to Walter White read in part:

> This case has been hanging fire in the Supreme Court of Kansas for a long time . . . and I wrote Attorney Scott at least two letters requesting a report on this case. The Newton Branch told me by letter that . . . Mr. Scott would not tell them anything and that there was a move on foot to establish a segregated swimming pool for Negroes. The Branch was opposed to this and told Mr. Scott that they were opposed. However, they believe that Mr. Scott is in favor of such a proposal. . . . I wrote Mr. Scott two more letters and I still have heard nothing from him.

Like Charles Houston in Washington and Marshall working out of New York, but without the education of either or the interplay of friendly minds to help hone his legal thinking, Elisha Scott worked in his sometimes mysterious ways as almost the sole legal arm of the black community in his part of the country. Things got lost on his desk that shouldn't have, and sometimes he looked less courageous than others, but he kept on fighting—against the exclusion of blacks from the swimming pool of Newton, from the kindergarten in Coffeyville, from the junior high schools and the movie houses of Topeka—though he never argued a landmark case in civil rights or civil liberties that got him to the Supreme Court of the United States. He was a foot soldier in the fight for racial equality, not a general, and it was not until after the Second World War that he received any reinforcements. Curiously, one of the first was a white, middle-class housewife who discovered the face of racial fanaticism that Elisha Scott had confronted so often. She never got over it.

A pretty, hazel-eyed, curly-headed brunette of thirty, Esther Brown lived with her husband, Paul, and their family in Merriam, Kansas, a suburban area southwest of Kansas City. White, Jewish, educated at the University of Chicago and Northwestern, Esther Brown had grown up across the river in Kansas City, Missouri, where completely segregated schools were the law. It did not occur to her in 1948 when she drove her black maid, Mrs. William Swann, to her home along the dirt roads of nearby South Park that the schools of Kansas ought perhaps to be desegregated. Certainly she did not know that the South Park school district, which sent its Negro children to a broken-down wooden grade school without plumbing, proper heating, or anything more than a tiny basement room for a cafeteria, was in violation of Kansas state law that permitted segregation only in cities of more than 15,000. But she was shocked by the sight of the school, by the dilapidated Swann home, and, indeed, by Mrs. Swann's whole precarious way of life, though she knew she was paying Mrs. Swann only fifteen dollars a week and that her husband earned only forty-five more as a garage mechanic.

One day, Mrs. Swann told Mrs. Brown that the white folks in her area were meaning to vote a bond issue for a nice new white $90,000 school; what did Mrs. Brown think the colored people ought to do about that? Esther Brown told her the Negroes ought to oppose the bond issue unless the school board agreed to improve that rickety old school set aside for them. Hat in hand, some South Park blacks took Mrs. Brown's advice and went to the white board. The whites responded by installing a new stop sign in front of the school for Negroes. "That really got me angry for the first time," Mrs. Brown recalled long after. She offered to appear before the school board in behalf of the South Park black community, and the offer was accepted. "I went before the most gruesome bunch of people I'd ever seen in my life—I mean these were real lynchers, from the look of it," said Mrs. Brown, whom they nevertheless initially treated with respect. As a gesture of good will, the board offered to install new light bulbs in the colored school and transfer to it the used desks from the old white school as soon as the new white school was finished. Esther Brown left the meeting "nauseated."

The bond issue passed despite Negro opposition. Esther Brown did not know any black people besides Mrs. Swann, but she found herself growing increasingly determined to do something about the black school in South Park. She began to rally the Negro community, and talk of legal action began. The white school-board president, owner of the local feed store which gave a good deal of credit to South Park Negroes who supplemented their scant incomes by growing anything they could in their spare time, caught wind of Mrs. Brown's role and asked her to attend a small meeting at the white school to discuss conditions at the black school. Mrs. Swann told her employer not to go alone, but Esther Brown went anyway and found herself surrounded by an auditorium full of 350 bristling whites. There was not a black face in the house. "All of a sudden we seem to have a racial problem in South Park," the board president declared. "Well, let me tell you that no nigger will get into South Park school as long as I live." Catcalls fell on Esther Brown, and the woman sitting behind her wanted to hit her and had to be restrained, but finally the room got quiet and it was clear that Mrs. Brown was supposed to speak. Terrified, she pulled herself together, stood up, and said, "Look, I don't represent these people. One of them works for me and I've seen the conditions of their school. I know none of you would want your children educated under such circumstances. They're not asking for integration—just a fair shake." More catcalls and many suggesting she go back where she came from. When she cried out that she had been invited to attend the meeting by the school-board head, he denied it and walked off the platform. A minister rose and called for restraint and got hooted down. "I stayed another hour, and when I finally got out of that room," said Mrs. Brown, "I was a changed woman."

She went on a one-woman crusade. The blacks did not know what to make of her. No white person had ever taken their side with such vehemence before. She went to the Kansas City, Kansas, NAACP and asked its black counsel to file suit. He did so, but with what struck her as great indifference. The South Park whites, having earlier promised to build a new black school as soon as the bonds for the new white school were paid off—in thirty years—now responded by gerrymandering the black neighborhood right out of the South Park school district. Esther Brown struck back. For one thing, she fired the first lawyer she had approached and hired Elisha Scott of Topeka to handle the case. Scott, by then, walked with a limp from an auto accident, and the very sight of him startled Esther Brown. "He was a little, bent-over man with a big mustache and big black-frame glasses," she recalled, "and he was disorderly and unorganized and a drunk and one of the ugliest men I'd ever seen—but I think he really cared."

He had, of course, been really caring since before Esther Brown was born. He had also spent a great deal of his own time and money on civil-rights cases and handling indigent clients, and so when he had to file papers and have briefs typed and pay his traveling costs, Elisha Scott did not think it wrong to ask this apparently well-heeled young white woman, who had sought his help, to meet his expenses. "He always wanted money, which surprised me," she said later. "I just assumed a Negro attorney would work for a civil-rights cause for nothing, but Elisha was always needing twenty dollars for a deposition or fifty dollars for a brief—and I didn't have it."

But she went and got it, and a lot more. When school opened in the fall, South Park Negroes boycotted their old rundown schoolhouse. Under Esther Brown's leadership, they set up private schools with qualified teachers in homes and churches around the area, and the white housewife started touring Kansas to raise money for the schools and the lawsuit. "If someone will put me up for the night," she wrote to the NAACP branches across the state, "I have a story to tell." And people she had never seen before got out their good china—"I ate more fried chicken than anyone alive"—and took her to the local church or "Y" to talk about South Park and what it meant to all of them. "I got to adore these people," she recalled, "who fed me and gave me clean sheets and took a chance on me. They were people with no ulterior motives who didn't know what to want, who didn't know what they were missing. Sometimes it seemed as if I cared more than they. I had to pull them, hold them, show them. . . ." She raised $6.21 one Sunday at a church in White City. She raised nearly $400 making a pitch at midnight, with thirty black children in tow, on stage at a Billie Holiday concert in Kansas City. She borrowed money for the gasoline that carried her to all her one-night stands, and when she wasn't on the road she got up early to fire the furnaces at the protest schools she had organized. She got threatened and insulted and a cross burned on her lawn. Her husband got fired from his job, her father-in-law called her a Communist behind her back, she had a miscarriage, and when she called the district attorney of Johnson County to report a threat to burn her house down, he agreed with her that it was unlikely and added, "But if they do, call me." His name was John Anderson and he later got to be the governor of Kansas.

Elisha Scott's handling of the South Park suit drove Esther Brown to distraction, but he got the job done, however late or inept it seemed to her. She appealed to Thurgood Marshall's office for help, and Franklin Williams was dispatched to work with Scott. They won the case, and the black children of South Park were ordered admitted to the white school. Before they went for the first time, Mrs. Brown bought a new dress for every little girl and a new shirt for every little boy. And she brought seven children from one especially destitute family to her home and bathed them and took them to Kansas City University Health Center for emergency dental care "which frightened the hell out of them." She had become, she realized, a full-fledged agitator. She continued to travel, declaring wherever she went, "We have to correct these conditions all over the state."

Flushed with victory in the South Park case, Esther Brown pushed the NAACP in Wichita, the biggest city in Kansas, to launch a suit against segregation. But she was beaten by the teachers, who feared for their jobs. She next invaded Elisha Scott's hometown, and by then not all of black Topeka was fearful of the challenge she posed. "I don't know if we could have done it without her," says Lucinda Todd, then secretary of the Topeka branch. In fact, the uprising had been in the air ever since Elisha Scott's boys, and others like them, had come home from the war.

Elisha Scott, Jr., and Charles Scott had served in the European theater of the Second World War and their brother, John Scott, had served on an aircraft carrier in the South Pacific. By 1948, all three had law degrees from Washburn and their names appeared under their father's on the family firm's letterhead. Elisha, Jr., went off to Flint, Michigan, to take over his uncle's practice, but the two younger boys built up the Scott office and carried on

Elisha's efforts in behalf of the race: John plunged into NAACP work, heading up the legal-redress committee, and Charles got into civic and religious work on a broad scale. They and other liberal veterans of both races joined in forming a local chapter of the American Veterans Committee, a progressive variation of the American Legion, and marched side by side in one Memorial Day parade, to the horror of old-line Topekans, who got the police to raid the AVC clubhouse and remove the slot machine, a principal source of revenue. The AVC nucleus included a number of Jewish staff members at the Menninger Foundation, who were seen as menacing "pinkos" from the East Coast, particularly after the group actively campaigned for Henry Wallace's Progressive Party in the 1948 election and helped the Scotts raise money to cover the costs of their action to de-Jim Crow the public pool in Gage Park and other legal measures. By then, too, a yet younger group of vocal Negro discontents such as Sam Jackson was coming of age. But as a whole the black community in Topeka still saw the Scotts and their crowd as troublemakers.

The displeasure was mutual. "Complacent and apathetic" is how Charles Scott describes the rank and file of colored Topeka then. His brother John suggests that most Negroes in town were still hoping for a turnaround in the employment situation and feared that any show of militancy on the civil-rights front would compound the problem. "The ruling ambition was to be able to finance a house and a car, go to church, and get their kids a decent education—and that was enough," adds John Scott, who would later go to work as an attorney for the Department of the Interior in Washington. "Anything or anybody who was going to interfere with that was rocking the boat. Bear in mind that the indigenous Midwestern Negro is very different from the Eastern or Southern Negro. Sectionalism applies to blacks as well as whites."

What this meant was that the aspiring black citizenry of Topeka suffered from the limbo status that E. Franklin Frazier acutely described in his most controversial book, *Black Bourgeoisie.* One qualified for the Negro middle class, Frazier noted, by means of one's education, the stability of one's employment, the prestige of one's employer, and one's willingness to conform to the behavioral patterns of the white community. This last characteristic, rather than income level, was critical, for it uprooted aspirants to the black bourgeoisie from their folk culture and drove them to place a priority on features and traits—such as light skin and conspicuous consumption—likely to ingratiate them with the white community. Yet the whites did not welcome them, black frustration and sense of inferiority festered, and a great many Negroes seeking the stamp of membership in the great American middle class became fringe people, living in a world of make-believe between the whites who would not accept them and their black brothers who seemed to have nothing to offer them but soul and woe.

That little leadership came from the blacks best trained to supply it was particularly apparent among the three dozen or so colored public-school teachers of Topeka, who wanted no part in any drive to desegregate the grade schools and rid the high school of its racist practices outside the classroom. They were hardly unique. Dependency of black teachers on white financial support for the continued practice of their profession had been nearly universal since the start of public education in America. Whites ran the schools, along with everything else, and blacks who did not approve of prevailing racial separatism could go seek their livelihood in other fields. This obligatory knuckling-under was demanded as well by the presumptively openhearted white philanthropic organizations of the North that shipped money and schoolmarms into the South after Reconstruction to keep alive among blacks the flame of learning that the restored white-supremacists would just as soon have quenched for good. The price for being allowed to maintain their do-gooding operations in the South was that the philanthropies could in no way encourage racial mingling or policies that would basically alter the humble position of the Negro. The Peabody Fund, for example, probably the most influential of the early philanthropic organizations, exerted heavy pressure on Congress in 1875 to remove the federal prohibition of segregated public schools from the proposed Civil Rights Act of that year. The Rosenwald Fund, which succeeded the Peabody as the most active white group in the education field, aligned itself firmly with Booker Washington's teachings and withheld its support from black militants. "It has not been necessary, of course, for the foundations to make explicit demands upon the Negro teacher or intellectual," Frazier remarked, for every black teacher or intellectual "realized that if he were to secure employment, he must indicate that his ideas of racial adjustment conformed to the social philosophy of the foundations."

It was hardly surprising, then, that as the NAACP reorganized itself in Topeka after the war, no black teachers joined it. It was a threat to them in more ways than one. Most obvious was its growing interest in ending segregated schools. Lena Burnett, wife of the late McKinley Burnett, who took over as president of the Topeka NAACP in 1948, remembers her Quincy Street neighbor Mamie Williams asking her in that era: "Do you think the white people would have me teach their children?" And Mamie Williams (who disclaims asking the question) was the best black teacher in town.

Even if some black teachers might have been retained, there was the unspoken fear that they might not measure up in open competition with their white counterparts. It was precisely such a fear that drove many members of the black bourgeoisie into tacit, if not active, approval of Jim Crow practices and institutions. Black teachers, professors, ministers, doctors, undertakers, and insurance men thrived in blacks-only enterprises, never knowing—and not particularly eager to find out—how they would have prospered if forced to plunge into the integrated mainstream.

McKinley Burnett was one member of the Topeka black bourgeoisie who curried favor with neither the white establishment nor the colored professional world, though he had to get along with both. Son of a slave, grandson of a white slaver, Burnett was fifty-two years old when he took over the leadership of the Topeka NAACP in 1948 and maneuvered it onto a collision course with white racism. He had worked in the Santa Fe shops for thirteen years and in the back of the Palace clothing store on Kansas Avenue for a time before landing a job with the government supply depot opposite Forbes Air Force Base, where his sub-literate white supervisor was continually asking Burnett to read to him the latest instructions or requisition forms of the day. When he urged the depot to hire colored secretaries, Burnett was marked as a troublemaker and ostracized. Things were a bit better when he moved to the big VA hospital on Gage Boulevard as stock clerk, one of the ranking black jobs on the 1,000-man staff of the institution, but Burnett's leadership role in the NAACP soon evoked hostility there as well. "Hostility was the *only* response that black pressure produced in the white community," commented his widow more than two decades later.

The black community was not notably more cordial. The NAACP meetings that Burnett chaired rarely drew more than a dozen or so people and usually degenerated into gripe sessions. But Burnett was a fighter. As the school year got under way in the autumn of 1948, Burnett and his main NAACP co-worker, a young father of seven named Daniel Sawyer, presented a petition to the Topeka Board of Education in behalf of what they called simply "The Citizens' Committee," since mention of the NAACP, it was presumed, would have earned the back of the school board's hand. The petition was a bold attack on the McFarland-Caldwell administration of the schools. Caldwell, as director of Negro education, was denounced as "a stumbling block to our progress" who had reduced the morale of colored teachers "to an all-time low" and "attempted to invoke social and economic sanctions on all who oppose his methods and policies of fostering more and more segregation in the senior high school." But Caldwell was not the principal target of the petition:

> . . . Our main complaint is against Dr. McFarland, whose willing tool he is. Dr. McFarland says: separate schools are here to stay. Regardless of added expense, the extra drain on a short supply of teachers . . . [r]egardless of the national trend toward integration; regardless of the fact that separation in our schools prevent[s] the educational processes from acting positively in the field of race relations, and sets up another barrier to American unity, and hampers our leadership in world affairs. Dr. McFarland says separate schools are here to stay, and separate secondary schools are in the plans. To which Mr. Caldwell says: Amen!
>
> There is one thing we have learned, however. Things and conditions don't remain static because a few well-placed people will it so. The world is in the midst of a mighty upheaval and conditions change in the twinkling of an eye. Consequently we believe the segregation policy in Topeka schools [is] subject to change. . . . We therefore pray that the Board will take cognizance of our petition and instruct its agents to adopt policies which will be an inspiration to all the people regardless of race, color or creed.

The school board was unmoved. McFarland, in the view of the NAACP people who came before him during the next two years, was skillful at patronizing the black petitioners. Topeka wasn't ready for integration, he held. The board itself was less suave. "They were just as insulting as they could be," Lucinda Todd recalls. "I remember Mr. Burnett standing up at one meeting and saying that we paid taxes just like everyone else—and that he paid the same twenty-five cents for a loaf of bread—and that he was entitled to the same rights as anyone else. This got one of the board members so angry that he jumped up and said, 'Let's go outside and settle this matter right now.' And Mr. Burnett, just as cool and dignified as could be, said, 'I don't settle these matters that way. I settle them by legal means.' "

In the fall of 1950, Burnett made his last attempt to win over the board. He came in front of the members before the school term began and restated his grievances. "I told them, 'It may sound rather abrupt,' " he later recalled, " 'but you've had two years now to prepare for this.' As soon as I sat down, one of the board members jumped up and roared, 'Is that a request or is that an ultimatum?' He roared so loud and so quick that it rather frightened me. . . ." But not enough to deter the course of action he had settled upon, for what Burnett had delivered to the Topeka school board was indeed an ultimatum. There had been time enough. On August 25, 1950, Lucinda Todd as secretary of the NAACP branch wrote to Walter White in New York, saying that the school situation in Topeka had grown "unbearable" and the branch was prepared to go to court to test the Kansas law that permitted it. Burnett in a separate letter to White reported that the school board had turned down his latest request to end segregation and "told us that they would not change their position till the law was changed and told us to go to the Legislature and have a new law drawn." But the Kansas law clearly gave the Topeka board the power to end school segregation any time it chose. "Words will not express the humiliation and disrespect in this matter," the resolute Burnett added.

Wheels began to turn in Thurgood Marshall's office. Robert Carter was in steady touch with Burnett's legal committee, headed by an ex-fireman named Charles Bledsoe, who had put himself through Washburn Law School by attending night classes for over half a dozen years, but whose letters to Carter suggested only a primitive grasp of the constitutional issues involved. Bledsoe invited John and Charles Scott to join him in drawing up the legal papers, and while the brothers were dubious—as was their father—over the psychological approach that the New York office was now taking, they deferred to more experienced heads. Their draft, after months of research, required a good deal of sharpening in New York.

While the legal paperwork moved ahead, Burnett tried to rally the black community behind the suit. For all his dedication, though, he was not a dynamic leader, and he was in bed a good deal of the time in a recurring struggle against leukemia. The white newspapers, as usual, gave very little coverage to black affairs in general and NAACP activities in particular. And black groups were openly hostile. One Negro PTA sent a letter to the school board endorsing its position in favor of retaining segregated grade schools. A group of colored teachers, including McFarland's aide Caldwell, was invited to the Scotts' law office, advised by Burnett that the suit was proceeding, and urged to lend support. "All it did was to draw the lines tighter," Mamie Williams remembers. "One of the NAACP people was outraged at the situation, saying, 'Imagine, our children have to go right by these white

schools and go to separate black schools'—as if that was a dreadful thing."
Comments J. B. Holland, then principal of the Monroe School: "If they were
going to sue for integration, I thought they should have gone all the way—for
teachers as well as pupils." No teacher joined Burnett's crusade.

But he had to have plaintiffs. Lucinda Todd, the NAACP branch
secretary, was one. She went over to the Lowman Hill elementary school, the
white one nearest her home, and asked to have her daughter, Nancy,
admitted. That would not be possible, she was told as she had expected to
be—it was an exercise the lawyers thought appropriate. Not all the plaintiffs,
though, came from the local NAACP membership. Indeed, the man they
picked to head the list was not a member. But Oliver Brown had other
important qualifications for the honor that most Topeka Negroes viewed as a
hollow one indeed. A thirty-two-year-old veteran, he had worked for several
years as a welder in the Santa Fe shops and had the advantage of union
membership to protect him against the possibility of economic reprisal. Then,
too, he was an assistant pastor and sexton at St. John AME, the
substantial-looking stone church at Topeka and Seventh, just a couple of
blocks from the capitol. The black Methodists were the establishment church
in Topeka, and few of its members had anything to do with the NAACP.

Lena Burnett remembers Oliver Brown as a diffident participant in the
suit. He had come once to give the opening prayer at an NAACP meeting
and then disappeared into a back room without joining the working session.
But his lack of militancy was viewed almost as a virtue by the NAACP
lawyers. A quiet, nice-looking, hard-working, somewhat withdrawn man, a
lifelong resident of Topeka whose wife had been the black beauty queen of
the high school just before the war, Ollie Brown would prove no lightning rod
to the white anger the suit would likely arouse. Recalls Mamie Williams, who
taught him at the Buchanan School: "He was an average pupil and a good
citizen—he was not a fighter in his manner." Adds Sam Jackson, who was a
law student at Washburn while the case was being prepared in the Scott
office, "He was no longer willing to accept second-class citizenship. Oliver
Brown wanted to be a whole man."

The case was officially filed with the United States District Court for
Kansas on February 28, 1951. Its title was *Brown v. Board of Education of
Topeka.*

Trial was set for June 25, just a month after *Briggs* was heard in
Charleston. On June 13, while the *Briggs* decision was being awaited, Robert
Carter sent a memo to Thurgood Marshall on his estimate of *Brown*:

> . . . The more I think about this case, the more importance I think it will have
> on our main objective of securing legal support for our attack on segregation.
> . . . Our possibilities for winning here seem much better than they are in South
> Carolina. . . .

He was half right.

# 17

# The Menninger Connection

Thurgood Marshall did not go to Topeka.

In Charleston, his had been the dominant personality, though he had left most of the work with the witnesses to Robert Carter. But the press of litigation at the Legal Defense Fund had become so great that the time was plainly past when Marshall could handle every major case himself. The drive against school segregation, it was decided, moreover, would require a small constellation of suits, presenting the question to the Supreme Court in a variety of civic settings, so that the Justices could not shrink from confronting it directly in at least one of them. Test cases were being explored in Atlanta, New Orleans, Virginia, and Delaware, among other places, and Marshall saw that he had to give over some of the responsibility he himself had shouldered until now to his lieutenants. Of them, Bob Carter was the most clearly qualified.

He was also the closest thing to a militant among the lawyers then involved in the drive for racial equality. His upbringing north of the Mason-Dixon Line had given him more than a glimpse of how white America lived, and all his life he would resent settling for anything less because he was born black.

He was not yet a year old when his father died in 1917 of a ruptured appendix, leaving Annie Carter a widow at the age of thirty-three with eight children to raise in the Central Avenue section of Newark, New Jersey. She had already lost one child, and four of the others would die from pneumonia, tuberculosis, and other diseases that strike the poor with special intensity, but Annie Carter never surrendered to despair. By day, she worked as a domestic; by night, she did the family's washing and ironing and took in outside laundry as well. She would not seek or accept government assistance because, as she would say on approaching her ninetieth birthday, "I wanted to be independent." She also wanted her children to have a better life than she did, and that meant they would all have to pull together during those growing-up years. "I told 'em I'd do my part and they had to do theirs," she says. "I felt a mother should live so her children wouldn't be ashamed of her—and the other way around."

Annie Carter sent her kids off to school neat and clean, if occasionally in the old clothes of her employers' children, which she accepted not as charity but as a form of payment for her services. The kindness of some whites for whom she worked prevented Annie Carter from ever becoming a hater. One woman in particular took an interest in her struggle to keep her family together. On any given day, she might offer Annie one of her daughter's dresses from the previous year or "come back from the grocery with a mess of potatoes and ham and cabbage and say to me, 'Annie, you take this home and cook it for your family.'" Eventually she was invited to the wedding of the family's daughter. "If you got to work for good people who thought you were human and trying to do the right thing, they'd try to help," she reflects. "But of course there wasn't no money ever in that kind of work."

Annie Carter channeled all her hopes and dreams in life into her children. And the principal beneficiary was her last-born, Robert. As the baby of the family, he got away with a few less chores than the others but did not squander the advantage thus permitted him. He was a serious-minded boy and a religious one in a churchgoing family that felt early on he was destined for the ministry. He was always reading the Bible—"There wasn't many things in it he didn't know," his mother notes—or some other book, though he was by no means unathletic: he liked to play tennis and swim but his lithe physique suggested he would never become a bruising athlete. "I knew I wasn't a physical kid," Carter recounts. "I knew I had to get an education." As a grade-school scholar, he did well indeed, being pushed by some of his teachers until one day in an eighth-grade English class he handed in a book report on Virgil's *Aeneid.* Required to explain his choice, young Bob defended his precocious reading taste by writing that he thought it would help him get into college—"only I spelled it 'colle*dge*' and the teacher read my paper out loud, without giving my name, and with so much sarcasm that she had the whole class in hysterics." It was a searing moment for the boy. Later, when the teacher learned that he was earnest indeed about going to college, she did her best to discourage him. "I didn't appreciate *that,*" Annie Carter remembers and told her little one, on whom the family's hopes now centered, "You go back and tell her your mama said you are *goin'* to college!"

At Newark's Barringer High School, which few Negroes attended, Bob Carter's first report card showed five 10s and one 9—almost perfect. "He was an A-plus student on the super-honor roll during all three and a half years in high school," says his sister Alma with retrospective pride. Most of those high-school years were spent in suburban East Orange, a growing town with a sizable black population, to which Annie Carter moved her household to escape the encroaching decay of downtown Newark. "Everything we'd built could have been lost in that old neighborhood," she says. "The children could have been hurt by it." At East Orange High, Bob found black companionship and a good deal more prejudice than he had faced at nearly all-white Barringer. In order to graduate, for example, every student had to pass a swimming test, but the high-school pool was closed to black youngsters except on Friday afternoons. Then one night the newspapers disclosed that the New Jersey Supreme Court had outlawed such restrictions; Bob Carter and a friend were the first ones in the pool the next morning.

Sending him to college was a family project, and they all took pride in his academic achievements at Lincoln University. His record there earned him a scholarship to Howard Law School, where he fell under William Hastie's tutelage. All Annie Carter's friends had had their hearts set on his becoming a minister and bemoaned his career decision to her. "I'd tell them, 'Well, they're all big liars—lawyers, ministers, what difference does it make?' " she laughs with gusto. The point was that after all their struggle her boy was becoming a professional man. She would live to see him argue before the Supreme Court of the United States and be elevated to the federal bench.

The Second World War almost upended Bob Carter's career. "I thought I was pretty well balanced regarding the race problem," he recounts in carefully chosen words, "but once I got in the Army, the thing was ground into my face everywhere I turned: blacks acting as lackeys to whites, and whites acting oppressively toward blacks." As a private in the Army Air Force, he was shipped to Daniel Air Force Base in Georgia, where Negroes were used to keep the field clean and the base commander took the view, as far as Carter saw, that it was a waste of time to educate colored troops. "While I was a private, there wasn't much I could do to fight the system," he says, "except to goldbrick, which I did." When black applicants were sought for officer-candidate schools, Carter applied, graduated, and got assigned as a trial judge advocate to Harding Air Force Base near Baton Rouge, Louisiana, where in no time his insistence on being treated as a full-fledged lieutenant in the American armed forces got him pegged as a troublemaker. He had the nerve to enter the officers' club, for one thing. For another, he did not appreciate a couple of racist remarks that were made to him by a pair of white enlisted men who passed him one day while he was in fatigues, and Carter pressed charges against them. Then there was the hassle with the colonel who came with clattering brass into the barracks washroom one night looking for some clothes hangers. "This sure is one helluva place," the colonel said to Carter, who was there in his pajamas, his rank undetectable. Lieutenant Carter agreed with that estimate—a reaction that infuriated the colonel, who had of course expected him to scurry about in quest of hangers. He shortly charged into Carter's room and chewed him out for bad manners; Carter told him to learn some manners of his own and quit pulling rank over such a small thing. In swift order, he was being denounced as an uppity nigger and instructed to live off the base, the way every other colored man connected with it had to, but he refused and promised to protest to Washington if the issue was forced. Transfer to Columbus, Ohio, followed, and for a time superior white officers tried to cozen him—"until they found out that I wasn't going to be anyone's stool pigeon and that I had some quite firm ideas about racial prejudice, after which they became very unfriendly," says Carter.

They kept yo-yoing him around the country. Finally, at a base in Michigan, he defended a black soldier charged with raping a white woman, and Carter effectively demonstrated that the alleged victim was a thoroughly practiced prostitute. "They were furious with me," he remembers, "and would have court-martialed me if they could have." In fact, effort was made to get him discharged in a category neither honorable nor dishonorable that would have put him back in draftable status. Carter appealed to his mentor from Howard, Bill Hastie, whose ties to the Secretary of the Army's office helped get the review board to quash the recommendation. Shortly thereafter he was mustered out and joined Thurgood Marshall's office.

Bob Carter had no special thirst for power. He was content at first and for a number of years to master his trade. Marshall saw him as a well-organized scholar with better than passable skill as a writer of legal briefs and began to lean on his talents. "He was a very good, very dedicated lawyer, and much more introspective than Thurgood," remarks William Coleman, "but he was not as good a lawyer." Carter's industriousness and basic skills were universally acknowledged, but some of those who worked with him were bothered by other traits. Some thought he took criticism badly. Some felt he was peremptory with junior lawyers. There were questions of a temperamental nature and stubbornness. Remarks one outsider who saw him close up over a number of years: "He was a man limited by rigidities of approach and his own doctrinaire framework." Comments another veteran NAACP legal counselor: "He was good—but not as good as he thought he was." The other side of the coin suggests that Carter stuck his neck out farther than most of the lawyers who participated in the NAACP effort and left himself a sitting target. Carter felt that Marshall wanted him to function as a gadfly within the Fund councils, and as a result he earned the rebuke of some, such as one professor who recalls, "Bob was frequently saying ill-considered things." Whether they were ill-considered or simply unconventional, they served to label Carter as more hot-blooded advocate than cool analyst. Yet a less fervent man might have buckled before the criticism that was directed at Carter for getting Kenneth Clark and the other social psychologists into the school cases with both feet. To the legal purists among them, the introduction of social science that Carter persistently favored seemed something of a gimmick and perhaps beneath the dignity of the profession. It was not Carter, perhaps, who suffered from a rigidity of approach.

As early as 1946, Carter had explored the argument that segregation *per se* was unconstitutional. That year, he authored an *amicus* brief in a case before the federal District Court in California—*Mendez v. Westminster*—in which separate schools for children of Mexican ancestry in Orange County were challenged as a violation of the Fourteenth Amendment. Though the separation was explained by the alleged language handicap of the Mexican-American youngsters, none of them was in fact given a language proficiency test, and school assignments were made on the basis of Latin-sounding last names. Surprisingly, the District Court held that separate-but-equal schools were unconstitutional, but the Court of Appeals for the Ninth Circuit ruled for the Mexican-American children on the ground not that *Plessy* was invalid but that there was no California statute that authorized segregated schools. Carter's brief was a useful dry run, though, for it tested the temper of the courts without putting the NAACP itself directly in the field and, as important, it drew added attention to the case in a number of the leading law reviews across the country.

It was not until 1950, though, that Carter began to come into his own at the Fund. Franklin Williams departed in the middle of the year and by then Carter had argued and won his first case before the Supreme Court—*McLaurin*. It seemed a key case at the time because it was the first one in which the NAACP felt it had isolated the segregation question, since there was no question that the University of Oklahoma was supplying the sixty-eight-year-old black graduate student with physically equal facilities even while segregating him within the white school. It was a tricky case, though, and Marshall had run into considerable opposition from his advisors, who felt the Court might well vote against the NAACP position. Carter argued it before the Court the same day that Marshall argued *Sweatt*. "I was frightened but arrogant," he remembers. The case came up with fifteen minutes left in the Court's day—just enough time for Carter to get his feet wet. He fielded a tough question from Justice Jackson, won overnight plaudits from his NAACP colleagues, and came on confidently the next day with the rest of his argument to win a unanimous opinion from the Court. His stock rose. "The feeling had been that if we could win *McLaurin*," Carter notes, "we could win it all." For if the Court were to hold that a state could not legally segregate anyone *inside* a public institution such as a university because of his race, how could it hold that it was legal to segregate him in a *separate* institution for that same reason?

Having sold Marshall on Kenneth Clark and the theory of blending psychology with the straight legal approach to desegregation, Carter now became the battlefront commander with full responsibility for bringing in experts who would not get the NAACP laughed out of court. In the Clarendon County case, Carter had had plenty of time to assemble his star scholars, but even so it had proven a formidable job. He had been unable to get some of the most eminent people he approached, and there were several dropouts along the way. The problem was compounded in the Topeka case, for it had seemed unwise to line up experts for *Brown* until the effectiveness of the social psychologists had been measured first in Charleston. On balance, it was decided that Kenneth Clark, David Krech, Helen Trager, and the others had done well enough in South Carolina to justify sticking with Carter's strategy.

There was just a month before the Topeka case was to open. Carter assigned his junior colleague Jack Greenberg to a crash program to find experts in the Midwest. There could have been no worse time for such a task than the beginning of June, when scholars traditionally decamp for their summer projects. Greenberg's last-minute enlistees, though, would leave a lasting mark.

The old Constellation in which they flew out to Kansas via Chicago was buffeted in the stormy weather, and by the time Bob Carter and Jack Greenberg got into Topeka on June 21, 1951, they were ready for a little freshening up at their hotel. Esther Brown, the Merriam housewife who had given so much of herself in rallying black Kansas behind the South Park desegregation case a few years earlier, had made most of the hotel arrangements for the expert witnesses the NAACP was bringing in for the *Brown* trial. The team of Carter and Greenberg, though, had given her a problem. The main downtown hotels, the Jayhawk and the Kansas, were Jim Crowed for whites only. She wrote the lawyers asking if they wanted to stay at a colored hotel. "Not knowing the situation in Topeka," Carter wrote back, "we do not view the prospect of staying at a colored hotel with happy anticipation. There is no reason for Jack to stay in a colored hotel . . . however, he feels that it would be advisable for the two of us to be together."

She booked them into a colored hotel. When the New York civil-rights lawyers checked in, they were stunned at its dirtiness. In the bathroom, Greenberg reached up for the light cord, yanked, and a small part of the ceiling came down on them. They promptly arranged to move to the home of one of the Topeka NAACP branch members.

It was just as well because the New York and Kansas lawyers had a lot of quick synchronizing to do. "We didn't know how the case was going to be presented," recalls John Scott. It was clear to the two men from the New York office that they could brush the Topekans aside only at their own peril. It was the kind of situation that Thurgood Marshall handled with a few big laughs, a couple of drinks, and a painless passing show of expertise. Neither Carter, with his quite deliberate speech pattern, nor Greenberg, whose staccato Eastern tones sounded alien to the Kansas ear, had the sort of personality to mesmerize the Topeka people, whose pride in their own skills and in their standing in the community would not let them relinquish a voice in directing the litigation.

"They listened to us," says Scott, "and took some of our suggestions, such as on the order of the local witnesses," but Carter, who struck them as a bit overbearing at first, soon established his command. "He knew what he wanted and implied that this was the way it was going to be," Scott remembers. In the background remained Elisha Scott, who found the legal theory of the case, with all these psychologists and other high-domed types being shipped into town, a lot of confounded nonsense.

At the pre-trial hearing the next day, Carter and Greenberg got their first look at two-thirds of the three-judge panel that would hear the case. It was both sobering and encouraging.

Judge Walter August Huxman, a member of the United States Court of Appeals for the Tenth Circuit and the sixty-three-year-old embodiment of almost everything Kansas prided itself on, presided over the windowless third-floor courtroom of the architecturally neuter federal office building on Kansas Avenue a couple of blocks north of the state capitol. Once, for two years during the Depression, he had been the governor of Kansas—a rare achievement for a Democrat. But, like most Kansas Democrats, and most Kansans, he was a conservative and a tight man with the dollar, especially the public's. "Personally, I believe in an old-fashioned kind of government," he would remark in his later years. "If you don't have the money for something, don't spend it." Even his mild social-welfare programs in the 1937–39 term he served in the statehouse, providing old-age assistance, aid to the blind and to crippled children, and a few other measures in keeping with the New Deal that the nation as a whole was embracing, earned him the voters' ingratitude after what observers in both parties agreed was an otherwise exemplary performance as governor. He had grown up on a farm near tiny Pretty Prairie in Reno County in south central Kansas, about thirty miles west of Wichita. It was an era when wheat fetched only thirty cents a bushel and corn a dime, and times would never be truly plush for the Huxmans. The lad had to scrape for an education, teaching for a time on the strength of his "common school" learning, attending the state teachers college at Emporia over summers until he could put aside enough to go to Kansas University for his law degree, waiting on tables and currying horses to meet his costs and then some. Then there were two decades as a country lawyer in Hutchinson, the county seat in his home territory, with spells as assistant county attorney, city attorney for Hutchinson, and a member of the state tax commission—none of which left Walter Huxman with a burning ambition for power. Rather, he loved the good life of Kansas, loved to fish and hunt duck and quail, and slowly accumulated a spread of 4,000 acres in the western part of the state for which he paid no more than $10 an acre.

On the bench, at the height of his judicial career, Walter Huxman was a flinty magistrate impatient with long trials and singularly lacking in pomposity about the exalted position he occupied. The Topeka courtroom in which he now sat was ringed with oil portraits of Kansas federal judges dating back to the beginning of statehood, but Huxman had always refused to pose for his. "Why should I have?" he would ask after retiring from thirty years of judging. "So future generations could pass by and ask, 'Who's that old sourpuss?' " "Sour" was not the word for him. "Dignified," "tough-minded," "expeditious," and "compassionate" would all apply. As a legal thinker, though, he came nowhere approaching the likes of a John Parker. His junior colleague at the pre-trial hearing, U.S. District Judge Arthur J. Mellott, was thought of as rather more the legal scholar and moralizer. Possessor of a full head of majestic white hair, a strong chin, and flashing blue eyes behind wire-rimmed glasses, Mellott looked every inch the titan of Midwestern rectitude. He was also a rock-ribbed prohibitionist and a Democrat. Their third colleague, who would not join the panel until the trial itself began the following Monday, was a recently named District judge, Delmas Carl Hill, who had been an Assistant U.S. Attorney and then state Democratic chairman for several years preceding his appointment. Eighteen years younger than Huxman, Hill had served as counsel to the state tax commission while the senior judge was governor, and before that had apprenticed as a lawyer in the John Brown country of Pottawatomie County, about twenty miles west of Topeka. It was a solid, sobersided panel of respected Kansans the NAACP faced.

Less comforting were the sight and demeanor of the opposing counsel. Lester Goodell was a tall, bony, dark-complexioned man who was always reminding people around Topeka of Abe Lincoln. To less sympathetic outsiders who saw him in court then for the first time, he looked rather like a hawk. As a quiet young man, he had acquired the reputation of competence while serving as prosecuting attorney for Shawnee County, of which Topeka was the seat, and gone on to establish a highly successful local practice that represented a fair number of individuals and firms among the city's merchant class. There was a margin of himself withheld, though, from out-and-out alignment with the policies and politics of his best-paying clients. "He was never merely the establishment's hired gun," remarks a Kansas law professor with the vantage point of seven years of well-placed legal service in the statehouse. Goodell, moreover, had been friendly over the years with Elisha Scott. "They would fight a lot in court and quote the Bible at each other pretty fierce," says John Scott, "but out of court they would drink together, play cards together, lend each other money, and send each other cases. I'm not sure Goodell's heart was really in this case."

There was another matter, too, that shadowed Goodell's performance as counsel to the Topeka Board of Education. Increasingly, the board had come under criticism for handing over total control of the schools to Kenneth McFarland, its eloquent, iron-handed superintendent. And for too much of the time McFarland was out of town delivering his we're-right-and-they're-wrong brand of super-American lectures in Miami, Florida, or South Bend, Indiana, under the sponsorship of General Motors or the *Reader's Digest*, proceeds from which went to supplement his $11,308 superintendent's salary and to help build up the McFarland horse-breeding farm on the western outskirts of town. By then the darling of the downtown financial community and a comforting evangel of hyper-patriotism at a time when McCarthyism was viewed as respectable by large sectors of the public, McFarland seemed on the threshold of a promising political career. But he overreached himself.

Three of the six members of the Board of Education that hired him were up for re-election that April of 1951, and a slate of candidates opposed to his allegedly high-handed superintendency began waging a strong campaign. The McFarland forces took full advantage of their incumbency. Voter meetings were called and held in the schools during school hours, and businessmen allied to the superintendent spoke out in behalf of his administration and the incumbent board candidates. Muscle was exercised on the faculty of the school system, which was charged with campaigning for the incumbents by sending messages home to the voters of Topeka via the youngsters they taught. This charge of inappropriate partisanship seemed to be confirmed by a five-column newspaper advertisement in which the Topeka Teachers Association endorsed the members of the Board of Education as upstanding civic leaders and expressed "complete confidence in our superintendent." The anti-McFarland camp struck back with an ad no smaller that was headlined, "Let's end the puppet government in our schools/Let's get politics OUT of our schools," and asserted: "Our children deserve a better school administration with a FULL-TIME SUPERINTENDENT."

At stake seemed to be the vigor with which the Board of Education would defend Jim Crow schools in Topeka. The previous November, Topeka NAACP lawyer Charles Bledsoe had written Bob Carter, ". . . one of our good friends of the white race has polled every member of the Board of Education; two of them were bitterly against integration, and four of them would welcome a law suit, in order to take the load off their shoulders. . . . We interpret this as meaning that the Board will not wage an all-out defense; but this is opinion only." The key to it all, from the viewpoint of the progressive elements of the black community, remained McFarland. "He held back the tide," Sam Jackson comments. "The school board might have gone along with desegregation when the NAACP came before it if McFarland had not resisted."

On Easter Sunday, March 25, 1951, Kenneth McFarland's standing as an eminent Topekan was shattered. The *Daily Capital* had caught wind of a bill slipping through the state legislature that would have destroyed the right of citizens to inspect the financial records of boards of education in the state. Loud protest headed off the undemocratic step, and the newspaper followed up with an inspection of the Topeka board's official financial audits. The results were a bombshell. "Thousands of dollars of Topeka public school money in the past five years have been spent in a manner considered improper by official auditors," began the front-page exposé in the *Capital*, "and repeated recommendations for tightening control over these funds have not been followed by administrative officials." Thousands of dollars of student-paid fees for activities—the total had come to $75,000 for the previous school year—were retained at the high-school office and spent by officials, often without properly accounting for the outlays, on a wide range of supplies and services, including furniture, typewriters, night-school and summer-school salaries, and an electric range installed in the superintendent's office suite. Among the funds considered improperly expended was a $3,000 purchase from a furniture company operated by the husband of McFarland's secretary, who also functioned as clerk to the school board and business manager of the Topeka schools. State law required that all purchases of more than $200 be made only by a contract duly executed by the school board itself—a provision, the *Capital* disclosed in a front-page story the following week, that had been ignored by McFarland's secretary-clerk-business manager in a number of cases.

Despite howls from the McFarland camp that it had been unfairly smeared, the majority of the voting public sensed that school affairs had been run with a certain arrogance, disregard of accepted financial procedure, and perhaps something worse. Charles Bledsoe wrote Jack Greenberg that "three said-to-be liberals were elected to the school board on April 3; two days later the superintendent announced his resignation as effective on the first of August, 1951." The whole question of financial impropriety would be allowed to drop quietly, and Kenneth McFarland retreated to his farm, which became his home base for an intensified schedule of public speaking under the GM banner.

If the NAACP attorneys had hoped Lester Goodell's defense of school segregation in Topeka would be muted by the outcome of the election results, by McFarland's resignation, or by Goodell's long acquaintance with the elder Scott, they would prove mistaken. From the start, the craggy lawyer with the gray tousled hair pounced on the Negro plaintiffs' counsel every chance he got. Early in the pre-trial hearing, Judge Huxman asked if either side intended to furnish expert witnesses, and when Carter explained their importance to his case, Goodell declared that he would certainly object to that since the determination of what constituted equal protection was "simply a question of law." Huxman avoided passing on the relevance or competency of such testimony ahead of time, but was mightily concerned about how much of it would assault his ears. How many experts did Carter have in mind? The NAACP attorney said about nine.

> JUDGE HUXMAN: Well, the Court feels that nine witnesses on that one issue is too many witnesses. In other words, the issue is whether segregation itself, I presume, is not a denial of due process, irrespective of whether everything else is equal, to that furnished in the white schools, is that not your general contention?
>
> CARTER: Yes, sir.
>
> JUDGE HUXMAN: Because of the effect it has upon the mind, upon the student, upon his outlook; I presume that would be your position.
>
> CARTER: That is absolutely correct, your honor.

Huxman proposed that Carter accept a limit of five expert witnesses, after whose testimony the court would reconsider whether to hear the four others, but in no case would the total exceed nine. Carter, having so swiftly established the main premise of his argument with the presiding judge, was not eager to jostle him, but there was too much riding on the case for him to yield readily. He was there primarily to build a record for the Supreme Court.

> CARTER: Well, I frankly think that we won't have more than nine, but I would just prefer not to be tied down. I am not going to—believe me, your honor, we are not going to parade a lot of witnesses here merely to keep you tied down.
>
> GOODELL: It would be under ninety, wouldn't it?
>
> CARTER: It will be under fifteen.
>
> GOODELL: Nine to ninety.

Goodell kept up his hectoring and small-arms fire throughout the morning. It was plain he meant to win or go down in flames trying.

The courtroom was hardly half-filled—strong testimony to the jumbled emotions of Topeka's black community over the NAACP case—when the three-judge panel took its place on the morning of June 25, 1951, to hear *Brown v. Board of Education.*

Carter led off by calling one of the recently defeated members of the school board, testifying in place of the board president, who had been out of town when a subpoena had been issued to him. The instant Carter began probing to learn why the school board favored segregation—a practice that it was entirely within its power to end—Lester Goodell was on his feet: "Object to that as incompetent, irrelevant and immaterial and invading the province of the court. . . ." Judge Huxman sustained the objection, and kept on sustaining it as Carter raised the same basic question in a variety of forms. The question upon which the case turned, Huxman finally lectured Carter, was what the school administrators of Topeka had been and were still *doing,* "and what they may think about it is immaterial, if they are furnishing adequate facilities. If they are doing that, then what they are thinking about is immaterial."

Carter gave up and called Kenneth McFarland for the first of his two appearances in the case. It was not a useful confrontation for either side. The defanged school superintendent seemed in no mood to be truculent. On his side, Carter limited his questioning to trying to establish that Topeka's black schoolchildren suffered hardships because many of them had to travel a considerable distance to the four colored elementary schools that served them when, had there been no segregation, each of them could have gone to the closest of the twenty-two elementary schools in town. His argument was somewhat dampened by the fact that Topeka supplied buses for the Negro children but did not do so for the white children. Carter asked a lot of questions about school hours until the defense objected and Judge Huxman charged the Negro attorney with going on "purely a fishing expedition." Carter tried to find out a bit about the bus schedules, but again toward no apparent purpose, and was eventually squelched by the bench. Finally, and perhaps in frustration, Carter tried to make a quick showing of unequal facilities by asking McFarland if there were any "special rooms"—rooms set aside for groups of children unable, for one reason or another, to fit into regular classrooms—in the colored schools. No, said McFarland, because there was no need for them. Was there any provision made for serving hot lunches in the elementary schools? No, said the superintendent, except for "health rooms" to feed undernourished children. And that failure to provide hot lunches applied to Negro children even though many of them were too far from home to make it there and back before classes resumed? Outside of the health rooms, McFarland acknowledged, there was no lunch provision for either colored or white children. Then he nicked Carter with, "You understand we have two health rooms for four colored schools, where we have only two health rooms for eighteen white schools." It would have been easier to fluster the Rock of Gibraltar. Having made no headway at all, the New York attorney yielded the floor to his co-counsel from Topeka, who, it had been agreed, would handle the testimony of the plaintiffs.

Most of the plaintiffs had been picked because their children had a long way to go to school, and their grievance in this regard was about the extent of the NAACP case on inequality. It did not make notably moving or convincing testimony.

John Scott, Elisha's thirty-two-year-old second son, who handled a lot of trial work for the family firm now that his father had been slowed down by age and his limp, put on Lena Mae Carper, a somewhat heavy-set woman whose husband ran the laundry room at the Kansan Hotel. Her ten-year-old daughter, she testified, had to walk about four blocks, crossing two major thoroughfares, to catch the school bus that took her to the Buchanan School twenty-four blocks distant. Sometimes the bus came fifteen minutes late in the morning, winters included, and Mrs. Carper would wait with her daughter in a small grocery store and then have to dart out to flag down the

bus. Often when it brought her daughter home in the aftern\
overcrowded. There were two schools, presently open to whi\
about only half as far from her home as the Buchanan Schoo\

The defense had no questions.

Then a child took the stand—chubby, alert Katherine Carp\
of the woman who had just testified. Kathy, who played the pian\ ..cd
to perform, had been eager to be a witness when the plaintiff pa.ents were
polled to find a willing youngster. John Scott began by urging the child not to
be nervous and assuring her that "these gentlemen up here are your friends."
Kathy proceeded to do very well indeed. Asked to describe the condition of
the bus when she caught it in the morning, she said, "It is loaded, and there is
no place hardly to sit." She spoke with a clear little voice that was audible
throughout the chamber. A bit later:

Q. . . . Katherine, I want you to tell these three gentlemen what the conditions
of the bus in the evening are when you go home.
A. Sometimes when I get on the bus it is loaded, and there is no place to sit.
Q. And are the children sitting on top of each other?
A. Yes, sir.
GOODELL: We object to this whole line of leading questions of counsel
testifying rather than the child.
JUDGE HUXMAN: They are slightly leading, but try not to lead the witness. The
objection is overruled.
Q. In your neighborhood, Katherine, do you live in a neighborhood with white
children?
A. Yes, sir.
Q. Do you play with them?
A. Yes, sir.
Q. What schools do they go to?
A. Randolph.
GOODELL: I object to that as incompetent, irrelevant and immaterial, outside
the issue.
JUDGE HUXMAN: Objection to this line of questioning will be sustained.

In view of the basic premise of the NAACP lawyers, which Judge Huxman
had quite accurately paraphrased at the pre-trial hearing, Scott's line of
questioning would seem to have been relevant. To avoid it was almost as if
the court could not quite bear having the antiseptic gauze of the law pulled
from the social infection beneath.

Then it was the turn of Oliver Brown, the principal plaintiff.

It is one of the idiosyncrasies of American constitutional law that cases
of profound consequence are often named for plaintiffs whose involvement
in the original suit is either remote or merely fortuitous. So it was with the
Brown of *Brown v. Board of Education*. Nothing in his background seemed to
suggest that he would stand against the tide of apathy and fear in the black
community of Topeka that had accepted segregated grade schools and
oppressive economic racism since long before Oliver Brown's birth in 1919.
He was a loving and dedicated father of three little girls and very definitely
the master in his own home, a one-story, five-room stone house at 511 First

.reet. It was not a very desirable neighborhood. Railroad tracks bisected the street, and the Browns lived nearly in the shadow of the Topeka Avenue viaduct that spanned the Kaw River a few hundred yards north of their home. It was a racially mixed neighborhood, with Negro, Indian, and Mexican families in the immediate area, but mostly it was white. And noisy, for it was very close to a Rock Island switching yard for the trains that were so vital a part of Topeka's—and the Brown family's—life.

To Oliver Brown's oldest daughter, Linda Carol, the noise became routine but not the size of the trains. "They always looked enormous to me," she remembers. "We used to make up games with the trains and got to know some of the trainmen in the switching yards. They would give us candy sometimes. I remember one very big, robust switchman who always waved at us three girls and yelled, 'Hi, boys!' and we'd always call back, 'Hi, Mary!' He reminded me of Santa Claus. But the most thrilling thing about living near there was when the Mid-America Fair came to town by railroad, and we'd always be the first to know because they'd bring the show cars up on a siding. We loved to see the red-and-yellow cars with the animals and the troupers' quarters and the silver flatcars with the words 'Royal American Shows' on the sides." Life for the Brown girls had its less spectacular pleasures as well. It was a daily highlight when their father would come back from his job as a welder repairing boxcars at the Santa Fe shops about half a mile east on First Street. He would toss his goggles aside, sometimes catch a quick nap to chase the fatigue that his job induced, and then joke with his youngsters over the dinner table, though he was normally a stern man. Friday nights were special times when they would pop corn and Oliver and Leola Brown would reminisce about their own childhood days, and afterward Oliver would be there to hear their bedtime prayers. It was a religious household—grace before meals, the Child's and later the Lord's Prayer before retiring, Sunday School each week without fail—and Oliver Brown gave what he could in time and energy to his work as part-time assistant pastor at St. John AME, the big church about seven blocks from their home.

Linda Brown attended the Monroe School about a mile away. To get to it, she used to walk between the train tracks for half a dozen blocks down First Street to the corner of Quincy, where she caught the school bus. There would generally be movement in the switching yards at that time of the morning, but still she preferred to walk on the grassy strips between the tracks rather than along the warehouse-lined edges of First Street, which had no sidewalks. One bright September morning in 1950 when Linda was seven years old and about to begin third grade, her father took her for a little walk in the neighborhood. They avoided the trains entirely as they headed west on First Street, past where the tracks veer north to the river, for three or so blocks and then turned south onto Western Avenue, a pleasant, tree-lined street of modest but well-kept homes. Her father led her by the hand along Western for three and a half blocks till they reached the Sumner School for white children. Prettier than the plain, dark-brick, and rather gloomy-looking Monroe School for colored children that she attended, Sumner had a little tower on one end topped by a fancy weathervane and at the other end a big wall sculpture of the sun beaming down on a flock of children running, skipping, jumping rope, rolling a hoop, and flying a kite. As they climbed the front steps, there was tension in Oliver Brown that his daughter could detect, even at her age. They were directed to the principal's office, and Linda waited outside the door for a few minutes while her father went in. He was upset when he came out, to judge by his tone of voice, and "quite upset" when he got home.

It is Linda's recollection that a registration notice for all the families in the Sumner School zone had been stuck in the door of every home, including the Browns', late that summer and that her father, simply fed up that September with the long trip that Linda had had to make each day to the Monroe School, tried to enroll her at Sumner in defiance of the segregation rule. When he was refused, according to later accounts of the incident based largely on Linda's recall, Brown took his case to the NAACP, which then began the case bearing his name.

Oliver Brown died in 1961 at the age of forty-two without ever giving a detailed account of his participation in the case, but it is almost certain that the many versions of the story that cast him in the role of heroic leader are inaccurate. This is not to say that he did not step forward when summoned—only that the fight had begun long before and that Oliver Brown was never in the vanguard. The local NAACP under McKinley Burnett, and with the forceful guidance of Esther Brown, almost certainly had taken the initiative in approaching Oliver Brown that summer, as it had several dozen other black parents whose children had to make particularly long trips to school. Litigation had been contemplated for several years, and Oliver Brown, though hardly an NAACP enthusiast, qualified as an ideal litigant. Some who knew him well attributed Brown's uncharacteristic participation in the case to his deep conviction that God had approved it.

Little Linda Brown was shielded from the case, for the most part. At no time did her father sit her down and tell her what it was all about. But she does remember going with him to an evening meeting at the Church of God, where the NAACP's Mac Burnett was a leader of the congregation, and being called up to the front of the room to stand on the podium while somebody demanded of the audience, "Why should this child be forced to travel so far to school each day?" She was not in the courtroom, though, that Monday morning in late June of 1951 when her father uneasily took the witness stand.

He was nervous. And he was not helped much by attorney Charles Bledsoe, whose inexperience was apparent. He left out basic steps in the examination, such as establishing what school Linda attended. Brown failed to speak up firmly enough until coaxed by Judge Huxman, and when he did, his discomfort showed as he said that Linda's school was fifteen blocks away and then corrected it to twenty-one. But then Oliver Brown pulled himself together and got his story out. Linda had to leave home at 7:40 a.m. to get to school by nine. She had to go through the dangerous Rock Island switching yards to get to the bus pickup point by eight o'clock, but often the bus was late and "many times she had to wait through the cold, the rain and the snow until the bus got there." It was a thirty-minute ride to school, and so if the bus was on time, Linda got to wait—sometimes as long as half an hour—in front of the school until it opened at nine. Bledsoe asked him whether his daughter would confront any such hazardous conditions if she attended the nearby Sumner School. "Not hardly as I know of," said Oliver Brown. And how far away was the Sumner School? Seven blocks. Was he a taxpayer, Bledsoe asked. Goodell objected, but the bench let the question stand. Yes, said Oliver Brown, he was a taxpayer. Well, wouldn't he consider it an advantage to have a school in the neighborhood which his children could attend? Goodell again objected and this time was sustained. Bledsoe, getting into the swing of it now, argued with the bench: "If the court please, I believe that is really a part of our case." Huxman dryly remarked that the court would take judicial notice that every parent would prefer to have his or her child attend a school closer to home than one far away. With that, Goodell took over for a brief cross-examination. He referred the witness to a large map of Topeka divided into school zones.

> Q. You say your child goes four blocks to the bus pick-up point?
> A. She goes six blocks to the pick-up point.
> Q. Six blocks, pardon me. Don't you know as a matter of fact that in many, many instances there are children that go to the white schools in this town that go thirty and thirty-five blocks and walk to get there?
> CARTER: I object to that.
> BROWN: Where at?
> CARTER: I see no materiality to this question.
> JUDGE HUXMAN: Objection will be sustained. That is not proper cross-examination of this witness.

With that, Oliver Brown was excused. It was 11:15 a.m. when he left the stand and passed into American history.

Seven other plaintiffs followed in swift and uneventful order, telling the same basic story. Among them was Lucinda Todd, who remembers, "I couldn't wait to get up there—we'd been fighting for this for so long. And so many in the black community had thought we were a bunch of crackpots."

The last of the plaintiffs to testify brought the court up short. He was a small, nice-looking man named Silas Hardrick Fleming, he lived in the Negro section behind the Santa Fe shops in east Topeka, and he explained that it was easier for his two boys to take the public bus than to ride the school bus to the Washington School a dozen blocks from their home. And there was one white school just two blocks from his home and another four or five blocks from it. Then he said he would like to explain to the court "why I got into the suit whole soul and body." Jack Greenberg remembers his heart jumping into his mouth. "We didn't know *what* he was going to say," he recalls. "Sometimes witnesses have a way of giving their lawyers very unpleasant surprises—such as saying they didn't really want to be witnesses or they were testifying against their will. We just held our breath." Then:

> GOODELL: We object to [a] voluntary statement.
> JUDGE HUXMAN: I can't hear what you say.

GOODELL: He wants to explain why he got in with the other plaintiffs to bring this lawsuit.

JOHN SCOTT: He has a right to do that.

JUDGE HUXMAN: Didn't you consent to be a plaintiff in this case?

THE WITNESS: That's right.

JUDGE HUXMAN: You did not?

JUDGE MELLOTT: He said he did, but he wants to tell the reason why.

THE WITNESS: I want to tell the cause.

JUDGE HUXMAN: You want to tell the court why you joined this lawsuit?

THE WITNESS: That's right.

JUDGE HUXMAN: All right, go ahead and tell it.

THE WITNESS: Well, it wasn't for the sake of hot dogs. It wasn't to cast any insinuations that our teachers are not capable of teaching our children because they are supreme, extremely intelligent and are capable of teaching my kids or white kids or black kids. But my point was that not only I and my children are craving light—the entire colored race is craving light, and the only way to reach the light is to start our children together in their infancy and they come up together.

JUDGE HUXMAN: All right, now you have answered and given us your reason.

THE WITNESS: That was my reason.

In order to secure its fall-back position in the school cases—that is, that segregation was illegal if for no other reason than that it invariably produced unequal educational facilities and curriculum—the NAACP legal corps had to have the Topeka system scrutinized for the inevitable disparities. The advantages enjoyed by the white schools proved to be largely cosmetic, but they nevertheless had to be documented in court.

To perform the task, Esther Brown approached a friend who headed a local social-service group called the Jewish Community Relations Bureau of Kansas City, who in turn enlisted the chairman of the department of education at the local University of Kansas City, an institution of exceedingly modest repute. Professor Hugh W. Speer, though, was well trained for the job the NAACP needed done. The department he headed specialized in training elementary-school teachers, and he had earned his doctorate at the University of Chicago by specializing in the evaluation of school programs and facilities. He had grown up in the town of Olathe, Kansas, about twenty miles southwest of Kansas City, and knew the temperament of the region. Before agreeing to the NAACP assignment, he dutifully obtained the blessing of the president of his school and then headed over to Topeka.

The reception he got there was not warm. Speer had of course considered whether the assignment might damage his professional standing and dismissed that as an unwarranted fear. But "one of the first points made to me in Topeka by two school administrators who wished to dissuade me," he later would write, "was that it *would* hurt me professionally." Kenneth McFarland advised him: "Look around the mountain on it first, Hugh." One of McFarland's assistants told him that the NAACP group in Topeka was not the kind of people he wanted to get mixed up with. He also said that the Board of Education had a very skillful and "mean" lawyer. "The same administrator was leaving Topeka to take a position in a large city where he had bought a new suburban home," Speer noted. "He was pleased to find a large new church nearby which was so popular that it had two services every Sunday morning and 'there was not a nigger or a Jew within ten miles.' "

Hugh Speer did not look with favor on such bigotry. He did his best to help Jack Greenberg secure additional expert witnesses and he himself enlisted Dr. James Buchanan, then the chairman of the graduate division of Kansas State Teachers College at Emporia, to join him in the survey of facilities. Buchanan agreed over the direct protest of the president of his college, who thought it would hurt the school's standing with the politicians of the state who funded it. On the witness stand, Speer endured nearly two hours of examination and cross-examination that revealed a remarkably imperturbable man who, while retaining his professionalism, was anything but a neutral observer in the courtroom combat.

Greenberg led him easily through his testimony, which was largely dry and straightforward. The white and colored teachers were about on a par in their professional training and in their pupil load. The colored schools were six years older on average than the white ones, which were therefore naturally valued somewhat higher for insurance purposes, but the auditorium and gymnasium facilities were about equal, and Speer made no serious claim of physical disparities in the school plant provided the Negro children. When it came to curriculum, though, Speer departed from the statistics-crammed testimony he had been giving and became a philosopher of education. If curriculum were defined merely as course offerings, he said, there were no significant differences between the white and colored schools, but "as commonly defined and accepted now," curriculum meant the total school experience of the child, the development of his personality and his social adjustment. His social skills and attitudes, his interests and sense of appreciation were all involved, "and the more heterogeneous the group in which the children participate, the better they can function in our multi-cultural and multi-group society." Then he cut through the jargon and loosed his most telling volley: "For example, if the colored children are denied the experience in school of associating with white children, who represent 90 percent of our national society in which these colored children must live, then the colored child's curriculum is being greatly curtailed. The Topeka curriculum or any school curriculum cannot be equal under segregation."

Having established such an argument, Greenberg then had Speer put endless testimony in the record on the physical features of every one of the fourteen schools—ten white and four colored—the professor had inspected and compared each colored school with the white one nearest to it to show that the white one was newer or otherwise physically superior. When Goodell objected that a similar disparity could be shown to exist between the older and newer white schools, Speer fell back to the segregation-*per-se* argument. The professor was plainly mixing his apples and oranges, but the court in no way discouraged him. At one point, Judge Huxman asked Speer if he were not stating that segregation denied to the colored children of Topeka "the opportunity to mingle and live with white children, which they would otherwise have and that, to you, is an important factor." It was less a question than a paraphrase of Speer's testimony—a sign of sympathy from the bench that helped brace Speer for Goodell's long cross-examination.

Warned by Topeka school people that the defense attorney could be "mean," Speer seemed determined to yield nothing to him. Goodell tried repeatedly to get Speer to say that once the factor of segregation was removed from the equation, the children at the older white schools were no less disadvantaged than the colored schoolchildren, but the professor kept insisting that segregation could not be eliminated as a factor in making such an overall evaluation. They went back over the curriculum question and Goodell tried the same technique: eliminate the racial factor and where did Speer come out?

> A.   In professional circles we have a term called the great *gestalt,* which means the sum is greater—the whole is greater than the sum of the parts, and when we start taking into account only the parts one by one, we destroy our *gestalt* and we cannot make a wise comparison.
>
> JUDGE MELLOTT: What was that word?
>
> THE WITNESS: *(Spelling)* G-e-s-t-a-l-t.

Goodell tried another tack, *gestalt*wise. Even if the Topeka grade schools were not to practice segregation, the adult community did not countenance racial commingling, so wouldn't the colored child have to endure a much greater emotional strain if he had got used to going to school with white children and then later "went downtown and couldn't eat in a white restaurant, couldn't go to a white hotel, couldn't do this and that—couldn't that make the impact greater and accentuate that very thing?" Greenberg jumped in to object. The court held the question to be "purely argumentative," but it was surely no more argumentative than Speer's insistence that segregation produced social maladjustment among schoolchildren. The difference was that Goodell's question assumed that there was nothing unnatural about a system in which a black man couldn't go into a white restaurant, couldn't go into a white hotel, couldn't do this and that. Implicit in it was the whole point of the lawsuit.

As Goodell was completing his cross-examination, the courtroom witnessed its saddest moment of the trial. The witness had been asked whether a Negro child who was obliged to attend a school in which he was heavily outnumbered by whites would not be emotionally upset, and Speer was explaining that

> we have adjoining our campus a demonstration school of 210 students in the elementary grades, and mixed in with them are about ten Negro children, so they are outnumbered in that proportion, and my observation is—and the reports I receive from my assistants are—that these children are very happy, very well adjusted, and they are there voluntarily. They don't have to attend.
>
> ELISHA SCOTT:   I object to that.
>
> JUDGE HUXMAN:   Mr. Scott, are you entered here as an attorney of record?
>
> ELISHA SCOTT:   I am supposed to be.
>
> JUDGE HUXMAN:   Go ahead.

ELISHA SCOTT: I object to that because he is invading the rights, and he is answering a question not based upon the evidence adduced or could be adduced—.

GOODELL: You just got here. You wouldn't know.

ELISHA SCOTT: Yes, I do know.

JUDGE HUXMAN: Objection will be overruled. You may answer.

"It was one of life's most embarrassing moments," Esther Brown would remember. All who knew him—and that included most of the courtroom—recognized that the bent little lawyer was almost certainly under the influence. His objection, interrupting a star witness for the black plaintiffs, made no sense. "He had just come into court and he was perspiring something terrible," Esther Brown recalled, "so he took off his coat and sat down at the counsel table next to his sons, who were having a fit at the sight of him. He knew it was to have been his day in court and that he had been shunted aside."

Walter Huxman, while tolerant, did not quite see the pathos of the moment. He remembered it well, though, nearly twenty years later: "Elisha was a character. . . . He came into court that day drunk as a lord and objected to something. His boys tried to pull him down and they led him outside in a little while. Now Judge Mellott was a strict prohibitionist, and after court that day he said to Judge Hill and me, 'Say, fellas, you don't think old Elisha was intoxicated back there in court, do you?' Well, Judge Hill, he was pretty liberal in that regard and I used to take an occasional highball, so we said, 'Oh, no, Arthur, he wasn't drunk.' We both figured that old Mellott just might push for a contempt-of-court charge against Elisha."

It cannot be said, therefore, that the small, brave ebony lawyer who had fought in the courtrooms of Kansas for the rights of Negroes for thirty-five years did not participate in the most important civil-rights case of his lifetime. It was not much of a contribution, but his sons were of course in the thick of the fight and he had had more than a little to do with that.

To add weight to Speer's already heavy, indeed almost leaden, testimony, Greenberg put on James H. Buchanan, the renegade dean from the state teachers college at Emporia, who compared the landscaping and other exterior physical features of the white and colored schools and stated that an attractive setting was important to a child's disposition to learn. Asked to compare the colored Monroe School, the one that Linda Brown attended, with the nearer white Sumner School, the one in which her father had tried to enroll her, Buchanan said, "Obviously Sumner is a better school than Monroe—a more up-to-date school, a newer school, as I have indicated."

Perhaps the white Sumner School was physically superior to the colored Monroe School in 1951 as Dr. Buchanan testified, but that was not the judgment seven years later when the Bureau of Educational Research at Denver University's School of Education made a study of every Topeka school at the request of the Board of Education. The twenty-three-year-old Sumner School was found to have a weak foundation, improper water-proofing, serious cracking in the walls, and very little playground space; it scored 459 out of a possible 1,000 points on the research group's rating system. The thirty-one-year-old Monroe School was found to be in an uncongenial neighborhood and the site needed extending, but the structure itself was held to be strong, safe, and roomy; it scored 498 on the rating system.

The NAACP's next witness proved easily the most magisterial of the experts Greenberg had collected. Horace B. English of Ohio State University had been a full professor of psychology for thirty years. He had been on the team that developed the famed alpha intelligence tests for the Army during the First World War. He had been president of the American Association for the Advancement of Science, chairman of the professional-ethics committee of the American Psychological Association, a consultant to the U.S. Forestry Service and the West Virginia department of education, a morale analyst for the American occupation forces in Japan after World War Two, and about two dozen other things. He had just brought out a new textbook on child psychology, a subject he had studied for nearly forty years, and he spoke with formidable authority in answer to Jack Greenberg's set-up questions. No, there was certainly no evidence that a person's ability to learn was related to the color of his or her skin. "But if we din it into a person that it is unnatural for him to learn certain things," Dr. English declared, "if we din it into a person that he is incapable of learning, then he is less likely to be able to learn." It was like the myth, he said, that women are unable to master mathematics. And "there is a tendency for us to live up to—or perhaps I should say down to—social expectations and to learn what people say we can learn, and legal segregation definitely depresses the Negro's expectancy and is therefore prejudicial to his learning." Was there any scientific evidence to support his claim that racial origin did not affect learning ability? A good deal, said English, and as one example he cited work he had done in the Second World War with a group of illiterate soldiers who were put into schools to be brought up to fourth-grade literacy standards: 84 percent of the whites and 87 percent of the Negroes successfully completed the work.

Defense attorney Goodell wanted to know whether the professor had ever tested Negro children who had gone to separate schools to determine the effect of segregation on their subsequent record of achievement.

A. I don't believe that I testified on that point, did I?

Q. I didn't say you did. I am asking you if you have ever done such a thing.

A. I have not done such a thing. I am not sure that it is relevant at all to my testimony.

Q. Well, is it possible that you could be in error in some of your conclusions here? Could you be mistaken about some of them?

A. Every man can be mistaken. Certainly I can.

Q. You could be mistaken, couldn't you?

A. Oh, yes.

Q. Have you given this expert testimony around the country in cases such as this?

A. No sir, never before. I teach it.

Q. Now, doctor, the ideal state, if I understand your testimony . . . would be where you had no segregation as far as educational process.

A.  I don't think I said anything about the ideal state.

Q.  Well, it would be better, in other words, is that right?

A.  I certainly believe that things would be better if we had no segregation, but that is not an expert opinion; that is my personal opinion. I didn't testify to that.

. . . .

Q.  And there are some outstanding Negroes in different fields or professions and—who have received their—part of their education—in the deep South in segregated schools?

A.  That is true.

Q.  And yet have achieved great places of importance, isn't that right?

A.  Education isn't the whole answer to ability; it is merely one factor. There are men who are big enough, white or black, to rise above unfavorable circumstances.

Goodell tried the same tactic with Wilbur B. Brookover, a social psychologist from Michigan State College, who testified that segregation persuaded Negro children that they were "a subordinate, inferior kind of a citizen." Had the professor heard of Mary McLeod Bethune of Sumter, South Carolina, who had become a Negro college president? Goodell wanted to know. Or Negro author Richard Wright from Mississippi? Or sociologist Charles Johnson? Or Walter White or George Washington Carver or Langston Hughes or W. E. B. Du Bois or Mordecai Johnson, all of whom had been at least partly educated at segregated schools? Certainly, said the professor, but such exceptions did not disturb his general view. Well, but wasn't it true that many white youngsters also undergo emotional stress and strain in school due to being left off the football team or not being invited to parties and the like? "The differences which you cite," answered Brookover, "are not enforced differences."

It was this point that was made with special stress by Greenberg's next-to-last witness of the day, but with two distinctions. The witness could claim a tie to Topeka's most famous cultural resource—the Menninger Foundation—and she was quite beautiful.

Dr. C. F. Menninger had begun practicing medicine in Topeka in 1890. A trip he took to the Mayo Clinic in Minnesota in 1908 lighted in him a vision of opening a similar center in Topeka, and with his sons Will and Karl to help him, the dream crystallized in 1920. "Dr. Karl," as the more restless and excitable of the brothers was called, was just back from Boston, where he had graduated with honors from Harvard Medical School and completed post-graduate psychiatric and neurologic study, with a Kansas City internship sandwiched in between. It was a time when mental institutions were widely known as "nuthouses," "looney bins," or by any of a number of other playfully pejorative terms that revealed the public's ignorance and fear. A mental hospital was regarded as a threat to the community, and in those early days Karl Menninger was obliged to work in what one medical magazine has called "compassionate conspiracy with sympathetic attendants and nurses" to smuggle his psychiatric patients into the hospital through disguised diagnoses.

By 1925, the Menningers had come out of the closet. They opened a sanatorium attached to their clinic, added a facility for mentally ill children the following year, and began to convince Topeka—and then the world— that a mental hospital could be a place for dynamic treatment and not simply a filth-strewn warehouse for discarding the chronically ill. The setting for the sanatorium was a farmhouse at the western end of Topeka, and previously withdrawn and apathetic patients were urged to leave their beds and undertake farm chores throughout the day. A family atmosphere began to evolve, patients became interested in one another, the doctors worked as a team, deepening their analyses and providing wider-ranging treatment. Suspicious Topekans were drawn into the Menninger enterprise as house- wives and businessmen volunteered their time and patients judged competent were allowed to participate in the community. In 1930, Karl Menninger published his first book, *The Human Mind*; aimed primarily at medical students and practitioners, it became a selection of the Literary Guild and a best seller, and "Dr. Karl" has been the nation's most successful expositor of mental health ever since. By 1933, the Menningers had begun teaching psychiatry, and within two decades their training program became the world's largest. During the Second World War, Will Menninger revolution- ized the Army's neuropsychiatric program, then led a post-war drive to get the state legislatures of the nation to end the deplorable condition of America's mental hospitals; his travels and fund-raising on behalf of the Menninger Foundation placed greater burdens than ever on his brother, Karl, who by then rivaled Alf Landon as Topeka's best-known and most highly regarded citizen. On three months' notice, Karl had agreed in 1946 to manage the transformation of Topeka's thousand-bed VA hospital into a massive pilot project in psychiatric care. By the time of the school-segrega- tion case in town, he headed a matchless institution with a professional staff of nearly 125 doctors, had written many books and articles that carried his reputation around the globe, and was the only Topekan to be a member simultaneously of the Chamber of Commerce, the American Civil Liberties Union, and the NAACP. He was a brilliant, warm, and somewhat irascible man of strong liberal leanings. He had welcomed European Jews to his staff in the Thirties when Nazism began its ten-year pogrom, and he had insisted that blacks be given a fair share of the jobs at his own clinic, the VA hospital, the Topeka State Hospital, and every other institution with which he worked.

In view of the NAACP's adoption of social psychology as a supplemen- tary weapon in its legal battle to end segregation, there was no institution in America that would have seemed a more natural and responsive ally in the *Brown* case than Topeka's very own Menninger Foundation. And whose voice decrying racial segregation as a form of mental cruelty would carry greater weight than Topeka's own good "Dr. Karl"? Why, then, did he not testify? He was a paid-up member of the NAACP and genuinely interested in its effort to gain equality for the Negro. McKinley Burnett, Topeka branch president, reported to Walter White on October 10, 1950, that "A committee from our branch had a meeting with two very wealthy and influential white men concerning our case a few days ago. They were Mr. Harry H. Woodring, former governor of Kansas and former Secretary of War under the late Franklin D. Roosevelt, and the famed psychiatrist, Dr. Karl A. Menninger. They are very much in accord with our cause and urged us to request legal aid from the national office. . . ." Both Woodring and Menninger, more-over, would speak after the *Brown* trial at an NAACP fund-raising dinner to help cover the costs of the litigation. This degree of participation suggests that Karl Menninger might have accepted an invitation to testify before the court. And his testimony could have been expected to hold special meaning for Judge Huxman, whose daughter had been a patient at the Foundation.

For all his strong convictions, though, some of Karl Menninger's close working associates believed that he did not wish to do anything to jeopardize his standing with the people who ran Topeka. Some Menninger confidants speak of the reported traumatic effects on "Dr. Karl" of his alleged rejection by a fraternity while he attended Washburn for two years—a social slight in his hometown that he wished never to risk again. In support of this theory, his longtime membership in the Topeka Country Club, where Jews and Negroes were unwelcome, has been cited. "He always wanted badly to be liked by the powerhouses in the community downtown," comments a prominent ex-member of the Menninger hierarchy. A lot of people want to be popular, so Menninger was hardly aberrant in that regard, but he perhaps had more reason than some to be uneasy about his standing in the community. For one thing, his brother, Will, was generally regarded as the more personable and easy-going of the pair. For another, Karl had divorced his first wife, who had been held in high esteem by many community pillars. For a third, the liberals he harbored at the Foundation—some of whom had joined the left-leaning American Veterans Committee and gone marching arm in arm with colored vets on Memorial Day—may have been fine doctors but they bred suspicion and dislike among Topeka's more ardent peach-preservers. And finally, of course, there remained a small portion of the town that never grew up and continued to believe that, as one ex-staff member puts it, "everyone at Menninger's is crazy and the usual treatment there consisted of having intercourse with the doctors." Thus, any reluctance Menninger might have had about mixing into the *Brown* case could have been rationalized as an act of omission in order to protect the Foundation's rear flank. A former colleague, Dr. Harry Levinson of Harvard, adds that Menninger "has strong feelings about doctors appearing as expert witnesses for one side or another, as he wrote in *The Crime of Punishment*, and believes issues settled by courts should be issues of law." But had the court summoned Menninger to testify as an *amicus*, Levinson suspects, the psychiatrist would have accepted. There is some evidence to support this view.

In answer to a direct inquiry about his non-participation in the case, Karl Menninger stated in January 1974: "I did not testify because I don't think I was asked to. I certainly wasn't intimidated by any suggestion that the people in Topeka would not like it." Letters in the Legal Defense Fund files suggest that the psychiatrist's memory may be either faulty or highly selective. On June 6, 1951, Professor Hugh Speer addressed a letter on his University of Kansas City letterhead to Dr. Menninger at the Menninger Clinic indicating that he was writing in his capacity as "an educational advisor to the counsel to the plaintiffs" in the forthcoming trial on segregation in the Topeka public schools and asking him to testify on its psychological effects. A copy of the letter was sent to Greenberg. On June 17, Speer advised Greenberg: "Dr. Menninger has not replied to my letter. There are no doubt many on his staff competent to testify. They may be hesitant to take the stand so close [to] home. Mr. Bledsoe [head of the legal-redress committee of the Topeka NAACP] says that Dr. Menninger stated he would testify if subpoenaed but did not wish to involve the clinic." Greenberg wrote back that before issuing a subpoena, it would be prudent to try to meet with Menninger "to discuss with him what testimony he is willing to give. I hope that he will be able to give us an appointment." But that letter was sent just a week before the trial was to begin and did not indicate whether Speer was to seek the appointment or Greenberg would pursue the matter from New York. In the rush of arrangements to be completed at the last minute, the matter was never pressed with Menninger.

But the Menninger name nevertheless did find its way into the trial, if by the back door.

Among those whom Greenberg had asked to testify was Arnold M. Rose, a University of Minnesota sociologist who had worked closely with Gunnar Myrdal on *An American Dilemma* and was credited with partial authorship of the book. Rose, who had first agreed to come and then declined, recommended a number of others who might serve the NAACP's purposes, among them a thirty-four-year-old sociologist with strong credits in psychology by the name of Louisa Pinkham Holt, then serving as an assistant professor in the psychology department at Kansas University. Her background proved interesting.

A distant relative of social-activist and cosmetician Lydia Pinkham, she was the daughter of parents deeply committed to equal rights. Her mother headed the Massachusetts League of Women Voters and the Massachusetts Civic League; her "rad-lib" father's basic teaching was "No sane person has a prejudice" and he quite specifically told his daughter he would not object if she chose to marry a Negro. Louisa Pinkham earned three degrees, including her doctorate, at Radcliffe, where she studied under scholars such as Talcott Parsons and Robert Merton, who would become leading sociologists of their time. She went on to study at the Boston Psychoanalytic Institute and do field research in public administration for the Federal Bureau of Prisons in West Virginia, settlement-house work in the South End of Boston, vocational counseling at the Family Society of Boston, and educational counseling at the National Institute of Public Affairs in Washington. In between, she taught sociology at Skidmore College in upstate New York and, after marrying a clinical psychologist named Robert Holt, held a part-time appointment at the school of psychiatry run by the Menninger Foundation, where her husband was moving up through the ranks.

During the 1947–49 span in which she taught at the Menninger Foundation, Louisa Holt was never more than an underling, but her husband's position and her own combination of brains and beauty—she is a strikingly attractive woman of medium height with pale blue-gray eyes accentuated by strong brows and possesses a deep Bette Davis voice—assured her of more than wallflower status at the great psychiatric clinic on Topeka's West 10th Street.

By the time Jack Greenberg wrote to her in early June of 1951, Mrs. Holt had left the Menninger Foundation to have her third child and then resumed teaching at Kansas University in nearby Lawrence, though her residence remained in Topeka, where one of her children attended the public schools and a second one was about to begin. Yet Louisa Holt's association with the Menninger center, though in the past and never more than peripheral ("Dr. Menninger had hired me to teach psychiatric students what they needed to know about sociology," she remarks in self-deprecation), now became very important to Carter and Greenberg as they prepared their witnesses for the trial. "We decided to mention the Menninger affiliation," she remembers, "because some of the Justices in the Supreme Court had been in analysis, according to the NAACP lawyers," and because of Judge Huxman's interest in the Foundation. No point was seen in asking Dr. Menninger's permission for her to testify; moreover, "I was in the throes of getting a divorce from Robert, so my testifying couldn't have hurt his standing with Menninger. Hell, the truth is that I didn't have much to lose."

On the afternoon of Sunday, June 24, the day before the *Brown* trial began, the expert witnesses gathered at the Scott law office. "We went around the table, each person indicating which area he or she wanted to discuss or stress," Louisa Holt remembers. "We wanted to avoid being repetitive, and by the time it came around to me, there weren't many areas left. But I knew what I wanted to stress—that separate-but-equal is a contradiction in terms and that government sanction heightened the inequity. And that was fine with the lawyers, who left it to us to shape the views we'd express so long as we didn't duplicate one another. We did a bit of rehearsing on how the questioning would proceed, and they asked me to come down to court on that first day of the trial just to get the sense of it. But the case zoomed right along and, to my consternation, they called me late in the afternoon of that first day. I was scared silly. I could feel my knees knocking on my way up there. The judges had been slumped way down in their seats—the session, after all, had been going on all day—but when I came up, you could see them lean forward in their seats to see what it was exactly that they had here. Now when I'm called upon to speak, I'm unpredictable—sometimes I'm articulate, sometimes not—but I had thought through what I wanted to say, and the lawyers were very helpful in running me through the easy opening questions on my credentials."

She did not speak for very long, but none of the hundred or more witnesses who testified in the cluster of cases that would eventually go down as a landmark in legal history under the collective name of *Brown v. Board of*

*The Marshalls of Baltimore*—Thurgood Marshall's mother, Norma, a schoolteacher, and father, William A., a dining steward, shown in the late 1940s.

*Architects of Victory*—Thurgood Marshall (left), chief counsel of the NAACP Legal Defense Fund, as he looked after his 1944 Supreme Court victory in *Smith v. Allwright,* the Texas white primary case; and Charles H. Houston, Marshall's mentor, who built Howard Law School into a crack academy for black lawyers.

*Legal Defense Fund Brain Trust*—James M. Nabrit, Jr. (top left), who led the District of Columbia case against segregation and later became president of Howard University; Robert L. Carter (top right), Thurgood Marshall's principal lieutenant during the *Brown* struggle; Jack Greenberg (bottom left), who succeeded Marshall as head of the Legal Defense Fund; and William T. Coleman, Jr., the Philadelphia attorney who served as key outside counselor to Marshall and later became president of the LDF, before joining President Ford's Cabinet as Secretary of Transportation.

*After the Battle*—The Legal Defense Fund team of lawyers and expert witnesses gather on the steps of the U.S. Court House in Richmond after the acrimonious trial in the Prince Edward County, Virginia, case in February 1952. Standing in front are the principal NAACP lawyers, Spottswood W. Robinson III (left) and Oliver W. Hill. Partially visible, just behind Robinson's left shoulder, is Kenneth B. Clark, who coordinated the efforts of psychologists and other social scientists serving as witnesses.

*The First Plaintiffs*—Mr. and Mrs. Harry Briggs, whose names led the list of black litigants in the Clarendon County, South Carolina, case; and the Reverend Joseph A. DeLaine, the minister-teacher who organized the agrarian uprising in the small town of Summerton in 1949.

*Jim Crow Schooling*—The Spring Hill elementary school in Clarendon County, where Mrs. DeLaine taught before the segregation case led to her dismissal.

*The Kansans*—Linda
Brown, right, daughter of
the principal plaintiff in the
Topeka case, shown in the
yard of the Monroe School
in 1953, when she was ten.
Below: Mamie Williams
(left), veteran Topeka
schoolteacher; Elisha Scott
(center), pioneer black
lawyer in the Southwest,
whose sons played a leading
role in the Topeka case; and
Kenneth McFarland,
superintendent of Topeka
schools and defender of the
racial status quo at the time
of the segregation case.

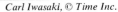

*Carl Iwasaki, © Time Inc.*

*Pariah*—U.S. District Court Judge J. Waties Waring, whose pro-Negro rulings in his Charleston federal court, including a sharp dissent in the *Briggs* case, earned him ostracism from the community in which he was born and lived most of his life.

*Charleston Evening Post*

*Milestone*—In the Delaware case, psychiatrist Frederic Wertham (middle) offered telling testimony on the corrosive effects of segregation on children of both races; the state Court of Chancery, presided over by Collins J. Seitz (below), became the first tribunal in the nation to outlaw segregated public schools, though it did so not on constitutional grounds but because the black schools were found to be unequal.

*Defenders of Segregation—*
John W. Davis (left), who at
the age of eighty led the
attorneys for the segregating
states in arguments before the
Supreme Court in 1952 and
1953; Robert McC. Figg, Jr.
(top), who argued the first
segregation case for South
Carolina at the Charleston trial;
and Paul E. Wilson, who as
Assistant Attorney General of
Kansas defended the state's
statute before the high court.

*The 1954 United States Supreme Court*—Front row, left to right: Felix
Frankfurter, Hugo L. Black, Earl Warren, Stanley F. Reed, and William O.
Douglas; back row: Tom C. Clark, Robert H. Jackson, Harold H. Burton,
and Sherman Minton.

*Education* spoke words that had a more detectable impact on the phrasing of the final decision in the case.

Q.   . . . [D]oes enforced legal separation have any adverse effect upon the personality development of the Negro child?

A.   The fact that it is enforced, that it is legal, I think, has more importance than the mere fact of segregation by itself does because this gives legal and official sanction to a policy which is inevitably interpreted both by white people and by Negroes as denoting the inferiority of the Negro group. Were it not for the sense that one group is inferior to the other, there would be no basis—and I am not granting that this is a rational basis—for such segregation.

Q.   Well, does this interference have any effect, in your opinion, on the learning process?

A.   A sense of inferiority must always affect one's motivation for learning since it affects the feeling one has of one's self as a person. . . . That sense of ego-identity is built up on the basis of attitudes that are expressed toward a person by others who are important—first the parents and then teachers and other people in the community, whether they are older or one's peers. It is other people's reactions to one's self that basically affects the conception of one's self. . . . If these attitudes that are reflected back and then internalized or projected, are unfavorable ones, then one develops a sense of one's self as an inferior being . . . and apathetic acceptance, fatalistic submission to the feeling others have expressed that one is inferior, and therefore any efforts to prove otherwise would be doomed to failure.

Q.   Now . . . would you say that the difficulties which segregation causes in the public school system interfere with a well—development of a well-rounded personality?

A.   I think the maximum or maximal development of any personality can only be based on the potentialities which that individual himself possesses. Of course they are affected for good or ill by the attitudes, opinions, feelings which are expressed by others and which may be fossilized into laws. . . . I feel, if I may add another word, I feel that when segregation exists, it's not something . . . directed against people for what they are. It is directed against them on the basis of who their parents are . . . it is not simply skin color. In the case of Walter White, for example, and sociologist Allison Davis, and his brother, [Lincoln University political scientist] John Davis, who are Negroes, their skin is lighter than mine—of course, I have been out in the sun—the definition does depend on who a person's parents were . . . and my understanding . . . of the American tradition, religious tradition as well as set of values and ethos, determining much of our most valued and significant behavior, hinges upon a belief of treating people upon their own merits, and we are inclined to oppose a view which states that we should respect people or reject them on the basis of who their parents were.

Q.   Now, Mrs. Holt . . . is the integration of the child at the junior high school level, does that correct these difficulties which you have just spoken of, in your opinion?

A.   I think it's a theory that would be accepted by virtually all students of personality development that the earlier a significant event occurs in the life of an individual, the more lasting, the more far-reaching and deeper the effects of that incident, that trauma, will be. The more—the earlier an event occurs, the more difficult it is later on to eradicate those effects.

"I felt damned good at the end," Louisa Holt recalls. "It was as if inspiration had somehow been granted to me. After the day was over, one of the mothers of the black families that were in the court came up to me and introduced her daughters and asked if the girls could shake hands with me. She told the kids, 'I want you children to remember this day for the rest of your lives.' I was really moved."

By then, Walter Huxman had heard quite enough expert witnesses. He urged the NAACP lawyers to wind up their case. A Notre Dame sociologist closed out the day's testimony by arguing that segregation drains the upward ambitions of blacks, and the next morning Carter and Greenberg finished their case with testimony by an aide of Professor Speer, who suggested that adolescence was a particularly difficult time to integrate children, as was the practice in Topeka.

Lester Goodell had no big surprises in store for the defense's case. The contractor for the buses that took the colored children to school said that he had been carrying out his work for thirty-five years, that every effort was made to meet the schedules, that the buses met state safety regulations, and that each run carried a student patrol to keep order. The school board's clerk–business manager, who had been given the front-page treatment for her irregular and unsanctioned purchases of equipment, declared that the colored schools were administered just as the white ones were—same books, same supplies, same curriculum, same teachers' salaries—and that some white children did indeed travel long distances to get to school. Finally, Goodell put on McFarland. It was his last hurrah as superintendent of schools and a public official now tumbled from his pedestal.

Q. Have you ever, as an administrator of schools, considered it part of your business to formulate custom and—social customs and usage in the community?

A. Mr. Goodell, I think that point is extremely significant. In fact, it's probably the major factor in why the Board of Education is defending this lawsuit, and that is that we have never considered it, and there is nothing in the record historically, that it's the place of the public school system to dictate the social customs of the people who support the public school system.

Q. Do you say that the separation of the schools that we have is in harmony with the public opinion, weight of public opinion, in this community?

A. We have no objective evidence that the majority sentiment of the public would desire a change in the fundamental structure.

Carter moved in fast on the cross-examination. How did the school superintendent know that the social customs of Topeka required separate schools at the elementary level? McFarland repeated what he had told Goodell—that there was no evidence to the contrary. Well, was it McFarland's understanding that the community had a different feeling about segregation above the grade-school level? Goodell bounced in to object that the law and the courts had prevented the practice of segregation above the grade-school level, so the matter was out of the school board's hands.

Q. I see. So, actually, you are not maintaining—you can't really say you are maintaining the schools in accord with social custom. You merely have kept constant the status quo as you found it when you came here. You are maintaining segregated schools merely because they were here when you arrived—that's all you can say, isn't that true?

A. We have, as I stated, no objective evidence that there is any substantial desire for a change among the people that the board represents.

Of great relief to the NAACP forces as the trial closed was that the defense had not been able to find—or chose not to look for—a Negro witness to speak out in favor of continued segregation. The colored teachers may have feared for their jobs if segregation were ended and the black community at large may have felt that Negro militants like the Scotts and McKinley Burnett and white militants like Esther Brown were pushing for racial integration before the town would accept it without rancor, but there was enough racial solidarity and pride in black Topeka not to buck the NAACP's standing up in court against The Man.

Five weeks later, Judge Huxman handed down the court's unanimous opinion. The physical facilities and all other measurable factors, Walter Huxman wrote, were comparable in the white and colored schools of Topeka. And since bus service was provided to the colored schools while none was furnished to the white ones, the court found "no willful, intentional or substantial discrimination" to exist in the operation of the Topeka public schools. Whether segregation itself constituted inequality was another matter. *Plessy* and *Gong Lum* had been cited as governing precedents by the defense, and so the question of law came down to evaluating how much the separate-but-equal doctrine had been eroded by the *Sweatt* and *McLaurin* decisions. Huxman's leanings seemed clear:

. . . If segregation within a school as in the *McLaurin* case is a denial of due process, it is difficult to see why segregation in separate schools would not result in the same denial. Or if the denial of the right to commingle with the majority group in higher institutions of learning as in the *Sweatt* case and gain the educational advantages resulting therefrom, is lack of due process, it is difficult to see why such denial would not result in the same lack of due process if practiced in the lower grades.

"It must, however, be remembered that in both of these cases," the opinion went on, "the Supreme Court made it clear that it was confining itself" to weighing equal protection when subjected to segregation in graduate schools only. And so, in an abrupt and pointed conclusion, the decision was rendered:

We are accordingly of the view that the *Plessy* and *Lum* cases . . . have not been overruled and that they still presently are authority for the maintenance of a segregated school system in the lower grades.

The prayer for relief will be denied. . . .

But in dealing the NAACP a unanimous defeat, the District Court offered it a consolation prize that would leave vibrations all the way to Washington. Attached to the opinion were nine "Findings of Fact" in the case. Finding VIII, echoing the testimony of the social scientists who had testified, especially Louisa Holt, read:

> Segregation of white and colored children in public schools has a detrimental effect upon the colored children. The impact is greater when it has the sanction of the law; for the policy of separating the races is usually interpreted as denoting the inferiority of the Negro group. A sense of inferiority affects the motivation of a child to learn. Segregation with the sanction of law, therefore, has a tendency to retard the educational and mental development of Negro children and to deprive them of some of the benefits they would receive in a racially integrated school system.

A few days later, Jack Greenberg wrote to Hugh Speer that he thought "Judge Huxman's opinion, although ruling against us, puts the Supreme Court on the spot, and it seems to me that it was purposely written with that end in view."

Huxman would admit as much long afterward. "We weren't in sympathy with the decision we rendered," he remarked in 1970 at his home on Pembroke Lane in west Topeka. "If it weren't for *Plessy v. Ferguson*, we surely would have found the law unconstitutional. But there was no way around it—the Supreme Court had to overrule itself."

# 18

# Jim Crow, Inc.

Sandy, marshy where not sandy, low-lying throughout, and remarkably good for growing things, the Eastern Shore is a 5,000-square-mile, bizarrely crenelated peninsula sculpted over millennia from the mid-Atlantic coastline by the steady wash of the ocean and the long, tapering fingers of Delaware and Chesapeake bays. The fortune-seekers from Europe who drove the Algonquin and the Lini-Lenape tribes from it in the seventeenth century—the Swedes first, then the Dutch, and finally the British—soon discovered that the moist climate, rich earth, and easy access to the place by sailing vessels made it ideal plantation country and attractive for smaller farms as well. It was too far north for citrus or other tropical fruit, but it was splendid for every variety of garden produce, tomatoes and strawberries especially, and such fruits of the sea as oysters and blue clams and menhaden proliferated not far offshore. Tobacco provided the staple that kept the colonizers financially afloat.

By the early part of the eighteenth century, the jagged piece of lush real estate had been dismembered and divided among three colonial jurisdictions. The narrow, sixty-mile-long tail at the southern end went to Virginia, to which it is not connected by land. The larger portion of the remainder, facing the great harbor of Baltimore across the Chesapeake, went to Maryland. The remaining section, a slender right-triangle with its hypotenuse formed by not quite 100 miles of uneven Atlantic coastline, was once deeded by the Duke of York to William Penn, at the southeastern corner of whose great colony it dangled like a vestigial organ, vaguely protecting the lower reaches of the Delaware River. But the Pennsylvania legislature offered inadequate protection and attention to the three Lower Counties, as the Eastern Shore sector of the colony was then known, and early in the eighteenth century they were granted their own identity and legislature. Delaware, second smallest of the original thirteen states, took a strong and constructive interest in the creation of the new nation. It fought hard for a union in which the rights of small states would not be swallowed up by their larger neighbors, and having won its point, the little state—its 2,000 or so square miles make it not quite twice as large as minuscule Rhode Island—became the first of the United States to ratify the Constitution. That act, on December 7, 1787, is perhaps Delaware's sole claim to distinction as a champion of democracy. Certainly it was long hostile to the Negro, probably longer and more defiantly so than any other state outside of the Confederacy.

In spirit if not in law, Delaware was a Southern state, though it took the Union's side in the Civil War. All but a tiny outcropping on the northern end of the state in fact lies south of the Mason-Dixon Line. More to the point, the two southern counties of Kent and Sussex, which between them make up three-quarters of Delaware, were slaveholding territory, and the farther south one traveled in Delaware, the deeper the allegiance to Dixie ways and attitudes one encountered. Kent and Sussex had enough votes to control the state legislature in a classic case of rural domination of urban-commercial interests, which were centered in Wilmington in New Castle County adjacent to New Jersey and Pennsylvania—the only city to speak of in the whole state. In 1860, Delaware voters registered a strongly pro-slavery preference, picking Breckinridge for President over Lincoln; it was, after all, a slaveholding state and not eager to discard a principal source of its wealth.

Pre-eminent among those Wilmington-area industrialists who acted decisively to hold the state out of the Confederacy was Henry du Pont, a strong Lincoln man, who saw that the fate of the growing gunpowder company launched by his grandfather, Eleuthère Irénée du Pont de Nemours, at a mill on Brandywine Creek in 1802, was linked to the survival of the Union. Indeed, the du Ponts became major suppliers of explosives to the Union military machine. But many Delawareans defected to the Confederacy as individual soldiers, and when peace came, Southern sentiment did not abate in Delaware, which was not obliged, like the Confederate states, to pay homage to the Radical Republicans who now took control of Congress and imposed a punitive Reconstruction on the uncontrite South. And so Delaware displayed a kind of defiant schizophrenia: having stayed in the Union throughout the war, it now spat upon the great Civil War amendments that corroborated the higher purposes of the terrible conflict. It refused to ratify the Thirteenth Amendment, which stripped the state of its slaves. It refused to ratify the Fourteenth Amendment, and its legislature declared its "uncompromising opposition" to all "measures intended or calculated to equalize or amalgamate the Negro race with the white race, politically or socially . . . and to making Negroes eligible to public offices, to sit on juries, and to their admission to public schools where white children attend." And it refused to ratify the Fifteenth Amendment, declaring that federal outlawing of prohibitions on the right to vote on the ground of race "would have a tendency to destroy the rights of the states . . . [and] would be an attempt to establish an equality not sanctioned by the laws of nature or of God." Downstate Delaware, which is to say three-quarters of the state, was not notably more sympathetic to Negro civil rights than they were in the Mississippi Delta.

By using county and local property-tax lists and poll taxes as the basis for voter qualification, the Delaware legislature kept the black man virtually disenfranchised. Colored schools were approved in fact and equality was proclaimed in principle, but they were funded largely by a tax levied against Negroes for that specific purpose and so were severely underfinanced. White schools were operated twice as many months as the colored schools, and as late as 1920, illiteracy among Negroes in Delaware ran as high as 20 percent, compared to 1.8 percent for whites. Ramshackle colored schools were openly approved by the state, and they might have stayed that way for another generation if Pierre du Pont of the state's great industrial family had not stepped forward in the early Twenties and contributed the better part of $2.6 million that went into a crash construction program of eighty-seven schoolhouses for colored children throughout the state. But so hostile to the educational advancement of the Negro did the balance of the state's citizens remain that by 1950 there was no four-year high school for Negroes anywhere in the state south of Wilmington.

As the twentieth century advanced, and particularly as the du Pont interests grew from those of a sizable munitions manufacturer that supplied 40 percent of all explosives used by the Allies during the First World War into a massive international miracle-maker of cellophane, rayon, nylon, Duco paints, Lucite plastic, and a hundred other products for better living and better profits through chemistry, the Wilmington area grew in population and soon had the votes to elect governors and other statewide officials and get out from under the thumb of the rural interests. But the era of "one man, one vote" had not yet arrived, and Kent and Sussex counties still wielded power in Delaware out of all proportion to their population. The big money, though, stayed in Wilmington, most of it in the hands of the du Pont interests.

An unspoken *quid pro quo* arrangement had evolved between the sophisticated Wilmington plutocracy and the downstate conservative farmers who still had the votes that passed the laws that ran the state. If Wilmington saw to it that statewide taxes were kept low and did not foist a lot of costly social-welfare programs on the southern counties—particularly anything that would materially benefit the black man—the legislature would rubber-stamp the fondest wishes of the high-powered corporation types, most of them linked by employment or family to the du Pont squirearchy. It worked. A small, elitist, well-trained corps of Wilmington lawyers, largely Anglo-Saxon Protestant and determined to keep it that way, put Delaware into the business of currying favor with American corporations so that they would make the state their headquarters, pay it franchising and income taxes (albeit modest in their rates but considerable in the agglomerate), bring it prestige, and, not incidentally, keep its able lawyers busy with well-rewarded labors. And so, starting at the close of the nineteenth century and in periodic revisions thereafter, Delaware has made itself exceedingly attractive to corporations domiciled within it by creating a corporate-law code characterized in a scornful analysis by the *University of Pennsylvania Law Review* as "containing a maximum number of enabling provisions and fettering the corporation with a minimum number of responsibilities to, for example, its creditors, its shareholders, and the public." Thus, in Delaware's be-nice-to-management climate, the myth that shareholders have a real voice in the policies of their companies has become particularly vaporous. The state legislature, privately described by the Wilmington legal elite as "just a bunch of farmers," never hesitated to approve the sweetheart corporation laws drafted or amended by the Delaware Bar Association, itself hardly an innocent bystander since the law thoughtfully provides that certain kinds of shareholder suits and management defenses can be undertaken only by counsel licensed to practice in the state of Delaware. To complete the tight fraternity, the state's Court of Chancery, the trial court for corporate matters, has historically been viewed as highly tolerant of management so long as it avoided outright venality in executing its functions.

In short, Delaware succeeded in establishing an environment of great comfort to corporations, which elsewhere found themselves being increasingly buffeted by the demands of unions, consumer interests, and political reformers. So well did the state succeed that the last time anyone counted, nearly one-third of the companies listed on the New York Stock Exchange were incorporated in Delaware, as were nearly one-half of the 100 largest corporations in America. Franchising taxes alone were yielding about $25 million a year—a good deal of money for a state whose entire population could fit into one corner of Brooklyn.

The principal beneficiary of this corporate nirvana, of course, was the E. I. du Pont de Nemours Company. It owned Delaware as no other private enterprise controlled any other state in the Union. This was true partly because of the smallness of Delaware. In 1950, the state's total population was just 318,000, more than two-thirds of it in New Castle County, half of whose residents lived in Wilmington proper. Du Pont liked keeping Delaware as its own duchy, over which it exercised its *droit de seigneur* with a relatively benevolent but nonetheless decisive hand. Blue-collar workers were long throttled as du Pont tolerated only relatively weak company unions lacking the clout of nationally affiliated locals. Ralph Nader would charge the company with maintaining its white-collar corps in "a state of dependency"—without contracts but under agreements that sharply limited its social, political, and professional mobility. New industries that might bring union labor to the state were discouraged by conditions and limitations, such as pollution controls, that were often not wielded against du Pont, its suppliers, and and its allies. And such social questions as urban planning, public transit, education, tax policy, and welfare benefits were viewed with pinchpenny stringency by state and municipal policy-makers who kept Delaware a relatively backward, unsightly, and poorly serviced state.

Thanks to the distinctly limp social concern that prevailed in the state, even the most liberal community in Delaware—Wilmington—remained a Jim Crow town in 1950, very much like Topeka, Kansas, but a bit worse. All the public schools were segregated, not just the grammar schools. There were no black nurses in the white hospitals, and not nearly enough hospital beds were available to Negroes, who made up 14 percent of the state's population. There were no black clerks in the banks or retail stores. Restaurants and movie theaters and hotels in downtown Wilmington were strictly segregated, and no black man served in the Delaware National Guard. The state college for colored people at Dover was not nationally accredited, and nothing approaching equal protection of the laws was practiced in any walk of life throughout the state, which functioned as a fossilized racist encampment on the traditionally white-supremacist Eastern Shore peninsula.

And the local Borgias patronized the whole arrangement. "It is fair to say that the du Ponts had never been identified with the movement for interracial justice in this state," asserts one of Delaware's most eminent jurists and a lifelong resident of Wilmington. "If you asked the du Ponts about their failure to employ more blacks, they would claim that they were just following the mores of the community and that they didn't set those mores—a patently absurd contention, given their concentration of power. The du Ponts may point with pride to what Pierre S. du Pont did to help the black schools, but that was an exception. The movement for racial justice did not come from above here."

It came largely through the efforts of a single white man who chose to pass up his slice of the du Pont-fertilized melon—and of a black man who was never offered one.

No Negro was admitted to the practice of law as a member of the Delaware bar until the astonishingly late date of 1929.

The black lawyer's name was Louis Lorenzo Redding. A native of Wilmington's east side, Redding was the son of one of the most respected Negroes in the community. Lewis Alfred Redding, born in rural Kent County, Delaware, in 1869, had graduated from Howard University in 1896 and come up to Wilmington in 1900, where he had a long career as a mail carrier and clerk in the post office. He was also a founder of the local black "Y," a trustee of the Bethel AME Church, where he ran the Sunday School for more than twenty-five years, and the longtime secretary of the Wilmington branch of the NAACP. His two daughters became schoolteachers. His younger son, Jay Saunders, became a professor of English and a prominent historian of Negro life in America, whose well-known books include *They Came in Chains* and *The Lonesome Road*. His older son broke the color line of the Delaware bar.

A short, dark man of great dignity and elocution that would be well regarded in Buckingham Palace, Louis Redding was groomed at Brown University in the Ivy League, where he did well enough to serve as a speaker at the commencement of the class of 1923 and earn a scholarship to Harvard Law School. One Christmas vacation during his law-school years, he wandered into the New Castle County courthouse in Wilmington and took a convenient seat. A guard shooed him out of it toward the section reserved for blacks. Redding refused to be shooed and was forcibly ejected from the premises. After Harvard, he taught for a short time at a church-run school in Florida and at Morehouse College in Atlanta and then came home to face the lion in its den. The tight, WASPish clan that kept the Delaware bar a closed guild of the right, white sort was said to have acted generally with uncommon severity in administering its licensing examinations. But Redding was admitted in 1929, with prominent notice of the fact in the Wilmington newspapers.

Black Delaware badly needed his services. Most of the best legal talent in the state hired out to the du Ponts and other corporate interests. There was little prestige and less money in handling black clients, whose legal problems were often either messily domestic or depressingly criminal. And white lawyers who did take on colored cases were often known to charge extortionate fees. Louis Redding did not do that. He fought, largely alone, for the civil rights and liberties of black Delawareans by throwing all his superior training and bottomless energy into representing them ably at the bar. By 1949, he was ready to challenge the government's racist establishment.

Thirty students at Delaware State College for Negroes applied that year for admission to the lily-white University of Delaware and were rejected. Delaware State was provided for colored youth, they were told. But Delaware State was little more than a fancified high school, as was the case with many of the nation's so-called Negro state colleges of the time, and nobody could have confused it with a seat of higher learning. The rejected students took their case to Louis Redding, who sent a letter to the prominent Delaware judge Hugh H. Morris, then president of the university's board of trustees, and asked him to convene the board to discuss its racial policy. "Judge Morris replied that he would call the board together when he felt it was necessary," Redding recalls. "I wrote back to him and told him it wasn't a case of whether he liked it or not, nor did it have anything to do with his personal feelings. I told him it was his duty to call the board together." Chastened, the board president did summon his board, which promptly confirmed the earlier action of university officials in refusing admission to the black applicants. Redding went to court with the eager aid of a young white lawyer named Jack Greenberg who had just joined Thurgood Marshall's shop in New York and whose wife was a Wilmington woman. Hearing the case was a remarkably astute judge who, at the age of thirty-six, had already been sitting for the better part of five years as the vice chancellor of Delaware, the second-ranking jurist in a state known for the high caliber of its bench.

Collins Jacques Seitz, like Louis Redding, was a Wilmington boy and a member of a minority. In the nineteenth century and earlier, the Delaware Negro's best friends were the Quakers, who largely manned the underground-railroad stations in Wilmington and rural New Castle County. Few other Protestant denominations looked kindly on the plight of the black man—certainly not the Methodists, who came to occupy a dominant position among the state's religious groups. They were not a great deal fonder of the Catholics, whose ranks swelled with the arrival of an increasing proportion of immigrants from non-Nordic lands. "The Catholics in Delaware are very sensitive about their religion," notes Redding. "You can't be with one for more than a few minutes before being made aware of his Catholicism." It was the Catholics of Delaware who became the spiritual successors to the Quakers in befriending—or at least tolerating—the Negro.

Collins Seitz grew up into a devout churchman. But he did not wear his faith or understanding of Christian brotherhood on his sleeve. After attending St. Ann's parochial school, he pursued a non-Catholic education:

Wilmington High School, the University of Delaware, and the University of Virginia Law School, where he compiled an outstanding record, became an editor of the *Virginia Law Review*, and landed a spot with the blue-ribbon Wilmington law firm of Southerland, Berl & Potter. His uncommon intellectual capacity, unhesitancy about doing his homework, and ability to write in easy-to-follow non-legalese on even the most complex of topics marked him from the start for a swift ascent that swept away the residue of religious narrow-mindedness mildewing the Delaware legal establishment.

Calm, clearheaded, unconniving, Seitz had one other quality that marked him off from most of his contemporaries at the Delaware bar: he was not all that interested in making money. And because there was so much of it to be earned in the good Wilmington firms, which handled a heavy volume of high-fee business for many of the nation's top companies that were domiciled in the state, it was sometimes difficult to find first-rate legal minds willing to serve as judges. Since, however, Delaware's corporation laws had come to be regarded as one of the state's most cherished assets, special care had to be taken in filling the posts of chancellor and vice chancellor. It was the Chancery Court alone among the tribunals of the state that functioned as an equity court with original jurisdiction over a wide range of legal problems affecting the multi-million-dollar lifelines of vast corporations. It was thus a high tribute to Collins Seitz when in 1946, at the age of thirty-one, he was designated vice chancellor of Delaware.

On the bench, Seitz proved nobody's puppet. Given the prominence of many of the companies that came before him as parties to an action, his opinions swiftly won national recognition for their ability to balance vigorously conflicting interests. He would eventually become pre-eminent among the state judges of the nation as the consummate arbiter of corporate law, and his court was sought out by attorneys eager to find a judge capable of untangling particularly labyrinthine disputes. A case he heard involving the Bata Shoe Company lasted 100 days, filled 15,000 pages of testimony, and featured French, German, and Czech citizens contending for control of the Delaware-based enterprise. One lawyer who confronted Seitz when he was well into his second decade on the Delaware bench was Louis Nizer, who was defending the directors of the giant Loew's entertainment empire, incorporated in Delaware, from an assault by dissident shareholders. Writing of the experience in his best seller *My Life in Court*, Nizer noted that Seitz's neatly parted, shining black hair and pale, clean-cut features gave him an almost boyish look. Then he added: "His chief characteristic is serenity, but even it cannot disguise his enthusiasm for his task as he listens to the argument with eager patience. Even if one had not read his lucid and learned opinions in other cases, one would be deeply impressed with the Judge before him. I have never seen greater concentration in repose."

The Chancery Court had other functions as well, some of them involving not millions upon millions of dollars but the most elemental sort of human problems, such as the custody of children, the guardianship of old people, the pardoning of criminals, and the civil rights of Negroes. It was before the vice chancellor of Delaware that Louis Redding and Jack Greenberg argued *Parker v. University of Delaware* in 1950. Seitz listened to the arguments, went to look at the white and colored colleges provided by the state, found the colored one "grossly inferior," and ordered the Negro plaintiffs admitted to the white university. As if in recognition of the severe nature of the inequity, the state did not appeal the Seitz decision. The University of Delaware became the first state-financed institution in America to be desegregated at the undergraduate level by court order.

It is no doubt too much to claim that Seitz's opinion sparked a chain reaction that led to the immediate lowering of racial barriers in Delaware, but it is a fact that things began to change, especially in Wilmington, not long afterward. In March of 1951, five downtown movie theaters opened their doors to Negroes for the first time. In July, the Delaware National Guard admitted an apprentice lens-grinder as its first black member, black nurses began being hired by hospitals, and by the fall a few blacks were appearing as clerks in retail stores and other businesses where they had never been accepted before. Of special note was the action of an elfin priest named Thomas A. Lawless, who ran the Salesianum School for Boys in Wilmington. Father Lawless, small as a jockey and hardly less spry though he was nearly sixty, returned to his native Delaware in the war years, took command of the school he had once attended, and soon noted that racism had not abated in the community. "The neglect of colored children in public schools of this state has been terrible," he told Negro journalist Carl Rowan. "Not second-rate schools, but third- and fourth-rate—that's what they've given them." His conclusion: "We want to develop intelligent leadership among colored people around here, so we must educate them in Catholic schools." In 1947, Father Lawless invited three Negro boys to come to Salesianum, but when his superior found out, the plan was overruled. "Imagine how I felt about that!" remarked the pipe-puffing, white-haired little cleric. But a few years later the diocesan hierarchy shifted, and Father Lawless was permitted to bring in five black boys. They did well, no disruption occurred, and the number of Negroes enrolled soon rose to several dozen.

To pay tribute to the work of Father Lawless, lay Catholic Collins Seitz addressed the commencement exercises at Salesianum in early June of 1951—an event that on its face should have been no more newsworthy than 10,000 other such graduation-day speeches given at that time of year across America. But the words of the vice chancellor of Delaware proved electric. He spoke out, as he was wont to do in his court opinions, with clarity and directness on a subject that was one of Delaware's great taboos—the subjugated state of its Negroes. What made Seitz's words more than rhetoric was the risk they entailed for their speaker: the vice chancellor had just been nominated by the governor to become the new chancellor of Delaware—an appointment that had to be approved by the State Senate. And the Senate remained, as it had historically been, in the grip of anti-black downstaters. Seitz nevertheless told his young listeners at Salesianum that they were headed into a world where too many lacked the courage of their convictions, and he illustrated the charge by dwelling on what he said was "the most pressing domestic issue today in Delaware, and in fact in the United States generally"—the condition of the Negro.

> . . . How can we say that we deeply revere the principles of our Declaration and our Constitution and yet refuse to recognize those principles when they are to be applied to the American Negro in a down-to-earth fashion? During election campaigns and in Fourth of July speeches, many speakers emphasize that these great principles apply to all Americans. But when you ask many of these same speakers to act or vote so that those great principles apply in fact to Negro-Americans, you may be accused of being unfair, idealistic or even pro-Communist.
>
> . . . A person has real moral courage when, being in a position to make decisions or determine policies, he decides that the qualified Negro will be admitted to a school of nursing [as had recently been done at St. Francis Hospital in Wilmington]; that the Negro, like the white, will receive a fair trial no matter what the public feeling may be; that every Catholic school, church and institution shall be open to all Catholics—not at some distant future time when public opinion happens to coincide with Catholic moral teaching—but now. Are these requests of our business, governmental and religious leaders too much to ask? I think not.

Such remarks, added to Seitz's *Parker* opinion the previous year, his own Catholicism, and his insistent support of such integration-minded clergymen as Father Lawless, put the downstate Democrats who held a narrow majority in the Delaware Senate in a decidedly sour frame of mind when they gathered eleven days later to pass upon the governor's selection for chancellor. They convened at two in the afternoon and proceeded to sit on their hands. Then they groused and grumbled and began to drift away from the chamber, only to be summoned back by the presiding officer, Republican Lieutenant Governor Alexis I. du Pont Bayard, a Wilmington lawyer and an adornment of the Delaware financial-legal powerhouse. Hours passed. Evening wore on. Senators went off to fulfill speaking obligations, but were brought back to the capitol at Dover under police escort when they were done. Midnight came and went. Bayard was not about to let Collins Seitz be thrown to the wolves of racism. Everyone recognized his excellence as a judge. His integrity was beyond question. The state needed him—at least the worldly Wilmington community did, and it made up two-thirds of the people of Delaware. No one has ever recorded what concessions had to be offered, what porkbarreling or patronage had to be approved, or what sheer political muscle was exercised, but at 1:19 a.m. on the morning of June 16, 1951, the Delaware Senate went into executive session. Six minutes later, Collins J. Seitz was, at thirty-seven, the chancellor of Delaware.

Four months later, he presided over the third in the series of four state cases brought by the NAACP to test the legality of segregated schools in America. For the first time, the NAACP lawyers went into court with what they felt was a better than fair chance to win.

There were two separate cases in Delaware, but the issues were identical.

In suburban Claymont, about nine miles north of Wilmington along the

Delaware River, the attractive combination grade school and high school accommodated 400 or so students on a landscaped fourteen-acre site with well-equipped playing fields and carefully tended ornamental shrubbery. Negro children were not permitted to attend it. Instead, they had to take a bus to downtown Wilmington's venerable Howard High School, an unlovely structure bounded by factories, warehouses, and badly deteriorating tenements. The trip took most of the colored children from Claymont fifty or more minutes each way. Howard, with nearly 1,300 pupils, had a pupil-teacher ratio of 24:1—one-third higher than the ratio at Claymont—and nearly 60 percent of the Claymont faculty members held master's degrees, compared with fewer than 40 percent at Howard. Claymont offered several subjects unavailable at Howard, such as public speaking, economics, Spanish, and trigonometry, and a wide range of extracurricular activities, such as an art club, a driver's-education group, a student newspaper, and a square-dancing group, not offered at Howard. Associated with Howard but nine blocks away was the rundown Carver vocational-training annex, to which students had to traipse in all kinds of weather. Everything considered, the trip into Wilmington seemed hardly worth it to Ethel Belton and seven other Negro parents of Claymont who brought the matter to the attention of Louis Redding in Wilmington in March of 1951. Redding urged the Claymont parents to ask the State Board of Education to admit their children to the local high school. They tried and were turned down.

Out west of Wilmington, about as far from it as Claymont, was the tiny rural village of Hockessin, a mile or two from the Pennsylvania state line. Back in 1945, Sarah Bulah of Hockessin had read in the Wilmington newspapers about a ten-month-old Negro baby that had been found abandoned in the city. Mrs. Bulah asked her husband, Fred, who worked as a foreman at a paper mill in nearby Yorklyn, if they might adopt the child. Mr. Bulah had fathered eight children in his first marriage, four of whom survived to adulthood, but Sarah, who was his second wife, was by now in her fifties and past child-bearing age. They fretted a bit about what health problems the abandoned infant might be suffering, but upon contacting welfare authorities in Wilmington, Mrs. Bulah found a plumply fit baby with whom she instantly fell in love. Officials were troubled by the lack of a bathtub in the Bulahs' home, but when the family agreed to have one installed the moment that war-caused material shortages permitted, the couple was awarded the child and named her Shirley Barbara.

In the autumn of 1950, Sarah Bulah got it into her head that there was something basically unjust about the fact that a bus passed right by her front door to take the white children of Hockessin to their pretty little school up on the hill while she had to drive her daughter, Shirley, two miles to the old one-room schoolhouse for colored youngsters down in the village. The differences between the schools bothered her a good deal less than the complete absence of transportation for the colored children. She had to get out the old Chevrolet she used for selling maybe sixty dozen eggs a week to her neighbors, and drive Shirley to the school and, in bad weather, stay with her until the teacher arrived. It was not right. If there was a bus for white children, there should be one for colored children. Or maybe the school bus for whites that went right by her door could stop for Shirley.

Sarah Bulah wrote the Department of Public Instruction for the State of Delaware in Dover. Weeks passed. Nothing happened. Then she wrote Elbert N. Carvel, the governor of Delaware. He answered with remarkable promptness. The same mail brought a letter from an assistant bureaucrat telling Mrs. Bulah what she already knew—that "we have no transportation facilities" for her daughter's school—and suggesting she apply for "the private allowance based on the distances as shown in Rule 18 of the enclosed Rules and Regulations." Unfortunately, Rule 18 applied only to families who lived farther away from a school than she did. Mrs. Bulah wrote more letters. She wanted that bus for white children that went right by her home twice a day to stop for Shirley. Finally she got a firm letter from the state superintendent of the Department of Public Instruction that said the State Board of Education had reviewed her case and decided that "bus transportation is an integral part of a school program, and that, since the State Constitution requires separate educational facilities for colored and white children, your children may not ride on a bus serving a white school." Delaware, in other words, was telling Sarah Bulah that colored children were not entitled to what white children were. She went to see Louis Redding.

"He said he wouldn't help me get a Jim Crow bus to take my girl to any Jim Crow school," Mrs. Bulah remembers, "but if I was interested in sendin' her to an integrated school, why, then maybe he'd help. Well, I thanked God right then and there." Redding went out to her home that very evening to meet with Fred Bulah and make sure he understood the risks involved. Impressed with the Bulahs' determination, Redding dictated a letter to go over Mrs. Bulah's signature to the chairman of the local school board, requesting Shirley's admission to the white school. It was forwarded to the state board, which told Mrs. Bulah that her request went against the law. So she sued to change the law.

Sarah Bulah was not overly popular with the black folks of Hockessin over her lawsuit. None of them joined her in it. Said her minister, Reverend Martin Luther Kilson of the Chippey African Union Methodist Church, who had come to his calling after completing a correspondence Bible course thirty years earlier: "I was for segregation. These folks around here would rather have a colored teacher. They didn't want to be mixed up with no white folks. All we wanted was a bus for the colored. Redding and some members of the NAACP encouched this issue of segregation. I hated to see them tamper with that little old colored school next to our church. It was so handy." Handy to Reverend Kilson, not to Sarah Bulah.

Redding's papers named as principal defendant in both the Claymont and Hockessin cases the members of the State Board of Education, first of whom in alphabetical order was Francis B. Gebhart. The two cases were thus called *Belton v. Gebhart* and *Bulah v. Gebhart*.

They were filed in U.S. District Court in Wilmington, where Redding asked for a special three-judge District Court to hear arguments. Delaware's Attorney General Hyman Albert Young argued, though, that since a state law was involved, the cases ought to be heard first in a state court—namely, the Court of Chancery. Nothing could have suited Redding better than to have the just-approved chancellor preside over the cases, yet the Negro attorney had hesitated to file in his court. "The University of Delaware case had made Seitz a lot of enemies," Redding recalls, "and we didn't want him to have this much additional heat on him by having to decide the school cases as well." But once the state itself had asked for the cases to be shifted to the chancellor's courtroom, the NAACP felt the pressure had been eased a bit on Collins Seitz, a man whose courage seemed to need little shoring up.

"I knew Thurgood Marshall well enough to call him when Jack Greenberg was finishing up here," recalls Columbia law professor Walter Gellhorn, "and tell him that it was about time his office stopped discriminating against white men and gave one a chance."

Jack Greenberg was not yet twenty-five years old in 1949 when he first walked through the door to the cramped offices of the NAACP Legal Defense Fund on West 40th Street in Manhattan. Twenty-five years later, he would still be with the Fund, running it out of a suite of Columbus Circle offices as big—if hardly as plush—as any Wall Street law firm's. Those who have worked closely with him over the years in which Greenberg has risen to become perhaps the most knowledgeable and successful civil-rights lawyer in America are agreed on several of his qualities: a supple and uncluttered mind, great intellectual energy eagerly exercised and methodically disciplined, the courage to take a position on a complex legal question and the stamina to stick to it, and the manipulative skills to keep a large organization of professionals working with dedication toward a goal beyond their own enshrinement. Most people who have worked with him also agree that Jack Greenberg is not a particularly lovable man. They do not say that he is a mean or unfriendly man—just that he seems to have little time for amenities. Close friends acknowledge there is a frostiness to his exterior, but say it hides, as one puts it, "a substratum of deep emotional commitment as to what kind of world this should be." Others who have watched him close-up for extended stretches suggest he is more bloodless technician than outraged freedom fighter.

As a youngster growing up in the Bensonhurst section of Brooklyn and later in a pleasant neighborhood near Bronx Park, Jack Greenberg saw few Negroes and knew almost none. Nor was there a strong civil-libertarian tradition in the family. His father was a certified public accountant, and it was thought that Jack might combine the practices of accounting and law. At DeWitt Clinton High School in the Bronx, his class yearbook predicted a career for him in business administration. His undergraduate days at Columbia were given over in part to training in the Navy Reserve, and it was not until he was serving as a lieutenant junior grade on a landing ship in the Pacific that he saw the face of racial injustice close-up. "The only blacks on board were three or four stewards' mates," he remembers. "They were our servants. It made me uncomfortable." His unsuccessful effort to get one of the black crew members another job on board was the beginning of a career devoted to helping end the Negro's status as the white man's servant.

At Columbia Law School, Greenberg won academic distinction, but the shaping part of his legal education was his work in the quasi-curricular program that Walter Gellhorn directed and called, blandly enough, "Legal Survey." It was nothing less than an apprenticeship in civil-liberties law, though in that Red-scare era after the Second World War it was given the protective coloration of a half-credit course. As a liberal young member of the conservative Columbia law faculty in the mid-Thirties, Gellhorn began attracting students eager to put their brains at the disposal of such social-activist groups as the labor unions, the American Civil Liberties Union, the American Jewish Committee, and the NAACP. As such groups came to Gellhorn with pressing problems requiring legal research, he would shape them into questions that his students could approach in seminar fashion, breaking down the components of the problem and then assembling the pieces in an action-oriented memorandum or a legal brief. It was real work for real clients, among whom Thurgood Marshall's office was episodically included, especially during the voting-rights cases.

"I thought well of Greenberg," Gellhorn recalls. "He came to Columbia in the immediate post-war era when the quality of the law school was very high. He was in speedy company. Toward the end, he said he wanted very much to get into *pro bono* work, and there just weren't many avenues open then. I was a director of the ACLU, so I knew how small a staff they had." But Gellhorn kept asking around in Greenberg's behalf while the young graduate took a post with the New York State Law Review Commission, where he scrutinized old and proposed new acts of the legislature and helped draft a few, including one that allowed prisoners paroled from a life sentence to get married. Among those Gellhorn approached was Thurgood Marshall, whose office seemed a particularly promising spot for Greenberg's legal talents.

Greenberg's coolness under fire was apparent even at the start of his legal career and developed, as Gellhorn watched it, into a highly valuable asset. "He doesn't get into a flap when the going gets rough," the Columbia professor notes, "and he can stand controversy without developing animosity. Perhaps more emotion was wanted in him by some, but this coolness of his—which Thurgood Marshall shared, by the way—was tactically correct, whether conscious or not. After all, they were asserting legal rights—not simply arguing moral positions—and they took as intellectual an approach as possible. An emotional one would not have been productive, especially in the South."

Thurgood Marshall filed Greenberg's name away, and when an opening developed in the Fund office he called Gellhorn back. "I asked him how Greenberg had done in his studies at Columbia," Marshall recalls, "and Walter paused and said, 'Why, I don't actually know.' " Greenberg had in fact been designated a Harlan Fiske Stone Scholar at Columbia Law School, but what impressed Gellhorn—and what he cited to Marshall—was

Greenberg's student work for the ACLU and the Japanese-American Citizens League in the "Legal Survey" course and the craftsmanship and care the young lawyer exhibited working on the New York State Code. That was the sort of training Marshall valued most highly.

From Greenberg's end, the idea of working for and with Negroes in an organization dedicated to widening the rights of black America seemed not at all peculiar. "The question of race never really entered into it," he says of his feeling about going to work for Thurgood Marshall. "It was a matter of human liberty. It was the principles that were involved." Beyond that, there was the intellectual challenge. Herbert Hill, another white man who went to work for the NAACP—in the labor field—after the war, recalls Greenberg's remarking after having been at the Fund for several years that his was the best job of any lawyer in the United States. "And he was right," adds Hill, "if the lawyer's prime interest was constitutional law."

Marshall put his new young white assistant to work researching the wisdom of using special three-judge federal courts as the Fund's principal avenue of litigation. After several weeks, Greenberg handed in his memo. It was technical, thickly detailed, exceedingly dry—but very solid. It was also characteristic of an attorney who would always resent the occasional snide cuts he absorbed from acquaintances in the profession to the effect that civil-rights law was the toyland of the legal world. Greenberg was also exposed early to the waywardness of human nature that sometimes cropped up and prevented too abstract an approach to his task. "Shortly after I went to work at the Fund," Greenberg recalls, "a woman came into the office and told me that her son had been sent to jail in Richmond—and it was a long sentence—for stealing a bag of peanuts. I was outraged and went and told Thurgood about it. He just sort of raised his eyebrows, but didn't say anything. I got busy on the case, and it turned out that the bag was one of those enormous burlap sacks that are used down there to haul peanuts to the market. The fellow had also stolen the truck it was in."

Greenberg learned rapidly how to direct his zeal, and his early collaboration with Louis Redding in Wilmington on the University of Delaware case boosted his standing at the Fund. "He was obviously a very bright lawyer, though perhaps with more of an intellectual than emotional commitment to his tasks," remarks Robert Carter, who worked closely with him in those early years before a bitter estrangement developed between the two a decade later. Though Carter had seniority at the start, it became clear in time that he and Greenberg were vying for the position of Marshall's heir apparent. The contrast between the two had less to do with their surface mannerisms than with what seemed to others to be going on inside them. Nor was that assessment divided along racial lines. A white observer who worked with and admires the lawyerly skills of both men remarks, "Carter was much more of a human being—not the mechanical and obsessive kind of man Greenberg is." Adds another white NAACP veteran: "His name may be Greenberg, but he's practically a—a WASP! He used to laugh at me for what he felt was my excessive involvement with Negro activities outside the office, like my going to speak at black churches." Others who worked with him closely saw him differently. Professor Louis Pollak suggests that the seemingly abstract manner Greenberg wears in public may be "a form of self-protection from the drain of emotional energy that his work could so easily cause—rather as with a surgeon." Adds Louis Redding, the black attorney, who has worked with Greenberg for a quarter of a century: "Jack is not a man to spill his guts over what's inside him. He's a very private individual. But there has never been any question in my mind over his genuineness about the Negro cause."

That relationship flowered during the fall of 1951 as the young white NAACP lawyer from New York rejoined the first black lawyer in Delaware history in arguing against segregated public schools before Chancellor Seitz, who had ruled in their favor in the University of Delaware case the year before. With the lessons of the Charleston and Topeka trials behind them and a sympathetic judge sitting, the NAACP attorneys mounted the strongest social and psychological attack yet on *Plessy*. Greenberg was not an unalloyed enthusiast about using social scientists as expert witnesses. "All the expert testimony really said," he comments, "was that if you stopped and thought about it, segregated people are clearly the worse off for it. Yes, it's hard to demonstrate this precisely, but doesn't common sense tell you as much?" Perhaps the eventual outcome would not have been altered without the social scientists, Greenberg adds, "but the real question is whether we would have brought the segregation cases when and how we did without them. The main function of the social-science testimony was to help the courts—and especially the Supreme Court—convey the confidence of its common-sense perceptions of what the nation knew about right and wrong in this regard." Human, not strictly legal, values were at stake.

Greenberg had his share of disappointments in trying to enlist witnesses for the Delaware cases. Among those who said no were Columbia sociologist Robert Lynd, co-author of the classic study *Middletown*, and black Haverford sociologist Ira De A. Reid. But the panel of experts who responded affirmatively was easily the strongest to appear for the NAACP since the *Sweatt* trial. Greenberg was able to put fourteen expert witnesses on the stand. Columbia's Otto Klineberg gave the court the essence of his career-long studies: Negroes had the same inherent learning capacity as whites. Ohio State's George A. Kelly, then president of the American Board of Examiners in Professional Psychology and a consultant to the U.S. Public Health Service, the Air Force, and the Surgeon General of the Navy, spoke of the fatiguing and otherwise punitive effects of the nearly two hours of bus-riding required of the Negro youngsters from Claymont who attended Howard High in Wilmington each day. Harvard psychologist Jerome Bruner, who was soon to gain recognition as one of the nation's leading writers and authorities on the learning process, addressed himself to the cancerous effect of segregation in producing frustration, apathy, and hostility among Negro schoolchildren. Stephen J. Wright, then professor of education and dean of the faculty at Hampton Institute and later president of Fisk University and then the United Negro College Fund, analyzed the virtues of the white high school in Claymont in contrast with the overall learning opportunity at

Howard High for Negroes; almost all the advantages, he found, rested with the former. A number of professors from Delaware whom Redding enlisted added their weight to the testimony. And Kenneth Clark reported on the results of his doll tests with a group of forty-one Delaware black youngsters, whose overall functioning, the psychologist now asserted more boldly than he had at the Charleston trial five months earlier, was impaired as a result of school segregation:

> The nature of that impairment seemed clearly indicated by the results in which it is seen that three out of the four—three out of every four youngsters—who when asked the question, "Which of these dolls is likely to act bad?", picked the brown doll. . . .
>
> Now, when you see that 100 percent of these youngsters correctly identify themselves with the brown doll . . . I think we have clearcut evidence of rather deep damage to the self-esteem of these youngsters, a feeling of inferiority, a feeling of inadequacy—evidence which was further supported by the kind of things which the youngsters said: "I suppose we do act kind of bad. We don't act like white people."

Such a quantitative approach to the psychological effects of segregation had its uses, but Greenberg wanted to add a qualitative evaluation by a prominent clinical psychiatrist with full medical credentials. If such an authority would first examine in depth a group of both black and white Delaware youngsters and then report to the court on how segregation affected them, the effect might be powerful. But psychiatrists were expensive, and to find one who would give a good deal of his time to such a project without charging for it seemed an unlikely prospect. Yet Greenberg did find one, and an eminent one at that, with a touch of genuine Viennese in his speech. The effect on the courtroom in Wilmington proved not only powerful but nearly hypnotic.

As a Bavarian-born medical student doing post-graduate work in Vienna, Frederic Wertham once visited the office of Sigmund Freud to convey the request of an American friend. Would the great doctor consider writing an article—"at any price"—for the American magazine the *New Republic*, then under the editorial direction of Walter Lippmann? Freud was cordial to young Wertham and offered to give him introductions around the city, but he could not accept the kind invitation from the magazine because he did not believe that psychiatry ought to be written about in a popularized way.

Frederic Wertham came to disagree sharply with the master on this question. As time went on, he would view himself as a forensic as well as a clinical psychiatrist whose most valuable contribution was to speak to and write for the layman about the lessons psychiatry offers in helping people sustain their will to survive.

Educated at Kings College in London, the University of Munich, and a number of other famed institutions on the Continent, Wertham came to the United States in 1922 at the age of twenty-seven and joined the staff of the

Johns Hopkins Hospital in Baltimore, where he worked for seven years and served as chief resident psychiatrist. It was while there that Wertham began to testify in court on criminal cases in which the sanity of the defendants was in doubt. He became friends with attorney Clarence Darrow, whose successful defense in the Loeb-Leopold case in Chicago on the ground of temporary insanity did much to introduce the concept that compulsively anti-social behavior required medical treatment, not capital punishment or indefinite confinement. In a number of grisly cases, Wertham testified on the mental state of the defendants, including one man charged with killing fifteen children.

After working with the National Research Council in Washington for a few years, Wertham came to New York City, where he would do his major work. He was named a senior psychiatrist with the Department of Hospitals and joined the medical faculty at New York University, which ran Bellevue Hospital, where Wertham at times directed the alcoholic ward, the children's ward, and the prison ward. At the same time, he organized and directed the clinic established in 1932 by the Court of General Sessions to give every convicted felon a thorough psychiatric examination prior to sentencing—the first such clinic in the country. The steady stream of reports he and his staff filed with the court and the appearances he was obliged to make on occasion to elaborate upon his clinic's findings for the enlightenment of the bench began to build Wertham's reputation as a leading forensic psychiatrist. And he started to write about violent behavior in human beings, which he showed was not instinctively programmed into their lives but was attributable to the severe tensions and traumas of their psychiatric circumstances—and was therefore generally treatable by medical science. His first book, *The Brain as an Organ*, a medical text, appeared in 1935 and was followed by half a dozen books written for laymen, many of them dealing with his own case studies in violence. His most successful and controversial book, *Seduction of the Innocent*, dealt with the corrosive effects of the popular media on children's personalities and behavior, especially gory comic books that seemed to lack any redeeming virtue while glorifying violence, sadism, and racism.

While he was at Johns Hopkins, and partly as a result of his friendship with Darrow, Wertham had come to understand that the racist strain in white America contributed to the disproportionately high incidence of pathological behavior among Negroes. Darrow, Wertham discovered, was a surprisingly prudish man who once was so loath to discuss a homosexuality case with the psychiatrist while his wife was present that he bustled her off into his bathroom, where, surrounded by baskets of fruits and flowers sent by well-wishers for the attorney's latest victory, Mrs. Wertham was soon forgotten and ended up napping in the tub. But there was nothing naïve about Darrow's understanding of the plight of the Negro. He had been one of the founding supporters of the NAACP, and he took on black clients that few successful white defense attorneys would have. In Wertham, he found a kindred spirit, for few psychiatrists of the day accepted even those Negro patients who could afford the often protracted examinations and therapy. At the Hopkins out-patient clinic, Wertham routinely dealt with black patients, and he occasionally did what almost no other psychiatrist in America would dream of doing: testify in a court of law in behalf of a Negro. Segregation, Wertham saw in Jim Crow Baltimore, did not promote good mental conditioning, to put it mildly. In New York and the North in general, he found, the situation was worse still. "The exploitation of the Negro in the South is a very direct and brutal one," he remarked in the mid-Forties. "In the North, it is very insidious—half-concealed—and in the long run really much more ruthless and deadly."

He knew what he was talking about. Starting in 1946, Wertham had been the guiding force to a group that grew to more than twenty men and women who contributed two or more evenings of each week to a free clinic at 133rd Street near Seventh Avenue in Harlem. Of more than 4,000 psychiatrists in the nation at the time, hardly a dozen were Negro, and thus black communities like Harlem, where 400,000 people were wedged into an area that should have accommodated perhaps 75,000, were virtually without badly needed psychiatric care. And the few highly trained people in the field who would take Negro patients could hardly be expected to provide their services for nothing. But Wertham did, along with the team of psychiatrists, psychologists, social workers, physiotherapists, registered nurses, speech and reading experts, and secretaries who took over two basement rooms with exposed pipes in the community house at St. Philip's Episcopal Church. They called it the Lafargue Clinic, after a black Cuban physician who worked in humane causes, and anyone could come to it for help. Those who could afford it were asked to pay a quarter per visit. There were no appointments. You just came. Patients would be interviewed in screened-off cubicles and their problems then analyzed after hours by the team that worked with Wertham.

It was to Lafargue that Jack Greenberg and Louis Redding ushered a group of thirteen Delaware children, eight of them black and five white. Kenneth Clark's tests had been limited to Negro youngsters, and so the inclusion of whites in the Lafargue group was of special value. They obtained the white children—"some of whom were very prejudiced," Wertham recalls—by explaining to their parents that the clinic was conducting experimental research in race relations. Segregation was not mentioned. Since Wilmington was only two hours by train from New York, it was possible for the Lafargue staff to examine the children on five different occasions. It took some time to win their confidence and put them at ease, for the trips were, of course, a major adventure. After the first session, Greenberg took the whole group to dinner at a Chinese restaurant, where, "as I recall, they ordered the most expensive dishes on the menu"—an almost certain indication of their normality.

During the individual and group interviews with the Delaware children, who ranged in age from nine to sixteen, the human cost of a segregated society revealed itself. The black youngsters in particular were responsive to the Lafargue clinicians, in part because they had so long bottled up feelings that they had not been able to discuss comfortably with their parents, whose own sense of insecurity, the children guessed or sensed, would have left them embarrassed by the subject of segregation. The Negro children who were bussed long distances to school were plainly unhappy about the fact. "I travel thirty miles a day to school," said one. "The white high school is twelve blocks away." The buses were often late and caused them to miss classes, some of them said. One thirteen-year-old reported, "When we get on the bus, the white children [outside] look at us and laugh." The tensions produced between the races by enforced segregation were apparent to the Lafargue people. "When you sit with the white people, they look at you so hard," said one thirteen-year-old girl. "If I have to go to segregated schools all the time," a boy added, "I won't know how to react to different people in life. . . . [You] have to be so careful about what you say, how you act. Seems you don't have a chance to act normal [and] natural." Prejudice as such was attributed by the Negro children principally to "the plain Americans." Wertham was struck by the phrase and pressed to learn who "the plain Americans" were. By a process of elimination, the psychiatrist soon deduced that the reference was to white Anglo-Saxon Protestants. "The others are the foreigners," the children chimed in. "They're much nicer to us. They treat us better—the Poles, the Italians, the Jews, the Catholics, the Germans. . . ." They cited, by way of example, the willingness of some Catholic schools to welcome black children and some Italian restaurant owners to serve their families. Such behavior was in dramatic contrast to the prevailing pattern of segregation they confronted—the restaurants they and their parents could not enter, the drugstore counters at which they could not sit, the movie theaters they could not attend. One sixteen-year-old girl recounted how she and a friend had gone job-hunting the previous summer and been told by one restaurant owner that he did not hire colored dishwashers.

The effects of segregation were by no means limited to the black children that the clinic examined. "In some of the white children we found a subtle, though definite tendency to identify themselves unconsciously with the Negro children," Wertham later reported. Among other white children, he found, segregation tended to confirm or sanction some of the worst prejudices absorbed from other sources in the community. One white child told Wertham's group that some of the youngsters in her class said they wanted to tie up colored children with their hands behind their backs and make them work—a not very practical arrangement. "The boys say that they [the Negro children] should work and we should play," she said. "I guess they got that from the comic books."

On October 22, 1951, before the chancellor of Delaware, Frederic Wertham reported all this and a good deal more, and Collins Seitz gave him all the time he wanted. Seitz had never heard of Wertham, but he recalls being struck by the precision and thoroughness of his testimony, which ran for more than an hour and took the form of a lecture to the court. Wertham did not abuse Seitz's receptivity with histrionics or overstatement. "Darrow would tell me no wisecracks and no theatrics," the psychiatrist recalls, "and just to present my findings straight and to the point." In Wilmington, Frederic Wertham told the court that segregation created a massive public-health problem and elaborated on his charge:

... I am basing it partly on a positive concept of mental health, by which I mean that it isn't enough to look at the child and say, "This little girl doesn't have nightmares, she gets by in school, she doesn't annoy anyone at home, she isn't a juvenile delinquent"—that is not enough. I hold the scientific opinion that if a rosebush should produce twelve roses and if only one rose grows, it is not a healthy rosebush. It is up to us to find out what is interfering with its growth and with its health.

Now the fact of segregation in public and high school creates in the mind of the child an unsolvable conflict, an unsolvable emotional conflict, and I would say an inevitable conflict. . . . One way to overcome such a conflict is to have a realistic rationalization about it, but . . . I have found that the children cannot find such a realistic rationalization for the simple reason that the adults don't give it to them and for the reason that the state itself, to the extent that I have searched for it and they have searched for it, cannot give an understandable explanation. So we place on these children a burden we don't take ourselves ordinarily, and they cannot solve it.

... I have come to the conclusion that the physical differences in these schools are not at all really material to my opinion. In other words, if I may express it graphically, if the state of Delaware would employ Professor Einstein to teach physics in marble halls to these children, I would still say everything I have said goes: It is the fact of segregation in general and the problems that come out of it that to my mind is anti-educational, by which I mean that education in the larger sense is interfered with. . . . Most of the children we have examined interpret segregation in one way and only one way—and that is they interpret it as punishment. There is no doubt about that. Now, whether that is true, whether the state of Delaware wants to punish these children, has nothing to do with it. I am only testifying about what is in the minds of children.

Wertham acknowledged that school segregation alone was not the culprit, but with conciseness he ticked off the reasons it was especially damaging: (1) It is absolutely clearcut; (2) the state does it; (3) it is discrimination of a very long duration, and (4) "it is bound up with the whole educational process, which I consider part of the mental health of the child. It hits the child at two very important moments of his life . . . where a child steps forward from the . . . more or less sheltered family [and in adolescence where for] the first time the person must find a social group for himself." The state, Wertham suggested in coming to a close, "identifies itself with its most bigoted citizens" in perpetuating school segregation, a practice that he said could affect the minds of children with severe force "if we continuously destroy their own ethical development by an act of government."

On cross-examination, Wertham disarmed Attorney General Young by admitting that non-segregated communities, such as New York, were also implicated in many of his remarks, for "although the state of New York does not practice segregation by law . . . there are schools, too, where there are mostly Negroes, and if they are not segregated by law, they are segregated by custom or prejudice . . . segregation anyway *de facto*." That satisfied Young, who then asked if the duration of segregation as a custom in a community did not make a difference to Wertham's analysis of the social pressures it caused. The psychiatrist answered:

We are dealing with the mind of a child and the emotions of a child of nine, who is late for a bus going to a segregated school, and the state decrees it, and the bus for white children passes and children stick out their tongues and say, "You nigger." What difference does it make if it is one year or one hundred years? Do I care where the tubercle bacillus comes from? The tubercle bacillus is the tubercle bacillus. . . . I am a doctor. I want to know what is good for a child, and I don't care how long they have done it.

Well, but segregation had been a fact of life in Delaware for a long time. Would ending it "cause or eliminate the effect of this emotional disturbance and this frustration that you say exists in Negro children"? Wertham shot back:

> . . . I don't think that laws are only there to tell people what to do or what not to do; I think laws are one of the best educational measures we have, and I think if this law were changed . . . it would be a very great educational factor, and I think many adults would say, "What? They changed the law? They must have something." I think the law very often is ahead of the people.

Wertham himself thought his best weapon was the concession that there was as much prejudice in New York as in Delaware. "That melted the judge's disbelief," he suspects, and contributed to the exceedingly loose tether Seitz kept on his testimony. "He seemed a very neutral judge," Wertham adds. "Darrow told me, 'You don't need a friend on the bench—just a fair-minded man.' "

The closest thing Attorney General Young could find to a defender of the Delaware school-segregation law was, perhaps not inappropriately, the state superintendent in charge of the Department of Public Instruction. His name was George R. Miller, Jr., and it was he who wrote the letter to the Bulahs telling them that their daughter, Shirley, could not ride the white school bus that went right by their house in Hockessin, even though the state provided no bus for Negro children. Superintendent Miller's emergence as the principal defender of the state program he was charged with directing was noteworthy only because of the doctoral thesis he had written in 1943 at New York University's School of Education.

Miller's advisor on his doctoral had been sociologist Dan W. Dodson, who testified for the NAACP in the *Bulah* and *Belton* cases. Professor Dodson thought it worth the time of Greenberg and Redding to review Miller's thesis. It was titled *Adolescent Negro Education in Delaware: A Study of the Negro Secondary School and Community (Exclusive of Wilmington)*. The exclusion was curious in view of the fact that Wilmington was the site of the only four-year high school for Negroes in the entire state. Otherwise, though, it was a quite valuable and skillful thesis, with a good deal of original fieldwork and surveys of public opinion. These were some of the things George Miller wrote in 1943 about colored schools of Delaware:

> In spite of the progress made in secondary education for Negroes they have a long way to go before the educational chasm between the two races can be bridged. Meanwhile the Negro must continue to face the requirements of American life at an enormous disadvantage.

. . . Negro youth have demonstrated their capacity for academic achievement in schools comparable to those available for white pupils. With the
resulting knowledge that the Negro is not necessarily condemned to subordinate
position by any innate disability of intellect, the Negroes seemed [in a report by
Franklin Frazier that Miller was citing with approval] dissatisfied with an inferior
social status. . . .

. . . There must be a fairer distribution of state and local funds among the
white and the Negro schools. . . . Segregation of the white and Negro for
educational purposes offers innumerable opportunities for discriminatory practices.

. . . Our record as a nation will be improved only as it benefits from the
potentialities of all of its people.

Things had not changed much regarding the inequities between the white
and colored schools in Delaware since George Miller composed that
indictment of the system he now directed. It must be said in his behalf that
on the witness stand he did shrink from admitting the disparity. About the
only step Miller could point to with flaccid pride was an act of the state
legislature three months earlier assuring equal per-capita outlays for white
and colored schoolchildren—a condition that in theory had been obligatory
since the *Plessy* decision fifty-five years earlier. Redding lacerated him on
cross-examination.

Q. How long has that situation [of equal per-capita outlays] existed, doctor?
A. Not very long. I think July 1, 1951, wasn't it, when that new law went into
effect, was implemented?
Q. Prior to that time the schools for Negroes and whites did not have available
to them equal funds?
A. I would say that is true.
Q. Isn't it true that under the law as it has existed since the adoption of our
state constitution Negroes and whites are entitled to equal educational
opportunities?
A. That's correct.
Q. So the mere fact that a law has been enacted providing for this doesn't
insure its effectuation, does it?
A. It does not.
Q. And haven't you said that previously the education offered for Negroes in
this state was not equal to the education offered for whites?
A. I said on the secondary level.
Q. . . . And is it not true that there is inequality on the elementary level?
A. Well, I would have to say yes. I am not being forced to say yes, you
understand. . . .

It was not an attractive sight to see a man stew in his own juices quite so
publicly.

After hearing three days of testimony, Chancellor Seitz wanted to see for
himself how the white and colored schools compared. He was accompanied
only by his clerk and the opposing attorneys. The three-car caravan moved
with such speed that Jack Greenberg found himself wondering whether a

traffic cop who might flag them down and ticket the judge would be held in contempt of court.

The contrast was overwhelming. Howard High and the Carver vocational annex in Wilmington were plainly rundown, and the state had already acknowledged that Carver was going to be abandoned and Howard itself refurbished. The eyes of the viewing party were not their only sense to be assaulted: the urinals at the Negro schools were not in working order and the smell was overpowering. The Claymont School for whites was in every way a more attractive, better-equipped, and more satisfactorily maintained place. But the contrast between the little two-room schoolhouse for colored children and the four-classroom school for whites in Hockessin where the Bulahs lived made an even greater impression on the chancellor.

"No. 29 [the white school] is so beautifully situated that the view immediately catches the eye," Seitz wrote in his opinion. "The landscaping is also outstanding." It was a point that the NAACP had stressed during the trial. "Its landscaping includes a pine watershed located at the rear of its school area to prevent the wash of rains and what-not," their expert witness had testified. "It has a multiflora rose border to lend beauty and some privacy to the rear of the school yard. Scattered throughout . . . are clumps of bushes, various types of trees, all of which lend a very restful and pleasing appearance to the entire school plant." Inside the building, Seitz noted other features: a fully equipped nurse's office, a basketball court, a big basement with ample storage facilities, and an auditorium where he came upon "a dancing class of little white children who gave a quite lovely performance. It was very impressive." Shirley Bulah's colored school had no dancing class. It had no auditorium. It had no nurse's office—just a first-aid kit. It did not have drinking fountains of the kind that the white school had or sanitary toilet facilities. It had, as Seitz wrote in his opinion, "one commode in a very small room which adjoins the space where the children's lunches, the janitorial materials and the school drinking-water bottles are kept." The colored school was also unlandscaped, Seitz remarked, "and apparently always has been."

It would take five months before the chancellor's opinion came down. Seitz normally worked with dispatch, but he could not write until the briefs were submitted by both sides. Delays in getting the transcript of the trial slowed the attorneys, and the state took all the time it could get to work out its plan to improve the educational facilities for its admittedly disadvantaged black children. Briefs were finally turned in toward the latter part of February 1952. The opinion was issued at the beginning of April.

"I found it inexcusable that the state would lend its support to dividing its citizens this way," Seitz reflects, and his opinion pulsed with moral outrage, though it never lapsed into the abrasive language that Judge Waties Waring indulged in in his last opinions on racial questions in South Carolina. The chancellor shared the finding of fact that Judge Huxman had made in the Topeka case regarding the psychological hardship caused by mandatory segregation of schoolchildren, but Seitz elaborated. Referring to Wertham as "one of America's foremost psychiatrists," the judge quoted and paraphrased him at length and concluded that the practice of racial separation "creates a mental health problem in many Negro children with a resulting impediment to their educational progress." He then added:

> Defendants say that the evidence shows that the state may not be "ready" for non-segregated education and that a social problem cannot be solved with legal force. Assuming the validity of the contention without for a minute conceding the sweeping factual assumption, nevertheless, the contention does not answer the fact that the Negro's mental health and therefore his educational opportunities are adversely affected by state-imposed segregation in education. The application of constitutional principles is often distasteful to some citizens, but that is one reason for constitutional guarantees. The principles override transitory passions.

Segregation *per se*, then, created inequality. But did that make it unconstitutional? Principled as he was, Seitz was hardly an iconoclast. "Could I make a reasonable inference at that time," he speculates at a distance of more than two decades, "that the Supreme Court, if presented with a case of public-school segregation, would have ruled it unconstitutional?" He examined the precedents with great intensity from *Plessy* to *Sweatt* and *McLaurin*. One case kept bothering him. "I wasn't writing on a clean slate," Seitz remarks. "You just couldn't ignore *Gong Lum*."

The NAACP lawyers had contended, ever since the Margold Report was drafted twenty years earlier, that Justice Taft's unanimous opinion of the Court in 1927 had avoided the main issue of whether segregation itself was legal and had merely ruled that the state of Mississippi was entitled to categorize Gong Lum's daughter Martha as "colored" and assign her to the colored school in her area. Lum, the NAACP said, had sued on the wrong issue; instead of challenging the whole system of segregation, he challenged only the way it was implemented with respect to his daughter. But Seitz could not put aside *Gong Lum* so readily. The Supreme Court had plainly ruled that Mississippi was acting well within its constitutional power in assigning an American of Chinese extraction to a "colored" school. "It is true that there was no proof in that case concerning the effect of such state-imposed segregation on Negroes," Seitz wrote. "But it seems to me that the very use of the 'separate but equal' doctrine in an elementary school case has implicit therein a recognition that in such a case there can be separate but equal educational opportunities in a Constitutional sense." He went on significantly:

> Of course, this could not be true were my finding of fact given Constitutional recognition, but if it were, the principle itself [of separate-but-equal] would be destroyed. In other words, the Supreme Court . . . has said a separate but equal test can be applied, at least below the college level. This court does not believe such an implication is justified under the evidence. Nevertheless, I do not believe a lower court can reject a principle of United States Constitutional law which has been adopted by fair implication by the highest court of the land. I believe the "separate but equal" doctrine in education should be rejected, but I also believe its rejection must come from that Court.

It looked as if Collins Seitz were going to come out just where Walter Huxman and the District Court in Kansas had. But the chancellor of Delaware saw a ready remedy available to the Negro plaintiffs that did not exist for the black children in Topeka, where the court had found the white and colored schools to be substantially equal. Seitz left the overruling of *Plessy* to the Supreme Court, but within the separate-but-equal doctrine he concluded that the Negro plaintiffs were being denied equal protection of the law by the inferior school facilities Delaware supplied to them. Claymont, he said, was "vastly superior," to the Howard-Carver school for blacks. The state's defense that such differences were inevitable in any comparison of urban and suburban schools the chancellor brushed aside because, he said, "it only goes to demonstrate the dreary fact that segregated education, as here provided, means that white children in the Claymont school district may have the benefits which flow from living in the suburbs, but Negro children similarly situated may not. . . . The cold, hard fact is that the state in this situation discriminates against Negro children."

The inequalities at the colored school in Hockessin were "depressing" to Seitz, and the state's denial of Mrs. Bulah's contention that her daughter should be allowed to ride the bus for white children so long as none was provided for blacks was indeed another reason why the facilities offered Shirley Bulah were unequal to those at the white school to which she now sought admission. "To suggest . . . that there are not enough Negroes to warrant the cost of a school bus for them," Seitz asserted, "is only another way of saying that they are not entitled to equal services because they are Negroes. Such an excuse will not do here."

Then Seitz delivered his thunderbolt. "It seems to me that when a plaintiff shows to the satisfaction of a court that there is an existing and continuing violation of the 'separate but equal' doctrine," he wrote, "he is entitled to have made available to him the state facilities which have been shown to be superior. To do otherwise is to say to such a plaintiff, 'Yes, your Constitutional rights are being invaded, but be patient, we will see whether in time they are still being violated.' " In short, he rejected the position taken by Judge Parker in the *Briggs* decision, where the state had promised to mend its ways and the court had given it six months to make a progress report. No, said Seitz, invoking the Supreme Court's decision in *Gaines* that the plaintiff's right to relief was a personal one, Shirley Barbara Bulah in Hockessin and Ethel Louise Belton and the nine other black plaintiffs in Claymont were entitled to immediate admission to the white schools in their communities.

For the first time, a segregated white public school in America had been ordered by court of law to admit black children. "This is the first real victory in our campaign to destroy segregation of American pupils in elementary and high schools," Thurgood Marshall announced to the press.

It was not the big breakthrough they had hoped for. It was in fact precisely the kind of technical victory Nathan Margold had seen as readily obtainable when he blueprinted the NAACP legal strategy in 1931: that segregation *as practiced*—not as a constitutionally sanitary concept—was illegal because it always failed to provide equality to the segregated Negro children. But it had taken more than two decades to get such a decision out of a state court, let alone the Supreme Court. Seitz's opinion, however, left no doubt as to his estimate of the social desirability and legal acceptability of segregation. If Huxman's decision in the Topeka case had sharply framed the question of segregation itself for presentation to the Supreme Court, Chancellor Seitz's decision had now put a big red ribbon around that frame and tied a bow on top.

It was a good thing, too, from where the NAACP lawyers sat, for in the interim between the hearing and the decision in the Delaware cases, the fourth and last of the state school-segregation cases had been both argued and decided. The result had given the pro-segregation forces of the nation new hope. It showed, too, that not for nothing had the capital of the Confederacy been located in Virginia.

# 19

## "Stick with Us"

In the middle of the twentieth century, in a remote county that time had left to dawdle amid the picturebook loveliness of the Virginia countryside, a leader arose among the black people. The blacks made up a bit more than half the population, but their hopes for obtaining justice from the whites remained nearly as slender and muted as those of their ancestors in bondage a century before. At the time of the events she inspired, this leader was sixteen years old and her beauty apparent to every eye. She did not claim, as Joan of Arc had, to be inspired by celestial voices. But some pious ones who knew her family well suggest that a messenger of the Lord, in the person of her uncle, who was a man of the cloth, helped inspire her unheralded emergence as leader of the Negroes of Prince Edward County. Her grand-mother's second husband, for one, disagrees with that view. He saw her growing up, and he says: "She had that grit in her herself."

Barbara Rose Johns was born in New York City in 1935, the oldest of five children of Robert and Violet Johns, who had come north from their rural Virginia home to find work. It was a hard time for most Americans, and for Negroes from Virginia with modest skills and less learning, Harlem was a forbidding place to seek a smile from fortune. Violet Johns worked as a domestic and her husband snatched what jobs he could while the family moved in with relatives in a roominghouse on 129th Street. After a while, they gave up and went home to Prince Edward County in Southside Virginia, at the northern end of the great Black Belt that formed an enormous scimitar curving southwestward for more than a thousand miles to the Mississippi and beyond. In Prince Edward, both their families owned some land, but farming was brutal without proper equipment and paid very little, so Robert ran a little general store that his older brother, the Reverend Vernon Johns, owned on The Road, as everyone called state highway 665 in the southwestern sector of the county known as Black Bottom. But there was not much money in running the store, either, and so the growing Johns family moved to Washington, where Violet found steady work and they lived in an apartment at Fourth and K streets Northeast not far from the Capitol. Barbara would walk by it often.

When war came, her father went into the Army, and the financial strain on her mother became even heavier, so the children were packed onto a train to live for the duration with their maternal grandmother back on the farm in

Virginia. As the oldest child, Barbara sensed that she had a special responsibility now as the train, filled with men in uniform, carried them southward 170 miles via Richmond toward the town of Farmville at the beginning of Southside Virginia. Her excitement was mingled with apprehension at the prospect of the free and open life in the country, so different from the city places where she had done most of her growing up. The tension passed quickly as all of the children fell into the ample embrace of their grandmother Mary Croner at her farmstead, which had already withstood more than its share of children's carrying-on. "I loved Ma Croner," says Barbara. "She was kind and open—and God's most patient woman."

She had little choice. Mary Croner had had a total of eight brothers and sisters in her own growing-up days on a Prince Edward farm, and after she married Charles Spencer and had nine children of her own, life was earnest. Her husband lived away in Sparrows Point, Maryland, as a construction worker during the week, and Mary coped alone with her brood. Then suddenly Charles Spencer was gone, killed in an accident on the job. The company sent some compensation, though, and the Widow Spencer paid $1,200 for the 106-acre farm on which they had been living and decided to work it for sustenance with the willing hands of her children. "We grew tobacco—maybe three, four acres of it—and corn, wheat, 'tater," she remembers. Tobacco was the key, the cash crop. "It's right hard to grow," she says. "You got to plow it, replant it, sucker it, top it, and worm it—and there weren't any sprayin' then. We sold it over in Farmville, mostly for cigars and chewin'." The 415 man hours of labor that went into an average acre of tobacco seemed barely worth the $150 or so that it brought in the Thirties. And, too, there was the cruel price that the weed exacted from the gray-brown soil. "It was kind of thin land," Mary recalls, "too thin to work, a lot of it was, and if you didn't fertilize it, the tobacco took too much out of the soil—and the thinner the soil, the more it took out."

Tobacco had been inflicting its toll on the earth of Virginia ever since the first Tidewater plantations were measured off in the seventeenth century. But land was plentiful then and the demand for tobacco in Europe high, so it did not matter that the soil was quickly exhausted. By the middle of the eighteenth century, though, the tobacco market had been glutted and much of the Tidewater land played out as settlers began pushing inland to the great Piedmont plateau. They came up the Appomattox River from Petersburg and found a gently undulating land of virgin oak and yellow pine on the ridges and slopes. The white men chopped out farms, and those who owned black slaves set them to the task, but it was not a place where great plantations flourished. Small harvests of tobacco were grown and shipped with timber down the river to Petersburg, and slowly the area was cleared.

In 1753, a chunk of 356 square miles of the inland earth was carved from Amelia County and named in honor of King George III's otherwise uncelebrated grandnephew, Prince Edward. Good for growing corn and wheat and hay in addition to peach and apple orchards, the land was given over only in small measure to the ravenous if profitable tobacco plant, and so the soil stayed fertile but the people stayed poor though they never starved.

In the first national census of 1790, the population of Prince Edward County was recorded as 8,100; in forty more years, it would reach 14,000—and stop. By 1900, it would inch up to 15,000 and then retreat, climbing back up to 15,000 by midcentury and then tailing off anew as the more vigorous of the young people emigrated in increasing numbers. All roads in Prince Edward led to the town of Farmville, the county seat of 3,000 to 4,000 souls on the Appomattox River, which formed the northern border of the county. Generals Lee and Grant, in that order, stopped at the local hotel in early April of 1865, shortly after the last battle of the Civil War had been fought along Saylor's Creek in the easternmost sector of the country; the two men were to meet at last a few days later and twenty-five miles to the west in the adjacent county of Appomattox.

Aside from Farmville, which in time turned into a busy marketplace and tobacco clearinghouse for several thousand square miles surrounding it, Prince Edward remained somnolently rural. Two-thirds of it was in forest land, most of it second-growth yellow Virginia pine, a tree that kept the county's lumber business in operation. Eighty percent of the cleared land was in corn and wheat and hay, as dairying became a cash crop along with the tobacco that grew everywhere but only in small stands. The black population, which had outnumbered the white by nearly two to one on the eve of the Civil War, fell off in the post-war days and more and more Negroes began to accumulate enough money to buy small spreads of their own. There were few large farms in the county—scarcely a dozen with as many as a thousand acres in 1950; most of them were a hundred or so acres, like Mary Croner's spread on the north side of the road between Hampden-Sydney, five miles south of Farmville, and the little settlement of Darlington Heights.

In 1932, Mary Spencer married Robert Croner, the man who share-cropped the big farm across the road from hers. Croner, a raw-boned widower, brought over his plow, two mules, and five children, and so there were fourteen young ones in the eight-room house, the boys and girls in separate quarters. "We made do," says Croner. "I bought me a wagon and we raised us some hogs, and we was all workin' the land. The land, it's a friend, and it was good when we could all work it. Mostly it was home to us."

Most of the Croner and Spencer children had struck out on their own by the time the batch of five belonging to Violet, Mary's second-born, moved in early in the Second World War. Barbara, the oldest of Violet Johns's children, fell right in with the family chores, including farm work. The worst of it was the tobacco. It was planted in rows about two and a half feet apart, spaced widely enough to let the sunlight reach the middle and lower leaves and to assure enough moisture to each plant. At 5,000 or more plants to the acre, the tobacco took a lot of tending. Barbara's specialties were topping them off after they sprouted twelve or fourteen leaves but before the flowers bloomed, and then gently tearing off the "suckers," the little shoots that grew off the leaves and sapped their vitality. "They were the most irksome, tiresome things to pull off when you were out in the blazing sun," she remembers. But she did it without complaining. "She didn't have a lot of put-on airs about her," says Ma Croner. "She was a country girl, not some flirty thing worrying about her clothes." She went to the little wooden schoolhouse on The Road right down at the foot of the Croner property, where seven grades were taught in one jumble of noise, and somehow she prospered as a student. She began to read and think and listen to her other grandmother, Sally Johns, a very direct, very independent spirit. "She wasn't an easy person to get close to," Barbara remembers, "but I think she was more of an influence on me than Ma Croner. She had no fear and was not the slightest bit subservient to whites."

It was Sally Johns's son Vernon, though, who lifted the girl's horizons. Where her father was a quiet and kindly man, her Uncle Vernon was a dazzlingly articulate and argumentative preacher who made as many enemies as friends with his thundering sermons that took no pity on the black man for his ignorance and docility in the face of the white man's malice. Vernon Johns was no mail-order minister, despite his deep rural background. In his late fifties during the war years, he was a widely traveled, high-spirited, thoroughly read man educated at Virginia Union in Richmond, Oberlin in Ohio, and Virginia Theological Seminary in Lynchburg, where he later taught homiletics and served for a time as president. An ordained Baptist minister, he pastored the Court Street Church in Lynchburg, one of the oldest black congregations in the South, and won a reputation as a dramatic pulpiteer. But his words did not often bring comfort. They shocked and unsettled and challenged. One of his sermons was included in the book *Best Sermons, 1926,* published by Harcourt, Brace; its editor noted that the Reverend Johns was "the first colored preacher to appear" in the annual volume.

It was the race war that attracted Vernon Johns's sharpest words. "The nastiest and deadliest problem before the world today," he declared early in his ministry, "is the insane hatred between races." He lashed out at the South: "It so happens in our country that the very section of it which is unquestionably the chief seat of orthodoxy is at the same time the dependable theatre of our most heartless inhumanities." Why, he asked, were the "perpetrators and abettors" of lynching left "at peace with their ritual-loving God"? He demanded: "When will Christian preachers either preach Jesus or save the public from further deception by unfrocking themselves of His name?" This was not the sort of ministering to divert a flock that had come to church to escape the realities that the Reverend Johns would not let lie. He moved on from Lynchburg, teaching and lecturing and preaching in many communities, including Farmville, where the Reverend Charles Henry Dunstan Griffin occasionally invited him to the pulpit of the First Baptist Church on Main Street, the biggest black congregation in Prince Edward County.

"He was beyond the intellectual scope of everyone around the county," his niece Barbara recalls. "I remember that white men would be at the store that he and my father ran together after the war and they'd listen to him speak and shake their heads, not understanding his language." No white man bested him in an argument, and Barbara Johns listened to his way with words and began to make it hers. "We'd always be on opposite sides in an argument," she says with fondness. "I'm afraid we were both very antagonistic." It was a crucial relationship for her as she grew into adolescence and became a reader. She read Booker Washington's autobiography and Richard Wright's *Native Son* and classics like *Little Women* and dipped into her uncle's library for H. G. Wells's *Outline of History*. By the time the family was reunited after the war, she had become an independent spirit, with a brain and tongue of her own, and a bit of a temper. Barbara's family moved into Vernon's store for a time while her father built their new home down The Road half a mile to the east. The store and the mill attached to it—"WE CHOP WHEAT AS FINE AS FLOUR," declared the big sign painted on its side, though in fact its biggest business was grinding cornmeal for hogs—were a social center for that outlying sector of the county, and whites and blacks alike, customers and salesmen, came to shoot the breeze or play cards and talk crops. Barbara would wait on customers after school and came to hold the white man in no special awe. Indeed, her mother would tangle almost daily with white customers who, in the manner of the Southland, unhesitatingly addressed her by her first name, no matter how slightly they knew her. Her daughter did not escape being wounded by such racial unetiquette. Barbara recalls that one white farmer's wife was a regular visitor to the store, where she would sit and socialize with the black proprietors in perfect ease. "I remember she had a daughter and I used to think she was such a beautiful girl," says Barbara. "She went to Farmville and got a job in the five-and-ten, and I came in one day and she just turned away. . . ."

She learned to shake off such rebuffs and kept growing inside herself. Her uncle stimulated her mental development, and Vernon's wife, Altona, a fine musician who taught public school in the county and later at Virginia State College, brought another dimension of culture into Barbara's life. Their bright, well-schooled daughters were frequent playmates of their cousin, and the girls wrote plays together that got staged at their grade school. But as Barbara reached her teenage years, there was less time for playing. Her mother had gone back to work in Washington—there were few opportunities outside of domestic service for a black woman to earn decent money in Prince Edward, and few maids' jobs in a place where most men of both races were dirt farmers—and her father was trying to make a living on the land, and so Barbara was now the lady of the Johns household. Charged with the cooking and the mending, looking after her younger brothers and sisters, and helping when she could with the farm work, she did not let her burdens pull her down. She was full of life and hope and beauty, for she had emerged from childhood as a quite lovely young woman, with high, rounded cheekbones, an almost Oriental cast to her striking eyes, and long, graceful legs. Pre-school chores systematically completed, she hurried down the pasture in front of her house each morning and caught the old bus that picked her up on The Road and jounced along to the Robert R. Moton High School in Farmville.

Moton would never be the same after she left it for the last time.

Before 1800, Virginia was the most populous and influential colony, and then state, in America. Its aristocracy supplied the infant nation with two generations of remarkable leaders, and its wealth and power seemed assured in the future. That Virginia's fortunes tumbled thereafter and the state became an economic and cultural backwater can be traced in significant measure to the commonwealth's most cherished social policy: maintaining the poor in the style to which they had become accustomed by, among other things, providing them with (1) as few public services as possible—especially free compulsory education—and (2) a baffling array of devices to remove all political power from their unwashed hands.

The men who ran the plantations ran the South. In Virginia, with its infinite waterways, every planter could sell his goods at his own dockside, or one not very far away, and so there was little need for the rise of towns or marketplaces. Few craftsmen or artisans pursued their trades independently in competition with slaves trained in similar skills. Authoritarian religion was unwelcome, and the prevailing Presbyterian and Episcopal faiths were honored to the extent that they did not interfere with the temporal mastery of the planters. Education, which the North and West saw early on as a vital requirement, was of small concern to those in control of the Old Dominion of Virginia. Throughout the existence of slavery, the planter had to fend off non-slaveholders who sought to tax the Negro as property and deny his owner the right to count him in the population basis upon which the Black Belt counties' numerical strength in the state legislature and at political conventions was calculated; the planter counterattacked by fighting to retain property qualifications for voting and to prevent the poor-white sectors of the state from being awarded an expanded quota of seats in the legislature.

In view of such tensions, proper Virginians were understandably unenthusiastic about the spread of learning among the rabble. Publicly supported schools to teach pauper children to read, write, and count were opened in scattered locations, but by 1845 there were no more than 10,000 children attending public schools in Virginia; that year in Massachusetts, which had a population slightly smaller than Virginia's, the total attending public schools was 158,000. By the middle of the century, the percentage of native whites of eligible age attending school in Virginia—12.26 percent—was the lowest in the nation except for California and Florida, which were frontier societies.

Civil war cost Virginia dearly. It was the principal battleground of the conflict, and the physical devastation was immense. Crops and livestock were widely seized, and fields laid waste. The secession of West Virginia in 1863 removed one-quarter of Virginia's population and 35 percent of its area. And the new state declined to bear any part of Virginia's state debt, which had swollen in the prosperous Fifties with the issue of railroad bonds. Added to that burden were the collapse of the state's economic institutions—slavery, the banks, credit—and the limitations of Virginia's agricultural system of relatively small farms and rolling terrain, which put it at a severe disadvantage in productivity and competition for markets with the new farming empire on the Western plains. Reconstruction measures, passed at bayonet point, expanded both public services and the state debt, but with the end of

Union occupation and dominance after the Hayes-Tilden Compromise, public education in Virginia suffered an acute and immediate setback. Universal public education was viewed as a carpetbagger invention, and taxes to support it were denounced as socialistic.

To assure that those who needed schooling the most—the poor-whites and the new black freedmen—would not get it, the re-enthroned Virginia aristocracy busied itself with a series of measures that effectively disenfranchised the lower orders. Voters were required to obtain registration certificates, often long before election day, and then retain them and present them at the polls—a great inconvenience for rural people unused to preserving written records. Petty larceny was added to the list of causes for disqualification from voting—a measure that fell with special severity on the destitute Negro. Out-and-out fraud, in the form of stuffed ballot boxes, boxes with false bottoms, manipulated counting of the returns, and the like, was widely practiced and scarcely ever punished. In 1893, the Virginia legislature bore down on illiterate voters by prohibiting their being assisted in marking their ballots. The cumulative weight of these oppressive devices was considerable, but they were not thought extreme or effective enough in curbing the poor, especially the poor-whites, who had shown alarming strength at the polls during the Populist movement in the closing decade of the nineteenth century. The Virginia elite fixed that.

Despite strong opposition, a state convention was held at the end of 1901 and into 1902 to redraw the Virginia constitution. Democracy in Virginia was dealt a nearly mortal blow. Poor-whites were advised that the preservation of white supremacy required that certain measures be taken to prevent the black voter from gaining political leverage between competing factions of white voters. That was a roundabout way of saying that white officials would no longer be tempted to steal or otherwise tamper with black votes because the state was about to do away with Negro voters altogether, or come as close as possible. The measures chosen for that purpose also served, of course, to disenfranchise tens of thousands of poor-whites. A literacy test was built into the new Virginia constitution along with a poll tax of one or two dollars a year. The anti-democratic bias that dominated the constitutional convention was so rampant that the state's General Assembly was denounced as "a wild rabble" inimical to the business interests of Virginia; a proposal to reduce the size of the legislature and limit its meetings to one session every four years narrowly missed passing. But in other areas the pervasive distrust of the voting public, or such of it as survived the chopping block, was carried into law: many formerly elective offices were converted into appointive ones, and the previous practice of electing the judiciary was abandoned. To clinch the argument that the new ground rules for Virginia-style democracy should not be ratified by the public, the convention's commanding figure, Carter Glass, future U.S. Secretary of the Treasury and U.S. Senator, asserted that "no body of Virginia gentlemen could frame a constitution so obnoxious . . . that I would be willing to submit its fate to 146,000 ignorant Negro voters." Great applause greeted gentleman Glass, and so the electorate was spurned.

The disenfranchisement machinery proved wonderfully efficient. In

1900, before the new rules went into effect, the total Virginia vote in the presidential election was 264,240; in 1904, with the new laws working, the vote was down to 130,544. By 1940, fewer than 10 of every 1,000 Virginians voted, compared with 147 at the beginning of the century. Virginia's government was more thoroughly controlled by a reigning oligarchy than that of any other state in the South. Between 1925 and 1945, only 11.5 percent of Virginians over twenty-one voted in the Democratic primaries, and Democrats appointed by the unshakably Democratic legislature ran the election machinery in every one of Virginia's 100 counties. Virginia Democrats, moreover, were not to be confused with Wilsonian or New Deal Democrats; they were rather like McKinley Republicans, with an occasional Coolidge progressive thrown in. Virginia Democrats supported taxes favorable to corporations and other business interests, strong curbs on organized labor, and tight restrictions on expansion of public-nuisance services such as education, health, and welfare. Slowly, the state debt had been retired, and by the 1920s the Virginia oligarchy rejoiced that its state was second to none in fiscal soundness. Current taxes for current services, that was the motto. It kept Virginia solvent—and most of its people ignorant and servile.

The First World War brought new prosperity to the state as Norfolk became the U.S. Navy's principal East Coast base, and adjacent Newport News became a great shipbuilding center. The New Deal brought still more federal jobs, and the expansion of the Washington bureaucracy had spillover benefits across the Potomac, where increasing numbers of federal employees worked and lived. Finally, grudgingly, the Virginia oligarchy began to recognize its social obligations. Money started to be directed, in small squirts, at the state's grossly deficient educational facilities.

In little Prince Edward County, where the clocks seemed to have no hands, there was finally a stirring in the Twenties. The six magisterial districts making up the county committed themselves at last to putting up real high schools for the white children—a substantial one in Farmville and a smaller one a few miles south at the crossroads of Worsham in the dead center of the county. In charge of the expanded public-school program, the county fathers placed wispy T. J. McIlwaine, the son of Presbyterian missionaries, who had lived in Japan until he was fifteen. McIlwaine had attended tiny Hampden-Sydney College, founded by the Presbyterian Church a few miles below Farmville in 1776, and afterward taught for four years in the Prince Edward schools before being elevated to county superintendent in 1918. He would keep the job for nearly four decades, long enough to watch his little empire grow steadily and then be torn apart by racial strife. "He was a milquetoast," remarks one black leader in the county. "And that's just what the white community wanted in that job—he wasn't a threat to anybody."

By his own lights, though, Superintendent McIlwaine served both races with Christian devotion. That he could not do as much for the colored people as for the whites was due to the prevailing sentiment of the county's rulers. "When I first came here, there was only one colored school in the county that went beyond the earliest grades," McIlwaine recounts. "It was a brick building known as Farmville No. 2—it had six teachers, one per grade." Almost everywhere else in the county, the blacks had to make do with one- or two-room schoolhouses that offered only a few grades, and no transportation to Farmville No. 2 was provided. McIlwaine acknowledges that there was reluctance among the whites to build schools for the Negroes. "The widespread feeling was that the whites were doing far more already for the colored people than their tax contributions warranted," he recalls. The same logic, of course, had deprived poor-white Southerners of adequate schools for generations, but in the case of the Negroes there was the added conviction that blacks simply did not need and could not benefit from increased schooling. "I was concerned about this situation," McIlwaine testified many years later. "The Negro schools had a shorter term. There were no compulsory-attendance laws at the time. The attendance was very poor. I made talks in the schools, urging parents to send their children . . . and apprising them of the fact that they could not expect their children to be educated if they sent them on Monday and waited until the following Thursday to send them back again." Gradually, the school term lengthened and black teachers began to be paid more than a pittance. In the mid-Twenties, seventh and eighth grades were added to the black elementary school in Farmville. In the early Thirties, after sustained pressure by Negro parents who for two years privately raised $900 beyond their tax payments to cover teacher salaries, the school board added tenth and eleventh grades to the black school. But no bus service to it was yet provided, and out in the county, Negroes who wanted a high-school education had to board in Farmville or go untutored past sixth grade.

Not until 1939 did Prince Edward put up a real high school for colored children. It was inadequate from the start. Built with federal funds from the Public Works Administration and an allocation from the State Literary Fund, as Virginia demurely dubbed its loan pool for school construction, the black high school was named for Robert Russa Moton, the most famous black native of the county; Moton succeeded Booker Washington as principal of Tuskegee and for a time inherited his megaphone as chief pleader for black virtue as prerequisite for white tolerance of the Negro. A one-story, U-shaped building put up for $40,000 on a triangular plot bounded on one side by the main access road to town from the south, the Robert R. Moton High School was planned to hold 180 children; the day it opened, 167 enrolled. The next year, there were 219. It did not have a gymnasium or a cafeteria or an auditorium with fixed seats or locker rooms or an infirmary, all of which white Farmville High had, and its teachers were paid substantially less, but it was a high school and in the early Forties the county finally provided bus service to it for outlying Negro children. It was hardly equality, but it was progress.

The eagerness with which Prince Edward's Negro population responded to the opening of Moton High belied widely parroted claims of the black man's resistance to mental stimulation. Though the Negro population in the county remained stable, enrollment at the black high school shot upward during World War Two and immediately afterward. By 1947, it stood at more than twice the number for which Moton was built. Something plainly had to be done about it. A survey undertaken by state authorities of all Prince Edward's school facilities concluded in late 1947 that Moton ought to be converted into an elementary school; the existing black grade school in Farmville should then be converted into a high school holding 600. No stopgap measures to meet the Moton overcrowding ought to be considered, the survey concluded. And so the county, calculating that it was already paying a higher percentage of its gross income for educating its children than fifty-six other counties in Virginia, decided to meet the Moton situation with stopgap measures. Three temporary outbuildings were put up within a year at a cost of $17,000. That was economical indeed for adding a shop and doubling the number of classrooms at the school. But there were a few things wrong with the additions. They were made of wood and covered with tarpaper, and so they leaked. And they were heated only with stoves, and so those who sat close to them in winter got very warm and those who sat far away from them had to wear their overcoats. Worst of all, they looked like oversized chicken coops. People called them "the shacks," and that was what they were.

State law would allow the tarpaper shacks to be used for no longer than five years. Meanwhile, the whites who ran the school board could leisurely explore the possibilities of a new building program and a bond issue to finance it. But black parents who were disturbed by the gross inadequacies of the Moton School were advised that the time was not ripe for a bond issue. It would take a while to woo public opinion, which meant white opinion. In the interim, the county school board said it was looking for a suitable site for the new colored high school it was going to build someday soon.

Such cavalier conduct by the white establishment of the county was traditional, for Prince Edward viewed its Negroes as a quiet breed, used to the long-prevailing rural way of life there and lacking the wit and stamina to alter it much. Those blacks who were dissatisfied did not stage protest meetings or march on the town hall; they simply left the county. Equal public-school facilities for colored were scarcely more conceivable to the whites than, say, ending segregation at the restaurants, movie theater, and bowling alley in Farmville. The blacks had their place and knew it. And liked it. "If the Negroes wanted a library or a swimming pool, we'd . . . help them get it," a prominent white resident of Farmville would tell a reporter from the *Saturday Evening Post* after the school crisis turned molten. "But they're not interested. They want pool rooms and dance halls. They're more interested in drinking and carousing than in reading or swimming. That's what they've got—and they're happy with it. We have a saying around here: be a Negro on Saturday night and you'll never want to be a white man again."

But as the Fifties began, the whites failed to notice that their local candidates for the road company of *Amos 'n' Andy* were suddenly being aroused and organized by black men who never brandished a cue stick.

His father, grandfather, great-grandfather, five uncles, and one brother were all ministers, and that is almost certainly why Leslie Francis Griffin did not rush to take up the cloth of God. It was something he had to come to when he was ready for it, not simply out of obligation, and he was not ready until the age of thirty-two.

Charles Griffin had come to Farmville in 1927 after pastoring at Central Baptist, one of the biggest churches in Norfolk. Fire had destroyed it, and the Reverend Griffin led his congregation of more than a thousand in a massive rebuilding drive that left him exhausted and in need of a less draining pastorate. The First Baptist Church in Farmville, oldest black congregation in Prince Edward County, was ideal. Located prominently at the corner of Fourth and Main streets, a few hundred feet from gentlewomanly Longwood College, Virginia's training academy for white female teachers, the church had apparently housed a white congregation up until the Civil War, when Yankees seized it and used it as a hospital. Thus contaminated, it was viewed by the community after the war as fit only for use by Negroes, who bought the sturdy, two-story brick building for about $1,000 in 1866. In his essay "Of the Faith of the Fathers" in his most important book, *The Souls of Black Folk*, W. E. B. Du Bois wrote in 1903 as if describing First Baptist in Farmville to the tee:

> The Negro church of today is the social centre of Negro life in the United States, and the most characteristic expression of Negro character. Take a typical church in a small Virginia town: it is the "First Baptist"—a roomy brick edifice seating five hundred or more persons, tastefully finished in Georgia pine, with a carpet, a small organ, and stained-glass windows. Underneath is a large assembly room with benches. This building is the central clubhouse of a community of a thousand or more Negroes. . . .

Reverend Griffin's church was a little smaller than that, the windows were a translucent white with stained-glass panels only around the edges, and it had competition from Race Street Baptist farther south in Farmville and such smaller outlying congregations as Triumph Church, white and imposing on its hilltop site in Darlington Heights, which the Croner and Johns families attended. But First Baptist was the wealthiest and most solid Negro church in the county, and the only one with more than one regular Sunday service.

Reverend Griffin's son Francis, ten years old when the family came to Farmville, grew into a high-spirited, two-fisted lad very much at home in the busy tobacco town. He played easily with the children of white families in the neighborhood, joining in sandlot baseball games and exchanging home visits and meals with them, until the inevitable day when young Griffin was told, with childhood's cruel candor, that such comradeship would have to end because his white friends' parents had decreed it. "It hurt like nothing before and very little since," Griffin recalls.

He went as far as he could in the Negro elementary school in town, then began to read widely on his own, influenced in part by the Reverend Vernon Johns, who had struck up a friendship with his father and preached once or twice a year at First Baptist. The differences in doctrine and personality between the two men did not escape Francis Griffin's notice as he sprouted into young manhood. His father, whom he thought a saintly man, was a devout believer with a faith that veered toward fundamentalism. "There was a time when he was sure that heaven was a literal, geographic place," the younger Griffin remembers, but the essence of his preaching was not so much heaven-directed as a call to the brethren to keep the faith until a new day dawned on earth without oppression and without poverty. First Baptist was a beacon in the storm, then, and the Griffin boy admired his father's ministry, even if it did seem more ethereal and less relevant than Vernon Johns's kind of Christianity. "I was impressed by his life," Francis Griffin remarks of his father, "and by his ability to stay calm and not to call for retaliation against our tormentors. He was a pacifist—non-violence was a part of his nature— but he was by no means a submissive man. He was well aware of all our problems and certainly viewed segregation as inconsistent with Christian ethics, but he didn't crusade against it. Like many another black theologian then, he would couch his message in terms of allegory to avoid being labeled a rabble-rouser."

Despite his admiration for his father, Francis Griffin lost interest in the church as his late teenage years arrived, and his father did not push him toward the ministry. There was a world to see, ideas to mull, and the hormones were running in the stocky young man, who worked in Farmville for a time as a doctor's helper and then, smitten with wanderlust, set out for the West Coast traveling by thumb or jumping freights and tangling with his share of railroad bulls. He hitchhiked back through the South—"which was quite a feat for a Negro then," Griffin recalls. "Once when I was having trouble getting a lift, I borrowed a crayon from a service station and wrote out a sign saying, 'Suppose I was your son?' The brakes started screeching for me fast." Back East, he tried a lot of things. He worked on fishing boats off the Florida coast, as a shipping clerk in New York, as a handyman at a Charlotte, North Carolina, department store, and home in Farmville a black stunt pilot taught him how to fly out of a pasture called Young's Flat near town. The two black aviators ran a short-haul passenger service out of the area and gave aerial sightseeing tours to mostly white customers. It was not the ministry, but young Griffin was at least involved now with the heavens.

Race relations in pre-World War Two Farmville were never far from the thoughts of the minister's son. He sensed his own militant tendencies and recognized the reigning white paternalism for what it was. "Things were fine so long as we stayed in our place," says Griffin. "I was treated as something of a privileged character—I don't know why—being included in sidewalk discussions with whites, probably because I could cope with them intellec-tually. But I didn't want this kind of favoritism. Occasionally the young blacks would make a show of rebellion—like refusing to get out of the way of oncoming whites while walking the streets—and fists would get thrown. Or we'd go into a restaurant sometimes and argue with them about not being served, but we never sat in. We'd throw down a challenge, but nobody was ready to push it to the point of a confrontation. The most we'd get was abuse for being smart, uppity niggers."

In the war, Francis Griffin was a foot soldier and then with the first Negro tank corps under George Patton in Europe. During his four years in service, his letters to relatives made clear that he had finally settled on his professional calling. He would become a minister. Purposefully now, he returned to civilian life, finished up high school down in North Carolina, where a favorite uncle lived, and enrolled at Shaw University, where he applied himself to his studies, joined the local NAACP branch, and found a wife. On weekends and holidays, he would return to Farmville and give an occasional guest sermon at his father's church. His skills as a preacher were apparent, as was the difference between his and his father's views of the uses of religion. "I felt that all forms of worship should be related to a form of action," says Griffin of the kind of social gospel he first encountered from the lips of Vernon Johns. "Too many people do no more than pray and expect the world to change. I didn't and don't think that a church is meant to be housed inside a building. Everything about life is a legitimate concern of my religion."

In temporal matters, Griffin similarly veered from the orthodox. He worked for Henry Wallace in the 1948 presidential campaign, and his feelings about the black man's struggle for a square deal in America intensified. He was struck, he recalls, by the story of how Moses went to Pharaoh to ask that the Israelites' quota of brick production be cut and of the response he got: same number of bricks, less straw to make them with. "The meaning had become clear to me," Griffin remembers. "We would have to do it for ourselves. Begging and pleading for relief was no way." When his father died in the fall of 1949 and the pastorate was offered to him, Francis Griffin was ready to accept it. He saw in the church an opportunity for the leadership he was now eager to exercise. At thirty-two, one term short of completing his studies at college, he was the new spiritual leader of the Negroes of Prince Edward County.

He did not wait for the county to come to him. True to his belief that the church has no walls, Reverend L. Francis Griffin, as he was now known, moved restlessly about the pine-scented countryside, meeting blacks he had not known before and solidifying ties with his parishioners. He drove mostly, arriving unannounced, being asked to supper, sometimes staying overnight, for he was an honored guest wherever he went, spreading the word that the Lord truly helped those who helped themselves. Once a month, he would come by the general store and mill that Vernon and Robert Johns operated out on The Road and find a receptive audience there. "He was tryin' to get the people to pull together, to understand," recalls Mary Croner. "He believed what he said, and he wasn't afraid to say what he believed. He had the right spirit—and he didn't look as if he would fly off the handle any moment." Before long, he found the required fifty people in the county to start a chapter of the NAACP, and he put out lines to Richmond lawyers Spottswood Robinson and Oliver Hill, who were roaming the state organizing a massive legal drive for equalized school facilities for blacks. Griffin's boyhood friend John Lancaster, who, like the minister, had succeeded to his father's occupation in the community, proved a key ally. Lancaster, the Negro county agricultural agent, had come back to Prince Edward with ideas similar to Griffin's about the black man's duty to lift himself by his own bootstraps; he, too, moved about the county worrying about the souls, as well as the crops, of its Negro residents. "He felt that all things in the farmers' lives ought to be in his domain," Reverend Griffin remarks.

The dual campaign of the minister and the farm agent to put steel into the backbone of every black brother and sister was not advertised to the white community, but it was of course apparent to the more conservative—and resistant—element among the colored people. The Parent-Teachers Association of Moton High School, the principal black institution in the county, provided the arena for the new leadership's assumption of power. Lancaster had been active in organizing the PTA at the end of the war and advising the white school board of the shortcomings of the Moton High plant. The PTA's posture was anything but militant, and its most influential member was a relatively wealthy contractor named Willie Redd, who argued that the route to progress was cooperation with the white leadership, not a sword's-point relationship. Redd's kind of cooperation, as it turned out, meant waiting until the whites were good and ready to act. The construction of the obviously inadequate and stopgap tarpaper shacks at Moton signaled to many Negroes that the white school board had little intention of facing the problem squarely, and a new mood settled over the PTA. Redd resigned, and Reverend Griffin assumed charge of the black PTA's drive for improved facilities—an effort that now seemed to focus the latent yearnings of the people.

Griffin, preacher at the First Baptist, president of the NAACP, and head of the Moton PTA, had one other prime collaborator besides Lancaster—Moton High's principal, M. Boyd Jones. Together, the three men were a formidable triumvirate, though it was the minister, as the only one not dependent on whites for the bread on his dinner table, who carried the flag. But the wrath of the white community would eventually fall on Jones, a native of Gloucester in the Tidewater, who had come to Farmville in 1947 to be principal of Moton. A graduate of Hampton Institute with a master's degree in education from Cornell, Jones came full of self-confidence and the conviction that a good Negro high school should equip its students to cope with the realities of the outside world and not settle for a disguised form of serfdom. That, too, was the way Griffin saw his church and Lancaster his job as farm agent.

County school superintendent McIlwaine, the tense little man who hired him as principal, acknowledged Boyd Jones's gifts as an educator. "He ran a taut school—but I think he had an undying hatred of whites." McIlwaine based that suspicion partly on the chronic complaints that he said Principal Jones lodged with him about Moton's inadequacies. It was a querulousness that seeped down to the faculty and student body and then out to the community at large, and that disturbed McIlwaine, who thought the principal's obligation was, like his own, to knuckle down and do the best job he could with what tools he was handed.

What riled Jones, of course, was that the tools he had to work with were not nearly as good as those available at the white high school in town. The leaky, chilly tarpaper shacks that exposed a lot of youngsters to colds in the winter were hardly the only problem. The school buses for colored children were mostly hand-me-downs from the white schools, and there were not enough of them, and some of them were always arriving late, so that the first class period of every day was marred by a steady stream of tardy pupils. Equipment to teach science was lacking, and when Jones asked for a single microscope, he found it and many of his other minimal requests slashed from the budget. Even if he had gotten the equipment the school needed, there was no place to store it, any more than the students had lockers for their clothes and books and lunches. The toilets were hopelessly inadequate, there was no cafeteria, and the auditorium was simply a very large room without fixed seats. Anybody traveling from one wing of the school to the other had to go through the auditorium and disturb any activity, such as drama or music, that was conducted there and required isolation. Because there were not enough buses for children remaining after school to participate in extracurricular activities, boys playing football had to practice during the regular school day, missing two class periods three times a week. They had to change clothes in a classroom, since there were no lockers, and after playing they had no shower room to use. The shop had nothing like the equipment at Farmville High, and the highest-paid teacher at Moton made less than the lowest-paid teacher at the white school.

Boyd Jones resented all that, and not the least of his reasons, he later explained, was that on his very first day at Moton "I was told by the Division Superintendent [McIlwaine] that he had available at that time $190,000 with which to renovate an old building they had there that they were going to use for the Negro high school. That fell through, for one reason or another—I don't know what happened." Promises were about all Jones got for his efforts, besides the tarpaper shacks and a belated increase in the authorized number of teachers to handle a student enrollment that by 1950 had passed 450. That year, the state legislature, at the behest of Virginia's new governor, John S. Battle, had established a $45-million kitty—the so-called Battle Fund—for school construction across the state and invited every county to submit a list of its needs. Prince Edward's school board, eager for the state funds but damned if it was going to tax itself to meet its pressing school needs, applied for a Battle Fund grant of just over $1.1 million, of which $800,000 was ticketed for a new colored high school. Word got back that Prince Edward could not realistically expect to get more than perhaps one-fourth of its request from the state. That left the problem right where it had been when the tarpaper shacks were put up as the expedient alternative to a bond issue that the white board was sure it could not sell to the county voters, hardly enthusiasts of black education.

Closely informed on the needs at Moton by Principal Jones, Reverend Griffin and others on the PTA committee appeared regularly before the white school board in 1950 and into 1951 to seek a firm commitment to a new colored high school. The board did not bother to tell the black PTA about its proposed $1.1-million building program lest Prince Edward's skittish voters object before the Battle Fund allocation was made. Even if the board had made the disclosure, it might have remained a relatively private matter in the black and white communities alike because the weekly Farmville *Herald*, the only paper covering the community and a dedicated mouthpiece of white supremacy, did not report on the meetings of the school board. The board spoke of finding a site for the hypothetical new colored high school and designated a committee for that purpose, but when it made no evident progress, Griffin and Lancaster offered their services to the board on behalf of the PTA, found an attractive sixty-three-acre spot south of town available for $8,000, and were told—six months later—that the purchase had been approved, provided a satisfactory price could be agreed to.

"I had no confidence that the white power structure would be moved," says Griffin, "but we went in time after time, only to come away without anything. I was trying to show the others that we weren't going to make any headway, but Boyd [Jones] disagreed with me. He thought the school board could be moved if we were persistent. I told him he was naïve but I'd go along until he could see it my way. We'd meet—he and John Lancaster and I were good social friends—and Boyd would say to me, 'Chief, let's take it easy—we can work it all out.' It's ironic that he should turn out to have been the one to get it right between the eyes."

Barbara Rose Johns was a quiet girl during her freshman and sophomore years at Robert R. Moton High School. Admired for her intelligence and attractiveness, she soon became a spirited participant in many school activities. She joined the chorus and the drama group and the New Homemakers of America, and then she was elected to the student council. These activities would take her out of the county from time to time to other schools in other parts of Virginia, and the more she saw of the outside world, the more dissatisfied she became with the facilities at Moton.

"The man who drove the bus I took, who was also my history teacher, had to make the fires in the shacks each morning to keep us warm," she remembers. "Some of us had to sit in our coats—it would bother me a lot." It bothered her still more that the school buses the black students rode were mostly ones discarded by the white schools when they bought new ones. "What really bothered us was the time some of the boys in the vocational program visited the shop at the white school and came back telling us how nice their whole school was—and how well equipped. The comparison made me very angry, and I remember thinking how unfair it was. I kept thinking about it all the way home, I thought about it a lot while I was in bed that night, and I was still thinking about it the next day."

She was in her junior year, eleventh grade, and in the full bloom of young womanhood. She felt old enough to try to do something about the injustice she saw being foisted on her and her schoolmates every day, but just what to do was not clear to her at first. Her parents and their generation seemed incapable of bold action now, for, having lived too long under the system that degraded them, they were, if not numb to it, unwilling to challenge it. Most of the other students at Moton seemed to have had their sense of outrage scooped out of them. One person she might have shared her anger with was her school principal, Boyd Jones. "I had great respect for him," Barbara recalls. "I liked his manner—he was straightforward and a fine person." Boyd Jones did not tell the students at Moton that every day in every way things were getting better. He leveled with them, and the brighter ones such as Barbara Johns knew about the PTA's thwarted efforts to improve conditions and get a new high school built. Beyond that, Principal Jones brought fresh ideas into the school. He introduced a course, for example, called "Consumer Buying" in the hope, he explained, that "these children would at least get some of the language that is in everyday usage with members of the other groups. . . . [T]he average Negro parent has had so little background with this sort of language whereas with white children it is common language in the family." It was the sort of down-to-earth thinking and action that made Boyd Jones widely respected among Moton students, who encountered too few articulate, forceful, and educated black men after whom they might pattern themselves. Barbara Johns lacked the nerve to approach Principal Jones with what was on her mind. But she did the next best thing.

Miss Inez Davenport, a music teacher at Moton, had been going with Boyd Jones for some time, and the couple were to marry before long. Barbara Johns studied with Miss Davenport and liked her, and one's music teacher seemed a good deal more accessible than one's principal. "I told her how sick and tired I was of the inadequate buildings and facilities and how I wished to hell—I know I wasn't this profane in speaking to her, but that's how I felt—something could be done about it. After hearing me out, she asked simply, 'Why don't you do something about it?' I didn't ask her what she meant—I don't know why. Soon the little wheels began turning in my mind. I decided to use the student council."

It was late in the autumn of 1950 when Barbara Johns broached the idea to Carrie Stokes, president of the Moton student body, and her brother John, who, besides being vice president, had lately been elected state president of the New Farmers of America, the Jim Crow equivalent of the 4-H Club, and had his picture run in the Farmville *Herald.* John was also a top student, a star on the track team, business manager on the school paper, and an orator of some promise. John and Carrie Stokes and two other student leaders met with Barbara Johns at her request in the bleachers on the scruffy Moton athletic field. She spoke to them slowly and quietly, John Stokes remembers, and with great effectiveness. "She opened our eyes to a lot of things," he would tell an interviewer a decade after the event.

Barbara Johns's listeners did not need much persuading. They, too, had done a fair amount of traveling and knew their school was inferior in many important ways. She asked the group to consider just why it was that their parents had made so little headway with the school board in trying to win improvements for Moton. "Then she said our parents ask us to follow them," John Stokes recalled, "but in some instances—and I remember her saying this very vividly—a little child shall lead them. She said we could make a move that would broadcast Prince Edward County all over the world." The group agreed to keep a close watch on PTA developments and to begin attending the school-board meetings at which Reverend Griffin's group appeared regularly to ask for progress reports and received—regularly—the runaround.

Each of the five student leaders who had been at the rendezvous in the bleachers brought one trusted friend to another student huddle a few months later. There was no progress on the school-board–PTA front. If things stayed that way, Barbara Johns proposed, in the spring the group assembled there should lead the entire Moton student body out on strike. And they would stay out on strike until the school board agreed to build them a new high school. It would require solidarity, like any other strike, and they would picket and carry protest signs, like any other strikers. Meanwhile, no word of their plans must get out, especially to Boyd Jones, who, however sympathetic he might be toward their ends, would be obliged to squelch the means the students proposed for gaining them. Everyone at the meeting agreed.

It was at the February 1951 meeting of the Prince Edward school board that Reverend Griffin's PTA group was told permission had been granted by the county's Board of Supervisors for purchase of a site for a new colored high school. But the black group was also told not to bother showing up at the monthly school-board meetings any more and that it would be advised when the transaction was completed.

By late April, nothing had changed. The site had still not been purchased. No plans for the new school had been announced. Moton High was still busting at the seams, and education there was separate and decidedly unequal. Barbara Johns's strike group firmed up its plans, an expanded corps of juniors and seniors was passed the word, and on Monday morning, April 23, 1951, shortly before eleven o'clock, Principal Boyd Jones received a phone call at his office in Moton High School. A muffled voice told him that two of his students were at the Greyhound bus terminal and about to get in trouble with the Farmville police if the principal did not speed to the rescue. The moment he left, Barbara Johns moved to the auditorium, where she met four other students and dispatched them to every classroom with message slips announcing a short assembly of the whole school at eleven a.m. That was the usual hour for assemblies, and Barbara signed the notes the way Boyd Jones generally did—with just the letter "J."

At the appointed moment in the auditorium, 450 students and a faculty of two dozen teachers less one principal hushed as the stage curtains opened. The student strike committee was seated behind the rostrum. Standing at it and in command of the suddenly murmuring room was Barbara Rose Johns. She asked the teachers to leave, and as the excitement grew, most of them obliged. And then the beautiful sixteen-year-old girl at the rostrum told her schoolmates what was in her heart. It was time that Negroes were treated equally with whites. It was time that they had a decent high school. It was time for the students themselves to do something about it. They were going to march out of school then and there and they were going to stay out until the white community responded properly. The Farmville jail was too small to hold all of them, and none of them would be punished if they acted together and held fast to their resolve. In the long run, said Barbara Johns, things would never be really equal until they attended school with white students on a non-segregated basis.

During the question-and-answer period that followed her spirited talk, Boyd Jones reappeared. John Stokes remembered that the principal "rushed into the auditorium in a kind of hysterical state" and pleaded with the students not to proceed with the walkout. Progress was being made with the school board, he insisted. When he had finished his appeal, Barbara Johns asked him to go to his office. He went. Whether out of respect for the orderly manner in which the students were conducting their grave deliberations or out of complicity with their cause—or both—the principal did not pull rank and snuff out the uprising in its larval stage. His exit left Barbara and the student committee very much in charge of the proceedings, and the details were arranged. Students were to stay on the school grounds for the rest of the day, either carrying picket signs, which had been made in advance and stored in the shop, or remaining at their desks but without opening their books or otherwise participating in lessons. Meanwhile, the student committee would seek an audience with the white superintendent of schools, T. J. McIlwaine.

The superintendent was not pleased to learn of the irregular developments at Moton. He declined to see the strike committee that day, nor would he come over to the school as requested by Principal Jones. The student uprising was a disciplinary situation and had to be resolved by the principal, said McIlwaine, who was convinced that Jones was implicated in the protest and probably its instigator. "The students had little to do with it," he remarked two decades later. "I went by the school on a number of occasions and the principal would be behind closed doors with the minister and the county agricultural agent. I found out that they planted someone at the bus station to say that there was trouble down there and so forth, and I told Jones I expected him to straighten out the situation. I don't have any question that it was a put-up job—an undertaking on the part of a very few. I don't think the Negroes in the county generally supported the move."

Ever after, Barbara Johns would swear that the Moton strike was organized solely by the students. "We knew we had to do it ourselves," she says, "and that if we had asked for adult help before taking the first step, we would have been turned down. Boyd Jones knew nothing about the strike before it began." There is only circumstantial evidence to suggest otherwise. How was it possible, for example, for the picket signs to be made ahead of time and stored in the shop without the faculty's knowledge? How could a principal who ran "a taut ship" not catch wind of what was brewing? How could that many teenagers keep a secret that long? Plainly, Boyd Jones was trapped between his convictions as a black leader and his obligations to his white employers. On the face of it, he honored his obligations, but his convictions kept showing through. "Once the strike was on," Barbara Johns remembers, "he kept telling us we were wrong to do it this way and we couldn't succeed. I felt that, as principal, he should stand up for us, and when he chewed us out, the expression on my face must have told him how disappointed I was with him. After one of those sessions in his office, he finished his reprimand, saw the look on my face, and said, sort of to the side: 'Continue on!' That buoyed me up tremendously, even though I couldn't tell the others about what he'd said. I felt my confidence in him as a good person had not been misplaced, but the other students were feeling that he was some kind of an ogre."

On the afternoon of the first day, the student strike committee asked Reverend Griffin to come to the school and give them some advice. Having gone this far, should they proceed without the approval of their parents? Griffin, who has always denied he played any part in the uprising before that day but never denied his complete sympathy with the students' efforts, suggested that the youngsters vote on the question. They voted not to seek their parents' blessings. And then they took the added momentous step of obtaining from Griffin the names and address of the NAACP's special counsel for the Southeastern region of the United States. The letter, typed on a plain sheet of white paper and signed by Barbara Johns and Carrie Stokes, school president, arrived in Richmond the next day. It read:

Gentlemen:

We hate to impose as we are doing, but under the circumstances that we are facing, we have to ask for your help.

Due to the fact that the facilities and building in the name of Robert R. Moton High School, are inadequate, we understand that your help is available to us. This morning, April 23, 1951 the students refused to attend classes under the circumstances. You know that this is a very serious matter because we are out of school, there are seniors to be graduated and it can't be done by staying at home. Please we beg you to come down at the first of this week. If possible Wednesday, April 25 between 9:00 a.m. and 3:00 p.m.

We will provide a place for you to stay.

We will go into detail when you arrive.

While they waited for the lawyers, the student strike leaders sought an audience with the chairman of the county school board, a prominent Farmville industrialist. He declined to talk to the black youngsters until they agreed to return to school. He added that nobody could say when they might get their new school because a bond issue had to be voted, and a demonstration such as the one they had launched would not improve its chances. Then the students visited Superintendent McIlwaine in his office at the county courthouse. As he recalls the meeting: "They sent a bunch of children over to see me. There wasn't enough room in my office, so we went upstairs to the county courtroom for the meeting. I sat behind the rail where the lawyers usually sit. The children seemed to be parroting questions that someone else had given them, but they were in no way disrespectful. Barbara Johns—her uncle was quite a radical—did a good deal of the talking. She was a nice-looking girl, tall and handsome. They were asking questions like why couldn't they go to the white high school, and I had to explain that we have to live by the laws and that it was just a matter of the Virginia statutes. I said we were going to get them a better school as soon as we could." The school superintendent left the meeting certain that the Negro students were pawns in an adult conspiracy. "I was disgusted," he said.

The students were no less so. They left the courthouse convinced they might as well have spoken to the planets. They resolved to hold to their course. When Barbara Johns got home, she went over to Ma Croner and told her, "Grandma, I walked out of school this morning and carried 450 students with me." "Took my breath away," the old woman recalled. "I said to her, 'You reckon you done the right thing?' 'I believe so,' she say. She say, 'Stick with us.' "

Bald, strapping Oliver Hill and reedy, monkish Spottswood Robinson were due to bring their legal roadshow to the federal District Court in Roanoke that Thursday morning, and so it would be no major problem to break the 163-mile drive from their office in Richmond to see the striking Farmville students who had written them for help. There was no doubt in the minds of the two NAACP lawyers that they would urge the youngsters to go back to classes and work through more orthodox methods, because, from what the attorneys knew of the intransigence of the white people of Prince Edward County, there was no less promising place in all Virginia to wage the fight for equal schools. Their judgment was not an idle one, for by the spring of 1951 no lawyer in America—with the possible exception of Thurgood Marshall— had logged more combat hours fighting for better schools for Negroes than Oliver Hill or Spottswood Robinson.

Hill was the older of the pair by eight years, and both were products of the Howard Law School. Hill was closer in temperament to his Howard classmate Thurgood Marshall, with whom he had formed a close, lifelong friendship. Each was large, outgoing, and fun-loving, and had a highly pragmatic mind that leaped at Charles Houston's conception of the black lawyer as a social engineer. "I went to law school so I could go out and fight segregation," Hill says simply.

He lost little time getting into the fray. In a mid-Thirties campaign that paralleled the work Thurgood Marshall was doing in Maryland, Hill opened an office in the city of Roanoke in south central Virginia, where he had grown up, and set about helping organize the state's Negro teachers in an NAACP-coordinated drive for equal salaries. It was a long, slow effort, waged in constant fear of reprisals by white school boards. Hill's hand was strengthened after Charlie Houston's 1938 victory in the *Gaines* case, which suggested the Supreme Court now meant to enforce the separate-but-equal doctrine in earnest. Black Virginia lawyers decided that if they had to live within the *Plessy* doctrine, the white school boards that were always pleading poverty were now going to have to pay the true price of genuinely equal but still separate school systems. The equalization campaign would be in three stages: first, teachers' salaries, then transportation, and finally school buildings and equipment. In 1939, Hill moved to his birthplace, Richmond, a better spot from which to run the school-equalization drive, and the following year, with a big lift from Thurgood Marshall, the principle of equal salaries was affirmed by the Supreme Court in upholding the Fourth Circuit's *Alston* decision, involving the black teachers of Norfolk. The precedent may thus have been firmly fixed, but Hill and his colleagues had to keep pushing white school boards throughout the state to give the black teachers their due and stop scheming up ways around the court-ordained parity.

In the early Forties, Hill widened the scope of his efforts. In Sussex County, for example, in the southern Tidewater, he interceded in the case of a group of children who lived forty miles from the nearest colored school, to which no transportation was provided by the state or local school board, but only seven or eight miles from the nearest white school in Stony Creek. "In that era, you either had to board your kids out near a school during the week or put up maybe seventy-five cents a day for private bus transportation—or even a dollar if you lived thirty or forty miles out," Hill explains. "Most people just couldn't afford it. Well, first I stood out on the road with my group and hailed the white bus driver and asked him if he could take them to the Waverly Training School—they weren't even called high schools because the feeling was what-for do the colored need high school if they're just going to be trained as cooks and farm workers—and the driver said hell, no. So I piled the whole bunch of kids into a truck and pulled 'em in to the white school at Stony Creek and told the principal we wanted to enroll them. I remember the eyes on that guy. He ran for the phone and got the district superintendent, who told him, 'Don't you go lettin' any niggers in there.' " It was the kind of fruitless knocking on the door that had to be done as a prelude to the massive legal action that followed.

To undertake it, Hill needed reinforcements. He got them in the form of two partners, jovial, heavy-set Martin A. Martin and frail, earnest Spotts-wood W. Robinson III, who had achieved the best academic record in the history of Howard Law School. James Nabrit, who taught him and then helped corral him for the Howard faculty for ten years, says, "Spot was the best student of the law I ever taught. He was a superb pleader and writer and yet a modest man. He didn't have much of a voice, but he did very well in court. He was always reading, always thinking, and worked harder than anyone I have ever known." Son of a Richmond lawyer who had first established a thriving real-estate business, Robinson himself proved a successful businessman-lawyer, dividing his time between teaching at Howard and specializing in realty law as a partner in the firm Hill had established before going into the Army in 1943. By the time Robinson quit Howard in 1949 to devote full time to his practice and NAACP work, Hill had come back from the war overseas and resumed fighting on the home front. The victories started coming now. In Fauquier County, about forty miles due west of Washington, a Negro who would not let his son walk to school along Route 29 because he said it was too dangerous found himself convicted in county court of violating the state compulsory-school-attendance law. Hill, suing on the ground that the county had failed to provide bus transportation for the black youngster, lost the case in the Virginia circuit court but won on appeal in the state's highest court. It was a vital precedent in the equal-transportation area, as *Alston* had been for equalizing salaries.

In 1948, Robinson was named special NAACP counsel in Virginia and set out with W. Lester Banks, state executive secretary for the association, on a fact-finding tour of the black school systems of the Old Dominion, spurring

Negro challenges to the unequal facilities and preparing for legal action. "The black people just wanted some leadership, someone to lean on," says Banks of the warm reception he and Robinson received as they logged 30,000 miles a year in his old Chevrolet. "It wasn't like in the Deep South, where people were still worried about getting lynched. But you knew you were up against a stone wall when it came to segregation and discrimination."

To turn the tide, Hill and Robinson began appearing before school boards all over Virginia, and when they were rebuffed, as they almost always were, they filed lawsuits—dozens of them. "We had actions going in seventy-five different school districts at one point," says Banks. Crisscrossing the state to meet a tight schedule of court appearances and school-board meetings, Robinson stuffed the trunk of Banks's car with legal files and law books and stayed up half the night banging out legal briefs to be filed first thing the next morning. The task was slightly complicated by a flaw in Robinson's character: he was a perfectionist. "He is the most thorough, most methodical man in the world," says Banks. "If he was going to cut a board ten inches long, he'd measure it fifteen times to make sure it was just right. He'd think nothing of sitting up to three or four in the morning to search out a point of law he needed. He was always looking for just the right case in every situation. He was a terrific worker—with a wonderful mind."

In late 1948, the effort started to pay off massively. They won a whole series of breakthrough decisions in U.S. District Court: lower salaries were ordered equalized in Chesterfield County, the black high school in King George County had to be brought up to par with the white one, and the black schools in Gloucester County had to be improved. In the first few days of 1949, Thurgood Marshall announced in New York that the Virginia campaign would speed up and be brought to no fewer than 124 separate school jurisdictions. White school boards were supposed to see the handwriting on the wall and submit with good grace. Few did. With Hill somewhat slowed as a litigator by his duties as a member of the Richmond City Council—he was the first Negro to be elected to that body—Robinson handled the lion's share of the court action while Banks continued as his advance man and traveling companion. By 1950, they had won declaratory judgments or injunctions from the courts in most of the counties where the NAACP had brought actions, but the follow-up and mop-up work was endless. In Gloucester County, for example, where the school board had claimed in court it had no money to equalize the black schools, a bond issue was turned down by the voters—with the *sub rosa* complicity of the school board, the NAACP charged—and the school authorities proceeded to put up brick facing over the pre-Civil War building that housed the black school, splash some cold-water paint around the inside, and claim it had provided a facility equal to the white school. The NAACP promptly brought the Gloucester school board back into federal court, where the judge found its members in contempt and fined them $1,000 each. When a similar failure to comply with an equalization decree occurred in Pulaski County, the NAACP argued that a contempt-of-court finding was insufficient and demanded immediate integration of the schools as the only solution. "That ole judge,"

Hill chortles, "he kept saying to us, 'I will not do it! I will not do it!' I thought he'd bust a blood vessel." In King George County, the NAACP men countered the school board's failure to obey a court order to equalize by trying to enroll a group of Negro children in the white school; they were met by a stony-faced bunch of farmers bearing pickaxes. In Arlington, the lawyer for the school board claimed that the Negro school had an advantage over the white one because of its superb view of the Army and Navy Country Club golf course; the NAACP lawyers pointed out that (1) the schoolchildren were not supposed to be gazing out the window, and (2) if they did, they would soon notice that no Negroes were allowed on that golf course.

Other forms of Jim Crow afflicted the NAACP's Virginia field team besides school segregation. There was the almost daily humiliation of trying to find a lunch or restaurant that would feed them. "You had to fight hard to avoid compromising with the system," Banks recalls. "One day back in 1949 or so, I remember we'd been working hard with the branch people in King and Queen County—we'd made several stops and were getting mighty hungry—so we pulled in at some lunch place in the little hamlet of St. Stephen's Church and, sure enough, they led us around to the take-out section in the back. That was what you'd have to do a lot: survive on take-out crackers and cheese. We'd do almost anything to avoid it. I think we waited half that afternoon before we found an old country store owned by a Negro who served us pork and beans." Robinson began to avoid the problem altogether by bringing along a neatly wrapped sandwich. Buying gasoline was another potentially hazardous daily episode for black men who stood on principle. "I'd make it my business to try to buy at Esso stations," Banks recounts, "because they were slightly more liberal in their policies, like not segregating their washrooms, than some of the other chains. I'd never buy at a segregated place—and you could get a hurt bladder that way waiting to get back home. One day, I found myself over on Eastern Shore and pulled into this Esso place. The fella had started puttin' the gas in when I noticed the signs: 'White Ladies,' 'Colored Women.' So I told the attendant to stop. The pump registered exactly thirty-eight cents. The owner comes out and wants to know what the trouble is, and the attendant tells him I don't like the segregated toilets. The owner explains, 'You're on Eastern Shore'—as if I didn't know and as if that made it okay."

The Virginia NAACP team welcomed the 1950 edict by Thurgood Marshall, endorsed by the board of directors of the association, to stop filing equalization suits and, on the strength of the *Sweatt* and *McLaurin* decisions, to sue only on the ground that segregation itself was illegal. "This equalization method of fighting them one case at a time failed to produce enough results," says Hill. "We were just grinding our wheels with all these suits." Perhaps, but the Washington *Post* estimated that the NAACP's Virginia equalization drive produced $50 million in higher teacher salaries, new buses, and improved schools for Negroes. With that sort of tangible, if painfully achieved, progress to show, there was real question as to how well rural blacks would respond to the relatively new tactic of trying to overturn the deeply entrenched practice of segregation.

The response outstripped the expectations of the NAACP leaders. "We had more than four hundred at one turnout at a church in Dinwiddie County where we were explaining the new strategy," Hill remembers. "There was this old man in the back wearing overalls and he gets up after hearing us out—he looked like he didn't know beans from Adam—and he says, 'Mr. Hill, I've heard you, and all I want to say is that we've known all along that you couldn't do it this way, a piece at a time, and we've just been waiting for leaders to tell us we had to go all the way.' "

White officials were less enthusiastic about the new NAACP strategy. In Cumberland County, immediately adjacent to Prince Edward on the north, Hill and Robinson appeared before the county school board in a 1950 equalization hearing that had been set in motion before the NAACP decided to take aim at segregation *per se*. The black lawyers were pushing for the removal of tarpaper shacks very much like those that had been put up at Moton High in Farmville, and, in Hill's words, "The whites told us, 'We'd like to do something to help you fellas, but you're pushin' too fast and we just don't have enough money.' So Spot says, 'Look, I know how you could do it overnight—all you have to do is let the colored kids into Cumberland High School.' At which point one of the school-board members jumps up and shouts, 'The first little black son of a bitch that comes down the road to set foot in that school, I'll take my shotgun to and blow his brains out.' "

Prince Edward was a lot like neighboring Cumberland County, only farther south. That was one good reason Hill and Robinson saw scant promise in a student strike there. But then neither had ever met Barbara Johns.

On Wednesday morning, April 25, the third day of the strike at Moton High School, buses loaded with students arrived at the regular starting time. But the students made no effort to go inside, nor did Principal Jones and the rest of the faculty, who were holding a conference at that hour in Jones's office, make any effort to herd the youngsters to their classrooms. The strikers headed instead five blocks up Main Street to the basement meeting room at Reverend Francis Griffin's First Baptist Church to hear the lawyers from the NAACP. Superintendent McIlwaine did not look kindly on the use of the county's buses to assist the strike activities in this manner. He did not understand why Principal Boyd and the faculty were closeted at the time the students were discharged from the buses and why the teachers did not direct the children back to school. Nor did he see why the students' protest posters and signs were left up inside and outside the building if Jones and his fellow black teachers were unsympathetic to the walkout.

Oliver Hill and Spottswood Robinson did not want to launch their first Virginia suit against segregated education itself in, of all places, Prince Edward County. A city would have been the logical place to start such an action, just as Norfolk was the site for the landmark *Alston* case on teachers' salaries. The white people in the cities were more open to change, the blacks more determined and financially able to seek it. Prince Edward, which Hill had first visited back in the late Thirties when Moton went up, was practically a slice of antebellum Virginia, and the lawyer considered the black leadership there as long-suffering and entirely lacking in the militancy needed to sustain a radical lawsuit. "We were going to tell the kids about the *Briggs* suit, which was about to begin in Charleston in a few weeks, and how crucial that would prove," Hill remembers, "but a strike in Prince Edward was something else again. Only these kids turned out to be so well organized and their morale was so high, we just didn't have the heart to tell 'em to break it up." Robinson coolly debated with the churchful of youngsters: what would they do if the county just flat-out refused to build a new high school for them? They would stay out indefinitely, came the answer. But suppose, Robinson asked, the officials began to enforce the truancy laws? No jail could hold all of them, the youngsters answered, ignoring the obvious retort that several jails could accomplish the feat. "It was apparent to us that they were not listening to anybody at this point," Robinson recalled.

The lawyers told the striking students that the only way the NAACP could get involved in their cause was to sue for the end of segregation itself—a giant step beyond the goal of the young strikers. "It seemed like reaching for the moon," says Barbara Johns. "It was all pretty hard to grasp. But we had great faith in Mr. Robinson and Mr. Hill." The lawyers urged the students to think it all over very carefully and to bring their parents with them to the mass meeting planned for the following evening at the high school. Only if the older generation was solidly behind the legal action would the NAACP proceed with it.

If white officialdom wished to dismiss the Moton uprising as a passing whim of the normally docile black community, the turnout for the meeting on the evening of the fourth day of the strike was hard to explain away—as hard as the thus far unbroken ranks of the strikers themselves. There were a thousand Prince Edward Negroes at Moton High that night. The NAACP lawyers were obliged by court schedules to be elsewhere that evening, but the association's main organizer and firebrand in the state—executive secretary Lester Banks—was there and in peak form. The only way they would achieve their full dignity as citizens, he told the enthusiastic crowd, was by integration; a new colored high school would not bring them equality even "if it were built brick for brick, cement for cement" the way the white school was. It had taken their children to demonstrate to the whites how deeply the Negroes felt about their second-rate schools, and now here was Banks proposing that the black adults of this backwoods county leapfrog over the equalization stage entirely and spearhead the most militant protest movement in all the Southland by suing to end segregation itself. Yet there was remarkably little opposition to the idea at the mass meeting.

A letter from Principal Jones urging that the strike be curtailed was received by every Moton parent on Monday, April 30, a week after the strike had begun. It spoke of the punishment that might be visited on their striking children, of "the tremendous disadvantage in their scholastic work" that the strike was causing, and of "the wrong impression" that it was creating. Circumstantial evidence indicated that Jones might have sent the form letter under duress, delaying it as long as he could and giving his friends Griffin and Lancaster time to prepare a counter-thrust. Jones began his written appeal this way: "We, the staff members of Moton High School, have been authorized by the division superintendent to write this letter to you. . . ." Many of the black parents receiving the letter grasped that its sender had had little choice. Griffin said later that he feared the Jones letter would cause a serious break in the ranks of black solidarity and many parents would accede to the principal's request, and so "I got out a letter that very same day," lugging the batch to the post office with the help of his friend John Lancaster. Quick work indeed. Griffin's letter summoned the Moton parents to an emergency meeting of the county-wide black PTA that Thursday evening, May 3. "It is necessary that all of us support the efforts being made to get our just rights," the Griffin broadside asserted. "We shall expect you to be present and to bring others with you. REMEMBER. The eyes of the world are on us. The intelligent support we give our cause will serve as a stimulant for the cause of free people everywhere."

Griffin, meanwhile, was driving all over the county canvassing Negro homes, where the lights were burning late those exhilarating nights, and getting signatures for a petition to the county board to integrate the high school. "I never felt that integration would truly work here," the minister commented long afterward, "but the suit had great tactical virtues. It carried us through a critical stage toward freedom and it was a means of rallying the black community. But I did not think the white power structure was going to yield." Farm agent John Lancaster later remarked, "It was hard for me to realize that this community was [as] aroused as it was. . . . It had been my feeling that a two-year campaign to get voters registered was the next thing we should do." But there were 600 farms in Prince Edward County that were owned by Negroes then—nearly as many as were owned by whites—and while there were almost no non-agricultural jobs in the county not controlled by whites, the relatively high proportion of independent black farmers no doubt encouraged the unprecedented showing of fortitude by the Negro community.

At the May 3 mass meeting held at Reverend Griffin's church, the newly militant Negroes ratified the desegregation plan. There were many speakers, but none more warmly received than Barbara Johns, who reviewed the events of the preceding fortnight and, to a roomful of nodding heads, urged that the NAACP lawyers be empowered to proceed. The consensus in support of that position seemed overwhelming. Spottswood Robinson had begun detailing the timetable of the lawsuit and instructing the students to return to school the following Monday when up stood J. B. Pervall, the former principal of Moton High, who had opposed the strike and more strongly opposed the radical turn of events. "I was under the impression that the students were striking for a new building," he declared. "You are pulling a heavy load, Mr. Robinson, coming down here to a country town like Farmville and trying to take it over on a non-segregated basis." It was an electric moment.

Lester Banks answered that the whole situation had been carefully explained the previous week. Robinson asked the crowd if it really wanted unsegregated schools and got back a wave of applause from all corners of the room. And then Barbara Rose Johns was on her feet and speaking for the last time that evening. Her head tossed back, her voice echoing with pride and power that had come perhaps too soon in life to her, she turned a searing look on the old Moton principal and told them all, "Don't let Mr. Charlie, Mr. Tommy, or Mr. Pervall stop you from backing us. We are depending upon you." More than a few eyes in that pulsing room shone with tears. There were reporters there and popping flashbulbs to record it all. The Old Black Joes of Prince Edward County had been routed—or suddenly rejuvenated. "Anybody who would not back these children after they stepped out on a limb is not a man," Francis Griffin declared in closing out the meeting. "Anybody who won't fight against racial prejudice is not a man. And to those of you who are here to take the news back to Mr. Charlie, take it—only take it straight."

On May 23, 1951, exactly a month after the two-week strike was started in Farmville, Spottswood Robinson filed suit at the federal courthouse in Richmond on behalf of 117 Moton students who asked that the state law requiring segregated schools in Virginia be struck down. First on the list of plaintiffs by happenstance was a fourteen-year-old ninth-grader named Dorothy E. Davis, daughter of a Prince Edward farmer. The case was titled *Davis v. County School Board of Prince Edward County.* The same day he filed it, Robinson boarded the train to Charleston for the *Briggs* trial that was to begin the following week.

A month later, in a closed-door, off-the-record meeting, a group of leading whites tried to persuade a group of leading blacks to drop the desegregation suit in exchange for a guarantee that a new colored high school would be put up as soon as possible. There was some sympathy for the idea among the blacks in the room, but Francis Griffin said there was now plenty of evidence that Negroes had as much native intelligence as whites and that the time had come for the separation of the races to end. One of his white listeners asked the militant minister where he had got hold of that notion about black and white brainpower; Griffin cited a sociology book, chapter and verse, and in the process clinched the point.

A few days later, despite a petition signed by 493 black citizens urging his retention, Boyd Jones was fired as principal of Robert R. Moton High School. He had not acted forcefully to squelch the strike, the school board said officially. Unofficially, whites said Jones had been an instigator. Under oath, he denied it. A week after Jones was dismissed, the school board applied to the state Literary Fund for $600,000 to add to the $275,000 grant it had received from the Battle Fund to build a new high school for Negroes. Within a month, the commonwealth of Virginia, determined to undercut the Negro position in the Prince Edward desegregation suit, granted the request. Efforts to build the new school, which had been languishing for years, now moved ahead at full speed.

It was all too much for the conservative element at Reverend Griffin's church. In midsummer, a move was afoot to depose him as pastor. Characteristically, Griffin met it head-on. On Sunday morning, July 28, he delivered a sermon entitled "The Prophecy of Equalization" and took his text from Isaiah 40:4–5, which begins: "Every valley shall be exalted, and every mountain and hill shall be made low. . . ." In forty-five minutes of the most powerful preaching of his life, he denounced colored ministers of the sort who "believe everything will be all right so long as they pay lip service to the accepted code, sidestep local gossip, and 'whoop it up' on Sunday." Then he asserted that

> when I look and see healthy colored babies, I think how God has brought them into the world properly and how the rotten system of the Southland will twist them into warped personalities, cringing cowards, unable to cope with the society into which they were unwillingly thrown and which they have a God-given right to enjoy.
>
> . . . When I think of the years of economic exploitation made on my people by the white race, and the hatred thrown against us, I must, in all sincerity, fight against such inhumanity to man with every ounce of energy given to me by God. . . .
>
> I would sacrifice my job, money, and any property for the principles of right. I offered my life for a decadent democracy [in the Second World War], and I'm willing to die rather than let these children down. No one's going to scare me from my convictions by threatening my job. All who want me to stay as the head of the church, raise your hands.

Almost every hand in the church was in the air.

More than half a year would pass before *Davis v. County School Board* came to trial in Richmond. Meanwhile, Barbara Johns was sent for her safety to finish high school in Montgomery, Alabama, where she lived with her Uncle Vernon, then the pastor at the Dexter Avenue Baptist Church. Boyd Jones moved to Montgomery, too, to pursue his doctorate at Alabama State College.

There were those up in Prince Edward County who said that Vernon Johns was the mastermind behind the strike, though he was in Alabama when it occurred. The outspoken minister was well remembered for his leadership of the county Negroes in the late Thirties, when he verbally lashed them into insisting that bus service be provided for their schoolchildren. It was fitting that his niece should have led the uprising a dozen years later. An intrepid man, the Reverend Johns returned to his native county in 1954 to raise livestock. His place as pastor of the Dexter Avenue congregation in Montgomery was taken by a much younger man. The new pastor was twenty-seven years old, and his name was Martin Luther King, Jr.

# 20

# The Pride of Virginia

Almost certainly, the outdoor privy at the little schoolhouse for colored children in that remote section of Prince Edward County had never had more eminent visitors than the two white men who were poking around it in the middle of the summer of 1951.

Archibald Gerard Robertson, age sixty-two, was one of the leading lawyers of the state. Long a partner of the Richmond firm of Hunton, Williams, Anderson, Gay & Moore, widely regarded as the best in Virginia and surely the biggest, Robertson was in addition the president of the board of directors of tony Sweet Briar College, president of the board of one of the major hospitals in Richmond, a director of and counsel to a child-adoption agency, and, the foregoing notwithstanding, a man who in private was given to referring to Negroes as "niggers." He did not call them that all the time, of course; he often modulated it to "nigras" and was quick to reassure Yankee visitors that "I'm no nigra-hater." Robertson's traveling companion that day in Prince Edward was James Lindsay Almond, Jr., age fifty-two, formerly judge of the Hustings Court in Roanoke for a dozen years, a two-term member of the United States House of Representatives, and for the previous three years the attorney general of the commonwealth of Virginia.

"Lindsay," Robertson called out to him, "you oughta come on over here and take a look at these nigra toilets."

The conscientious state official made his inspection. The privy, he discovered, was "just awful." When Almond emerged, there was Archie Robertson doubled up with laughter. "If you ever run for governor," the private attorney told the attorney general, "I just may use this against you."

It was no laughing matter to Lindsay Almond, who later did run for governor and won. "The nigra had been badly treated educationally—and he knew it," comments the tall, courtly Almond, whose full head of flowing hair had begun turning white. But in Almond's view, the legitimacy of the black man's grievance scarcely justified the extreme remedy proposed by the NAACP. As soon as the Prince Edward desegregation case was filed in Richmond, Attorney General Almond declared that the state would intervene and bring all its resources to bear in defense of the dual school system. "Governor Battle was a lawyer, too, and a profound one," remarks Almond, "and we all realized that, though there had been a good deal of litigation going on involving the schools, this Prince Edward case was the key one, that the die had been cast here, and that Virginia law and Virginia policy were on the mat."

Robertson's law firm had been hired by the Prince Edward school board to defend it in the segregation suit, and one of Almond's assistant attorneys general accompanied the Richmond lawyer to Charleston to watch Robert Figg defend South Carolina's school law in the *Briggs* trial in May. What they saw alarmed them. Figg was a good lawyer, no doubt, but he seemed to feel that precedent was so clearly on the state's side that there was little or no need to counter the expert witnesses brought into court by the NAACP. "Our decision was that up here," says Robertson, "we were going to create issues of fact, not just of law. We were determined to show that segregation and discrimination were not the same thing."

After Almond and Robertson surveyed the situation in Prince Edward from stem to privy, the attorney general told the governor that they had no chance of prevailing in the case under the separate-but-equal doctrine. The governor promptly agreed to grant funds to Prince Edward to equalize the colored facilities. The decision was not a matter of gross cynicism, as the Virginians viewed it. For while it was true that 1950 state-wide figures showed that not quite two-thirds as much money was being spent per Negro schoolchild as per white one, the gap had been narrowing markedly. In some cities, new construction had provided colored youngsters with schools that were obviously superior to what the whites had. Lawyer Robertson, a native of Staunton, where Woodrow Wilson was born in the heart of the Shenandoah Valley, was a man who grew up surrounded by ex-slaves as servants; he believed that Virginia had nothing at all to apologize for in its racial record. "We were very proud of our history in this regard," he reflected in his eighty-second year. "After the War Between the States, this gentle, highly educated people, amid all its desolation and poverty, was trying to pull itself together, and we had loosed on us a horde of nigras who were utterly unprepared for freedom. It was the white people who paid the taxes and maintained civilization—the Negroes were an albatross around our necks, but we brought them up along with us and equalized the teachers' salaries and gave them as good schools as ours whenever we built new ones. Why, this Prince Edward case was instigated by the NAACP, which was going all over the country looking for cases. . . ."

Lindsay Almond's version of Virginia history was a bit more candid than Robertson's. "The Negro came out of slavery and was placed within a caste system, and he accepted it," Almond notes. "My forebears, people who were honest and Christian, felt kindly disposed to the nigra, but in no way wanted mingling and disapproved entirely of the amalgamation of the races because it would have endangered both. We believed strongly in separate schools, churches, and recreational facilities for the nigra. The Constitution called for equality, but it really wasn't there, and at the grass-roots level, people didn't favor it and didn't recognize the principle. While I was attorney general, there were many cases of voting discrimination and I had to tell our people, 'Look, I can't defend these actions.' " The NAACP, to Almond's way of thinking no less than Robertson's, had fired up the Negroes of Virginia, but

Almond recognized "the justness of what they were seeking." To the attorney general, the black man's claim to legal equality was undeniable, but it was to be a separated equality—one that flatly rejected the NAACP argument that separate-but-equal schooling was necessarily discriminatory—and it was to take time. "We looked toward a very slow, evolutionary process, at the end of which the nigra might take his place alongside the white man," says Almond. "Meanwhile, there remained a profound, deep-rooted basis for segregation in Virginia."

Virginia, in short, was preparing to defend segregation not only because it felt that constitutional law and precedent were on its side but also because it felt that the customs and preferences of the people made the practice morally right. The Old Dominion's lawyers studied the proceedings of the South Carolina, Kansas, and Delaware school-segregation trials and concluded that the other states had been far too ready to yield courtroom initiative to the NAACP lawyers. The Virginians planned massive retaliation. Kenneth Clark's doll testing, for example, struck Lindsay Almond at the time as "crackpot" and worthy of sharp rebuttal, but in none of the first three state trials had the defense put on eminent witnesses to try to debunk NAACP testimony on the psychological damage allegedly caused or severely compounded by school segregation. Virginia officials began to understand the omission only after they began preparing for the trial. "My job was to get the expert witnesses for our side," recalls Archibald Robertson. "It was a very frustrating thing. I must have talked to more than a hundred sociologists, psychologists, historians, and so forth. We tried Odum, too. I talked with them freely, off the record, in total candor, and afterwards I would ask them, 'Would you be willing to testify to that in court?' And most of them said that their views would likely prove so unpopular among their colleagues that it might well ruin their careers to testify. Then I asked my friend George Modlin, president of the University of Richmond, for names and he suggested Henry Garrett at Columbia."

Garrett had all the ribbons Robertson badly wanted in an expert rebuttal witness. Then fifty-eight years old, he had been on the Columbia faculty for nearly thirty years, the last dozen of them as chairman of the psychology department. He had been president of the American Psychological Association, an advisor to the Secretary of War, and the author of a number of respectable if not very profound scholarly articles and at least one textbook of wide repute. But beyond that, he was a native of Halifax County in Southside Virginia, barely forty miles southwest of Prince Edward, had received his public-school and undergraduate college education in Richmond, and had taught mathematics for two years at John Marshall High School in the Virginia capital. Here, Robertson thought, might be a sympathetic soul.

The lawyer called the psychologist, who was spending his Christmas vacation in Gainesville, Florida. Garrett listened carefully and then invited Robertson to come see him soon at his Columbia office. For the fact was that Henry Garrett was convinced that the Negro was inferior to the white man, that the black race was immature anthropologically, and that in pressing for the end of segregation, the Negro was unwisely trying to break the evolutionary cycle of the South's effort to bring him up in the world. In later years, Garrett would turn pamphleteer and argue bluntly that in terms of heredity, physiology, and cultural history the Negro suffered badly when compared with the white man. "Despite glowing accounts of ancient African achievements," he would write, "over the past 5,000 years the history of Black Africa is a cultural blank." Physiologists were finding evidence, he argued, that the Negro's brain was not significantly smaller than the white man's but less fissured, less complex, and less thick in the frontal lobes where reasoning and abstract thinking go on. And while environment no doubt played a part in the IQ scores recorded by test groups of both races, advanced research, as Garrett saw it, suggested that human intelligence was determined 90 percent by hereditary factors. There was no escaping the meaning of the intelligence-test performances that showed a Negro "overlap" of between 5 and at best 25 percent—that is, the collected literature on the subject showed that only between 5 and 25 percent of the Negroes tested did better than the average white person taking the same test. "Given roughly the same opportunity and background," Garrett comments, "the Negro still performs less well than the white, even after 50 years of social progress, and the relative gaps remain as wide as ever."

The Columbia psychologist greeted Richmond attorney Robertson cordially in New York, heard him out, was assured that the state was making serious efforts to equalize the school facilities for both races, and said yes, he would testify for Virginia at the coming trial. He did not fear for his standing in the academic world. He had his tenure on the faculty. He had garnered his share of honors. And besides, by then he had pretty well decided to get out of New York. "I liked the city during my first ten years there," he recalls. "We had lived on Claremont Avenue in a university-owned apartment, and you could walk over to Riverside Drive in those days and stay till midnight to watch the activities on the river. I grew increasingly disenchanted with the city, though, as places like the Drive became off-limits. People were being beaten up there during the day."

Word soon escaped that Garrett was going to Richmond to testify in behalf of the maintenance of segregation. He was summoned to the office of the dean of the graduate faculties, where, as Garrett remembers it, he was told that the university faced "a pretty explosive situation" in its relationship with the surrounding Harlem community and that his testifying in Virginia might well embarrass Columbia. Garrett telephoned Robertson's law firm in Richmond and reported that the heat was being applied to him to back off. The lawyers asked President Modlin at the University of Richmond to send off a letter to his counterpart at Columbia, Dr. Grayson Kirk, to protest the threatened infringement of Garrett's academic freedom. The psychologist recounts: "I was then summoned to Dr. Kirk's office and he questioned me about my intentions. I said yes, I planned to testify and that so long as equal facilities were provided, segregation was in the best interests of both races at that time. He said, 'Well, I happen to agree with you, but I wouldn't say so.' It was agreed that if I chose to testify, I had to make it clear that I was not talking for the university or in my official capacity as head of the psychology department." * It was a tense moment for the Virginians while Garrett reconsidered the situation. "We had to sit down and talk with him like a Dutch uncle," Lindsay Almond recalls. "He was very worried and upset when he started getting that pressure applied to him up North." Convinced of the sincerity of Virginia's expanding efforts to equalize its schools for both races, Garrett stuck to his agreement to testify.

Finally the pro-segregationists had a social scientist of national reputation who would come into court and lend the dignity of academia to their cause. "He was our star witness," Almond says, "and the backbone of our defense."

He was more the biceps, actually. The backbone of Virginia's defense belonged to Archie Robertson's senior law partner, T. Justin Moore, a high-powered corporation lawyer who functioned as chief counsel for the Prince Edward school board. A native of Louisiana, Moore had come up to the University of Richmond for his undergraduate schooling, graduated Phi Beta Kappa—later serving as national president of the academic fraternity— and gone on to Harvard Law School, where he excelled. Admitted to the Virginia bar in 1913, he began the kind of corporate practice that would have made him a rich man at a young age if he had joined a Wall Street firm in New York; as it was, he would die a millionaire, though barely. Instead of a vast fortune, Justin Moore earned gilded status in his adopted hometown. He was the chairman of the board of deacons at the First Baptist Church. He relaxed after work or on weekends at the Hermitage Country Club and the Country Club of Virginia and took luncheon and athletic exercise during the work day at the downtown Commonwealth Club. He was rector of the board of trustees—chairman is the more usual term—of the University of Richmond, then in its one hundred and nineteenth year. And he was long a director and general counsel of Virginia Electric and Power Company, the state's biggest utility, and on several occasions turned down its presidency. Indeed, his knowledge of byzantine utility regulations made him the South's leading authority on the subject and one of the top utility lawyers in the country. In Richmond, he was widely considered a brilliant businessman and eagerly sought for directorships of banks and corporations. "He worked harder and loved his work more than any man I ever knew," says Archibald Robertson.

That Justin Moore was a forceful and determined man, no one who knew him disputes. But he was not a beloved figure in Richmond. "He had a lot of enemies here," remarks a former partner. "He was a very strong

---

* Grayson Kirk contradicts Henry Garrett's account of their exchange. In an interview on October 14, 1971, the retired president of Columbia said: "I have no recollection of such a conversation with Dr. Garrett. I barely knew the man and saw him perhaps two or three times while he was on campus." Dr. Kirk added that he knew of Dr. Garrett's racial views, "but it's absolute nonsense to suggest that I agreed with his views or that I was or am a racist. I knew many leaders of the Harlem community—some of them were friends of mine." Dr. Kirk also said he had no memory of any chastening correspondence with President Modlin of the University of Richmond. Dr. Modlin, however, says that he recalls writing a letter to Dr. Kirk "concerning the pressures being exerted on Dr. Garrett, but, unfortunately, we are unable to locate the letter in our files."

character, and there are people who feel he walked over them on his way up." Many successful men have had as much said of them. In Justin Moore's case, the aggressiveness was exhibited in his bare-toothed display of advocacy in the Prince Edward segregation case. "He put the drive and force into this thing," says John W. Riely, a younger partner in Moore's firm who logged well over a thousand hours working on the school case and the litigation that followed it. Moore's firm was not in the Prince Edward case as a charitable undertaking, Riely notes—and that may explain the authoritative, resourceful way in which the commonwealth's legal effort was conducted and the relentless fashion in which Moore and Robertson stalked opposing witnesses in the courtroom. "We all knew that these guys were going to be playing for keeps," says Robert Carter, who joined Oliver Hill and Spottswood Robinson at the NAACP's counsel table for the trial. "They were out to cut our throats—and we, theirs."

Presiding over the special three-judge U.S. District Court that convened on February 25, 1952, to hear *Davis v. County School Board* was one of the most colorful members of the appellate level of the federal judiciary—Armistead Mason Dobie, a seventy-one-year-old bachelor with a somewhat squeaky voice that he persisted in using endlessly when others so equipped would have chosen to remain sagely silent.

A native of Norfolk, where his father had been the superintendent of schools, young Armistead—an honored Virginia patronymic that was "ideal for a sleeping car," Dobie once said, "but hell for a boy"—began his forty-year love affair with the University of Virginia at the turn of the century. His garrulousness, once estimated to run at the rate of 10,000 words a minute, made him a campus character, and his unforgettable performance on the steps of the famed Rotunda, during which he fulfilled his ragging duty as a pledge to playful Phi Delta Phi by giving deadly accurate imitations of leading faculty members, made him a celebrity. The public mimicking of professors is said to have become an annual tradition at Charlottesville from then on. Dobie unquestionably had a zany streak in him. In Europe one summer, he bought half-ownership of a dancing bear and administered its bookings with Hurok-like zeal.

A quipster, a celebrant of the richness of the English language, a shrewd investor in the stock market, a *bon vivant* and an epicure who became a devoted golfer to keep himself in shape, Armistead Dobie was, above all, a lover of the law. After earning an advanced degree at Harvard, he came back to the University of Virginia, where he had taken his law degree as well as his undergraduate training, and spent the next thirty-two years on the faculty of the law school, the last seven of them as its dean. He was lionized as a lecturer who was as entertaining as he was acute, and was renowned for his minting of such hyperboles as "the scream of a consumptive gnat" and "as pure as the new-fallen snow on a convent roof." He became an expert on federal procedure, bailments and carriers, and the Virginia criminal code—a wide range of expertise for any legal scholar—and wrote books on them. And no football pep rally was complete without a few bristling words from Dr.

Dobie urging the Orange and Blue Cavaliers to demolish the Generals of Washington & Lee the next day. His elevation to the U.S. District Court in 1939 was both popular and unexpected. Because Virginia's Senators Harry Byrd and Carter Glass were avowed enemies of the New Deal, President Roosevelt had balked at granting them the traditional senatorial privilege of approving the selection of new members of the federal bench from their state. Roosevelt's son Franklin, Jr., had studied under Dobie and recommended him to his father, whose nomination of the Virginia law dean delighted the otherwise hostile Senators and was speedily confirmed. Within a year, Dobie was elevated to the Court of Appeals for the Fourth Circuit, which, composed also of Judges John J. Parker and Morris A. Soper, won a reputation for excellence surpassed only by the Second Circuit under Chief Judge Learned Hand.

Besides his indisputably wide and deep knowledge of the law, Judge Dobie was distinguished by two characteristics on the Fourth Circuit. He would dissent just six times in some 1,400 cases that he heard in his more than fifteen years on the bench, and four of the six dissents were upheld by the Supreme Court, reversing Dobie's brethren on the Circuit. Such a record suggested that Dobie was not very likely to go off half-cocked in reviewing so grave a matter as the legality of segregation. In view, too, of his colleague John Parker's long and careful decision in *Briggs*, the NAACP lawyers saw small chance of Dobie's ruling for them in the Prince Edward case. But his other chief judicial characteristic—peculiarity, one might even term it— assured that the Richmond trial would be presided over in a quite different fashion from the way Parker ran the Charleston hearing. Where Judge Parker was reserved and dignified, Dobie was given to chirpily interrupting counsel with an irreverent question, some judicial prompting to underscore a point, or an irresistible impulse to wisecrack. It made him a refreshing personality on the bench, but it did not do much for the concentration of the lawyers working in front of him. "I revere the memory of the man," comments Lindsay Almond, who studied under him, "but Judge Dobie could break into the heart of your argument with a quip. . . ."

Dobie's junior colleagues on the bench hearing the Prince Edward case were a pair of straight-laced fellow Virginians. District Judge Sterling Hutcheson, a native of Mecklenberg County adjacent to Henry Garrett's Halifax County on the state's southern tier, had served for eleven years as U.S. Attorney for the Eastern District of Virginia before being named to the federal bench in 1944. Fifty-seven years old when the Prince Edward school case was heard, he was viewed as a quiet, even-tempered jurist who rarely raised his voice, even in anger. Judge Hutcheson was no stranger to NAACP lawyers Hill and Robinson, who had won a series of important school-equalization suits in his court starting in 1948. The final member of the special three-judge court was fifty-two-year-old Albert Vickers Bryan, a native of Alexandria who served that Washington suburb as city attorney for two years and then became commonwealth attorney, or state prosecutor, for that sector of Virginia for twenty years before being appointed to the U.S. District Court in 1947.

All three judges, then, were lifelong Virginians deeply versed in federal and state law and not given to apostasy. "There was never any doubt about the outcome of the trial," says Oliver Hill. "We were trying to build a record for the Supreme Court."

The Reverend Francis Griffin and the Prince Edward delegation that kept the Richmond courtroom packed throughout the five-day trial did not know their hopes for victory were groundless. "We weren't sophisticated," Reverend Griffin notes. "Our people were very enthused—they had hopes that this one trial would settle it all."

From the beginning, and right up until the last few words, the white Virginia lawyers dominated the trial in that historic Richmond court where both Aaron Burr and Jefferson Davis once stood trial for treason.

Spottswood Robinson, whom the white lawyers respected as an able attorney and skillful Richmond businessman, opened for the NAACP with a short, dry statement of the plaintiffs' twofold purpose: to have the Prince Edward colored schools declared unequal and the Virginia segregation statute declared unconstitutional. Then Justin Moore took the floor and delivered a long, bristling statement that yielded nothing to his opponents. Virginia had embarked on "a tremendous program of public education" twenty years earlier, and the new Battle Fund, named in honor of the governor, was but the latest installment in this ongoing effort, the burden of which "I may say without any improper inference . . . necessarily falls principally on the white population." In Prince Edward, the defendant school board was struggling manfully to provide the colored people with better schools. The board, he said, playing fast and loose with the facts, had acquired land for a new colored high school "long before this case was instituted." The new school now being built would give Prince Edward's Negroes educational facilities that were superior to what the whites had. Moore did not say that the money to build the school had not been forthcoming from either the county or the state until the Negro children had gone on strike at Moton High School and the suit had been filed.

But the real issue in the case, Moore correctly told the court, was not whether the Prince Edward schools were equalized, for "the charge of inequality is included just as a matter of precaution." The heart of the case was whether segregation itself was discriminatory and therefore illegal. In the previous school-segregation cases, expert testimony had gone into the record unchallenged on the alleged personal damage inflicted by the continuance of segregation, but

> [w]e are prepared to show by competent evidence that that sort of thing, at the present time at least, is purely speculative, that it is not based on a sound scientific basis, and we give notice to these gentlemen right now, if they don't already know it, that we intend to challenge that proposition if they attempt to present evidence on that, as has been done in some of these cases. . . . [T]here is no foundation whatever for the fundamental theory on which this case is built—namely, that equal facilities and advantages cannot be provided regardless of the amount of money that is spent. . . .

The law governing the equal-protection aspect of the case, moreover, had been "settled beyond peradventure of doubt," the best corporation attorney in Virginia declared. Moore cited District Court opinions by all three judges now hearing him that had upheld the separate-but-equal principle as applied to public schools in Virginia, and for good measure he reminded them of the *Briggs* opinion by their distinguished associate Judge Parker. Then he came to his masterfully patronizing close:

> . . . in these eighty years, as will be shown here, there has been an outstanding piece of work done in building up the Negro in every way—socially, politically and economically—where today he occupies a position of importance in economics and politics, in many ways, all due to the opportunities that have been given to him in this land in which we live and love. . . .

Attorney General Lindsay Almond then weighed in with a few hundred orotund words "to proudly proclaim" to the court that "in the reasonably near future" the state would wipe out every remaining discrimination in the field of high-school education "to which any reasonable man could make any complaint."

It looked as if the commonwealth threatened to drown the NAACP in old-style Southern rhetoric.

Robert Carter opened for the plaintiffs with a determined effort to pin down the Prince Edward school superintendent, T. J. McIlwaine, on the inferior equipment and curriculum at Moton and on the educational effects of segregation, but the witness kept dematerializing like a will-o'-the-wisp every time the black lawyer came too close. The superintendent acknowledged a few inequalities—the library at the white high school, for example, had about twice as many books as the one at Moton and the facilities for teaching science at Moton were definitely inferior—but he yielded little else of substance. When Carter asked why such academic subjects as physics, world history, geography, trigonometry, and Latin and such vocational subjects as shorthand, woodwork, machine shop, electricity, and mechanical drawing were available at the white school but not at Moton, McIlwaine blandly said that there had been no demand for them at the Negro school. Carter then read a number of passages from official publications of Virginia's Department of Education regarding the scope and goals of the public-school programs in the state, all of which called for preserving, improving, or extending the tenets of democracy and encouraging cooperation among students of all types. Though McIlwaine acknowledged the desirability of such goals, he nimbly dodged Carter's efforts to assert that they were in direct conflict with the state's Jim Crow school law.

Spottswood Robinson took over, put on a photographer and a statistician to authenticate masses of documents that the NAACP was submitting to the court in support of its claim of inequality at Moton, and then brought on Thomas Henderson, dean of the college and professor of education at Virginia Union University, a Negro school in Richmond founded at the close of the Civil War. Henderson, a veteran of the Hill-Robinson-Banks school-equalization campaign in Virginia, had testified in many of the cases brought throughout the state by the NAACP over the previous four years, and he confidently spelled out the advantages that white Farmville High had over Moton. These included location in a quiet neighborhood, compared with Moton's site hard by a principal highway; a far more attractive physical plant, valued at nearly four times the cost of Moton's; asphalt floors that made it much easier to keep clean; an industrial-arts shop, a gymnasium, an auditorium with fixed seats, and a cafeteria; a faculty that averaged eleven years of experience, compared with four years at Moton, and was paid 50 percent more than the Moton teachers; and a transportation system that provided fifteen buses for 854 white students requiring such service in the county, compared to nine buses for 811 Negroes—and six of the nine buses for Negroes had previously been used to carry white children. Unable to restrain himself and ever the pedagogue, Judge Dobie intruded on Henderson's testimony several times to plug the old-fashioned virtues that he thought were being overlooked in the witness's presentation. Teachers' salaries and training were not all that important, the judge suggested in one of his disruptive sallies:

> JUDGE DOBIE: It is also true, based on my forty years of academic work, that some of the rottenest teachers I ever sat under, who were a disgrace to the profession, were the highest paid. I think you will agree that some of the—.
> A. That is true.
> JUDGE DOBIE: And the personality and the charm and the number of books he has read are of more importance than the degree he has. Wouldn't you agree with that?
> A. I don't know that I can agree with all the latter part, but—.
> JUDGE DOBIE: Some of them can teach and some can't, and you can't make a silk purse out of a sow's ear. Neither can you make a teacher out of some people if they sat under the most magnificent teachers in the world for 762 years—isn't that true?
> A. That is quite true. May it please the court, I am still a dean, your honor, and I am trying—.
> JUDGE DOBIE: Yes, and I have the advantage over you. I don't mean to decry training in education—it is extremely important—but it is by no means all the picture. My experience has been that we have paid too much attention to that and entirely too little to the personality of the teacher.

Polonius was alive, well, and wearing robes in Richmond, Virginia.

Oliver Hill took the floor for the first time and put on Boyd Jones to recount his side of the student strike at Moton and the conditions that prompted it. Jones spoke vividly of the overcrowding at the school, of how the shortage of buses meant that half the student body straggled in late each morning, of his continuing efforts to obtain better equipment, of the four years in which he had been given promises of a new school without a single concrete step being taken to fulfill them, and of the strike and his ignorance of it beforehand. On cross-examination, Robertson skillfully set up the ex-principal. The white defense lawyer got Jones to acknowledge that the Prince Edward school board that was supposedly so unresponsive to the needs at Moton had in fact increased the faculty from fourteen to twenty-five teachers and doubled the classroom space, albeit by use of temporary tarpaper-covered structures, during Jones's four-year principalship. Then the lawyer hammered at Jones's role in the strike. Wasn't it true that the students' final examinations were to come shortly after the date of the strike? Jones said yes.

Q. So it occurred at the most critical time, scholastically, in the whole session?
A. I would say it was a critical time.
Q. And you knew not one thing about it coming until it broke?
A. That's exactly right.
Q. You had no information whatsoever?
A. That's exactly right.
Q. Do you think it is rather strange [that] a principal of the high school such as that could have such a thing get under way without your having any intimation of it?
A. I don't think so.
Q. You did not instigate it, did you?
A. No, sir, I did not.
Q. You did not encourage it, did you?
A. No, sir, I did not.

Jones went on to describe steps he had taken to defuse the strike, such as meetings with the student leaders and parent groups and his letter to every Moton family, but said he could not control the students in this matter, particularly since they apparently had the support of their parents.

Q. Did it ever come to your attention that your inability to control that situation impaired your efficiency to such an extent that you were no longer justified [in] being retained as principal of that school?
A. No.
Q. That never occurred to you?
A. No, and it still doesn't occur to me.
Q. . . . [D]id you seek the advice of any of the officials or employees or counsel of the National Association for the Advancement of Colored People?
A. No, sir.
Q. Is it not a fact that they were the instigators of this entire trouble there at the time of the rebellion?
A. So far as I know, there is no evidence to show it.

At the beginning of the second day of the trial, Carter put on the NAACP's first expert witness, John Julian Brooks, formerly professor of education at New York University and then director of the New Lincoln School, a private secondary school with a highly heterogeneous student body, which for most of its history had been affiliated with Columbia's Teachers College. As promised, Justin Moore pounced at once as soon as Carter asked the witness to comment on the educational effects of segregated schools. Such testimony, the defense attorney objected, was surely "immaterial and irrelevant and has nothing to do with constitutional rights . . . [but] with legislative policy." Dobie acknowledged some sympathy with Moore's claim, but said the court preferred to compile a full and open record, "and we will decide what it is worth. I do that with a good deal of biological and anthropological and psychological and other-logical considerations. . . ."

Brooks offered the by-now familiar testimony on the withering effects of school segregation on Negro children and then braced for Moore's cross-examination, which was long, unsubtle, and, in Brooks's case, singularly unavailing. The educator had been raised in Asheville, North Carolina, and taught public school in Atlanta for nine years, thus gaining a familiarity with Southern folkways that Moore and Robertson would pointedly note to be lacking in the NAACP's other experts. Brooks would not agree to Moore's suggestion that racial prejudice existed everywhere in about the same degree and cited his own experience in a Northern school that had been desegregated in an atmosphere of distrust and anxiety; within a very short time, the hostility had sharply diminished and black youngsters were winning the respect of whites and being elected to positions of leadership. Regarding the Prince Edward situation, Moore asked, did Brooks seriously mean that even if the Negro students were provided with the finest building in the state, a faculty with splendidly qualified teachers paid well above the state average, and brand-new buses, they could not obtain educational opportunities equal to those of the whites?

> A. My opinion, sir, is that these are fine things, and I am proud Virginia is doing them, but the large teaching salaries, shining buses, fine brick buildings, are poor compensation for humiliation, lack of self-respect, and a restricted curriculum.
> Q. Well, you only answered my question in part.
> A. The answer is No.

Squelched, Moore wondered if Brooks's overall view of the social customs of Virginia would not also call for the abolition of laws against intermarriage. Carter objected that no one was proposing such a step and that it was beyond the scope of the case. Dobie upheld him.

Dobie's initial ruling to allow expert testimony on the alleged effects of segregation permitted Carter's star social scientist, M. Brewster Smith, chairman of the psychology department at Vassar, to sketch out at some length the growing body of evidence "beyond any reasonable doubt" that environment rather than racial inheritance was the prime factor in any individual's learning ability. As to racially separate schools,

> . . . the effects of segregation in this sphere are such as to make the Negro, on the average, more like the common, prejudiced conception of a Negro, as a stupid, illiterate, apathetic but happy-go-lucky person. In other words, the effects of segregation . . . help perpetuate the pattern of segregation and prejudice out of which these effects arise. . . . Children, whether they be white, Negro, or any background, who grow up knowing that they are despised by the people around them, are thought not as good as the people around them, are going to grow up with conceptions of themselves as being, in some way, not worthy. . . . [S]egregation is, in itself, under the social circumstances in which it occurs, a social and official insult and . . . has widely ramifying consequences on the individual's motivation to learn. . . .

Justin Moore sailed into thirty-three-year-old Professor Smith. He had never lived in the South and therefore knew little by firsthand experience about Virginia customs, Moore's questions implied. Intelligence tests showed there still to be considerable gap between white and Negro learning capacity, did they not? In achievement, not necessarily capacity, said the Vassar professor. Did it not occur to the learned professor that, in speaking about "official insults," the white people of Virginia might be insulted if their preferred social customs were taken away from them? Smith said he did not see how stripping away his ability to relegate members of another race to an inferior position was an insult to the integrity or self-respect of the white Southerner. Suppose the white Southerner disagreed and chose to ignore a court order to end segregation on the ground that the great majority of his fellow citizens favored retaining the practice? Smith answered:

> . . . what we know of the psychology of prejudice leads us to believe that if a clear-cut, straightforward change is proposed from that height [i.e., the courts], that the population will be very likely to go along with it, rather than with a gradual, pussyfooting sort of approach that in no way speaks firmly to those who are most deeply prejudiced. . . .

Moore's predatory instincts found their most tempting prey in Carter's next witness, who was not the sort to be readily befriended, as Moore himself had been, by the First Families of Virginia.

Isidor Chein had taught psychology at City College of New York from 1937 to 1950 and then become director of research of the Commission on Community Interrelations of the American Jewish Conference, a non-profit, Zionist-oriented organization aimed at advancing the welfare of Jews and all other minority groups in America in the belief, Chein explained, that "the fate of the Jews is bound up with the fate of all minority groups." Chein had been summoned to tell the court the results of a survey he had taken with a colleague, Max Deutscher, and published in the *Journal of Psychology* in 1948 under the title "The Psychological Effects of Enforced Segregation: A Survey of Social Science Opinion." Chein and Deutscher had sent out a questionnaire to 849 social scientists whose field of specialization suggested that they were likely to hold informed opinions on the subject of the inquiry; these included the entire membership of the American Ethnological Society, all the members of the Division of the Personality and Social Psychology of the American Psychological Association, and all the members of the American Sociological Society who concentrated on social psychology or race relations. Of those sent questionnaires, 517, or 61 percent, responded. Of those sent the questionnaire, 8.4 percent were Southerners or at Southern institutions; of the responses, 6.2 percent came from the South. The survey included three questions and produced these responses:

1. *Does enforced segregation have detrimental psychological effects on members of racial and religious groups which are segregated, even if equal facilities are provided?* Response overall: 90 percent said yes, 2 percent said no, 8 percent said they had no opinion or did not answer the question. Southern respondents: 91 percent said yes, 6 percent no, 3 percent no opinion or no reply.

2. *Does enforced segregation have a detrimental effect on the group that enforces the segregation, even if that group provides equal facilities to the groups that are segregated?* Response overall: 83 percent said yes, 4 percent said no, 13 percent had no opinion or did not answer. Southern respondents: 84 percent said yes, 6 percent said no, 10 percent no opinion or no reply.

3. *What is the basis for your opinions?* Multiple answers were provided for; 29.2 percent said they relied on their own research, 61.1 percent on the research of others, 65.5 percent on their own professional experience, and 47.6 percent on the professional experience of others.

The numbers were overwhelming and the fact that they had been published in a leading professional journal lent them the imprimatur of high authority. Justin Moore did not try to tear them down—he would leave that to his rebuttal witnesses; instead, he went after the man. His cross-examination began this way:

Q. Dr. Chein, just how do you spell your last name?
A. C-H-E-I-N.
Q. What kind of name is that? What sort of racial background does that indicate?
A. The name is a poor English version of Hebrew which designates "charm."
Q. What is your racial background?
A. As Dr. Smith has testified, I could not give an honest answer to that because of the complexity of the concept. I think what you want to know is am I Jewish.
Q. Are you 100 percent Jewish?
A. How do I answer that?
Q. I don't know—you know.
A. In all honesty, the framework of the question is not one which can be, as far as I know, intelligently answered. All of my—both of my parents and all of my ancestors, as far back as I know, were Jewish.
Q. That answers my question. I simply wanted to find out what was the story about that. Where were you born?
A. In the United States, in New York City.
Q. Were your parents native born in the United States?
A. No.
Q. Where were they born?
A. In Poland.
Q. How long had they lived in this country when you were born?
A. I am not sure—for some 20 years, I think. I was the youngest child.

The distaste in the lawyer's questions was palpable, and he gained little in subtlety as he put Chein through the wringer. Wasn't segregation rampant in New York City as a matter of practicality? Wasn't prejudice rife? Wasn't it true that among Negroes "a very sharp prejudice" was exhibited by those with a light skin color toward those with a very dark one? Wasn't the survey of social scientists that he reported on seriously deficient in Southern respondents? Didn't he realize that the average white child growing up in the average home in Virginia became accustomed to certain ways of thinking and acting "with respect to persons of another race or group" and that no statute could much affect that child's fundamental attitude? Along with opposing segregation, didn't Chein also favor killing the ban on racial intermarriage? The last question was left unobjected to by NAACP counsel, though Judge Dobie had earlier ruled it beyond the scope of the case, and Chein, struggling to keep his composure throughout what Dobie characterized from the bench as "a pretty gruelling cross-examination," said unwaveringly: "I know of no reason why individuals should not be able to follow their own choice in terms of skin color. I do not think that is a relevant factor." Moore kept after him. Wasn't it true that a group could be discriminated against without suffering a sense of inferiority? Now take the Jews, they were discriminated against, were they not?

A. Yes.
Q. Is it your view that that has resulted in the Jew feeling any inferiority as to status?
A. Yes, sir.
Q. You really believe that?
A. I not only believe it, I have evidence to that effect. But this is to a much less marked degree than in the case of the Negro. As a matter of fact, in the social science literature the notion of self-hate first appeared in connection with a study of Jews. Jews are also people just like Negroes and other white people, people of other religious groups. They react to the same kind of social and psychological forces. If the weight of society bears against them, then they tend to share in the viewpoint of society. . . . [T]hese full stereotypes which they acquire of themselves are given additional force in the case of the Negro by the fact that the state is saying these are true, by implication. . . . Suppose all people here hated my guts—if you will excuse the inelegant expression. Suppose they all hated me? I can take the position and support myself by saying, "Well, all of these people do not understand me. They are out of step; I am not out of step." It would be perhaps an irrational thing to do to say everybody else is wrong and I am right, but I would have that recourse available to me. But suppose the United States Government says to me—or suppose the government of New York State, in which I live, says to me, "Dr. Chein, you are just no good." . . . I can no longer say that all of these people are wrong, because the government is giving sanction, it is embodying in its practices, it is saying what these people are saying is true, and so the government is saying this to me and I cannot balance the government against people.
Q. You agree that the Japanese and Chinese have great pride of race?
A. There are Japanese and Chinese who do.
Q. Do you not agree that the average Japanese or Chinese has pride of race?
A. I am not too familiar with the Chinese and Japanese groups.
Q. Do you know of any reason why the Negro in America should not be just as proud of his race as the Japanese or Chinese?
A. I certainly do know a reason.
Q. What?
A. Because the state is saying to the Negro that he should have no pride in his race.

After Reverend Griffin of Farmville testified that prior to filing of the lawsuit the black PTA in Prince Edward had not been advised of any tangible steps or commitment by the defendant county school board to build a new colored high school, the NAACP put on the mainstay of its corps of social psychologists—Kenneth Clark.

In his third and most expansive appearance in the school-segregation cases, Dr. Clark showed the benefits of his growing experience on the witness stand. He was, by now, a skilled performer in explaining the abstract concepts he wanted to put across. "Segregation is prejudice concretized in the society," he stated, "and in my work with Negro youth and in my interviewing them, I find this is the way they interpret it: Segregation is a mist, like a wall, which society erects, of stone and steel—psychological stone and steel—constantly telling them that they are inferior and constantly telling them that they cannot escape prejudice. Prejudice is something inside people. Segregation is the objective expression of what these people have inside."

Clark had not used his doll tests on Prince Edward children, given their age. Instead, fourteen Moton High students had been brought up to Richmond on Monday, the first day of the trial, and the psychologist had interviewed them at the law offices of Hill and Robinson. Clark's testimony on the results of the interviews lacked the arithmetical precision of his doll tests, yet it seemed more persuasive because of the unquantified approach.

Asked what they thought of their school, the Moton students in every instance responded with a negative comment, Clark reported to the court. They reacted to the school as "a symbol of some stigma." They all believed the white school to be better, and many felt whites consciously wished to keep Negroes in an inferior status. The most pronounced characteristic he observed in the Moton students, he said, was "an excessive preoccupation with . . . the race struggle," much of it attributable, no doubt, to the strike and the conflict it symbolized. Indeed, Clark added, probably the most detrimental consequence of segregation is the degree to which it obsesses everybody with race.

Clark's direct testimony ended the second day of the trial, and Justin Moore had overnight to prepare his cross-examination. It proved no less jagged than the one the defense counsel inflicted on Clark's former City College colleague Isidor Chein. Moore began, as he had with all the expert witnesses, by asking about their origins. When Clark said he was born in the Panama Canal Zone, Moore followed with:

Q. In view of your reference to Panama, I must inquire if you know—you appear to be of rather light color—what percentage, as near as you can tell us, are you white and what percentage some other?

A. I haven't the slightest idea. What do you mean by "percentage"?

Q. I mean are you half-white, or half-colored, and half Panamanian, or what?

A. I still can't understand you.

Q. You don't understand that question?

A. No. My parents were not born in Panama. My mother and father are from the West Indies. My father was born in Jamaica and so was my mother. They met in Panama, and I was the result.

Q. So you are, really, a West Indian?

A. I was not born in the West Indies; I was born in the Panama Canal Zone. . . .

Moore wanted to know if his attendance at black Howard University had given Clark any feeling of inferiority, and Clark said it was at Howard that "I first became aware of what it really meant to be a Negro in America." It was while there that he got turned away from a restaurant for the first time. It was at Howard, he told the court, that he led a group of fellow students on a march to the Capitol "to see if we could not get them to treat us like loyal Americans, which we felt we were, by just giving us food in the public restaurant there." Oh, yes, after having grown up in New York, he found Howard and segregated Washington "an education in race relations which will stay with me for the rest of my life."

Moore, burned, turned to Clark's interviews with the Prince Edward students. Who brought the youngsters to Richmond? Clark said he did not know for sure, though Lester Banks of the NAACP made the arrangements. Well, did Clark know what was said to the youngsters by way of explaining their pending interviews with him? No, he did not. Leaving the strong inference that the students might well have been coached beforehand, Moore then asked if Clark didn't think that the strike and the lawsuit had been much on the students' minds for months and months and that their response to his questions reflected that. Clark acknowledged that that was probably so. Moore then lured Clark into conducting a sample interview with him while the lawyer posed as one of the black children. Part of it went:

CLARK: "I would like to ask you some questions. Tell me about your school."
MOORE: "Well, it is not much good."
CLARK: "Will you tell me about it?"
MOORE: "Well, we don't have all the things that they have got over at the other school. That is what my parents say."
CLARK: I don't remember one of them saying that, by the way. Not one of them volunteered information.
MOORE: I just want to see how you put on the test.
CLARK: "What about the white school?"
MOORE: "I hear at home that it is fine. I have never been over there."
CLARK: "You hear that it is fine?"
MOORE: "Yes, that is what I hear."
CLARK: "Why is that?"
MOORE: "Well, they have got more money, I suppose, for it."
CLARK: "Who has more money?"
MOORE: "The School Board."
CLARK: "Well, what do you think can be done about it?"
MOORE: "Well, I think we may get a better school if we keep on fighting about it."
CLARK: "Do you think that things will get better?"
MOORE: "Oh, yes, I think they are going to get better if we keep NAACP working for us."
CLARK: "Tell [me] what you think of white people."
MOORE: "Oh, some of them good, some of them bad. I think that is about the way most of my friends feel about it."
CLARK: "What do you think of colored people?"
MOORE: "Oh, the same way—some of them good, some bad."
CLARK: "What do you think we can do to make things better?"

MOORE: "Well, just work harder."
CLARK: "Do you think it will get better eventually?"
MOORE: "Oh, yes, I think it is getting better all the time."
CLARK: That was the briefest interview we have ever had.

Archibald Robertson, Moore's co-counsel, thought it devastating the way Moore "put on a moronic face and the accent of a little darkey" in posing as one of Clark's interviewees. "But it wasn't done in a nasty way," he added; the purpose of the gambit had been simply to trivialize Clark's methods. "It brought the house down," Robertson recalled. "Everyone there enjoyed it—except maybe the other side."

Moore then waded in for the knockout punch. Did Clark seriously contend that such an interview, even if expanded some, proved anything at all except that the students wanted to complain about their school? Weren't Clark's findings simply the inferences he chose to draw from the students' remarks? When Clark said that he had not identified himself to the students and thought it strange that none of them asked who he was, Moore snapped: "Did it ever occur to you that the reason for that was that somebody had explained to them what they were coming in for and whom they were going to see?" Clark fought back grimly, but the cross-examiner was making his mark. Then he overstepped himself and got caught:

Q. Are you familiar with the fact that one of the primary purposes of the NAACP, as it has been announced repeatedly by their representatives, as reported in the press, has been to stir up and foment critical situations that will call attention to this racial problem?

A. I am not—.

OLIVER HILL: Just a moment. If counsel is going to ask a question, I think he should ask it accurately, and I challenge Mr. Moore to state any place where the NAACP has been reported as being its policy to foment anything. We unquestionably are trying to break up segregation, and everybody will admit that. But if he is going to ask the question, let him ask it fairly.

MOORE: You yourself were reported in the Richmond press, just after the Mosque [theater] case . . . as urging the people in Richmond to create these situations that focus attention on differences in race treatment, and you know you were.

HILL: I dispute that, and I dispute the fact that even the press reported any such thing. I did say—and I say it now—that I urged people to exert themselves to carry on their rights—whatever their rights were, under the law, they should press for them. And going to the Mosque, being segregated, is a denial of their rights, and they ought to go there and not be segregated, and refuse to be segregated, and I say it here.

It is not easy to say whether Armistead Dobie had lost control of his courtroom or the Hill-Moore clash was so spontaneous and fascinating that no judge could have checked it. In a saloon, the two lawyers would plainly have been rolling in the sawdust in another instant. But the passion ebbed, Clark denied he was aware the NAACP had a policy of stirring trouble, and Moore settled down to a long and unchecked series of questions that probed at the genuineness of the psychologist's claim that the Virginia Negro, even if given equal facilities and equipment, could not obtain an equal, though segregated, education.

Q. . . . [W]hy can't the Negro have pride of race? Why does he want, I suggest, to be in the category of what I believe someone has described as a "sun-tanned white man"?

A. . . . I don't think it is the desire of a Negro to be a "sun-tanned white man." I think it is the desire of a Negro to be a human being and to be treated as a human being without regard to skin color. He can only have pride in race—and a healthy and mature pride in race—when his own government does not constantly and continuously tell him, "Have no pride in race," by constantly segregating him, constantly relegating him to a second-class status.

With Clark's testimony, the plaintiffs rested their case—and Justin Moore's talons retracted. His had been a memorable display of partisan advocacy, and its excessive nature was not lost on at least one of his colleagues. "There was right much tension during the trial," remarks Lindsay Almond, who functioned more as observer than co-counsel, "and Mr. Moore was under too much tension. He was a very intensive worker, and he was in high gear all the time. As a corporation lawyer, he had a fine legal mind, but he was not a great trial lawyer. I remember once watching Clarence Darrow argue a case and I had occasion after the trial to compliment him on how he had handled the cross-examination. He thanked me and said, 'My idea of an effective cross is to drive the nail in *and clinch it.*' Justin Moore didn't do that. He spent much too much time on trivial points and irrelevant points instead of focusing on the main issue."

A far more scorching verdict on Moore's performance was rendered in the *New York University Law Review* by Edmond Cahn in the same 1955 essay in which he also roasted Kenneth Clark's doll-test findings in *Briggs* as illogical, confusing, and unconvincing. But there was balm, too, for Clark in Cahn's added words: "As any healthy-minded person reads the Virginia trial record, it is impossible not to contrast the altruism and sober dignity of the [social] scientists with the behavior of defendants' counsel, who, by his manner of espousing the old order, exposed its cruelty and bigotry. Here was a living spectacle of what racial segregation can do to the human spirit."

In midmorning on the third day of the Prince Edward trial, the defense began its case and held the floor for more than two days. Nine of its twelve witnesses came from various sectors of Virginia's education apparatus, and their collective testimony amounted to the claim that the black people of the state were being well served by prevailing arrangements.

The chairman of the Prince Edward school board testified that progress had been made in planning a new colored high school, to be erected within the five-year life of the temporary tarpaper structures that had been built as a stopgap.

A leading Richmond architect discussed the blueprints for the new high school, which he said had been well along in the drafting stage at the time of the strike and the suit. The state supervisor of school buildings added that in a number of Virginia cities and counties the facilities for colored schoolchildren surpassed those for whites.

T. J. McIlwaine, the feathery Prince Edward school superintendent, held the stand for nearly two hours in an effort to explain away the inequalities between the white and Negro schools. There had been no foot-dragging on the bond issue to finance the new colored high school—only a realistic appraisal of the county voters' likely reluctance to pass it in view of the fact that Prince Edward already ranked ninth among Virginia's 100 counties in the proportion of its assessed valuation spent on public schools. He did not say that the property assessments in many rural counties were historically and notoriously low. He said that while it was true that many of the school buses used for Prince Edward colored children had been handed down from the white schools, all were in excellent repair and perfectly safe. He did not explain why, if the buses were in such good shape, they could not have continued in use at the white schools. He said that teachers' salaries were markedly higher at the white school because of a regular bonus paid by Farmville's Longwood College, a state institution, to those faculty members who helped train the future teachers enrolled there. He did not deny that a bonus was real money, that colored teachers in Farmville were not eligible for the same benefit, or that the Longwood salary supplements left white teachers of similar training and experience far better paid. He did admit that there had been overall educational inequalities between the races during his thirty-three-year tenure as county superintendent but they were now being rapidly corrected. As to the fired Boyd Jones—well, the ex-principal had been a chronic complainer since the day he arrived in Farmville and there was small doubt in McIlwaine's mind that Jones had encouraged, if not actually instigated, the strike.

The supervisor of accounts and records at the Virginia Department of Education trotted out bundles of statistics to prove that Negroes were getting their fair share of the state's school outlays. The state's superintendent of public instruction reinforced that assertion, noted that Virginia's segregated system could hardly be all bad if many Negroes from non-segregating states voluntarily attended the state's all-black colleges, and predicted that any immediate court-mandated end of segregated schools would be "a catastrophe" for education in Virginia because "you cannot legislate custom" and the people of Virginia "are in no sense prepared for a drastic change."

A similar doomsday forecast was made, though in more tempered language, by Colgate W. Darden, Jr., former governor of Virginia and for the preceding five years president of the University of Virginia. With Olympian authority, he traced the troubled course of public education in Virginia from its hopeful start in Thomas Jefferson's day through the dark ages that did not end until after his own boyhood at the beginning of the twentieth century, when he was taunted by wealthier children as a "free cat" for attending the local public schools as if on a dole. Desegregation would "seriously weaken" the people's commitment to newly healthy public education in Virginia, said the ex-governor. Besides, the Negro had made "phenomenal" progress under segregation, which was the only way the taxpayers would have approved a meaningful public-school program. With statesmanlike moderation, Darden acknowledged that "in the past there has been too intimate an association between segregation and discrimination for us not to be forewarned of its danger" and yet, he added a bit later in quoting Toynbee, the Negro had more than likely benefited from all the obstacles he had had to overcome. Lest his views be mistaken for those of a liberal, the former governor wound up by rejecting Oliver Hill's contention, offered in the cross-examination, that harmonious community relations would be improved by ending segregation:

> . . . I don't believe that knowing people better necessarily leads you to like them more, nor do I believe that the interchange of information between people will prevent war. Europe is a breeding ground of war, and their people have known one another for centuries. So I don't believe that knowing a fellow necessarily makes you like him—you may know so much about him that you do not like him. . . .

A paean to progress was sung, too, by the president of Longwood College, who had previously been in charge of public instruction in Virginia and noted that as recently as twenty-five years earlier only eighty-three Negro teachers in the entire state were college graduates and there was but one accredited rural high school for colored students. By 1952, a higher proportion of Virginia's more than 5,000 Negro teachers held college degrees than of white teachers. Such splendid progress, he said, would be set back "at least half a century" by desegregation. Besides, as he viewed the colored children on the streets of Farmville, they had hardly suffered because of the separate schools: "If anything . . . the Negro groups are a little bit happier, from my casual observations. Maybe that is due to the fact that the Negro race has a fine sense of humor. . . ." The dean of the department of education at the University of Virginia wound up the list of prominent witnesses from the academic establishment with the startling confession that he opposed segregation. A native New Mexican who was educated in Colorado, he nevertheless summed up the case for not abruptly abandoning the dual school system:

> . . . It seems to me that education is the intellectual and moral penicillin by which the bacteria of segregation are being destroyed, and to the degree that Negro children are given equal opportunities to learn, and to the extent that all children in Virginia are provided better schools, segregation, in my opinion, is in fact in the process of being abolished.

The commonwealth concluded its determined defense by bringing on three experts from the world of psychology whose task was to shoot away the underpinnings of the NAACP's carefully built-up argument in all four state trials that forcible segregation inflicted grave mental damage on Negro schoolchildren. To find professionally competent authorities of unchallengeable integrity who would testify to the opposite had proven no easy job for the defense lawyers, but they were a resolute band.

William H. Kelly, a child psychiatrist, was director of the Memorial

Foundation and Guidance Clinic in Richmond, a sizable private diagnostic and treatment center supported in part by state and federal funds. Dr. Kelly had run a similar clinic in Lansing, Michigan, the state in which he grew up, was educated, and received most of his early professional training. It could not be claimed that he was a lifelong cracker willing to go to the wall in defense of Dixie's finest traditions. Segregation, said Dr. Kelly, was inherent in the daily life of almost all cultures and was not a discrete factor that in itself produced personality distortions. Kenneth Clark's doll tests, like most projective tests, said Kelly, could be interpreted in many ways. The performance of the children tested could be sharply affected by such factors as the sex and skin color of the person giving the test; the chance for manipulating the results was considerable, and such tests as well as the interviewing method used on the Moton students lacked standardization and had none of the claim to scientific validity that applied to measurable findings in chemistry or physics. Racially separate schools could indeed provide equal learning opportunities, said Dr. Kelly, and the end of segregation could best be realized by a gradual process.

For Robert Carter, such testimony threatened to adulterate the humane ingredients he had fought so hard to have added to the NAACP's case against segregation. Carter fenced with Dr. Kelly in his cross-examination, made little headway, but then at the end won a surprising and critical concession:

> Q. As a psychiatrist, do you feel that racial segregation is a social situation that has some effect upon personality development of the individual?
> A. Yes, I do.
> Q. As a psychiatrist, do you think that social situation is adverse or beneficial to the personality?
> A. I would have to say that it is adverse to the personality.

John Nelson Buck, a clinical psychologist, had put in more than twenty years administering personality tests to every patient who entered Lynchburg State Colony, a state-operated mental hospital. His research work, he explained to the court, included development of what he called the H-T-P test, involving freehand drawings in pencil and then crayon of a house, a tree, and a person, followed by extensive questioning of the patient, in order to determine his personality configuration. In short, he knew all about such techniques as Kenneth Clark's doll test and interviewing sessions, and he thought neither they nor any of the other findings of the plaintiffs' expert witnesses had "any substantial validity as applied to the public school situation in Prince Edward County." He found Dr. Chein's poll of social scientists to be based on "unhappily worded" questions of "a somewhat superficial level" that could be answered in no other way. Indeed, Buck said he himself would have answered the two prime questions in the affirmative as most of the respondents had, though he did not favor the swift end of segregation in Virginia. As to the fourteen high-school students Clark interviewed, they, too, "could scarcely have answered otherwise"—that is, he thought the questions were loaded.

But on cross-examination Carter again won important mitigation:

Q. . . . in your opinion as a clinical psychologist, do you feel that racial segregation has an adverse effect on a healthy personality development?

A. As an abstract statement—as a generality, let us put it that way—I should say yes. I think that anything that sets up artificial barriers, restricting communication between individuals in a given community, is perhaps, at least theoretically, bad. But I think that such a statement must be modified by the situation which exists, obviously, and there are many, many situations. I don't think a generality can actually be given.

At the end came Virginia's star witness, Columbia psychologist Henry Garrett.

A tall, freckled man of such gentility and self-possession that he bordered on the haughty, Professor Garrett had arrived in Richmond only the night before to be on hand for the fifth and final day of the trial. "We were scared to death when we saw him in the courthouse," recalls Bob Carter. "We had heard reports that he might be coming. He had taught Kenneth and Mamie Clark while they were working on their doctorates, and he had a formidable reputation at that time."

There had been no great love lost between the older white psychologist and the two young Negro ones who studied in his department. Garrett had found Kenneth Clark "none too bright"—"he was about a C student, but he'd rank pretty high for a Negro"—and seriously deficient in imagination, though very hard-working. Otto Klineberg had ardently championed Clark's doctoral candidacy and worked closely with him on his thesis, and the rest of the department, eager to avoid accusations of bias, leaned over backward to approve his work, Garrett said. He himself was Mamie Clark's thesis advisor and found her "a nice little woman" who was taking no chances with her academic work and often called Garrett at home to ask exactly how to proceed. Of Garrett, Clark would say: "He was a model of mediocrity. He taught me statistics in the most boring and elementary way. I never thought much of him." When the two men met in the hall outside the Richmond courtroom that Leap Year Day in 1952, as Clark remembered the encounter, Garrett "apologized and said the only reason he had agreed to testify was that the state officials had promised him they were definitely going to make the schools equal."

But there was nothing apologetic about his testimony. Under examination by Justin Moore, Garrett noted that "the principle of separation in education . . . is long and well established in American life"—boys and girls were taught in separate schools, Catholic children attended parochial schools and Jewish children went to Hebrew schools, and there were separate classes for slow learners and quick ones—and did not in itself produce any stigma. To Vassar psychologist Brewster Smith's earlier testimony for the plaintiffs that, from a psychological view, segregation was "inherently an insult to the integrity of the individual," Garrett responded:

The term "insult" . . . it seems to me, is fairly strong language in the situation in which it is used. I think an idealistic person, who is likely to let his sympathies go beyond his judgment, may be so strongly prejudiced on the side of abstract goodness that he does not temper the application of the general principle with a certain amount of what might be called common sense. The Farmville situation is fairly far removed, it seems to me, from an abstract term of that sort.

The "mere act of segregation of students," as Moore termed it in his questioning, had no particular relevance to the personality development of the Farmville youngsters, said Garrett—"unless you consider something which is . . . abstractly right is always and irrevocably right." As to Isidor Chein's survey on the effects of segregation, Garrett was openly scornful. He called the questionnaire "blunderbuss" in character—that is, lacking in all nuance and specificity, since it failed to explain what sort of segregation was referred to, whether it was practiced by law or custom, and in what way or ways it might be "detrimental" to personality—and commented: "I am surprised he did not select his sample well enough to have gotten a hundred percent [response endorsing the harmful effect of segregation]. . . . I would not like to make a bet, but I could wager that I could send a questionnaire and phrase it rightly and get almost any answer I wanted."

Garrett was hardly more generous in assessing Clark's interviews with the Moton students: "I think if you call in a group of children who are members of a school that a year before struck for two weeks, if you do not get answers which say, 'We don't think our school is good,' 'We don't think we have been well treated' and so on, you should be very much surprised." To close, Moore asked him if a Negro could not get a satisfactory education under segregation, and Garrett replied:

> Provided you have equal facilities. It seems to me that in the state of Virginia today, taking into account the temper of its people, its mores, and its customs and background, that the Negro student at the high school level will get a better education in a separate school than he will in mixed schools.

Carter had obtained the court's permission for Clark to sit beside him at the counsel table to help him prepare the cross-examination. "I was very tight," Carter recalls as he arose to face the formidable witness for the defense. "Mostly, I didn't want to give him a platform to make any more points than he already had. I didn't do very well with him." Garrett agrees. "I felt sorry for the boy," he says of Carter's cross-examination. "He didn't know what to ask me. I was being just as easy as I could with him. . . . He was very courteous to me, but it was clear he didn't know what he was doing." It was not at all clear to Kenneth Clark, who disputes them both: "I think Bob did just fine with him—in fact, I think he made Garrett our witness by the job he did."

Carter's performance was neither triumph nor tragedy, but it did put a few rips in the Columbia psychologist's billowy sails. If Chein's questionnaire was as loaded a "blunderbuss" as Garrett claimed, how was it that so many experts in the field—people presumably capable of detecting the limitations of the questions—took the trouble to answer it? If the sort of projective tests that Kenneth Clark used were so unreliable and open to varying interpretations, how was it that Garrett's own recently published psychology textbook said that such tests were proving "useful" and showing "considerable promise" in providing insights into personality trends and problems? If the customs of Virginia were so unbending in their adherence to segregation, how was it that Attorney General Lindsay Almond's *amicus* brief in the *Sweatt* trial two years earlier had predicted that admission of Negroes into the graduate schools of the South would provoke massive withdrawals from the schools and violence, yet the Supreme Court's decision had triggered no such things in Virginia or anywhere else? Finally, there was this exchange in which Carter won a key admission from the witness, as he had from the two preceding ones, and then a revealing elaboration:

> Q. Do you consider, Dr. Garrett, that racial segregation, as presently practiced in the United States, and in Virginia, is a social situation which is adverse to the individual?
>
> A. It is a large question. In general, wherever a person is cut off from the main body of society or a group, if he is put in a position that stigmatizes him and makes him feel inferior, I would say yes, it is detrimental and deleterious to him.
>
> Q. . . . [D]o you know of any situation involving racial segregation of Negroes . . . where this stigmatism has not been put on the separation?
>
> A. I think, in the high schools of Virginia, if the Negro child had equal facilities, his own teachers, his own friends, and a good feeling, he would be more likely to develop pride in himself as a Negro, which I think we would all like to see him do—to develop his own potentialities, his sense of duty, his sense of art, his sense of histrionics. . . . [T]he Negroes might develop their schools up to the level where they would not [want to] mix, themselves; and I would like to see it happen. I think it would be poetic justice. They would develop their sense of dramatic art, and music, which they seem to have a talent for—[and] athletics, and they would say, "We prefer to remain as a Negro group." . . .

By the time the NAACP's rebuttal witnesses were produced on the afternoon of the last day of the trial, the court's admirable patience was about exhausted. The defense's objections that new evidence and not rebuttal testimony was being offered were, in essence, upheld, and the NAACP witnesses, including Mamie Clark and Horace English of Ohio State, were able to offer little of substance before being rushed off the stand. But the final rebuttal witness, Alfred McClung Lee, chairman of the department of sociology and anthropology at Brooklyn College, sounded a closing note of defiance. After dismissing as propaganda the claim that desegregation would set back educational progress in Virginia for half a century, Professor Lee cited his own experience to the contrary at a mixed school in Detroit; then he braced for the usual *ad hominem* assault by Justin Moore:

> Q. Doctor, I would like to find out the answer to one question. What is the extent of your experience in educational lines in the South and particularly in Virginia?
>
> A. Well, my first ancestor came to Virginia in 1610. Many others came to Virginia after that.

Q. . . . Have you ever had any experience in teaching or in educational work in Virginia or in the South?

A. As a matter of principle I will not teach in a segregated school.

Q. You think that is a complete answer to my question?

A. That is—yes.

Q. You intend it to be?

A. I was offered a job at the University of Texas. I turned it down on that basis.

Robinson offered a brief, cold summation for the plaintiffs. Carter followed, stressing that all three of the defense's expert witnesses had conceded the adverse effects of segregation. Moore for the defense emphasized, as he had at the outset, the prior rulings of all three judges sitting on the case in upholding the separate-but-equal doctrine in equalization cases; he also declared that the social-science testimony of the plaintiffs had been effectively discredited by the expert witnesses put on by the state.

The last two lawyers to speak closed out the trial on the note of intense conviction that marked the five-day-long proceedings. Reaching well up into the higher spheres of demagoguery, the attorney general of Virginia angrily objected to the suggestion that the citizens of his state might indulge in massive violation of the law if the court were to void school segregation—a suggestion that none of the plaintiffs' lawyers or witnesses had in fact made. But Lindsay Almond then went on to state that, rather than disobey a court desegregation decree "that our people, literally and morally, are not prepared to accept, for they believe and they know out of the experience of the years that separation with equal facilities is morally defensible, in addition to being legally defensible," the people of Virginia would simply close down their schools. Not that he was making threats, he hoped the court understood. The Prince Edward conflict, Almond said, "was fomented by agitation and propaganda by the NAACP under the tutelage and direction of counsel in this case to the point where not even the powers of the Creator could . . . break down these inequalities." Segregation was a legitimate exercise of the police power of the commonwealth, and "If separation violates the constitutional rights of a Negro, it, by the same token and at the same time, in the same manner and to the same extent, violates the constitutional rights of the white race. . . ." It was up to the legislature, anyway, and not the courts to determine whether segregation was a discriminatory practice.

Oliver Hill had the last word. It was an angry word and eloquent with the fire that had raged inside him for nearly twenty years of fighting racism in his native state.

How could the state argue, asked Hill, that just a little inequality remained in Virginia's schools—and that would soon be fixed—when in Prince Edward County, after thirty-three years of the same administration, "the superintendent cannot come in here in this court and say a single time, during his whole thirty-three years, when any Negro child had an equal opportunity with the white child in his community"? How much time did they want? The vaunted progress in school equalization that Virginia now boasted about had come as a result of compulsion by the federal District

Courts, whose decrees in a number of counties had still not been obeyed. As to the argument that segregation is really a legislative matter,

> . . . I wonder how people can stand up in any court and talk freely and openly and make any such statement as that when they know that the legislative process in this state and in this nation has been thwarted by a willful and small group of people. They know as well as I know that the Congress of the United States cannot express its will on questions involving civil rights because the Senators of this state and other Southern states will refuse to permit the Congress to express its sentiments. . . .

Would it not therefore be commendable, especially so long as the United States Supreme Court hesitated to dictate to the states in matters of this nature, if "a Virginia court was to say that in this year of our Lord 1952 we have got to face the issue, we cannot any longer avoid it, and there is only one way for human beings to go—that is in a line of respect for each other as individuals"? Hill had sharp words for Professor Garrett's closing remarks on the wonders that separate and truly equal schools might achieve in helping the Negro develop talents allegedly unique to his race:

> That is foremost in the minds of these people who want segregated schools: Let a Negro develop along certain lines. Athletics, that is all right. Music, fine—all Negroes are supposed to be able to sing. Rhythm—all Negroes are supposed to be able to dance. But we want an opportunity along with everybody else to develop in the technical fields. We want an opportunity to develop in the business and commerce of this nation. In other words, we want an opportunity to develop our talents, whatever they may be, in whatever fields of endeavor there are existing in this country. . . . I submit that in this segregated schools system, you do not have that opportunity. . . .

The court was unpersuaded.

Its decision came just one week after the close of the trial. Racial separation in Virginia, the judges found, rested "neither upon prejudice nor caprice nor upon any other measureless foundation" but had "for generations been a part of the mores of her people. To have separate schools has been their use and wont." So important was school segregation to the state that it was the only such racial separation provided for in the Virginia constitution, said the court, as if that were somehow an endorsement of its validity. Maintaining separate systems did not amount to "social despotism, the testimony points out, and suggests that whatever its demerits in theory, in practice it has begotten greater opportunities for the Negro." Greater than what, the judges did not say. "We have found no hurt or harm to either race," the court concluded. The defendant Prince Edward school board was ordered to pursue "with diligence and dispatch" its equalization of facilities for Negro students. "Both local and state authorities are moving with speed to complete the new program," the court concluded in declining to set a timetable for equalization. "An injunction could accomplish no more."

The opinion was written by Judge Bryan with Dobie and Hutcheson concurring.

Here there was no spirited dissent, like the one by Judge Waring in the South Carolina case. In Virginia, there was unanimity.

Here there was no finding of fact, as there had been by the trial court in the Kansas case, that segregation inflicted mental anguish and psychological damage upon those against whom it was directed. In Virginia, the court found segregation a venerable custom of the people that harmed neither race and indeed benefited the Negro.

In Virginia, the lawyers of the South had rallied and fought to uphold its way of life with much the same fury and skill that its soldiers had brought to the early Virginia campaigns of the Civil War. But in its legal combat, as in the earlier military one, the South would find both time and numbers against it, not to mention the gathering verdict of mankind.

# 21

# The Best Place to Attack

In the years just after the Second World War, the capital of the United States—gleaming citadel of democracy triumphant, pillar of strength to the poor and powerless, provider of succor to the battle-scarred and war-weary— was as thoroughly segregated a community as any in the nation, and nobody white seemed to mind much. For Washington, as everyone knew, was a Southern town.

On the face of it, things were much better there for the Negro than almost anywhere else in America. Since the coming of the New Deal, the federal bureaucracy had expanded enormously, and blacks for the first time began to be hired in substantial numbers for jobs at the bottom of the governmental totem pole. By 1950, 46,000 colored people residing in the District of Columbia worked for the government—more than one out of every three employed Negroes. Half of them were categorized as clerks; many of them held less exalted jobs, such as janitor. But a lot of blacks were at least on the federal payroll, which brought to them a measure of security and prestige available in such quantity in no other American city. And to service the federal household, many other black hands were at work. More than 2,000 Negro taxi drivers and chauffeurs transported the white upper echelons of government, nearly 2,500 cooked in the city's restaurants and clubs, 8,000 served its meals and liquor, and thousands more cleaned and tended its public lodgings.

The lure of jobs had sent the District's black population zooming. Between 1930 and 1950, it more than doubled, reaching about 280,000 in the latter year; Washington was 35 percent black. The colored community's professional elite was also relatively the largest in the nation. It numbered 300 Negro physicians and surgeons, 150 lawyers and judges, 50 electrical engineers, nearly 2,000 schoolteachers, and more than 150 professors and faculty members at the country's largest black university. Skilled work requiring less educational training was also available to Washington blacks as it was not, for example, to the Negroes of Topeka. Nearly 800 black men worked as masons and stonecutters out of 11,000 Negroes holding jobs in the construction industry; some 200 black women worked as bookkeepers. And while the average Washington colored family earned only 63 percent as much as the average Washington white family in 1950—a bit better than the national proportion—it did vastly better than most Southern families, black or white. The average Negro family in the District earned one-third more than the average for *all* families in South Carolina. And while just 600 black families in all of South Carolina earned $5,000 a year or more, the District's black population, only one-third the size of South Carolina's, included 9,000 families in the $5,000-and-over category. And so they kept coming to Washington.

But the gap between the haves and the have-nots of black America was nowhere else as apparent as in Washington. Housing, thoroughly segregated, was in short supply in the city generally after the war, and in the black ghetto the overcrowding ranged from severe to desperate. There were no worse slums in America. Crime in the black neighborhoods was rampant; the "numbers" game and prostitution were a way of life; health conditions were appalling. Schools were old and on double and triple sessions in many places. Juvenile vandalism was spreading. Many of the District's biggest employers outside of the federal government, the telephone and transit companies among them, made clear they would not hire Negroes for anything beyond menial jobs. The 100 black firemen and 325 black police officers in the District were rigidly separated from the rest of their forces. Almost no restaurant outside the ghetto served blacks, so that any Negro who worked downtown but lacked access to a cafeteria in a government agency had to go miles both ways to get lunch or bring it with him. Without access to toilet facilities, black parents could not take their children shopping in the well-stocked downtown stores. The city's playgrounds and recreational areas were strictly segregated, too, and it seemed to matter little that 1,500 black boys and girls were confined to a few patches of ground at jammed Dunbar High School while across the street scarcely a dozen children a week frolicked in a spacious and well-equipped playground for whites only. The District's Board of Recreation declined to accept transfer of ownership of golf courses and swimming pools from the Department of the Interior because of the proviso that the facilities had to be desegregated. And the National Theatre, the only legitimate house in the capital for touring Broadway plays, shut its doors in 1948 rather than yield to growing demands that it admit Negroes.

Washington was where the flutter of national conscience alighted gingerly upon the racial customs of the South, and the landing made a gentle impact indeed. People of Southern birth or recent ancestry dominated the civil service, the federal departments and bureaus and cubbyholes, the local business and financial community, and the congressional committees that held the power of the purse for the District in a manner to keep taxi fares to and from Capitol Hill at rock bottom and the quality of public facilities not much higher. Liberals came and went in Washington, but the abiding power remained with the Jim Crow bloc, prominently including the nation's military establishment, which strongly influenced racial attitudes in the area. The clubby brass, weaned at West Point and Annapolis on an elitist and nearly lily-white creed, potent with victory in the great global war just ended, and armed now with thermonuclear weaponry and multi-billion-dollar budgets, was not overly concerned that its right-wing, anti-Negro attitudes detracted from America's standing at such ideological bazaars as the United Nations. One member in good standing of the military elite—Major General Ulysses S. Grant III, grandson of the President and war hero—was named soon after the war to head a mammoth redevelopment program for Washington under the banner of the National Capital Park and Planning Commission. When the elaborate surveys were done and plans unfurled for lovely new parks and playgrounds and schools and other public buildings and a network of connecting highways, it was noted in small print that the colored population dispossessed in the process would be relocated "in the rear of Anacostia"—that is, as far from the shadow of the Washington Monument, and access to the central facilities of the community, as was possible. "Segregation is the accepted pattern of the community," blithely remarked an official of the National Capital Housing Authority. Liberal Congressmen intervened to scuttle the plan, just as Dixiecrats did to stymie efforts to give the District meaningful home rule, a benefit that would have handed considerable power to the unenfranchised blacks who were effectively without voice in the government of their city.

It was the Jim Crow school system, though, that most deeply affected the racial attitudes of the city. In Washington, as everywhere that segregation held sway, the schools were recognized as the principal purveyor of cultural values and community tradition. No other public facility or institution touched as many lives or had greater impact on the future. Separate schools for Negroes carried with them a legacy of social untouchability and psychological inferiority, and so their very presence in a community held the promise of yet another generation of second-class citizenship. Washington, however, had been obliged by its status as the federal city to serve its black schoolchildren more justly than the rest of the sovereign South. Even before the Civil War had ended, Congress had established a separate public-school system for the city's colored population. The language of the 1864 enabling act did not make separate schools mandatory; it merely assumed their preferability and alluded to the dual system in all subsequent legislation affecting the District schools.

Small outcry was heard at the time the colored schools were established, for nowhere south of the Mason-Dixon Line had public schools for blacks existed prior to that time, and many communities in the North either banned blacks from their school system or arranged for separate schools, whether by law or by custom. The very provision of free public schools for the District's swiftly growing colored population was viewed in the Reconstruction era as an act of social responsibility. Subsequent passage of the Fourteenth Amendment with its demand on the states of equal protection of the laws was evidently not viewed by Congressmen as inconsistent with the continued maintenance of segregated schools in the District, for the system was reconfirmed in 1874 by legislation that gave white residents of the District the privilege of placing their offspring "at any one of the schools provided for the education of white children in said portion of the district he or she may think proper to select . . . and any colored resident shall have the same rights with respect to colored schools." The legality of the practice was affirmed by a 1910 decision of the Court of Appeals for the District of Columbia, holding that the school board had the power to assign a child who was even one-sixteenth Negro to a colored school.

The Negro schools in the capital were more nearly equal to the white schools than in any of the segregating states, but they were scarcely palaces of learning. With the great influx of Negroes beginning in the Thirties, the gap in the quality of the two school systems started to widen. In other communities, needed school facilities were traditionally paid for by local property taxes. In Washington, where nearly half the property was tax-exempt, the schools were dependent upon Congress for their building needs, and Dixiecrats who dominated the committees that governed the District were not eager to pay for new black schools. The war put a freeze on school-building, though not the rise of the black population, and the scarcity of building materials in the immediate post-war period left the District colored population with a critical classroom shortage while white children were rattling around in half-empty schools in some places. Per-pupil outlays in 1947 were $160.21 for whites and $120.52 for Negro children. Many black youngsters were offered no kindergarten classes at all. Nearly 44 percent of the black elementary-school classes had forty or more children in them, while fewer than 1 percent of the white grade-school classes were that clogged. Black junior-high schools built to hold, at most, 6,500 students were attended by 8,400, many of them on double sessions. And when new colored schools were built, they tended to be confined to the same neighborhoods where the old schools were, thereby further entrenching residential segregation.

Carl F. Hansen, who came to Washington in 1947 as an executive assistant to the District's superintendent of schools, a job he would himself hold a decade later, was astonished to learn with what low regard Negro education was treated. He was reprimanded by his white superiors for going to lunch with his counterpart from the colored branch of the system, which Hansen found to be viewed as "only a dimly outlined appendage of the white structure." It was widely understood in Washington that any family which could afford it would send its children to private school. Few black families could afford such an expenditure, but those at the top of the Negro social scale, and especially those with federal jobs, often succeeded in getting their children transferred to the newer or least crowded colored schools in the District. Worst off of all, of course, were the plain black people, the ones without a pipeline to the white community and without stature in the highly stratified world of colored Washington.

One such plain black man, who ran a barbershop on U Street near 15th in the Northwest section, got angry enough at the haughty whites who controlled the city and at the Negroes who he felt lorded over the black rabble to defy both groups and start a minor revolution.

Gardner Bishop began to resent white people deeply when he was still a small boy shining their shoes in his father's barbershop in Rocky Mount,

North Carolina. His father, as Bishop recalls, did little to discourage his powerful animosity.

Young Bishop did not dislike them all equally, of course. There were some quite decent ones, like the Kyser family that owned the pharmacy next to his father's shop. The Kysers' boy Kay would grow up to become a famous bandleader and radio personality. And there were a lot of nice enough white boys who came over to the best swimming place in town, on the riverside in the black section, and acted friendly. But there were too many deep and abiding wounds. Like the time the influenza epidemic hit town and Bishop's father had to shut his shop. His white customers would come to the Bishop home to be barbered, but none of them would take off his hat on crossing the threshold—not until it was his turn in the chair.

Young Bishop was not much fonder of the black men in his community whom both races acknowledged as the colored leaders. They were ministers mostly, but Bishop thought they were out to feather their own nests more than to spread the faith or to look the white man in the eye and demand justice of him. A forceful speaker, the boy won some prizes as a debater while in high school, and there was talk of sending him on a scholarship to the colored state college in Orangeburg, South Carolina. But he had a deep fear of the violence-prone whites in that area, and so he turned down the chance for a college education and joined the black throngs who began heading north as the Great Depression hit. He arrived in Washington in 1930 and got a job cutting hair in a barbershop for whites. One of his customers told him an off-color joke in which a Negro was the butt; Bishop reciprocated with a joke in which the white man played the fool—and that was the end of the barber's working relationship with the white world. You earned more money cutting white men's hair, but Gardner Bishop, a large, barrel-chested, handsome man with a wide face and a wicked tongue, retained his pride and fed his long-smoldering fury by offering the service of his scissors to the black world only, and mostly to the little people, the street people, who did not try to let him know at every turn that they were better than he. He was known as "the U Street barber" throughout the underside of black Washington, and "Bish," as his friends called him, came to understand the ragtag life of the drunks and the addicts and the pimps and their prostitutes, the world where "the numbers" and the latest crap game provided the day's only hope for a financial lift, the streets and alleys where fatherless children multiplied and grew into desperate little vandals—the part of Washington, in short, that the white establishment wanted to bulldoze out of existence and the black establishment was eager to disown. "It was double Jim Crow," says Bishop, who came to despise its perpetrators in both races.

Bishop and his world of the urban walking wounded were not the stuff out of which the NAACP built its membership. Their powerlessness, as much as anything else, was what defined them. Not that Bishop was incapable of his own brand of occasional protest. Early one cloudy Sunday morning in the late Thirties, for instance, he took his four-year-old daughter Judine out for a walk and noticed that the whites-only playground near his house was empty.

No harm, he thought, in giving his child a few minutes on one of the swings reserved for the bottoms of white small-fry. In the middle of the forbidden ride, the law arrived in the form of a District cop who noted that the little girl's joy was in violation of the sign posted at the entrance to the playground, limiting it to whites. Gardner Bishop wanted to punch the policeman in the worst way, but instead he said: "She can't read." The cop thought that was too much sass to take from a black man, pulled Bishop down to the stationhouse, and told the sergeant to "book this nigger." His lip cost the U Street barber a ten-dollar fine.

By the time his daughter was a teenager, the deprivations routinely imposed upon black Washington were brought home yet more heavily to Bishop. Judine was getting reduced school time now at Browne Junior High School, where the enrollment was twice what the school had been built to handle and double sessions were ordered. What made the situation particularly galling was that nearby Eliot Junior High for whites had several hundred unoccupied places as more and more white families put their children in private schools or began the exodus to the Maryland and Virginia suburbs that would turn Washington into a city two-thirds black within twenty years. Enough Browne Junior High parents were sufficiently angered by the reduced quality of education being offered blacks throughout Washington to file a suit in the name of Marguerite Carr, daughter of the president of the Browne PTA. Black attorney Belford Lawson, who had first won fame in colored Washington for his work with the New Negro Alliance in the late Thirties, was hired to handle the case, and a mass meeting of the Browne PTA was summoned to seek wide support and financial backing for the legal action. Gardner Bishop, the U Street barber, went to that meeting, and he was not impressed.

The truth was that Bishop had never before been to a PTA meeting, was not even a dues-paying member of the PTA, and deeply resented the sort of upper-crust blacks who ran the PTA with the blessing of the teachers. They were the same sort who belonged to the NAACP and the other civic and social-uplift organizations—professional people, government people, people with jobs in white neighborhoods, people with learning. They spoke grandly, the way Belford Lawson did in explaining the lawsuit that charged white officials with illegally preventing black children in badly overcrowded schools from being transferred to schools for whites that had plenty of room. Nothing in the laws Congress had passed made segregated schools obligatory in Washington, Lawson argued. The case was duly filed in the spring of 1947 against the superintendent of schools and bore the title of *Carr v. Corning*. Gardner Bishop and the poor people with him were unconvinced by the legal tactics. "We knew the case wasn't going to work," he says of their gut reaction, "but nobody asked us what we thought because we were nothin'! Nobody gave us a chance to speak. What we wanted was relief, not lawsuits with $500 fees for the lawyers."

Over the summer, an effort was made to relieve the overcrowding at Browne Junior High by designating two rundown white schools in the vicinity as annexes, but the colored children who took shop and other classes in the satellite buildings had to travel many blocks to and from the main building in every sort of weather. Resentment ran deep among the poorer Browne parents, who groped for a way now to organize and act. "I had more mouth than anyone else," says Bishop, "and I worked for myself, so there wasn't much chance of being punished by the whites. Ignorant as I was, these people believed in me, and I had to do it." Denied access to the school building itself because they were not members of the PTA, Bishop's followers found a hospitable church to meet at and set to work. "We didn't have no president, we didn't have no vice president, we didn't have no nothin'—and we were mad at everyone—the whites, the highfalutin' blacks, the Board of Education—everyone." They took the name Consolidated Parents Group, Inc., puzzled over the same numbers the PTA had compiled showing the inequities of black education in the District, and then went along with Bishop's conclusion: "We needed whites on our side to oppose whites if we were going to get anywhere."

With winter coming on, Bishop piled forty youngsters into taxis that had been volunteered for their use and drove them down to the offices of the Board of Education, whose members were about to begin their weekly deliberations at three in the afternoon. The arrival of so many colored children was disconcerting enough, but when the large, angry black man who was leading them asked, without any prior warning, to address the board, confusion reigned. No, he could not just barge in and obtain a hearing from the august school board, Bishop was told—and anyway, what was so confounded important? "These are children from the Browne Junior High School," the barber explained, "and there's not going to be a one of them—or anyone else—at that school tomorrow, so I just wanted to explain who was doin' it and why." They let him speak, Bishop recalls, "but they sat there like a bunch of fools, not believing a word they heard." That night, the ragtag legion that Bishop headed was on the telephone and knocking on front doors to organize people who had never taken concerted civic action before. The next day, almost all the 1,800 students who normally attended Browne Junior High stayed home. And they stayed home the next day, too, and the day after that.

Pickets were out, demanding better schools, insisting that half-empty white schools be turned over to the black community, and soon the white press began to cover the uprising and comment sympathetically on it. The Board of Education started to feel the hot breath of civic resentment and began to treat Bishop's group like full-fledged citizens with legitimate grievances. Negotiations were opened. The Consolidated Parents held fast. Membership rose to nearly 300, despite efforts by the NAACP to discourage the strike. The president of the school board, a white woman who had never before had contact with the poor colored community, found Bishop a devoted and sincere leader and asked to address his group. "A charming woman," Bishop recalls, excepting her from his gallery of hated white-establishment types. She looked around the packed meeting room at the burbling, curious colored crowd and remarked to Bishop, "These are fine-looking people"—as if relieved that they had not all just been shanghaied from the

Congo bush, the cotton fields of Alabama, the gutters of the "Gold Coast," or some other blighted section of the capital.

Winter deepened, the strike went into its second month, the Board of Education was growing increasingly embarrassed, and the black parents began to lose enthusiasm. Some token measures were offered by the whites: vocational shops, for example, would be built in Browne, so that the annex buildings would no longer have to be used. But no wholesale transfer of white schools for black use was proposed, not in the middle of the school year, at any rate; besides, the transfer Bishop's group demanded would throw white and colored children into close contact and clashes would surely follow, it was predicted. Time was running out on the U Street barber who had emerged from obscurity to become an embattled leader of the colored masses of the capital. He had nothing to show for all his efforts except a fistful of press clippings.

Then, one evening late in February of 1948, Gardner Bishop steeled himself for a visit to the enemy camp. The enemy was not white but blacks attending an NAACP meeting in a Methodist church to hear a talk by Charles Houston, the well-known and widely admired civil-rights lawyer. These were the high and mighty of his own race, and Bishop resented them fiercely, but he needed help. He waited until the meeting was over, caught Houston on the way out, introduced himself, and told the lawyer he had a problem. "I know you, Bishop," Houston said warmly, "and I'd like to help." He wrapped an arm around the barber, who welcomed the gesture as a sign both of respect and of warning to the others in the crowd not to come between the two men.

They went to Houston's home that very evening and met again the next day. "He wanted to know everything about us," Bishop recalls, "how we got our printings and mailings done, who paid for what, what we were really after. He seemed terribly concerned—and terribly ignorant about us. He had never been associated with our kind of people before." Finally, Houston asked Bishop how much money his group had in its treasury. The answer was $14. "Well, you've got yourself a lawyer," Houston said, and proceeded to work out a face-saving scheme whereby Bishop would convene a mass meeting of his group and call the strike off on the understanding that Houston would file a whole series of lawsuits and take other actions aimed at winning equal facilities for the black schoolchildren of Washington. It was as if Houston, who once had been a member of the school board, suddenly legitimized the efforts of Bishop's group. The end of the strike marked the beginning of an unlikely collaboration between the outspoken, unlettered barber and the formidable lawyer who was even then preparing to argue before the Supreme Court of the United States that residential covenants against blacks violated the Constitution.

"Charlie became us—a part of our group," recalls Bishop. "There was no fake or make-believe about it. I'd come by his place and we'd sit up till three or four o'clock in the morning talking about everything. He wanted to find out about life in the gutter, and he found out plenty. Charlie would tell me I was too bitter. 'You hate too bad,' he'd say. 'Just hate a little.' " They would meet or talk three or four times a week as Bishop began to devote himself to a wide range of protest activities planned by or with Houston, whose standing as a lawyer prevented his taking to the barricades in so open a manner. Houston explained to Bishop that a suit against segregated schools in Washington would collide inescapably with the historical record which showed Congress had repeatedly passed acts sanctioning the practice and so no claim could be made that Washington's Negroes had been deprived of due process of law under the Fifth Amendment. And the Fourteenth Amendment's promise of equal protection pertained only to the usurpation of citizens' rights by state governments; it did not cover residents of the District of Columbia. Houston's strategy, then, was to file a series of equalization suits calling for improvement at every level of learning: kindergarten classes had to be offered to black children if they were offered to white children; elementary-school class sizes had to be the same; colored junior-high schools could not be on double sessions when the white ones were not; colored senior-high schools were entitled to all the equipment, courses, classroom space, and athletic facilities that the white ones had. Petitions and legal briefs proliferated. Gardner Bishop was all over black Washington, gathering depositions from people who had never heard the word before.

It was a cumbersome process, and many who participated in it were discouraged by the failure to obtain overnight results. "A lot of people thought you filed a case and bing! the next morning it was all settled." The ranks of the Consolidated Parents thinned, and Bishop had only a few dozen ardent members still working with him. But he also had Charlie Houston. The two men used each other in a mutually agreeable manner. Houston knew the ins and outs of official Washington, when and where budgetary hearings were held, what levers to push and whose ears to pull. And Bishop went everywhere as spokesman for the black parents of Washington who were fed up with the humiliation visited upon their children by cruel rules and icily administered regulations. The age of the pickaninnies was over. The mean-spirited District Board of Recreation, besieged to desegregate its playgrounds and swimming pools, inch by inch began to give ground. Bishop and his minions went out and gathered 50,000 signatures for a petition to convert white Central High School, most venerated in the District but only 60 percent full, to a black high school replacing all-black Cardozo High School, where the enrollment was 60 percent *over* capacity. Strong appeals to Congress resulted in larger building appropriations in 1949, and a lawsuit forced the school board to admit colored children to the District's Kendall Green school for deaf-mutes, where sign language had first been used in teaching, instead of shipping them to integrated special schools in Maryland or Pennsylvania. Throughout the non-stop agitation, the barber and the lawyer worked hand in glove. "I'd be in his office," Bishop remembers, "and he'd call in his secretary to take down what I was saying about whatever it was we were fighting for just then, and she'd go type it up and he'd work on it, rewriting it and saying, 'No, this doesn't sound like Bishop,' and showing it to me and I'd add something or take something out, and finally I'd send it to the papers." Houston would speak at fund-raising rallies wherever Bishop could arrange them. Other money came from sources as diverse as wealthy out-of-town white liberals, including the Marshall Field interests, and the poor black neighborhoods of the District, where raffles and chitlin' parties yielding maybe three or five dollars were run by charwomen and prostitutes eager to be of help. If there was ever any extra money, it went to send black children to summer camp.

Late in 1949, Houston was hospitalized with a heart ailment. He summoned Bishop to the hospital, where, the barber recalls, Houston's father "cursed me out" for helping bring on the heart condition. "He won't let go," said William Houston of his son's commitment to the fight for black rights. From his bed, Houston worried not about his own health but about how Bishop could afford to give all the time he did to the fight. Bishop in fact had three barbers working in his shop, "so it wasn't any big thing for me to run over to Cardozo High, say, and arrange my pickets for the day, and then get on back to the shop. People used to get haircuts then all the time—a barber could always make a living." But Houston's illness inevitably took its toll on Bishop's spirit. And in February of 1950 the Court of Appeals for the District of Columbia ruled—as Houston and Bishop had always supposed it would—against the black plaintiff in *Carr v. Corning*. Segregated schools were constitutional, said the court in a two-to-one opinion, though in eloquent dissent Judge Henry Edgerton declared that "enforced racial segregation in schooling is even more arbitrary" than enforced segregation in housing, which the Supreme Court had outlawed in the Washington case of *Buchanan v. Warley* in 1917 because it served no legitimate public purpose. Then, taking dead aim at *Plessy*, Edgerton added:

> . . . School segregation is humiliating to Negroes. Courts have sometimes denied that segregation implies inferiority. This amounts to saying, in the face of the obvious fact of racial prejudice, that the whites who impose segregation do not consider Negroes inferior. Not only words but acts mean what they are intended and understood to mean. . . . Segregation of a depressed minority means that it is not thought fit to associate with others. Both whites and Negroes know that enforced racial segregation in schools exists because the people who impose it consider colored children unfit to associate with white children. . . .

The judge filled his dissent with damning data from an exhaustive, Congress-ordered study of the District's public schools undertaken in 1948–49 by retired Columbia Teachers College expert George Strayer and twenty-two associates—a project prompted in part by the tireless protests of Gardner Bishop and his people's crusade. But the majority on the Court of Appeals noted that the Strayer Report, pinpointing the disparity between white and black schools, was not part of the record in the case and that even if it had been, it could not have changed the court's holding that separate-but-equal education was legal.

Two months later, Houston was back in the hospital. An orderly telephoned the dying lawyer's request to Bishop that he come to his bedside. "He told me that it looked as if he wasn't ever going to practice again the way he had," the barber recalls, "and that the important thing was for us to carry on the fight. He told me to go see Jim Nabrit at Howard to take over the equalization cases he'd been working on for so long. Well, I didn't want to do that. Nabrit was a big shot, and I didn't know him—and I didn't want to know him. I figured that our man was dyin' and we had no money and I was tired. . . ." But his colleagues in what was left of Consolidated Parents set up the appointment, and Bishop reluctantly made his way to the Howard campus, a place where he felt singularly uncomfortable, and to the office of James Madison Nabrit, Jr., professor of law, secretary of the university, and its next president.

"I explained it all to him," says Bishop, "including Charlie's wish that he should take over the lawsuits and continue the fight." None of the equalization cases had yet reached the hearing stage, but several of them were due to be heard imminently. Nabrit thought they were bad cases to pursue and that the equalization strategy was a lost and wasteful cause. He turned Bishop down, and the barber, unsurprised, concluded that few Charlie Houstons were put on this earth. But Nabrit interrupted Bishop's swift exit to say that if the barber wanted to arrange for a group of plaintiffs to challenge segregation itself, he would be happy to handle it. True, the Court of Appeals had just upheld the custom in *Carr v. Corning*, but the Court of Appeals was not the Supreme Court, and there were no plans to appeal *Carr* to the Justices. In short, James Nabrit thought the time had come to take larger legal risks than either Charles Houston or Thurgood Marshall in New York had thought prudent.

Gardner Bishop considered the matter, then shook hands with his new lawyer.

In the year 1910 in the town of Americus in the southwestern part of Georgia, a local Negro became so worked up at the news that Jack Johnson, the splendid black heavyweight boxer, had defeated Jim Jeffries, "The Great White Hope," that he managed to get himself beaten up by whites, hog-tied, and dragged out to the colored section of town, by which time life was no longer in him. They took him to an open lot and set fire to his body, and throughout the night white people came to pick off pieces of his clothing and his corpse and carry away their ghastly souvenirs. From a house not 200 yards distant, a small black boy watched in transfixed horror—Jim Nabrit, the minister's son.

When the Nabrits moved across the state to Augusta, on the South Carolina line, there were ever fresh reminders to the boy that to be black was to be vulnerable to the white man's worst whims. To reach school near the Savannah River, young Nabrit had to walk three and a half miles each way each day, and each trip brought him through a settlement of poor-white cotton-mill workers, whose children regularly punched, stoned, or otherwise pelted the minister's son. "I didn't attribute it to my color, though," Nabrit would recall sixty years later. "I just assumed they'd treat any stranger that way."

His college years at Morehouse in Atlanta were relatively free of racial incident, save for his being arrested because he once had the cheek to leave a streetcar by the front door. He played on the football team, monitored a dormitory and worked in the registrar's office to help pay his tuition, and did well enough academically to qualify for almost any white graduate school in the country. Nabrit's father wanted his son to follow him into the ministry. His mother wanted him to become a dentist. The young man decided on the law despite the counsel of family and friends noting that there were only two black lawyers in all of Georgia just then and that the entire legal system in the state was stacked against the Negro. Such grim facts spurred rather than discouraged Nabrit, who headed off to Northwestern Law School in Chicago and sat right up front where the bright white boys were usually seated instead of at the back of the classroom where blacks were expected to languish before expiring academically.

For the first six weeks, several of his professors declined to call on the persistent colored student whose upraised hand was hard but not impossible to ignore. Occasionally, Nabrit recalls, one of his professors "would recognize me, let me speak, and then go right on as before—as if he had just been clearing his throat when he called on me." His fellow students used to stamp their feet against the floor whenever Nabrit tried to ask a question in class. But then one day his whole class was given a true-false examination on a 700-page introductory textbook that was required reading for every first-year man. The black student got every question right, a feat never before achieved and duly noted by the dean in posting the grades. Things changed after that. Nabrit did not hesitate to clash with his professors, who seemed to him smugly certain that the ways of the law were fixed for all time. They listened respectfully to Nabrit's carefully prepared recitations on such radically explosive cases as *Dred Scott* and *Plessy*, commended him for his ingenuity, but advised the young man that he simply did not understand the judicial process. Undaunted, Nabrit applied himself yet harder. His grades won him top rank in his class and an editorship on the law review, and his white classmates picked him as their representative on the student council. For his academic distinctions, he was given a job in the law library to help meet his expenses, which were a continuous problem. Summers he would work as a redcap at Union Station or as a hotel clerk until he was able to land a job as an assistant in the office of Chicago's black Congressman, William Dawson. Still, the money ran out between his second and third years at Northwestern, and Nabrit had to take a job teaching English and political science and coaching at little Leland College in Louisiana. For all his money problems, in Chicago he still found time to do voluntary work with the Legal Aid Society—work, he says, that "made so clear to me how the law was applied unevenly and in a racist manner."

At graduation time, the first-ranking member of the law-school class sat around with his white classmates and listened to them discussing their immediate futures. One was going to work as an attorney for the biggest stockyard in town. A second was going to work for the Illinois Central. Another was joining a big downtown bank. Several others were going to clerk for well-known judges. "It just never occurred to any of them that a Negro would be eligible for these jobs," Nabrit remarks. "I figured I'd better go see the dean about all that." The dean said he had been just about to send for Nabrit because he was eager to learn what the excellent young man's plans were. Stay in touch, the dean advised—and that was that. Jim Nabrit did not return to Northwestern for thirty-nine years. When he came back, it was as the president of Howard to accept an honorary degree.

Nabrit's swift success as partner in a black law firm in Houston, representing Indians with oil wells and specializing in other real-estate matters, did not dim his interest in civil-rights law. His activities in Texas, especially those that involved his firm in the voting-rights cases of *Nixon v. Herndon* and *Nixon v. Condon*, put Nabrit in contact with Charles Houston and William Hastie, the Washington cousins who were in the midst of turning Howard Law School into a crack academy for defenders of the race. In time, they lured him to Howard, and Nabrit began sketching out and then teaching the first full-scale course in civil rights ever offered by an American law school. A dedicated professor, he helped produce such Howard law graduates as NAACP mainstays Robert Carter and Spottswood Robinson and yet kept in constant touch with Charlie Houston and Thurgood Marshall, offering his counsel as the legal drive picked up steam in the late Thirties and throughout the Forties. Nabrit himself argued and won the 1939 Supreme Court decision of *Lane v. Wilson*, upsetting Oklahoma's effort to circumvent the 1915 decision of *Guinn v. United States*, which outlawed the "grandfather clause" from the state's voting law, and he contributed importantly to the massive legal effort by the nation's top black civil-rights attorneys that led to the 1948 triumph of *Shelley v. Kraemer*, overturning court-enforced racial covenants in housing.

A member of the NAACP Legal Defense Fund's inner circle of advisors, Nabrit watched the agonizing progress of Spottswood Robinson and Oliver Hill in their Virginia campaign to equalize the black schools, and soon the Howard professor began to press Thurgood Marshall to strike at segregation itself. It was a position that Marshall's younger assistants, including Carter and Franklin Williams, urged on their chief, but Marshall was not eager to push the Supreme Court for decisions he feared it was not yet ready to render. He challenged *Plessy* at every opportunity in the graduate- and professional-school cases of the late Forties, but always he argued within the *Plessy* doctrine as well, demanding equal facilities for blacks or immediate admission to the white ones—a formula that yielded him a string of unbroken, if sharply limited, successes climaxing in the *Sweatt* and *McLaurin* decisions. But Nabrit saw that the ultimate risk of challenging *Plessy* head-on, without giving the Court any escape hatch, had to be faced if any massive gain in black education was to be realized in his generation. When Gardner Bishop came to him in the spring of 1950 to carry on the fight for better Negro schools in the District of Columbia, Nabrit insisted that desegregation was the only real solution. When *Sweatt* and *McLaurin* were announced a few months later, he was sure that the *Plessy* doctrine had been sufficiently eroded to risk mounting a direct drive on segregation itself, equal schools or no equal schools, and despite the Court of Appeals ruling in *Carr v. Corning* just that February. That fall, with Bishop's cooperation, the opportunity presented itself.

On September 11, 1950, Bishop led a group of eleven Negro schoolchildren to brand-new John Philip Sousa Junior High School, a spacious glass-and-brick structure located across the street from a golf course in a solidly residential section of Southeast Washington. It had forty-two bright classrooms, a 600-seat auditorium with all the trimmings, a double gymnasium, a playground with seven basketball courts, a softball field, and no Negroes. Some of the classrooms were empty, and Bishop asked that the black youngsters he shepherded be admitted to them. He was refused, and his charges began the school year, as they always had before, at all-Negro schools. One of the children was twelve-year-old Spottswood Thomas Bolling, Jr., whose widowed mother worked as a $57.60-a-week bookbinder for the government's General Services Administration. Young Bolling attended not Sousa but Shaw Junior High. It was forty-eight years old, dingy, ill-equipped, and located across the street not from the velvet green of a golf course but from The Lucky Pawnbroker's Exchange. Its science laboratory consisted of one Bunsen burner and a bowl of goldfish. Bolling's name led the list of plaintiffs for whom Nabrit brought suit against C. Melvin Sharpe, president of the Board of Education of the District of Columbia.

Nowhere in the pleadings of *Bolling v. Sharpe*, which Nabrit filed in early 1951 in U.S. District Court, was any claim made that young Bolling and the other plaintiffs were attending schools unequal to those provided white children. Their plainly inferior facilities were entirely beside the point, as Nabrit framed the case. He based it entirely upon the fact of segregation itself. The burden of proof, he argued, was not upon the black plaintiffs but upon the District government to show that there was any reasonable basis for or public purpose in racial restrictions on school admission. He dwelt at length upon the Supreme Court's wartime decisions on the relocation of Japanese-Americans as an emergency measure—temporary deprivations of civil rights and liberties that the Justices excused only in the face of a presumed dire threat to the nation's security. "Pressing public necessity may sometimes justify the existence of such restrictions; racial antagonism never can," Hugo Black had written in the 1944 case of *Korematsu v. United States*. "The educational rights which petitioners assert are fundamental rights protected by the due-process clause of the Fifth Amendment from unreasonable and arbitrary restrictions," Nabrit went on and cited a 1923 Supreme Court decision that, in passing, elaborated on the "liberty" which the amendment protected. Upholding the right of children to study German in the public schools, the Court wrote in *Meyer v. Nebraska*:

> While this Court has not attempted to define with exactness the liberty thus guaranteed, the term has received much consideration and some of the included things have been definitely stated. Without doubt it denotes not merely freedom from bodily restraint but also the right of the individual to contract, to engage in any of the common occupations of life, *to acquire useful knowledge,* to marry, establish a home . . . and generally to enjoy those privileges long recognized at common law as essential to the orderly pursuit of happiness of free men. . . .

The established doctrine is that this liberty may not be interfered with under the guise of protecting the public interest, by legislative action which is arbitrary or without reasonable relation to some purpose within the competency of the state to effect. Determination by the legislature of what constitutes proper exercise of police power is not final or conclusive but is subject to supervision of the courts. [Emphasis supplied by Nabrit.]

The enabling acts of Congress could not therefore be cited as sufficient basis for maintaining segregated schools in the District, said Nabrit. Besides, if Congress had truly intended to enforce segregated schools instead of merely to honor the prevailing customs of the post-Civil War era, it would have made separate schools mandatory in the strong and unmistakable language used by the Southern states that wrote the practice into law at about that time. But if the congressional acts were nevertheless now held to compel the District to maintain separate schools, Nabrit added in a daring departure from previous arguments against segregation, then those acts were in fact bills of attainder, defined by the Court in 1867 as any legislative act "which inflicts punishment without a judicial trial"; such acts, aimed at particular individuals or specified classes, had not been uncommon in English history and were prohibited by Article I, section 9, clause 3 of the United States Constitution. Finally, Nabrit invoked the powerful dissent of Judge Edgerton in *Carr v. Corning*, which said in part:

Appellees [the District of Columbia school officials] say that Congress requires them to maintain segregation. . . . I think the question irrelevant, since legislation cannot affect appellants' constitutional rights.

When the Fifth Amendment was adopted Negroes in the District of Columbia were slaves, not entitled to unsegregated schooling or to any schooling. Congress may have been right in thinking Negroes were not entitled to unsegregated schooling when the Fourteenth Amendment was adopted. But the question what schooling was good enough to meet their constitutional rights 160 or 80 years ago is different from the question what schooling meets their rights now. . . .

It was a forceful argument that went beyond anything which Thurgood Marshall had yet attempted. Just why he had not became clear in the District Court's handling of Nabrit's new challenge. The Washington school board counter-punched that *Bolling v. Sharpe* should be tossed out of court because the Negro plaintiffs acknowledged that they were attending a junior high school and had never been denied that privilege. In *Carr v. Corning*, the board added, the Court of Appeals had only recently ruled that segregation as provided for in the District of Columbia by Congress was legal. And it was apparent that in originally establishing separate schools for Negroes, Congress was not seeking to punish colored children by a veiled bill of attainder, as Nabrit had concocted, but was in fact seeking to extend to them educational opportunities they had never before enjoyed.

United States District Court Judge Walter M. Bastian agreed with the Board of Education. Nabrit's complaint, he ruled in April 1951, had failed to state a claim upon which relief could be granted. Since no claim of unequal school facilities had been raised, only the constitutionality of segregation itself was challenged—and that, said Bastian, had just been plainly ruled upon in *Carr*. The law had thus come full circle. In 1896, in *Plessy*, the Supreme Court had cited congressional approval of separate schools in the District of Columbia as one legitimizing reason to uphold segregation. Now, fifty-five years later, the courts turned history upside down and were citing *Plessy* to justify segregated schools in the District of Columbia.

While James Nabrit, without the blessings of the NAACP, plunged ahead with his frontal attack on segregation and readied his case for a hearing before the United States Court of Appeals, Thurgood Marshall continued to play a more cautious hand. In the twelve months following Nabrit's initial setback in *Bolling v. Sharpe*, Marshall and his staff argued the state cases in South Carolina, Kansas, Delaware, and Virginia. The outcome produced a disconcerting chorus of voices which suggested to Marshall that his decision of the previous summer to drop the equalization strategy and go after segregation *per se* had been premature.

Not long before the *Briggs* decision, even the more moderate elements in the South were proclaiming their implacable opposition to desegregation. Governor Byrnes of South Carolina, after pushing his big school-equalization bond issue through the legislature, announced that if the federal courts outlawed public-school segregation, he would order the schools closed and converted to a private system. Within a few months, the public would pass a referendum by a two-to-one margin giving the legislature standby power to perform the shutdown—an implied threat to the courts that any decree they might issue would be in vain.

Judge Parker's cool, careful opinion in *Briggs* spared any immediate confrontation with the state government and provided the pro-segregationist forces with a fresh and authoritative citation in defense of *Plessy*. Thurgood Marshall was prepared for the defeat in South Carolina, but he did not expect to get his ears pinned back for it the following month on the front page of the nation's largest Negro newspaper. In the July 7, 1951, issue of the Pittsburgh-based *Courier*, which also circulated a popular national edition in black Washington and New York, Negro lawyer Marjorie McKenzie devoted her weekly column, "Pursuit of Democracy," to a sharp rebuke to Marshall and his staff.

Terming the three-judge District Court's decision in *Briggs* "a serious legal setback in the civil rights fight," McKenzie called the suit "a bare bones challenge to the legality of segregation under the states' police power" and said that "the NAACP high command" which had decided to make the frontal assault "got a bare bones answer which infuses new vigor in the moribund *Plessy v. Ferguson* doctrine of 'separate but equal.'" The NAACP lawyers, she wrote, should have stuck to the equalization formula that had produced the *Sweatt*, *McLaurin*, and *Henderson* victories the previous year in the Supreme Court, which pointedly did not overrule *Plessy*, "[a]nd we have no reason to believe that it is any nearer such a declaration now." In McKenzie's view, the Court perhaps did not intend ever to pronounce *Plessy* dead with a flourish of trumpets to mark its passing. The Justices seemed bent, rather, on a low-key, non-inflammatory course that was producing progress in black education and, under the *Gaines* principle, slowly opening the doors to white schools. "Those who have thought it wise to let the ancient *Plessy* [doctrine] fade away, look upon the NAACP's strategy moves with honest irritation and alarm," said the *Courier* columnist, who added that *Briggs* and the coming round of test cases in other states "involve risk where none was necessary."

McKenzie sounded much like the Cassandras who had predicted defeat in *Sweatt* and *McLaurin*, Marshall said in rebuttal. "All of our cases have involved risks," he added. The decision to challenge segregation directly had been made not by some cabal of NAACP bigwigs behind closed doors but by the national convention on the recommendation of the legal staff, which had consulted with the presidents of the state conferences. In Clarendon County, South Carolina, the local Negroes were strongly behind the all-out assault on segregation; there was "unanimity among them against any weak-kneed approach to this problem." He concluded:

> . . . It is completely unrealistic to believe that the South will voluntarily . . . without affirmative action on our part, equalize school facilities or any other governmental facilities. If we had not threatened to challenge the legality of the segregation system and if we do not continue the challenge to segregated schools, we will get the same thing we have been getting all these years—separate but never equal.

The president of the New Orleans NAACP weighed in with a few words supporting Marshall: "We want our rights now, not a century hence."

McKenzie fired off another salvo two weeks later. It was her considered opinion, she said, that the Supreme Court was not ready to overturn *Plessy*: "It seems foolish to force the Court to rule on the point it has avoided. . . . We must not confuse what we think the Court 'ought' to do with what the Court customarily does." The Court, in the graduate-school cases, had laid down "a standard of equality that can be realized only under a non-segregated system. The Court has shown us a sure-fire route to success. Why should we abandon that route in so short a time, before we have tried it in elementary and secondary education?" The answer, of course, was that the equalization effort had already been going on for nearly twenty years, beginning with the teachers'-salaries cases launched by Thurgood Marshall and others in Maryland and Oliver Hill and others in Virginia. The answer was that what you won in one town or school district or county or state had to be rewon all over again in the next one, where a whole new set of facts had to be presented and argued to establish the lack of equality. That was what Spottswood Robinson and Oliver Hill had shown in their exhausting campaign across the hills and valleys of Virginia for the previous five years. The very decision in *Briggs*, moreover, which McKenzie said had dealt "a serious legal setback" to the civil-rights struggle had in fact ordered the defendant school board to equalize the colored schools as rapidly as possible. How, then, had the Negro cause been set back by Marshall's strategy?

Other events and critics more discerning than McKenzie clouded Marshall's skies as the year 1951 lengthened and the pace of activity on the segregation question quickened. The *Brown* decision by Judge Huxman came out of Topeka in August and, on the face of it, was another defeat for the NAACP, though neither Marjorie McKenzie nor any other prominent black commentator chose to characterize it as such. But the Kansas court's finding of fact, based on the NAACP's expert testimony, that segregation was damaging to Negro children seemed a silver lining that justified the introduction of the social-science strategy. Down in Charleston, South Carolina, the potential impact of the Kansas decision was duly noted. Robert Figg, chief counsel in *Briggs* for the state and the defendant Clarendon County school board, wrote in a letter to Governor Byrnes: ". . . The [Kansas] decision seems to supply to the appellants a factual finding which they could not get from the court in our case, and the pendency of the appeal from that judgment may adversely affect our motions, and cause the [Supreme C]ourt to decide that the whole matter should be ready to come up for review now. . . ." Figg's concern was that the six-month breathing spell that the District Court had given South Carolina to make a progress report on its efforts to equalize the colored schools in Clarendon might not be honored by the Supreme Court, to which Marshall had promptly appealed the *Briggs* decision. But so long as the District Court retained jurisdiction of the case, the Justices showed no readiness to bring the case up for argument as they reconvened in October for their regular fall term. To South Carolina, no news from Washington was good news.

In October, moreover, two developments out of South Carolina produced no pleasure in Thurgood Marshall's office.

In Summerton, the house that belonged to the Reverend Joseph A. DeLaine, who had led the uprising of the Clarendon Negroes, went up in flames. Though no one was ever charged with arson, there was circumstantial evidence that the blaze was set in reprisal for the minister's civil-rights activities. Members of the all-white Summerton fire department were on hand as the wooden house burned to the ground, but they made no effort to put out the flames because DeLaine's house, they said, was beyond the town limits. And it was—by 100 feet. At the time, the minister was serving as pastor to a congregation in Lake City in adjacent Florence County, to which he had been assigned temporarily for safety's sake.

The other piece of news from the state had far deeper meaning to the NAACP's legal prospects. On October 16, Governor Byrnes announced that if and when the Supreme Court agreed to hear the Negro suit against segregated schools in South Carolina, the state's case would be argued by a man he described as "one of the ablest constitutional lawyers in the nation." Byrnes had understated the matter.

To his wife, John W. Davis was "the most perfect husband any woman ever had." To his valet, giving lie to the old saw, he was very much a hero. To King George V of England, he was "the most perfect gentleman" the monarch had ever met. To Oliver Wendell Holmes, who sat for thirty years on the Supreme Court, no advocate who ever argued before him was "more elegant, more clear, more concise, or more logical." So apparent were his qualities that in 1924 the Democratic Party nominated him for President of the United States while he barely lifted a finger. Indeed, few lives have been more exemplary of the impulses that distinguish Americans as a people, and yet, for all the grace and virtuosity of the man, few schoolboys' hearts ever quickened at the mention of John William Davis.

The reason was not hard to find. The values for which Davis would stand unbending throughout the eighty-one years of his life—the sanctity of property, the immutability of laws, the obligation of the individual to sink or swim on his own—had been challenged by other principles in the nation's running struggle with itself to define what makes a just society. Part of that ultimate definition, it became clear in the aftermath of the Second World War, would hinge on settling the status of black Americans. John Davis's role in that settlement was determined by one of the few shortcomings in his otherwise sterling character: all his life he was a gentleman racist.

Davis came out of the small boomtown of Clarksburg in the West Virginia hills. Weaned on straight Calvinism, he was the son of a pro-slavery, Jeffersonian Democrat lawyer of old Virginia stock who taught his boy that liberty and property were sacred and inseparable and that government was no man's salvation. The apple never fell nearer the tree. John Davis grew up a staunch conservative who, along with his father, viewed such measures as women's suffrage, child-labor laws, mine safety regulations, and a federal anti-lynching bill as meddlesome mischief put forward by egalitarian reformers and yet more perfidious levelers. In the beginning, he agreed with his father's view that the Republican Party had become the plaything of the marauding, monopoly-minded rich who were to be opposed as tyrants. In time, the younger Davis would go to work for the economic royalists of America, clubbing and yachting with J. P. Morgan and his likes while protesting that as a lawyer he remained a free moral agent.

Taught fundamentalist law at Washington & Lee, he proved a precocious student. There were blended in him the ease, warmth, and mellowness of the South and the more rigorous stuff of the North—energy, industry, and decisiveness—that, together, produced a formidable attorney-at-law. It was an era, unlike the corporate age that followed, when much of the law's real work was played out in the public forum of the courtroom, and John Davis proved a lion at the bar, albeit a decorous one. Fire-eating might be good showmanship and attract clients, but Davis's brand of unflappable advocacy was classically underplayed. He mastered the facts at issue, knew the record inside out in a case on appeal, simplified the main points in his presentation, dealt courteously with his adversaries lest he gain them sympathy—and had the courage to sit down and stay down when he had no more to say to the court. He had no tricks up his sleeve. He was not a legal innovator. A lawyer, he insisted, was simply a highly skilled technician "who does not build or erect or paint anything. He does not create. All he does is lubricate the wheels of society by implementing the rules of conduct by which the organized life of men must be carried on." As his biographer, William H.

Harbaugh, would note, Davis adhered "absolutely to the principle that the lawyer's duty was to represent his client's interest to the limit of the law, not to moralize on the social and economic implications of the client's lawful actions."

For a dozen years, his client was the public, and he served it brilliantly. He was an instant leader during his two-year term in the West Virginia House of Delegates and so skilled a legal draftsman during his sole term (1911–13) in the U.S. House of Representatives, where he was co-author of the Clayton Antitrust Bill, that Woodrow Wilson named him his Solicitor General. Legal scholars and historians have suggested there was never a better one. Davis won forty-eight of the sixty-seven cases he argued in the government's behalf during five masterful years before a Supreme Court that leaned obliquely rightward away from Wilsonian progressivism. Necessarily, Davis began to take on the coloration of a liberal as he argued and won antitrust actions against Standard Oil, United States Steel, and International Harvester; defended acts of Congress aimed at ending child labor and setting minimum wages and hours; and defeated peonage practices in Alabama and the "grandfather clause" in Oklahoma's voting statute. It was in this last matter that the NAACP entered a Supreme Court case for the first time—on the side of Solicitor General Davis as an *amicus curiae*. Thirty-seven years later, in the last case he ever argued before the Court, he would stand against the NAACP at the climactic moment of its fight to end segregation.

Leaving Washington to pass the last two years of the Wilson administration as its ambassador to the Court of St. James's, Davis proved so gracious and winning a personality that a small armada flying the Stars and Stripes escorted him out of the harbor at Southampton on his homeward voyage. John Davis was recognized at home and abroad as a statesman. A dignified, articulate moderate, he had been a dark horse for the 1920 presidential nomination until Wilson privately branded him a standpatter. But in 1924, with the leaderless party badly splintered, Davis was a logical compromise candidate. Opposing him, battered warhorse William Jennings Bryan acknowledged Davis's high character but insisted "the Presidency ought to go only to those who champion causes." On the one hundred and third ballot in dank Madison Square Garden, John Davis was nominated. On the campaign trail, he seemed vague and lacking in force. The one issue in which he showed courage was his delayed, hesitant denunciation of the high-riding Ku Klux Klan—a step to which he was driven by liberals in his party, headed by Al Smith, and by the earlier outcry against the Klan from independent candidate Robert La Follette. Davis's anti-Klan stand and his defense of Negro rights while he was Solicitor General won him black votes, but cost him badly needed support in the South and among conservative Democrats everywhere. That well-known champion of causes, Calvin Coolidge, stayed home in the White House and won in a cakewalk. Harvard law professor Felix Frankfurter wrote Davis's political epitaph in the *New Republic* by noting that he was "a man of great ability" but searingly adding, "what's he done with it? . . . What meaning has he?"

In truth, John W. Davis never really opposed the prevailing social and economic order. The compromises with liberalism that he had had to make as a public servant were behind him when he came to Wall Street as a peerless corporation lawyer, for thirty-four years heading the technically superb and socially elitist firm of Davis, Polk, Wardwell, Sunderland & Kiendl. Earning $275,000 in even the worst Depression years and generally a good deal more, he lived the life of a supercharged prince while serving as the elegant mouthpiece of entrenched capitalism. Among clients he represented before the Supreme Court were Eastman Kodak, RCA, International Paper, the New York Telephone Company, P. Lorillard, Western Union, M-G-M, the Delaware-Lackawanna and other railroads, many banks including the Atlanta and Richmond Federal Reserve, oil companies, insurance companies, real-estate interests, natural-gas pipelines, and trade associations of window-glass manufacturers, cement manufacturers, and almost every other form of profit-making activity licensed in America. He fought the New Deal in and out of court with rare passion, himself winning the 1935 case in which the Supreme Court invalidated sections of the anti-Depression Frazier-Lemke Act granting moratoriums on the repayment of farm mortgages.

Davis was not without interest in civil liberties and other matters affecting the public welfare, but such cases consumed relatively little of his time during his long career as a private practitioner. As a young lawyer, he once defended Socialist labor leader Eugene Debs against charges of inciting a riot in connection with a strike by West Virginia coal miners. In later years, he represented the Associated Press in several cases involving freedom of the press, a number of fellow lawyers unjustly charged with crimes, and a Chinese immigrant who confessed to murder after being held incommunicado for a week by law officers. Near the end of his life, he was of counsel to Alger Hiss and Robert Oppenheimer, each pilloried for intimacy with or unreported knowledge of Communist agents while holding positions of great sensitivity in the American government. But neither before nor after his five-year career as Solicitor General was there anything to indicate Davis's support of the black man's fight for justice. What evidence there was all pointed in the opposite direction. While still back in West Virginia, he represented a young white man who, Davis wrote, had shot "a darkey here some days since—not fatally, unfortunately for the good of the community but fortunately for my client." Though he privately questioned the wisdom of voting rights for Negroes, Davis succeeded in suppressing his racial prejudices while arguing before the Supreme Court against Oklahoma's "grandfather clause"—so well, in fact, that his wife sardonically remarked that he was "in danger of winning." In later years, he declined to sit on either the board of directors or the legal-advisory committee of the NAACP and turned down a request by Roger Baldwin of the ACLU for help in the defense of the Scottsboro Boys. He opposed the Costigan-Wagner anti-lynching bill of 1935 and Harry Truman's civil-rights program thirteen years later. In private, he defended the poll tax, never spoke out against all-white primaries, never threw his considerable prestige into any effort to obtain a better shake for the Negro from the American judicial system. And while the partners and associates at Davis, Polk who honor his memory deny any insinuation of racism in the man, citing examples of small kindnesses and private philanthropic acts he performed for several Negroes, Davis was at best indifferent to the blacks and at worst a closet white-supremacist in certain habits of thought and manner. His biographer notes that, like many men of his generation, "Davis made mildly derogatory comments about Negroes in passing. ('I am busier than a nigger at election' was the most common.)" His correspondence, too, discloses a strong hint that he believed the gulf between the races ran far beyond skin color and involved "differences in the intellectual processes, in tastes and in aptitudes."

Altogether, John Davis had participated one way or another in more than 250 cases heard by the Supreme Court of the United States—more than any other lawyer in the twentieth century—and many hundreds more in the lower courts. He was in his seventy-ninth year when Governor Byrnes, who had first met him while a young Congressman during the Wilson years, asked Davis to defend South Carolina's segregation laws against the NAACP onslaught. Davis, who vacationed regularly at a South Carolina resort community, was pleased to accept. That the great lawyer was still in command of most of his powers, even at that advanced age, is suggested by his performance the following year in what is widely regarded as his most celebrated victory, *Youngstown Sheet & Tube v. Sawyer*, in which a divided Supreme Court denied President Truman the power to seize the nation's steel mills as an emergency measure during the Korean conflict.

The entry into *Briggs* of so formidable an advocate on the other side did not much cheer Thurgood Marshall. As a law student at Howard, he had gone to hear the disciplined eloquence and withering logic of John Davis addressing the Supreme Court in a sonorous baritone that carried vibrantly to the corners of the chamber. With Davis as chief counsel for the Jim Crow South, the NAACP's legal corps would be tested severely now. To hone the edge of his attack, Marshall turned more and more to outside advisors who might bring new ideas to the Legal Defense Fund's thinking or punch holes in it the way Davis could be expected to do.

On November 10, for example, Marshall's staff got the sort of roughing up it welcomed at a strategy session attended by Columbia's Herbert Wechsler, one of the nation's most highly regarded legal scholars. Wechsler's troubling questions dominated the meeting and could not be wished away. The cornerstone of the NAACP's attack on *Plessy* was that segregation was, on its face, discriminatory and therefore a denial of equal protection. But *Plessy* had a certain nagging "intellectual strength," Wechsler argued, in its insistence that to segregate two people is not a deprivation of equal protection since each person is equally affected by the action. Why was segregation more discriminatory against blacks than it was against whites? *Plessy* held that there was no discrimination if the law imposed reciprocal limitations on the segregated parties. The result, Wechsler argued, may be a deprivation of the liberty of both parties—a violation of Fifth Amendment rights under the due-process clause—but not necessarily a denial of equal protection. Indeed, the question posed by state-enforced segregation was not one of discrimination at all, Wechsler would later write:

. . . Its human and its constitutional dimensions lie entirely elsewhere, in the denial by the state of freedom to associate, a denial that impinges in the same way on any groups or races that may be involved. . . . But if the freedom of association is denied by segregation, integration forces an association upon those for whom it is unpleasant or repugnant. Is this not the heart of the issue involved, a conflict in human claims of high dimension, not unlike many others that involve the highest freedoms[?] . . . Given a situation where the state must practically choose between denying the association to those individuals who wish it or imposing it on those who would avoid it, is there a basis in neutral principles for holding that the Constitution demands that the claims for association should prevail?

This was a stern sort of challenge that served to drive off heavy reliance on the necessarily emotion-charged arguments and testimony of the social scientists. Wechsler's concern over "neutral principles" of adjudication brought the issue back to cold legal logic. Robert Carter noted in rebuttal that segregated black and white children were not wronged equally. Marshall added that the Court would have to take judicial notice that the reigning political and law-making powers in segregated communities were not Negroes—that segregation was in fact imposed on black people. But was it so plain, Wechsler countered, that a Negro child attending a segregated school was worse off than a Negro child attending a non-segregated school where he might feel the full brunt of white prejudice? Could it not reasonably be argued that the Negro child attending a non-segregated school would be doubly frustrated by the limited economic and social opportunity that would later confront him in a world where *de facto* segregation prevailed? Kenneth Clark responded: "Which is better—to be sick or to be dead? Segregated school is a sort of fatality." But was a colored child any less injured in a segregated school, Wechsler persisted, than he was in a completely hostile white school? Clark conceded the point.

No effort was made to grapple with such large and thorny questions in the first stage of the Legal Defense Fund's appeal of the *Brown* decision filed the following week with the Supreme Court. Indeed, the rules of the Court specified that such applications for review—called a "Statement as to Jurisdiction" in cases appealed directly from special three-judge District Courts—ought to be a relatively concise assertion of the legal questions in dispute and not a full-dress discussion; the latter would be made in briefs submitted prior to oral argument before the Justices in the event they granted the appeal—or, to use the language applied in cases such as *Brown* and *Briggs,* in the event the Court noted its "probable jurisdiction." Even so, the application for appeal in *Brown* was surprisingly skimpy and lackluster, casual almost, given the momentous issue at stake. Emphasis was placed on the difficulty of teaching democratic ideals in a segregated school system: no child could "attend separate schools and learn the meaning of equality." Rather than attacking *Plessy* as false doctrine, the NAACP application for appeal put almost all of its eggs in baskets labeled *Sweatt* and *McLaurin*: they were said to be the governing precedents now. And since the District Court in Kansas had found as a fact that state-sanctioned segregation had a detrimental effect on colored children, it "logically follows, therefore, that the injuries which segregation causes in the elementary grades is more far-reaching and devastating and affects more people than is the case with respect to graduate and professional education." Only at the close of the statement were a few undifferentiated precedents cited to support the charge that the Kansas law was the sort of racial classification lacking in legitimate legislative objective that the Court had many times struck down. Omitted from the list of precedents were two of the most pointed and pertinent: *Strauder v. West Virginia,* the luminous 1879 decision overturning the state's denial of jury service to Negroes, and *Buchanan v. Warley,* the 1917 decision outlawing residential-segregation laws.

As the year turned, the Court was still sitting on the *Brown* appeal.

Meanwhile, the NAACP kept scheduling think sessions to refine its strategy. Each new flock of devil's advocates had its sobering effect. One typically unsettling view came in mid-January from Paris, where Louis Pollak, a former clerk to Justice Rutledge and later an advisor to Marshall's office while working in the *pro-bono*-minded Paul, Weiss law firm, was now an attorney with the State Department and attached to the American delegation to the United Nations General Assembly. Pollak thought the Supreme Court was likely to affirm the District Court's opinion in *Briggs* and "continue to find that specific instances of segregation are also in fact unequal and hence unconstitutional in every case where there is an element of inequality demonstrable from the record." Then he added, partially echoing the view of Marjorie McKenzie in the *Courier* the previous summer:

> I am troubled by what the Court may do if asked directly either to repudiate or to reaffirm *Plessy* in a case where the record contains nothing beyond a segregation statute and compliance therewith. A possible technique the Court might employ to avoid the issue in that situation would be to place the burden of proof on the state authorities in every segregation situation—simply declaring that segregation is *prima facie* discriminatory and that . . . it would be up to the state in each instance to demonstrate the equality of the segregated facilities.

That Pollak may have been on to something was suggested at the end of January as the Supreme Court took its first official step in the segregation cases.

Right on schedule, the defendant Clarendon County school board had filed its obligatory progress report in *Briggs* on December 20 with the three-judge District Court that had heard the case in Charleston and retained jurisdiction pending an assessment of the board's efforts to equalize the black schools.

The report was convincing. A bid had been accepted for a new $261,000 high school in Summerton, and Governor Byrnes had used his influence in Washington to get clearance for building materials that were in short supply nationwide. The new high school would be ready by the following September. Plans were also being drawn up for two new colored grade schools to replace the little old schoolhouses still dotting the county; no colored grade school would have less than one teacher per grade henceforth.

Meanwhile, teachers' salaries, school equipment, and curricula had all been equalized, and bus transportation was now being supplied to the colored schoolchildren on the same basis as to the whites. Everything humanly possible to do was being done to equalize the black schools. In fact, a survey showed that the white Summerton elementary school was in severe need of repair or replacement, but that project was being shelved until the colored schools were brought up to, and beyond, equality.

Instead of making a final disposition of the case on the strength of the defendants' report, the District Court announced on January 8, 1952, that it would send the report to the Supreme Court, where the case had been appealed, and wait for the Justices to act on the appeal. In short, they were passing the buck.

The Supreme Court, though, passed it right back. On January 28, in a *per curiam* opinion, the Court said:

> . . . Prior to our consideration of the questions raised on this appeal, we should have the benefit of the views of the District Court upon the additional facts brought to the attention of that court in the report which it ordered. The District Court should also be afforded the opportunity to take whatever action it may deem appropriate in light of that report. In order that this may be done, we vacate the judgment of the District Court and remand the case to that court for further proceedings. . . .

By vacating the judgment, the Court in effect dismissed the NAACP appeal for the time being but left the door open for further appeal in light of the District Court's final disposition of the case. Two of the Justices disagreed with the Court's action. At the end of the order was this paragraph:

> Mr. Justice Black and Mr. Justice Douglas dissent. . . . They believe that the additional facts contained in the report to the District Court are wholly irrelevant to the constitutional questions presented by the appeal to this Court, and that we should note jurisdiction and set the case down for argument.

The two most ardent supporters of a judicially expansive Court were thus going on record to say that the time had come to face up to *Plessy*. Hugo Black and William Douglas were holding that the equality or lack of it in the measurable physical properties of the Clarendon schools was not the point of the *Briggs* case, and they were ready to hear arguments on the constitutionality of segregation itself. The rules of the Court provided, however, that four Justices had to vote to take a case before it could be heard on appeal. At the moment, all Thurgood Marshall could count on to get his case heard was the support of the Court's two judicial-activists.

In expunging the *Briggs* case from its docket, the Justices were left now with only one school-segregation appeal before them—the Kansas case of *Brown v. Board of Education.* As the other school cases worked their way up to the Court, they would take their places on the docket underneath *Brown*. It was not merely a matter of chronology, for *Briggs* had reached the Court first and could be restored to the docket ahead of *Brown* if the Justices so chose. But *Brown* did not come to the Court from the South, and that, as events would prove, was all to the good so far as the Justices were concerned.

On March 3, with Judge Parker presiding and Judge Dobie sitting in place of the retired Judge Waring, the U.S. District Court held its rehearing of *Briggs*. The defendants' attorney, Robert Figg, contended that the state and Clarendon school board had acted with maximum speed and good faith to equalize the colored schools. Thurgood Marshall agreed—except for one thing: the schools were still segregated, and thus unequal. And "every day they are not equal," the NAACP legal chieftain argued, "these plaintiffs are losing rights, for which they cannot be adequately compensated."

> JUDGE DOBIE:   Well, what can we do about that? It is fairly obvious—I will take judicial notice of it—that you can't have teachers in schools before you have schools. Now, if these defendants in this case have done everything that they could reasonably do to carry out the decree of the court [to equalize the schools], they can't do any more at this stage, can they?
>
> MARSHALL:   No, sir, they cannot physically do more. It is impossible for them to build those schools overnight.
>
> JUDGE TIMMERMAN:   Well, do you want us to put them in jail for not doing something that you know they can't do?
>
> MARSHALL:   It is something they can do, sir. They could break down the segregation.
>
> JUDGE DOBIE:   Let that alone.
>
> JUDGE PARKER:   That is the same question [that we decided in the negative at the first hearing].
>
> MARSHALL:   Then, as I say, sir, at the present time there is no relief that we can get that would be adequate if that question is closed. . . .

But Marshall had a suggestion. The court could order desegregation within the framework of its ruling of the previous June. "I am not saying to strike it down on the basis of segregation *per se*, but on the basis that the facilities that are being offered to Negroes are not equal as of today." Marshall was hedging. He was adopting precisely the strategy that his legal critic Marjorie McKenzie had prescribed: Don't ask for a grandstand proclamation that segregation is unequal; just get the court to desegregate on the ground of inequality.

Judge Parker was not receptive. The court, he said, had ruled earlier that South Carolina's segregation law was valid; the problem was not the law but the way the law had been administered in Clarendon County. Furthermore, asked Judge Timmerman, what did Marshall propose—to move 2,500 colored children into schools currently occupied by perhaps 300 white children? "If they were already filled up, wouldn't there be a problem of sitting somebody on somebody else's lap?" Not at all, said Marshall; "it would be a problem of shifting some of the white children by district lines . . . and mixing them, or sharing the school equally. . . . [T]hey wouldn't all go to the white school."

That casually suggested formula, multiplied thousands of times over, would haunt the entire nation for the next generation. Just how little thought Marshall and his colleagues had given to the question of how segregation ought to be dismantled if and when the courts ordered an end to the practice may be inferred from the South Carolina court's naked disbelief of what the

NAACP lawyer was now proposing. Did he really expect the court to order that the several hundred white schoolchildren in the district should be mixed indiscriminately with the black children who outnumbered them nine to one? Would any white parent permit such a thing? Here was the basic peril that had been present all along in making *Briggs* the first segregation suit instead of one of the last. "We really had the feeling then that segregation itself was the evil—and not a symptom of the deeper evil of racism," explains Robert Carter more than twenty years later. "Thus, we attached no importance then to the ratio of blacks to whites in the Clarendon schools. It wasn't our concern to figure out how integration would work. We minimized the social consequences in that immediate environment—that wasn't the issue for us. The box we thought we were in was segregation itself, and most of the nation saw it that way, too."

Ten days after the second *Briggs* hearing, the District Court ruled. While the colored schools had not yet been equalized, there was "no doubt that as a result of the program in which the defendants are engaged, the educational facilities and opportunities afforded Negroes within the district will, by the beginning of the next school year beginning in September 1952, be made equal to those afforded white persons." No purpose could be served "by disrupting the organization of the schools so near the end of the scholastic year." Nor did the court ask the defendants to make additional progress reports. It relied instead on their good-faith fulfillment of the equalization program.

Just how much good faith was floating around in South Carolina was suggested at the close of the courtroom proceedings when one of the local white attorneys remarked to Thurgood Marshall, in a voice tinged with unmistakable venom, "If you show your black ass in Clarendon County ever again, you're a dead man."

The outcome of *Briggs*, coupled with the unanimous setback in the Prince Edward case announced by Judge Dobie's three-judge District Court in Richmond the previous week, left Marshall's Southern front tattered. While he and his staff prepared to re-appeal *Briggs* to the Supreme Court, their efforts were opened to wholesale second-guessing the following month at a massive conference at Howard University, summoned to celebrate the twentieth anniversary of Charles Thompson's *Journal of Negro Education.* What Marshall heard there might have given pause to a less determined man.

Some 300 lawyers, social scientists, and civil-rights leaders and workers gathered at the three-day Howard colloquium in mid-April of 1952 to discuss "The Courts and Racial Integration in Education." Just a few days before the sessions opened, there had finally been a cheering piece of news in Chancellor Seitz's Delaware decision ordering the white schools in Claymont and Hockessin desegregated within the *Plessy* doctrine. It was exactly the sort of opinion that Louis Pollak and Marjorie McKenzie thought was the best Marshall and the NAACP lawyers could hope for from the Supreme Court in the near future. Their view was given added fuel now at Howard.

Harry Ashmore of the Arkansas *Gazette*, a leading white liberal of the

South, acknowledged virtue in the thinking of "a new generation of Negro leaders, far more militant than their predecessors" for whom "the school issue has been seized upon as an opportunity to exploit the whole of their racial grievances." But Ashmore took sharp issue with the basic assumption of the conference that, according to its prospectus, "Negroes are determined, and all but the most reactionary whites are resigned to the fact, that enforced segregated schools must go in the very near future." Not so, said the spirited newspaperman. Conservatives, who make up the bulk of the South's white population, "are a long way from being resigned to the abandonment of segregation in the public schools." Governor Byrnes was speaking for "an overwhelming majority of his constituents" when he declared he would sooner abandon public education than lower the color bar in a single school. The Supreme Court, moreover, was entirely aware of Southern sentiment in the matter, and its gingerly treatment of the segregation question bespoke that awareness. And there was the "eternal problem of every jurist—should a court hand down a decision that may very well be, in view of popular opinion, unenforceable?"

A cautionary tale was told as well by one of Thurgood Marshall's newer and most astute outside advisors, John P. Frank, then an associate professor at Yale Law School. Frank, who had clerked for Justice Black and later written a well-received book about him, was perhaps more familiar with the constitutional and legislative history involved in the segregation cases than any of the NAACP's other advisors. He was co-author of an important article on the subject, titled "The Original Understanding of 'Equal Protection of the Laws,'" in the *Columbia Law Review* in 1950 and had made valuable contributions to the hard-hitting *amicus* brief by the *ad hoc* group of law professors who sided with the NAACP in *Sweatt.* After noting that "A judge cannot be blamed if he shrinks from precipitating a race riot," John Frank told the Howard crowd it was plain that the Supreme Court was stalling on both *Briggs* and *Brown* and he wondered if the Justices were not likely to delay a good deal longer in a presidential election year. Unquestionably, the NAACP "should not hesitate in its just demands for fear of reaping the whirlwind" because "judicial victories will not be won without asking for them." But "Vigor is not recklessness," Frank asserted. "The most daring army guards its lines of retreat. So should a litigation strategist." It would be a mistake to push the attack on segregation itself to the exclusion of victories won on lesser grounds (that is, equalization). For if the Court were pushed "inescapably" to a decision on the validity of school segregation where no other element of discrimination is present, "it may decide in behalf of segregation; and the morale and prestige loss to the anti-segregation forces from such a decision would be incalculable."

Will Maslow, former field director of the President's Committee on Fair Employment Practices (FEPC) and general counsel of the American Jewish Congress, wondered whether, in view of Governor Byrnes's defiant position in South Carolina, it was the wisest strategy to push the segregation fight in the Deep South. Might it not be better to chip away in the border areas first, seeking victories like "this magnificent decision in Delaware"? Then Marjorie

McKenzie, terming herself "the loyal opposition," rose to repeat the views she had expressed the previous year in the *Courier* and declared that the conference they were holding, while "a wonderful thing," was too late by nearly two years. It should have been held in the immediate wake of the *Sweatt, McLaurin*, and *Henderson* decisions in 1950. And with so broad-based a group present, the resulting plan of action would have removed the fight from the sole control of "one point of view, from one organization"—a not very subtle thrust at Thurgood Marshall and his Legal Defense Fund.

Marshall hardly shrank from the challenge. He urged his listeners not to stand in fear of the Jimmy Byrneses of the world, reminded them that similar threats and fright tactics had been used by the South when *Sweatt* was being argued, and quite properly noted that the equalization strategy had not been abandoned as a route of retreat. He did not say so, but he indeed had just used it at the rehearing in *Briggs* the month before and got nowhere with it; in Delaware, though, it had worked.

At the conference, Marshall won firm backing for his all-out attack from Horace Mann Bond, then serving as the first black president of Marshall's alma mater, Lincoln University, as well as from Howard's president, Mordecai Johnson, and economist Robert Weaver, who would become the first Negro ever to serve in the Cabinet of an American President. But the real counter-blast in support of the no-holds-barred attack on *Plessy* came from the one lawyer in the room who had already taken that stand in court—James Nabrit. He spoke with more eloquence and conviction than anyone else heard throughout the gathering.

"I am at a loss to understand why all this talk about the collateral undertakings and these excursions off on the side issues giving the Court holes to duck into," the Howard law professor declared. Citing Roscoe Pound's dictum that "Law makes habits, it does not wait for them to grow," Nabrit easily deflected every sniping shot at the all-out tactics he himself had embraced while Marshall continued to hedge. Those who argued that the Court should not be pushed into something it did not yet wish to do and should therefore be given hatches through which to escape, said Nabrit, must be either joking or ignorant of the Court's methods. The Justices did not need any help in avoiding a showdown on *Plessy* if they wished to avoid it. It was precisely the job of those in the room to force the Court's hand—and to do so now. Had their gains been so great under the cautious strategy they had used for so long? Did they have so much to lose? Did they expect a more liberal Court in the future? To those who suggested that perhaps the attack ought to be brought in the border states rather than South Carolina or Mississippi, Nabrit asserted: "This is the same as saying, 'White people in those states are so mean and treat Negroes so badly that they are accustomed to no rights, so let them suffer.'" Of those who said blood would run in the streets if the segregation fight was waged in the face of intransigent white-supremacists, Nabrit demanded, "Suppose it does? Shall the Negro child be required to wait for his constitutional rights until the white South is educated, industrialized, and ready to confer these rights on his children's children?" No, he thundered, "Wherever the Negro is laboring under constitutional disabilities in the South, there is the best place to attack. The attack should be waged with the most devastating forces at hand. . . . The Supreme Court will have to worry over community attitudes. Let us worry over the problem of pressing for our civil rights. . . . Let the Supreme Court take the blame if it dares say to the entire world, '*Yes*, democracy rests on a legalized caste system. Segregation of races is legal.' Make the Court choose. . . . "

That the Court was manifestly not ready to choose was the opinion offered the following month in a relatively short but brilliantly comprehensive note in the esteemed *Yale Law Journal*, which noted Kenneth Clark's doll tests with skepticism. "A North-South breakdown of the results fails to establish any statistically significant difference in the preference for the white doll or self-identification with it," the magazine remarked, lancing Clark's findings where they were most vulnerable. Nor did his tests isolate school segregation as the source of emotional disturbances in Negro children. And even if they did, "there is no way to prevent the Court from insisting that proof of a deleterious psychological impact in one case does not prove it for other cases." Finally, the source of the Court's go-slow policy in facing up to the segregation question "may be its fear of precipitating widespread social unrest and possible violence."

The net result of all this speculation and brainstorming was a far stronger and more determined effort by Thurgood Marshall to convince the Supreme Court to strike down segregation. On May 10, the NAACP's lawyers filed a new statement of jurisdiction with the high court to take up *Briggs*, now that the District Court had finished with it. The appeal application had all the force of legal logic and muscularity of language that the matter-of-fact *Brown* appeal had lacked. It said, in effect: The last time we came before you Justices on this profound question, you agreed with us that George McLaurin was "handicapped in his pursuit of effective graduate instruction" by the restrictions the state had placed upon him solely because of his race—restrictions that, in your words, "impair and inhibit his ability to study, to engage in discussions and exchange views with other students, and, in general, to learn his profession." We have carefully adhered to the logic of your thinking in *McLaurin* and ask now that you extend it to students required to attend separate public schools for no reason other than the color of their skin. Just as McLaurin was handicapped by segregation inside the school he attended, so are these plaintiff children irreparably harmed by their segregation in separate schools. We have produced abundant expert testimony by social psychologists and others describing the nature of the humiliation and self-hatred caused by this unnecessary and unjustified practice of the state of South Carolina, yet the court below has dismissed the burden of our unchallenged evidence, just as it has chosen to dismiss the force of your opinion in *McLaurin*. The court below was unable to distinguish permissible personal customs and mores from governmental actions that have been proscribed many times by this Court. You have repeatedly invalidated racial discrimination in other areas—in residential segregation, whether by statute *(Buchanan v. Warley)* or by restrictive covenants *(Shelley v. Kraemer)*, and in segregation of interstate passengers, whether by statute *(Morgan v. Virginia)* or carrier regulation *(Henderson v. United States)*. You have shown no greater tolerance for distinctions based on race affecting the right to vote, whether imposed by statute *(Lane v. Wilson)* or by political party *(Smith v. Allwright)*, the right to engage in a gainful occupation *(Yick Wo v. Hopkins)*, the right to fair representation by a labor organization *(Steele v. Louisville & Nashville Railroad)*, the right to serve on a jury *(Strauder v. West Virginia)*, and the right to a fair criminal trial where Negroes have been habitually barred from juries *(Hale v. Kentucky)*. It is therefore all the more incumbent upon the Court to come to the relief of colored schoolchildren against whom this state-mandated discrimination is inescapably directed. "On occasion courts have denied that enforced segregation of Negroes in American life is a badge of inferiority, thus closing their eyes as judges to what they must know as men." The fact is that the Negro attending public school in South Carolina is segregated against his will and forced into ostracism plainly bespeaking the white majority's belief in his inferiority—a state of imposed degradation that affects his thoughts and actions at almost every moment. Segregation as practiced in America has been "universally understood" to impose on Negroes this badge of inferiority, and the contrary dictum in *Plessy v. Ferguson* can no longer stand in the face of a wealth of evidence flatly contradicting it.

In their short statement opposing jurisdiction, South Carolina's lawyers summed up their case for segregation in this single sentence: "We have failed to discover any decision, federal or state, in the period immediately after the adoption of the Fourteenth Amendment or since then, or any action of the Congress, which has cast any doubt upon the power of a state under that amendment in regulating its public schools to provide separate schools for the pupils of the two races."

On June 9, 1952, the Supreme Court noted probable jurisdiction in both *Briggs* and *Brown* and set them down for argument at the beginning of the fall term in October. Votes of the Justices in noting jurisdiction or granting applications for a writ of *certiorari*—the usual way cases reach the Court—are almost never made public. In this case, according to the memory of Tom Clark, one of the three Justices of that court who were still living twenty-two years later, the vote finally to hear the school-segregation cases was probably unanimous. According to the one documented source available to the public—Harold Burton's docket book (on file at the Library of Congress), in which he recorded the votes taken at the closed-door conferences of the Court—the vote was not quite unanimous. Burton recorded Justice Jackson as having voted to hold over the cases, while Chief Justice Vinson was recorded as not having voted. Since only four votes were needed for the Court to hear a case, not much was to be read into the Jackson or Vinson position, nor could the outcome of the case be foretold from the disposition of the Justices at that time, for very often Justices who voted not to take a case wound up siding with the appellants and those voting to hear a case ended up voting against them.* All that the vote to take

* It would have been particularly rash to predict Justice Jackson's final position on the segregation cases from his vote at the June 7, 1952, conference. He believed that the Court

the segregation cases meant for certain was that the Court felt it could no longer, in good conscience, forestall considering the question.

On July 12, the NAACP appeal in the Virginia case of *Davis v. County School Board of Prince Edward County* was filed with the Supreme Court.

On August 28, the Supreme Court of Delaware upheld Chancellor Seitz's decision in *Belton v. Gebhart* and *Bulah v. Gebhart.*

On October 8, just days before oral argument was scheduled to be heard by the Justices in *Brown* and *Briggs*, the Supreme Court postponed it, noted jurisdiction in *Davis* as well, and put it down for argument with the other school cases on December 8. That was a good month after the presidential election returns would be in.

Shortly after the October postponement, Harold B. Willey, the clerk of the Supreme Court, telephoned Professor James Nabrit at Howard. Nabrit's case of *Bolling v. Sharpe*, the District of Columbia school-segregation suit, was still awaiting a hearing before the Court of Appeals. Chief Justice Vinson, Willey told Nabrit, wanted him to petition the Court to have his case brought up with the three other segregation cases scheduled for argument in December. The Chief Justice's request was tantamount to an order. Ordinarily, Nabrit would have been delighted with the development, but in view of his more militant legal position—attacking segregation *per se* without any reliance on the equalization strategy favored by conservatives such as Marjorie McKenzie and urged as a back-up position by knowledgeable scholars such as John Frank—it seemed possible that the Court's order to join all the cases might introduce an element of tension into the Negro camp. On November 10, the Court granted *certiorari* in *Bolling* and put it down for argument after the Virginia case.

On November 13, less than a month before the four segregation cases were set for argument, Albert Young, the attorney general of Delaware, applied to the Court for a writ of *certiorari* in the pair of cases he had lost in

---

should hear the cases, but he evidently disagreed with his brethren on the timing and on the manner in which the several cases ought to be consolidated. That spring, he had sent Frankfurter a handwritten note on *Brown*, which was then No. 436 on the Court's 1951 Term docket, and suggested a memorandum that the Justices might issue upon taking the cases:

> For 436—something like this?
> "The writ of certiorari is granted.
> "The Court recognizes the Constitutional issues herein however decided are of far-reaching effect on many states and interests. It has been a frequent practice in such situations to accommodate cases presenting similar issues for hearing together in order that the Court may have the benefit of argument from different settings and aspects. A number of cases raising the same or related issues are [proceeding] in this or lower courts. This case is continued to the Oct 1952 term when it[s] time for hearing will be given further consideration in the light of the foregoing policy."

It is possible that Jackson proposed such a memo at the Court conference and was voted down by the other Justices, who were evidently ready to proceed with *Briggs* and *Brown* and add the other cases as they came to the Court. In any event, Jackson knew that his vote to hold the cases would not affect their being taken, since the three members of the Court preceding him in the voting on June 7—Minton, Clark, and Burton—had already voted to hear the cases, and Jackson knew that at least two of those voting after him—Black and Douglas—would also vote to take them, as they had at the beginning of the year when the rest of the Court was not yet prepared to do so.

the state courts. Eight days later, he received a call from Court clerk Willey, who sent a memo reporting its outcome to Chief Justice Vinson:

> I have just spoken to Mr. Young, the attorney general of Delaware, on the telephone. He objects to the advancement of the Delaware case for hearing with the other segregation cases in December on the ground that there would not be time for him to prepare an adequate brief. If certiorari is granted, he is willing that the case take its normal course.

But the Court was ready to hear all the segregation cases together now, and if that gave Delaware barely two weeks to prepare for its appearance before the Justices, that was Delaware's problem. Willey advised Young that, like it or not, his case had been set down for argument right after the District of Columbia case and he was to submit his briefs not later than three weeks after the argument.

"We felt it was much better to have representative cases from different parts of the country," says Justice Tom Clark, "and so we consolidated them and made *Brown* the first so that the whole question would not smack of being a purely Southern one."

And so on December 9, 1952, in the waning days of the presidency of Harry Truman, fifty-six years after segregation was approved in *Plessy*, ninety years after the Emancipation Proclamation, 163 years after the ratification of the Constitution, and 333 years after the first African slave was known to have been brought to the shores of the New World, the Supreme Court convened to hear arguments on whether the white people of the United States might continue to treat the black people as their subjects.

# Part III On Appeal

It is a maxim among these men, that whatever has been done before may legally be done again; and therefore they take special care to record all the decisions formerly made, even those which have through ignorance or corruption contradicted the rule of common justice and the general reason of mankind. These under the name of precedents, they produce as authorities and thereby endeavor to justify the most iniquitous opinions. . . .

—SWIFT, *Gulliver's Travels*

# 22

# Going for the Jugular

John W. Davis, the most accomplished and admired appellate lawyer in America, never doubted that he would successfully defend the constitutionality of segregated schools before the Supreme Court.

South Carolina had turned the case over to Davis without any strings attached. Governor Byrnes and Robert Figg, the best lawyer in Charleston and maybe the whole state, kept in touch with Davis at his giant New York law office but made no effort to second-guess him. Nor did Davis have any special strategy in mind; unvarnished, the state's case looked immensely strong to him. Never had he had a case in which the precedents were stacked so heavily on his side, he would tell his colleagues from time to time. There was circumstantial evidence, moreover, that the Justices were in no rush to give the separate-but-equal doctrine an early burial. If they were, why would they have remanded *Briggs* to the District Court for a rehearing after sitting on it for half a year? And while he did not scorn the competence of the black lawyers ranged against him, they hardly sent shivers through him. As to the social-science strategy that the NAACP had built into its case, Davis wrote Figg: "I think I have never read a drearier lot of testimony than that furnished by the so-called educational and psychological experts." Later, he remarked of the extensive piece of field research in Philadelphia by Helen Trager and her team: ". . . if anything were needed to discredit these high-flying psychologists, I think it could be found in Mrs. Trager's 'Projected Play Techniques' from which she developed the astounding conclusion that even at five years of age white children realized that they were white and black children realized that they were black. Presumably they should have been found to ignore the evidence of their senses. . . ."

With a pool of ninety-five lawyers to choose from in the 104-year-old firm he headed, Davis asked for the initial help of a forty-nine-year-old senior associate, William R. Meagher (pronounced "mar"), who had joined the firm ten years earlier. When he was first hired, Meagher had met Davis and disclosed that it had been his privilege to cast his very first vote for President for Davis in 1924. "And he sat back," Meagher remembers, "and said, 'Well, now, Mr. Meagher, that's one vote that'll never do the country any harm.'"

Davis's presidential stature was never made into a big thing at the firm, though it placed him beyond the back-slapping comradeship of his colleagues. "He was a very fine gentleman," says Meagher. "You would never think to intrude on his private life." He was a superb storyteller and masterful user of the language in both written and spoken form. His learning was prodigious: he could quote quite as comfortably from the Koran or Talmud as from the Bible or Shakespeare. One of his partners, Taggart Whipple, remarks, "He could recite you a page of Dickens without even thinking about it." And he was handsome as well—six feet tall, slim until old age softened him a bit, with a headful of beautiful silver hair.

Meagher, pleased to be invited into the *Briggs* case, shared Davis's doctrinal approach to it. "He had great reverence for the Constitution," says Meagher. "Today, you'd call him a strict-constructionist. Quite simply, he felt that if segregation was to be outlawed, it had to be done either by an act of Congress or by amending the Constitution." So long as Congress had not acted under the enforcement powers granted it in Section 5 of the Fourteenth Amendment, segregation duly enacted by the states could not be undone by mere judicial fiat, since that, Meagher explains, "would have been judicial legislation, destroyed the separation-of-powers concept, and been an unconstitutional intrusion by the federal government into the affairs of the states." Davis, in short, was a fervent Jeffersonian—and, like the master of Monticello, a country boy of remarkable urbanity.

Even at his advanced age, John Davis was used to putting in twelve-hour days on the job, and the segregation case was part of that routine. "He was in it up to his eyebrows," says Whipple, who joined Davis on the case in its later stages. "He was no figurehead." Davis was indeed the architect for the entire South Carolina brief, though he wrote only the opening and closing sections. He used what he could from Figg's earlier effort to get the Supreme Court to deny the NAACP's *Briggs* appeal. However, instead of leading off with the precedents in the state's favor, he reversed Figg's approach and stressed South Carolina's efforts "to wipe out all inequalities between its white and colored schools"—a program that Davis contended had mooted the NAACP's case. He brushed into the brief the clear, forceful strokes of language that were his hallmark and that served to give his words the tone of revealed wisdom. The history of the Fourteenth Amendment "compels the conclusion that it has no such scope as is claimed by appellants," he wrote. The right of a state to classify its public-school children by race "has been so often and so pointedly declared by the highest authorities that it should no longer be regarded as open to debate. . . . There is no conflict of opinion among them which needs to be resolved. Only an excess of zeal can explain the present challenge." Typical of the historical evidence that added to the supreme confidence radiating from Davis's brief was the assertion that of the thirty-seven states in the Union at the time of the adoption of the Fourteenth Amendment, "23 continued, or adopted soon after the Amendment, statutory or constitutional provisions calling for racial segregation in the public schools"—apparently overwhelming testimony to the contemporary view that the new amendment did not rule out such arrangements.

The social-science tack in the NAACP's approach to the case presented a new challenge to Davis. He sent out to the bookstore for a copy of *Readings in Social Psychology*, the 1947 textbook published by Henry Holt, to which Kenneth and Mamie Clark had contributed a chapter titled "Racial Identification and Preference in Negro Children." Davis studied the chapter, compared it carefully with Kenneth Clark's testimony in Charleston, and decided to exploit the apparent contradictions between the two. After quoting the Clarks' article—"The southern children . . . in spite of their equal favorableness toward the white doll, are significantly less likely to reject the brown doll (evaluate it negatively) as compared to the strong tendency for the majority of the northern children to do so"—Davis noted in his brief:

> . . . While these experiments would seem to indicate that Negro children in the South are healthier psychologically speaking than those in the North, Dr. Clark appears to disagree. In any case, the results obtained in the broader sample of experiments completely explode any inference that the "conflicts" from which Professor Clark's Clarendon County subjects were found to suffer are the result of their education in segregated schools.

Carrying his argument further, Davis said that since studies by Clark and Trager among others suggested that the Negro youngster was psychologically pre-conditioned to racial awareness at a tender age, it was a tricky and difficult question to determine whether it was better for him to attend a separate school with members of his own race or a school "with children whom he regards as superior." Only after a "most careful and painstaking consideration" involving "study of the accumulated data which the most thorough, impartial and scientific research can supply" should the matter be settled—and then it was a question for the legislative and educational authorities of the states to decide, not the courts.

After cannonading the social-science evidence against him, Davis then took the offensive, as if to say that both sides could play at that game. But his own zeal let him stray from candor. "This Court may judicially notice the fact," he addressed the Justices in his brief, "that there is a large body of respectable expert opinion to the effect that separate schools, particularly in the South, are in the best interests of children of both races as well as of the community at large." But it was not a fact, and the great difficulty encountered by the Southern lawyers in enlisting reputable social scientists to appear in the school-segregation cases testified to the opposite "fact." Davis had to cite Edgar Knight, a professor of education at the University of North Carolina, whose 1922 study *Public Education in the South* offered a derogatory view of South Carolina's brief experience with racially mixed public schools in the Reconstruction era. It was as if Davis preferred not to notice that the world had changed a great deal since 1922, not to mention 1870. He then quoted E. R. Crow, the superintendent of schools in the small city of Sumter, South Carolina, as an "expert" on the undesirability of desegregation, though Thurgood Marshall had shattered Crow on cross-examination at the *Briggs* trial and got him to admit to a life-long belief in the separation of the races. Davis went on to quote at length from Howard Odum's speech "The Mid-Century South: Looking Both Ways," which Figg had failed to get introduced into the record at the trial, just as he had failed to induce the famed scholar to testify. The great lawyer wound up his tenuous claim to authority in support of segregation by the well-known device of quoting his sources out of context. Davis picked up a sentence from Myrdal's *An American Dilemma* that read, "Negroes are divided on the issue of segregated schools," and a few additional sentences explaining their concern over possible ill-treatment in mixed schools as the reason—as if this in any way contradicted the overwhelming indictment of brutalizing racial practices that the Swedish sociologist documented for more than a thousand pages and said had reduced the black man in America to a pathological state. Finally, Davis quoted Du Bois's article titled "Does the Negro Need Separate Schools?" from the 1935 *Journal of Negro Education* yearbook and stressed the black author's remarks that there was "no magic" in mixed schools and that the Negro parent who forced his youngsters into schools where they would be unfairly and perhaps inhumanly treated was doing them no favor. Ignored was Du Bois's obvious intention to instill in Negroes pride in their own schools so long as it was clear that the country was not ready to honor its duty and commitment to treat them as full equals. Ignored, too, was the unmistakable warning with which Du Bois had ended the article Davis cited: "I know that this article will forthwith be interpreted by certain illiterate 'nitwits' as a plea for segregated Negro schools and colleges. It is not. It is simply calling a spade a spade. . . ."

When the NAACP's brief reached his desk, Davis went through it and found little to concern him. He wrote to Figg that in Marshall's brief

> great play [is] made of the doctrine of reasonableness and the assertion that race is not a reasonable basis [for school segregation]. The weight of the precedents should be enough to answer this assertion. It may catch, however, some of the wavering brethren on the Court. It seems wise, therefore, to give them some stiffening. With this end in view I have lifted bodily from your brief in the court below so much as defended the public policy. It shows at least that notwithstanding the appellants' learned witnesses, there is still a large conflict of opinion on the subject. I have not cast it in the form of a defense of reasonableness, not wishing to adopt the battleground which the appellants evidently prefer. . . .

Figg and Governor Byrnes expressed their pleasure in the handiwork of their Wall Street lawyer. About the only point that troubled Figg was the preference in the Davis brief to spell Negro with an uncapitalized "n"— which was the custom in the South and was widely practiced still in the North. The *New York Times* had not adopted the capital N as its official style until 1950. "Our colored brethren appear to be sensitive on this point," Figg noted.

Another clue to the state of John W. Davis's mind, if not his art, was to be found in his pleasurable comment to Figg that the Supreme Court had turned down the application of the National Lawyers Guild, a professional group of mostly Negro and liberal white attorneys who disapproved of the lily-white and highly conservative policies of the American Bar Association, to file an *amicus* brief in the school-segregation cases. "I have always thought the *amici curiae* were the lowest form of animal life and I have rarely consented to have them filed in any case where I was concerned. If I were going to make an exception, it would certainly not be in favor of the National Lawyers Guild. They are a crowd of 'pinkos' and self-advertisers and, like the American Civil Liberties Union, they try to horn into every case that arouses public interest. I am against all such. . . ."

About the only source of concern in the segregationist camp was the Kansas sector of their line.

Davis and Figg had established close ties with Justin Moore's firm in Richmond as the Virginia lawyers prepared their briefs for the Court, and the Delaware and the District of Columbia cases were both still mired in the lower courts as summer ended and the date neared for argument before the Justices. From Kansas, though, there came only ominous silence. That was a problem because the Kansas case now led off the docket, and any softening of resistance by officials there might leave the entire segregationist bloc vulnerable.

The concern of the lawyers for South Carolina and Virginia was well founded. In early October, with the original date for argument before the Justices little more than a week away, the attorney for the Topeka Board of Education wrote the clerk of the Supreme Court that the board "does not desire to file a brief in the above case and will not present oral argument at the time the case is set for argument." But the Court suddenly rescheduled the argument for early December and added the Delaware and District of Columbia cases to the docket. Still, no brief from Kansas showed up as October dwindled. Justin Moore wrote to the assistant attorney general of Kansas who was more or less watching over the *Brown* situation—Paul E. Wilson—that the Southerners felt "it would be most unfortunate for your Kansas case, which is the first case in the group to be called, to go by default. . . ." But that was precisely what was happening. Harold R. Fatzer, attorney general of Kansas, believed that since the state's school-segregation law merely permitted cities of 15,000 or more people to operate separate schools and did not command the separation, the *Brown* case was essentially a local matter for Topeka to handle as it wished.

In Topeka, though, a different view emerged. The citizens' uprising that had swept the forces of School Superintendent Kenneth McFarland from power the previous year and elected three relatively liberal members to the school board now had prompted the general feeling that segregation ought to be abandoned in the very near future. Gradually, perhaps, but abandoned. There was no enthusiasm in town, therefore, for defending the *Brown* suit. After the Court had rescheduled the arguments for December, the Topeka school board reconsidered its earlier decision and, by a three-to-two vote (with one abstention) in early November, reaffirmed it. The board announced that it would not defend the suit and thought that since it was a Kansas statute that was under attack, the defense ought properly to be conducted by the attorney general of Kansas. Attorney General Fatzer kept insisting it was the school board's duty.

In late November, the Supreme Court itself settled the Kansas squabble. It virtually ordered the attorney general to participate:

> Because of the national importance of the issue presented, because of its importance to the state of Kansas we request that the State present its views at oral argument. If the State does not desire to appear, we request the Attorney General to advise whether the State's default shall be construed as concession of invalidity.

Fatzer wired the Justices that "It is not within the prerogative of a public official in the executive department of the state government to concede the invalidity of any act passed by the state legislature" and assured them that Kansas would show up in court at the appointed time to argue the legitimacy of its segregation law.

Prior commitments and an inflexible schedule were given by Fatzer as the reasons he could not handle the case himself, though his actions left him open to the inference that he had no stomach for the job. On November 28, just ten days before the arguments in the Supreme Court of the United States, Fatzer handed the job to his assistant Paul Wilson, a man not measurably more enthusiastic about the assignment than his boss. "While I believed that the state of Kansas should have done something about its segregated schools long before *Brown v. Board of Education* was begun," says Wilson, "I then believed—and now believe—that in the framework of our federal system the solution to this problem properly belonged on a state legislative level. I know all the counter-arguments, and some of them are difficult to refute. The problem is essentially one of man's inhumanity to man. Unfortunately, the law is not very good at dealing with problems of this kind."

By Eastern standards, Paul Wilson was a hayseed. His background and practice as a lawyer did not seem to qualify him very well for the role thrust upon him as a reluctant dragon defending his state's Jim Crow public schools. He was the stocky, thirty-six-year-old son of a modestly successful farmer from near the little town of Lyndon, seat of Osage County, about twenty miles south of Topeka. Fewer than a thousand people lived in the vicinity of Lyndon, among them "no blacks, no Mexicans, no Indians, no Jews, and only a few Catholics," Wilson recalls. His parents, people "of rather meager educational accomplishment," wanted better things for their son. At the University of Kansas, he took his bachelor's degree and a master's in political science, went to Washburn in Topeka for his law degree, served in the Army during the Second World War, and came home to be a lawyer. There was not a great deal of private lawyering for a young fellow to do in rural Osage, so Paul Wilson ran for and was elected Osage County Attorney for two terms before being named general counsel to the Kansas Department of Social Welfare. After a year, he joined the attorney general's staff in 1951 and so was a newcomer when the assignment to defend *Brown* was given to him. He had never argued before the Supreme Court. In fact, he had never argued before any appellate court, in or out of Kansas, though he had conducted his share of local trial work. And he had never set foot in Washington, D.C.

Without relevant experience, without any staff help—illness had reduced the attorney general's office manpower just then—and with almost no time to explore the nuances of the case, Wilson set to work over the Thanksgiving weekend in his office in the state capitol. He had a key to the State Law Library, also located in the capitol, a promise from a local printer to move the brief ahead of all other work as soon as it was ready, and the confidence that "the precedents were all on our side" in both the federal and Kansas courts. But he had a foreboding from the beginning that it was "quite likely that the case would result in striking down segregation. History and the social conscience had simply overtaken the law." But to overturn segregation, Wilson was convinced, the Supreme Court "would have to make new law."

Working steadily, sleeping little, Wilson turned out a concise, direct, and clearly competent brief. Kansas was not coming before the Supreme Court, it said, to argue the economic, sociological, ethical, or religious desirability of school segregation. Its only concern in appearing was to defend the state's right to permit such a practice. He spelled out the history of the school laws, traced how they had been upheld in the state courts, and challenged the NAACP reading of the relevant Supreme Court cases. *Sweatt* and *McLaurin* were the keys to their hopes, but nothing in them truly diluted the *Plessy* doctrine; the acts of separation in both those cases had prevented the plaintiffs from receiving equal educational opportunities. No doubt the separate-but-equal doctrine was susceptible to abuse, Wilson wrote, and it had often resulted in unequal practices, but "it is the impossibility of equality under such a doctrine, and not the difficulty of administering and applying the same with equality, that would make such a doctrine unconstitutional *per se.* The situation in Topeka is one where substantial equality has been reached." *Plessy* had been inarguably reaffirmed by a unanimous Court in *Gong Lum* and no amount of insistence to the contrary by the black plaintiffs could erase the words of the 1927 decision upholding the power of the state of Mississippi to classify its schoolchildren by race:

> . . . Were this a new question it would call for very full argument and consideration but we think that it is the same question which has been many times decided to be within the constitutional power of the state legislature to settle without intervention of the federal courts under the Federal Constitution.

Finally, Wilson came down hard against the heavy reliance of the Negro side on the finding of fact in Judge Huxman's *Brown* opinion that mandatory school segregation tended to damage the psyche, morale, and learning ability of colored children. The judge had not found that segregation damaged these particular plaintiffs in that fashion, Wilson argued, and opposing counsel had made no effort to claim such damage in behalf of their clients. Nor was there evidence or any finding that the black youngsters in the case interpreted segregation as a practice that denoted their inferiority.

On December 6, with the required forty copies of his forty-four-page brief in his suitcase, Paul Wilson boarded the Santa Fe train for Chicago and switched there to the B&O for the major part of the twenty-eight-hour

Topeka-to-Washington trip. It was his first real opportunity to catch his breath and think about what he would say to the august Court, a prospect that, now that he thought about it, left him more than a little queasy. In the drawing room he had to himself for the journey, he spread out his papers and began jotting down thoughts on how he would present his case. In Washington, his colleagues among the pro-segregation state lawyers were hardly less apprehensive about how the unknown Kansan would perform in the lead-off position.

On his arrival at the Carlton Hotel in the capital, Wilson found a phone message waiting for him—from the opposing lawyers, who were staying across the street at the Statler. Robert Carter of the NAACP had called to say hello and obtain a copy of his brief. Wilson agreed to come to Thurgood Marshall's suite. The visit lasted about twenty minutes and left Wilson with the feeling that his adversaries were "agreeable people and apparently competent lawyers." Retiring from the enemy camp, he headed back across the street to the Carlton rooms occupied by John W. Davis and his associates. "I think that it was feared I might either concede the invalidity of the Kansas statute," Wilson surmises, "or make no argument in its defense." His spirited brief ended such speculation, and Wilson spent most of Sunday, December 7, 1952, closeted with Davis. The old master went over the Kansas brief with the novice appellate lawyer, discussed the outline of his argument to the Court, and helped him anticipate questions that the Justices might put to him and frame answers that might be favorably received. "Throughout the conference," Wilson recalls, "there was no hint of impatience or condescension or superiority." The impression of the great lawyer that he came away with was, rather, one of "gentleness, civility, learning, and poise."

The procedure is exceedingly simple.

The nine Justices, emerging simultaneously as a berobed *ensemble* from behind the curtains in back of their great mahogany bench, take their seats in high-back, black leather swivel chairs that place their occupants several exalted heads higher than anyone else in the hushed chamber. Then counsel for the appellant begins his argument, standing at a lectern directly below and in front of the Chief Justice of the United States.

In most cases of any magnitude in that era, each side had one hour to present its case to the Court. In recent years, that allotment has been cut in half but the basic procedure has not changed. Whoever delivers the opening argument may stop before his time is up and reserve the balance of his allotment for rebuttal. During the last five minutes of each attorney's argument, a white warning light on the lectern goes on. When his time is up, a red light goes on and the Chief Justice may well cut off the long-winded counsel in midsentence. At any time during anyone's argument, any Justice may interrupt with a question, and the time required to answer it is taxed against the speaker's allotted hour—a disconcerting arrangement for the inexperienced lawyer who is under the impression that he is there to make a speech, not persuade the Court in what Justice William Brennan has characterized as "a Socratic dialogue between Justices and counsel."

Brennan has said that "my whole notion of what a case is about crystallizes at oral argument." Chief Justice Hughes wrote: "I suppose that, aside from cases of exceptional difficulty, the impression that a judge has at the close of a full oral argument accords with the conviction which controls his final vote." A less subjective estimate of the importance of the oral argument before the Court is offered by Philip Elman, whose legal career includes seventeen years in the Solicitor General's office, perhaps the best perch in Washington for observing the habits of the Justices. "As a generalization," Elman ventures, "I would say the greater the issues involved in a case, the less oral arguments are likely to affect it. In lesser cases, effective counsel can sway a Court that hasn't made up its mind. Overall, though, it is safe to say that you may well lose your case with a bad oral argument but it is difficult to win it by a strong one."

There are several primers on how to star before the Supreme Court. One of them is an article based on a witty address that Justice Jackson delivered to the California state bar the year before *Brown* was argued. Another is a 700-page how-to opus titled *Supreme Court Practice* by Robert L. Stern, for some years Elman's colleague and superior in the Solicitor General's office, and Eugene Gressman. But the best and pithiest of all is the address that John W. Davis delivered to the Association of the Bar of the City of New York in 1940. It was called simply "The Argument of an Appeal" and offered the fledgling—and even the veteran—appellate lawyer ten secrets to success:

(1) *Change places, in your imagination of course, with the Court.* "If the places were reversed . . . think what it is you would want first to know about the case. How and in what order would you want the story told? . . . what would make easier your approach to the true solution?" In passing, Davis urged the lawyer not to speak so softly or indistinctly or monotonously "as to make the mere effort at hearing an unnecessary burden." Justice Jackson noted on this score that the acoustics of the Supreme Court were "wretched" and those with low voices risked poor transmission of their words. "On the other hand," Jackson added, "no judge likes to be shouted at as if he were an ox."

(2) *State first the nature of the case and briefly its prior history.* One never knew if the Justices had read the briefs beforehand.

(3) *State the facts.* And do so with candor, "the telling of the worst as well as the best, since the court has the right to expect it, and since any lack of candor, real or apparent, will wholly destroy the most careful argument." Justice Wiley Rutledge elaborated on the point in 1942: "Do not try to dodge or minimize the facts which are against you. If you can't win without doing this—and it is seldom you can by doing it—your case should not be appealed. It is equally bad to give evasive answers to questions at oral argument. Conversely, few things add strength to an argument as does candid and full admission." Stern and Gressman in *Supreme Court Practice* add that "unfavorable facts should be fairly stated, and accompanied by any further . . . argument which will minimize their force. But don't let the Court hear them for the first time from opposing counsel."

(4) *State next the applicable rules of law on which you rely.* But the

recitation of precedents alone is no way to argue a case; "the advocate must be prepared to meet any challenge to the doctrine of the cases on which he relies and to support it by original reasoning. Barren citation is a broken reed. What virtue it retains can be left for the brief." In a case like *Brown*, where conflicting lines of precedent were invoked by opposing counsel, it was plain that the advocate had to try to persuade the Court by principle as well as legal doctrine. Stern and Gressman write that "except when there is a recent Supreme Court case directly in point, counsel should emphasize the appeal to reason, rather than try to overwhelm the Court with authority." Justice Jackson was more pointed still: ". . . if the one or two best precedents will not convince, a score of weaker ones will only reveal the weakness of your argument. I always look with suspicion upon a proposition with a page full of citations in its support. And if the first decision cited does not support it, I conclude the lawyer has a blunderbuss mind and rely on him no further."

(5) *Always go for the jugular vein.* There is too little time to fool with minor points, Davis declared; get right to the heart of your case. Stern and Gressman add in this regard that dwelling on lesser points lays the counsel open to sharp questions from the bench and shows his vulnerability. Jackson remarked: "The impact of oral presentation will be strengthened if it is concentrated on a few points that can be simply and convincingly stated and easily grasped and retained."

(6) *Rejoice when the Court asks questions.* "If you value your argumentative life, do not evade or shuffle or postpone, no matter how embarrassing the question may be or how much it interrupts the thread of your argument." Justice Brennan has written that the questioning process "is the way we get answers to things that are bothering us about the case." Chief Justice Hughes noted that "well-prepared and experienced counsel . . . would much prefer to have the opportunity of knowing the difficulties in the minds of the court and of attempting to meet them than to have them concealed and presented in conference when counsel are not present." Stern and Gressman stress that it is "much more important to answer questions fully and accurately . . . than to complete the prepared argument on points which may not bother the Justices at all." Justice Jackson wrote that "A question argumentative in form should not be attributed to hostility, for oftentimes it is put, not to overbear counsel, but to help him sharpen his position." Besides, any question from the bench "is clear proof that the inquiring Justice is not asleep. If the question is relevant, it denotes he is grappling with your contention even though he has not grasped it. It gives you opportunity to inflate his ego by letting him think he has discovered an idea for himself."

(7) *Read sparingly and only from necessity.* "A sentence here or a sentence there, perhaps, if sufficiently pertinent and pithy, but not, I beg of you, print by the paragraph or page." Said Jackson: "We like to meet the eye of the advocate, and sometimes when one starts reading his argument from a manuscript he will be interrupted, to wean him from his essay. . . . If you have confidence to address the Court only by reading to it, you really should not argue there."

(8) *Avoid personalities.* To criticize sharply the court below is to run the risk of offending "the quite understandable *esprit de corps* of the judicial body. Rhetorical denunciation of opposing litigants or witnesses may arouse a measure of sympathy for the persons so denounced." And controversy between the counsel only irritates the Court, never really persuades it.

(9) *Know your record from cover to cover.* At any moment, you may have to correct your adversary or answer an inquiry, and the more readily and firmly you do so, the more confidence with which the Court will listen to what else you have to say.

(10) *Sit down.* And when you do this before your time has expired, "a benevolent smile overspreads the faces on the bench and a sigh of relief and gratification arises from your brethren at the bar who have been impatiently waiting for the moment when the angel might again trouble the waters of the healing pool and permit them to step in." Davis himself almost never took his full hour before the Court. "He was a great believer in economy of expression," says Taggart Whipple. "He was a man secure in his own supreme abilities." The ultimate display of his control and discipline may have come when Davis was arguing before the Justices on the morning that Calvin Coolidge, the man who beat him in the presidential election, was being inaugurated. Upon finishing his oral argument early as was his wont, Davis said with lordly grace, "I make a gift of my remaining time to the Court"—and the nine Justices trooped over to the Capitol earlier than they might have to witness the swearing-in. Davis himself, no doubt, repaired to "the waters of the healing pool."

At Thurgood Marshall's office, everyone was at battle stations as early as August when drafts of the briefs in *Brown* and *Briggs* were roughed out. After the Virginia case was added by the Court, it was clear that the NAACP Legal Defense Fund was now locked in an all-out struggle with the forces of white supremacy by whatever name it wore.

For a whole week beginning September 8, the office was turned into a writers' workshop as Marshall's regular staff and a small group of close outside counselors—Jim Nabrit from Washington, Bob Ming from Chicago, Spot Robinson and Oliver Hill from Richmond, Judge Bill Hastie and Bill Coleman from Philadelphia, and Lou Pollak from New York among them—combed through the three briefs with intense care and kept redrafting them. Robinson stayed for two weeks to refine the writing.

There were two main questions for the NAACP lawyers to resolve: (1) Should we attack *Plessy* head-on, simply telling the Court that by every known standard of law and humanity it must be reversed, or should we try to dismiss it as irrelevant? (2) How much should we rely on the body of social-science testimony gathered in the courts below?

With the clock ticking now, Marshall's men fought hard among themselves to resolve these two basic trouble spots. The sharp attack on *Plessy* in the *Briggs* statement of jurisdiction was muted as Marshall decided not to go through the middle of the line but to make an end-run on the separate-but-equal doctrine. But he varied the method a bit in each of the three state cases.

In the Kansas case, the NAACP argued in effect that *Sweatt* and *McLaurin* had replaced *Plessy* and *Gong Lum* as the governing decisions, so that the latter pair could simply be disregarded—no need to overrule them. The logic went like this: (a) unequal educational opportunities for Negroes are illegal under the Fourteenth Amendment; (b) *Sweatt* and *McLaurin* established that such opportunities are defined not solely by physical or curricular factors but by intangible ones as well, including racial discrimination that may put the student at a disadvantage in the pursuit of knowledge; (c) the District Court in Topeka found as a fact that segregation placed Negro students at an educational disadvantage by stunting their motivation to learn, and therefore (d) it should have ruled that segregation in Topeka public schools was illegal. As to *Gong Lum*, the NAACP position remained fixed: the Court in 1927 did not give a full airing of the state's right to make racial distinctions in its public school system nor had any claim or showing been made by the plaintiff that segregation invariably produced unequal learning opportunities; all that Lum had attacked was the right of Mississippi to classify his daughter as "colored."

In the *Briggs* brief, both *Plessy* and *Gong Lum* were dismissed as inapplicable in a scant two pages. *Plessy*, the brief said, "was decided upon pleadings which assumed the possibility of attainment of a theoretical equality within the framework of racial segregation, rather than on a full hearing and evidence which would have established the inevitability of discrimination under a system of segregation." The Court should be governed by its own rulings just two and a half years earlier in *Sweatt* and *McLaurin*, which, though dealing with graduate schools, framed the basic constitutional question that applied at every level of the learning ladder: does state-imposed segregation destroy equality of educational benefits? It was a forceful statement, but it left the way open to the inevitable rebuttal that while the Court had found inequality created by the particular kinds of state-imposed segregation in *Sweatt* and *McLaurin*, it did not follow from those cases that all forms of segregation imposed inequality. That was precisely what Paul Wilson of Kansas argued in reply.

In the Virginia case, the NAACP brief took what seemed to be both its most cautious and its most daring stand. Growing out of the exhausting experiences of Robinson and Hill in trying to get the state to equalize its black schools, the brief insisted that the Supreme Court order prompt desegregation in Prince Edward County since the separate schools for Negroes there had been found to be unequal. This was the solution that Chancellor Seitz had applied in the Delaware cases. But the NAACP's brief went beyond that stopgap measure, which would have achieved desegregation without upsetting the *Plessy* doctrine or Virginia's segregation laws. "Notwithstanding Virginia's efforts in this case, it is clear that her racial policy in public education cannot be permitted to endure," the brief concluded. "For many years Negro children in Prince Edward County have suffered educational deprivations at the hands of the state. It is clear that they will continue to suffer as long as racial segregation in public schools is practiced."

Nowhere in any of the briefs, though, was it asserted point-blank that *Plessy* was bad law and that the time had come to inter it.

How—or if—to use the social-science material in the briefs for the Supreme Court was a yet more divisive issue within the NAACP ranks. The testimony that had been given at the trial level in the state cases had of course already been brought to the Supreme Court's attention in the form of the transcripts of the hearings sent up to the Justices with the appeal applications. How much of that testimony, and what other outside authorities, ought to be worked into the briefs themselves for final argument were different questions. The skepticism among the Legal Defense Fund lawyers that had first greeted the social-science approach when Bob Carter enlisted Kenneth Clark at the outset of the state cases had never entirely died. In two of the cases—Kansas and Delaware—the testimony had helped produce findings by the courts that state-enforced school segregation diminished educational opportunities. But the Supreme Court offered a far sterner test than the courts below, and the seemingly self-contradictory findings of Clark's doll tests, as prominently noted in the *Yale Law Journal* the previous spring, did little to stir enthusiasm among the NAACP lawyers, many of them professors, for heavy reliance on the social-science testimony.

Pollak and Coleman had registered their sharp reservations from the first. Ming oscillated between love of and scorn for the idea. Nabrit thought it was basically irrelevant to the clear-cut constitutional issue, though he admired Clark's character. One newcomer to the inner council, a thirty-year-old Columbia law professor named Jack B. Weinstein, who had been Jack Greenberg's classmate at law school, was particularly unimpressed by the social-science approach. "I may have used the word 'crap' to describe the doll tests," recalls Weinstein, who later became a U.S. District judge in New York, "which I'm afraid upset Kenneth at one of our meetings. I thought it absurd to try to couch our argument in terms of dubious psychological data. I was afraid of it, frankly, especially since some of the Justices were well informed in the area and liked to dress up their opinions in terms of sociology. I thought we ought to build our case on the general movement of the common law, historical evidence, and the trend of the nation in the wake of the Second World War. I didn't want us to build our case on a gimmick."

Faced with such acidic arguments, Carter proceeded a step at a time. He asked Clark to prepare a summary of the social-science testimony given in the trial courts. He did not know what use, if any, the rest of the staff would finally decide to make of it. While the briefs themselves were being drafted by the lawyers without reference to the social-science material, Clark set to work with Isidor Chein and Stuart W. Cook, then chairman of the psychology department at New York University. What emerged was a careful 4,000-word summation of the state of social-scientific knowledge of segregation and its effects. The language was low-key, and Myrdal's was the only name to appear in the text itself, which gained its weight of authority from thirty-five footnotes that plainly suggested there was in fact a good deal of research data on the question. The basic line of approach was the same Clark had taken in his paper for the Midcentury White House Conference on Children in 1950—and the same he had presented in three of the four state trials: segregation tends to create feelings of inferiority and personal humiliation in black youngsters, whose sense of self-esteem is soon replaced with self-hatred, rejection of their racial group, and frustration. Anti-social and delinquent behavior may be the aggressive, hostile result. "These reactions are self-destructive," the statement noted, "in that the larger society not only punishes those who commit them, but often interprets such . . . behavior as justification for continuing prejudice and segregation."

Clark and his two writing partners reached beyond this material now and stressed that the effects of segregation on the white community were no less toxic. It produced "a distorted sense of social reality" in white children as well as confusion, conflict, and "moral cynicism." It blocked communication between the races and tended to feed mutual suspicion, distrust, and hostility. Since a broad body of evidence now existed showing that "much, perhaps all, of the observable differences among various racial and national groups may be adequately explained in terms of environmental differences," there was no sound reason why desegregation should not proceed with a minimum of conflict. Studies of housing developments, the armed forces, and industry (among those cited in this last area were "The Pattern of Race Relationships in the Pocahontas Coal Field" and "Attitudes of White Department Store Employees Toward Negro Co-Workers," which both appeared in the *Journal of Social Issues*) showed that the desegregation process worked with least friction when (1) "the change is simultaneously introduced into all units of a social institution to which it is applicable—*e.g.,* all of the schools in a school system or all of the shops in a given factory" and (2) "consistent and firm enforcement of the new policy" is practiced by those in authority. The statement concluded with the candid confession that "The problem with which we have here attempted to deal is admittedly on the frontiers of scientific knowledge."

Carter was exceedingly pleased with Clark's paper. And because the statement did not speak of doll tests or any other clinical methods—and offered only the damning conclusions—the other lawyers saw its usefulness. At their gathering during the second week of September, it was decided to use the statement as an appendix to the *Briggs* brief. To give it added authority, they hit upon a device that had been used successfully in *Sweatt* in the form of the law professors' *amicus* brief. They would try to get several dozen leading figures in the field to sign the Clark-Chein-Cook statement. But little time remained before the briefs were due at the Court. Both to speed things and to enhance their chances of obtaining as many signatures as possible, Clark and Chein practiced a small piece of duplicity. Their letters of solicitation began:

> In line with the idea that social science knowledge should be made available wherever it can be of practical value, several of us have collaborated in preparing the enclosed statement summarizing the evidence of the effects of segregation

and the consequences of desegregation. When we started to work on this summary, we had no clear idea as to how the statement might be used. . . .

The letter went on to say that shortly after the supposedly casual project had been begun, NAACP lawyers had learned of it and now asked that the statement be included as an appendix to their brief in the pending school-segregation cases. "In order that this should not appear to be the private notion of the few of us who prepared the statement, we felt that it should bear the signatures of those who are in substantial agreement with its content," the letter concluded. To get several dozen social scientists to agree to any proposition without protracted haggling and to do so practically overnight would normally be the intellectual equivalent of the combined labors of Hercules, and so Clark and Chein added: "The time available for this particular use of the statement does not permit revisions. It must be in the hands of the printers by the end of this week." A stamped, self-addressed envelope was enclosed.

They ended up with thirty-five names, including those of some of the most eminent social scientists in America. Nine of them had testified for the NAACP in the school or graduate-school cases: Jerome Bruner of Harvard, David Krech of Berkeley, Robert Redfield of Chicago, Otto Klineberg of Columbia, M. Brewster Smith of Vassar, Alfred McClung Lee of Brooklyn College, Kenneth and Mamie Clark, and Chein. Among the other signers were Gordon Allport and Samuel Stouffer of Harvard; Robert Merton, R. N. MacIver, and Paul Lazarsfeld of Columbia; Hadley Cantril of Princeton; Charles S. Johnson, then the president of Fisk; Arnold Rose of Minnesota; and Allison Davis of Chicago, said to be the first black man ever to attain full professorship at a major unsegregated university.

John W. Davis was not impressed. He wrote to Figg in Charleston on September 29 that "I have read the brief and appendix submitted by our opponents and there seems to be nothing in them which requires special comment. I think it perfectly clear from interior evidences that the witness Clark drafted the appendix which is signed by the worthy social scientists. I can only say that if that sort of 'guff' can move any court, 'God save the state!'"

Guff or not, Thurgood Marshall had decided to go with it. But he suffered from none of the confidence that seemed to overflow Davis's office. During the two-month delay of the arguments caused by the last-minute additions of the Virginia, Delaware, and District of Columbia cases, the NAACP camp was in a state of suspended animation. The briefs were written and sent to the Court. The opposing briefs were pondered and preparation for the oral arguments proceeded. "All arguments were framed to meet Felix Frankfurter's position," recalls Jack Greenberg. "In terms of the oral argument, you had to address yourself to him—he was just more demanding than any of the other Justices, and you had to be ready with tight answers on all technical points, like justiciability and whether all remedies had been exhausted by the parties."

During the waiting period, suspense grew at the Fund office over the position that the lame-duck Truman administration would now take in the segregation cases. Dwight Eisenhower had been elected President in a near-landslide, and for the first time in twenty years the Republicans would be in command of the executive branch. The oral arguments, though, were to be held more than a month before the Eisenhower inauguration, and *Brown* therefore provided the final occasion for improving on the record of largely unfulfilled promises and goals of the Truman administration in the civil-rights field. Only a determined effort by liberals in the Justice Department, however, brought the government into the case at the last minute.

Under Solicitor General Philip Perlman, the conservative Baltimore Democrat, the government had intervened forcefully in *Shelley v. Kraemer*, the 1948 case outlawing judicial enforcement of restrictive covenants, and pleaded error in *Henderson v. United States*, the 1950 decision striking down Jim Crow arrangements in dining cars on trains traveling interstate. In *Henderson*, the government brief went so far as to urge the overturning of *Plessy* in no uncertain terms. But by the spring of 1952, as *Briggs* was being weighed for argument by the Supreme Court, Perlman drew the line. "He thought it was all right to mix the races in law and graduate schools," recalls Philip Elman, the Solicitor General's assistant who wrote the United States briefs in both *Shelley* and *Henderson*, "but to mandate integrated public schools would wreck the whole system in the South and lead to open revolt." Elman wrote Perlman a strong memo urging the government to file an *amicus* brief, but the Solicitor General was adamant and declined to take the question to Attorney General J. Howard McGrath. Thurgood Marshall came down from New York to pry Perlman loose from his negative position, but had no success. In May, though, the picture began to change.

Under fire for sitting on his hands while departmental scandals festered at Justice, McGrath was forced out of office and replaced by a Pennsylvania federal judge who had served in Congress with Harry Truman—James P. McGranery. A rather flighty figure whom some ranking officials at Justice viewed as close to irresponsible, McGranery dismayed Solicitor General Perlman, who clashed with the new Attorney General almost at once and shortly resigned. In his place as Acting Solicitor General went Robert Stern, whose ideological views on the segregation issue were akin to those of Philip Elman. Stern and Elman went to McGranery and asked him to put the government into *Brown*. They pointed out that what they were urging was no new position for the government to be taking. Without any great hair-tearing, McGranery replied, "Okay, boys, go ahead in with it."

Elman fashioned a thirty-two-page brief that turned out to be a good deal more useful to the Justices than all ten briefs filed in the five cases by the litigants. "It's the thing I'm proudest of in my legal career," says Elman, who later became a member of the Federal Trade Commission and a law professor at Georgetown. Elman's brief, signed by him and McGranery, was a distinctly mixed bag in the view of both the NAACP and the segregation-ists. For the Court, though, it proved ventilating.

Elman began with a short anthem to American ideals. The United States government had a stake in *Brown*, he wrote, because the proposition that all men are created equal was no mere rhetoric. He invoked Harlan's dissent in *Plessy* with its glowing reminder that the Constitution was color-blind. Segregation was a particularly serious matter in Washington, he said—"the window through which the world looks into our house."

Then the U.S. brief got down to the first of its three basic propositions: the Court did not necessarily have to face up to the question of overruling *Plessy* in order to decide *Brown.* In three of the state cases—South Carolina, Virginia, and Delaware—inequalities in the black schools have been found, and the Court could grant relief by ordering the immediate admission of the Negro children into the superior white schools until such time as the colored schools were equalized. In short, the logic of the Delaware decision could be applied to South Carolina and Virginia without upsetting *Plessy.* In the Kansas situation, the U.S. brief adopted much of the NAACP's reasoning: nothing in *Plessy* should have prevented the District Court from concluding that the Topeka colored schools were unequal if it found (as it had) that segregation produced unequal and inferior treatment of colored pupils. Nothing in *Plessy* limited the definition of equality to physical facilities. Thus, where segregation was deemed to produce damaging effects on those segregated, *Plessy* could in effect be invoked against itself and segregation in Topeka ruled a violation of separate-but-equal treatment. And in the District of Columbia case, *Bolling v. Sharpe,* Elman said that the Justices could hold off consideration since no testimony had been taken in the District Court hearing. The Court could, furthermore, construe the congressional acts regarding separate schools in the District as neither approving nor disapproving of segregation but merely as assuming its practice. The case could then be remanded to the District Court, which could find that the practice was not based on any mandate from Congress; if the school board then persisted in the practice without authorization from Congress, a legal issue different from and less grave than the Fifth Amendment violation charged by the Negro petitioners would be raised.

Elman thus pointed out to the Justices the way to an escape hatch. But if the Court wanted to come to grips with *Plessy* at last, he wrote, then it must rid the nation of the noxious precedent. Separate-but-equal was plainly a contradiction in terms, and a great body of precedent as well as "the facts of every day life" challenged the Court's holding in *Plessy* that racial classification did not constitute a "badge of inferiority" except in the minds of colored people. *Strauder v. West Virginia* had eloquently ruled against imposing racial restrictions on Negroes and not on other groups in the community or state. *Gaines, Sweatt,* and *McLaurin* forbade the denial of equal educational advantages to Negroes, and nothing in the Fourteenth Amendment could conceivably be taken to distinguish between graduate schools and public schools in the application of that principle. Then, both to bolster his case and to pick up votes on what he took to be a reluctant Court, Elman cited other decisions written by the sitting Justices. In Vinson's *Shelley* opinion, he noted, the Chief Justice had written that, whatever else the framers of the Fourteenth Amendment had had in mind, their basic aim was to preserve the individual's political and basic civil rights from discriminatory action at the hands of the states. In Justice Black's opinion in *Takahashi v. Fish and Game Commission*, a 1948 case outlawing a California statute that withheld commercial fishing licenses from non-citizens, the Court had held that the Fourteenth Amendment embodied "the general policy that all persons lawfully in this country shall abide 'in any state' on an equality of legal privileges with all citizens under nondiscriminatory laws. . . ." And in *Smith v. Allwright*, upsetting the white primary, Justice Reed had written that "when convinced of former error, this Court has never felt constrained to follow precedent." *Plessy* was such an error. It was filled with holes in logic, not the least of them the *non sequitur* that the alternative to segregation was "enforced commingling" of the races. On the contrary, it was segregation which interfered with the individual's right to exercise his voluntary choice of associates; "to remove such an interference is to enlarge individual freedom, not to limit it."

If the Court reversed *Plessy*, Elman wrote in the pregnant closing action of his brief, it did not have to order that segregation be abandoned overnight. "The practical difficulties which may be met in making progressive adjustment to a non-segregated system cannot be ignored or minimized," the brief allowed. "A reasonable period of time will obviously be required to permit formulation of new provisions . . . in areas affected by the Court's decision. School authorities may wish to give pupils a choice of attending one of several schools, a choice now prohibited." A program "for orderly and progressive transition" to be carried out "within a specified period" would serve to reduce any community antagonisms that might arise from a desegregation order. "An appropriate tribunal to devise and supervise execution of such a program is a District Court, which could fashion particular orders to meet particular needs." Such local federal courts could work with an advisory committee of lawyers and other citizens in setting the desegregation schedules and could require the school districts to submit progress reports "at reasonable intervals."

The Court's basic problem in approaching the school cases, Elman believed, was how to rule for the Negro plaintiffs on the constitutional issue and yet withhold immediate relief, which many of the Justices feared would produce an epidemic of civil disobedience and perhaps a great deal of bloodshed. It was not a reading of the Court that Elman invented. A former clerk to Felix Frankfurter, Elman had remained on intimate terms with him. From that relationship, the Solicitor General's top civil-rights attorney derived useful insights into the disposition of the Court. Yet, remarks Elman, "when we filed our brief in early December, I went on the NAACP's shitlist as a gradualist. They just didn't know how to count the votes on the Court. Marshall and his team were lacking a sense of subtlety about the Justices' concerns. It had been a mistake to push for the overruling of segregation *per se* so long as Vinson was Chief Justice—it was too early. When Marshall and his staff felt I had betrayed them, they failed to grasp that our brief had been done the Frankfurter way, bearing in mind the key problem and how it vexed the Court."

That Chief Justice Vinson might prove an obstacle to the NAACP's hopes was suggested to Elman in part by a telephone call he received late in November from Clerk of the Court Willey. Attorney General McGranery had asked the Court for thirty minutes at the oral argument in which to present the government's position "in view of the serious constitutional issues involved and their obvious large national importance." But the Chief Justice, Willey advised Elman, "did not want any political speeches by McGranery" and had turned down the Attorney General's request. Elman's brief alone would have to speak for the United States government.

"When the day arrives," Justice Robert Jackson remarked in his 1951 address on advocacy before the United States Supreme Court, "shut out every influence that might distract your mind. . . . Friends who bear bad news may unintentionally disturb your poise. Hear nothing but your case, see nothing but your case, talk nothing but your case. If making an argument is not a great day in your life, don't make it; and if it is, give it everything in you."

Thurgood Marshall was taking no chances. He left for Washington ten days before the *Brown* arguments and turned his suite at the Statler into a combination of field office, campaign headquarters, and open-house fiesta. It was essential that he be as loose and fresh as possible during the three-day courtroom ordeal he was captaining. He had been in fifteen previous Supreme Court cases, either as chief counsel making the oral argument or with a decisive hand in fashioning the brief, and won thirteen times. But *Brown* was more important than all of the cases that had gone before it, and everyone in the NAACP organization knew it. Marshall's post-war pace had been ceaseless. "He's aged so in the past five years," his wife remarked earlier in 1952.* "His disposition's changed—he's nervous now where he used to be calm. This work is taking its toll of him. You know, it's a discouraging job he's set himself." Marshall's longtime friend and advisor William Hastie adds: "He drove himself to and beyond the limits of the human anatomy. He was at the point of exhaustion in trying to dispel the sense of defeatism that had inflicted itself on so much of black America."

Marshall's way of unwinding was not to drink buttermilk and get a lot of sleep. Nothing gave him more pleasure than presiding over a salon in his

---

* The aging process was no doubt spurred in February of 1952 when Marshall and Jack Greenberg were greeted by a Saturday-night torchlight parade of the Ku Klux Klan upon their arrival in Orlando, Florida, to defend a young black originally charged, along with three others, with beating up a white man, leaving him on the side of the road near the town of Groveland, and kidnapping and raping his wife. Marshall stayed at the home of a black resident and Greenberg at a white hotel, out of deference to local custom. Klan members circled Greenberg's hotel with trucks and torches throughout the night. Though the state never produced medical evidence that the white woman had in fact been raped, though corroborating identification of the defendant was lacking, though footprints found near the scene matching the defendant's were said to have been planted there, and though Marshall gave one of his finest courtroom performances, the all-white, all-male jury found the defendant guilty and doomed him to the electric chair. Marshall, stunned by the verdict, came out of court fighting back tears and promised the convicted man's mother, "Don't worry, darling, we're going to stick by you. We are going to keep on fighting." And he did. Twice the NAACP appealed the so-called "Groveland Case" to the Supreme Court, which declined to hear it. Eventually, the governor, LeRoy Collins, commuted the death sentence.

Washington hotel in the days before a Supreme Court argument. The flow of traffic, food, drink, and ideas was constant. "We'd rarely get any sleep," he recalls. "We'd fuss 'n' fight all night." But always, always he was sharpening his ideas, gaining confidence, working himself up emotionally. Before 1952, the NAACP legal crowd would bivouac at a colored hotel, and Marshall would reserve the biggest suite in the house with a dining room and kitchen. "It all seemed very luxurious," Jack Greenberg remembers, "but of course we piled in a lot of people." By 1952, though, the color line was beginning to crack in downtown Washington. The Hecht Company department store had started to serve Negroes in its restaurant, a number of theaters had ended their Jim Crow rules, and several of the major hotels were accepting black guests, though the enlightened innkeepers preferred to slot Negroes into rooms on the lower floors so they would not be conspicuous on the elevators. There was no way, however, to muffle the high spirits and continuous stirrings in Marshall's Statler suite as the best black lawyers in America prepared for the battle of their lives.

To bring themselves to a fine fighting edge, the NAACP attorneys traditionally went through a dry run of their oral arguments at Howard Law School, alma mater for so many of them, a night or two before the actual performance in the Court. Generally held in the biggest meeting hall in the building, the sessions were closed to the public, but every member of the law school, faculty and students alike, and any friendly lawyer in Washington, in or out of government, were invited to attend. "It was run just like a court, and there was no nonsense about it," says James Nabrit. The NAACP lawyer handling a case would present his argument, and then the half-dozen or so mock judges, selected from the Washington people on hand, would riddle the attorney with the toughest questions they could pose. Afterward, a long *post mortem* would be devoted to assessing the performances. "There was a kind of tenseness to it," says Nabrit, "for we all knew that these were questions that might have to be answered satisfactorily before the Justices themselves in the next day or two."

Marshall did not participate in the dry run before *Brown*. Instead he hovered like a father hen, warming and nourishing and nudging. And he never stopped asking questions, even if it made him look unschooled to outsiders. Philip Elman remembers, "He'd buttonhole us at those moot-court sessions at Howard or at his hotel room and ask us what questions we thought he was likely to get from the Court. Sometimes it was like pulling teeth to get the points across to him—all subtleties seemed to be lost on him. But then he'd get up in the Court and do a perfectly creditable job."

On the day of an argument, waiting to go on before the nine Justices, Marshall was generally very edgy and irritable—until his turn came.

The home of the Supreme Court of the United States is at once the most elegant and most preposterous building in Washington. Not that it is ugly to behold. It is surely stately and imposing. It bespeaks the dignity and majesty of the law. Designed as a monument to the seemingly congealed spirit of the Greek and Roman lawgivers from whom much of Anglo-American jurisprudence is derived, the Supreme Court building was put up in the middle of the Depression for a bit under $10 million—a steal at the price. A generation later, any decent regional suburban high school would cost nearly as much. It is longer than a football field on both its east-west and north-south axes, four stories high in most places—and nearly all marble, outside and in. This is how, with palpable pride, the official government pamphlet describes a small part of it:

> Marble steps, inside the entrance hall, lead to the main corridor. The walls are shadowed on either side by double rows of marble columns, which rise toward a richly colored coffered ceiling with rosettes—a harmonious crown for the monolithic shafts and polished stone. . . . Medallions decorating the frieze of this corridor include profiles of the Roman goddess Juno, the Greek god Zeus, and legislators Solon and Moses, alternating with various symbolic carvings, including armor, the helmet, the open book with torches, the scale and the lamp, the lion's head flanked by fasces, the owl, and the eagle.

There is nothing wrong with all this splendiferousness except that it is icily forbidding and largely alien to the spirit and mood of the United States of America. It seems more of a gigantic sarcophagus—a sort of Tomb for the Unknown Soldier of the Peloponnesian War—than the home of the keepers of the flame of the living Constitution. It is as if America wished to proclaim itself the reincarnation of Greece of the Golden Age or Rome at its imperial height—a status attained, as lives of nations are measured, virtually overnight.

Whatever their manifold virtues, it is worth recalling that both the Greeks and the Romans were highly stratified societies, as arrogant as they were enlightened, and highly partial to human slavery. Compassion was not a high Greco-Roman value. The great motto below the pediment on the front of the Supreme Court building—"Equal Justice Under Law"—has been carved into a setting that speaks of a civilization built upon sharp distinctions among mankind. The words, though, could scarcely have been more fitting to describe the business that drew the nation's attention to that monumental structure on December 9, 1952. The moment had come to determine whether that credo carved above its gates meant not what it seemed to say but something less fixed and noble, something more nuanced and nimble. Could "Equal Justice" truly be read to mean "Separate But Equal Justice"?

The courtroom itself is a great cubic sanctum of deeper hues and warmer materials than the rest of the building. The highest tribunal of the land measures ninety-one feet from its front doors, which are always open, to the back, eighty-two feet between side walls, and forty-four feet high. The chamber is edged by twenty-four stout columns of light-sienna marble imported from northern Italy. The walls are of an ivory-veined marble from Spain. The Justices' bench, the desks of the Court's clerk and marshal at either end (but at a lower level), the 160 or so seats for the public, and the chairs and tables within the space up front reserved for the press, members of the Supreme Court bar, and the rival counsel, are all in mahogany. The wine-red rug complements the rich, dark velour hangings behind the bench through which the Justices pass to take their places. Only the carved panels above the columns defy the muted atmosphere of the rest of the chamber. The east and west panels feature, among other favorites from someone's bloated notion of the mythicized past, the "Genii of Wisdom and Statecraft," a winged figure tagged "Divine Inspiration," and a cast of opposing contenders—"Corruption," "Deceit," "Slander," and "Despotic Power" versus "Charity," "Peace," "Harmony," and "Security." The north and south panels offer an all-time, all-star cast of great lawgivers, including Hammurabi, Solomon, Confucius, Mohammed, Augustus, Justinian, Charlemagne, King John (which seems like crediting Moses for parting the Red Sea), St. Louis, Blackstone, Napoleon, and John Marshall. Marshall is the only thing uniquely American about the room, except for the large flag in the corner.

For all its trappings and grandeur, the Supreme Court becomes an astonishingly intimate and informal arena once the minds and tongues of its members begin to function upon the clashing ideas offered up to them by the adversaries of the day. The Justices are nine men of varying personality, perception, and intellect, and the differences among them invigorate the arguments that too often turn into dreary oratory by lawyers either ill-prepared or under-equipped to argue their cases with winning conviction.

This day, though, no one was unprepared. Every seat in the Court was taken—about 300 all together, perhaps half of them occupied by Negroes. Four hundred more people lined the main corridor seeking admittance. The five cases to be argued came from one state in the Deep South, one state in the upper South, one border state, one Midwestern state, and one great metropolis which happened to include the site on which the Court itself stood. At stake was the question of what schools would be attended by more than 10 million white children and nearly 2.5 million black children in the segregating communities of the nation. Beyond that was the standing of all black Americans in their own eyes and in the eyes of their white countrymen. The rest of the world looked on as well.

Robert Carter went first. He argued in the name of Oliver Brown, the Topeka railroad welder and part-time minister, whose oldest daughter, Linda, was at the moment in fifth grade at the Monroe elementary school. The big clock on the wall behind the Justices read 1:35 p.m.

Carter did well enough at first. "It is the gravamen of our complaint," he asserted, that the appellants were being deprived of the equal protection of the laws "because the act of separation and the act of segregation in and of itself denies them equal educational opportunities which the Fourteenth Amendment secures." He added, "Here we abandon any claim . . . of any constitutional inequality which comes from anything other than the act of segregation itself." That act, he said in summarizing the testimony in the trial court, "tended to relegate appellants and their group to an inferior caste . . . lowered their level of aspiration . . . instilled feelings of insecurity . . . retarded their mental and educational development." No state had the authority to use race as a factor in determining how it would offer public education to its citizens. "It is our position that any legislative or governmental classification must fall with an even hand on all persons similarly situated."

Justice Minton had a question, an innocuous one. Was the finding in the court below that the only basis of classification in the case was race or color? The Topeka school officials conceded as much, said Carter, who then moved ahead to note that the Kansas statute at issue used the word "discrimination" to describe the practice it approved. The District Court had found as a fact that public-school segregation had "a detrimental effect upon the colored children" and that the impact of that effect was all the greater because it was sanctioned by law. It was precisely this sort of disadvantage, Carter stressed, that the Justices had confronted in *Sweatt* and *McLaurin* and struck down. If they had done so in those cases, it was difficult to see how they could logically decline to extend that principle to segregated public schools.

So far, so good. And then it was lunchtime. No matter who was saying what at any juncture of his presentation, the Court in those days always adjourned at 2 p.m. for lunch. It convened at noon, recessed at 2:00, reconvened at 2:30, adjourned at 4:30. Four hours of intense engagement was enough for any one day.

Soon after lunch, Carter sailed into a storm. Justice Reed asked an easy question—was there any evidence to suggest a lesser learning ability of the children in the segregated schools? Carter met it by saying that the findings of the court were that the learning ability of the segregated youngsters was impaired by segregation itself. Justice Burton followed with a creampuff: "Is it your position that there is a great deal more to the educational process, even in the elementary school, than what you read in the books?" Said Carter: "Yes, sir, that is precisely the point." Chief Justice Vinson wanted to clear up a few points on the degree of equality between the white and colored schools of Topeka as determined by the District Court. Physical equality was not really at issue, Carter replied, but the court below had decided as if only that ground could be applied in determining what was or wasn't equal protection. The Kansas court had said explicitly that it felt constrained to rule as it did because in *Sweatt* and *McLaurin* the Justices had chosen not to reach the question of whether *Plessy* and *Gong Lum* still governed. "It is our position that *Plessy v. Ferguson* is not in point here," declared Carter, "that it had nothing to do with educational opportunities whatsoever." Nor was *Gong Lum* governing, since the petitioner there had not contested the state's power to enforce racial classification in its schools—a question never squarely presented to the Court before now. That was too much for Felix Frankfurter, who pounced upon the NAACP lawyer:

> Mr. Carter, while what you say may be so, nevertheless . . . the Court, in *Gong Lum*, did rest on the fact that this issue had been settled by a large body of adjudications going back to what was or might fairly have been called an abolitionist state, the Commonwealth of Massachusetts. . . .

The reference was to *Roberts v. City of Boston*, on which *Plessy* and, through it, *Gong Lum* were in substantial measure based. Did Carter really think that a Court like the one that had unanimously decided *Gong Lum*—including,

Frankfurter noted, such civil-libertarians as Justices Holmes, Brandeis, and Stone—would let its decision rest on an implied concession by the petitioners that the legality of segregation itself was not involved? Didn't the lawfulness of segregation really underlie the whole *Gong Lum* decision?

Frankfurter's explosive question sent Carter reeling. In effect, the Justice was asking the lawyer if he was really contending that *Gong Lum* did not mean what it plainly said. Implied in the question was rejection of the NAACP's wishful reading of the pivotal opinion. Carter scrambled for cover. The words poured out of him in random order while he seemed to grope for a coherent reply. Without saying it in so many words, he tried to suggest that the Court in *Gong Lum*, including the eminences Frankfurter cited, had dodged the question even as it approved the school board's right to classify the Chinese-American child as colored. The only further question the Justices had hinted that they would have entertained in that case, said Carter, was whether the colored school to which Miss Lum had been assigned was equal to the white one where she was denied admission. But that question had not arisen in the litigation. Frankfurter was not to be put off, though.

> JUSTICE FRANKFURTER: Yes. But the Court took as settled by a long course of decisions that this question was many times decided that this power was within the constitutional power of the state legislatures—this power of segregation.
> CARTER: Yes, sir.
> JUSTICE FRANKFURTER: The more specific question I would like to put to you is this. Do we not have to face the fact that what you are challenging is something that was written into the public law and adjudications of courts, including this Court, by a large body of decisions and, therefore, the question arises whether, and under what circumstances, this Court should now upset so long a course of decisions? Don't we have to face that . . . and is anything to be gained by concealing that central fact, that central issue?
> CARTER: Well, I do not think, your honor, that you have to face that issue. . . . [T]his Court in the *Sweatt* case, it seems to me very carefully to have decided that it did not have to face the question because *Plessy v. Ferguson* was not involved. . . .
> JUSTICE FRANKFURTER: . . . But a long course of legislation by the states, and a long course of utterances by this Court and other courts in dealing with the subject, from the point of view of relevance as to whether a thing is or is not within the prohibition of the Fourteenth Amendment, is from my point of view almost as impressive as a single decision. . . . I do think we have to face in this case the fact that we are dealing with a long-established historical practice by the states. . . .

Before so declarative a view, Carter saw no recourse but to retreat. He conceded that he had been attempting to take "the narrow position with regard to this case and to approach it in a way that I thought the Court approached the decision in *Sweatt* and *McLaurin*." But if the Court did not favor that approach now, said Carter, "I have no hesitancy in saying that the issue of 'separate but equal' should be faced . . . and should squarely be overruled." Having ventured that far, Carter promptly returned to his earlier tack. The Court did not really have to overrule the separate-but-equal doctrine at the elementary-school level because it had never decided that it applied at that level. Frankfurter could not swallow that.

> JUSTICE FRANKFURTER:  Are you saying that we can say that "separate but equal" is not a doctrine that is relevant at the primary school level? Is that what you are saying?
> JUSTICE DOUGLAS:  I think you are saying that segregation may be all right in street cars and railroad cars and restaurants, but that is all we have decided.
> CARTER:  That is the only place that you have decided that it is all right.
> JUSTICE DOUGLAS:  And that education is different, education is different from that.
> CARTER:  Yes, sir.
> JUSTICE DOUGLAS:  That is your argument, is it not? Isn't that your argument in this case?
> CARTER:  Yes.

Plainly, Douglas was trying to be helpful, but it was a leaky preserver he tossed overboard to Carter, who grabbed at it. Frankfurter persisted: "But how can that be your argument when the whole basis of dealing with education thus far [in this Court] has been to find out whether it—the 'separate but equal' doctrine—is satisfied?" The Court had not really applied that test in *McLaurin*, said Carter, for there was no separation there. But that was playing with words, for if McLaurin had not, in a manner of speaking, been separated from his white schoolmates in classes, the library, and the cafeteria, no legal action would have been brought. The separation was a matter of degree, and in each of the school cases beginning with *Gaines*, said Frankfurter, the Court had measured to see if equality prevailed under conditions of separation. Having delivered himself of his own deep concerns in the case in front of him, Frankfurter then desisted long enough to let Carter try to put the pieces back together. Slowly, the lawyer worked his way back to the basic NAACP position: *McLaurin* was a very different story from *Gaines*, for in *McLaurin* the Court had found that the manner of the black man's separation from his schoolmates impaired his ability to learn.

Off the ropes now, Carter sparred a bit with Justice Reed, who wanted some clarification of *Gaines*. In another moment, though, Felix Frankfurter was back to throttling Carter's mind. The little Justice's questions were often the most probing and revealing of any put by the bench—a tribute to both his intellect and his training as a Harvard law professor who had greatly savored the give-and-take with a classroom of alert young minds. As an interrogator for the Court, he could be remorseless, to the discomfiture of even the ablest counsel. In his searching inquiries during oral arguments rather than in his written opinions, which sometimes reflected as much self-torture as enlightenment, Frankfurter may have made his most valuable contribution to the Court. And in his unwillingness to let a limp answer get by, he demonstrated the purpose and virtue of the oral argument. Reading Carter's contentions in a brief, Frankfurter might merely have pronounced them humbug and turned the page; in Court, out loud, Carter could try to answer the Justice's objections. Now Frankfurter had another blockbuster for the black attorney—a more philosophical one:

. . . Now, unless you say that this [segregation] legislation merely represents man's inhumanity to man, what is the root of this legislation? What is it based on? Why was there such legislation and was there any consideration that the states were warranted in dealing with—maybe not this way—but was there anything in life to which this legislation responds?

Translated from convoluted Frankfurterese, the question meant: was there any legitimate basis for these segregation laws? But his manner of putting the question—i.e., was it *merely* man's inhumanity to man?—fogged his apparent intent, and Carter did not take the lead offered to him. He said that race was the only basis for the law in Kansas and went off on an historical tangent, helped by the Chief Justice, who put in a few quick factual questions on dates. Finally, Carter circled back and, in words that still sounded a bit shell-shocked, neared the point of Frankfurter's question:

. . . [O]ur feeling on the reach of equal protection, the equal protection clause, is that as these appellants, as members of a minority group, whatever the majority may feel that they can do with their rights for whatever purpose, that the equal protection clause was intended to protect them against the whims, as they come and go.

Frankfurter brightened at that none too robust reply. How could the Court establish that this was the intention of the equal-protection clause? He was plainly leading Carter now. The Court had repeatedly held that to be the purpose of the clause, said Carter. There was *Shelley v. Kraemer*, for example. Frankfurter jumped in at once so the point would not be lost: "Impliedly it prohibited the doctrine of classification, I take it?" The Court had done that time and time again, said Carter, and in many cases that had nothing at all to do with Negroes; he cited a decision in which the Court had denied the right of a state to treat a foreign corporation as unequal to a domestic corporation. "Meaning by that," asked Frankfurter to clinch it, "that there was no rational basis for the classification?" Carter said that was what he meant. Then he reserved the rest of his time for rebuttal.

Paul Wilson climbed to his feet for the first time before the Supreme Court and proceeded to deliver a perfectly able, if somewhat simplistic argument for the state of Kansas as he followed closely the arguments he had made in his brief.

He quickly sketched in the history of the school-segregation statute, stressed that it was permissive only and not mandatory, and that in fact it affected only twenty schools in the entire state at that moment. It was "sheer sophistry" to suggest that *Plessy* and *Gong Lum* did not apply now to *Brown*, he went on, and if the Court chose to overturn segregation, it would be saying that twenty-one states, Congress, and many courts in the land had been wrong for the past seventy-five years. But Justice Burton thought that far too pat. He asked: "Don't you recognize it as possible that within seventy-five years the social and economic conditions and the personal relations of the nation may have changed so that what may have been a valid interpretation of them seventy-five years ago would not be a valid interpretation of them constitutionally today?"

WILSON:   We recognize that as a possibility. We do not believe that this record discloses any such change.

JUSTICE BURTON:   But that might be a difference between saying that these courts of appeals and state supreme courts have been wrong for seventy-five years.

WILSON:   Yes, sir.

The Kansas lawyer then addressed himself to the most vulnerable part of his defense—the finding of fact by the District Court that segregation was detrimental to Negro schoolchildren. This "psychological reaction," he said, was something apart from "the objective components of the school system— and something that the state does not have within its power to confer upon the pupils." Nor did the court's finding apply "to these specific appellants," who had to show that they had been deprived of some benefit conferred on the rest of the population or subjected "to some detriment that the rest of the population does not suffer" before they had any genuine claim to relief.

Having consumed no more than half of his allotted time but delivered himself of all he had to say, Wilson sat down.

What had made his argument against the finding of fact ironic was that only in Kansas, of the four state school-segregation cases that had been argued, did the NAACP fail to dispatch a Kenneth Clark or a Frederic Wertham to examine local Negro schoolchildren and testify on how segregation affected them. Yet Topeka was a city teeming with psychologists and psychiatrists.

In rebuttal, Carter asserted that the Kansas court's finding of fact made necessary a reversal of its decision—a position the United States *amicus* brief had also taken. But suddenly Carter found himself in trouble with the bench again, this time from an unexpected source. Justice Hugo Black was puzzled by Carter's contention that the finding of fact was a solid reason for the Supreme Court to reverse, for what would the lawyer say if the court below had made a contrary finding? Was he implying that segregation might be legal in some places and not in others, depending upon the findings of the nearest federal court? Carter had put himself in the bind by trying to counter Wilson's argument, and now he had to back-pedal furiously to avoid Black's thrust. "Now, of course, under our theory, you do not have to reach the finding of fact or a fact at all in reaching the decision," Carter said, "because of the fact that we maintain that this is an unconstitutional classification based upon race and, therefore, it is arbitrary."

At 3:15, Bob Carter sat down. It had not been easy. To play by the NAACP strategy book, he had stuck to the *Plessy*-doesn't-matter argument until he was nearly destroyed by it. It was rather as if Carter had gone out on patrol for the rest of the black lawyers, got shot at from all sides, and managed to get back to the trenches alive with some valuable information. For what the probes from the bench—and especially by Frankfurter— seemed to suggest was that the Justices were fully aware that the past decisions of the Court directly or indirectly upholding *Plessy* were at sharp odds with its line of decisions outlawing race as a reasonable basis for a state to classify its citizens.

It was a point that did not escape Thurgood Marshall as he moved to the lectern next to argue *Briggs*.

In some of his appearances before the Court, he was good; in others, he tended to be a bit on the dull side. On this day, he was at his best. He took the offensive from the start and he held it throughout the argument.

The lawyers on the other side, Marshall noted wryly, did not seem to think much of the expert witnesses the plaintiffs had produced. Nor, it seemed, had the District Court in Charleston thought too much of them, for its decision ignored their testimony almost completely—testimony that stood uncontradicted. But both his adversaries and the court below were in grave error, for what the entire body of social-science evidence, starting with Robert Redfield's testimony in *Sweatt* (and read into the record in *Briggs*), had demonstrated was that there was no real difference in the learning potential of white and Negro children—and without a contrary showing by the state of South Carolina, its law classifying school youngsters by race was without a basis in reason or in law. Not only had the state failed to give a good reason for its racial-classification law; its adoption had also proven exceedingly harmful to the colored children who had been segregated without legitimate cause.

As to Judge Parker's decision holding that school segregation was properly a matter of legislative policy for each state to decide for itself, Marshall asserted that this view ran directly counter to many opinions of the Court and most emphatically against the intentions of the framers of the Fourteenth Amendment, which had been passed precisely to protect the rights of Negroes from usurpation by the states. It was not sufficient to say that the majority of people in South Carolina, as spoken for by their legislature, approved the practice of segregation and therefore it was legal and proper. As far back as 1823, said Marshall, the Court had struck down a South Carolina law under which free Negro sailors who came to Charleston could be detained in jail so long as their ship was in port—a practice countenanced in the name of public safety and necessity. Said the Court's opinion:

> . . . But to all this the plea of necessity is urged; and of the existence of that necessity we are told the state alone is to judge. Where is this to land us? Is it not asserting the right in each state to throw off the federal constitution at its will and pleasure? If it can be done as to any particular article it may be done as to all; and, like the old confederation, the Union becomes a mere rope of sand.

And that was a decision nearly half a century before the adoption of the Fourteenth Amendment. In the intervening years, the Civil War had been fought to re-establish federal supremacy over willful claims by any state to run its affairs as it saw fit, regardless of the federally guaranteed rights of minorities.

Now if the Justices found that extension of the principle laid down in their *Sweatt* and *McLaurin* decisions—namely, that intangible factors such as reduced career prospects and intramural restrictions upon their movements denied Negro students equal educational opportunities—was too narrow a ground for overturning segregation, there was another very substantial body of law that would serve the purpose. Among other examples of it, he cited Justice Holmes's 1927 opinion in *Nixon v. Herndon*, the first of the Texas white-primary cases, which noted: "States may do a good deal of classifying that it is difficult to believe rational, but there are limits, and it is too clear for extended argument that color cannot be made the basis of a statutory classification affecting the right set up in this case." The Court, Marshall declared, "has repeatedly said that these distinctions on a racial basis or on a basis of ancestry are odious and invidious, and those decisions, I think, are entitled to just as much weight as *Plessy v. Ferguson* or *Gong Lum v. Rice.*"

When Chief Justice Vinson and Justice Frankfurter put questions to him on the relevance of *Plessy* and its antebellum antecedent *Roberts v. City of Boston*, Marshall stayed on the offensive:

> . . . I can not conceive of the Roberts case being good for anything except that the legislatures of the states at those times were trying to work out their problems as they best could understand. And it could be that up in Massachusetts at that time they thought that Negroes—some of them were escaping from slavery and all—but I still say that the considerations for the passage of any legislation before the Civil War and up to 1900, certainly, could not apply at the present time. I think that every race has made progress, but I do not believe that those considerations have any bearing at this time. . . .

There then followed this exchange, with Marshall at his rough-hewn best:

> JUSTICE FRANKFURTER: Do you really think it helps us not to recognize that behind this are certain facts of life, and the question is whether a legislature can address itself to those facts of life in despite of or within the Fourteenth Amendment, or whether, whatever the facts of life might be, where there is a vast congregation of Negro population as against the states where there is not, whether that is an irrelevant consideration? Can you escape facing those sociological facts, Mr. Marshall?
>
> MARSHALL: No, I cannot escape it. But if I did fail to escape it, I would have to throw completely aside the personal and present rights of those individuals.
>
> JUSTICE FRANKFURTER: No, you would not. It does not follow because you cannot make certain classifications, you cannot make some [other] classifications.
>
> MARSHALL: . . . [S]o far as the appellants in this case are concerned, I cannot consider it sufficient to be relegated to the legislature of South Carolina, where the record . . . shows their consideration of Negroes. . . . I think that when an attack is made on a statute on the ground that it is an unreasonable classification, and competent, recognized testimony is produced, I think then that the least that the state has to do is to produce something to defend their statutes.
>
> JUSTICE FRANKFURTER: I follow you when you talk that way.

A few moments later, Marshall stressed that he was not asking the Court to command the admission of the plaintiffs to any specific school or for the Justices otherwise to mix into the everyday workings of the local communities. "The only thing that we ask for is that the state-imposed racial segregation be taken off, and to leave the county school board, the county people, the district people, to work out their own solution of the problem to assign children on any reasonable basis they want to assign them on." Frankfurter indicated he thought that might lead to gerrymandering and, in so saying, revealed one of the gravest problems troubling him about the case: "I think that nothing would be worse than for this Court—I am expressing my own opinion—nothing would be worse, from my point of view, than for this Court to make an abstract declaration that segregation is bad and then have it evaded by tricks." Marshall suggested that gerrymandered school districts would be readily apparent to any court and outlawed; the main thing, first of all, was to have the principle of racial classification struck down and then to give the local districts time to proceed in good faith—"it might take six months to do it one place and two months to do it another place."

At the close, Justice Jackson asked Marshall if his argument about the reach of the Fourteenth Amendment would not apply to Indians as well as Negroes.

> MARSHALL: I think it would. But I think that the biggest trouble with the Indians is that they just have not had the judgment or the wherewithal to bring lawsuits.
> JUSTICE JACKSON: Maybe you should bring some up.
> MARSHALL: I have a full load now, Mr. Justice.

John W. Davis succeeded him at the lectern. The Justices, Davis's colleagues like to remember, leaned forward in their places, eagerly attentive.

He was as good as his precepts. He was clear. He was direct. He was cutting. His sentences had beginnings, middles, and endings. And there was a Victorian elegance to his language that added authority to his every assertion.

He had three points to make, he said, basically adhering to his brief. First, South Carolina had complied with the mandate of the court below and equalized its schools or was well on the way to doing so. Second, the right of a state to classify its public-school pupils by race was "not impaired or affected" by the Fourteenth Amendment. Third, the social-science testimony offered by the plaintiffs, "be its merit what it may, deals entirely with legislative policy, and does not tread on constitutional right. Whether it does or not, it would be difficult for me to conceal my opinion that that evidence in and of itself is of slight weight and in conflict with the opinion of other and better informed sources."

Though the Court made a practice of peppering the advocates before it with questions—Justice Frankfurter spoke fifty-three times, for example, during Thurgood Marshall's argument immediately preceding—John Davis was interrupted only twice during his remarks. The first time it was by Justice Burton, who asked the same question he had put to Paul Wilson earlier:

> What is your answer, Mr. Davis, to the suggestion . . . that at that time [of the adoption of the Fourteenth Amendment] the conditions and relations between the two races were such that what might have been unconstitutional then would not be unconstitutional now?

DAVIS:   My answer to that is that changed conditions may affect policy, but changed conditions cannot broaden the terminology of the Constitution. The thought is an administrative or a political one, and not a judicial one.

JUSTICE BURTON:   But the Constitution is a living document that must be interpreted in relation to the facts of the time in which it is interpreted. Did we not go through with that in connection with child labor cases, and so forth?

DAVIS:   Oh, well, of course, changed conditions may bring things within the scope of the Constitution which were not originally contemplated, and of that perhaps the aptest illustration is the interstate commerce clause. Many things have been found to be interstate commerce which at the time of the writing of the Constitution were not contemplated at all. . . . But when they come within the field of interstate commerce, then they become subject to congressional power, which is defined in the terms of the Constitution itself. So circumstances may bring new facts within the purview of the constitutional provision, but they do not alter, expand, or change the language that the framers of the Constitution have employed.

That brought Felix Frankfurter out of his respectful and unaccustomed silence:

Mr. Davis, do you think that "equal" is a less fluid term than "commerce between the states"?

DAVIS:   Less fluid?

JUSTICE FRANKFURTER:   Yes.

DAVIS:   I have not compared the two on the point of fluidity.

JUSTICE FRANKFURTER:   Suppose you do it now.

DAVIS:   I am not sure that I can approach it in just that sense.

JUSTICE FRANKFURTER:   The problem behind my question is whatever the phrasing of it would be.

DAVIS:   That what is unequal today may be equal tomorrow, or vice versa?

JUSTICE FRANKFURTER:   That is it.

DAVIS:   That might be. I should not philosophize about it. But the effort in which I am now engaged is to show how those who submitted this amendment and those who adopted it conceded it to be, and what their conduct by way of interpretation has been since its ratification in 1868.

JUSTICE FRANKFURTER:   What you are saying is that, as a matter of history, history puts a gloss on "equal" which does not permit elimination or admixture of white and colored in this aspect to be introduced?

DAVIS:   Yes, I am saying that.

In ticking off the precedents that he said supported his position, Davis began with *Plessy*, added *Cumming, Berea College*, and *Gong Lum*, and then reached out to undercut Marshall's position by claiming *Gaines, Sipuel, Sweatt*, and *McLaurin*, all four of which he said were, in granting Negroes relief, "decided solely on the basis of inequality" under the separate-but-equal concept.

For the NAACP's social scientists, the old gladiator reserved his most lethal thrusts. It seemed to him, said Davis, that "much of that which is handed around under the name of social science is an effort on the part of the scientist to rationalize his own preconceptions. They find usually, in my limited observation, what they go out to find." He mocked Kenneth Clark's doll test on sixteen children in Clarendon County as "that intensive investigation," the results of which "we are invited to accept as a scientific conclusion," and then cited the seemingly conflicting data in the textbook chapter the Clarks had written. He went on to say, as he did in the South Carolina brief, that many learned authorities approved of segregation, but the only one he cited by name was Du Bois, whom he called "perhaps the most constant and vocal opponent of Negro oppression of any of his race in the country." To invoke Du Bois's words in support of mandatory school segregation—words from an article in which Du Bois explicitly disclaimed that he had any such intention—was an act of intellectual fraudulence beyond any advocate's permissible range of selective citation. But no one called Davis on it.

He closed, well before his hour was up, on a note of winged oratory:

> . . . Is it not a fact that the very strength and fiber of our federal system is local self-government in those matters for which local action is competent? Is it not, of all the activities of government, the one which most nearly approaches the hearts and minds of people—the question of the education of their young?
>
> Is it not the height of wisdom that the manner in which that shall be conducted should be left to those most immediately affected by it, and that the wishes of the parents, both white and colored, should be ascertained before their children are forced into what may be an unwelcome contact?
>
> I respectfully submit to the Court, there is no reason assigned here why this Court or any other should reverse the findings of 90 years.

For all his forensic virtuosity, Davis had left untouched Marshall's main point, and in rebuttal now the NAACP lawyer came on powerfully to stress the omission. The most significant factor running through all these arguments, he said, "is that for some reason, which is still unexplained, Negroes are taken out of the mainstream of American life in these states. There is nothing involved in this case other than race and color, and I do not need to go to the background of the statutes or anything else. I just read the statutes, and they say 'white' and 'colored.' " Under the Constitution, the individual rights of minority members may not be relegated to the mercies of the majority, even one exercising its most mature judgment, said Marshall. In *Sweatt*, the state of Texas had produced a public-opinion poll showing that most of the people wanted to maintain segregation, yet the Court ruled in effect that such a preference trampled on the rights of the Negro plaintiff.

Marshall failed to point out how vulnerable Davis was in his selection of authorities to support his claim that segregation was a socially desirable policy where it existed. He let the Du Bois distortion stand uncorrected. But he asked why the state had not produced its own expert witnesses in the District Court. Frankfurter wondered why that should have been necessary, since he and his judicial brethren were perfectly capable of reading Myrdal or any other cited work on their own without the author's appearance and testimony in court. Marshall replied, "But I think when you take judicial notice of Gunnar Myrdal's book, we have to read the matter, and not take portions out of context. Gunnar Myrdal's whole book is against the argument [for segregation]." Then he added:

... it seems to me that in a case like this that the only way that South Carolina, under the test set forth in this case, can sustain that statute is to show that Negroes as Negroes—all Negroes—are different from everybody else.

JUSTICE FRANKFURTER: Do you think it would make any difference to our problem if this record also contained the testimony of six professors from other institutions who gave contrary or qualifying testimony [*i.e.,* different from your professors' testimony]? Do you think we would [have] a different situation?

MARSHALL: You would, sir, but I do not believe that there are any experts in the country who would so testify. . . . I know of no scientist that has made any study, whether he be anthropologist or sociologist, who does not admit that segregation harms the child.

He amiably countered Justice Reed's supposition that the school-segregation statutes might have been passed to avoid racial friction. Did not a state legislature have to weigh the disadvantages to the segregated group, Reed wanted to know, against "the advantage of the maintenance of law and order"? Yes, Marshall said, but it was worth noting who did the weighing: there was no Negro legislator now serving in any of these segregating states. And what might have been prudent law in 1895 was not necessarily such today "because people have grown up and understand each other" and were living and working together and fighting wars together now. The real arbiter of balancing the individual rights of minority-group members against the majority's repressive claims in the name of law and order, he said, was not the legislature of any state but the Constitution of the United States as interpreted by the nine men he now addressed.

Spottswood Robinson, the finest legal technician Howard Law School had ever produced, delivered an able but rather listless and somewhat obscure argument that sought to narrow the ground of the Virginia case to such a degree that it would have avoided the main issue altogether.

He belabored the details of the case, dwelling on the inequalities and arguing for relief under what he acknowledged to be the *Gaines* formula: since what the white school officials had provided for the Negro children at Moton High fell short of equality, the colored plaintiffs were entitled to prompt admission to the white schools—and the officials should thereafter be forbidden to assign children to schools on the basis of race. It was not a very well-organized presentation, and it seemed almost submissive in contrast to the triple-fisted vigor of his opponent, the redoubtable Justin Moore of Richmond.

Moore's brief contained several instances of the same sort of overkill he had exhibited in the District Court trial. The Prince Edward County school board, he wrote in his formal presentation to the Justices, had planned a bond issue to finance the new Negro high school in Farmville: "This program was pushed along as rapidly as possible. . . . The Negro pupils, however, blocked this attempt at financing by a two-week strike, which their principal testified he was unable to control." This statement was a manifest distortion of the events. No bond issue had ever been formally decided upon or announced by the school board; its failure to schedule one was, indeed, one of the reasons for the student strike. Moore, moreover, in reviewing the testimony of the social scientists, implied that Kenneth Clark's remarks in court showed him to be an unstable zealot: "His experiences at Howard so warped his judgment that, because of segregation alone, his entire career was changed." Such a statement bore almost no true relationship to Clark's courtroom testimony, which had come in response to Moore's standard tactic of trying to show that the NAACP witnesses had spent little or no time in the South and therefore were ill-equipped to comment authoritatively on its customs.

Before the Court, Moore gratuitously added to his distortion of the events in Prince Edward. "The record indicates—and the matter was argued in the District Court—that the strike was really inspired by outsiders," said Moore. No such evidence existed in the record or anywhere else. As to the money to finance the new high school, said Moore, that had been obtained firmly in June of 1951, right after the end of the strike. "You see," he told Chief Justice Vinson, "they [the school-board members] were on the program of the bond issue when the strike created such a public sentiment that it was felt that they could not carry that through." That was another demonstrable misstatement of the events. The money for the new Negro high school was made available by the state only after the strike and as a transparent device to head off or at least undercut the desegregation suit.

His splenetic excesses aside, Moore delivered a commendably vigorous argument. The record created by Virginia's long string of expert witnesses and the opinion of the District Court gave him a lot to work with, and Moore proceeded boldly. There had been no finding by the Virginia court that segregation harmed Negro children. The basis for the segregation law was found to be not in caprice or prejudice but in the history and mores of the people of Virginia. He swung out, as Davis had not bothered to, at the NAACP contention that many Supreme Court decisions had struck down racial classifications and restrictions and that school segregation should similarly be ended. Such cases as *Strauder, Nixon v. Herndon, Smith v. Allwright,* and *Shelley,* said Moore, were easily distinguishable from the segregation cases because the former all involved the complete denial to the Negro of his claimed rights; no such denial existed under a genuinely separate-but-equal school system, the likes of which Virginia had been conscientiously building in recent years. He scorned the NAACP's expert witnesses and praised his own, denounced the social-science appendix which the NAACP had submitted with its brief as merely "a means to rehabilitate" its expert witnesses, and encouraged Justice Reed's suggestion that the Virginia legislature might well have been seeking merely to promote the greatest good for the greatest number when it established racially separate schools.

Moore dug in his heels when Jackson pursued him with questions that seemed to disclose the Justice's grave doubts on the limits of judicial power in such dangerous terrain as segregation. Suppose Congress were to pass an anti-segregation law under the enforcement section of the Fourteenth Amendment—would that not be a proper way to proceed constitutionally?

No, said Moore, that would not be valid; only a constitutional amendment would serve. For it was plain that the Fourteenth Amendment had not been intended to cover such purely local matters as schools, which were solely the business of the states and their legislatures, and no mere act of Congress could add this area to federal supervision.

In rebuttal, Spottswood Robinson did far better than he had earlier. He genteelly suggested that the true basis for the Virginia segregation laws was not at all what Moore had indicated in his colloquy with Justice Reed. Historical examination discloses, he said, that "the segregation laws themselves were intended to—and have, in fact, in Virginia accomplished—were intended to limit the educational opportunities of the Negro and place him in a position where he could not obtain . . . opportunities and benefits from the public educational program equal to those which flowed to white students." He cited the remarks of Carter Glass, a leader of the 1901–02 Virginia constitutional convention, who bluntly admitted that the purpose of the new laws was to discriminate against and remove power from the Negro. And the current statistics showed—despite his adversaries' claims to the contrary— that Virginia was still discriminating against Negro schoolchildren; for every dollar per white child it currently had invested in school buildings and sites, for example, it had invested only sixty-one cents per Negro child.

Robinson displayed his impressive command of legal history and scholarship in exploring with Justice Jackson why he thought, contrary to Justin Moore's view, the Court was fully empowered to outlaw public-school segregation without an enforcement act of Congress or the need to adopt a new constitutional amendment. For the Constitution itself was law, and any amendments to it were also, and thus legal scholars applied the term "self-executing" to describe the use of direct constitutional authority by the judiciary in cases where Congress had not further legislated to enforce prohibitions or rights originating under the fundamental law of the land. In many cases, the Court had assumed the self-executing nature of various sections of the Constitution. Perhaps most prominently, the Court had greatly expanded—without specific supplementary legislation by Congress— the reach of the Fourteenth Amendment in the last quarter of the nineteenth century to bring corporations under the shield of the due-process clause and thereby hastened nationwide industrial expansion. When state regulatory commissions set railroad shipping rates that struck the Justices as too low, they were not dependent upon acts of Congress as the basis for judicial intervention; instead, they held that the railroads had been unduly deprived of property under the self-executing due-process provisions of the Fourteenth Amendment. Similarly, the Court was fully capable of reviewing cases said to arise under the equal-protection clause of the amendment. To Justice Douglas's question of whether the Court had ever held that the Fourteenth Amendment was not executed unless Congress had first acted, Robinson said, "No, I do not think so."

Historical considerations consumed much of the oral argument in the District of Columbia case. The principal question was the motives of the

Congressmen who passed the laws that seemed to invite continuation of Jim Crow schools.

The fight led by Gardner Bishop, the U Street barber, was brought to its climax before the Supreme Court by James Nabrit, who shared the oral argument with a colleague of long standing, fifty-eight-year-old black Washington attorney George Edward Chalmers Hayes. A native of Richmond but a Washington resident since he was four, Hayes was a Brown University alumnus who had taken his law degree at Howard in 1918 and taught at the Negro law school steadily since 1924 while enjoying a successful private practice. General counsel of Howard University, he had served a term on the District's Board of Education but was not reappointed in 1949 because his views on segregated schools and related racial questions were considered abrasive. He had been involved in his share of civil-rights litigation, including cases fighting Jim Crow theaters and restaurants in the capital.

A man of powerful voice and large, riveting eyes with wrathful-looking brows, Hayes led off the argument in *Bolling v. Sharpe* by reciting the bold strategy that Nabrit and he had settled on from the outset. They had been aided by other Howard law professors who in effect had turned the case into a massive extracurricular faculty project outside the supervision of Thurgood Marshall's office. Congress had certainly been mindful of the practice of school segregation in the District, said Hayes, but close reading of its enactments showed that the lawmakers had never made it mandatory. The practice itself was left to the discretion of District of Columbia officials, who were violating the due-process provisions of the Fifth Amendment by denying Negro children the liberty to attend unsegregated schools. Echoing Robinson's charge in the Prince Edward case, Hayes declared that the purpose behind segregation was "pure racism" and that "it could have no other conceivable purpose." That troubled Chief Justice Vinson. Could that charge really be levied against the federal lawmakers who first countenanced school segregation in the District? Their ranks were composed of many of the men who had framed the Civil War amendments, which served principally to protect the interests of the freed Negroes. What was done by Congress, Hayes answered, "was a matter of politics . . . it was done as an expedient." The people in the District, he was suggesting, had been permitted their racial preferences in the interests of town-and-crown amity.

Under the rules of Supreme Court practice that permit the oral argument of either side to be divided between two lawyers, Nabrit took over the second part of the hour to press the point that the Civil War amendments "have removed from the federal government any power to impose racial distinctions in dealing with its citizens." Surer on his feet than any of the other Negro attorneys except Marshall and a good deal more precise in his language than the Legal Defense Fund chief, Nabrit was crisp and direct. The individual liberties of citizens had never been entrusted to the hands of legislators, he asserted, citing the Bill of Rights as towering evidence, and when Congress or the states threatened those liberties on whatever pretext, it was up to the Supreme Court to scrutinize such acts with the utmost suspicion. As an example, he pointed to the so-called Japanese-exclusion cases during the Second World War; the Court had permitted the removal of Japanese-Americans from West Coast military areas as a regrettable but forgivable deprivation of liberty because of the war emergency, but it denied to the government power to confine indefinitely those same citizens so long as their loyalty was not demonstrably in doubt. Declared Nabrit:

> . . . [W]e ask nothing different than that we be given the same type of protection in peace that these Japanese [-Americans] were given in time of war. . . . We are simply saying that liberty to us is just as precious, and that the same way in which the Court measures out liberty to others, it measures to us, and Congress itself has nothing to do with it. . . . I assert that there is absolutely no basis that can be produced that would be accepted in our country in 1952 that would justify Congress making such a racial basis for the exclusion of a student from a high school in the District of Columbia.

The case for retaining Jim Crow schools in the capital was argued with great energy if not much finesse by a forty-six-year-old career man in the Corporation Counsel's office. Beefy, good-natured Milton Korman, an ex-football player at Central High and George Washington University in the District, had joined the District's legal department in 1937 and specialized in handling the school board's problems. Civil-rights activists found him excessively zealous in the defense of Jim Crow, but Korman, a civic-minded man with a special fondness for showing up at fires in running coat, boots, and helmet to lend a hand to the District's professional fire-fighters, insisted he was simply doing his job the way any good lawyer would. The school-segregation question, he reflects from the perspective of twenty years, "was a legal issue—not a sociological one. We had a mandate from Congress to run separate schools—we didn't have a choice. Separate public schools had been established in the District before the Civil War ended and the amendments had been put through. These were slaves who had just been freed and come in off the fields. The District was trying to do its best for these people who had been in bondage. But there was no intention to invite them into their homes or to share their schools."

It was that position Korman argued to the Justices. In excruciating detail, he reviewed the congressional statutes that he said evidenced beyond doubt the lawmakers' intention to authorize a dual school system. The failure of the repeated efforts by Senator Sumner to get segregated schools banned in the District clinched the point that Congress knew just what it was doing. Separate schools were established not out of the racial prejudice that George Hayes had cited, said Korman, but out of "a kindly feeling. . . . [T]here was and there still is an intention by the Congress to see that these children shall be educated in a healthful atmosphere, in a wholesome atmosphere, in a place where they are wanted, in a place where they will not be looked upon with hostility, in a place where there will be a receptive atmosphere for learning for both races without the hostility that undoubtedly Congress thought might creep into these situations."

What measure of persuasiveness Korman may have achieved in his argument to that point was gravely damaged when, about midway through it, he pulled an astonishing gaffe that had Hayes and Nabrit elbowing each other with disbelief at the counsel table. To counter the argument in the United States brief that Washington, as America's window on the world, should not be the scene of discriminatory practices such as school segregation, Korman said he wished to read a few words to the Court from an opinion by the Justices of another era. He began quoting:

> No one, we presume, supposes that any change in public opinion or feeling, in relation to this unfortunate race, in the civilized nations of Europe or in this country, should induce the Court to give to the words of the Constitution a more liberal construction in their favor than they were intended to bear when the instrument was framed and adopted. . . .

Supreme Court decisions, he went on quoting, could never be "the mere reflex of the popular opinion or passion of the day." Unfortunately, in seeking to stiffen the courage of the Justices to sustain what he suspected was a not terribly popular practice, Milton Korman had chosen to cite to them the most denounced and discredited decision in all the annals of the Supreme Court—*Dred Scott v. Sandford.* The Civil War had been fought to reverse the findings of that opinion, and the passage of the Thirteenth, Fourteenth, and Fifteenth amendments served conclusively to rid it of any remnant of present-day authority.

Winding up his infelicitous presentation, Korman made another gift to his black adversaries. The only way to end school segregation in the District, he said, was by action to that effect in the halls of Congress. Then he noted that there had been many moves in the direction of "breaking down segregation in all fields" across the country, and in the District itself Negroes were now enjoying admission to many theaters, restaurants, hotels, playgrounds, hospitals, and other facilities where recourse to congressional remedial action had not been necessary. Nabrit, in rebuttal, promptly seized upon Korman's recitation of improved racial relations in the capital to argue that whatever justification Jim Crow schools might have had when established no longer applied and that no vexing problems or friction would result from prompt desegregation. Nabrit concluded on the most eloquent note sounded on the Negroes' side throughout the three days of oral argument:

> The basic question here is one of liberty, and under liberty, under the due process clause, you cannot deal with it as you deal with equal protection of laws, because there you deal with it as a quantum of treatment, substantially equal.
>
> You either have liberty or you do not. When liberty is interfered with by the state, it has to be justified, and you cannot justify it by saying that we only took a little liberty. You justify it by the reasonableness of the taking.
>
> We submit that in this case, in the heart of the nation's capital, in the capital of democracy, in the capital of the free world, there is no place for a segregated school system. This country cannot afford it, and the Constitution does not permit it, and the statutes of Congress do not authorize it.

In the last of the five school cases heard by the Court, Attorney General

Albert Young of Delaware went first because he had lost in the state courts and was the appellant now before the Justices. Chancellor Seitz had acted precipitously in ordering the Claymont and Hockessin schools desegregated, Young argued, for the state had had every intention of equalizing the black schools involved. But nothing Young said could change the fact that even if Howard High in Wilmington were improved, colored students in Claymont would still face a ten-mile bus ride to and from it each day. Young's brief had also committed some damaging errors that NAACP co-counsels Louis Redding and Jack Greenberg effectively rebutted. Young had contended that the social-science testimony introduced by the original black plaintiffs had not related to the Delaware scene—the same argument that Paul Wilson had made in the Kansas case—but in fact Frederic Wertham and Kenneth Clark had produced an impressive body of clinical evidence dealing with the effects of segregation on both black and white youngsters in the Wilmington area. And four of the social scientists who testified before Seitz were affiliated with the University of Delaware.

Redding and Greenberg, who at the age of twenty-eight was making his first appearance before the Supreme Court, kept their arguments short and localized, for all the relevant constitutional issues had been cited by then in the previous arguments. They held that the temporary relief granted their clients by the courts below was not sufficient and that the state ought to be permanently enjoined from segregating its students. As for Chancellor Seitz, he had had in front of him no evidence of any firm future plans by the state to equalize the Negro schools—only vague allusions by the attorney general. Seitz had been right to order immediate desegregation, and the amicable feeling that had marked the relationship between the white and Negro pupils affected by the chancellor's decree, which had gone into effect at the beginning of that current school term, demonstrated the hollowness of the state's contention that segregation laws were still necessary to prevent serious racial friction.

At 3:50 p.m. on Thursday, December 11, Greenberg rested.

On his way out through the big doors to the Supreme Court building, John W. Davis was heard to remark to Justin Moore, his litigating colleague from Virginia, "I think we've got it won, five-to-four—or maybe six-to-three."

Among the others filing out from the Court that day was the Reverend Joseph A. DeLaine of Clarendon County, South Carolina, who had sparked the Negro uprising there. Through the Reverend James Hinton, head of the South Carolina NAACP, DeLaine had acquired a precious ticket to the Court proceedings—one of just a few dozen that Thurgood Marshall was allotted for the occasion. The minister had followed the entire argument with rapt attention. His eyes had kept wandering over the Justices to sense their reaction to what was being said and for a clue as to how each would vote. Most of all, he had watched the pouchy-eyed man in the middle. "I was afraid of Vinson's face," he remembers.

# 23

# At Loggerheads

In the two and a half years since they had last sat down to decide a major racial case, the Justices of the Supreme Court had not grown closer. Indeed, the philosophical and personal fissures in their ranks had widened since they had agreed—unanimously—to side with the Negro appellants in *Sweatt, McLaurin,* and *Henderson* in the spring of 1950. That had been a rare show of unanimity. By the 1952 Term, the Court was failing to reach a unanimous decision 81 percent of the time, nearly twice as high a percentage of disagreement as it had recorded a decade earlier.

Behind this erosion of unity was intensified disagreement among the Justices over the role the Court ought to exercise in defining, challenging, and striking down the excesses of governmental power. In the fifteen years since Roosevelt had proposed his court-packing scheme to check the continuing invalidation of the New Deal's progressive social legislation, the Court had undergone a complete evolutionary cycle. No one remained from the pre-1937 Court, and the thirteen Justices appointed in the interim had all been Holmesian liberals in the sense that they opposed the Court's intrusion into the legislative process by cutting down urgently needed economic-recovery measures. As transformed by Roosevelt, the Court saw its duty as narrowly cabined: the people's representatives, however imprudent their policies might seem to the Justices, were not to be thwarted by the private policy views of the nine men who comprised the least democratic branch of government. The Court had been converted from hunting dog to watchdog and rather encouraged, in the process, to laze around the porch.

The swollen girth of government had grown well past the stage of manageability as emergency economic measures adopted to counter the Depression were followed by emergency wartime measures that placed national worries far above the cares and claims of individual citizens. America's security was enthroned as the pervasive national value. And as hot war gave way to the Cold War in a doomsday-dreading nuclear age, the psychological fallout settled upon the formerly sanctified freedoms of the Bill of Rights and the Fourteenth Amendment, which suddenly seemed to many Americans to offer shelter to those who questioned the nation's basic policies and values and thereby threatened its very survival in a broken, hostile world. Temperate patriots and mindless jingoists alike saw in every manifestation of dissent the incubus of disloyalty and the need for its obliteration.

By the end of 1952, this collision of individual civil liberties with the pervasive demands of national security had turned Holmesian liberalism on its ear at the Supreme Court. The doctrine of judicial restraint that had invited the Justices to find constitutional rationalizations for the new economic initiatives taken by government in the Thirties and Forties now operated to reduce the fierceness of the scrutiny with which they examined the new governmental security and loyalty programs. The passivity of the Court and its seemingly diminished independence were mirrored in the Vinson-Truman relationship, which bordered on the symbiotic. The President and the Chief Justice remained poker-playing pals, reportedly spoke to each other regularly at night from bedside telephones, and brought their families together for Thanksgiving dinner at the White House.

Thus, the Vinson Court, with a majority solidly composed of the four Truman appointees—Burton, Clark, Minton, and the Chief—and Reed, the least scintillating of the remaining Roosevelt designees, and joined about half the time by Frankfurter and Jackson, the virtuosos of judicial restraint, took a strongly pro-government slant. In 1950, in *American Communications Association v. Douds*, the Court speaking through Vinson had upheld a provision of the Taft-Hartley Law that denied the protections of the act to any labor organization unless each of its officers filed an affidavit swearing he was "not a member of the Communist party or affiliated with such party, and that he does not believe in, and is not a member of or support any organization that believes in or teaches, the overthrow of the United States Government by force or by any illegal or unconstitutional methods." The anti-libertarian trend continued in the 1951 case of *Feiner v. New York*, in which the Court found against a university student who had made a street-corner speech in behalf of the Young Progressives of America. His sharp words, including the assertions that President Truman was "a bum," the American Legion was "a Nazi Gestapo," and Negroes should rise up in arms to obtain their rights, stirred the crowd of seventy-five or so, several of whom made their strong disagreement with the speaker known to two policemen who circulated among the listeners. As "angry mutterings" grew in the crowd, the policemen arrested the speaker, who was booked on a charge of disorderly conduct. Vinson, for six of the Justices, said the student speaker had surely been free to speak his mind but not to incite to riot; it was for the reaction his speech engendered that Feiner was at fault. Black, calling the decision "a dark day for civil liberties in our nation," noted that it was precisely against such threats as those which greeted Feiner's harangue that speakers needed police protection, for if instead "the police throw their weight on the side of those who would break up the meetings, the police become the new censors of speech."

The First Amendment suffered its most jolting setback at the hands of the Vinson Court in *Dennis v. United States*. In that 1951 case, the Justices upheld the conviction of eleven leaders of the American Communist Party for teaching and advocating the forceful overthrow of the United States government, even though no overt revolutionary acts were attributed to the defendants. The intent of the accused was what mattered most, Vinson wrote for the six-man majority; in curbing free speech on the ground of national security, the government was not obliged to wait "until the *putsch* is about to be executed, the plans have been laid and the signal is awaited. . . ." Only Black and Douglas dissented. Despite the guarantees of the First Amendment, American citizens were thus sent to jail for what they thought and said, not what they had done.

By 1952, the witch-hunt was spreading. A six-man majority, with Minton writing the opinion, upheld a New York law which said that any schoolteacher's membership in organizations which the State Board of Regents believed to advocate the forceful or otherwise illegal overthrow of the government was "prima facie evidence for disqualification for appointment to or retention in" any school position. Guilt by association had been sanctioned by the Justices. Black, Douglas, and Frankfurter dissented.

From the 1946 through the 1952 terms of the Court, in twenty-eight major cases dealing with free-speech claims against federal and state governments, the polarization of the Justices was clearly illustrated. The Court as a whole favored the free-speech claimants in only 25 percent of the state cases and 17 percent of the federal cases. Vinson, Reed, and Minton *never* favored the libertarian position in any of the federal cases and Burton did just once, while Black and Douglas upheld the free-speech claimants in *every* federal case and Black failed to in only one state case. Jackson and Frankfurter were in the middle, though the latter was plainly the more libertarian of the pair. A similarly prosecutorial bias was revealed in the Court's voting pattern in cases dealing with the due-process claims of criminal defendants.

In other areas, the division between the Justices was less extreme, but the general pattern of alignment was unmistakable. From 1949, when Clark and Minton joined the Court, through the 1952 Term, the Vinson bloc of Reed, Burton, Clark, Minton, and the Chief voted together in non-unanimous cases nearly three-quarters of the time. At the other end of the Court, Black and Douglas voted together in 61 percent of the non-unanimous cases. And oscillating between the two poles were Jackson and Frankfurter, who voted together in 69 percent of the non-unanimous cases.

It was perhaps the most severely fractured Court in history—testament, on the face of it, to Vinson's failure as Chief Justice. Selected to lead the Court because of his skills as a conciliator, the low-key, mournful-visaged Kentuckian found that the issues before him were far different from, and far less readily negotiable than, the hard-edged problems he had faced as Franklin Roosevelt's ace economic troubleshooter and Harry Truman's Secretary of the Treasury and back-room confederate.

Fred Vinson's lot as Chief Justice, then, had not proven a happy one. True, he commanded a majority of the Justices in most cases, but even that hold had been lost earlier in 1952 in the landmark steel-seizure case of *Youngstown Sheet & Tube v. Sawyer*, when he carried only two other Justices in defending Truman's takeover of America's steel mills as an action justified by national-security factors in the midst of the Korean War. All the Roosevelt appointees to the Court except his fellow Kentuckian, Reed, looked down on Vinson as the possessor of a second-rate mind, and in contrast to the Roosevelt quartet, the Chief glowed dimly indeed. It was hardly surprising that Court scuttlebutt had it, according to William K. Bachelder, one of Justice Minton's clerks during the 1952 Term, that several of Vinson's colleagues "would discuss in his presence the view that the Chief's job should rotate annually and . . . made no bones about regarding him—correctly—as their intellectual inferior."

But if the Big Four of the Court were united in their disdain for Vinson, they themselves faced off in hostile pairs: Jackson-Frankfurter vs. Black-Douglas. Jackson, convinced that Black had intervened with Harry Truman to prevent his succeeding Stone as Chief Justice in 1946, had flown at the Alabaman in open rage that was slow to die. Frankfurter viewed much of Douglas's writing and thinking as slipshod and governed by "pre-posses-sions" that he had brought to his facile consideration of cases that deeply troubled Frankfurter. Douglas found many of Frankfurter's anti-libertarian opinions to be tortured apologias and once wrote him, "We all know what a great burden your long discourses are." Frankfurter, moreover, was forever proselytizing the three members of the Vinson majority who were not put off by his pedantic manner—Reed, whom he used as an intellectual punching bag of sorts; the sweet-tempered Burton, who was sometimes the Court's swing man on tough cases; and Minton, surely the least introspective member of the Court, yet genuinely appreciative of Frankfurter's solicitous overtures to him. But Frankfurter, seeking to influence the direction of the Court by tirelessly pollinating among the wavering Justices, had scant luck with the anti-intellectual Vinson and even less with his satellite, Tom Clark, whom Frankfurter had not very artfully patronized during the Texan's first term on the Court. The tension lines ran every which way. Minton found Jackson pompous and Black prone to demagoguery. Douglas remained aloof from nearly everybody save Black. Black and Frankfurter thought Reed often lacked the courage of his convictions. Burton, a strait-laced teetotaler who never smoked or cursed, found his neighbor on the bench, the Rabelaisian Minton, somewhat on the uncouth side and did not enjoy having his robe sprayed when the tobacco-chewing Hoosier missed the spittoon provided for him behind the bench. And so it went.

What, then, could be expected of the deeply divided Vinson Court as it convened on the morning of December 13, 1952, to deliberate on the transcendent case of *Brown v. Board of Education*? The earlier racial cases—*Sweatt* and *McLaurin*—they had managed to cope with by chipping away at the edges of Jim Crow but avoiding the real question of *Plessy's* continued validity. The Court could no longer dodge that question, though it might continue to stall in resolving it. Hovering over the Justices were all the repressive bugaboos of the Cold War era. The civil rights of Negroes and the civil liberties of political dissenters and criminal defendants were prone to be scrambled together in the public mind, and every malcontent was a sitting target for the red tar of anti-Americanism. No sector of the nation was less hospitable to both civil-liberties and civil-rights claimants than the segregating states of the South, and it was the South with which the Justices had primarily to deal in confronting *Brown*.

No function of American government has been both more open and yet more cloaked than the decision-making process of the Supreme Court.

The final position taken by each Justice on every case is of course a matter of public record, stated in open court by the Justices themselves, who present their decisions in reasoned written opinions that fill the shelves of law libraries. The record of the cases in the lower courts before they reached the Justices is likewise an open book, and the oral arguments in the Supreme Court are open to the public and often widely covered by the press.

But the most vital part of the Court's deliberations is and has traditionally been conducted with probably greater secrecy than any other group of decision-makers has ever managed to maintain in Washington. The Justices generally heard oral arguments for a period of two weeks and then repaired to their chambers for the next two weeks to study the cases they had just listened to, write opinions, and contemplate the merits of the latest batch of applications that flow ceaselessly to them from petitioners seeking a hearing before the nation's highest court. On Saturday mornings of the weeks in which oral arguments were held, the Justices convened to present to each other their views of the cases they had heard the preceding week. It is in these conferences, held on Fridays in more recent years, that the Court's decisions have been thrashed out. And it is these conferences of which the public hears nothing.

This secrecy is largely to the good, for their temporary insulation from public pressure allows the Justices freedom to weigh the issues before them without regard to any immediate external factors or need to please. Such freedom is essential because the Court does not function as a committee of the whole; each Justice is responsible for his own vote and cannot rely on the fellowship of his judicial brethren as a substitute for judging. He himself is ultimately held accountable for his voting record, for the Supreme Court is truly nine separate judges, each guided principally by his own intellect, philosophy, and conscience, but each of course open to the subtle (and sometimes not so subtle) play of will and conviction exercised on him by the collective judgment of his eight colleagues. Each, to be sure, has the confidential help of bright, recent law-school graduates who clerk for him for a year or two and ease the research burden. But the clerks come and go, and the Justices abide, often unto death, obliged to do their own homework, mostly in solitude. They can turn to no outside scholars or experts—only to their clerks, who are usually novices in constitutional law, to the Supreme Court library, and to their brother Justices. A partner at any good-sized law firm has greater research and manpower facilities available to him. It is, in many ways, a grave and lonely job.

The secret conclaves would be signaled a few minutes before the meeting hour by a ritualistic clatter in the hallways. Each Justice possessed a small cart with metal wheels, and his secretary or clerks would pile it high with the briefs for the fifty or sixty cases due to be discussed at that Saturday's conference. Then his messenger (who was also his chauffeur, valet, and lunchtime waiter) would push the heavily loaded little vehicle rattling down the hall to the holiest sanctuary in the vast marble building—the Justices' conference room on the first floor, just behind the courtroom.

It was less ornate than most rooms in the building. Oak-paneled, but without decorative cornices on the woodwork, the conference room was dominated by a rectangular table, about a dozen feet long, that stood in the middle of the chamber and was covered in green felt, like a pool table. From floor to ceiling, the walls were lined with volumes recording the results of every case on appeal ever decided by the federal courts. At one end of the room was a fireplace, and over its mantel hung a portrait of the fourth and most revered Chief Justice of the United States. At the other end of the room, near the head of the conference table, stood a small table with a telephone on it. If you looked out the windows, you could see a row of trim, two-story townhouses directly across Second Street. To the far right, the Folger Shakespearean Library is visible; to the left, streets funneling toward Union Station. It is not a distracting vista. The room itself is a functional, not a ceremonial, one. The function is to determine the law of the land.

And so the nine men assembled on the morning of the second Saturday of December of 1952 to discuss together for the first time their disposition toward the five school-segregation cases. They did not wear their robes to conference. They came, as always, in conservative business suits, like mortal men accustomed to dispensing power. Before they began, and despite the not altogether fraternal feelings they bore one another, each Justice shook the hand of every other Justice—a total of thirty-six handshakes—as if to say that whatever divided them, more united them.

The ceremony swiftly concluded, the thirteenth Chief Justice of the United States took his seat at the head of the long table. Fred M. Vinson, at the age of sixty-two, was in his seventh year as the presiding member of the great court. At the far end of the table, beneath the painting of John Marshall, sat the senior Associate Justice, sixty-five-year-old Hugo Black, well into his sixteenth year of service on the high tribunal and widely recognized as one of the most able men ever to serve on it. On the side of the table to the Chief Justice's right sat Stanley Reed, Robert Jackson, and William Douglas. Across from them, and frankly a bit cramped, sat the remaining four Justices: Harold Burton, Tom Clark, Sherman Minton, and Felix Frankfurter. At sixty-nine, Frankfurter was the oldest of the nine; Douglas and Clark, both fifty-three, were the youngest. Their average age was not quite sixty-two, their average length of service stood at nine and a half years—both figures a bit under the average for the Court's history. Four came from the South: Black from Clay County, Alabama; Clark from Dallas; and Vinson and Reed both from small towns in eastern Kentucky. Two came from the Northeast: Jackson from upstate New York and Frankfurter from Massachusetts (via New York and Vienna). Two came from the Midwest: Burton from Cleveland and Minton from downstate

Indiana. The West could claim only Douglas, a native of Minnesota who grew up in Yakima, Washington, and went to college in that state before coming East to seek his fortune; at the time of his appointment, he was considered a resident of Connecticut. All nine had been appointed by Democratic Presidents, and all but Burton were themselves Democrats.

Their junior-most member, Justice Minton, sat nearest the door, as was the Court's custom, and as the glorified gatekeeper it was he who received or dispatched messages, since there was never anyone else in the conference room when the Justices assembled. No clerks, no secretaries, no messengers —just the nine of them. They came at eleven, worked till one, took a half-hour for lunch, returned and stayed as long as need be, generally till five or five-thirty. The Chief Justice spoke first as they took up each case on the docket; a good deal of his power as presiding member of the Court stemmed from this initial opportunity to evaluate the issues as he saw them in any given case and to attempt to direct the thinking of his colleagues along channels of his choosing. The other Justices spoke after him in descending order of seniority. Each man said his piece without interruption until they had all spoken, and then the floor was opened to cross-discussion. If they were ready to vote at the close of the discussion, each Justice would state his vote, but in the reverse order of the initial go-around; that is, the newest Justice voted first, presumably in order to be influenced as little as possible by his seniors.

More titular head of the Court than its authentic leader, Fred Vinson had not often proven persuasive in convincing his eight colleagues to resolve their differences even when he himself was of firm mind on the case before them. And on the explosive segregation cases, his mind was apparently far from settled.

Vinson's stature as a defender of humanitarian values was middling at most. As a Congressman, he was progressive and strongly in favor of pro-labor legislation. He declined to back off from Al Smith as head of the Democratic ticket in 1928, though he had been told his loyalty to the Catholic standardbearer would likely cost him his House seat (and it did, for one term). But there was little in his record during thirty years as a federal legislator, executive, and judge to suggest his concern for the rights of black Americans, save for three Supreme Court opinions he authored—*Shelley, Sweatt,* and *McLaurin,* of which he was said to be extremely proud. Yet *Sweatt* and *McLaurin* were tightly drawn opinions that artfully avoided the essence of the segregation problem, and *Shelley,* written two years earlier, had begun to look to a lot of legal scholars and Court-watchers the way it did to Anthony Lewis of the *New York Times,* who describes it as "a piece of lawyer's law, a sort of crooked case, that had no lasting impact on its time." Just how lacking in conviction Vinson's *Shelley* opinion may have been is suggested by a dissent he wrote later in the 1952 Term. In *Shelley,* the Court had held that court enforcement of an anti-Negro housing covenant among a group of white private-property owners was a form of discriminatory state action that violated the Fourteenth Amendment. But did that mean that other white signatories to a covenant could not collect damages from a fellow white who broke the agreement and sold to a black family? In *Barrows v. Jackson*, three white covenanters from California claimed that their property value had been reduced by their neighbor's sale of his home to a Negro family. The Court majority held that, as in *Shelley*, court-compelled payment of alleged damages would in effect be state action that enforced discriminatory practices. Vinson, dissenting alone for the first and last time on the Court, argued that the rights of the Negro family were in no way involved in the dispute between the white property-owners, and the obligations of the white signatories to the private covenant had to be honored. In other words, Vinson's position was that no court could dispossess a Negro family that bought a house from a white signatory to a restrictive covenant, but that the white selling party could be sued by the other co-signatories. Had his *Barrows* dissent prevailed, it would plainly have emasculated the effect of the *Shelley* opinion.

Vinson's reluctance to advance Negro rights beyond a line he judged not to be intrusive on white sensibilities was signaled by one other telltale dissent not long before the school-segregation cases came up for a vote at the end of 1952. In the 1944 case of *Steele v. Louisville & Nashville Railroad* (won for the petitioner by Charles Houston), the Court had held that the all-white Brotherhood of Locomotive Firemen could not force the railroads to enter into contracts discriminating against non-member Negro firemen, for, once a union had been designated as the statutory representative of a craft under the Railway Labor Act, it was obliged to represent fairly and equally the entire membership of the craft and not use its power to drive out black workers, whom the union barred from membership. Now, in the 1952 case of *Brotherhood of Railway Trainmen v. Howard*, another of the all-white railway unions had been charged with illegally inducing a railroad to fire its Negro "train porters" and to replace the colored workers with white members of the brotherhood. The white union said that the Negroes, who actually performed trainmen's duties but were never so categorized or paid as much as whites doing the same work, had never been regarded as formally belonging to the trainmen's craft, and so the white brotherhood had merely been using its statutory bargaining power under the Railway Labor Act to protect its own members. The Court, speaking through Black, held that the brotherhood, as the federally designated bargaining agent for its craft, was not free to practice "lawless invasions of the rights of other workers." Chief Justice Vinson dissented, along with Reed and Minton.

A passionate plea for Negro rights would therefore have been out of character now for the Chief Justice as he led off the conference.

There are no minutes or other formal record of what was said at that conference, but notes on it by two Justices who were in attendance—Burton and Jackson—have survived, and while they are often cryptic and sometimes illegible, they match sufficiently in a number of places to offer a useful guide to the posture of the Court. Fred Vinson, the Burton and Jackson notes seem to agree, was almost certainly not ready to support the abolition of segregation.

"Body of law back of us on separate but equal," Jackson recorded

Vinson as telling the conference. And, "Congress pass no statute contrary." Burton, in his microscopic hand, had Vinson saying: "However construe it Congress did not pass a statute deterring & ordering no segregation." The Chief Justice found it "Hard to get away" from the contemporary view by its framers that the Fourteenth Amendment did not prohibit segregation, Burton noted. "Hard get away long established acceptance [of segregation] in DC," Jackson jotted. "For 90 years segregated schools in city." Both men noted that Vinson was struck by the failure of Justice Harlan's eloquent dissent in *Plessy* to mention school segregation—a highly significant omission, Vinson stressed, in view of Harlan's authorship of the unanimous *Cumming* decision three years later, when the Court inferentially upheld Georgia's right to classify its schoolchildren along racial lines. Jackson and Burton also noted that Vinson was cool to the argument that the basic responsibility in the segregation matter belonged to Congress and thus the Court was let off the hook. "Don't think much of idea that it is for Congress & not for us to act," Burton wrote. "If they *do not act* that leaves us with it—It would be better if it would act." In a more telling note, Burton added parenthetically: "(May act for DC—probably *not* for the states)." That is, Vinson evidently was persuaded that Congress had the power to ban segregation in the District of Columbia but not in the states—this despite the enforcement provisions of Section 5 of the Fourteenth Amendment.

Then Vinson took up each of the five cases. The South Carolina case troubled him especially. Jackson records the Chief's position this way: ". . . Not close eyes as to seriousness of problem as to time. Face complete abolition of public school system in South—serious." Burton has him noting that Thurgood Marshall "says will be necessary to take time for it [presumably meaning the court-mandated equalization of black schools] to be made effective." The greater the number of Negroes in any community, the graver the problem, Vinson believed. "Courage is needed . . . also wisdom," Burton additionally quotes him. Then, at the end of his notes on Vinson's remarks, Burton wrote: *"Aff?"* That meant Burton thought the Chief was leaning toward affirming the lower-court rulings—that is, toward upholding the constitutionality of segregation.

There are a number of other clues, of varying degrees of reliability, that suggest Vinson was not prepared to overturn segregation. Burton kept a detailed diary and noted in it a year and a half later that he believed Vinson would have voted to retain segregation. Frankfurter, writing to Reed at about the same time, stated a similar view of Vinson's position. Reed told one of his 1953 Term clerks, John D. Fassett, that he expected Vinson to vote to uphold segregation. Over in the Solicitor General's office, top civil-rights lawyer Philip Elman had heard that the Chief Justice did not favor overruling *Plessy*; few in Elman's office believed the Vinson Court would or could take a united stand on the school-segregation cases. Toward the close of the Court's 1952 Term, Vinson asked his clerks to prepare a memorandum on the enforcement problems that might be encountered if the Court were to order desegregation; the clerks, with whom the Chief Justice did not discuss the cases except in the most oblique fashion, feared the assignment meant that

Vinson was trying to marshal all the arguments he could against a desegregation decree by emphasizing the great difficulties that enforcement of it might present.

Little evidence has been uncovered to suggest that Vinson was willing to vote against segregation. His papers, according to his son, Fred, Jr., contain no evidence at all of his thoughts on *Brown*. Only his closest colleague on the Court, Tom Clark, believes Fred Vinson would not have voted to retain segregation—"not the way Vinson was writing then," says Clark, alluding to *Sweatt* but choosing to overlook Vinson's dissents in *Barrows* and *Brotherhood of Railway Trainmen v. Howard.*

A shrewd politician and a legal pragmatist, the Chief Justice was thus exceedingly wary about brushing aside the long-standing customs of the South—his South—no matter what constitutional justifications could be assembled in behalf of overturning *Plessy*. He saw the problem as essentially political and social in nature, not legal, and believed no step should be taken by the Court without its collective eye firmly fixed on the potentially drastic consequences. In the continuing absence of congressional action, he seems to have doubted that the time was yet ripe for the Justices to act. He much preferred a waiting game, taking the whole problem one small step at a time. And, at the moment, he wanted to see how Governor Byrnes of South Carolina, a man he had dealt with and respected during the New and Fair Deals, and other Southern officials would carry out their pledges to equalize the colored schools under the *Plessy* formula.

Justice Hugo Black spoke second at the conference. His vote was never really in doubt.

He was the one man on the Court to come from the heart of Dixie, and a proud regionalist he was. He had a good many relatives back in Alabama, and his son Hugo, Jr., was doing well in law practice in Birmingham, the city in which the Justice had first risen to fame as judge and lawyer. But when the moment came, Hugo Black did not hesitate to burn his bridges to the Southland, though it hurt him to do so.

In a sense, he had committed himself to the black man's fight for justice as early as a dozen years previous. His record till then was mixed but promising. Mostly, it had been a matter of disclosing his sympathies without unduly ruffling the ranks of the white-supremacists. As a local police judge, he had administered the law with an even hand for whites and blacks alike—a remarkable departure from Alabama custom. And he had won stripes as a humanitarian in Washington by challenging the big financial interests in the name of the proverbial man in the street, who, it turned out in that age, more often than not had a hole in his shoe. Hugo Black was the only member of the Senate to call out against Herbert Hoover's use of force to drive off the protesting veterans of the Bonus Army who had flocked to Washington to make their grievances known. Hugo Black was the only member of the Supreme Court to attend the controversial Marian Anderson concert in front of the Lincoln Memorial. But he had functioned as a wily politician all those pre-Court years and made his share of bargains with expediency. He had joined the Klan, for however brief a time, to enhance his political acceptability. He had filibustered against the anti-lynching bill when he was in the Senate. And when Walter White and Charles Houston approached him as head of the education subcommittee with an amendment to guarantee that funds dispensed under a federal-aid-to-education bill would be allocated without discrimination to white and colored schools in the South, he rejected the proposal and argued that such a measure would surely lose the bill much needed Southern votes and thus hurt the children of both races. "Education is the answer to the race question, not legislation," he said oracularly.

On the Court, his earliest votes suggested that, free of a segregationist constituency, he would vote his conscience. He took the Negro's side in the *Gaines* decision in 1938 and the Oklahoma "grandfather clause" case of *Lane v. Wilson* in 1939, but he truly crossed the Swanee with the unanimous opinion he wrote for the Court in the 1940 case of *Chambers v. Florida*, delivered on Lincoln's Birthday. Reluctant to have the Court interfere with judicial proceedings in the states, Black had voted originally not to hear the case. "But the evidence of oppression and injustice would not down," according to one of Black's 1953 Term clerks, Charles Reich, later to serve as a Yale law professor and write the best-selling treatise *The Greening of America.* "The opinion Black wrote, after great internal struggles, was a turning point . . . [a precursor to] much of what was to become his mature judicial philosophy." The case had involved several Negroes who, after almost ceaseless questioning for six days and nights without aid of counsel, family, or friends, confessed to murdering a white man. The Court found a glaring denial of due process under the Fourteenth Amendment, and Black's opinion declared that the Court was there to stand as a haven for the weak and helpless victims of prejudice. He declined thereafter to cast the Court in a passive role or himself as a humanitarian neuter. The Justices' highest duty was to protect the rights and liberties of the individual citizen, not to weigh them meticulously against the claimed needs and readily rationalized intrusions by government, as Felix Frankfurter proposed. Excessive deference to the other branches of government was tantamount to a betrayal by the Court of its most sacred duty.

By 1947, his libertarian activism had expanded and he was proclaiming that a close reading of history showed that the framers of the Fourteenth Amendment had intended it not merely as a series of majestic generalities but as a guarantee to every citizen that he would have the same freedoms from and protections against intrusion in his life by state governments as he had from federal intrusions under the Bill of Rights. To the Frankfurter camp of narrow-constructionists, it was a shockingly latitudinarian reading of constitutional history and it never did command support from a majority of the Court. But Black stuck to his view and pressed the argument that strict adherence to the Bill of Rights was the highest form of national security. He wrote in his courageous 1951 dissent in *Dennis v. United States*:

> . . . I cannot agree that the First Amendment permits us to sustain laws suppressing freedom of speech and press on the basis of Congress' or our own

notions of mere "reasonableness." Such a doctrine waters down the First Amendment so that it amounts to little more than an admonition to Congress. . . . Public opinion being what it now is, few will protest the conviction of these Communist petitioners. There is hope, however, that in calmer times, when present pressures, passions and fears subside, this or some later Court will restore the First Amendment liberties to the high preferred place where they belong in our free society.

His study of post-Civil War history had also convinced Black that the whole legislative package of the era—the three constitutional amendments and their various enforcement measures, taken together—was profound testimony that the lawmakers of that day had intended to place all racially discriminatory measures by government under perpetual ban. And the segregation of white and colored schoolchildren was just such an impermissible state regulation, to the mind of Hugo Black, who said as much now to his fellow Justices.

Besides the strength of his convictions and the plain-spoken eloquence with which he expressed them in his written opinions, Black was known to be a powerful figure on the Court because of the effectiveness of his remarks at the Justices' conferences. He generally spoke at length and with great clarity; the notes kept by Burton and Jackson suggest he did both this day as he called on his brethren to strike down segregation. He was familiar with all the arguments of the South that the end of segregation would lead directly and fatally to the mixture of the races, Black told the conference. But he had lived a long time in the South and he did not need scholars or philosophers to tell him what the purpose of segregation was. Its purpose, he said he was compelled to admit, was to discriminate against Negroes in the belief that they were inferior beings, and the Civil War amendments had been drawn to protect all Americans from precisely that sort of discrimination. "Segregation *per se* is a violation of the Fourteenth Amendment," he declared, according to both Burton and Jackson, and the practice should be overruled unless the Court felt its prior rulings plainly prevented that conclusion.

For himself, Black did not underestimate the difficulties that lay ahead. The effects of the Court's ruling against the practice would be "serious" and perhaps "drastic." He agreed with Vinson that South Carolina might well abolish its public schools as Governor Byrnes had threatened, and one of the most regrettable features of an anti-segregation ruling would be to put the federal courts on the battlefront and make their injunctive powers the crucial weapon. But the principle to be decided in *Brown* could not be avoided for such reasons. At the end of his notes on Black's remarks, Burton wrote: "*Rev.*" Black had stated his intention to vote to reverse the decisions of the courts below (the Delaware case excepted) and declare segregation illegal.

Black's position was an open secret among the inner circle of Court-watchers. Over at the Justice Department, Philip Elman had heard that "Hugo was telling the brethren that you cannot constitutionally defend *Plessy*, but if and when they overruled it, it would mean the end of Southern liberalism for the time being. The Bilbos and the Talmadges would come even more to the fore, overshadowing the John Sparkmans and the Lister

Hills. The guys who talked nigger would be in charge, there would be riots, the Army might have to be called out—he was scaring the shit out of the Justices, especially Frankfurter and Jackson, who didn't know how the Court could enforce a ruling against *Plessy*. But Hugo was determined to overrule it on principle." Justice Clark recalls that Black wondered aloud about the wisdom of framing the Court's decree in a way not to treat the cases as class actions, thereby limiting the results to the specific plaintiffs involved and minimizing the potential upheaval caused by the Court's decision. It was a wistful notion, for it was plain that what the Court was now weighing would unavoidably affect millions of lives across America, not a few hundred.

Several other pieces of evidence suggest the unequivocal position Black had taken from the start. Douglas, in his autobiographical book *Go East, Young Man*, would testify twenty-two years later that Black had voted to overturn segregation at the 1952 conference (though a more accurate statement, in view of other evidence, might be that Black was prepared to vote that way had the Justices in fact polled themselves that day). Disinclined to lobby with his fellow Justices in the segregation matter, partly out of fear that excessive partisanship on his end might drive his ideological foe Frankfurter and his personal foe Jackson into the enemy camp, Black said and wrote little during and after the case that might inflame passions on the subject. Toward the end of 1960, though, he wrote to his friend Edmond Cahn at New York University Law School: "I want to say one thing about *Brown*. . . . My decision in that case was not the result of brushing aside history nor on the theory that time had made something unconstitutional that had not been so since the Fourteenth Amendment was adopted. Some articles that have been written indicating [that position] . . . are not in accord with my own views." Finally, Black himself directly verified his position at the 1952 conference in a sharp reaction to a paper written eighteen years later by a political scientist at the University of Kentucky named S. Sidney Ulmer. Seeking to reconstruct the secret conference solely on the basis of Burton's sometimes indecipherable and quite often cryptic notes, Ulmer studied Burton's last two paragraphs on Black's remarks—

> Have to say seg of *itself*
> violates amendment unless long
> line of decisions prevents
> Didn't go all the way that
> was intended in old cases.
>    Will vote that way—if
> majority the other way—to segregate
> them would be [illegible] of change      Rev.

—and translated them this way in the paper he was preparing to deliver to the Southern Political Science Association in Atlanta: "[Black] was prepared to say that segregation by race violated the amendment (unless a long line of decisions prevented him from doing so). In the event that a majority voted otherwise regarding segregation, then Black retained the option of changing his position." In the Justice's copy of Ulmer's essay retained in the Black

Papers at the Library of Congress, the parenthetical clause and the last eight words of the quoted passage are underscored and the word "no" in Black's handwriting is penciled in the margin. Then Black wrote to Ulmer to say that the passage did not accurately reflect his position and that he doubted "if Justice Burton's reports of the meeting justify any such inference." Ulmer wrote back in an effort to get Black to elaborate, but the Justice declined to. In a letter dated September 8, 1970, however, he told Ulmer that "if you are saying that under any circumstances I would have voted to continue to hold that segregation was constitutional then your statement is not correct." Ulmer struck the offending passage from his paper.

Black, according to his widow, burned all his own conference notes for fear they might be used by future historians, as he felt Ulmer had used Burton's, to draw unjustified conclusions. The internal workings of the conference, he thought, should remain inviolable.

From his voting record on the Court, sixty-eight-year-old Stanley Reed seemed likely to favor overturning *Plessy.* He had written two of the most important opinions of the Court in racial cases—*Smith v. Allwright* in 1944 and *Morgan v. Virginia* in 1946—and while he did not participate in *Shelley,* he had joined in *Sweatt, McLaurin,* and *Henderson.* And yet, speaking third at the conference, he said he opposed abolishing segregation.

Toward the end of the 1952 Term, the Court considered another racial case that reportedly provoked a reaction from Reed suggestive of his down-to-earth view of the segregation issue. In *District of Columbia v. John R. Thompson Co., Inc.,* the Justices voted unanimously in the spring of 1953 that restaurants in the District which refused service to Negroes were violating a universally ignored but still valid 1873 municipal statute banning such a practice. The Court, through Douglas, spurned arguments that the law had fallen into disuse so long before that it would now be unenforceable. Reed went along, but, according to several clerks who served that term, his misgivings were apparent. Reed, an austere and very proper Southern gentleman, lived with his wife at the Mayflower Hotel in downtown Washington, and the couple did not cook in. The decision in *Thompson,* then, could have had immediate impact on the Reeds' lives. The Justice was reported to have exclaimed, upon returning from the conference at which the *Thompson* vote was taken: "Why—why, this means that a nigra can walk into the restaurant at the Mayflower Hotel and sit down to eat at the table right next to Mrs. Reed!"

In correspondence and conversations later that year with John Fassett, one of his 1953 Term clerks, Reed made his position in the school-segregation cases plain enough. He did not accept the proposition that segregation was necessarily an act of discrimination, as the NAACP lawyers insisted it was. Nor did he believe the segregation cases had been properly brought under the equal-protection part of the Fourteenth Amendment. Equal protection, Reed thought, could be obtained by the Court's insistence that the colored schools be equalized—that is, by strictly enforcing *Plessy.* The only ground he saw as a constitutionally plausible basis for reversing was that segregation was a denial of due process, but he did not happen to believe that was so.

At the December 13, 1952, conference, Reed said, according to Burton: "Negroes have not thoroughly assimilated/must try our best to give Negroes benefits. Must start with the idea that a large opinion [holds] that separation of races is for benefit of both. . . . Must allow time—10 years in Va perhaps/every year helps." Jackson recorded Reed's views this way:

> Knows some desire keep Negro for laborer.
> Race out of slavery a short time ago
> When are the changes to be made?
>     Great progress in the South.
> Agree Constitution not fixed. When changes?
>     If body of people think unconstitutional.
> Can not say time come when 17 states are denying
>     equal protection or due process.
> 10 years would make really equal.
> Uphold segregation as constitutional.

Burton, too, wrote "Uphold Seg" at the end of his notes on Reed. And in his letter to Reed on May 20, 1954, Frankfurter referred to Reed's intention, as of the December 1952 conference, to vote to uphold the practice.

More than any of his brethren on the Court, Felix Frankfurter could be said to have worshipped the law. There were times when he seemed to conceive of it not as a body of rules for human behavior but as an immaculate, shimmering essence with an exalted life of its own divorced from and beyond the reach of mere wayward mortals. The Supreme Court, to Felix Frankfurter, was hallowed ground, its resources to be spent frugally, never dissipated in hollow proclamations beyond its power to enforce.

If the Court was to retain its majesty, it dared not venture where it had no business—onto the battlefields of the legislature and into the back rooms where current policy was carpentered in a swirl of sawdust and smoke. The Court was to remain above the battle, reaching down to tip the balance only when or if one side or the other was in open violation of the great organic law of the land. Frankfurter put it characteristically in his concurring opinion in *Dennis v. United States* in which he voted to jail eleven Communist leaders by holding the protections of the First Amendment subsidiary to a congressional statute that seemed to intrude upon them in the name of national security:

> Courts are not representative bodies. They are not designed to be a good reflex of a democratic society. Their judgment is best informed, and therefore most dependable, within narrow limits. . . .

The power of the Supreme Court, he once said, was "inherently oligarchic," and it was therefore to be dispensed with proper "humility" since it was the least representative of the three branches of government. Its decisions were to be reached not on the feelings of the Justices but on "rational standards" that were to be both "impersonal and communicable." The correlation between a Justice's visceral response to and his vote in any case before him had best be zero. As he put it in *Dennis*: "In finding that Congress has acted within its power, a judge does not remotely imply that he favors the implications that lie beneath the legal issues. . . ." And he added, as if to show he was still a true-blue libertarian: "When legislation touches freedom of thought and freedom of speech, such a tendency is a formidable enemy of the free spirit. . . ." There was something very nearly masochistic in his frequent insistence that he could not reach judgments on the bench which he would readily have favored as an unrobed private citizen. In one case, he declared that as a judge he could not yield to his personal revulsion from capital punishment. In another, when a condemned man had not died in the electric chair due to a mechanical failure, he supplied the fifth vote to send the prisoner back for a second try, explaining that he could not rid himself of the conviction that if he had held the repeat performance to be a form of cruel and unusual punishment, "I would be enforcing my private view rather than that consensus of society's opinion. . . ." He would often vote to avoid hearing difficult cases, and he was wont to draft dissents or concurrences on the narrowest grounds possible. Typical was the 1952 teacher-loyalty-oath case of *Adler v. Board of Education of New York*, in which six Justices upheld the oaths, Black and Douglas judged them unconstitutional, and Frankfurter avoided the substantive issue by holding that the Court should have declined jurisdiction in the case because those who brought it—many of them parents who were not directly affected by the oath requirement—lacked sufficient legal standing or interest to invoke judicial protection.

There seemed to be a lack of fiber in this sort of reluctant judging. But Frankfurter's many admirers saw in his insistent restraint a higher form of moral behavior, stemming, as Reinhold Niebuhr put it,

> from a consistent political and legal philosophy, neither liberal nor conservative, but based on confidence that the vital forces of a free society, sometimes conflicting, sometimes overlapping and sometimes convergent, will gradually adjust the political forms to the social realities, and will do so more successfully if they are not impeded by judicial fiat.

Another school of thought suggests, however, that Frankfurter's notably self-conscious conduct as a Justice owed something to his origins. He had, after all, been a passionate, nationally known civil-libertarian before coming to the Court as he defended victims of the notorious Palmer Raids, fought superbly in behalf of Sacco and Vanzetti, argued in favor of minimum wages for women in the Supreme Court case of *Adkins v. Children's Hospital*, and was an advisor to both the NAACP and the ACLU. He himself may have offered a clue to his contrastingly cautious behavior on the Court when, asked by a friend why he had not spoken out on the Roosevelt court-packing plan in 1937, he replied: "Fundamentally, because through circumstances, in the making of which I have had no share, I have become a myth, a symbol, and promoter not of reason but of passion. I am the symbol of the Jew, the 'red,' the 'alien.' In that murky and passionate atmosphere anything that I may say becomes enveloped. . . ." An immigrant who had been chosen as a guardian of the nation's most cherished credos and canons, he wanted to avoid divisive actions whenever possible. Thus, in the second flag-salute case, he explained his reluctance to outlaw the compulsory-salute regulation in public schools by noting:

> One who belongs to the most vilified and persecuted minority in history is not likely to be insensible to the freedoms guaranteed by our Constitution. Were my purely personal attitude relevant I should wholeheartedly associate myself with the general libertarian views in the Court's opinion, representing as they do the thought and action of a lifetime. . . .

When Chief Justice Stone designated him in 1944 to write the Court's eight-to-one opinion in *Smith v. Allwright*, Frankfurter stepped aside at Jackson's suggestion that the reception given the decision would be "greatly weakened" if it were written by Frankfurter because his being a Jew "may grate on Southern sensibilities."

One result of this deferential demeanor and voting pattern was to reduce Frankfurter to an apologist for some very bad, perilously authoritarian law-making; by 1952, he was able to write the majority opinion in *Beauharnais v. Illinois*, upholding a sweeping state censorship law that made it illegal to publish any writing or exhibit any picture, drama, or film that "portrays depravity, criminality, unchastity, or lack of virtue of a class of citizens, of any race, color, creed or religion . . . [or] exposes the citizens of any race, color, creed or religion to contempt, derision, or obloquy or which is productive of breach of the peace or riots." Frankfurter considered this drastic statute as merely a "group libel law," suggested that state legislatures had to be free to exercise "choice of policy," and held that the Court should accept "the trial-and-error inherent in legislative efforts to deal with obstinate social problems." That struck Black and the other three Roosevelt appointees who joined his dissent as noxious pettifoggery: "State experimentation in curbing freedom of expression is startling and frightening doctrine in a country dedicated to self-government by its people."

Thus, Felix Frankfurter was snagged on a dilemma of his own insistent making as he approached the school-segregation cases. To follow his humanitarian impulses, he would have to violate a number of his favorite and most assiduously pronounced doctrines. For the Court to outlaw segregation, it would suddenly have to demolish the long-standing prerogatives of twenty-one state legislatures. The Court would then have to intervene massively, one way or another, to make sure its edict was being followed; it would have to become, so to speak, a national board of education—a role that Frankfurter had vigorously urged the Court to shun in the first flag-salute case some years earlier. There were other problems, too. Like Black, he had studied the history of the Fourteenth Amendment, but Frankfurter came to a far different conclusion: in all likelihood, the framers of the amendment had not intended to outlaw segregation. And, as he had pointedly noted in grilling Robert Carter during the oral argument in *Brown*, neither contemporary nor subsequent courts nor state legislatures had interpreted the amendment as proscribing the practice. And, like Vinson, he was struck by Justice Harlan's failure to mention schools in his *Plessy* dissent; the Great Dissenter, Frankfurter guessed from Harlan's opinion for the majority in *Cumming*, would probably have voted to sustain segregated schools had he been confronted with a case framed as *Brown* now was.

But Felix Frankfurter favored the black man's fight for justice. He had voted on the black man's side in virtually every case involving Negro rights since he had come to the Court. None of the previous cases, though, had presented him with anything like the difficulties that *Brown* did. To cope with the problem, he followed his own advice offered in 1948 to Justice Rutledge while the Court was considering a case dealing with a state's right to forbid Jim Crow rules on an excursion boat traveling in international waters. His earlier work with the NAACP had convinced him, he told Rutledge, "that the ugly practices of racial discrimination should be dealt with by eloquence of action, but with austerity of speech. . . . By all means, let us decide with fearless decency, but express our decisions with reserve and austerity. It does not help toward harmonious race relations to stir our fellow colored citizens to resentment by even pertinent rhetoric or by a needless recital of details of mistreatment which are irrelevant to a legal issue before us." Even more to the point if applied now to *Brown*, Frankfurter had added: "Nor do we thereby mean whites, both North and South, from what so often is merely the momentum of the past in them."

Thus, he had encouraged Vinson to keep the language of the *Sweatt* and *McLaurin* opinions moderate and had not voted to bring up *Briggs* when it was first appealed. But there was a difference in his mind between proceeding slowly and malingering, as he felt Vinson had begun to do in failing to call for a decision on whether the Court should take the segregation cases. When earlier in the year Jackson sent him a draft memorandum on how the Court might take the cases but postpone scheduling them for argument, Frankfurter wrote back on the bottom of Jackson's note: "Certainly, something like the above. We ought not be doing the cowardly thing of 'passing' from week to week!" *

When the Court took the segregation cases in June, Frankfurter set to work in his fashion to win the only result he thought would stand both the Court and the country in good stead: a unanimous opinion. But just what common denominator could be found for the divided Court remained to be seen. He assigned one of his 1952 Term clerks, Alexander Bickel (who, like Frankfurter, was an immigrant from *Mitteleuropa*, a graduate of City College of New York and Harvard Law School, and a highly skilled writer), to a special term-long research project: Bickel was to read through the *Congressional Globe* and the equivalent records, wherever extant, of the state legislatures during the immediate post-Civil War years to determine if there was anything in the history of the legislative debates over the framing of the Fourteenth Amendment that foreclosed the Court from now striking down segregation. Then Frankfurter himself began trying to formulate in his mind the outlines of the sort of decree the Court might fashion if it voted to end

* See footnote on page 539 for the text of the Jackson memorandum.

segregation. More and more, he was convinced that *how* the Court presented its ruling would be no less important than the substantive content of the opinion. And increasingly, too, he was convinced that any desegregation process that the Court might order should not be a drastic one, instant and universal; it would probably have to allow the South time to make the adjustment. Yet that acknowledgment presented him with another problem: if and when the Court declared that any plaintiff had a constitutional right to attend an unsegregated school, how in the name of equity and humanity could it countenance delay in the attainment of that right? Frankfurter began to write notes to himself on the subject against the day he might need to gather his thoughts on paper; one of the penciled notes that survive in the *Brown* file in his papers at Harvard bears the heading "Segregation" and reads:

> Is equity to be unmindful to the psychological truth that change, especially drastic change, takes time? Is equity to be heedless of the lessons of experience but accommodati[ng] in practice to formal condemnation of deeply rooted social habits and their displacement by new habits [illegible word] an evolutionary process best promoted when firmly designed but not precipitously expressed. . . .

More than normally, the irrepressible Justice began to reach out to build a consensus among the brethren—a function that should naturally have fallen to the Chief Justice, who seemed in this case disinclined to exercise it. Frankfurter mended his fences with Black, his ideological arch-rival on the Court, and observers noted the pair were getting along far better in this period than they had in years. He may well have intensified his efforts to win Reed, Burton, and Minton to his way of thinking. Reed he communicated with heartily, almost airily. He showed up frequently for the tea served on fine china each afternoon in Sherman Minton's chambers. And one of Burton's clerks recalls of Frankfurter, "He was always coming by and telling us what a great guy Harold was—and then he'd go in and try to get his vote."

Three of Frankfurter's clerks offer a composite assessment of the Justice's position as *Brown* now came up for formal action by the Court. "His main concern during the '52 Term," recalled Alexander Bickel, who was there then, "was to prevent the Court from taking a premature vote." All that an early vote would have proven was that no consensus had yet jelled; all it would have produced was a number of clashing opinions that might have reduced the Court's standing and ignited racial warfare in the South. Frankfurter was perhaps more open in this period with Philip Elman, who had clerked for him between 1941 and 1943. "He used to talk to me about the segregation question a good deal," Elman recalls. "He personally was deeply against it, but his first concern was the Court, and he had a fear that the whole thing was moving along too fast. He'd hear that view from Jimmy Byrnes, with whom he had become good friends when Byrnes was on the Court, and he admired Byrnes as an able administrator and a man of action when Byrnes had been in the Senate and working for the White House. And so the Justice would listen when Byrnes insisted the South was really and finally moving to improve the black schools and that to outlaw segregation might kill the public-school system in the South." Both Frankfurter and his closest colleague on the Court, Jackson, were therefore inclined to procrastinate to see how well Byrnes and other Southern leaders whom they took to be high-minded were really succeeding in equalizing the colored schools. Besides, if the schools were not made more nearly equal, how could any desegregation process that the Court might eventually order be realistically carried out? And so Frankfurter cast himself in the dual role of both a brake on the Court's decision-making process and the prime forger of an alliance between its seemingly indissoluble factions; the two jobs went together. But in the view of another of the Justice's former clerks, William Coleman, who worked for Frankfurter during the 1949 Term and was the first Negro ever to clerk at the Court, there was never any doubt how the Justice himself was disposed on *Brown.* "From the day the cases were taken," says Coleman, "it was clear how he was going to vote. Now it may be true that he felt if there had been any honorable way of delaying it *now*, then maybe the Court should do that. But I know for a fact—well, let's not say 'fact'—that he was for ending segregation from the start."

What Frankfurter said at the December 1952 conference of the Justices would seem to support these impressions, though the notes by Burton and Jackson are inconclusive. Frankfurter often spoke and wrote in arabesqued phrases that scarcely lent themselves to being recorded accurately by colleagues noting them down on a scratch pad. Burton's notes are relatively extensive but not very lucid, yet they do make it clear that Frankfurter was ready to vote then and there to end segregation in the schools of the District of Columbia. He reminded the brethren that he "has never had close living relations to Negroes but much to do with the problem—Was asst counsel to NAACP/also belong to the Jewish minority. *Intolerable* that Gov. should permit *seg. in DC life.*/but deprecates needless *force* in changing this." Jackson noted of Frankfurter's remarks: "Prepared today to vote segregation in D.C. violates due process."

But the states presented a far thornier thicket, and Frankfurter apparently played it cagily in his comments to the conference. On the one hand, he said he found nothing in his reading of the equal-protection clause that limited the Court to considering only physical facilities in weighing whether a state was treating its citizens equally. To say that equal rights meant only physical things would be "arbitrary." On the other hand, he could not say that the Court was guilty of having long misread the Constitution with regard to the intention of the framers, whose ultimate hopes for the reach of the Fourteenth Amendment were open to ambiguous interpretation. Burton notes him saying in this context: "What justifies us in saying that what *was* equal in 1868 is not equal now[?]" To help answer that question and, though he did not say it in so many words, to stall for time, he suggested that the Court "Ask counsel to demonstrate what it is that justifies saying it [segregation] is all wrong." Jackson quotes him as remarking on this part of the problem: "With states can not treat as sociological problems." Frankfurter wound up by proposing that all the cases be set down for reargument and that the incoming Eisenhower administration, which would be charged with the job of enforcing any decision the Court reached, be invited to submit a brief and participate in the oral argument to set forth its ideas on desegregation procedure. March might be a suitable time for the reargument.

Probably no man who ever sat on it was less inclined to view the Supreme Court as a fraternity of high priests than William Douglas. The comradeship of his brother Justices was of remarkably little interest to him—a great irony, of course, since none of the 100 men who have served as Justices was destined to sit on the Court longer than Douglas has.

He struck many around the Court as a cold, highly introverted, sometimes downright unfriendly man, though few have contested his brilliance and productivity. A quick study with a highly absorbent, restless mind, Douglas employed only one clerk each term, had relatively little to do with him, and was not inclined to generous recognition of the fellow's contributions. His clerks tended to find him distant and indifferent to their well-being, though he was known at least once to have plunked down a bottle of Scotch on a clerk's desk as a birthday gift and then marched swiftly off, lest the showing of thoughtfulness be taken as a sign that he had thawed. Said one clerk: "I kept thinking that Douglas was another of those liberals who loved humanity in the abstract, but couldn't stand people in particular."

One price Douglas paid for his glacial personality was lack of fiercely admiring disciples who, like the clerks to Frankfurter and Black, might spread kind words and the judicial views of their mentors throughout the world of legal scholarship and the law profession in general. What would emerge instead was a widespread impression of Douglas as a fervent champion of individualism—perhaps the greatest in the Court's history—but also as a Justice lacking in judicial detachment, as a man sometimes prone to have his mind made up before he heard the arguments in a case, as an activist not easily reconciled to the thought that any social wrong that might come before the Court could be without a judicial remedy. He was open to the charge of conceiving of the Court not as a reviewing body but as a countervailing center of power to rectify the failures of the other branches of government. A speedy writer, he seemed a victim almost of his own facility. Few of his opinions were termed "landmark" and few of his dissents resonated with the conviction that his fellow libertarian Hugo Black brought to his writing. Disquisitions on the nuances of the law left him impatient if not downright bored, and one sensed he would much prefer to be off mountain climbing or horseback riding or writing another of the seventeen books credited to him by the end of his thirty-fifth year on the Court.

On the school-segregation cases, he registered not the slightest doubt as to how the Court should act. He and Black had dissented early in 1952 when the rest of the Justices voted to send the South Carolina case back down to the District Court for final disposition. And in October, when the Court agreed to postpone argument in the South Carolina, Kansas, and Virginia cases until December so that the District of Columbia and Delaware cases could be joined with them, Douglas had dissented alone—a sign, perhaps, that Frankfurter was winning Black to his let's-go-slow position. "Very simple for me," is how Jackson records Douglas's first comment at the December conference. "*State* can't classify by color for education," Burton has him saying. But the two sets of notes seem in conflict over how Douglas felt about stretching out the decision-making process. "Can't play factor of time," is how Jackson quotes him. But Burton writes: "Simple—Const. question—will take a long time to work it out. . . ." Whether the "it" meant the Court's opinion or the nation's acceptance of it and the desegregation process itself is unclear, though the latter interpretation is more likely. All that Douglas himself has disclosed publicly on the subject is that at the 1952 conference he favored reversing the lower-court opinions upholding segregation. He was not enthusiastic about Felix Frankfurter's suggestion that the cases ought to be reargued, though he thought he saw some value in that for the District of Columbia case.

His unhesitating stand against segregation, free from the kind of homeland tug that the South still exercised on Hugo Black, was probably admirable in the abstract to Felix Frankfurter's way of thinking but it did not contribute much to solving the Court's dilemma. Like a lot of Douglas's work, Frankfurter seemed to find it impetuous and unstatesmanlike in view of the need for the Court to present a united front to the nation on so grave a question. Douglas was a polarizing influence from this standpoint. Writing to his friend Judge Learned Hand two years later, Frankfurter promised to tell him someday the full story of how the Court had managed to resolve *Brown* and added, in an apparent allusion to Douglas and perhaps Black: "But I will tell you that if the 'great libertarians' had had their way we would have been in the soup."

At the age of sixty, his ambitions to be President or Chief Justice now largely behind him, Robert Jackson remained the most intellectually charming member of the Court. The commendable and difficult job he had done as chief counsel for the United States at the International Military Tribunal at Nuremberg had made him a world figure, and his work at the Court had demonstrated his firm command of constitutional law in all its sinuous complexity. Off the bench, he enjoyed life in exurban McLean, Virginia, at his manorial home, Hickory Hill, later owned by John and then Robert Kennedy; he loved to fish and ride and hike and go camping and to take a belt of his favorite brand of bourbon. What he did best of all, though, was write. Probably only Holmes matched or surpassed him as a stylist. It was Jackson who penned the ultimate aphorism on the Court's uniqueness: "We are not final because we are infallible, but we are infallible only because we are final."

A partial clue to Justice Jackson's posture toward the segregation cases may be found in his admirable 1941 book, *The Struggle for Judicial Supremacy*, in which he wrote:

. . . Legal learning is largely built around the principle known as *stare decisis*. It means that on the same point of law yesterday's decision shall govern today's decision. Like a coral reef, the common law thus becomes a structure of fossils. . . . Precedents largely govern the conclusions and surround the reasoning of lawyers and judges. In the field of common law they are a force for stability and predictability, but in constitutional law they are the most powerful influence in forming and supporting reactionary opinions. The judge who can take refuge in a precedent does not need to justify his decision to the reason. He may "reluctantly feel himself bound" by a doctrine, supported by a respected historical name, that he would not be able to justify to contemporary opinion or under modern conditions.

Such a conviction freed Jackson from the sort of constricting doctrinal devotion that made Frankfurter seem a far more consistent jurist. It also seemed to free Jackson from the obligation to follow his own prior judicial positions. In a 1950 opinion, he could thus bluntly warn Congress to leave men's minds alone in its zeal to check the domestic spread of Communism by repressive laws, yet the very next year he voted with the Court majority upholding the Smith Act that punished Communist leaders not for any overt acts they took toward overthrowing the government but because of their conspiratorial speech and teachings. In one case, he would scorn Harlan Stone's doctrine that the First Amendment, or any part of the Constitution, could occupy a "preferred position" among the rights and protections granted by the great document; in other cases, he himself seemed to espouse a preferred position for the Fourth Amendment, outlawing unreasonable searches and seizures. He was proud of his dissent in *Korematsu*, one of the Japanese-American relocation cases during the Second World War, but he was on the majority side in the companion (and not readily distinguishable) *Hirabayashi* case. He was, in short, often as inconsistent and unpredictable as he was brilliant.

As Jackson reviewed the legal arguments in *Brown*, he saw no basis in the prior uses of the law for overruling segregation. By his own lights, though, this hardly shut the door on such a ruling. Nor did he doubt, according to a memo he wrote fifteen months later, that the continued practice of segregation was not wise or fair public policy. Yet he shared Frankfurter's belief that the Court's decision could hardly take the form of a simplistic rendering of his own—or the rest of the Justices'—personal convictions in the matter. He saw little help in the extra-legal sociology and psychology that the black lawyers had introduced into the case; all that struck Jackson as rather too subjective and unmeasurable. And he was worried about how a Court decision outlawing segregation would affect the nation's respect for "a supposedly stable organic law" if the Justices were now, overnight as it were, to alter an interpretation of the Fourteenth Amendment that had stood for more than three-quarters of a century. Even if he could have put that concern aside, he had doubts that a seemingly "ruthless use of federal judicial power" would have much effect in truly abolishing Jim Crow practices.

The Justice asked his two 1952 Term clerks for an advisory memorandum on the segregation cases. The two clerks later seemed to disagree on whether their memos were intended to be a playback of Jackson's own views or a statement of the varying positions Jackson might adopt in the case, and internal evidence suggests that they may have been neither but were instead invited statements of each clerk's personal views of the case. One memo, initialed "DC" on the bottom for clerk Donald Cronson, a Chicago Law School graduate, was titled "A Few Expressed Prejudices on the Segregation Cases," and stated that, according to its author's prejudices, "there is no doubt that Plessy was wrong" and should have been decided along the lines of Harlan's dissent. But to say that *Plessy* was wrongly decided did not dispose of the matter, the Cronson memo went on, because the decision had resulted in the growth of important institutions—"not only rules of law, but ways of life"—and under those circumstances, Cronson said, he questioned "the wisdom or propriety of overruling the case, right or wrong." He acknowledged that there was perhaps not much justification for keeping an incorrect ruling on the books, but "where a whole way of life has grown up around such a prior error, then I say that we are stuck with it—until such time as Congress sees fit to act. . . ." The Court, Cronson thought, should confess error in *Plessy*—just how, he did not say—and "straighten out the mess so that Congress may by legislation prohibit segregation." If Congress chose not to do so, even after being advised by the Court that segregation was unconstitutional, then surely the Court should not do so by a sweeping decree, Cronson concluded.

The second memo was less ambiguous. It was titled "A Random Thought on the Segregation Cases" and is of historical interest because of the initials at the bottom—"whr"—which stand for William H. Rehnquist, who nineteen years later became the one hundredth man to sit on the Supreme Court. His memo threatened for a time to cost him that seat. The memo, Rehnquist advised the Senate while it was weighing his nomination to the high court in 1971, had been written at Justice Jackson's request and represented Jackson's views on the segregation cases. The Justice wanted the memo, Rehnquist said, to arm himself when speaking at the conference of the Justices. The informal nature of the memo, Rehnquist reflected, made him think that it had been "prepared very shortly after one of our oral discussions on the subject." The first half of the two-page Rehnquist memo is a gratuitous thumbnail sketch of the Court's earlier tendency to read its own economic views into the Constitution. The second half of the memo bemoaned the possibility of the Court's reading its own social views into the Constitution by now voting to outlaw segregation. Rehnquist wrote in part, allegedly paraphrasing the position Jackson was about to state to his fellow Justices:

> . . . Urging a view palpably at variance with precedent and probably with legislative history, appellants seek to convince the Court of the moral wrongness of the treatment they are receiving. I would submit that this is a question the Court need never reach. . . . If this Court, because its members individually are "liberals" and dislike segregation, now chooses to strike it down, it differs from the McReynolds court only in the kinds of litigants it favors and the kinds of special claims it protects.

To those who argue that personal rights are more sacrosanct than property rights, the memo added, "the short answer is that the Constitution makes no such distinction." Then it continued:

> . . . One hundred and fifty years of attempts on the part of this Court to protect minority rights of any kind—whether those of business, slaveholders, or Jehovah's Witnesses—have all met the same fate. One by one the cases establishing such rights have been sloughed off, and crept silently to rest. If the present Court is unable to profit by this example, it must be prepared to see its work fade in time, too, as embodying only the sentiments of a transient majority of nine men.
>
> I realize that it is an unpopular and unhumanitarian position, for which I have been excoriated by "liberal" colleagues, but I think *Plessy* v. *Ferguson* was right and should be re-affirmed. . . .

If Rehnquist was telling the truth to the Senate in 1971* and the words in

---

* There is much evidence, both internal and external, that casts doubt on Rehnquist's account of the nature of his memorandum. After it was published in *Newsweek* at the time of the Senate confirmation hearings, some liberal Senators and civil-rights proponents took the memo at face value—that is, as a statement of Rehnquist's own views, since it bore his initials and an informal, rather personal-sounding title, "A Random Thought on the Segregation Cases"—and challenged his suitability to be appointed to the Court in view of his having apparently favored the upholding of segregation. Faced with growing resistance to his nomination, Rehnquist sent a letter on December 8, 1971, to Senate Judiciary Committee Chairman James Eastland which said that to his best recollection after some nineteen years, "the memorandum was prepared by me at Justice Jackson's request; it was intended as a rough draft of a statement of his views at the conference of the Justices, rather than as a statement of my views." Rehnquist went on to say that Jackson had asked him to assist "in developing arguments which he might use in conference when cases were discussed. He expressed concern that the conference should have the benefit of all of the arguments in support of the constitutionality of the 'separate but equal' doctrine, as well as those against its constitutionality." The clear implication was that Rehnquist's memo was intended to add armor to Jackson's defense of *Plessy*. Rehnquist wound up his explanation to the Senate by stressing that the memo was very unlike most of those normally done by the clerks of the Court in analyzing cases, that the style of the memo was hardly that of a clerk addressing the Justice he worked for but was prepared by Rehnquist "as a statement of Justice Jackson's tentative views for his own use at conference," and that Rehnquist himself fully supported (in 1971) "the legal reasoning and the rightness from the standpoint of fundamental fairness of the *Brown* decision."

Of the two living people who might have corroborated Rehnquist's explanation to the Senate, one offered elaborations that seemed to conflict with the Rehnquist account, and the other sharply denied it.

Rehnquist's fellow clerk, Donald Cronson, by then an executive with Mobil Oil in the company's London office, cabled a message to Rehnquist that Republican Senate Minority Leader Hugh Scott placed in the *Congressional Record* for December 9, 1971. Cronson wrote, "It is my recollection that the memorandum in question is my work at least as much as it is yours and that it was prepared in response to a request from Justice Jackson. . . ." That was the first piece of information supplied by Cronson which did not quite mesh with Rehnquist's explanation: Rehnquist had not suggested that the memo was a collaborative effort. Cronson went on to say that prior to the memo which bore Rehnquist's initials at the end, "another memorandum was prepared of which I still have a copy. It is my recollection that I actually typed the first memorandum, although it is possible that you did. It was in any case the result of collaboration between us." Cronson then described the first memo, which he said contended that *Plessy* had been wrongly decided but that the Court should leave it to Congress to implement any change in the practice of segregation—that is, the memo titled "A Few Expressed Prejudices on the Segregation Cases" and carrying Cronson's initials at the end, which survives in Justice Jackson's papers. Later, Cronson said, Jackson asked for a second memo "supporting the proposition that *Plessy* was correctly decided. The memorandum supporting *Plessy* was typed by you, but a great deal of the content was the result of my suggestions . . . and it is probable that the memorandum is more mine than yours."

Cronson's explanation raises at least three questions: (1) Why did Rehnquist fail to his undated memo even remotely reflected Jackson's views, then the Justice must have undergone a considerable change of heart about presenting them to his colleagues at the Court conference on December 13, 1952, for little in Burton's notes on Jackson's remarks resembles any of the thoughts attributed to him in the Rehnquist memo. And nothing in the memo that Jackson himself prepared on the subject in February 1954 remotely suggests that he ever thought that *Plessy* had been rightly decided.

---

mention the first memo in his letter to the Senate? (2) If Jackson had requested two memos reaching opposite conclusions on the rightness of *Plessy*, why did Rehnquist claim that the second memo—the one bearing Rehnquist's initials—represented Jackson's view of the case? Cronson did not suggest that Jackson had changed his mind after the first memo, only that he wanted a second memo reaching the opposite conclusion. (3) If Rehnquist and Cronson had collaborated on both memos to the extent that Cronson suggests (and Rehnquist never suggested), why did each memo carry the initials of just one of the clerks, why were the styles of the memos so different, and why would Rehnquist not want to inform the Senate that another man was co-author of the memo that was the subject of such controversy—especially if, as Cronson put it, the memo was "more mine than yours"?

The other person who might have corroborated Rehnquist's explanation of the memo was Mrs. Elsie Douglas, Jackson's secretary and confidante for the nine years preceding his death in October 1954. She told the Washington *Post* that by attributing the views of a pro-segregation memo to Jackson, Rehnquist had "smeared the reputation of a great Justice." She challenged Rehnquist's assertion that Jackson would have asked a law clerk to help prepare the remarks he would deliver at a conference of the Justices, especially in view of Jackson's acknowledged gift for spontaneous eloquence and his splendid oral performances before the Court while Solicitor General and while serving at the Nuremberg war-crimes trials. She told *Newsweek* that Rehnquist's account was "incredible on its face."

Without resort to the statements by Cronson or Mrs. Douglas, Rehnquist's attribution to Jackson of the views in the 1952 Term memo bearing Rehnquist's initials is challenged by internal evidence in both the Rehnquist and Cronson memos:

(1) The titles of both memos are strikingly inappropriate to the use Rehnquist claims Jackson had in mind: as a draft of the Justice's views for presentation to his fellow Justices. Is it possible that Cronson would have titled his memo "A Few Expressed Prejudices on the Segregation Cases" or Rehnquist would have called his "A Random Thought on the Segregation Cases" if either or both had been drafted for use by the Justice at conference? The Justices, one would think, would hardly be inclined to conceive of their considered views as either "prejudices" or "a random thought." But such titles would be entirely appropriate if Justice Jackson had simply asked each of his clerks to put down informally his own personal views on the case for the Justice's consideration.

(2) Is it possible that Jackson would have bothered to deliver so crude and elementary a summary of the Court's historic position on property rights and its preferential treatment of business interests—the subject of the first half of the Rehnquist memo? Every member of the Vinson Court except Burton was a veteran New Dealer, entirely familiar with the court-packing fight and the Court's pre-1937 biases.

(3) Is it possible that Jackson would have disaparaged, as Rehnquist indicates in the memo that the Justice planned to, "150 years of attempts on the part of this Court to protect minority rights of any kind—whether those of business, slaveholders, or Jehovah's Witnesses" when Jackson himself wrote many a decision protecting minority rights? Among the most eloquent was Jackson's opinion in the second flag-salute case, *West Virginia Board of Education v. Barnette* in 1943, which took the side of the Jehovah's Witnesses and concluded with one of the Justice's most memorable passages: "If there is any fixed star in our constitutional constellation, it is that no official, high or petty, can prescribe what shall be orthodox in politics, nationalism, religion, or other matters of opinion or force citizens to confess by word or act their faith therein. . . ."

(4) Is it possible that so confident and civilized a man as Robert Jackson would have told his brother Justices anything remotely approaching what Rehnquist writes at the end of his memo purportedly reflecting Jackson's views—namely, "I realize that it is an unpopular and unhumanitarian position, for which I have been excoriated by 'liberal' colleagues, but I think *Plessy* . . . was right and should be affirmed"? The "I" in that passage, according to Rehnquist, was supposed to be Jackson, not his clerk, but when and where might Jackson have been excoriated by his "liberal" colleagues? And what colleagues might those be? Surely not his

According to Burton's notes, Jackson began his comments to the Justices with the aside that if they were going to take their time to thrash the cases out, it would be better for them not to take a vote that day. Burton's diary entry for that date indicates that the suggestion was adopted: "We discussed the segregation cases thus disclosing the trend but no even tentative vote was taken." Burton's notes on Jackson's presentation are hard to decipher, but they seem to say that Jackson had found nothing in his reading of legislative

---

fellow Justices, who would hardly have spoken ill of him for expressing genuine convictions. A far more plausible explanation might be that the "I" of the memo is Rehnquist himself, referring to the obloquy to which he may have been subjected by his fellow clerks, who discussed the segregation question over lunch quite regularly, who were almost unanimous in their belief that *Plessy* ought to be reversed, and who were, for the most part, "liberal." Support for this surmise is lent by an article that Rehnquist wrote in the December 13, 1957, issue of *U.S. News & World Report.* Under the title "Who Writes Decisions of the Supreme Court?" it says, as part of a complaint against the leftward bias of the clerks: "Some of the tenets of the 'liberal' point of view which commanded the sympathy of a majority of the clerks I knew were: extreme solicitude for the claims of Communists and other criminal defendants, expansion of federal power at the expense of State power, great sympathy toward any government regulation of business. . . ." The telltale use of quotation marks around the word "liberal" adds to the suspicion that the "I" of the Rehnquist memo was never meant to be Robert Jackson speaking to his brethren. That Rehnquist was ideologically a pole apart from his fellow clerks that year is suggested by the comment of Harvard law professor Donald Trautman, who clerked for Justice Frankfurter that term. "As I knew him, he was a reactionary," Trautman told the *Harvard Law Record* of October 24, 1971, at the time of Rehnquist's Court appointment. "I would expect him to be a reactionary today, but you never know what a person will do once he's appointed."

(5) While Rehnquist claimed his memo was intended to convey Jackson's words and thoughts, it would be difficult to support such a claim for the companion Cronson memo, which is plainly a memo from a clerk to his Justice, as evidenced by the paragraph that begins, "One of the main characteristics to be found in *your* work on this Court is a reluctance to overrule existing constitutional law . . . [emphasis added]."

(6) In his disclaimer to the Senate, Rehnquist did not say that he agreed with the *Brown* decision when it was made, only that he agreed with it in 1971, when he was being scrutinized for appointment to the Supreme Court—and when "an unpopular and unhumanitarian position" in favor of segregation might well have cost him his seat on that Court. That Rehnquist may once have felt otherwise about the outcome in *Brown* can be inferred from a passage in an article by Rehnquist in the *Harvard Law Record* of October 8, 1959, a dozen years before his appointment:

> . . . There are those who bemoan the absence of *stare decisis* in constitutional law, but of its absence there can be no doubt. And it is no accident that the provisions of the constitution which have been most productive of judicial law-making—the "due process of law" and "equal protection of the laws" clauses—are about the vaguest and most general of any in the instrument. The Court in *Brown v. Board of Education* . . . held in effect that the framers of the Fourteenth Amendment left it to the Court to decide what "due process" and "equal protection" meant. Whether or not the framers thought this, it is sufficient for this discussion that the present Court [the one that decided *Brown*] thinks the framers thought it.

It remains to be said that William Hubbs Rehnquist has been, from the first dawning of his political awareness, a forceful, outspoken conservative with a low threshold of tolerance for civil-liberties claimants and the civil rights of minorities. "The Justice's views on the law, the Constitution, discrimination and crime seem indistinguishable today from those [that] friends recall in his late adolescence," wrote veteran Washington correspondent Warren Weaver, Jr., in an article on Rehnquist in the October 13, 1974, issue of the *New York Times Magazine.* "While most people's views evolve and shift as they grow older, Rehnquist's conservative outlook seems to have been adopted and then flash-frozen while he was an undergraduate at Stanford. . . . A law-school classmate at Stanford, an unabashed liberal, recalls: 'Rehnquist was very consistently more than just conservative. . . .' Another fellow student observed: 'Bill was the school conservative. A lot of us had mixed views about him. He was very sharp, a brilliant student, but

or judicial history that suggested segregation had been thought unconstitutional anywhere along the line. He thought Thurgood Marshall's brief contained more sociology than law, and he had his doubts that racism could be overcome in America "by putting children together." Still, he thought the Court might be able to justify the abolition of segregation on political grounds, though he did not see how the Justices could claim a judicial basis for the decision. He would likely go along with such a politically framed decision provided it gave the segregating states "reasonable time" to adjust to the ruling. But if the Court were to rule that the South had been acting illicitly all along, he would have trouble going along.

Jackson's 1953 Term clerk E. Barrett Prettyman, Jr., elaborates: "Justice Jackson was wary. He wanted to make sure that the Court was going to shoot straight. He didn't want it to accuse the South of behaving unconstitutionally all those years, especially since the history of the Fourteenth Amendment didn't really point to the conclusion that *Plessy* should be reversed. In short, he wanted the Court, in ending segregation, to admit that it was making new law for a new day."

Had it been practicable, Jackson's preference might have been to follow the essence of the Cronson memo and urge the Court to shape an advisory opinion holding: (1) the *Plessy* doctrine had been attenuated and neutralized by a whole line of cases, most recently *Sweatt* and *McLaurin* (but others as well in the areas of transportation, restrictive housing covenants, and voting rights); (2) if the Court in *Plessy* had meant to deny Congress's power to outlaw segregation under Section 5 of the Fourteenth Amendment, then the Court had erred; but (3) in the absence of congressional initiative in the

---

so far-out politically that he was something of a joke.' " In private law practice in Phoenix, he gave a speech in 1957 denouncing Justices Black and Douglas, among others, as "left-wing" and called them down for "making the Constitution say what they wanted it to say." He was an ardent supporter of fellow Arizonan Barry Goldwater's political fortunes, and as a Phoenix civic leader Rehnquist spoke out forcefully against a local anti-discrimination ordinance and asserted in opposition to a 1967 desegregation program in the city's schools that "we are no more dedicated to an 'integrated' society than we are to a 'segregated' society." As an Assistant Attorney General and head of the Office of Legal Counsel in the Nixon administration, he was well known as the Justice Department's most ardently prosecutorial advocate of wiretapping, government surveillance, preventive detention, and other so-called law-and-order techniques of a totalitarian cast. In 1970, he drafted for the White House a proposed constitutional amendment prohibiting bussing to achieve desegregation. In the Supreme Court, he has consistently voted to constrict civil rights and civil liberties, opposing the claims of, among others, women seeking abortions, poor people who had to wait a year before qualifying for public medical services, aliens applying for civil-service jobs and lawyer's licenses, and Negroes seeking expanded school-desegregation efforts in Denver, Richmond, and Detroit. He has voted to retain the death penalty, to permit warrantless searches for narcotics of people stopped for minor traffic offenses, and to authorize government agents to lure a defendant into a crime if he was deemed to have a "predisposition" to commit it anyway. In antitrust cases, he usually sided with business against government; in labor cases, he usually sided with management against unions. In September 1974, he gave a speech characterizing himself as a "libertarian" in the sense of one who conceives minimum-wage and maximum-hour legislation as interfering impermissibly with an employer's freedom of choice.

Taking the careers and judicial assertions of both men in their totality, one finds a preponderance of evidence to suggest that the memorandum in question—the one that threatened to deprive William Rehnquist of his place on the Supreme Court—was an accurate statement of his own views on segregation, not those of Robert Jackson, who, by contrast, was a staunch libertarian and humanist. The Senate confirmed Rehnquist's nomination, 68 to 26.

matter, the Supreme Court ought not to intrude, for it lacked the administrative machinery and specialized local knowledge to oversee the desegregation process, not to mention the will to do so. Jackson felt strongly that Congress had shunned its responsibility and he had implied as much in one of his questions during the oral argument. The idea of an advisory opinion was thus appealing to Jackson but not to Frankfurter, who mentioned it skeptically to Elman. The worst thing the Court could do, in Frankfurter's view, was to get up on its hind legs and then get right down again; better not to have heard the cases at all than to issue an opinion implying a moral imperative to cure a social evil but confessing the Court's incapacity or indisposition to attend to the matter until Congress had done so first.

Jackson, then, was keeping his options open. His reluctance to see any real judicial basis for overturning segregation—and his flirtation with the sort of advisory opinion that the Court had insisted since John Marshall's day it could not constitutionally issue to the other branches of government—were almost certainly why Frankfurter, in his May 20, 1954, letter to Reed, listed Jackson as a probable vote to affirm segregation as of the 1952 Term. That was one good reason why Frankfurter badly wanted to hold off a vote.

Harold Burton, the handsome, sixty-four-year-old Ohioan, was not notably smart or articulate or facile, but no member of the Court worked more conscientiously to compensate for the gifts nature forgot to bestow. He was a conservative, highly moral Midwesterner without being sanctimonious about it, and he did not rely on his clerks to do his homework for him. "He tried to divest himself of every prejudice before working out his positions by himself," recalls Raymond S. Troubh, a 1953 Term clerk, who found him to be a saintly man without an ounce of guile. Clerks to other members of the Court shared Troubh's admiration. "If I had my life at stake," says Jackson's '53 Term clerk, Barrett Prettyman, "and wanted to come before the fairest judge in the world, Burton would have been my choice." At Burton's death in 1958, Frankfurter's ex-clerk Alexander Bickel wrote for the *New Republic* that while many judges managed to be "honest, open-minded, conscientious, selfless and humble . . . few could have done so in our time to the degree that Justice Burton did."

Since his solo dissent in *Morgan v. Virginia* during his first term on the Court, Burton had increasingly aligned himself with the black man's ever lengthening petition for equal rights. And on the school-segregation cases, his vote was not really in doubt. His packed diary, filled with the minutiae of his life (including his weight after a daily swim in the Senate pool), gives no clue to his thinking on the subject, but a letter to Frankfurter dated September 25, 1952, suggests where he stood on *Brown*, as well as promoting the inference that Frankfurter had been working on him:

Dear Felix:
    I thank you for this glimpse into your inner consciousness.
    I have been increasingly impressed with the idea that under the conditions of 50 or more years ago it probably could be said that a state's treatment of

negroes, within its borders, on the basis of "separate but equal" facilities might come within the constitutional guaranty of an "equal" protection of the laws, because the lives of negroes and whites were then and there in fact *separately* cast and lived. Today, however, I doubt that it can be said in any state (and certainly not generally) that compulsory "separation" of the races, even with equal facilities, *can* amount to an "equal" protection of the laws in a society that is lived and shared so *"jointly"* by all races as ours is now.

At the Justices' conference two and a half months later, Burton was still of that view. Jackson records him as saying: "Agree should be done in easy way as possible. *Sipuel, Sweatt* control. Gives force enough to upset segregation." Next to his own name, Burton wrote in his notes: "Rev & time/& reargue DC." Douglas in his autobiography says Burton was ready to reverse at the 1952 conference.

One odd thing bobs up in Harold Burton's papers preserved in the Library of Congress. His diary carefully lists the title of every case the Court heard on a given day and the attorneys who argued them, along with a short rating of each lawyer's performance. Beside the name of each NAACP lawyer in *Brown*, all of whom he rated from "good" to "excellent," he also wrote: "(colored)."

In his three years on the Court, Tom Clark had clung tightly to Fred Vinson's robe tails. Clark voted the way the Chief did about 90 percent of the time. No two other Justices came so close to functioning in unison. "He was strongly deferential to the Chief Justice," notes a former Clark clerk of that period.

The closeness of the two men involved more than their judicial outlook. Both intimates of Harry Truman, they shared with the President a pragmatic, non-intellectual, and highly politicized sense of the world around them. At the Court, Clark generally sat at Vinson's table in the Justices' dining room, where the talk, especially when ex-semi-pro baseball player Sherman Minton joined them, was as likely to be about Stan Musial's batting average as the vicissitudes of the Fourteenth Amendment. There was reason, therefore, to suspect that Clark would share Vinson's attitude toward the school-segregation cases, and, to an important degree, he probably did. But by the end of 1952 there were increasing signs that Tom Clark was standing on his own two judicial feet. The most important evidence was his vote earlier in the year to strike down Truman's seizure of the nation's steel mills. That vote was perhaps the turning point in Clark's career as a Justice, for not only did it burn his bridge to his principal political patron in the White House but it also placed him on the opposite side of the Court, on the first occasion of any consequence, from Fred Vinson.

Though he had agreed, as Attorney General in 1948, to put the Truman administration on the Negro's side in *Shelley v. Kraemer*, had stayed on that side in his votes since coming to the Court, and was regarded by his clerks as "a very unprejudiced human being," Clark was apparently not yet ready to take a clear stand on *Brown* as the Justices first met to consider it. "You may be ready in your own mind to decide on a case," Clark reflected twenty years later, "but think it wiser to hold off—till the circumstances are different."

Jackson's notes of the conference record Clark as remarking, "Have led states on to believe separate but equal OK." Burton noted that Clark said he was "inclined to go along with delay."

Clark's hesitation was doubtless compounded by his reading of the likely reaction if the Court were to command proud Texas to desegregate its schools—and to do it promptly forthwith. Frankfurter, a keen observer of his colleagues' voting inclinations, listed Clark—along with Vinson, Reed, and Jackson—as probable dissenters if the Court had voted to overturn *Plessy* in the spring of 1953.

Sherman Minton, it was once said of him by Felix Frankfurter, was "an almost pathological Democrat." Justice Douglas referred to him as "Mr. Mainstreet." There were few bohemians in "Shay" Minton's native state of Indiana, and fewer still in the towns where he grew up and first practiced law just across the Ohio River from Louisville. His party regularity was what defined him as a United States Senator, and his strict adherence to precedent and a sometimes myopically literal reading of the law marked his service on the Court of Appeals for the Seventh Circuit. He proved, accordingly, a not very adventurous or reflective member of the Supreme Court, on which many legal scholars soon came to the conclusion he had been misplaced. More than any other Justice, he was moved by a strong presumption of constitutionality toward actions of the legislative and executive branches, and he evidenced an almost palpable aversion toward anything he thought smacked of judicial lawmaking by the appellate courts.

As a civil-libertarian, then, Minton had earned low grades. It was said of him by Court underlings that he was so mean-spirited a man that he would not have considered acting favorably on a writ of *habeas corpus* unless it reached him with blood on it. His position on the civil rights of the Negro was more complex. As a Senator, he had pushed for the NAACP's anti-lynching bill. When told that the measure trespassed on states' rights, Minton is said to have responded, "But I am more interested in human rights." Yet his votes on the Seventh Circuit reflected little of the liberal social commitments that had characterized his service in the Senate. On the Supreme Court, his record before and during the period when *Brown* was under consideration was spotted. He had dissented with Vinson and Reed in *Brotherhood of Railway Trainmen v. Howard* earlier in 1952, and in the spring of 1953 he would dissent alone in the final Texas white-primary case to come before the Court—*Terry v. Adams*, the so-called "Jaybird" case. Minton's "Jaybird" dissent suggests something of the limitations of his thinking.

For more than fifty years, the Jaybird Democratic Association of Fort Bend County just southwest of Houston had been holding a primary election every May. The Jaybird election was not conducted as an official act of the Democratic Party, though the qualifications to vote in it were precisely the same as those for the county-operated primaries—except for one thing: Negroes were excluded. Jaybird Association officials acknowledged in court that their intention was to restrict the voting to whites, and the record showed that whoever won the "private" Jaybird primary invariably won the regular state-sanctioned primary, which had been opened to Negroes by *Smith v. Allwright*. The Jaybirds contended that no state action was involved in their preferential polling, but Hugo Black, writing for the Court, demurred: "For a state to permit such a duplication of its election processes is to permit a flagrant abuse of those processes to defeat the purposes of the Fifteenth Amendment. The use of the county-operated primary to ratify the result of the prohibited election merely compounds the offense." Alone, Minton disagreed: "This record will be searched in vain for one iota of state action sufficient to support an anemic inference that the Jaybird Association is in any way associated with . . . the Democratic Party of the county or state." The Jaybirds, he said, were merely a political pressure group. It seemed beyond his conception that a state, by its failure to act as well as by its overt actions, might violate the plain intent of the Constitution's commandment against racial tests in voting. And yet it was Minton who authored the Court's opinion, handed down at about the same time as the Jaybird decision, in *Barrows v. Jackson*, the case expanding the definition of state action in *Shelley* to prevent white signatories to restrictive covenants from collecting damages from other signers who sold their property to Negroes. Minton, in short, seemed something of an enigma on how the law could be used to answer the race question.

Stanley Reed indicated in 1953 that he hoped Minton might join him in opposing a Court vote to upset *Plessy*, and over at Justice, Elman had heard that neither Vinson nor Minton wanted to overrule segregation. But at the Court conference in December, Sherman Minton took a surprisingly strong and unmistakable position. It was true, he said, that a body of constitutional law had grown up to surround the separate-but-equal doctrine with an aura of legitimacy, but the Court had been chipping away at the protective covering for some time now. Classification of American citizens on the basis of race was unreasonable, he said. Segregation in and of itself was unconstitutional, he said. And he was ready to vote that way that day.

At its first full-dress consideration of *Brown*, then, the Supreme Court of the United States was of several minds as to whether, how, and when it ought to strike down state-imposed segregation in the nation's schools.

Four of the Justices—Black, Douglas, Burton, and Minton—had stated their willingness to vote in favor of ending the practice. One, Reed, was ready to vote to affirm it. The others apparently did not say how they would vote, except for Frankfurter's indication that he was ready to overturn Jim Crow schools in the nation's capital. Vinson and Clark were troubled by the uproar the Court might stir in voting down segregation and feared protracted domestic strife; they plainly preferred a wait-and-see stance. Jackson, according to his clerk who later succeeded to the Supreme Court, thought *Plessy* had been rightly decided and was ready to take the "unhumanitarian" position that it should now stand; according to all other evidence, he did not admire *Plessy* and would not oppose a Court vote striking it down unless a majority insisted on declaring that segregation had been wrongly held to be constitutional all along.

And so they were divided. But given the gravity of the issue, they were willing to take their time to try to reconcile their differences. They clamped a precautionary lid on all their discussions of *Brown* as the year turned and Fred Vinson swore in Dwight David Eisenhower as the thirty-fourth President of the United States. The Justices seemed to make little headway toward resolving the problem, but they all knew that a close vote would likely be a disaster for Court and country alike. The problem of welding the disparate views into a single one was obviously complicated by the ambivalence afflicting the Court's presiding Justice. As spring came and the end of the Court's 1952 Term neared, Fred Vinson seemed to be in increasingly disagreeable and edgy spirits. Says one of the people at the Court closest to him then: "I got the distinct impression that he was distressed over the Court's inability to find a strong, unified position on such an important case."

What evidence there is suggests that those on or close to the Court thought it was about as severely divided as it could be at this stage of its deliberations.

Frankfurter thought the Court was divided five-to-four in favor of reversing *Plessy*, with himself in the majority.

Burton thought the Court stood at six-to-three for reversing.

Jackson counted anywhere from two to four dissenters if the Court voted to reverse, with himself in the majority camp, provided that an opinion palatable to him was drafted by Black or whoever might write for the Court.

During the last week of the term in June, the law clerks of all the Justices met in an informal luncheon session and took a two-part poll. Each clerk was asked how he would vote in the school-segregation cases and how he thought his Justice would vote. According to one of their number, a man who later became a professor of law: "The clerks were almost unanimous for overruling *Plessy* and ordering desegregation, but, according to their impressions, the Court would have been closely divided if it had announced its decision at that time. Many of the clerks were only guessing at the positions of their respective Justices, but it appeared that a majority of the Justices would not have overruled *Plessy* but would have given some relief in some of the cases on the ground that the separate facilities were not in fact equal."

Into that breach stepped Felix Frankfurter.

His clerk and ardent admirer Alexander Bickel remembered the dynamic little Justice returning from a conference of the Justices toward the end of the term in a state bordering upon exultation. "He said it looked as if we could hold off a decision that term, that no one on the Court was pushing it, that no vote had actually been taken throughout the term—and that if we could get together some questions for discussion at a reargument, the case would be held over until the new term."

But the questions, of course, had to be plausible. The Court must not look to the litigants or the nation beyond as if it were stalling. Frankfurter and Bickel set to work roughing out the questions, and the Justice sent the draft to the other members of the Court on May 27, 1953, with an attached memo reading in part:

> . . . These questions, I think, do not offend against the suggestion that we ought not to disclose our minds. Certainly as an entirety, they look in opposite directions. Some give comfort to one side and some to the other, and that is precisely the intention. Insofar as the questions dealing with remedies may indicate that a decision against segregation has been reached by the Court, I think it is not undesirable that an adjustment be made in the public mind to such a possibility. I know not how others feel, but for me the ultimate crucial factor in the problem presented by these cases is psychological—the adjustment of men's minds and actions to the unfamiliar and the unpleasant. . . .

With a few minor changes, the Frankfurter-Bickel draft of the questions was accepted by the divided Court as a stopgap measure. On June 8, all five segregation cases were unanimously restored to the docket for reargument on October 12, and the parties to the litigation were asked to discuss "the following questions insofar as they are relevant to the respective cases":

> 1. What evidence is there that the Congress which submitted and the state legislatures and conventions* which ratified the Fourteenth Amendment contemplated or did not contemplate, understood or did not understand, that it would abolish segregation in public schools?
>
> 2. If neither the Congress in submitting nor the states in ratifying the Fourteenth Amendment understood that compliance with it would require the immediate abolition of segregation in public schools, was it nevertheless the understanding of the framers of the amendment (a) that future Congresses might in the exercise of their power under Sec. 5 of the amendment, abolish segregation, or (b) that it would be within the judicial power, in light of future conditions, to construe the amendment as abolishing such segregation of its own force?
>
> 3. On the assumption that the answers to questions 2(a) and (b) do not dispose of the issue, is it within the judicial power, in construing the amendment, to abolish segregation in public schools?
>
> 4. Assuming it is decided that segregation in public schools violates the Fourteenth Amendment,
>
> (a) would a decree necessarily follow providing that, within the limits set by normal geographic school districting, Negro children should forthwith be admitted to schools of their choice, or
>
> (b) may this Court, in the exercise of its equity powers, permit an effective gradual adjustment to be brought about from existing segregated systems to a system not based on color distinctions?
>
> 5. On the assumption on which questions 4(a) and (b) are based, and assuming further that this Court will exercise its equity powers to the end described in question 4(b),
>
> (a) should this Court formulate detailed decrees in these cases;
>
> (b) if so, what specific issues should the decrees reach;
>
> (c) should this Court appoint a special master to hear evidence with a view to recommending specific terms for such decrees;

---

* There were in fact no state conventions held to ratify the Fourteenth Amendment; it was voted on only by the state legislatures. Bickel attributed the error to himself.

(d) should this Court remand to the courts of first instance with directions to frame decrees in these cases, and if so, what general directions should the decrees of this Court include and what procedures should the courts of first instance follow in arriving at the specific terms of more detailed decrees?

The Attorney General was invited to take part in the oral argument—an invitation not extended for the first argument the preceding December—and to file a new brief.

Jim Crow was still alive.

# 24

# The Six-Month Summer

Over the names of Walter White and Thurgood Marshall, the NAACP dispatched emergency telegrams on June 9, 1953, to several hundred well-heeled supporters of civil-rights and civil-liberties causes. The message read:

UNITED STATES SUPREME COURT TODAY DEFERRED JUDGMENT ON FIVE HISTORIC CASES CHALLENGING RACIAL SEGREGATION IN ELEMENTARY AND HIGH SCHOOLS. . . . POSTPONEMENT COMES AFTER THREE YEARS LEGAL ACTIONS . . . COSTING $58,000. . . . WORK MADE POSSIBLE ONLY THROUGH CONTRIBUTIONS FROM CITIZENS WHO UNDERSTAND SIGNIFICANCE TO NATIONAL LIFE AND IMPACT UPON WORLD STRUGGLE. FUNDS ENTIRELY SPENT. HIGHEST COURT NOW REQUESTS PREPARATION OF ANSWERS WITHIN THREE MONTHS TO MANY BROAD QUESTIONS REQUIRING LEGAL ARGUMENT ON HISTORIC CONSTITUTIONAL FACTORS, SOCIOLOGICAL DATA AND AUTHORITATIVE OPINION. NO MONEY AVAILABLE MEET EMERGENCY.

OPPORTUNITY FOR DECENT PUBLIC EDUCATION AFFECTING NEARLY THREE MILLION NEGRO AMERICAN CHILDREN DEPENDS UPON RESOLUTION THIS DILEMMA. $15,000 NEEDED IMMEDIATELY TO FORESTALL POSSIBILITY THESE YOUNGSTERS MUST WAIT DECADES BEFORE EQUAL OPPORTUNITY ESTABLISHED. PLEASE SEND YOUR TAX-DEDUCTIBLE GIFT TODAY TO . . .

Among those receiving the urgent wire was Allen Wardwell, a partner in the giant Wall Street law firm of Davis, Polk, Wardwell, Sunderland & Kiendl. That made him an intimate associate, of course, of his partner John W. Davis, who was leading the pro-segregation lawyers. Wardwell naturally passed the NAACP telegram on to Davis, who thought it was pretty rich that a partner of his would be solicited for such a purpose. It was too good a joke not to share, and so Davis sent a copy of the wire down to James F. Byrnes in the governor's mansion at Columbia, South Carolina, along with a short, ironic note. Wardwell "unfortunately" felt that he could not "contribute to the end in view," Davis quipped. "I send it on the possibility that you might be willing to take his place or select some other person similarly disposed."

There is no record of how broadly Jimmy Byrnes smiled upon reading that. But later correspondence between him and Davis indicates that the governor set his agents to work checking out Washington sources to see if such gifts to the NAACP were in fact lawfully tax-deductible. The South was using every weapon at its disposal.

The lack of money did not slow the NAACP effort. While the nation's black newspapers promptly opened a strong fund-raising drive on their pages, Thurgood Marshall gathered his troops for a morning-after assessment of the situation.

It could not be said that the Legal Defense Fund had frittered its scarce financial resources on baubles. The Fund, cramped in its sector of the main NAACP office on 40th Street near the Public Library, had recently moved into its own headquarters at 107 West 43rd Street, a seedy five-story building just a short stroll from Times Square. Wedged into the little offices on the third floor were six lawyers, as many secretaries, a bookkeeper, a switchboard operator, and a file clerk. The place, frankly, was a dump. Winos were forever congregating in front of it downstairs. Burglars were forever coming up the fire escape and in through the back windows at night to grab any visible typewriter. And the smell of urine was noticeable in and around the scissors-gate elevator. But these inelegant surroundings were to become, during the summer and autumn of 1953, the nerve center of a remarkable intellectual effort affecting the fate of black America.

As Felix Frankfurter had anticipated, the Court's intentions were not entirely clear from the five questions it had now put to the litigants in *Brown*. Thurgood Marshall's staff, while hopeful, was of two minds about the delay and what it meant. Jack Greenberg, perhaps because he was young and still new and born white, was among the more sanguine of the Fund personnel. "We thought we basically had the case won," Greenberg recalls. "Not automatically, by any means, but the questions suggested a clear frame of mind to us. Why would the Court have asked help in framing a remedy if the Justices weren't contemplating a remedy? They were asking us to help figure out pragmatically how to do it, so the implication seemed to be that the injustice of segregation was by then established in their minds. We were quite encouraged."

But Robert Carter, perhaps because he was older and a Fund veteran and born black, was not so optimistic. The Court's questions, he says, "shook us—not completely—but they shook us. Where we had been 75 percent confident, we now were down to 50 or 55 percent confident." It seemed plain to Carter that the Court, in reaching a decision on so sweeping and potentially convulsive a social issue, was trying to demonstrate to the nation that an exhaustive investigation of the legal and historic background had preceded its judgment day and that nothing precipitous or impulsive had been done. "The questions seemed by design—a design in which we saw the hand of Felix Frankfurter—to give the Court an out as well as maximum flexibility in shaping an opinion," Carter remarks. "The Justices, with their answered questions before them, could always cite the intentions of the framers of the Fourteenth Amendment. But we had no real idea why the questions had been invented. Nor did anybody at the office ever feel we were just going through an exercise. We took it all very seriously, knowing that we had to deliver—or the Court wouldn't. We had a lot to do. It was a very exhilarating time, that summer."

Marshall himself indulged in scant speculation. The Court had spoken, and his job was now plain. The historical evidence did not all have to line up on his side just so long as there was enough of it to show how far the Court and Congress and the Presidents had all strayed from the original ennobling intentions of the Radical Republicans who had guided the nation during the ten years following the Civil War. Or as Marshall put it in his disarming vernacular: "A nothin'-to-nothin' score means we win the ball game."

A mammoth research job loomed, without much time to do it. The Fourteenth Amendment could not be examined in a vacuum. It was the centerpiece in a decade of unprecedented congressional ferment, and to understand the intentions of its framers, one had to comb through the spoken and written words of hundreds of lawmakers. And since there were thirty-seven states in existence at the time the amendment was ratified, the understanding of legislators, governors, and other public officials in every one of them would have to be examined as carefully as time and manpower allowed. It was a job for scholars—constitutional experts, historians of the period, authorities on the South and the Negro—and one of such complexity as to dwarf the efforts by Kenneth Clark and his social-science experts. The Court's timing, moreover, could not have been worse. Most scholars had long since made their summer plans. What chance did Marshall have of lining up top people for his crash research program? And whom should he get?

To head up his research task force, which would number more than 200 by the time the brief on reargument was filed with the Court, Marshall turned to a friend with just the right combination of inter-disciplinary skills and knowledge—forty-one-year-old John A. Davis, then a professor of political science at Marshall's alma mater, Lincoln University. A native of Washington, D.C., Davis had graduated from Williams College and done advanced work bridging law and political science at Wisconsin and Columbia. In his early twenties, he had become involved as a civil-rights worker with the New Negro Alliance in Washington, where he connected with Marshall, Houston, Hastie, Lawson, and the rest of the black legal elite. At Lincoln, he had taught Bob Carter and recommended him to Dean Hastie's attention at Howard Law School. The work of his brother, Allison Davis, a prominent anthropologist at the University of Chicago and one of the first to argue that standard IQ tests were culturally biased, had given John insight into the social sciences. He was "full of ideas," says Carter, "at home with lawyers as well as scholars," and willing to work, though Marshall could not pay him anything like the fifty dollars a day he was due to earn as a consultant to the State Department that summer. That Davis was not a widely renowned scholar or the author of any major book mattered less than the enthusiasm he brought to his task. For the summer he took a five-dollar-a-day room at the Hotel Paris on New York's West End Avenue at 96th Street—a hostelry that, whatever its other deficiencies, boasted a swimming pool. "But I never got back in time to use it," says Davis. They all worked into the night regularly that summer.

Davis was given a desk and a phone and a secretary at the Fund office on West 43rd Street and started puzzling over how to organize his task. "I talked with everyone I knew in constitutional history, Reconstruction history, the history of education, and Negro history—and the leading political scientists concerned with civil rights," he recalls. After breaking the overall project into manageable sectors, Davis began to search for leading scholars to prepare research papers that would serve as the grist for a series of late-summer mini-conferences of leading authorities in each field; the essence of the papers, as then tempered by the judgments of the other experts in each field, would in turn form the nucleus for part of the final brief. At once, Davis ran into problems.

His first choice to write on the constitutional history was Dartmouth's Robert Carr, professor of government who had written books on judicial review and civil rights and, equally to the point, had served as staff director of President Truman's Civil Rights Committee. But Carr was about to become president of Oberlin College and could not spare Davis any time. Then there was Columbia's renowned Henry Steele Commager, whose ten books constituted a cosmic *oeuvre* of a kind rapidly going out of style among the younger generation of historians. Davis had studied under Commager at Columbia, knew that the white-maned historian was the very embodiment of the liberal academic establishment, and thought that his work in preparing *Documents in American History*, the classic reference book in the field, would have qualified him additionally to cope with the avalanche of documents that had to be untangled by NAACP researchers before summer ended. Commager, though, was over at Oxford, England. More troubling was what he wrote to Davis about the nature of the NAACP's request. He "greatly feared" that what Davis had had in mind for him "is not a valid point," Commager wrote. "The framers of the amendment did not, so far as we know, intend that it should be used to end segregation in schools." He cited two well-known law-review articles on the subject, by way of suggesting he knew what he was talking about, and closed: "I strongly urge that you consider dropping this particular argument as I think it tends to weaken your case."

That was about the last thing the Fund office wanted to hear just then. It was not as if they had any choice about facing the question; the Supreme Court had commanded it. And here was one of the foremost historians in America saying they probably didn't have a leg to stand on. "I had a great deal of respect for the man," Robert Carter comments of the Commager letter. "His rejection of our position was a real blow—it put us right down on the ground." Davis was less perturbed. Commager, for all his medals, was not the most insightful member of his breed, as Davis saw it. "He could tell you every damn thing about a constitutional case—except what was decided by it. So when he turned us down, I rationalized, 'Well, he really doesn't know that much about it.'"

The same could not be said about Carl Swisher, Johns Hopkins political scientist and author of a leading work of American constitutional history. Swisher, teaching that summer in Claremont, California, said he would have no time for research or writing along the lines Davis had suggested. And, like Commager, he offered a disquieting comment with his rejection: "I have some doubt as to what historical investigation of the point in question would show, and I should not want to offer even a comment thereon without opportunity for careful investigation and thought." Another glancing blow that Davis shook off: "Swisher was probably too much of an accommodationist to the Court's post-1877 decisions—too much of an apologist to be of any value to us, except to show how the other side's mentality was running in the case."

Not surprisingly, Davis began reaching for those he knew, starting with his boss, Horace Mann Bond, then finishing his seventh year as president of Lincoln. Bond, in his notable career, had combined the scholarship and militancy of a Du Bois with the leadership, patience, and pragmatism of a Booker Washington to emerge as the most prominent black educator in America after Howard's Mordecai Johnson. At the age of thirty, he had published a major scholarly work that at the same time was a scorching rebuke to the nation's professed ideals—*The Education of the Negro in the American Social Order*, a thickly documented study pinpointing the grossly deficient finances provided for colored schools and arguing that, thus hobbled, education could do little to relieve the ill health, economic dependence, or family disorganization of America's blacks. But he was scarcely a radical. Bond's 1934 book despaired of an early end to segregated schools—an attitude Du Bois had adopted at about that time—and called instead for a massive, though very gradual, program of equalization through federal funding. His thinking took a more controversial turn with the publication in 1939 of *Negro Education in Alabama: A Study in Cotton and Steel*, an important contribution to social history, then undergoing a badly needed purge of the saga-strewn version of the post-Civil War South as victimized by a conspiracy of the shiftless and incompetent black man, the cunning and malicious carpetbagger, the thieving and merciless scalawag, and the vindictiveness of politically opportunistic Radical Republicanism. Bond demonstrated that most white Alabamans, far from being selfless defenders of the lost cause of the Confederacy, were politically unrepentant and economically desperate, riddled by class distinctions, and thus easily exploitable by Northern capital that brought the steel industry and railroads to the state. With them came Yankee fiscal imperialism, the restoration of white supremacy, and the terror-induced resubjugation of the Negro. Thus, Bond understood how black education had been caught in the crossfire of politics and economics—precisely the areas that NAACP researchers needed to know about in fashioning their argument for the Supreme Court. Bond, moreover, had had firsthand experience dealing with Southern officialdom during his six-year tenure as president of Fort Valley State College, a state-backed shoestring school in central Georgia that Bond converted into a vital center for rural Negroes, who were instructed there in everything from better teaching techniques to raising poultry and canning vegetables. He did the job without either antagonizing or buttering up Georgia whites, and his subsequent elevation to the presidency of academically outstanding Lincoln in Pennsylvania anointed Bond as a major black intellectual leader. White America, of course, had never heard of him or his books.

"I called him on the phone," John A. Davis recalls, "and said, 'Horace,

I'm in trouble. None of these guys around here has any sense of the real political strategies that were involved back then.' I knew him well, of course. I was a headstrong professor and he was a college president trying to keep his school going and growing. Being somewhat dependent on the state legislature for funds, he was not eager for his faculty and students to rile up local officials, yet I remember being astonished when he called me one night and said, 'Professor Davis'—he always called me that or just 'Davis'—'we're going over to integrate the Oxford Hotel, and you'd be welcomed if you chose to join us.' I was dumfounded." Horace Bond's son Julian did not need to rebel from his father to become a militant twenty years later.

Bond took up Davis's invitation with enthusiasm. His packed response to Davis sketched out a major research program full of leads and speculations that a group of younger scholars began pursuing. Later in the summer, Bond came to New York, conferred with Davis, assembled the research material gathered at his direction, and locked himself into a cheap hotel room on West 43rd Street to hammer it all together—a charged monograph on the effects of the Fourteenth Amendment on the development of public education. Bond was convinced that the NAACP's key to answering the Court's leading question was the course followed by the ex-Confederate states which had to adopt the amendment in order to be re-admitted to the Union by the Radical Republicans dominating Congress. None of the states had a word about segregated schools in their newly framed constitutions, which Bond viewed as *prima facie* evidence of their understanding that the amendment had outlawed Jim Crow schools and other forms of racial discrimination. "He kept saying that it was like dropping a pebble in the water," Davis recalls, "and Congress was that pebble and the waves kept going out farther and farther from it. To get back into the Union, the rebel states knew they had to toe the mark."

It was an argument that would finally be woven into the NAACP brief, yet it was as much a hypothesis as a scholarly conclusion, for five of the ten rebel states thus re-admitted adopted segregated school systems within a year of ratifying the amendment and all the others followed within varying periods. What did that swingover to segregation mean? Did it mean that the ex-rebel states had known that the Fourteenth Amendment forbade the practice and that the only way they could be re-admitted to the Union was to present racially immaculate, discrimination-free constitutions for congressional approval? That was Bond's contention, but it ran into complications. One of them was that it implied the state legislatures that proceeded to institute Jim Crow schools did so in knowing violation of the Constitution— an arguable proposition since most of the Southern state legislatures were by no means controlled by diehard Confederates but by shifting alliances of at least nominal allegiance to the Republican Party. The public school systems of the South, moreover, were in their fetal stage at this period, and Southern lawmakers may well have seen little connection between the strictures of the Fourteenth Amendment and the establishment of a system of public education, resented as a costly innovation at a time when economic survival was the principal concern of the region. To Negroes, too, judging by the remarks of blacks serving in Reconstruction legislatures and Congress, mixed schools were not the crucial thing; what mattered was that blacks, fresh from bondage and badly in need of basic learning, should be offered free public schools of any kind on a sustained basis. Such ambiguities cast a fog over Bond's brainstorm and were to plague the historical findings of NAACP researchers all summer.

As early as mid-July, Davis was convinced that the most his researchers would find was that the evidence, like that produced by so enlightened a scholar as Horace Bond, was largely inconclusive. And that would give Thurgood Marshall the "nothin'-to-nothin' " stalemate he thought would be enough to win. But Davis also pushed on a more aggressive tack, the one Marshall and Spottswood Robinson had begun to take at the first oral argument before the Court the previous December. In a memo to Carter, Davis suggested that the second part of the Court's second question—had the framers of the Fourteenth Amendment intended to empower the judiciary to outlaw segregation "in light of future conditions"?—could be effectively answered "by a document which shows that the intent of those who would segregate was to make things unequal. Such an intent would impose a duty on the Court in terms of the equal protection clause."

Toward documenting that anti-Negro intent of Jim Crow lawmakers, Davis's team was reinforced by two ranking historians. Though he was in Tokyo that summer, C. Vann Woodward of Johns Hopkins, whose massive *Origins of the New South, 1877–1913* had recently been acclaimed by the profession as a masterpiece, wrote Davis that he would be pleased to participate. Woodward, a white native of Arkansas, would go on to greater fame as the author of a far slimmer volume, *The Strange Career of Jim Crow*, and the ranking historian of the post-Reconstruction South. Davis had written Woodward that "It is our feeling that the Court's questions reveal either historical ignorance or historical unreality . . . [and] imply a kind of Elmo Roper or George Gallup approach to history." Woodward's only concern in producing a paper for the NAACP—it ended up dealing with how the idealistic and humanitarian goals of Reconstruction had given way before the money-making pragmatism of Northern and Southern whites alike—was that "I should feel constrained by the limitations of my craft. . . . I would stick to what happened and account for it as intelligently as I could. . . . You see, I do not want to be in a position of delivering a gratuitous history lecture to the Court. And at the same time I do not want to get out of my role as historian."

It would not be the only time that summer that Davis would have to face the tough question of whether historians, presumably dedicated to as objective a version of the truth as possible, and lawyers, presumably seeking to shape as forceful and partisan a case for their clients as possible, could really work together in an effort such as the NAACP brief to the Supreme Court. "We wanted the historians to look at the whole thing from the viewpoint of the blacks and their aspirations, not from some cloud," acknowledges Carter, who coordinated all the paperwork and helped put it together. "All history is a distortion of sorts, depending on the historian's myopia and precepts." That, though, was not quite how Carter's colleague Davis put it to reassure Woodward. "Your conclusions are your own," Davis wrote. "If they do not help our side of the case, in all probability the lawyers will not use them. If they do help our argument, the present plan is to include them in the overall summary argument and to file the whole work as a brief in an appendix. No matter what happens, your work will be of real educational value to the men who must argue before the Court. . . ."

Another star historian whom Davis enlisted was Howard's John Hope Franklin, whose 1947 history of black America, *From Slavery to Freedom*, was generally regarded as the most candid and inclusive account of its kind. Franklin, who was later to turn down the presidency of Howard to remain a practicing historian and eventually become chairman of the department at the University of Chicago, was first contacted that summer by Marshall. "Thurgood made it clear that I had no choice in the matter whatever," Franklin recalls. "It was merely a matter of beginning as soon as I could." What emerged at summer's end was a Franklin monograph on, as he put it, "the way in which the Southerners defied, ignored, and worked against every conception of equality laid down in the Fourteenth Amendment and subsequent legislation." Its use in the final NAACP brief would sting the segregating states. The South Carolina brief called it "this catalogue of inflammatory labels. . . ."

More top-grade brainpower flowed into the NAACP camp early that summer when, without being asked, William Coleman, the tough-minded black Philadelphia lawyer, phoned Marshall and asked to coordinate the research in the various states—a task that in most cases had to be done in the state capital, where archives and official accounts of legislative and other governmental proceedings were generally stored. From his experiences as an editor of the *Harvard Law Review*, a clerk to Felix Frankfurter, and an associate at the Paul, Weiss firm in New York, Coleman had a growing network of acquaintances in the profession who shared with him a notably high-caliber intellect—young lawyers and legal scholars who had been, in effect, the law-school All-Americans of their day. "Sitting here in my office one afternoon," Coleman remembers, "I figured I knew someone in each of the thirty-seven states who could do a superior research job for us. Thurgood said fine." Indeed, Marshall was delighted to obtain such gifted assistance from across the nation. Among those Coleman would enlist was a white Alabaman who made it plain that he was unsympathetic with the NAACP's anti-segregation efforts but would, out of respect for Coleman as well as his own intellectual curiosity, undertake the research.

The most critical of the areas to be researched from the Negro's standpoint was what Congress had said and done about segregation in fashioning the Fourteenth Amendment, which passed both houses over-whelmingly in the middle of 1866 and was pronounced ratified by three-fourths of the states two years later. In *Plessy*, decided by the Court thirty years after Congress had passed the amendment, the Justices held that the measure had no doubt guaranteed Negroes equality but it had by no means voided all state-imposed "distinctions based on color" since such distinctions were not necessarily discriminatory except in the mind of the Negro. A separate equality was lawful.

To determine whether the framers of the amendment had thought that segregation was indeed discriminatory, Davis and Marshall needed the nation's most authoritative scholar on the Fourteenth Amendment. The two experts probably most deeply versed in the subject shared a pair of traits that presented problems to the NAACP. Both lived on the West Coast: Jacobus tenBroek, whose 1951 book *The Antislavery Origins of the Fourteenth Amendment* had established his reputation, taught political science at Berkeley. And Howard Jay Graham, whose meticulous articles in various law reviews and journals had gained wide attention in the field, was a bibliographer at Los Angeles County Law Library. And there was the other problem: tenBroek was totally blind and Graham was stone-deaf.

The disabilities of the two men had to be weighed. TenBroek explained to Davis on the phone how he worked and what kind of assistance he would need—conditions that made his cooperation almost impossible on such short notice and with so little time to complete the project. Jay Graham, on the other hand, was about to begin a year's leave from his library post to be a Guggenheim Fellow and extend his studies on the Fourteenth Amendment. His scholarly research was indeed the love of his life. At college, where he got by well enough as a lip-reader, he had had ambitions to become a professor and teach history. But the severity of his handicap, he eventually realized, would prevent such a career and caused him to turn to library work, which, according to colleagues at the Los Angeles County Law Library, he came to scorn in his frustration. He had worked in the acquisitions section of the library, eagerly buying books and materials on his favorite field of study, the anti-slavery period—a practice that his superiors were forced to curtail. His later work as a bibliographer left him isolated from colleagues, with whom he communicated on a scratch pad that he always carried. Regarded as a gifted man with a short fuse, he was haunted by the hunch that he might have reached the uppermost rung of the intellectual world but for a grim trick of nature. When the NAACP invited his help, he therefore responded to the self-validating enterprise with unreserved enthusiasm. He called it "an honor and privilege" to serve and left the fee for his services entirely up to Marshall, to whom he wrote: "I didn't undertake the job for money, but to help redress an evil and errors that go back far beyond our lifetime. It promises to be one of the most satisfying experiences of my life. . . ."

Soon he was suggesting that the only truly systematic way to organize the contents of the *Congressional Globe* during the years in question was to commit the essence of every relevant speech to punchcards—that is, to computerize it all—an undertaking that he thought could be done for no more than $3,000. Marshall gulped, wrote back that it was no doubt a fine idea but such money was not available, and urged Graham to do the best he could by conventional methods. Doggedly, the scholar went at the job. "Without him," Carter recalls, "we would have felt very vulnerable."

Graham scrutinized the evolution of the Fourteenth Amendment and focused on its anti-slavery origins and the egalitarian principles that guided its champions in the Capitol. To complement that effort, Davis enlisted an historian in midsummer who would put in more time and stay with the project longer than any of the non-legal scholars—Alfred H. Kelly, the tall, blond, blue-eyed, forty-six-year-old chairman of the history department at Detroit's Wayne University. A native of Pekin, Illinois, in the center of the state, where Southern sympathies ran deep in his growing-up years, Kelly was co-author of *The American Constitution: Its Origins and Development*, a well-regarded work of history that had appeared five years earlier. The NAACP invitation, he recalls, "struck a certain point of idealism in me about the role of the Negro in American life. It just seemed to me that the constitutional and statutory impediments to Negro equality were an outrage —almost as bad as slavery in their way." But Kelly, like Woodward, was determined not to let the humanitarian aims of the project prostitute his standards as an historian. He went to work at a public library across the street from his college in downtown Detroit and concentrated on the work of the so-called Joint Committee of Fifteen, the nine Representatives and six Senators who shaped most of the Reconstruction legislation for the Thirty-ninth Congress, which sat in 1865 and 1866, the crucial years. What had those key lawmakers said about segregation—and what had they really intended with regard to the protection of the black man's rights?

As the dog days of August began to slip by, the findings by Graham, Kelly, and others included a number of troubling revelations that brought heightened anxiety to the NAACP offices.

The proclaimed equality of all men and their inalienable right to life, liberty, and the pursuit of happiness had made the Declaration of Independence one of history's undying humanitarian statements. But no such exalted declarations had found their way into the much more businesslike Constitution. Part of the reason for the omission, of course, was the continuing toleration of human slavery in the new republic. Viewed as a unit, the decade of legislation beginning with adoption of the Thirteenth Amendment in 1865 and culminating in passage of the Civil Rights Act of 1875 may reasonably be said to have closed the gap between the promise of the Declaration and the tactful, tacit racism of the Constitution.

For a generation before the outbreak of civil war, abolitionist leaders had shaped the equalitarian doctrines that would find their way into the laws of the land but only after the guns stopped in 1865. Anti-slavery theorists began arguing in the 1830s that Article IV of the Constitution—the so-called comity clause declaring, "The citizens of each state shall be entitled to all privileges and immunities of citizens in the several states"—was in fact nothing less than a proclamation of national citizenship, to which were implicitly attached the natural rights and civil liberties of all men first promised in the Declaration. That claimed national citizenship covered all Americans, it was said, black as well as white. In the Forties, Charles Sumner and other abolitionist stalwarts were asserting that "equal protection before the law" was an absolute cornerstone of American nationhood, and the phrase "equal protection," a variant of some of the more exalted ideology to emerge from the French Revolution, was sounded by Sumner as he argued the first school-segregation case, *Roberts v. City of Boston*, in 1849. By the Fifties, Ohio's abolition-minded Congressman John A. Bingham, the future draftsman of the Fourteenth Amendment, was taking the floor of the House to declare, "It must be apparent that the absolute equality of all, and the equal protection of each, are principles of our Constitution [as] . . . universal and indestructible as the human race." Slavery itself was increasingly denounced as a manifest deprivation of liberty without due process in both the substantive and the procedural senses of the term.

The passage of the Thirteenth Amendment, all sides in Congress agreed, had given the Negro his liberty, but had it given him more? Was he thereafter, and automatically, a citizen? TenBroek's studies of the congressional debates preceding passage of the abolition amendment argued that proponents of the measure had plainly intended a revolution in federalism and creation of a national citizenship by giving Congress the power to enforce the anti-slavery edict. In the view of such Republican leaders as Thaddeus Stevens in the House and Lyman Trumbull in the Senate, the Thirteenth Amendment had not only commanded freedom from bondage but also proclaimed for every American federal protection for a wide range of natural and constitutional rights. Democrats and conservative Republicans, while outnumbered, challenged so sweeping a reading of the amendment, denied that it had granted citizenship to the Negro, insisted there was no such thing as national citizenship, and said that because civil rights remained within the sovereign discretion of the separate states, Congress could not possibly legislate to protect them.

Imposition of the Black Codes by the unrepentant white South threw the question into yet sharper relief. Under the codes that went into effect in the latter part of 1865, Negroes were widely compelled to work for arbitrarily limited pay, were drastically restricted in their mobility, were forbidden to carry arms and to testify against whites, and were often segregated on conveyances and in public places—in short, driven back as close to bondage as the South thought it could get away with. Congress struck back by invoking the enforcement section of the Thirteenth Amendment and passing the Civil Rights Act of 1866. The shaping of that bill and its metamorphosis into the Fourteenth Amendment were at the heart of the answers to the Supreme Court's questions on segregation in 1953.

As introduced on the Senate floor on January 5, 1866, by Judiciary Committee Chairman Trumbull of Illinois, the Civil Rights Bill declared: "All persons born in the United States, and not subject to any foreign power, are hereby declared to be citizens of the United States, without distinction of color, and there shall be no discrimination in civil rights or immunities among the inhabitants of any state or territory of the United States on account of race, color, or previous condition of servitude. . . ." The Thirteenth Amendment had endowed the Negro with citizenship as a necessary incident of his freedom, Trumbull argued, and now Congress was both confirming that and exercising its duty to guarantee the Negro his natural rights as a citizen, among them freedom from discriminatory laws.

The Black Codes were of course prime examples of such bias-inspired legislation, and the Civil Rights Bill aimed at destroying them. It would do this, according to language in the bill that came just after the sweeping "no discrimination in civil rights or immunities" pledge, by guaranteeing to every American inhabitant, citizen or not

> . . . the same right to make and enforce contracts, to sue, be parties, and give evidence, to inherit, purchase, lease, sell, hold, and convey real and personal property, and to the full and equal benefit of all laws and proceedings for the security of person and property, and shall be subject to like punishment, pains, and penalties, and to none other, any law, statute, ordinance, regulation, or custom to the contrary notwithstanding.

But were these specifically enumerated rights and immunities the *only* ones intended to be covered by the expansive-sounding "no discrimination" language at the beginning of the bill? Or were these enumerated rights simply specific examples of such civil rights and immunities, listed here to make clear the intention of the bill to negate the Black Codes? If the bill had been passed in this original form, with its broad anti-discrimination language intact, all future segregation laws offered by the states might well have been snuffed out by the congressional prohibition.

Senate conservatives began lambasting the bill at once, attributing an all-inclusive scope to the term "civil rights" and arguing that such a proposal would utterly destroy the power of states to make race the basis of any kind of statutory discrimination or classification. Anti-miscegenation laws and Pennsylvania's requirement of segregated schools were cited as examples of regulations that would be proscribed by the new federal bill. "Monstrous" is what Senator Edgar Cowan, a conservative Republican of Pennsylvania, called such an iron-fisted intrusion on the states by federal power. Some of the Radical Republican leaders, like Lot Morrill of Maine, acknowledged the revolutionary nature of the Civil Rights Bill and asked one of its detractors, "Is the Senator from Kentucky utterly oblivious to the grand results of four years of war?" But the more seemly tactic in the Radical Republican camp, which was not yet sure of the strength of its majority and at any rate was not eager to polarize Congress in the healing time after a terrible fratricidal war, was to gloss over the revolutionary nature of the bill, as Senator Jacob Howard of Michigan did in asserting that its purpose was simply "to secure to these men whom we have made free the ordinary rights of a freeman and nothing else. . . . There is no invasion of the legitimate rights of the states." The bill passed in the Senate, 33 to 12, with the broad "no discrimination" provision intact.

In the House, though, James Wilson of Iowa, chairman of the Judiciary Committee, reported out the bill and at once seemed to narrow its range. While it assured every citizen of equality in his civil rights, said Wilson, the words of that pledge had to be clarified. "Do they mean that in all things civil, social, political, all citizens, without distinction of race or color, shall be equal?" he asked. "No. . . . Nor do they mean that all citizens shall sit on the same juries, or that their children shall attend the same schools. These are not civil rights or immunities." But the opposition did not read the bill as narrowly as Wilson. Representative Andrew Jackson Rogers, arch-conservative Democrat of New Jersey and a member of the Committee of Fifteen overseeing Reconstruction legislation, declared that the "no discrimination" clause would surely eliminate such measures as Kentucky's law punishing Negroes unequally for committing rape, Indiana's law forbidding Negroes to acquire real estate, and Pennsylvania's requirement of separate schools for Negroes. "Civil rights," Rogers insisted, included "all the rights that we enjoy," and the scope of the words "privileges and immunities" was hardly less expansive. An Ohio conservative argued that the bill as written would wipe out his state's school-segregation law since it "did not, of course, place the black population on an equal footing with the whites. . . . " An Indiana Representative, challenging the applicability of the Thirteenth Amendment, demanded to know how either slavery or involuntary servitude could be read into a state law written "to deny to children of free Negroes or mulattoes . . . the privilege of attending the common schools of a state with the children of white men." Moderate Republican Henry Raymond of New York, who not incidentally was the editor of the *New York Times* just then, agreed with Rogers that the bill's reach probably exceeded any reasonable grant of power that might be read into the Thirteenth Amendment.

The end came for the "no discrimination" clause when House Radical leader John Bingham, a member of the Joint Committee of Fifteen, rose to discuss the rights bill and asked that the offending language be jettisoned. Bingham had drafted the Fourteenth Amendment, which the Joint Committee had presented to Congress only a few days earlier, and the relationship between the two measures had apparently been much on his mind. The Civil Rights Bill, said Bingham, did indeed propose to strike down "by congressional enactment every state constitution which makes a discrimination on account of race or color in any of the civil rights of the citizen," and since practically every state had at least some discriminatory laws, the right way to prohibit them was by a further amendment to the Constitution. Whether he meant the Fourteenth Amendment specifically, he did not say. After some jockeying and despite added disclaimers by Wilson on the potency of the bill, it was finally reported back to the House floor minus the "no discrimination" clause, which, Wilson acknowledged, "might give warrant for a latitudinarian construction not intended." The House passed the watered-down measure, 111 to 38, the Senate concurred, and both houses voted to override Andrew Johnson's veto. The President was evidently less worried about the potentially expansive language that remained in the bill—"the inhabitants of every race . . . shall have the same right . . . to . . . full and equal benefit of all laws and proceedings for the security of persons and property"—than about the assumption by Congress of power to protect even the specifically enumerated anti-Black Code rights in the bill (i.e., that the Negro should have "the same right" as the white man to make and enforce contracts, to sue and testify in court, to buy and sell and hold real estate, and not to suffer more severe punishments for crimes) against abuse by state governments. If Congress could intervene in the business of the states to that extent, why could it not go further and strike down all discriminatory measures by the states?

Many in Congress evidently believed that the entire question would be placed beyond constitutional dispute by the new Fourteenth Amendment. As introduced by Bingham, its first version began:

> The Congress shall have the power to make all laws which shall be necessary and proper to secure to the citizens of each State all privileges and immunities of citizens in the several States [Article IV, Section 2]; and to all persons in the several States equal protection in the rights of life, liberty, and property [Fifth Amendment].

Bingham's bracketed references were offered by way of reassurance that the amendment was not very revolutionary, since the genesis for this national bill of rights against state incursions was plainly in the Constitution already. All that the new amendment would do, Bingham and other Radical leaders said soothingly, was to arm Congress with the express power to enforce the federal guarantee of equality; it did not, as the conservatives charged, transfer all sovereignty over civil rights from the states to the federal government.

For strategic reasons, perhaps, the first section of the new amendment was represented by some of its backers as having no more ennobling an aim than to place the specifically enumerated guarantees of the Civil Rights Act beyond constitutional challenge. Some leading Radicals, including Thaddeus Stevens, went on to suggest that the amendment was offered partly to place the Civil Rights Act guarantees beyond the reach of future Congresses that might be tempted to dilute or remove them. Whether that interpretation was offered in an excess of either candor or guile is unclear, but if it succeeded in softening the opposition of conservatives, it also managed to harden the resolve of radicals, who noted that the proposed language of the amendment, beginning with "the Congress shall have the power . . . ," still left the protection of the rights in question to the mercies of Congress—and congressional majorities had a way of shifting. It was not strong enough as worded.

The amendment was left to brew for six weeks and then emerged, under Bingham's hand, in approximately the form in which it was to be adopted, beginning with these crucially changed words: "No state shall make or enforce any law which shall abridge the privileges or immunities of citizens of the United States; nor shall any state deprive any person of life, liberty, or property without due process of law; nor deny to any person the equal protection of the laws." Here, plainly, was language that placed the natural rights of every American inhabitant beyond the power of Congress to impair or destroy by either taking or withholding legislative action. Congress, under the fifth section of the redrafted amendment, was apparently to enforce the guarantees of the first section in the event a state violated the absolute commandment of the Constitution not to deny those critical privileges and immunities to any of its residents. Even without congressional action, though, the self-executing command against state usurpation of those rights could presumably be enforced by the federal judiciary, like any other such imposition of federal supremacy prescribed in the Constitution. That principle of judicial enforceability of Fourteenth Amendment rights was unmistakably illustrated by the Supreme Court in *Strauder v. West Virginia*, eleven years after the adoption of the amendment, in striking down a state prohibition against Negroes on juries.

That the framers of the new amendment intended it to go well beyond the specifically enumerated rights of the Civil Rights Act of 1866 was strongly suggested by its sweeping language and the grand, hard-to-pin-down terms that had not been part of the rights bill. The amendment's key phrases, "due process" and "equal protection," had a majesty to them that could be taken as narrowly applicable only by those in willful opposition. Senator Howard, acting as co-chairman of the Joint Committee of Fifteen, declared that the amendment "abolishes all class legislation in the states, and does away with the injustice of subjecting one caste of persons to a code not applicable to another. . . ." Co-chairman William Pitt Fessenden, Senator from Maine, denied that the first section of the amendment had been drawn merely to protect the constitutionality of the Civil Rights Act—or, indeed, had any connection with it. To illustrate how the amendment was far more than a prop to the Civil Rights Act and would go well beyond it in mandating equal protection, Senator Timothy Howe of Wisconsin cited an outrageously discriminatory Florida school law which provided that whites and Negroes would be taxed for white schools but only Negroes would be taxed for the colored schools; most of the money raised by the tax for colored schools, moreover, would go to pay state superintendents who would have absolute power over whether a Negro might be allowed to attend any given school in his area. Could any Congressman, Howe asked, hesitate to amend the Constitution to place a "positive inhibition upon exercising this power of local government to sanction such a crime . . . ?"

Howe's example was notable for several reasons. It was one of the few instances during the congressional debates on the amendment when its supporters got very specific. They much preferred to use the generalized language of Bingham, who spoke of "the inborn rights of all persons" that would be protected by the addition to the nation's organic law. Such a tactic was almost certainly intentional if not downright evasive, for the Radical Republican leadership was probably not eager to advertise just how far-reaching the amendment was or might be taken to be. The Fourteenth Amendment corroborated the outcome of the Civil War—and could not have passed Congress had the outcome of the war been different—by installing the glorious language of the Declaration of Independence as the supreme law of the land, in every state. It did not assume that masters would naturally choose to treat their former slaves as legal equals or that non-slaveholding whites would like the idea any better. In the end, the constitutional guarantee of the Negro's rights was cast not in the negative anti-discrimination form that had originally been proposed in the Civil

Rights Bill, but in the positive, broad language of equal protection and due process. In writing a constitution, you do not outlaw murder; you guarantee the right to life.

Senator Howe's denunciation of the Florida school law was also notable, as litigants in *Brown v. Board of Education* reviewed the congressional debates eighty-seven years later, because it was one of the very few references to the effect of the amendment on public schools. During the Civil Rights Bill debate, there had been a number of such references, and there was considerable evidence that many Congressmen believed that the bill as originally framed would have eliminated racially segregated schools. But elimination of the "no discrimination" language seemed to have ended that debate. Under the "equal protection" language of the amendment, however, the question seems to have been left unresolved. Indeed, it was scarcely raised. Howe's railing against the Florida school law was due not to the fact that it sanctioned separate schools but to its grossly unequal provisions for colored education. More than likely, school segregation was not much on the lawmakers' minds: compulsory public education in America at that time was still in its rudimentary stage. The provision of any public education at all for the newly freed slaves was viewed by the abolitionist bloc as a major advance in the South.

Public education, in fact, had been strongly resisted by the antebellum South even as the idea grew in the North and in the frontier states, where it was seen as a great uplifting force and harbinger of a bright future. The values that Horace Mann, Henry Barnard, and other apostles of compulsory common-school education preached in the first half of the nineteenth century—the school as the seedbed for civic-mindedness and a sense of national unity, for the spread of humanitarian and egalitarian values, for the homogenization of immigrants and all the varying religious and racial strands of the people, for enhancing human efficiency and building a wiser electorate in a land where universal manhood suffrage would be practiced—were almost all unwelcome in the plantation South. Elitist planters were no more inclined to send their offspring to school with the children of the white rabble than they were to put rebellious thoughts in the heads of their enslaved darkeys by providing them with even the most basic sort of formal education. A broad-based, well-informed electorate with all sorts of fool notions about the equality of men was about the least appetizing prospect the masters of the pre-war South could have contemplated. Community facilities of any sort, paid for by planters' tax dollars, were rare throughout Dixie, where the widely dispersed populace had few meeting grounds and those who ran its politics saw no harm at all in keeping the region a cultural wasteland. Even Virginia, where the Jefferson legacy might have encouraged public education, made no real provision for it until the middle of the nineteenth century; fewer than one out of ten Southern children between the ages of five and fifteen attended formally organized schools in the two decades before the war. As Congress sat down to write the Fourteenth Amendment, no Southern state could be said to have had a public school system worthy of the name.

In deep financial distress, the South was not anxious to correct its educational backwardness during the last third of the century. Only Kentucky would pass a compulsory-school-attendance law by the year 1900. The Freedmen's Bureau, as an emergency measure, had begun to teach the Negro basic reading, writing, and ciphering skills in the immediate aftermath of the war when it was estimated that no more than one freedman in ten had managed to snatch even the most primitive sort of education. But the desperate need of the ex-slaves for food and clothing and shelter, the constantly shifting population, widespread illness and epidemics, the lack of classrooms and books, and the failure of many Negroes to grasp the practical applications of book learning all conspired to limit the achievements of the Freedmen's Bureau program at the time Congress was mulling the amendment. When the bureau's federal funding ended, the ex-Confederate states balked at assuming the burden of carrying on the colored schools. The financially reduced upper classes were unhappy about being taxed to educate their former slaves, though it was the labor of those very blacks, of course, that had brought the gentry its former wealth. The lower-class whites were equally resentful that their black social inferiors should now be offered, free of charge, an education—the sort of privilege formerly reserved for their social betters. Poor-whites, moreover, were openly hostile to the idea of enhancing the Negro's skills and thereby making him a more formidable economic competitor, and propertied whites still badly needed the blacks to work the land, a task for which they needed little schooling. The equal-protection requirement of the Fourteenth Amendment served, no doubt, to deter many Southern states from forsaking public education for Negroes entirely, for white children were increasingly benefiting from the growth of the Southern public school system. What support the South did give to colored schools was grudging and minimal. A major share of the financial load was carried by Northern-based philanthropies that brought some light to the darkness but served as well both to relieve the states of their obvious responsibilities and to inculcate a severely restricted life outlook among the colored children. Had they lifted the eyes of the blacks too far above the cotton fields, the Northern schoolmarms would soon have been sent packing. Fifty years after ratification of the Fourteenth Amendment, "equal protection" in Southern schools meant that scarcely one-third as much was spent on the education of each black child as on each white one.

By all available evidence, then, the framers of the Fourteenth Amendment would have been familiar with public education only as a developing concept in most states, not only the South. Whether those schools were segregated mattered a good deal less, to most contemporary supporters of the Negro's rights, than that schoolhouses and teachers be provided in sufficient numbers and with adequate financing to improve his skills and economic opportunity. At the time the amendment became law, the practice and nature of school segregation varied widely. Thirteen states either had no segregation laws or specifically forbade the practice (the six New England states plus Iowa, Michigan, Minnesota, Nebraska, New Jersey, Oregon, and Wisconsin). Eight states either provided for separate schools or left it up to local communities to adopt that practice if they wished (California, Kansas, Missouri, Nevada, New York, Ohio, Pennsylvania, and West Virginia). Five states outside the old Confederacy either directly or by implication excluded colored children entirely from their public schools (Delaware, Indiana, Illinois, Kentucky, and Maryland). Only five states could reasonably have been said to have abandoned segregated schools in the immediate wake or as a result of the Fourteenth Amendment—Connecticut, Florida, Louisiana, Michigan, and South Carolina—and three of those subsequently restored the practice. What changes there were in the public schools in the decade following adoption of the amendment were directed not toward the abolition of segregation but toward strengthening or equalizing the school rights of the colored children. In Indiana, for example, where no schools had been provided for Negroes before the amendment, the state superintendent of public instruction ruled that "whatever distinctions may have been previously made in the rights and privileges of citizens by our laws, they have been set aside by the amendations of our National Constitution and the Civil Rights Bill." Negroes, in other words, had as much right to attend public schools as whites—but not the *same* schools, as Indiana saw it.

Thus, the historical evidence seemed to demonstrate persuasively that neither the Congress which framed the Fourteenth Amendment nor the state legislatures which adopted it understood that its pledge of equal protection would require the end of segregation in the nation's public schools. But it is quite another—and unwarranted—matter to conclude that that Congress and those states contemplated that the amendment would not or could not, at some future time, require the abolition of segregation. For, as many historians and commentators have noted, the framers of the Constitution did not contemplate any number of legislative or judicial steps that future social and economic conditions would dictate. Agricultural price supports, social-security payments, and minimum-wage laws are obvious examples of legislative measures never envisioned by the Founding Fathers but nevertheless framed by a future Congress and sanctioned as constitutional by the Court. Similarly, the framers of the Fourteenth Amendment never said that they intended it to apply to corporations as "persons." Yet the Court later in the nineteenth century was to apply just such an apparently unintended—but not explicitly prohibited—use of the amendment to the property rights of corporations, which proved to be the major beneficiaries of the enactment while the Negro's rights under it were construed so narrowly as to become nearly inoperative.

It is scarcely surprising, then, that as the NAACP's scholars uncovered this highly ambiguous evidence, spirits alternately rose and ebbed at the Legal Defense Fund's New York headquarters.

From Los Angeles, Jay Graham checked in with the not very encouraging news that he had found almost no discussion at all during the congressional debates on school segregation, and what he had found was of little help. He was particularly troubled by Representative Wilson's insistence during the phase of the debates dealing with the "no discrimination" clause that the Civil Rights Bill was not intended to outlaw separate schools. That negative reference, Graham reported, was "unfortunate, particularly since he was House manager of the . . . bill." Out in Detroit, historian Alfred Kelly was seriously troubled by the removal of the "no discrimination" clause from the Civil Rights Bill, which he, along with many other scholars, still believed to be the keystone to the Fourteenth Amendment. "Now from the NAACP standpoint, this was very damning, as I saw it," Kelly remembers. "The bill was amended specifically to eliminate any reference to discriminatory practices like school segregation, and I was really stumped at that point in trying to figure out how to answer the Court's question, because it looked as if a specific exclusion had been made, and so here I was caught between my own ideals as an historian and what these people in New York wanted and needed."

Other troubling evidence began accumulating from those researching the understanding of the state legislatures that ratified the amendment. Loren Miller, the NAACP's West Coast attorney and one of Marshall's most astute advisors, put the matter concisely when he wrote him on August 8:

> My own research into California, Oregon and Nevada historical and judicial attitudes toward the separate school issue has led me to the tentative conclusion that none of them believed that the Amendment struck down separate schools but that all of them recognized the equalitarian impact of its commands. Its impact on separate schools was recognized only as it became plain that such schools denied that equalitarianism. . . .

The harder they looked, the more trouble spots the NAACP team found. Since twenty-four of the thirty-seven states in the country had either required or allowed segregated schools at the time of the amendment, it seemed highly unfavorable that so little discussion during the congressional debates and those in the state legislatures had been devoted to the effect of the amendment on Jim Crow schools. If Congress and state legislators had understood that the amendment was to wipe away the practice, surely there would have been more than a few howls.

And no one in the NAACP camp had come up with a persuasive rebuttal to the fact that Congress had permitted segregated schools in the District of Columbia from 1864 onward—and that, though the matter was debated thoroughly between 1871 and 1875, Congress had declined to include a prohibition against segregated schools in the Civil Rights Act of 1875. If, furthermore, the framers of the Fourteenth Amendment had truly intended to wipe away all racial discrimination as the climax of the anti-slavery crusade, as tenBroek, Graham, and other scholars believed, why had the Negro not been granted suffrage by the amendment, as all sides held he had not been? Why, in fact, had the Fifteenth Amendment been necessary at all if the reach of the Fourteenth was all that its most expansive interpreters insisted? Could it be reasonably claimed that segregation had been outlawed by the Fourteenth when the yet more basic emblem of citizenship—the ballot—had been withheld from the Negro under that amendment? To answer that the true intentions of the legislators of that day could be fathomed only by viewing their handiwork over the 1865–75 decade was no doubt a reasonable contention, but it somewhat begged the Supreme Court's question for the *Brown* reargument.

Adding to the complex data the NAACP had to rebut or rationalize were the determination and resources of their adversaries. That the South was not sparing the horses in its preparations for the second Court argument of *Brown* was clear to Thurgood Marshall, who wrote to a friend in mid-August:

> . . . Incidentally, one of the evidences of our general problem of fighting governmental agencies is that the Attorney General of Virginia had written to the Attorney General of each of the [thirty-six other] states which considered the Fourteenth Amendment and, in turn, each of these Attorneys General are doing the research for them without cost or obligation.

Considering their difficulties, Marshall's staff was scarcely woebegone when it received a request from the new Attorney General of the United States, Herbert Brownell, Jr., to agree to postponing the reargument until early December so that the Justice Department could complete its own comprehensive research on the Court's questions. Aside from being able to use the extra time to fashion as convincing an historical presentation as possible, Marshall could not afford to say no and thereby risk antagonizing the government, now under the control of Republicans who were by no means certain to behave half so kindly as the Truman administration.

By September, the research was flowing into the NAACP office from all over the nation, and the director-counsel of the Legal Defense Fund, as Marshall was now known, studied most of it himself before channeling it to other hands. The mimeograph machine was going all the time, churning out a cross-flurry of monographs, memos, and rough drafts. Everyone was working late all the time, and food consisted of sandwiches, coffee, and beer, with an occasional *gemütlich,* if somewhat heavy, meal at the nearby Blue Ribbon restaurant when notable visitors came to town. "The mood was hectic, driving, disordered, and anxious," recalls John A. Davis. "We knew we were going to be made or broken within a couple of months," Robert Carter remembers feeling. "I think we all felt that we might be making history," says Alice Stovall, who managed the office.

And through it all, Marshall kept pushing them without ever becoming abrasive about it. "I have *never* seen a man work so long and so hard," recounts John Hope Franklin, who logged a lot of hours around the office that fall during the never-ending series of conferences. "It was nothing for him to say at one a.m., 'How about a fifteen-minute break?'" Typical, too, was the letter Marshall sent to the NAACP's counsel for the Southwest, U. Simpson Tate, who had mailed in his findings on the Texas legislature's handling of the Fourteenth Amendment. Marshall was pleased with Tate's material but felt there was room for improvement: "It seems to me that you had better make a pretty careful check of whatever books are available concerning this problem and let us know about that also. Whatever you do, please do not let up but keep digging until we are sure that we have everything that will do us any good."

Toward the end of September, Marshall brought the whole operation together in a giant conference running for three days and nights at the Overseas Press Club. Nearly a hundred scholars and lawyers broke into smaller seminars, each attacking a different aspect of the questions the Court had asked. But the key session was devoted to the papers by Jay Graham and Alfred Kelly on the troubling relationship between the Civil Rights Act of 1866, which had been specifically stripped of its broad "no discrimination" language, and the Fourteenth Amendment, created in its immediate aftermath and conceived, as many historians believed, simply to constitutionalize the rights act. At the center of the controversy was Kelly, a tall, hearty Midwesterner with a radio-announcer's voice and a favorite blue suit that one office regular that summer recalls "was rather brighter than most blue suits."

The paper he delivered on what he called "the damning modification of the Civil Rights Bill in the House and its apparent identity in purpose with the Fourteenth Amendment" was "not adequate by any standard," in Kelly's own estimate. "I didn't understand the relationship between advocacy and history at that point," he says. "I was trying to be both advocate and historian within the same paper. I just should have spelled out the problem for them." But the problem looked nearly insurmountable to Kelly just then; "I didn't see the good argument that might be available to us," he adds by way of acknowledging that his summer study had dwelt so much on the trees that the contours of the forest itself had gone unnoticed. "I did get the devastating facts on the table, though," Kelly suggests. Those "facts" so discouraged some of the NAACP advisors that the conference became mired over choosing a strategy to overcome the historical evidence that the framers of the Fourteenth Amendment had apparently had segregation itself very little on their minds in light of the far more appalling inequities burdening the black man just then.

No one was more troubled about the historical findings than William Robert Ming, Jr., the forty-two-year-old black native Chicagoan who was then a full professor at the University of Chicago law school and one of Thurgood Marshall's most gifted consultants. A sharp legal logician, a forceful and often eloquent debater, and a sometimes bareknuckled infighter, Ming vibrated with confidence born of an outstanding career in teaching and government. He had moved from nearly all-black Howard Law School to nearly all-white Chicago Law School, where one of his students in a federal-procedure course was Ramsey Clark, later U.S. Attorney General. "He was a very bright man," Clark recalls of Ming, "and the kids loved him. They and the faculty people were 'proud' of him in a kind of unintentionally patronizing way. He had a real zest for life, though he was perhaps overly sophisticated in his approach to the law."

Ming's approach to the problem presented by the findings of Kelly and Graham was quite direct. He thought that the textual evidence, based on the pronouncements of Congressmen and the wording of the various drafts of the Civil Rights Bill and the Fourteenth Amendment, was so scanty or unconvincing that the NAACP ought not even to attempt an argument based on the framers' immediate intent. Perilous as the idea might be, Ming urged that the Court's question be, in effect, bypassed and the historical case argued in terms of the approach suggested in Jay Graham's paper—namely, by invoking the overall spirit of humanitarianism, racial equalitarianism, and social idealism that had fueled the abolitionist movement and, by obvious implication, had shaped the objectives of the Radical Republicans who wrote the amendment. The papers by Vann Woodward and John Hope Franklin, arguing that the original equalitarian intentions of the post-Civil War amendments had been eroded in ensuing decades by unbearable political and economic pressures and extra-legal tactics, strongly supported this general position. The historians present were generally enthusiastic over this broad approach to the Court's questions. "We were putting the intellectual establishment on notice," comments John A. Davis, "that we rejected the conventional Columbia school of thinking on Reconstruction and its aftermath. That school argued that the country had turned away from the words of the Fourteenth Amendment to bind up regional wounds and to make the country whole again. It was a step rationalized on grounds of alleged Negro incompetence and pressing economic need by the white South. The fastening of the Jim Crow caste system on America was thus justified by this school of historians who did not want to turn their backs on their fathers or face the moral issues raised by that forfeiture of Negro rights. We were saying to all of them, 'No, goddammit, now you're going to have to face the truth.' "

Alfred Kelly left that September conference with a $400 fee (plus expenses) for his efforts and the expectation that the next word he received about the school-segregation cases would come on the front pages of the newspapers. But just ten days or so later, in early October, Thurgood Marshall rang him up. "In the curiously winning manner so characteristic of the man," Kelly later recounted, "he informed me that since I wasn't doing anything anyhow, I might as well come on down to New York for four or five days and waste my time there. My help, he said with careful flattery, was needed very badly on the brief. My vanity thus touched to the quick, I came."

Marshall had been uneasy about the so-called "broad approach" favored by the September conference. In close consultation then with William Coleman, who knew the mind of Felix Frankfurter better than any of the other NAACP advisors did, Marshall was fearful about looking evasive to the Court. He called his inner circle together—Carter, Greenberg, and Motley of the office staff, Spot Robinson from Richmond, Louis Redding from Wilmington, Jim Nabrit from Washington, Bob Ming from Chicago, psychologist Ken Clark, and research project director John Davis—and invited Kelly and John Hope Franklin in for a four-day intensive re-examination of the historical evidence. "I never worked for harder taskmasters," Franklin recalls. He and Kelly were pumped with question after question on the detailed events of the period. "I soon sensed that the role I was expected to play was that of devil's advocate," Kelly noted, "of a foil to prepare them all for the main event."

During the intensive sessions, Kelly was struck by two not quite contradictory qualities in the black men who sat around the table with him. "If I had ever entertained any lurking white-man's suspicion of the intellectual adequacy of this group of lawyers, all but one or two of whom were Negroes, these men soon kicked it out of me," Kelly later said. "Without exception, they were razor-keen, deadly at argumentation, and, as far as a layman who knew some law could tell, thoroughly competent in their profession." But there was that other quality that frankly surprised Kelly: "In a sense, these men were profoundly naïve. They really felt that once the legal barriers fell, the whole black-white situation would change. I was more skeptical, but they were convinced that the relationship between the law and society was the key. There was a very conservative element in these men then in the sense that they really believed in the American dream and that it could be made to work for black men, too. Thurgood Marshall was—and is— an American patriot. He truly believed in the United States and the Constitution, but that the whole system was tragically flawed by the segregation laws. Wipe away those laws and the whole picture would change. Marshall and his colleagues were no rebels. They felt that the social order was fundamentally good. What they wanted was the chance to share in it like men."

While the October conference progressed mostly in the evenings, Kelly and Ming were isolated with a stenographer for three exhausting days in a suite at the main NAACP office on 40th Street, where they turned out a draft for the historical sections of the brief. Ming did most of the writing while Kelly kept sharpshooting at his history and constitutional law. "We got on famously," says the historian.

With the Ming draft in hand, the conference broke up on a Saturday night after having resolved, as Carter noted in a letter to Kelly a few days later, "to take the position that segregated schools would necessarily be violative of the intended reach of the Fourteenth Amendment even though very little, or nothing, was said specifically about segregated schools as such" during the congressional debates. Bill Coleman came up to New York on weekends to work over the Ming draft with Marshall while other hands developed the less troubling parts of the brief. Kelly kept sending in suggestions of key speeches that might be worked into the brief to support "the broad approach," but Marshall remained uneasy. He sent out copies of the draft and started getting unsettling feedback. His West Coast advisors were particularly direct. Graham wrote that he liked what had been done with Kelly's material: ". . . it seems to me an excellent job—it has organization, balance, and—by skirting the weak points and by cleverly using the argument from silence the way lawyers customarily do in matters of this sort—it comes out with the conclusion you need and want." So much for the good news. Then Graham said, "[F]or these very reasons, one can't snip out segments of Kelly's narrative and combine them into a legal brief, as has been attempted here, apparently by different hands working on different segments of the problem. You destroy one carefully worked out presentation without achieving another, because there is no real mastery of the material as a whole, no coherence or progression. The plan simply breaks down." Loren Miller chipped in:

> The section devoted to the debates . . . is namby-pamby. It is hesitant and unconvincing, a fault that seems to me to stem from the fact that too little stress is laid on the underlying philosophy of the proponents of the Civil Rights Acts and framers of the Amendment. . . .
>
> It also seems to me that the point should be made that to the proponents of the Civil Rights Act and the framers of the Amendment, segregation was, per se, discrimination . . .

and he cited specific passages in the debates where the segregated schools of Pennsylvania were recognized as having discriminated "as between the two classes of children." Marshall himself recognized the shortcomings of the brief. He sent the latest draft to Kelly on October 30, remarked that it was "not in good shape," and added:

> After kicking around the debates in three or more different drafts we ended up with a draft which is merely a rehash of your paper. The obvious criticism to this approach is that as it now appears in our brief it is more of a historical document than an argument. I am still convinced that there must be some way to redo the debates, yet I must confess that I have not come up with the idea yet. . . .

Marshall might well have meant to characterize the troublesome section of the brief in just the opposite fashion—more of an argument than an historical document. He wanted more grit in there. Would Kelly come back to New York for yet another session, this time with John Frank of Yale Law School? The Ming draft was just too generalized and seemed to Marshall to fudge on the central question of the framers' intentions. "I gotta argue these cases," Marshall told Kelly, "and if I try this approach, these fellows [the Justices] will shoot me down in flames."

During the early November sessions with Frank and Marshall, Kelly has recounted, "I am very much afraid that . . . I ceased to function as an historian and instead took up the practice of law without a license. The problem we faced was not the historian's discovery of the truth, the whole truth, and nothing but the truth; the problem instead was the formulation of an adequate gloss on the fateful events of 1866 sufficient to convince the Court that we had something of an historical case. . . . It is not that we were engaged in formulating lies; there was nothing as crude and naïve as that. But we were using facts, emphasizing facts, bearing down on facts, sliding off facts in a way to do what Marshall said we had to do—'get by those boys down there.'" And yet Kelly would become increasingly convinced with the passing years that the last-minute interpretation he came up with on the two sorest points in the historical evidence was essentially the correct one.

The hardest problem was John Bingham's speech calling for the removal of the broad "no discrimination in civil rights and immunities" clause from the Civil Rights Bill. In calling for the deletion, Bingham, the former abolition theorist, had openly acknowledged that the bill as drafted would have prohibited statutes such as school segregation. Since that broad language was in fact deleted from the final form of the bill and since many of the proponents of the Fourteenth held that the amendment had no purpose beyond constitutionalizing the Civil Rights Act, it had therefore seemed to Kelly, Marshall, Ming, and others in the NAACP camp that they could not reasonably argue that the framers intended the amendment to prohibit school segregation. But the more Kelly pondered Bingham's remarks—and the fact that a few days earlier Bingham had presented a draft of the Fourteenth Amendment to the House—the clearer the picture became to him: Bingham's objection to the "no discrimination" clause was based solely on the apparent lack of constitutional authority for so sweeping a congressional enactment, Kelly suggested. That shortcoming could be cured only by a new amendment to the Constitution, Bingham indicated, and Kelly took that to be a reference to the Fourteenth Amendment that Bingham himself had drafted and was eagerly promoting. If that were the case, then a whole new interpretation, far more favorable to the NAACP, could be put on Bingham's speech on the Civil Rights Bill—namely, that once the Fourteenth Amendment had been passed by Congress and ratified by the states, then constitutional power would exist for a sweeping congressional prohibition of discriminatory statutes by the states, segregation included. And since the amendment, as finally redrafted by Bingham to remove its dependency on Congress, itself became a direct prohibition on the states, Kelly believed it could plausibly be claimed to have outlawed all discriminatory legislation, just as the original draft of the Civil Rights Bill would have done.

One hurdle in the way of that reading of Bingham's intentions was a later speech by Thaddeus Stevens, the most powerful man in the House and a strong ally of Bingham. Among other things, Stevens said that a principal purpose of the Fourteenth Amendment had indeed been to re-enact and therefore insure the constitutionality of the Civil Rights Act (even shorn of its broad "no discrimination" language)—an apparent concession to those who wished to interpret the amendment narrowly. But Kelly concluded that the apparently damaging portion of Stevens's speech had to be considered against the larger political picture and the clear drift of Stevens's generally radical utterances. Stevens did not mince words except when there might be a political dividend in it, as there may indeed have been in passing off the new amendment as less of an earthquake than its opponents claimed. When Bingham had first presented the amendment, Stevens had said—in words that latter-day conservatives and segregationists preferred to glide over—that it plainly meant "where any state makes a distinction in the same law between different classes of individuals, Congress shall have the power to correct such discriminations and inequality" and that under the amendment ". . . no distinction would be tolerated in this purified Republic but what arose from merit and conduct."

"It was like a light breaking through," Kelly remembers. "Here finally was a really plausible interpretation. Thurgood got up from his chair and began pacing excitedly around the room, as if to say, 'Hot damn! Here's something finally that we can use that isn't manipulating the facts.'"

As Thurgood Marshall ran against the clock now toward his most fateful rendezvous with the Supreme Court, he did not abandon the qualities that had set him apart as a leader. "What impressed me most about Thurgood," says John Frank, who had first met Marshall while teaching law at Indiana University in the late Forties, "was that he had worked his way through the hell and the tedium and the travel and the endlessness of all those cases long before he ever came to this great day. I remember him particularly vividly at some kind of a meeting in Indianapolis when I taught at Indiana. We were not then approaching the millennium or anything like it. It was just little people with grim problems in somebody's living room. . . . What I felt then is what I remember now: that it was a good thing that someone would come to us this way. What impressed me at the meetings in 1953 was Thurgood's good humor, and his calm, and the steadiness of his judgment."

That judgment was particularly notable for its negative as well as its positive uses. William Coleman remembers that Marshall was a good deal less taken with the research material uncovered in the states than Coleman himself had been. "Thurgood had the greatest ability an advocate can have in this regard," says Coleman. "He knew how and when to reject things—the way a painter does. He had the knack for looking over a memo and saying, 'Yeah, page five is great for us, but page seven can kill us.'"

He had another knack of incalculable value: he kept everybody feeling he or she was contributing and he reduced friction to a minimum among men who were in no way his intellectual inferiors.

There was Carter, careful and conscientious and efficient, keeping a thousand loose ends from getting knotted. There was Coleman, a superb technician, bringing his clinical intellect to bear on the language of the brief itself. There was Spottswood Robinson, habitually cautionary, battling fatigue and the loud, bold policy-forging of Bob Ming. Recalls one regular at the NAACP councils: "Ming might say, 'They *got* to listen to us,' and Spot would say, 'No, they *don't* got to listen to us. . . .'" For all the dogmatism of his style, Ming's mind was supple and his position on the cases fluid, and Marshall knew how to get the most out of him—and when to stop taking. Others added vital ingredients. Nabrit supplied "a kind of drive and poetry" to the sessions, remarks another insider. And a pair of youngish Columbia professors, Jack Weinstein and Charles L. Black, Jr., brought, besides their insights, first-rate writing skills to the homestretch drive.

What struck Weinstein and Black was Marshall's great gift for keeping his crew feeling good. "I never had so much fun in my life as during those sessions," remarks Black. "It was exactly the opposite of the image the South would later try to project of a bunch of hard-eyed conspirators." Adds Coleman, "There were no prima donnas in that room—only a lot of high spirit." A good deal of the humor, not unnaturally, stemmed from the racial predicament that had brought them together. Some of it was harmlessly sophomoric. When most of the men at one of the conferences had ordered chocolate milkshakes and one of the white professors in attendance ordered a vanilla one, Marshall pounded the table and roared, "We'll have no white chauvinism around here!" On another occasion, the group was discussing the question of the Supreme Court's power to rule in the segregation cases. Suddenly Marshall leaned forward in his place, looked around as if addressing the Justices, and said, "White bosses, you can do *any*thing you want 'cause you got de power!" Marshall was forever telling jokes on himself, as he had done all his professional life. A lot of them were one-liners, like the one he told of his appearance before a particularly crusty Southern judge who demanded of him, "What do you want from this court?" and Marshall said, "Anything I can get, your honor."

While most of Marshall's humor served to relieve the growing tension, part of it had the reverse effect, especially when it seemed to be aimed, consciously or not, at discomforting some of the white participants. Alfred Kelly, especially, was not prepared for Marshall's more mordant thrusts. Marshall once playfully asked one of the secretaries, who had been a trifle slow in bringing in some papers, if she had forgotten who "de H.N." was around there. Kelly recoiled upon learning that H.N. stood for "head nigger." Another time, Marshall was going through an old Midwestern newspaper from the post-Civil War period they had been dealing with and he came across a story about a colored worker who somehow had fallen from the track during railroad construction and hurt himself landing in a ditch. "Nigger in a Pit," the headline said. Marshall kept reading the headline out loud, over and over, savoring the sound of it: "Nigger in a pit, nigger in a pit. . . ." Or he would describe his great-grandfather as "the most worthless nigger there ever was" and toss off double-edged gags like one he once foisted on a white associate who had run out of matches and borrowed Marshall's cigarette lighter but couldn't get it lighted. Marshall took it back and lit it for him, needling, "No way you can operate that—this here's a lighter I had made special for people who say niggers ain't mechanical."

One day the playfulness seemed to be missing when they sat around the conference table puzzling silently over a particularly difficult problem. Looking over at Kelly, Marshall said softly, "Alfred, I like you. And it's very good of you to come here and work this way." Then he took off his glasses and added, voice rising, "But know one thing, Alfred—when we niggers take over the power, every time a white man takes a breath, he's gonna have to pay a fine!" A great stillness hovered over the room until the large man subsided in his chair and the discussion picked up again. Kelly, an easy mark for such shocking gambits, perfectly well grasped the serious part of Marshall's needling. To Kelly, Marshall was saying, without saying it, "Look here, don't you see now how the white man has rigged the law to deprive us Negroes of a fair shake? How'd *you* like to be in *our* place?" Remarks Kelly: "The frustration and anger in the man would come welling up in those rare moments, as if he sensed the appropriateness of reminding us what it was all about—of the need to dramatize for us the whole catastrophe of black-white relations in America." Marshall's intramural use of the word "nigger" seemed to serve a similar end. It sorely bothered a few of the black NAACP lawyers who otherwise held Marshall in high regard. Kelly, after a while, came to understand what Marshall was up to: "That word seemed to epitomize for him the entire tragedy of the black man's situation, but he wasn't somber about it. He could invest the word with as much humor as sadness."

At least one white man in that company was Marshall's match at brandishing gallows humor. Charles Black was a native of Austin, Texas, where he had been taught to play the harmonica by an aged ex-slave. In time, Black fell under the spell of jazz, which he suspects was part of the emotional lure to him of the black man's cause. The element of racial protest in jazz and the blues was plain to the young Texan, who grew up in Austin surrounded by statues of Confederate heroes. After taking his bachelor's degree at the University of Texas, where anti-racist students were then in short supply, Black came east to Yale. He earned a master's degree in English before swinging over to the law school, where he became a minor legend by avoiding lectures, not studying for exams until the last possible moment, and then doing so well that he was invited to join the *Yale Law Journal*—but declined the honor. As a young law professor at Columbia, Black also wrote poetry, studied the trumpet, haunted Greenwich Village, and socialized with some of his students—habits that earned him the reputation of an oddball among the more conservative members of the Columbia law faculty, which was no hotbed of permissiveness. Intense and effusive, Black seemed to be drifting in those years. "There was a fair sense of social injustice gnawing at him," recalls Jack Weinstein, who had the office next to Black's at Columbia in the early Fifties. When Bob Carter came to address a campus group which Black was advising, the professor was struck by the black lawyer's earnestness and volunteered his services. His work with the NAACP thereafter did not greatly enhance Black's standing with the more orthodox members of the Columbia law faculty, who did little to try to keep him when Yale made an offer. "He was an original," says Columbia's Walter Gellhorn, "and Herb Wechsler and I and some others wanted to keep him. But the feeling among a majority of our colleagues was that Charlie was not a terribly effective teacher in those days. I think a very bad error in judgment was made in not keeping him here. He has turned out to be a very original and useful writer and free spirit." At Yale, Black would also become one of the nation's recognized authorities on admiralty law.

His arrival at the NAACP inner councils stirred some curiosity. Black was, after all, a white Texan. "It took us a few sessions to believe he was really on our side," Carter remarks. After the first one, Thurgood Marshall could not restrain his curiosity. "We're glad to have you with us, Professor Black," said Marshall, according to one who was on hand, "but what is it exactly that brings you here?" Black, as expansive in his way as Marshall, replied: "Well, I'll tell you, Mr. Marshall, I come from deep, deep in Texas—so deep that I can't even remember hearing the word 'Republican' before I was eleven years old. But well before then, I'd heard of this really terrible organization way up North called the N-A-A-C-P. It was an awful place with a great big office all the way up there in New York, they said. And the worst thing of all about it was that right in that big office there was this room, this special secret room, a room with no windows and no doors and walls about a foot thick—and the only way you could get in was with a combination to this huge lock. And inside that room, they said, there was nothing but hooks on the walls—hundreds and hundreds of hooks—and do you know what was hanging on each and every one of those hooks?" Marshall, foaming with curiosity now, asked what. "Why, they said that on each of those hooks was a key to the bedroom of a Southern white woman. And so I figured *that's* an organization I wanna get involved in!"

Black threw all his passionate brilliance into the NAACP effort that fall as he joined in the brief-drafting and spoke up strongly to urge Marshall not to invite the Court to frame a decree implementing desegregation on a gradual basis if it should vote to outlaw Jim Crow schools—an issue the Justices had raised in the fourth of their five questions to the litigants. Black did not balk at seeing his prose tinkered with or discarded. "Everything was torn to pieces," he recalls. But Black's gift for clear, vigorous, and moving prose was evidenced in this sort of passage that he contributed to the final brief:

> These infant appellants are asserting the most important secular claims that can be put forward by children, the claim to their full measure of the chance to learn and grow, and the inseparably connected but even more important claim to be treated as entire citizens of the society into which they have been born. We have discovered no case in which such rights, once established, have been postponed by a cautious calculation of conveniences. The nuisance cases, the sewage cases, the cases of the overhanging cornices, need not be distinguished. They distinguish themselves.

Black did not blink when, later that fall, Marshall once looked at him and said, "You are a Negro."

Spottswood Robinson, whose balanced judgment, scrupulous care, clarity of expression, and remarkable recall made him Marshall's most valuable all-around associate, locked himself away from the world and went over the whole thing a final time, ironing out the bumps. What emerged was both a 235-page legal brief and an eloquent manifesto of the black man's claim to a long-deferred equality. Bristling with conviction, the consolidated brief presented the NAACP side in all four of the state cases combined. It deserves a place in the literature of advocacy.

The historical evidence in Congress and the states, declared the NAACP brief, showed that the Fourteenth Amendment was intended, in and of itself, to prohibit all forms of state-imposed racial discrimination. Even if the historical evidence were otherwise, the brief added, it was clear that segregation laws violated all the conventional tests for a reasonable basis to state classification of citizens. Whatever appeal the separate-but-equal doctrine may have had at the time it was sanctioned in *Plessy*, "it stands mirrored today as the faulty conception of an era dominated by provincialism, by intense emotionalism in race relations . . . and by the preaching of a doctrine of racial superiority that contradicted the basic concept upon which our society was founded. Twentieth century America, fighting racism at home and abroad, has rejected the race views of *Plessy v. Ferguson* because we have come to the realization that such views obviously tend to preserve not the strength but the weakness of our heritage." There was no longer any question, furthermore, that "furnishing public education is now an accepted governmental function," and equality was not provided by a system of separate schools, the only purpose of which was the perpetuation of an inferior status among black Americans.

The Court in *Plessy* had approved the enforcement of racial distinctions, the brief contended, because it said it found them in accordance with "the established usages, customs and traditions of the people"—and that was precisely what was wrong with the Court's opinion, the NAACP asserted, using its "broad approach," because

> . . . the very purpose of the Thirteenth, Fourteenth and Fifteenth Amendments was to effectuate a complete break with governmental action based on the established uses, customs and traditions of the slave era, to revolutionize the legal relationship between Negroes and whites, to destroy the inferior status of the Negro and to place him upon a plane of complete equality with the white man. . . . When the Court employed the old usages, customs and traditions as the basis for determining the reasonableness of the segregation statutes designed to resubjugate the Negro to an inferior status, it nullified the acknowledged intention of the framers of the [Fourteenth] Amendment, and made a travesty of the equal protection clause. . . .

Drawing upon the collective work of the scholars they had enlisted, the NAACP lawyers sketched out a slashing account of the history of segregation in the wake of the Compromise of 1877, which, they said, handed control of the Republican Party "to those who believed that the protection and expansion of their economic power could best be served by political conciliation of the southern irreconcilables, rather than by unswerving insistence upon human equality and the rights guaranteed by the postwar Amendments." Once the Redeemers of white supremacy took over in the South, they brought massive peonage, disenfranchisement, segregation, and terror to the colored masses, the brief argued, and *Plessy* legitimized that caste system. Thus the Negro "was effectively restored to an inferior position through laws and through practices, now dignified as 'custom and tradition.' " The fact was, the brief thundered, that

> . . . Segregation was designed to insure inequality—to discriminate on account of race and color—and the separate but equal doctrine accommodated the Constitution to that purpose. Separate but equal is a legal fiction. There never was and never will be any separate equality. Our Constitution cannot be used to sustain ideologies and practices which we as a people abhor.

The states defending segregation in *Brown* were encouraged when the Supreme Court set the cases down for reargument.

"We felt the posing of the five questions would strengthen our position," recalls J. Lindsay Almond, then attorney general of Virginia. "We knew what the contents of the debates over the Fourteenth Amendment had been—we knew that Congress had allowed segregated schools in Washington. We thought our research would give the Court the basis on which to lodge its interpretation of the Constitution consistent with our position."

The Virginia and South Carolina lawyers gathered at the Davis, Polk law offices in New York in mid-June a week after the Court's reargument order had come down. While all present recognized that the Court, throughout its history, had felt free to veer from what had likely been the original intentions and understanding of the framers of the Constitution—the Court's expansive interpretation of the interstate-commerce clause, they agreed, was an obvious case in point—the segregation issue as viewed from historical perspective seemed far more resistant to Court tampering. John W. Davis, presiding, said that the framers of the Fourteenth Amendment had "so clearly understood" that it was not applicable to schools that the South was on safe ground to argue that it was now "not properly within the judicial power . . . to construe the amendment so as to abolish segregation."

The research load was divided. Davis's office would explore the congressional debates on the amendment, and the Virginians in Justin Moore's Richmond firm would follow through on the ratification process in the states. They would cooperate fully, of course, but Virginia insisted on filing its own brief, partly out of state pride, partly because it still felt that the stronger record it had produced through its expert witnesses in the trial court might make its case a more attractive one in the eyes of the Supreme Court.

Half a dozen summer trainees from the Davis firm, most of them crack law students, camped out for weeks in the New York Public Library combing through the congressional debates, and several of them made extended sorties to the Library of Congress. "We didn't find a scintilla of evidence to the effect that the framers intended the amendment to outlaw segregated schools," says William Meagher, Davis's associate on the case. "And the evidence in the states was the same. Why, in New York State there was a permissive school-segregation law on the books as late as 1909. And of course there was the fact that the Congress that had voted for the amendment had also permitted segregated schools in the District of Columbia. Mr. Davis felt that the judicial and legislative authority was so much in support of his case that, unless the Court was going to disregard all that history and all the judicial precedent, he had the case won." Meagher himself was convinced that the Court's questions signaled that the Justices were still open-minded on the whole issue. "We thought it was pretty plain from those questions what was bothering them," Meagher adds—the lack of legal or historical justification to overturn segregation, whether or not they wanted to do so on humanitarian grounds.

The humanitarian aspect of the question was put to one side in the interest of professionalism by Davis's other principal associate in preparing the brief on reargument—New Hampshire-born and New England-educated Taggart Whipple. "I felt we had a just and solid case," Whipple remembers, "that we were not merely raising a cry in the dark nor a medieval prospect. I wasn't concerned with the sociological judgment but with the legal precedent only. The more I got into it, the more it seemed to me that, based on authority, we had a strong case—and that the subject area was the kind of thing that the Court had traditionally felt ought to be settled by the people most directly concerned—the local communities. There was no wringing of hands among us over whether segregation was, *per se,* discrimination. We had no internal struggle over the substantive legal points."

It was perhaps not surprising that the Virginia brief, prepared by born and bred white Southerners, was more spirited than the South Carolina brief turned out by Davis's New York office. The tone throughout the Virginians' argument was a match for the certitude of the NAACP brief. Reading the two briefs in succession, a moderately astute Martian would have concluded that each side had examined totally different historical evidence. It was beyond dispute, declared the Virginia brief, that the Civil Rights Act of 1866 did not outlaw school segregation. Representative Wilson, who was chief sponsor of the bill in the House, had made that clear. And of course the "no discrimination" clause had been scrubbed from the bill before its passage. But then Virginia made the jump in its argument that set it apart from any further resemblance to the NAACP account of the congressional debates. The reason for passage of the Fourteenth Amendment, said the Virginians, was "simply" to constitutionalize the Civil Rights Act, and so Congress kept the amendment "within the same bounds" as the rights bill. Regulation of schools was "outside those bounds." Such a statement was based, of course, on as conclusionary a selection of the remarks made during the debates as the NAACP had indulged in, and it failed to acknowledge that the generalized language of the Constitution had historically been subjected to far more expansive interpretation than specific statutes such as the rights bill. In short, Virginia was having no part of the NAACP view that even though the rights bill itself did not outlaw segregation, that was no reason for the Court to hold that the Fourteenth Amendment could not be interpreted in 1953 to find the practice a denial of equal protection.

The other historical evidence seemed to clinch the matter for Virginia. Its brief maintained that in not one of the thirty-seven states then in the Union was there "any substantial evidence" that the Fourteenth Amendment had been thought to outlaw school segregation (the South Carolina brief said it could find even circumstantial evidence in no more than five states, three of which later went over to Jim Crow schools). And if the Fourteenth Amendment had had the grand intentions that the appellants' lawyers had claimed for it (i.e., outlawing all racial discrimination), there would have been no need for the Fifteenth Amendment—a somewhat risky and not very accurate assertion since the NAACP had argued that all three post-Civil War amendments were to be taken in their totality if one wished to understand the full intentions of the framers. Nor, said the Virginians, had Congress acquired the power to prohibit school segregation by the fifth section of the Fourteenth Amendment ("The Congress shall have power to enforce, by appropriate legislation, the provisions of this article") since the provisions of the first section could not be expanded to include school segregation, a practice the framers had never intended to outlaw. Indeed, the privilege of attending public school was not a right that any citizen derived from any part of the Constitution, and to suggest that school segregation offended the Fourteenth Amendment was a twentieth-century "afterthought."

As to the decisions of the Court in classification cases upon which the NAACP was relying as precedent for reversing *Plessy*, the Virginians asserted that all of these—from *Strauder* and *Yick Wo* to *Shelley* and the Texas primary cases—were readily distinguishable from the segregation question because all those prior cases involved "absolute deprivations" of Negro rights while *Plessy*, pledging a separate equality, could not be so characterized. And *McLaurin*, Virginia argued, was a different sort of case in which the Court had found that "there was separation but not equality"—a slick way of avoiding the Court's holding that it was precisely the sort of separation imposed on McLaurin that constituted the inequality. But the Virginians, for all their confidence in the historical and judicial evidence, could do little to cover their point of gaping vulnerability: what real justification was there in 1953 for a state to segregate its schoolchildren? "The record in this case abounds with testimony as to the reasonableness of school segregation," the Virginia brief insisted. But, on examination, all that that testimony came down to was the claim by a number of state officials and a pair of Virginia-born white psychologists that separate schools were "in the best interests of both races" and that "the general welfare" of the state would likely be harmed by ending the practice. If Virginia had produced documentary evidence to show that all Negroes were so mentally and morally inferior that the very presence of any of them in the same schools with white children would pollute the learning atmosphere, the state might have been able to argue legitimately that a reasonable basis existed for segregation. No such evidence was ever unearthed.

The Davis firm's brief in the South Carolina case was more concise and less strident, but it did not blanch in declaring that it was "the expressed intent of the framers" of the Fourteenth Amendment not to abolish segregated schools—a claim lacking documented foundation, just as the opposite claim could not have been (and finally was not) made by the NAACP.

The Kansas and Delaware briefs echoed the positions in the two Southern briefs for the most part. Delaware was rather more adamant about it. "The original reason for allowing segregation in the public schools undoubtedly was the feeling that there was such a degree of prejudice that the system of mixed schools did not work and that the school system and education of the people as a whole would suffer," the Delaware brief of Attorney General Albert Young stated. "There is nothing in the record to show to this Court that the situation has changed sufficiently to invalidate this reason." Two things were noteworthy in such a statement. First, there were no historical grounds for suggesting that "the system of mixed schools did not work" in the segregating states because in none of them had truly mixed schools ever really been established widely or on a sustained basis. Second, even if that statement had been historically valid for the years immediately after slavery, could it be said that the Supreme Court should have continued to acknowledge the legitimacy of "such a degree of prejudice" nearly a century after the freeing of the slaves?

The government of the United States, newly under the command of Dwight Eisenhower, was not sure how to deal with the school-segregation cases. Republicans were in command as well of both houses of Congress for the first time in twenty-two years, and they rather liked the feeling. Eisenhower had managed to carry four Southern states (Florida, Tennessee, Texas, and Virginia), and the political strategists guiding the party's newly minted fortunes were not eager to see them dissipated by a strong administration stand in favor of desegregation.

None of Eisenhower's Cabinet members or White House advisors was more politically astute than his Attorney General, Herbert Brownell, a New York corporate lawyer and an intimate of Thomas E. Dewey. It was Brownell's responsibility to recommend the government's course in *Brown*. Shortly after the Court's reargument order, Brownell, a chilly ramrod, summoned his principal aides to a meeting in his office. Among them were Deputy Attorney General (later Attorney General and Secretary of State) William P. Rogers, Assistant Attorney General (later Solicitor General) J. Lee Rankin, Assistant Attorney General (later Chief Justice of the United States) Warren E. Burger, and two Truman-administration holdovers specializing in civil rights, Robert Stern and Philip Elman of the Solicitor General's office. "Their prevailing attitude," recounts Elman of his new Republican superiors, "was expressed by Rogers, who said in effect, 'Jesus, do we really *have* to file a brief? Aren't we better off staying out of it?' Stern and I told them that the Court's invitation to appear at the reargument was tantamount to a command. And there was no point in declining to submit a brief by way of avoiding taking a position on the merits because the question was sure to be raised at the oral argument in view of the prior administration's record of having come out for overruling *Plessy*."

For a time, Brownell made no move at all other than to pull the case out of the Solicitor General's office and bring it directly under his own wing in the person of Rankin, a native Nebraskan (like Brownell) who had practiced in Lincoln for the previous twenty years and could be counted on to honor the chain of command. An uneasy relationship formed in those midyear months between Rankin and Elman. To Elman, the Republicans seemed unsophisticated and sanctimonious. "They've been out in the wilderness [so long] . . . they've come to believe their own propaganda," he confided to Felix Frankfurter. "Rankin, for example, thinks that there is a distinguishing characteristic of the 'New Deal–Fair Deal' type of person. Such a person, he told me, believes in the philosophy that the end justifies the means. The Republicans—and this too was said with a straight face—do not share that philosophy."

Principled or otherwise, by a month after the first meeting in Brownell's office, the Attorney General had apparently not made up his mind on the segregation cases. Though Rankin was plainly in charge "of whatever-it-is that we'll be doing," Elman advised Frankfurter in mid-July, "the fact is that as of now the Government of the United States of America has done almost nothing in response to the Court's invitation." Part of the reason was indecisiveness at the top. "Eisenhower was committed to the abolition of segregation," says one of his closest and most powerful White House assistants of that period, "but he did not believe that this ought to be the result of any summary court order applying to immediate termination of every vestige of segregation." While the President favored prompt desegregation of colleges and secondary schools, according to this knowledgeable assistant (who declines to be named), "he thought that in the primary schools a more gradual approach would diminish the probability that severe and very likely violent opposition would result in the event that little children were forcibly intermingled." The assistant adds that "Eisenhower's advisors differed among themselves" and that "the Department of Justice was more eager to promote a definitive resolution of the matter than was the Executive."

By the end of July, the government was finally ready to move. Having dithered for the better part of two months, Brownell acted first to get more time from the Court, and in view of the Justices' jumbled feelings on the cases, they did not seem to mind postponing the reargument for two months. Chief Justice Vinson, not eager for the showdown, granted the request. At the Department of Justice, Rankin gave the go-ahead to Elman, whose work earlier that year in the *Thompson* case, in which the Court had voted to uphold a nineteenth-century statute prohibiting Jim Crow restaurants in the District of Columbia, apparently pleased the Assistant Attorney General. Elman, with a staff of eight under him, produced a massive brief of more than 600 pages. It managed to avoid saying outright on any of them that school segregation was wrong and ought to be outlawed then and there by the Court—but it came very close. When it left his desk to go to Brownell's office and then the White House, Elman's brief "to my best recollection" stated that segregation was illegal and ought to be stopped. But Brownell later advised Anthony Lewis of the *New York Times* that the Elman draft "did not include any such conclusion . . . when it reached my desk and, so far as I know, never did include it. Mr. Rankin . . . and I agreed at all times that since the brief was filed in direct response to questions asked of the department by the Court, it should answer those questions solely."

That the government's written argument did not come out foursquare against segregation was not of great concern to Elman, who titled the new document a "Supplemental Brief" to the Justice Department's 1952 brief and proceeded on the assumption that nothing in the 1953 brief was intended to weaken the unequivocating stand of the earlier one. "No attempt has been made to re-examine other questions briefed and argued at the last term," Elman wrote on the second page of the new brief, which he described a few lines earlier as "an objective non-adversary discussion of the questions stated in the Court's order of reargument."

Elman's brief, filed in late November, did not seem very objective to the South. Examination of all the historical evidence, said the United States brief, disclosed that there were so few specific mentions in Congress or the ratifying state legislatures of the Fourteenth Amendment's possible or intended effects on education that it was impossible to draw "a definite conclusion" regarding the framers' intentions or the understanding of them in the states. Nor would the government grant that any "persuasive inference" could be drawn from congressional approval of school segregation in the District of Columbia at the time of the amendment's passage or later. The Fourteenth Amendment was not much alluded to during the congressional debates over Charles Sumner's civil-rights bills that would have outlawed segregation in the District as well as the states. What evidence there was suggested that Congressmen who declined to vote to prohibit segregation in public schools might have been persuaded by the declarations of their Southern colleagues that such an action would doom public education in the South—a none too sturdy institution as it was. Then, too, it was important for the Court now weighing the wisdom of continued segregation to recall the state of public education at the time of the amendment:

> In 1868 public schools had been hardly begun in many states and were still in their infancy. School attendance was, as a general matter, not compulsory. The Negroes had just been released from bondage and were generally illiterate, poor, and retarded socially and culturally. To educate them in the same classes and schools as white children may have been regarded as entirely impracticable. It is possible that state legislatures—while recognizing in the Fourteenth Amendment a clear mandate of equality—may have considered separate schools for colored children as a temporary practical expedient permitted by the Amendment. Many proponents of Negro education regarded separate schools as a more effective means of extending the benefits of the public school system to the colored people. . . .

History, then, would not aid the Court in determining "the application of the Amendment to the question of school segregation as it exists today, when school attendance is compulsory and there are no considerations of an educational character which warrant separation of children of different races in public schools." What the legislative history did suggest was that the Congress which proposed it understood not that the Fourteenth Amendment would abolish segregated schools but that it "established the broad constitutional principle of full and complete equality of all persons under the law, and that it forbade all legal distinctions based on race or color."

In short, the government essentially agreed with the NAACP.

The summer of 1953 provided a welcome respite for the members of the Supreme Court. The previous term had ended with the segregation cases dangling in irresolution and the painful intra-Court clash over the fate of Julius and Ethel Rosenberg, convicted of atomic espionage.

Never before in American peacetime had civilians been executed for espionage. On seven occasions, the Supreme Court had acted on motions by the Rosenbergs' lawyers. On the first one, in October of 1952, only Justice Black voted to grant *certiorari* to review the trial and conviction. On the final occasion, at a special session of the Court in mid-June of 1953, Black had been joined by Douglas, who had granted a short stay of execution so that the Court might review the applicability of a 1946 atomic-energy act that provided for the death penalty in espionage cases only on recommendation of the jury—and no such recommendation had been made in the Rosenbergs' case. Vinson wrote for a six-to-two majority, holding that the 1946 act had not mitigated a 1917 espionage act. Frankfurter neither concurred nor dissented, but wrote an enigmatic memo promising to elaborate at a later date; he finally dissented—after the switch had been pulled on the Rosenbergs at Sing Sing. At one point during the motions before the Court, Jackson had joined the old Roosevelt civil-libertarian bloc of Black, Douglas, and Frankfurter, though in the end he sided with the anti-libertarians, of whom only Burton cast a single pro-Rosenberg vote during the course of the Court's ordeal in the charged, divisive case. The net effect of the Justices' deliberations had been to strain further their ideological and personal relationships.

Summertime was generally slow at the Court. Most of the Justices would be out of town until September. In their chambers, the new crop of clerks would be reviewing "cert" applications for recommended disposition by the Justices at the beginning of the October term. At least one outgoing clerk, though, spent the summer of 1953 wrapping up a piece of important unfinished business that was to have its value in the Court's final deliberations on *Brown.*

Alexander Bickel was one of the most gifted young men ever to clerk for Felix Frankfurter. There was a quality of intensity and mental agility about the twenty-eight-year-old Harvard Law graduate that the Justice admired, and Bickel's skill as a writer added to his usefulness. Early in the 1952 Term, Frankfurter had given the clerk an open-ended assignment: he was to do appropriate background reading and then go over every word spoken during the congressional debates in order to advise the Justice on the original understanding of the framers of the Fourteenth Amendment—a project that precisely presaged the research that would be carried on by the litigants and Elman's crew of government lawyers the following summer.

It took Bickel nearly a year to complete his assignment. He was never under any deadline pressure from Frankfurter, who made it clear that he wanted the best piece of work of which the clerk was capable. "But I suppose if it looked as if a decision had to be reached that term, I would have been speeded up," Bickel remarked. He kept beavering away at the project throughout the term. The Court library trundled in a new cartful of *Congressional Globe*s every time Bickel finished another batch of note cards on his typewriter. The cart of *Globe*s beside his desk became a part of Bickel's furniture that year.

Bickel finished up his project late in August, his last piece of work before leaving Frankfurter's employ. The Justice was so impressed by the Bickel memorandum that, after doing a bit of polishing, he had it set in type in the Court's basement print shop and distributed among the Justices a few days before the *Brown* reargument in early December. It was one way the Justice apparently hoped to sway his brethren, though the Bickel memo was hardly free of the ambiguities confronting any scholar trying to resurrect the past at the distance of nearly a century. Indeed, it was his dissection of the ambiguities, especially as encountered in the sometimes filmy words of Representative John Bingham, who played the critical role in the shaping of both the Civil Rights Act and the Fourteenth Amendment, that made Bickel's nuanced reading of the debates particularly useful. In effect, Bickel disputed the conclusions of all three participants to the *Brown* litigation—the NAACP, the pro-segregationists, and the government—as well as those of earlier historical commentators for tending to oversimplify Bingham's position.

It was by no means certain, Bickel contended, that Bingham's key intervention in moving to strip the Civil Rights Bill of its "no discrimination" clause was based solely on his belief that Congress lacked constitutional authority for such a step. Bickel found evidence that Bingham was concerned about the ends sought as well as the means used in the bill. The congressman, "a man not normally distinguished for precision of thought and statement," as Bickel remarked, indicated that he sought to make the bill less "oppressive" and less "unjust" in urging that it be stripped of its blanket civil-rights coverage. And if Bingham had objected to the bill on policy as well as strictly legal grounds, then the argument by Alfred Kelly, John Frank, and other scholars that Bingham promoted the Fourteenth Amendment mainly to cure the constitutional infirmities of the Civil Rights Bill would be thrown into serious question. On the other hand, Bickel was not smitten by the argument, to be insisted upon by the South's lawyers in *Brown*, that it was the intention of Bingham and other framers of the amendment to do no more than constitutionalize the rights bill, though it surely had that effect as a minimum. In a trenchant letter transmitting his noteworthy memorandum, Bickel wrote to Frankfurter:

> . . . Section 1 of the Amendment was passed to the refrain of assurances and accusations that it embodied the Civil Rights Act. Little regard was had for language by a Congress not notable for the presence in its membership of very many brilliant men. A blunderbuss was simply aimed in the direction of existing evils in the South, on which all eyes were fixed. There were a few muted warnings that the language was broad, but in the hurry of it in the end no one cared much. The dangers to which broad language might lead were distant anyway. It was preposterous to worry about unsegregated schools, for example, when hardly a beginning had been made at educating Negroes at all and when obviously special efforts, suitable only for the Negroes, would have to be made. . . . In any event, it is impossible to conclude that the 39th Congress intended that segregation be abolished; impossible also to conclude that they foresaw it might be, under the language they were adopting. What was in Bingham's mind, God alone knows, and in any event Bingham was unable to impart it to the House.

But that was not the end of it so far as Bickel was concerned in suggesting how the legislative history might affect the Court's handling of the school-segregation cases. It was doubtful that an explicit "no discrimination" provision going beyond the enumerated rights in the Civil Rights Bill as finally enacted could have passed the Thirty-ninth Congress, Bickel suspected, nor was it likely that the plenary grant of legislative power in the first Bingham draft of the amendment ("The Congress shall have power to make all laws . . . necessary . . . to secure to the citizens of each state all privileges and immunities of citizens in the several states . . . and to all persons . . . equal protection in the rights of life, liberty, and property") would have attracted a majority in both houses. "But may it not be," Bickel wrote in a revision of his memo that appeared in the *Harvard Law Review* two years later, "that the Moderates and the Radicals reached a compromise permitting them to go to the country with language that they could, where necessary, defend against damaging alarms raised by the opposition, but which at the same time was sufficiently elastic to permit reasonable future advances?" Or, as he put it in his farewell letter to Justice Frankfurter: "I think the legislative history leaves this Court free to remember that it is a *Constitution* it is construing. I think also that a charitable view of the sloppy draftsmen of the Fourteenth Amendment would ascribe to them the knowledge that it was a *Constitution* they were writing."

In summary, then, the Bickel-Frankfurter memo as circulated to the Justices held that the legislative history, while revealing no evidence that the framers of the amendment had intended to prohibit school segregation, did not foreclose future generations from acting on the question, either by congressional statute or by judicial review.

The second-busiest clerk at the Supreme Court that summer, in all likelihood, was John Fassett, Justice Stanley Reed's new assistant. A native of the Hamptons on eastern Long Island and a graduate of Yale Law School, where Reed himself had gone, Fassett was put to work chasing down various data that the Justice asked for in helping to strengthen his view that the *Plessy* doctrine was not, in and of itself, a denial of equal protection to segregated Negro schoolchildren. It was not a position that Fassett favored, but he went about his task with diligence. "I was there to assist him," he says in retrospect. "I recognized that it was going to be a difficult decision for him."

Most of the summer, Reed was away from Washington, visiting part of the time with his kin in and around Maysville, Kentucky, but he kept peppering his staff for memos on the segregation cases. First he wanted a rundown on all Court cases in the previous decade involving alleged denial of due process by a state government or one of its subdivisions. Then he wanted a comparison of crime among whites and Negroes in comparable-sized cities tabulated according to whether Jim Crow was practiced in them or not (e.g., Louisville vs. Cincinnati, New Orleans vs. San Francisco, Baltimore vs. Pittsburgh). In mid-August, he wrote in to ask for an updating of attitudes of other nations toward segregation as manifested in the evolving draft of the United Nations Declaration and Covenant on Human Rights. The UN had expressed no interest in the abolition of segregation, Reed was convinced, and remarked in his letter, " 'Segregation' as now presented does not mean 'discrimination' to me. . . ." Earlier in the summer, he had written, "If anyone thinks segregation is discrimination they have decided the segregation issue against segregation. That is the argument of the N.A.A.C.P. The S.C. rule for 75 years has been 'separate but equal.' No discrimination. . . ."

Justice Reed returned to Washington to stay just before Labor Day. He soon met with Fassett, who gave him the results of the UN and crime research projects and then inquired whether the Court was going to deal directly with the issue of the continued vitality of *Plessy*. "He replied in the affirmative," Fassett recalls, "and added, '*They* know they have the votes and they are determined to resolve the issue.'" Fassett, who was less outspoken in his opposition to Reed's view of the case than the Justice's clerks had been in previous terms, ventured the thought that "the result *they* sought to achieve was desirable." Reed replied that "he did not conceive that to be the criterion of the Court's function, and he asked me whether I was also in favor of 'krytocracy.' He directed me to one of his favorite sets of books, the Oxford English Dictionary, from which I learned that 'krytocracy' means government by judges."

It was during that initial conversation that Reed disclosed his expectation that Chief Justice Vinson and at least one other member of the Court, perhaps Justice Minton, might join him when the crucial vote was taken in *Brown*.

All such bets on the alignment of the Court ended abruptly a few days later when the single most fateful judicial event of that long summer occurred. In his Washington hotel apartment, Fred M. Vinson died of a heart attack at 3:15 in the morning of September 8. He was sixty-three.

All the members of the Court attended Vinson's burial in Louisa, Kentucky, his ancestral home. But not all the members of the Court grieved equally at his passing. And one at least did not grieve at all. Felix Frankfurter had not much admired Fred Vinson as judge or man. And he was certain that the Chief Justice had been the chief obstacle to the Court's prospects of reaching a humanitarian and judicially defensible settlement of the monumental segregation cases. In view of Vinson's passing just before the *Brown* reargument, Frankfurter remarked to a former clerk, "This is the first indication I have ever had that there is a God."

# 25

# Arrival of the Superchief

Fred Vinson was not yet cold in his grave when speculation rose well above a whisper as to whom President Eisenhower would pick to heal and lead the Supreme Court as it faced one of its most momentous decisions in the segregation cases. The members of the Court themselves were hardly immune from this instant epidemic of curiosity.

The day after the funeral, Harold Burton noted in his diary that he and Justice Jackson had discussed the subject. Burton, as the only Republican on the Court, became by that fact alone an immediate candidate for elevation to the Chief's chair by a Republican President. Jackson confided that he would be happy if the mantle were to pass to Burton, though both men agreed that Earl Warren, governor of California, was the most logical candidate. At breakfast on Saturday morning, September 12, with Justice Black, Burton again discussed the subject. Black echoed Jackson's satisfaction with the thought of Burton's elevation to Chief, according to Burton's diary, and there is scant reason to doubt the sincerity of either Jackson or Black, for Burton's personality was surely the least abrasive of any on the Court. His intellectual capacity, however, hovered near the bottom, and his assumption of the Chief's spot would almost surely have invited a mortal clash for his judicial soul by the Big Four Roosevelt appointees. The Washington *Post* that Saturday morning carried a United Press article stating that Jackson, in view of his widely recognized brilliance and conservative swing in the post-war era, was a leading contender to take Vinson's place, and Burton told Black that that would be fine with him. Burton was too kind a man to have been needling Black with such a remark, so one is left to conclude that the earnest Justice from Ohio did not know how unappealing the elevation of Robert Jackson to Chief Justice would have been to Hugo Black. Black confined his response to the thought that no Democrat was likely to be chosen and that, at any rate, it was better for the Court to reach outside for a new Chief. Warren, they both agreed, would be the best choice.

Eisenhower, in his memoirs, recorded the qualities he ranked highest in considering candidates to head the Court: character and ability that would inspire "respect, pride, and confidence of the populace" came first. Then he looked for high ideals, a moderately progressive social philosophy—a middle-of-the-roader, in other words, in his own image—and a substantial ration of common sense. Judicial experience would be helpful but not essential. The nominee should give geographic and religious balance to the Court and should not be older than sixty-two (which happened to be Eisenhower's age). Both the FBI and the American Bar Association, furthermore, had to clear the man.

Such criteria, as well as other practical considerations, helped whittle the list rapidly. Harold Burton was an admirable man, but nothing about his performance on the Court suggested that he had the stature or the temperament to lead it. And he was sixty-five. Robert Jackson was surely an outstanding jurist, but his latter-day conservatism could not erase from long Republican memories the skilled service he had rendered to the New Deal; there had been flashes of pettiness and airs of grandeur, moreover, that plainly had distanced him from a number of the brethren. Other eminent judges were considered. Arthur T. Vanderbilt, chief justice of the New Jersey Supreme Court and a solid Republican, had impressive credentials. His health, though, was said to be questionable; he might better be considered for an Associate Justiceship when the time came. John J. Parker of the Fourth Circuit Court of Appeals was a universally admired judge, but he was sixty-eight—twenty-three years older than when he was nominated to the Court by Herbert Hoover. (His appointment, furthermore, would have obliged the Court's presiding official to abstain from voting on the appeal of his own decision in the *Briggs* case.) A number of other federal judges offered attractive credentials, but in the final analysis Eisenhower seemed to want a man fully versed in the rough-and-tumble of practical affairs to run the Court, a forceful administrator who could end its squabbling and restore its dignity by forging a new era of unity.

John Foster Dulles, his deeply committed Secretary of State, was sounded out by the President, but expressed his thanks and clear preference for combatting further territorial encroachments by the infidels of global Communism. It was more of a perfunctory offer, perhaps, than a serious bid to Dulles, whose relish of his worldwide task must have been obvious to the President. A far more likely choice would have been the three-term governor of New York, Thomas E. Dewey, then but fifty-one years old. Leader of the progressive Eastern wing of the Republican Party for a dozen years, Dewey through his political manager, Herbert Brownell, was widely credited with having stage-managed the entire Eisenhower presidential drive. Brownell, of course, had been rewarded with the Attorney General's post. Dewey seemed to have most, if not all, of the qualifications Eisenhower wanted in his Chief Justice, yet more than likely he was never offered the high honor. According to some accounts, he asked not to be considered for it. There was perhaps something of the city slicker about Tom Dewey that may have cooled Eisenhower to him for the Court job; or perhaps his two unsuccessful runs for President served to tarnish him in Eisenhower's mind as a partisan figure rejected by the national electorate and therefore not likely to be a binding force as leader of the Court.

Whatever reservations, if any, the President may have had about nominating the governor of the nation's largest state to be Chief Justice, he seems to have had few about the governor of the second-largest state.

Earl Warren had been well into his second term as California's chief executive when John Gunther's *Inside U.S.A.* appeared in 1947 and pronounced him a genial second-rater. Warren was "honest, likeable, and clean," wrote Gunther; he was a kindly and well-balanced man, one of your friendly, upright Californians "with little intellectual background, little genuine depth or coherent philosophy; a man who has probably never bothered with abstract thought twice in his life. . . ." Gunther's ultimate judgment of Warren's prospects was that "he will never set the world on fire or even make it smoke. . . ."

That estimate was not widely amended the following year after Warren had run, with great reluctance, for Vice President on the Dewey ticket. He had not conveyed a notably more dimensioned image of himself to the American public, though he had been so highly regarded in California that the Republicans *and* Democrats had nominated him for re-election as governor in 1946. To the nation at large, in the dawn of the television age, Earl Warren registered as an able and amiable public servant whose utterances achieved the approximate vibrancy of vanilla tapioca. There was, to be sure, an admirably wholesome, sort of Smokey-the-Bear robustness behind that broad smile of his, but one sensed in him a trustworthiness and a purposeful bustle more in keeping with a lifelong Eagle Scout than a dynamic statesman. Flint and fire seemed missing. That bland, foursquare, and elusive personality would militate against a serious run for the White House, though Warren went through the motions in 1952 and might well have succeeded in the event of an Eisenhower-Taft stalemate. But those who, like Gunther, confused low-voltage magnetism with simple-mindedness in Earl Warren failed to note how thoroughly the man had been steeped in the pressure cooker of American power politics and how skillfully he had managed not merely to survive but to emerge from it as a master pragmatist whose ideals, strange to say, had been tempered, not shattered, by the ordeal.

His father was a Norwegian immigrant, brought to America in his infancy soon after the Civil War. He never really prospered in the new land. At the time his son Earl was born in Los Angeles in 1890, Matt Warren was a $70-a-month repairman on the Southern Pacific's rolling stock. He joined the upstart American Railway Union (for whites only), got in trouble for it, and had to find work where he could. That turned out to be Kern City, California, on the outskirts of the boisterous railroad town of Bakersfield, and it was here that Earl Warren grew up. His was not a sheltered childhood. Dollars were scarce in the Warren household, and the boy always had a job, delivering ice or groceries on a mule-drawn wagon, serving as a mechanic's helper, or speeding all over town on his bike as a $2.50-a-day summer "callboy" rousting out railroad crewmen from front-porch rockers, saloon poker games, and whorehouse cribs. In time, he managed to accumulate $800 and went off to college in Berkeley; he would spend most of the next forty years in the San Francisco Bay area.

Earl Warren flourished amid the good companionship of his college days. His friendships, not any book he ever read or professor who taught him, were what mattered to him most, he would say later. He lingered at

Berkeley for his law degree as well and persisted in his studies long enough to win a doctorate in jurisprudence. His thesis dealt with the corporate liability of directors in the state of California, but corporate law held small allure for him. After an interlude in the Army during World War I—he wound up a first lieutenant on the merit of his skilled instruction in the many uses of the bayonet, though he never saw combat—he went to work as an assistant to the city counsel of Oakland. In a year, he was installed a few blocks away in the Alameda County Courthouse as an assistant district attorney, putting in sixteen-hour days for $150 a month. Five years later, in 1925, local bosses gave him an interim appointment as district attorney of the third-largest county in California; he would stay on for thirteen years, winning re-election three times. He never hesitated to prosecute some of those same bosses when he discovered they had long profited from street-paving contracts. From the start, it was widely recognized that Earl Warren was incorruptible. For the duration of Prohibition, he even stopped drinking.

He was not only honest; he was a remarkably efficient and fair-minded prosecutor. He fought the bootleggers and bunco artists and organized crooks with fearless zeal by enlisting and training a crack staff of investigators and assistants who were expected to bring the same sort of dedication to their task as Warren, who worked till midnight five days a week when need be. He held daily briefings for the office staff and pushed hard for friction-free teamwork between the legal people and the less exalted law-enforcement troops, the cops and deputy sheriffs charged with doing the dirty work. Every Saturday at 8:30 a.m. sharp, he had staff members in from the outlying sectors of the county for updating and to maintain close coordination among his charges.

The district attorney's office handled both criminal and civil prosecutions, and so the range of Warren's work was large. It included one case brought against a local railroad that Warren argued and won before the Supreme Court in Washington. He taught his lawyers how to draw up a proper brief, accurate and forceful without overstating the case. He taught them how to persevere and keep digging for the facts that would put a felon in jail, not how to beat him into a confession. It was said that the DA's office in Alameda County in the years Earl Warren ran it never extracted an involuntary confession from a defendant. Anyone who wanted to see his lawyer before submitting to police interrogation was permitted to do so. No conviction ever won by Warren's office was thrown out on appeal by a higher court. Insists a lawyer who apprenticed in that office during the Warren years, "None of us was ever asked to prosecute a defendant if we weren't sure of his guilt."

He was chary with praise, yet commanded keen loyalty from his staff. He possessed three particular gifts that helped weld them to him. He could make and stick to a decision. He had an almost supernatural sense of when to move in on a situation and when to hold back. And he had a seemingly flawless knack for remembering names, so those under him were not just so many spear-carrying functionaries; they were his people.

In 1938, he stepped up to attorney general of California. He shut down the dog tracks, the slot machines, the bingo games, and the bookmaking parlors all over the state. He went after bigger racketeers, labor-union thuggery, and once descended upon Los Angeles, commandeered a small fleet of police boats, and decommissioned four floating casinos bobbing blissfully in a bay twenty miles offshore. He started to win a national reputation as both a highly effective enforcer of the law and a humanitarian who understood that it could not be used as a club to extract good behavior from troubled souls. He told a national convention of peace officers in 1939:

> . . . The one relic that we have of barbarism . . . is our belief that we can take men who are weak in character, men who have got into trouble . . . hold them in jail for a period of time with absolutely nothing to do except commune with other people with the same or greater weaknesses, and then turn them out on society and expect them to be better.

For all his virtues, he was not flawless. As war came on, he was caught up by patriotic zeal and foreboding that combined to make him an unflinching advocate of oppressive tactics unlike anything he had ever before countenanced in defending the security of the public. Soon after Pearl Harbor, Warren began sounding alarms about the potential menace to the civilian defense effort of the 110,000 Japanese-Americans on the West Coast, any or all of whom, so far as loyal white Americans knew, might be fifth-columnists. In February 1942, he declared before a conference of district attorneys and sheriffs that he thought it strange there had been absolutely no reports of sabotage efforts in California and attributed to the yellow peril "a studied effort not to have any [reports] until the zero hour arrives." Soon he was testifying before a special House committee taking testimony in California on the wisdom of removing from their homes these Americans of Japanese extraction, two-thirds of them citizens, and interning them. Warren favored the move, explained that the Nisei had an "entirely different" cultural background from that of other Americans, including those of German and Italian extraction, and produced maps of the California coast showing that "virtually every important strategic location and installation" from Marin County to the Mexican border had one or more Japanese-American landowners in the immediate vicinity. Some airplane factories were "entirely surrounded by Japanese land ownership or occupancy. It is a situation fraught with the greatest danger and under no circumstances should it ever be permitted to exist."

President Roosevelt ordered the step, liberal columnist Walter Lippmann blessed it, Tom Clark was dispatched by the Justice Department to oversee the compulsory relocation, and the Supreme Court, in a six-to-three opinion by its foremost civil-libertarian, Hugo Black, eventually sanctioned it as a war emergency measure. But it was as much a racist-inspired move as a military one. The Japanese-Americans were forcibly uprooted from their homes and their land, from their fishing boats and their shops, and had to sell them and their cars and their furniture at any price they could get before being transported a hundred or more miles inland to refugee camps and detention centers, where they stayed for most of the war. By June of 1943, in his first year as governor of California, Earl Warren was telling his fellow governors convened in Ohio:

> . . . If the Japs are released, no one will be able to tell a saboteur from any other Jap. We are now producing approximately half of the ships and airplanes of the country on the Pacific Coast. To cripple these industries or the facilities that serve them would be a body blow to the war effort. We don't want to have a second Pearl Harbor in California. We don't propose to have the Japs back in California during this war if there is any lawful means of preventing it.

He nearly got his wish. Not until the closing months of the war were the Nisei permitted to return to the Coast and pick up the pieces of their lives. By then, Warren and many others had begun to regret the massive deprivation of liberty that had been perpetrated without any justifying evidence of disloyalty. He called emergency meetings of state officials to ensure that the returning Japanese-Americans would be reintegrated into their communities peaceably and with full protection of the law. But Earl Warren would not publicly express his regret over the relocation process until more than thirty years afterward, in his posthumously published autobiography scheduled for release in late 1976.

Aside from that large blemish, Warren's record as governor was nearly a model of enlightenment. He shook the party hacks out of the trees and installed efficient administrators throughout the state government on a non-partisan basis. He raised unemployment benefits and shortened the waiting time to qualify for them. He increased old-age pensions and heartily endorsed them as a citizen's right, not a dole. He put through a higher minimum-pay scale for teachers. He overhauled the state penal system, created a state mental-hygiene department, and, as soon as war shortages permitted, launched a massive public-works program of schools, highways, hospitals, and parks, all urgently needed by a state that was adding residents at the rate of nearly 10,000 a week during many of his years in the governor's mansion. And yet he was able to balance the state budget, keep taxes stable, and maintain the building projects on a pay-as-you-go basis from 1943 until 1949, when he asked the legislature for the first billion-dollar state budget in American history. Parts of his liberal legislative program were denied him: he tried repeatedly to put through the nation's first compulsory-medical-care program, beginning as early as 1945, and had no better luck plumping for a state FEPC. He called for a buildup of publicly owned hydroelectric power resources. He opposed a relaxation of labor laws that would have allowed young women to work the midnight shift at canning plants during the war—a back-door union-busting gambit, in Warren's eyes. He spoke out forcefully against Joseph R. McCarthy in 1950 soon after the Wisconsin Senator charged the State Department with harboring unnamed Communists by the dozens (or perhaps hundreds), and continued to oppose McCarthy while others in his party approved or stood mute. And he voted against the imposition of a loyalty oath on the faculty members of the University of California as an unnecessary and discriminatory measure.

All of which made Earl Warren a rampaging commissar in the view of many conservatives; yet there was plenty in the Warren record for them to admire. He had denounced the New Deal for its "impractical experimentation and the unbridled waste of public funds" in the mid-Thirties. He had taken a hard line on Communist-dominated labor-union activities. He had opposed the appointment of a prominent liberal law professor from Berkeley to the state supreme court. He spoke out with conviction in favor of states' rights, believing that efficient local government could achieve a great deal more than a bloated federal bureaucracy. He was a prudent manager of public funds, as evidenced by his debt-free works projects and balanced budgets. He was a firm believer in law-and-order and placed a high priority indeed on national security, even if it cost some Americans (such as the Nisei) their civil liberties. His apparent economic and political liberality was not without its mitigating features. His avowal of public power expansion, for example, sprang in large measure from Warren's recognizing the peculiar nature of arid southern California's water problems, which had dictated much of the state's pattern of economic development. "Most of our power potential," he explained, "is inseparably connected with water conservation for all purposes: irrigation, flood control, navigation, salinity control, municipal purposes, recreation and conservation of wildlife. It must be developed in projects that serve all of these purposes." Few private power companies had the money, jurisdictional authority, or desire to pursue such undertakings. Warren's actions on the loyalty-oath program were similarly open to ambiguous interpretation: he had fought the compulsory oaths when imposed only on college professors, but he supported the oaths when administered to all state employees. Earl Warren was resistant to being politically typecast. He tended to approach every legislative proposal or policy question with a fresh view and embraced or spurned it on its own merits. It was that openness and non-partisanship that made him so attractive to so many California voters of every political coloration.

To Dwight Eisenhower, who had first met Warren at the 1952 Republican national convention, the husky, handsome California governor "seemed to reflect high ideals and a great deal of common sense." As President now, preparing to name the fourteenth Chief Justice of the United States, Eisenhower found much to admire in Warren's long public record. He had never served on the bench, it was true, but he had worked with great distinction for thirty-two years, enforcing, fashioning, administering, and interpreting the law. He knew the pulsebeat of the people and the practical problems of its leaders. And on a number of important policy questions, his ideas meshed with Eisenhower's: support of state jurisdiction over offshore oil lands, for example, and full approval of the Court's vote to strike down Truman's seizure of the steel mills—in both of which Fred Vinson had favored the federal government. It was a fact, too, that the Warren-led California delegation had voted on principle—and against the governor's presidential ambitions—to seat pro-Eisenhower delegates at the 1952 Republican convention, a step that probably sealed the Eisenhower victory, though Ike always insisted he owed Warren nothing. Politically savvy Herbert

Brownell must have known better. And it was Attorney General Brownell who flew to California on September 27, 1953, to discuss with Earl Warren his readiness to put aside his political career and move almost at once to Washington, where the Court was to convene the following week for the fateful 1953 Term.

He was sixty-two years old when nominated. And he gave the Court lineup transcontinental span; no other Justice then came from west of the Mississippi save Tom Clark of Texas. Congress was in recess until the turn of the year, and so his appointment would have to be an interim one. "The President called me on a Wednesday [September 30] and asked me to be there for the opening of the new term the following Monday [October 5], so I had four days to finish up in Sacramento," Warren recounted. "He said he understood that there were some very important cases pending—he didn't specify—and he wanted me to accept an interim appointment so that there would be a full Court sitting to hear these cases. It was not the way I would have wanted to leave behind an administration of eleven years, but the President said he felt it was essential that I make the move at once."

Felix Frankfurter was reportedly outraged that Eisenhower would name a mere politician to head the Court. Alpheus T. Mason, McCormick Professor of Jurisprudence at Princeton, spoke for many Court-watchers in the academic community in denouncing the Warren selection by noting that "a first-rate appointment to the vacancy created by the death of Chief Justice Vinson might have helped the nation forget President Truman's string of conspicuously bad additions to the highest court." John O'Donnell, conservative columnist of the nation's best-selling newspaper, the New York *Daily News*, wrote: "The selection is not a good one for the nation for the simple reason that a better Chief Justice could be found among a score of top-flight jurists. After all, the charming, competent Governor—a truly honest and upright man—never sat on a bench in his life, not even for five minutes in a police court."

But to most Americans who followed such matters, the selection seemed an appropriate one. Earl Warren had always carried himself with exemplary dignity. His private behavior was beyond reproach, and there had never been a whisper of scandal about his conduct of public office. A Bible-reading Baptist, he spoke unblinkingly of God and country and the sanctity of the home. He was a doer. He was an optimist. He was in the American grain. And he looked and sounded the way a Chief Justice should.

Black America, contemplating what effect the coming of the burly, white-haired, Nordic son of California might have on the Supreme Court's ultimate decision in the segregation cases, might have found a hopeful clue on the front page of the nation's largest Negro newspaper the previous year. During the pre-convention skirmishes in the spring of 1952, the weekly *Courier* asked the leading contenders for the Republican presidential nomination for their views on civil rights. In the issue featuring Eisenhower's response, the *Courier* headlined the story in two-inch-high type: "IKE'S BLIND SIDE." The story itself began: "General Dwight D. Eisenhower, 'the grass roots' candidate of the Republican Party, this week was running a sorry last in the presidential campaign where civil rights are concerned." Eisenhower had "voiced complete ignorance on the subject, except to express his firm belief in states' rights," the *Courier* reported. Asked point-blank whether he favored fair-employment legislation by the states, Eisenhower fudged and went spiraling off in a gush of disconnected phrases that made nothing perfectly clear except that he believed in laws. What did he think about the tremendous added costs to education of the dual systems maintained by the segregating states? "You brought up a feature of this thing that I have not even thought about," said Eisenhower. "I did not know that there was an additional cost involved." What about a Negro in his Cabinet—Ralph Bunche, for example? He had not thought about that, and whether there might be a place to use Ralph Bunche he was not sure, but he did indeed admire Dr. Bunche "and when I was president of Columbia, we called him up and gave him an honorary degree. I could not say anything more than that, because we think a great deal of our honorary degrees at Columbia."

The *Courier* interview with Earl Warren was headlined: " 'One Law for All Men'—Warren; Californian First Presidential Candidate to Advocate Full Civil Rights Program." The article quoted Warren as declaring: "I am for a sweeping civil rights program, beginning with a fair employment practices act. . . . I insist upon one law for all men." He said that the nation must not fear the word "welfare" and that "We must not shrink from the known needs of social progress." And he adopted as his own the Republican civil-rights plank of 1948, calling for anti-lynching and anti-poll-tax legislation.

Dwight Eisenhower's principal contribution to the civil rights of Americans would prove to be his selection of Earl Warren as Chief Justice—a decision Eisenhower would later say had been a mistake. The President was on hand, at any rate, on Monday, October 5, when just after noon the clerk of the Supreme Court read aloud the commission of the President that began, "Know ye: That reposing special trust and confidence in the wisdom, uprightness and learning of Earl Warren of California, I do appoint him Chief Justice of the United States. . . ." Warren stood up at the clerk's desk to the side of the bench and read aloud his oath of office. At the end, Clerk Harold Willey said to him, "So help you God." Warren said, "So help me God." Then he stepped quickly behind the velour curtains and re-emerged a moment later through the opening in the center to take the presiding seat. His entire worthy career to that moment would be dwarfed by what followed.

In California, he had functioned like a monarch. He ran a government staffed by tens of thousands. There was a never-ending round of appointments and meetings and speeches. His public relations busied a battery of flacks. There was a mansion—and a limousine and highway patrolmen and an airplane on call at the snap of his fingers.

In Washington, he had to function suddenly in near-isolation. His immediate staff consisted of one secretary, two aged messengers, and three law clerks. The entire payroll of the Supreme Court carried fewer than 200 names, most of them clerks, guards, and janitors. There were no appointments except the business of the Court. And there were no speeches. Public relations consisted of making sure one's robe bore no ketchup stain. There was no mansion, no limousine—just power.*

The power of the Chief Justice, however, did not come automatically with the gavel. Fred Vinson had found that out and died frustrated by the realization. But Earl Warren was not a Fred Vinson, as Felix Frankfurter and the rest of America would discover in the ensuing sixteen years. Warren respected his brethren on the bench, but he did not stand in awe of them. Behind the photographs of him as a chortling charmer—a sort of year-round Santa Claus in pinstripes or dark serge—was a deadly serious man who had always been a prodigious worker. He put all pomp and pageantry aside upon coming to the Supreme Court and, unlike Vinson, avoided getting caught up in the social whirl that could easily have distracted him from the considerable task he faced. From his earliest days as an assistant district attorney, he had displayed a high aptitude for accumulating, absorbing, and analyzing data. It was a skill he never lost, though in the press of work as chief executive of the most dynamic state in the nation, he had inevitably come to call upon the judgment of many others. In the monastic privacy of the Court now, he freshly honed his own intellect.

"It is a process of self-education," he said, after leaving the bench, of his on-the-job training as America's ranking jurist. By chance, he had begun reading Albert J. Beveridge's four-volume biography of Chief Justice John Marshall over the Labor Day weekend preceding Vinson's death. "But I didn't have time for that once I was sitting," Warren noted. "You pick up the pieces as you go—through the briefs themselves, the Supreme Court Reports, consultation with my colleagues—but that's all, there was no outside consultation. We didn't talk with anyone on the outside about the cases." His lack of judicial experience would surely have slowed a less confident man. Warren, if hardly seeking to make a virtue of his limitations as legal scholar and judicial philosopher, understood the Supreme Court to serve a function beyond the letters of the law, and it was that higher purpose—as ultimate framer of just solutions to profound disputes—that most appealed to him. "There's no such thing as an expert here," he said, after retirement, in an interview granted in the chambers he maintained at the Court until his death. "We hear such a wide diversity of cases, no one can be an expert in all the fields."

Justices, then, were generalists in the law, not specialists in torturing it to avoid discomforting decisions. The law was there to be used, not limply saluted, and it fell to the Court to declare how broadly it could be applied. Warren's frame of reference had little to do with the long-standing dispute between Black and Frankfurter over judicial restraint. His frame of reference was the back rooms of police stations, the pressing needs of pensioners, the thirst of arid valleys, the health of the bodies and minds of the people. All his

* In the spring of 1954, however, on the theory that the Chief Justice of the United States as head of one of the national government's co-equal branches should not have to ride a bus, catch a taxi, or hitch a ride to work, Congress authorized a limousine and chauffeur for Mr. Warren.

life, he had been a man of action, and he did not swerve from that upon donning the robes of Chief Justice. It was not, for him, an honorary position that promoted passive tendencies. It was a new chance to serve—his nation now, not just his native state—and he meant to serve vigorously. "Earl Warren was the closest thing the United States had had to a Platonic Guardian, dispensing law from a throne without any sensed limits of power except what was seen as the good of society," Anthony Lewis would write. "Fortunately he was a decent, humane, honorable, democratic Guardian."

He began by disarming everyone at the Court with his friendliness and unpretentiousness. Within a few weeks, he knew everybody's name, from the watchmen on up. He always had a moment for a short chat and a hearty laugh. He sought the counsel of Hugo Black and asked him to preside over the first conference of the Court in the new term. He was deferential to Felix Frankfurter, who in turn sought to influence the new Chief. He could admire Robert Jackson's intellectual charm and ribald *bons mots*. He shared William Douglas's West Coast upbringing and social concerns. And by his warmth and dignity he established swift rapport with the Court's lesser lights: he commanded their respect as he tendered them his own. Within a few weeks, it was clear to all of them that the Chief was tending to business with the sort of dedication Frankfurter and Burton admired. The sour mood of the past began to lift. A fresh breeze was blowing through the marble corridors of the Court, and everyone knew that it came from California.

At one o'clock in the morning of Monday, December 7, 1953, a seventy-six-year-old black man named Arthur J. Smith took his place proudly outside the front door of the Supreme Court. He was the first on line.

A retired employee of the State Department, Mr. Smith showed up for his night-long vigil in overcoat and fedora. He brought a sandwich to fortify him against the thirty-degree weather. By 2 a.m. he had been joined by a third-year law student from Howard. After daybreak, the line included the Reverend J. A. DeLaine of Lake City, South Carolina, organizer of the *Briggs* case. "There were times when I thought I would go out of my mind because of this case," the Reverend told an early-bird reporter for the *Afro*. But he added, "If I had to do it again, I would. I feel that it was worth it. I have a feeling that the Supreme Court is going to end segregation."

In the reserved seats later that morning, Thurgood Marshall's mother, Norma, was on hand, and his wife, "Buster," in the last year of her life, and his early mentor, Carl Murphy, president of the *Afro*. The school-segregation cases were called at 1:05 p.m. The Honorable Earl Warren presided. Argument lasted for three days.

The order of the cases had been shuffled for the reargument. Since the circumstances and state laws involved were so similar, the South Carolina and Virginia cases were joined and they led off the docket.

Spottswood Robinson went first for the NAACP. The scholarly Richmond attorney did far better than he had the year earlier. Briskly and forcefully, he spelled out the basic historical argument of the Negro litigants as it had been thrashed out by several hundred scholars putting their heads together for thousands of hours during the previous six months. The Fourteenth Amendment, Robinson declared, had been aimed at achieving "complete legal equality" for Negroes and the prohibition of all state-imposed caste laws; school-segregation statutes were plainly this sort of proscribed law and therefore had to be struck down.

Throughout his argument, Robinson kept referring to the "broad purpose" of the framers of the amendment. He did not say that the framers had had segregated schools on their minds, but that in the only specific reference to the subject during the congressional debates, Representative Rogers of New Jersey had declared that the amendment would ban such separate schools and nobody had risen to contest that claim. The key to the debates, said Robinson, reflecting the Alfred Kelly argument that the NAACP inner council had settled upon, was John Bingham, the Ohio Representative who precipitated the quashing of the "no discrimination" language in the Civil Rights Act of 1866 only because he felt that there was no constitutional authority for so sweeping a measure—a condition about to be remedied by the Fourteenth Amendment that Bingham had introduced a few days earlier. It was that brightly varnished rendering of Bingham's position that Felix Frankfurter's clerk Alexander Bickel had objected to as oversimplified and perhaps unjustified in the memorandum which he had prepared for the Justice and which Frankfurter had circulated among his brethren. Frankfurter, though, did not jump on Robinson's version of the Bingham position; rather, he wanted to know, in opening up the question from the bench, how the Court was to weigh the individual utterances of Congressmen. Having read several thousand pages of briefs that went over the same historical evidence and come out with sharply varying interpretations, Frankfurter was undoubtedly speaking in candor for all the Justices.

> JUSTICE FRANKFURTER: I grant you we solicited and elicited that. But I just wondered, now that we have got it, what are we going to get out of it? The fact that a man . . . says, "This is a terrible measure and if you pass it we will do this and that," does that tell me that this measure does do this and that?
>
> ROBINSON: To this extent, sir. So far as the statement standing alone is concerned, I would attribute no value to it. But when a man makes that statement and he is joined in it by others [or] he is not disputed by anyone, we have a condition of general understanding that is demonstrated by the overall statements pro and con in that particular connection. I think we get assistance.
>
> JUSTICE FRANKFURTER: You think if an opponent gives an extreme interpretation of a proposed statute or constitutional amendment in order to frighten people on the other side, and the proponents do not get up and say, "Yes, that is the thing we want to accomplish," that means they believe it, do you?

But Robinson stuck firmly by his guns. He had mastered his material, and he called up the relevant parts when the quizzing from the bench required it. And he did not let the questioning throw him off the track he had set out to take. His side had not been able, he asserted, "to find anything in history that discloses, as our opponents contend, that the rights which are embraced in, and the prohibitions imposed by, the Fourteenth Amendment are no larger than those which are embraced in or imposed by the Civil

Rights Act of 1866." The Court in *Strauder* had noted in 1879: "The Fourteenth Amendment makes no effort to enumerate the rights it designs to protect. It speaks in general terms, and those are as comprehensive as possible." Justice Reed wanted to know whether congressional legislation wiping out segregated schools would have helped Robinson's case. "Oh, yes," the attorney said, "I think if we had a congressional act, sir, that we probably would not have to be here now. However, I do not think that legislation by Congress in any wise detracts from the power of the judiciary to enforce the prohibitions of the Fourteenth Amendment." Only toward the end, in his comment that the contemporaneous actions of the states showed they understood that the amendment invalidated school-segregation laws, did Robinson's words ring hollow. Yet he escaped with that claim unchallenged from the bench.

Thurgood Marshall, who followed Robinson to the lectern, had no such luck. Indeed, he was assaulted so rapidly and steadily that he seemed to come unhinged. It was one of his least creditable performances before the Court.

Marshall had come prepared to review the Court's prior rulings on racial classification laws, on cases interpreting the reach of the Fourteenth Amendment, and on the so-called *Plessy* line of decisions—terrain that had been rehearsed at length in the first oral argument the year before. The Court was not in the mood to hear it all hashed over anew. After Marshall had made his intentions known but before he launched into the cases, Justice Jackson intruded. "I do not believe the Court was troubled about its own cases," he said. "It has done a good deal of reading of those cases." What Jackson wanted to know was Marshall's view of the propriety of the Court's exercising its judicial power to overturn the segregation laws under challenge. It was the very question Marshall had burlesqued back at his New York office by insisting white folks had the power to do anything they wanted. That did not seem the ideal answer at this moment of confrontation with the well-honed mind of Robert Jackson. The question hung in the air: In the absence of congressional action on the subject, was it right for the Court to overrule segregation after the passage of so many years?

Instead of noting, as the NAACP's brief did, that "This Court has repeatedly declared invalid state statutes which conflicted with section 1 of the Fourteenth Amendment, even though Congress had not acted," Marshall groped. He sailed off into some incoherent remarks about *Strauder* and the *Slaughterhouse* cases, which he said interpreted the amendment broadly—a thought that was disconnected from Jackson's question. Then he made matters worse by invoking an 1871 federal statute that said anyone acting under color of state law or custom to deprive a citizen of his rights and immunities was liable in a lawsuit; the law declared itself to be aimed specifically at enforcing the Fourteenth Amendment. But this was really very little help to the NAACP position and merely begged the question. For the NAACP's basic argument was that the amendment was a flat and total prohibition on discriminatory action by the states—a self-executing edict that was of course to be invoked by the federal courts whenever necessary. If the courts' authority to move against infringements of the Fourteenth Amendment was derived from congressional statutes such as the one Marshall had cited, then they would also be obliged to wait for passage of a federal law declaring that school segregation was a caste practice of the type outlawed by the amendment. Frankfurter riddled Marshall: "I do not know what that act [of 1871] has to do with this, our problem. If your claim prevails, it must prevail by virtue of what flows out of the Fourteenth Amendment, as such."

Slowly, painfully, Marshall dug his way out of the hole. The only way his opponents could win, he said, was to prove that the amendment had *not* been intended to cover schools. And his opponents had forfeited such a possibility by having erroneously claimed that the *McLaurin* decision was merely another in the separate-but-equal line of cases when in fact it was no such thing but rather a recognition of the broad reach of the amendment to effect higher education. And if the Court had found unconstitutionality in *McLaurin*, there was no reason whatever why it could not extend its ruling to cover public schools as well.

Frankfurter would not go along with such thinking, however. He read *McLaurin* differently. The basis of that decision, he said, was the determination that McLaurin, isolated from his classmates as he was, had been denied equal treatment. "Your position in these cases is that that is not arguable, that you cannot differentiate, you cannot enter the domain of whether a black child or a white child gets the same educational advantages," Frankfurter asserted—that is, the Court did not have to weigh the particular merits of McLaurin's or anyone else's claims of mistreatment; the very act of separation was a denial of equal protection. When Marshall acknowledged as much, Frankfurter shot back, "Well, therefore, you reject the basis of the *McLaurin* case." Marshall was torn in his response. For the Court in *McLaurin* had not declared that the act of separation in and of itself created inequality; it had found McLaurin to have been cruelly and unreasonably separated—and therefore denied an equal educational opportunity. Marshall failed to make the obvious point that if the Court had found it intolerable for a Negro to be cruelly separated within a white school, it could and should now find it no less intolerable for him to be separated by being ordered to attend school with other blacks only.

Frankfurter had jumped all over Robert Carter at the oral argument the previous year when the NAACP attorney claimed that *Plessy*, a railroad case, really had had nothing to do with school segregation and that *Gong Lum* could readily be distinguished from *Brown* because the 1927 case had not specifically challenged the state of Mississippi's right to segregate its schoolchildren. Marshall this time said straight out that both *Plessy* and *Gong Lum* had been wrongly decided. Each flew in the teeth of the Court's previous landmark holdings in *Strauder* and *Slaughterhouse*, both of which had declared unequivocally that the purpose of the amendment had been to grant equality to Negroes. But such an argument was of little help to the Court, as Marshall's masterful adversary pointed out almost as soon as he took over the lectern. The basic question facing the Court, said John W.

Davis, was not whether the amendment was designed to grant equal protection to the Negro—everyone acknowledged that—but whether segregation, under terms of equal facilities, was a denial of that pledge.

At the age of eighty, Davis was making the last of his 140 appearances before the Court. He came in his cutaway, a throwback to a more formal era, and he was reduced by age to consulting his notes more often than he ever had, but there was nothing antique about the working of his mind or tongue. No one else in the cases came near matching him for bite, eloquence, or wit. Early in his remarks, he summed up the Court's dilemma in trying to evaluate the answers it had received to the five questions it had put to the parties:

> Now, your honors then are presented with this: we say there is no warrant for the assertion that the Fourteenth Amendment dealt with the school question. The appellants say that from the debates in Congress it is perfectly evident that the Congress wanted to deal with the school question, and the Attorney General, as a friend of the court, says he does not know which is correct. So your honors are afforded a reasonable field for selection.

That brought laughter from the Court. Little of it lingered, though, as he paraded the evidence that, in his hands, seemed to destroy the NAACP's interpretation of the congressional history. From its first act in this area, the Freedmen's Bureau Bill, Congress had countenanced racially separate schools, and the same Thirty-ninth Congress that had passed the Fourteenth Amendment had legislated to donate lots and distribute funds to the schools for Negroes which had previously been established in the District of Columbia. It had been suggested by "the learned Attorney General," said Davis, alluding to the government's brief, that those acts of Congress affecting the District of Columbia schools

> were mere routine performances, that they came very late in the congressional session, that they were not even honored by having any debate.
>
> Apparently, to have a law which is really to be recognized as a congressional deliverance, it must come early in the session, it must be debated, and the mere fact that it is passed by unanimous consent and without objection more or less disparages its importance as an historical incident. I have never, that I can recall, heard a similar yardstick applied to congressional action.

He was no less devastating in dismissing the NAACP's claim that the states understood that the amendment had outlawed school segregation. Nor could Congress have gained the power to outlaw the practice under Section 5 of the amendment, since all that Congress had been empowered to enforce were the rights embraced by the first section of the amendment—and the right to attend unsegregated schools was not among them. The Court, moreover, had ruled not once but seven times over the years in favor of the separate-but-equal doctrine, and "somewhere, some time, to every principle there comes a moment of repose when it has been so often announced, so confidently relied upon, so long continued, that it passes the limits of judicial discretion and disturbance." But even if legal precedent were not deemed governing, Davis went on, could it genuinely be contended that the state of

South Carolina had acted unreasonably in classifying the schoolchildren of Clarendon County along racial lines? He then graphically warned the Court of the problem it would confront at once if it ordered the schools desegregated in a heavily Negro district such as the one in Clarendon, where there were 2,800 black pupils and 300 white ones:

> Who is going to disturb that situation? If they were to be reassorted or commingled, who knows how that would best be done?
>
> If it is done on the mathematical basis, with 30 children as a maximum . . . you would have 27 Negro children and three whites in one schoolroom. Would that make the children any happier? Would they learn any more quickly? Would their lives be more serene?
>
> Children of that age are not the most considerate animals in the world, as we all know. Would the terrible psychological disaster being wrought, according to some of these witnesses, to the colored child be removed if he had three white children sitting somewhere in the same schoolroom?
>
> Would white children be prevented from getting a distorted idea of racial relations if they sat with 27 Negro children? I have posed that question because it is the very one that cannot be denied.
>
> You say that is racism. Well, it is not racism. Recognize that for sixty centuries and more, humanity has been discussing questions of race and race tension, not racism. . . . [T]wenty-nine states have miscegenation statutes now in force which they believe are of beneficial protection to both races. Disraeli said, "No man," said he, "will treat with indifference the principle of race. It is the key of history."

As he neared the end of his argument, the drain on him became apparent to Chief Justice Warren, who looked down on the great old advocate from a distance of just a few feet. "Mr. Davis was quite emotional," Warren recalled later. "In fact, he seemed to me to break down a few times during the hearing." With deep conviction, Davis wound up pleading for the integrity of states' rights and the good intentions of his client. "Your honors do not sit, and cannot sit, as a glorified board of education for the state of South Carolina or any other state," he declared. South Carolina had not come before the Court "as Thad Stevens would have wished—in sack cloth and ashes. . . . It is confident of its good faith and intention to produce equality for all of its children of whatever race or color," as it had done in equalizing the schools of Clarendon County. So much had been gained in race relations, he said, adding,

> I am reminded—and I hope it won't be treated as a reflection on anybody—of Aesop's fable of the dog and the meat: The dog, with a fine piece of meat in his mouth, crossed a bridge and saw [his] shadow in the stream and plunged in for it and lost both substance and shadow.
>
> Here is equal education, not promised, not prophesied, but present. Shall it be thrown away on some fancied question of racial prestige?

Thurgood Marshall remembered seeing tears on the cheeks of John W. Davis as he turned away from the Court for the final time in his life. Attorney General Lindsay Almond of Virginia, sitting at the counsel table with him, recalls that Davis was emotionally overwrought at the end. He had stated the

South's case as effectively as it could be done. But his day was past. "He thought the case could be viewed as a strictly legal matter," reflects Robert Figg, who had argued *Briggs* in Charleston. "I don't think he ever realized the swirl of social and political events affecting it."

For the commonwealth of Virginia, Justin Moore was less predatory than had been his fashion throughout the litigation and therefore the more effective.

The Civil Rights Act of 1866 had had specific and limited goals, he said, of which the prohibition of school segregation was clearly not one. And the Fourteenth Amendment, he claimed, had no purpose beyond writing the Civil Rights Act into the Constitution. The great states of the North and West had segregated their schools both before and after the amendment, and all the history was plainly on the side of the South. As to the relevance of *McLaurin*, the Court had been quite right in its decision because the Oklahoma Board of Regents had misapplied the *Plessy* doctrine in treating the black student as a leper once he had been admitted to the state university. But because Oklahoma had been unreasonable in imposing its restrictions, it did not follow that Virginia's segregation law was an inhumane statute, and cruelly applied. Moore had been battered the year before by Robinson on that very point, and though the white lawyer had no more or new evidence to introduce in support of his contention, he nevertheless argued with force that Jim Crow schools served both races well in his state, as Virginia's expert witnesses had claimed at the trial. To challenge that position, he implied, was to be ignorant of the facts of life:

> We recognize that there are a great many people of the highest character and position who disapprove of segregation as a matter of principle or as ethics. We think that most of them really do not know the conditions, particularly in the South, that brought about that situation.

Attorney General Almond took the prize for fulsome rhetoric in his follow-up remarks to Moore's more than adequate defense of Virginia. The courtly official told the Justices that in seeking to end segregation, his opponents

> are asking you to disturb the unfolding evolutionary process of education where from the dark days of the depraved institution of slavery, with the help and the sympathy and the love and respect of the white people of the South, the colored man has risen under that educational process to a place of eminence and respect throughout this nation. It has served him well. . . .

That help, sympathy, love, and respect stopped short, of course, of admitting him to their schools, but no member of the Court thought it seemly to suggest as much.

Thurgood Marshall had saved some of his time for rebuttal and had had overnight to recover from his shell-shocked performance on the first day of the reargument. On the counterattack, he did a great deal better.

The heart of the South's defense, as expounded by Davis and Moore, was that prejudice had nothing to do with the practice of segregation: it was simply something that served both races well. Marshall swatted hard at that. The South's only justification "for this being a reasonable classification," he said, "is (1) that they got together and decided it is best for the races to be separated and (2) that it has existed for over a century." Neither argument held any water, he said, and stressed that segregation was not a policy that had been mutually agreed upon by both races but was simply imposed upon the Negro. As to John Davis's contention that the Negroes' main concern in bringing these cases was prestige, Marshall replied: "Exactly correct. Ever since the Emancipation Proclamation, the Negro has been trying to get what was recognized in *Strauder v. West Virginia*, which is the same status as anybody else regardless of race." He confessed that he had committed a gaffe the previous day in encouraging the impression that the Court in *McLaurin* had strengthened the separate-but-equal doctrine. McLaurin's constitutional grievance was a denial of equality, said Marshall, but the only inequality he had suffered was segregation itself; thus, "what we really ask this Court is to make . . . explicit what [we] think was . . . implicit in the *McLaurin* case." Then Marshall seemed to stand back from the fray for a moment, check the battlefield, and launch his last salvo; his words were as informal and loosely grammatical as John Davis's were polished and precise, but they were hardly less effective for it:

> . . . I got the feeling on hearing the discussion yesterday that when you put a white child in a school with a whole lot of colored children, the child would fall apart or something. Everybody knows that is not true.
>
> Those same kids in Virginia and South Carolina—and I have seen them do it—they play in the streets together, they play on their farms together, they go down the road together, they separate to go to school, they come out of school and play ball together. They have to be separated in school.
>
> There is some magic to it. You can have them voting together, you can have them not restricted because of law in the houses they live in. You can have them going to the same state university and the same college, but if they go to elementary and high school, the world will fall apart. . . .

The school-segregation laws were nothing but Black Codes, Marshall declared, and the only way for the Court to uphold them now was "to find that for some reason Negroes are inferior to all other human beings." What the South was guilty of was "an inherent determination that the people who were formerly in slavery, regardless of anything else, shall be kept as near that stage as is possible, and now is the time, we submit, that this Court should make it clear that that is not what our Constitution stands for."

The government of the United States spoke next as a friend of the Court. It took its place, as the Justice Department brief had signaled it would, on the side of the Negro.

The Justices had concurrent jurisdiction with Congress for enforcing the dictates of the Fourteenth Amendment, stated Assistant Attorney General J. Lee Rankin, who was plainly nervous in his debut before the Court. That Congress had chosen not to act to outlaw school-segregation laws had in no way reduced the Court's responsibility in the matter. No evaluation of the historical data presented by the litigants had any weight, furthermore, if divorced from an understanding of the state of public education in the Reconstruction era. The overriding concern of the day, as Rankin paraphrased it, was: "What are we going to do to educate the Negro? He is a free man, he is a part of our citizenry like any white man. He has no background for education. Many of them are of mature years, as well as the children." The provision of the essentials of schooling came ahead of any such niceties as whether segregated schools might have been proscribed by an expansive reading of the amendment. Even by the time public education developed into a universal, compulsory practice throughout the nation, it was still not a constitutionally guaranteed civil right, Rankin added, but once a state did decide to offer public education—as all had—then "it must do it equally . . . on the same basis . . . to all citizens."

All of that sounded resolute enough, but Justice Douglas noted that the government brief fell short of an outright declaration to the Court that Jim Crow schools ought to be found illegal. Rankin acknowledged the point, said that was so because the government was simply answering the questions the Court had asked, and that, for the record, "it is the position of the Department of Justice that segregation in public schools cannot be maintained under the Fourteenth Amendment, and we adhere to the views expressed in the original brief of the Department in that regard."

Justice Jackson had a far more troubling question to put to the government: If the Court were to oblige it and outlaw segregated education, precisely how should it be done? Rankin stuck to the plan offered in the U.S. brief: the cases ought to be sent back down to the District Courts, which would oversee the actual desegregation process "according to criteria presented and set out by this Court." School districts would have no more than a year to formulate and present to the lower courts a desegregation plan that would be carried out "with deliberate speed." That, though, did not really help Jackson, who said, in underscoring the exceedingly painful task that confronted the Court:

> . . . What criteria are we going to lay down? I am all for having the District Courts frame decrees and do all the rest of the work that we can put on them, but what are we going to tell them . . . ?
>
> What are we going to do to avoid the situation where in some districts everybody is perhaps held in contempt of court almost immediately because that judge has that disposition, and in some other districts it is twelve years before they get to a hearing? What criteria do you propose?

This was precisely the problem troubling Jackson and Frankfurter perhaps more than the constitutional basis for outlawing the practice. Nothing could be worse for the Court than to issue a ringing declaration of human and civil rights—and then throw up its hands and dump the entire problem into the laps of the rest of the nation. Thurgood Marshall, in his rebuttal comments, had stressed that black America could brook no delay beyond a single year at most in the desegregation process. But the government had not urged that the black child's right should be granted immediately or given him under a uniform nationwide timetable. Such considerations as a community's possible reluctance to vote funds for the maintenance of its forcibly desegregated public schools could not just be ignored. Rankin could do no better than to guess that the problem would have to be worked out on a case-by-case basis in the courts below, which would be charged with determining "whether or not the equities of the particular situation are such that the defendant [school district] has established . . . that it is unreasonable under those conditions to require them to act more rapidly than they propose. . . ."

Jackson remained unconvinced. With noteworthy prescience, he remarked: "I foresee a generation of litigation if we send it back with no standards, and each case has to come here to determine it standard by standard."

Reargument in the remaining three school cases was abbreviated and anti-climactic.

In the Kansas case, Justice Frankfurter was at his most pestiferous in wondering at length whether the Topeka school board's launching of a desegregation program had not rendered the entire matter moot. Robert Carter noted that only two of the four colored schools in the city had thus far been desegregated. Assistant Attorney General Paul Wilson said, "The state of Kansas is here to defend its statute." And defend it he did, insisting quite as firmly as his counterparts in the Southern states that the historical evidence was all on the side of the segregating camp. Carter told the Justices that Wilson had raised no points they had not heard before and so he would not take their time other than to note that he still had clients with a constitutional grievance.

Since the Fourteenth Amendment applied only to the states and not to the District of Columbia, the second round of briefs and reargument in *Bolling v. Sharpe* was mainly a rerun of the first year's encounter. The school board's attorney, Milton Korman, who had not precisely enshrined himself as a second Blackstone by invoking *Dred Scott* to bolster his case at the first argument the previous year, got into similar hot water this time out. Or, more precisely, black attorneys James Nabrit and George Hayes had put him there by suggesting to the Court that Korman might have no legal standing since eight of the nine members of the District of Columbia school board had been replaced since the case was first filed and it was by no means clear that the board still favored the policy of segregated schools. Korman muttered and sputtered about that as the second day of the reargument came to a close; the next noon, when Court resumed, he produced documents showing that the board did indeed stand solidly behind him as its legal representative. In the process, he used up a substantial portion of his time, to the delight of Nabrit and Hayes. As he had in the first argument, Nabrit provided the Negro side with its most memorable moment of oratory; he concluded his remarks:

> . . . America is a great country in which we can come before the Court and express to the Court the great concern which we have, where our great

government is dealing with us, and we are not in the position that the animals were in George Orwell's satirical novel *Animal Farm*, where after the revolution, the dictatorship was set up and the sign set up there that all animals were equal, was changed to read, "but some are more equal than others."

Our Constitution has no provision across it that all men are equal but that white men are more equal than others.

Under this statute and under this country, under this Constitution, and under the protections of this Court, we believe that we, too, are equal.

Not quite two decades later, James Nabrit would retire as president of Howard University, battered by student charges that he had not been a militant enough black leader.

Albert Young, attorney general of Delaware, led off the last case on the docket by allying himself with the South Carolina, Virginia, and Kansas readings of the historical evidence. For the Court to rule against segregation, he said, would require it to go plainly counter to the intentions of the framers of the Fourteenth Amendment. His own state's policy of separate schools was the wisest and most workable one for the citizens of Delaware. But, as he had at the first argument, Young made a telltale remark that revealed the vulnerability of his otherwise forceful presentation:

This Court is not in a position to judge to what extent the prejudices and tensions which gave rise to the segregation laws . . . have abated in any particular state or district, or to judge the wisdom of abolishing segregation in public schools of that state.

But were "prejudices and tensions" ever sufficient to justify racial classification laws and the curtailment of civil rights by any state or school district? Was it not the very purpose of the state to defend its citizens against prejudice and tensions in maintaining domestic tranquility?

When Jack Greenberg rose to close out the three-day reargument, Frankfurter and Jackson pounced on him, as Albert Young had urged, for having failed to cross-file an appeal of the state court's decision to desegregate the Claymont and Hockessin schools. The Delaware courts had held that the original black plaintiffs were attending unequal schools and ordered that they be admitted to the white schools on that ground, not because segregation itself was illegal. As Greenberg began to argue that his clients were still "under a cloud" because the state segregation law remained intact, Frankfurter snapped, ". . . I do not understand that you can object to a decision below on a ground that you have not appealed from." The young NAACP lawyer replied that he had believed that "we could urge other grounds for the affirmance of the judgment below"—a position he and Louis Redding had taken in their brief at the first oral argument when the question was not raised by the Court. Frankfurter answered dryly: "I am glad to get your observations, but I might suggest I do not think the nature of the issues has been changed." Jackson added that probably the most the Court could do was affirm the decree of the Deleware courts "but you probably will have the benefit of anything said in any other case that is helpful."

The Court then called its regular 2 p.m. recess of half an hour, during which the NAACP legal corps hurriedly gathered and decided to pull Greenberg from the lineup. When Court reconvened, Thurgood Marshall was at the lectern. He quickly ticked off several precedents to support the NAACP contention that in not having cross-filed, it had not jeopardized its hope for affirmance of the ruling below on far broader grounds than the Delaware courts had ventured. The four state cases, he noted, had in effect been consolidated and the constitutional issue was identical in all. And he closed out with seven or eight minutes of impromptu rebuttal of Albert Young's remarks—a tribute to Marshall's experience and calm at a moment of possible crisis.

At 2:40 p.m. on December 9, 1953, the Court adjourned the second argument in the school-segregation cases.

"We are inclined to count Justice Frankfurter, Justice Jackson and Justice Reed as indicating a leaning toward our point of view by their questioning," Robert Figg, counsel of record for the state of South Carolina, wrote to a friend the day after the reargument ended. "The rest of the Court preserved a stony, and somewhat quizzical, silence. We think that Justice Clark would vote with us if the vote would decide the issue either way. We are inclined to cede Justice Black and Justice Douglas to the other side. We hope that if our figuring is right, we can get another vote out of the Chief Justice or Justice Burton or Justice Minton. Mr. Davis says that he feels we will win the case, and that he is prepared to concede only Justice Black and Justice Douglas. . . ."

At the reargument, Earl Warren had said very little. The Chief Justice had put no substantive questions to any of the attorneys. Nor is it likely that he had given any indication of his views to the other Justices before they convened at the Saturday-morning conference on December 12. But then, speaking first, he made his views unmistakable.

Nearly twenty years later, he would recall, "I don't remember having any great doubts about which way it should go. It seemed to me a comparatively simple case. Just look at the various decisions that had been eroding *Plessy* for so many years. They kept chipping away at it rather than ever really facing it head-on. If you looked back—to *Gaines*, to *Sweatt*, to some of the interstate-commerce cases—you saw that the doctrine of separate-but-equal had been so eroded that only the *fact* of segregation itself remained unconsidered. On the merits, the natural, the logical, and practically the only way the case could be decided was clear. The question was *how* the decision was to be reached."

At least two sets of notes survive from the Justices' 1953 conference discussion of the segregation cases—extensive ones by Justice Burton and exceedingly scratchy and cryptic ones by Justice Frankfurter. They agree on the Chief Justice's remarks. The cases had been well argued, in his judgment, Earl Warren told the conference, and the government had been very frank in both its written and its oral presentations. He said he had of course been giving much thought to the entire question since coming to the Court, and after studying the briefs and relevant history and hearing the arguments, he could not escape the feeling that the Court had "finally arrived" at the moment when it now had to determine whether segregation was allowable in the public schools. Without saying it in so many words, the new Chief Justice was declaring that the Court's policy of delay, favored by his predecessor, could no longer be permitted.

The more he had pondered the question, Warren said, the more he had come to the conclusion that the doctrine of separate-but-equal rested upon the concept of the inferiority of the colored race. He did not see how *Plessy* and its progeny could be sustained on any other theory—and if the Court were to choose to sustain them, "we must do it on that basis," he was recorded by Burton as saying. He was concerned, to be sure, about the necessity of overruling earlier decisions and lines of reasoning, but he had concluded that segregation of Negro schoolchildren had to be ended. The law, he said in words noted by Frankfurter, "cannot in 'this day and age' set them apart." The law could not say, Burton recorded the Chief as asserting, that Negroes were "not entitled to *exactly same* treatment of all others." To do so would go against the intentions of the three Civil War amendments.

Having established how he wanted the decision to come out, the Chief Justice then stressed that he thought it would be "[u]nfortunate if we had to take precipitous action that would inflame more than necessary." Conditions in the Deep South must be carefully considered by the Court in framing its opinion and decree, though he suspected the problem would be less acute in Kansas and Delaware, whose ethnic composition did not differ much from that of unsegregated California, with its 520,000 Negroes, 120,000 residents of Japanese extraction, and 100,000 of Chinese extraction. It would take all the wisdom of the Court to decide the cases in a manner that produced "a minimum of emotion and strife." How they did it would be vital. It was essential that it be done in a tolerant way.

Unless any of the other four Justices who had indicated a year earlier their readiness to overturn segregation—Black, Douglas, Burton, and Minton—had since changed his mind, Warren's opening remarks meant that a majority of the Court now stood ready to strike down the practice.

But to gain a narrow majority was no cause for exultation. A sharply divided Court, no matter which way it leaned, was an indecisive one, and for Warren to force a split decision out of it would have amounted to hardly more constructive leadership on this transcendent question than Fred Vinson had managed. The new Chief Justice wanted to unite the Court in *Brown*. His carefully considered remarks on this day were thus noteworthy not only for what he said but also for what he did not say—and for how he had stated the substance of his position.

He did not pretend that the historical evidence submitted to the Court by the bushel in the reargument had beamed much new light or provided solid footing to justify overturning *Plessy*. Had he argued otherwise, he would have distanced himself from Jackson and Frankfurter, at least.

He did not accuse the South of having acted illegally or immorally in practicing segregation; all he said was that the practice was no longer justifiable. Had he stated the matter more negatively, he would have distanced himself from Black, Reed, and Clark, at least.

He recognized that a number of Court precedents of long standing would be shattered in the process of overturning *Plessy*, and he regretted that necessity. It was the sort of reassuring medicine most welcomed by Burton and Minton, the least judicially and intellectually adventurous members of the Court.

He recognized that the Court's decision would have wide repercussions, varying in intensity from state to state, and that they would all therefore have to approach the matter in as tolerant and understanding a way as possible. Implicit in this was a call for flexibility in how the Court might frame its decree.

But overarching all these cushioning comments and a tribute to both his compassion as a man and his persuasive skills as a politician was the moral stance Earl Warren took at the outset of his remarks. Segregation, he had told his new colleagues, could be justified only by belief in the inferiority of the Negro; any of them who wished to perpetuate the practice, he implied, ought in candor to be willing to acknowledge as much. These were plain words, and they did not have to be hollered. They cut across all the legal theories that had been so endlessly aired and went straight to the human tissue at the core of the controversy.

Hugo Black was absent from the conference due to a serious illness in his family back in Alabama, but he had left word that his view of the cases had not altered. The second Justice to speak, then, was Stanley Reed, who also made it plain, despite the new Chief's resolute remarks, that his views remained what they had been—against closing up Jim Crow schools.

He could understand the Chief's attitude, Reed said. He could grant that the Constitution was a dynamic document and that what had been constitutionally justifiable at the time of *Plessy* might no longer be so. It was undeniable, furthermore, that the equality of the Negro had not been realized under the separate-but-equal formula. But that did not mean that it could not be achieved under that formula. Equal protection in the form of equal schools was possible and could of course be commanded by the courts, as it had been in the South Carolina and Virginia cases. To him, said Reed, the only plausible legal ground for the Negro's suit against segregation was a denial of due process, but he did not agree that it was in fact a denial of liberty to say that people must separate to go to school. No one had suggested to the Court, he added, by way of countering Warren's moral challenge, that segregation was permissible because the Negro belonged to an inferior race. Of course, there was no such thing as an inferior race, he said without apparently suggesting what other ground the Court might then rely upon to justify the continued practice of forced separation.

Felix Frankfurter's remarks, as recorded somewhat incoherently by Burton, were not entirely straightforward, though surviving documents (discussed below) establish beyond much question that he had by then made his mind up to vote against segregation. But it must surely have been a painful decision for him for some of the very reasons Warren had already noted. Neither history nor legal precedent—masters to whom he was greatly dedicated—was of much help to him, so Frankfurter had evidently had to resolve in his own mind that neither was an insuperable barrier in this case to the humanitarian goal his deepest conception of justice cried out for him to reach.

The members of the Court had best curb their tongues in discussing this extraordinary problem, Frankfurter remarked to the brethren by way of urging them to confine their deliberations to the room they were in or to exchanges among themselves. They had best not put any time limitation on when the decision should come down. It was too bad history had conspired to make the Court the trustee of that incorrigible constitutional changeling, the due-process clause, and therefore impose upon the Justices a policy-making function unlike that borne by any other court in any other nation. Wherever they all finally came out on the segregation case, he told them, they dared not be self-righteous.

William Douglas said he agreed with Warren. The historical evidence had cast a mixed light on the questions they had put to the litigants, but in this day, segregation by race or color could not be sanctioned. The Court should not try to anticipate too much in its opinion and would have to recognize that adjustments might be necessary in dealing with the issue afterward; the important thing was to decide the basic principle during the current term of the Court.

Robert Jackson's position remained complex. The historical evidence had deepened his conviction that segregation could not be abolished in a judicially defensible way. The Court's problem was to find a judicial basis for "a congenial political conclusion," and he did not see how that could be done. As a political decision, he could go along with it, but he would insist that it be so defined or he would have to protest. Almost certainly, Jackson was telling the conference that he would file a separate concurring opinion if whoever wrote the opinion of the Court feigned that the Justices were doing anything other than declaring new law for a new day. Nor would it do, he insisted, simply to "throw in the hopper" the main decision against segregation and leave the rest of the problem—namely, how the desegregation process should be managed—to another fight. This, perhaps, was a slap at Douglas's proposal for settling the basic constitutional principle during the current term and remaining flexible on the question of implementation.

Harold Burton made no notation of his own position as he had at the conference on the cases the year before. But nothing in his extensive papers has ever been uncovered to suggest that in the intervening period he had swerved from his intention to vote against segregation. "I think he had made his mind up early," says one of his 1953 Term clerks, Raymond Troubh, "but he never discussed it with us—he was somewhat of a secretive man." Occasional clues that appear in his diary during the ensuing months suggest he was entirely supportive of the Chief Justice's efforts to mass the Court behind a single opinion.

Tom Clark did a lot of talking at the conference this day. He had been closer than anyone else on the Court to Fred Vinson, but had functioned in his shadow. The passing of the Kentuckian seemed to liberate Clark from the sort of instinctively prosecutorial, pro-government mentality he had displayed since coming to the Court. His growth process toward being an earnest and workmanlike member of the Court who could think for himself was greatly accelerated by the arrival of Earl Warren.

He had experienced the race problem more intimately than any member of the Court except Hugo Black, Clark told the conference. He had lived with it and did not underestimate the possibilities of a violent reaction if the Court did not handle the segregation decision properly. The matter could not be settled by a brief policy statement or by flat decree that the practice cease at once. Clark was frank enough to say that he had been surprised by the legislative history, since he had always thought that one of the avowed purposes of the Fourteenth Amendment had been to abolish segregation. The evidence appeared to be otherwise and was obviously of no use to the Court in support of a decision against segregation. He was willing to go along with such a decision, however, so long as the relief provisions of the Court's ultimate decree were carefully worked out in a way to permit different handling of the problem in different places. This seemed to be a good deal more positive statement than Clark had made at the conference the year earlier when Vinson was plainly steering the Court with his foot jammed heavily on the brake.

Speaking last, Sherman Minton was hardly less forceful than either Warren or Douglas in favoring the end of segregation. The concept of a separate equality had been read into the Constitution by the Court in *Plessy*, "a weak reed today," and now it should be read right out of it. The world in 1953 was very different from that of the 1860s, said Minton, and no justification remained for racial barriers except, as the Chief Justice had said, an avowed belief in Negro inferiority. In terms of remedying the practice, he would just as soon leave that up to the District Courts to settle in keeping with local conditions.

Thus, the Court's array showed Warren that he had a piece of work to do. A solid five-man bloc was apparently ready to declare against segregation on principle. But even its members were not entirely agreed on just how it should be done. Douglas and Minton seemed to favor a short, simple statement of principle which did not try to face the varying problems that would arise in different areas. Black apparently wanted to narrow the scope of the opinion to something less than a cosmic declaration of human rights. Burton and Warren seemed flexible on the timetable that would be laid down for implementing the Court's action.

Beyond the openly committed group, Warren could apparently count on Clark—but only if the opinion of the Court assured the segregating states a good deal of latitude and enough time to respond in as painless a fashion as possible; whether such an opinion could be fashioned without yanking all its teeth first remained to be seen. Frankfurter sounded as if he would go along, but he was known to savor writing concurrences that often served to dilute the impact of the majority opinion. And Jackson had all but promised to write a concurring opinion if the majority did not acknowledge that it was acting in a frankly unjudicial way—a scarcely reasonable request to make of the brethren. Reed, finally, seemed fixed on voting to uphold segregation while insisting that every state was obliged to equalize its colored schools straightaway.

But Earl Warren did not want dissents or concurrences if he could help it. He wanted a single, unequivocating opinion that could leave no doubt that the Court had put Jim Crow to the sword. It was clear to him at the December 12, 1953, conference that he would not be able to unify the Court behind such an opinion if he polled the Justices there and then. "We decided not to make up our minds on that first conference day," he recounted later, "but to talk it over, from week to week, dealing with different aspects of it—in groups, over lunches, in conference. It was too important to hurry it."

Warren's highest hope, for a single unanimous opinion, did not look especially bright. It rested in large part on his overcoming the philosophical reservations of both Felix Frankfurter and Robert Jackson, men who could talk, write, and think rings around the Chief Justice. Neither was likely to curl up at Warren's mere bidding.

Frankfurter had been the most disputatious and yet the most influential member of the Vinson Court. His intellect and zeal would have made him a formidable force in any group of nine men. Plainly, though, they did not intimidate Earl Warren, an imperturbable voyager of utmost self-confidence. Warren knew his strengths and his limitations, and neither set obliged him to lock horns with Frankfurter; indeed, quite the contrary. The new Chief, certainly during this first term on the Court, seemed bent on a policy of kindly accommodation with the spirited little Justice, and in the school-segregation cases, at least, there is strong evidence to suggest they worked together toward a mutually sought end.

Some time during the 1953 Term, and more than likely in the weeks just after the reargument of *Brown*, Frankfurter committed to paper two pages of thoughts that offer insight into the intellectual and humanitarian forces tugging at him. The memorandum, undated, was discovered in the Frankfurter Papers at Harvard University and has not previously been published. It was the sort of memo he might compose in longhand any time after arising, as he was wont, at five or so in the morning, bring into the office with him at eight-thirty or nine, have typed, and then pop into the file for standby use if and when he decided to write an opinion on that case. The memo began with a characteristically breast-beating, yet nonetheless genuine, assertion of the agonies of the judicial function at such trying moments:

> Only for those who have not the responsibility of decision is it easy to decide these cases. This is so because they present a legal issue inextricably bound up with deep feeling on sharply conflicting social and political issues. The legal issue derives from the established practice of exercising judicial authority when appeal is made to vague provisions in the Civil War Amendments. While it has now been settled beyond question that some of the guaranties of the Constitution are not judicially enforceable, *e.g.*, the guarantee of a republican form of govern-

ment, amendments to the Constitution introduced in the reconstruction period, no less vague and no more appropriate for judicial judgment, serve as the basis for adjudication. The inevitable result is that issues are cast in legal form for disposition by this Court that are embroiled in explosive psychological and political attitudes.

That, in essence, is about what he said at the December 12, 1953, conference of the Court. The Court as an institution had been saddled with so grave a responsibility in the segregation cases that its foremost proponent of judicial restraint had retreated to his private wailing wall. There he found more woe in the clash between his private instincts and his public obligations as a Justice:

> However, it is not our duty to express our personal attitudes toward these issues however deep our individual convictions may be. The opposite is true. It is our duty not to express our merely personal views. However passionately any of us may hold egalitarian views, however fiercely any of us may believe that such a policy of segregation as undoubtedly expresses the tenacious conviction of Southern States [is] both unjust and short-sighted, he travels outside his judicial authority if for this private reason alone he declares unconstitutional the policy of segregation.

But as a man of wide learning and omnivorous reading habits, he knew full well what had been the basis for the adoption and spread of Jim Crow laws. He thought that basis had been eroded:

> Equally so he cannot write into our Constitution a belief in the Negro's natural inferiority or his personal belief in the desirability of segregating white and colored children during their most formative years. To attribute such a view to science, as is sometimes done, is to reject the very basis of science, namely, the process of reaching verifiable conclusions. The abstract and absolutist claims both for and against segregation have been falsified by experience, especially the great changes in the relations between white and colored people since the first World War. The inequities and hardships of a policy of segregation have in the short period of thirty odd years undergone great amelioration. The promising results of this tendency afford no ground for complacency. But it is fair to say that the pace of progress has surprised even those most eager in its promotion.

This happy trend meshed with the constitutional mandate:

> The outcome of the Civil War, as reflected in the Civil War Amendments, is that there is a single American society. Our colored citizens, like the other components which make up the American nation, are not to be denied the right to enjoy the distinctive qualities of their cultural past. But neither are they to be denied the right to grow up with other Americans as part of our national life. And experience happily shows that contacts tend to mitigate antagonisms and engender mutual respect.

It was one thing for such a process to unfold naturally; it was another for it to be made obligatory by the courts:

> The legal problem confronting this Court is the extent to which this desirable and even necessary process of welding a nation out of such diverse elements can be

imposed as a matter of law upon the States in disregard of the deeply rooted feeling, tradition and local laws, based upon local situations to the contrary. The basis of such legal compulsion, if the Constitution requires it, is a provision of the Fourteenth Amendment, whereby a State is forbidden to "deny to any person within its jurisdiction the equal protection of the laws."

That concept of equal protection was a dynamic one, for, however much he preferred to sail by the fixed star of court-made precedent and libertarian restraint, Felix Frankfurter never believed that a just interpretation of the law could be rendered based upon a view of society from out of the judge's coat closet:

> But the equality of laws enshrined in a constitution which was "made for an undefined and expanding future, and for a people gathered and to be gathered from many nations and of many tongues," *Hurtado v. California*, 110 U.S. 516, 530, 531, is not a fixed formula defined with finality at a particular time. It does not reflect, as a congealed summary, the social arrangements and beliefs of a particular epoch. It is addressed to the changes wrought by time and not merely the changes that are the consequences of physical development. Law must respond to transformation of views as well as to that of outward circumstances. The effect of changes in men's feelings for what is right and just is equally relevant in determining whether a discrimination denies the equal protection of the laws.

There was no more. But it was enough to show how he had unchained his thinking from legalistic orthodoxy and was considering the segregation cases against a frame of reference as broad as all of American history. He had taken judicial notice, without saying so, of psychological and sociological premises that could not be pinned down like case law. His memo was all but bereft of legal citations; its sole reference to a decision of the Court was a cosmetic usage. He was ready to say, if he chose to mobilize the thoughts in the memo, that the Court was free to reinterpret the Constitution on the strength of "changes in men's feelings for what is right and just"—which was really the only justifiable ground for its intrusion into the deeply held convictions of the white people in command of the segregating states.

There is other extant evidence that Frankfurter was strongly committed to a desegregation decision by this time and was working with Warren in massing the Court toward that end at as early a date as possible. On December 17, 1953, the Friday following the initial conference discussion of the cases, Justice Burton noted in his diary: "After lunch the Chief Justice told me of his plan to try [to] direct discussion of segregation cases toward the decree—as providing . . . the best chance of unanimity in that phase." In other words, even though some members of the Court might hold out against a vote to end segregation or might insist on writing a concurrence, Warren felt that once the majority's will was made firm and final, all the Justices would want to stand with institutional solidity behind the decree of the Court implementing the decision. Anything short of that might serve only to invite massive resistance in the segregating states.

That Frankfurter was in accord with Warren's approach is testified to by a five-page memo he circulated to the Court on January 15, 1954, in the hope that it might "stimulate good thoughts in others." (The secretiveness with which the school cases were being deliberated by the Justices is suggested by the last line of Frankfurter's covering note: "I need hardly add that the typewriting was done under conditions of strictest security.") The memo contained ten numbered points beginning with: "A decree in this case in favor of the appellants of necessity would be drastically different from decrees enforcing merely individual rights before the Court." In earlier cases involving segregation in higher education, the Court's decisions affected only a small number of litigants and so the problem "was amenable to individual treatment. This is not so in the situations before us." While it was true, of course, that the Court formally had before it "only individual claimants, standing on their individual rights," the Justices were being "asked in effect to transform state-wide school systems in nearly a score of states." Even assuming the best will in the world, it was plain that "declaration of unconstitutionality is not a wand by which these transformations can be accomplished." To guide the process, Frankfurter urged, the Court had best define what was implied by the term "integrated schools":

> . . . Integration that is "equal protection" can readily be achieved by lowering the standards of those who at the start are, in the phrase of George Orwell, "more equal." "Integration" could be achieved in a way to lower the standards of those now under discrimination. It would indeed make a mockery of the Constitutional adjudication designed to vindicate a claim to equal treatment to achieve "integrated" but lower educational standards. Surely we can take as a starting point that in enforcing the Fourteenth Amendment the Court is, broadly speaking, promoting a process of social betterment and not contributing to social deterioration. Not even a court can in a day change a deplorable situation into the ideal. It does its duty if it gets effectively under way the righting of a wrong. When the wrong is a deeply rooted state policy the court does its duty if it decrees measures that reverse the direction of the unconstitutional policy so as to uproot it "with all deliberate speed." *Virginia v. West Virginia*, 222 U.S. 17, 20.

Different ratios of white to colored pupils might suggest different formulas for working out the process from community to community, Frankfurter added in a key retreat from doctrinally pure equalitarianism. "The Court does not know that a simple scrambling of the two school systems may not work. It surely cannot assume that scrambling is all there is to it. . . . It is surely entitled to suspect that spreading the adjustment over time will more effectively accomplish the desired end. . . ." No doubt, differing opinions as to the desirable pace and scope of the court-ordered integration process would breed future litigation; the Court's responsibility was to keep such litigation to a minimum. But the worst thing the Court could do would be to declare segregation unconstitutional and let it go at that; such a course would be "the most prolific breeder of litigation and chaos." The Court would have to make clear that any inequality begotten by a segregated school system could not stand and must be terminated "as soon as this can be done" without disrupting the school system or lowering the educational standards "for any sizable group."

Just who should dig out the facts and oversee the desegregation process in any given school district was a difficult question, but one thing was clear to Frankfurter: the Supreme Court itself must not attempt to do it. "Since a social policy with entangling passions is at issue, the facts ought to be dug out by an active, disinterested digger-out-of-facts." The parties to *Brown* as well as the Attorney General's office had proposed that the remedial process be superintended by the U.S. District Courts. Frankfurter ventured a more unusual method, hinted at in the last of the five questions he had formulated for the Court as the basis of the reargument: the appointment of a "master," a neutral officer of the Court "undistracted by other judicial duties," who would be free to move about the community searching out facts and proposing remedies. Frankfurter acknowledged that it might not be easy to find qualified "masters" even if the Court cloaked them with great moral authority, and, in the long run, perhaps the District Courts would be the most prudent overseers of the process. His principal purpose in the memo, he wound up, was to spur thinking on the subject among the brethren.

It was precisely the sort of open-ended, moderate statement to ease the lingering anxieties of a Tom Clark—of everyone on the Court, really, who feared that explosive consequences would grow out of the decision. They were all now at last confronting the reality of the monumental decision that lay not far ahead. Warren went to them individually and talked about it. He was bringing them together on the question by including them all in trying to formulate an equitable set of ground rules for the desegregation process. On the very day Frankfurter circulated his memo, the Chief hosted a luncheon for all the Justices, who rarely ate *en masse*. The menu featured duck, Mr. Justice Frankfurter dissenting for some pheasant. At the conference of the Court the next day, Burton reported to his diary, the segregation cases were again discussed, though he gave no indication of the drift. Frankfurter's memo, presumably, had provided useful grist.

It is more than likely that one reason Earl Warren was not pushing his fellow Justices unduly in the segregation cases during the early weeks of 1954—aside from good sense and practical politics—was that he had not yet been confirmed as Chief Justice by the Senate.

Congress had reconvened after the turn of the year, and the Warren nomination, it was assumed, would win swift approval from the Senate Judiciary subcommittee assigned to weigh it, followed by automatic confirmation by the upper chamber itself. But that process was interrupted by the maverick antics of the subcommittee's chairman, Senator William Langer of North Dakota, a man virtually unknown to Warren. Weeks crawled by without any action on the Warren nomination. Reports circulated in Washington that enemies of Warren were determined to cause him trouble because he had opposed the loyalty oath at the University of California. Other rumors, reported in the *New York Times* by James Reston on February 17, held that some Southern Senators would try to block confirmation because they feared Warren was planning to vote to end school segregation. But the real reason for the delay proved to be Senator Langer's abiding annoyance with federal administrations for constantly overlooking the good citizens of North Dakota every time they named someone to high office. On February 19, the chief counsel of Langer's subcommittee read aloud ten unevaluated "charges" against Warren from various detractors. Among the charges was that he was "biased toward the AFL labor monopoly," had allowed "organized crime to establish its national headquarters in California," and while governor had owned and operated an "escrow racket." Langer said he planned to schedule an open hearing on the charges, which Vice President Richard M. Nixon and Senate Republican leader William Knowland, Warren's fellow Californians, promptly dismissed as absurd. Dismayed by Langer's conduct, Warren could do nothing but cool his heels and tend to the Court's business. Lacking confirmation, though, he would have been imprudent to force the segregation cases with the Court.

Among those who in all likelihood would have rebelled at any effort to whip him into line was Robert Jackson, who in mid-February remained unconvinced that the Court would produce a majority opinion that spoke as candidly as he wished it to on *Brown*. As Frankfurter had done earlier, Jackson sketched out his thoughts on the school cases in a memorandum, dated February 15, 1954. It was a good deal longer and more developed than Frankfurter's memo and clearly suggests that Jackson was preparing to write a separate concurrence or perhaps to join in one with Frankfurter.

The Jackson memo began with the bite and directness typical of his style:

> Since the close of the Civil War the United States has been "hesitating between two worlds—one dead, the other powerless to be born." War brought an old order to an end but as usual force proved unequal to founding a new one. Neither North nor South has been willing really to adapt its racial practices to its professions. The race problem would be quickly solved if some way could be found to make us all live up to our hypocrisies.

He ruminated a bit on the nature of racism, noting, "This Court can not eradicate these fears, prides and prejudices on which segregation rests." Nonetheless, he lamented the victimization of the black man:

> . . . in the South the Negro not only suffers from racial suspicions and antagonisms present in other states and in other countries, but also, I am convinced, has suffered great prejudice from the aftermath of the great American white conflict. The white South retains in historical memory a deep resentment of the forces which, after conquest, imposed a fierce program of reconstruction and the deep humiliation of carpet bag government. The Negro is the visible and reachable beneficiary and symbol of this unhappy experience, on whom many visit their natural desire for retaliation.

Nevertheless, the Negro had made "one of the swiftest and most dramatic advances in the annals of man." Whether the "real abolition of segregation will be accelerated or retarded by what many are likely to regard as a ruthless use of federal judicial power," Jackson wrote, "is a question that I cannot and need not answer." He added:

> That Negro segregation in the schools has outlived whatever original justification it may have had and is no longer wise or fair public policy is a conclusion congenial to my background and social and political views. . . .

But we can not oversimplify this decision to be a mere expression of our personal opinion that school segregation is unwise or evil. We have not been chosen as legislators but as judges. . . . This Court must face the difficulties in the way of honestly saying that the states which have segregated schools have not . . . been justified in regarding their practice as lawful. And the thoughtful layman, as well as the trained lawyer, must wonder how it is that a supposedly stable organic law of our nation this morning forbids what for three quarters of a century it has allowed.

Jackson then said that there was little in the nation's legislative or judicial history that provided the Court with a strong basis for outlawing school segregation. The Fifth Amendment had never been invoked before the Civil War in behalf of Negro claims that slaves were denied their liberty without due process of law. The Fourteenth Amendment could hardly be said to have given the Negro the blanket rights his lawyers now claimed, since it had been necessary to pass the Fifteenth Amendment to protect his right to vote. The fact was that the Constitution was mute about education and segregation, and the acts of Congress and the several states offered no comforting evidence that the nation in the last century understood the Fourteenth Amendment to have prohibited school segregation. "A long line of judicial decisions [was] almost unanimous in the view that the matter was one left to solution by each state—at least in the absence of Congressional action." Custom, "a powerful lawmaker," has reinforced the practice of segregation, and the Supreme Court, in common with all courts, was reluctant to use judicial power to try to recast social usages.

. . . But we decide today that the unwritten law has long been contrary to a custom deeply anchored in our social system. Thus despite my personal satisfaction with the Court's judgment, I simply can not find, in surveying all the usual sources of law, anything which warrants me in saying that it is required by the original purpose and intent of the Fourteenth or Fifth Amendment.

The only way the Court could, "with intellectual honesty," justify its decision to end segregation, Jackson asserted, was on the ground that the majestic generalities of the Constitution "have a content and a significance that vary from age to age," to quote Cardozo. After citing thirteen prior reversals by the Court based on changing conditions, Jackson considered and dismissed "extra-legal criteria from sociological, psychological and political sciences" that had been urged upon the Justices as reasons to end segregation. He did not doubt that segregation was painful to Negroes, said Jackson, adding:

However that may be, and if all the woes of colored children would be solved by forcing them into white company, I do not think we should import into the concept of equal protection of the law these elusive psychological and subjective factors. They are not determinable with satisfactory objectivity or measurable with reasonable certainty. If we adhere to objective criteria the judicial process will still be capricious enough.

The Court, furthermore, was obliged to consider the feelings of those who were to be coerced out of segregation as well as those who had been coerced into it. "While the prosegregation emotion may seem to us less rational than antisegregation emotion," he wrote, "we can hardly deny the existence of sincerity and passion of those who think that their blood, birth and lineage are something worthy of protection by separatism."

Public opinion in recent years, though, had undergone a "profound change" in this area and the "awful consequences of racial prejudice revealed by . . . the Nazi regime" had caused "a revulsion against the kind of racial feeling" that had led to the Japanese-American relocation cases during the Second World War. But Jackson did not think that the Justices, who had "pondered this [segregation] problem, as we have pondered no other in my experience on the Court," ought merely to defer to public opinion, for then "the judicial process has counted for naught."

There was only one truly valid reason to warrant the Court's decision, Jackson said in conclusion, and that is "not a change in the Constitution but in the Negro population." Today, Negroes were "a different people" from those "[l]ately freed from bondage" who had had no chance "to show their capacity for education or assimilation, or even a chance to demonstrate that they could be self-supporting or in our public life anything more than a pawn for white exploiters." Then, with candor that might have rocked the Southland, he added:

> Whatever may have been true at an earlier period, the mere fact that one is in some degree colored no longer creates a presumption that he is inferior, illiterate, retarded or indigent. Moreover, assimilation is under way to a marked extent. Blush or shudder, as many will, mixture of blood has been making inroads on segregation faster than the courtroom. A line of separation between the races has become unclear and blurred and an increasing part of what is called colored population has as much claim to white as to colored blood. This development baffles any just segregation effort.

Jackson did not define what a "just segregation effort" might be, but wound up noting that education, once regarded as a privilege bestowed upon a fortunate few, had become "a right and more than that a duty, to be performed not merely for one's own advantage but for the security and stability of the nation." That right and that duty could no longer be encumbered by discriminatory or otherwise oppressive conditions.

It was a remarkable memorandum, both for its forthrightness and for demonstrating, at least in rough form, how the Court might fulfill the condition Jackson had laid down in conference for his going along with the majority opinion—that is, by admitting there was no judicial basis for its decision. Now he had framed his statement and would await the majority opinion. Whatever its virtues, though, the Jackson memo left a good deal to be desired as a state paper. As a Justice of the Supreme Court, he was obliged to be judicious if not altogether judicial. Some of the problems with his memo were suggested to Jackson in a courageous reply memo by E. Barrett Prettyman, Jr., his only clerk that term. The exchange is instructive.

The most important thing about the Court's decision, Prettyman offered, was that the nation as a whole accept it as "honestly arrived at, confidently espoused, and basically sound." The American people should feel that the decision was based on certain truths, even if they were not yet prepared to accept those truths fully, and that it was a decision "as far as possible . . . based upon *law*." And:

> . . . If they receive the decision in this way, segregation should die in relatively short order, no matter how many legal skirmishes ensue. On the other hand, if the country feels that a bunch of liberals in Washington have finally foisted off their social views on the public, it will not only tolerate but aid circumvention of the decision.
>
> Therefore, I think that your opinion should *begin*, not with doubts and fears—not with a negative attitude, but with a clear and affirmative statement of your legal position. You have stated this position in only two out of 23 pages, and these two pages are almost at the end of the opinion. They are almost an afterthought.

Prettyman then sketched out a possible restructuring of the opinion, noted spots that seemed to him to need elaborating, pointed out internal inconsistencies, and added these bracing remarks:

> . . . I say this in all frankness: if you are going to reach the decision you do, you should not write as if you were ashamed to reach it. . . . The fact that you cannot explain exactly how you know the races are sufficiently equal or that you cannot say just when they reached sufficient equality, should not make your decision apologetic. Some one must make these decisions, and under our system the burden is on the courts. . . .
>
> You indicate several times . . . that abolition of segregation by this Court may well be an empty gesture. This may be only too true. But it seems to me in a case of this magnitude, the very attitude of the Court is important, and that attitude should be one of faith rather than futility. If segregation is no longer legal, *of course* the country will not tolerate it—that would be a much better tone in your opinion. After all, this is a great country, and its people are great, and they will not tolerate lawlessness if they are convinced it *is* real lawlessness. How can you expect them to be convinced if you are not yourself?

It is doubtful if any of the many excellent young men who have come fresh out of the law schools or soon thereafter to serve the Justices of the Supreme Court ever served more faithfully or usefully than Barrett Prettyman served Robert Jackson. What part Prettyman's memo played will never be known, but it is a fact that Jackson, having written this much on the segregation cases, wrote no more.

Nothing he had heard or read during the reargument had convinced Justice Stanley Reed that the Court should declare segregation unconstitutional.

From December to February, Reed put his clerks, John Fassett and George V. Mickum III, to work researching for the dissent he intended to write. Fassett pursued historical data and a footnote on segregation in the armed forces that Reed planned to use by way of showing that in an area where the executive branch had decided to move against segregation, it had done so by a gradual process. Mickum set to work gathering material on the attitude of the Catholic Church toward segregation. The Justice confided to

Fassett that the new Chief Justice was with the majority and that, in all likelihood, Reed would be casting a lone dissent. The clerk tactfully wondered aloud to the Justice whether a solo dissent might not be both a useless gesture and a disservice to the Court as an institution. Fassett's fellow clerk, Mickum, who had grown up in the District of Columbia, did not share Fassett's disagreement with Reed on the merits of the case.

During the Court's two-week recess in February, Justice Reed roughed out the essence of his dissent on a yellow legal pad and handed it to Fassett for typing and comment. Reed's words read:

> If "equal protection," in fact and now, is accepted as a true touchstone by which to judge the constitutionality of segregation, the argument is finished. There are so many places in the South that have not carried out their responsibility to give separate but equal educational facilities that Negro residents of these communities would have and would receive constitutional remedies as do the citizens of S.C. [South Carolina] case.
>
> But, of course, equal protection is not the touchstone. It would not bring school integration to the District of Columbia. It would not through the coercion of the Constitution make all white or integrated rural schools equal white and integrated urban schools, it would not put the white schools of a slum ward on a par with those more favorably considered by certain school boards. The Equal Protection Clause does not assure by constitutional command equal public facilities to all citizens whether State or Nation. If it did, many of our ideals would be achieved, all families would have available gas, water and electricity, would live "out of the mud" and would have a job. What the clause does do is to give each citizen an opportunity to obtain facilities substantially equal to his neighbor for himself. That right has been fully protected and equipped by the Court (cite with catchword explanation Sweatt-McLaurin-Equal salary equal money per pupil—Canada [*Gaines*]). (Examine equal protection cases in other lines.) Equal protection and due process have many close associations (cite cases which say not much difference) but the issue in segregation is whether segregation violates due process. . . .
>
> Public policy is declared by Congress (Reed's case on Mo. purchase), not this Court. If we could declare policy we might have decided that due process commanded no capital punishment, no legal prohibition of labor unions (Cormack Amendment), universal suffrage, outlawry of liquor. Provide a striking down of private property based on Das Kapital, etc. short 200 words or less.

Fassett flyspecked the memo from beginning to end with critical remarks. "In essence, my argument was that his reasoning was unclear to me, particularly his transition from equal protection to due process," Fassett recalls. "I felt that while a logical and persuasive argument based on historical materials could be made to support the separate-but-equal doctrine, his approach evaded the issue." Fassett argued that it was irrelevant that the Court's striking down of segregation would not make all schools across the country equal; the point was that all students within the same district ought to be treated equally. The provision of gas, water, and electricity had never been made a universal free service of government as public education had, so that analogy seemed weak to the clerk. The equal-protection clause did not say anything about "substantially equal," he added—a point that Thurgood Marshall had made in answer to a Reed question during the reargument.

"During the course of this discussion," Fassett remembers, "I referred to the importance of a decision rejecting segregation to our country's position in the community of nations. I do not recall the Justice's exact words, but their substance was that he had heard a lot on that subject and had been giving it considerable thought."

Earl Warren was confirmed as Chief Justice on March 1, 1954. No Senator voted against him, not even William Langer of North Dakota.

By the time the Senate gave him its blessing five months after he had come to the Court, the new Chief Justice had won the admiration of his brethren for traits of character if not breathtaking legal acumen. "It must have been enormously difficult to come from the life he had late been leading to the cloistered atmosphere of the Court," remarks Earl Pollock, one of his clerks that first term, "and he was the first to say that he was no legal scholar, but he was a very endearing, very complex, and very human man. I liked him very much."

His colleagues on the bench seemed to like him for the way he had applied himself to the job. For one thing, he was a good listener in a city of talkers. For another, he had become, since the *Brown* reargument, a lucid interrogator during the Court's oral sessions. "Before you sit down," he would say to the advocate before him, "I would like to hear you on—" and then specify often enough precisely the terrain the lawyer had hoped to avoid. And, according to James Reston in the *New York Times* of March 4, 1954, word had seeped out to the press that the Chief's conduct of the Court's conferences displayed a number of traits that were greatly welcomed: "an ability to concentrate on the concrete; a capacity to do his homework; a sensible, friendly manner, wholly devoid of pretense, and a self-command and natural dignity so useful in presiding over the court."

His intitial voting record, moreover, did not place Warren at either end of the Court and hardly qualified him as a devoted civil-libertarian. Early in his first term, he joined a narrow five-to-four majority in *Irvine v. California*, in which the Court upheld a gambling prosecution based on evidence obtained from a microphone planted in the bedroom of the defendant. Jackson's opinion, while condemning the police action, found no ground for reversing the conviction, but he was joined by Warren, who had been a California law-enforcement officer for twenty-two years, in suggesting that the Justice Department investigate the case to see if the police had not violated the civil-rights statutes. Black, Douglas, Frankfurter, and Burton dissented. In a yet more startling and unlibertarian vote later in the term, Warren was part of a six-man majority in *Barsky v. Board of Regents*, in which the Court declined to overrule New York medical authorities who had suspended a prominent physician's license to practice because he refused to produce the records of a group called the Joint Anti-Fascist Refugee Committee, subpoenaed by the House Un-American Activities Committee, which suspected it of fellow-traveling. Only Black, Douglas, and Frankfurter dissented from this late spasm in the finally ebbing Red witch-hunt. Justice Jackson in particular must have been comforted by having the Chief with him in both cases.

Some time between late February and late March, the Court voted at one of its Saturday conferences on the school-segregation cases. The date is in doubt because the Justices had agreed that the case was of such magnitude that no word ought to leak out before the decision was announced. As a result, no record of the vote seems to have been written down in any of the docket books that each Justice maintained. The tally sheet in Burton's docket book records no vote beyond the one to take the cases in June of 1952. One of Tom Clark's clerks recalls that his tally book, which had a built-in lock on it as did all the Justices' books, was generally available to his clerks who wished to look through it and see the disposition of the Court on any given case. But there was no tally sheet on *Brown* in Tom Clark's docket book that term, the clerk recalls.

Warren himself gave conflicting information on the date of the vote. On direct inquiry by the author, the retired Chief Justice replied on June 16, 1971: "I don't think we took a vote on it till the end of February—and then I took my time writing the opinion." And in response to a written query, he wrote on November 20, 1973, that "the formal vote in the *Brown* case was taken around the middle of February 1954." The slight discrepancy suggests that neither he nor any other official of the Court recorded the precise date—a departure from custom. (His lack of precision may also have meant, of course, that he had not bothered to check his records for the date.) But there is added evidence that there was no written record: in the May 1974 issue of *Ebony*, staff writer Jack Slater reported that in an interview for an article marking the twentieth anniversary of the *Brown* decision, Warren said: ". . . Eventually there were so many briefs that we decided to depart from the usual procedure and consider the case as it developed. And so, week by week, we discussed it, from the middle of November to the latter part of March, when we took a vote. There was no divisiveness and no arguing."

Late March seems the more likely moment for the vote. In February, he still had not been confirmed by the Senate, and while such a consideration might have been irrelevant to him, Earl Warren was a man dedicated to the formal procedures of democracy, and it is likely that he greatly preferred to confront his eminent fellow judges, convoked to decide a case of surpassing magnitude and grave national importance, only after having been fully and properly invested with the authority of his high office. The vote was apparently eight to strike down segregation and one, Reed, to uphold it. But it was far from certain still whether Jackson was going to file a separate concurrence or whether Frankfurter might or whether the two of them might agree on one; their thoughts on the cases were certainly close enough, to judge by their uncirculated memos. Warren, of course, wished to avoid concurring opinions; the fewer voices with which the Court spoke, the better. And he did not give up his hope that Stanley Reed, in the end, would abandon his dissenting position. The Chief assigned himself the all-important task of writing the majority opinion.

Before Warren put pencil to paper, it is almost certain, the Justices had agreed on the basic compromise formula for deciding the case. The Court would rule segregated schools unconstitutional before the close of the 1953 Term, but it would hold the cases over for reargument the following term in order to get the detailed views of the litigants on the most fitting way for the constitutional decision to be implemented. There would be no decree, then, at the current term. That would give the South nearly a year to condition itself to the Court's edict. But on the basic issue itself, the Court had voted to declare Jim Crow an outlaw. Beyond that, speculated Alexander Bickel, who remained on close terms with Justice Frankfurter and would write at length on the Court in books and magazines during the next two decades: "There is little doubt in my mind that at whatever conference the decision was taken in 1954, Justices Frankfurter, Black and Jackson left the room with a mutual understanding of the general form that the eventual decree of the Court would take—that it would provide for gradual enforcement and not forthwith as was the usual practice." Warren himself later offered a less revealing summation of the Court's consensus by the time he sat down to write: "There was no particular disagreement about the course of settling only the constitutional question then or that the question of implementation could well stand additional argument."

On March 30, fate intruded anew on the Court's deliberations. Justice Jackson, who had seemed in good spirits and robust health to that moment, was felled by a serious heart attack. He was hospitalized, with the immediate prospect that he would not return to the Court before the end of the term.

Whether the Chief Justice was aware that the stricken Justice had composed a draft for a concurring opinion, an opinion that Warren did not want written, is not known. (Prettyman surmises that he did know.) Jackson's illness, at any rate, seemed to reduce the likelihood that he would be inclined to make the effort to turn out a persuasive concurrence. The Court might, of course, have chosen to hold over its major cases until Jackson was fully recuperated, but a decision in the segregation cases had already been put off for quite some time; besides, the full Court had already voted on *Brown.* At the April 3 conference, the Justices therefore decided to hear out the rest of the calendar without Jackson and hold over for reargument cases of special importance and those in which the Court was evenly split. Warren then went to work on the draft of the *Brown* opinion.

By mid-April, he had something to show Earl Pollock, the clerk who probably worked most closely with him on the opinion. It was a delicate task but one that Warren must have relished. "If there were three things of great value and stimulation to him," recalls Pollock, who later became a prominent Chicago attorney, "they were (1) equality, (2) education, and (3) young people." The writing process itself went smoothly. "The opinion never greatly changed after the first draft," Warren disclosed. "The speed with which it was prepared was almost breathtaking," adds Pollock. "I think his feeling was: let's get it done and out, now that we have a solid Court."

Pollock's account seems corroborated by the chronology traceable in surviving documents. Warren apparently did not circulate his draft of the opinions—one covering the state segregation cases, the other the District of Columbia case—until Friday, May 7, the date of a memo he dispatched to members of the Court. The attached drafts, the Chief wrote, were offered as "a basis for discussion of the segregation cases" and "were prepared on the theory that the opinions should be short, readable by the lay public, non-rhetorical, unemotional and, above all, non-accusatory." His aspirations were those of a statesman, not a poet.

The drafts of the Warren opinions were carried by the Chief himself to those Justices who were in their chambers when the proofs came up from the print shop. Earl Pollock brought Hugo Black his copy while the Justice was playing tennis at his home in Alexandria and carried Sherman Minton's to his rarely seen apartment. No copies were allowed to float around Washington unaccounted for.

The Chief did not have long to wait for the returns to come in. Burton's response was probably among the most immediate and most enthusiastic: he told his diary on May 8 that he had read the Chief's drafts and written him "my enthusiastic approval—with a few minor suggestions. He has done, I believe, a magnificent job that may win a unanimous Court. . . ." Black, Douglas, Minton, and Clark, it is likely, had only minor suggestions to make and, to one degree or another, shared Burton's pleased response. It was with the three remaining members of the Court that Warren could have anticipated problems: any of them might still choose to write his own opinion.

But Felix Frankfurter had, from the beginning, been working for a unified Court. Nothing could have been worse, for the Court or the nation itself, than a flurry of conflicting opinions that would confuse and anger the American people. And nothing could have been better than a unanimous, low-key, but utterly resolute opinion. So long as the Chief was willing to fashion his opinion in a frank, carefully modulated way, Frankfurter had intended to go along. And all the signs were that if the Chief's opinion had not filled Frankfurter's minimum requirements, he would have discussed the problems with Warren fully and the latter would have given him every consideration. Relations between the two men at that time were "superb," in the opinion of Frank E. A. Sander, one of Frankfurter's clerks that term. That judgment would seem to be confirmed indisputably by a letter Frankfurter wrote to Jackson in the hospital on April 15; in passing, Frankfurter mentioned that on the previous day he had had "another experience with the Chief, confirming all the others." The matter had to do with a long-neglected piece of Court business unrelated to any of the cases before the Justices. "E.W. was properly outraged over the indifference," Frankfurter told Jackson, "and showed the understanding that comes from caring for the real responsibility that that problem implies. What a pleasure to do business with him."

Rumors survive that Frankfurter drafted a dissenting opinion in *Brown* or perhaps a concurrence, but none of his clerks ever saw it if he did. The only documentary evidence that he was even considering a concurrence is the short, undated memo discovered in his papers and cited in its entirety earlier in this chapter. But he was habitually composing such memos against the day when he would decide whether he would write in any given case before the Court. He may not have made up his mind to go along with the Chief's *Brown* opinion until after visiting Jackson at the hospital on Monday, May 10, but since Frankfurter had received his copy of the draft only a few days earlier, he can scarcely be characterized as having been a holdout.*

Warren personally delivered his draft opinions to Jackson's hospital room and left them for the ailing Justice to study. "I think he was greatly relieved by the Chief's opinion," says Barrett Prettyman, who was with Jackson at the time.

Jackson gave his trusted clerk his copy of the draft and asked him to read it. "I went out in the hall and went over it," Prettyman recounts. "When I came back in, he asked me what I thought of it. I said that I wished that it had more law in it but I didn't find anything glaringly unacceptable in it. The genius of the Warren opinion"—and Prettyman makes clear that he does not rate Warren's performance on the Court generally in the genius category—"was that it was so simple and unobtrusive. He had come from political life and had a keen sense of what you could say in this opinion without getting everybody's back up. His opinion took the sting off the decision, it wasn't accusatory, and it didn't pretend that the Fourteenth Amendment was more helpful than the history suggested—he didn't equivocate on that point."

All those features made Warren's opinion attractive to Jackson, who would probably have preferred a more gracefully executed piece of writing for so important an occasion but was willing to settle for one whose principal virtue seemed to be its temperate tone. Jackson did work up two suggested insertions in the opinion and offered them orally to the Chief Justice when he returned to the hospital later that same day. One of the proposed additions Warren declined to accept because he felt it could be interpreted as being directed toward segregation in general, not only in public education, and as Prettyman puts it, "He wanted the decision to be narrowly circumscribed." But the Chief did accept a one-sentence insertion from Jackson, noting the professional success of Negroes in many fields of endeavor—a far cry from their compulsory benighted state at the time the Fourteenth Amendment was under debate. Jackson, moreover, was still in a weakened state from his heart

---

* In his otherwise estimable biography, *Lawyer's Lawyer: The Life of John W. Davis* (Oxford University Press, 1973), University of Virginia historian William H. Harbaugh discusses the decision-making process in *Brown* in a manner unsatisfactorily casual. He writes: ". . . on May 12, five days before the decision was rendered, Frankfurter, the last holdout, indicated that he would probably sign it." Harbaugh's source note cites S. Sidney Ulmer's essay "Earl Warren and the Brown Decision," *Journal of Politics*, XXXII (August 1971). Professor Ulmer's essay, however, was based solely on the papers and diary of Justice Burton in the Library of Congress, and nothing Ulmer cites—or I have found—in the Burton papers supports his and Harbaugh's conclusion that Frankfurter was "the last holdout" or any sort of holdout. He may have had a number of textual suggestions for the opinion-writer; he usually did. But that would scarcely have qualified him as a resistant signer. That Frankfurter was strongly committed to the decision months before Warren circulated his opinion was evidenced by the mid-January 1954 memorandum on the implementation decree (cited above) that the Justice circulated to the Court; he would hardly have been working on a decree to implement a decision he did not favor.

condition and would have been likely to activate his concurrence memorandum only if Warren's opinion had seemed to him a piece of irresponsible butchery.

Having decided to join in the Chief's opinion, Jackson was absolutely determined that the Court should give it solid backing. Even if he were not fully recuperated, he would try to make it to the courtroom on the day the Chief was ready to read the opinion.

On May 12, Burton wrote in his diary: ". . . The Chief Justice also read to me his latest revision (slight) of his drafts in the *Segregation* cases. It looks like a unanimous opinion. A major accomplishment for his leadership. . . ." The entry invites the inference that the Chief had by then won over the Court's would-be dissenter, Stanley Reed.

To his brethren, Reed was anything but a petulant loner. On the contrary, he was an amiable, even-tempered colleague, and the rest of the Justices recognized that his position in the segregation cases stemmed from a deeply held conviction that the nation had been taking big strides in race relations and that the Court's decision to outlaw separate schools threatened to impede that march, if not halt it altogether. There was never a breakdown in the dialogue between Reed and the Chief Justice, who, in addition to all their other contacts during the Court's regular business, lunched together along with the genial Burton at least twenty times between the December conference at which the cases were first discussed and the middle of May. At the end, Warren put it to him directly, according to Reed's clerk, George Mickum, who was on hand at one of the Chief Justice's final interviews with the Kentuckian.

"He said, 'Stan, you're all by yourself in this now,'" Mickum recalls. " 'You've got to decide whether it's really the best thing for the country.' He was not particularly eloquent and certainly not bombastic. Throughout, the Chief Justice was quite low-key and very sensitive to the problems that the decision would present to the South. He empathized with Justice Reed's concern. But he was quite firm on the Court's need for unanimity on a matter of this sensitivity."

After the Chief Justice had left, Reed asked Mickum, who had been raised in a community with segregated schools, how he felt about the Justice's going along with the rest of the Court. Mickum, a man not notably more convinced of the natural equality of the Negro than Reed himself was, suggested that the demands of conscience seemed to require his going beyond the knowable facts in the case and asking himself, as Warren had, what was best for America. "I think he was really troubled by the possible consequences of his position," Mickum adds. "Because he was a Southerner, even a lone dissent by him would give a lot of people a lot of grist for making trouble. For the good of the country, he put aside his own basis for dissent." The only condition he extracted from Warren for going along, Mickum believes, was a pledge that the Court implementation decree would allow segregation to be dismantled gradually instead of being wrenched apart.

The Warren opinion was "finally approved" at the May 15 conference,

Burton noted in his diary. The man from California had won the support of every member of the Court.

Not long before the Court's decision in *Brown* was announced, Warren told *Ebony* magazine twenty years later, he had decided to spend a few days visiting Civil War monuments in Virginia. He went by automobile with a black chauffeur.

At the end of the first day, the Chief Justice's car pulled up at a hotel, where he had made arrangements to spend the night. Warren simply assumed that his chauffeur would stay somewhere else, presumably at a less expensive place. When the Chief Justice came out of his hotel the next morning to resume his tour, he soon figured out that the chauffeur had spent the night in the car. He asked the black man why.

"Well, Mr. Chief Justice," the chauffeur began, "I just couldn't find a place—couldn't find a place to . . ."

Warren was stricken by his own thoughtlessness in bringing an employee of his to a town where lodgings were not available to the man solely because of his color. "I was embarrassed, I was ashamed," Warren recalled. "We turned back immediately. . . ."

# 26

# Simple Justice

In the press room on the ground floor, reporters filing in at the tail end of the morning were advised that May 17, 1954, looked like a quiet day at the Supreme Court of the United States.

All of the opinions of the Court were announced on Mondays in that era. The ritual was simple and unvarying. The Justices convened at noon. Lawyers seeking admission to the Supreme Court bar were presented to the Court by their sponsors, greeted briefly by the Chief Justice, and sworn in by the clerk of the Court. Then, in ascending order of seniority, the Justices with opinions to deliver read them aloud, every word usually, without much effort at dramaturgy. Concurrences and dissents were read after the majority opinion. And then the next case, and then the next. There was no applause; there were no catcalls. There were no television or newsreel cameras. There were no questions from the newsmen in the audience. There was no briefing session in the press room or the Justices' chambers after Court adjourned. There were no weekly press conferences. There were no appearances on *Meet the Press* the following Sunday. There were no press releases elaborating on what the Court had said or meant or done. The opinions themselves were all there was.

The routine was generally so cut-and-dried that most veteran newsmen covering the Court did not bother going upstairs to hear the opinions being read by the Justices in none too sonorous voices. The quicker way to learn what the Court was up to was to wait by the phones and typewriters in the press room. As soon as the reading of a decision began in the courtroom, a message to that effect was dispatched by pneumatic tube to the press room, where printed copies of that opinion—and that opinion only—were taken from an office safe and distributed to the thirty or so reporters on the premises. They could read it a lot faster to themselves than could the Justice delivering it out loud in the courtroom. That saving in time mattered, since the decisions of the Court often made the front pages of the evening papers that were already beginning to come off the presses. Too often, the pressure to get the gist of the Court's decisions to the media caused the intention of the Justices to be garbled in those first dispatches. Many of the cases before the Court, after all, dealt with matters of great complexity, and the nuances of constitutional law did not make easy front-page reading. But the news this day would not be garbled.

Had they been on the lookout for clues, reporters might have found one to suggest that they were on hand for an historic day. Justice Robert Jackson, just seven weeks after having suffered a serious heart attack, returned to the Court that morning, well before the normal recuperative period had expired. Looking thinner, older, and wan from his ordeal, he arrived as unobtrusively as possible: by a little-used entrance and then the Justices' private elevator en route to the robing room near the Court itself.

Word of Jackson's imminent return had preceded him that morning among some of the clerks to the other Justices. In Tom Clark's chambers, clerk Ellis H. McKay, a thirty-year-old native of western Pennsylvania and graduate of the University of Pennsylvania Law School, compared notes with twenty-five-year-old Ernest Rubenstein, who had grown up in New York City and excelled at Yale's School of Law. Justice Clark had said almost nothing about the school-segregation cases to his clerks during that term, and those clerks who were privy to any part of the opinion-writing in *Brown* (such as Earl Pollock working with the Chief Justice, Barrett Prettyman with Justice Jackson, John Fassett and George Mickum with Justice Reed, and Frank Sander, who was permitted a quick advance reading of the opinion by Justice Frankfurter) were constrained from discussing the subject at the clerks' daily luncheon sessions, which normally were non-stop bull sessions on the business of the Court. McKay had to go down to the Court's basement print shop on the morning of May 17 to pick up copies of an opinion Justice Clark was to deliver that day. While in the shop, he spotted a very large wrapped package of opinions that was not marked with the docket number of the case, as was customary. Its size and mysterious anonymity he reported to Rubenstein, who in turn had heard about Jackson's return to the Court. These unmistakable signs of big doings were confirmed by Justice Clark, who stopped for a moment on his way to the robing room just before noon and said to the clerks, as Rubenstein recalls, "I think you boys ought to be in the courtroom today." More often than not, the clerks would work while the Court was in session; in most cases, they were thoroughly familiar with the opinions being read. In many instances, they had helped draft them. This day was different, though. Justice Clark did not tell Rubenstein and McKay why. He did not have to.

They stood in the alcove on the left side of the great ceremonial room. Rubenstein recalls watching Dean G. Acheson, the retired Secretary of State, come before the Court that noon to sponsor his son's membership with the words, "Mr. Chief Justice, I have the honor to move the admission of David Campion Acheson of the bar of the District of Columbia. I am satisfied that he possesses the necessary qualifications." Since the qualifications were none too rigid—membership for three years in the highest court of a state or territory, written endorsement by two members of the Supreme Court bar, and a $25 fee—there was no shortage of lawyers applying for the certificate, which, when tastefully framed and prominently installed on the office wall, added cubits to their stature in the eyes of clients. On May 17, 1954, young Acheson was one of 118 lawyers to be admitted to the bar of the nation's highest court. Also being admitted that morning was Roman Lee Hruska, an

Omaha lawyer then serving his first term in the House of Representatives and to be elevated later that year to the United States Senate, where he would pass more than twenty years in uncelebrated mediocrity. What was remarkable about the otherwise monotonous admission ceremony was the enthusiasm which the Chief Justice somehow brought to it. As each candidate for the Court's bar appeared before him, Earl Warren smiled broadly, pronounced the lawyer's name distinctly, and bade him or her a brief but hearty and apparently genuine welcome. A large man made larger still by his black silk robe, he had a full head of white hair and spoke in a flinty bass that combined to project massive majesty and strength. But there was a saving warmth that kept him from ever quite seeming forbidding.

At about half after noon, the admission ceremony concluded, the Chief Justice turned to Justice Clark, who read the opinion of the Court in case No. 464 on the docket, *United States v. Borden Company.* The Court affirmed a judgment that Borden had not engaged in monopolistic practices in the sale of milk in the Chicago area. Justice Douglas went next with No. 398, *Capital Service, Inc. v. National Labor Relations Board,* in which the Court held that the federal government was not entitled to collect an indemnity from an employee found guilty of negligence. Douglas also read the Court's opinion in No. 449, dealing with the right of a bakery workers' union to picket retail stores.

Down in the press room, as the first three routine opinions were distributed, it looked, as predicted, like a very quiet day at the Court. But then, as Douglas finished up, Clerk of the Court Harold Willey dispatched a pneumatic message to Banning E. Whittington, the Court's dour press officer. Whittington slipped on his suit jacket, advised the press-room contingent, "Reading of the segregation decisions is about to begin in the courtroom," added as he headed out the door that the text of the opinion would be distributed in the press room afterward, and then led the scrambling reporters in a dash up the marble stairs.

"I have for announcement," said Earl Warren, "the judgment and opinion of the Court in No. 1—*Oliver Brown et al. v. Board of Education of Topeka.*" It was 12:52 p.m. In the press room, the Associated Press wire carried the first word to the country: "Chief Justice Warren today began reading the Supreme Court's decision in the public school segregation cases. The court's ruling could not be determined immediately." The bells went off in every news room in America. The nation was listening.

It was Warren's first major opinion as Chief Justice. He read it, by all accounts, in a firm, clear, unemotional voice. If he had delivered no other opinion but this one, he would have won his place in American history.

Considering its magnitude, it was a short opinion. During its first part, no one hearing it could tell where it would come out.

These four state cases had reached the Court by different routes, the opinion began, but had been consolidated because each dealt with "minors of the Negro race" who sought admission to public schools closed to them under "the so-called 'separate but equal' doctrine announced by this Court in *Plessy v. Ferguson,* 163 U.S. 537." The Justices had heard reargument that "exhaustively" considered the circumstances surrounding the adoption of the Fourteenth Amendment, the reach and intention of which were at the core of the segregation dispute. "This discussion and our own investigation convince us," announced Warren, "that although these sources cast some light, it is not enough to resolve the problem with which we are faced. At best, they are inconclusive." Thurgood Marshall had won his "nothin'-to-nothin' " standoff on the historical question.

Another reason why the amendment's history did not much help the Court resolve the issue was the primitive nature of public education at the time of its adoption, the Chief Justice said. In the South, where the movement to free common schools supported by general taxation had not yet taken hold, the education of white children was largely in the hands of private groups, while education of Negroes was almost non-existent, "and practically all of the race were illiterate. In fact, any education of Negroes was forbidden by law. . . . Today, in contrast, many Negroes have achieved outstanding success in the arts and sciences as well as in the business and professional world." It was not surprising, then, that "there should be so little in the history of the Fourteenth Amendment relating to its intended effect on public education."

Warren then turned to the Court's understanding of the amendment. In the first cases coming to it soon after the adoption of the amendment, "the Court interpreted it as proscribing all state-imposed discriminations against the Negro race," the Chief Justice said, citing in a footnote the *Slaughter-house Cases* and *Strauder v. West Virginia* decisions and quoting from the latter the well-known passage that "the law in the States shall be the same for the black as for the white. . . ." That was the way the Court had originally construed the reach of the amendment; "separate but equal" did not surface as a doctrine of the Court until two decades later, and when it did, it involved not education but transportation. "American courts have since labored with the doctrine for over half a century."

Having established that *Plessy* was a relative johnny-come-lately, Warren sounded as if he were about to direct criticism at it for its departure from the Court's earlier view of the amendment as prohibiting all racial discriminations under law. But he did not do that. Indeed, he seemed to take pains to establish the longevity of the separate-but-equal doctrine, which he said in a footnote had apparently had its genesis in *Roberts v. City of Boston* in 1849. He did not choose to note that the Massachusetts case had antedated the Fourteenth Amendment by nineteen years, though he did indicate that the state legislature had ended school segregation six years after the decision. With scrupulous fairness, though, the note added: "But elsewhere in the North segregation in public education has persisted until recent years. It is apparent that such segregation has long been a nationwide problem, not merely one of sectional concern." The Court was clearly taking pains not to level a finger at the South.

Six times after *Plessy*, the Court had dealt with cases involving the separate-but-equal doctrine in the field of education, the opinion continued. In two of the cases, *Cumming* and *Gong Lum*, "the validity of the doctrine itself was not challenged," the Chief Justice noted. He cited *Berea College v. Kentucky* in a footnote without comment, though he might have remarked that in that case, too, the doctrine itself was involved only tangentially. In the more recent cases—*Gaines, Sipuel, Sweatt,* and *McLaurin*—it had not proven necessary to re-examine "the doctrine to grant relief to the Negro plaintiff." In fact, the Court in *Sweatt* had "expressly reserved decision on the question of whether *Plessy v. Ferguson* should be held inapplicable to public education." But that question was now presented directly to the Court in the instant cases, where the courts below had found that the Negro and white schools had been—or were being—equalized in terms of the school buildings, curricula, qualifications and salaries of the teachers, and other "tangible" factors. To settle the question of *Plessy*'s applicability, said Warren, the Court could therefore not compare merely the tangible factors: "We must look instead to the effect of segregation itself on public education."

Without in any way becoming technical and rhetorical, Warren then proceeded to demonstrate the dynamic nature and adaptive genius of American constitutional law:

> In approaching this problem, we cannot turn the clock back to 1868 when the Amendment was adopted, or even to 1896 when *Plessy v. Ferguson* was written. We must consider public education in the light of its full development and its present place in American life throughout the Nation. . . .
>
> Today, education is perhaps the most important function of state and local governments. Compulsory school attendance laws and the great expenditures for education both demonstrate our recognition of the importance of education to our democratic society. It is required in the performance of our most basic public responsibilities, even service in the armed forces. It is the very foundation of good citizenship. . . .

Having declared its essential value to the nation's civic health and vitality, he then argued for the central importance of education in the private life and aspirations of every individual:

> . . . Today it is a principal instrument in awakening the child to cultural values, in preparing him for later professional training, and in helping him to adjust normally to his environment. In these days, it is doubtful that any child may reasonably be expected to succeed in life if he is denied the opportunity of an education. Such an opportunity, where the state has undertaken to provide it, is a right which must be made available to all on equal terms.

That led finally to the critical question: "Does segregation of children in public schools solely on the basis of race . . . deprive the children of the minority group of equal educational opportunities?"

To this point, nearly two-thirds through the opinion, Warren had not tipped his hand. Now, in the next sentence, he showed it by answering that critical question: "We believe that it does."

At 1:12 p.m., the Associated Press sent out its second bulletin: The Chief Justice, it said, was attacking segregation in schools, but he "had not read far enough into the court's opinion for newsmen to say that segregation was being struck down as unconstitutional."

Earl Warren read on.

In *Sweatt v. Painter*, the Chief Justice declared, the Court had relied on "those qualities which are incapable of objective measurement" in holding that the all-black law school did not provide the plaintiff with an educational opportunity equal to that offered white students at the University of Texas. In *McLaurin v. Oklahoma State Regents*, similarly, the treatment given to the plaintiff caused him to suffer by affecting him in such intangible areas as ". . . his ability to study, to engage in discussions and exchange views with other students, and, in general, to learn his profession." Now Warren swept aside the argument by the South that unsegregated higher education, involving mature young people, was quite a different story from compulsory schooling in the more formative years. Extending the *Sweatt-McLaurin* line of logic, he asserted: "Such considerations apply with added force to children in grade and high schools." In the only soaring passage in the opinion, he went on:

> To separate them from others of similar age and qualifications solely because of their race generates a feeling of inferiority as to their status in the community that may affect their hearts and minds in a way unlikely ever to be undone.

To brace this compassionate declaration, he invoked the finding of the Kansas court, which in turn had been based largely on the testimony of the witness Louisa Holt: Segregation, with its detrimental effect on colored children, had a still more severe impact "when it has the sanction of the law; for the policy of separating the races is usually interpreted as denoting the inferiority of the Negro group. A sense of inferiority affects the motivation of a child to learn. Segregation with the sanction of law, therefore, has a tendency to retard the educational and mental development of Negro children. . . ."

This finding flew directly in the face of *Plessy*. And here, finally, Warren collided with the 1896 decision. But he did so in such an economical and uncontentious way that the basic dishonesty of *Plessy* was allowed to escape censure and seemed instead to be dismissed as simply no longer fashionable thinking. *Plessy* had said that "the underlying fallacy" of the Negro plaintiff's complaint was its "assumption that the enforced separation of the two races stamps the colored race with a badge of inferiority. If this be so, it is not by reason of anything found in the act, but solely because the colored race chooses to put that construction upon it." Warren, in response now to this piece of enshrined disingenuousness, said simply: "Whatever may have been the extent of psychological knowledge at the time of *Plessy v. Ferguson*, this finding [by the Kansas court in *Brown* that segregation denotes inferiority and diminishes learning motivation] is amply supported by modern authority. Any language in *Plessy v. Ferguson* contrary to this finding is rejected."

To buttress such a brisk dismissal of *Plessy*'s essence, Warren added a footnote—the eleventh in the opinion and destined to become one of the most debated in the annals of the Court. Footnote #11 was merely a list of seven works by contemporary social scientists, all of which had been cited in the NAACP briefs during litigation of the school cases. First on the list, and the highest tribute to his contribution to the overall NAACP effort, was "K. B. Clark, *Effect of Prejudice and Discrimination on Personality Development* (Midcentury White House Conference on Children and Youth, 1950)." A bit farther down on the list was "Deutscher and Chein, *The Psychological Effects of Enforced Segregation: A Survey of Social Science Opinion,* 26 J. Psychol. 259 (1948)." It was Isidor Chein's reward for withstanding the personal and professional assault made on him on the witness stand in Richmond by Justin Moore in the name of the commonwealth of Virginia. The footnote wound up with two massive books: "[E. Franklin] Frazier, *The Negro in the United States* (1949). . . . And see generally Myrdal, *An American Dilemma.*"

To Warren, it had seemed an innocuous enough item to insert in the opinion. "We included it because I thought the point it made was the antithesis of what was said in *Plessy,*" he later commented. "They had said there that if there was any harm intended, it was solely in the mind of the Negro. I thought these things—these cited sources—were sufficient to note as being in contradistinction to that statement in *Plessy.*" Then he added, by way of stressing that the sociology was merely supportive and not the substance of the holding, "It was only a note, after all." Warren's clerk Earl Pollock, one of those closest to the writing of the opinion, puts it more bluntly: "The only reason to have included footnote # 11 was as a rebuttal to the cheap psychology of *Plessy* that said inferiority was only in the mind of the Negro. The Chief Justice was saying in effect that we know a lot more now about how human beings work than they did back then and can therefore cast doubt on that preposterous line of argument."

But the footnote apparently provoked at least mild concern among several members of the Court, especially the last part of the listed authorities. "I questioned the Chief's going with Myrdal in the opinion," recalls retired Justice Tom Clark. "I told him—and Hugo Black did, too—that it wouldn't go down well in the South. And he didn't need it." Myrdal's compendious assault on the brutalities of American racism had by then, a decade after its publication, become a dagger in the flesh of the white South; its author, moreover, was both foreign and leftward-tilting in his political orientation and therefore prone to ready vilification throughout the old Confederacy. That two of the three Southerners on the Court may have cautioned Warren* against the very mention of Myrdal's scholarly masterwork underscored both the wisdom and the necessity of the Chief Justice's insistence on making the opinion as bland and non-accusatory as possible. Any pointed language would almost surely have shattered the unanimity Warren had won. "You know," adds Justice Clark, "we don't have money at the Court for an army and we can't take ads in the newspapers, and we don't want to go out on a picket line in our robes. We have to convince the nation by the force of our opinions."

It was this very need not to offend, though, that seemed to make the

---

* Warren's clerk Earl Pollock believes that if any of the other Justices had objected strongly to the footnote—especially Hugo Black—it would most likely have been struck by the Chief Justice.

inclusion of footnote #11 forceless and therefore gratuitously obnoxious. Alexander Bickel, capsulizing the criticism that was to descend on the inclusion of the footnote, commented: "It was a mistake to do it this way. If you're going to invoke sociology and psychology, do it right. Invoking Kenneth Clark was a mistake because of the vulnerability of the doll tests, which John Davis had so effectively demolished. Yes, the Court was justified to have included such references as a Brandeisian move, but it should not have been just dropped in like that. No matter how it had been done, no doubt, the enemies of the opinion were certain to seize upon it and proclaim the ruling unjudicial and illegal. The opinion therefore should have said straightforwardly that *Plessy* was based on a self-invented philosophy, no less psychologically oriented than the Court was being now in citing these sources to justify the holding that segregation inflicted damage. It was clear, though, that Warren wanted to present as small a target as possible, and that was wise. He did not want to go out to the country wearing a Hussar's uniform."

The balance of the Chief Justice's opinion consisted of just two paragraphs. The first began: "We conclude"—and here Warren departed from the printed text before him to insert the word "unanimously," which sent a sound of muffled astonishment eddying around the courtroom—"that in the field of public education the doctrine of 'separate but equal' has no place. Separate educational facilities are inherently unequal." The plaintiffs and others similarly situated—technically meaning Negro children within the segregated school districts under challenge—were therefore being deprived of the equal protection of the laws guaranteed by the Fourteenth Amendment.

The concluding paragraph of the opinion revealed Earl Warren's political adroitness both at compromise and at the ready use of the power of his office for ends he thought worthy. "Because these are class actions, because of the wide applicability of this decision, and because of the great variety of local conditions," he declared, "these cases present problems of considerable complexity. . . . In order that we may have the full assistance of the parties in formulating decrees," the Court was scheduling further argument for the term beginning the following fall. The attorneys general of the United States and all the states requiring or permitting segregation in public education were invited to participate. In a few strokes, Warren thus managed to (1) proclaim "the wide applicability" of the decision and make it plain that the Court had no intention of limiting its benefits to a handful of plaintiffs in a few outlying districts; (2) reassure the South that the Court understood the emotional wrench desegregation would cause and was therefore granting the region some time to get accustomed to the idea; and (3) invite the South to participate in the entombing of Jim Crow by joining the Court's efforts to fashion a temperate implementation decree—or to forfeit that chance by petulantly abstaining from the Court's further deliberations and thereby run the risk of having a harsh decree imposed upon it. It was such dexterous use of the power available to him and of the circumstances in which to exploit it that had established John Marshall as a judicial statesman and political tactician of the most formidable sort. The

Court had not seen his like since. Earl Warren, in his first major opinion, moved now with that same sure purposefulness.

He turned next to the District of Columbia case, *Bolling v. Sharpe*, and disposed of it in similar fashion in six paragraphs.

"Classifications based solely upon race must be scrutinized with particular care, since they are contrary to our traditions and hence constitutionally suspect," the Chief Justice asserted, pursuing a line of argument that had been basic to the entire NAACP legal effort but that Warren had not bothered to introduce into the opinion on the state cases that he had just delivered. As source for his warning against racial classifications, he cited with unspoken irony the Court's decisions in *Korematsu v. United States* and *Hirabayashi v. United States*, upholding the mass wartime removal of Japanese-Americans from their West Coast homes—an act of dishonor that Earl Warren had promoted as vigorously as any other man in the nation. Now he declared that such a wholesale deprivation of due process of law was involved in the imposition of segregated education in the District of Columbia, where the protections of the Fourteenth Amendment did not extend. In thus invoking the Fifth Amendment guarantee against denial of life, liberty, or property without due process by the federal government, Warren elaborated for just a moment on the nature of that denial:

> Although the Court has not assumed to define "liberty" with any great precision, that term is not confined to mere freedom from bodily restraint. Liberty under law extends to the full range of conduct which the individual is free to pursue, and it cannot be restricted except for a proper governmental objective. Segregation in public education is not reasonably related to any proper governmental objective, and thus it imposes on Negro children of the District of Columbia a burden that constitutes an arbitrary deprivation of their liberty in violation of the Due Process Clause.
>
> In view of our decision that the Constitution prohibits the states from maintaining racially segregated public schools, it would be unthinkable that the same Constitution would impose a lesser duty on the Federal Government. . . .

It was 1:20 p.m. The wire services proclaimed the news to the nation. Within the hour, the Voice of America would begin beaming word to the world in thirty-four languages: In the United States, schoolchildren could no longer be segregated by race. The law of the land no longer recognized a separate equality. No Americans were more equal than any other Americans. Jim Crow was on the way to the burial ground.

"I felt good—and clean," remembers Tom Clark's clerk Ernest Rubenstein, looking out on that historic tableau from an alcove of the Court. "It was so right."

Stanley Reed's clerk George Mickum saw tears on his Justice's face as the last words of the two opinions were spoken. It was Reed whose yielding at the end of the Court's deliberative process had given the decision its extra, crucial dimension: the Justices had spoken as one. A unanimous opinion of the Court inspires a measure of respect and obedience that even a single dissent bespatters. A single opinion says that the nine men have in union apprehended truth and now reveal it; more than one opinion suggests that truth may be glimpsed from many angles—or that there is none, only conflicting opinion among mere mortals, and that another season may bring a different outcome. "I am not unaware of the hard struggle this involved in the conscience of your mind," Felix Frankfurter wrote to Stanley Reed three days later. "I am not unaware because all I have to do is look within. As a citizen of the Republic, even more than as a colleague, I feel deep gratitude for your share in what I believe to be a great good for our nation."

A few weeks later, when Reed's other clerk that term, John Fassett, said goodbye to the Justice, he asked him which had been the most important case the Court had decided during the fifteen years he had sat on it. "He replied that there was no question in his mind but that the segregation case so ranked," Fassett recalls, "and that if it was not the most important decision in the history of the Court, it was very close."

The great wave of enthusiasm for the decision that first rippled over much of the land bore with it Reed's glowing estimate of *Brown.* There was instant recognition that far more than a narrow judicial pronouncement had been made. Something basic in American lives and values had been touched. "In its 164 years the court had erected many a landmark of U.S. history," declared that week's *Time.* "None of them except the Dred Scott case (reversed by the Civil War) was more important than the school segregation issue. None of them directly and intimately affected so many American families."

It was not only how many people the decision affected that mattered; it was the way it affected them—inside. Having proclaimed the equality of all men in the preamble to the Declaration of Independence, the nation's founders had then elected, out of deference to the slaveholding South, to omit that definition of equalitarian democracy from the Constitution. It took a terrible civil war to correct that omission. But the Civil War amendments were soon drained of their original intention to lift the black man to meaningful membership in American society. The Court itself would do much to assist in that process, and *Plessy* was its most brutal blow. Congress passed no civil-rights laws after the Court-eviscerated one of 1875, and those that remained on the books were largely ignored by the states and unenforced by federal administrations that ranged in their attitudes from the racism of the Wilson regime to the largely ineffectual friendship of the Truman presidency. Since the expedient demolition of Reconstruction, white America had lost enthusiasm for the ennobling language of equalitarianism. The Negro, technically liberated from bondage, was expected to shift on his own. But he was no more welcomed in the North and the West than he was embraced in the South, which derived a perverse solace for its own troubled fortunes by kicking around his black hide. Denied high skills or advanced learning, he remained a superfluous and lower order of American being, excess baggage in the nation's rush to prosperity and greatness. At most, he was there to keep the American dream brightly polished and fetch cool libations for its white beneficiaries. The law, as interpreted by the Supreme

Court, had pronounced it permissible—indeed, it was normal and expected —to degrade black America.

It was into this moral void that the Supreme Court under Earl Warren now stepped. Its opinion in *Brown v. Board of Education*, for all its economy, represented nothing short of a reconsecration of American ideals. At a moment when the country had just begun to sense the magnitude of its global ideological contest with Communist authoritarianism and was quick to measure its own worth in terms of megaton power, the opinion of the Court said that the United States still stood for something more than material abundance, still moved to an inner spirit, however deeply it had been submerged by fear and envy and mindless hate. "What the Justices have done," editorialized the Cincinnati *Enquirer*, "is simply to act as the conscience of the American nation." The Court had restored to the American people a measure of the humanity that had been drained away in their climb to worldwide supremacy. The Court said, without using the words, that that ascent had been made over the backs of black America— and that when you stepped on a black man, he hurt. The time had come to stop.

The reaction within the black community was muted. There was no dancing on the tables in Harlem. Race leaders such as Ralph Bunche were pleased but cautious in their comments. Commendatory editorials appeared throughout the black press, to be sure, along with calls for prayers of thanksgiving, but the mood of overall wariness in colored America was suggested by the *Courier*'s columnist Nat D. Williams, writing out of Beale Street in Memphis. "There was no general 'hallelujah, 'tis done' hullabaloo on Beale Street over the Supreme Court's admission that segregation in the public schools is wrong," wrote Williams. "Beale Streeters are sorta skeptical about giving out with cheers yet." Too many proclamations of white America's good intentions had reached black America's ears in the past to permit premature celebration now. There was added hesitation, no doubt, in expressing open glee lest it be taken as a sign of gratitude and thereby provide whites the emotional satisfaction over a deed well done. For, upon analysis, all the Supreme Court had truly and at long last granted to the black man was simple justice.

Not everyone agreed, of course.

The white-supremacists of the South were swift and shrill in their outcry. Governor Herman Talmadge of Georgia asserted that the Court's decision had reduced the Constitution to "a mere scrap of paper." The Justices "had blatantly ignored all law and precedent and usurped from the Congress and the people the power to amend the Constitution, and from the Congress the authority to make the laws of the land." Senator Byrd of Virginia called the decision "the most serious blow that has yet been struck against the rights of the states in a matter vitally affecting their authority and welfare." Governor Umstead of North Carolina was "terribly disappointed." Governor Byrnes of South Carolina was "shocked." Senator Eastland of Mississippi was defiant: the South, he said, "will not abide by or obey this legislative decision by a political court." Any effort to integrate Southern schools would lead to "great strife and turmoil."

More mellow and modulated voices, though, were heard in the South as well. Governor Thomas Stanley of Virginia said the *Brown* decision called for "cool heads, calm study, and sound judgment." He promised to consult "leaders of both races" in his state. Dean Frederick Ribble of the University of Virginia Law School said he thought the problems implicit in the decision would be met "in good will and in full accord with the spirit and the letter of the law." At the University of North Carolina, the South's foremost social scientist, Howard Odum, said: "The South is likely to surprise itself and the nation and do an excellent job of readjustment. We might want to delay a little so we can get ready, but in my opinion, the South for the most part will take it in stride." The Louisville *Courier-Journal* editorialized that "the end of the world has not come for the South or for the nation. The Supreme Court's ruling is not itself a revolution. It is rather acceptance of a process that has been going on a long time. People everywhere could well match the court's moderation and caution." Said the Atlanta *Constitution*: "It is no time to indulge demagogues on either side or those who are always ready to incite violence and hatred. . . . It is a time for Georgians to think clearly."

By declining to proclaim a crash deadline for the end of segregation, the Court had plainly succeeded in muting the initial response to its decision in the South. The region's most vocal extremists had nothing firm yet at which to direct their fire. But there were early signs elsewhere that Earl Warren's opinion, for all its moderation and caution, lacked the depth and persuasiveness ideal to withstand the criticism that would be directed at it even by those who strongly approved of its purpose. In the *New York Times* of May 18, 1954, columnist James Reston offered his instant analysis of *Brown*; the headline to his piece—"A Sociological Decision"—was a bellwether of the rebuke that would grow in the following months and years, even as the influence of the decision itself multiplied. The Court had rejected "history, philosophy and custom" in basing its decision on "the primacy of the general welfare," wrote Reston, one of the clearest-sighted newsmen in America. "Relying more on the social scientists than on legal precedents—a procedure often in controversy in the past—the Court insisted on equality of the mind and heart rather than on equal school facilities. . . . The Court's opinion read more like an expert paper on sociology than a Supreme Court opinion."

Though overstated, Reston's view was invited by Warren's own insistence that the opinions be "short, readable by the lay public, non-rhetorical, unemotional and, above all, non-accusatory." Those were all admirable qualities to bring to the delicate task. The price paid for them, however, was a loss of persuasiveness and judicial authority. There were at least four major contentions that the Court might have put forward in part or in whole as building blocks in the *Brown* opinion:

(1) Instead of dismissing the historical evidence surrounding the adoption of the Fourteenth Amendment as inconclusive with regard to segregated schools, the Court might have noted that the overall purpose of the three Civil War amendments had been, by wide assent, to provide full

citizenship to the Negro and to wipe away all state-imposed discriminations against him. That this explicit purpose had been the Court's initial understanding of the equal-protection clause, *Brown* did in fact note, but it did so with almost whispered modesty, relying solely on the oft-quoted lines from *Strauder* and declining to quote from the *Slaughterhouse Cases* and other pertinent precedents. The Warren Court might profitably have said that it was to this original understanding of the Fourteenth Amendment that it was now returning; instead, it merely noted that *Plessy* had postdated these early cases. In noting that the primitive state of public education had made the legality of segregated schools an unlikely concern of the framers of the amendment, *Brown* might also have made the obvious point that the Court had not hesitated to apply the amendment to many issues and many litigants evidently not contemplated by the framers at the time of its adoption—the protection of corporations was perhaps the most prominent example—since the Constitution had been interpreted from the first not as a static but as an organic body of basic principles, to be prudently applied to ever new civic and political needs as time and technology required.

(2) Having gingerly introduced *Strauder*'s ringing endorsement of the Fourteenth Amendment as prohibiting all state-imposed racial discrimination, the Court failed entirely to narrate the impressive catalogue of ensuing decisions that struck down racial-classification laws. Only in *Bolling v. Sharpe* did the Warren opinion explore the subject, and then it relied on the two Japanese-American relocation cases, which in fact upheld, albeit with extreme reluctance, the totalitarian step. The whole family of voting-rights cases, beginning with the "grandfather clause" decision in *Guinn v. United States* in 1915, was directly relevant. All such classification laws could be legitimized only by a rational purpose behind the state action; vague allusions to protecting the public safety were not sufficient, as the Court had asserted in throwing out Louisville's ghetto-building residential-segregation law in *Buchanan v. Warley* in 1917. And if segregated housing was illegal, why was not segregated schooling also? To justify separate schools, the South would have had to demonstrate in rational terms—not merely by allusions to imposed custom—why all Negro children were unfit to mingle with white ones. No such showing had been made in any of the cases, as the Court could have noted.

(3) Though fair on its face, the separate-but-equal doctrine had been implemented, in the fifty-eight years since the Court legitimized it, in a manner that blatantly deprived Negroes of equal educational opportunities. The documentary evidence of this habitual inequality in terms of measurable, tangible factors was overwhelming—and a classic instance of a law that, however fair in theory, had been administered "with an evil eye and an unequal hand, so as practically to make unjust and illegal discriminations between persons in similar circumstances," to quote the Court's 1886 decision of *Yick Wo v. Hopkins*. Here was a famous precedent that antedated and yet exactly anticipated the *Plessy* doctrine, and was available to doom it.

(4) Warren's opinion had given *Plessy* itself the merest nudge of the elbow. It failed entirely to challenge, in explicit words, the 1896 assertion that

"enforced segregation of the two races stamps the colored race with a badge of inferiority . . . not by reason of anything found in the act, but solely because the colored race chooses to put that construction upon it." Most Americans had never heard of or read a line of the *Plessy* decision, and to air a few of its mendacious words and rebut them by common-sense reasoning, not merely by vague reference to contrary "modern authority," would have added conviction to *Brown*. The Court might have inquired rhetorically, for example, why segregation laws were in fact imposed in the first place if the white majority did not believe the Negro to be inferior. And what message other than his own low worth might a human being conceivably be expected to read into segregation that was, as *Plessy* acknowledged, "enforced" upon him? To say, as *Plessy* did, that Jim Crow laws neither imposed nor implied inequality was cruelly deceitful, and *Brown* might have said just that without invoking Myrdal or anyone else. More effective yet, it might have offered testimony on the corrosive effects of segregation by not only Kenneth Clark, a Negro, Isidor Chein, a Jewish New Yorker, and Gunnar Myrdal, a Swedish socialist, but also such well-regarded writers and scholars as W. J. Cash, a native and longtime resident of the Carolinas, Howard Odum *(Southern Regions of the United States)*, and John Dollard *(Caste and Class in a Southern Town)*.

Even without probing at the blatant and undocumented psychologizing in *Plessy*, Warren might have riddled the 1896 decision for arguing, "The object of the [Fourteenth] amendment was undoubtedly to enforce the absolute equality of the two races before the law, but in the nature of things it could not have been intended to abolish distinctions based upon color, or to enforce social, as distinguished from political, equality or a commingling of the two races upon terms unsatisfactory to either." In the nature of *what* things? Where in the amendment was any such differentiation noted between political and other kinds of equality? The amendment called for equal protection of *all* the laws. The amendment said nothing about separate-but-equal protection. *Plessy* was based not on constitutional precedent but on the thin air of racism—and so the Court might have asserted in *Brown*.

But Earl Warren was not out to pick a fight. He was not going to the front, as Bickel put it, in a Hussar's uniform. A more stirring or incandescent opinion might have enthroned Warren as a righteous deliverer of the oppressed, but it would more than likely have cost him the unanimity of the Court. And a provocative opinion, launched by a divided Court, would almost certainly have set the South on fire with anger and defiance. Or so the Chief Justice was convinced. As presented to the nation, *Brown* did what Earl Warren, operating by instinct as much as design, wished it to.

Arthur Krock, the senior pundit of the *New York Times*, was not disturbed by the bleached-out quality of the language, the thinness of the legal materials, or the evident reliance on psychological considerations that went into the opinion. Indeed, he was astounded because never before, in his view, had the Court "so simply and briefly disposed of an issue of such magnitude." The unanimity of the Court was "remarkable," he wrote, confounding experts who had anticipated as many as nine separate opinions.

"The fundamental divisions on political philosophy and legal interpretation that have manifested themselves among the present Justices were submerged," Krock wrote in tribute to Warren. "If further arguments had not been called for," he added astutely and probably with inside knowledge, "dissents would have materialized." At the end, he counseled that "those who have been pressing for the decision that came today should be foremost in cooperating with those who are confronted with its incalculable consequences at first hand."

Those who had pressed most assiduously for the *Brown* decision were not lamenting that Earl Warren did not write with the passion of Frederick Douglass. In New York, Thurgood Marshall, twenty-one years after leaving Howard Law School, had won the victory of a lifetime. "I was so happy I was numb," he later recalled. Nobel laureate Ralph Bunche was so excited when the news started moving across the AP wire that he cashed a $35 check at the Chemical Bank and left the money on the counter. "On the basis of early bulletins," he ventured, collecting himself and thanking a bank guard who retrieved the money, "this decision appears to be an historic event in the annals of American democracy." Out in Chicago, black scholar Allison Davis saw the decision as a triumph for the entire nation, not only the Negro part of it: "When this decision is implemented, it will result in a tremendous increase in the fund of ability and skill available to our country. . . . [T]he survival of the United States seems to depend upon its developing the ability of millions of our citizens whose capacities have been crippled by segregation."

At NAACP headquarters, Executive Secretary Walter White grabbed the spotlight. Wiping out housing and job discrimination was next on the agenda, he told a crowded press conference at which Marshall played obedient second fiddle. At his New York apartment, retired federal judge Waties Waring, the South Carolina expatriate, told the press that *Brown* would make history and "erase the shame" of earlier decisions of the Court. That evening, he had over his friend Walter White, and Robert Carter, who had helped argue *Briggs* in Charleston, and some other black and white guests, who shared drinks and listened to appropriate words by the South African writer Alan Paton. Few Americans had written more profoundly about racism than Paton, the title of whose best-known work provided a fitting anthem for that memorable day: *Cry, the Beloved Country*.

The next day's *Times* quoted Thurgood Marshall as predicting that school segregation in America would be entirely stamped out in no more than five years. And by the hundredth anniversary of the Emancipation Proclamation, he exuded, all forms of segregation in America would be eliminated.

Five weeks later, the governor of Virginia, who had greeted the *Brown* decision with moderate words and the pledge to consult with leaders of both races, declared: "I shall use every legal means at my command to continue segregated schools in Virginia."

One year and two weeks would pass between the Court's decision in *Brown* and its issuance of a decree explaining how it wished the process of desegregation to unfold. No one could claim the Justices were acting precipitously.

Further argument had been put down for the early part of the Court's 1954 Term—late October was the most likely date. Over the summer, Felix Frankfurter and Earl Warren exchanged chatty letters, dealing with the segregation question among others. Frankfurter advised the Chief that he had heard from Governor (and ex-Justice) Byrnes of South Carolina, who was apparently making soothing noises and taking a wait-and-see attitude by way of urging the Court to act with similar moderation in fashioning its desegregation directive to the South. Warren advised Frankfurter that he was pleased that Byrnes sounded conciliatory but he could not escape the thought that "he could have been much more helpful, had he been as restrained in recent years." As to the scheduling of the final round of argument in *Brown*, Warren wrote, "I agree with you that it would be sound judgment to place the cases on the calendar shortly after the fast-approaching 'sound and fury' "—a reference to the national elections. Fate, though, once again intervened to protract the litigation.

Robert Jackson, advised by his doctors that he would have to slow down if he wanted to live to a benign old age, chose not to rein in his restless energies. He did not want to function as half a man. Soon after the Court reconvened in the fall, he suffered a second heart attack. It was fatal. He had been a remarkably zestful, charming, civilized man who, for all his achievements, was never able to occupy the seats of power he had most coveted—the White House or the center chair on the Court. He died at sixty-two.

The Court's most important business, of which *Brown* was foremost, now had to mark time. To fill the vacancy, President Eisenhower on November 8 nominated another New Yorker who was every bit Jackson's match as a lawyer—John Marshall Harlan, fifty-five-year-old grandson of the Justice with the same name who had served on the Court for thirty-four years. Of the elder Harlan's many famous dissents, none was more luminous than his sole vote against the Court in *Plessy*. It had been in that dissent that he declared the Constitution to be color-blind and that segregation was indeed a brand of servitude, no matter how the Court tried to minimize it. If there was any single name from the annals of the Court likely to whip up fear and loathing among white-supremacists at that moment, it was that of John Marshall Harlan. The nomination of his namesake to the Court that would set the timetable for desegregation was not Dwight Eisenhower's most tactful stroke. The Southern bitter-enders in the Senate sat on the Harlan nomination for more than four months. The tall, straight-backed lawyer, who at the time of his appointment had been sitting for a year on the United States Court of Appeals for the Second Circuit, took his seat on the high court at the end of March.

The South's concern and annoyance proved somewhat misdirected, for Harlan II, as legal historians sometimes refer to him, turned out to be the conservative conscience of a highly activist Court and, to traditionalists, the ideal follow-up to the Warren appointment. A Princeton graduate and

Rhodes Scholar, Harlan had gone into practice in the mid-Twenties with a top Wall Street law firm that encouraged its members to engage in public service as well as make money. Harlan thus held such varied posts as Assistant U.S. Attorney for the Southern District of New York, counsel for the New York City Board of Higher Education, and chief lawyer for the New York State Crime Commission while also developing into his firm's top trial lawyer with competence in a wide range of fields, including corporate and antitrust matters of numbing complexity. During the Second World War, he headed a handpicked corps of American civilians serving in England to help oversee bombing operations for the Eighth Air Force. On his return to civilian life, he was widely acclaimed as a leader of the New York City bar and headed up its judicial-ethics committee. His qualifications for the nation's highest court were beyond dispute. But until the Dixiecrats vented their spleen, Harlan had to stand aside—and *Brown* with him.

During the fifty-four-week cooling-off period between the Court's pronouncements on school segregation, rancor in the South was modulated, as the Justices had hoped, but apprehension grew rather than subsided during the long wait. The dimension of the issue at stake could not be mistaken.

Technically, the Supreme Court rules only on the cases before it. It functions by precept and example. It examines previously pronounced constitutional principles and then attempts to square them with the particular set of facts presented by the case before it. The rest of the federal judiciary, of course, is expected to follow suit in disposing of similar cases. But the Court does not issue blanket orders to the nation. All it says is that, faced with the same set of facts in a new case, it will probably settle the issue the same way it did the previous time. That assurance does not relieve grieved plaintiffs of the bother, expense, and often heartache of bringing an action to obtain the results that the Court, by its previous rulings in similar cases, implies it would reach anew.

But the school-segregation cases were not like most other cases that came to the Court. To start with, the Justices had reviewed earlier Court rulings on the question and pronounced them no longer applicable. Times and the nation had changed. The Court, then, had no ready example of its own devising to lean upon in determining how the mechanics of desegregation ought to be arranged. Beyond that was the realization that, however narrowly the Court tried to confine its implementation decree, the great social question at issue would pry it open and seek to apply it universally. The place of every black child the Court now ordered admitted to school on an unsegregated basis would be taken by 10,000 others. Would each of them have to go to court, too? For if Harry Briggs in Clarendon County, South Carolina, or Linda Brown in Topeka, Kansas, began to attend school with white children, how could that right be withheld from any black child in the Mississippi Delta?

Should the Court ignore, moreover, or did it really have to take cognizance of the prevailing racial attitudes in segregating communities as it handed down its orders? What judicial notice might it or should it take of the likely difference in parental responses in Topeka, where true integration would place 2 or 3 Negroes in every classroom with 22 or 23 white youngsters, and Summerton, South Carolina, where the process would place 2 or 3 white children in every classroom with 22 or 23 black youngsters? And if the Justices did recognize the difference, under what principle of law might the Court rule that the higher the ratio of black children in a school system, the longer a period of adjustment would be allowed to extend? How, indeed, could any period of delay be legally justified by the Court? Once having been told by the Court that their children had the right to attend unsegregated schools—and assume the full membership in American society emblemized by that right, most Negro families naturally wanted the process to begin as soon as possible. Every day a black youngster was denied admission to desegregated schools—and the educational advantages derived from them— was a fresh deprivation of his constitutional rights, and a day that child could not repurchase at any price.

The segregating South, for its part, wished to postpone the commanded commingling of schoolchildren as long as possible. It wanted every black family who would disturb the settled racial customs of the region to have to fight in court for the privilege of seating its children in the same classrooms with whites—and the longer and costlier the courtroom ordeal, the fewer blacks likely to press their Court-given rights. The South would yield, to be sure, but in its own sweet time. It was neither fair nor reasonable, the region indicated, to expect the South's prompt abandonment of its most strongly held customs and beliefs.

Between the newly proclaimed rights of the Negro and the freshly voided prerogatives of the South, the Supreme Court now had to negotiate without seeming to. It did not quite develop into a collision of unmovable object and irresistible force, largely because of moderating influences on both sides.

Among the more enlightened moderates on the Southern white side was Harry Ashmore, executive editor of the Arkansas *Gazette* in Little Rock, who was well regarded in the black community as a decent, liberal thinker. The day before the *Brown* decision came down from the Court, the University of North Carolina Press, probably the most broad-minded book-publishing enterprise in the South, brought out Ashmore's extremely timely book *The Negro and the Schools.* Though it carried his byline, the book was really a composite effort by forty scholars and commentators funded by the Ford Foundation. What the book had to say was immediately seized upon by both camps as the desegregation fight moved into its new phase of recommending to the Court how the process should unfold.

The depth of the American public's concern with education was what made the desegregation of schools an explosive issue, for, as Ashmore wrote, "Interest in the schools is universal, and it is an interest that directly involves not only the taxpayer but his family, and therefore his emotions. Those who are indifferent to all other community affairs tend to take a proprietary interest in the schools their children attend, or will attend, or have attended." Since that was so, said Ashmore, drawing his examples from the non-South, the most important factor in integrating the public schools was "community attitudes." He went on: "It is axiomatic that separate schools can be merged only with great difficulty, if at all, when a great majority of the citizens who support them are actively opposed to the move. No other public activity is so closely identified with local mores." The attorneys general of the South read those words, underlined them, and called them to the attention of the Supreme Court in the briefs submitted to it for the final round in *Brown*. Ashmore had based his findings on communities where segregation was not legally required but was extra-legally countenanced. How much more severe the problem of desegregation was likely to be in the South, where, without much question, "a great majority" of the citizenry actively opposed the step. The process must not be shoved down our throats, said Southern officials, invoking Ashmorean moderation.

But there was grist in Ashmore for the Negro side as well. "One thing that stands out in these case histories," he wrote, "is the frequency with which those who have had experience with integration—professional educators and laymen alike—have steeled themselves for a far more severe public reaction than they actually encountered." Not only that, but there was evidence to counter the proponents of gradualism who argued that it minimized public resistance to integration. Ashmore noted that "some school officials who have experienced it believe the reverse is true. A markedly gradual program, they contend, particularly one which involves the continued maintenance of some separate schools, invites opposition and allows time for it to be organized." Whatever the merits of the gradualist approach, it was clear that unsavory pressures mounted in the community whenever policies remained unsettled for a protracted period. It was important, furthermore, to understand that resistance to integration was not always specifically racist in origin:

> . . . In many cases the basis of objection might be the demonstrable fact that the great majority of American Negroes are still slum-dwellers; many a parent who proudly considers himself wholly tolerant in racial matters will object to having his child associate with classmates of inferior economic and social background. . . .

Most of the findings in the Ashmore book were no surprise at Thurgood Marshall's NAACP Legal Defense Fund office. While Ashmore's task force of researchers was exploring the state of black education, Kenneth Clark had undertaken a parallel effort on integration for the NAACP by way of answering the fourth of the five questions the Supreme Court had put to the parties for the *Brown* reargument—assuming segregation was found illegal, could and should the Court order Negro children admitted to integrated schools at once, or might it and ought it to do so by "an effective gradual adjustment"? Clark asked leading social scientists around the nation to send him case studies, news clippings, and any other data relevant to desegregation efforts, public and private, in the recent past. This flow of data, added to his own studies and the gatherings of NAACP field researcher June Shagaloff, Clark worked up into a richly detailed survey paper that he titled

"Desegregation: An Appraisal of the Evidence." It filled an entire issue of the quarterly *Journal of Social Issues*, the official publication of one division of the American Psychological Association. Clark's findings now became the focus of NAACP legal strategists, who, having won the constitutional phase of the fight in the May 17 decision, were no longer squeamish about getting the advice of the psychologists. Clark's, after all, was the first name cited in Warren's footnote #11. And the working out of an implementation decree was as much a matter of social engineering as of legal process. But Clark's advice, for all his enhanced overnight stature in the wake of the Warren opinion, proved a source of contention within the NAACP ranks.

Clark's most significant position, perhaps, was one that contrasted sharply with the Ashmore group's conclusions about the importance of favorable "community attitudes" as a prelude to the integration process. Where the South's lawyers latched on to this finding and cited deeply hostile community attitudes as a prime reason to delay desegregation, Clark in effect advised NAACP planners that that line of argument was so much baloney. He did not put it quite that way in his paper. What he said, in the classic jargon of his field, was: "The hypothesis that attitudinal and other subjective changes are necessary antecedents to behavioral changes is not supported by the empirical data examined in this survey. On the contrary, these data suggest that situationally determined behavioral changes generally precede any observable attitudinal changes." Translated from academese, that meant Clark found people who were faced with altered conditions were likely to change the way they acted before the way they thought. Practically speaking, that meant those opposing desegregation were likely to go along with its being imposed on them, even if they did not much like the idea, but if the process did not begin until those opposing the idea changed their minds about it, the wait might be a long one.

One of Clark's contributors, Gordon Allport of Harvard, whose major work, *The Nature of Prejudice*, had just appeared, argued that the Southern white masses knew deep down that segregation was un-American but were impaled by their own prejudices. "When we try to solve the conflict to accord with their consciences as Americans, we naturally arouse all the protests and threats and dying gasps of their prejudices," wrote Allport. "But let the backbone come from the Supreme Court, and it will strengthen the moral backbone of those who now live in conflict. . . . People do accept legislation that fortifies their inner conscience. . . . Protests are short-lived and readjustment rapidly sets in. Let the line of public morality be set by authoritative pronouncements, and all the latent good in individuals and communities will be strengthened. . . ." This view, which Clark embraced and the NAACP adopted without ever quite putting it that way in public, conflicted directly with the dictum in *Plessy*, which had insisted: "Legislation is powerless to eradicate racial instincts or to abolish distinctions based upon physical differences, and the attempt to do so can only result in accentuating the difficulties. . . ."

Clark himself formulated five requisites for "the accomplishment of efficient desegregation with a minimum of racial disturbance":

A. A clear and unequivocal statement of policy by leaders with prestige and other authorities.

B. Firm enforcement of the changed policy by authorities and persistence in the execution of this policy in the face of initial resistance.

C. A willingness to deal with violations, attempted violations, and an incitement to violations by a resort to the law and strong enforcement action.

D. A refusal of the authorities to resort to, engage in or tolerate subterfuges, gerrymandering or other devices for evading the principles and the fact of desegregation.

E. An appeal to the individuals concerned in terms of their religious principles of brotherhood and their acceptance of the American traditions of fair play and equal justice.

Firmness of the authorities in demanding compliance was the key to it for Clark, who cited, among many examples, the words of one battalion commander from the Deep South who described the success of the desegregation process in the U.S. Army's European Command in 1952 this way: "We got the order. We got detailed instructions for carrying it out and a time limit to do it in. And that was it."

Clark's findings stressed what Ashmore had far more gingerly suggested —that gradual integration could be a lot more painful than prompt and total integration. The longer the process was drawn out, the greater the likelihood that opposition would gather itself. Immediate desegregation of Catholic schools in St. Louis, for example, had been achieved more effectively than in Washington, D.C., where the process unfolded more gradually. The likelihood of violence developing, Clark added, had far less to do with the expressed racial virulence among whites prior to desegregation than with the disinclination of police to intervene effectively once the process was begun; slack law-enforcement encouraged violence. The size of an institution or jurisdiction undergoing desegregation, furthermore, had little to do with the ease or difficulty of the process. What evidence there was suggested, in fact, that the larger a community, the easier the process.

As the first Southern communities desegregated their schools voluntarily over the summer of 1954 following *Brown*, Clark monitored the process and remained in the midst of Thurgood Marshall's inner circle. First reports, mostly from the border states, were encouraging. Washington officials pushed hard to convert the capital's Jim Crow school system to an integrated one by the opening of the new term. Baltimore put its freedom-of-choice school-attendance policy on a non-racial basis, so that nearly 3,000 black students were going to previously all-white schools during the 1954–55 school year. Louisville swung over all its schools in a single semester, and St. Louis spread the process over two. Twenty-five counties in West Virginia, eleven junior colleges in Texas, and one small community in Arkansas desegregated. And in Delaware, Wilmington and other places where 28 percent of the state's Negro population lived began the process.

One of the more unlikely communities in Delaware to have started racially mixing its schoolchildren before it had to was the little agricultural town of Milford in downstate, Southern-minded Sussex County. The Milford board of education opened up a white school to ten Negroes. In no time, a strong resistance movement developed. More than 1,500 whites attended a heated rally at the local American Legion Hall, picketing began, and violence threatened. Black leaders were asked to consider withdrawing the Negro youngsters voluntarily, but they declined, arguing that with desegregation about to begin in many places, it was essential for the first blacks who experienced the abuse of die-hards to stand fast and not be intimidated. The local school board, fearing the worst, closed the schools temporarily and appealed to state authorities to intervene. Milford looked like a test-tube example of the sort of resistance that might lie ahead in the surliest sectors of the Southland. The NAACP dispatched Kenneth Clark to investigate toward the end of September.

Aside from being trailed in a car soon after reaching the area, Clark suffered no firsthand brushes with lawlessness, but he caught more than a whiff of the mob in the Milford air. His talks with local officials, black leaders and students, and some of the more brutish white element reconfirmed his faith in the conclusions he had reached for the NAACP during his 1953 survey of desegregation patterns. Indecisive in the face of heavily marshaled and vocal opposition, the Milford school board had succumbed to the threat of violence. Bloodshed was prevented not so much by the board's backing down in the face of the mob as by a firm law-and-order stand by the Milford mayor and police chief. The black youngsters themselves had been received without friction at the formerly all-white school, but adult pro-segregationists fanned the flames from the sidelines as local and then, more damagingly, state officials wavered. The lessons of Milford, Delaware, were clear to Clark as he reported back to Marshall after his three-day mission to the front lines: only unflinching community leadership, strictly enforcing its will and policy, would assure successful desegregation in areas of entrenched enmity to the changeover.

Clark's preference for iron-hand-at-the-helm desegregation, carried out as swiftly as possible, was congenial to many within the NAACP councils that summer. The road that had taken them this far had been long and steep and obstacle-strewn; they were all naturally eager to be at their destination. Typical of this attitude was Spottswood Robinson's analysis of strategy alternatives, transmitted in midsummer to NAACP advisor Jack Weinstein at Columbia Law School:

> The time factor is undoubtedly one of the most important considerations. I think that we must build our argument to demonstrate that transition from a segregated to a nonsegregated system most effectively occurs when immediately ordered and implemented and that, absent circumstances of an extraordinary character, desegregation of a public school system can be accomplished by school officials acting diligently and in good faith within a maximum of one calendar year. Since the law was made clear on last May 17, it would seem that completed desegregation by September 1955 would work no real hardship and would create no substantial administrative problems. . . .

Clark's recommendation, as seconded by Robinson, was both legally and emotionally justifiable, but it struck Weinstein, for one, as perhaps rather rash and, in the long run, perhaps not the most prudent course. He shared his concerns with his erstwhile Columbia associate Charles Black, Jr., who had moved to Yale:

> . . . Kenneth [Clark], as you know, takes the position that it is unwise to attempt any preparation of the people in a locality for desegregation. He feels that a direct order from above, calling for immediate desegregation, is best. I have a good deal of doubt about his conclusion, not only because its implications with respect to the democratic process against authoritarianism is quite disturbing, but because I think his data is far from conclusive. In this respect I think we must consider not only recent examples but also what happened after the Civil War.

Marshall himself was admittedly uncertain about whether to take the militant route and demand immediate desegregation across the board—the Clark-Robinson position—or to return to the Court with a more moderate, gradualist position. His own instincts were for the former, but the constitutional lawyer in him argued that the Justices would surely look more kindly on the NAACP's brief if it took a "realistic" view. In late September, Marshall sent a memo to his New York-area inner circle (Carter, Greenberg, Clark, Weinstein, Black, Louis Pollak, and William Coleman) suggesting that they were on a "merry-go-round" with regard to the implementation decree. "It will, of course, not do us any good to take the exact same position we took last year," he wrote in urging them all to review Clark's research on desegregation. "On the other hand, I am not certain as to what position we should take this year."

NAACP branches throughout the South were due to report to Marshall by the beginning of October on desegregation attitudes and progress, if any, in their areas. He wanted as wide a sampling as possible before settling on a policy that was to be more than mere personal willfulness. His task was made no easier in mid-October by a pair of back-to-back letters he received from William Coleman, who along with Robinson was perhaps the advisor he leaned on most heavily. Coleman sent him a rough draft for a section of the implementation brief and tried to work it around Kenneth Clark's data and conclusions. But his own effort, in Coleman's opinion, was a failure because "I just cannot bring myself to stress that material in the brief since I think it will not persuade the Court and, in fact, will irritate it. . . ." After staying awake half the next night, Coleman dispatched a longer, stronger letter to Marshall. In it, he said he kept coming back to the position that "we would be much better off under a decree which would permit the States to file for Court approval plans which would permit . . . gradual effective transition."

Coleman proceeded to spell out how it might well be to the NAACP's advantage to take the gradualist view, though on the face of it that might seem the timid course. The Court, he noted, had exercised "great statesmanship" even though Marshall & Co. might be irritated with the long delays and multiple arguments that had marked the whole *Brown* litigation. Similar statesmanship on the NAACP's part would require the black camp to offer a delay in the swingover to integrated schools instead of demanding it at once.

Such a show of sweet reasonableness might very well help lure the Southern states into submitting plans and a timetable of their own for carrying out desegregation instead of truculently resisting NAACP demands for immediate integration and obliging the Court to impose a program of its own upon defiant multitudes. If the South went for the bait, "the Court would feel that the [state] officials would be in the position where they would have to carry out the plans since they could not argue impossibility, the plans being their own."

It was a shrewd and accurate reading of the Warren strategy. And it was clearly advice that Coleman did not relish giving. "God knows that I am not a gradualist," he wrote, but he thought "it would be a pyrrhic victory to get a forthwith decree and yet two or three years will elapse before the first child goes to a school in South Carolina on a non-segregated basis. . . . I realize that as a great constitutional lawyer who has spent the major part of his adult life . . . trying to establish the principles which the Court finally accepted, it is difficult for you to even contemplate taking a position which would be construed as a retreat." But in his own judgment, Coleman concluded, it was not a retreat but calculated wisdom.

The South, digging in for the siege, was beset by no such nuanced skull-wracking. Anger and frustration were apparent in the last-ditch briefs that began moving to the Court in mid-November from the attorneys general of the Southern states which were participating in the final round of argument. Virginia, proud and unapologetic throughout the litigation, perhaps best relayed the region's sentiments.

The Court's May 17 decision had been based not on solid reasoning or legal precedent but on "psychological evidence," Virginia charged. And so long as the Court was so concerned with the psyche, it had best consider also the state of mind of white Virginians who "feel a sense of bewilderment that traditions and systems that have operated with judicial approval since 1870, and, in fact, since 1619, can be so readily swept away." More than time would be needed to bring about integrated education in Virginia: "It will require a complete change in the feelings of the people," the brief declared and invoked the Ashmore book on the importance of favorable community attitudes as a prelude to successful desegregation. As a measure of the depth of hostility to the Court's decision, the brief cited the text of a resolution, passed two months after *Brown* came down, by the Prince Edward Board of Supervisors, the county's governing body, stating that it was "unalterably opposed to the operation of nonsegregated public schools in the Commonwealth of Virginia," that it believed the operation of such schools to be not only impractical but impossible in Virginia, and that it intended to use "its power, authority and efforts to insure a continuation of a segregated school system. . . ." More than half the counties in the state had passed such resolutions by the time the Court heard the final round of arguments.

Going beyond what it had said in the first two arguments, Virginia now urged the Court to consider "the general level of educational capacity and attainment between the two races" as well as "general standards of health and morals." And it trotted out statistics to reinforce the unmistakable innuendo that Negroes were a lower order of humanity. In standard eighth-grade silent-reading tests given to 31,000 Virginia schoolchildren of both races, the lowest quarter of the white test group performed at a higher level than the top quarter of the Negro group. In IQ tests given to Virginia high-school seniors, the bottom quarter of the whites averaged 71.2 while the highest quarter of the Negro group averaged 63.9. Tuberculosis, an infectious disease, was twice as prevalent among Negroes as among whites, and Negroes, composing 22 percent of Virginia's population, contracted about 80 percent of all reported cases of venereal disease in the state. One out of every fifty white children born in Virginia was illegitimate; one out of five black children was.

That the degrading treatment in the form of economic, political, and social exploitation suffered by Virginia's Negroes for nearly three and a half centuries had been the white population's lasting contribution to those statistics was in no way acknowledged, of course. Nor was there any reference to figures just released by the federal government stating that it would cost $2 billion to bring black school buildings up to the level of white ones throughout the segregating South—and that current operating budgets would have to rise by $200 million a year to equalize teaching, transportation, and supplies at the nation's colored schools. What Virginia did say quite eloquently was that the Court must not set a deadline for the desegregation process, but "must permit a now indeterminable period to elapse before requiring integration of the races in Virginia's public schools." The state had "no plan or panacea that will result in complete solution of this problem. We do not foresee a complete solution at any future time."

Of the six segregating states that chose to join the final *Brown* argument—Arkansas, Florida, Maryland, North Carolina, Oklahoma, and Texas—Florida submitted the most extensive and spirited brief and offered some wrinkles that seemed to have been beneath Virginia's dignity.

Like the Old Dominion, Florida pursued the "community attitudes" argument that Ashmore's non-partisan group had espoused. The only hope to end segregated schooling in the Sunshine State without destroying public education itself was for "the Court to restrain the use of coercive measures where necessary until the hard core of public opinion has softened. . . ." After all, the school-segregation law had been "rigidly" enforced for the previous sixty-nine years in Florida, and "an immediate inrush of turbulent ideas" might cause "a tornado which would devastate the entire school system"—easily the best use of regional imagery in any of the Southern briefs. But this entire line of argument that a change in public opinion had to precede desegregation failed to acknowledge that if hostile public opinion might alone justify delaying the integration process, the hostility was likely to prove permanent.

To measure public opinion, Florida spent $10,000 on a poll which showed that three-quarters of "the white leaders" in the state disagreed in principle with the *Brown* decision, that 30 percent disagreed "violently," and—most ominous—only 13 percent of the peace officers polled said they would enforce state attendance laws at racially mixed schools. Only time would change matters, Florida said and cited many instances in which the Court had granted a good deal of time for the implementation of its decrees. These ranged from eight months in the 1911 antitrust case of *United States v. American Tobacco Company* to nine years in the so-called *Gaseous Nuisance Cases* that began in 1907 when Justice Holmes, writing for the Court, granted the Tennessee Copper Company "a reasonable time" to complete plant changes that would reduce the gaseous discharges destroying forest, orchard, and crop lands in five counties of Georgia.

The South's skill at erecting legal barriers to slow the desegregation process was foreshadowed by Florida's suggested "plan" to implement the Court's decision. Under it, even the most ungainly camel in Islam would have had an easier time passing through the eye of a needle than a black child getting into a white school in Florida. First, the petitioner would have had to show that admission to the white school had been sought within a "reasonable" (undefined) time before the beginning of the school term and that "all other administrative remedies such as appeal to the State Board of Education" had been exhausted in the event the local school board turned down the petitioning black schoolchild. Then "the court of first instance" (presumably the U.S. District Court) would conduct hearings and take testimony to determine, among other things, whether (1) state school authorities and the legislature had had "a reasonable amount of time" (undefined) to reorganize the state school structure; (2) sufficient progress had been made to overcome "practical, administrative problems" that naturally arose in integrating schools; (3) citizens' educational and interracial committees were improving the climate of racial relations in the communities affected in litigation; (4) "a strong degree of sincere opposition and sustained hostility on the part of the public to granting the petitioner's application . . . would cause a disruption of the school system or create emotional responses among the children which would seriously interfere with their education"; (5) the black petitioner's application "was made in good faith and not for capricious reasons" and was "not motivated . . . solely by a desire for the advancement of a racial group on economic, social or political grounds, as distinguished from his personal legal right to equality in public school education. . . ." Throughout this obstacle course, the burden of proof would have rested entirely upon the Negro petitioner, while local and state officials would have had a vast repertoire of vague and arbitrary standards at their disposal to thrust into the desegregation machinery anywhere along the line and jam it.

Having proposed that horror chamber of legal restraints, Florida then wound up its brief by asserting, "The Court stands not in need of the whip and the scourge of compulsion to drive our people to obedience. . . ."

Three of the parties to the litigation—the states of Kansas and Delaware and the District of Columbia—reported in their briefs that they had already made substantial progress in desegregation and that the Court need not bother directing implementation decrees toward them. Topeka claimed that it was in the second year of a three-year changeover to integrated schools and that 123 colored youngsters were already attending previously all-white schools (though 711 remained at all-black ones).

Washington's desegregation plan, while massive on the face of it, provided an important escape hatch for white students. In the name of educational continuity, all District students were allowed to remain through graduation at the schools in which they were currently enrolled. That device—the so-called "option plan"—served to freeze the student bodies at the white schools, since few whites were eager to transfer to black schools, and tended to invite hostility toward black youngsters who chose to desegregate the white schools. The net effect of the "option plan," as black attorneys Nabrit and Hayes argued, was to nullify the Court's decision by stigmatizing the black students at previously all-white schools as interlopers and placing the burden of desegregation on the Negro children instead of the school-district officials. The Delaware brief called attention to the ugly events at Milford and urged a gradual transition to desegregated schools. How the process could be made more gradual than at Milford, where only ten Negro schoolchildren had been involved, the state did not say.

Mediating between the positions of the Southern states, which did not want the Court to tell them when or how to desegregate, and the Negro plaintiffs in *Brown,* who insisted that the process begin by the fall term of 1955 and be completed by the fall term of 1956—the compromise position that Marshall reached between the Clark-Robinson and the Coleman views within the NAACP camp—was the United States government. The final U.S. brief in *Brown* took essentially the same position Philip Elman had adopted in the first government brief for the 1952 arguments: the Court could be flexible in setting down a timetable for desegregation and ought to let the District Courts oversee the process, since they were a lot closer to varying local conditions that might dictate a faster or slower pace. In urging the Court to bear in mind that school segregation was not an isolated phenomenon but "part of a larger social pattern of racial relationships," the third government brief in *Brown* stressed that the Justices had best proceed cautiously since the social institution they had just outlawed had "existed for a long time in many areas throughout the country." Precisely at that point in the brief, an insertion was apparently made by the President of the United States, according to Anthony Lewis, who covered the Supreme Court for the *New York Times* and says he saw Mr. Eisenhower's handwriting on a draft copy of the Justice Department's brief. Eisenhower, according to Lewis, made this contribution to the brief:

> —an institution, it may be noted, which during its existence not only has had the sanction of decisions of this Court but has been fervently supported by great numbers of people as justifiable on legal and moral grounds. The Court's holding in the present cases that segregation is a denial of constitutional rights involved an express recognition of the importance of psychological and emotional factors; the impact of segregation upon children, the Court found, can so affect their lives as to preclude their full enjoyment of constitutional rights. In similar fashion, psychological and emotional factors are involved—and must be met with

understanding and good will—in the alterations that must now take place in order to bring about compliance with the Court's decision.

The wording was almost surely drafted by White House lawyers, or perhaps Attorney General Brownell himself, but the sentiment accurately reflected the hands-off-the-South attitude that President Eisenhower would exhibit throughout his White House tenure.

But the American government's brief was hardly an open invitation to Southern defiance of the Court's decision. "Popular hostility, where found to exist, is a problem that needs to be recognized and faced with understanding," said the brief, in which Elman's determined hand was still visible, "but it can afford no legal justification for a failure to end school segregation. Racial segregation in public schools is unconstitutional and will have to be terminated as quickly as feasible, regardless of how much it may be favored by some people in the community. There can be no 'local option' on that question, which has now been finally settled by the tribunal empowered under the Constitution to decide it." Citizen-education programs, pupil-placement tests, and remedial instruction were among the steps suggested to facilitate the civic and administrative problems the process was likely to bring.

The government's key suggestion to the Court was not to enslave itself to the calendar. Surely the Court ought to make clear to segregating school districts that they could not delay integration indefinitely, but "we do not think it would be feasible" for the Justices to specify outside time limits to the desegregation process. "Apart from the fact that there is no way of judging at this point what integration will involve in the particular area," said the brief, "maximum periods tend to become minimum periods. The Court should not enter any order which might have the practical effect of slowing down desegregation where it could be swiftly accomplished." In other words, setting a deadline had the negative effect of encouraging segregation to continue until the last minute.

What the Court ought to do, said the government, is to insist upon "an immediate and substantial start toward desegregation" everywhere. The lower courts should at once direct the defendant school boards "to submit within 90 days a plan for ending, as soon as feasible, racial segregation of pupils in public schools, subject to their authority or control." The burden should be on the defendants "on the question of whether, and how long, an interval of time in carrying out full desegregation is required." The lower courts should require the defendant school districts to submit detailed periodic reports showing the progress made in ending segregation. Finally:

> The responsibility for achieving compliance with the Court's decision in these cases does not rest on the judiciary alone. Every officer and agency of government, federal, state, and local, is likewise charged with the duty of enforcing the Constitution and the rights guaranteed under it. . . .

The command of this concluding passage, ensuing events would suggest, seemed to have escaped the attention of the President of the United States.

The NAACP's hopes that at least some of the Southern states might submit a desegregation plan to the Court were unfulfilled on the eve of the final round of argument in *Brown*. The closest thing to a plan was Florida's blueprint for intransigence, which the NAACP's reply brief called "not a plan for granting rights, but a plan for denying them just as long as can possibly be done without a direct overruling of the May 17th ruling." Indeed, all that the Southern states seemed to care about in their remarks to the Court, the NAACP argued, were reasons for delaying desegregation: ". . . the affirmative problem gets virtually no attention."

But the settlement of Negro rights could not be postponed, the NAACP brief insisted. Nor was there any reason "for supposing that delay can minimize whatever unpleasant consequences might follow from the eradication of this great evil"—a view that clearly reflected Kenneth Clark's thinking. To the contention that community attitudes in the South had to change before integration could be contemplated, the NAACP said that this was no more than arguing that desegregation should be delayed "just as long as the conditions exist which [the South] formerly regarded as sufficient grounds for imposing segregation as a matter of legal right." In short, the whites wanted to keep denying the blacks their rights until the former, of their own volition, decided to stop the bullying. It was not sufficient for the South that the Court had commanded the practice to cease.

That the Court's decision would have wide effects on the public school systems of many states was no reason to delay granting the "personal and present rights" of the black plaintiffs, the NAACP brief insisted. There was obviously nothing in "mere numerousness as such which has any tendency whatever to create or destroy rights to efficacious legal relief. Behind every numeral is a Negro child, suffering the effects spoken of by the Court on May 17. It is a manifest inconsequence to say that the rights or remedial needs of each child are diminished merely because others are in the same position." In response to Virginia's contention that Negro children on average had far lower academic and moral standards, the NAACP brief lashed back: "That the Negro is so disadvantaged educationally and culturally in the states where segregation is required is the strongest argument against its continuation for any period of time. Yet those who use this argument as a basis for interminable delay in the elimination of segregation in reality are seeking to utilize the product of their own wrongdoing as a justification for continued malfeasance." Besides, average differences in student groups had no relevance to the individual rights of pupils; current academic disabilities could be compensated for through homogeneous grouping of students by academic proficiency and other administrative measures. No excuses could be tolerated for postponing the enjoyment of constitutional rights once declared by the Court, for the Constitution was not a document that applied in some sections of the country more than others. Beyond that, *Brown* was a great beacon in the black man's struggle for equality, the NAACP said in its last written words in the school-segregation cases, because

> . . . The fate of other great constitutional freedoms, whether secured by the Fourteenth Amendment or by other provisions, is inevitably bound up in the

resolution to be made in these cases. For delay in enforcement of these rights invites the insidious prospect that a moratorium may equally be placed on the enjoyment of other constitutional rights.

Still riding on the momentum of the May 1954 decision, Marshall and his associates performed with marked confidence and vigor in the final round of argument before the Court that began on April 11, 1955, and lasted for thirteen hours and twenty minutes spaced over four days.

Robert Carter, arguing the Topeka case, and Louis Redding, handling Delaware, both asked for "forthwith" decrees from the Court—that is, an order for immediate desegregation—and James Nabrit, winding up his five-year involvement with the District of Columbia case, offered the Court a sample of the wording he proposed for a decree ending Washington school segregation just as promptly, and without any "option plan" favoring white students. Now was the moment for a firm decision by the Court, said Nabrit. A strong directive by the Justices "will be complied with by the South where I have lived all my life and . . . thus, in spite of all their protestations and the attitude which many of them generally genuinely have, they will follow a decision of this Court just as other Americans follow the law."

Spottswood Robinson was just as steadfast in pushing the Court for desegregation of the Prince Edward schools in Virginia. If a school district as large and heavily Negro as the District of Columbia was already well on its way to a truly integrated school system, there was no reason why Prince Edward should not begin the process by the following September. The rights asserted in these cases, Robinson said, were the rights of children "and if they are ever going to be satisfied, they must be satisfied while they are still children." The period for attending public schools was a short one, and every delay was an irredeemable one. Not only was unfriendly public opinion among whites irrelevant to promptly granting Negroes their rights, but it was against precisely such "local hostilities and prejudices and customs and all that our opponents rely on" that the Fourteenth Amendment was passed in the first place to protect the black man.

Marshall took over the lectern and kept up the forceful NAACP offensive. The exact same sort of dire predictions of civil uprisings and closed schools and possible bloodshed that were now being made by the segregating states in the face of the *Brown* decision had been made before in the voting-rights cases, especially *Rice v. Elmore* in South Carolina, and *Sweatt*; nothing had come of them because the courts held firm, and all studies of the subject showed that a firm hand by authorities resulted in obedience by the public. The results of the public opinion polls that Florida and Texas had taken on the *Brown* decision in their states were not surprising, any more than they were predictive of how the individual citizen would actually behave once confronted with a firm decree by the Court to send his child to a desegregated school:

> . . . He would not like to go to school with the Negro, he would not like to have his children . . . go to school with the Negro, but that is not saying he won't. And that is not saying that he would prefer for his child to grow up and be an

imbecile [rather than] going with the Negroes. It does not say that. It says that in the context of an area where segregation has not only been considered lawful but it has been considered on a very high level, to ask somebody . . . whether or not you want to destroy [his] present system, his answer would be no.

As to the reportedly large gap in the educational levels of the two races, Marshall argued that was merely a dodge to avoid desegregation. The solution was simple, he explained in his blunt argot: "Put the dumb colored children in with the dumb white children, and put the smart colored children with the smart white children—that is no problem."

The fact was, Marshall declared, that the Justices would have to act decisively now to let the segregating states know that they could not defy the will of the Court. He cited a report by an official state commission set up by Virginia that stated its intention to formulate "a program within the framework of the law designed to prevent enforced integration of the races in the public schools." Marshall bristled: "That is what they are working on—and they are coming to this Court, asking to be given time to work on that. . . ." The South was devoting its efforts to circumvent the decision, not to figure out how best and faithfully to bow to it. For that reason, it was vital that the Court set a fixed date for the end of segregated schools everywhere: "[T]here is no local option on the Fourteenth Amendment in the question of rights—that just because there is a Southern area involved or border area involved, that is no reason to delay it." If the Court left the timing of the entire process in the hands of the District Courts, as the government brief had recommended, "the Negro in this country would be in a horrible shape. He, as a matter of fact, would be as bad, if not worse, off than under the 'separate but equal' doctrine. . . ."

To lead its final volley before the Court, the South could no longer call upon the matchless expertise of John W. Davis. The great advocate had died a few weeks earlier at his South Carolina vacation retreat at the age of eighty-one.* But Davis had made clear right after the *Brown* decision was announced the previous spring that he was bowing out. "We have met the enemy and we are theirs," he wrote to Robert Figg on May 20, 1954. Confessing his surprise and shock at the unanimous opinion, Davis added, "But looking at the matter philosophically, perhaps a unanimous opinion was better than a split Court." After graciously complimenting Figg for his part in the litigation, Davis noted, "I have no stomach for personal participation in the Court's effort to frame a decree." He declined a fee of $25,000 from the state of South Carolina for his part in the litigation—it was his way, he said, of reciprocating for the kindness and good times he had enjoyed so often in that land of grace and comfort—and accepted instead a sterling-silver tea service.

To lead off the Southerners' final stand, S. Emory Rogers, the feisty little Summerton attorney and scion of the plantocracy, spoke in behalf of

* Besides Davis and Justice Jackson, two others less directly active in *Brown* but much involved with it died in the half-year preceding its final act—Walter White, longtime executive secretary of the NAACP, and Vivian Burey Marshall, Thurgood Marshall's wife for twenty-five years.

Clarendon County. He spoke with such feeling and aggression that it looked, for a moment or two, as if Earl Warren might hold him in contempt of the Supreme Court of the United States.

Rogers advised the Court that its decision of the previous spring had presented the people of his county with "terrific problems." Clarendon was *not* the District of Columbia, he asserted, and what racial relations prevailed in the densely populated capital of the United States could not be transplanted to his county in the form of overnight desegregation, as the NAACP attorneys had asked. "We are tied to the land," Rogers said. "Our district is composed of the old plantation section of the county, fronting along a deep curve in the Santee River. It is for that reason that our Negro population is so large in that district and our white population so small. There has not been very much change in the texture of the population over the years." Integration in Clarendon, therefore, would not be what most people had in mind when the term was used: "It would actually be the sending of the few white children that we have there to the Negro schools. . . ." The Court had spoken, in its 1954 decision, of the impossibility of turning the clock of progress back to 1868, when the Fourteenth Amendment was adopted, or to 1896 and *Plessy*, but "I do not believe that in a biracial society," said Rogers, "we can push the clock forward abruptly to 2015 or 2045." Clarendon would work within the framework of the law, but local attitudes could be changed only slowly down there, and so "we are asking that these cases be sent back without instructions . . . to the lower court. . . ."

The Justices had some things to say about that:

JUSTICE FRANKFURTER:   Would it not be fair to say that attitudes in this world are not changed abstractly, as it were, by reading something—that attitudes are partly the result of working, attitudes are partly the result of action?

ROGERS:   I think so.

JUSTICE FRANKFURTER:   Would that be a fair statement?

ROGERS:   Yes, sir, I think so. Our sociologists have had a very difficult time in saying what attitude comes from or how it can be changed. But it does have to be in the society as it works.

JUSTICE FRANKFURTER:   But you do not fold your hands and wait for an attitude to change by itself?

ROGERS:   No, sir. You cannot. That has not been done here. That is not being done in this district. We have made progress and greater progress will still be made, I am sure. But to simply say you have to change your attitude is not going to change it.

After a brief exchange with Justice Harlan, Rogers felt the decorous wrath of Chief Justice Warren, who wished to know if the South Carolina lawyer's request for an open decree—i.e., one that did not specify when and how Clarendon had to desegregate schools—was based on the assumption that his school district would "immediately undertake to conform to the opinion of this Court of last year and to the decree. . . ."

ROGERS:   Mr. Chief Justice, to say we will conform depends on the decree handed down. I am frank to tell you, right now in our district I do not think that we will send—the white people of the district will send their children to the Negro schools. It would be unfair to tell the Court that we are going to do that. . . . But I do think that something can be worked out. We hope so.

To Earl Warren, this was close to heresy. You did not "work out something" with the decrees of the Supreme Court; you obeyed them. That is what a government of laws meant. That is what the social contract was all about. And Warren had been a law-enforcement officer his entire professional life. There seemed to be a pugnacity in Rogers's remarks, however candid, that plainly rubbed the Chief Justice, who looked down on the low-slung attorney and said, "It is not a question of attitude—it is a question of conforming to the decree. Is there any basis upon which we can assume that there will be an immediate attempt to comply with the decree of this Court, whatever it may be?"

> ROGERS: Mr. Chief Justice, I would say that we would present our problem, as I understand it, if the decree is sent out—that we would present our problem to the District Court, and we are in the Fourth Circuit. . . . I feel we can expect the courts in the Fourth Circuit and the people of the district to work out something in accordance with your decree.
>
> CHIEF JUSTICE WARREN: Don't you believe that the question as to whether the district will attempt to comply should be considered in any such decree?
>
> ROGERS: Not necessarily, sir. I think that should be left to the lower court.
>
> CHIEF JUSTICE WARREN: And why?
>
> ROGERS: Your honors, we have laid down here in this Court the principle that segregation is unconstitutional. The lower court, we feel, is the place that the machinery should be set in motion to conform to that.
>
> CHIEF JUSTICE WARREN: But you are not willing to say here that there would be an honest attempt to conform to this decree, if we did leave it to the District Court?
>
> ROGERS: No, I am not. Let us get the word "honest" out of there.
>
> CHIEF JUSTICE WARREN: No, leave it in.
>
> ROGERS: No, because I would have to tell you that right now we would not conform—we would not send our white children to the Negro schools.
>
> CHIEF JUSTICE WARREN: Thank you.

Eyewitnesses of the exchange differ in their accounts of it, but most agree that Rogers poked his forefinger toward the Chief Justice in urging the deletion of "honest" from Warren's question and that the Chief Justice grew quite flushed. "We thought he might charge Rogers with contempt," Attorney General Almond of Virginia recalls.

A couple of face-saving questions followed from the bench, and then Rogers was excused, to be replaced by the more suave and convincing Robert Figg, the best courtroom lawyer in Charleston. At the outset, he made clear that South Carolina did not challenge the Court's decision, but that an abrupt command to desegregate the public schools might drive the people to seek other means to educate their children. All aspects of life in Clarendon County were totally segregated—not as in the District of Columbia, where schools were almost the last institution to be integrated, Figg noted. In South Carolina, a biracial society had been deeply ingrained from the start. It would be punitive of the Court now suddenly to find this way of life illegal and demand that it be changed at once.

The Chief Justice had a question for Mr. Figg: "I wonder if the decision of May 17 last year would be of much value to these people if they waited until 2045 for that change in the attitude of these people?" Figg coolly implied that no such timetable was in his mind, that there had in fact been real progress in his region—much more so than many people realized—and that it was not so far behind other sections of the nation. Take New Jersey, he said, where forty-three school districts had still maintained segregated schools in 1947, when a statewide crackdown began, and by 1951 there were still three segregated districts. And New Jersey was a place far more receptive to integration than South Carolina.

For Virginia, Justin Moore's partner, Archibald Robertson, followed up with a two-fisted counterattack. He began by noting that 55 out of the state's 100 counties had passed resolutions opposing desegregation and added the by now familiar argument that community attitudes had to change before integration could proceed. Virginia had not been convicted of any wrongdoing, Robertson said, and since it had taken the Court nearly sixty years to change its mind about the legality of segregation, surely Virginians were likewise entitled to time to change their collective minds.

There was not a shred of contrition in Robertson as he boldly took up the argument from the state's brief to the effect that white Virginia families were naturally hesitant to send their children to school with Negroes, whose educational capacity and attainment were so low by contrast and whose "incidence of disease and illegitimacy is just a drop in the bucket compared to the promiscuity." He added: "I know that it may be said, 'Well, that is your fault—you denied them opportunity, you denied them equality. It is the result of environment.' We think that is irrelevant in this case. We are not aware of any unfairness or inequality, and we are not responsible for that."

In his steady drumbeat of reproach, Robertson hinted to the Court the nature of the defiance it might expect from the South. The Justices, he said, "can tell Virginia what *not* to do, but what I apprehend and what I think presents a much more difficult problem—this Court cannot tell Virginia what kind of public schools to operate. . . . [W]e would not for one minute say that [Virginians] would disobey the Court, defy the Court and continue segregated schools against the mandate of this court, but there are more difficult and subtle ways of doing it which we as counsel in this case do not know how to meet. They could refuse to vote the money, refuse to support necessary laws, and repeal usual public attendance laws."

The attorneys general of seven Southern states then drilled the Court with cautionary advice. Virginia's Lindsay Almond led off, noting that the lives of 50 million Americans were intimately bound up with the Court's decision and that the "forthwith" decree that the NAACP was asking the Justices to issue would arm it with the power to destroy what the Court in *Brown* had said was perhaps the most important function of state and local government—public education. He did not know what the solution was to desegregating the schools in Prince Edward, but, whatever it might be, he said, "it will not . . . in the lifetime of those of us hale and hearty here, be enforced integration of the races in the public schools of that county."

Florida told the Court that in its decision the previous year it had basically accepted the Negro contention that psychological and sociological reasons conspired to make segregation damaging. Now the Court ought to consider such factors as they affected the white population and provide a grace period for transition to unsegregated schools. "Give the people a chance through the democratic process to change the attitudes . . . of the community," said the state's attorney general (and later chief justice of the Florida Supreme Court), Richard W. Ervin. "If it does not work, you can . . . come back to a deadline timetable."

North Carolina's legal spokesman, I. Beverly Lake, began by shifting the entire burden of domestic tranquility in his state onto the shoulders of the Court for having had the gall to outlaw segregation. He declared that "whether or not the children of this state will or will not attend public school after this year and whether or not the people of North Carolina will or will not continue to live side by side in peace and friendliness will depend in a large measure on the decrees about to be issued." If the Court commanded the immediate admission of colored children to white schools, "it would in all probability be a death blow [to public education], and if not . . . would put those schools in turmoil and confusion from which only the enemies of our country could derive satisfaction." The state conceded not a farthing's worth of culpability in the matter. A decree ordering immediate admission of Negro pupils to white schools, Lake "respectfully" submitted, was beyond the Court's power: "The federal Constitution does not confer upon the federal government, as a whole, authority to impose upon state officials affirmative duties in the administration of the states' schools, and it certainly does not give that power to the federal courts. . . ."

Spokesmen for Arkansas, Oklahoma, and Maryland followed, arguing in a more subdued manner but all asking the Court to act cautiously. Texas, through its attorney general, John Ben Shepperd, wound up with a whoop for the South. "Texas loves its Negro people," he said, "and Texas will solve their problems in its own way." Great strides had been made in "human understanding" and raising educational levels during the past decade.

> We see no reason to pluck local affairs out of local hands.
>
> The question [of desegregation] is more basic than laws and systems. This touches the deepest roots of human emotion. It touches mothers and fathers and children in an area of deepest sensitivity. It comes dangerously close to interference in the sacred, inviolable relationship between parent and child and the right of parents to bring up their children in their own customs and beliefs.
>
> Texas does not come here today to argue the cause of other states. . . . It argues only that in Texas, a man-made cataclysm must be made slowly and with wisdom. Our argument may be summed up in eight words, the simplicity of which I believe this honorable Court will appreciate: It is our problem—let us solve it.

The concluding *amicus*, Solicitor General Simon E. Sobeloff, speaking for the government of the United States, urged the Justices to instruct the courts below to insist that the segregated school districts make at least a prompt beginning to the integration process and "effectuate the Court's decision as speedily as feasible." Justice Black wanted to know what "feasible" meant in this context. Soboloff said, a bit limply, " 'Feasible' means like any other question of fact—a determination after considering all relevant factors." Public attitudes were among those factors, to be sure, but that did not mean that "whether or not a constitutional right shall be vindicated by a court shall depend upon a public opinion poll. . . ."

Justice Black disclosed his possible leaning toward a narrow decree by asking the Solicitor General if he thought that the Court's decision would better serve the nation "if there were a direct immediate order that these individuals should be admitted in these schools and nothing more." In other words, suppose the Court did not frame a decree that in effect established machinery for desegregation everywhere? Suppose the Court simply ordered that these several hundred black plaintiffs be admitted to the white schools or otherwise mingled with the white schoolchildren in their communities and let the cases stand as precedent? Soboloff answered that such a solution "would be settling a much narrower question" and he granted, "Perhaps from one point of view, that is desirable. But I think both sides want to have the situation settled in the light of these administrative problems, which they say and which we all recognize will happen if a great number will apply." In other words, having reached the decision it did on May 17, 1954, the Court could not confine its effect to a few scattered locales, the Solicitor General implied. The genie was out of the bottle forever.

Thurgood Marshall closed out the argument for black America. He insisted that "there is nothing before this Court that can show any justification for giving this interminable gradual adjustment. I am particularly shocked at arguments of the impotency of our government to enforce its Constitution." The burden was not on the Negro to show that gradualism would not work; the burden was on the states to show why Negroes should not at once be granted the rights due them under the Court's decision. Why should those seeking to delay desegregation "be given advantage brought out by their own wrongdoing"?

To Virginia's objections to the low academic and health standards of Negroes, Marshall said that "it is interesting to me that the very people . . . that would object to sending their white children to school with Negroes are eating food that has been prepared, served and almost put in their mouths by the mothers of those children, and they do it day in and day out, but they cannot have the child go to school."

To Florida's argument that its people were entitled to desegregate using their own hourglass, Marshall suggested that a measure of Florida's good faith and reliability was its refusal—after five years of protracted litigation—to admit a Negro to the law school at the University of Florida. The Court had settled that right in *Sweatt* in 1950. "I think it is quite pertinent to consider how long it would take, without a forthright decree of this Court, [for Florida] to get around to the elementary and high schools."

To North Carolina's strong plea for mark-time desegregation to save its celebrated school system, Marshall said that the argument to postpone enforcement of a constitutional right "is never made until Negroes are involved. And then for some reason this [Negro] population of our country is constantly asked, 'Well, for the sake of the group that has denied you these rights all of this time,' as the attorney general of North Carolina said, 'to protect their greatest and most cherished heritage, that the Negroes should give up their rights.' If by any stretch of the imagination any other minority group had been involved in this case, we would never have been here."

He challenged the contention that prejudice was not the basic impulse in the gradual adjustment requested by the states. He said the notion that integration could be readily arranged in communities where there were few Negroes but would take a long time where there were many Negroes was plain racism. Texas had brought maps into court to show the widely varying concentration of Negroes in the state and suggest that different integration timetables should apply in different places accordingly. "I am sure that the state of Texas does not . . . administer their own constitution in varying [ways] in various sections of the country," Marshall said, but that was how Texas wanted the federal Constitution to be administered.

The South had been waiting with arms crossed until the Court now followed up its great pronouncement of May 17, 1954, said Marshall. And that pronouncement "will mean nothing until the time limit is set."

The members of the Court had been contemplating the implementation problem for the better part of two years when they assembled after the third argument in *Brown*. They looked naturally now to the Chief Justice as their leader.

The main lines of the decree had taken shape in Earl Warren's mind by the time he had left Washington for his trip back to California during the summer of 1954. He had asked to borrow Justice Reed's extensive file of materials on desegregation and its problems, among them Harry Ashmore's just published book. Reed's clerk John Fassett delivered the materials and had an extensive talk with the Chief, the gist of which he reported in a memo to Reed:

> . . . As I understood it, his [Warren's] inclination at this time, with which I agree, was to send the cases back to the trial court for the entry of appropriate decrees. Such action would have the dual advantages of allowing more time for compliance and also would better allow for local variations in the mode of compliance depending upon the intensity of the problem in the area. I take it that he agreed that reasonable attempts to start the integration process is all the Court can expect in view of the scope of the problem, and that an order to immediately admit all negroes in white schools would be an absurdity because impossible to obey in many areas.

Later that summer, Warren designated six clerks to prepare an advisory report on desegregation and how it might best be accomplished. The group, of which Justice Harlan's holdover clerk from Justice Jackson—Barrett

Prettyman—was a member, worked away at the project throughout the 1954 Term, absorbing all available literature and undertaking fresh research, such as mapping out every home in a typical Southern city—Spartanburg, third-largest city in South Carolina, was the guinea pig—to see how readily the existing white and colored school districts could be integrated. They also developed eight other maps of school tax and attendance districts in six other states to demonstrate to the Justices the effects of various desegregation plans. The day before the Court heard the final round of oral arguments, the clerks filed their recommendations with the Court; the six young lawyers essentially agreed that:

(1) *The cases should be remanded to the District Courts to supervise the execution of the Supreme Court decree.* The District Courts were "closer to the particular circumstances of each case, and may be regarded less as interlopers than this Court would be, in exercising direct supervision. . . ." Earl Warren turned out to agree with that.

(2) *The Court should formulate a simple decree.* It might read something like: "The defendants are hereby enjoined from determining the admission of the plaintiffs to schools on the basis of a racially segregated school system." If any general guidelines to the desegregation process were to be given, they should be not part of the decree but in a separate opinion. Mostly, Earl Warren did not agree with that.

(3) *The Court should provide guidelines to the courts below.* Five of the six clerks agreed on that. Without instructions, the District Courts would be left far out on a limb, and that was not right since "The remand will cast a heavy enough burden upon them." If the Supreme Court put down standards, then the lower courts could far more readily "point to a superior authority in undertaking what will often be unpopular action" and would be better able to judge whether local districts were making *bona fide* efforts at compliance or simply using "the jargon of educators which may or may not be a guise for evasion." A lack of guidelines would increase confusion and encourage delay. Earl Warren more or less agreed with that.

On the crucial question of timing, however, the clerks were of four different minds. One clerk opposed all gradualism; he argued that it would be an extreme injustice to condemn half a generation of Negro schoolchildren to a segregated system, would "greatly weaken the Court's moral position," and would not pacify militant segregationists. The other five clerks agreed that a Court order of immediate desegregation was "impractical" and was likely to be ignored by almost all elements in the South as clearly arbitrary and unreasonable. On the other hand, all five clerks felt that "the mere passage of time without any guidance and requirements by the courts produces rather than reduces friction. It smacks of indecisiveness, and gives the extremists more time to operate." One of the five clerks thought it best to leave the matter of timing entirely in the hands of the District Courts "in light of local conditions and sentiment." Another of the five, while encouraging immediate compliance, would have allowed school districts to submit plans contemplating no desegregation at all for several years just so long as the process itself was completed within twelve years (i.e., one full school cycle). The three remaining clerks opposed that drawn-out scheme on the ground that "we see nothing to be gained by sanctioning years of inaction; we fear that this would increase opposition, inhibit communities ready to move more quickly, and insult those officials who have already begun to desegregate." This trio favored, instead, allowing segregated school districts one year of grace, during which they did not have to do any integrating at all but could complete whatever planning and administrative changes were necessary; after the year, though, they would have to take some "immediate" steps toward desegregation that would be sufficient to support a finding by the supervising District Courts of good-faith compliance. Even if the desegregating districts then proceeded at the pace of only one class per year, consuming twelve years to integrate their entire systems, that would be permissible, though the Court should not advertise so conciliatory an attitude in its decree.

Among those most interested in the clerks' efforts was Felix Frankfurter, who had been pondering the mechanics of desegregation and passing around memos on the subject to his brethren for a year and a half. An early advocate of the idea that the Court might appoint "masters" to oversee the desegregation process, Frankfurter had apparently backed off from that notion by November of 1954, when he drafted a proposed decree that favored returning the cases to the District Courts, which would work out detailed decrees that "should take into account prevailing local attitudes and customs, but in no event may the desegregation process take longer than one school cycle of twelve years." He had not made up his mind to the wisdom of having the lower courts establish a terminal date in their decrees, but he called for periodic progress reports to be made to the courts by desegregating school boards, which were to establish "compact, nongerrymandered districts" and not to refuse Negro students admission "to any school where they are situated similarly to white students in respect to distance from school, natural or manmade barriers or hazards, and other relevant educational criteria."

By April 14, 1955, at the close of the Court's marathon final oral arguments in *Brown*, Frankfurter had composed a final memo to his fellow Justices that included some of the language from his memo of the previous November, including his conviction that the Court must not function as a "super-school board" in monitoring the desegregation process. Now, though, he saw two major alternatives: a "bare bones" decree permanently enjoining segregation of the named plaintiffs and those similarly situated (i.e., other Negro children in the same school districts), or a far more loosely worded decree that would allow the lower court to take into account local attitudes in exercising "the power of equity to enforce any decree and not merely issue a *brutum fulmen* [a futile threat]." The "bare bones" alternative, the sort of thing Hugo Black felt worth seriously considering, still left open the question of whether the Supreme Court ought to fix a terminal date for the mandatory desegregation. Frankfurter leaned away from that because any date "would necessarily have to be arbitrary or surely be considered as such. . . ." If, however, the Justices adopted the second alternative, the lower courts were entitled, said Frankfurter, to receive a set of implementation standards from the Court that would help guide them, allow for local difficulties, "and yet not serve as the mere imposition of a distant will."

The Justices convened in conference on April 16, 1955, to try to settle the delicate and highly ramified issue. Earl Warren, presiding, showed in his opening remarks that he had picked and chosen eclectically from the blended caution and resoluteness of the Justice Department brief, from the bifurcated conclusions of the six-clerk research committee the Court had appointed, from the canny ruminations of Felix Frankfurter, from the fervent fears of the Court's Southern contingent—Black, Reed, and Clark—and from the most astute outside commentators on the problem, such as Harry Ashmore. His suggestions, as recorded in the notes of Burton and Frankfurter, leave little doubt that he was the Court's driving force in resolving the *Brown* decree.

The Chief Justice began by saying he had not reached a fixed opinion and he was entirely open to an extended discussion, over as long a period of time as they needed, such as the one they had carried on in settling the basic constitutional question the year before. In other words, he wanted a unanimous Court again and he would wait it out again if need be. But he was quite clear on some things the Court should *not* do, he said. The Court should not appoint a master nor suggest to the District Courts that they do so, though they of course had that power. The Court should not fix any date for the completion of desegregation nor should it suggest to the lower courts that they should do so, though they could if they wished to. The Court should not require the courts below to call for a desegregation plan from the defendant school districts, though it was of course perfectly feasible for the lower courts to enter such an order. He himself would recommend putting down no procedural requirements, said Warren, for the Supreme Court was a court of equity—in short, the Court should not be, as Frankfurter had insisted, a "super-school board."

What the Chief Justice did favor was a combined opinion and decree citing a number of factors that the courts below should take into consideration. This would be a more useful mechanism than a formal decree, for it would give the lower courts guidance without too narrowly circumscribing them. It would be "rather cruel" to shift the burden of implementation back to the lower courts and let them flounder without any guidelines from above. Among the factors he would suggest that the lower courts take into consideration were financial problems and problems involving the physical plant within any given school district; he would *not* suggest mentioning "psychological" or "sociological" attitudes. In approving any plan offered by a desegregating district, the lower court had to consider whether a serious effort was being made to get the process started and whether genuine progress was being made. Overall, the Court's main goal should be, according to Burton's notes of the Chief's remarks: "Give District Courts as much latitude as we can but also as much support as we can."

Hugo Black, speaking second, told the conference that he had no fixed ideas, either, but the ones he did have were somewhat different from the

Chief Justice's. One thing he was sure of, though: the Court should do "everything possible to achieve a unanimous result" in settling the matter.

In general, according to Burton, Black thought that "the less we say, the better off we are." He was brought up in an atmosphere distinctly hostile to federal officials, he said, and the Deep South was only just beginning to manifest respect for their authority; the caution of the region was rooted in the race question, and what progress there had been would be dissipated if the desegregation process was forced harshly upon the South. One of his law clerks came from Lowndes County, outside of Montgomery, Alabama, said Black, and was convinced that Negro and white children would not go to school together "in this generation." Frankfurter's notes have Black saying: "Nothing more important than that this Court should not issue what it cannot enforce." The Court, he said, should take a lesson from Prohibition, which the government had finally abandoned because of its unenforceability. It was futile, moreover, for the Court to think that in these cases, at a single stroke, "we can settle segregation in the South." Black said he was not fond of "class action" lawsuits, partly because many who are included in the class do not really want to be. His preference, therefore, would be to treat the five cases composing *Brown* not as class actions but as cases involving only the individual plaintiffs named, whom the defendant school boards would be required to admit to formerly all-white schools. This would at least get the desegregation process under way. He had little confidence in leaving the whole question in the laps of the District Courts, said Black, because he knew all the Southern judges in the federal system and none of them, so far as he could tell, was in favor of the Court's *Brown* decision. The best that the Court could hope for at the moment, he foresaw, was glacial movement in the integration process.

Stanley Reed, the last man on the Court to vote for ending school segregation, seemed a good deal more sanguine about its prospects than Hugo Black. Admitting that he did not know the Deep South as Black did, Reed said he nevertheless felt firmly that a considerable part of the Southern population was willing to give the whole matter "sympathetic consideration." He believed that once some schools opened on a desegregated basis, the pace of the process would pick up and go along more easily. He himself favored a short opinion, but was undecided as to what sort of instructions or guidelines ought to be offered the lower courts. Reed thought it best to conceive of the cases as class-action suits, but there was no need to state as much in the Court's opinion-decree.

Felix Frankfurter said he greatly welcomed the "candid relaxed way" in which the Justices were discussing the general direction in which they should proceed. Such a remark was, of course, a warm tribute to Warren's leadership, though Frankfurter did not have to spell it out that way. Though the segregation cases were indeed lawsuits, they were of a different sort from most, and the environments in which they arose could not be ignored. He did not agree with Thurgood Marshall's contention that the Court should not take into account local attitudes in framing its decree. His own guess was that desegregation would proceed by gradual infiltration of the border states and then spread to the deeper South; developments during the previous eleven months supported that projection. Frankfurter thought the question of labeling the cases before them as class actions was probably extraneous because even if the Court's decree was restricted to the names of the plaintiffs, the same demand for desegregated schools would surely be made by other Negroes in the district. What was most important, he wound up, was the feeling that the Court's decree transmitted; a sympathetic view of the problems involved had to be balanced with a clear reminder that the Justices constituted the Supreme Court for all of the United States, including the South.

William Douglas did not have much to add. He was inclined to agree with Black in opposing the class-action label and favored limiting the decree to the individual plaintiffs. However worded, the Court's opinion should give a push to the desegregation process and not leave the matter at a mere declaration that segregated schools were no longer constitutional.

Harold Burton was somewhat more expansive in his views of the case and rather close to the Chief Justice. These were plainly class suits, as he saw it, and the problem they all raised was that of the continued legality of the race line, not merely of putting a few colored children in school with whites.

Tom Clark, too, thought the Court's decree should not limit the reach of the cases to the named plaintiffs. Plainly, Negroes all over were going to try to obtain the rights that the Court had said were theirs, though no doubt many would remain at wholly colored schools because of their distrust of whites.

Sherman Minton, like Hugo Black, said he thought it vital that the Court remain unanimous in this phase of the case. He felt it important that they not talk big in the opinion and small in the decree—that would be weaseling, he said. The Court's main goal should be to get the desegregation process started without, in the process, revealing its own impotence to make it happen.

The newcomer to the Court, John Marshall Harlan, was not reticent. Even before his confirmation by the Senate, he had begun applying his intellect to the issue. "Justice Harlan was immediately interested in the problem of the decree," recalls his first clerk, Barrett Prettyman, "and wrote me from New York asking that I send him within a few days not only an analysis of all the briefs but whatever views I wished to express on the merits—which of course I did." In conference now, he said that most of his own thoughts had already been expressed by others, but he did wish to emphasize a few points. He was surprised and pleased by the apparent unanimity of the Court and wished for that solidarity to be maintained as a sign of political statesmanship. Then, he was deeply impressed by Black's remarks on the difficulty of making rapid headway in the Deep South, and it was important to consider such a *caveat* in settling on the time factor in the decree. He thought the Justices might be mistaken in underestimating the value of a gracefully written opinion to transmit the Court's basic approach to the whole issue in preference to handing down a decree that might come across as too cold and heavy-handed. Harlan favored combining the opinion and decree in a single statement that placed no time limit on desegregation.

That matter of the time limit remained the most difficult one of all. Any date was necessarily an arbitrary one. Any date, except perhaps one in the twenty-first century, was certain to antagonize the South. And wholesale defiance of whatever date the Justices might settle on would gravely undermine the authority of the Court and the entire judicial system. But what kind of equal justice under law was it that granted some Americans their rights but then told them they would have to wait a while, perhaps a long while, before they might exercise them? Thurgood Marshall's words could not be tuned out. The very numerousness of Negroes should not be used against them to postpone their rights. The objection of whites to having their children mingle with colored children was not a valid reason to hold off the process.

And yet more than reason was involved here, as all the Court grasped. The Justices stood at the very interface of man's susceptibility to destructive private impulse and his longing for reasoned social order. Here was a classic instance of what Freudian psychology calls the collision of id and superego. Unless the two forces are resolved, chaos follows. But law, in a democracy, cannot impose that resolution by the force of the state alone. Democracy is too unruly for that. That is its great weapon against the would-be tyrant; that is the agony it imposes on the most enlightened reformer. Law in a democracy must contend with reality. It has to persuade. It has to induce compliance by its appeal to shared human values and social goals. How well law succeeds in winning, however reluctantly, the abandonment of unjust private advantage is perhaps the severest, and best, measure of that society's humanity. Few nations in history have ever aspired to such a massive reconciliation of public needs and private impulses. It is, frankly, a cumbersome process; no ruler would turn to it gladly. Yet America has known no other, and perhaps no other process is possible in so pluralistic a society. But the process breaks down without leaders who understand that it must be primed and lubricated to function well. Earl Warren was such a leader. He moved at ease in the ample territory between authoritarianism and a civic listlessness beloved by those who prefer the sashes of office to the peril of leading.

In settling down to the punishing task of drafting an opinion of the Court, Earl Warren seized upon a phrase far too subtle to have been his own invention but one that he recognized as useful in solving the dilemma of how to spur the desegregation process without fixing a firm timetable for its completion. In the first argument of the cases in 1952, the U.S. government brief had suggested that the Court might instruct segregating school districts to abolish the practice "with deliberate speed." The phrase was inserted by Philip Elman, former clerk and continuing confidant to Justice Frankfurter, who had used the term in two opinions he had written in the mid-Forties and had introduced it again in the memo he had distributed to the Court in January of 1954 in anticipation of the Justices' grappling with the implementation question (see Chapter 25). Frankfurter had borrowed the phrase from his idol, Oliver Wendell Holmes, who had used it in writing the Court's opinion in the 1918 case of *Virginia v. West Virginia,* dealing with a controversy between the two states over how much and when Virginia ought to be repaid a fair share of the state's public debt at the time West Virginia broke off from it:

> . . . A question like the present [one] should be disposed of without undue delay. But the state cannot be expected to move with the celerity of a private businessman; it is enough if it proceeds, in the language of the English Chancery, with all deliberate speed.

Precisely where in English Chancery law the term originated, Frankfurter did not know. It was precisely the sort of thing that gnawed at the scholar in him. Three years later, he was still trying to trace the quotation. He confided to his friend Mark De Wolfe Howe at Harvard Law School that he had made "the most assiduous search to find Holmes's authority" and had asked British scholars "to authenticate the phrase"—without luck. Howe evidently did no better, for Frankfurter wrote his still closer friend (and former student) at Harvard Law, Paul A. Freund, in midsummer of 1958, noting that Freund had recently written that " 'deliberate speed' was a phrase [Holmes] took from English Chancery practice. I wonder if you know that Mark Howe and I, between us, have spent not a little time in trying to find in English Reports or treatises substantiation for Holmes's attribution, and all to no avail. . . . Yet, it cannot be that Holmes pulled it out of the air."

But Holmes might have been mistaken in recalling how the phrase got into his head. It might well have come, instead, from the lines written in 1893 by the British metaphysical-symbolist poet Francis Thompson, whose best-known work, titled "The Hound of Heaven," began:

> I fled Him, down the nights and down the days;
>   I fled Him, down the arches of the years;
> I fled Him, down the labyrinthine ways
>   Of my own mind; and in the mist of tears
> I hid from Him, and under running laughter.
>       Up vistaed hopes I sped;
>       And shot, precipitated
> Adown Titanic glooms of chasmed fears,
>   From those strong Feet that followed, followed after.
>       But with unhurrying chase,
>       And unperturbed pace,
>   Deliberate speed, majestic instancy,
>       They beat—and a Voice beat
>       More instant than the Feet—
> "All things betray thee, who betrayest Me."

Whatever the precise genesis of the phrase, it appealed to Warren when Frankfurter suggested its appropriateness to *Brown.* The ironic use in combination of contradictory or incongruous words for epigrammatic effect—such as "cruel kindness" or "wise fool"—is a rhetorical device known to linguists as "oxymoron." Though this sort of thing was normally as foreign to Earl Warren's guileless writing as a horde of umlauts, it appealed to him, he later explained, "because we realized that under our federal system there were so many blocks preventing an immediate solution of the thing in reality that the best we could look for would be a progression of action—and to keep it going, in a proper manner, we adopted that phrase." Perhaps, too, the phrase seemed an apt description of the pace set by the tortoise in his fabled race with the hare; and the tortoise, moving with all deliberate speed, of course triumphed.

On May 31, 1955, the last day of the 1954 Term, Chief Justice Earl Warren delivered the unanimous opinion of the Supreme Court implementing its previous decision in *Brown v. Board of Education.* It ran just seven paragraphs. Nowhere in it did the words "segregation" or "desegregation" appear.

Warren began by recalling the Court's opinion of May 17, 1954, "declaring the fundamental principle that racial discrimination in public education is unconstitutional" and added: "All provisions of federal, state, or local law requiring or permitting such discrimination must yield to this principle."

Then he turned to the manner in which relief was to be accorded. He noted that the Court had found it "informative and helpful" to hear from a number of states in its consideration of the complexities involved in the "transition to a system of public education freed of racial discrimination." Substantial steps toward that goal had already been taken by several states, Warren also noted. And then he got to the nuts and bolts of the problem. First, the Chief Justice established firmly that the Court was not about to usurp local prerogatives in commanding the end of segregation:

> Full implementation of these constitutional principles may require solution of varied local school problems. School authorities have the primary responsibility for elucidating, assessing, and solving these problems; courts will have to consider whether the action of school authorities constitutes good faith implementation of the governing constitutional principles. Because of their proximity to local conditions and the possible need for further hearings, the courts which originally heard these cases can best perform this judicial appraisal. Accordingly, we believe it appropriate to remand the cases to those courts.

The opinion then walked the tightrope between acknowledging the relevance of community attitudes and yielding to them the right to delay the exercise of anybody's constitutional rights. The courts below, in fashioning their decrees, Warren wrote, were to be guided by "equitable principles" that traditionally had been marked by "a practical flexibility" in the shaping of remedies. At stake in the cases before them was "the personal interest of the plaintiffs in admission to public schools as soon as practicable on a nondiscriminatory basis." But "practicable" was a relative term:

> . . . To effectuate this interest may call for elimination of a variety of obstacles. . . . Courts of equity may properly take into account the public interest in the elimination of such obstacles in a systematic and effective manner. But it should go without saying that the vitality of these constitutional principles cannot be allowed to yield simply because of disagreement with them.

The courts below were then ordered to "require that the defendants make a prompt and reasonable start toward full compliance with our May 17, 1954 ruling." Once that start had been made, additional time might be granted for carrying out the desegregation process in an effective manner, but the burden would then rest with the defendants to show that the extension was "in the public interest and is consistent with good faith compliance at the earliest practicable date." Among the "problems related to administration" that the courts were free to consider in determining the timetable were those "arising from the physical condition of the school plant, the school transportation system, personnel, revision of school districts and attendance areas into compact units to achieve a system of determining admission to the public schools on a nonracial basis, and revision of local laws and regulations which may be necessary in solving the foregoing problems." (The opinion said nothing about community attitudes or public opinion.) During the transition period, the courts below were to retain jurisdiction of the cases. Finally, the Court wound up with its ambiguous catch phrase that told the nation to make haste slowly in this momentous business:

> The judgments below, except that in the Delaware case, are accordingly reversed and the cases are remanded to the District Courts to take such proceedings and enter such orders and decrees consistent with this opinion as are necessary and proper to admit to public schools on a racially nondiscriminatory basis with all deliberate speed the parties to these cases.

The Delaware judgment, ordering the immediate admission of the plaintiffs to schools previously attended only by white children, was affirmed on the basis of the May 17, 1954, opinion, but was sent back to the Delaware Supreme Court "for such further proceedings" as that court deemed necessary. The decree concluded with the Court's traditional flourish: "It is so ordered."

The Court did not fix a date for the end of segregation, as Thurgood Marshall had so vigorously requested.

It did not direct the courts below to require the defendant school boards to submit a desegregation plan within ninety days, as the federal government had recommended.

It did not even credit Oliver Wendell Holmes's 1918 opinion with the phrase "all deliberate speed," as Frankfurter strongly urged Warren that it should have.

And by almost any measure, it gave the South a great deal more of what it had asked at the final round of arguments than it gave to the Negro. Yet the Court's implementation decree in the school-segregation cases—legal scholars have come to call it *Brown II*, as they have labeled the May 17, 1954, decision *Brown I*—did not reduce the moral compulsion to end Jim Crow as soon as possible. It recognized, though, that what is possible in the everyday business of nations is rarely determined by what Felix Frankfurter called, in the Court's back-room deliberations over *Brown II*, "the mere imposition of a distant will."

The two *Brown* opinions, taken as a unit, did in fact launch the desegregation process. It began, as any tactician might have recommended, in the border states and then seeped deeper into the South, starting generally in the cities. Wisely or not, the Supreme Court avoided making the process seem like a revival of Reconstruction, for, practically speaking, it placed effective control of the undertaking in the hands of Southerners themselves— the fifty-eight federal judges manning the twenty-eight United States District Courts and two Court of Appeals circuits, the Fourth and Fifth, serving the South. These men, whatever their limitations, however ill-disposed they were to dismantling the most fiercely held tradition of their region, were mostly a blend of Old South aristocrats and New South urbanites; they were not backwoods lynchers or potbellied sheriffs or closet Klansmen. They were, generally speaking, about the best of the white South. And perhaps the nine men in Washington knew that only the white South could truly liberate the black South. Perhaps all the Supreme Court could do, short of risking massive insurrection, was to proclaim to the nation that the enforced separation of human beings by race was neither God's will nor the purpose of the Constitution as amended after the Civil War. Perhaps the most the Justices could do, in plainer language, was to say that segregation was wrong and then rely on the best instincts of the American people to figure out how to eradicate the practice.

On Thursday, June 2, 1955, two days after the Court delivered *Brown II*, Thurgood Marshall phoned his earliest sponsor, Carl Murphy, president of the *Afro-American*. It was Murphy who twenty-two years earlier had put his newspaper and his standing at the top of Baltimore's black community behind efforts to rebuild the moribund local branch of the NAACP. In the process, he had taken a strong liking to the lanky young attorney just out of Howard Law School. Now, the harvest of many years was in sight. The two men spoke about it.

MURPHY: Carl Murphy.

MARSHALL: Hey, how ya doin'?

MURPHY: Fine, thank you.

MARSHALL: After you've thought now, what do you think of Tuesday's decision?

MURPHY: Well, I was disappointed in the beginning . . . [when] I read the first paragraph, and then I read all the good faith, deliberate speed, prompt start, and I come to the conclusion that we got a package.

MARSHALL: That's what we've been saying.

MURPHY: That's absolutely what I think. They didn't put a time limit on it, but my thought is that we can go with this.

MARSHALL: I'm sure of it. I was telling the guys up here—the guys kept on woofin' and I told them—I said, you know, some people want most of the hog, other people insist on having the whole hog, and then there are some people who want the hog, the hair, and the rice on the hair. What the hell! The more I think about it, I think it's a damned good decision! . . .

MURPHY: I talked with Carter before. . . . He said *Plessy v. Ferguson* is out . . . and [Warren has] cut the ground from under them by saying if you have segregation in these schools, it's unlawful and therefore the burden is on you to get 'em lawful.

MARSHALL: And the laws have got to yield! They've got to yield to the Constitution. And yield means yield! Yield means give up!

MURPHY: I'm not enthusiastically happy, Thurgood, but I'm happy.

MARSHALL: Well, you know, the more you think of it, it had to be anticlimactic, anyhow. . . .

MURPHY: What are you going to do, Thurgood?

MARSHALL: We're going to—actually adopt—what we're going to do state by state, that's what I hope. For example, we're going to treat Georgia one way, we're going to treat Maryland another way. But now if Maryland doesn't act right, then we treat Maryland like we treat Georgia. . . . And we're going to give West Virginia a chance. Virginia we're going to bust wide open!

MURPHY: I don't see any reason why, if we beat Virginia and Carolina, the rest of them aren't going to wake up.

MARSHALL: You're darned right they are. You can say all you want but those white crackers are going to get tired of having Negro lawyers beating 'em every day in court. They're going to get tired of it. . . .

Those crackers, as events would prove, lived not only in Little Rock and New Orleans and Clinton, Tennessee, and Selma, Alabama, but also in Englewood, New Jersey, and Denver, Colorado, and South Boston, Massachusetts. In fact, they live everywhere in the United States where the black man sets foot. But now they are not the law. Now the law says that, like them or not, white America may not humiliate colored Americans by setting them apart. Now the law says that black Americans must not be degraded by the state and their degradation used as an excuse to drive them further down. That is what *Brown v. Board of Education* accomplished. It took the better part of four centuries.

# 27

# Visible Man: An Epilogue Twenty Years After

Exorcism is rarely a pretty spectacle. It is frequently marked by violent spasms and protracted trauma, and so it has been in the two decades since *Brown* signaled the beginning of the nation's effort to rid itself of the consuming demons of racism. We are too close to this unfolding process to view it with objectivity, but the bruising post-*Brown* years have clearly marked the onset of the third major stage in the history of black-white relations in America.

During the first, blacks were openly classified as property, and even those who were not held in legal slavery were generally regarded as having been placed on earth to do the bidding of white men. The Thirteenth Amendment technically ended that state of formal subjugation in 1865. The second stage promoted the colored man to the category of marginal human being, evidently of the same species as the white man and technically entitled to the same rights and protections, but an unfortunately witless, lecherous, odoriferous sort whose very presence was an eyesore as the nation reached for greatness. Denied learning, denied all but the most primitive vocational training, denied access to the political and social institutions that functioned as a giant ethnic melting pot for the European peoples who stocked American shores, the Negro hobbled into the twentieth century as a reviled scapegoat for the frustrated, a target for the sadistic, and an inconvenient reminder of past sins and current indifference. It seemed only natural that he should have been segregated as a pollutant. Not until the Supreme Court acted in 1954 did the nation acknowledge that it had been blaming the black man for what it had done to him. His sentence to second-class citizenship had been commuted; the quest for meaningful equality—equality in fact as well as law—had begun.

It is more the business of melodrama than social analysis to suggest that a single moment or event can change the course of history. It is not suggested here that *Brown*, alone, was such a moment or event. The Court's decision might more aptly be called the cresting wave of a tidal movement unleashed by the great economic earthquake of 1929. Not until then did the nation seriously acknowledge that its most sacred obligation went beyond the protection of capital to the well-being of its citizens. People were no longer infinitely discardable, and the New Deal of Franklin Roosevelt became the first national administration to treat black Americans as recognizably human. Worldwide conflicts with fascism and Communism added to the country's consciousness that its colored citizens had not been precisely beneficiaries of the social order; a system that tolerated so much human spillage was plainly in need of repair. Full employment and an extended economic boom unlike any the world had ever known contributed to the growth of tolerance in post-war America; there was work for all, though no one was handing cushy jobs to colored people. The good times reached into the South, which now embraced full-scale industrialization and lost much of its economic and psychological isolation from the rest of the country. The electronic communications revolution advanced the national homogenization process. Radio, television, the movies, and the phonograph brought an insistent mass culture of shared sights, sounds, and attitudes to every region, every social class, every income level, and every ethnic category in the land. If the common denominator was not very high and did as much to imbed as uproot racial stereotypes, all this cross-fertilization reduced much of what provincialism remained in the country and gave wide exposure to the achievements of such Negroes as Ralph Bunche, Richard Wright, Louis Armstrong, and Jackie Robinson. Evidence was accumulating that black Americans had much to offer their country if given the opportunity to grow up in decent surroundings and make their way like everyone else. Revulsion over incidents of racial violence grew. The clergy, longtime protector of Jim Crow religion in much of the nation, turned moral as well as pious and began to call for racial equality and act in ways to help achieve it.

It was in this receptive soil that the Supreme Court planted the seed of *Brown.*

Every colored American knew that *Brown* did not mean he would be invited to lunch with the Rotary the following week. It meant something more basic and more important. It meant that black rights had suddenly been redefined; black bodies had suddenly been reborn under a new law. Blacks' value as human beings had been changed overnight by the declaration of the nation's highest court. At a stroke, the Justices had severed the remaining cords of *de facto* slavery. The Negro could no longer be fastened with the status of official pariah. No longer could the white man look right through him as if he were, in the title words of Ralph Ellison's stunning 1952 novel, *Invisible Man.* No more would he be a grinning supplicant for the benefactions and discards of the master class; no more would he be a party to his own degradation. He was both thrilled that the signal for the demise of his caste status had come from on high and angry that it had taken so long and first exacted so steep a price in suffering.

Lawsuits are proceedings too technical and lengthy to form the basis for a mass movement, though they may set that movement in motion. Direct action is required. The mass movement sparked by *Brown* was unmistakably thriving as soon as six months after the Court handed down its implementation decree. It began in the Deep South, in Montgomery, Alabama, when a forty-three-year-old seamstress and active NAACP member named Rosa Parks refused to move to the back of a city bus to make room for a white passenger. Within days, and thanks to the leadership of Mrs. Parks's pastor, the Reverend Martin Luther King, Jr., all blacks were staying off the buses of Montgomery in a massive show of resentment over the continuing humiliation of Jim Crow. With dignity, resolve, and courage that inspired blacks everywhere in America, Montgomery's Negroes made their boycott stick for more than a year. At the end of it, the Supreme Court struck down Jim Crow laws in public transportation just as it had in public education; *Plessy v. Ferguson*, a case dealing with transportation, not schools, was now technically overruled. The boycott movement soon spread throughout the South, where suddenly intrepid leadership began to emerge everywhere. Lunch counter sit-ins started in North Carolina in 1960, and soon in hundreds of communities blacks were making personal statements of protest—and risking their necks—to demonstrate the depth of their demand for equal treatment as human beings.

The Supreme Court had taken pains to limit the language of *Brown* to segregation in public schools only. The less terrain covered by the decision, the better, Chief Justice Warren had believed. But it became almost immediately clear that *Brown* had in effect wiped out all forms of state-sanctioned segregation. Bowing to *Brown*, the Fourth Circuit Court of Appeals under Chief Judge John Parker ruled in the spring of 1955 that Baltimore could no longer segregate its bathing beaches or public recreation facilities. The Supreme Court affirmed Parker's Baltimore decision in November of 1955 on the same day it reversed a Fifth Circuit opinion upholding a separate-but-equal golf course for black residents of Atlanta. That year, courts in Michigan and Missouri cited *Brown* as authority for ending segregated housing at municipally run developments. And the Supreme Court itself, in its brief *per curiam* decision, leaned primarily on *Brown* when it struck down Montgomery's Jim Crow buses in 1956.

Legal scholars were distressed that the Court seemed to be so casual about invoking *Brown*, which after all had avoided lawyerly discussion of the development of racial-classification case law and instead depended almost entirely on the peculiar importance of public education in order to justify the outlawing of segregated schools. How could the negative psychological effects of separate schools on student motivation to learn be invoked to justify the ending of Jim Crow buses, beaches, and golf courses? The scholars no doubt had a point, but the Court seemed to believe it had a higher obligation to preserve domestic tranquility than to write logically or judicially irrefutable opinions. It continued to say as little as possible every time it struck down another racial-classification law, apparently broadening the premise of *Brown* to hold that all forms of racial segregation were discriminatory and therefore humiliating and therefore a violation of equal protection.

Over the next dozen years, the Warren Court handed down decision after decision that followed the path *Brown* had opened. Segregation was outlawed in public parks and recreation areas, on or at all interstate- and intrastate-commerce facilities (waiting rooms and lunch counters as well as the carriers themselves), in libraries and courtrooms and the facilities of all public buildings, and in hotels, restaurants, and other enterprises accommodating the public. It was declared unlawful to list on a ballot the race of a candidate for public office. Black witnesses could no longer be addressed by their first names in Southern courtrooms. Sexual relations between consenting blacks and whites were removed from the criminal decalogue, and in 1967, with barely a murmur of objection in the land, the Court ruled in *Loving v. Virginia* that state laws forbidding that most detestable of all rites—the joining of a white and a Negro in holy matrimony—were unconstitutional. Within that same dozen years after *Brown*, the Court also handed down monumental decisions in two other areas of critical importance to Negroes. In voting rights, the anti-gerrymandering opinion of *Gomillion v. Lightfoot* in 1960, overturning an effort to peel black voters away from Tuskegee, Alabama, was followed by the far more sweeping "one man, one vote" decisions of *Baker v. Carr* in 1962 and *Reynolds v. Sims* in 1964, requiring massive legislative reapportionment that resulted in significantly increased representation of urban centers, where Negroes were concentrated. In the area of criminal justice, the Court under former Alameda County District Attorney Warren significantly improved the ability of accused criminals to defend themselves; *Escobedo v. Illinois*, *Miranda v. Arizona*, and *Gideon v. Wainright* were the landmarks. When the states of Alabama and Virginia tried to shut down the operations of the NAACP within their borders, the Court prevented such blatantly repressive measures. And when peaceful but vocal civil-rights demonstrators were locked up by the hundreds for allegedly disturbing the peace and trespassing, the high court in most instances freed them of such charges.

Once mandated or approved by the Court, desegregation progressed at a relatively rapid rate and in a relatively peaceable manner in most areas—from the restaurants of Washington to the buses of Montgomery to the ballparks of the Texas League. One area alone was excepted: the schools. Streetcars and eating places and amusement parks were, after all, settings for transients who shared proximity for a limited period of time; schools were something else. There the contact would last for six or eight hours daily; it was from interaction with one another as much as attention devoted to lesson books or lectures that schoolchildren derived the essence of their education. And so it was the schoolhouse that became the arena for the South's fiercest resistance to the desegregation order of the Supreme Court.

On July 15, 1955, the first of the five school-segregation cases to travel up to the Supreme Court—*Briggs v. Elliott*—was acted upon by the three-man District Court to which it had been remanded by the Justices. The durable John Parker, then in his thirtieth year on the federal bench, wrote the opinion of the court in the South Carolina case and set a standard for evasiveness by school districts throughout the South. All that the Supreme Court had decided in *Brown*, declared Parker, was that

> a state may not deny to any person on account of race the right to attend any
> school that it maintains . . . but if the schools which it maintains are open to

children of all races, no violation of the Constitution is involved even though the children of different races voluntarily attend different schools, as they attend different churches. Nothing in the Constitution or in the [*Brown*] decision of the Supreme Court takes away from the people the freedom to choose the schools they attend. The Constitution, in other words, does not require integration. It merely forbids discrimination. It does not forbid such discrimination as occurs as the result of voluntary action. It merely forbids the use of governmental power to enforce segregation. . . .

This so-called "Parker doctrine" was widely seized upon by Southern courts to approve a variety of maneuvers designed to deflect the impact of *Brown* in those states and school districts that did not turn to outright defiance of the Court. Some communities followed the lead of Baltimore in giving students a "freedom of choice" form of desegregation; instead of rezoning the district and assigning blacks and whites together to their nearest neighborhood schools, pupils were allowed, regardless of where they lived, to transfer to any school they chose so long as there was room. But in many communities where freedom-of-choice (also known as "local option" or "open enrollment") was theoretically practiced over the next dozen years, relatively few black families would have the nerve to send their children to white schools where they were not wanted. A yet more effective dilatory tactic was the wide adoption of "pupil placement" laws across the South—a technique that was fair on its face but proved strongly segregative in practice. And the Supreme Court did not, in that era, rule out "pupil placement" practices so long as desegregation proceeded at least at a trickle. Tokenism was the order of the times, and just enough of it served to insulate most of the South from the Court's wrath. The District Courts were extraordinarily lenient in granting delays and accepting plans providing for the most fragmentary sort of desegregation.

Many parts of the South wanted nothing whatever to do with desegregation. The more rabid elements in the region were abetted no end in that resolve by the so-called Southern Manifesto issued in the spring of 1956 by 101 Congressmen from the eleven states of the old Confederacy. (The only Southern Senators to rise above the demagoguery of the hour and not sign were Lyndon Johnson of Texas and Estes Kefauver and Albert Gore of Tennessee, three of the better spirits ever to serve in the upper house.) The Court's "unwarranted" decision in *Brown*, said the manifesto, was "a clear abuse of judicial power" and substituted the Justices' "personal political and social ideas for the established law of the land." The men of Dixie concluded their ejaculation of bile with a pledge "to use all lawful means to bring about a reversal of this decision which is contrary to the Constitution."

Such orgiastic declarations of defiance, it must be noted, had not been instantly forthcoming after *Brown* was announced. The interval suggests that the Court had badly misplaced its hope that time would temper the Southern response. As Kenneth Clark and many social psychologists who studied desegregation patterns had warned, gradualism was no guarantee of heightened acceptability. Indeed, the evidence was to the contrary. Throughout the balance of the Fifties, the South interpreted "all deliberate speed" to mean "any conceivable delay," and desegregation was far more a figment in the mind of the Supreme Court than a prominent new feature on the American social landscape. The reasons why the command of the Justices went unheeded extended beyond Southern intransigence. Much of the nation remained in calculated disregard of *Brown* because neither the President nor the Congress came to the aid of the Court. Congress, of course, was still run by the very Dixiecrats who conceived the Southern Manifesto, so it was unlikely that the Court could look there for enforcement legislation to bolster the desegregation process. But President Eisenhower might reasonably have been expected to urge his country to accept the Court's decision. Yet this soldier of rectitude never did that, except in the most offhand way. Word traveled in circles closest to the Court that the Justices were deeply resentful over the White House's failure to lend its great persuasive powers to supporting the rightness of the *Brown* decision. "If Mr. Eisenhower had come through," comments retired Justice Tom Clark, "it would have changed things a lot."

To stand above this battle was to side with the legions of resistance, and Dwight Eisenhower, either by design or by obtuseness, comforted and dignified those who were ranged against the Court. He refused ever to say whether he agreed with the *Brown* decision. "I think it makes no difference whether or not I endorse it," he said in 1956. "The Constitution is as the Supreme Court interprets it; and I must conform to that and do my very best to see that it is carried out in this country." His very best did not include any effort to counter the Southern Manifesto. That same year, as a few Southern school districts began token integration amid reports of planned student boycotts, Eisenhower was asked by the press if he would dip into his "tremendous reservoir of good will among the young people" and offer them some advice as to how they ought to conduct themselves at this important moment. "Well, I can say what I have said so often," said the President. "It is difficult through law and through force to change a man's heart. . . . We must all . . . help to bring about a change in spirit so that extremists on both sides do not defeat what we know is a reasonable, logical conclusion to this whole affair, which is recognition of equality of men." But that was to suggest that there were indeed "extremists on both sides" who were equally culpable when in fact the "sides" consisted of those who insisted on obedience to the law of the land and those who would defy it. Repeatedly, the President stressed the limits of the law's power to transform the minds of men. "As I have always believed, we have got to make certain reforms by education," he said. "No matter how much law we have, we have a job in education, in getting people to understand what are the issues here involved." Never did the President of the United States participate in that educational process, though; never did he urge the country to obey *Brown* not only because it was a decision of the nation's highest court but because it was right.

In 1956, federal court orders in the Autherine Lucy case involving the University of Alabama and in the desegregation of the high school in Mansfield, Texas, were defied, and the President did nothing about it. In 1957, Governor Orval Faubus of Arkansas posted National Guardsmen at the entrance of Little Rock's Central High School to prevent the court-ordered admission of a handful of Negro students. Eisenhower finally had to act when talks with Governor Faubus led nowhere. He reluctantly dispatched crack paratroopers, who stood watch while a few anxious black youngsters came to school at the white man's fortress. Even then, the President did not use the dramatic confrontation at Little Rock to say that lawlessness could not be tolerated in America any longer; even then, he did not follow up and call upon the country to move ahead with desegregation.

Still, the Eisenhower administration was not totally devoid of concern for the Negro. In 1957, Congress passed its first civil-rights act since 1875. From most accounts, the act owed its existence not to the President, whose ineptness nearly submarined it, but to his Attorney General, Herbert Brownell, one of the very few pro-civil-rights people in the Eisenhower high command. The tepid bill provided for the creation of a Civil Rights Commission with no power other than to recommend legislation, a new Civil Rights Division in the Justice Department, and, most important, the right of the Justice Department to bring suits on behalf of Negroes denied the right to vote.

Once equipped with its new power in the voting-rights area, the Eisenhower Justice Department proved something less than a tiger in the bush. It filed a grand total of ten cases during the more than three years it held power after the 1957 rights bill was passed. Administration pressure meanwhile on the South to desegregate its schools may be gauged by the fact that during the first four years after *Brown* was decided, a total of 750 school districts underwent at least token desegregation, almost all of them voluntarily. During the last three years of the Eisenhower administration, 1958 to 1960, when one might not unreasonably have asked the South to demonstrate less deliberation and more speed in the integration process, a total of 49 school districts were desegregated.

Ike, the amiable, peace-loving warrior who had led the West's great crusade in Europe against the forces of darkness, had proven unwilling to muster a comparable moral effort in his homeland when the hour called for it.

John F. Kennedy was the first American President who genuinely committed his administration to broad action taken specifically to improve the position of the Negro. Whether he and his activist brother Robert, the Attorney General for the thousand days of the Kennedy administration, did as much as they might have or as much as has been claimed is not at issue here; what is incontestable is that for the first time the White House was an active and willing participant in the widening struggle to win the Negro his civil rights. That burden no longer rested, as it had until that time, almost entirely upon the Supreme Court and the rest of the federal judiciary.

Kennedy people began using the civil-rights weapons at their disposal soon after taking office. Federal protection was extended to freedom riders protesting segregated waiting rooms and lunch counters in bus, train, and air terminals. The Justice Department petitioned the Interstate Commerce

Commission, a quasi-independent regulatory body, to issue a blanket order against segregation at bus and railroad facilities, and within a few months the edict was approved. Enforcement was rapid. The government moved to enter a number of school-desegregation suits on the side of Negro petitioners as a friend of the court. The pace of desegregation itself picked up: 31 districts in 1961, 46 districts in 1962, 166 districts in 1963. For the first time, the Deep South began to desegregate. The most spectacular cases occurred at the college level, with ranking Justice Department officials prominently involved in the desegregation of the University of Alabama, where clench-fisted Governor George Wallace briefly blocked the doorway, and the University of Mississippi, where two died before James Meredith officially matriculated.

The Justice Department filed forty-five voting-rights-infringement cases under the 1957 Civil Rights Act during the fewer than three years John Kennedy was in office, and young blacks and whites from the North began penetrating the rural South to help register long-reluctant and long-silent Negroes. The federal government chose not to extend its protective umbrella to this perilous private effort, but unofficially monitored the drive and encouraged it. All branches of the federal government were urged to step up substantially their hiring of blacks, and federal contractors were similarly pushed. In late 1962, Kennedy signed an executive order prohibiting racial discrimination in all housing that received direct federal subsidies and in the much vaster part of the home-building market financed by federally guaranteed mortgages.

This last step was overdue and illustrated the margin of restraint that Kennedy insisted upon in the civil-rights area. Though no dynamo during his six years in the House and eight years in the Senate, he had prospered nicely by not provoking the Dixiecrats. As President, Kennedy remained uneager to antagonize Congress by too ardent an espousal of black men's rights lest the Southern lawmakers scuttle his entire legislative program. Thus, he delayed for more than two years before signing the anti-discrimination order in housing that he promised during his election campaign could be readily accomplished by a single stroke of the presidential pen. Instead of hailing the move when it finally was made, civil-rights advocates lamented that it had taken so long and did not have more teeth in it—a sure sign that the glamorous young President had ignited expansive hopes and perhaps unfulfillable expectations in this area.

In the spring of 1963, black initiatives escalated the widening civil-rights campaign. New young Southern Negro leadership settled upon a strategy of non-violent confrontation with the segregation-forever cadres, personified by Birmingham's porcine commissioner of fire, police, and education (*sic*), Eugene "Bull" Connor. Birmingham proved a fateful battleground all that year. It won nationwide attention on Good Friday, April 12, when the Reverend King led a hymn-singing column of Negroes on a protest march against the repressive racism of Birmingham, where blacks had as much trouble getting a cup of coffee at a lunch counter as a decent job. King had promised to lead a "kneel-in" on Easter Sunday—when black worshippers would pray on the steps of whites-only churches throughout the city—and refused to obey an injunction Connor obtained to prevent all such protest marches. King's group was met with snapping police dogs that Good Friday in a spectacle relayed across America by television news cameras as the reverend and two fellow ministers were jailed. It was the thirteenth time that King had been arrested since taking the lead in the civil-rights movement.

Throughout the spring, the protest marches and demonstrations continued, manned in substantial measure by young blacks, many of them schoolchildren. And "Bull" Connor arrested them by the hundreds. Peaceful demonstrations gave way to rocks and bottle-throwing, and soon bombs were going off in colored neighborhoods. Robert Kennedy sent his gifted Civil Rights Division chief, Assistant Attorney General Burke Marshall, to Birmingham to try to negotiate a peace settlement between blacks and the city's financial leaders, who were alarmed at the increasingly infamous name the city was winning for itself by its intransigence on the race question. A shaky pact was no sooner worked out than the city exploded with riots and more bombings. Just a week later, Governor Wallace, calling for law and order, announced that he would defy a federal-court directive to admit two Negroes to a summer session at the University of Alabama. In the event, Wallace backed down, but it took the federalization of the Alabama National Guard to make him.

That confrontation pushed John Kennedy beyond the limit of patience with the defiantly segregationist South. He went on television that evening and delivered by far the most moving words on the deprivations of black America that had ever been heard in the land on the lips of a high federal official. "We are confronted primarily with a moral issue," President Kennedy declared. "It is as old as the Scriptures and is as clear as the Constitution." He went on:

> If an American, because his skin is dark, cannot eat lunch in a restaurant open to the public; if he cannot send his children to the best public school available; if he cannot vote for the public officials who represent him; if, in short, he cannot enjoy the full and free life which all of us want, then who among us would be content to have the color of his skin changed and stand in his place?
>
> Who among us would then be content with the counsels of patience and delay? One hundred years of delay have passed since President Lincoln freed the slaves, yet their heirs, their grandsons, are not fully free. They are not yet freed from the bonds of injustice; they are not yet freed from social and economic oppression. And this nation, for all its hopes and all its boasts, will not be fully free until all its citizens are free.
>
> We preach freedom around the world, and we mean it. And we cherish our freedom here at home. But are we to say to the world—and much more importantly to each other—that this is the land of the free, except for the Negroes; that we have no second-class citizens, except Negroes; that we have no class or caste system, no ghettos, no master race, except with respect to Negroes?

Now the time had come for the nation to fulfill its promise, said John Kennedy, for the events of Birmingham were not isolated ones. "The fires of frustration and discord are burning in every city, North and South," he said—and a week later he sent Congress the most potent civil-rights bill in history. Kennedy had played politics with the South's congressional leaders, but it had not won him notably more legislation than he might otherwise have obtained. He had gone along with the appointment of a number of white-supremacist federal judges in an effort to bargain with Southern power, and it was plain that his call for a strong civil-rights bill would end that fragile working relationship between the White House and the entrenched Southern bloc on the Hill. Yet some President had to take that step sooner or later. John Kennedy took it on June 19, 1963.

Kennedy's civil-rights bill bore this heading: "An act to enforce the constitutional right to vote, to confer jurisdiction upon the district courts of the United States to provide injunctive relief against discrimination in public accommodations, to authorize the Attorney General to institute suits to protect constitutional rights in public facilities and public education, to extend the Commission on Civil Rights, to prevent discrimination in federally assisted programs, to establish a Commission on Equal Employment Opportunity, and for other purposes." Arbitrarily administered literacy tests and other devices to keep the Negro disenfranchised were to be put under vigorous federal inspection. Hotels, theaters, restaurants, and other places of business open to the public would no longer be able to discriminate—a prohibition that the Supreme Court had struck down in 1883 in overturning portions of the Civil Rights Act of 1875. The Kennedy bill also denied employers license to discriminate in their hiring practices and labor unions the power to keep blacks from their membership roster. And to oversee this disestablishment of racism, the Justice Department would be massively empowered now to go to court in the name of black Americans who could ill afford the time, energy, and cost of suing sovereign states and their subdivisions whose laws and policies effectively frustrated the desegregation process.

The filibustering South began warming up its tonsils in the event the bill ever emerged from committee, while Kennedy set to work on a lobbying drive to win broad national support from business, labor, and the professions for the sweeping rights bill. When black leaders proposed a mass March on Washington later that summer to show their own solidarity and add their insistent demand for the rights bill and other federal action, the Kennedy people were edgy. Any display of violence or provocative conduct was viewed as likely to imperil the bill's chances. But the March could not be headed off. It proved the soaring moment of the first post-*Brown* decade. Two hundred thousand people gathered on the Mall on August 28 to hear the words of the prophet of the civil-rights movement, the man whose bearing and bravery had won the respect of the world:

> . . . I have a dream that one day this nation will rise up and live out the true meaning of its creed. . . .
>
> I have a dream that one day on the red hills of Georgia, the sons of former slaves and the sons of former slaveowners will be able to sit down together at the table of brotherhood.

I have a dream that one day even the state of Mississippi, a state sweltering with the heat of injustice, sweltering with the heat of oppression, will be transformed into an oasis of freedom and justice.

I have a dream that my four little children will one day live in a nation where they will not be judged by the color of their skin but by the content of their character.

I have a dream that one day every valley shall be exalted, every hill and mountain shall be made low, the rough places will be made plain, and the crooked places will be made straight, and the glory of the Lord shall be revealed and all flesh shall see it together. . . .

But even then, other black voices were rising to preach a different message. Those Negroes whose idea of protest was to link arms at an interracial rally and sing "We Shall Overcome" were just trying to crawl back to the plantation, Malcolm X was telling black audiences now. "You need somebody who is going to fight," he had declared at the height of the Birmingham upheavals. "You don't need any kneeling in or crawling in." The black man was afraid to bleed in his own defense, said Malcolm, but that would no longer do. It was time for all blacks to recognize that the white man was their oppressor and they had too long been lambs before this marauding wolf. Blacks had to assume command of their own destinies.

Intellectual spokesmen such as James Baldwin also transmitted a growing sense of rage in black America as Negroes, with their heightened sense of selfhood, began to turn on their tormentors and declare the pace of progress a dawdle. But even this new militancy itself was a measure of how much America had changed in the decade since *Brown*. Before 1954, what black man would have stood up in the nation and cursed the white man as a loathsome predator without expecting swift retribution? Black rage was newly permissible among the emotions being registered in American public rhetoric. It angered and frightened whites. It both emboldened and confused blacks, caught between the non-violent, integrationist preachments of Martin Luther King and Malcolm's increasingly strident black nationalism.

In January of 1964, the Twenty-fourth Amendment, outlawing the poll tax, was pronounced adopted—a step hastened, no doubt, by the contrition of a nation grieving the tragedy in Dallas two months before. But John Kennedy's great legacy to the black man's drive for equality was the civil-rights bill that the new President took up as his own and pushed with all his manipulative might through the halls of Congress. The tenth anniversary of *Brown* arrived while the bill was still pending. A head count then showed that only 1.17 percent of black schoolchildren in the eleven states of the Confederacy were attending public school with white classmates, and Malcolm X could stand up and proclaim that there had been no progress since the *Brown* decision. But it was evident that a great deal had changed. Almost everywhere, laws requiring or permitting racial segregation of any kind had been or were being stripped from the books and integration was growing in all walks of life. The hundred daily lashes of petty humiliation which the hand of the state had administered to every Negro for so long were truly ending. Attention turned now to the worsening *de facto* segregation of the North. In the early Sixties, for the first time a federal court charged a Northern community—New Rochelle, New York—with districting its schools to segregate its black children. Chic liberals who took cheap shots at scoring Southern racism would now have to answer to the virulent variety in their own backyards.

During Lyndon Johnson's first months in the White House, Malcolm X demeaned him as "a Southern cracker—that's all he is." Perhaps black leaders feared that the new President would prove the reincarnation of the last man named Johnson to occupy the White House. Perhaps it was the leftover cracker in his speech. As it turned out, Lyndon Johnson, whose mastery of legislative technique featured glad-handing that could become bone-crushing, got Congress to do a great deal more for the rights of Negroes than John Kennedy could probably ever have accomplished. Kennedy's ghost, though, was alive in the land; black America was the principal beneficiary of his martyrdom.

The Senate passed the landmark 1964 Civil Rights Act precisely a year to the day after Kennedy sent it to Congress. It was a mighty weapon if only the executive branch chose to use it. Over the next ten years, with sharply varying degrees of enthusiasm, the federal government put the 1964 rights bill to a great deal of use. The Justice Department would bring legal actions against more than 500 school districts during the decade. The Department of Health, Education, and Welfare, charged in 1965 with suspending federal education aid to school districts that discriminated racially, would file more than 600 actions. Justice, furthermore, was to undertake more than 400 anti-discrimination suits against hotels, restaurants, taverns, gas stations, truck stops, and other establishments catering to the public, and many times that number of businesses complied voluntarily with the 1964 act when the Justice Department registered its displeasure with their policies. Before 1964 was over, the Supreme Court had ruled unanimously, in the case of *Heart of Atlanta Motel v. United States*, that the rights act was constitutional.

Having outflanked the Dixiecratic power base in the Senate, Lyndon Johnson kept pushing civil-rights measures through Congress throughout the next four years. The legislative branch now joined in the drive for black equality that the judiciary had led during the Eisenhower years and the executive branch had fostered during the Kennedy years. In 1965, the Voting Rights Act closed remaining loopholes in the 1964 measure and further restricted "tests and devices" used to foil would-be black voters. Such legislation, adding federal registrars and observers to the continuing efforts of civil-rights workers in the field, most effectively led by the Student Nonviolent Coordinating Committee, produced extraordinary results. As of 1961, only 1,250,000 Negroes, or one-quarter of the South's voting-age blacks, were registered to vote. By 1964, the number had reached nearly two million; in the next ten years, another 1,330,000 blacks were added to the South's voting rolls, and no one seeking office could afford to ignore their collective strength at the polls.

In 1965 as well, the Elementary and Secondary Education Act was passed, making sizable federal funds available to local school districts and providing the government with a mighty financial club to enforce compliance with the desegregation orders of federal courts; under the 1964 Act, any state or local government practicing discrimination was not eligible to receive federal aid. The education bill was part of a proliferating series of imaginative new federal programs aimed at declaring war on poverty and ignorance. Together—aid to schools, Model Cities, the Office of Economic Opportunity, VISTA, Head Start, and others—Johnson labeled them steppingstones to a Great Society that he mapped out in his expansive rhetoric. No sector of the nation stood to gain more from the Great Society program than black America.

Everywhere, the color line was now being crossed. Robert Weaver, named Secretary of Housing and Urban Development, became the first black Cabinet member in 1966. That same year, Edward Brooke of Massachusetts, a Republican, became the first Negro to be elected to the United States Senate since Reconstruction. Constance Baker Motley, after twenty years as a member of the NAACP Legal Defense Fund office, became the first black woman named to the federal bench. Bill Russell became the first black coach of a major-league sports team, the Boston Celtics of the National Basketball Association. Bill Cosby, the first black to be given a starring role in a television dramatic series, won an Emmy award for his work in *I Spy*, and Julian Bond, with a little help from the Supreme Court, first took his seat in the Georgia House of Representatives as leader of a new generation of black politicians.

In 1967, the President named a Negro to the court that had touched off the civil-rights revolution. Kennedy had appointed Thurgood Marshall to the U.S. Court of Appeals for the Second Circuit in 1961 amid reports that Judge William Hastie of the Third Circuit was in line for elevation to the Supreme Court. But when the first vacancy occurred, the politically attuned President found the time not ripe to select a Negro for the high court and chose instead Assistant Attorney General Byron R. White. The next and final Kennedy appointment went to Secretary of Labor Arthur Goldberg to fill "the Jewish seat" being vacated by Felix Frankfurter. In 1965, Lyndon Johnson put a bear hug on Thurgood Marshall to come off the bench and become Solicitor General, a position that would presumably give him exposure to a breadth of social problems and better qualify him for the ultimate reward in the offing. It came when Justice Tom Clark stepped down in 1967. Marshall, at fifty-nine, became the ninety-sixth man to serve on the nation's highest court—and the first Negro. He was no stranger when he got there.

In 1968, his last year in office, Johnson won a major addition to the battery of civil-rights laws he was to obtain from Congress. The Fair Housing Act of that year made it unlawful to refuse to sell or rent—or to refuse to negotiate for the sale or rental of—a dwelling because of race or religion; to advertise the sale or rental of any dwelling in any way "that indicates any preference, limitation, or discrimination" based on race, religion, or national origin; to pretend to anyone for such reasons that "any dwelling is not available for inspection, sale, or rental when such dwelling is in fact so available"; and to deny any person "access to or membership or participation in any multiple-listing service, real estate brokers' association" or other organization established to help sell or rent dwellings. Here was a law so sweeping that, if properly enforced and policed, it would go far toward ending the ghettoization of black America. It said in unmistakable language that any Negro who could meet the asking price must not be denied the purchase or rental of any dwelling on the market anywhere in the nation. And the Justice Department in fact filed or joined in some 200 cases involving violations of the Fair Housing Act during the first six years it was in force, a number of the cases affecting large apartment complexes. But this effort was as the dropping of a single vial of purifier into the Mississippi River. No serious effort was being made in those years to apply the housing act or dramatize its scope, and most people in America were unaware that any such federal law existed.

Lyndon Johnson, whose extraordinary civil-rights and anti-poverty programs should have made him a beloved patron saint to black America, nevertheless wound up substantially discredited and sharply reviled. His own ambitions and obsessions proved uncontainable as he allowed his most humane impulses—and America's financial resources—to be leeched by a war on the other side of the world. The wide-ranging domestic programs the President set in motion, moreover, were underfunded for the goals they envisioned and were too slackly or imprudently directed. The whole enterprise was spread too thin, and the expected overnight results were impossible to obtain.

When enemies of the Great Society eagerly began to snipe at the programs as pie-in-the-sky, the President, ever more deeply mired in his Vietnam misadventure, was too distracted to manage his admirable and innovative domestic undertakings. The nation was suddenly spinning out of orbit. A severe case of frustration was inflaming emotions and polarizing the people as they had not been since the Civil War. And the plainer it became that here was a war America could not win, the more shrill and bitter the division grew.

Paralleling the deepening turmoil over Vietnam was the escalation of the black revolution at home. Negro leadership now passed into steadily more radical and impatient hands as the tiny black bourgeoisie proved ill-equipped to cope with the convulsive changes and soaring expectations of the colored masses. Self-hatred gave way to black-is-beautiful, and pride turned aggressive and menacing toward white America. Desegregation itself was now sharply questioned; it was one thing not to be quarantined by law from the rest of the nation, but it was quite another, and unacceptable, thing to be forced to mingle with it on terms of the white man's choosing. Integration as a social solution to the problems of black America was based on the premise, wrote Stokely Carmichael and Charles V. Hamilton in *Black Power* in 1967, that "in order to have a decent house or education, black people must move into a white neighborhood or send their children to a white school. This reinforces, among both black and white, the idea that 'white' is automatically superior and 'black' is by definition inferior. For this reason, 'integration' is a subterfuge for the maintenance of white supremacy." The middle-class values and institutions that ruled America clinked hollow to the new black leaders, who found few models worth emulating among their white country-men.

To inarticulate ghetto-dwellers, still trapped by poverty and ignorance, yet now seemingly free to express their discontent over the accumulated debris of their existence, all the angry words of the young black intellectuals heaped tinder in a parched forest. At the first show of provocative white behavior, they put their rundown sections of the city to the torch and then stoned the agents of the power establishment who came to put the fires out. They rioted in dozens of communities when the warm weather came. In 1965, it was Watts, the sidetracked black quarter of Los Angeles, where arrest of a twenty-one-year-old Negro for drunk driving set off a five-day fiery mayhem that required 13,000 National Guardsmen to quell; thirty-four died, more than 1,000 were injured, 200 businesses were totally destroyed, and property damage was estimated at $40 million. The riots continued for three years. In 1968, after the assassination of Martin Luther King in Memphis on April 4, rioting was reported in 125 American cities. Nearly 70,000 troops were called up to restore peace; forty-six were killed, all but five of them black, 3,500 were injured, 20,000 were arrested, and damage was calculated at $45 million.

The cities seemed on the verge of anarchy. Yet black America, in all its fury, had chosen to inflict most of the damage on itself, as if to purge what it hated most about its way of life.

Whites viewing this volcanic display of black power, most of it seemingly destructive and self-immolating, shrank from the hellish scenes. Racial tension, supposedly a Southern phenomenon, was now undeniably a national problem and far more combustible in its urban variety in the North and Midwest and West. The old Brotherhood Week platitudes were being spat upon. The old alliances were dead. The only brothers these rampaging hordes seemed interested in were black ones. Liberals to them were worse than Klansmen because they lent false hope within a corrupt system. Whitey was a pig. Blacks demanded their own hairdos back and gloried in their own kind of dress and food and talk and music. They demanded black studies and black dormitories and preferential treatment for any coveted opening, to compensate for all the generations of exploitation. Power to the people meant black people, and the Black Panthers, conceived as a protection society against white police brutality, came on like unleashed killers ready to spatter The Man up against the wall.

All this churning aggressiveness inspired as much resentment as fear in white America. What, after all, did these people want? They could not continue to rape and rob with impunity; they could not keep shooting up with dope and living off welfare handouts and expect whites to welcome them to their neighborhoods. Cool assessment of the severe social and economic problems at the root of the race war was hard to hear above the din. Whites were confronted by a black uproar in their streets, by soaring crime rates, by an endless war they could not win and dared not lose, by a younger generation that wore its hair long and despised much of what its parents believed in, by an environment gone to grime, by assassinations and demonstrations and rancor all around, and by an economy beginning to go haywire.

And that was how Lyndon Johnson went away. Gone, too, by then, were the Kennedy brothers and the Reverend King and his Beelzebub, Malcolm, and Medgar Evers, the black NAACP leader of Mississippi, and too many other good men of both races. A new leader, promising to bring the nation back together, became President.

Whatever other crimes history may finally assign to Richard Nixon, he was hopelessly guilty of debasing the Queen's English. It was not that he was especially ungrammatical, but that he never uttered a memorable phrase, never rose above the most banal selection of words, and seemed to think the use of slang might somehow endear him to the masses. It was thus the height of eloquence for Nixon during his 1968 campaign for the presidency to assure black America that he thought it was entitled to "a piece of the action."

But it was hard to mistake Richard Nixon for a friend of the colored people. Nothing in his political past suggested that he was concerned with civil rights or the complex racial problems besetting the country. Indeed, he came to the White House on a platform bedecked with cryptic racism. He would end the internal strife in America by restoring "law and order" in the streets. He would name "strict-constructionists" to the Supreme Court to replace the criminal-coddling Justices who thought hoodlums deserved as much protection as their victims. He thought all the mismanaged giveaways of the Great Society had to be curbed and the long-neglected rights of the sovereign states had to be restored.

He meant what he said. His accession to power signaled a crackdown on rebelliousness in all forms. Black rioting fell off sharply. Peace demonstrations declined as well, the more so after bullets fired by National Guardsmen ended the student display at Kent State University in Ohio. But if violence ebbed, hope did, too, in the disadvantaged sectors of the population. Richard Nixon seemed inclined to roll back the gains scored by black America or, at the least, to check them; in the process, he would strengthen his standing in the more conservative cantons of Dixie. This "Southern strategy" worked too well; eventually, the rest of the nation would turn its back on him.

He began by phasing out the anti-poverty programs as rapidly as was feasible. Away with Model Cities and offices of economic opportunity and all such inflationary flotsam. He slashed federal spending for education and school lunches. He talked about a guaranteed annual wage and welfare reform but did not bother pushing Congress for his social legislation the way Lyndon Johnson had. He picked Warren Burger, a moderate conservative, as Chief Justice and then for a second vacancy on the Court nominated two Southern judges, neither of whom was destined to rival Robert E. Lee for flawless character. The first of his Southern choices, while judicially competent, was found to have committed several financial improprieties stemming from cases on which he had sat; the second was found both judicially incompetent and apparently sympathetic to white supremacy. The President settled for Harry Blackmun, a Midwestern judge who was a pale carbon of the Chief Justice. Two years later, he named Lewis Powell, a moderate, upright, and skilled Richmond lawyer,* and William Rehnquist, the bright, very conservative law-and-order Assistant Attorney General, to fill two more vacancies. Gone now were Earl Warren, Hugo Black, Abe Fortas, and John Marshall Harlan—three liberals and a constructive conservative, and four of the ablest men ever to sit on the Court. His four appointees by no means did all the President might have wished, but the spirit of the highly activist, humanitarian Warren Court had departed. The Nixon bloc, voting together more often than any foursome since Harry Truman's sodden appointees, commanded the Court.

It was in the quarter-hearted way the Nixon administration applied the anti-discrimination laws of the Johnson era that its indifference to the claims of black America was perhaps most obviously measurable. A 1974 report by the U.S. Civil Rights Commission, for example, reviewed federal-government enforcement of the 1968 Fair Housing Act and concluded: "Present programs often are administered so as to continue rather than reduce racial segregation." State and local officials were, with impunity, using zoning regulations, building codes, and highway construction to keep out or remove poor and minority-group families from many suburban areas, the commission found. Private real-estate brokers were, with still less fear of federal intrusion, steering buyers to all-white or all-black neighborhoods, and white real-estate boards were widely refusing to admit black brokers, who as a result were denied access to lists of homes for sale.

In school desegregation, the administration's policy was more than Fabian; it became downright obstructionist, and those in the Justice Department and HEW who disagreed with it either left or were purged.

Just how this foot-dragging went on was documented by a report issued in September 1974 by the Center for National Policy Review, an outcropping of the law school at Catholic University of America in Washington. Titled "Justice Delayed and Denied," the 117-page report noted that HEW had begun reviewing cases in Northern and Western communities in earnest in 1968 to see if school-desegregation guidelines were being met; if not and the districts did not remedy the situation, federal funds were to be cut off. In 1968, HEW initiated 28 such community reviews. In 1969, the first Nixon year, the number dropped to 16; in 1970, to 15; in 1971, to 11; in 1972, to 9; in 1973, to one; in 1974, to zero—all at a time when the Office of Civil Rights staff was growing. The average length of an HEW investigation was thirty-two months—before a decision was made whether to advise a district it was in non-compliance. If a district under investigation became the target of private litigation, the HEW investigation was suspended, as if the district should therefore be immune from federal hectoring. HEW also had an odd

---

* He was a member of the same firm as Justin Moore and Archibald Robertson, who handled the state's case in the original Virginia school-segregation suit, *Davis v. County School Board of Prince Edward County.*

sense of priorities; it preferred to review small or medium-sized cities involving relatively few Negroes rather than large cities with severe compliance problems affecting tens of thousands of black students.

When an HEW review finally did point to the need for a cutoff of federal funds, the department's Office of the General Counsel sat on the case, sometimes for years, insisting that the evidence be airtight before proceeding with a reprimand and possible punitive measures. So dilatory was Nixon's HEW that in February 1973 a federal District judge had to order the department to begin enforcement proceedings against seventy-four Southern school districts found in non-compliance in 1971 or which had reneged on their desegregation plans, and to commence proceedings against forty-two other Southern districts in probable non-compliance. The Center for National Policy Review concluded its report by declaring "there is little question that the Nixon Administration's negative policy declarations have impaired enforcement action and demoralized the HEW civil rights staff. . . . All of this means that minority citizens face continued disappointment of their legitimate expectations that the federal government will protect their children's rights. This situation could be altered—by a Congress prepared to exercise its oversight responsibilities to assure that its laws are obeyed by the executive branch, by new political leadership committed to the rule of law and ready to appeal to people's aspirations rather than their fears, by federal officials determined to be faithful to their oaths of office. . . ."

The HEW record in desegregation amply demonstrated what the Nixon people meant when they suggested in 1970—in the memorable words of the resident (and solitary) White House intellectual, Daniel Moynihan—that "the time may have come when the issue of race could benefit from a period of benign neglect . . . in which Negro progress continues and racial rhetoric fades." But it was not just neglect that Nixon offered the Negro; it was downright opposition, most notably in an effort to reverse the mandates of the Supreme Court by trying to push a constitutional amendment through Congress prohibiting bussing of schoolchildren to achieve desegregation.

"Bussing" replaced "law-and-order" as the white-backlash code word of the early Seventies. There was, to be sure, a good deal to be said on both sides of the question, though it cannot be said the President did anything to elevate the level of the public discussion; rather, he played to the galleries for all the emotion he could wring from the heated subject. Few whites had objected when, before *Brown*, black children were bussed all over the map to segregated schools far from their homes while white children were generally within easy walking distance of their neighborhood school. Topeka had been a classic example: black children were bussed to the four colored schools in town, usually passing one or more white schools en route; white youngsters attended eighteen schools scattered conveniently around the city and needed no buses. Thus, bussing to maintain segregation had been happily countenanced by white parents, but the prospect of bussing their own youngsters for the purpose of integration produced bared teeth. Why should any child have to forgo a nice white neighborhood school to take an exhausting bus ride to an older school with broken equipment and inexperienced teachers in a black neighborhood? It was well known, moreover, that Negro children had far lower educational standards than whites, who would therefore likely suffer both academic malnutrition and the constant threat of a shakedown at the point of a switchblade.

Blacks, for their part, were also finding fault with bussing; going to a white-majority school was no automatic ticket to paradise. Their white classmates often snubbed them and left them out of extracurricular activities. Their white teachers often assumed they could not handle the intellectual challenge and had them "tracked" into heavily black classes where low academic expectations prevailed. And their white principals were said to be far quicker to charge them with infractions of the rules and seek their expulsion than they were with wayward whites.

The President proclaimed his opposition to "forced integration" by bussing. It was a popular stand with both races. Unfortunately, it placed him in opposition to the Supreme Court, which sanctioned bussing as one of a number of ways that school districts could get on with the long-delayed business of desegregation.

In Earl Warren's last term as Chief Justice, the Court made clear that, whatever it had meant in *Brown II* by ordering the nation's school districts to desegregate "with all deliberate speed," the "deliberate" part of that phrase had about expired. In *Green v. County School Board of New Kent County, Virginia*, the Court punctured the "freedom of choice" scheme prevalent in much of the South as an evasive device. Though in theory the open-enrollment system allowed black parents to send their children to schools in white neighborhoods, only about 10 percent of black families exercised that option, even when free transportation was available. The system was flawed because it cast the black child in the role of interloper; almost no whites, moreover, exercised their "freedom of choice" by going to black schools, and so many all-black schools remained until the Court spoke in *Green.* The key to the acceptability of any school-district plan submitted in compliance with the original *Brown* decision was, quite simply, how effectively it was accomplishing desegregation. Freedom-of-choice plans had obviously functioned to perpetuate segregated schools. "The burden on a school board today," said the Court, "is to come forward with a plan that promises realistically to work . . . until it is clear that state-imposed segregation has been completely removed . . . root and branch." The time to come forward with such a plan, said the Justices, was now.

At its next term, the Court was presided over by Richard Nixon's choice to lead it, Warren Earl Burger. The new President was apparently not warm to the drift of the Warren Court's *Green* decision. Things would be different now under Burger. A temperate outlook would be most welcome at a time when the issue was being disputed by what Nixon on September 26, 1969, called "two extreme groups"—namely, "those who want instant integration and those who want segregation forever." A few weeks later, the President learned, to his distress, that his new Chief Justice was among the former group of extremists. Writing a short, blunt opinion for a unanimous Court in *Alexander v. Holmes County (Mississippi) Board of Education*, Burger asserted:

"Under explicit holdings of this Court, the obligation of every school district is to terminate dual school systems at once and to operate now and hereafter only unitary schools." There was no confusing the timetable of the Court. Fifteen years of deliberate speed were more than enough. Compliance was now required "at once."

In rural areas of the South, where white and black lived interspersed, effective compliance could readily be attained simply by assigning children of both races to the nearest schoolhouse, no matter which color it had previously served. And indeed throughout much of the rural South, including the most virulent white-supremacist country in Mississippi, the process began to be accomplished, and without violence. The Justice Department, while maintaining a very low profile, spread word that it was not eager to press the crown of thorns upon Dixie but the Court's command was unmistakable and a beginning would have to be made everywhere. But in urban areas, where the races lived largely apart, going to the neighborhood school meant remaining in a racially unmixed setting because of *de facto* segregation. Had the Court intended to outlaw schools that were segregated by social conditions as well as by state and local laws? And if so, how could desegregation be accomplished if not by massive bussing, pairing of schools, use of non-contiguous zones, and similar devices that worked against the long-honored concept of the neighborhood school? The Court addressed itself to those questions in 1971.

Charlotte, the biggest city in North Carolina, and surrounding Mecklenburg County made up the most populous school district in the state. In June of 1969, when black litigants began to press for desegregation, only 29 percent of the district was Negro, but two-thirds of the 21,000 colored children in the Charlotte-Mecklenburg district attended schools that were either entirely black or nearly so. An expert appointed by the District Court—after the school district itself offered an inadequate plan—proposed a comprehensive desegregation plan that involved considerable reshuffling of students by pairing schools (e.g., transferring grades one to three at an all-black school to an all-white school and shifting grades four to six from the all-white school to the all-black school), drastic gerrymandering, carving school-attendance zones out of non-contiguous areas, clustering schools, and a considerable amount of bussing, though not a great deal more than the district itself was already practicing. In April of 1971, the Supreme Court, in an opinion again unanimous and again written by Chief Justice Burger, ruled in the case of *Swann v. Charlotte-Mecklenburg Board of Education* that, all things being equal, it was desirable to assign pupils to schools nearest their homes, but "all things are not equal in a system that has been deliberately constructed and maintained to enforce racial segregation." It was not enough now for such a community to come forward with a "racially neutral" assignment plan based on existing residential patterns that in themselves had developed around segregated schools in the past, because

> such plans may fail to counteract the continuing effects of past school segregation resulting from discriminatory location of school sites or distortion of school size in order to achieve or maintain an artificial racial separation.

Thus, while every school in every community did not have to reflect the racial composition of the school district as a whole, the district was obliged to undertake as much desegregation as possible; the preservation of neighborhood schools was not sacrosanct. Remedial steps, like some of those proposed in the plan the District Court had approved for Charlotte, might be "administratively awkward, inconvenient and even bizarre in some situations and may impose burdens on some," but that price had to be paid in the interest of eliminating dual school systems. Bussing specifically was approved as a constructive way to attain maximum desegregation, provided it did not place an undue hardship on pupils. Some 40 percent of all schoolchildren in the nation already traveled to school by bus each day, the Court remarked; it could not be said that to achieve desegregation by bussing necessitated a radical departure from custom.

The NAACP Legal Defense Fund, by then under the command of Jack Greenberg for ten years, moved swiftly to follow up the *Swann* breakthrough by pushing similar cases elsewhere. President Nixon himself moved to circumvent *Swann*. He instructed Justice Department officials to start drafting a constitutional amendment against bussing to nullify the Court's decision. The South, by contrast, obeyed the Court. By the 1972–73 school year, 46.3 percent of the black children in the eleven Southern states were attending schools in which the majority of children were white. No other sector of the nation had achieved anything near that degree of desegregation.

Two years later, the laggard North and West were put on notice by the Court that they, too, had to comply. Outside the South and border states, in 1972–73 only 28.3 percent of Negro children were attending schools where the majority of students were white. Ghettoization in most cities was growing more severe; the largely unused Fair Housing Act of 1968 had made no dent in the pattern, and the white middle-class exodus to suburbia left more and more cities with a lopsided population composed of a slim economic elite, blue-collar whites too poor to move, and an inner core of blacks. In Denver, the situation was less severe than elsewhere, but local officials had plainly rigged the black Park Hill area to confine its residents to heavily black schools and blamed the result on *de facto* segregation. In the Legal Defense Fund-sponsored case of *Keyes v. Denver School District No. 1*, the Supreme Court ruled in June of 1973 by a seven-to-one vote (Justice Rehnquist dissenting) that the district could not disclaim responsibility for its policies that served, as effectively as any openly Jim Crow statute might have, to keep 38 percent of the city's Negro school population racially isolated. Among the policies cited were the building of a new school in the heart of the black area instead of on the fringe, gerrymandering student-attendance zones to include blacks and exclude whites from the Park Hill district, establishment of optional zones on the outer edge of the black area so that whites were free to choose their school (almost always the nearest white one), and excessive use of mobile classrooms so that children in crowded black schools would not have to be assigned to available classrooms in white schools. The Court held that "a finding of intentionally segregative school board actions in a meaningful portion of a school system, as in this case, creates a presumption that other segregated schooling within the system is not adventitious." Once partial segregation by design was shown, the burden was on the authorities to show that the entire system was not so infected. As in *Swann*, the Court said that past segregative practices obliged the school district to go well beyond providing a racially neutral assignment plan in the future.

Court-ordered desegregation had now reached beyond the South. The rest of the nation could no longer pretend that so long as it did not have segregation laws on its books, it was exempt from the *Brown* imperative. In 1954, the Court had spoken not against "segregation" but "racial discrimination" in any form that resulted in separate schools.

In his last eighteen months in office, the Nixon Court finally gave the President two school decisions that must have pleased him. In March of 1973, all four Nixon appointees voted together and were joined by Eisenhower holdover Potter Stewart in a five-to-four opinion that headed off a revolution in the funding of public schools in America.

Since the Court had held in *Brown* that state-ordered discrimination resulting in racially separate schools was a denial of equal protection, why wasn't a state-approved disparity in the per-pupil funds spent in that state a similar denial of equal protection? Why, in other words, should a child living in a poor school district be provided with a less costly public education than a child living in a wealthy one? Or to put it yet another way: once a state made school attendance compulsory and required each community within it to operate free public schools, wasn't that state obliged to assure every one of its schoolchildren a public education on equal terms with every other? What else did equal protection of the laws mean if not that? Just these troubling questions were raised in a case coming to the Court from San Antonio, Texas.

Edgewood, a poor section in the heart of San Antonio, had a population 90 percent Mexican-American, 6 percent Negro, and the rest white. Its property-tax rate of $1.05 per each $100 of assessed valuation yielded just $26 for the education of each pupil in the district; to this was added $108 in federal funds and $222 from the state of Texas's so-called Foundation Program (to provide the foundation for at least a minimal public education). That brought the total per-pupil outlay in the Edgewood area to $356. In the Alamo Heights section of San Antonio, the richest part of town, where the population was 18 percent Mexican-American, less than 1 percent black, and the rest white, the prevailing tax rate was 85 cents per $100 of assessed valuation, well under the rate in Edgewood. But the average family's property was worth so much more in Alamo Heights that the local school tax yielded $333 per pupil. To this, the federal government added $36 and the state Foundation Program $225 (slightly *more* than it gave in Edgewood), bringing the per-pupil outlay there to $594. That meant that for every dollar spent to educate a child living in the wealthiest section of San Antonio, only 60 cents was spent on a child living in the ghetto of the same city. Was that equal protection of the laws? Why shouldn't Texas either have supplemented Edgewood's meager property resources or added a good deal less to the Alamo Heights per-pupil kitty?

A sharply divided Court said, in *San Antonio Independent School District v. Rodriguez*, that the state was not discriminating in a suspect fashion against any identifiable class. The deprivation permitted by the Texas school-funding method was relative, not absolute. The whole thrust of the state-aid program, moreover, was "affirmative and reformatory" and part of a system that bore a rational relationship to a legitimate state purpose—namely, providing a basic education for every pupil in Texas while encouraging local community participation and control. Besides, asked Justice Powell's lengthy opinion, where would the Court draw the line? If local taxes for local schools were unconstitutional because they provided unequal benefits, would not the same hold true for local police and fire protection, hospitals, and other public health services? It was a good question. To raise it, though, was not to answer it. Lurking unspoken in the background was the profoundly unsettling question of how far government in a capitalist nation dared to venture toward wiping away the advantages of private wealth in order to provide truly equal public services.

Of the dissenting opinions, Justice Thurgood Marshall's was, not surprisingly, the most outspoken. He asserted that "the majority's holding can only be seen as a retreat from our historic commitment to equality of educational opportunity and as unsupportable acquiescence in a system which deprives children in their earliest years of the chance to reach their full potential as citizens." Once a state conferred any right upon its citizens, the Fourteenth Amendment required that "the right must be available to all on equal terms"—that was what *Brown* had said with regard to public education. The Texas system did not narrow the gap between the haves and the have-nots; indeed, it widened it.

Marshall's position failed to carry the Court by but a single vote. The issue, though, appeared almost certain to come before the Justices again. Just a month after the San Antonio case was decided, the New Jersey Supreme Court ruled, in essentially the same kind of case, that the state constitution's requirement of a "thorough and efficient system" of public education for all schoolchildren was not met by a financial system based on a widely varying property-tax base. Property taxes are regressive, said the highest court of New Jersey, and impose financial burdens on poor districts in inverse proportion to the residents' ability to pay them. The court instructed the New Jersey legislature to devise a new and more equitable method of funding public education in the state. By 1975, California and Connecticut were also under state-court orders to restructure their school-funding arrangements, and at least eleven states had passed reform measures aimed at reducing the disparity in per-capita pupil outlays between their wealthiest and poorest municipalities. Thus, the insistence in *Brown* on equal educational opportunity had begun to open up once undreamed-of routes to that goal outside the Fourteenth Amendment. The states themselves were redefining the meaning of equality in citizenship without being leaned upon by the Supreme Court.

Having declined to extend the reach of *Brown* in the San Antonio school-tax case, the Court predictably shrank from a no less revolutionary step in the last school case it was to consider during the Nixon administration. The decision came twenty years and sixty-nine days after *Brown I*—and just a month before Nixon was shamed out of office. It was, in a way, his final gesture of neglect of black America, for the Court's five-man majority again included all four Nixon appointees.

The Charlotte and Denver cases had involved school districts in which Negroes were in a distinct numerical minority. There were plenty of whites in those communities with whom to integrate. But what could or should be done in districts where blacks were in the majority? Detroit was a striking example. A city of broiling racial relations during much of the century, the motor capital was being abandoned by tens of thousands of whites. By 1973, the school population in Motown was 70 percent black. When legal action was launched in 1970 to force greater desegregation, 69 of the city's schools were 90 percent or more white and 133 schools were 90 percent or more black.

Lower courts found that the Detroit school board, like the one in Denver, had adopted or sanctioned policies that intensified segregation. It had not been a simple matter of letting human dynamics operate by themselves. The Detroit Board of Education had created and altered attendance zones and feeder patterns from the elementary to the secondary schools in a way "naturally and predictably perpetuating racial segregation of students." It had bussed Negroes to predominantly black schools "which were beyond or away from closer white schools with available space." It had constructed most new schools in either overwhelmingly all-Negro or all-white neighborhoods so that they opened as predominantly one-race institutions. And it had established optional-attendance areas in neighborhoods in which Negro families had recently begun to settle so that white students were permitted to transfer to predominantly white schools nearer the city limits. Because public education in Michigan was constitutionally defined as a function of the state and because the state board of education exercised superintendency over municipal officials, Detroit Negroes sued Governor William G. Milliken for relief.

In a sweeping opinion, the U.S. District Court for Eastern Michigan held that an adequate system of desegregated schools could not be established within the Detroit school district's geographic limits and that a multi-district metropolitan area plan, mixing 503,000 students, most of them white, in fifty-three suburban school districts (among them, deluxe Grosse Pointe) with Detroit's 276,000 students should be undertaken promptly. The Court of Appeals upheld the decision. Suburban whites, who had fled from the crime-infested city, stormed. They objected that municipal and school-district lines could not be so blithely disregarded and that massive bussing would destroy the basic American concept of neighborhood and community schools. A similar case in Richmond, Virginia, had reached the Supreme Court in 1973 but was left unresolved when the Justices split four-to-four, Justice Powell not participating because he had in the past served as counsel to the Richmond schools. The Detroit case, though, was even more typical of the urban regions across the nation succumbing to the bull's-eye population pattern—a black inner-city core surrounded by rings of mostly white suburbs; America was rushing headlong back to the segregated-school arrangement that had existed in the South before *Brown*. But now the scale was many times vaster: instead of rigidly separate black and white schools within the same community, racially separate whole communities were growing within a single metropolitan area. Was the segregative effect any different? Was the legal principle any different from that in *Brown*?

In *Milliken v. Bradley*, a closely divided Supreme Court decided on July 25, 1974, that the broad metropolitan plan integrating inner-city and suburban schoolchildren was not justified. Detroit would have to get as much integration as it could by scrambling, sincerely, its rapidly dwindling white pupil population among the city's blacks—a directive certain to speed the white flight to suburbia. The Court clearly implied that involving the suburban districts in Detroit's segregation problem was punitive to the out-lying whites. More troubling, it denied the organic cohesiveness of metropolitan regions and the responsibility of satellites for the problems of the urban core around which they economically and often culturally revolved. Chief Justice Burger's majority opinion said that since no official acts by the suburban school districts had been responsible for or contributed to the discriminatory practices of the Detroit board, the courts were not free to reach across district boundaries to disrupt the deeply rooted tradition of local control of schools.

Such "talismanic invocation of the desirability of local control of education" did not address itself to the root problem, responded Justice White in the most biting and carefully reasoned of the three dissenting opinions.* The Court majority had declined to state why, in ordering remedies in a school-segregation case, courts were obliged to stop at the district line. Nothing in *Brown* or *Swann* imposed such a crippling condition. It was the state, after all, that was commanded by the Fourteenth Amendment not to deny equal protection to its citizens, and racially separate schools, the Court had settled in *Brown*, constituted such a denial. The courts, said White, "must be free to devise workable remedies against the political entity with the effective power to determine local choice"—in this case, the state of Michigan. Municipalities and school districts are not sovereign entities but merely creatures chartered by the state; thus, the state should have been ordered by the Court to fashion an interdistrict remedy that was well within both its power and its constitutional obligation.

Justice Douglas, in his thirty-fifth year on the Court, said sharply that the majority's opinion, coupled with *Rodriguez*, the San Antonio school-tax case decided the year before, "means that there is no violation of the Equal Protection Clause though the schools are segregated by race and though the Black schools are not only 'separate' but 'inferior.' So far as equal protection is concerned we are now in a dramatic retreat from the . . . decision in 1896

---

* The fourth dissenter, Justice William J. Brennan, did not file an opinion.

that Blacks could be segregated in public facilities provided they received equal treatment." *Rodriguez*, in other words, had approved unequal schools; now, in the Detroit case, the Court was accepting separate ones as well. Between the two decisions, the Negro was worse off than he had been under *Plessy*, Douglas was asserting. The interdistrict plan for desegregating metropolitan Detroit presented "no new principles of law," he added. "Metropolitan treatment of metropolitan problems is commonplace." He cited sewage, water, and energy problems, and might well have added transit (e.g., the Metropolitan Transit Authority of New York).

The man who had successfully led the plaintiffs' case in *Brown* twenty years earlier offered the most memorable words of dissent. In his seventh year on the Court, Justice Thurgood Marshall did not pull his punches. He said that the evidence in the Detroit case "showed that Negro children had been intentionally confined to an expanding core of virtually all-Negro schools immediately surrounded by a receding band of all-white schools. . . . We deal here with the right of all of our children, whatever their race, to an equal start in life. . . . Those children who have been denied that right in the past deserve better than to see fences thrown up to deny them that right in the future. Our nation, I fear, will be ill-served by the Court's refusal to remedy separate and unequal education, for unless our children begin to learn together, there is little hope that our people will ever learn to live together." In his profound unhappiness with the decision, Marshall said that after "twenty years of small, often difficult steps" toward the constitutional ideal of equal justice under law, "the Court today takes a giant step backwards." He concluded:

> Desegregation is not and was never expected to be an easy task. Racial attitudes ingrained in our nation's childhood and adolescence are not quickly thrown aside in its middle years. But just as the inconvenience of some cannot be allowed to stand in the way of the rights of others, so public opposition, no matter how strident, cannot be permitted to divert this Court from the enforcement of the constitutional principles at issue in this case. Today's holding, I fear, is more a reflection of a perceived public mood that we have gone far enough in enforcing the Constitution's guarantee of equal justice than it is the product of neutral principles of law. In the short run, it may seem to be the easier course to allow our great metropolitan areas to be divided up each into two cities—one white, the other black—but it is a course, I predict, our people will ultimately regret. I dissent.

By the mid-Seventies, encouraged by the Court's liberating suburbia of any obligation to share its wealth and classrooms with nearby urban blacks, the white exodus from cities of every size was turning into a full and blatant gallop. The very concept of school integration was thus being severely imperiled by a new generation of massive residential segregation beyond apparent reach of the law.

Thurgood Marshall was at least somewhat justified, then, in his gloom over the Detroit case, but there was other evidence everywhere twenty years after *Brown* that the drive for black equality in America was not abating.

Americans more than most people tend to believe that progress must be upward linear, steadily and unbrokenly upward, or it is not progress at all. The conduct of human affairs, though, does not move that way. It runs in cycles and must be viewed from a longer perspective than most of us are capable of—in terms of years and decades and lifetimes. Yet even in the relatively short span since May 17, 1954, a great deal has occurred to raise hope that history may yet judge the United States to have been a humane nation, not a continuously cruel one.

The years since *Brown* have established the federal government as an active participant in the effort to guarantee the equal rights of all citizens. The pace and enthusiasm of that participation have varied a good deal because for twelve of the twenty years since the Court acted, the executive branch of the government has been under the direction of Presidents who have been unsympathetic to the civil-rights cause. If Dwight Eisenhower and Richard Nixon had used the power of the White House to insist that the nation meet its moral obligations to black Americans, racism in the nation might long since have become a fugitive. It is nevertheless in retreat. And if black interests were surely not served by the Supreme Court's important decisions in the San Antonio and Detroit cases, the narrowness of those decisions must be kept in mind. The switch of a single vote would have produced a different and hugely promising result. Other men, appointed by Presidents perhaps more kindly disposed to the earnest petitions of social justice, will one day join the Court.

Black Americans, meanwhile, are no longer merely the wards of the courts. They are voting now in massive numbers everywhere, no less so than whites. If they have been ghettoized, they are at least benefiting by the concentration of elective might. More than 3,000 Negroes held public office across the nation in 1974—767 of them on local school boards, 108 of them as mayors (of, among other cities, Los Angeles, Detroit, and Newark), 17 as members of the United States Congress. In Mississippi, long regarded as the red-hot center of racial bigotry, black voter registration rose from 22,000 in 1964 to 300,000 ten years later—and no one seeking state office there hollers "nigger" any more.

Despite all the bends in the road, school desegregation overall has not retreated. Nearly half the black children in the South in 1974 were attending schools in which a majority of the students were white, and fewer than 10 percent still attended schools without any whites. A four-year study of Southern schools receiving federal desegregation-aid funds showed that by 1974 black male students in high schools had gained half a grade level in their academic standing. Added the U.S. Office of Education report: "Fears that white achievement has suffered because of Southern school desegregation appear to be unfounded." The University of Alabama, where the court-ordered admission of two blacks in 1963 brought the federal-state relationship to the flash point, was enrolling 600 Negroes in 1974, half its powerful football team was black, and Governor Wallace, whose racism had modulated, was on hand to crown the university's 1973 Homecoming Queen, a black woman. In once hatred-contorted Birmingham, instead of bombing black churches, they were listening to the local symphony orchestra inaugurate the city's new multi-million-dollar complex of 3,000-seat concert hall and 800-seat theater. In Jackson, Mississippi, public swimming pools were integrated in the summer of 1975. It was a new South. And across the nation, Negroes in the 25-to-29-year-old age category—those who began school at the time of the *Brown* decision and in its immediate wake—had attended school for 12.4 years on the median; whites in the same age category had attended for 12.7 years. In relative terms, the young black was taking giant steps in education.

Those cultural gains were slowly but steadily being translated into economic progress as well. In earning power, the Negro was still worth only three-fifths as much as a white man in America, but that proportional figure was not indicative of what was happening to individual blacks. Negroes with an education and skills were advancing briskly all along the line, moving into better and higher-paying positions in nearly all job categories. The situation was brightest for younger blacks; those in the 25-to-34-year-old category were earning 80 percent of what whites of the same age did, though they often had to moonlight to do it. Negroes without an education and skills useful to a technologically mature economy were falling farther and farther behind, with scant prospect of catching up. Still, the number of Negroes living at or below the poverty level had dropped from an appalling 56 percent in 1959 to a still intolerable 33 percent by the early Seventies—nothing to celebrate, but strong movement in the right direction. How far Negroes had to go before exerting real economic influence on America was told by another set of numbers. Blacks, comprising 11.3 percent of the American population, owned only 1.2 percent of the business equity and but one-tenth of one percent of the value of all stock holdings in the nation in 1974.

The civil-rights movement itself was fractured and seemingly spent as an identifiable crusade. Instead, individual blacks were stepping forward to claim their rights. A new kind of black leader, more poised and confident, was surfacing, stressing the Negro's economic needs. The NAACP seemed on the brink of being declared as superannuated as the term "colored people"; its high command, after devoted and durable service, was suddenly very old. Yet the fight waged by the NAACP's remarkable offspring, the Legal Defense Fund, moved ahead on all cylinders.

In the first half-dozen years after *Brown*, while the federal government lagged badly in its enforcement efforts, the Legal Defense Fund, Inc., had never faltered in pressing the desegregation drive in countless courtrooms throughout the South. In the Kennedy years and after, alumni of the Fund's *Brown* campaign moved to the federal benches—Robert Carter, Constance Motley, and Jack Weinstein were United States District Court judges in New York; Spottswood Robinson was on the U.S. Court of Appeals for the District of Columbia; William Hastie, though retired, still sat occasionally on the Third Circuit Court of Appeals, of which he had been the chief judge (a post in which he had been succeeded by Collins Seitz, the former chancellor of Delaware), and Thurgood Marshall, of course, sat on the nation's highest court. A new crop of lawyers at the Fund carried on with more energy and success than ever under Jack Greenberg, who in 1974 marked his twenty-fifth year in the organization. Dozens of Fund lawyers and affiliated attorneys were pushing several hundred cases across the nation to widen black rights. In New York, the Fund was charging the state legislature with gerrymandering political districts to deny blacks their fair representation. In Alabama, it was winning the right of black youngsters not to be expelled from schools for alleged misbehavior without a hearing by the board of education. In Washington, it was carrying on six employment-discrimination lawsuits in behalf of 13,000 black steelworkers and challenging the federal government for working out too soft a settlement with the nine big steel companies involved. It had appealed to the Supreme Court for injunctive relief and got turned down in behalf of an Arkansas Negro to whom a leading white real-estate developer refused to sell a home lot. But it had just won a sweeping federal court order requiring the Georgia Power Company to double its black work force from 9 to 17 percent. In Mississippi, it was following up on a pathbreaking decision by the Fifth Circuit Court of Appeals that the 1,500 black residents of the little town of Shaw (total population: 2,500) were plainly being denied equal protection by the community's failure to provide them with certain municipal services (e.g., 98 percent of the homes fronting on unpaved roads belonged to Negroes, as did 97 percent of those not served by sanitary sewers). Greenberg was preparing to apply the decision to other communities where blacks were being denied public services. And in Philadelphia, William Coleman, then president of the Legal Defense Fund, won settlement of a four-year-old employment-discrimination case he brought in behalf of eighty-eight blacks against the General Electric Company, which agreed to hire one-third more Negro workers at its Philadelphia-area plants.*

Beyond the law, America was beginning to honor black culture and demonstrate genuine admiration for both its outward forms and its animating force. The "Afro" was no longer an outlandish hairdo or frizzy emblem of protest but was understood widely to be a source of pride and an object of beauty. Whites with curly hair were growing their own, and the "soul" handshake was not the exclusive greeting of black brothers. Negro performers and black casts were multiplying in television programming, though they were still placed mostly in comic or crime situations, and every group scene in a commercial had at least a token black. Black performers were dominating the sports world, and black music, language, and style were almost everywhere far more a source of joy and admiration than a target of scorn or denigration. The new Babe Ruth was black, and the nation applauded just the same.

There was, however, no sugarcoating the fearsomely high rate of crime, drug use, and joblessness that hung over the ghettos in unholy trinity. That the three were intimately linked and formed a paralyzing cycle of despair was beginning to be widely recognized in white America. But psychological

---

* Early in 1975, Coleman, one of Thurgood Marshall's closest advisors during the *Brown* litigation, became the second Negro to serve in a presidential Cabinet. Gerald Ford named him Secretary of the Department of Transportation.

explanation of black lawlessness was no more sufficient to excuse it than the generations of white oppression that had nurtured it. As black America's economic status improved, its respect for the law was now required to keep pace. Sympathetic liberals were fond of saying that those without rights of their own could hardly be expected to respect the rights of others. But once those rights were won, the black man's obligations as citizen were plain. Equal protection of the law is a two-way street.

The nation as a whole, though, still had a major piece of work in front of it before it could acclaim black equality a reality, whether Negroes chose to exercise it in the form of full membership in integrated communities—a goal reachable only by rigorous enforcement of civil-rights laws by federal, state, and local authorities—or of economically healthy black communities whose members prefer, but are not forced, to live apart from whites. Among the nation's most pressing social priorities as it looked toward its third century was the rebuilding of its slums and ghettos, ideally with the muscle and skills of their own underemployed inhabitants. There were signs, despite a depressed national economy, that the rehabilitation of battered black neighborhoods might in fact become America's next great public-works project. In New York late in 1974, as a prominent example, responsible planners unveiled a visionary ten-year blueprint to rebuild Harlem—with more than 50,000 apartments, thousands of new jobs, and two major commercial and retail arteries—at an estimated cost of $6.6 billion. The price of one year of the Vietnam war at its height could yet buy four or five such rebuilt Harlems.

Unless or until the nation decided to put its massive resources at the disposal of black Americans, they were still forced in too many places to cope with spiraling segregation in housing and, with it, education. In New York in the 1974–75 school year, more than half of the state's minority-group pupils were attending "grossly segregated" (more than 90 percent minority-group enrollment) schools, and the State Board of Regents had pointedly disavowed the use of racial enrollment quotas or ratios in judging a school district's compliance with the Supreme Court mandate to integrate as much as possible. In Chicago, twenty years after *Brown*, 259 out of 537 schools had enrollments 90 percent or more black (109 were 90 percent or more white); the number of all-black schools had risen from 128 in 1972 to 144. In Washington, the white abandonment of the city had nearly reached the terminal stage: 96 percent of the public-school children in the nation's capital, site of one of the five desegregation cases decided by the Supreme Court in 1954, were black. Yet black spirit was not broken. "You can have a beautiful lesson without integration," said one Negro principal. "It's just not true that you need whites to have a good school."

In the other four communities where the cases comprising *Brown* arose, the goal of thoroughly integrated schoolhouses had not yet been realized after twenty years. But it was not beyond reach and was no longer a hopeless dream.

In Topeka, Kansas, the former Linda Brown was a divorced working mother living in an integrated housing complex with her two children, who attended a public school that was 35 percent black. More than half of the 1,700 black grade-school students in the city were concentrated in just six of the thirty-four elementary schools in town, four of them 60 percent or more black. Parents of both races were balking at city-wide bussing that could readily accomplish far more thorough desegregation, and a new suit outside of NAACP auspices was in the courts to force the situation.

In Delaware, the residential pattern in the greater Wilmington area had heavily altered and become like that in Detroit. The white withdrawal, the coming of urban renewal, the upheaval wrought by thruways had all contributed to converting the city's population to nearly half black; the schools were about 90 percent black. Pressed by desegregationists, the Delaware legislature had passed a statewide school-redistricting program, but the Wilmington district boundaries had explicitly been retained, thereby locking the city's blacks into nearly all-Negro schools. Louis Redding, the veteran NAACP attorney, was leading a court fight to upset the sweet-and-sour state law and mingle Wilmington's black youngsters with suburban whites.

In Prince Edward County, Virginia, where white intransigence had been so strong that the public schools were closed entirely from 1959 to 1964, most white schoolchildren—about 1,000 of them—were attending the private white academy while 1,728 black youngsters went to the public schools. But the whites were drifting back to the public schools: in 1969, only two dozen of them enrolled in the overwhelmingly black public schools; five years later, the whites numbered 358 and the upward trend was expected to continue.

Only in School District No. 1 in Clarendon County, South Carolina, site of the first of the school-segregation cases to reach the Supreme Court of the United States, had nothing much changed. In August of 1974, twenty years and three months after the Court had crowned with glory the black agrarian revolt he had sparked in his hapless native county, the Reverend Joseph A. DeLaine died of cancer at the age of seventy-six in Charlotte, North Carolina, where he had lived out his old age in exile. In the area of Manning, the Clarendon county seat, where the reverend was born and the population was about evenly divided between black and white, about one out of every three white children in the area was attending one of the public schools, which were three-quarters black. But in the Summerton area, in the school district where Reverend DeLaine had organized the *Briggs* case and paid so dearly for it, the public school system twenty years later had an enrollment of more than 3,000 black youngsters—and just one white child.

Perhaps, as the school district's attorney, Emory Rogers, had intimated to the Supreme Court at the oral argument in 1955, integration would not come to that defiant, time-shrouded end of Clarendon County, South Carolina, until well into the twenty-first century. But to almost everywhere else in America it had already come, and more was due.

# Appendix: Text of the Decisions

BROWN V. BOARD OF EDUCATION OF TOPEKA*

Opinion on Segregation Laws Delivered May 17, 1954

No. 1. Appeal from the United States District Court
for the District of Kansas.†

MR. CHIEF JUSTICE WARREN delivered the opinion of the Court.

These cases come to us from the States of Kansas, South Carolina, Virginia, and Delaware. They are premised on different facts and different local conditions, but a common legal question justifies their consideration together in this consolidated opinion.[1]

In each of the cases, minors of the Negro race, through their legal representatives, seek the aid of the courts in obtaining admission to the public schools of their community on a nonsegregated basis. In each instance, they have been denied admission to schools attended by white children under laws requiring or permitting segregation according to race. This segregation was alleged to deprive the plaintiffs of the equal protection of the laws under the Fourteenth Amendment. In each of the cases other than the Delaware case, a three-judge federal district court denied relief to the plaintiffs on the so-called "separate but equal" doctrine announced by this Court in *Plessy v. Ferguson*, 163 U.S. 537. Under that doctrine, equality of treatment is accorded when the races are provided substantially equal facilities, even though these facilities be separate. In the Delaware case, the Supreme Court of Delaware adhered to that doctrine, but ordered that the plaintiffs be admitted to the white schools because of their superiority to the Negro schools.

The plaintiffs contend that segregated public schools are not "equal" and

---

* Supreme Court of the United States, 347 U.S. 483 (1954).

† Together with No. 2, *Briggs et al. v. Elliott et al.*, on appeal from the United States District Court for the Eastern District of South Carolina, argued December 9–10, 1952, reargued December 7–8, 1953; No. 4, *Davis et al. v. County School Board of Prince Edward County, Virginia, et al.*, on appeal from the United States District Court for the Eastern District of Virginia, argued December 10, 1952, reargued December 7–8, 1953; and No. 10, *Gebhart et al. v. Belton et al.*, on certiorari to the Supreme Court of Delaware, argued December 11, 1952, reargued December 9, 1953.

cannot be made "equal," and that hence they are deprived of the equal protection of the laws. Because of the obvious importance of the question presented, the Court took jurisdiction.[2] Argument was heard in the 1952 Term, and reargument was heard this Term on certain questions propounded by the Court.[3]

Reargument was largely devoted to the circumstances surrounding the adoption of the Fourteenth Amendment in 1868. It covered exhaustively consideration of the Amendment in Congress, ratification by the states, then existing practices in racial segregation, and the views of proponents and opponents of the Amendment. This discussion and our own investigation convince us that, although these sources cast some light, it is not enough to resolve the problem with which we are faced. At best, they are inconclusive. The most avid proponents of the post-War Amendments undoubtedly intended them to remove all legal distinctions among "all persons born or naturalized in the United States." Their opponents, just as certainly, were antagonistic to both the letter and the spirit of the Amendments and wished them to have the most limited effect. What others in Congress and the state legislatures had in mind cannot be determined with any degree of certainty.

An additional reason for the inconclusive nature of the Amendment's history, with respect to segregated schools, is the status of public education at that time.[4] In the South, the movement toward free common schools, supported by general taxation, had not yet taken hold. Education of white children was largely in the hands of private groups. Education of Negroes was almost nonexistent, and practically all of the race were illiterate. In fact, any education of Negroes was forbidden by law in some states. Today, in contrast, many Negroes have achieved outstanding success in the arts and sciences as well as in the business and professional world. It is true that public school education at the time of the Amendment had advanced further in the North, but the effect of the Amendment on Northern States was generally ignored in the congressional debates. Even in the North, the conditions of public education did not approximate those existing today. The curriculum was usually rudimentary; ungraded schools were common in rural areas; the school term was but three months a year in many states; and compulsory school attendance was virtually unknown. As a consequence, it is not surprising that there should be so little in the history of the Fourteenth Amendment relating to its intended effect on public education.

In the first cases in this Court construing the Fourteenth Amendment, decided shortly after its adoption, the Court interpreted it as proscribing all state-imposed discriminations against the Negro race.[5] The doctrine of "separate but equal" did not make its appearance in this Court until 1896 in the case of *Plessy v. Ferguson, supra,* involving not education but transportation.[6] American courts have since labored with the doctrine for over half a century. In this Court, there have been six cases involving the "separate but equal" doctrine in the field of public education.[7] In *Cumming v. County Board of Education,* 175 U.S. 528, and *Gong Lum v. Rice,* 275 U.S. 78, the validity of the doctrine itself was not challenged.[8] In more recent cases, all on the graduate school level, inequality was found in that specific benefits enjoyed by white students were denied to Negro students of the same educational qualifications. *Missouri ex rel. Gaines v. Canada,* 305 U.S. 337; *Sipuel v. Oklahoma,* 332 U.S. 631; *Sweatt v. Painter,* 339 U.S. 629; *McLaurin v. Oklahoma State Regents,* 339 U.S. 637. In none of these cases was it necessary to re-examine the doctrine to grant relief to the Negro plaintiff. And in *Sweatt v. Painter, supra,* the Court expressly reserved decision on the question whether *Plessy v. Ferguson* should be held inapplicable to public education.

In the instant cases, that question is directly presented. Here, unlike *Sweatt v. Painter,* there are findings below that the Negro and white schools involved have been equalized, or are being equalized, with respect to buildings, curricula, qualifications and salaries of teachers, and other "tangible" factors.[9] Our decision, therefore, cannot turn on merely a comparison of these tangible factors in the Negro and white schools involved in each of the cases. We must look instead to the effect of segregation itself on public education.

In approaching this problem, we cannot turn the clock back to 1868 when the Amendment was adopted, or even to 1896 when *Plessy v. Ferguson* was written. We must consider public education in the light of its full development and its present place in American life throughout the Nation. Only in this way can it be determined if segregation in public schools deprives these plaintiffs of the equal protection of the laws.

Today, education is perhaps the most important function of state and local governments. Compulsory school attendance laws and the great expenditures for education both demonstrate our recognition of the importance of education to our democratic society. It is required in the performance of our most basic public responsibilities, even service in the armed forces. It is the very foundation of good citizenship. Today it is a principal instrument in awakening the child to cultural values, in preparing him for later professional training, and in helping him to adjust normally to his environment. In these days, it is doubtful that any child may reasonably be expected to succeed in life if he is denied the opportunity of an education. Such an opportunity, where the state has undertaken to provide it, is a right which must be made available to all on equal terms.

We come then to the question presented: Does segregation of children in public schools solely on the basis of race, even though the physical facilities and other "tangible" factors may be equal, deprive the children of the minority group of equal education opportunities? We believe that it does.

In *Sweatt v. Painter, supra,* in finding that a segregated law school for Negroes could not provide them equal educational opportunities, this Court relied in large part on "those qualities which are incapable of objective measurement but which make for greatness in a law school." In *McLaurin v. Oklahoma State Regents, supra,* the Court, in requiring that a Negro admitted to a white graduate school be treated like all other students, again resorted to intangible considerations: ". . . his ability to study, to engage in discussions and exchange views with other students, and, in general, to learn his profession." Such considerations apply with added force to children in grade and high schools. To separate them from others of similar age and qualifications solely because of their race generates a feeling of inferiority as to their status in the community that may affect their hearts and minds in a way unlikely ever to be undone. The effect of this separation on their educational opportunities was well stated by a finding in the Kansas case by a court which nevertheless felt compelled to rule against the Negro plaintiffs:

> Segregation of white and colored children in public schools has a detrimental effect upon the colored children. The impact is greater when it has the sanction of the law; for the policy of separating the races is usually interpreted as denoting the inferiority of the negro group. A sense of inferiority affects the motivation of the child to learn. Segregation with the sanction of law, therefore, has a tendency to [retard] the educational and mental development of negro children and to deprive them of some of the benefits they would receive in a racial[ly] integrated school system.[10]

Whatever may have been the extent of psychological knowledge at the time of *Plessy v. Ferguson,* this finding is amply supported by modern authority.[11] Any language in *Plessy v. Ferguson* contrary to this finding is rejected.

We conclude that in the field of public education the doctrine of "separate but equal" has no place. Separate educational facilities are inherently unequal. Therefore, we hold that the plaintiffs and others similarly situated for whom the actions have been brought are, by reason of the segregation complained of, deprived of the equal protection of the laws guaranteed by the Fourteenth Amendment. This disposition makes unnecessary any discussion whether such segregation also violates the Due Process Clause of the Fourteenth Amendment.[12]

Because these are class actions, because of the wide applicability of this decision, and because of the great variety of local conditions, the formulation of decrees in these cases presents problems of considerable complexity. On reargument, the consideration of appropriate relief was necessarily subordinated to the primary question—the constitutionality of segregation in public education. We have now announced that such segregation is a denial of the equal protection of the laws. In order that we may have the full assistance of the parties in formulating decrees, the cases will be restored to the docket, and the parties are requested to present further argument on Questions 4 and 5 previously propounded by the Court for the reargument this Term.[13] The Attorney General of the United States is again invited to participate. The Attorneys General of the states requiring or permitting segregation in public education will also be permitted to appear as *amici curiae* upon request to do so by September 15, 1954, and submission of briefs by October 1, 1954.[14]

*It is so ordered.*

1. In the Kansas case, *Brown v. Board of Education,* the plaintiffs are Negro children of elementary school age residing in Topeka. They brought this action in the United States District Court for the District of Kansas to enjoin enforcement of a Kansas statute which permits, but does not require, cities of more than 15,000 population to maintain separate school facilities for Negro and white students.

Kan.Gen.Stat. § 72–1724 (1949). Pursuant to that authority, the Topeka Board of Education elected to establish segregated elementary schools. Other public schools in the community, however, are operated on a nonsegregated basis. The three-judge District Court, convened under 28 U.S.C. §§ 2281 and 2284, found that segregation in public education has a detrimental effect upon Negro children, but denied relief on the ground that the Negro and white schools were substantially equal with respect to buildings, transportation, curricula, and educational qualifications of teachers. 98 F.Supp. 797. The case is here on direct appeal under 28 U.S.C. § 1253.

In the South Carolina case, *Briggs v. Elliott*, the plaintiffs are Negro children of both elementary and high school age residing in Clarendon County. They brought this action in the United States District Court for the Eastern District of South Carolina to enjoin enforcement of provisions in the state constitution and statutory code which require the segregation of Negroes and whites in public schools. S.C.Const., Art. XI, § 7; S.C.Code § 5377 (1942). The three-judge District Court, convened under 28 U.S.C. §§ 2281 and 2284, denied the requested relief. The court found that the Negro schools were inferior to the white schools and ordered the defendants to begin immediately to equalize the facilities. But the court sustained the validity of the contested provisions and denied the plaintiffs admission to the white schools during the equalization program. 98 F.Supp. 529. This Court vacated the District Court's judgment and remanded the case for the purpose of obtaining the court's views on a report filed by the defendants concerning the progress made in the equalization program. 342 U.S. 350. On remand, the District Court found that substantial equality had been achieved except for buildings and that the defendants were proceeding to rectify this inequality as well. 103 F.Supp. 920. The case is again here on direct appeal under 28 U.S.C. § 1253.

In the Virginia case, *Davis v. County School Board*, the plaintiffs are Negro children of high school age residing in Prince Edward County. They brought this action in the United States District Court for the Eastern District of Virginia to enjoin enforcement of provisions in the state constitution and statutory code which require the segregation of Negroes and whites in public schools. Va.Const., § 140; Va.Code § 22–221 (1950). The three-judge District Court, convened under 28 U.S.C. §§ 2281 and 2284, denied the requested relief. The court found the Negro school inferior in physical plant, curricula, and transportation, and ordered the defendants forthwith to provide substantially equal curricula and transportation and to "proceed with all reasonable diligence and dispatch to remove" the inequality in physical plant. But as in the South Carolina case, the court sustained the validity of the contested provisions and denied the plaintiffs admission to the white schools during the equalization program. 103 F.Supp. 337. The case is here on direct appeal under 28 U.S.C. § 1253.

In the Delaware case, *Gebhart v. Belton*, the plaintiffs are Negro children of both elementary and high school age residing in New Castle County. They brought this action in the Delaware Court of Chancery to enjoin enforcement of provisions in the state constitution and statutory code which require the segregation of Negroes and whites in public schools. Del.Const. Art. X, § 2; Del.Rev.Code § 2631 (1935). The Chancellor gave judgment for the plaintiffs and ordered their immediate admission to schools previously attended only by white children, on the ground that the Negro schools were inferior with respect to teacher training, pupil-teacher ratio, extracurricular activities, physical plant, and time and distance involved in travel. 87 A.2d 862. The Chancellor also found that segregation itself results in an inferior education for Negro children (see note 10, *infra*), but did not rest his decision on that ground. *Id.,* at page 865. The Chancellor's decree was affirmed by the Supreme Court of Delaware, which intimated, however, that the defendants might be able to obtain a modification of the decree after equalization of the Negro and white schools had been accomplished. 91 A.2d 137, 152. The defendants, contending only that the Delaware courts had erred in ordering the immediate admission of the Negro plaintiffs to the white schools, applied to this Court for certiorari. The writ was granted, 344 U.S. 891. The plaintiffs, who were successful below, did not submit a cross-petition.

2. 344 U.S. 1, 141, 891.

3. 345 U.S. 972. The Attorney General of the United States participated both Terms as *amicus curiae.*

4. For a general study of the development of public education prior to the Amendment, see Butts and Cremin, A History of Education in American Culture (1953), Pts. I, II; Cubberley, Public Education in the United States (1934 ed.) cc. II-XII. School practices current at the time of the adoption of the Fourteenth Amendment are described in Butts and Cremin, *supra,* at 269–275; Cubberley, *supra,* at 288–339, 408–431; Knight, Public Education in the South (1922), cc. VIII, IX. See also H. Ex. Doc. No. 315, 41st Cong., 2d Sess. (1871). Although the demand for free public schools followed substantially the same pattern in both the North and South, the development in the South did not begin to gain momentum until about 1850, some twenty years after that in the North. The reasons for the somewhat slower development in the South (*e.g.,* the rural character of the South and the different regional attitudes toward state assistance) are well explained in Cubberley, *supra,* at 408–423. In the country as a whole, but particularly in the South, the War virtually stopped all progress in public education. *Id.,* at 427–428. The low status of Negro education in all sections of the country, both before and immediately after the War, is described in Beale, A History of Freedom of Teaching in American Schools (1941), 112–132, 175–195. Compulsory school attendance laws were not generally adopted until after the ratification of the Fourteenth Amendment, and it was not until 1918 that such laws were in force in all the states. Cubberley, *supra,* at 563–565.

5. *Slaughter-House Cases,* 16 Wall. 36, 67–72 (1873); *Strauder v. West Virginia,* 100 U.S. 303, 307–308 (1880): "It ordains that no State shall deprive any person of life, liberty, or property, without due process of law, or deny to any person within its jurisdiction the equal protection of the laws. What is this but declaring that the law in the States shall be the same for the black as for the white; that all persons, whether colored or white, shall stand equal before the laws of the States, and, in regard to the colored race, for whose protection the amendment was primarily designed, that no discrimination shall be made against them by law because of their color? The words of the amendment, it is true, are prohibitory, but they contain a necessary implication of a positive immunity, or right, most valuable to the colored race,—the right to exemption from unfriendly legislation against them distinctively as colored,—exemption from legal discriminations, implying inferiority in civil society, lessening the security of their enjoyment of the rights which others enjoy, and discriminations which are steps toward reducing them to the condition of a subject race." See also *Virginia v. Rives,* 100 U.S. 313, 318 (1880); *Ex parte Virginia,* 100 U.S. 339, 344–345 (1880).

6. The doctrine apparently originated in *Roberts v. City of Boston,* 59 Mass. 198, 206 (1850), upholding school segregation against attack as being violative of a state constitutional guarantee of equality. Segregation in Boston public schools was eliminated in 1855. Mass. Acts 1855, c. 256. But elsewhere in the North segregation in public education has persisted in some communities until recent years. It is apparent that such segregation has long been a nationwide problem, not merely one of sectional concern.

7. See also *Berea College v. Kentucky* 211 J.S. 45 (1908).

8. In the *Cumming* case, Negro taxpayers sought an injunction requiring the defendant school board to discontinue the operation of a high school for white children until the board resumed operation of a high school for Negro children. Similarly, in the *Gong Lum* case, the plaintiff, a child of Chinese descent, contended only that state authorities had misapplied the doctrine by classifying him with Negro children and requiring him to attend a Negro School.

9. In the Kansas case, the court below found substantial equality as to all such factors. 98 F.Supp. 797, 798. In the South Carolina case, the court below found that the defendants were proceeding "promptly and in good faith to comply with the court's decree." 103 F.Supp. 920, 921. In the Virginia case, the court below noted that the equalization program was already "afoot and progressing" (103 F.Supp. 337, 341); since then, we have been advised, in the Virginia Attorney General's brief on reargument, that the program has now been completed. In the Delaware case, the court below similarly noted that the state's equalization program was well under way. 91 A.2d 137, 149.

10. A similar finding was made in the Delaware case: "I conclude from the testimony that in our Delaware society, State-imposed segregation in education itself results in the Negro children, as a class, receiving educational opportunities which are substantially inferior to those available to white children otherwise similarly situated." 87 A.2d 862, 865.

11. K. B. Clark, Effect of Prejudice and Discrimination on Personality Development (Midcentury White House Conference on Children and Youth, 1950); Witmer and Kotinsky, Personality in the Making (1952), c. VI; Deutscher and Chein, The Psychological Effects of Enforced Segregation: A Survey of Social Science Opinion, 26 J. Psychol. 259 (1948); Chein, What Are the Psychological Effects of Segregation Under Conditions of Equal Facilities? 3 Int. J. Opinion and Attitude Res. 229 (1949); Brameld, Educational Costs, in Discrimination and National Welfare (MacIver, ed., 1949), 44–48; Frazier, The Negro in the United States (1949), 674–681. And see generally Myrdal, An American Dilemma (1944).

12. See *Bolling v. Sharpe, Post*, p. 497, concerning the Due Process Clause of the Fifth Amendment.

13. "4. Assuming it is decided that segregation in public schools violates the Fourteenth Amendment

"*(a)* would a decree necessarily follow providing that, within the limits set by normal geographic school districting, Negro children should forthwith be admitted to schools of their choice, or

"*(b)* may this Court, in the exercise of its equity powers, permit an effective gradual adjustment to be brought about from existing segregated systems to a system not based on color distinctions?

"5. On the assumption on which questions 4*(a)* and *(b)* are based, and assuming further that this Court will exercise its equity powers to the end described in question 4*(b),*

"*(a)* should this Court formulate detailed decrees in these cases;

"*(b)* if so, what specific issues should the decree reach;

"*(c)* should this Court appoint a special master to hear evidence with a view to recommending specific terms for such decrees;

"*(d)* should this Court remand to the courts of first instance with directions to frame decrees in these cases, and if so what general directions should the decrees of this Court include and what procedures should the courts of first instance follow in arriving at the specific terms of more detailed decrees?"

14. See Rule 42, Revised Rules of this Court (effective July 1, 1954).

## BOLLING V. SHARPE*

District of Columbia: Companion Case

MR. CHIEF JUSTICE WARREN delivered the opinion of the Court.

This case challenges the validity of segregation in the public schools of the District of Columbia. The petitioners, minors of the Negro race, allege that such segregation deprives them of due process of law under the Fifth Amendment. They were refused admission to a public school attended by white children solely because of their race. They sought the aid of the District Court for the District of Columbia in obtaining admission. That court dismissed their complaint. The Court granted a writ of certiorari before judgment in the Court of Appeals because of the importance of the constitutional question presented. 344 U.S. 873. . . .

We have this day held that the Equal Protection Clause of the Fourteenth Amendment prohibits the states from maintaining racially segregated public schools.[1] The legal problem in the District of Columbia is somewhat different, however. The Fifth Amendment, which is applicable in the District of Columbia, does not contain an equal protection clause as does the Fourteenth Amendment which applies only to the states. But the concepts of equal protection and due process, both stemming from our American ideal of fairness, are not mutually exclusive. The "equal protection of the laws" is a more explicit safeguard of prohibited unfairness than "due process of law," and, therefore, we do not imply that the two are always interchangeable phrases. But, as this Court has recognized, discrimination may be so unjustifiable as to be violative of due process.[2]

Classifications based solely upon race must be scrutinized with particular care, since they are contrary to our traditions and hence constitutionally suspect.[3] As long ago as 1896, this Court declared the principle "that the constitution of the United States, in its present form, forbids, so far as civil and political rights are concerned, discrimination by the general government, or by the states, against any citizen because of his race." [4] And in *Buchanan v. Warley*, 245 U.S. 60, . . . the Court held that a statute which limited the right of a property owner to convey his property to a person of another race was, as an unreasonable discrimination, a denial of due process of law.

Although the Court has not assumed to define "liberty" with any great precision, that term is not confined to mere freedom from bodily restraint. Liberty under law extends to the full range of conduct which the individual is free to pursue, and it cannot be restricted except for a proper governmental objective. Segregation in public education is not reasonably related to any proper governmental objective, and thus it imposes on Negro children of the District of Columbia a burden that constitutes an arbitrary deprivation of their liberty in violation of the Due Process Clause.

---

* Supreme Court of the United States, 347 U.S. 497 (1954).

In view of our decision that the Constitution prohibits the states from maintaining racially segregated public schools, it would be unthinkable that the same Constitution would impose a lesser duty on the Federal Government.[5] We hold that racial segregation in the public schools of the District of Columbia is a denial of the due process of law guaranteed by the Fifth Amendment to the Constitution.

For the reasons set out in *Brown v. Board of Education*, this case will be restored to the docket for reargument on Questions 4 and 5 previously propounded by the Court. 345 U.S. 972. . . .

*It is so ordered.*

1. *Brown v. Board of Education*, 347 U.S. 483.

2. *Detroit Bank v. United States*, 317 U.S. 329; *Currin v. Wallace*, 306 U.S. 1, 13–14; *Steward Machine Co. v. Davis*, 301 U.S. 548, 585.

3. *Korematsu v. United States*, 323 U.S. 214, 216; *Hirabayashi v. United States*, 320 U.S. 81, 100.

4. *Gibson v. Mississippi*, 162 U.S. 565, 591. Cf. *Steele v. Louisville & Nashville R.R. Co.*, 323 U.S. 192, 198–199.

5. Cf. *Hurd v. Hodge*, 334 U.S. 24.

# Sources and Acknowledgments

Of the many strands from which this book was composed, the most basic were of course the legal briefs, transcripts of trials, hearings and arguments, and the opinions of the courts in the cases discussed. Most of the cases are cited in the index on page 824 for further consultation, but I have not—in the interest of readability—indicated the precise whereabouts of every quoted passage in the original record; those interested in pursuing the subject ought, at any rate, to consult the cited documents in full and not risk dealing with the parts out of context. Assembling the legal record in the lower courts was a considerable project in itself; my task in dealing with the arguments before the United States Supreme Court was lightened by the publication, shortly after I began the research, of the book *Argument*, edited by Leon Friedman (Chelsea House, 1969), containing a verbatim transcript of those proceedings, which was otherwise unavailable except in the Supreme Court building.

By far the most essential of the private correspondence and legal memoranda consulted were the case files of the NAACP Legal Defense Fund, Inc., in New York, without which I would not have attempted the book. The correspondence files of three other participants in the case were also illuminating—William T. Coleman, Jr., Robert McC. Figg, Jr., and Jack Weinstein. The chapters on the legal activities of the NAACP during the 1930s make generous use of that association's papers and archives on file in the Manuscript Division of the Library of Congress; discussion of the activities in the case of John W. Davis, principal attorney for the segregationist side in arguments before the Supreme Court, was enriched by consulting his collected papers at Sterling Memorial Library, Yale University.

A more intimate view of the men who decided these cases was gained by interviews with the late Chief Justice Earl Warren and Associate Justice Tom C. Clark. In addition, considerable use was made of the legal papers and correspondence of Associate Justices Hugo L. Black, Harold H. Burton, and Felix Frankfurter in the Manuscript Division of the Library of Congress and of the *Brown* file in the Frankfurter Papers at Langdell Law Library, Harvard. Of the judges who heard the cases in the courts below, I interviewed Walter A. Huxman and Collins J. Seitz and drew upon the transcribed reminiscences of J. Waties Waring on file at Columbia University's Oral History Project. Valuable other documentation was supplied to me by the family and biographer of Associate Justice Robert H. Jackson, by one of the law clerks of Associate Justice Stanley Reed (with the Justice's knowledge), and by the son of Chief Justice Fred M. Vinson. Associate Justice William O. Douglas, the only member of the Court that decided *Brown* who was still sitting at the time I completed the book, declined to see me but answered one inquiry by letter.

Of the printed sources, most vital by far were the annals of the *Journal of Negro Education*, which both reported on and campaigned vigorously for the desegregation drive from its first issue in 1932 through the consummation of *Brown*. Considerable use was made, too, of the files and back issues of these newspapers and magazines: *Afro-American, Amsterdam News*, Charleston *News & Courier*, Columbia (S.C.) *State, Courier* (of Pittsburgh), Manning (S.C.) *Times*, New York *Post, New York Times*, Philadelphia *Bulletin*, Richmond *Times-Dispatch*, Time Inc., Topeka *Capital-Times*, Washington *Post*, and Wilmington *News-Journal.*

The resources of the following institutions were similarly of high value: Butler Library and the Law School Library, Columbia University; Langdell Law Library, Harvard University; Founders' Library, Howard University; Kansas Historical Society, Topeka; Schomburg Collection, New York Public Library; Law Library, New York University; University of North Carolina Library; Ridgefield (Conn.) Library; Rutgers University Library; South Carolina Historical Society, Charleston; Library, United States Supreme Court; and Sterling Library, Yale University. The essential institution, though, was the Library of Congress.

The basic reading list appears in the bibliography; many other books were consulted, but to list them all would serve no purpose. Similarly, hundreds of articles and clippings were drawn upon, but in the interest of conserving space only the most important are cited in the chapter notes.

Finally, liberal use has been made of the firsthand recollections of individuals who were interviewed for this book, in perhaps two dozen locations, most of them in person, some by telephone or mail. The complete list is below. Several of the people whom I interviewed were connected with the Supreme Court. Neither they nor I, it is worth adding here, felt that we were making a radical departure from the tradition of confidentiality that has grown up around the deliberations of the Justices. Chief Justice Warren and Associate Justice Clark agreed to see me with the stipulation that I limit my inquiries to their own views of the case and not delve into the give-and-take among the brethren. And I did not approach the two dozen former law clerks to the Court who were kind enough to help me until I had first consulted all the papers cited above; my inquiry of the clerks was thus in the nature of corroboration of the picture I had by then developed of each Justice's position in the case. More than twenty years have passed, moreover, since the initial *Brown* ruling—a sufficient span, I believe, to insulate the current Court from the flash of controversy that first greeted the decision. It is one thing to insist that the Court and its family must go about their internal deliberations out of public view and with concern first and most of all for the principles at issue; it is another thing, though, I think, to hold that those deliberations must never be exposed to the light of history.

A great many people were very kind to me during the long research that went into this book—a tribute, I am sure, more to the surpassing importance of the subject than the credentials of the author. I was a stranger to most of them, and their generosity with time and candor made my task both easier and more meaningful. Among these are all whom I interviewed (see below), but I must single out Robert L. Carter, now a member of the federal bench for the Southern District of New York, who was especially giving of his time, and at a very difficult moment in his life. I am appreciative as well for the help of those in charge of the libraries at the newspapers, periodicals, and educational institutions listed above; in several instances, institutional policy would have prevented my inspection of news clippings, but friends arranged for that privilege on the premises.

Among those who provided research assistance, I am particularly grateful to Phyllis Kluger for extensive investigation into the history of Negro education in the United States; her massive memorandum had many uses. Others who provided research help were Roger Newman (a constant source of useful suggestions), Richard

Rhodes, Ann Barringer, Leonard Ellis, Jan Rubin, and Joan Berman Arbeiter. Six lawyers kindly lent me the use of their brains, their firms' law libraries, or both: Jay D. Arbeiter, of Baer & Arbeiter, Metuchen, New Jersey; Blaine V. Fogg, of Skadden Arps Slate Meagher & Flom, New York, who first suggested this undertaking to me in 1967; James C. Freund and Stuart Shapiro, of Skadden Arps; and especially Lawrence G. Goodman, of Shereff Friedman Hoffman & Goodman, New York, and Michael Meltsner, professor of law at Columbia.

For permission to use private documents and materials in the book, I must thank, above all, Jack Greenberg, director-counsel of the NAACP Legal Defense Fund, Inc., who opened his doors and the Fund's files to me from the first—an act of confidence and kindness upon which the rest of this undertaking was built. In addition, I am grateful to the late Alexander M. Bickel, William T. Coleman, Jr., John D. Fassett, Robert McC. Figg, Jr., Paul A. Freund, William E. Jackson, Philip B. Kurland, retired Justice Stanley Reed, Fred M. Vinson, Jr., and Judge Jack Weinstein for their permission to quote or refer to materials not otherwise available.

More personally, I owe an unrepayable debt to the late David Segal, who encouraged my career as a writer at a time when it was not foremost in my thoughts; while an editor at Harper and Row, he contracted for this book, and I moved gladly with him to Alfred A. Knopf, Inc. After his death, I was urged to carry on the project, however long it might take, by Knopf's editor in chief and irrepressible talent-nurturer, Robert Gottlieb. He and Knopf senior editor Charles Elliott responded to the manuscript with a warmth and an alacrity that made the editing process congenial. I was blessed also with an excellent copy editor, Paul Hirschman, and a typist of rare skill—Doris K. Schubert of Ridgefield, Connecticut. And, finally, I was fortunate to share most of this adventure with my wife, Phyllis, who kept me on course when I was tempted to abandon the journey and whose enthusiasm heightened the rewards of this profoundly instructive—and moving—experience for me.

R.K.

# Selected Bibliography

The chapter notes indicate where a book was of particular use or relevance. Where a paperback edition is cited in addition to the hardcover edition, the author used the paperback in his reading; in such cases, page references in the chapter notes refer to the paperback edition cited.

Abraham, Henry J., *Justices and Presidents: A Political History of Appointments to the Supreme Court* (New York: Oxford University Press, 1974).

Allport, Gordon W., *The Nature of Prejudice* (Boston: Addison-Wesley, 1954; Doubleday Anchor paperback, 1958).

Aptheker, Herbert, ed., *A Documentary History of the Negro People in the United States* (New York: Citadel, 1951; 6th Citadel paperback edition).

Ashmore, Harry S., *The Negro and the Schools* (Chapel Hill: University of North Carolina Press, 1954; paperback).

Atkinson, David N., *Mr. Justice Minton and the Supreme Court, 1949–1956*, unpublished doctoral thesis in political science, University of Iowa, 1969.

Baker, Liva, *Felix Frankfurter: A Biography* (New York: Coward, McCann & Geoghegan, 1969).

Bardolph, Richard, *The Negro Vanguard* (New York: Holt, Rinehart & Winston, 1959; Vintage paperback).

Beard, Charles A., *An Economic Interpretation of the Constitution of the United States* (New York: Macmillan, 1913, 1935; Free Press paperback, 1965).

Bennett, Lerone, Jr., *Before the Mayflower: A History of the Negro in America, 1619–1964* (Chicago: Johnson, 1962; Penguin paperback, 1966).

Bergman, Peter H., *The Chronological History of the Negro in the United States* (New York: Harper & Row, 1969).

Berman, Daniel M., *It Is So Ordered: The Supreme Court Rules on School Segregation* (New York: W. W. Norton, 1966).

Bickel, Alexander M., *The Least Dangerous Branch: The Supreme Court at the Bar of Politics* (Indianapolis: Bobbs-Merrill, 1962).

——, *The Supreme Court and the Idea of Progress* (New York: Harper & Row, 1970).

Black, Hugo L., *A Constitutional Faith* (New York: Alfred A. Knopf, 1968).

Bland, Randall W., *Private Pressure on Public Law: The Legal Career of Justice Thurgood Marshall* (Port Washington, N.Y.: Kennikat Press, 1973).

Blaustein, Albert P., and Clarence Clyde Ferguson, Jr., *Desegregation and the Law: The Meaning and Effect of the School Segregation Cases* (New Brunswick: Rutgers University Press, 1957; Vintage paperback).

Bond, Horace Mann, *The Education of the Negro in the American Social Order* (Englewood Cliffs, N.J.: Prentice-Hall, 1934; republished by Octagon Books, New York, 1966).

Bradshaw, Herbert Clarence, *History of Prince Edward County* (Richmond, Va.: Dietz, 1955).

Breitman, George, ed., *Malcolm X Speaks* (New York: Merit, 1965; Grove Press Black Cat paperback, 1966).

Brunsman, Howard G., and U.S. Bureau of the Census, *Census of Population: 1950: Vol. II, Characteristics of the Population, Part 8, Delaware; Part 9, District of Columbia; Part 16, Kansas; Part 40, South Carolina; Part 46, Virginia* (Washington: U.S. Government Printing Office, 1952).

Bullock, Henry Allen, *A History of Negro Education in the South* (Cambridge: Harvard University Press, 1967).

Carmichael, Stokely, and Charles V. Hamilton, *Black Power: The Politics of Liberation in America* (New York: Random House, 1967; Vintage paperback).

Carter, Dan T., *Scottsboro: A Tragedy of the American South* (Baton Rouge: Louisiana State University Press, 1969).

Cash, W. J., *The Mind of the South* (New York: Alfred A. Knopf, 1941; Vintage paperback).

Clark, Kenneth B., *Prejudice and Your Child* (Boston: Beacon Press, 1955; Beacon paperback, 1963).

Clayton, James E., *The Making of Justice: The Supreme Court in Action* (New York: E. P. Dutton, 1964; Cornerstone paperback, 1965).

Corwin, Edward S., *The Constitution and What It Means Today* (Princeton: Princeton University Press, 1920; Atheneum paperback, 4th edition, 1967).

Davis, David Brion, *The Problem of Slavery in Western Culture* (Ithaca: Cornell University Press, 1966).

Dollard, John, *Caste and Class in a Southern Town* (New Haven: Yale University Press, 1937; Anchor paperback, 1957).

Douglas, William O., *Go East, Young Man, The Early Years: The Autobiography of William O. Douglas* (New York: Random House, 1974).

Du Bois, W. E. Burghardt, *Autobiography of W. E. B. Du Bois* (New York: International Publishers, 1968; paperback edition).

——, *Black Reconstruction in America, 1860–1880* (New York: Harcourt, Brace, 1935; Atheneum paperback, 1969).

——, *The Crisis Writings*, edited by Daniel Walden (New York: Fawcett, 1972).

——, *The Souls of Black Folk* (Chicago: A. C. McClurg, 1903; Fawcett paperback, 1961).

Elkins, Stanley M., *Slavery: A Problem in American Institutional and Intellectual Life* (Chicago: University of Chicago Press, 1959; paperback, 1968).

Fax, Elton C., *Contemporary Black Leaders* (New York: Dodd, Mead, 1970; Apollo paperback).

Fenderson, Lewis H., *Thurgood Marshall: Fighter for Justice* (New York: McGraw-Hill/Rutledge Books, 1969).

Fox, Stephen R., *The Guardian of Boston: William Monroe Trotter* (New York: Atheneum, 1970).

Franklin, John Hope, *From Slavery to Freedom: A History of Negro Americans* (New York: Alfred A. Knopf, 1947; Vintage paperback, 1969).

Frazier, E. Franklin, *Black Bourgeoisie* (New York: The Free Press, 1957; Collier paperback, 1962).

——, *The Negro Church in America* (New York: Schocken, 1964; paperback, 1964).

——, *The Negro in the United States* (New York: Macmillan, 14th edition, 1969).

Friedman, Leon, ed., *Argument: The Oral Argument Before the Supreme Court in Brown v. Board of Education of Topeka, 1952–1955* (New York: Chelsea House, 1969).

Friedman, Leon, and Fred L. Israel, *The Justices of the United States Supreme Court, 1789–1969: Their Lives and Major Opinions*, 4 vols. (New York: Chelsea House/ R. R. Bowker, 1969).

Garraty, John A., ed., *Quarrels That Have Shaped the Constitution* (New York: Harper & Row, 1962; Harper Colophon paperback, 1966).

Genovese, Eugene D., *The Political Economy of Slavery* (New York: Pantheon, 1965; Vintage paperback).

Gordon, Asa H., *Sketches of Negro Life and History in South Carolina* (Columbia: University of South Carolina Press, 1929, 1971).

Gossett, Thomas F., *Race: The History of an Idea in America* (Dallas: Southern Methodist University Press, 1963; Schocken paperback, 1965).

Gottman, Jean, *Virginia at Mid-Century* (New York: Henry Holt, 1955).

Green, Constance McL., *Eli Whitney and the Birth of American Technology* (Boston: Little, Brown, 1956; paperback).

———, *The Secret City: A History of Race Relations in the Nation's Capital* (Princeton: Princeton University Press, 1967; paperback, 1969).

Greenberg, Jack, *Race Relations and American Law* (New York: Columbia University Press, 1959).

Grier, William H., and Price M. Cobbs, *Black Rage* (New York: Basic Books, 1968; Bantam paperback, 1969).

Hansen, Carl F., *Danger in Washington: The Story of My Twenty Years in the Public Schools in the Nation's Capital* (West Nyack, N.Y.: Parker Publishing, 1968).

Harbaugh, William H., *Lawyer's Lawyer: The Life of John W. Davis* (New York: Oxford University Press, 1973).

Harlan, Louis R., *Separate and Unequal: Public School Campaigns and Racism in the Southern Seaboard States, 1901–1915* (Chapel Hill: University of North Carolina Press, 1958; Atheneum paperback, 1968).

Harris, Middleton, with the assistance of Morris Levitt, Roger Furman, and Ernest Smith, *The Black Book* (New York: Random House, 1974).

Herskovits, Melville J., *The Myth of the Negro Past* (New York: Harper & Bros., 1941; Beacon paperback, 1958).

Hill, Herbert, and Jack Greenberg, *Citizen's Guide to Desegregation: A Story of Social and Legal Change in American Life* (Boston: Beacon Press, 1955).

Hopkins, Vincent C., *Dred Scott's Case* (New York: Fordham University Press, 1951; Atheneum paperback, 1967).

Jackson, Robert H., *The Struggle for Judicial Supremacy* (New York: Alfred A. Knopf, 1941; Vintage paperback).

Jordan, Winthrop D., *White Over Black: American Attitudes Toward the Negro, 1550–1812* (Chapel Hill: University of North Carolina Press, 1968).

Kellogg, Charles Flint, *NAACP: A History of the National Association for the Advancement of Colored People, Vol. I, 1909–1920* (Baltimore: Johns Hopkins Press, 1967).

Key, V. O., Jr., *Southern Politics* (New York: Alfred A. Knopf, 1949; Vintage paperback).

Klineberg, Otto, ed., *Characteristics of the American Negro* (New York: Harper & Bros., 1944).

———, *Negro Intelligence and Selective Migration* (New York: Columbia University Press, 1935).

Kozol, Jonathan, *Death at an Early Age: The Destruction of the Hearts and Minds of Negro Children in the Boston Public Schools* (Boston: Houghton Mifflin, 1967; Bantam paperback, 1968).

Lewis, Anthony, *Gideon's Trumpet* (New York: Random House, 1964; Vintage paperback).

Lewis, Anthony, and The New York Times, *Portrait of a Decade: The Second American Revolution* (New York: Random House, 1964).

Logan, Rayford W., *Howard University: The First Hundred Years, 1867–1967* (New York: New York University Press, 1968).

Mason, Alpheus Thomas, *The Supreme Court from Taft to Warren* (Baton Rouge: Louisiana State University, 1958; Norton paperback, 1964).

McCloskey, Robert G., *The American Supreme Court* (Chicago: University of Chicago Press, 1960; paperback, 1969).

McFarland, Kenneth, *Eloquence in Public Speaking* (Englewood Cliffs, N.J.: Prentice-Hall, 1961).

Meltsner, Michael, *Cruel and Unusual: The Supreme Court and Capital Punishment* (New York: Random House, 1973).

Menninger, Karl A., *A Psychiatrist's World* (New York: Viking Press, 1959).

Miller, Kelly, *"Radicals and Conservatives" and Other Essays on the Negro in America* (New York: Schocken, 1968).

Miller, Loren, *The Petitioners: The Story of the Supreme Court of the United States and the Negro* (Cleveland: World Publishing, 1966; Meridian paperback, 1967).

Miller, Merle, *Plain Speaking: An Oral Biography of Harry S. Truman* (New York: G. P. Putnam's Sons, 1974).

Miller, Nyle H., Edgar Langsdorf, and Robert W. Richmond, *Kansas* (Topeka: Kansas State Historical Society, 1961).

Mills, Nicolaus, ed., *The Great School Bus Controversy* (New York: Teachers College Press/Columbia University, 1973).

Myrdal, Gunnar, *An American Dilemma* (New York: Harper & Bros., 1944; McGraw-Hill paperback, 1964).

Odum, Howard W., *Man's Quest for Social Guidance: The Study of Social Problems* (New York: Henry Holt, 1927).

——, *Southern Regions of the United States* (New York: Agathon Press, 1969; orig. pub. by University of North Carolina Press, 1936).

Peirce, Neal R., *The Deep South States of America* (New York: W. W. Norton, 1974).

Peltason, J. W., *Fifty-eight Lonely Men: Southern Federal Judges and School Desegregation* (New York: Harcourt, Brace & World, 1961).

Pfeffer, Leo, *This Honorable Court: A History of the United States Supreme Court* (Boston: Beacon Press, 1965; paperback, 1967).

Pritchett, Herman C., *Civil Liberties and the Vinson Court* (Chicago: University of Chicago Press, 1954).

Quarles, Benjamin, *Frederick Douglass* (Washington: Associated Publishers, 1948; Atheneum paperback, 1968).

Rawley, Joseph A., *Race and Politics: "Bleeding Kansas" and the Coming of the Civil War* (Philadelphia: J. B. Lippincott, 1969).

Redding, Saunders, *The Lonesome Road: The Story of the Negro's Part in America* (Garden City, N.Y.: Doubleday, 1958).

Rodell, Fred, *Nine Men: A Political History of the Supreme Court of the United States from 1790 to 1955* (New York: Random House, 1955; Vintage paperback).

Rossiter, Clinton, *1787: The Grand Convention* (New York: Macmillan, 1966; NAL Mentor paperback, 1968).

Savage, Henry, Jr., *The Santee: River of the Carolinas* (New York: Rinehart, 1946).

Schrag, Peter, *Voices in the Classroom: Public Schools and Public Attitudes* (Boston: Beacon Press, 1965; paperback, 1967).

Sheldon, Charles M., *In His Steps* (New York: Grosset & Dunlap, 1972).

Silberman, Charles H., *Crisis in Black and White* (New York: Random House, 1964; Vintage paperback).

Smith, Bob, *They Closed Their Schools: Prince Edward County, Virginia, 1951–1964* (Chapel Hill: University of North Carolina Press, 1965; paperback).

Speer, Hugh W., *The Case of the Century: A Historical and Social Perspective on Brown v. Board of Education* (unpublished, 1968). Written with the aid of a federal grant, it is available in a photocopy of the manuscript from Document Reproduction Service, Bethesda, Md.

Stampp, Kenneth M., *The Era of Reconstruction, 1865–1877* (New York: Alfred A. Knopf, 1965; Vintage paperback).

——, *The Peculiar Institution: Slavery in the Ante-bellum South* (New York: Alfred A. Knopf, 1956; Vintage paperback).

Stern, Robert L., and Eugene Gressman, *Supreme Court Practice* (Washington: Bureau of National Affairs, 4th edition, 1969).

Strother, D. B., *Evidence, Argument and Decision in Brown v. Board of Education*, unpublished doctoral thesis in speech, University of Illinois, 1958.

Taper, Bernard, *Gomillion Versus Lightfoot: Apartheid in Alabama* (New York: McGraw-Hill, 1962; paperback).

tenBroek, Jacobus, *Equal Under Law* (New York: Collier paperback, 1965; orig. pub. as *The Antislavery Origins of the Fourteenth Amendment*, University of California Press, 1951).

Van Doren, Carl, *The Great Rehearsal: The Story of the Making and Ratifying of the Constitution of the United States* (New York: Viking Press, 1948; Compass paperback, 1961).

Vose, Clement E., *Caucasians Only: The Supreme Court, the NAACP and the Restrictive Covenant Cases* (Berkeley: University of California Press, 1959; paperback, 1967).

Wallace, David Duncan, *South Carolina: A Short History, 1520–1948* (Columbia: University of South Carolina Press, 1951).

Warren, Charles, *The Supreme Court in United States History* (Boston: Little, Brown, 1922).

Washington, Booker T., *Up from Slavery* (New York: Airmont Publishing, 1967).

Washington, Joseph R., Jr., *Black Religion: The Negro and Christianity in the United States* (Boston: Beacon Press, 1964; paperback, 1966).

Weaver, John D., *Warren: The Man, the Court, the Era* (Boston: Little, Brown, 1967).

White, Walter, *A Man Called White: The Autobiography of Walter White* (New York: Viking Press, 1948; Indiana University Press paperback, 1970).

Wilkinson, J. Harvie III, *Serving Justice: A Supreme Court Clerk's View* (New York: Charterhouse, 1974).

Williams, Roger M., *The Bonds: An American Family* (New York: Atheneum, 1971).

Woodward, C. Vann, *The Burden of Southern History* (Baton Rouge: Louisiana State University Press, 1960, 1968; NAL Mentor paperback, 1969).

——, *Origins of the New South, 1877–1913* (Baton Rouge: Louisiana State University Press, 1951; paperback).

——, *The Strange Career of Jim Crow* (New York: Oxford University Press, 1955, 1967; paperback, 1966).

# Interviews and Correspondence

In most cases, these interviews were conducted in person and on the date and in the community cited. Some of the interviews were conducted by correspondence, indicated by the notation (C) below, and some by telephone, indicated by the notation (T) below. Each person interviewed is briefly described by his or her role in the *Brown* cases and/or occupation; when more than one position is cited, the first one listed generally indicates the interviewee's role at the time of the cases. LDF stands for NAACP Legal Defense Fund, Inc.

Adams, Sherman, former Assistant to President Eisenhower; (C) November 6, 1973, Lincoln, New Hampshire.

Almond, J. Lindsay, attorney general and governor of Virginia; January 5, 1972, Washington, D.C.

Bachelder, William K., law clerk to Justice Sherman Minton; (C) June 28, 1974, Newport Beach, California.

Banks, W. Lester, executive secretary, Virginia Conference of NAACP Branches; April 4, 1971, Richmond, Virginia.

Bell, Derrick, assistant counsel, NAACP Legal Defense Fund (LDF), 1960–66, and professor of law, Harvard; March 25, 1971, Cambridge, Massachusetts.

Bickel, Alexander M., law clerk to Justice Felix Frankfurter, law professor, Yale; August 20, 1971, New Haven, Connecticut. (Deceased.)

Bishop, Gardner L., a barber by trade and organizer of Parents Consolidated, Inc., the group that brought the District of Columbia school-segregation case of *Bolling v. Sharpe*; August 22, 1974, Washington, D.C.

Black, Charles L., Jr., professor of law at Columbia and then Yale, advisor to LDF; July 29, 1971, New Haven, Connecticut.

Black, Elizabeth (Mrs. Hugo L.), widow of the Justice and formerly his secretary; (C) November 18, 1973, Alexandria, Virginia.

Boone, Reginald, Charleston shipyard worker and owner of home where LDF lawyers stayed during *Briggs* trial; (T) October 19, 1971, Charleston, South Carolina.

Boulware, Harold, attorney for NAACP in South Carolina and local counsel for plaintiffs in *Briggs v. Elliott*; October 18, 1971, Columbia, South Carolina.

Briggs, Mr. and Mrs. Harry, and Harry, Jr., residents of Summerton, South Carolina, and plaintiffs in *Briggs v. Elliott*; November 29, 1971, New York City.

Brown, Esther (Mrs. Paul), civil-rights worker in Kansas City area and chief white organizer of school-desegregation suits there; May 31, 1969, New York City. (Deceased.)

Brown, Inza, longtime secretary to attorney Elisha Scott of Topeka; October 22, 1970, Topeka, Kansas.

Brown, Linda (Mrs. Charles Smith), principal infant plaintiff in *Brown v. Board of Education of Topeka*; October 25, 1970, North Topeka, Kansas.

Bulah, Sarah, plaintiff in Delaware segregation case; (T) July 15, 1974, Hockessin, Delaware.

Burnett, Lena (Mrs. McKinley), widow of president of Topeka NAACP during *Brown*; October 24, 1970, Topeka, Kansas.

Carter, Annie, mother of LDF lawyer Robert L. Carter; June 18, 1971, Philadelphia.

Carter, Robert L., assistant LDF counsel from 1944 to 1958, U.S. District Court judge; various interview sessions between January 23, 1971, and May 14, 1971, New York City.

Clark, Kenneth B., professor of psychology at City College of New York and chief LDF advisor in the social sciences; November 4, 1971, New York City.

Clark, Ramsey, former U.S. Attorney General, son of Justice Tom C. Clark; November 18, 1971, New York City.

Clark, Tom C., Associate Justice of the U.S. Supreme Court; October 8, 1971, Washington, D.C.

Coleman, William T., Jr., close advisor to LDF, later its president, and Secretary of Transportation in the Ford administration; July 21, 1971, Philadelphia.

Conway, Richard T., law clerk to Justice Sherman Minton; (C) June 25, 1974, Washington, D.C.

Croner, Mary and Robert (Mr. and Mrs.), farmers; Mrs. Croner is maternal grandmother of Barbara Johns, the teenager who led the student strike in Farmville, Virginia, that sparked the Prince Edward school-segregation case; April 8, 1971, Darlington Heights, Virginia.

Davis, John A., professor of government at City College of New York and head of non-legal research in reargument of *Brown* during summer of 1953; December 4, 1971, New Rochelle, New York.

DeLaine, Joseph A., minister and teacher who led black agrarian uprising in Clarendon County, South Carolina, in late 1940s and early 1950s; extensive correspondence beginning November 1, 1971, (C) and (T) Charlotte, North Carolina. (Deceased.)

Douglas, William O., Associate Justice of the U.S. Supreme Court; (C) October 3, 1974, Washington, D.C.

Drummond, Forrest S., chief librarian of Los Angeles County Law Library; (T) October 8, 1974, Los Angeles.

Dugger, Ronnie, founding editor of the *Texas Observer*; (T) June 2, 1974, Austin, Texas.

Elman, Philip, civil-rights specialist in office of U.S. Solicitor General from 1947 to 1960, member of Federal Trade Commission, professor at Georgetown Law Center; August 19, 1971, Washington, D.C.

Emerson, Thomas I., Yale law professor; (T) June 25, 1974, New Haven, Connecticut.

Ernst, Morris L., private attorney specializing in civil liberties and member of President Truman's Civil Rights Committee; November 4, 1971, New York City.

Fassett, John D., law clerk to Justice Stanley Reed; September 19, 1974, New Haven, Connecticut.

Figg, Robert McC., Jr., Charleston attorney and special counsel for the state of South Carolina in *Briggs v. Elliott*, dean of University of South Carolina law school; October 17, 1971, Columbia, South Carolina.

Flemming, Billie, proprietor of Flemming and DeLaine Funeral Home, Manning, South Carolina, and nephew of Rev. Joseph A. DeLaine; (T) October 22, 1971, Manning, South Carolina.

Fortas, Abe, attorney and former Associate Justice, U.S. Supreme Court; (C) January 14, 1974, Washington, D.C.

Frank, John P., professor of law at Yale and advisor to LDF, formerly clerk to Justice Hugo Black; (C) November 19, 1971, Phoenix, Arizona.

Franklin, John Hope, professor of history at Howard University, advisor to LDF, and chairman of history department at University of Chicago; (C) October 23, 1973, and November 28, 1973, Stanford, California.

Gardner, Warner, solicitor of Department of Interior following Nathan Margold, Washington attorney; December 27, 1973, Washington, D.C.

Garrett, Henry E., professor of psychology at Columbia University and chief expert witness in the social sciences for Virginia in Prince Edward segregation case; April 9, 1971, Charlottesville, Virginia.

Gellhorn, Walter, professor of law at Columbia University, sometime advisor to LDF and prominent civil-libertarian; October 14, 1971, New York City.

Gibson, James, farmer in Clarendon County, South Carolina; October 19, 1971, Summerton, South Carolina.

Greenberg, Jack, assistant LDF counsel and, after 1960, director-counsel of LDF; various interviews between July 12, 1968, and March 3, 1971, New York City.

Griffin, L. Francis, pastor of First Baptist Church in Farmville, Virginia, and spearhead of NAACP desegregation effort in Prince Edward County; April 8, 1971, Farmville.

Harris, Louis, pollster and consultant to LDF; December 28, 1971, New York City.

Hastie, William H., second cousin of Charles Houston; professor and later dean of Howard Law School; chief judge, U.S. Court of Appeals for the Third Circuit; and longtime informal advisor to LDF; June 18, 1971, and June 30, 1971, Philadelphia.

Hawkins, Carl S., law clerk to Chief Justice Fred Vinson; (C) July 2, 1974, Provo, Utah.

Hill, Herbert, labor director of NAACP; March 2, 1971, New York City.

Hill, Oliver W., NAACP attorney for Virginia and co-counsel for plaintiffs in Prince Edward segregation case; April 4, 1971, Richmond, Virginia.

Holland, J. B., teacher and principal in Topeka, Kansas, for thirty years; October 23, 1970, Topeka.

Holt, Louisa (Mrs. Louisa Pinkham Howe), psychologist and witness for plaintiffs in Topeka segregation case; March 25, 1971, Quincy, Massachusetts.

Huston, Luther A., *New York Times* staff reporter covering Supreme Court from 1951 to 1957; October 1, 1971, Washington, D.C.

Huxman, Walter A., former governor of Kansas, judge for U.S. Court of Appeals for the Seventh Circuit and presiding judge at *Brown* trial; October 24, 1970, Topeka, Kansas. (Deceased.)

Indritz, Phineas, chief counsel for American Veterans Committee and legal advisor to LDF during restrictive-covenant cases; March 15, 1971, Washington, D.C.

Jackson, Samuel C., student leader at Topeka High School, later head of Topeka NAACP, Assistant Secretary of Housing and Urban Development in Nixon administration; June 11 and 21, 1969, Washington, D.C.

Jackson, William E., son of Justice Robert Jackson and New York attorney; October 6, 1971, New York City.

Johns, Altona T. (Mrs. Vernon), wife of well-known preacher and aunt of Barbara Johns; (C) July 28, 1971, (T) June 15, 1971, Petersburg, Virginia.

Johns, Barbara (Mrs. William Powell), leader of student strike at Robert R. Moton High School in Farmville, Virginia, that sparked Prince Edward case; May 14, 1971, Philadelphia.

Jones, M. Boyd, principal of Robert R. Moton High School, Farmville, Virginia; (C) October 29, 1971, Virginia Beach, Virginia.

Kelly, Alfred H., professor of history at Wayne State University in Detroit and key advisor to LDF during *Brown* reargument; December 28, 1971, New York City.

Kiene, Thomas, writer and executive editor, Topeka *Capitol-Journal*; October 23, 1970, Topeka, Kansas.

Kirk, Grayson, president of Columbia University; October 14, 1971, New York City, and (C) October 21, 1971.

Koger, A. Briscoe, graduate of Howard Law School and Baltimore attorney who began practice in mid-1920s; February 6, 1974, Baltimore.

Korman, Milton, assistant corporation counsel for District of Columbia and chief counsel for District Board of Education in *Bolling v. Sharpe*; October 7, 1971, Washington, D.C.

Krech, David, professor of psychology at University of California and expert witness in *Briggs* trial; (C) December 17, 1973, Berkeley, California.

Lawson, Belford V., Jr., Washington attorney and counsel for plaintiff in *Henderson v. U.S.*; March 17, 1971, Washington, D.C.

Lawson, Mr. and Mrs. Henry, NAACP leaders in Summerton, South Carolina, area in 1970s; October 19, 1971, Summerton.

Levinson, Harry, psychologist, director of division of industrial mental health at Menninger Foundation, later professor at Harvard Business School; March 25, 1971, Cambridge, Massachusetts.

Lewis, Anthony, *New York Times* reporter covering Supreme Court during Warren era, "op-ed" page columnist; October 22, 1973, New York City.

Lovett, Edward P., junior partner of Charles Houston during 1930s; (T) March 15, 1974, Washington, D.C.

Marshall, Elizabeth, aunt of Thurgood Marshall; February 7, 1974, Baltimore.

Marshall, Thurgood, director-counsel of LDF, Associate Justice of the U.S. Supreme Court; December 28, 1973, Washington, D.C.

Massey, Mrs. J. S., friend of McKinley Burnett, Topeka NAACP president; October 24, 1970, Topeka, Kansas.

McIlwaine, T. J., longtime superintendent of schools for Prince Edward County, Virginia; April 8, 1971, Farmville, Virginia.

McKay, Ellis H., law clerk to Justice Tom Clark; (T) September 15, 1974, New York City.

McKenzie, Marjorie (Mrs. Belford Lawson), columnist for the *Courier*, largest black weekly in nation at time of *Brown*; March 17, 1971, Washington, D.C.

Meagher, William R., associate counsel to John W. Davis representing South Carolina in *Briggs*; August 27, 1971, New York City.

Meltsner, Michael, assistant LDF counsel beginning in 1961, professor of law at Columbia; February 25, 1971, and March 3, 1971, New York City.

Menninger, Karl A., psychiatrist and co-founder of Menninger Foundation; (C) January 9, 1974, Topeka, Kansas.

Mickum, George V., III, law clerk to Justice Stanley Reed; (T) October 20, 1974, Washington, D.C.

Modlin, George M., president of Richmond University; (C) April 23, 1971, Richmond, Virginia.

Montgomery, Eugene, executive secretary of South Carolina NAACP conference; October 19, 1971, Orangeburg, South Carolina.

Moon, Henry Lee, public-relations director of the NAACP and editor of *The Crisis*; July 22, 1971, New York City.

Morgan, Ray, Kansas state correspondent for Kansas City *Star* since 1947; (T) July 15, 1974, Topeka, Kansas.

Moss, Elizabeth Murphy, daughter of Carl Murphy and vice president and treasurer of *Afro-American*; February 6, 1974, Baltimore.

Nabrit, James M., Jr., co-counsel for plaintiffs in *Bolling v. Sharpe*, professor and dean of Howard Law School, secretary and president of Howard University; October 30, 1971, Washington, D.C.

Nabrit, James M., III, assistant LDF counsel starting in mid-1950s; March 11, 1971, New York City.

Paul, James C. N., law clerk to Chief Justice Fred Vinson; (C) July 10, 1974, New Brunswick, New Jersey.

Payne, A. J., minister of Baltimore's Enon Baptist Church for fifty years, and his wife, Odell, friend of Marshall family; February 6, 1974, Baltimore.

Pearson, Conrad O., co-counsel in *Hocutt v. Wilson*, first college-desegregation case argued under NAACP auspices; (C) June 28, 1971, and January 16, 1974, and (T) Durham, North Carolina.

Perry, Marian Wynn (Mrs. Alfred Yankauer), assistant LDF counsel, 1945–49; March 25, 1971, Newton, Massachusetts.

Pollak, Louis H., professor of law and dean at Yale, LDF advisor; June 25, 1971, New Haven, Connecticut.

Pollock, Earl E., law clerk to Chief Justice Earl Warren; (T) August 19, 1974, Chicago.

Poston, Ted, reporter for *Amsterdam News*, later for New York *Post*, where for years he was only black newsman on a major New York daily; July 22, 1971, New York City. (Deceased.)

Prettyman, E. Barrett, Jr., law clerk to Justice Robert Jackson; September 30, 1971, Washington, D.C.

Randall, Robert L., law clerk to Justice Stanley Reed; (C) July 5, 1974, Washington, D.C.

Redding, Louis L., veteran NAACP attorney and private practitioner in Wilmington, Delaware, counsel for blacks in Delaware segregation cases; December 8, 1971, Wilmington.

Richburg, Joseph, teacher, farmer, and barber in Clarendon County, South Carolina; October 19, 1971, Summerton, South Carolina.

Riely, John W., assistant counsel for state of Virginia in reargument and further argument of Prince Edward County segregation case; April 3, 1971, Richmond, Virginia.

Robertson, Archibald G., co-counsel for state of Virginia in Prince Edward segregation-case trial and appeal; April 3, 1971, Richmond, Virginia.

Robinson, Spottswood W., III, special counsel for the Southern region of NAACP, Richmond attorney, co-counsel for plaintiffs in Prince Edward case, judge on U.S. Court of Appeals for the District of Columbia; March 16, 1971, Washington, D.C.

Rogers, S. Emory, counsel to Clarendon School District No. 22 School Board, defendant in *Briggs*, later head of White Citizens' Councils for South Carolina; October 19, 1971, Summerton, South Carolina, and (C) October 19 and December 17, 1971.

Ross, Mr. and Mrs. Merrill, teachers in the Topeka schools; October 23, 1970, Topeka, Kansas.

Rowe, Frederick, law clerk to Justice Tom Clark; (C) June 25, 1974, Chevy Chase, Maryland.

Rubenstein, Ernest, law clerk to Justice Tom Clark; July 23, 1974, New York City.

Sander, Frank E. A., law clerk to Justice Felix Frankfurter; (C) January 24, 1974, Cambridge, Massachusetts.

Scott, Charles, son of Elisha Scott, leader of black Topeka, co-counsel in *Brown*; interviews throughout week of October 21, 1970, Topeka, Kansas.

Scott, Mr. and Mrs. John; he is son of Elisha Scott and served with his brother Charles as local counsel to plaintiffs in *Brown*, later an attorney in U.S. Department of Interior; August 18, 1969, Washington, D.C.

Seitz, Collins J., chancellor of Delaware, chief judge of U.S. Court of Appeals for the Third Circuit; December 8, 1971, Wilmington, Delaware.

Solomon, Maisie, housewife and domestic worker in Summerton, South Carolina; October 19, 1971, Summerton.

Steel, Lewis, assistant NAACP counsel during 1960s; March 3, 1971, New York City.

Stovall, Alice, secretary to Thurgood Marshall, LDF office manager; April 20, 1969, New York City.

Taylor, William L., assistant LDF counsel in late 1950s, staff director of U.S. Civil Rights Commission; August 1, 1968, Washington, D.C.

Thompson, Charles H., founder and editor of the *Journal of Negro Education*, professor and dean at Howard; March 16, 1971, Washington, D.C.

Tidwell, Winfred, teacher and principal in Topeka schools in 1960s and 1970s; October 22, 1970, Topeka, Kansas.

Todd, Lucinda (Mrs. Alvin C.), secretary of Topeka branch of NAACP, plaintiff and witness in *Brown* trial; October 23, 1970, Topeka, Kansas.

Troubh, Raymond S., law clerk to Justice Harold Burton; (T) August 23, 1974, New York City.

Vinson, Fred M., Jr., son of Chief Justice Vinson and Washington attorney; October 7, 1971, and December 27, 1973, Washington, D.C.

Waddy, Joseph C., law partner to Charles Houston in 1930s and 1940s, U.S. District Court judge; September 30, 1971, Washington, D.C.

Wallace, Harry L., law clerk to Justice Sherman Minton; (C) June 21, 1974, Washington, D.C.

Warren, Earl, Chief Justice of the United States; June 16, 1971, Washington, D.C., and (C) November 20, 1973. (Deceased.)

Wechsler, Herbert, professor of law at Columbia, sometime advisor to LDF; November 31, 1973, New York City.

Weinstein, Jack, professor of law at Columbia, close advisor of LDF, U.S. District Court judge; March 31, 1971, Brooklyn, New York.

Wertham, Frederic, psychiatrist, head of Lafargue Clinic, and principal expert witness at Wilmington trial in Delaware segregation cases; October 28, 1971, New York City.

Whipple, Taggart, associate counsel with John W. Davis for South Carolina's brief on reargument of segregation cases before Supreme Court; October 12, 1971, New York City.

Whitehead, Matthew J., professor of education at Howard, expert witness for plaintiffs at *Briggs* trial, dean of District of Columbia Teachers College; March 18, 1971, Washington, D.C.

Wilkins, Roy, executive secretary of the NAACP; May 15, 1974, New York City.

Williams, Franklin H., assistant LDF counsel from 1945 to 1950, U.S. ambassador to Ghana, director of Phelps Stokes Fund; March 22, 1971, New York City.

Williams, Mamie, longtime teacher and civic leader in Topeka; October 24, 1970, Topeka, Kansas; (C) November 3, 1970.

Wilson, Paul E., assistant attorney general of Kansas and counsel for state in *Brown*; (C) December 3, 1973, and January 3, 1974, Lawrence, Kansas.

Wimmer, James R., law clerk to Justice Sherman Minton; (C) July 2, 1974, Chicago.

Workman, William D., political reporter and editor of Columbia *State*; October 18, 1971, Columbia, South Carolina.

Young, H. Albert, attorney general of Delaware and counsel for school districts and state in Delaware segregation cases; (T) July 15, 1974, Wilmington.

# Notes

The source of much of the material in the text is given in the text itself and not repeated here; this is particularly true of material extracted from the briefs, arguments, and opinions of the cases discussed. These notes are intended to credit only the principal published sources and interviews drawn upon in each chapter. The books and interviewees are listed in detail in the preceding sections.

## PART I / UNDER COLOR OF LAW

## Chapter 1 / Together Let Us Sweetly Live

*Books:* Brunsman and Bureau of Census, *Census of Population: 1950*; Frazier, *The Negro Church in America*; Gordon, *Sketches of Negro Life . . . in South Carolina*; Green, *Eli Whitney and the Birth of American Technology*; Harlan, *Separate and Unequal*; Savage, *The Santee*; Wallace, *South Carolina: A Short History*; and Washington, *Black Religion*. Wallace's 753-page "short" history is a condensation of a four-volume work.

*Interviews and Correspondence:* Briggs, Harry, Liza, and Harry, Jr.; DeLaine, Joseph A.; Figg, Robert McC., Jr.; Flemming, Billie; Gibson, James; Lawson, Mr. and Mrs. Henry; Montgomery, Eugene; Richburg, Joseph; Rogers, S. Emory; and Solomon, Maisie.

*Articles and Documents:* Letter, Boulware, Harold, to Joseph A. DeLaine, March 8, 1949; Charleston *News & Courier*, generally and especially article headlined "Side Issue to Segregation Case," March 7, 1954; (Pittsburgh) *Courier*, article headlined "S.C. Victimizes Preacher, Foe of School Bias," front page, December 22, 1951; DeLaine, Joseph A., extensive personal papers and documents, especially his memorandum to parents of Scott's Branch schoolchildren, Summerton, September 10, 1949, letter to Clarendon County Board of Education, July 9, 1949, and his article "The Clarendon County School Segregation Case" in *A.M.E. Review*, 1954 (otherwise undated); Greider, William, "Landmark City After 16 Years," Washington *Post*, September 3, 1970; Manning (S.C.) *Times*, in general and particularly June 27, 1951, and various articles on local history, September 14, 1955, and October 17, 1956; Pett, Saul, Associated Press dispatch from Summerton, June 12, 1954, appearing in Charleston *News & Courier*; Rowan, Carl T., series of eleven articles titled "Jim Crow's Last Stand" appearing daily from November 29 to December 9, 1953, in Minneapolis *Tribune* (see especially articles 1 and 9); United States Department of Agriculture Soil Conservation Service (with South Carolina Agricultural Experiment Station), "Land Resource Map of South Carolina," 1966; United States Department of Agriculture, South Carolina Cooperative Reporting

Service (with South Carolina Experiment Station), "The Agriculture of Clarendon County, South Carolina," County Statistical Series No. 31; *Voice of Missions*, pub. of AME Church, "Like Father, Like Son," December 1953. Rowan's articles are particularly noteworthy.

## Chapter 2 / Original Sin

*Books:* Aptheker, *A Documentary History of the Negro People*; Beard, *An Economic Interpretation of the Constitution*; Bennett, *Before the Mayflower*; Cash, *The Mind of the South*; Davis, *The Problem of Slavery in Western Culture*; Du Bois, *Black Reconstruction*; Elkins, *Slavery*; Franklin, *From Slavery to Freedom*; Frazier, *The Negro in the United States*; Genovese, *The Political Economy of Slavery*; Harris, *The Black Book*; Herskovits, *The Myth of the Negro Past*; Hopkins, *Dred Scott's Case*; Jordan, *White Over Black*; Myrdal, *An American Dilemma*; Quarles, *Frederick Douglass*; Rossiter, *1787: The Grand Convention*; Silberman, *Crisis in Black and White*; Stampp, *The Era of Reconstruction* and *The Peculiar Institution*; tenBroek, *Equality Under Law*; Van Doren, *The Great Rehearsal*; and Woodward, *The Burden of Southern History.*

*Quotations*

p. 37—The Douglass speech is quoted in full in Aptheker, 333.

p. 45—The Schurz report is cited by Frazier, 128.

## Chapter 3 / The Special Favorite of the Laws

*Books:* Du Bois, *Black Reconstruction* and *The Souls of Black Folk*; Franklin, *From Slavery to Freedom*; Friedman and Israel, *The Justices of the Supreme Court* (see especially sketches on Samuel Miller by William Gilette, 1011, John M. Harlan by Louis Filler, 1281 ff., and Henry Billings Brown by Joel Goldfarb, 1553 ff.); Garraty, *Quarrels That Have Shaped the Constitution* (see Chapter IX, "The Case of the Prejudiced Doorkeeper" by Alan F. Westin, 128 ff.; Chapter X, "The Case of the Louisiana Traveler" by C. Vann Woodward, 145 ff.; and Chapter XVI, "The School Desegregation Case" by Alfred H. Kelly, 243 ff.); Greenberg, *Race Relations and American Law*; Jackson, *The Struggle for Judicial Supremacy*; Miller, *The Petitioners*; Pfeffer, *This Honorable Court*; Washington, *Up from Slavery*; Woodward, *The Burden of Southern History*, *Origins of the New South*, and *The Strange Career of Jim Crow*. A special debt is acknowledged to the works of Professor Woodward.

*Articles:* Among the many articles in scholarly journals dealing with *Plessy*, I found especially useful Bernstein, Barton J., "Case Law in *Plessy v. Ferguson*," *Journal of Negro History*, XLVII, No. 3 (July 1962), 192–198; Bernstein, Barton J., "*Plessy v. Ferguson*: Conservative Sociological Jurisprudence," *Journal of Negro History*, XLVIII, No. 3 (July 1963), 196–205; *Columbia Law Review*, unsigned note titled "Is Racial Segregation Consistent with Equal Protection of the Laws? *Plessy v. Ferguson* Re-examined," May 1949, 629–639; Levy, Leonard W., and Harlan Philips, "The Roberts Case: Source of the 'Separate But Equal Doctrine,' " *American Historical Review*, LVI (1951), 510–518; Pollak, Louis H., "Racial Discrimination and Judicial Integrity," *University of Pennsylvania Law Review*, November 1959, 1–34; Waite, Edward F., "The Negro in the Supreme Court," *Minnesota Law Review*, March 1946, 220–304; and *Yale Law Journal*, unsigned note titled "Segregation in Public Schools: A Violation of 'Equal Protection of the Laws,' " June 1947, 1059–1067.

*Quotations*
p. 51—Du Bois passage from *The Souls of Black Folk*, 111.
p. 51—Washington passage from *Up from Slavery*, 30.
pp. 70–71—Excerpts from Washington's Atlanta speech from *Up from Slavery*, 135 ff.

## Chapter 4 / Not Like Bales of Hay

*Books:* Bennett, *Before the Mayflower*; Du Bois, *The Crisis Writings* (edited by Danie! Walden), *Autobiography*, and *The Souls of Black Folk*; Fox, *The Guardian of Boston*; Franklin, *From Slavery to Freedom*; Gossett, *Race*; Harbaugh, *Lawyer's Lawyer*; Harris, *The Black Book*; Kellogg, *NAACP*; Miller, *The Petitioners*; Woodward, *Origins of the New South* and *The Strange Career of Jim Crow*. Kellogg's multi-volume work-in-progress promises to be the definitive history of the NAACP; he draws on other accounts as well as adding valuable new documentation.
*Quotations*
p. 94—From *The Souls of Black Folk*, 54.
p. 95—*Ibid.*, 22.
pp. 95–96—From *The Autobiography of W. E. B. Du Bois*, 250.
p. 99—From *The Crisis Writings*, 118.

## Chapter 5 / Coming of Age in Nigger Heaven

*Books:* Baker, *Felix Frankfurter*; Bennett, *Before the Mayflower*; Du Bois, *The Crisis Writings*; Franklin, *From Slavery to Freedom*; Friedman and Israel, *The Justices of the Supreme Court*; Green, *The Secret City*; Kellogg, *NAACP*; Logan, *Howard University*; Mason, *The Supreme Court from Taft to Warren*; McCloskey, *The American Supreme Court*; Miller, Kelly, *Radicals and Conservatives*; Miller, Loren, *The Petitioners*; Rodell, *Nine Men*; and White, *A Man Called White*.
*Interviews:* Hastie, William H.; Lovett, Edward P.; Nabrit, James M., Jr.; Thompson, Charles H.; and Waddy, Joseph C.
*Articles and Documents:* See Charles Houston file in the archives of Founders' Library, Howard University; for Houston's pre-Howard days, I have drawn largely on interviews and "A Sketch of the Life of Charles H. Houston" by Geraldine R. Segal, a master's thesis, University of Pennsylvania, 1963. There is remarkably little material in print—in any form—on Houston.
*Quotation*
p. 111—Du Bois's editorial, "Returning Soldiers," *The Crisis*, XVII (May 1919), 13–14 (quoted in *The Crisis Writings*, 259–261).

## Chapter 6 / Exhibit A

*Books:* Carter, *Scottsboro*; Franklin, *From Slavery to Freedom*; Frazier, *The Negro in the United States*; Hill and Greenberg, *Citizen's Guide to Desegregation*; Logan, *Howard University*; Miller, *The Petitioners*; Vose, *Caucasians Only*; and White, *A Man Called White*. The Hill-Greenberg book, a small one, contains the fullest previous history of the Legal Defense Fund and its desegregation efforts.
*Interviews and Correspondence:* Carter, Robert L.; Clark, Kenneth B.; Davis, John A.; Fortas, Abe; Gardner, Warner; Gellhorn, Walter; Hill, Herbert; Hill, Oliver W.; Lawson, Belford V., Jr.; Lovett, Edward P.; Marshall, Thurgood; Nabrit, James M., Jr.; Perry, Marian Wynn; Redding, Louis L.; and Wechsler, Herbert.
*Articles and Documents:* On Houston and Howard, see especially Bunche, Ralph, J., "A Critical Analysis of the Tactics and Progress of Minority Groups," *Journal*

*of Negro Education*, IV, No. 3 (Summer 1935), 309–320; Davis, Arthur P., "E. Franklin Frazier (1894–1962): A Profile," *Journal of Negro Education*, XXXI, No. 4 (Fall 1962), 429–435; Hastie, William H., "Charles Hamilton Houston, 1895–1950," *Journal of Negro History*, XXXV, No. 4 (October 1950), 355–358; and Segal, "A Sketch of the Life of Charles Houston." On Nathan Margold, see his file in NAACP Papers at the Manuscript Division, Library of Congress, especially his own biographical statement and pages 41–93 of his unpublished report titled "Preliminary Report to the Joint Committee Supervising the Expenditure of the 1930 Appropriation by the American Fund for Public Service to the N.A.A.C.P."; various articles about the Garland Fund appeared in the New York press, beginning with one in the *New York Times*, July 24, 1922, and concluding with a report on the Fund's dissolution in the New York *Herald Tribune*, June 20, 1941. On John Parker's career and nomination to the Supreme Court, see especially tributes to him by the bar at the beginning of 253 F. 2d; Du Bois, W. E. B., "The Defeat of Judge Parker," *The Crisis*, XXXVII (July 1930), 225 ff.; *New York Times*, May 8, 1930; and Richmond *Times-Dispatch*, March 29, April 28, April 30, and May 8, 1930. On the Crawford murder case, see *Amsterdam News*, June 22, 1935; Dabney, Virginius, "Virginia's Crawford Case," Baltimore *Sun*, February 16, 1934; Loudon County (Va.) *Times-Mirror*, January 14 and 21, February 4, 1932, October 19 and 26, November 2, 9, 16, and 23, December 21, 1933, and January 4 and February 1, 1934; and Washington *Post*, November 7 and 8, 1933; see also White, *A Man Called White*, 152–156, for an interesting but highly partisan account.

*Quotations*

p. 132—Margold Report excerpt taken from Hill and Greenberg, 57.

p. 133—This quotation and other paraphrased material taken from original Margold Report in NAACP Collection, Library of Congress.

p. 142—Greensboro *Daily News* clipping quoted in Vose, 35.

## Chapter 7 / The Raw Deal

*Books:* Du Bois, *Autobiography*; Green, *The Secret City*; Logan, *Howard University*; Miller, *The Petitioners*; and White, *A Man Called White*.

*Interviews and Correspondence:* Hastie, William H.; Hill, Oliver W.; Lawson, Belford V., Jr.; Marshall, Thurgood; Pearson, Conrad O.; and Perry, Marian Wynn.

*Articles and Documents:* On *Hocutt v. Wilson*, see records for Superior Court of Durham County, North Carolina, complaint (March 16, 1933), answer (March 24, 1933), and judgment (March 28, 1933); also, Durham *Morning Herald*, February 14, March 24, 25, 26, and 29, 1933; Greensboro *Daily News*, March 14 and 28, 1933; Raleigh *News & Observer*, March 17, 18, 25, 26, 28, and 29, and April 1, 1933; University of North Carolina *Daily Tarheel*, March 24, 26, and 30, 1933; and letter from Conrad Pearson to Walter White, February 6, 1933, NAACP Collection, Library of Congress. On William Hastie, see Hastie, "Position of the Negro in the American Social Order: Outlook for 1950," *Journal of Negro Education*, XVIII, No. 3 (Summer 1949), 595–602; Philadelphia *Bulletin*, September 30, 1962, and June 1, 1971; Philadelphia *Daily News*, February 6, 1967; Philadelphia *Inquirer*, October 16, 1949; Pollak, Louis H., remarks at dinner honoring Hastie held at Philadelphia Museum of Art, May 15, 1971; Seitz, Collins J., "Honorable William Henry Hastie: Magnanimity of Mind and Spirit," *Shingle*, pub. of Philadelphia Bar Ass'n, May 1971, 101–102; and Time Inc. file, unpublished profile by Gene Moore, December 11, 1963. On Houston, see *Afro-American* stories on September 15 and December 15, 1934, and February 16, 1935; articles by Houston in *The Crisis*, including

"TVA: Lily-White Reconstruction" (with John P. Davis), XLI (October 1934), 290 ff., "Educational Inequalities Must Go," XLII (October 1935), 300 ff., and "How to Fight for Better Schools," XLIII (February 1936), 52 ff.; articles about him in *Journal & Guide*, February 3, 1934; Washington *Post*, April 10, 1931; Washington *Star*, December 25, 1934; and Washington *Tribune*, July 7, 1933. Also, Houston's letters to Roy Wilkins, March 21, 1934; to his father, January 4, 1936; and to Walter White, September 13, October 12, November 2, 4, and 7, 1934, and February 9, March 19 and 30, April 10, and July 31, 1935, all in NAACP Collection, Library of Congress. On *Journal of Negro Education*, see especially IV, No. 3 (Summer 1935) in its entirety.

*Quotations*
   p. 162—Houston to White, September 13, 1934, Library of Congress.
   pp. 162–163—Houston to White, February 9, 1935, Library of Congress.
   p. 163—Undated intra-office memo in Houston's handwriting, Library of Congress.
   pp. 164–165—Motion-picture scenario of South Carolina schools, interoffice memo by Houston, June 16, 1935, Library of Congress.
   p. 166—Roosevelt quotation in White, *A Man Called White*, 170.
   p. 170—Du Bois article, *Journal of Negro Education*, IV, No. 3 (Summer 1935), 335.
   p. 171—Long's pioneering article is worth reading in its entirety, *Journal of Negro Education*, IV, No. 3 (Summer 1935), 336–350.
   p. 172—Thompson article in same issue of *Journal of Negro Education*, 419–433.

## Chapter 8 / Uncle Fearless's Nephew

*Books:* Bland, *Private Pressure on Public Law*; Fax, *Contemporary Black Leaders*; Fenderson, *Thurgood Marshall*; Friedman and Israel, *The Justices of the Supreme Court* (see portrait of Marshall by John P. MacKenzie, 3063–3092); Redding, *The Lonesome Road*; and White, *A Man Called White*. There is no adequate treatment of Marshall in any of the above; MacKenzie's cameo is the best synopsis of his career in book form. Fenderson, written for youngsters, is recommended for children of all colors.

*Interviews:* Ernst, Morris L.; Hastie, William H.; Hill, Herbert; Hill, Oliver W.; Koger, A. Briscoe; Lawson, Belford V., Jr.; Marshall, Elizabeth; Marshall, Thurgood; Meltsner, Michael; Moss, Elizabeth Murphy; Payne, Rev. and Mrs. A. J.; and Thompson, Charles H.

*Articles and Documents:* On Marshall's career, the *Afro-American* files in Baltimore probably carry the most extensive collection anywhere of articles about the attorney, a native son; clippings on Marshall's mother, Norma, and Mrs. Lillie Jackson were also useful, as was Marshall's letter to *Afro*, November 9, 1950, setting straight his bar-examination score. Among other sources consulted were *Howard Magazine*, "Mr. Civil Rights," January 1963, 4–8; *Newsweek*, "Mr. Justice Marshall," June 26, 1967, 34–35; Poston, Ted, "New Man on the Bench," New York *Post*, October 7, 1962; Poston, "On Appeal to the Supreme Court," *Survey*, January 1949; Ross, Irwin, "Thurgood Marshall," five-part series in New York *Post*, June 13–17, 1960; Segal, "Portrait of Charles Houston," 68; Taper, Bernard, "A Reporter at Large: A Meeting in Atlanta," *New Yorker*, March 17, 1956, 80 ff.; *Time*, cover stories December 21, 1953, 15–18, and September 9, 1955, 23–24. See also Marshall file in NAACP Collection, Library of Congress, including letter from Marshall to Lillie Jackson and Carl Murphy, February 1, 1936. On *Murray v. Pearson*, the fullest account of the trial appeared in *Afro*, June 22, 1935; see also Baltimore *Sun*, June 18, 1935, and Mencken, H. L., "The Murray Case," *Sun*,

September 23, 1935; extensive correspondence on the case may be found in the NAACP Collection, Library of Congress, especially Marshall to Houston, January 4 and October 11, 1934; Houston to Marshall, November 22, 1934; Hillegeist, W. M., to Donald Murray, February 9, 1935; Murray to Board of Regents, University of Maryland, March 5, 1935; Pearson, R. A., to Murray, December 14, 1934; and Lawson, Belford V., Jr., to Houston and to William Gosnell, December 5, 1934.

*Quotations*

    p. 188—Pearson letter of December 14, 1934, NAACP Collection, Library of Congress.

    p. 188—Hillegeist to Murray, February 9, 1935; Murray to Board of Regents, March 5, 1935. Both in NAACP Collection, Library of Congress.

    p. 193—*Crisis*, October 1935, 300 ff.

## Chapter 9 / Stalking the Law of the Jungle

*Books:* Bickel, *The Least Dangerous Branch*; Du Bois, *Autobiography*; Fenderson, *Thurgood Marshall*; Franklin, *From Slavery to Freedom*; Friedman and Israel, *The Justices of the Supreme Court* (see especially John P. Frank's sketch on Hugo L. Black, 2321–2346); Jackson, *The Struggle for Judicial Supremacy*; Lewis, *Gideon's Trumpet*; Myrdal, *An American Dilemma*; Pfeffer, *This Honorable Court*; and Rodell, *Nine Men.*

*Interviews:* Banks, W. Lester; Hill, Oliver W.; Marshall, Thurgood; Moon, Henry Lee; Robinson, Spottswood W. III; Waddy, Joseph C.; and Wilkins, Roy.

*Articles and Documents:* On *Murray* appeal, *Afro*, January 25, 1936, and Baltimore *Sun*, January 16, 1936. On Baltimore County school-equalization suit, *Afro*, October 12, 1935, and February 15 and 22 and September 19, 1936; Baltimore *Sun*, September 14 and 15, 1936; correspondence, Hershner, John T., to Marshall, September 9, 1935, and Marshall to Walter White, October 3, 1935, and September 16, 1936, NAACP Collection, Library of Congress. On Marshall's teacher-equalization drive in Maryland, see *Journal of Negro Education*, 1936–39, *passim*. On Houston's tenure as NAACP counsel in New York, *Afro*, April 9, 1938; *Amsterdam News*, February 8, 1936; Associated Press dispatch on Houston arguing case to desegregate University of Tennessee school of pharmacy, March 22, 1937, in many papers; Houston, writing in *Crisis*, "How to Fight for Better Schools," February 1936, 52, 59, "Don't Shout Too Soon," March 1936, 79 ff., and "Cracking Closed University Doors," November 1936, 364, 370; articles about him in Philadelphia *Independent*, March 21, 1937; Segal, "Sketch of Charles Houston," 65 and 67; correspondence, Houston to Walter White, May 28, 1936; Houston intra-office memo on *Gaines* trial, July 10, 1936; Houston to Roy Wilkins on anti-lynching drive and other matters, March 2, 1938; Houston to Marshall, January 8 and 18, 1938; Houston to White and Marshall, October 19, 1936, and Houston to his father, April 14, 1938; Houston, application to Employers' Liability Assurance Corp., May 31, 1938, all in NAACP Collection, Library of Congress. On Marshall's early career with the NAACP and relationship with Houston, see correspondence, Marshall to Houston, October 2, 1935, and May 25, 1936; Houston to Marshall, July 11, 1935; Marshall to NAACP Legal Committee, June 9, 1936; Marshall to law-office staff, October 17, 1937; Marshall intra-office memo, June 23, 1938; Marshall to Walter White, August 24, 1938, and January 30, 1939, all in NAACP Collection, Library of Congress.

*Quotations*

    p. 199—Marshall memo to office, October 17, 1937, Library of Congress.

p. 208—*United States v. Butler*, 297 U.S. 1 (1936).
p. 209—Jackson, *The Struggle for Judicial Supremacy*, 172.

## Chapter 10 / One of the Gang

*Books:* Bennett, *Before the Mayflower*; Bland, *Private Pressure on Public Law*; Fenderson, *Thurgood Marshall*; Franklin, *From Slavery to Freedom*; Frazier, *The Negro in the United States*; Friedman and Israel, *The Justices of the Supreme Court* (see especially Philip B. Kurland's sketch of Robert H. Jackson, 2543–2571); Greenberg, *Race Relations and American Law*; Mason, *The Supreme Court from Taft to Warren*; Miller, *The Petitioners*; Myrdal, *An American Dilemma*; Redding, *The Lonesome Road*; Rodell, *Nine Men*; and White, *A Man Called White*.
*Interviews:* Hastie, William H.; Hill, Herbert; Hill, Oliver W.; Lovett, Edward P.; Marshall, Thurgood; Moon, Henry Lee; Nabrit, James M., Jr.; Poston, Ted; Redding, Louis L.; Thompson, Charles H.; Waddy, Joseph C.; Wechsler, Herbert; Wilkins, Roy; and Williams, Franklin H.
*Articles and Documents:* On Marshall, see his articles in *The Crisis*, "Equal Justice Under Law," July 1939, 199–201, "The Gestapo in Detroit," August 1943, 232 ff., and "Negro Status in the Boilermakers Union," March 1944, 77–78; text of prepared addresses by Marshall to Wartime Conference of the NAACP at Metropolitan Community Church, Chicago, July 13, 1944, and meeting of the National Newspaper Publishers' Association at Tuskegee Institute, January 23, 1954, and extemporaneous remarks he delivered to Columbia Law School students, April 16, 1969 (attended by author); correspondence including Marshall to Walter White, August 24, 1938, and January 30 and March 8, 1939; Marshall to William H. Hastie, re *Alston* case, July 21, 1939; Phillips, Utillus R., head of Memphis NAACP branch, to Marshall, April 1, 1939; miscellaneous documents including Marshall's expense account for four-day trip to Richmond in connection with *Alston* case, March 9, 1939; intra-office memo, undated, on Marshall's May 1939 speaking engagements, and memo on his hectic itinerary for week of March 24–31, all in NAACP Collection, Library of Congress. Other articles consulted: *Afro*, October 15, 1938, and June 3, 1944; Allen, Oliver, "Chief Counsel for Equality," *Life*, June 12, 1955, 141 ff.; *Amsterdam News*, November 22, 1946; *New York Times*, July 1, November 20 and 23, 1946; Poling, James, "Thurgood Marshall and the Fourteenth Amendment," *Collier's*, February 23, 1952, 28 ff.; Ross, Irwin, "Thurgood Marshall," New York *Post*, June 15, 1960; and Wechsler, Herbert, "Toward Neutral Principles of Constitutional Law," *Harvard Law Review*, LXXIII, No. 1 (November 1959), 1–35. Poling's article is the best and most extensive on Marshall that I found anywhere. On Houston, see Chicago *Defender*, December 7, 1945; letter from Frankfurter, Felix, to Francis Biddle, May 4, 1942, Frankfurter Papers, Library of Congress; Houston, "Foul Employment Practice on the Rails," *The Crisis*, October 1949, 269 ff.; Segal, "Sketch of Charles Houston," 41; and Washington *Post* and Washington *Star*, December 4, 1945, on his resignation from FEPC.
*Quotation*
p. 222—From Marshall's speech to black newspaper publishers at Tuskegee, January 23, 1954.

## Chapter 11 / A Foot in the Door

*Books:* Baker, *Felix Frankfurter*; Black, *A Constitutional Faith*; Clayton, *The Making of Justice*; Corwin, *The Constitution and What It Means Today*; Friedman and

Israel, *The Justices of the Supreme Court* (see especially Albert M. Sacks's sketch of
Felix Frankfurter, 2401–2419, and Richard Kirkendall's sketch of Fred M. Vinson,
2639–2649); Green, *The Secret City*; Greenberg, *Race Relations and American Law*;
Mason, *The Supreme Court from Taft to Warren*; Miller, *Plain Speaking*; Pfeffer,
*This Honorable Court*; Pritchett, *Civil Liberties and the Vinson Court*; Rodell, *Nine
Men*; and Vose, *Caucasians Only*. I am especially indebted to Pritchett and Vose.
*Interviews:* Carter, Robert L.; Clark, Ramsey; Clark, Tom C.; Elman, Philip; Ernst,
Morris L.; Indritz, Phineas; Perry, Marian Wynn; Vinson, Fred M., Jr.; and
Williams, Franklin H.
*Documents:* A few selections from Chief Justice Vinson's Papers were made available
to me by his son, Fred M. Vinson, Jr. See also "In Memory of Honorable Fred M.
Vinson," a tribute to him at the beginning of 346–347 U.S.

## Chapter 12 / The Spurs of Texas Are Upon You

*Books:* Atkinson, *Mr. Justice Minton and the Supreme Court*; Berman, *It Is So
Ordered*; Bland, *Private Pressure on Public Law*; Franklin, *From Slavery to
Freedom*; Hill and Greenberg, *Citizen's Guide to Desegregation*; Logan, *Howard
University*; Miller, *The Petitioners*; Myrdal, *An American Dilemma*; Pritchett, *Civil
Liberties and the Vinson Court*; and White, *A Man Called White*. Franklin and
Miller, cited in nearly every chapter in Part One, are indispensable to a clear
understanding of black American history; White, while very useful, must be read
with his partisanship constantly in mind.
*Interviews:* Carter, Robert L.; Clark, Ramsey; Clark, Tom C.; Coleman, William T.,
Jr.; Dugger, Ronnie; Elman, Philip; Emerson, Thomas I.; Gellhorn, Walter;
Greenberg, Jack; Hastie, William H.; Lawson, Belford V., Jr.; Marshall, Thur-
good; Nabrit, James M., Jr.; Perry, Marian Wynn; Redding, Louis L.; Robinson,
Spottswood W. III; Thompson, Charles H.; Waddy, Joseph C.; and Williams,
Franklin H.
*Articles and Documents:* On *Sweatt v. Painter*, see the full record below, including
"Appendix to Petition and Brief in Support of Petition for Writ of Certiorari to the
Supreme Court of the State of Texas," 339 U.S. 629 (1950); also, Caliver, Ambrose,
"Education of Negro Leaders," U.S. Office of Education *Bulletin*, 1946, 1–65, and
New York *Post* dispatch from Austin, May 12, 1947, on Marshall's attitude. On
Hastie, see Lewis, Roscoe E., "Role of Pressure Groups in Maintaining Morale
Among Negroes," *Journal of Negro Education*, XII, No. 3 (Spring 1944), 469, and
correspondence, Hastie to White, January 4 and February 11 and 18, 1939, and
Hastie to Marshall, August 3, 1939. On Houston, see Segal, "A Sketch of Charles
Houston," 57–62, and, among other obituaries and tributes, *Black Dispatch*, May 6,
1950; Cleveland *Call & Post*, April 27, 1950; *Journal of Negro History* (by William
H. Hastie), XXXV, No. 4 (October 1950); Philadelphia *Tribune*, May 23, 1950; and
Washington *Post*, April 23 and April 25 (editorial), 1950.
*Quotations*
pp. 280–281—Frankfurter to Vinson, May 19, 1950, Vinson Papers.
p. 281—Black to Vinson, May 18, 1950, Vinson Papers.

PART II / THE COURTS BELOW

## Chapter 13 / On the Natural Inferiority of Bootblacks

*Books:* Bland, *Private Pressure on Public Law*; Dollard, *Caste and Class in a Southern
Town*; Garraty, ed., *Quarrels That Have Shaped the Constitution*; Gossett, *Race*;

Herskovits, *The Myth of the Negro Past*; Jackson, *The Struggle for Judicial Supremacy*; Jordan, *White Over Black*; Key, *Southern Politics*; Klineberg, ed., *Characteristics of the American Negro*; Klineberg, *Negro Intelligence and Selective Migration*; Myrdal, *An American Dilemma*; Odum, *Southern Regions of the United States*; Wallace, *South Carolina: A Short History*; and Woodward, *The Strange Career of Jim Crow.*

*Interviews:* Carter, Robert L.; Coleman, William T., Jr.; Elman, Philip; Hastie, William H.; Hill, Herbert; Hill, Oliver W.; Nabrit, James M., Jr.; Pollak, Louis H.; and Williams, Franklin H.

*Articles and Documents:* Klineberg, Otto, "Cultural Factors in Intelligence-Test Performance," *Journal of Negro Education*, III, No. 3 (Summer 1934), 478–483; letter from Marshall to Walter Gellhorn, June 13, 1950, describing lawyers' conference on June 26–27, 1950, to decide on challenge to segregation *per se;* NAACP, minutes of board of directors, 1950, see annual Report of the Special Counsel; Roche, John P., "Education, Segregation and the Supreme Court," *University of Pennsylvania Law Review*, May 1951, 949–959; Rogers, Warren, *Look*, October 17, 1967, 115; Thompson, Charles H., "Southern Intransigence and the Sweatt and McLaurin Decisions," editorial in *Journal of Negro Education*, XIX, No. 4 (Fall 1950), 427–430 (see also *JNE* 1950–51 *passim* on desegregation); and Viteles, Morris, "The Mental Status of the Negro," *The Annals of the American Academy*, Vol. 140 (1928), 166–177 (see especially bibliography). On William Coleman, Philadelphia *Bulletin*, April 27, 1948, and October 5 and 24, 1965; Philadelphia *Inquirer*, October 10, 1965. On Judge Waties Waring, see especially transcript, Columbia University Oral History Project, pp. 11, 236, 267, and 344 among others; also, Charleston *News & Courier* file, especially articles on June 9, 1945, November 27, 1950, November 7, 1954, and January 12 and 13, 1968; (Pittsburgh) *Courier*, October 21, 1950; July 7, 1951, and February 23, 1952; Grafton, Samuel, "Lonesomest Man in Town," *Collier's*, April 29, 1950, 48 ff.; Leland, Jack, memo to author on St. Cecilia's Society and Charleston Light Dragoons, October 24, 1971; *Pee Dee Advocate*, South Carolina weekly, October 26, 1950; Poston, Ted, article on Waring's posthumous revelations about threats, New York *Post*, January 13, 1968; Richmond *Times-Dispatch*, February 27 and April 20, 1950, and January 18, 1968; St. Louis *Post-Dispatch*, October 28, 1950; Tobias, Rowena W., "Lost Cause, 1948," *Nation*, August 14, 1948; Waring, Elizabeth Avery, "Mrs. Waring Meets the Press," *American Mercury*, May 1950; Warren, Anne Waring, "The South Re-visited," New York *Post*, July 5, 1960; and Wechsler, James A., columns in New York *Post*, November 14, 1964, and January 18, 1968.

*Quotations*

pp. 287–288—Warren Rogers's account of this scene appeared in *Look*, October 17, 1967.

p. 291—Kelly's report appears in Garraty, ed., *Quarrels That Have Shaped the Constitution*, 257.

p. 300—The Democratic Party oath appears in Key, *Southern Politics*, 631.

p. 301—Charleston *Evening Post* editorial of October 13, 1950.

p. 304—One of Carter's letters of explanation was sent, for example, to Kenneth Clark, dated November 24, 1950. Marshall's corroboration of the tactics he used is given in a letter from him to Franklin Williams, December 8, 1950, in answer to a query from Williams. Both letters are in the NAACP Collection, Library of Congress.

p. 306—Sumner, William Graham, *Folkways* (Boston: Ginn & Co., 1906), 285.

p. 311—Odum, Howard W., *Social and Mental Traits of the Negro*, doctoral thesis

published by Columbia University Press as part of Columbia University Studies
in History, Economics and Public Law, Vol. 37 (1910–11); see especially pp.
39–41 quoted here, but virulent racist attitudes abound in it.

p. 313—Myrdal, *An American Dilemma*, 205.

## Chapter 14 / The Doll Man and Other Experts

*Books:* Ashmore, *The Negro and the Schools*; Clark, *Prejudice and Your Child*;
Dollard, *Caste and Class in a Southern Town*; Friedman and Israel, *The Justices of
the Supreme Court* (see Walter F. Murphy's sketch of James F. Byrnes, 2517–2533);
Myrdal, *An American Dilemma*; and Silberman, *Crisis in Black and White.*

*Interviews and Correspondence:* Boone, Reginald; Boulware, Harold; Carter, Robert
L.; Clark, Kenneth B.; Figg, Robert McC., Jr.; Krech, David; Marshall, Thurgood;
Montgomery, Eugene; Poston, Ted; Robinson, Spottswood W. III; Rogers,
S. Emory; Whitehead, Matthew J.; and Workman, William D.

*Articles and Documents:* On Kenneth Clark and his psychological tests, Clark,
Kenneth B., with Mamie P., "Segregation as a Factor in the Racial Identification of
Negro Pre-School Children: A Preliminary Report," *Journal of Experimental
Education*, Spring 1940, 101–103; Clark, Kenneth B., "Effect of Prejudice and
Discrimination on Personality Development," Report for Mid-century White
House Conference on Children and Youth, Children's Bureau—Federal Security
Agency, 1950; Clark, Kenneth B. and Mamie P., "Racial Identification and
Preference in Negro Children," chapter in *Readings in Social Psychology*, ed. by
Theodore Newcomb and Eugene Hartley (New York: Henry Holt, 1947); Clark,
Kenneth B. and Mamie P., "Emotional Factors in Racial Identification and
Preference in Negro Children," *Journal of Negro Education*, XIX, No. 3 (1941),
341–350; Clark, Kenneth B., "The Social Scientist as an Expert Witness in Civil
Rights Litigation," *Social Problems*, I, No. 1 (1953), 5–10; *Current Biography*,
September 1964, 19–22; Founders' Library Archives, Howard University; New
York *Herald Tribune*, March 3, 1946; New York *Post*, March 22, 1964, profile by
Ted Poston; *New York Times*, June 15, 1964, and April 21, 1970; Philadelphia
*Tribune*, May 29, 1941; and Radke, Marian J., and Helen G. Trager, "Children's
Perceptions of the Social Roles of Negroes and Whites," *Journal of Psychology*,
XXIX (1950), 3–33. On Thurgood Marshall, see Marshall, Thurgood, "The
Supreme Court as Protector of Civil Rights: Equal Protection of the Laws," *Annals
of the American Academy*, Vol. 275 (May 1951), 101–110; McBee, Susan, "A
Single-Minded Dual Personality," *Life*, November 12, 1965; New York *Compass*
and *New York Times*, December 22, 1950, on Korean War treatment of black
soldiers; *Newsweek*, "Mr. Justice Marshall," June 26, 1967. On Robert Carter's
efforts to obtain expert witnesses for *Briggs* trial, most of the material is drawn from
correspondence files of the NAACP Legal Defense Fund, especially Kilpatrick,
William H., to Carter, October 17, 1950; Robinson, Elsa E., to Carter, May 21,
1951; Klineberg, Otto, to Carter, May 14, 1951; Allport, Gordon, to Carter,
October 26, 1950; Krech, David, to Carter, March 23 and May 14, 1951, and Carter
to Krech, May 11 and May 23, 1951; Rhine, J. B., to James A. Dombowski,
October 21, 1950. On Robert Figg and the South Carolina defense team:
Charleston *News & Courier*, May 27, September 18 and 27, 1948, and February 5,
1955; Charleston *Post*, November 12, 1939, and August 28, 1940, and memo for
AP, December 12, 1956; Figg's correspondence, especially Callison, T. C., to Figg,
February 8 and April 9, 1951; Figg to James F. Byrnes, April 23, 1951; Odum,
Howard W., to Figg, May 15, 1951; Thurmond, J. Strom, to Figg, May 28, 1951,

and Figg to J. Walter Brown, June 4, 1951; Kempton, Murray, columns in New York *Post*, March 28 and 30, 1956; and Timmerman, George Bell, Sr., *Georgia Bar Journal*, May 1958, 483 ff.

*Quotations*

p. 320—Dollard, *Caste and Class in a Southern Town*, 425.

p. 325—Myrdal, *An American Dilemma*, 777.

p. 327—The compilation on Jim Crow practice in the nation is drawn largely from Konvitz, Milton R., "The Extent and Character of Legally-Enforced Segregation," *Journal of Negro Education*, XX, No. 3 (Summer 1951), 425–435. Konvitz was a member of Marshall's LDF staff before the school-segregation cases began.

p. 332—Whitehead's letter to Carter of May 16, 1951, resides in the NAACP Legal Defense Fund files on *Briggs*.

## Chapter 15 / Charleston Detour

*Interviews and Correspondence:* Briggs, Mr. and Mrs. Harry, and Harry, Jr.; Carter, Robert L.; Clark, Kenneth B.; Coleman, William T., Jr.; Figg, Robert McC., Jr.; Gibson, James; Krech, David; Marshall, Thurgood; Poston, Ted; Robertson, Archibald G.; Robinson, Spottswood W. III; and Whitehead, Matthew J.

*Articles and Documents:* For full text of *Briggs* trial, see Transcript of Testimony at Trial on Civil Action No. 2657 (filed December 22, 1950) in the United States District Court for the Eastern District of South Carolina, Charleston Division; opinion of the three-judge trial court, see *Briggs v. Elliott*, 98 F. Supp. 529 (1951); for full record, see entire file numbered 103 F. Supp. 920 (1952), 342 U.S. 350 (1952), 347 U.S. 497 (1954), and 132 F. Supp. 776 (1955). Charleston *News & Courier* coverage, May 28–30, 1951; see also Poston, Ted, in New York *Post*, June 3, 1951. On Judge Waring's views of the trial, transcript of his interviews, Columbia University Oral History Project; see editorial on his death, Charleston *News & Courier*, January 13, 1968. On Kenneth Clark's testimony, Cahn, Edmond, "Jurisprudence," *New York University Law Review*, XXX (January 1955), 150–169; van den Haag, Ernest, and Ralph Ross, Chapter 14, "Prejudice About Prejudice," *The Fabric of Society*, 1957, see especially 163–166; van den Haag, Ernest, "Social Science Testimony in the Desegregation Cases: A Reply to Professor Kenneth Clark," *Villanova Law Review*, VI (Fall 1960), 69–79; Clark's rebuttal appears in Appendix IV of the paperback edition of *Prejudice and Your Child*, 185–205. Carter's concern about Kesselman was expressed in his letter to J. H. Walls, October 25, 1950, NAACP Legal Defense Fund file. Figg's views of the trial and his concluding strategy were expressed in his letter to Walter J. Brown, June 4, 1951.

## Chapter 16 / Prairie Fire

*Books:* Brunsman and Bureau of Census, *Census of Population: 1950*, Vol. II, Part 16, Kansas; Frazier, *Black Bourgeoisie*; McFarland, *Eloquence in Public Speaking*; Menninger, *A Psychiatrist's World*; Miller *et al.*, *Kansas*; Myrdal, *An American Dilemma*; Quarles, *Frederick Douglass* (see especially Chapter 15); Rawley, *Race and Politics*; Schrag, *Voices in the Classroom*; Sheldon, *In His Steps*; and Speer, *The Case of the Century*.

*Interviews:* Brown, Esther; Brown, Inza; Brown, Linda; Burnett, Lena; Holland, J. B.; Huxman, Walter A.; Jackson, Samuel C.; Kiene, Thomas; Levinson, Harry; Massey, Mrs. J. S.; Morgan, Ray; Ross, Mr. and Mrs. Merrill; Scott, Berdyne;

Scott, Charles; Scott, John; Tidwell, Winfred; Todd, Lucinda; and Williams, Mamie.

*Articles and Documents:* On Kansas and Topeka, Greater Topeka Chamber of Commerce, infinite documents, studies, reports; Landon, Alf M., "New Plain Talk from Kansas," *New York Times,* February 1, 1971; McFarland, Kenneth, Annual Report, 1950–51, Board of Education, Topeka, to Kansas State Department of Public Instruction; Rowan, Carl T., "Jim Crow's Last Stand," Minneapolis *Tribune,* November 30, 1953; Schwendemann, Glen, "Wyandotte and the First 'Exodusters' of 1879," *Kansas Historical Quarterly,* XXVI, No. 3 (Autumn 1960), 233–249; Schwendemann, "The 'Exodusters' on the Missouri," *Kansas Historical Quarterly,* XXVII, No. 1 (Spring 1961), 25–40; Shepherd, Charles Lawrence, "A Study of the Educational Status of the Negro in Kansas," master's thesis, Kansas State Teachers College, Emporia, 1934; Larry Smith & Co., Topeka Area Planning Study, Economic Base Report for Topeka-Shawnee County Regional Planning Commission, October 1969; and Snell, Joseph W., and Don W. Wilson, "Birth of the Atchison, Topeka, and Santa Fe Railroad," Kansas State Historical Society, 1968. On Kenneth McFarland, see biographical references *passim* in his book, *Eloquence in Public Speaking;* biographical sketch in history of Topeka schools, Topeka Board of Education Archives; biographical sketch by his office; letter to author from his secretary, Hazel Ellis, July 12, 1974; phonograph records distributed by Edward N. Miller & Associates, Inc., Grand Rapids, Michigan, "Wake the Town and Tell the People," 1961, and "Liberty Under Law," undated; among newspaper clippings, see especially Topeka *Daily Capital,* March 25 and April 1, 1951. On Elisha Scott, see Ripley, John W., "The Strange Story of Charles M. Sheldon's *In His Steps,*" *Kansas Historical Quarterly,* XXXIV, No. 3 (Autumn 1968), 1–25, and memo from Thurgood Marshall to Walter White, July 22, 1937, NAACP Collection, Library of Congress. On Esther Brown, see Williams, Franklin, and Earl L. Fultz, "The Merriam School Fight," *Crisis,* May 1949, 140 ff.; Williams, Franklin, "Merriam, Kansas: Since the Parents Fought," *Crisis,* December 1949, 370 ff.; Kansas City *Call,* June 17, 1949, and June 4, 1970; Kansas City *Times,* May 26, 1970; and Washington *Post,* October 4, 1968. On NAACP Legal Defense Fund preparations of *Brown* for trial, I relied heavily on the Fund's correspondence files, especially Burnett, McKinley, to Franklin Williams, September 3, 1948, and Burnett to Walter White, September 1 and December 11, 1950; Todd, Lucinda, to White, August 29, 1950; Carter, Robert L. to Charles Bledsoe, September 18 and November 21, 1950, and Bledsoe to Carter, November 20 and 24, 1950; Bledsoe to Jack Greenberg, April 6, 1951; Speer, Hugh W., to Greenberg, May 30, 1951; and Carter to Marshall, memo, June 13, 1951.

*Quotations*

pp. 376–377—The occupational figures are extrapolated from the detailed 1950 Bureau of Census report, Vol. II, Part 16, on Kansas.

p. 393—NAACP petition was submitted to the Topeka Board of Education dated September 13, 1948, and signed by Daniel S. Sawyer in the name of "The Citizen's Committee" (*sic*) in order not to alienate the school board and local white and black sensibilities; the NAACP in that era was viewed as a radical organization in Topeka.

## Chapter 17 / The Menninger Connection

*Books:* Menninger, *A Psychiatrist's World;* and Speer, *The Case of the Century.*
*Interviews:* Brown, Esther; Brown, Linda; Burnett, Lena; Carter, Annie; Carter,

Robert L.; Coleman, William T., Jr.; Greenberg, Jack; Hastie, William H.; Holt, Louisa; Huxman, Walter A.; Levinson, Harry; Menninger, Karl A.; Nabrit, James M., Jr.; Scott, Charles; Scott, John; Steel, Lewis; Todd, Lucinda; Williams, Franklin H.; and Wilson, Paul E.

*Articles and Documents:* For full text of *Brown* trial, see transcript of proceedings filed in United States District Court, State of Kansas, October 16, 1951; opinion of three-judge trial court, see *Brown v. Board of Education*, 98 F. Supp. 797 (1951); for full record, see entire file numbered 344 U.S. 141, 344 U.S. 1 (1952), 345 U.S. 972 (1953), 347 U.S. 483 (1954), and 349 U.S. 294 (1955). Associated Press, biographical sketch of Walter Huxman, May 13, 1937; Bureau of Educational Research, School of Education, University of Denver, 1958 Report on physical plant of Topeka schools, 67–69 and 101–103; Kansas City *Star*, March 29, 1967, on Hugh Speer; *MD*, XIV (June 1972), "The Remarkable Menningers," 189–195; *New York Times*, February 12, 1961, "The Case of Linda Brown"; and *Yale Law Journal*, "Segregation in Public Schools: A Violation of 'Equal Protection of the Laws,' " prompted by *Mendez v. Westminster*, LVI (1947), 1059–1067. Correspondence on Menninger: Speer, Hugh W., to Karl A. Menninger, June 6, 1951; Speer to Jack Greenberg, June 17, 1951; Greenberg to Speer, June 19, 1951; Bledsoe, Charles to Robert L. Carter, November 24, 1950; Menninger to author, January 9, 1974. Also, Greenberg to Louisa Holt, June 13, 1951, and Holt to Greenberg, June 16, 1951. All letters except Menninger-author are from NAACP Legal Defense Fund files.

## Chapter 18 / Jim Crow, Inc.

*Interviews:* Bulah, Sarah; Carter, Robert L.; Clark, Kenneth B.; Coleman, William T., Jr.; Gellhorn, Walter; Greenberg, Jack; Hill, Herbert; Marshall, Thurgood; Meltsner, Michael; Pollak, Louis H.; Redding, Louis L.; Seitz, Collins J.; Wertham, Frederic; Williams, Franklin H.; Young, H. Albert.

*Articles and Documents:* On Delaware as a sanctuary for corporations, see especially *University of Pennsylvania Law Review*, "Law for Sale: A Study of the Delaware Corporation Law of 1967," CXVII (1969), 861–898, and Spruance, John S., "Why Firms Incorporate in Delaware," Wilmington *News*, August 23, 24, and 25, 1967. On Delaware's racial history, see state's briefs on appeal in *Belton v. Gebhart* and *Bulah v. Gebhart*, also Miller, George R., Jr., "Adolescent Negro Education in Delaware: A Study of the Negro Secondary School and Community (Exclusive of Wilmington)," doctoral dissertation, School of Education, New York University, 1943; Wilmington *Journal*, March 10, 1950, March 9, July 7, September 21, October 22 and October 24, 1951; Bill Frank column in Wilmington *News*, February 18, 1950, October 4, 1951, and June 11, 1969; Wilmington *News* stories, March 17, June 4 and 18, and October 25, 1951. On Louis Redding, Wilmington *Journal*, October 30, 1961, and September 15, 1971; Wilmington *News*, March 19, 1929, and September 16, 1971. On Collins Seitz, see Nizer, Louis, *My Life in Court* (1961), 501–502; Seitz's speech to Salesianum High School for Boys, June 4, 1951; Wilmington *Journal*, June 10, 1966, and March 24 and November 30, 1971; and Wilmington *News*, February 28, 1966, and Bill Frank's column, March 2, 1966. On Frederic Wertham and the Lafargue Clinic, see Brown, Earl, "Timely Topics," *Amsterdam News*, February 15, 1947; "Clinic for Sick Minds," *Life*, February 23, 1948; Lobsenz, Norman M., "Human Salvage in Harlem," *Coronet*, March 1948; New York *Post*, February 24, 1947; *Time*, December 1, 1947; Tuck, James L., "Here's Hope for Harlem," *This Week*, January 26, 1947; Wertham, Frederic, "Psychological Effects of School Segregation," *American Journal of Psychotherapy*,

VI (January 1952), 94–103, and Wertham, "Nine Men Speak to You: Jim Crow in the North," *Nation*, CLXXVIII, No. 24 (June 12, 1954). On the origin and course of the school-segregation cases in Delaware, see Rowan, Carl T., Minneapolis *Tribune*, November 30 and December 2, 1953. For a transcript of the trial and Chancellor Seitz's opinion, see *Belton v. Gebhart*, 32 Del. Ch. 343, 87 A2d 862, affirmed 91 A2d 137 (Delaware).

## Chapter 19 / "Stick with Us"

*Books:* Bradshaw, *History of Prince Edward County*; Brunsman and Bureau of Census, *Census of Population: 1950*, Vol. II, Part 46, Virginia; Gottman, *Virginia at Mid-Century*; Key, *Southern Politics*; Peirce, *The Deep South States of America*; Smith, *They Closed Their Schools*; and Woodward, *Origins of the New South.* I am especially indebted to Smith, the only book I have discovered that focuses on the plaintiffs in any of the segregation cases; it does not deal, however, with either the NAACP involvement or the trial and subsequent appeal of the case.

*Interviews and Correspondence:* Banks, W. Lester; Croner, Mary; Croner, Robert; Griffin, L. Francis; Hill, Oliver W.; Johns, Altona T.; Johns, Barbara Rose; Jones, M. Boyd; McIlwaine, T. J.; Nabrit, James M., Jr.; and Robinson, Spottswood W. III.

*Articles and Documents:* On Prince Edward County, see Dabney, Virginius, "Southern Crisis: The Segregation Decision," *Saturday Evening Post*, November 8, 1952, 40 ff.; Division of State Planning and Community Affairs, State of Virginia, "Prince Edward County: Projections and Economic Base Analysis," June 1970; Goodman, Irv, "Public Schools Died Here," *Saturday Evening Post*, April 29, 1961; Governor's Office, Office of Administration, Division of Planning, State of Virginia, "Economic Data Survey of Prince Edward County," September 1967; Steck, John C., "The Prince Edward County, Virginia, Story," Farmville, Virginia, *Herald*, 1960; U.S. Department of Agriculture, Soil Conservation Service, "Soil Survey of Prince Edward County," Series 1949, No. 4, June 1958; and Virginia Electric & Power Co., "Prince Edward County, Virginia: An Economic Study," December 1967. On Oliver Hill, Richmond *News-Leader*, June 27, 1950, January 11, 1952, and February 12, 1955; Richmond *Times-Dispatch*, June 18 and 19, 1950, March 12, 1953, March 30 and April 2, 1969. For an example of Vernon Johns's eloquence in the pulpit, see his "Transfigured Moments" in Newton, Joseph Fort, ed., *Best Sermons, 1926* (Harcourt, Brace). On Spottswood Robinson, *New York Times*, January 9, 1949, and July 28, 1961; Richmond *Times-Dispatch*, July 28, 1961, October 4, 1963, and April 2, 1967; Washington *Post*, "Virginia Affairs" column by Benjamin Muse, June 6, 1954, and March 30, 1958; and Washington *Star*, October 2, 1963.

*Quotations*

p. 461—Du Bois, *The Souls of Black Folk*, 142.

p. 470—The Johns-Stokes letter, dated April 23, 1951, was first published in the Richmond *Times-Dispatch*, April 2, 1967. Its text is not included in Smith's book, published in 1965, because Robinson felt it would violate the lawyer-client confidential relationship. Its existence serves to refute the charge by Prince Edward and other Virginia white-supremacists that the student strike was inspired by outside agitators, presumably Robinson, Hill, and Banks.

p. 479—Full text of Griffin's sermon in Richmond edition of *Afro-American*, July 28, 1951.

# Chapter 20 / The Pride of Virginia

*Interviews and Correspondence:* Almond, J. Lindsay; Carter, Robert L.; Clark, Kenneth B.; Garrett, Henry E.; Hill, Oliver W.; Kirk, Grayson; McIlwaine, T. J.; Modlin, George M.; Riely, John W.; and Robertson, Archibald G.

*Articles and Documents:* Cahn, Edmond, "Jurisprudence," *New York University Law Review*, XXX (January 1955), 163; Chein, Isidor, and Max Deutscher, "Psychological Effects of Enforced Segregation: A Survey of Social Science Opinion," *Journal of Psychology*, XXVI (1948), 259–287; Garrett, Henry E., "Heredity: The Cause of Racial Differences in Intelligence," pamphlet published by Patrick Henry Press, Kilmarnak, Virginia, 1971. On Armistead Dobie, see Bryan, James III, "Court Card," *Saturday Evening Post*, December 28, 1940; Richmond News-Leader, May 17, 1939, February 1, 1956, and January 18, 1963; Richmond *Times-Dispatch*, August 8 and 9, 1962; and "In Memoriam Honorable Armistead M. Dobie," tribute to him by the bar at United States Court of Appeals for the Fourth Circuit, Richmond, on January 18, 1963, reported at the beginning of 311 F. 2d. For full text of *Davis v. County School Board* trial, see transcript of record of Civil Action No. 1333 in the United States District Court for the Eastern District of Virginia, Richmond Division, on complaint filed May 23, 1951; for full text of opinion, 103 F. Supp. 337. On Justin Moore, Richmond *News-Leader*, February 6, 1951, March 11 and 17, 1958; Richmond *Times-Dispatch*, August 9, 1953, and March 13, 1958. On Archibald Robertson, see the speech he delivered before Forum of University of Pennsylvania Law School, March 16, 1956. On Henry Garrett, see also Richmond *News-Leader*, May 10, 1963, and Richmond *Times-Dispatch*, April 27, 1956, July 30, 1961, and April 26, 1963.

# Chapter 21 / The Best Place to Attack

*Books:* Green, *The Secret City*; Hansen, *Danger in Washington*; and Harbaugh, *Lawyer's Lawyer.*

*Interviews and Correspondence:* Bishop, Gardner L.; DeLaine, Joseph A.; Figg, Robert McC., Jr.; Indritz, Phineas; Korman, Milton; Lawson, Belford V., Jr.; McKenzie, Marjorie; Meagher, William R.; Nabrit, James M., Jr.; and Whipple, Taggart.

*Articles and Documents:* Letter, Figg, Robert McC., Jr., to James F. Byrnes, September 13, 1951; text of proceedings at Howard University national conference on "The Courts and Racial Integration in Education," held April 16–18, 1952, *Journal of Negro Education*, XXI, No. 3 (Summer 1952), 229–444; McKenzie, Marjorie, columns "Pursuit of Democracy" in *Courier*, July 7, 1951, July 28, 1951, and February 9, 1952 (see rebuttal by Thurgood Marshall in *Courier*, July 14, 1951); NAACP Legal Defense Fund intra-office transcript of conference of November 10, 1951, highlighted by Wechsler's disturbing questions; *Time*, December 21, 1953, see page 15 on Bolling, Thomas Spottswood; Wechsler, Herbert, "Toward Neutral Principles of Constitutional Law," *Harvard Law Review*, LXXIII, No. 1 (November 1959), 34; and "Grade School Segregation: The Latest Attack on Racial Discrimination," *Yale Law Journal*, LXI (May 1952), 731–744. This Yale piece and the one cited in the notes to chapter 17 are the two most incisive and yet comprehensive notes of the many dozens to run in the legal journals during the first post-World War II decade.

*Quotations*

p. 524—Marshall's rebuttal, *Courier*, July 14, 1951.

p. 531—Pollak to Carter, January 13, 1952, in LDF files.

p. 539—Jackson's memo is in the Jackson Papers and is used here by courtesy of William E. Jackson and Philip B. Kurland.

p. 540—Willey to Vinson, November 21, 1952, United States Supreme Court Library.


PART III / ON APPEAL

## Chapter 22 / Going for the Jugular

*Books:* Friedman, ed., *Argument*; Harbaugh, *Lawyer's Lawyer*; and Stern and Gressman, *Supreme Court Practice.*

*Interviews and Correspondence:* Carter, Robert L.; Clark, Kenneth B.; Coleman, William T., Jr.; DeLaine, Joseph A.; Elman, Philip; Greenberg, Jack; Hastie, William H.; Korman, Milton; Marshall, Thurgood; Meagher, William R.; Nabrit, James M., Jr.; Pollak, Louis H.; Redding, Louis L.; Robertson, Archibald G.; Robinson, Spottswood, W. III; Weinstein, Jack; Whipple, Taggart; and Wilson, Paul E.

*Articles and Documents:* On Supreme Court oral arguments, see Davis, John W., "The Argument of an Appeal," lecture delivered October 22, 1940, before the Association of the Bar of the City of New York, and Jackson, Robert H., "Advocacy Before the United States Supreme Court," *Cornell Law Quarterly*, XXXVII, No. 1 (Fall 1951), 1–16; Stern and Gressman contains many references to other such instructive essays. On Davis, see correspondence, Davis to Robert McC. Figg, Jr., September 24 and October 11, 1951, and September 3 and 29 and October 16, 1952, Davis Papers, Manuscript Division, Yale University Library; also "Matter of John W. Davis: An Amicus Brief," a useful compendium reciting Davis's cases before the Supreme Court, presented to him by his law firm on his seventy-fifth birthday. On Marshall, see Brooks, Tom, "Thurgood Marshall: The Man and the Office," *Tuesday*, November 1965, 15, and Poling, James, "Thurgood Marshall and the Fourteenth Amendment," *Collier's*, February 23, 1952. On William Robert Ming, see *Afro*, July 10, 1973. Paul E. Wilson's account of his role in *Brown* was first recited in his article "Brown v. Board of Education Revisited," *Kansas Law Review*, XII (1964), 509–524, and was supplemented by letters to Harbaugh (see *Lawyer's Lawyer*) and the author.

*Quotations*

pp. 556–557—This same language appears in Isidor Chein's letter to Robin Williams, dated September 15, 1952, and Kenneth Clark's letter to Bingham Dai, dated September 17, 1952, both in the LDF files. The other letters soliciting signers for the social-science statement contained identical or similar language.

p. 563—From the U.S. Government Printing Office pamphlet titled "The Supreme Court of the United States," 1961.


## Chapter 23 / At Loggerheads

*Books:* Atkinson, *Mr. Justice Minton and the Supreme Court*; Baker, *Felix Frankfurter*; Black, *A Constitutional Faith*; Clayton, *The Making of Justice*; Douglas, *Go East, Young Man*; Jackson, *The Struggle for Judicial Supremacy*; Lewis, *Gideon's Trumpet*; Pritchett, *Civil Liberties and the Vinson Court*; and Wilkinson, *Serving Justice.*

*Interviews and Correspondence:* Bickel, Alexander M.; Black, Elizabeth; Clark, Tom C.; Coleman, William T., Jr.; Elman, Philip; Fassett, John D.; Hawkins, Carl S.;

Lewis, Anthony; Prettyman, E. Barrett, Jr.; Rubenstein, Ernest; Troubh, Raymond S.; and Vinson, Fred M., Jr.

*Articles and Documents:* On Hugo Black, see Ulmer, S. Sidney, address to annual meeting of Southern Political Science Association, November 5, 1970, and Black's letters to Ulmer of August 7 and 21 and September 8, 1970, Black Papers, Manuscript Division, Library of Congress; also, Reich, Charles, "Mr. Justice Black and the Living Constitution," *Harvard Law Review*, LXXVI (1963), 673–679. I am indebted to Gerald T. Dunne for the insights in his chapter on *Brown* in his forthcoming book on Justice Black. Harold Burton's conference notes and diaries are in the Manuscript Division, Library of Congress; see especially his diary entry for May 8, 1954. On William Douglas, see especially Viorst, Milton, "Bill Douglas Has Never Stopped Fighting the Bullies of Yakima," *New York Times Magazine*, July 14, 1970. On Felix Frankfurter, see especially his letters to Grenville Clark, March 6, 1937; Hugo Black, December 15, 1939; Stanley Reed, May 20, 1954; Learned Hand, July 21, 1954; and John Marshall Harlan, July 18 and 31, 1956. Robert Jackson's conference notes are in the Jackson Papers, as are the Rehnquist and Cronson memos written by them while in the Justice's employment; as a background to the Rehnquist controversy, see *Congressional Record* for the Senate, December 8 and 9, 1971, and *New York Times*, December 9, 1971. I wrote to Justice Rehnquist asking for an appointment to discuss his understanding of Justice Jackson's views in *Brown*; in a letter to me on November 19, 1973, he declined to see me on the ground that whatever confidentiality had been imposed upon him by his earlier relation with Justice Jackson was probably heightened by his own presence on the high court.

*Quotations*

p. 597—Niebuhr's quotation, *Harvard Law Review*, LXXVI (November 1962), 21; other tributes to Frankfurter in that issue are also instructive. The expression of self-consciousness over his religion is found in Frankfurter's letter to Grenville Clark, March 6, 1937.

p. 598—Jackson's suggestion to Stone that Frankfurter had best not write the Court's opinion in *Smith v. Allwright* is found in Mason, *Harlan Fiske Stone*.

p. 599—Frankfurter to Harlan the Younger, July 31, 1956; his note to Rutledge is included in Baker, *Felix Frankfurter*, 312.

p. 600—Frankfurter's penciled notes are in the *Brown* file at Harvard Law Library in Langdell Hall. I have done my best to decipher them, as did his former clerk, Alexander Bickel, not long before his death. The notes are undated.

pp. 603–604—Jackson, *The Struggle for Judicial Supremacy*, 295.

pp. 610–611—Burton to Frankfurter, Burton Papers, Library of Congress.

p. 615—Frankfurter memo to his brethren, Frankfurter Papers, Library of Congress.

## Chapter 24 / The Six-Month Summer

*Books:* Garraty, ed., *Quarrels That Have Shaped the Constitution* (see Chapter 16); Harbaugh, *Lawyer's Lawyer*; Stampp, *The Era of Reconstruction*; and tenBroek, Jacobus, *Equal Under Law* (originally published as *The Antislavery Origins of the Fourteenth Amendment*).

*Interviews and Correspondence:* Adams, Sherman; Almond, J. Lindsay; Black, Charles L., Jr.; Carter, Robert L.; Clark, Ramsey; Coleman, William T., Jr.; Davis, John A.; Elman, Philip; Fassett, John D.; Frank, John P.; Franklin, John Hope; Gellhorn, Walter; Greenberg, Jack; Kelly, Alfred H.; Meagher, William R.; Nabrit, James M., Jr.; Nabrit, James M. III; Riely, John W.; Stovall, Alice;

Weinstein, Jack; Whipple, Taggart; Wilson, Paul E.; and Young, H. Albert. *Articles and Documents:* There is a vast body of literature on the origins of the Fourteenth Amendment, as the Court well knew in proposing its questions to the parties in *Brown*. To see what use they made of it, one should consult, first of all, the extensive briefs on reargument, especially the United States government's brief, authored principally by Philip Elman, and the LDF's consolidated brief in the four state cases. The main doctrinal dispute is not between the segregationist and Negro sides but between the differing views of the pivotal role of John Bingham; see especially Kelly, Alfred H., "The Fourteenth Amendment Reconsidered: The Segregation Question," *Michigan Law Review*, LIX, No. 8 (June 1956), 1049–1086, and compare with Bickel, Alexander M., "The Original Understanding and the Segregation Decision," *Harvard Law Review*, LXIX, No. 1 (November 1955), 1–65. Other important articles are Fairman, Charles, "The Attack on the Segregation Cases," *Harvard Law Review*, LXX (1956), 83–94 (see especially 86); Frank, John, and Robert Munro, "The Original Understanding of 'Equal Protection of the Laws,' " *Columbia Law Review*, L (February 1950), 131–169; Graham, Howard Jay, "The Early Antislavery Backgrounds of the Fourteenth Amendment," *Wisconsin Law Review*, No. 3 (April 1950), 479, and No. 4 (May 1950), 610, and Graham, "The Conspiracy Theory of the Fourteenth Amendment," *Yale Law Journal*, XLVII (1938), 371, and XLVIII (1939), 171. Alfred Kelly's account of the summer of 1953 was presented in a paper he called "An Inside View of *Brown v. Board of Education*," delivered to the annual convention of the American Historical Association on December 28, 1961, and excerpted by *U.S. News & World Report*, February 5, 1962, in a manner that put Thurgood Marshall and his team of attorneys in the most unfavorable light possible. Among the letters used to reconstruct the LDF efforts that summer were Commager, Henry Steele, to John A. Davis, June 22; Swisher, Carl, to Davis, July 26; Bond, Horace Mann, to Davis, August 29; Bond to Robert L. Carter, July 8; Davis to Carter, memo, July 16; Davis to C. Vann Woodward, July 16 and August 7; Woodward to Davis, July 21; Miller, Loren, to Marshall, August 8 and November 3; Brownell, Herbert, Jr., to Marshall, July 24, and Marshall to Brownell, July 29; Marshall to U. Simpson Tate, July 27; Marshall to Alfred H. Kelly, October 30; and Graham, Howard Jay, to Marshall, October 23. All are from the LDF files. I also consulted but did not cite William Coleman's extensive file of correspondence that summer with researchers exploring the Court's questions with regard to the state legislatures.

*Quotations*

p. 617—NAACP telegram to Wardwell, Davis Papers, Yale.

p. 636—Marshall's unease was expressed in a letter to John Finerty, August 17, 1953.

pp. 644–645—In acknowledging the accuracy of this anecdote, Professor Black asked me not to use it in the book for fear that it would be misinterpreted; I have chosen not to honor that request because (1) I did not obtain the anecdote from him, (2) he confirmed it, and, much more important, (3) it wonderfully exemplifies the gallows humor of those men at that time and demonstrates the absurd length to which white detractors of the Negro would go in propagating the myth of his hypersexuality.

p. 651—Elman letter to Frankfurter, July 15, 1953, Frankfurter Papers, Library of Congress. Invited several times by the author to discuss their concerns that summer before putting the government into the case, Messrs. Rankin and Brownell declined, the former emphatically, saying he planned to discuss the matter in his own book someday.

p. 651—Brownell's disclosure to Lewis is given in Lewis's *Portrait of a Decade*, page 27.

p. 654—Bickel's fascinating letter to Frankfurter, of which only a fragment is here given, is in the Frankfurter Papers at Harvard.

pp. 655–656—The account of Justice Reed's thinking that summer is taken from a private memoir by one of his clerks, John D. Fassett.

## Chapter 25 / Arrival of the Superchief

*Books:* Abraham, *Justices and Presidents*; Friedman, ed., *Argument*; Friedman and Israel, *The Justices of the Supreme Court*; Harbaugh, *Lawyer's Lawyer*; and Weaver, *Warren*. Leo Katcher also wrote a biography of Warren, published in 1967, the same year as Weaver's; I found Weaver's more reliable, though neither book is more than a gloss on Warren's extraordinary career.

*Interviews and Correspondence:* Bickel, Alexander M.; Clark, Tom C.; Fassett, John D.; Figg, Robert McC., Jr.; Greenberg, Jack; Korman, Milton; Meagher, William R.; Mickum, George V. III; Nabrit, James M., Jr.; Pollock, Earl E.; Prettyman, E. Barrett, Jr.; Rowe, Frederick; Rubenstein, Ernest; Sander, Frank E. A.; Troubh, Raymond S.; and Warren, Earl.

*Articles and Documents:* In most instances in this chapter, I have supplied the dates of cited documents in the text. Since heavy reliance is placed upon Justice Burton's conference notes and diary in the Library of Congress, I am indebted to S. Sidney Ulmer, who has published several papers and essays drawing largely on the Burton Papers; in view of the Justice's microscopic and sometimes indecipherable script, such corroborating inspection is both necessary and reassuring. See Ulmer, "Earl Warren and the Brown Decision," *Journal of Politics*, XXXII (August 1971), and Ulmer, "The Saliency of Negro Claims for Earl Warren's Response Behavior: 1953–1968," a paper delivered to the Southern Political Science Association, November 5–7, 1970, mimeographed (see especially page 8 on Chief Justice Warren's remarks in conference, December 12, 1953). On the reargument, see especially *Afro*, December 10, 1953. On Chief Justice Warren, I consulted hundreds of items and wish to cite the *Courier*, April 19 and June 14, 1952, on the Eisenhower and Warren presidential candidacies; *Ebony*, May 1974, page 129, in a story by Jack Slater for incident on which this chapter concludes; Eisner, Richard A., "Earl Warren: The Individual and the State," unpublished undergraduate thesis in American studies, Yale University, 1956; *New York Times* staff writers Arthur Krock, "In the Nation," September 18 and October 1, 1953; Anthony Lewis, "A Man Born to Act, Not to Muse," *New York Times Magazine*, June 30, 1968, and "A Talk with Warren on Crime, the Court, the Country," *New York Times Magazine*, October 19, 1969; James Reston, analytical columns on September 30, 1953, and February 18 and March 5, 1954; and Alden Whitman's obituary of Warren, July 10, 1974; Rodell, Fred, "It Is the Warren Court," *New York Times Magazine*, March 13, 1966; Smith, Beverly, "Earl Warren's Greatest Moment," *Saturday Evening Post*, July 24, 1954, 17 ff.; *Time*, June 28, 1968; Warren, Earl, *New York Times*, October 31, 1970, and December 20, 1972; and Washington *Post*, July 13, 1974, for Robert Joffee's dispatch from San Francisco on report that Warren's autobiography will express regret over the Japanese-American relocation actions.

*Quotations*

p. 678—Figg expressed the prevailing sense in the Southern camp of the Court's disposition in a letter to Eugene S. Blease, December 10, 1953.

pp. 683–685—Justice Frankfurter's undated memo, Harvard Law Library. Though neither Alexander Bickel, a 1952 Term clerk to the Justice, nor Frank Sander, a 1953 Term clerk, recalls ever having seen the memo, I rely on circumstantial evidence and Bickel's surmise in approximating the date.

p. 686—Frankfurter memo to his brethren is in both the Library of Congress and the Harvard collections of his papers.

pp. 688–691—Both the Jackson memo and the Prettyman reply are in the Jackson Papers, made available to me by courtesy of William E. Jackson and Philip B. Kurland, his designated biographer. The Prettyman memo is undated.

p. 692—Justice Reed's rough draft for a dissent is taken from John D. Fassett's private memoir, based upon files he maintained with the Justice's blessing.

p. 696—Frankfurter's letter to Jackson, in the Library of Congress, is especially noteworthy in view of Frankfurter's later falling out with the Chief Justice.

## Chapter 26 / Simple Justice

*Books:* Allport, *The Nature of Prejudice*; Ashmore, *The Negro and the Schools*; Berman, *It Is So Ordered*; Blaustein and Ferguson, *Desegregation and the Law*; Friedman and Israel, *The Justices of the Supreme Court* (see Norman Dorsen's sketch of John Marshall Harlan, 2803–2820); Greenberg, *Race Relations and American Law*; Hill and Greenberg, *Citizen's Guide to Desegregation*; Lewis, *Portrait of a Decade*; Peltason, *Fifty-eight Lonely Men*; and Smith, *They Closed Their Schools.*

*Interviews and Correspondence:* Almond, J. Lindsay; Bickel, Alexander M.; Clark, Kenneth B.; Clark, Tom C.; Elman, Philip; Fassett, John D.; Huston, Luther; McKay, Ellis H.; Mickum, George V., III; Pollock, Earl E.; Prettyman, E. Barrett, Jr.; Rogers, S. Emory; and Rubenstein, Ernest.

*Articles and Documents:* Clark, Kenneth B., "Desegregation: An Appraisal of the Evidence," *Journal of Social Issues*, IX, No. 4 (1953), entire issue; Clark's report on desegregation in Milford, Delaware, in September 1954 is in the LDF files. Justice Frankfurter's letter to Justice Reed, May 20, 1954, offering the writer's impression of the Court's disposition on *Brown* a year earlier, and his letter to Paul A. Freund, July 22, 1958, ruminating on Holmes's use of "all deliberate speed," are in the Library of Congress. The *New York Times*'s massive coverage of the *Brown* decision in its May 18, 1954, issue shows why it is the leading newspaper in the United States.

*Quotations*

p. 706—Chief Justice Warren's remarks on Footnote #11 were made to the author in an interview in his chambers. I made no tape of this or any other interview I had, but typed up my notes at the first possible moment.

p. 713—Of the great volume of commentary on the *Brown* opinion, none was more instructive to the author than the clashing views in Herbert Wechsler's by now famous essay, "Toward Neutral Principles of Constitutional Law," in the *Harvard Law Review*, November 1959, and Louis H. Pollak's spirited "Racial Discrimination and Judicial Integrity: A Reply to Professor Wechsler," *University of Pennsylvania Law Review* of the same month and year (both cited earlier). Pollak's essay is of special interest because it includes a suggested text of the *Brown* opinion, were he to have written it, that would have gone a long way to meet the objections of Professor Wechsler and other scholars who have faulted Chief Justice Warren's opinion not for its conclusion but for the way it got there. See also Black, Charles L., Jr., "The Lawfulness of the Segregation Decisions,"

*Yale Law Journal*, LXIX (January 1960), 421–430, the most moving and, to me, most persuasive discussion of the rightness of the decision.

p. 718—Ashmore, *The Negro and the Schools*, 83.

p. 720—Clark, "Desegregation," *Journal of Social Issues*, IX, No. 4 (1953), 54.

p. 721—Robinson to Weinstein, July 21, 1954.

p. 722—Weinstein to Black, June 17, 1954, from Weinstein's files.

p. 722—Marshall's memo to Black, Clark, Coleman, *et al.*, September 27, 1954, Marshall to Coleman, September 24, 1954, and Coleman to Marshall, October 14, 1954, all from Coleman's files.

pp. 726–727—Lewis, *Portrait of a Decade*, 29.

p. 736—Fassett's memo to Reed, undated, comes from the former's private memoir.

pp. 737–738—Memo titled "Law Clerks' Recommendations for Segregation Decree," dated April 10, 1955, Frankfurter Papers, Harvard.

pp. 739–749—Burton's conference notes were supplemented by typed and extensive notes by Frankfurter, which made the reconstruction of this session both easier and more authoritative. Frankfurter's notes are at Harvard.

p. 744—Warren's casual explanation of the "all deliberate speed" phrase, *New York Times*, December 20, 1972.

pp. 746–747—Transcript of the Marshall-Murphy telephone conversation is from the morgue at the *Afro-American* in Baltimore, where numerous courtesies were extended to me.

## Chapter 27 / Visible Man: An Epilogue Twenty Years After

*Books:* Bergman, *Chronological History of the Negro*; Blaustein and Ferguson, *Desegregation and the Law*; Breitman, ed., *Malcolm X Speaks*; Carmichael and Hamilton, *Black Power*; Greenberg, *Race Relations and American Law*; Grier and Cobbs, *Black Rage*; Lewis, *Portrait of a Decade*; Mills, ed., *The Great School Bus Controversy*; Peltason, *Fifty-eight Lonely Men*; Silberman, *Crisis in Black and White*; and Smith, *They Closed Their Schools*.

*Articles and Documents:* The leading authority for the desegregation process is the annals of the now defunct *Southern School News*, a prime source for historians and analysts of the post-*Brown* era. A newer periodical, covering the problems of other minorities as well as blacks, is *Integrated Education*, published bimonthly through the School of Education, Northwestern University. The leading scholar on desegregation is Robert B. McKay of New York University Law School, who is preparing a book on the post-*Brown* period; early articles by him on the subject appeared in the June 1956 issue of the *New York University Law Review* and the December 1957 issue of the *Virginia Law Review*. Some of the articles drawn upon in this chapter: *New York Times*, survey articles on the twentieth anniversary of *Brown*, see especially May 12 and 13, 1974, and November 21, 1974, on the Harlem rehabilitation plan; *U.S. News & World Report*, "After Twenty Years: New Turns in the Black Revolution," May 20, 1974, "Ten Years of Civil Rights: Report by Chief Enforcer," September 23, 1974, and "Blacks Find That 'Making It' Doesn't Solve All Their Problems," October 14, 1974; *Wall Street Journal*, front-page leader by Pamela G. Hollie on racial situation in Topeka two decades after *Brown*, May 2, 1974; Wilkins, Roger, "The Sound of One Hand Clapping," *New York Times Magazine*, May 12, 1974; and Washington *Post*, Outlook section, May 12, 1974.

*Indexes*

# Index of Principal Cases Cited

# Index of Subjects and Names

A  NOTE  ABOUT  THE  AUTHOR

Richard Kluger was born in Paterson, New Jersey, and grew up in
New York City. He attended the Horace Mann School and
graduated from Princeton University. He worked as a copy editor
for the *Wall Street Journal*, a reporter for the New York *Post*, and
literary editor of the New York *Herald Tribune* (editing its book
supplement, *Book Week*). After serving as executive editor of
Simon & Schuster, editor in chief of Atheneum, and publisher of
Charterhouse, he decided to devote himself full-time to writing.
He has published two earlier books, the novels
*When the Bough Breaks* (1964) and *National Anthem* (1969).
He is married, has two sons, and lives in Connecticut.

　　*Simple Justice* took him seven years to complete.

A NOTE ON THE TYPE

This book was set by computer in a face called Times Roman,
designed by Stanley Morison for *The Times* (London) and first
introduced by that newspaper in 1932.

Among typographers and designers of the twentieth century,
Stanley Morison has been a strong forming influence, as
typographical adviser to the English Monotype Corporation, as a
director of two distinguished English publishing houses, and as a
writer of sensibility, erudition, and keen practical sense.

The book was composed, printed, and bound by The Colonial
Press, Clinton, Massachusetts.

Typography and binding design by Camilla Filancia

# SUPREME COURT OF THE UNITED STATES

Nos. 1, 2, 4 and 10.—October Term, 1953.

| | |
|---|---|
| Oliver Brown, et al.,<br>Appellants,<br>1      v.<br>Board of Education of To-<br>peka, Shawnee County,<br>Kansas, et al. | On Appeal From the United States District Court for the District of Kansas. |
| Harry Briggs, Jr., et al.,<br>Appellants,<br>2      v.<br>R. W. Elliott, et al. | On Appeal From the United States District Court for the Eastern District of South Carolina. |
| Dorothy E. Davis, et al.,<br>Appellants,<br>4      v.<br>County School Board of Prince Edward County, Virginia, et al. | On Appeal From the United States District Court for the Eastern District of Virginia. |
| Francis B. Gebhart, et al.,<br>Petitioners,<br>10      v.<br>Ethel Louise Belton, et al. | On Writ of Certiorari to the Supreme Court of Delaware. |

[May 17, 1954.]

Mr. Chief Justice Warren delivered the opinion of the Court.

These cases come to us from the States of Kansas, South Carolina, Virginia, and Delaware. They are premised on different facts and different local conditions,